CLASSICAL AND MEDIEVAL LITERATURE CRITICISM

Guide to Gale Literary Criticism Series

For criticism on	Consult these Gale series
Authors now living or who died after December 31, 1999	*CONTEMPORARY LITERARY CRITICISM (CLC)*
Authors who died between 1900 and 1999	*TWENTIETH-CENTURY LITERARY CRITICISM (TCLC)*
Authors who died between 1800 and 1899	*NINETEENTH-CENTURY LITERATURE CRITICISM (NCLC)*
Authors who died between 1400 and 1799	*LITERATURE CRITICISM FROM 1400 TO 1800 (LC)* *SHAKESPEAREAN CRITICISM (SC)*
Authors who died before 1400	*CLASSICAL AND MEDIEVAL LITERATURE CRITICISM (CMLC)*
Authors of books for children and young adults	*CHILDREN'S LITERATURE REVIEW (CLR)*
Dramatists	*DRAMA CRITICISM (DC)*
Poets	*POETRY CRITICISM (PC)*
Short story writers	*SHORT STORY CRITICISM (SSC)*
Literary topics and movements	*HARLEM RENAISSANCE: A GALE CRITICAL COMPANION (HR)* *THE BEAT GENERATION: A GALE CRITICAL COMPANION (BG)*
Asian American writers of the last two hundred years	*ASIAN AMERICAN LITERATURE (AAL)*
Black writers of the past two hundred years	*BLACK LITERATURE CRITICISM (BLC)* *BLACK LITERATURE CRITICISM SUPPLEMENT (BLCS)*
Hispanic writers of the late nineteenth and twentieth centuries	*HISPANIC LITERATURE CRITICISM (HLC)* *HISPANIC LITERATURE CRITICISM SUPPLEMENT (HLCS)*
Native North American writers and orators of the eighteenth, nineteenth, and twentieth centuries	*NATIVE NORTH AMERICAN LITERATURE (NNAL)*
Major authors from the Renaissance to the present	*WORLD LITERATURE CRITICISM, 1500 TO THE PRESENT (WLC)* *WORLD LITERATURE CRITICISM SUPPLEMENT (WLCS)*

ISSN 0896-0011

Volume 78

CLASSICAL AND MEDIEVAL LITERATURE CRITICISM

Criticism of the Works of World
Authors from Classical Antiquity through the
Fourteenth Century, from the First Appraisals
to Current Evaluations

Jelena Krstović
Project Editor

THOMSON
✳
™
GALE

Detroit • New York • San Francisco • San Diego • New Haven, Conn. • Waterville, Maine • London • Munich

Classical and Medieval Literature Criticism, Vol. 78

Project Editor
Jelena O. Krstović

Editorial
Jessica Bomarito, Kathy D. Darrow, Jeffrey W. Hunter, Michelle Lee, Rachelle Mucha, Thomas J. Schoenberg, Lawrence J. Trudeau, Russel Whitaker

Data Capture
Francis Monroe, Gwen Tucker

Indexing Services
Zott Solutions, Inc.

Rights and Acquisitions
Edna Hedblad, Jacqueline Key, Shalice Shah-Caldwell

Imaging and Multimedia
Dean Dauphinais, Robert Duncan, Leitha Etheridge-Sims, Lezlie Light, Michael Logusz, Dan Newell, Kelly A. Quin, Denay Wilding

Composition and Electronic Capture
Kathy Sauer

Manufacturing
Rhonda Dover

Associate Product Manager
Marc Cormier

LIBRARY OF CONGRESS CATALOG CARD NUMBER 88-658021

ISBN 0-7876-8025-7
ISSN 0896-0011

Contents

Preface vii

Acknowledgments xi

Literary Criticism Series Advisory Board xiii

Preface

Since its inception in 1988, *Classical and Medieval Literature Criticism (CMLC)* has been a valuable resource for students and librarians seeking critical commentary on the works and authors of antiquity through the fourteenth century. The great poets, prose writers, dramatists, and philosophers of this period form the basis of most humanities curricula, so that virtually every student will encounter many of these works during the course of a high school and college education. Reviewers have found *CMLC* "useful" and "extremely convenient," noting that it "adds to our understanding of the rich legacy left by the ancient period and the Middle Ages," and praising its "general excellence in the presentation of an inherently interesting subject." No other single reference source has surveyed the critical reaction to classical and medieval literature as thoroughly as *CMLC*.

Scope of the Series

CMLC provides an introduction to classical and medieval authors, works, and topics that represent a variety of genres, time periods, and nationalities. By organizing and reprinting an enormous amount of critical commentary written on authors and works of this period in world history, *CMLC* helps students develop valuable insight into literary history, promotes a better understanding of the texts, and sparks ideas for papers and assignments.

Each entry in *CMLC* presents a comprehensive survey of an author's career, an individual work of literature, or a literary topic, and provides the user with a multiplicity of interpretations and assessments. Such variety allows students to pursue their own interests; furthermore, it fosters an awareness that literature is dynamic and responsive to many different opinions. Early commentary is offered to indicate initial responses, later selections document changes in literary reputations, and retrospective analyses provide the reader with modern views. The size of each author entry is a relative reflection of the scope of the criticism available in English.

An author may appear more than once in the series if his or her writings have been the subject of a substantial amount of criticism; in these instances, specific works or groups of works by the author will be covered in separate entries. For example, Homer will be represented by three entries, one devoted to the *Iliad,* one to the *Odyssey,* and one to the Homeric Hymns.

CMLC continues the survey of criticism of world literature begun by Thomson Gale's *Contemporary Literary Criticism (CLC), Twentieth-Century Literary Criticism (TCLC), Nineteenth-Century Literature Criticism (NCLC), Literature Criticism from 1400 to 1800 (LC),* and *Shakespearean Criticism (SC).*

Organization of the Book

A *CMLC* entry consists of the following elements:

- The **Author Heading** cites the name under which the author most commonly wrote, followed by birth and death dates. Also located here are any name variations under which an author wrote, including transliterated forms for authors whose native languages use nonroman alphabets. If the author wrote consistently under a pseudonym, the pseudonym will be listed in the author heading and the author's actual name given in parenthesis on the first line of the biographical and critical information. Uncertain birth or death dates are indicated by question marks. Single-work entries are preceded by a heading that consists of the most common form of the title in English translation (if applicable) and the original date of composition.

- The **Introduction** contains background information that introduces the reader to the author, work, or topic that is the subject of the entry.

- A **Portrait of the Author** is included when available.

- The list of **Principal Works** is ordered chronologically by date of first publication and lists the most important works by the author. The genre and publication date of each work is given. In the case of foreign authors whose works have been translated into English, the list will focus primarily on twentieth-century translations, selecting those works most commonly considered the best by critics. Unless otherwise indicated, dramas are dated by first performance, not first publication. Lists of **Representative Works** by different authors appear with topic entries.

- Reprinted **Criticism** is arranged chronologically in each entry to provide a useful perspective on changes in critical evaluation over time. The critic's name and the date of composition or publication of the critical work are given at the beginning of each piece of criticism. Unsigned criticism is preceded by the title of the source in which it appeared. All titles by the author featured in the text are printed in boldface type. Footnotes are reprinted at the end of each essay or excerpt. In the case of excerpted criticism, only those footnotes that pertain to the excerpted texts are included. Criticism in topic entries is arranged chronologically under a variety of subheadings to facilitate the study of different aspects of the topic.

- A complete **Bibliographical Citation** of the original essay or book precedes each piece of criticism.

- Critical essays are prefaced by brief **Annotations** explicating each piece.

- An annotated bibliography of **Further Reading** appears at the end of each entry and suggests resources for additional study. In some cases, significant essays for which the editors could not obtain reprint rights are included here. Boxed material following the further reading list provides references to other biographical and critical sources on the author in series published by Thomson Gale.

Cumulative Indexes

A **Cumulative Author Index** lists all of the authors that appear in a wide variety of reference sources published by the Thomson Gale, including *CMLC*. A complete list of these sources is found facing the first page of the Author Index. The index also includes birth and death dates and cross references between pseudonyms and actual names.

Beginning with the second volume, a **Cumulative Nationality Index** lists all authors featured in *CMLC* by nationality, followed by the number of the *CMLC* volume in which their entry appears.

Beginning with the tenth volume, a **Cumulative Topic Index** lists the literary themes and topics treated in the series as well as in *Nineteenth-Century Literature Criticism, Twentieth-Century Literary Criticism,* and the *Contemporary Literary Criticism* Yearbook, which was discontinued in 1998.

A **Cumulative Title Index** lists in alphabetical order all of the works discussed in the series. Each title listing includes the corresponding volume and page numbers where criticism may be located. Foreign-language titles that have been translated into English are followed by the titles of the translation—for example, *Slovo o polku Igorove* (*The Song of Igor's Campaign*). Page numbers following these translated titles refer to all pages on which any form of the titles, either foreign-language or translated, appear. Titles of novels, dramas, nonfiction books, and poetry, short story, or essay collections are printed in italics, while individual poems, short stories, and essays are printed in roman type within quotation marks.

Citing *Classical and Medieval Literature Criticism*

When citing criticism reprinted in the Literary Criticism Series, students should provide complete bibliographic information so that the cited essay can be located in the original print or electronic source. Students who quote directly from reprinted criticism may use any accepted bibliographic format, such as University of Chicago Press style or Modern Language Association style.

The examples below follow recommendations for preparing a bibliography set forth in *The Chicago Manual of Style,* 14th ed. (Chicago: The University of Chicago Press, 1993); the first example pertains to material drawn from periodicals, the second to material reprinted from books:

Sealey, R. J. "The Tetralogies Ascribed to Antiphon." *Transactions of the American Philological Association* 114, (1984): 71-85. Reprinted in *Classical and Medieval Literature Criticism.* Vol. 55, edited by Lynn M. Zott, 2-9. Detroit: Gale, 2003.

Bourne, Ella. "Classical Elements in *The Gesta Romanorum.*" In *Vassar Medieval Studies* edited by Christabel Forsyth Fiske, 345-76. New Haven: Yale University Press, 1923. Reprinted in *Classical and Medieval Literature Criticism.* Vol. 55, edited by Lynn M. Zott, 81-92. Detroit: Gale, 2003.

The examples below follow recommendations for preparing a works cited list set forth in the *MLA Handbook for Writers of Research Papers,* 5th ed. (New York: The Modern Language Association of America, 1999); the first example pertains to material drawn from periodicals, the second to material reprinted from books:

Sealey, R. J. "The Tetralogies Ascribed to Antiphon." *Transactions of the American Philological Association* 114. (1984): 71-85. Reprinted in *Classical and Medieval Literature Criticism.* Ed. Lynn M. Zott. Vol. 55. Detroit: Gale, 2003. 2-9.

Bourne, Ella. "Classical Elements in *The Gesta Romanorum.*" *Vassar Medieval Studies.* Ed. Christabel Forsyth Fiske. New Haven: Yale University Press, 1923. 345-76. Reprinted in *Classical and Medieval Literature Criticism.* Ed. Lynn M. Zott. Vol. 55. Detroit: Gale, 2003. 81-92.

Suggestions are Welcome

Readers who wish to suggest new features, topics, or authors to appear in future volumes, or who have other suggestions or comments are cordially invited to call, write, or fax the Associate Product Manager:

Associate Product Manager, Literary Criticism Series
Thomson Gale
27500 Drake Road
Farmington Hills, MI 48331-3535
1-800-347-4253 (GALE)
Fax: 248-699-8054

Acknowledgments

The editors wish to thank the copyright holders of the criticism included in this volume and the permissions managers of many book and magazine publishing companies for assisting us in securing reproduction rights. We are also grateful to the staffs of the Detroit Public Library, the Library of Congress, the University of Detroit Mercy Library, Wayne State University Purdy/Kresge Library Complex, and the University of Michigan Libraries for making their resources available to us. Following is a list of the copyright holders who have granted us permission to reproduce material in this volume of *CMLC*. Every effort has been made to trace copyright, but if omissions have been made, please let us know.

COPYRIGHTED MATERIAL IN *CMLC*, VOLUME 78, WAS REPRODUCED FROM THE FOLLOWING PERIODICALS:

Analecta Bollandiana: Revue Critique d'Hagiographie, v. 91, 1973. Reproduced by permission.—*Comparative Drama,* v. 25, spring, 1991. Copyright © 1991, by the Editors of *Comparative Drama*. Reproduced by permission.—*Hispanic Review* v. 61, summer, 1993. Reproduced by permission.—*Journal of Early Christian Studies,* v. 3, fall, 1995. Copyright © 1995 by the Johns Hopkins University Press. Reprinted with permission of the Johns Hopkins University Press.—*Kentucky Romance Quarterly,* v. 28, 1981. Copyright © 1981 by Helen Dwight Reid Educational Foundation. Reproduced with permission of the Helen Dwight Reid Educational Foundation, published by Heldref Publications, 1319 18th Street, NW, Washington, DC 20036-1802.—*Latomus: Revue d'Études Latines,* v. 43, 1984; v. 1, July-September, 1991. Both reproduced by permission.—*Medievalia et Humanistica: Studies in Medieval and Renaissance Culture,* 1973. Copyright © 1973 by Rowman & Littlefield Publishers, Inc. Reproduced by permission.—*Neophilologica Fennica,* v. 45, 1987 for "Hrabanus' *De Laudibus Sanctae Crucis* and *The Dream of the Rood*" by Matti Kilpiö. Reproduced by permission of the publisher and the author.—*Neuphilologische Mitteilungen: Bulletin of the Modern Language Society,* v. 77, 1976 for "The Pater Noster Battle Sequence in *Solomon and Saturn* and the *Psychomachia* of Prudentius" by John P. Hermann. Copyright © 1976 Modern Language Society, Helsinki. Reproduced by permission of the publisher and the author.—*Proceedings of the PMR Conference,* v. 3, 1978. Copyright © 1978 by Villanova University. Reproduced by permission.—*Rhetorica: A Journal of the History of Rhetoric,* v. 9, winter, 1991. Copyright © 1991 The International Society for the History of Rhetoric. Reproduced by permission.—*Romance Quarterly,* v. 33, August, 1986. Copyright © 1986 by Helen Dwight Reid Educational Foundation. Reproduced with permission of the Helen Dwight Reid Educational Foundation, published by Heldref Publications, 1319 18th Street, NW, Washington, DC 20036-1802.—*Speculum: A Journal of Medieval Studies,* v. 46, October, 1971; v. 67, April, 1992. Both reproduced by permission.—*Traditio: Studies in Ancient and Medieval History, Thought, and Religion,* v. 38, 1982. Reproduced by permission.—*Transactions and Proceedings of the American Philological Association,* v. 99, 1968. © American Philological Association. Reprinted with permission of The Johns Hopkins University Press.

COPYRIGHTED MATERIAL IN *CMLC*, VOLUME 78, WAS REPRODUCED FROM THE FOLLOWING BOOKS:

Banniard, Michel. From "Rhabanus Maurus and the Vernacular Languages," in *Latin and the Romance Languages in the Early Middle Ages*. Edited by Roger Wright. Routledge, 1991. Reprinted, Penn State Press, 1996. Reproduced by permission of the Editor.—Carpenter, Dwayne E. From *In Iberia and beyond: Hispanic Jews between Cultures*. University of Delaware Press, 1998. Copyright © 1998 by Associated University Presses, Inc. All rights reserved. Reproduced by permission.—Chazelle, Celia. From *The Crucified God in the Carolingian Era: Theology and Art of Christ's Passion*. Cambridge University Press, 2001. Copyright © 2001 Cambridge University Press. Reprinted with the permission of Cambridge University Press.—De Jong, Mayke. From "The Empire as Ecclesia: Hrabanus Maurus and Biblical *Historia* for Rulers," in *The Uses of the Past in the Early Middle Ages*. Edited by Yitzhak Hen and Matthew Innes. Cambridge University Press, 2000. Copyright © 2000 Cambridge University Press. Reprinted with the permission of Cambridge University Press.—Keller, John Esten. From *Alfonso X, El Sabio*. Twayne Publishers, Inc., 1967. Reproduced by permission Thomson Gale.—Malamud, Martha. From *A Poetics of Transformation: Prudentius and Classical Mythology*. Cornell University Press, 1989. Copyright © 1989 by Cornell University. Used by permission of the publisher, Cornell University Press.—McCarthy, William J. From *Diakonia: Studies in Honor of Robert T. Meyer*. The Catholic University of America Press, 1986. Copyright © 1986 The Catholic University of America Press. All rights reserved. Used with permission: The Catholic University of America Press, Washington, DC.—O'Callaghan, Joseph F. From *Alfonso X and the*

Cántigas de Santa Maria. Brill, 1998. Copyright © 1998 by Koninklijke Brill, Leiden, The Netherlands. Courtesy of Brill Academic Publishers.—Smith, Macklin. From **Prudentius's** Psychomachia *: A Reexamination.* Princeton University Press, 1976. © 1976 Princeton University Press. 2004 renewed PUP. Reprinted by permission of Princeton University Press.

PHOTOGRAPHS AND ILLUSTRATIONS APPEARING IN *CMLC*, VOLUME 78, WERE RECEIVED FROM THE FOLLOWING SOURCES:

Alfonso X, photograph. The Library of Congress.—Anger, engraving by Hieronymus Cock (ca. 1510-1570). Brueghel, Pieter the Elder (c. 1515-69) (after). Private Collection/Bridgeman Art Library. Reproduced by permission.—Manuscript illumination of heretics and Jews unable to hear the word of God. From "Rabanus Maurus, *De Universo*," photograph by Gianni Dagli Orti. © Gianni Dagli Orti/Corbis. Reproduced by permission.

Gale Thomson Literature Product Advisory Board

The members of the Thomson Gale Literature Product Advisory Board—reference librarians from public and academic library systems—represent a cross-section of our customer base and offer a variety of informed perspectives on both the presentation and content of our literature products. Advisory board members assess and define such quality issues as the relevance, currency, and usefulness of the author coverage, critical content, and literary topics included in our series; evaluate the layout, presentation, and general quality of our printed volumes; provide feedback on the criteria used for selecting authors and topics covered in our series; provide suggestions for potential enhancements to our series; identify any gaps in our coverage of authors or literary topics, recommending authors or topics for inclusion; analyze the appropriateness of our content and presentation for various user audiences, such as high school students, undergraduates, graduate students, librarians, and educators; and offer feedback on any proposed changes/enhancements to our series. We wish to thank the following advisors for their advice throughout the year.

Alfonso X
1221-1284

(Also known as Alfonso el Sabio) Spanish poet, historian, prose writer, nonfiction writer, translator, and editor.

INTRODUCTION

As King of León and Castile, Alfonso X ushered in a thirteenth-century Spanish Renaissance that emphasized the cultivation of poetry, music, painting, architecture, history, science, and games. Called "El Sabio," or "The Learned," by his subjects, Alfonso wrote a Spanish history and a world history, and composed or commissioned a code of laws that, in its essentials, is still in effect today. His many treatises on astronomy earned him another sobriquet, "The Astronomer." His masterpiece is *Cantigas de Santa María* (1279; *Songs of Holy Mary*), a collection of poems that also features illuminated miniatures that complement the devotional texts and are considered without parallel for their presentation of common people engaged in ordinary life. In founding a school of translation in Toledo, he was responsible for bringing some of the greatest Arabic classics and Arabic versions of Greek classics to the West. He elevated Castilian to the official language with his decree that literature and charters would no longer be written in Latin. Politically, as king, Alfonso is regarded as having been less than successful; he did not manage to become Holy Roman Emperor, although he strove for the position for seventeen years, and was ultimately challenged by one of his sons for power. Alfonso's reputation has suffered from his characterization by sixteenth-century historian Juan de Mariana as a man who, while meditating on the stars, lost the earth. Many scholars adamantly disagree with this evaluation while acknowledging that Alfonso is best remembered for helping to develop a Spanish national culture and for his many accomplishments in war, politics, and the judiciary.

BIOGRAPHICAL INFORMATION

Alfonso was born in Toledo in 1221, the first of thirteen children of Ferdinand III and Beatrice of Swabia. As the eldest son, he received the finest of educations and spent most of his youth in Galicia. In his twenties he participated in important military campaigns, expelling Arabs from Murcia and capturing Seville. In 1249 Al-

fonso married Violante, the daughter of the King of Aragon, James the Conqueror. Violante and Alfonso would ultimately have five sons and five daughters. While still a prince, in 1251, Alfonso produced the *Calila e Digna,* a translation from the Arabic work *Kalila wa-Dimna,* and began work on his immensely influential code of laws. Alfonso began his reign as king in 1252. In 1253 he attacked Portugal, followed by Gascony in 1254, the same year that he commenced the *Cantigas.* Alfonso produced a summary of Roman law, the *Espéculo,* in 1255. The first several years of the decade of the 1260s were largely taken up by several wars against Arabs, ending in 1266 with the unification of Murcia and Castile. The last years of Alfonso's life were marred by battles of succession; his second son, Sancho, attacked his father, who was forced to fall back to Seville, where he died in 1284.

MAJOR WORKS

Scholars have always recognized that Alfonso did not personally write everything that is attributed to him; instead, he often served as a kind of executive editor, overseeing numerous scholar-scribes laboring on projects that he had commissioned. One such project, primarily the work of two Jewish scholars in his employ, was a set of astronomical tables, *Las Tablas Alfonsinas,* completed in 1262. These planetary tables were not bettered for centuries. Alfonso's highly acclaimed code of laws, largely the product of his own hand, is entitled *Las Siete Partidas* (1265). Alfonso worked on two histories during the 1270s, though neither was completely finalized. *La Crónica General* is a history of Spain, while *La Grande e General Estoria,* the oldest work of its kind written in the vernacular, covers the entire known world back to the times of the Old Testament. *Libros del saber de la astrologia,* consisting of some sixteen treatises on astrology and astronomy, largely translations of Arabic works, were completed in the late 1270s. *Cantigas de Santa María* was written in Galician-Portuguese instead of Castilian. It contains 427 lyric and narrative poems describing miracles performed by St. Mary, accompanied by finely detailed illustrations. In 1283, the year before his death, Alfonso wrote *Libro de Ajedrez, Dados e Tablas,* which helped to advance the popularity of chess, dice, backgammon, and other games of leisure.

CRITICAL RECEPTION

Alfonso X enjoys an excellent reputation among scholars. Frank Callcott (see Further Reading) notes how extraordinary it is that Alfonso found time to write and edit at all, considering the many pressing matters of politics and war he faced as king. Numerous scholars are also interested in Alfonso's biography. Connie Scarborough studies the *Cantigas de Santa Maria* with emphasis on those pieces dealing with curing illness and relieving suffering. Scarborough notes, as does John Esten Keller in another essay, that Alfonso frequently provides autobiographical details—in this case, of his own ill health. Richard P. Kinkade writes further of the King's suffering in his study of five particular cantigas. Joseph F. O'Callaghan, too, reads the *Cantigas* as partially autobiographical. He goes so far as to claim they are a form of poetic biography, "unique in the annals of medieval Europe." Keller also studies the *Cantigas* for what they reveal of thirteenth-century daily life. Keller notes: "Students of folklore, thematology, and comparative literature recognize the *Canticles* as a rich mine of motifs and themes, some of which appear nowhere else." Further, he praises them as "the apogee of perfection in three distinct artistic media": pictorial art, music, and literature. The pictorial art is analyzed by George D. Greenia, who assesses the importance of the miniatures of the *Cantigas* and praises Alfonso for "remarkable subtlety in merging" lyrics and images, while what is known of the music is discussed in an essay by Roger D. Tinnell.

Alfonso's creation of a national language is another area of great interest to scholars. Herbert A. Van Scoy discusses how Alfonso's inclusion of word definitions contributed greatly to the Castilian language. Dorothy Clotelle Clarke analyzes Alfonso's poetics, including the types of verse he favored, his polymetric combinations, and his rimes, which she calls "almost perfection itself." Clarke credits him with being largely responsible for laying the framework for Spanish metrics. She asserts that Alfonso "uncannily sensed lasting qualities in verse technique, kept his work amazingly free from mannerisms, from naïve embellishments and primitive awkwardness in metric structure, and was sufficiently prolific to be able to channel Spanish metric practice into ways both practical and artistic."

Albert I. Bagby, Jr. is one of several historians writing about Alfonso's treatment of Jews in his writings. Bagby contends that under Alfonso's reign, Jews were treated better than in any other period of Spanish history, adding the caveat that the King was still "a man of his time and circumstance" and that he held common anti-Semitic attitudes. Dwayne E. Carpenter concentrates on ostensibly incidental references to Jews in the *Cantigas* and concludes that their tone is consistently negative. Carpenter finds that although Alfonso does not go out of his way to malign Jews, he also does not advance positive portrayals, but, Carpenter adds, "Alfonso is not an anomaly in this regard, and we distort history and the man if we attempt to discover a tolerance that is inherently absent."

PRINCIPAL WORKS

Calila e Digna [translator] (prose) 1251

Espéculo (essay) 1255

Las Tablas Alfonsinas [editor] (nonfiction) 1262

Las Siete Partidas (nonfiction) 1265

La Crónica General (history) c. 1270

La Grande e General Estoria (history) c. 1270

Libros del saber de la astrologia (nonfiction) c. late 1270s

Cantigas de Santa María (poetry) 1279

Libro de Ajedrez, Dados e Tablas (nonfiction) 1283

Principal English Translations

Songs of Holy Mary of Alfonso X, The Wise: A Translation of the Cantigas de Santa Maria (translated by Kathleen Kulp-Hill) 2000

CRITICISM

Herbert A. Van Scoy (essay date October 1940)

SOURCE: Van Scoy, Herbert A. "Alfonso X as a Lexicographer." *Hispanic Review* 8, no. 4 (October 1940): 277-84.

[*In the following essay, Van Scoy discusses how Alfonso's efforts to coin concise and concrete definitions helped Castilian to become a national language in Spain.*]

Even a casual reader of the prose of Alfonso X is struck by the extraordinary number of definitions which are found throughout the context. Thousands of Latin, Arabic, Greek, Syriac and Spanish words are defined clearly and accurately with a nicety of expression and a choice of language which many a modern lexicographer might envy. The presence of this vast number of definitions is even more noteworthy when one considers that this policy of including definitions of foreign, learned or unusual words is to be found only in the works of Alfonso X and not in the other didactic prose works of the Middle Ages, or even of later periods.[1] The annals and the chronicles immediately following Alfonso X and the works of Juan Manuel, although didactic in nature, contain no definitions. The works by the Aragonese Juan Fernández Heredia, written during the first half of the 14th century, parallel somewhat the historical writings of Alfonso X. In Heredia one finds frequent use of synonyms and a large amount of explanatory material but no definitions.[2] Neither does medieval French show the tendency to define words on the scale to be noted in the Alphonsine works. The few definitions to be found in French prose at this time can scarcely be compared to the varied and complete forms used in the Spanish definitions.[3] There was no conscious effort on the part of the French writers to substitute French for Latin, or to establish a national language as was the intent of Alfonso X, and consequently there was less need for explanation and definition of words.

The presence of these definitions in the works of Alfonso X, inserted with such consistency and with such a conscious desire to produce an accurate and polished definition, deserves some explanation, and there are several reasons, both theoretical and practical, for their inclusion.

The Middle Ages enjoyed a repose which was the result of a conception of the world as a perfect harmony, arranged by God. In attempting to maintain this harmony the sharp division between myth and reality, between spiritual and material things was lost. This attitude toward the world naturally led to the encyclopedic spirit, the desire to harmonize all streams of knowledge into one body. Spain responded to this movement with the works of Alfonso X. In contrast to the situation in other countries, Alfonso controlled an extensive territory because of the Reconquest and because of political expansion. Here there was a feeling of national unity, a common pride in the country and what had been achieved. Because of this common cause Castilian was spread over all of this territory. It was possible for Alfonso X to use a language which could be understood easily throughout the whole country. This monarch took a deep pride in Castile and in the Castilian language. The extravagant praise of Spain which begins, "La península de España es como el paraíso de Dios," is well known. One feels the pride behind the expressions: "en el nuestro lenguaje de Castiella," "nos de Castiella dezimos," "en nuestro romance," "llamamos en lenguaje de Espanna." This emphasis upon the national character of the language is so frequent that it must be considered as ever present in the mind of Alfonso X and of his collaborators. Such expressions could never have been used by a French writer. In France there was an encyclopedic idea of culture, but not the imperial idea of politics, of culture and of life as is expressed by Alfonso X in Spain.

Curious definitions of *Francia* and *franco,* not located in any vocabulary or source, may possibly be explained by Alfonso el Sabio's love of a harmonious whole, and the regret which he felt at the breaking of the old unity of the Holy Roman Empire.

> Francia la antigua fue otrossi una partida de Alemanna, e por essol pusieron nombre Francia, que quiere dezir tanto como tierra que fue apartida e frannida d'Alemanna.[4]

Later he repeats this same thought and says,

> este nombre Francia le fue dado de *frangere* que dizen en el latin por franner o crebantar.[5]

> Franco, dezimos en el lenguage de Castiella por quebrantadura y partida.[6]

It is possible that Alfonso might have been thinking of his frustrated desire to become Holy Roman Emperor, which would have given him opportunity to put his imperialistic ideas into practice.

With this theoretical attitude of harmonization which resulted in a strong national spirit it was natural for Alfonso X to apply his principle of unification to Castilian. The duality of Latin and Spanish was not compatible to such a man, so for the historical reasons already mentioned, and because he wanted to teach his people in the language which they could understand, Alfonso X turned to Castilian instead of to Latin as the language for his works. He believed that Castilian was the proper instrument to disseminate the culture which he was gathering and unifying, and deliberately broke with the tradition which believed that erudite and scientific works should be written in Latin. In fact, "lo castellano se concibe como un no querer ya ser latino."[7] In thus supplanting Latin by Spanish is found the principal reason for the large number of definitions. Because Spanish lacked the vocabulary to translate most of the works which were used, it was necessary to build words, to bring in learned words, or to explain uncommon words to the reader. Whenever the scribe came into contact with such words he felt it his duty to define them in order to make them a part of the Castilian language.

In addition to this basic reason for defining words there were certain other considerations which made definitions either desirable or necessary. In the case of the *Siete Partidas,* a legal text, the aim was clarity and completeness, so that there could be absolutely no doubt about the meaning of certain terms. The following definitions illustrate this tendency to ramify in order to establish a legal meaning of a word:

> Por esta palabra armas non tan solamente se entienden los escudos, et las lorigas, et las lanzas, et las espadas, et todas las otras armas con que los homes lidian, mas aun los palos et las piedras.[8]

> Por esta palabra vestimiento se entienden todos los paños de vestir, quier sean de varon o de muger, quier los visten cada dia o en tiempo de solaz.[9]

Here the definitions have been given, not because the words are new or unusual, but to establish a definite meaning in case of litigation.

At other times it is not the newness of the word but its oldness which makes a definition necessary. New forms entering from other languages were crowding out older words. When the scribe felt this to be the case he designated the words as "palabras antiguas" and defined them.

> Debe el cabdiello siempre traer homes consigo que sepan bien la tierra a que llaman agora adalides que solian antiguamente haber nombre guiador.[10]

> Merino es antiguo nombre de España que quiere tanto decir como home que ha mayoria para facer justicia sobre algunt lugar señalado, asi como villa o tierra.[11]

Many of these definitions reveal the substitution of Arabic words for older Castilian ones and point out the change in progress;

> Almocadenes llaman agora a los que antiguamente solien llamar cabdiellos de las peonadas.[12]

Corredura is replaced by *algara, talega* by *arguena,* etc.

As an internationalist Alfonso X did not hesitate to incorporate a large number of foreign words into the Castilian vocabulary. These, of course, made definitions necessary. Reflecting this tendency are the definitions of such Italian words as: *potestad, catan, valvasor;* French borrowings, *chantre, dean, preste, saluaje,* etc.; Germanic words as *bandera, banido;* Arabic words as: *adalid, algara, alguazil, alferez,* and a host of scientific terms for which there were no Castilian words.

Coexistent with these practical reasons for defining words may be mentioned the pleasure that the medieval mind experienced in possessing knowledge and in transmitting this knowledge. The abundance of didactic literature at this period, filled with digressions and explanations, gives ample evidence of this tendency. In the works of Alfonso X defining words was a policy, but none the less one which was very agreeable. One does not have to read very deeply between the lines to sense the pleasure that the scribe felt in handling words, and in creating a definition which was clear, concise and accurate. It is easy to detect the desire on the part of the scribe to apply his personal experience to the problem at hand in order to make the definition something concrete and human, rather than an abstract explanation. This joy in defining and explaining often led to definitions which apparently had no other motive. The following is an example of this:

> Porpola otrossi todos saben que es panno de seda, e a este nombre dun marisco en cuya sangre la tinnen, a que dizen otrossi porpola.[13]

The writer says "todos saben" but goes ahead to explain *porpola* to show his knowledge of the word, and for the pleasure derived from passing on this knowledge.

Many of the sources which were used by Alfonso X contained copious glosses in the margin, or interlinear explanations. The presence of these glosses was a constant inspiration for definitions, and the scribes in most cases acknowledged their indebtedness with such expressions as: "como dize el maestro Pedro," "dizen los departidores," "el glosador dize," "segun dize Rabano," etc.

In summary, it may be concluded that the large number of definitions in the works of Alfonso el Sabio may be attributed to the need for defining words which had to be brought into the language with the substitution of Castilian for Latin, to the desire for establishing a legal meaning for words, to the necessity of explaining scientific and philosophic terminology new to Castilian, and to the need for explaining foreign words. In addition to these reasons the prolixity of explanation in the sources which the collaborators of Alfonso X had constantly before them, and the psychological traits of the medieval mind which made association with words a pleasure contributed to the definition of such a large number of words.

Now that we have considered the reasons which Alfonso X had for including so many definitions in his works, let us examine the technique or procedure which was followed. In the *Siete Partidas* Alfonso el Sabio makes a statement which reveals the pattern and procedure to be followed.

> Significamiento et declaramiento de palabra tanto quiere decir como demonstrar et espaladinar claramente el propio nombre de la cosa sobre que es la contienda, o si tal nombre no hobiese, mostrar la o averiguar la por otras señales ciertas.[14]

According to this the usual practice was to define an object by naming it. If the name of the object was lacking, or not entirely clear, then it was necessary to resort to "otras señales ciertas." These other methods of clarifying a word were: use of etymologies, explanation, and description of the object.

In defining a word Alfonso el Sabio and his collaborators had three positions which might be taken. Sometimes their attention was fixed upon the word itself, sometimes upon the object under consideration, and again upon the representation which the word suggested. In general it can be stated that when the attention was on the word the result was what may be called real definition; if the emphasis was upon the object or the concrete meaning of the word, description was necessary, while if the thought was upon the connotation of the word, then explanation was used. In actual practice it is sometimes difficult to make a fine distinction between definition, description and explanation, since many definitions combine something of each of these elements.

In the light of this it is interesting to notice how the various manners which Alfonso used to define a word may be grouped to agree with the emphasis upon the word, the object, or the connotation. This variety and flexibility of definition is one of the most pleasing aspects of the lexicographical work of Alfonso X, and emphasizes the great improvement over the rigid and dry definitions of the Latin glossators. When the scribe was thinking of the word itself he used such forms as: 'tanto quiere dezir,' 'por esta palabra se entiende,' 'tanto muestra como,' 'muestra como.' When the object under consideration received the emphasis, it was necessary to

use a phrase or word which would designate and point out. In this case 'llamar,' 'ser,' 'poner nombre,' 'nombrar,' etc., were employed. In order to stress the connotation or action implied by the words the following forms were used: 'es quando,' 'es cosa que,' 'es para,' 'quando,' etc.

Although the reading of quite a large number of definitions is necessary to establish this relationship, an example of each type of definition will serve as illustration.

> Cantigo quiere dezir tanto como cantiga o cantar de alabança.[15]

The word *cantigo* is the important consideration here, and neither description nor explanation is involved. In the following definition the object itself has the center of attention; therefore it is pointed out and described.

> Calizes son llamados aquellos vasos en que fazen el sacrificio del cuerpo de Nuestro Sennor Ihesu Christo.[16]

The word *confirmar* calls to mind the action related to it, so explanation is employed.

> Confirmar es quando se dobla aquello que fue firmado, deziendo o faziendo por que se confirme.[17]

In many instances the definition begins from one angle and then becomes more inclusive or more concrete so that a single definition is not necessarily restricted to only one of the forms mentioned above.

Occasionally the writer used forms expressing negation. "Non la llaman sinon," "non es otra cosa que," "non quiere al dezir sinon"; e.g.

> Cerca non quiere al decir sinon cosa que cieñe en derredor.[18]

Throughout the works of Alfonso X can be noticed the desire to be concrete rather than abstract. For Alfonso X nouns are not so much concepts as they are something real. In conformance with his philosophy Alfonso wanted his words to be a mirror of everything in existence. When he deals with an abstract noun he first attempts to reduce it to a state of concreteness by saying, 'es cosa que,' as for example,

> Fe es cosa que por la cual verdaderamente cree el home lo que non puede veer.[19]

> Uso es cosa que nace de aquellas cosas que home dice o face, et que siguen continuadamente por grant tiempo et sin embargo ninguno.[20]

This formula is a part of nearly every definition of an abstract noun.

Alfonso el Sabio's love of words for themselves, and his understanding of the importance of clear meanings made him strive always to give an accurate and concise signification of the word. Whenever possible he tried to reduce these words to a concrete status, and to draw upon personal experience and literary technique to produce a definition which would not only satisfy the requirements of definition, but also be expressed in the most polished language possible. These definitions reveal better than any other phase of his work Alfonso's conscious desire to establish Castilian as the national language, and the extent and the success of his plan. Through them one sees very clearly the state of the language of the thirteenth century. By extracting these definitions from the works of Alfonso X, and making a single volume of them, one reconstructs, in reality, the first dictionary to be written in a Romance language.[21]

Notes

Much of the material contained in this study was gathered at the Wisconsin Seminary for Medieval Spanish Studies which is carrying on a broader study of the works of Alfonso X.

1. It is interesting to note that the New World historians made some use of definitions in order to explain a number of terms found in the New World which were unfamiliar to readers in Spain. The following examples from the *Conquista de Nueva España* by Francisco López de Gómara are representative of this practice: "Andan en estas lagunas docientas mil barquillas que los naturales llaman acalles, que quiere decir casas de agua . . . Los españoles las dicen canoas, avezados a la lengua de Cuba y Santo Domingo." "Está la ciudad repartida en dos barrios; al uno llaman Tlatelulco, que quiere decir isleta; y al otro Méjico, que quiere decir manadero."

2. A check of the words defined in the *Primera Crónica* against Parts I and III of the *Gran Crónica de España* of Heredia, which used the Alphonsine work as one of its sources, reveals no definitions and very few explanations in common. The following definition of *legion* from the *Primera Crónica* compared to the discussion of the same word in the First Part of Heredia's *Gran Crónica* shows the wide difference in technique and the lack of interest in actual definition in Heredia's work. "Legion quiere dezir companna en que a seys mil et seyscientos et sessaenta et seys omnes." From Heredia, "Acordaron de enuiar en Espanya . . . una legion de caualleros que son vi mil e vi C lxvi."

3. [See Gautier de Metz and Jehan Bonnet.]

4. *Primera Crónica*, p. 6, line 18 *a*, Menéndez Pidal edition.

5. *Ibid.*, p. 368, line 11 *a*.

6. *General Estoria*, Part III, Ms. Escorial Y.I. 8, f. 96 *c*.

7. A. Castro, *Glosarios latino-españoles de la Edad Media*, p. lxv.

8. *Siete Partidas*, VII, Título 33, Ley 7, Academy edition.

9. *Ibid.*, VII, Título 33, Ley 8.

10. *Ibid.*, II, Título 23, Ley 19.

11. *Ibid.*, II, Título 9, Ley 23.

12. *Ibid.*, II, Título 22, Ley 5.

13. *General Estoria*, I, p. 431, line 53 *b*.

14. *Siete Partidas*, VII, Título 33, Ley 1.

15. *General Estoria*, I, p. 355, 10 *b*.

16. *Siete Partidas*, I, Título 4, Ley 54.

17. *Septenario*, Escorial Ms., f. 77 *a*.

18. *Siete Partidas*, I, Título 4, Ley 28.

19. *Ibid.*, I, Título 4, Ley 28.

20. *Ibid.*, I, Título 2, Ley 1.

21. A. Castro, *op. cit.*, p. lxv: "Alfonso el Sabio compuso el primer diccionario greco-latino-español, sólo que lo dispersó a lo largo de su inmensa producción . . . Podrían agruparse millares de glosas. Nada mengua a tan espléndido esfuerzo el que aquí y allí D. Alfonso forje falsas etimologías . . . Eso no obstante, es el primer y el mejor de los glosadores latino-románicos de la Edad Media."

Dorothy Clotelle Clarke (essay date April 1955)

SOURCE: Clarke, Dorothy Clotelle. "Versification in Alfonso El Sabio's *Cantigas.*" *Hispanic Review* 23, no. 2 (April 1955): 83-98.

[*In the following essay, Clarke analyzes Alfonso's metrics in the* Cantigas *and credits his verse techniques with helping to advance the development of Spanish poetry.*]

With his customary insight, Menéndez y Pelayo[1] summarized the great value of the versification in the *Cantigas*[2] of Alfonso el Sabio (1226-1284):

> Pero las *Cantigas,* no sólo importan por su valor lingüístico y por su contenido hagiográfico, sino por la extraordinaria variedad y relativa perfección de sus for-

mas métricas. Son, tomadas en conjunto, la más antigua manifestación lírica conocida hasta hoy en ninguna de las literaturas de la Península, y no muy posterior a las pocas muestras que tenemos del metro épico castellano. Por ellas habrá que comenzar cuando alguien intente hacer una prosodia histórica que todavía nos falta. . . .

La metrificación de las *Cantigas* es tan varia y abundante que abarca desde los versos de cuatro y cinco sílabas hasta los de diez y siete, sin que falte, por supuesto, el endecasílabo anapéstico, vulgarmente llamado *de gaita gallega,* mezclado con otros de mejor sonido. La variedad de combinaciones es estraordinaria, y muy notable la soltura artística del versificador, que venciendo las trabas de una lengua naciente, se empeña en arduas filigranas métricas, y atina a veces con un género de perfección técnica que parece enteramente moderna.

It is, in fact, surprising to find that the *Cantigas* could have been the source of the fundamentals of Castilian metric practice in formal poetry.[3] That is to say that Alfonso's ability to select, at almost the very dawn of Peninsular formal poetry, lasting qualities in so intricate an art as that of versification is indeed admirable. All presently known verse forms employed in Castilian before the Golden Age are found in the *Cantigas.* And there is in the collection a foreshadowing, as Menéndez y Pelayo indicates, of Golden Age and modern lines. Alfonso's system of verse measure—syllable count[4]—was the one followed almost exactly in subsequent Castilian poetry. Alfonso's rhythmic patterns[5] have lived to the present time and his strophe forms could have been prototypes for a number of basic Castilian strophes.[6] His great fondness for polymetric combinations[7] is of particular significance.

A review of some of the details of the Alphonsine and the formal Castilian metrics will illustrate the intimate relationship between the two and will, in part at least, constitute the beginning suggested by Menéndez y Pelayo of "una prosodia histórica que todavía nos falta."[8]

Only Perogrullo would state that both poetries base verse measure on syllable count, but it is of interest to notice that Alfonso's method of counting syllables was essentially that employed by Berceo (late 12th century to mid-13th), whose poetry antedated Alfonso's by only a few years. The only differences that I have been able to discover are that Alfonso was perhaps more liberal than Berceo in his use of apocope and enjambment and that the two poets may have followed slightly different rules for apocope.[9]

John D. Fitz-Gerald[10] lists about a hundred words from Berceo's *Vida de Santo Domingo de Silos* in which apocope of the final unstressed vowel or syllable appears, and further states (p. 56) that "An examination of the list of imperfect hemistichs will show that by the use of apocope many of them may easily be reduced to the norm." In the *Cantigas* apocope of the final unstressed vowel is so common that in many cases it practically serves the purpose of the synaloepha developed in fifteenth century Castilian—it gives elasticity and smooth flow to the verse and eases the poet's task of fitting words to verse length. There seems to be no rule to regulate the number or kinds of words apocopated in either Alfonso or Berceo. Apparently in Galician-Portuguese any final unaccented vowel followed by an initial vowel[11] or a verse end could be apocopated, particularly in certain verb forms and other common words, although final *a* seems to show great resistance to the practice. However, since many words were never apocopated, complete rules for apocopation in the *Cantigas* are not clear. In regard to the Castilian, Fitz-Gerald (p. 55, n. 1) quotes Hanssen's statement: ". . . hai pocos ejemplos de la apócope de la *a* final." He also says that in Berceo Romanic final syllables-*ce* (*-ze*), *-de, -io, -se,* and *-te* are sometimes apocopated. And I might add that in Berceo apocopation was not necessarily followed by a vowel or a verse-end, but was also sometimes followed immediately by a consonant of a word in the same hemistich. It may be said, then, that Alfonso was somewhat more modern than Berceo in his use of apocope, which in the *Cantigas* was almost equivalent to the synaloepha of later centuries, though of course more limited in use, and that Berceo's apocope was true apocope in the strictest sense.

As in Berceo's work, hiatus in the *Cantigas* is required between contiguous vowels of separate words when apocope is not employed. Hiatus is much more frequent than apocope.

For Berceo, Fitz-Gerald (p. 64) says of dieresis (dialysis) and syneresis (synizesis): ". . . the poet was virtually untrammelled in his use of dialysis and synizesis. In this usage, the poets of the *cuaderna vía* (to judge them all by our poem) were but continuing the liberty of their Latin predecessors.

"That they were not absolutely free has been admitted in the course of this argument. To summarize briefly the exceptions that I have noticed to this virtual freedom, they are the diphthongs *ie* < *ĕ* in the Latin, and *ue* < *ŏ* in the Latin . . . ; and root-diphthongs like the Latin *au* in *claustrum* and the Germanic *ai* in *laid*."

Alfonso also had some freedom in the use of dieresis and syneresis. However, additional restriction seems to have been felt: a diphthong after the accented syllable of the word might not be split unless the combination came originally from vowels of separate syllables.[12]

Alfonso's freedom in the use of run-on is almost shocking. Certainly no modern poet could be more lavish or more daring in taking advantage of this license. Division of a word between hemistichs or lines is common, as is the division of a phrase between lines or strophes. And not unknown is the division, even, of a word between strophes: "Et querría // T'eu ueer con él, ca sería" (p. 474b. See also 368a, 370a, 371b, 382b, 405a, 405b, 408a, 408b, 410a, 410b, 411a, 411b, etc.).

There arises the question of the application, in the *Cantigas*,[13] of the Ley de Mussafia:[13] measuring a verse length by counting the actual number of syllables present in the line instead of counting, as in the usual Spanish manner, to the last accented syllable and then adding one syllable to the count whether or not a syllable is actually present. The question arises because Alfonso so frequently employs in the same poem oxytones and paroxytones having the same actual number of syllables, as in No. 7, in which the oxytones are accented on the eighth syllable and the paroxytones on the seventh:

> Porende uos contare
> d'un miragre que achei
> que por hũa badessa
> fez a Madre do gran Rei
> ca, per com' eu apres' ei,
> éra-xe sua essa.
> Mas o demo enartar
> a foi, porque emprennar
> s'ouue d'un de Bolonna
> ome, que de recadar
> auía, et de guardar,
> seu feit' e sa besonna.

Since many poems among the *Cantigas* combine oxytones and paroxytones in the Castilian manner[14]—the paroxytonic having one actual syllable more than the oxytonic—, it is to be doubted that Alfonso differed from Berceo and other Castilian poets in the counting of his syllables. Any combination of different line lengths in a poem should probably be considered a phase of Alfonso's fondness for polymetric patterns.

Although Alfonso wrote lines ranging in length from two (No. 276) to seventeen (No. 5) syllables, his favourite was undoubtedly the octosyllable,[15] which has in the *Cantigas* the same characteristics, save for the frequent hiatus, as does the modern Castilian octosyllable: primary accent on the seventh syllable; either oxytonic or paroxytonic ending; movable secondary accent, generally falling in or near the middle of the verse. When one considers the gracefulness and rhythmic flow of this verse in the *Cantigas,* one is not surprised to find that the octosyllable became the "Spanish meter par excellence."

Strangely enough, the lines of next importance in the *Cantigas*—as in later Spanish—are probably the hendecasyllable and the heptasyllable. The pattern of Alfonso's hendecasyllable, naturally, was not that of the Ital-

ianate hendecasyllable that found a permanent place in Castilian when it was introduced in the sixteenth-century by Boscán and Garcilaso. Alfonso's hendecasyllables are frequently oxytonic and they usually have a variable rhythmic pattern, in contrast to the more modern Spanish paroxytones and proparoxytones adhering to specific rhythmic patterns:

> Rosa de beldad e de parecer,
> et Fror d'alegría et de prazer;
> Dona en mui pïadosa seer,
> Sennor en toller coitas et doores.
> Atal Sennor deu' ome muit' amar
> que de todo mal o pode guardar,
> et pode-ll' os peccados perdõar
> que faz no mundo per máos sabores.

(No. 10)

There are a few poems in the collection, however, in which a secondary accent is maintained on a fixed syllable throughout, or nearly throughout, the poem, as, for example, in No. 240, which has an accent consistently on the fourth syllable, and in No. 211, which has an accent on the fifth, or the poem on p. 599, which amounts to a five-plus-six:

> En a loar et dizer o seu ben
> et non cuidar nunca en outra ren;
> ca, pois que peccan per seu máo sen,
> roga por eles a do bon talan.

(No. 240)

> Faz-los muit' apostos porque aiamos
> sabor de sabel-os et os creamos,
> et faz-los fremosos porque queramos
> cobijçar d'auer a ssa companýa.

(No. 211)

> Ben uennas, Mayo, et con alegría;
> porén roguemos á Santa María
> que a seu Fillo rogue todauía
> que él nos guarde d' err' e de folía.

(p. 599)

The twelve-syllable line is frequent. The hemistichs sometimes have a relatively set pattern, as in Nos. 123, 145, 209, 223:

> Ca ela poder á de säude dar
> et uida por sempr' a quen ll'a demandar'
> de coraçon. Et d'esto quer eu contar
> un mui bon mjragre, assí Deus m'aiude.
>
> Por todo o mund' ela miragres faz;
> mais d' ũa sa casa, cabo Monssarraz,
> que chaman Terena, sei ben que assaz
> faz muitos miragres a quen ý recude.

(No. 223)

More often the pattern is varied within a poem. A close resemblance to the *verso de arte mayor* is often achieved (Nos. 79, 307, for example). In fact, I see no difference between the verse form of some of these poems and the fifteenth century *arte mayor* except regularity of syllable count in Alfonso's work. The likeness to some eighteenth century variations of the *arte mayor*[16] is striking:

> Ca ela foi uírgen en a uoontade
> e foi-o na carne con tan gran bondade,
> por que Deus do cëo con sa dëidade
> en ela pres carne que él non auía.
>
> (p. 573)

The nine- and the thirteen-syllable lines, which in Castilian were obliged to wait until the late nineteenth century for full recognition,[17] were by no means excluded from the **Cantigas**. In addition to their use in combinations (see below) they both solo:[18]

> E d'esto uos quero contar
> un gran miragr' e mui fremoso
> que fezo a Uírgen sen par,
> Madre do gran Rei grorïoso,
> por un ome que seu auer
> todo iá despendud' auía
> por fazer ben et máis ualer,
> ca non iá en outra folía.
>
> (No. 25)

> E d' est' un miragre fremoso uos direi
> que auëo na Clusa, com' escrit' achei,
> que fez Santa María; e creo e sei
> que mostrou outros muitos en aquel lugar.
>
> (No. 73)

The shortest line used as the sole verse-length in a poem is the hexasyllable, which appears in both the patterns later found in Castilian particularly during and after the Golden Age: the *serranilla* (No. 192) (having the secondary accent usually on the second syllable),[19] and the ordinary hexasyllable (Nos. 250, 319) (having fluctuating secondary accent):

> E d' esto contado
> uos será per mí
> miragr' e mostrado
> quant' end' aprendí
> fremos' aficado . . .
>
> (No. 192)

> Ca tan muitas graças
> deu, et pïadades,
> a ela seu Fillo,
> que enfermidades
> de muitas maneiras
> toll'; e ben creades
> que a quen a chama
> non é uagarosa.
>
> (No. 319)

The heptasyllable is more frequently than the hexasyllable the sole measure in a poem. It has no fixed inner accent. Its structure corresponds to that of the modern heptasyllable.

Lines of twelve or more syllables are generally divided by caesura, but more frequently than not the position of the caesura, and therefore of the principal inner accent, fluctuates within a poem, as in the following:

fourteen syllable:

> O caualeiro fez todo quanto ll' él mandou,
> e tod' ess' ano sas *Aues-Marías* rezou,
> senon poucos dias que na cima én leixou
> con coita das gentes que ýan con él falar.
>
> (from No. 16)

twelve syllable:

> Os iudeus ouueron d' esto gran pesar,
> et a César se foron ende queixar,
> dizendo que o auer querían dar
> que pola uenda foran én receber.
>
> (from No. 27)

thirteen syllable: (see above). The principle of the movable caesura was one of the main characteristics of the Castilian *verso de arte mayor*.[20] It involves the use of compensation between hemistichs, which was sometimes in Castilian carried over to include compensation between lines.[21] However, some poems do, like the Castilian *cuaderna vía,* divide the line at a fixed place and so we find verses like some of those mentioned above and:

seven-plus-seven:

> E pois foi na ygreia et o altar catou,
> aquela rauia grande toda se ll' amansou;
> e pois dormió un pouco, a Uírgen a fillou
> pela mão et dísse-ll':—Eu te uenno sãar.
>
> (from No. 372)

five-plus-six:

> Ben uennas, Mayo, et con alegría;
> porén roguemos á Santa María
> que a seu Fillo rogue todauía
> que él nos guarde d' err' e de folía.
>
> (p. 599)

eight-plus-six:

> E pois que sonnou aquesto, foi lógo desperto;
> ar uiú-a espert' estando, de que foi ben certo;
> e por saber máis que era, fez sas orações
> que lle dissesse seu nome et dar-ll'-ía dões.
>
> (from No. 85)

Solo verse types not heretofore mentioned are the decasyllable (Nos. 15, 120, 280), the fourteen-syllable (Nos. 16, 23, 64, 95, 117, 119, 136, 137), and the fifteen-syllable (No. 36).

The *zéjel*,[22] one of the principal minor strophes of the fifteenth century *cancionero*[23] poets, was by far Alfonso's favourite strophe for the **Cantigas.** Most of the *cantigas* have, basically, the *zéjel* rime scheme (*aaab, cccb, dddb,* etc.), although the poems of shorter lines usually alternate unrimed lines with the rimed:[24]

> Porend' a Sant' Escritura,
> que non mente nen erra,
> nos conta un gran miragre
> que fez en Engraterra
> a Uírgen Santa María,
> con que judeus an gran guerra
> porque naceu Jesu-Cristo
> d'ela que os reprende.
>
>   (No. 6)

Each strophe is followed by the refrain (*estribillo*), which also serves as introductory strophe (*cabeza*) to the poem. This use of the *cabeza* and *estribillo*[25] was exceedingly popular in the mid-fifteenth century *cancionero* poetry.

Variations of the *zéjel* in the **Cantigas**[26] are numerous and include that in which alternating rime replaces the monorimed sequences, or other rimes are inserted between the original monorimed lines: *abababac, dedededc,* etc. (Nos. 156, 157, 180); that in which use is made of longer monorimed sequences (Nos. 95, 283); that in which there is an insertion of an extra rime between two lines having the constant rime: *aaabab, cccbcb,* etc. (No. 239); that in which there is omission of one line: *aab, ccb,* etc. (No. 250); that using the rime scheme later characteristic of the *octava real: abababcc* (No. 35); several that might be prototypes of the *copla de arte menor* (p. 576); and numerous others.

Among the strophes less popular with Alfonso el Sabio in the **Cantigas,** but which became strophes of primary importance in Castilian are: the *redondilla*—though not octosyllabic in the **Cantigas,** however (Nos. 230, 326, p. 589); the *pareado* (No. 260); the *copla de pie quebrado* (No. 300); monorimed quatrains similar to the *cuaderna vía* strophe but having different lines (p. 599); a form closely resembling the *romancillo* (No. 401); and above all, a *romance*[27] (No. 308). This last is the earliest example of a *romance,* metrically speaking, that I have been able to find. It is divided into nine stanzas of twelve lines each and each stanza is followed by the *cabeza-estribillo.* The rime (including that of the four-line refrain) is *-ar* in the even-numbered lines. Odd-numbered lines are free. The first stanza is:

> E d' est' un muj gran miragre
> uos quer eu ora mostrar
> —De todo mal pod' a Uírgen
> a quen a ama sãar—
> que mostrou en hũa vila

> que Rara sõen chamar,
> —De todo mal pod' a Uírgen
> a quen a ama sãar—
> qu' é en terra de Sosonna,
> et per com oý contar,
> por hũa moller a Uírgen
> que non ouue nen á par.

This poem is exceedingly important because it indicates the presence of the *romance* form in Spain as early as the thirteenth century and strengthens the theory of the learned origin of the *romance.* Góngora,[28] among others, wrote *romances* similarly divided by a refrain at set intervals.

Of almost equal interest in the matter of the *romance* is the poem on pp. 582-584. It is a six-stanza monorimed poem of seven-plus-seven-syllable lines. Apparently a refrain was intended at the end of each stanza. If the lines of this poem were considered as independent lines, the poem would be metrically a perfect *romancillo* of the Golden Age:

> Bẽeita es, María, filla, madr' e criada
> de Deus teu Padr' e Fillo; est' é cousa prouada.
> Bẽeyta foi a ora en que tú gẽerada
> fuste et a ta alma de Deus santiuigada;
> e bẽeyto o dia en que póis fuste nada
> e d' Adam o peccado quita e perdõada;
> e bẽeytos los panos ú fust' enuurullada,
> e outrossí a teta que ouuiste mamada;
> e bẽeyta a agua en que fuste bannada
> e a santa uianda de que fust' auondada;
> e bẽeyta a fala que ouuiste falada.
> e outrossí a letra de que fust' ensinada.

Variations in strophe length and rime scheme are too numerous to list here, but they indicate a genuine Spanish tendency in two important characteristics found in poetry to this day: fondness for inventing new strophic patterns[29] and delight in an abundance of polymetric forms.

One of the surprising phases of Alfonso's polymetric combinations is his frequent wedding of lines—those having an even number of syllables with those having an odd number of syllables—traditionally, until recent years, considered incompatible in Castilian.[30] Also, he was not always satisfied with finding a suitable single mate for one type of line—he created whole families,[31] each of assorted lengths and types. The lines were arranged into definite strophic patterns and each strophe of a poem was an exact replica in pattern of the others. Combinations that were not so long in becoming acceptable to the Castilian ear were also freely employed.[32]

Did Alfonso also use free verse? See p. 584, "Nénbresse-te, Madre."

Rime in the **Cantigas** is pure consonance.[33] Alfonso's rime is almost perfection itself. One may find an occasional flaw in verse length—possibly due to careless copying—but rarely, if ever, in rime or rime pattern. A pattern set in the first strophe of a poem is strictly followed in subsequent strophes. Even the distribution of oxytones and paroxytones[34] is exactly copied from the first strophe in all following strophes in a poem. Some poems are rimed entirely in oxytones, some entirely in paroxytones, but most are rimed in a combination of the two. Oxytones and paroxytones were considered entirely distinct types of rime and their relative position in a strophe was never changed in a poem once the pattern was set. Alfonso's practice in this matter may be related in some way to the French rule for alternation of masculine and feminine rimes. Castilian poets apparently did not make any distinction between the two types—only in the eighteenth century was attention given to the use of the oxytone in a set position, as in the *octava italiana* and its related forms.[35] Although he seems to have favoured the oxytonic, Alfonso used both types of rime in all lengths of verse, as was the custom in Castilian until the Golden Age poets frowned on the presence of oxytonic rime in Italianate verses, although they occasionally permitted proparoxytonic rimes.

Rime schemes,[36] in typical Spanish fashion, varied exceedingly, though most of them seem to have stemmed from the rime scheme of Alfonso's favourite, the *zéjel,* as noted above.

As the work appears in the Academy edition, on which this study is based, numerous poems contain unrimed lines alternating with rimed lines, or, in a few poems, two consecutive unrimed lines alternating with one rimed line. Ribera[37] considers such distribution an error and claims that unrimed lines are merely hemistichs of the complete line, whose end is marked by the rime. In favor of his argument one might add that the unrimed line always *precedes* the rimed line as if dependent upon it for rime (cf. the Castilian *romance*), as a first hemistich of a divided line precedes the second. On the other hand, the fact should be made clear that with few exceptions the lines as distributed in this edition are perfectly counted syllabically. Moreover, unrimed lines of a poem are absolutely consistent in type of ending—that is, they are either all oxytones or all paroxytones.[38] In other words, unrimed lines are, except for rime, completely independent. In fine, if the unrimed lines had not become completely separated from the rimed, they were at least close to the final breaking-off point. The possible independent existence of the unrimed lines seems more obvious when the latter are compared with the numerous first hemistichs of lines having movable caesura. If Alfonso did not consider these unrimed lines independent, why was he so careful to perfect them in most poems, while he used movable caesura consistently in others? Perhaps he was influenced by the mediaeval Latin church hymn, particularly in the octosyllable, which Valmar[39] suggests as the model for similar lines

in Alfonso's work. Perhaps, as modern scholars suggest, music was the controlling factor, though Le Gentil[40] says of Alfonso: ". . . de toute façon, il se préoccupait peu de faire coincider les accents phonétiques de son texte avec les frappés musicaux." Perhaps we are merely witnessing the birth of the short line in Hispanic formal poetry. This problem is hardly different from that concerning the origin of the *romance* meter in Castilian, for which the theory of an original eight-plus-eight line was long accepted.[41]

This marked struggle for a more workable and more graceful grouping of words and phrases, for independence of the hemistich, is quite in keeping with the remarkably modern character of Alfonso's metrics in other respects already discussed: syllable-count, run-on, use of almost all verse lengths later employed in Spanish and preferences almost identical with those of Spanish poets of following centuries, choice of a fertile basic strophe (*zéjel*) and liberal variation of it, interest in other strophic patterns destined to attain primary importance, modern rime. A consideration of such details brings us to the conclusion that a sturdy foundation for Spanish metrics had been laid and the framework constructed before the end of the thirteenth century, and that Alfonso X, who was largely responsible for this early advancement, uncannily sensed lasting qualities in verse technique, kept his work amazingly free from mannerisms, from naïve embellishments and primitive awkwardness in metric structure, and was sufficiently prolific to be able to channel Spanish metric practice into ways both practical and artistic.

Notes

1. "Las cantigas del Rey Sabio," *La ilustración española y americana* (Madrid), XXXIX (1895), 163.

2. *Cantigas de Santa María de Don Alfonso el Sabio,* ed. Real Academia Española (Marqués de Valmar), 2 vols. (Madrid, 1889). In the present study I follow the line division indicated in this edition. However, Julián Ribera's statement (*La música de las Cantigas. Estudio sobre su origen y naturaleza* [Madrid, 1922], pp. 105-106) regarding verse division should certainly be taken into account: ". . . en el estribillo no hay que dividir los versos por el lugar en que aparezcan rimas interiores; y nunca se deben subdividir las estrofas sin rimas. . . . Por no atenerse a estos dos principios, han solido medirse mal los versos de las Cantigas, y, por consecuencia, se ha desconocido su verdadera forma. En la edición de Valmar aparecen versos de doce sílabas divididos como si cada uno fueran dos de 6 + 6; los de 13, en dos de 6 + 7; los de 14, en dos de 7 + 7 y muchas veces 8 + 6, alguna vez 5 + 9, y todos los versos de 16

en dos, 8 + 8, y los de 24, en 8 + 8 + 8, aun cuando no se vean rimas ni asonancias en ninguna cesura, ni aun en las del estribillo." See further discussion of this matter on pages indicated above. Henri Collet y Luis Villalba ("Contribution à l'étude des *Cantigas* d'Alphonse le Savant," *Bulletin Hispanique*, XIII (1911), 273) remarked: ". . . Ensuite, la musique des *cantigas* oblige l'analyste à considérer tout vers décomposable en ses deux hémistiches, ce qui explique assez bien les assonances internes et certaines libertés apparentes de la structure générale."

3. For a detailed account of important sources of Peninsular metrics consult Pierre Le Gentil, *La poésie lyrique espagnole et portugaise à la fin du moyen âge. Deuxième partie: Les formes* (Rennes: Plihon, 1953). This work (cf. index) discusses many aspects of Alfonso's *Cantigas* and their importance in the development of Spanish metrics.

4. Introduced earlier in the century in the *cuaderna vía* by Berceo or his contemporaries.

5. Rhythmic patterns were undoubtedly influenced by the music to which the poems were sung. See Collet y Villalba, op. cit., pp. 274, 288; Ribera, op. cit., Le Gentil, op. cit.

6. Le Gentil, op. cit., p. 313: "Les *genres à forme fixe* que l'on cultive au XVᵉ siècle dans la Péninsule ne sont pas des genres nouveaux. Ils sont l'aboutissement d'une lente évolution, qui s'amorce déjà dans les vénérables *Cantigas* d'Alphonse X."

7. But see quotation from Ribera in n. 2, above.

8. Several aspects of Alfonso's metrics have interested scholars: Francisco Pérez Beyer, in his notes to Nicolás Antonio's *Bibliotheca Hispana Vetus* (Vol. 2, Madrid, 1788), p. 80 calls attention to the numerous metric forms of the *Cantigas* and lists many of them. Federico Hanssen devoted several studies to Alfonso's metrics: "Los versos de las Cantigas de Santa María del rey Alfonso X," *Anales de la Universidad de Chile*, CVIII (1901), 337-373, 501-546; "Metrische Studien zu Alfonso und Berceo," *Deutscher wissenschaftlicher Verein zu Santiago de Chile*, V (1903); "Los alejandrinos de Alfonso X," *Anales de la Universidad de Chile*, CXXXIII (1913), 81-114; "Los endecasílabos de Alfonso X," *Bulletin Hispanique*, XV (1913), 284-299; "Die Jambischen Metra Alfons des X," *Modern Language Notes*, XXIX (1914), 65-68. The Marqués de Valmar, in the Academy edition of the *Cantigas*, includes a chapter (VII) on the "Versificación de las *Cantigas*" (reprinted in his *Estudio*

histórico, crítico y filológico sobre las Cantigas del Rey Don Alfonso el Sabio [Madrid, 1897]). Much light has been shed on the subject by the recent work of Higinio Anglés, *La música de las Cantigas de Santa María* (Barcelona, 1943). Studies by Julián Ribera, Collet and Villalba, and Pierre Le Gentil are mentioned elsewhere in this article.

9. Extant manuscripts of some of Berceo's work, undoubtedly not too reliable, however, show considerable fluctuation in verse length not found to any appreciable extent in the *Cantigas*. Poor copy may be at fault.

10. *Versification of the Cuaderna Vía as Found in Berceo's Vida de Santo Domingo de Silos* (New York, 1905), pp. 54-55.

11. A very few forms, such as the imperfect subjunctive, could be apocopated before a consonant. Compare Alfonso's vowel apocope with Nebrija's "ahogamiento de vocales": "Acontece muchas vezes que cuando alguna palabra acaba en vocal i si se sigue otra que comiença esso mesmo en vocal, echamos fuera la primera dellas. . . . A esta figura . . . nos otros podemosla llamar ahogamiento de vocales . . ." (Antonio de Nebrija, *Gramática castellana,* ed. Pascual Galindo Romeo and Luis Ortiz Muñoz, [Madrid, 1946], Libro II, ch. vii, 47). Nebrija's statement would make one wonder if the early system of apocopation as found in the *Cantigas* was continued even after the development of synaloepha in Spanish poetry.

12. Cf. dieresis in Encina: D. C. Clarke, "On Juan del Encina's *Una arte de poesía castellana,*" *Romance Philology,* VI (1953), 255-256.

13. Adolfo Mussafia, "Sull' antica metrica portoghese," *Sitzungsberichte . . . der Kaiserlichen Akademie der Wissenschaften* (Vienna), X (1896). See also review by Carolina Michaëlis de Vasconcellos in *Literaturblatt für germanische und romanische Philologie* (Leipzig), XVII (1896), 308-318. Le Gentil (op. cit., pp. 342, 343) states: ". . . normalement, troubadours et trouvères évitent de traiter les rimes masculines et les rimes féminines comme si elles étaient interchangeables: on les trouve réparties à des places correspondantes dans chaque strophe, en règle générale. . . .

"Je ne sache pas que la *loi de Mussafia* ait trouvé une application dans les *Cantigas* du Roi Savant. En revanche, à en juger par les transcriptions toutes récentes de Higinio Anglès, les finales graves peuvent s'y substituer aux finales aiguës selon l'équivalence posée plus haut, l'application pouvant d'ailleurs révéler une certaine recherche artistique."

14. Proparoxytones do not appear in rime position in the *Cantigas.*

15. Possibly influenced by Latin hymns—see ch. VII in ed. of *Cantigas* (see note 2, above).

16. Consult D. C. Clarke, "Some Observations on Castilian Versification of the Neoclassic Period," *Hispanic Review,* XX, (1952), 223-239.

17. See Julio Saavedra Molina, *Tres grandes metros: el eneasílabo, el tredecasílabo y el endecasílabo* (Santiago, 1946).

18. Examples are: nine-syllable verse, Nos. 25, 68, 80, 92, 146, 168, 230, 283, p. 567, p. 590; thirteen-syllable (with fluctuating inner accent), Nos. 73, 78, 141 (with accent on the sixth syllable and structure resembling the French Alexandrine), No. 110 (with accent usually on the sixth syllable), No. 93.

19. This form appears in the *Libro de Buen Amor* and also in fifteenth century Castilian poetry.

20. See D. C. Clarke, "El esdrújulo en el hemistiquio de arte mayor," *Revista de Filología Hispánica,* V (1943), 263-275.

21. See Aurelio M. Espinosa, "La compensación entre versos en la versificación española," *Romanic Review,* XVI (1925), 306-329; and "La sinalefa y la compensación en la versificación española," *Romanic Review,* XIX (1928), 289-301 and XX (1929), 44-53.

22. Ribera (op. cit., p. 105) defines the *zéjel* thus: "una estrofilla temática, generalmente un dístico, a la cabeza de cada cantiga, que es el estribillo que canta el coro; luego una estrofa compuesta de tres versos monorrimos, seguidos de un cuarto con rima común, para el cantor solista." He states that the form "nació en Andalucía a fines del siglo IX o principios del X." He also stresses: ". . . hay que tener presente:

"1.° Que la rima es esencial al verso; por tanto, donde no haya rima podrá verse cesura que señale una fracción de verso, pero no verso entero.

"2.° Que las Cantigas pertenecen a la lírica coral (no a la monódica), en la que el estribillo está dedicado al coro y, para facilitar a éste el recuerdo de la letra, suelen ponerse en las cesuras de ese estribillo rimas interiores, que no constituyen característica de verso entero." On the *zéjel* see also: "Discurso del señor don Julián Ribera y Tarragó," *Discursos leídos ante la Real Academia Española en la recepción pública del señor D. Julián Ribera y Tarragó el día 26 de mayo de 1912* (Madrid, 1912); Hans Spanke, "Die Theorie Riberas über Zusammenhänge zwischen frühromanischen Strophenformen und andalusisch-arabischer Lyrik des Mittelalters," *Volkstum und Kultur der Romanen, Sprache, Dichtung, Sitte* (Hamburg), III (1930), 258-278; P. Le Gentil, op. cit., and "A propos de la 'Strophe zéjelesque,'" *Revue des Langues Romanes* (Montpellier), LXX (1949), 119-134; and Isabel Pope, "El villancico polifónico," in *Cancionero de Upsala,* ed. Rafael Mitjana and Jesús Bal y Gay (Mexico, 1944), 15-43.

23. See D. C. Clarke, "Miscellaneous Strophe Forms in the Fifteenth Century Court Lyric," *Hispanic Review,* XVI (1948), 142-156.

24. See Ribera's statement, n. 2, above. See also works by P. Le Gentil, n. 22, above.

25. See Le Gentil, works cited in n. 22, above, and H. R. Lang, "Las formas estróficas y términos métricos del Cancionero de Baena," *Estudios eruditos "in memoriam" de Adolfo Bonilla y San Martín* (Madrid, 1927), I, 485-523.

26. Cf. Ribera, *La música . . . ,* p. 108.

27. Octosyllabic verse in which the even-numbered lines assonate in the same assonance throughout the poem and the odd-numbered lines are left free.

28. Examples in Luis de Góngora y Argote, *Obras completas,* ed. Juan Millé y Giménez and Isabel Millé y Giménez (Madrid, 1943), pp. 72, 106, 118.

29. See D. C. Clarke, "Miscellaneous strophe forms . . ." and "Some observations . . ."

30. In the order in which they appear in the *Cantigas* are the following "incompatible" combinations: 17-14 (No. 5), 8-7 (Nos. 6, 7, 28, 108, 116), 6-5 (No. 32), 8-9 (Nos. 70, 103, 112, 125, 160, 171, 239, p. 591), 11-12 (Nos. 21, 96), 10-11 (No. 109), 11-8 (No. 143), 8-5 (No. 190), 11-4 (No. 390).

31. In the order in which they appear in the *Cantigas* are the following "families" of lines: 8-6-5 (No. 11), 6-5-7 (Nos. 20, 57), 8-5-7 (No. 18), 11-8-7-6 (No. 26), 8-6-7 (No. 33), 11-15-9 (No. 38), 9-7-6 (No. 49), 9-8-6 (No. 72), 8-6-3-9 (No. 81), 7-9-8-6 (No. 89), 10-4-11 (No. 97), 9-5-7 (No. 100), 7-6-12 (No. 134), 12-15-14 (No. 187), 10-11-5-6 (No. 255), 8-7-2 (No. 276), 16-15-6-7 (No. 285), 12-6-11 (No. 317), 7-4-6 (No. 380), 11-13-16 (p. 593).

32. In the order in which they appear in the *Cantigas* they are: 9-7 (Nos. 1, 24, 87, 237, 400), 12-6 (Nos. 9, 79), 8-12 (Nos. 12, 91, p. 601), 11-7 (Nos. 30, 41), 8-6 (Nos. 40, 51, 66, 85, 94, 98, 153, 195, 363, 399, p. 584), 8-4 (Nos. 46, 106, 300, 340, p. 572), 11-13 (No. 52), 14-12 (No. 77), 11-5 (Nos. 139, 279), 9-11 (No. 162).

33. That finding suitable rimes must have cost Alfonso some labor at times is suggested in No. 202, in which the Virgin herself had to be called on to perform a miracle so that a rime-word might be found by one of her devotees: "Esta é como un clérigo en París fazía hũa prosa a Santa María et non podia achar hũa rima, et foi rogar a Santa María que o aiudasse ý, e achó-a logo et a Magestade lle disse: 'Muitas graças.'"

34. Proparoxytones do not appear in rime position.

35. Exceptions are sporadic. See D. C. Clarke, *A Chronological Sketch of Castilian Versification* . . . (Berkeley, 1952), p. 305.

36. See discussion of strophe forms, above.

37. See n. 2, above.

38. Unrimed lines are nearly always paroxytones— only occasionally oxytones.

39. Ch. VII of the introduction to the *Cantigas.*

40. *La poésie lyrique* . . . , p. 414.

41. See D. C. Clarke, "Remarks on the Early *romances* and *cantares,*" *Hispanic Review,* XVII (1949), 89-123.

John Esten Keller (essay date October 1958)

SOURCE: Keller, John Esten. "Daily Living as Presented in the *Canticles* of Alfonso the Learned." *Speculum* 33, no. 4 (October 1958): 484-89.

[*In the following essay, Keller explains that the manuscripts of the* Cantigas *are invaluable for their depiction of everyday life in the Middle Ages.*]

King Alfonso X of Castile, known as "el Sabio" (the Learned) needs no introduction to mediaevalists. His contributions to the writing of history—*Estoria de España* or *Primera Crónica general* and *General Estoria*[1] are well known; the many translations from the Arabic done at his command, such as *Los libros del saber de astronomía,* the *Lapidario,* and the *Libro de ajedrez, dados, y tablas*[2] made themselves felt abroad as well as in Spain during the Middle Ages and even into the Renaissance; his legal code, *Las Siete Partidas,*[3] became one of the most widely distributed geographically of all legal codices, and even helped to shape to some extent the laws of the United States of America. Less known, however, is a work of literary merit, *Las Cántigas de Santa María,*[4] often referred to in English as *The Canticles of Holy Mary.*

Those mediaevalists who have studied the *Canticles*— and their number is small, even when one takes into consideration the Spaniards themselves—know that in the pages of the four extant codices lies some interesting and extremely valuable information. The *Canticles* are unique in a number of ways and offer a variety of materials not found elsewhere. Musicologists consider these songs important to the development of music and regard the illustrations of musicians and their instruments (MS.B.1.2. or E.2 of the Escurial) as one of the best of such illustrations surviving from the Middle Ages. Students of folklore, thematology, and comparative literature recognize the *Canticles* as a rich mine of motifs and themes, some of which appear nowhere else. Historians and sociologists are looking to the songs to solve certain problems of history and for a better understanding of daily life in the thirteenth century. Professor Evelyn S. Proctor of St Hugh's College, Oxford, in discussing the *Canticles*[5] points to a number of historical facts established by mentions made of them in these songs. The history of Spanish art, and to some extent of mediaeval European art, rests upon King Alfonso's songs. Professor José Guerrero Lovillo of the University of Seville has recently published a brief, but enlightening treatise upon the rise of the art of miniatures in Spain[6] in which he traces the influence of French miniature art upon King Alfonso's artists and shows how the Spanish techniques and concepts then blossomed into something quite different from the original French models.

By and large, however, mediaevalists have overlooked what the *Canticles* have to offer, at least insofar as daily living is concerned.

Las Cántigas were composed by King Alfonso X or by his order, to record the miracles of the Blessed Virgin. They were written, it should be remembered, in Galician-Portuguese and not in Castilian. During Alfonso's time, and indeed for many years after, this tongue was considered most apt for the composition of lyric poetry. Castilian, for the most part, was used for narrative poetry and, of course, for works in prose.

King Alfonso liked to refer to himself as "Our Lady's Troubadour." He must have devoted a great deal of time to the *Canticles.* Apparently he had the great collections of miracles of the Virgin examined, for many of his canticles seem to have been taken directly from such collections as those of Vincent of Beauvais or Gautier de Coincy. As the composition of the *Canticles* continued across the years of Alfonso's reign, the standard miracles no longer sufficed and more and more miracles of native vintage were inserted. Evelyn Proctor lists those miracles said to have occurred in the Spanish and Portuguese shrines of the Virgin in Puerto de Santa María, Salas, Villa Sirga, Terena, and Montserrat.

In all there are 353 miracles in the four surviving manuscripts of the *Cántigas.* Any larger number given fails to take into account the fact that certain miracles are duplicated from manuscript to manuscript and even in certain single manuscripts. They are presented in one manuscript in three different media (Escurial MS.T.1.I), that is in verse, in music, and of great importance to those interested in the mediaeval way of life, in remarkable miniatures. This codex contains full-page sets of miniatures, each divided into six panels. In each of the panels can be seen one of the major events in the miracle so illustrated. The animals, people, angels, demons, and saints are depicted, in the opinion of most artists who have seen them, with great fluidity and spontaneity of movement. Their dress and actions reveal a great deal. The backgrounds upon which the characters move, however, are much more revealing as to the life of those times.

Another codex of the **Canticles** (MS. Banco Rari 20, formerly II.I.2.13) of the National Library of Florence also contains miniatures, although its ninety pages of these illustrations fall far short of the 212 found in the above-mentioned tomes of the Escurial. Furthermore, many of the miniatures were never finished, and some are no more than the preliminary sketches. However, this very incompleteness has contributed to knowledge. Students of mediaeval art can see in these unfinished minitaures a great deal about the manner in which the pictures were made. Some scholars, Professor Guerrero Lovillo among these, believe that the miniatures were the work of several artists and that there may have been a kind of production-line procedure in vogue at that time. The Florentine codex, incidentally, contains no music, although space was left for it; however, the canticles of this codex appear in another and larger codex (B.1.2, or E2) with music, and therefore the music for these songs is not actually missing.

The state of preservation of all four codices is remarkable. It is immediately apparent that great care has been accorded them. Indeed, King Alfonso so loved the songs that he made provision for their safekeeping in his last will and testament. Guerrero Lovillo cites the passage in his archaeological study of the **Canticles.**[7] "Likewise we order," reads the testament, "that all the books of the **Songs in Praise of Holy Mary** be in that church where our body will be buried, and that they cause them to be sung on the feasts of Holy Mary. And if that one, who may inherit what is ours according to law and our will, should desire to own these books of the **Songs of Holy Mary,** we command that he give for them good payment to the church from which he removes them so that he may own them with our grace and without sin."

When Philip II had the **Canticles** removed from Seville's cathedral, where Alfonso was buried, he provided good custodians in his library at the Escurial, and to this day the **Canticles** remain in almost perfect preservation.

The **Canticles** contain such a wealth of material concerning daily life in mediaeval Spain that one hardly knows where to begin. Some of the miracles took place in cities, and the miniatures in this case show an amazing amount of detail as to the life in streets and plazas, in churches, in palaces, or in private homes. Professor Guerrero Lovillo's archaeological study contains all 212 miniatures from MS.T.1.I., reproduced in black and white rather than in the beautiful colors of the original. One can, therefore, refer to these reproductions in a discussion of individual canticles.

Canticle IV is very valuable. It shows a school in progress, with the children seated on the floor listening to their teacher reading from a book. After the class the scholars took communion, and all this is clearly seen in the miniature. According to the story of this miracle, a Jewish pupil received the holy wafer from the image of the Virgin on the altar. For this his father, a glass maker, cast him into the furnace used in this trade. The details of the furnace are clearly visible, as are those of the meal of the Jewish family when the child tells his parents about having received communion.

Canticle XXV shows the establishment of a money-changer; XXVIII depicts a city under siege by Moors, with siege machinery, men in armor, and many of the weapons of war; XXXI takes place on a farm, and there is a good deal of detail as to vehicles, mangers, and farm animals; XXXIII is one of several canticles relating storms at sea and offers remarkable pictures of ships; XXXIV tells of a Jew who threw a picture of the Madonna into a latrine, and the arrangements as regards such facilities are clearly shown; gamblers and all that takes place in a tavern appear in LXXII; one sees an artist at work on a scaffold high in the nave of a church in LXXIV.

The two examples of miniatures [discussed] here were chosen almost at random, but they will, it is hoped, give some idea of what the pictures were like. Both come from the manuscript of the Escurial (T.1.I.). In their full color, with gold and silver illumination, these, like all the miniatures, are naturally much more impressive.

Canticle XVIII is one of some twenth-five that contain just beneath the pictures a kind of summary in Castilian of the Galician-Portuguese poem. It is quite possible that King Alfonso planned such a summary for the entire set of miniatures. If such was the case, the plan was not carried out.

This canticle concerns itself with what may be regarded as one of the popular miracles of the Alfonso the Learned, one drawn surely from Spain's own folklore. We read that a woman whose business was the production of silk in the city of Segovia appealed to the Virgin when the silkworms were afflicted with some sort of disease. Each section or panel of the page, it will be noted, bears a kind of caption describing, in Galician-Portuguese, what is taking place. The three bands of miniatures are to be viewed from left to right. In the first panel the woman can be seen kneeling before the altar of the Virgin. In her hand she extends a tray filled with sick worms. The caption ("How the woman prayed to Holy Mary that if she would save the worms she would give her a robe") plainly explains what is taking place. The woman is wearing a characteristic garment, one seen in many of the miniatures, and even on this page in the fourth and fifth panels where other women appear. The altar design is in tile, but the altar cloth, which repeats the design that frames the entire page, bears a fringe at its lower extremity and is therefore a cloth and not ceramic. The chapel is of simple design with little in the way of decoration save the pattern in tile and cloth already mentioned.

In the second panel one can see the woman leaving the chapel. Some time has passed, and according to the caption, she has been remiss as to her promise ("How, being before the altar, she remembered the robe she had promised to Holy Mary, and she was in grief because of it").

Panel three shows us the woman after she has hurried home to begin the promised robe ("How the woman returned home and found that the silkworms were weaving the robe"). In the fourth panel we see her with a number of Segovians whom she has summoned ("How she went out into the street to call the people, and the worms began to weave a second robe"). The woman then took one of the robes, in the fifth panel, and went with it to the chapel ("How the woman gave to the priests that robe which the worms had made").

The final panel ("How King Alfonso took one of the robes for his own chapel") shows the king with some of his courtiers, standing in the church with the robe in his hand. The king's appearance in the miniatures is frequent, and he apparently preferred to have himself depicted as a young man, even though before all the canticles had been written and illustrated, he was past middle age.

Note in the third panel the silkworms upon the frame where they were kept. The mulberry leaves can just be seen in the illustration. In the colors of the original they are clearly visible. The frame with the worms is painted at right angles to the viewer, for the artists wanted the worms to be seen distinctly, and had the frame been shown horizontal to the floor, they could hardly have been seen. This technique, incidentally, is followed in the *Libro de ajedrez, dados y tablas* (*Book of Chess, Dice and Backgammon*), in which all the game boards appear at right angles so that the moves can be easily seen.

A close examination of the silkworms will show how realistically they are portrayed, except, of course, for their size, which is entirely out of proportion to the woman. This magnification was necessary if the worms were to be seen.

Of passing interest, at least, is the image of the Virgin and the Child Jesus. No mention is made in the canticle of its having moved or changed its position in any way. A casual glance will show that the image in the first and second panels (those in the first band at the top) is different from the two pictures of the image in the last two panels. At the top the Virgin holds the Child quite close to her face, a little closer in the second panel than in the first, almost as if she were about to kiss him. In the last two panels the Child is sitting placidly with his arms in his lap, and his head is not pressed to the Virgin's at all. There is even another difference in the last two panels: at the left the Virgin's right hand rests upon her knee and her left hand is on the shoulder of the Child; in the right and final panel her left arm is thrown completely around his shoulders, indeed her hand seems to be covering his left shoulder, while her hand extends to his lap. This phenomenon is repeated many times in the miniatures.

Canticle CVII is another taken from the Spanish scene, and again the city is Segovia. The story survives today in Spain among the folk. A large and poorly executed picture of one of its incidents may be seen painted alfresco on a wall in the cloister of the cathedral of Segovia near the niche labeled as the resting place of Marisaltos, heroine of the miracle.

According to the canticle, Marisaltos, who earned this sobriquet from the leap she made, was a young Jewess who yearned to be a devotee of the Virgin. In the first panel we see her under arrest ("How they seized a Jewess of Segovia who had fallen into error"). She was sentenced by her people in the second panel ("How they led her to be hurled down from a peak that was there"). In the background stands the great Roman aqueduct which, strangely enough, the artists have painted not with Roman arches, but with the well-known horseshoe arch of the Moors. No one, by the way, has explained this mistake, although it has been suggested that Alfonso's artists did not see the aqueduct and drew it from a description, or perhaps saw it and did not draw it until enough time had elapsed to permit the error they made in its depiction.

Panel three shows the Jewess falling toward the earth from the high peak ("How they cast her down and she was not hurt because she called upon Holy Mary"). In panel four she has landed safely ("How she arose unharmed praising Holy Mary greatly"). Above her in the sky the Virgin extends a hand downward. In panel five the Jewess speaks to the Christians ("How she entered the church of Holy Mary and related the miracle to the people"). In the last panel one can see Marisaltos sitting in the font as the priest showers her with baptismal water ("How that Jewess was made Christian").

This page of miniatures is more detailed than the one dealing with the miracle of the silkworms. Much of the city can be seen in the first panel, as well as in the second; windows, the barbican, arched doorways, roofs with characteristic tiles, the aqueduct, the costumes of Marisaltos' compatriots with their exaggerated Semitic features, seen again and again in the miniatures.

[There is a] tree in the background and the flowers on the mountainside, some of which have been identified as flowers that still grow in that region of Spain. The altar, again covered in tile, and the elaborate altar cloth are worthy of note, and quite different from the ones depicted in Canticle XVIII.

After Alfonso's death Spanish miniatures, according to Guerrero Lovillo, passed into decline. Certainly none in the following century, or even in the next, equalled those of the *Canticles.* Indeed, none, insofar as regards the portrayal of daily life, has been found to compare with them. When all the miniatures in the codices of the Escurial and of the National Library of Florence, as well as the codex that presents the musicians and their instruments, have been thoroughly studied, we will have a considerable amplification in our concepts of what the life of man was in the second half of the thirteenth century.

Notes

1. *Primera Crónica general,* ed. Ramón Menéndez Pidal, in *Nueva Biblioteca de Autores Españoles,* v (Madrid, 1906); Alfonso el Sabio, *General Estoria, Primera Parte,* ed. A. G. Solalinde (Madrid, 1930).

2. *Los libros del saber de astronomía,* ed. M. Rico y Sinobas, five volumes (Madrid, 1863-67); *Lapidario del Rey Don Alfonso X,* ed. in facsimile J. Fernández Montaña (Madrid, 1881); *Libro de ajedrez, dados y tablas,* ed. in facsimile J. G. White, *The Spanish Treatise on Chess Play written by order of King Alfonso the Sage in the year 1283,* 2 vols. (London, 1913).

3. *Las Siete Partidas del Rey Don Alfonso el Sabio,* published by the Real Academia de la Historia, 3 vols. (Madrid, 1807).

4. *Cántigas de Santa Maria,* ed. Leopoldo Augusto de Cueto, Marqués de Valmar, 2 vols. (Madrid, 1889).

5. *Alfonso X of Castile, Patron of Literature and Learning* (Oxford, 1951), pp. 24-46.

6. *Miniatura gótica castellana siglos XIII y XIV* (Madrid, 1956).

7. *Las Cántigas, estudio arqueológico de sus miniaturas* (Madrid, 1949), p. 14.

John Esten Keller (essay date 1967)

SOURCE: Keller, John Esten "The *Cantigas de Santa María.*" In *Alfonso X, El Sabio,* pp. 64-95. New York, N.Y.: Twayne Publishers, Inc., 1967.

[In the following excerpt, Keller provides an overview of the Cantigas, *including sections on language, sources, and versification.]*

I ALFONSO'S AFFINITY WITH THE *CANTIGAS*

Superlatives begin to come to mind when the **Cantigas de Santa María, Canticles of Holy Mary,** are mentioned. And superlatives mount when one reflects that these *cantigas,* or canticles, to use an English equivalent, are the apogee of perfection in three distinct artistic media. In the area of pictorial art they are unsurpassed in the excellence of their marvellously colored miniatures and illuminations; unmatched in variety and beauty in their music; and unequaled in their literary and thematic content and manner of presentation. It is reasonable to believe that Alfonso expended more time and money upon the production of the **Cantigas de Santa María** than upon any of his other contributions. The **Cantigas** have been called the most clear, accurate, and faithful witness of thirteenth-century life and belief; the most noble attempt to teach a rough society the virtues of dependence upon divine grace; one of the richest of sources of medieval folklore—folk music, folk motif, folkways and even to some extent, folk speech; and an important aid to the unravelling of Spanish history. Nor would the list of enthusiastic plaudits end here if there were space or need to expand it.

In the production of the **Cantigas de Santa María,** Alfonso was again following an ancient and venerable tradition, this time the gathering of miracles of the Blessed Virgin. Collections in Latin had appeared earlier in most of Europe, and collections in the vernaculars had become common by the twelfth and thirteenth centuries. In Spain, for example, the contemporary *Liber Mariae* of Gil de Zamora had appeared in Latin, and the already mentioned *Milagros de Nuestra Señora* of

Berceo in Spanish. Like Berceo, by the way, Alfonso X represented living and practicing devotion to the Virgin. When the king rode into battle, her image went with him attached to his saddle; he bestowed goodly sums upon various of her shrines, and even went so far as to champion her miracles over those of St. James himself, Spain's patron saint.[1] Alfonso, like Berceo, dubbed himself the Virgin's troubadour. He wrote (and I translate):

> And I desire to sing the praise
> of the Virgin, the Mother of Our Lord,
> Holy Mary, who is the best
> thing that He created; and therefore I
> wish to be evermore her troubadour,
> and I beseech her to desire me for her
>
> Troubadour and to wish my singing
> to receive, because in it I wish to reveal
> the miracles which she wrought;
>
> (Prologue B, vv. 15-23)

> (*E o que quero é dezir loor*
> *da Virgen, Madre de nostro Sennor,*
> *Santa Maria, que ést' a mellor*
> *cousa que el faz; et por aquest' eu*
> *quero seer oy mais seu trobador,*
> *e rogo-lle que me queira por seu*
>
> *Trobador e que queira meu trobar*
> *reçeber, ca per el quer' eu mostrar*
> *dos miragres que ela fez; . . .*)[2]

It would be interesting to know just when Alfonso began his *Cantigas,* or the planning for their assembling. In 1257, which many scholars believe is the date of completion of the first one hundred of the miracles, the King was in his thirty-sixty year and in the fifth of his reign. The work of gathering, editing, and actually setting down in writing may have started much earlier. We do know, at least, when this work ended, for the entire corpus of over four hundred *cantigas,* representing the definitive edition, was finished either in, or just prior to, 1279.[3] If one is willing to accept the beginning date of 1257, Alfonso by 1279, had been intermittently or steadily at work on the *Cantigas* for nearly a quarter of a century. Probably he started before 1257, for the very mechanics of producing one hundred of these canticles, replete with musical notation, illustrative miniatures, and carefully penned in the excellent and demanding calligraphy of the age undoubtedly required many months, and even years. It is logical to think that Alfonso started on this masterpiece before 1257 for other reasons. One of these is the close personal association between the content of some of the songs and his own life. Some twenty-eight refer either to the King himself, to members of his family, or to people who lived at his court. And of these, several treat happenings which took place when he was very young or even before he was born. One such miracle (222) tells that his father,

Ferdinand, while still a small boy, was cured by the Virgin while King Alfonso VIII, Ferdinand's father, was warring in Gascony against England's Henry II. Another (256) is told about the miraculous healing of Alfonso's mother, Queen Beatriz, when Alfonso was six years old. Is it not easy to conjecture that Alfonso might have listened to these miracles at his mother's or his father's knee, or have had them from the mouths of relatives or servitors? They are not found in the chroniclers or elsewhere and would be lost but for the *Cantigas.* Certainly they are reminiscent of the kind of anecdotes in family repertories. It is not at all unlikely, then, in fact it is quite probable, that Alfonso may have been collecting miracles of the Virgin long before the first one hundred appeared in a volume of the *Cantigas de Santa María.*

In the past, possibly owing to that scholarly reticence which leads the expert to avoid making statements as to the authorship of medieval works, some writers hesitated to attribute the composition of the *Cantigas* to the King's personal creativity. Of late, and after careful consideration of content and manner of presentation, medievalists are admitting that he possibly, and even probably, was the author and composer, of many, if not all. *Trobar,* "the composing of lyrical pieces in verse according to the art of the troubadours," was regarded in Alfonso's time as the highest expression of literary genius. Most gentlemen and nobles wrote songs, not all with poetic excellence, but at least with true zeal. Recall the two thousand songs mentioned in Chapter 3, and the fact that these are the production of two hundred definitely known and named poets. Recall, too, that this kind of gentlemanly activity continued into the fourteenth and fifteenth centuries, resulting in even vaster *cancioneros* which also contain the personal creations of kings and princes. Alfonso, known and esteemed for his erudition, would not have avoided the composition of songs, and it is safe to believe that he composed a considerable portion of the *Cantigas de Santa María.* Moreover, in the Prologue to the *Cantigas,* written in the first person, as are some of the *cantigas* themselves, we read:

> Since the writing of verse is an art
> which entails deep understanding,
> a troubadour, therefore,
> should be endowed with this virtue
> and enough powers of reason
> to be able to understand
> that which he wishes to say
> and then come to express it well,
> for good songs are made this way.
>
> While my own poems are perhaps ill-planned
> in some points, still I propose to expand
> upon a thing or two I do know, and,
> through powers such as I have been conferred,

may God, the Source of Knowledge, stand
me in good stead (oh poet, hear his word).

(*Porque trobar é cousa en que jaz
entendimento, por en queno faz
á-o d'aver e de razon assaz,
per que entenda e sábia dizer
e que entend' e de dizer lle praz,
ca ben trobar assi s'á de ffazer.*

*E macar eu estas duas non ey
com'eu querria, pero provarei
a mostrar ende un pouca que sei,
confiand' en Deus, ond' o saber ven,
ca per ele tenno que poderei
mostrar do que quero algũa ren.*)

(*Prologo*, vv. 1-12)

These lines show not only that Alfonso wrote them in
the first person, but reveal also the mental equipment
and skills required for *ben trobar*, "excellent troubadour
style."

Perhaps the entire vast body of the **Cantigas de Santa
María** may be too much to attribute to one busy king,
and perhaps it is too varied in meters; perhaps, too, the
fact that some of the miracles about Alfonso are told in
the third person could lead to the belief that he was not
their composer; but the number which are written in the
first person should not be denied his authorship. Could
some professional poet in the King's service have
described Alfonso's own emotions and actions so effectively in the first person? In the Learned King's case
this hypothesis can hardly be accepted. Besides, there is
still more evidence of Alfonso's personal hand in the
Cantigas, for he is portrayed again and again in the
miniatures. Now medievalists know that the appearance
of a king's picture in the preface of a book he sponsored
is a common occurrence; but it is uncommon, and even
rare, for a monarch to be portrayed with frequency,
caught almost photographically, as it were, by the artists who depict him engaged in a variety of activities.
In number 142, for instance, we see the king mounted
on a mule watching his hawks bring down herons. In
number 169 the King tells as a first-person account the
story of a church in the Moorish quarter of Murcia, the
city which he conquered before his coronation. The
miniatures reveal him as a prince receiving the Moorish
delegation, and later as a king. A few lines of this *cantiga* will suffice to show the personal tone of the story
itself:

And of that I will relate a great miracle, which I saw
after God gave me Murcia, and which I heard
many Moors tell who dwelt there previously
and held the land due to our sinning, . . .

(*E daquest' un miragre direi grande, que vi
des que mi Deus deu Murça, e oý outrossi*

*dezir a muitos mouros que moravan ant' y
e tīian a terra por nossa pecadilla, . . .*)

(*cantiga* 169, vv. 8-11)

It is as though Alfonso were writing a report about his
rule in Murcia. Nothing could be more personal.

This intimacy of the King's life in the **Cantigas** is one
that has no parallel in other collections of miracles. The
importance of such a presentation is quickly apparent.
It is responsible for unexpected details and bits of
information which historians have found invaluable in
dating events of Alfonso's reign. The noted scholar,
Evelyn Proctor, who has studied the **Cantigas** from the
historian's point of view, makes this quite clear. In
discussing number 235, which relates a miracle that
saved Alfonso's life when he lay dying in Valladolid,
she writes: ". . . it might more justly be described as
the king's complaint of the treachery of his nobles and
his own difficulties, disappointments, and illnesses, for
it is only after a long catalogue of woes and in the
seventeenth stanza that we reach the king's illness at
Valladolid. Every incident given can be identified and
dated, and the poem provides an historical epitome
from 1272 to 1278."[4]

The intimacy is responsible likewise for what must
have been a strong bond of rapport between the King
and various elements among his people—within the
middle and lower classes, and the nobility. Since the
miracles and hymns were probably sung in the churches,
as well as in the royal chapel, at court, and possibly in
public places during festivals, many common people
must have heard them and, thus, these songs would
have served to bring the King closer to the commoner.
And the fact that even the lowliest peasant might be the
protagonist in a *cantiga* added to this bond of rapport.

Alfonso, then, was deeply involved in the **Cantigas de
Santa María** during most of the period of his reign. He
seems to have composed a good many of the songs, or,
as some believe, all of them. He thought highly enough
of these miracles to have a volume of them prepared
and presented to his cousin, Louis IX of France. The
possibility of Alfonso's direct participation should not
be overlooked because it makes the **Cantigas de Santa
María** his most intimate and truly creative literary
production.

II The Manuscripts of the *Cantigas*

According to the definitive edition of Walter Mettmann,
there are four hundred and twenty-seven *cantigas* written to honor the Blessed Virgin, or to relate the miracles
she performed for her devotees. Of these, however,
only two hundred and seventy-three are actual miracle
stories and, therefore, real brief narratives. The rest are

Cantigas de loor, "songs of praise," which sing her glories, laud her virtues, or stress her beneficence. They are distributed throughout the text at more or less regular intervals. The first appears directly after the King's Prologue, which is also, as we have seen, a piece of lyric verse. Then each tenth *cantiga* throughout the repertoire of miracles is a *cantiga de loor.* Furthermore, in the last one hundred *cantigas* only numbers 404, 405, 407, and 408 are miracles, for the rest are simply hymns to Our Lady and could better be relegated to a history of hymnology and song. So much for the actual number and classification of the *cantigas.*

Four manuscripts[5] of the **Cantigas de Santa María** have survived and may be described as follows: Codex j.b.2 of the Escorial, the largest of all and the one which contains forty miniatures revealing musicians playing their instruments; Escorial T.j.I, the most lavishly illustrated with full-page miniatures numbering over one hundred; Biblioteca Nacional 10069, more often referred to as *To,* signifying Toledo, since it originally belonged to the Cathedral Library at Toledo; and MS Banco Rari of the Biblioteca Nazionale of Florence, formerly known as II. I. 213, also illustrated with beautiful miniatures. A very complete description of these can be found in the edition of Walter Mettmann, cited previously. This edition, incidently, supersedes that of the Marqués de Valmar, published in 1889 with a lengthy and very valuable study by Mussafia.[6]

III THE LANGUAGE OF THE *CANTIGAS*

The particular variety, or rather the level, of Galician-Portuguese found in the **Cantigas de Santa María,** follows that erudite development designed by the troubadours as the vehicle of their professional versifying. As mentioned earlier, the troubadours of Spain, whether native speakers of Galician or Spaniards from some other area, employed for their lyrics a dialect of Portuguese spoken in Galicia. So had the troubadours of France preferred the language of Provence. Castilian, Léonese, and Aragonese poets considered it preferable to write in Galician, in their opinion a softer and more apt language for lyric verse. This Galician was not the highly flexible and mature vehicle that Portuguese would become in later ages, but it was, owing to its contacts with Provençal and Catalan, a language of cultural status. It was, then, a Galician refined by poets into a literary medium; it contained the vocabulary of courtly love and, since it was modeled upon the poetry of the Provençal singers, it had turns of phrase and even some syntactical elements not truly native. In spite of this artificiality of phrase and word, however, the language of the Spanish troubadours retained something of its own popular flavor and could be understood by the people to whom the songs were sung, whether they were Galicians or not. It was a Portuguese dialect, admittedly, and people who knew any dialect of Portuguese could understand it. And, since Spaniards were able to understand Portuguese, the language of Old Galicia offered no linguistic problems of moment. Old Spanish and Old Portuguese, even Old Galician, were all in the same stage of development, and contained many similarities not found in their counterparts today. All in all, Galician was a very apt vehicle for troubadour poetry in the Iberian Peninsula. Spanish and Portuguese lyric poets would not relinquish it in favor of pure Portuguese or Spanish for some two hundred years past Alfonso's time.

In employing Galician in the **Cantigas de Santa María,** Alfonso may have actually created a new genre represented solely by this single literary work. For lack of a better name, Martín de Riquer has called it the *canción sacra gallego-portuguesa,* "sacred Galician-Portuguese song."[7] Only the **Cantigas de Santa María** sing in sacred verse the glories of the Virgin and of divine love; the other *cancioneros* offer material of a different tone, indeed, and their very philosophy is far removed from Alfonso's in his **Cantigas.** Three varieties of troubadour verse are usually listed. In the *cantiga de amor* the poet sings of his profane love for a lady who has stolen his heart and who has literally enslaved him. Such poetry is an adaptation of the Provençal *cansó,* and like its model it is conventional, rhetorical, and burdened by the details of the lover's vassalage to his haughty lady whom he addresses as *mia senhor.* The second variety of Galician troubadour poetry is known as the *cantiga de amigo.* In this a lovelorn lass sighs for her absent *amigo,* "lover." Sometimes he is present, and she beseeches him to reciprocate her amorous passion. This is a more primitive kind of verse and is, therefore, even in the conventional versification of the troubadours, fresher and more delightful. After all, it sprang from pure native folksong, recognized by experts as something common to all peoples close to the soil, and is represented in those *jarchas* of the Mozarabs in Andalusia . . . . The last of the varieties of the troubadour's poetry is the *cantiga de escarnio* or *de mal dizir,* "song of mockery" or "libel," in which the poet attacks institutions he dislikes or slanders his enemies, both male and female, in terms often so obscene that medieval legislative action was taken against those who offended too greatly in their verses.[8]

Only the Learned King, it seems, used Galician-Portuguese for sacred song; but even though he did so, he strayed far from the rules of formal troubadour poetry, at least in some of his *cantigas.* The very content of the **Cantigas de Santa María** demanded this. The miracles, directed toward all classes of society, even toward members of the lowest levels, are simple and naïve accounts of the Virgin's wonder-working powers. Such an approach was the best, if the songs were to be relished and understood by untutored folk. A large proportion of troubadouresque formality, rhetoric, and conventionality had to be omitted. The words of a peasant woman as she beseeches the Virgin to remove the head of barley that has penetrated her child's body could hardly be set into the formal phraseology of the troubadours (*cantiga* 315). And how could conventional verse become the vehicle of a miracle relating the death of a dragon whose blood, spewed out upon its killer, infects him with leprosy (189)? No, Alfonso did not always abide by the poetic models he chose as the medium for his miracles, although in the case of the *cantigas de loor,* he was more successful in following such rules. When he used Galician-Portuguese, he was simply employing the only poetic medium then considered worthy of literary art. Those who had, a century earlier, written saints' lives had employed the meter of the *mester de juglaría* of the epic poets because that was the medium then esteemed as the best for literature.

The newness of the genre Alfonso created lay, not in its adherence to the conventions and forms of the Galician-Portuguese troubadours, although adherence was there; nor did this newness lie in the popular and folkloristic content of the *Cantigas,* for miracles in Spain had for decades, even centuries, been the subject of popular poetic treatment. It was rather a strange, new, and surprisingly successful blending of erudite forms and meters with popular, pious, intimate, and informal subject matter. If one could visualize a folk ballad set into the poetic measures of an Italian sonnet, he might draw a reasonably well-defined conception of what Alfonso had achieved in the *Cantigas de Santa María.*

IV The Subject Matter and the Sources of the *Cantigas*

Classifications of the subject matter of the *Cantigas* have been prepared by scholars but none is definitive, and few are even adequate, for the vastness and the variety of the miracles is too great to permit completeness in either of these areas of investigation. Calcott and Bell, the Marqués de Valmar, and Mussafia have attempted to classify the themes and motifs, the last to a greater extent. So has Valbuena Prat, although in a much more general way.[9] The present writer has nearly finished the rather onerous task of preparing a motif-index of the *cantigas* made in accordance with the world-standard index of Stith Thompson. I have found that from the viewpoint of thematology classification may simply not be feasible or perhaps even possible.

The same lack of completeness can be seen in source studies of these miracles. Some sources, it is true, can be identified and even proved; for example, the already alluded to miracles concerning the life of Alfonso, members of his family or his friends. Others can be no

more than surmised; many simply cannot be traced; this is especially true of scores of motifs which are derived from the folklore of the people. The subject matter of the *Cantigas* is not limited to Iberia. Alfonso's Suabian mother brought with her when she came to Spain to marry King Ferdinand a Germanic retinue made up most probably of noblemen and ladies in waiting, cooks, butlers, chamberlains, dressmakers, physicians, poets, and artists. Such people would have brought with them, along with their language and culture, a store of popular German lore and folkways among which would surely have been found accounts of miracles. One can hazard the guess that at least one of the *Cantigas de Santa María* came to Alfonso from some member of this transplanted German court, or perhaps Queen Beatriz herself related it to her son. *Cantiga* 74 is entitled *Como Santa Maria guareceu o pintor que o demo quisera matar porque o pintava feo* ("How Holy Mary protected the painter whom the demon wished to slay because he painted him ugly"). It might well have originated in Germany from a proverb well-known to this day in that country, but not found in the repositories of Spanish maxims. This German proverb translated into English is, "Never paint the devil on a wall," a thing that the painter in the *cantiga* did with frightful results. It is likely that in Germany the proverb gave rise to the miracle, or that, in reverse, the miracle might have given rise to the proverb, for either could have been the parent of the other. It is quite possible, then, that the miracle came from Germany fully developed, and that it quickly made its way into the growing Alfonsine repertoire. If so, a bit of Germanic lore helped to shape one of the *Cantigas.*

Some miracles of a nonliterary category might well have come from other foreign languages, for Alfonso's court swarmed with writers and artistic people from far and wide—France, England, Italy, Portugal, Byzantium, Moorish Spain, and Islamic lands beyond the sea. Delegations came occasionally from as far off as Egypt. One such mission deserves special mention, as it is definitely connected with the *Cantigas.* The *Crónica de los Reyes de Castilla,* "Chronicle of the Kings of Castile," Chapter IX, reports that each year on the anniversary of the death of King Ferdinand, delegations came to Seville to honor the King.[10] One was sent by the Sultan of Egypt, Alvandexaver. "And they brought presents to this King Don Alfonso of many fabrics, priceless, and of diverse natures, and many jewels, rich and exotic. And they brought likewise an elephant and an animal which they call *azorafa,* and an ass which was striped, for it had a white band and then another one black, and they brought other beasts and animals of many kinds." A delightful parallel to this account in the chronicle is to be found in the *Cantigas de Santa María,* for in one of the songs of praise (29) we see the strange beasts kneeling to Our Lady. The *azorafa* is, as might be expected, a giraffe, which can be seen in the miniature so correctly depicted that there can be no doubt that the artist used a living animal as a model. The elephant is also there, and the "ass with stripes," as well as a camel and what may be a gnu. Visible also is either a rhinoceros or hippopotamus, half-concealed behind the other mammals. Sundry exotic birds complete the group of worshipful creatures, and among these are an Egyptian ibis and flamingoes.

Incidentally, the aforementioned chronicle states on the same page that the king of Granada also sent delegations to honor the Learned King's father, offering additional proof of the close ties existing between Moslem and Christian Spain. The influence of Moorish story upon the *Cantigas* can only be surmised, but it can be stated with certainty that many *cantigas* described Moslem activities in Alfonso's time and in the centuries before him.

A few of the definitely known sources were the richly illustrated *Miracles de la Sainte Vierge*, "Miracles of the Holy Virgin," of Gautier de Coincy; the *Speculum Historiale*, "Mirror of History," of Vincent de Beauvais, a copy of which, according to the chronicles, was actually sent to Alfonso by the king of France, for Alfonso mentions this fact in his last will and testament; the *De Miraculis Beatae Mariae Virginis*, "Of the Miracles of the Blessed Virgin Mary," of unknown authorship; the *Liber Mariae*, "Book of Mary," of Gil de Zamora, who seems to have assisted the Learned King in the writing of some of his histories: the *De Miraculis Beatae Virginis Mariae* of Walter of Cluny; the *Scala Coeli*, "Ladder of Heaven," of Johannes Gobius; the *Liber Miraculis Sanctae Mariae Dei Genetrix*, "The Book of St. Mary, the Mother of God," possibly composed by Patho; the *Mariale Magnum*, "Greatness of Mary," attributed without authority to St. Isidore of Seville; and most probably the *Milagros de Nuestra Señora* of Gonzalo de Berceo.

The Marqués de Valmar suggests many other themes of foreign origin, as does Mussafia.[11] I have mentioned in several articles Alfonso's debt to various collections of miracles and to folklore.[12] I might repeat here a few of the more pertinent of these observations from an article in *The Southern Folklore Quarterly*. Some of the miracles resemble stories from Holy Scripture, although they have been reworked and greatly altered, with new characters and new settings. *Cantiga* 241 is an excellent example. A young man, during the festivities of his wedding day, lost his balance and fell several stories to the street. Mortally wounded, he was carried to the shrine of the Virgin where he was completely and instantaneously healed. The tale parallels that of Eutychus in Acts 20: 9-12; Eutychus fell from a window and was resuscitated by St. Paul. Another of this type is

cantiga 143 in which a merchant is bound hand and foot and cast overboard by sailors who dislike him. They tie the other end of the rope to the vessel's side so as to be able to retrieve the body and report the man's death as an accidental drowning. Three days later they haul the body aboard, only to find that he has not died. The Virgin had caused a bubble to form around him. Similarities between this story and that of Jonah are obvious.

In the same article I pointed out that earlier pieces of medieval literature furnished Alfonso with material for his *Cantigas*. Number 98 is the story of an invisible force which prevented the entry of a sinful woman into the church at Valverde, a tale quite reminiscent of one of the events in the life of St. Mary the Egyptian . . . . And there is the *cantiga* (103) about a monk who listened to the song of a little bird while three centuries passed.

Now all the *cantigas* discussed thus far, save that of the exotic animals, have appeared in some collection of miracles either in Latin, in a vernacular tongue, or in the Bible. Others, however, must be attributed to folklore in Spain and these, of course, are not to be found in other collections of the Virgin's miracles. Take, for example, the story of Marisaltos, Jewess of Segovia, as treated in *cantiga* 107. Condemned to death by her people because she has become a Christian convert, she is cast down from a cliff, but is saved by the Virgin who brings her safely to earth. This miracle is still told in Spain and Spanish America. The miniature depicts these events, as does a fresco painting on the wall of the cloister of Segovia's Cathedral. This is an instance, then, of a local folk legend.

Other *cantigas* are very much a part of local lore, too. Such erudite collectors as Gautier de Coincy used no such miracles, but Alfonso, who realized the rapport to be had with his people by including miraculous occurrences which many of them had witnessed or heard about, added stories of this variety. One tells of a woman who believed that a serpent had entered her body and was alive in her stomach. The Virgin at the Shrine of Our Lady of Porto told her to go to Cadiz and pray at the Cathedral, which she straightway did. After the prayer had been said, the woman vomited up a red snake. I have heard a similar folk tale in Kentucky from a mountain woman minus, of course, the Virgin's aid and the Spanish setting. Number 18 sings of some remarkable silkworms in Segovia which wove two lengths of silk cloth to be used in robes for the Virgin's image. A furrier (49) so as to leave his hands free to work, placed a needle between his lips and teeth. It became lodged in his throat and he was in agony for days until he dragged himself to the shrine of Our Lady to pray and be cured. Many more miracles of folkloristic background occur in the **Cantigas,** but few have been studied. When more of the autochthonous aspects of these songs have been examined, our knowledge of the Spanish Middle Ages in the areas of belief, tale, folk medicine, folk music and folk arts and crafts will be vastly broadened.

A few words, too, should be devoted to the contribution of the **Cantigas** to our understanding of daily life in the thirteenth century.[13] Here, as in the case of folkloristic elements in the **Cantigas,** there is great wealth of detail. The scenes of many of the miracles were cities and towns and, therefore, the miniatures give a remarkable picture of plazas, streets, alleys, churches, palaces, monasteries and nunneries, private homes, the houses of Jews and Moors, in short, of whole cross-sections of city life. In *cantiga* 4 one sees something rare and quite instructive, for the first panel reveals a schoolroom with a monk, who is the teacher, and students, all of whom are boys. They sit on the floor while the pedagogue explicates a book. Later the pupils go to the chapel for Holy Communion. One, who is a Jew, does not participate, but instead stands before the image of the Virgin while his companions receive the Sacrament. During this time the image of Our Lady extends her hand from the altar and gives the young Jew a holy wafer. At home—and here again we are privileged to see an unusual sight—the Jewish father, a glassmaker, rebukes his son and casts the lad into the heated glass-furnace from which he is saved by the Virgin. This picture of a Jewish home and glass factory is one of great value. The event, by the way, took place, according to the *cantiga,* in Canterbury.

Cantiga 25 opens to the eye of the reader the establishment of a moneychanger; 28 shows a city under attack by the Moors with siege machinery, men in armor and many of the weapons of war; 34 is the story of a Jew who threw a portrait of Our Lady into a latrine, thereby depicting just what these facilities were like; number 13 gives all the details of a medieval execution by hanging from a tree, while in number 175 a youth hangs from a man-made gallows; something closely resembling a baseball game appears in 42; and a thirteenth-century variety of bullfight can be studied in 144.

Rural scenes are quite plentiful as are seascapes, with many varieties of civilian and military crafts. Pilgrimages are depicted, dances, funerals, cavalry battles, infantry attacks, Moorish incursions—a mighty panorama of life as it was lived by medieval man.

One last matter should be mentioned in connection with the **Cantigas,** and this is their subjectivity, their deep consciousness of environment and of people, and especially of the latter's reaction to environment. Américo Castro, one of the greatest and most controver-

sial Spanish scholars of modern times, believes that this subjectivity and personal reaction to physical surroundings is a product of the quasioriental, quasioccidental culture of Spain, and that without the Moors the **Cantigas** (and for that matter many other monuments of Spanish literature), could not have been written. To support this phenomenon in the **Cantigas** he compares the objective treatment of the *cantiga* used by Gautier de Coincy with the "Hispano-Islamic" handling of it in the **Cantigas de Santa María.** His point is well taken, although many of the most outstanding scholars today will have none of Castro's suggestions.[14]

When all the miniatures in the three codices containing them have been studied in their entirety, scholars will be able to understand more clearly the way of life and the thought of their medieval ancestors.

V VERSIFICATION OF THE *CANTIGAS*

In turning to the versification of the **Cantigas,** one should recall two important facts. They are true songs with full musical notation and were certainly intended to be sung in the Spanish churches, probably at court and at gatherings of the aristocracy, and possibly in the public square or in the country—wherever celebrations of the feasts of the Virgin were held. The second fact is this: Alfonso used as the basis for his *cantigas* an erudite poetry devised by the troubadours of Galicia who had modeled their own art upon the poetic conventions of Provence. We have mentioned that in the miracles, which are narratives in verse, the king and his poets wandered somewhat far afield from the troubadouresque rules and patterns, but that in the *cantigas de loor,* or songs of praise, they made greater efforts to conform to poetic regulations. In these hymns, then, the King followed the troubadour tradition in which the poet sang the adoration and high praises of the earthly lady who possessed his heart and soul. This poetry of the troubadours in Provence and France and in Portugal, Galicia and the rest of Spain, reflected the philosophy of courtly love which in the twelfth, and to a smaller degree in the thirteenth century, had been in great vogue in much of Western Europe, and which would linger on in the Iberian Peninsula, to remain in popularity until well into the fifteenth century.

Alfonso, instead of lauding the physical, amatory, and other charms of a mortal woman, sang in his sacred *cantigas* the praises of Our Lady, and in a spirit of gratitude, deep respect and spiritual love, related her miracles. He regarded her, and not some earthly lady, in his songs as the exemplification of the perfect qualities of womanhood. If an amorous tone occasionally obtains in his hymns and miracles, it is but a reflection of the troubadour school of poetry under whose rules he wrote.

It is to Dorothy Clotelle Clarke of the University of California that we owe a truly masterly article on the versification of the *Cantigas* of Alfonso.[15] She writes of the wide range of meters found in these songs and of the remarkable fact that in them one finds possible sources for all Spanish meters. "That is to say that Alfonso's ability," she writes, "to select, at almost the very dawn of Peninsular formal poetry, lasting qualities in so intricate an art as that of versification is indeed admirable. All presently known verse forms employed in Castilian before the Golden Age are found in the *Cantigas*. And there is in the collection a foreshadowing, as Menendez y Pelayo indicates, of the Golden Age and modern times. Alfonso's system of verse measure—syllable count—was the one followed almost exactly in subsequent Castilian poetry. Alfonso's rhythmic patterns have lived to the present time and his strophe forms could have been prototypes for a number of basic Castilian strophes. His great fondness for polymetric combinations is of particular significance." An equal amount of originality in musical notation and melody, closely connected, of course, to versification will be examined briefly in the section of this chapter devoted to the music of the *Cantigas*.

The most frequently used poetic form in the *Cantigas* was the *zéjel*,[16] of Arabic origin according to some or, as others believe, of Mozarab precedence, and borrowed by the Arabic poets of Andalusia from their Christian subjects. But the form is known to have appeared also in Hebrew and Christian liturgies, and parallels exist in the Franco-Provençal *virelai*, the Catalonian *goig* and the Castilian *villancico*. In a typical *zéjel* the thematic refrain, called in Spanish the *estribillo*, is repeated before each strophe. In the *Cantigas* the *estribillo* may contain two or more verses, for greater variety in this aspect is permitted. Even the lines themselves vary greatly from two syllables (*cantiga* 276) to seventeen (*cantiga* 5), but the favorite was the octosyllable, perhaps the most popular of all even in Spain today. Gilbert Chase mentions two *estribillos* that were very much used. "Many of them consist of four-line stanzas (rhyme scheme, BBBA), with a refrain in the form of a rhymed couplet (AA) coming before and after each stanza. Others have a four-line refrain (ABAB) and a six-line stanza with alternating rhyme."[17]

A typical example of a long-lined *estribillo* (*cantiga* 5) must be seen in the original language, if it is to be properly understood and its metrification savored:

> *Quena coitas deste mundo ben quiser soffrer,*
> *Santa Maria deve sempr' antesi põer.*

> (Who wishes to endure the cares of this world
> ought ever to place Holy Mary before him.)

And a shorter *estribillo* is that found in *cantiga* 11:

> *Macar ome per folia*
>   *aginna caer*

>   *pod' en pecado*
> *do ben de Santa Maria*
>   *non dev' a seer*
>   *desesperado.*

                            (vv. 1-6)

> (Although a man through folly
>   is able to fall
>   into sinfulness,
> he should not despair
>   of the goodness
>   of Holy Mary.)

Dorothy Clarke shows that variations in the *zéjel* are indeed numerous and include alternating rhyme which replaces the mono-rhymed sequences. Sometimes other rhymes are inserted between the original monorhymed lines: *abababac, dededec* (numbers 156, 157, 180). Some use longer monorhymed sequences (95, 283), and there are some in which there is the insertion of an extra rhyme between two lines having consonant rhyme: *aaabab, cccbcb* (239). She refers to a variety of other examples.

"Among the strophes less popular with Alfonso el Sabio in the *Cantigas*," she goes on to say, "but which became strophes of primary importance in Castilian are: the *redondilla*—though not octosyllabic in the *Cantigas* (Nos. 230, 326, p. 589); the *pareado* (No. 260); the *copla de pie quebrado* (No. 300); monorhymed quatrains similar to the *cuaderna vía* strophe but having different lines (p. 599); a form closely resembling the *romancillo* (No. 401); and above all, a *romance* (No. 308)." This *romance* is the earliest version of this form that she had found in the poetry of the Iberian Peninsula.

In a typical *zéjel*, as has been mentioned above, the last verse in the *estribillo* sets the pattern of rhyme for the last verse in the strophe. In *cantiga* 14 this is well represented. For convenience I have italicized the last word in the *estribillo* and the last word in the following strophe.

> Con razon é d' averen gran pavor
> as bestias da Madre daquel Sennor
> que sobre todas cousas á *poder.*

> E dest' un gran miragre foi mostrar
> Santa Maria, a Virgen sen par,
> en Prazença, per com' oý contar
> a omees bõos et de *creer.*

                            (vv. 3-9)

> (With reason wild beasts fear the
> Mother of that Master who
> has power over all things.

> And about this a great miracle
> Holy Mary, the Virgin without peer,

revealed in Placencia, as I hear,
to good and faith-filled men.)

Dr. Clarke discusses a great many other metrical forms of importance, not all of which can be given here. She states that the hendecasyllable is most important, and then the heptasyllable, although the former was not the same form as the Italianate made famous later by Boscán and Garcilaso. She shows examples of twelve-syllable lines (*cantigas* 123, 145, 209, and 223) and of fourteen in *cantiga* 16; and she reveals that canticle 240 has a rare accent on the fourth syllable, while 211 is accented consistently on the fifth; occasionally the pattern varies within a given poem. An example of something closely resembling the *arte mayor* current in the fifteenth century is to be seen, she says, in numbers 79 and 307, for example—the only difference between the form as used by Alfonso and the later writers being the regularity of syllable count in the former. Nine- and thirteen-syllable lines, not known in Castilian until the late nineteenth century, appear in the **Cantigas** (25 and 73), she also reveals.

"The shortest line used as the sole verse-length in a poem," she proves, "is the hexasyllable, which appears in both the patterns later found in Castilian, particularly during and after the Golden Age: the *serranilla* (No. 192) having fluctuating secondary accent: . . ." She goes on to indicate that there are examples of the decasyllable (*cantigas* 15, 20, and 280), the fourteen-syllable (12, 23, and others), and the fifteen-syllable (36).

Among her other discoveries is what appears to be a perfect *romancillo* (420) of the type much in vogue in the Golden Age.

The rhyme itself of the **Cantigas** is pure consonance—not assonance—with an almost perfect rhyme pattern, for a pattern set down in the first strophe is faithfully continued in all the other strophes. And the rhyme scheme, too, is rich in variety.

Some who read the songs of Alfonso X find a few which appear to be unartistically written. As will be pointed out in section six of this chapter, which is devoted to the music of the **Cantigas**, so close are the ties between the poems and the music that what appears to be a lack of artistry disappears if one hears the music as he reads the words. Excellent musical recordings have been prepared in recent years, and these are listed in the Bibliography.

Perhaps the thoughts of Menéndez y Pelayo on the **Cantigas de Santa María** are the most cogent and valuable that can be used to indicate in a general way the value and importance of Alfonsine versification. This great Spanish scholar early in his career studied the **Cantigas** and recognized them for the remarkable heritage they hold in store. "But the **Cantigas**," he wrote, and I translate, "not only are important for their linguistic value and for their hagiographical content, but for the extraordinary variety and relative perfection of their metrical forms. They are, taken as a whole, the oldest manifestation known until this day in any of the Literatures of the Peninsula, and not very posterior to the few remains which we have of Castilian epic meter."[18]

VI THE MUSIC OF THE *CANTIGAS*

No student of musicology, I can only avail myself of the expert knowledge of those who do know the area. With their aid I have prepared the following brief synthesis of the music of the **Cantigas**.

Gilbert Chase, in his well-known study of Spanish music, said: "It is known that Spanish kings and nobles employed Moorish-Arabian musicians in their palaces. Some of the miniatures of the **Cantigas** of Alfonso the Wise of Castile, for example, show Moorish musicians playing various instruments together with Spanish musicians."[19]

Certainly, Alfonso, a musician himself, imported, as was the custom of medieval royalty, many jongleurs and troubadours from Europe as well as many musicians from Moorish Spain and probably North Africa. Gilbert Chase discusses one of the miniatures in which the king is seen with his scribes and musicians. Another miniature comes to mind in support of Chase's observations. This is one of the canticles of praise entitled *Esta e a primeira cantiga de loor de Santa Maria ementando os VII goyos que ouve de seu fillo*, "This is the First Song of Praise of Holy Mary Showing the Seven Joys which She Had from her Son," in ms. T.j.I. The King sits in the center of the picture and turns the pages of a book which rests upon a writing desk at his side. He points, as a teacher might, and seems to be explaining what is in the book. At his left, sitting on the floor, is a scribe who is a priest, as is indicated by his tonsure; at the King's right sits another scribe or secretary, who may be a layman. Both hold open books, and one may see on their pages the words of a song and the lines of the musical score ready for the notes. At the far right of the miniature stand three clerics. One holds a book and the others, looking at it, are in the act of singing. To the far left three musicians, tuning their viols, stand awaiting the king's command. Here, as in the case of the miniature cited by Chase, we may have an example of the actual "trying out" of a *cantiga*. From what is depicted it would seem that Alfonso has just dictated a song to his scribes and that the three singers are practicing it, while the three musicians wait their turn to give it instrumental interpretation.

Incidentally, it should be recalled, j.b.2 provides a remarkable rich depiction of musicians and instruments. Seventy-odd musicians, both Christian and Moslem, are portrayed playing instruments ranging from a wide variety of the percussion type to the family of the strings (lutes, viols, *vihuelas,* etc.), to organs, the hurdy-gurdy and others. One sees two varieties of guitars—the *guitarra morisca* and the *guitarra latina* as well as the rebec, sets of silver bells and hammers with which to play them, transverse flutes, trumpets of various sorts, harps and bagpipes, castanets, and so on.

The actual melodies of the *cantigas* were drawn, no doubt, from a variety of sources. Some belong to the music of the Church whose liturgies furnished melodies; others are taken from Moorish and Arabic and even Hebrew music; many are songs used by the Galician-Portuguese and Franco-Provençal troubadours; perhaps some were brought by professional musicians, singers, and composers from as far away as Italy, England, and the Germanies. One wonders if some of the Suabian musicians, who could have accompanied Princess Beatriz to Spain when she came to marry King Ferdinand, might not have supplied still others. Perhaps most important and fecund of all was the volume of songs originating with the Spanish people themselves. Regional songs abounded then as they do today, and the songs of many social strata and professions must have also existed: harvest songs of farmers, the songs of shepherds and cowboys, sailors' chanties, soldiers' ballads, watchmen's songs, and hunters' and fishermen's ditties may have all contributed. "The interplay of popular and artistic elements," writes Chase, "has nowhere been more significantly revealed than in Spanish music."

When after centuries of oblivion the *Cantigas* were studied at last by nineteenth-century musicologists, they were not understood and therefore were criticized as being of poor musical quality. The same was the fate of the songs of the Provençal and French troubadours, for no one could appreciate their true beauty which was concealed behind a system of musical notation not properly deciphered. Ribera in Spain had tried to prove that the *Cantigas,* as well as other Spanish lyrical pieces, stemmed from Arabic music, and although this may be considered in a small part true, in that Arabic melodies were doubtless taken into the *Cantigas,* the notation, even of these, is western.[20] The person who finally managed to decipher the system of notation used by the thirteenth-century scribes at Alfonso's court is Higinio Anglés, perhaps Spain's greatest musicologist. I translate: "The repertory of the four hundred and twenty-three *Cantigas de Santa María,*" he writes, "as presented in the extant texts, is to the present time, the most important repertory in Europe as regards medieval sacred lyric. The melodies have no relationship at all

with the oriental music of the Arabs. . . . The notation of the *Cantigas* . . . is most perfect, although until very recently it has been unknown by musicologists."[21]

Apparently many musicians and students of music had studied the Alfonsine songs, and all had been surprised at their "poor" quality. But this was owing to the mistaken belief that they could be studied and translated in accordance with the rules of musical notation made by modern musicologists. Anglés finally saw that no established regulations could be followed in the case of the *Cantigas,* and that it would be necessary to use the original transcription, as it appeared in the codices, and to develop his own techniques of understanding and transcribing what the medieval scribe had penned. "Thanks to his form of notation we can today assert that the Spanish melodies offer a rhythmic variety and a melodic richness which admit no comparison with other European repertories," continues Anglés.[22]

Anglés had, alongside his interest in medieval music, a lively interest in Spanish folk song, in particular, and European folk song, in general. He gathered and studied hundreds, and found that modern folk songs and the way they are sung by the folk performers in the villages and mountains and plains, contain much of the same melodic richness, and often a good deal of the form and actual melody, as the canticles in King Alfonso's *Cantigas de Santa María.* "In them, [the *Cantigas*]," he writes, "the rhythmic element of the folk song rules, as we do not find it in the lyrics of the troubadours and minnesingers. . . . Specialists had believed until recently that medieval monody must have had a close relationship with the polyphony of its epoch, and, since in this polyphony only the ternary measure was practiced, this rhythm alone was possible in the monody. But the notation of the *Cantigas* reveals just the opposite. In them is presented the ternary measure which combines with the binary; again melodies exist which can be sung with only the binary."[23]

This discovery of Anglés will eventually have even a more telling effect upon the study of the music of the troubadours, from which so many of the *Cantigas* came. For their music, like the *Cantigas,* had been subjected to the rules of medieval polyphony, because scholars had believed—and many still do believe—that polyphony was the key to understanding, and obviously this was a mistake in dealing with monody. These specialists had for years sought some manuscript that might offer a clue, or better still, an actual guide to the understanding of monody. "Well then," Anglés tells us, "these manuscripts which we looked for and never found, have just been discovered: they are the Spanish manuscripts of the Court of Castile and León; they are the manuscripts of the *Cantigas* of Alfonso el Sabio."[24]

Beyond this point in the technical discussion of Anglés, who is the expert acknowledged by musicologists as the best in the field, I cannot go, for this would require the skills of a trained student of the very science of music; however, I can, even as a layman, see, as can any reader, something at least, of the magnitude of Anglés' work and what it means to the entire study of the medieval lyric. I can also see what his discoveries mean to the case in point, that is, the **Cantigas de Santa María,** all of which definitely points to the native Spanish folkloristic quality of the Alfonsine melodies.[25]

VII THE PICTORIAL ART OF THE *CANTIGAS*

One cannot discuss the **Cantigas de Santa María** effectively solely from a literary viewpoint, for the miracles and hymns in the book are inextricably interwoven with the pictorial and musical presentations. Therefore, although no student of medieval art, I must perforce offer at least a general treatment of the artistic qualities of the miniatures, just as I did in the case of the musical notations in Section VI.

The pages of the most lavishly illustrated codex of the **Cantigas,** Escorial T.j.I, are large and measure four hundred and eighty-five millimeters in height by three hundred and twenty-six in width. Each page of miniatures is divided into six panels or compartments, save for one which contains eight, and in each panel some part of the action of that *cantiga* is depicted. The closest modern parallel to these techniques is that used in comic books with their divisions and labels. The labels in the miniatures are captions which appear above each panel in beautiful calligraphy, with the letters in deep blue or brilliant red. The six panels of each page of miniatures are framed together, as though they were a single picture, by a band of designs repeated again and again in brilliant colors, and these designs are believed to take their origin from ceramics and painted sculpture of the period. There is great variety and much artistic excellence in these frames—but more about this particular aspect later. The six-panel division, it should be stated, though carried out in almost every single one of the pages of miniatures, nonetheless does not actually limit the sequences of action to six parts. Some panels are further divided within themselves, with various means employed to accomplish this result. *cantiga* 9 in the fourth panel shows what at first glance appears to be two monks, the first of whom is facing a lion, the second a group of armed robbers. In actuality the same monk faces lion and robbers, for his two adventures are divided within the panel by a line of trees and mountain slopes. In *cantiga* 64, also in the fourth panel, two entirely different scenes are created by the device of a wall and a column which serve as lines of demarcation.

Sometimes, to add greater dimension to the miniatures, the artists depict characters, either animal or human,

beyond the framework of a panel. In describing number 119, Charles Nelson says that "Panel Four is so closely connected with the action of Panel Three that the two can be treated almost as one drawing. These two panels combined are probably the two most outstanding of the **Cantigas** as to related actions, continuity and visualization. The chief demon is shown on the rooftop directing the capture of the High Judge and, at the same moment of time, is shown directing the demons and their disposal of the Judge in Panel Four. . . . This is an astonishingly high level of achievement in the art of animation for the thirteenth century."[26]

I might add that my own observation of number 63 is also pertinent here. In a battle scene which begins in panel three one sees Christian knights charging. The usual band of roseates separates this panel from panel four, but across the line of division, action is continued in an interesting fashion. The rear of a horse is seen in panel three, and the rest of the animal mounted by a knight appears in panel four, as though no line of demarcation were there to prevent its charge. Movement and its continuation are admirably produced here.

Perhaps a good, if not professional, way to arrive at an understanding of the pictorial presentation of the **Cantigas de Santa María** is to choose one set of typical miniatures—one page of the book, that is—and to describe its content. *Cantiga* 157, which can be seen in black-and-white reproduction in an available book, serves conveniently as a point of reference.[27] The border or frieze of design surrounding this particular page of miniatures is, in this case, composed of four-petaled roseates in alternating scarlet and azure on a background ranging from pearl gray to shades of lavender and pink and pale red. The panels, which the eyes are supposed to examine from left to right and from top to bottom, represent a continuum of movement. Those on the left, however, in which the king and his group of companions appear, show little movement, whereas the ones to the right offer scenes of lively action. The alternation of these—the static or near-static scene first, then a scene of action, then another of static reality, and so on until the last—produces quite successfully the concept of fluidity and continuity.

In the first panel Alfonso himself, identified by a plum-colored robe and a hat on which is clearly visible the lion of León, appears against the background of subdued blues worn by his companions and the natural color of the mules and greyhounds. Mules, by the way, at least when one was hunting, were considered in those times as less skittish and safer than horses. Alfonso is portrayed, as he always is in the **Cantigas,** as a rather handsome young man, well proportioned, with a face pleasant and, if not actually plump, at least not thin. His eyes are large and set wide apart. The King has just loosed a falcon upon some herons, and his hand and arm are still raised as the hawk soars upward. In panel two the hawk has wounded a heron which can be seen hurtling toward the surface of the river. Another heron rests on the water, and still a third flies across the sky. The falcon climbs still higher and crosses the borders of the panel to invade the caption, thereby giving a feeling of great dimension and space. In this, we see a nascent impressionism side by side with realism.

The first caption reads: *Como el Rey don Alffonso lançou un falcon a huna garça,* "How King Don Alfonso loosed a falcon upon a heron"; the second caption is this: *Como o falcon firiu a garça e britoull' a ala e caeu a garça no rio,* "How the falcon struck the heron and broke its wing and the heron fell into the river."

Panel three reveals that the King called for a volunteer to retrieve the heron, since the dogs coud not be sent into the turbulent waters. The caption reads: *Como el começou a dezir a vozes quen' entrara pola la garça,* "How he began to call loudly for someone to go in after the heron." His companions here are revealed in fine detail. There are eight mounted men and two footmen, and these latter are holding two greyhounds on leashes.

Panel four is a scene of lively action and violent movement. The caption reads: *Como un omne entrou pola garça e agua o samorgullou ben tres vezes,* "How a man went into the water after the heron and the water drew him down." A hawk sweeps across the sky over the struggle in the river which is bounded by high banks and verdant trees. Two dogs, not greyhounds, but retrievers, watch from the shore on which grow some four separate species of wildflowers. The man, though under the water, can be seen clearly, for the artists have depicted him as though they were peering through glass at his underwater struggles, much as one looks into an aquarium today.

In panel five the caption reads: *Como deu a garça al Rey e el Rey e todos loaron muyto Sancta Maria,* "How he gave the heron to the King and the King and all the others greatly praised Holy Mary." The pictorial action in the miniatures parallels that described in the poetic narration. The man screams and implores the Virgin's aid. The King's companions all cry out that his life is as good as lost; but Alfonso says that Our Lady will not fail to render assistance, and this proves to be true. Panel six shows the man climbing the steep bank, the heron in his hand, and the caption reads: *Como Sancta Maria fez sayr o omne do rio con sa garça na mano,* "How Holy Mary makes the man leave the river with the heron in his hand." Add to this double form of presentation—visual in the miniatures and written in

the verses—the added attraction of a musical melody of great beauty, and one can readily see the power of such a threefold presentation to the eye, the ear, and the mind.

Color is not as riotous on this page of miniatures as in some, but its use is equally tasteful and effective. The king's pinkish or plum-colored robe is the focal point in the three perpendicular left-hand panels and attracts the eye to him. The three perpendicular right-hand panels strike a telling contrast with those on the left. The sky and the river are in pastels, it is true, but the river has deeper shades designed to delineate waves. The foliage of the trees and all the grasses and shrubs are dark green; the tiny blossoms are predominantly white. All this surrounded and framed by the brilliantly colored roseates in scarlet and azure produces a delightful overall presentation, rich, eye-catching, that closely parallels and, therefore, enhances the verbal account.

All the miniatures in this Escorial manuscript, as well as in those of Toledo and Florence, are polychromatic. Shades of red, blue, yellow, green, and brown and black predominate, but pastels abound. Gold illumination is very common, used primarily to set off haloes, royal and celestial crowns, crosses, lamps, altar-pieces and the columns of churches; but golden bedsteads, especially those of Alfonso and other royal personages, and tables and doorways are also to be found. Medieval artists were able to obtain striking illuminations by using finely beaten gold-leaf laid over a coating of Armenian bole, a red clay which imparted a very special glow to such work.

It is believed that each miniature was a composite of the work of several, or even of many artists' work. Calligraphers set down the captions; apprentices probably were given the task of drawing and painting the friezes in the frames; and other apprentices may have been allowed to sketch some of the general and conventionalized background scenes. Possibly some of the better artists drew only the first bare charcoal sketches. One can see such beginnings in the Florentine manuscript in which some of the miniatures appear in varying stages of completion. Perhaps after the sketches had been finished, the painters made their contributions. Some of these Florentine miniatures also contain human figures which at first glance seem to be complete; but a closer scrutiny reveals the absence of hands and faces, always difficult to portray. No doubt these awaited the finishing touch of that specialist who could most accurately and skilfully paint them in. The incomplete manuscript, by the way, may be a boon rather than a misfortune, for in it may lie important sectors of the history of medieval miniature production, proving that each page was produced in assembly-line fashion. Dr. Guerrero Lovillo[28] believes that he has identified the style of at least three separate unidentified artists through a careful study of what he thinks are three different manners and techniques of depicting the human body and face. Whether any of these styles is the work of one of three painters whose names have come down to us may never be known, for though three are named in contemporary documents, there is no indication of what part each painter played in any Alfonsine project.

With this general explanation and the description of one of the pages of miniatures presented, other more specific aspects and characteristics can be taken up. Dr. Guerrero Lovillo offers the suggestion that the idea for the depiction and designing of the miniatures may have come from the ivory dyptichs of thirteenth-century France and Spain.[29] These, though no longer possessed of their brilliant coloration, are known from the faded and chipped remains of paint upon them to have been polychromatic. Each is framed by a border of carved roseates or other designs identical to some of those found in the friezes in the **Cantigas.** And each is a sculptural representation of some miracle. Furthermore, each dyptich is divided into six panels, each of which depicts in ivory the events taking place. Other scholars have suggested that stained-glass windows, also portraying miracles, might have served the king and his artists as models when they planned the miniatures. Then, too, since Paris at the time was a center of the art of making miniatures, as attested in Dante's *Paradiso,* the Alfonsine miniatures may be no more than a hispanization of this French art.

One might even suggest still another inspiration for the artists who created the miniatures for the **Cantigas.** Might not a dramatization of such miracles as could have lent themselves to dramatic presentation have suggested much to the artists? We have seen . . . that drama dealing with miracles was common in medieval Europe, both in Latin and in the vernaculars. Could there not have been in Spain dramatizations of some of the Virgin's miracles? After all, in France about 1265 Rutebeuf had produced his *Miracle de Théophile,* "Miracle of Theophilus," in which the Virgin saved the soul of Theophilus who had sold it to the devil. If so much French influence is felt in other Spanish artistic manifestations, why not drama based upon the miracles of Our Lady? The miracle of Theophilus, by the way, is one of those included in the **Cantigas de Santa María.** Nor is it difficult to imagine this miracle acted out in Spain. Indeed, many others might just as easily have been adapted to dramatic form. In so far as I know, however, no one has suggested this possibility. Nor has anyone pointed out, aside from this writer,[30] that at times the stone images of the Madonna and the Child in certain of the **Cantigas** can be seen to assume different positions in separate panels. Now these different positions are not due to the fact that the images are sup-

posed to move, for in the case I am discussing they are no more than parts of the background scene. And yet, in *cantiga* 18, for example, the images do indeed change position. A glance at the page of miniatures will show that the images in the first and second panels at the top of the page are in a different posture from those in the last two panels at the bottom. At the top the Virgin is clasping the Child tightly against her face—a little closer in the second panel at the top than in the first—almost as if she were about to kiss Him. In the last two panels, the Child is sitting placidly in his mother's lap, and his head is not even near that of the Virgin. Still other differences are manifest on the page. In the left bottom panels, the Virgin's right hand is resting upon her knee and her left is on the Child's shoulder. If an artist were sketching as he watched a dramatic presentation of a miracle, he might have caught the actress, who represented the statue, in different positions as she shifted about in order to rest. I have no proof of any of this, of course, but it seems a fairly good explanation of the images' altered positions.

Realism—almost photographic realism—is an outstanding characteristic of Alfonsine miniatures. Life in these illustrations is depicted in all of its shades and colors, in its beautiful and uplifting aspects, as well as in its base and ugly ones. One sees angels with pastel-shaded wings ministering to mortals (*cantiga* 7), and driving away devils (3); the Virgin banishes demons and resuscitates a monk (11); a beautiful landscape, one of scores to be found, can be seen in 121. But ugliness in appearance, as well as in action, often comes to the eye—even the gross and the scurrilous: *cantiga* 17 may be the worst, for in it is depicted a young man having sexual intercourse with his own mother, while later she disposes of their offspring by dropping it into an open latrine; in number 38 there appears a group of young rascals carousing, drinking, and throwing dice; in another (124) a man is first stoned, then speared and finally slashed across the throat from which his life's blood gushes; a naked penitent is revealed kneeling before the font, while the priest pours baptismal water over him. His genitalia and the darkness of his pubic hair are perfectly visible (46).

In this realism, of course, there was no attempt at the pornographic: it was simply a depiction of life as people were used to seeing it. Naked penitents did kneel in churches; men did have their throats cut; perhaps pregnant women were stabbed in the abdomen and their children removed right in the street by a form of Caesarian section (284). The **Cantigas,** a book of miracles, but all the same a book of secular and not ecclesiastical production and conception, portrayed what there was to portray, and little apparently was concealed or disguised.

Astonishingly minor details appear in these pictures. A scene laid in a forest will contain varieties of fauna and flora. Violets, mosses, and tiny wild flowers, as well as shrubs and trees, can be noted, although sometimes it requires a magnifying glass to see them. In 44 a pair of quail hide among tussocks of grass, rabbit hounds pursue and catch their prey, and falcons dive after larks. Realism, and certainly not impressionism, is the forte of the *Cantigas de Santa María,* though the latter is often present.

The artistic composition of the miniatures is handled with consummate skill. Whole scenes and panoramas on land and on sea are laid down as the backdrops for miracles. The groupings of figures is artistic, and their attitudes and poses reveal their emotions and reactions to events (175); hands are thrown up in horror (4); faces are twisted in fear or glow with laughter (38); a man grimaces and turns his head while his foot is amputated (37).

If perspective is lacking, the very absence of it produces pleasing effects. The passengers on a ship, for example, appear far too enlarged for verisimilitude, but this is so that they can be seen in complete detail, and the effect is not at all displeasing (172]. Occasionally, the artists saved themselves work, much as they do today, by concealing the bare feet of individuals behind walls, stones, or grass, so as to avoid the necessity of painting these appendages, always difficult to portray faithfully (22).

The human figure, in the main, is so well depicted that one feels positive that the artists used living models. The movement of limbs, as well as their position beneath garments is graphically displayed and all proportions of the human body are carefully presented. And the nude, though not seen in many of the *canti-gas*—for that matter rare in all medieval manuscripts—is well represented. Guerrero Lovillo cites *cantiga* 60 in which are seen the nude Adam and Eve in the Garden, and says that their figures are not well portrayed. He is quite correct, for they are stiff and massive-limbed. But other nudes or near-nudes have the realistic photographic quality already alluded to. In number 22 there is a truly handsome young man, standing before his enemies in *bragas,* "underwear," and a skin-tight undershirt. His arms, neck, and torso are shapely, and his bare thighs and calves display the play and bulge of muscle in his tense stance. Young gamblers appear in number 38 and in 76 with powerfully thewed limbs and well-defined pectoral muscles. In number 46, mentioned above, a naked penitent, middle-aged and bearded, kneels fully revealed even to his genitalia. In 95 one sees a nude man sitting on the edge of a bed in which a nude woman reclines, her lower extremities under the cover. Both are well and realistically portrayed. A demon in the background is so muscular as to be of heroic proportions.

The plastic artistry in the *Cantigas de Santa María* is, then, an important milestone in the history of Spanish painting. One understands Alfonso's preoccupation with the book's final disposition, even in the great confusion and sorrow of his last illness, and why he felt constrained to mention it in his last will and testament. I translate:

> Likewise we order that all the books of the *Songs of Praise of Holy Mary* be in that church where our body shall be interred, and that they be sung on the feast days of Holy Mary. And if that one who inherits legally and by our will what is ours, should wish to own these books of the *Songs of Holy Mary,* we order that he therefore make good compensation to the church from whence he removes them so that he may have grace without sin.[31]

The *Cantigas*—at least manuscript T.j.I—remained in the Cathedral of Seville, where the King's body was interred. Philip II had the collection removed to his library in the Escorial where it is displayed today in a glass case together with Alfonso's astrolabe and other of his possessions.

Notes

1. I have treated in some detail the rivalry between the shrines of the Virgin Mary and the famous Tomb of Saint James at Compostela in "King Alfonso's Virgin of Villa-Sirga, Rival of St. James of Compostela," *Middle Ages-Reformation-Volkskunde, Festschrift for John G. Kunstmann* (Chapel Hill, N. C., 1959), pp. 75-81.

2. All quotations from the *Cantigas de Santa María* are taken from the new and definitive edition of Walter Mettmann listed in the Bibliography.

3. Professor Evelyn Proctor of St. Hugh's College, Oxford, discusses the dating of the manuscripts in her excellent book entitled *Alfonso X of Castile, Patron of Literature and Learning* (Oxford, 1951), pp. 44-46.

4. Proctor, pp. 37-38.

5. Mettmann, pp. vii-xxiv, gives an extremely detailed paleographical description of the four codices of the *Cantigas de Santa María.*

6. Leopoldo A. de Cueto, Marqués de Valmar, *Cantigas de Santa María* (Madrid, 1889).

7. Martín de Riquer, *Historia de la Literatura Universal,* I (Barcelona, 1957), p. 326.

8. Chapter 6, which treats of Alfonso's poetry exclusive of the *Cantigas de Santa María,* gives more detailed information about this variety of poetry.

9. See Frank Calcott, *The Supernatural in Early Spanish Literature* (New York, 1923); A. F. G. Bell, "'Las Cantigas de Santa María' of Alfonso X," *Modern Language Notes* X (1915), 338-48. For Mussafia's classification consult the Introduction to the edition of the *Cantigas* of the Marqués de Valmar; Angel Valbuena Prat, *Historia de la Literatura Española*. I (Barcelona, 1946), 124-28.

10. *Crónicas de los Reyes de Castilla* I (Madrid, 1953), ed. by Cayetano Rosell, and published as Vol. 66 of the *Biblioteca de Autores Españoles*.

11. Marqués de Valmar, Introduction.

12. The most helpful of my articles on this matter is "Folklore in the *Cantigas* of Alfonso el Sabio," *Southern Folklore Quarterly* XXIII (1959), 175-83.

13. John E. Keller, "Daily Living as Presented in the *Canticles* of Alfonso the Learned," *Speculum* XXXIII (1958), 484-89; and the same author's "Daily Living as Revealed in Alfonso's *Cantigas*," *Kentucky Foreign Language Quarterly* VII (1960), 207-10.

14. Américo Castro, *The Structure of Spanish History* (Princeton, N. J., 1954), pp. 361-68.

15. Dorothy Clotelle Clarke, "Versification in Alfonso el Sabio's *Cantigas*," *Hispanic Review* XXIII (1955), 83-98.

16. See Gerald Brenan, *The Literature of the Spanish People* (New York, 1957), pp. 63-68; 466-70.

17. Gilbert Chase, *The Music of Spain* (New York, 1941), p. 24.

18. I translate here from R. Menéndez Pidal, "Las Cantigas del Rey Sabio," *La Ilustración Española y Americana* XXXIX (1895), 163.

19. Gilbert Chase, p. 26.

20. Julián Ribera, *La Música de las Cantigas* (Madrid, 1922).

21. Higinio Anglés, *La Música de las Cantigas de Santa María del Rey Alfonso el Sabio* (Barcelona, 1943), p. 11.

22. Anglés, p. 11.

23. *Ibid.*

24. Anglés, p. 12.

25. Two excellent phonographic recordings have been made recently: *Las Cantigas de Santa María del Rey Alfonso el Sabio*, produced by Experiences Anonymes in *Music of the Middle Ages*, Vol. III—The Thirteenth Century with Russell Oberlin, Countertenor and Joseph Iadone, Lutist; and *Spanish Medieval Music: Twelve Cantigas de Santa María, Liturgy of Santiago de Compostela, Mass in Honor of the Blessed Virgin* produced by Pro Música.

26. Charles L. Nelson, "Literary and Pictorial Treatment of the Devil in the *Cantigas de Santa María*." (Unpublished Master's thesis, University of North Carolina, 1964), pp. 45-47.

27. José Guerrero Lovillo, *Las Cantigas, Estudio Arqueológico de sus Miniaturas* (Madrid, 1949) reproduces all the miniatures of the Escorial Codex, but not, alas, in color. Still, even in black-and-white reproduction one can see a surprising amount of detail and gain at least some idea of the remarkable richness of this Alfonsine book.

28. Guerrero Lovillo, pp. 34-35.

29. Guerrero Lovillo, pp. 22-23.

30. J. E. Keller, "Daily Living as Presented in the *Canticles* of Alfonso the Learned," *Speculum* XXXIII (1958), 488.

31. Guerrero Lovillo, p. 19, quotes these lines from the King's will.

Selected Bibliography

PRIMARY SOURCES

1. BOOKS BY ALFONSO OR WRITTEN UNDER HIS PATRONAGE

Calila e Digna. Critical edition by John E. Keller and Robert W. Linker (Madrid: Consejo Superior de Investigaciones Científicas, 1966). This edition presents both surviving manuscripts and in a long introduction studies the sources, influences, and content of eastern and western versions.

Cantigas de Santa María. Walter Mettmann, ed. (Coimbra: Acta Universitatis Conimbrigensis, 1959-64). Three volumes. This, the definitive edition, offers the most up-to-date study on the *Cantigas*.

Cantigas Profanas: The best editions are the following:

Cancioneiro da Ajuda. Carolina Michäelis de Vasconcellos, ed. (Halle: Niemeyer, 1904).

Cancioneiro da Biblioteca Nacional (Antiguo Colocci-Brancuti). Elza Pacheco Machado and José Pedro Machado, eds. (Lisbon: 1949-1958).

Cancioneiro Portuguez da Vaticana. Theophilo Braga, ed. (Lisbon: Imprenta Nacional, 1900).

Crónica General o Sea Historia de España que Mandó Componer Alfonso el Sabio y se Continuaba bajo Sancho IV en 1289. Ramón Menéndez Pidal, ed. (Madrid:

Bailly-Balliere, 1906). This is found in Vol. V of *Nueva Biblioteca de Autores Españoles.* Reedited by him with the collaboration of A. G. Solalinde, Manuel Muños Cortés, and José Gómez Pérez (Madrid: Editorial Gredos, 1955).

Fuero Real. Marcelo Martínez Alcubilla, ed., in *Códigos Antiguos de España* (Madrid: López Camacho, 1885).

General Estoria. Primera Parte. Antonio G. Solalinde, ed. (Madrid: Molina, 1930). *Segunda Parte,* Solalinde, Lloyd A. Kasten, and Victor R. B. Oelschläger, eds. (Madrid: Consejo Superior de Investigaciones Científicas, 1957).

Lapidario, Reproducción Fotolitográfica. Prologue by José Fernández Montaña (Madrid: La Iberia, 1881). Excellent color facsimile.

Libro de Ajedrez. Das Spanische Schachzabelbuch des Königs Alfons des Weisen von Jahr 1283. Prologue by John G. White (Leipzig: Karl W. Hiersemann, 1913). Excellent facsimile in black and white.

Libro del Saber de Astronomía. Manuel Rico y Sinobas, ed. (Madrid: E. Aguado, 1863-67). Five vols.

Libro de las Cruces. Lloyd A. Kasten and Lawrence B. Kiddle, eds. (Madrid: Consejo Superior de Investigaciones Científicas, 1961).

SECONDARY SOURCES

1. DOCTORAL DISSERTATIONS AND MASTERS' THESES

Elise F. Dexter. "Sources of the *Cantigas* of Alfonso el Sabio" (diss. Wisconsin, 1926).

Charles L. Nelson. "Elements of Humor in Medieval Spanish *Exempla*" (diss. North Carolina, 1965). Studies the major collections of *exempla,* but the section on *Calila e Digna* is most pertinent to Alfonso X.

———. "Literary and Pictorial Treatment of the Devil in the *Cantigas de Santa María*" (thesis, North Carolina, 1964). Gives a detailed treatment of artistic techniques in the *Cantigas.*

John H. Nunemaker. "Index of Stones in the Lapidary of Alfonso X with Identification in Other Lapidaries" (diss., Wisconsin, 1928). Helpful because it covers points not covered elsewhere.

Theodore H. Shoemaker. "Alfonso X as Historian" (diss., Wisconsin, 1941). A valuable supplement to Alfonsine historiography.

2. BOOKS

Altamira, Rafael. *A History of Spain* (New York: Macmillan, 1918).

Anglés, Higinio P. *La Música de las Cantigas de Santa María del Rey Alfonso el Sabio. Facsímil, Transcripción y Estudio Crítico* (Barcelona: Diputación Provincial de Barcelona: Biblioteca Central, 1943). This monumental study opens up new vistas and new approaches to the study of medieval musical transcription.

Atkinson, William C. *A History of Spain and Portugal* (London: Whitefriars Press, 1960). An excellent short history by a professor familiar with Spanish literature.

Ballesteros y Baretta, Antonio. *Alfonso el Sabio* (Barcelona: Salvat Editores, 1963). This 1,142-page book is the definitive study of the life of the Learned King. Some small part of it is a treatment of his literary and scientific works.

Brenan, Gerald. *The Literature of the Spanish People* (New York: Meridian Books, 1957). Readable, sound, up to date. One of the very best general treatments of medieval Spanish letters, and especially good for poetry.

Castro, Américo. *The Structure of Spanish History* (Princeton: Princeton University Press, 1954). Provocative commentary. A controversial study of many aspects of Spanish literature by one of the great scholars.

Chandler, Richard E. and Kessel Schwartz. *A New History of Spanish Literature* (Baton Rouge: University of Louisiana Press, 1961). A very useful and reliable book. Literature is treated by genre rather than by chronological approaches.

Chase, Gilbert. *The Music of Spain* (New York: W. W. Norton, 1941). The treatment of Alfonsine and medieval music is brief, but sound.

Cueto, Leopoldo A. *Cantigas de Santa María de Alfonso el Sabio* (Madrid: Real Academia Española, 1889). Copious notes, good introduction, indispensable for background.

Curtius, Ernst R. *European Literature and the Latin Middle Ages* (New York: Pantheon Books, 1948). An excellent English translation from German of this important book. Curtius's is the most useful study of the unbroken tradition of Latin literature in the Middle Ages which was so influential upon medieval literatures.

Denomy, Alexander J. *The Heresy of Courtly Love* (New York: McMullen, 1947). The most up-to-date and best general study in English.

Díaz-Plaja, Guillermo. *Historia General de las Literaturas Hispánicas* (Barcelona: Editorial Barna, 1951). This great work is a series of studies by experts in the many genres discussed, brought together and edited by Díaz-Plaja. Invaluable for concise and reliable discussions.

Fisher, John H. *The Medieval Literature of Western Europe, A Review of Research, Mainly 1930-1960* (New York: The New York University Press, and London:

University of London Press, 1966). This book gives in Chapter 8 and in Chapter 10 comprehensive bibliographies of Spanish and Portuguese medieval literatures.

González Palencia, A. *Historia de la España Musulmana* (Barcelona: Editorial Labor, 1945). Concise, but authoritative and useful.

————. *Moros y Cristianos en la España Medieval* (Barcelona: Editorial Labor, 1945). A very good treatment of the two cultures.

Green, Otis H. *Spain and the Western Tradition* (Madison: University of Wisconsin Press, 1963). Masterly treatment of many aspects of Spanish literature. Vols. I, II, and III have been published.

Guerrero Lovillo, José. *Las Cantigas. Estudio Arqueológico de sus Miniaturas* (Madrid: Consejo Superior de Investigaciones Científicas, 1949). Unsurpassed in detail and replete with excellent sketches and black-and-white reproductions of the miniatures.

Holmes, Urban T. *History of Old French Literature* (New York: F. S. Crofts, 1937). The best and only complete history of Old French literature in English. Very fine bibliographies.

Las Siete Partidas, trans. Samuel Parsons Scott (New York: Commerce Clearing House, Inc., 1931). A monumental piece of scholarship which makes this Alfonsine work available to English readers. Excellent introduction and background of law.

Menéndez y Pelayo, Marcelino. *Orígenes de la Novela* (Buenos Aires: Espasa Calpe, 1946). These three volumes offer one of the most complete studies of the rise and development of Spanish fiction.

Milá y Fontanals, Manuel. *De la Poesía Heroica-Popular Castellana* (Madrid: Consejo Superior de Investigaciones Científicas, 1959). This recent translation of the French original is updated. Invaluable for an understanding of medieval lyrics.

Millares Carlo, Agustín. *Historia de la Literatura Española hasta Fines del Siglo* XV (México: Antiguo Librería Robredo, 1950). This is the best general history of Old Spanish literature with chapters followed by excellent bibliographies.

Northup, George T. Revised by Nicholson B. Adams. *An Introduction to Spanish Literature* (Chicago: University of Chicago Press, 1960). A useful, standard, and valuable work. One of the most up to date of such studies.

Proctor, Evelyn S. *Alfonso X of Castile, Patron of Literature and Learning* (Oxford: Clarendon Press, 1951). An excellent treatment of Alfonso X from the viewpoint of an eminent historian.

Riquer, Martín de. *Historia de la Literatura Universal* (Barcelona: Editorial Noguer, 1957). Concise in its treatment of individual works, this three-volume book is nonetheless valuable and filled with good criticism and stimulating ideas.

Sarmiento, Juan Ríos. *La Vida y los Libros de Alfonso el Sabio* (Barcelona: Editorial Juventud, 1943). This modest book for students in Spain contains valuable information and is attractively presented.

Solalinde, A. G. *Antología de Alfonso el Sabio* (Buenos Aires: Colección Austral, 1940). Brief selections with adequate introductory remarks for each.

Waddell, Helen. *The Wandering Scholars* (New York: Doubleday, 1955). This study of the Goliards and of the Latin poetry of the Middle Ages is sound and very readable. Excellent renditions of the Latin verse in English.

3. PERIODICAL ARTICLES

Asín Palacios, Miguel. "El Juicio del P. Mariana sobre Alfonso el Sabio," *Al-Andalus,* VII (1942), 479. Gives valuable critical appraisal of Alfonso by one of Spain's great modern scholars.

Bohigas Balaguer, Pedro. "La Visión de Alfonso X y las Profecías de Merlin," *Revista de Filología Española,* XXV (1941), 383-98. Connects Alfonso X with the non-Hispanic materials of Merlin's prophecies.

Castro, Américo. "Acerca del Castellano Escrito en Torno a Alfonso el Sabio," *Filologia Romanza* I, Fasc. 4 (1954), 1-11. Shows the quality and style of Alfonsine prose as found in the greatest Alfonsine manuscripts.

Cerulli, Enrico. "Il Libro della Scala e la Questione delle Fonti Arabospagnuole della *Divina Commedia,*" *Studi e Testi,* 150 [of the Vatican], (1949), 574. Attempts to analyze and explain the reasons for believing that Hispano-Arabic texts influenced Dante.

Clarke, Dorothy Clotelle. "Versification in Alfonso el Sabio's *Cantigas,*" *Hispanic Review,* XXIII (1955), 83-98. A complete treatment of all the verse forms in the *Cantigas.*

Domínguez Bordona, Jesús. "*El Libro de los Juicios de las Estrellas,* traducido para Alfonso el Sabio," *Revista de la Biblioteca, Archivos y Museo del Ayuntamiento de Madrid,* VIII (1931), 171-76. A brief but scholarly note.

Fitzmaurice-Kelly, James. "Some Early Spanish Historians," *Transactions of the Royal Historical Society,* I, 3rd Series (1907), 139-56. Includes Alfonso's histories as well as some treatment of those histories before his times.

Johnson, Mildred E. "*Las Siete Partidas* as a University Catalogue," *Hispania,* XXXVI (1951), 91-93. A brief note on the curriculum mentioned by Alfonso in the *Partidas.*

Keller, John E. "Daily Living as Presented in the *Canticles* of Alfonso the Learned," *Speculum,* XXXIII (1958), 484-89. Treats of various aspects of rural and urban life and offers two illustrations in black and white from Alfonsine minatures in the *Cantigas.*

————, "Folklore in the *Cantigas* of Alfonso el Sabio," *Southern Folklore Quarterly,* XXIII (1959), 175-83. Using some twenty-odd of the *Cantigas,* this article treats most of the major classes of folklore to be found in these songs.

————, "The Lapidary of the Learned King," *Gems and Gemology,* (Winter 1957-58), 105-10 and 118-21. Translates several of the chapters in the *Lapidaries* and explains the importance of this Alfonsine work.

Lollis, Cesare de. "Cantigas de Amor e de Maldezir di Alfonso el Sabio, Rei di Castiglia," *Studi di Filologia Romanza,* II (1887), 31-66. Successfully proves by internal evidence that the Alfonso of León and Castile mentioned as an author in the *Cantigas Profanas* is Alfonso X and no other Alfonso.

London, Gardiner. "Bibliografía de Estudios sobre la Vida y Obra de Alfonso X el Sabio," *Boletín de Filología Española,* II (1960), 18-31. The most complete bibliography, but even so, lacking in many items.

Menéndez Pidal, Gonzalo. "Como Trabajaron las Escuelas Alfonsíes," *Nueva Revista de Filología Hispánica,* V (1951), 363-80. A fine explication of Alfonsine collaborators based upon the testimony of primary sources.

Millás Villacrosa, José. "El Literalismo de los Traductores de la Corte de Alfonso el Sabio," *Al-Andalus,* I (1933), 155-87. A detailed description and study about the style and techniques of Alfonso's translators.

Proctor, Evelyn S. "Materials for the Reign of Alfonso X of Castile, 1252-1284," *Oxford Essays in Medieval History Presented to Herbert Edward Salter* (Oxford, 1934), 104-21. A masterly brief study of these matters by one of England's greatest modern historians.

Rey, Agapito. "Correspondence of the Spanish Miracles of the Virgin," *Romanic Review,* XIX (1928), 151-53. Explains the correspondence of miracles in the *Cantigas,* the *Milagros* of Berceo and certain other collections of miracles of the Virgin.

Ruiz y Ruiz, Lina A. "Gonzalo de Berceo y Alfonso X el Sabio: los *Milagros de Nuestra Señora* y las *Cantigas,*" *Universidad de San Carlos,* XXIV (1951), 22-90. A lengthy comparative study of the content of the two works.

Solalinde, A. G. See the long list of articles, studies, and anthologies of this scholar in Gardiner London's *Bibliografía* mentioned above.

Steiger, Arnald. "Alfonso X, el Sabio y la Idea Imperial," *Arbor,* VI (1946), 389-482. Studies in great detail Alfonso's attempts to gain the title of Emperor of the Holy Roman Empire, showing the legality of Alfonso's claims.

Trend, John B. "Alfonso el Sabio and the Game of Chess," *Revue Hispanique,* LXXI (1933), 393-403. A brief study of the techniques and importance of Alfonso's famous book on chess.

Urrestarazu, Sinesio. "*Las Cantigas* de Alfonso X el Sabio: una Modificación a la Historia de la Música," *Revista de las Indias,* XVII (1943), 221-60. New and valuable remarks on the influence of Alfonso's *Cantigas.*

Van Scoy, Herbert. "Alfonso X as a Lexicographer," *Hispanic Review,* VIII (1940), 227-84. Valuable and informative remarks about Alfonsine vocabulary and the breadth of Alfonsine lexicography.

Albert I. Bagby Jr. (essay date October 1971)

SOURCE: Bagby Jr., Albert I. "The Jew in the *Cántigas* of Alfonso X, El Sabio." *Speculum* 46, no. 4 (October 1971): 670-88.

[*In the following essay, Bagby discusses the implications of the largely unfavorable portrayal of Jews in the* Cantigas.]

The history of the Jewish people in any country and in any century must be described as ridden with chaotic upheaval.[1] Their situation in Spain was little different, whether under Visigothic, Roman, Moorish, or Spanish-Christian rule. Still, if one were to select one period in Spanish history which could be considered favorable to the Jews, it would have to be the reign of Alfonso X,[2] since every historian, chronicler, and scholar—whether Moslem, Christian, or Jew—who treats the subject testifies that Alfonso's reign was ideal for Jews as well as for other races and nationalities, especially those who could make intellectual and professional contributions.[3]

Alfonso's court abounded in scholarly Jews whose pens were busy and whose words were influential. Their task consisted of making available in the vernacular cultures that were cherished but inaccessible to most Spaniards. While it is not possible to prove just how far they influenced the intellectual development of the Wise King,[4] various pieces of evidence point to the fact that their influence upon him was great indeed. We do know that Alfonso X's father-in-law, Jaime I of Aragon, "recibió la ciencia de Rabí Mosé Ben Nahman," and that Alfonso's wife, Queen Violante, had in her entourage

Don Todros ha-Leví Abu-l-Afiya, horseman and poet,[5] who sings the King's praises in one of his poems.[6] Ishaq Ben Cid and Yehuda Ben Mosé, authors of the *Tablas,* which are called "Alfonsies" in honor of Alfonso, suggest in Chapter 1 that his reign be taken as the starting point of a new era.[7]

During this period the Jews set about to accomplish that which would bring the greatest reward in Castilian society: economic gain and social prestige.[8] As medical doctors they had no rivals. Also, they were employed by wealthy Christians and Moslems as financial administrators of their affairs and as tax collectors. These obligations led often to the penetration of Jews into high places in the political, economic, social, and even religious life of the country. Thus, because they were frequently offered places of distinction in preference to Christians, the Jews came to be deeply resented by the general populace.

There were, it cannot be denied, Christian scholars and savants around Alfonso in his enlightened court. But historical fact bears out that, as both *infante* and *rey,* Alfonso the Wise chose to be surrounded by Jewish minds in every sphere of Spanish life with the possible exception of the purely social.[9] And, scholars[10] have traditionally maintained that under Fernando III and his son Alfonso X, the Jews received better treatment than in any other period of history except the present. González López tells us that with the Jewish minorities in particular, the Spanish monarchs followed a policy of "protection," under which the minorities were granted numerous privileges. It is further said that

> El Rey Sabio concedió amplia libertad religiosa a la población judía de los reinos de Castilla. Llevado de su celo por ella, dispuso en las Cortes de Valladolid (1285) que los cristianos que no pagasen sus deudas a los acreedores judíos incurrían en ciertas penalidades.[11]

Such favorable intervention on behalf of the Jewish population produced considerable protest on the part of the Spanish Christians, especially since the Jews and *mudéjares*[12] were acquiring great wealth. Thus, in the very year in which the above decrees were made, and again in 1267, Alfonso had to balance the account by levying certain limitations on the exercise of usury, which the Jews as moneylenders were often accused of practicing.[13]

Américo Castro, who has brought to light the significant place the Jews had in the formation of Hispanic culture and letters, sees their influence upon Spain's history as largely a result of the favorable conditions that existed for them in that country in the thirteenth and fourteenth centuries, particularly under Alfonso. To Castro, who cites Jewish scholars in support of this widely held

thesis, Alfonso's Spain was a haven for Jews—not only the select intellectuals, but the middle-class merchants as well.[14]

Even the Jews themselves consider that the Golden Age of their history was in Spain, beginning in the year 1038, the date marking the beginning of the decline of Babylonian Jewry. According to Margolies and Marx, Jewish philosophy, poetry, and culture began from that date to rise toward its zenith during the reign of Alfonso X.[15] It is significant, however, that modern Jews feel their good treatment was a means to an end, for good treatment came only from the monarchs and the nobility loyal to those monarchs. The populace and the Church—envious of Jewish privileges, successes, and riches—campaigned vigorously against their welfare, and even the legal treatises of the thirteenth century are considered only moderately favorable to the Jews.[16]

The question we are seeking to answer here is, whether or not the writings of Alfonso, which inevitably reflected his personal feelings, corroborate this testimony in his behalf, or whether he perhaps followed a double standard with regard to his Jewish subjects. As champion of enlightenment, was he—as scholars throughout history have held—truly a friend of the Jews? We shall look for the answer in two of his most important works: *Las Siete Partidas,*[17] his monumental legal codex, and the *Cántigas de Santa Maria,*[18] songs in praise of the Virgin Mary.

Before a discussion of the works themselves is undertaken the problem of authorship deserves some comment.

Concerning the *Siete Partidas,* whose sources are too numerous to discuss here,[19] Américo Castro stated that regardless of how much editorial help Alfonso had (and some of it was Jewish help), he must be regarded as the author, or at least the supervising editor, of these laws. Thus, the statements about Jews and Moors would either have been his own or have had his approval.

The same is true of the *Cántigas,* although there is considerable evidence that Alfonso borrowed little from the other volumes of miracles circulating in Europe at the time. Agapito Rey has published a table which reveals that of the thirty poems in the *Cántigas* which deal with the Jews, only eight appear in other Spanish collections of miracles.[20] And John Keller, in *Alfonso X, El Sabio,* summarizes the evidence in favor of Alfonso's authorship. First, it was characteristic of noblemen of the period to write songs as evidence of their literary genius, and Alfonso was widely esteemed for his scholarship. It is likely, therefore, that he would have wished to demonstrate that ability.

Second, in the Prologue to the *Cántigas,* written in the first person, the king acknowledges that while the poetry therein may be weak, his intention is to "expand upon a thing or two I do know," with God's guidance. This claim lends a personal touch to the narration, especially when a number of the *Cántigas* themselves are written in the first person, and many of the events described can be verified and dated, some as having occurred during his era.[21]

Third, Alfonso is frequently depicted in the miniatures which accompany the poems—again, an intimacy not likely unless the king had been personally involved with the writing of the poems.[22] Thus, the evidence is sufficient for us to accept him as the probable author.

Now let us return to a discussion of the *Partidas.* The portion of the codex significant to this study deals with the regulations governing the lives and rights of Jews within Spanish society. It is quite clear that Alfonso, even while attempting to excerise justice, is bound by tradition as he sets forth rules for the Jews.[23] Alfonso explains the particulars of the word Jew:

> A party who believes in, and adheres to the law of Moses is called a Jew . . . The reason that the Church, emperors, kings, and princes permitted the Jews to dwell among them, and with Christians, is because they always lived, as it were, in captivity, as it was constantly in the minds of men that they were descended from those who crucified Our Lord Jesus Christ.[24]

A cursory glance at some of the legal stipulations affecting the lives of Jews may be of value here. Concerning how Jews should pass their lives among Christians, the *Partidas* state that it should be "quietly and without disorder, practicing their own religious rites and not speaking ill of the faith of our Lord Jesus Christ. . . . Moreover, a Jew should be careful to avoid preaching to, or converting any Christian. Whoever violates this law shall be put to death and lose all his property" (Law II, p. 1433).

Alfonso's *Partidas* also provided that "no Jew can hold any office or employment by which he may be able to oppress Christians" (Law III, p. 1434). Fear of treason was justified, as we shall see in the discussion below of *Cantiga 2* (pp. 684-685). These laws were not always strictly enforced, however, and because of their abilities, Jews did enjoy many of the privileges of responsibility which by law they should not have enjoyed.

The law stated, as it did in Visigothic times, that Jews were not to be coerced into conversion, but rather, led to acceptance of the Christian faith through preaching. (Indeed, converted Jews came to enjoy many privileges enjoyed by Spanish-Christians, such as high offices and

dignities.) Furthermore, any Jew or Jewess who voluntarily became a Christian could be protected from other Jews who might wish to persecute them, and the offending Jews would be burned (Law VI, p. 1435).

Concerning penalties to be levied on Christians who became Jews, Alfonso wrote:

> Where a Christian is so unfortunate as to become a Jew, we order that he shall be put to death just as if he had become a heretic; and we decree that this property shall be disposed of in the same way that we stated should be done with that of heretics.
>
> (Law VII, p. 1435).

The law also specified that Christians could not live with nor have social dealings with Jews; nor could they work for them, bathe with them, or receive any medicine from them except by approval of an "intelligent person, such as a Christian physician" (Law VIII, p. 1436).[25] Jews who chose to live with Christian women were guilty of "great insolence and boldness," and would be put to death (*idem.*).

Law X decreed that Jews and Jewesses must wear some distinguishing mark to separate them from the rest of the populace. If they failed to do so and were apprehended, they would have to pay ten maravedis of gold, and if unable to pay, would receive ten lashes (Law XI, p. 1437).[26]

Scott suggests, unconvincingly to this writer, that the rigidity of these laws was really a product of a desire during the Visigothic period to please the clergy and the rabble, who were always clamoring for the persecution of heretics and infidels (see Scott, note 1b, p. 1437). Such a statement implies that Alfonso's personal feelings are not reflected here. One must remember, however, that Alfonso in all his wisdom and openmindedness was quite zealous in the faith—pious, reverent, and deeply dedicated to the Virgin, as his *Cántigas* well demonstrate.

Furthermore, as one explores the subject matter of the *Cántigas,* he will observe that many of the laws set down in the *Siete Partidas* are paralleled in the songs. Was Alfonso here, too, writing merely to please the clergy and the rabble; or was he, in his songs to the Virgin, also expressing his personal feelings toward those whom he and those of his time considered to be the Holy Mother's greatest foe?

The *Cántigas* should illustrate what the *Siete Partidas* have already established: that Alfonso El Sabio, for all his wisdom and understanding, was to a great extent a man of his time and circumstance, a man of flesh and blood who neither could hide nor tried to hide his feelings of prejudice where these complemented or supported the higher ideals of his faith.

Out of the total number of 427 *cántigas,* the figure of the Jew appears in 30. We have divided these 30 presentations into five more or less arbitrary categories—the criterion for their selection being the repetition of certain adjectives describing the Jew in each of the songs. That is, a grouping of the expressions Alfonso used to describe the Jew led to a logical formulation of the categories suggested. They are as follows: (1) the Jew as an archenemy of Christianity; (2) the Jew as the devil's disciple; (3) the Jew as a symbol of avarice; (4) the Jew as a traitor; and (5) the Jew as a Christian convert. While these categories overlap to a certain extent, they are reasonably satisfactory for illustrating the above-mentioned theses.

Interestingly, the only three benevolent treatments the Jew receives, compared to twenty-seven unsympathetic ones, do not present him as possessing any inherent virtue. His only positive trait is that when placed in a difficult situation, he has the wisdom to call upon the Virgin. Significant also is the fact that, even in the positive characterizations, no positive adjective or qualification worthy of note is used to describe the Jew.

THE JEW AN AN ARCHENEMY OF CHRISTIANITY.

This category is the largest and contains sixteen *cántigas.* While only the most representative ones have been selected for analysis here, other related *cántigas* are listed at the end of this section.

Cántiga 12 (I, 37-38) is told as follows: In Toledo, during the August Feast, the Archbishop enters the sanctuary to sing the Mass, and suddenly the voice of a woman (the Virgin) is heard speaking in sorrowful tones: "Oh, my God, how perfidious are the Jews, who killed my Son who was their own, and with whom they still want not peace." The Archbishop tells the people what he has heard, and they cry out: "This indeed hath the wicked Jewish people done." They all hurry to the Jewish quarter of town where they find the Jews abusing and spitting upon a waxen image of Christ. Next the Jews place the image of Christ upon a crude, handmade cross. The text of the *cántiga* is vague as to the outcome: we are merely told in the last two lines that "E por est' ouveron todos de morrer, / e tornou-xe-lles en doo seu solaz" (ll. 33-34). However, the pictorial representation, as will be seen later, supplies the needed clarification.

What is outstanding about this account is that the characterization of the Jew comes from the mouth of the Virgin herself. Alfonso does not make clear whether the Virgin actually appears in the form of a woman, or whether they merely hear her voice;[27] but it is clear that it is she, and that she is meant to be seen as experiencing the sorrow, not only as Saint Mary, but also as the

mother of a flesh-and-blood man. She is both a divine and a human symbol. What surer vehicle to arouse the people's sympathy for her and bitterness and rage against the Jews could Alfonso have used than a mother's anguish over her child?

> Ay Deus, ai Deus,
> Com' é mui grand' e provada / a perfia dos judeus
> que meu Fillo mataron, seendo seus,
> e aynda non queren con ele paz.
>
> (ll. 16-19)

Having suffered His rejection by His own people once, must she suffer it again? The author conveys the enormity of the act in her words, "meu Fillo mataron, seendo seus."

Alfonso has made effective use of the Holy Mother in the story to reflect the feelings of his own people toward the Jews. There is, so to speak, a powerful human vitality in this account which has at its center the divine, yet earthly, mother-figure of the Virgin Mary. Such *vitalismo* is integral to many of Alfonso's *cántigas.*

The pictorial representation of *Cántiga 12* clarifies the ending and supports the negative depiction of the Jews. The Jews themselves, portrayed in panels 5 and 6 with the grotesqueness of caricature—mean faces, crooked noses, some of them bearded—are seen being slain by Christians in battle dress, wielding blades, apparently the manner in which they meet their fate in the story.

Cántiga 12 has shown the Jews as profaners of the Christian religion through their mistreatment of the image of Christ. *Cántiga 34* (I,100-101)[28] deals with a similar theme—this time, with the Jews as people who dishonor the image of the Virgin. The poem is short but significant, and merits examination.

In the city of Constantinople, a Jew steals a beautiful and unusual picture of the Virgin. Hiding it under his cloak, he takes it to his house and places it in a hidden chamber where he secretly insults it. But the Virgin allows the devil to murder the Jew for his deed. Meanwhile, a good and wise Christian finds and rescues the picture from its place of filth, and washes it carefully to cleanse it. He then takes it to his house and places it in a worthy spot, rendering it due honor.

To any virtuous Christian, a statue of the Virgin Mary is an object of admiration and worship. The lesson of this *cántiga,* then, is what happens to the individual who dares to defile such an image.

The Jew here is the archetype of evil, the Christian the archetype of good. Both are "flat characters," to use E.M. Forster's phrase,[29] stereotypes whose behavior never takes on shades, even, of the color to which each is true. Both characters are symbols and perform their "natural" acts; each received his just reward, the Jew at the hands of Satan himself.

Many of Alfonso's characters are types, too graphic, too definitely biased, too puppet-like in their actions. They have no compensating virtues, no qualities which raise them above the single quality which they are created to represent. In many cases (e.g. *Cántiga 109*) these characters are the butt of ridicule. But while they are not exemplary of the highest literary art, they do contribute to a special kind of art, no matter how much that art rests upon prejudice against a minority.

Alfonso could not have used a more accurate representation of the Spanish concept of evil in the thirteenth or fourteenth century than the figure of the Jew. The role played by him in this *cántiga* would be understood at every level of Spanish society, by peasant and aristocrat alike. Likewise, a Christian character as the embodiment of good would be clearly understood by the Spaniards. Therefore, if Alfonso were trying to please his public, he had all the tools necessary at his command in this *cántiga*: the evil Jew performing the foul crime, the good Christian avenging the deed, the devil himself coming to carry away his own.

The pictorial representation reveals the Jew in the first panel skulking among some buildings on the street, holding the picture of the Virgin with the child Jesus. With characteristic black beard, crooked nose, and bulging eyes, he is the very embodiment of one who is accursed. Panel 2 shows him in his home with the picture as he is being attacked by the devil from behind and panel 3 shows him between two devils as he is being dragged away, already slain. The remaining three panels focus on the good Christian—handsome, well-groomed, and richly garbed—as he restores the picture of the Virgin to its rightful place in the church.

Cántiga 286 (III, 89-90) deals with two Jews who make fun of a good Christian "whose actions are above reproach." While the good man is kneeling at the portal of a church to pray, a dog bites and so harasses the man that he has to give up his praying. Meanwhile, two Jews, finding the situation amusing, have begun to tease him: "Viu do(u)s judeus que logo / se fillaron a riir; do que o can lle fezera / e muito o escarnir" (ll. 26-27). Humiliated by their teasing, the good Christian man pleads with the Virgin to rescue him:

> Ai, Sennor, destes judeus
> me dá, se te praz, dereito, / ca son ẽemigos teus
> que mataron a teu Fillo, / que era ome e Deus,
> e por ti me escarnecen, / como tu podes veer.
>
> (ll. 30-33)

The Virgin, defender of those who follow her in the faith, rescues the man from his plight by causing a gate to fall on the Jews. The people who have witnessed the scene are pleased with the outcome and praise the Virgin for her intervention.

If the punishment seems harsh, it must be realized that one can only understand such an attitude by placing himself within the context of thirteenth-century Spain. Alfonso is merely reflecting attitudes which no doubt existed and which he evidently shared, or wanted his people to believe he shared.

Cántigas 4 and *6* are not original with Alfonso. Both appeared first in Berceo's *Milagros de Nuestra Señora* and in Gautier de Coincy's *Miracles de la Sainte Vierge*. Both stories were popular ones which had been making the rounds in European literature during the Middle Ages. Even while not original creations of Alfonso, however, he could very well have omitted them from his collection had he felt them to be an unfair treatment of the Jews; but he did not.

In *Cántiga 4* (I, 11-14) a Jewish glassmaker's son partakes of the Host on Easter Sunday. The Virgin herself administers the communion. When the boy tells his father what has happened, the father goes berserk and immediately seizes his child and throws him into the furnace. But the Virgin protects the child, and the people throw the father into the furnace instead.

While the Jews in the **Cántigas** ordinarily were content with rejecting or insulting the Virgin and her Son, this one in his outrage attempts murder. The outcome is inevitable, for the Virgin in the **Cántigas** will not permit such treatment of one who has shown her veneration. Thus we see that the angry mob has meted out its own justice, a justice in keeping with the law of the land.[30]

Because *Cántiga 6* bears much resemblance to the one just treated, a complete analysis of it will not be presented. Briefly, however, it deals with a fatherless Jewish boy who, because he has learned to sing the "Gaude Virgo Maria," and sings it everywhere, incurs the displeasure of the Jewish populace. One Jew, particularly enraged, takes the boy home with him, kills him, and hides his body in the basement. The boy's mother, invoking the Virgin's help, locates the boy, who has been resurrected. Supported by the rest of the Christians, they fall upon the Jews, throw the murderer into the furnace, and kill the rest mercilessly. Again the law is fulfilled.

Although it is known that Alfonso did not paint the miniatures, he must surely have examined each carefully and can therefore be regarded as having approved of what each depicted. In the illustrations for *Cántiga 4*, which contain the usual six panels, the last three panels show the Jew casting his son into the furnace while the horrified mother looks on in grief. There is a wild, evil look in the eyes of the father. The last panel shows the murderous Jew, with his long black beard and beaked nose, roasting in the furnace.

Similarly, the pictorial presentation of *Cántiga 6* shows the Jew in the third panel driving his ax into the boy's head; he has the same evil look, black beard, and crooked nose. He is surrounded by four other Jews, his accomplices, who smirk with delight at what he is doing. The last panel shows the murderer burning in the furnace while the Christian people watch.

Although Alfonso borrowed these two stories from other collections of miracles, it is clear that he chose two which suited his purpose, and created or directed the pictorial representations to elicit from the reader the responses he wished him to have.

The other eleven *cántigas* which illustrate this category[31] make only brief mention of Jews, so they will not be discussed here. But in each case the mention is negative. The various adjectives and expressions employed by the author in presenting the Jew as the "archenemy of Christianity" include the following: they are "scorners," "unbelievers," "false people," "enemies of Christ"; they are "bad", "mean," and "false unbelievers"; they both try to kill and do kill; and they mistreat and spit upon images of Christ and the Virgin and commit unending perfidy against the religion of Christ. Furthermore, as is evidenced by the miniatures, the Jews were usually drawn as physically ugly, an indication of inward ugliness.

THE JEW AS THE DEVIL'S DISCIPLE.

Picture in your mind a scale to measure good and evil. At the end marked "Good" stand the Virgin and her Son; at the opposite end, labeled "Evil," stands Satan. In between, up and down the scale, appear various characters, such as good Christian laymen, apostles, and other biblical figures to fill in the picture of righteousness. From the midpoint to the other extremity, following the leader of darkness, appear his natural disciples— Moors, skeptics, and heretics of various hue, including the Jews. Alfonso must have had something akin to this concept in his mind when he wrote the **Cántigas,** for he was surely aware there was no better way to portray the Jew negatively than to depict him either as the devil's advocate or as one associated directly with him.[32]

There are four *cántigas* which illustrate the character of the Jew as a minion of Satan. *Cántiga 109* is the outstanding example, but numbers *3, 108,* and *425* belong in this category also.

Cántiga 3 (I, 9-10) is Faustian in character, and the Jew is represented, if not as Mephistopheles, at least as a servant of the devil. The story tells of a man who delivers a letter to Theophilus, offering him power from the devil. The good man succumbs to the temptation and rejects God and the Virgin; but in the end, as his name ("beloved of God") would indicate, he repents and is forgiven.

The ambassador of the Prince of Darkness, by whom Theophilus is instructed and encouraged in his wrongdoing, is a Jew:

> Theophilo . . . fora fazer
> per conssello dun judeu
> carta por gãar poder
> cono demo, e lla deu.

> (ll. 18-21)

The pictorial representation of this *cántiga* is significant with regard to the parallel drawn between the devil and the Jew. The last two panels are especially pertinent; in the first, Theophilus is shown in his home conferring with the Jew; in the second he is kneeling in submission before Satan as the Jew examines the letter. Nearby are numerous apprentices of the devil, horned and grotesque in appearance, and the Jew seems to be addressing Satan. The implication is clear enough.

Cántiga 109 (II, 25-26) is the most explicit statement of the Jew's being in league with the devil. The story tells of a good man on his way to the town of Salas. Five devils have conspired to attack him. As he journeys, he is stopped by the five, but two clerics see the man and rescue him from his tormentors, taking him to the sanction of the church. There he is safe, for the devils agree among themselves that the Virgin is one who is capable of protecting her own.

While the devils consider their loss, a Jew happens along and prevails upon them to explain why they have never threatened him or his people. One of the devils unhesitatingly replies that, since the Jews are already a possession of the Devil's and strive to do his bidding, there is no need to try to ensnare them. It is only those who bear the mark of baptism that they prey upon. Apparently the Jew is satisfied with the devil's answer.

If the Jew meant to imply by his question that Jews were not persecuted because they were above such treatment, the suggestion was quickly dealt with, for the devil spoke frankly:

> Diss' un demo: "Ca meus
> sodes e punnades de me servir . . .
> Por esto non vos fazemos mal,
> ca sodes todos nossos sen al."

> (ll. 37-41)

The miniature illustrating the events of the *cántiga* reveal the Jew only in panel 5, where, with the typical crooked nose and black beard, he stands in the background, a perplexed look on his face, observing the Christian inside the church.

The appearance of the Jew in this *cántiga* is actually an added artistic device. The Jew himself, and the episode of which he is a part, are incidental to the main plot and do not affect the outcome of the story. The basic plot—a good Christian attacked by several devils and then saved by two clerics through the Virgin's intervention—is really complete without the episode of the Jew, and satisfactorily teaches the lesson summarized in the two-line moral: "Razon an os diabos de fogir / ant' a Virgen que a Deus foi parir" (ll. 3-4).

The appearance of the Jew is surprising and enhances the artistry of the *cántiga*. It adds substance to the plot and, in an incidental manner, reemphasizes the virtue of the man the devils are harassing. Whether Alfonso put the clever retort in the mouth of the devil for artistic purposes or because he personally believed that the Jew was in league with the devil and knew that many Spaniards felt so, too,[33] need not be studied here; the fact is that the Jew was definitely depicted by Alfonso as belonging to Satan.

THE JEW AS A SYMBOL OF AVARICE.

Since historical accounts often vary according to the prejudices of the historian, history itself either may or may not bear out the testimony of the *Cántigas* that the Jews were usurers in the worst sense. Alfonso, and by extension the Virgin, shows no sympathy for Jewish characters in their financial transactions.

There are five *cántigas* which illustrate this conclusion well. *Cántigas 25* and *27* particularly are representative and will be examined here; others which depict the Jew as greedy are numbers *51, 85,* and *312.*

In *Cántiga 25* (I, 70-75) the harsh treatment received by the Jew is a consequence of his greed and dishonesty in a financial transaction. A Christian needs a loan, and the Jew offers to lend him money on the condition that the loan be protected by some form of collateral.[34] When the Christian's word alone is not enough, he offers as co-signers Jesus and the Virgin. From the Jew's own lips we learn that while he cannot believe in them ("non quer'eu creer en eles"), he will nonetheless make the loan in their names, for he knows that they are good "security risks."

Thus, even while rejecting Jesus and the Virgin as divine, the Jew thinks highly of them. This would be a point in his favor, were it not for the fact that this Jew

is doing no particular honor to Christianity; his recognizing the worth of Mary and Jesus is strictly a business proposition. Nor is he contradicting his own religion in recognizing Mary and Jesus as "saints" and Jesus as a "prophet" (see ll. 41-43). The development of the story, supported by the pictorial representation, shows clearly that Alfonso's intent is to depict this Jew's lack of integrity.

We are told that the loan must be paid within a given period, as is customary. The Christian asks of Christ that He pay off the debt for him if business takes him too far away to meet the deadline with the Jew. The Christian invests the money wisely, and is successful in his business. But the time expires for repayment of the loan, and the Christian recognizes the difficulty of his situation, for he must get the money to the lender by the following day. Knowing that he cannot do so in time, he places the money in a chest, throws it into the sea, and asks God to see it to its rightful destination: "Ai, Deus, tu o guia."

The Jew sees the chest arrive in port, floating upon the water and, ignorant of its contents, he is eager to open it. His desperation in retrieving it is comical; it is obvious that Alfonso intended satire here. First, the moneylender sends his servant, also a Jew, who fails to retrieve the chest from the water. The Jew's anxiety in losing the chest is reflected in his harsh words to his servant:

> Sol duas nozes
> non vales, que fuste temer
> o mar con mui gran covardia.
>
> (ll. 107-9)

He then plunges into the sea himself, and, after a great struggle, manages to save the chest. His joy over succeeding in this endeavor is equally comical:

> e fillou-a con alegria,
> ca non sse podia soffrer
> de saber o que y jazia.
>
> (ll. 118-20)

When the Jew examines the chest and finds that it contains his money, he decides to hide it under his bed and tell no one. But first he carefully counts the money to see if it is all there.

The climax ensues when the Christian arrives in town, and the Jew requests of him money. The good man is again in anguish, for he sees himself being deceived by the wily moneylender, and retorts: "Fiel bõo tenno que t'ey pagado." He then warns the Jew that the Virgin will reveal what has transpired, and the Jew will not be able to withstand the truth.

At this point the Jew agrees to withdraw his charge if the merchant's story is confirmed by the Virgin. Apparently he is certain that nothing will come of it.

> Diss' o judeu: "Desso me praz;
> pois vaamos aa eigreja,
> e se o disser en mia faz
> a ta omagen, feito seja."
>
>   (ll. 148-152)

Once they are in the church the Jew is confronted with his evil deed both by the offended merchant and by the Virgin herself. The merchant, pleading to the Virgin, asks that she

> faças parecer
> do judeu ssa aleivosia,
> que contra mi cuida trager,
> do que lle dar non deveria.
>
>   (ll. 162-65)

From the mouth of the Virgin comes a direct indictment of the Jew:

> A falssidade dos judeus
> é grand'; e tu, judeu maldito
> sabes que fuste receber
> teu aver, que ren non falia,
> e fuste a arc' asconder
> so teu leito con felonia.
>
>   (ll. 169-74)

The result of this case, Alfonso tells the reader, should be very pleasing to all Christians; for their greatest enemy has been humiliated and has had to recognize his mistake. The Jew casts himself upon the floor in total submission, acknowledges Mary and her Son Jesus, and is converted to the Christian faith. Such a complete reversal—from total evil to total good—is quite an accomplishment, and typical of the feats performed by the Virgin in the *Cántigas.*

Alfonso must have considered this particular characterization highly significant, for it is one of the few *cántigas* that occupies two full pages of miniatures—that is, twelve instead of six panels—to depict in painstaking detail the main sequences. The Jew appears in ten out of twelve and is portrayed as might be expected: a scraggly beard, a large crooked nose, and either a smirk or an evil look on his face. The Christian is handsome and wears beautiful garments. In the first panel the Jew is reclining in leisure as he listens to the Christian's plea for money. In panel 2, in the presence of the Virgin, his look is one of skepticism. In panel 5 we see him directing his half-naked servant, an ugly man with a black beard, to retrieve the chest from the water. In the next panel the Jew is clinging to the chest, his eyes bulging. In panel 8 he is seen wearing the same expres-

sion, counting his money and shoving the chest under the bed. Only in the last panel, when he is seen naked in the baptismal basin, does he appear submissive.

In every respect, Alfonso has made of this *Cántiga* a masterpiece of character analysis. Here the Jew is a perfect example of Alfonso's "round" character, one whose cunning, motivation, conduct, and values are revealed in plot and dialogue. Here the character is raised above the status of the single quality he represents to the level of the individual. This is the more valuable character portrayal and contributes greatly to the quality of the *Cántigas.*

In *Cántiga 27* (I, 80-82) we have another excellent characterization of the Jew as a symbol of avarice. The story is different but the center of attention is, again, money.

Here a group of Christian apostles, who are dedicated to God, purchase a synagogue from the Jews and transform it into a Christian church. The Jews, seeing this, regret having made the sale and go to the Emperor Julian, asking that they be allowed to purchase the synagogue back at the selling price. The apostles, however, feel they have acted rightly in acquiring the church for the worship of the Virgin. After hearing both sides, the Emperor closes the church for forty days, after which it is to be reopened and examined for signs that will determine the matter one way or the other. After the waiting period has expired. the Emperor's committee examines the church and encounters St Peter inside before the altar. St Peter causes a painting of the Virgin to appear before the Jews. Upon seeing it, the Jews decide to leave, lest they have to contend with the Virgin. Thus, the church remains in Christian hands.

It is hardly possible to single out a *cántiga* which limits itself strictly to one single negative aspect of the Jew. This one is unquestionably permeated with the prejudices discussed in the previous section, but we feel that the role money plays in the story is of equal interest. Within the financial framework there are two aspects to be considered.

First, the Jews are clearly willing to sell their place of worship for a good price. But when they see the purpose for which the synagogue has been bought, they adopt a dog-in-the-manger attitude. They do not want to preserve the synagogue for their own religious purposes, but neither do they want the Christians to use it for their worship.

Second, they want the synagogue back, but only on their own terms. Legally, the Jews had no right to the church unless the Christians were interested in reselling. Therefore, as arbitrator Julian, should not have hesitated in his judgment. But his decision reflects some pagan or anti-Christian bias, for he is willing to give the Jews an even chance.[35]

Alfonso is definite in his opinion of the ruler: "emperador cruel, que a Santa Maria no foi fiel" (ll. 65-66), a ruler inclined to take the part of Jews over Christians. He has the wisdom, however, and perhaps the curiosity, to let "the heavens" determine the case.

The Jews in the *cántigas*, for all their evil qualities, are not stupid. After St Peter confronts them with the face of the one to whom they are indirectly doing injury, they instantly realize the futility of their position:

> Os judeus disseron:"Pois que a Deus praz
> que esta omagen a Maria faz,
> leixemos-ll' aqueste seu logar en paz
> e non queramos con ela contender."
>
> (ll. 55-58)

With these words, the Jews surrender their case in favor of the Virgin.

The miniature representing *Cántiga 27* is quite revealing in its details. Panel 1 shows the apostles, easily identifiable throughout because of the halos above their heads, pouring what appears to be big nuggets of gold or big coins into the tunic of one of the Jews. The Jews are smiling with satisfaction at the receipt of payment. The last panel shows the Jews in the church, fainting and falling in every direction, stunned by the appearance of the Virgin's image on the wall.

This category, illustrated by five *cántigas*, offers the reader insight into Alfonso's estimation of the Jew as shrewd and greedy. Such adjectives as "furtadores," "usureros", "aleivosos," "avaros y mentirosos," and the phrase "andan con felonia" are all attributes of people devoted to financial exploitation.

There was a historical incident of great import in Alfonso's time which explains the King's awareness of the possibility of exploitation by the Jew. (The account is given in relation to *Cántiga 348* on pages 685-686). But Chapman suggests that while both the clergy and the general public were hostile toward the Jews because of their wealth, this wealth was largely exaggerated. Further, the fact that the Jews, *marranos* (converted Jews), and *mudéjares* (converted Moslems) often served as the collectors incited public opinion against them. Once when Jews were replaced in this capacity by Christians because of the bitter hatred for them, the people found that this did not solve the problem, for the fault lay in the system. This is not to say that the Jews were entirely innocent of the accusations levelled against them, but that they were less guilty than supposed.[36]

THE JEW AS A TRAITOR.

By some historians the Jew has been considered one of the great traitors in Spanish history. In *Cántiga 2* (I, 7-8) Alfonso reminds the reader of the epic and fateful year 711, which saw Visigothic Spain overrun, pillaged, and almost completely conquered by the Moorish hordes whose domination kept the country in constant upheaval and cultural ferment for centuries to come. Alfonso had not forgotten, almost five hundred years after it occurred, that at the root of the Moorish successes stood the figure of the Jew. Histories, chronicles, and legends will forever remind Christian Spaniards of the act of high treason committed by Count Julian, which placed the proud and noble houses of Spain under the humiliation of Moslem domination. It is, then, this significant crossroads in Spanish history which is being painfully called to mind by Alfonso in the second of his canticles to the Virgin. Let us examine this song in careful detail.

The *cántiga* tells us that the Virgin, well pleased with one of her prelates, gives him a beautiful tunic to wear which will do her honor. Alfonso, as he is named, worships the Virgin day and night and dedicates his compositions and preaching to her so that the praising and worship of Mary will return to Spain. A main obstacle to the growth of Christianity in Spain has been the Jewish faith, and in this context the Jews are singled out in one stanza of the *cántiga:*

> sa loor tornada
> foi en Espanna de quanta
> a end' avian deytada
> judeus e a eregia.
>
> (ll. 22-35)

Not only has Christianity's growth been thwarted; the Virgin's faith has actually been "deytada"—cast out of Spain—by intervention of the Jews. Recall the circumstances of Rodrigo's defeat at the shores of the Guadalete by the Berber-Moorish chief, Tarik.[37] However insignificant it may seem, then, this *cántiga* carries tremendous historical and social significance within its few lines.

Cántiga 348 is also a striking portrayal of the Jew as a traitor, and in this instance the victim is probably Alfonso X himself. The story tells us that "a king of Spain" was having difficulties financing his wars against the Moors in Andalucia. In the past, the Virgin had provided, but the cost of the campaigns was becoming so excessive that the king feared he would have to suspend his attacks. But one night the king dreamt that he had cried out in his sleep to the Virgin for funds, and that she had answered that provision would be made. Alfonso was directed to an area where supposedly he would find a great cache of hidden treasures. But despite his efforts, he was unable to locate the site. A year later, when the king mustered his weary hosts against Granada,[38] the Virgin appeared to him personally, showing him a place where he had not looked before. The monarch's reward was astonishing—great quantities of gold, silver, precious stones, and fine garments. According to the Virgin, the treasure had been buried by the Jews: "Ca mui gran tesouro / te darei que ascondudo / jaz sso terra, que meteron / y muy peyores ca mouros" (ll. 47-48).

The fact that Alfonso is vague about the identity of the monarch involved in this *cántiga* can be seen as an effort on his part to employ diplomacy. But one may infer from evidence in the *cántiga* that the king involved was either Alfonso himself, or his father Fernando III.

Spanish kings, in their efforts against the Moors, were constantly in need of money to finance their wars, and Alfonso was no exception.[39] In fact, because of his political aspirations and foreign interests, he was probably in greater financial need than most. The Virgin explains that money exists, and is simply to be found in the hands of the Jews—an enemy worse, actually, than the one Spanish Christendom is fighting. The Moors, at least, are a declared enemy, while the Jews, who illicitly hide away great sums of money while enjoying favored positions in the kingdom, are the surreptitious enemy.

As traitor, then, the Jew is greatly to be feared.

THE JEW AS A CHRISTIAN CONVERT.

Of the thirty *cántigas* that deal with Jews, only three depict him positively, and in each case the positive characterization is the result of the Jew's conversion. Two out of the three (i.e., numbers *89* and *133*) somewhere make negative reference to the Jew; only *Cántiga 107* makes no negative reference whatsoever.

Let us look, then, at number *107* (II, 19-21), since it is the exception. The story is as follows: in the city of Segovia a Jewess, accused of some crime, is taken out by the people to be thrown off a high cliff to her death. The woman in her plight calls upon the Virgin, and the Virgin intercedes. When the Jewess is cast down, no harm comes to her; she floats to earth at the foot of the cliff. Immediately afterwards she becomes a Christian.

Even before the conversion, the characterization of the Jewess is positive from the beginning to the end. The only reference to her wrongdoing is that "achada que foi en err." Besides, in all six panels of the miniature she is drawn as a beautiful woman with a kind face, while the other Jews surrounding her have the character-

istic malign expressions. (There appear to be one or two Christian bystanders in the pictures also, and these, as usual, are depicted as handsome.)

It is not made clear whether the woman had broken Christian or Jewish law, but we may safely assume that it was Jewish since it was they who wanted to throw her from the cliff.

> Os judeus que a levaron
> na camisa a leixaron
> e logo a espenaron
> dizendo: "Alá yrá!"
>
> (ll. 36-39)

This reaction from her tormentors comes just after she has promised the Virgin that "sse ficar viv' e sãa, / logo me farei crischaã" (ll. 31-32). Her rejection of her Jewish tradition would understandably anger her fellow Jews, for the Jewess calls upon the Virgin, not out of the anxiety of the moment, but out of an already-developing propensity to believe, it seems.

We are given no reason to believe that her plea is for reasons of convenience, for when her life is spared, immediately she rushes to a church and exclaims, "Acá . . . / Vĩid' e batiçar-m-edes" (ll. 59-61). No one doubts her sincerity, and

> tan tost' aquela gente
> a batiçou mantenente;
> e foi sempre ben creente.
>
> (ll. 66-68)

This Jewess, then, is given a place beside other Christians.

The purpose of this paper has been to study and evaluate the attitude of Alfonso X toward the figure of the Jew as revealed in the **Cántigas de Santa Maria** and the **Siete Partidas**. Alfonso seemed in most cases to be almost completely influenced by adverse sentiments toward the Jews.

Jews, of course, were well known all over Spain, for they were citizens in every city and in many villages. Virtually every Spaniard, with the possible exception of peasants in remote rural areas, had seen Jews and had even had dealings with them. And Spanish legend, folklore, and even history were filled with tales of Jewish treachery and unreliability—usually, though not always, exaggerated.

Because the Jews composed a hated minority, it is not strange that some seven percent of the stories in the **Cántigas** are concerned with them. They made good villains in stories for popular consumption. They were excellent foils for Christian characters; they provided made-to-order antagonists to Christian men and women and to the Blessed Virgin Mary; and they became the butt of satire, caricature, and animus.

But King Alfonso's personal sentiments, as revealed in his literary treatment of them, emerge quite sharply defined also. True, his prejudices lent themselves conveniently to a certain didacticism which, as ardent champion of the Faith, the King wished to make evident to his people. But there is in the *Cántigas* little of the tolerance one associates with this monarch in his dealings with the educated and highly trained Jewish physicians, scientists, and government figures. Although his great love of learning led him to close his eyes to the widespread racial and religious prejudice which existed at that time in Spain, this love did not preclude his suspicion and social denigration of Jews in his *Cántigas.* This contrast in the King's sentiments about and actions with regard to these minorities is noteworthy.

We have seen that, out of the 427 *cántigas* which Alfonso either wrote or supervised, thirty deal extensively with the character of the Jew. Of these, only three are sympathetic, in the sense that in each the Jew relinquished his own religion in favor of Christianity. Only as a convert, then, has the Jew appeared sympathetically. Throughout the other poems, numerous negative adjectives are used in describing him. Although one might have suspected that the Jew ranked low on the social scale, the intensity of the unsympathetic treatments and of the unusually ugly pictoral representations is surprising.

Evidently, Alfonso's experience with the Jew was less than satisfactory. For where in the *Cántigas* is the Jew of Alfonso's court? Why has the Jew who had done so much for Spanish society, and for the King personally in his renaissance of learning, been neglected in the King's poems? The double standard of Alfonsine sentiment toward the Jew—that is, the high regard he had for the scientific, legalistic, and other erudite and cultural contributions of this people as opposed to his prejudice, fear, and scorn for them—is amplified by legal evidence. In the *Siete Partidas,* the king made it clear that this minority group was not to be accorded rights and privileges equal to those of his Christian subjects. High regard for Jewish capabilities was reserved for a mere handful of individuals useful to the King in his erudite and scientific activities.

In the role of literary raconteur, a monarch is more than king or scholar. He reveals something of his inner self. In the *Cántigas* Alfonso gives a detailed description of a country's peoples and customs, of a king's interests and duties; but, most important of all, whether consciously or unconsciously, he has to reveal a king's attitudes. It is here, in the *Cántigas,* that we find more than a king clothed in ermine and velvet, more than a scholar wrapped in the cloak of learning, more than an example of the Christian faith; we find here a flesh-and-blood, practical man, swayed by the attitudes of his day.

Notes

1. Since the word *Cántigas* is written with an acute accent in mediaeval Galician Portuguese, it will appear that way throughout this study.

2. No work of importance has come to my attention which portrays as hazardous the lot of the Jew in the thirteenth century.

3. Desiring to promote his own renaissance of learning, Alfonso X drew upon the same sources which the Moors—whose holdings in Spain were now reduced to the kingdom of Andalucia—had drawn upon: namely, the Jews. See Américo Castro, *España en su Historia: cristianos, moros y judíos* (Buenos Aires, 1948), pp. 347-349. Hereinafter this work will be referred to as *España.*

4. *Ibid.,* pp. 482-483.

5. *Ibid.,* pp. 483.

6. *Idem.*

7. *Idem.*

8. *Ibid.,* p. 503.

9. Those who can definitely be proved to have aided in the research sponsored by Alfonso were Yehudá el Cohenese, Semuel el Leví, Rabi Çag el de Toledo, don Xosse, and don Abraham, alfaquí, the King's physician. *Ibid.,* pp. 496-497.

10. See Américo Castro, Valbuena Prat, Martín de Riquer, Antonio Ballesteros y Beretta, Evelyn Procter, Emilio González López, and Antonio Solalinde, for example. Even the authoritative *Cambridge Medieval History* credits Spain with being the most important refuge for Jews existent at that time in Europe: "They were strongly protected in the interests of science and literature in the time of Alfonso X . . . and played a great part in financial affairs both public and unofficial." See C. H. McIlwain, "Medieval Estates", *The Cambridge Medieval History,* planned by J. B. Bury and edited by J. R. Tanner, C. E. Previte-Orton, and Z. N. Brooke, 8 vols. (Cambridge, 1932), VII, 661. Nevertheless, the author notes that the legislation of the *Siete Partidas* "subjected the Jews . . . to the most minute and galling restrictions."

11. Emilio González López, *Historia de la civilización española* (New York, 1959), p. 159.

12. The *mudéjares* were Moslems who had been converted to Christianity.

13. González López, p. 159.

14. See *España,* pp. 481-484.

15. Max L. Margolies and Alexander Marx, *A History of the Jewish People* (Philadelphia, 1956), p. 69.

16. See *The Universal Jewish Encyclopedia,* ed. Isaac Landman, 10 vols. (New York, 1943), IX, 689-690. Jewish historian Heinrich Graetz finds Alfonso X's reign definitely *not* benevolent toward Jews, on the other hand. (There were four legal treatises or books written either by Alfonso or under his direction, the most important of which was the *Siete Partidas.* The other three are the *Setenario,* the *Fuero Juzgo,* and the *Espéculo de las Leyes.*) Graetz is probably referring to the *Partidas* when he says that Alfonso X's statutes were "anti-Jewish." But he quotes the monarch out of context in places. See his *History of the Jews,* 6 vols. (Philadelphia, 1894), IV, 194.

17. Trans. Samuel Parson Scott (New York, 1931). Hereinafter referred to as *Partidas.* All of the translations of the *Partidas* are taken from Scott.

18. Ed. Walter Mettmann, 3 vols. (Coimbra, Portugal: Acta Universitatis Coníbrigensis, 1959-1964).

19. See John E. Keller's discussion, *Alfonso X, El Sabio,* Twayne's World Author Series, XII (New York, 1962), pp. 120-122.

20. The eight *cántigas* are *2, 3, 4, 12, 25, 27, 34,* and *51.* "Correspondence of the Spanish Miracles of the Virgin," *Romanic Review,* XIX (1928), 151-153.

21. The incorporation in the *cántigas* of events in which the author participated or which took place during his lifetime is called "integralismo" by Castro. See his discussion in *España,* pp. 341-346.

22. Keller, pp. 66-69.

23. His opening statement concerning them is that even though they are a people who do not believe in the religion of Christ, "yet, the Great Christian sovereigns have always permitted them to live among them." It is unlikely that Fernando III could have contributed this portion to the *Siete Partidas,* for scholarship that accords him a hand in the work credits him only with beginning the codex. The portion dealing with the Jews is in the last Book. In any case, Alfonso X, even while apparently tolerant of Jews, seems to be admitting that it is more out of tradition than anything else.

24. *Partidas,* VIII, Title XXIV, Law I, p. 1433.

25. The Hebrew physicians of the Middle Ages were the most learned and skillful of the time. While the commoners were left to the care of amateurs,

the nobles and royalty (Alfonso was no exception) kept Jewish physicians in their palaces and placed every confidence in their ability. Alfonso did so before and after this law was adopted.

26. In almost every country, whether Christian or Moslem (but especially Christian), these victims of popular hatred were impelled to wear a particular costume or garment as a mark of obloquy. It was sometimes a robe, sometimes a hat; the latter was the distinguishing mark in Spain. The color was usually yellow. The Jews depicted in the miniatures often wear these homely garments.

27. Panels 1 and 2 of the frame suggest that the voice of the Virgin might have come "from on high," for of the Virgin herself we can seen only a statue upon the altar, holding the child Jesus. It is not reasonable to think that the voice comes from the statue, since the congregation of faithfuls is looking about at random and not directly at the statue.

28. The *estribilho* is helpful in the characterization of the Jew: "Gran dereit' e que fill' o demo por escarmento / quen contra Santa Maria filla atrevemento."

29. *Aspects of the Novel* (New York, 1954), p. 67.

30. In the *Siete Partidas* Alfonso says of those who try to harm a Jew who becomes a Christian: ". . . if any Jew or Jewess should voluntarily desire to become a Christian, the other Jews shall not interfere with this in any way, and if they stone, wound, or kill any such person, . . . and this can be proved; we order that all the murderers . . . shall be burned. But where the party was not killed, but wounded, or dishonored; we order that the judges of the neighborhood, where this took place shall compel those guilty of the attack . . . to make amends for the same; and also that they be punished for the offense which they committed, as they think they deserve. (Law VI, p. 1435.)

31. *Cántigas 22, 71, 91, 135, 149, 187, 238, 390, 415, 419,* and *426.*

32. For a detailed study of the devil in the *Cántigas,* see Charles L. Nelson, "Literary and Pictorial Treatment of the Devil in the Cantigas of Santa Maria" (unpublished M. A. thesis, Department of Romance Languages, University of North Carolina, 1964).

33. Charles E. Chapman writes, in *A History of Spain* (New York, 1918), that it was not uncommon for the Jews to be thought of as being in communion with the devil. He says: "Moslems and Jews continued to be the most famous physicians of Castillo . . . The most marked characteristic of

the cultivation of the natural sciences was in their extravagant applications with a view to . . . obtain vast wealth through supernatural agencies. Thus chemistry tended toward alchemy, . . . whereby base metals might be turned into gold . . . Chemists and alchemists came to be considered as practicers of magic arts in more or less intimate communion with the Devil" (p. 183).

34. B. W. Barron indicates, in *A Social and Religious History of the Jews* (New York, 1937), that for all that is said of the Jews' greed, they were among the fairest in lending throughout the Middle Ages, charging 33% per annum. During the same period other lenders asked as much as 43%, and by the sixteenth century, after the Jews were expelled from Spain, Christian lenders went as high as 240% (II, 16-25).

35. Curiously, Alfonso set the story in the fourth century during the reign of Flavius Claudius Julianus. Although Julian was reared under Christian tutelage, he early left the new religion for paganism. No overt persecution of Christians existed during his reign, but they were virtually prohibited from holding high office. See John Henry Freese and Thomas Kirkup, "Julian", *Encyclopaedia Britannica*, 1962 ed., XIII, 177-178.

36. See *A History of Spain,* pp. 143, 158.

37. Chapman's statement about this historical happening is vague. He says merely that while it has never been ascertained, "It seems likely that . . . the Spanish Jews plotted for a Moslem invasion of Spain" (p. 32), since the subsequent invasion found support among them. But such reliable historians and critics as Claudio Sánchez Albornoz (*La España musulmana: según los autores islamitas y cristianos medievales,* 2 vols. [Buenos Aires, 1960], I, 33-39), A. González Palencia, (*Historia de la España musulmana* [Barcelona, 1932]), E. Lévi Provençal (*Histoire de l'Espagne musulmane,* 3 vols., 2d. ed. [Paris, 1950-53]), Stanley Lane-Poole and Arthur Gilman (*The Story of the Moors in Spain* [New York, 1898], pp. 8-14) establish that Count Julian's conspiracy and treason are a matter of undeniable historical fact.

When King Witiza, who favored tolerance for the Jews (see Rafael Altamira, *A History of Spain* [New York, 1918], p. 85), was deposed in favor of the warrior-noble Rodrigo, the sympathizers of King Witiza—mainly the entire Jewish population, but also a few Christian noblemen—conspired to rid the kingdom of Rodrigo's rule. Count Julian, a Jew, hated Rodrigo. So Julian, in league with the Arab ruler Musa, marched to meet Rodrigo's army at the Guadalete in the year 711.

Although Rodrigo's troops numbered 100,000 (see Sánchez Albornoz, *La España musulmana,* I, 34-35), his army was routed because of rampant treachery on the part of his Jewish troops and followers of Witiza. In a single, decisive battle, Visigothic Spain became the Moorish Spain of Al-Andalús, and the course of Spanish history was changed completely—largely due to the treachery of one well-placed Jew and his fellows.

38. According to Altamira, the few territorial gains Alfonso X made during his reign were in Granada, in the following areas: the district of Cádiz, from Morón, to Medina Sidonia and Rota; Niebla and part of Algarve; and the fortress of Cartagena. These victories narrowed on the west and east the former coastal frontiers of the kingdom of Granada (p. 232).

39. Amid the chaos resulting from Sancho IV's rebellion against Alfonso was an historical happening of the utmost importance in understanding what inspired Alfonso's depiction of the Jew in this *cántiga.* In the year 1278 Alfonso X laid siege to Algeciras under circumstances made difficult for lack of supplies. Hope for Alfonso's armies rested in the money which was to be forthcoming from his Jewish collector of rents and taxes, don Zag de la Malea (collector for Leon and Castile). The key to national survival, then, was in Jewish hands. Don Zag and other Jews were able to subsist because of royal protection, and it was not difficult to see that the winds were blowing in favor of Sancho. Sancho requested the funds for his own political ambitions while Alfonso and his armies lay weak, poor, and sickly. Don Zag turned all the money over to Sancho while Alfonso's armies and fleet suffered complete disaster at Algeciras. Alfonso dismissed Dog Zag from his post, but the damage was done. See Castro, *España,* p. 351.

Roger D. Tinnell (essay date 1981)

SOURCE: Tinnell, Roger D. "Authorship and Composition: Music and Poetry in *Las Cantigas de Santa Maria* of Alfonso X, El Sabio." *Kentucky Romance Quarterly* 28, no. 2 (1981): 189-98.

[*In the following essay, Tinnell explores the question of the extent to which the* Cantigas *should be regarded as the work of Alfonso.*]

Controversy surrounds the four hundred and twenty-odd **Cantigas de Santa Maria.** What musical type served as the model for the *cantigas,* for example, was it an

Arabic *zéjel?* Higinio Anglés has insisted that the melodies of the *cantigas* have no relation to Arabic melodies, this in spite of Julián Ribera y Tarragó's attempts to force the *cantiga* melodies to correspond with Arabic poetical metres. Gustave Reese admits that the miniatures which accompany the *cantigas* do indeed prove the Arabic influence on instruments in the peninsula, but he denies proof of Arabic influence on the music itself.[1] Scholars have searched for the musical origin of the *cantigas* in the Provenzal or Catalan conductus, in troubadour melodies,[2] in Hebrew melody,[3] in both secular and liturgical models.

It was not until the turn of the present century and the research[4] of Pierre Aubry that musicologists recognized that the musical notation of the *cantigas* was mensural notation and, therefore, decipherable, and musicologists are still at odd ends as to how exactly the music sounded. Thirteenth-century musical notation had included no expressive marks. How, then, did the music sound in performance? Was it very "popular,"[5] or was it restrained in expression? How much spontaneous improvisation was allowed in its performance? Who performed the *cantigas* and on what instruments?[6] Also, what were the sources for the miracles described in the songs[7] and how did the source affect the melody? Who set these miracles to verse and who composed the music for the *cantigas*, troubadours in Alfonso's court, priests, the king himself? John Keller, Adolfo Salazar, Nan Cooke Carpenter, and Alan Deyermond, among others, feel that the poetry and/or the music of the *cantigas* are at least in part the product of the hand of Alfonso X himself.[8] We shall glance at what we know of the origins of music in Spain and of the musical environment in thirteenth-century Castile in particular and point to possible answers to some of these questions, particularly those of authorship and composition.

Wall painting at Osuna shows men blowing large, straight trumpets, the Phoenicians who founded Cadiz loved musical entertainment, and the Hebrews who arrived in Iberia had already a strong musical tradition. Greek ceramics discovered at Ampurias show dancing girls and instrumentalists; the Roman theater at Merida contains a statue of Mercury with a great lyre, and the silver disc commemorating Trajan's rule is decorated with cherubs with lyres.[9] We know that Visigothic kings kept *mimos,* that probably Byzantine church music influenced Spanish church music,[10] and that the sixth-century Council of Toledo complained of the dancing in churches, that Saint Leander of Seville (d. 599) composed, as did Saints Eugenius, Ildefonsus and Julian, and that Arab conquerors pursued the musical pleasures in Spain after their fierce religious fervor had abated (there was a flourishing school of music in eleventh-century Cordoba). The Spanish Christian Church was one of the first to introduce hymns into the liturgy,[11] and the mozarabic liturgy (the Toledan heresy), now indecipherable, was not suppressed until the eleventh century. In the late Middle Ages, Spanish nobles surrounded themselves with poets, musicians, artists, and thinkers from all parts of the known world. But, though we know the names of over six hundred singers and instrumentalists between 1290-1400 in Catalonia-Aragon alone,[12] and know, too, that musical tradition in Spain was an ancient one by the time of Alfonso's reign, and that musical cross-fertilization was astounding in its complexity, we have no clear idea as to what all this strumming and pounding and singing sounded like. Unfortunately, most non-liturgical music was never written down,[13] and much of the liturgical work which was committed to paper is now undecipherable. Aquitanian (mensural) notation did not appear in Spain until the late twelfth-early thirteenth centuries, earlier mozarabic neumes are still undecipherable, and even individual notes were written differently by different scribes in different parts of the peninsula; the neumes *scandius, punctus, podatus, clivis* and *torculus* were written in nine, ten, thirteen, seventeen and twenty-eight ways respectively.[14] We have some snatches of information about interpretation of pre-twelfth-century Spanish notation: sixteen Mozarabic melodies were transcribed into Aquitanian notation in an anonymous 12th-century hand in the margin of an 11th-century San Millán de la Cogolla manuscript. Unfortunately, the original Mozarabic neumes were erased, so no comparison can be made. Cardinal Cisneros (1436-1517), Archbishop of Toledo, incorporated into his *Intonarium toletanum* (a volume of one hundred and nineteen folios printed in black and red ink on paper, with mensural notation on red five-line staves) a *Hymnal* which contained several "reconstructed" Mozarabic melodies. But Cardinal Cisneros had been unable to find anyone who knew how to decipher the neume notation of the Mozarabic Codices of the Cathedral of Toledo, so his reconstructed melodies are untrustworthy models.[15] Even with the aid of decipherable Aquitanian mensural notation, many problems still remain unsolved for the modern musicologist. Any attempt to answer such questions as: How was the music embellished?; What did an accompanist do?; How many instruments were used in a performance?; and, What instrument was used for what kind of song?; must recognize as of primary importance the musical environment of the period and the literary and musical tradition of poet, composer and performer.

One way to investigate performance is to observe the performer. In Spain it was the *juglar* who sang, played and told tales of heroic deeds, recited saints' lives and entertained a public. There were many different kinds of audiences, and many kinds of *juglares*. A *Domini imperatoris joculator* did not sing for the same audience as an ordinary entertainer. Nor, of course, was the *juglar* necessarily a he. Twelve of the sixteen miniatures in the *Cancionero de Ajuda,* for example, show a female entertainer with the juglar. The Archpriest of Hita in the *Libro de buen amor* (vv. 470-1) talks of females who performed, and many of these women were quite well-known.[16] The *juglar* and his art were important parts of life at all levels. Entertainers such as a Cítola or Cornamusa or Malanotte flashed brightly in the church, marketplace, castle, townhouse, and at the dinner tables of kings and prelates (so brightly that one poet asked:

> Decid, amigo, sois flor . . .
> gayo o martin pescador . . .
> o tamboril, o trompeta,
> o menestril, o farante,
> o bancal, poyal o arquetta
> o tañedor de la flaute?).[17]

Words most often used to describe the effects produced by a good *juglar* include *solaz, solazar, solacia,* etc. In the **Siete Partidas** Alfonso X placed "cantares et sones et strumentos" high among the cures for "pesares" and "cuidados" (**Las Siete Partidas** II, 6, 21). The much-discussed question of the origins of the *juglar* in Spain can not be dealt with here other than to note that Menéndez Pidal finds that the death of one *Cardelle joculero* in the eleventh century marks the first recorded use of the word *juglar* in Spain,[18] and that French fashion was followed and gave rise to a clearly codified distinction between *trovador,* a cultured creator of fine poetry, and *juglar,* a simple performer of another's music.

Alfonso X, el Sabio's court was home to many troubadours and *juglares* and as such was torn by jealousies and rivalries among these musicians. Guiraut Riquier, one of the Provenzal troubadours who lived in Alfonso's court, wrote a *Suplicatió*[19] lamenting that idiots with monkeys and puppets were being called *juglares.* He beged the king to order that the word *juglar* be used only for those who played well and gave momentary pleasure, and that the word *trovador* be used only for those who knew how to create good verses and whose solace and teachings endured even after their deaths. Riquier versified the king's response in a *Declaratió.* After a brief etymological discussion of names, Alfonso pointed out that, though in France everyone was called a *juglar,* in Spain each type of performer had a special classification: he who played an instrument well was a *juglar,* frequently in the company of the *juglar* was the female *juglaresa* or *juglara,* the performer who mimicked was a *remedador,*[20] ill-talented performers in public places were *cazurros* or *zaharrones* or *zamarones,* certain masked figures were called *cagarrones* or *caharrones,* knife throwers were *trasechadores,* fools were known as *bufones, albardanes* or *truhanes,* and men who went about dressed in animal hair were known as *caballeros salvajes.*[21] He

who with courtesy and science knew how to conduct himself well among the wealthy and to play instruments, sing *novas* or recite poetry, possessed the mastery of the sovereign troubadour, he was the *don doctor de trobar.*

In Spain, the *juglar* served a troubadour, travelled with him and played his master's compositions. The *juglar* might perform with a troubadour in a *tensón,* for example, but it is clear from the *tensones* which survive that the *juglar* was the inferior and even an object of ridicule. Apparently at great banquets *juglares* performed at every dish and were given gifts (some quite rich) at each performance. They also travelled with the great and near-great to relieve the pains of travel, and they performed at weddings, wakes, religious ceremonies, coronations, etc. They sang, also, in public places and were, like the travelling cleric and student, active agents in the diffusion of the literature of their day. Provenzal troubadours and *juglares* were very popular in Alfonso's court and they must have strongly influenced both court and popular literary-musical traditions. Italian, Muslim, German,[22] Scottish, Persian, Egyptian, Tartan and even Bohemian artists also brought new ideas and styles into Spain.

The cosmopolitan air of Alfonso's great court on the occasion of an important affair must have been remarkable, with many artists singing in their own languages, using their own melodies and rhythms, dancing their own dances, and playing their own favorite instruments, instruments such as the *vihuela de peñola* or the *viheula de arco,* the two most important varieties of the vihuela, the principal instrument of the peninsula, or other stringed instruments such as the *cedra,* the *cítola,* the *rabé* (a primitive violin), the Germanic or Celtic *farpa,* the *rota* (a small harp), the various kinds of psalteries (with up to seventy-eight strings), the lute, the *bandurria* and the dulcimer. Instrumentalists blew into various kinds of flutes, trumpets and bagpipes (some of them quite mechanically complex),[23] and pumped portative organs. Drums were low instruments and were thumped in unison with the other percussion instruments such as the cymbals, tambourine and castanets.[24] We have some hints as to what instruments were used for what type of music; the Arcipreste de Hita, for example, tells us that Arabic music did not use bowed instruments.

> Arávigo non quiere la viuela de arco,
> Cinfon ía é guitarra non son de este marco,
> Cítola é odreçillo non aman *ataguylaco;*
> Mas aman la taverna é sotar con vellaco.
>
> Albogues é bandurria, caramiello é çanpoña
> Non se paga del arávigo, quanto dellos Boloña:
> Como quier que por fuerça dísenlo con vergoña,
> Quien lo desir fesiere, pechar deve caloña.[25]
>
> (LBA [Libro de Buen Amor], 1516-1520)

The combination of all these instruments and instrumentalists, languages and songs, performers and performing techniques must have made for frequent chaos and tumult: Ramón Muntaner says that at the coronation of the Aragonese Alfonso IV in 1328 the 256 newly-knighted *caballeros* all played instruments, that there were 300 pairs of horns and more than 1,000 (can he be exaggerating for effect?) *juglares, caballeros salvajes,* etc.[26] In 1461 Miguel Lucas talks of a solemn mass in which everyone was astonished by the noise of *atables, dulzainas, tamborinas, panderos,* and *cantares.*[27] The *Cantigas de Santa Maria* are amply illustrated with miniatures showing *juglares* and other entertainers singing, playing and dancing. Number 194, for example, tells how the Virgin helped a *juglar* beset by robbers.[28] Number 8 relates how the Virgin caused a candle to descend onto a *juglar*'s viola (there are, however, few references to instruments in the verse themselves).

Alfonso X, el Sabio, the man who caused the cantigas to be written, was proud of his glorious court, a court that was not great politically nor militarily but which excelled in its artistic brilliance, a brilliance which was in itself a kind of thirteenth-century Spanish renaissance.[29] He was especially proud of his cultured musical background.[30] In his book *Septenario,* he described his warrior-king-father, Fernando, as a man who knew everything a good caballero should know; Fernando surrounded himself with good *juglares* and troubadours, and he knew how to distinguish between good and bad performances.[31] Alfonso loved music of all kinds, delighting in Provenzal as well as Galician lyrics and song,[32] and he was so enamoured of the musical art that he founded a chair in music at the University of Salamanca.[33]

At the first of the *Cantigas* manuscript is a miniature showing Alfonso himself surrounded by scribes and musicians. His hand is raised, and it would seem that he is dictating poetry or story or music or all three to the scribes and that the instrumentalists and singers are perhaps trying out the king's musical ideas.[34] The king surrounded by his court is a common formulaic pattern in Gothic painting and literature: Joinville's description of France's Louis IX seated in a garden dressed in black silk with white peacock feathers on his head and surrounded by his nobles all seated on rich rugs[35] is a good example of the king seen as center. Despite the tendency among critics to regard the above-mentioned miniature as proof that Alfonso himself composed all or part of the *cantigas,* the historian must bear in mind that there would not necessarily appear in the *Cantigas* mention of any artist other than the king. The bond between artist and patron in the thirteenth century was still fundamentally feudal and the professional artist was taken for granted. The work done in the court appertained to him for whom it was done, rather than to him who did it.[36]

There is no doubt that Alfonso X was a driving force behind the composition and creation of the *Cantigas de Santa Maria* and that they were an expression of *his* ideals, interests and attitudes.[37] They were, in effect, an expression of his own mind. But, even if he had composed all or some of the *cantigas* himself, there is no reason to believe that the work would have been entirely or even principally his own. The principle of constitutive unity[38] important in the formation of the medieval church was of equal weight in the court. There was not a crowd of mutually independent musicians and poets in Alfonso's court, but a community of artists whose mutual influence and borrowings must have been complete. Mozart remarks[39] in his letters that some of his best melodies came to him in snatches of tunes heard through open windows and through walls in boarding houses and in public places where groups of musicians of all kinds were rehearsing, composing and performing. We can expect no less expansive environment in Alfonso's court.[40] As he is seen in the miniature I have mentioned, Alfonso must have sat in his court and suggested a song, perhaps based on a model then popular. Rival troubadours must have vied for the honor of selecting the perfect melody for the king. Alfonso may have suggested an appropriate musical idea and must have received in turn suggestions of musical turns of phrase, delightful possibilities. Instrumentalists and singers must have interpreted each song according to their own training and experience and therefore their own musical taste.[41] Alfonso's *Cantigas de Santa Maria* are surely the product of religious devotion, but first and foremost they reflect his keen delight in music and poetry and the diversity and excellence of his court. They are, like all great Gothic monuments,[42] the product of a community of minds functioning as one.

The questions, then, of who composed the *cantigas'* melodies and who wrote their verses are somewhat false questions. The court composed their songs and the court versified their miracles. In the miniature in question, Alfonso may have his hand raised not so much to dictate to the court, but in an attempt to regain some sort of order in the chaotic exuberance of talented professionals whose diversity of training and experience was matched only by the extent and diversity of Spanish musical tradition and which was outshone only by the glory of the Virgin to whom they raised their songs.

Notes

1. Higinio Anglés, *La Música de las Cantigas de Santa Maria del Rey Alfonso el Sabio,* 3 vols. (Barcelona: Diputación Provincial de Barcelona,

1958-64), Vol. 2, p. 11. Julián Ribera's views are found in his *La música árabe y su influencia en la española* (n.p., 1927), *La música de las Cantigas: Estudio sobre su origen y naturaleza* (Madrid: RAE, 1922), and in *La música andaluza medieval en las canciones de trovadores, troveros y minnesinger,* 3 vols. (Madrid, 1923-25). Gustave Reese, *Music in the Middle Ages* (New York: Norton, 1940), pp. 245-46. See, also, Dorothy Clotelle Clarke, "Versification in Alfonso el Sabio's *Cantigas,*" *Hispanic Review,* 23 (1955), pp. 83-98.

2. Anglés points out that the *cantiga* was in vogue in Spain even before the arrival in Alfonso's court of Provenzal troubadours (such as G. Riquier) and avows that the music of the troubadours "distaba mucho de la gracia y delicadeza de las *cantigas* de Alfonso el Sabio . . ." (p. 6).

3. Ann Livermore, in *A Short History of Spanish Music* (New York: Vienna House, 1972), argues that the Spanish melismatic traditions may be Semitic in origin (p. 6), and Joseph Dahmus, in *A History of Medieval Civilization* (New York: Odyssey, 1964), cites the Hebrew influence on medieval music as one of the most important (p. 639). F. B. Artz, in *The Mind of the Middle Ages* (New York: Knopf, 1965), points out that Christian musical tradition had inherited from the Jews an "elaborate style of chanting which often used a number of notes to one syllable and also adorned the chant with ornaments like the repeated alleluias at the end of a Psalm . . ." (p. 92).

4. Pierre Aubry, *Iter Hispanicum* (n.p.: Societe Internacionale de Musique Gregorienne, 1907).

5. Livermore (p. 1) points to *alegría* as the keynote to all Spanish music. I. J. Katz, "The Traditional Folk Music of Spain: Explorations and Perspectives," in *Yearbook of the International Folk Music Council* (1974), notes that there is evidence that secular music practices influenced the *Antiphoner of Leon,* and he calls the *Cantigas* the earliest *Cancionero* with music of the "popular" type (pp. 66-67).

6. A great variety of performance techniques in modern transcriptions of the *Cantigas* are heard in the many recordings of the *Cantigas* listed in Roger Tinnell, "An Annotated Discography of Recordings of *Las Cantigas de Santa Maria* of Alfonso X, el Sabio," *La corónica,* 6 (1977), pp. 46-48; "Supplement to 'An Annotated Discography of Recordings of Music from the Middle Ages in Spain: Additional Recordings of *Las Cantigas de Santa Maria* of Alfonso X el Sabio and of the

songs of Juan del Encina," *La corónica,* 7 (1978), pp. 62-63; and "New Recordings of *Las Cantigas de Santa Maria,*" *La corónica,* 8 (1980), pp. 215-16.

7. John E. Keller, *Alfonso X, el Sabio* (New York: Twayne, 1967), cites many sources of the miracles which occur in the *Cantigas,* among them local folklore, happenings in the royal court, German proverbs, other miracle texts such as Gautier de Coincy's *Miracles de la Sainte Vierge,* Vincent de Beauvais' *Speculum Historiale,* Gil de Zamora's *Liber Mariae,* etc. (pp. 73-78).

8. John E. Keller, in "Folklore in the *Cantigas* of Alfonso el Sabio," *Southern Folklore Quarterly,* 23 (1959), p. 175, states that "Alfonso himself is quite probably the author of some of the poems." In his 1967 Twayne book Keller expands his analysis and avers that Alfonso "possibly, and even probably, was the author of and composer of many, if not all (the *cantigas*) . . ." (p. 66). Keller founds his premise on the facts that Alfonso was a learned gentleman who surely composed (his biographer Gil de Zamora said that Alfonso was a good composer), that the personal tone of many of the *cantigas* argues for the king's touch, that Alfonso appears so frequently in the miniatures, and that many of the *cantigas* are written in the first person (pp. 68-69). Also noting that many of the *cantigas* are written in the first person, Adolfo Salazar writes that this frequent appearance of the first person shows us that "era él (Alfonso) mismo el compositor de sus melodías," *La múica de España* (Madrid: Espasa-Calpe, 1972), p. 118. Nan Cooke Carpenter, in *Music in the Medieval and Renaissance Universities* (Norman, Oklahoma: University of Oklahoma Press, 1958), agrees with Salazar and goes further to say that Alfonso "himself wrote the words and music for some of these songs . . ." (p. 93). A. D. Deyermond, in *A Literary History of Spain: The Middle Ages* (New York: Barnes and Noble, 1971) says that ". . . very many of them (the *cantigas*) may be individual compositions by the king . . ." (p. 93). A. I. Bagby, in "Further Notes on the Moslems under Alfonso X," *Kentucky Romance Quarterly,* 24 (1977) argues that those who deny Alfonso's composition of the *cantigas* "may not have acquainted themselves with . . . recent scholarship" (p. 3).

9. Livermore gives a concise survey of these historical proofs of the long tradition of music in Spain.

10. Katz affirms that there is strong evidence to suggest that Byzantine church music affected the *Antiphoner of Leon* and he notes that both H. Anglés

and M. Schneider argue for the importance and profundity of Byzantine influence on Spanish church music (pp. 166-67).

11. The Council of Compostela in 1031 ordered all priests to be well-versed in psaltery, chants and hymns (cited in Livermore, p. 13).

12. Higinio Anglés, "Cantors und Ministers in den Diensten der Koenige von Katalonien-Aragonien im 14. Jhdt.," in *Bericht uber den musikwissenschaftlichen Kongress in Basel*, 1924 (n.p. 1925), p. 56.

13. Dahmus laments these secular melodies "lost in the dust of time . . ." (p. 641).

14. Livermore, p. 14.

15. See Higinio Anglés, "Early Spanish Musical Culture and Cardinal Cisnero's *Hymnal* of 1515," in *Aspects of Medieval and Renaissance Music*, ed. Jan La Rue (New York: Norton, 1966), pp. 3-16. On pp. 14-16 Anglés reproduces the music of seven hymns from the Cisneros *Hymnal*.

16. Ramón Menéndez Pidal, in *Poesía juglaresca y orígenes de las literaturas románicas* (Madrid: Instituto de Estudios Políticos, 1957), delights in retelling some of the adventures of the scandalous La Balteira. For more ample views of female troubadours, see Lucy A. Sponsler, *Women in the Medieval Spanish Epic and Lyric Traditions* (Lexington, Kentucky: University of Kentucky Press, 1975), and Meg Bogin, *The Women Troubadours* (New York: Paddington Press, 1976).

17. *Cancionero de Antón de Montoro*, quoted in Menéndez Pidal, p. 4, n. 3.

18. Ibid., p. 102.

19. See Ibid., pp. 10-12, for an interesting discussion of this *Suplicatió* and the answering *Declaratió*.

20. See *cantiga* no. 293 for a description of a *remedador* who imitated a bird's song. All numbers here refer to the numbers used in Walter Mettmann, *Alfonso X, O Sabio. Cantigas de Santa Maria* (Coimbra: Acta Universitatis Conimbrigensis, 1959-64).

21. See Menéndez Pidal for his information on the *caballero salvaje* and a photograph (p. 27) of the modern *caballero salvaje* in Salamanca, pp. 24-27.

22. In *Alfonso X*, Keller discusses the probability that Alfonso's Suabian mother and her retinue must surely have brought with them, along with their language, a store of popular German lore and folkways among which would have been found accounts of miracles (p. 73). Keller continues with an argument (pp. 73-74) for a German origin for the miracle related in *cantiga* no. 74. See, also, J. F. Alemparte, "Fuentes germánicas en las *Cantigas de Santa Maria*, de Alfonso X el Sabio," *Grial*, 31 (n.d.), pp. 31-62.

23. Emanuel Winternitz, in *Musical Instruments and Their Symbolism in Western Art* (New York: Norton, 1967), talks about the bagpipes in the *cantiga* illuminations and calls the bagpipe with two separate pairs of drones and a double chanter "an unusually complex combination for the period," p. 72. Winternitz remarks, too, on the interesting cross-fertilization of instruments as shown in the juxtaposition of the eastern rebec and the occidental portative organ.

24. There were literally hundreds of instruments popular in medieval Spain. Others most commonly mentioned include the *guitarra latina* and the *guitarra morisca*, the *medio cañón, cañón entero, axabeba, albogues, añafil morisco*.

25. *LBA*, 1516-1520. See also *LBA*, vv. 1227-36.

26. *Corónica del Condestable Miguel Lucas*, cited in Menéndez Pidal, p. 45.

27. Cited in Menéndez Pidal, pp. 45-46.

28. Miniatures show choruses (no. 1) juglares and dancers in a religious vigil (no. 5), *soldaderas* (no. 93), etc.

29. An idea well-expressed in Juan Ríos Sarmiento, *La Vida y los Libros de Alfonso el Sabio* (Barcelona: Editorial Juventud, 1943).

30. In *Alfonso X*, Keller notes that Alfonso had received the best of educations as befitted a prince, see Ch. 2.

31. See Menéndez Pidal, pp. 79, 114. He quotes from *Memorias para la vida de Fernando III*: ". . . et entendía quien lo fazía bien et quien non."

32. Antonio Ballesteros y Baretta, in *Alfonso el Sabio* (Barcelona: Salvat, 1963), feels that Alfonso developed his love for Galician language and culture at least partly because his tutor was Galician and because Alfonso perhaps spent time in Galicia.

33. The chair of "un maestro en órgano" probably meant the teaching of the science of polyphonic music. See Higinio Anglés, "Hispanic Musical Culture," *Musical Quarterly*, 23, p. 518.

34. Several critics discuss this famous miniature and reach the conclusion that Alfonso is dictating. See, for example, Keller's *Alfonso X*, pp. 83-84, and Menéndez Pidal, pp. 180-83.

35. Cited in George Henderson, *Gothic* (Baltimore: Penguin Harmondsworth, 1967), p. 81. In *Alfonso X*, Keller notes that Alfonso sent a copy of the *Cantigas* to this same French king (p. 69).

36. Henderson, p. 35.

37. Just as Henry III was the light behind the Palace of Westminster (see Henderson, p. 38).

38. Ibid., p. 43.

39. Eric Blom, ed., *Mozart's Letters* (Baltimore: Penguin, 1968).

40. Joseph T. Snow, in "Alfonso X y la *Cantiga* 409: Un nexo posible con la tradición de la 'Danza de la Muerte,'" in *Studies in Honor of Lloyd A. Kasten* (Madison, Wisconsin: Hispanic Seminary of Medieval Studies, 1975), asserts that the *cantigas* offer a "visión panorámica de su sociedad," (p. 264).

41. John E. Keller, in "Verbalization and Visualization in the *Cantigas de Santa Maria,*" in *Oelschlager Festschrift* (Chapel Hill: Estudios de Hispanofila, 1976), discusses the differences he finds between the events recounted in the *cantigas* and the events depicted in their accompanying miniatures. Keller stresses the active relationship between Alfonso and the painters, and we can expect no less active relationship between Alfonso and his musicians, pp. 271-76.

42. Robert I. Burns, S. J., in "Christian Islamic Confrontation in the West: the Thirteenth-Century Dream of Conversion," *The American Historical Review,* 76 (Dec., 1971), pp. 1386-1434, likens the *Cantigas* to a Gothic cathedral and ranks them with the contemporary masterpiece of Aquinas and Dante (p. 1413). On pp. 1414-28, Burns offers black and white reproductions of the miniatures (taken from the Escorial Ms.) which accompany *cantigas* 46, 63, 83, 99, 95, 126, 167, 169, 176, 181, 183, 185, 192. On pp. 1429-31, Burns gives brief summaries of the stories of each of these *cantigas*. José Guerrero Lovillo, in *Las Cantigas, estudio arqueólogico de sus miniaturas* (Madrid: Consejo Superior de Investigaciones, 1949), appends black and white reproductions of all the miniatures.

Connie Scarborough (essay date August 1986)

SOURCE: Scarborough, Connie. "Alfonso X: Monarch in Search of a Miracle." *Romance Quarterly* 33, no. 3 (August 1986): 349-54.

[*In the following essay, Scarborough concentrates on specific instances in the* Cantigas *that address the Virgin Mary's curing of illnesses and relieving of suffering.*]

Alfonso X caused the ***CSM*** [***Cantigas de Santa Maria***] to be continually expanded and enlarged throughout his adult life. He completed in 1257 the first "edition" of the ***Cantigas***—the Toledo Codex—containing the first 100 songs. A second, larger version containing 194 *cantigas* is extant in Escorial ms. T.J.I. A third, unfinished manuscript containing 113 *cantigas* and completed by 1279 is in the Biblioteca Nazionale in Florence. It has been suggested that these two manuscripts together comprise the second "edition" of the ***Cantigas*** (i.e., 300 songs). The last and most complete version, contained in Escorial ms. B.I.2, comprises approximately 420 poems and was completed between the years 1279 and 1281.[1] We must therefore view the ***CSM*** as an ongoing *project* rather than as a single, full-blown literary corpus. This perception of the ***CSM*** as project is, of course, in keeping with the Learned King's dedication to other scholarly ventures such as his historical, scientific, legal, and recreational writings.

Why then single out the ***CSM*** as uniquely distinct from Alfonso's other scholarly projects? Firstly, I must emphatically support scholars such as John Keller, Joseph Snow, Philip Vandry, etc., who designate the ***CSM*** as Alfonso's most personal work. Joseph Snow has called Alfonso the "master architect-designer"[2] of the ***CSM.*** In his "Self-Conscious References and the Organic Narrative Pattern of the ***CSM*** of Alfonso X," Snow convincingly demonstrates that internal references to other poems in the collection as well as references to the work as a whole reveal a "single intelligence" (i.e., editor) at work ordering the content and sequence of the *cantigas*. He contends that Alfonso is creating a larger narrative beyond the ***CSM*** itself, i.e., a quest for salvation.[3] In yet another penetrating article, "The Central Rôle of the Troubadour *persona* of Alfonso X in the ***Cantigas de Santa Maria,***" Snow focuses on the *loores,* appearing as every tenth poem in the ***CSM.***[4] These *loores,* or songs of praise, reveal especially, according to Snow, the personal and emotional relationship between Alfonso and his poetic subject, Mary. "He places before us an 'Alfonso' he saw in himself and wished others to see, an 'Alfonso' that does not get a chance to surface in the many prose works which bear his name and *imprimatur*" (p. 305). I would like to carry these assessments of Alfonso's personal involvement in the ongoing compilation of the Virgin's miracles and songs of praise to a further, related conclusion.

Most students of the ***CSM*** perceive, in some degree, the monarch's sense of personal devotion and belief in the Virgin as revealed through numerous first-person narrations and/or the king's personal participation in the events of various miracles. Many would also agree that Alfonso wrote as one means of assuring the Heavenly Queen's mercies and intercession to achieve his own salvation. He wrote also, I and other critics believe, to fulfill certain deeply felt personal needs and as a means of spiritual comfort. Beyond the texts of the *Cantigas* themselves, further support for such a view is founded in our historical knowledge that Marian devotion was strong in Alfonso's family. We also know that, as a child, Alfonso was influenced by accounts of the cure of his mother, Beatriz, from a serious illness by the intervention of the Virgin.[5]

A close examination of the subject matter and sequence of the *CSM* holds a further key to the precise nature of Alfonso's beseeching the Virgin for comfort and support. Generally, in the first two "installments" of the *CSM* (the Toledo ms. and Escorial T.J.I.), Alfonso relies heavily for the rendition of his songs on miracles appearing in written sources, both those composed in the European vernaculars and in Latin, as well as on well-known Marian lore circulating in oral tradition. However, a shift in sources, and also to a degree in subject matter, is observed in the *cantigas* after no. 200. Those *cantigas* numbered from 200 to the end of the most complete manuscript—no. 420 in Escorial ms. B.I.2—have settings which are often more local and contemporary and tend to involve *directly* Alfonso and members of his family or court.

A key element involved in this change of orientation and the one upon which I wish to focus here is the curing of illness and relief from bodily suffering. For example, in the first 200 *cantigas* for which written sources have been determined and identified, only six are directly related to cures.[6] There are a number, however, which involve resuscitation from the dead. I will not here classify these miracles as involving cures, the latter category being reserved for restoration to full health and relief from physical pain. Other miracles involving cures which cannot be traced to prior or contemporary written sources are reproduced from the cult-lore of localized shrines. As I have stated, this focus on local settings is much more common as the *cantigas* proceed in numerical sequence according to Alfonso's design for expanding his collection.

A related consideration are the some 28 poems within the collection which deal with Alfonso and/or members of his family and court.[7] These poems with Alfonso and his family serving as protagonists are, too, more frequent as one moves in sequence through the collection—or, in other words, as one proceeds from earlier to later dates of composition. In the monarch's life, these dates (1257-1281) were three decades of ongoing additions and refocusing in the collection.

A *cantiga* pertinent to this discussion, the plot of which I have already mentioned, is no. 256—"Como Santa Maria guareceu a Rea Dona Beatriz de grand' / enfermidade, porque aorou a sa omage con grand' esperança." This *cantiga* relates the Virgin's miraculous intervention in the cure of Alfonso's mother. The fact that Alfonso wrote, or supervised, the composition of a

cantiga involving an important and potentially tragic event of his childhood firmly establishes his sense of very close contact with the Virgin's power to effect miraculous cures. In *cantigas* dealing with Alfonso's immediate family, the collection also includes a cure effectuated for his father, Fernando (no. 221). As a child, Alfonso had learned firsthand of the miraculous cure of his mother. However, the illness and cure of Fernando occurred when Fernando himself was a child. Thus, in *Cantiga* 221, Alfonso is refashioning family lore. According to the Learned King's account, Fernando fell very ill and, being unable to eat or sleep, lay very near death. His mother, Alfonso's grandmother, decided to take her son to the Virgin's shrine at Onna (Oña) to ask the Heavenly Queen to heal him. The Virgin takes pity on the ill child, whose condition begins to improve immediately. Within fifteen days, according to Alfonso's account, the child Fernando is restored to good health.

We have just seen that near the midpoint of his compilation of the Virgin's miracles (*Cantigas* nos. 221 and 256), Alfonso includes cures of both his mother and his father. he thus presents himself in the very midst of his collection as the heir, both literally and figuratively, to a tradition of the Virgin's restoring health to members of his family. Beyond this tradition and taking into account an original premise that Alfonso wrote in part to effectuate his own salvation, what then of his increasing focus on the curing of illness? And, of more importance, why the progressive concentration on cures of the King's personal afflictions?

To attempt to answer these questions, let me first examine, as have Joseph Snow and Evelyn Proctor, the series of miracle narratives dealing with the Puerto de Santa Maria shrine, all of which appear late in the collection (328, 356-59, 364, 366-68, 371-72, 375-79, 381-82, 385, 389, 391-93, and 398 in Mettmann's edition).[8] In this group, we encounter a very high incidence of cures serving as the primary element of plot. In *CSM* 357, for example, a sinful woman is cured of a twisted mouth and paralyzed limbs after she confesses her sins; in 368, a woman is freed of a snake which had lived in her stomach for three years, causing her to be deathly ill; in 378, a couple's young daughter is cured of a continual bleeding from her eyes when they bring her to Puerto; in 389, a former abbot's son is cured because the abbot and his wife promise two ducks to the Virgin of Puerto; in 391, a devout man's paralytic daughter is cured when he takes her in pilgrimage to Puerto; and, in 393, a young man with rabies is cured when his grandfather brings him to Puerto. Even animals are included, as we read in 375, where the Virgin cures the horse belonging to Alfonso's scribe. This increased concentration on cures, especially in connection to a locally famous shrine, reaches a climax with a miracle relating the King's own cure through the intercession of the Virgin. *Cantiga* 367 relates that Alfonso became ill en route on a pilgrimage to Puerto de Santa Maria.

Since I am here focusing on the concept of cures in the *CSM,* it is especially pertinent to note in *Cantiga* 367 Alfonso's motive for his pilgrimage to Puerto. The Virgin earlier had cured him of an illness in Sevilla, and he travels to Puerto in a show of thanksgiving to her. While on this pilgrimage, Alfonso's legs swell very badly and his doctors cannot effect a cure. However, when the King calls on the Virgin, his legs are restored to a healthy condition and he leads the court in singing praises to Our Lady.

This particular cure of Alfonso within the series of Puerto de Santa Maria miracles is only the last of several recounted in the entire collection. Evelyn Proctor uses the adjective "frequent" when referring to Alfonso's illnesses as portrayed in the *CSM* (Proctor, p. 37). Very recently John Keller and Richard Kinkade have studied *Cantiga* 209—the King's account of his very lengthy illness in Vitoria.[9] This illness can be dated from the chronicles, which relate an extended and nonproductive period spent by the King in Vitoria during the winter of 1276-77 (Proctor, pp. 39-40). The narration of Alfonso's own cure in *Cantiga* 209 is especially germane to the present discussion of the Learned King's progressive interest in the dissemination of miraculous cures. Keller and Kinkade point out, especially relying on the visual narrative contained in the miniatures accompanying *Cantiga* 209, that in this poem one "actually experiences much of the king's own suffering as he fights for his life" (Keller and Kinkade, p. 348). Indeed, the heading (title) in the manuscript for this *cantiga* establishes that Alfonso's life was in moral danger and that his physical suffering was intense: "Como el Rey Don Affonso de Castela adoeçeu en Bitoria e ouv' hũa door tan grande, que coidaron que morresse ende . . ." (Mettman, I, 660-61). Moreover, that the King's miraculous cure is effectuated by placing the Book of the *Cantigas* on his chest, physically, as well as metaphorically, attests to the monarch's personal belief in the *Cantigas* not only as an instrument to win the salvation of his soul but also as a remedy for the present maladies of his body. In fact the text relates that the King even *rejected* more accepted (standard) means of relieving his anguish such as the hot cloths (*panos caentes*) the doctors ordered to be placed on him in favor of this remedy of his own devising. Quite literally, it is the *book* of the *Cantigas,* and by extension the lyric, narrative, pictorial, and musical (artistic) creations therein contained, in which the Monarch places supreme confidence.

Another example of the King's numerous bouts with illness is related in *Cantiga* 235—"[E] sta é como Santa Maria deu saude al Rey Don Affonso / quando foi en Valadolide enfermo que foi juygado por morto." This is a most personal poem, not only because the King deals with his own illness, but because he also takes the opportunity to list a long series of personal complaints and problems with his nobles before he even begins to

deal with his current sickness. In *Cantiga* 235, the King tells of a revolt of the nobles (probably the one of 1272-74) and another of his previous illnesses in Requenna (dated in August, 1273). He goes on to relate that he fell ill again on a journey to visit the Pope and became sick yet another time in Montpellier on his return trip. According to Evelyn Proctor, the illness at Montpellier accounts for a six-month gap in our records of Alfonso's activities between his audience with Pope Gregory in May of 1275 and his return to Castile in December of 1275 (pp. 37-38). He then recalls his illness in Vitoria (the subject of *Cantiga* 209 already discussed) at a time when he was also threatened by an attack from the King of France (1276-77). After the recapitulation of these hardships and illnesses, Alfonso turns to the main theme of this *cantiga,* i.e., his illness in Valladolid (dated in the spring of 1278) (Proctor, pp. 38-40). The King falls so ill that he is presumed dead, but the Virgin intervenes to assure his full recovery by Easter day. Immediate parallels can of course be drawn between the resurrection of Christ at Easter and Alfonso's return to good health.

Later in the collection—*Cantiga* 279—Alfonso recounts still another of his bouts with illness and the cure which he attributes to the Virgin. In this *cantiga,* as well as the others here discussed, Alfonso emphasizes the great pain and suffering he was enduring ("tan gran mal e . . . tan gran door") as well as the fear of being near death ("Que me faz a mort', ond' ei gran pavor") (Mettman, II, 80). The poetic narrative even mentions that his color had turned to a shade of green during this illness. The inclusion of such non-flattering details marks this *cantiga* with a very personal touch. Alfonso, as author or editor, did not mince words when describing his physical afflictions. This vivid accounting of suffering attests to the King's desire for relief. Also, in no. 279, Alfonso refers to himself as the Virgin's *trovador* with the favor he obviously hopes to receive from his lady being restoration to good health and alleviation from pain.

We have seen that Alfonso vividly portrayed illnesses and their miraculous cures by the Virgin, especially in the latter half of the *CSM.* He also includes a number of his own personal cures as examples of the Virgin's mercies shown to the suffering. That Alfonso repeatedly includes himself among the physically afflicted and that he openly expresses his desire to be relieved from pain indicate that the Learned King hoped to achieve more than the reward of his soul's salvation by composing the *cantigas.* His concerns, especially in *cantigas* where the composition date can be determined as late in the King's life, are also for prompt relief from ever-more-frequently occurring periods of ill-health. By his concentration on illness and cure Alfonso presents himself to us in a very personal guise. Situations of suffering, those of others but especially his own, also reveal a growing preoccupation on the monarch's part with the prospect of approaching death. In addition, as evident in the *cantigas* focused on here today, he was concerned about and dreaded the physical torments which would precede his demise. The act of composing the **CSM** of course denotes Alfonso's concern for his soul's salvation, but the *man* Alfonso revealed in the lyric and narrative songs also shows great concern for his physical well-being and freedom from suffering.

Notes

1. See Walter Mettman's introduction to his edition of the *CSM* (Vigo Edicións Xerais de Galicia, 1981), I, 17-36. All subsequent references to the *CSM* are taken from this edition.

2. Joseph Snow, "Self-Conscious Awareness and the Organic Narrative Pattern of the *CSM* of Alfonso X," in Joseph R. Jones, ed., *Medieval, Renaissance and Folklore Studies in Honor of John Esten Keller* (Newark, Delaware: Juan de la Cuesta, 1980), p. 54.

3. Snow, p. 60. Also, on p. 62, Snow states that in the *CSM,* Alfonso's "own search for the reward of eternal salvation is the central story."

4. *Bulletin of Hispanic Studies,* 56 (1979), 305-16.

5. Snow, "The Central Róle . . . ," p. 306.

6. Elise F. Dexter, "Sources of the *Cantigas* of Alfonso el Sabio," Diss. University of Wisconsin, 1926.

7. Evelyn S. Proctor, *Alfonso X of Castile: Patron of Literature and Learning* (Oxford: Clarendon Press, 1951), p. 32.

8. Joseph T. Snow, "A Chapter in Alfonso's Personal Narrative: The Puerto de Santa María Poems in the *CSM,*" *La Corónica,* 8 (Fall 1979), 11.

9. John E. Keller and Richard P. Kinkade, "Iconography and Literature: Alfonso Himself in *Cantiga 209,*" *Hispania* 66 (1983), 348-52.

Richard P. Kinkade (essay date April 1992)

SOURCE: Kinkade, Richard P. "Alfonso X, *Cantiga* 235, and the Events of 1269-1278." *Speculum* 67, no. 2 (April 1992): 284-323.

[*In the following essay, Kinkade documents a late, disastrous decade for Alfonso, referring to the narrative of Cantiga 235 and other historical evidence.*]

Of the more than four hundred poems written in praise of the Virgin Mary either by Alfonso the Wise (1221-84) or at his behest and known collectively as the ***Cantigas de Santa María,*** five in particular, *Cantigas* 209, 235, 279, 366, and 367, are of inestimable benefit to the

historian for the explicit descriptions they provide of the king's ill health and suffering.[1] *Cantiga* 235 is the most valuable of these informative compositions both for its broad historical perspectives and for its rigorous chronological ordering of significant episodes; it provides information that allows us to review and reassess what is undeniably the most crucial period of Alfonso X's reign as king of Castile.

Spanning a decade-long period from 1269 to 1278, *Cantiga* 235 recounts a sequence of events which encompass a bleak series of personal disasters for the Wise King, including the treachery of his relatives, the rebellion and renunciation of feudal obligations to the crown by many of Castile's most powerful nobles, a cycle of nearly fatal illnesses, the abandonment of his cherished claims to the throne of the Holy Roman Empire, and the deaths in the same year of his son and heir to the throne, Fernando, and his daughter Leonor. *Cantiga* 235 stands as a stark chronological recitation of betrayal and illness in twenty-one stanzas, punctuated by a methodical chorus reminding the reader that ingratitude is one of life's greatest iniquities. Like most of its companion pieces, *Cantiga* 235 opens with a narrative title: "This is how Saint Mary bestowed health upon King Alfonso when he was so sick in Valladolid it was thought he would die," followed by the refrain, "Gratitude properly expressed is a thing of great value, while he who is ungrateful is guilty of falseness and great evil." To fully comprehend the magnitude and scope of the events which took place during this period and the new interpretation we are now obliged to give them in light of *Cantiga* 235, I will first examine the narrative content of the poem and then compare the evidence contained therein with the historical circumstances of Alfonso's reign. A brief synopsis of each of the twenty-one eight-line stanzas follows.

The anonymous narrator recounts "a great miracle" that happened to Alfonso (1), who praised the Virgin Mary above all else (2) and pleaded with her that he might die in her service. So sincere was his desire in this wise that in a dream one night she granted him his wish (3). Thereafter, many things came to pass. Alfonso became the target of a conspiracy to dethrone him by many of the nobles (4), most of whom were relatives who owed him a debt of gratitude which they disdained to recognize (5). But the Virgin vowed that she would frustrate the plot against him (6), and in fact she did avenge him. Later, in Requena, when he was so sick it was thought he would die, she cured him with a miracle, the first of many benefits she would bestow upon him within the context of his wish to expire in her service (7). Afterward, when he went to see the pope in Beaucaire and was so sick he almost died, she again restored his health (8), and once more on his return journey to Castile, when he was near death with the same sickness in Montpellier, the Virgin healed him (9). Such was the nature of her cure that he was able to make great progress on his return to Castile (10), where he was given a warm welcome by those who later conspired against him (11). These rebellious nobles swore among themselves to overthrow him and divide the kingdom among themselves, but their plot was thwarted by God, who raised the king on high and crushed his opposition (12).

For the next year and a month Alfonso was sick in Vitoria, where the king of France moved against him with an army that God dissolved like salt in water (13). After many months of trials and tribulations in Castile, the Son of God allowed Alfonso to avenge himself on his enemies (14), some of whom were burned at the stake while others went to hell (15). Later the king urgently wanted to take up arms against the invading Moorish forces, but the Virgin was determined not to let him go until he was better and therefore caused him to be overcome with a persistent fever (16). This time, when it was thought he would die, he traveled to Valladolid, where the Virgin healed him (17). Before restoring him to health, however, she brought him once again to the point of death, then performed a miraculous cure on Easter Day (18). The final three stanzas sing the praises of the Virgin (19-21).

Cantiga 235 reports five separate occasions when the king was desperately ill and subsequently healed by the Virgin. Each time, according to his own wish to die in her service, the Virgin would bring him to a point near death, then effect a miraculous cure. In view of their frequency and magnitude, Alfonso's ailments must have constituted a major impediment to his successful management of the affairs of state and one of the principal causes of the political chaos which characterized the turbulent decade between 1269 and 1278. The most recent medical research indicates that the king's malady was in all likelihood a squamous-cell carcinoma of the maxillary antrum, a slow-growing cancer which inexorably spread through the bony structure of his face, alternately exerting great pressure from the accumulation of fluid within the sinus followed by a rapid remission of symptoms when the abscess drained.[2] During the winter of 1276-77 and again during the summer of 1280, the pressure was so great that the king's right eye was forced from its orbit.[3]

Armed with these facts, I wish to reconsider Alfonso's activities up to and during the decade 1269-78. The events of *Cantiga* 235 and its major themes of treachery, ingratitude, vengeance, and miraculous healing will serve as a historical frame of reference.

The key words in *Cantiga* 235, treachery and ingratitude, were to be lifelong companions of Alfonso, whose overly generous disposition and trusting nature, all too often bordering on naïveté, were scarcely qualities

which would assure him the support and backing of a fiercely competitive and habitually unscrupulous nobility. Moreover, Alfonso's constant preoccupation with an imperial title and the expenses occasioned by his need to maintain appearances in the game of politics then being played out in the courts of Europe weighed heavily against him at home during the course of the year 1268, as he showered lavish gifts upon his supporters while waiting for a favorable decision from Pope Clement IV, which was never to come. He had also been forced to renew the conflict against his old nemesis, Ibn al-Ahmar, king of Granada; and in the spring of 1268 the cortes of Jerez had to deal with a monetary crisis in Castile, brought about by a devaluation of the coinage necessitated by the expenses related to these campaigns.[4]

Late in the fall of 1266 Alfonso had been visited in Seville by his five-year-old grandson, Prince Dinis (1261-1325), offsprng of the king's illegitimate daughter Beatriz and Afonso III of Portugal.[5] Dinis, who like his grandfather would be known in years to come for his exceptional poetic ability and enthusiastic support of the arts,[6] had come ostensibly to be knighted by the king of Castile, but in reality, and no doubt coached by his parents, he contrived to petition Alfonso to release Portugal from certain feudal obligations incurred several years earlier.[7] It must have seemed a small favor to the monarch of Castile and León, who doted on his favorite grandchild. Alfonso granted the request in spite of the angry protests of many of his noble advisers, who considered it a foolish act and one which, while diluting the king's authority, indirectly weakened their own prerogatives.[8] This seemingly innocent gesture and the ensuing treaty with Portugal a few months later, in which the concessions made to Prince Dinis were formalized, were to have unforeseen and serious repercussions. Within a short time the resentful nobles, angered by among other things the king's apparent insensitivity to the issue of Castilian territorial integrity, began to organize a conspiracy against him led by the king's brother Felipe and by Nuño González de Lara, Felipe's uncle by marriage, who was governor of the frontier and a boyhood friend and relative of Alfonso's by marriage to the king's cousin, Teresa Alonso de León.[9] These two were soon joined by Lope Díaz de Haro, lord of Vizcaya, and Esteban Fernández de Castro, governor of Galicia. In all, the powerful and influential rebels represented not only the royal house but the three most significant families of the realm, the Laras, the Haros, and the Castros.[10] The king spent the rest of the year 1267 and nearly all of 1268 in Andalusia, primarily in the cities of Jerez, Seville, and Córdoba, far from the growing conspiratorial alliance in the north. At the same time, the death of Pope Clement IV on 29 November 1268 had precipitated a nearly three-year papal interregnum during which Alfonso was forced to wait and watch, absorbed in an attempt to discern what direction his imperial pretensions might take.

The year 1269 found Alfonso increasingly concerned with events in Castile, which now required his presence in that region. By the middle of the summer he felt obliged to leave Andalusia and take up residence in Toledo.[11] Much of the rest of the year was filled with diplomatic negotiations and final arrangements for a royal wedding to be celebrated later that fall in Burgos. The marriage of Fernando (1255-75), heir apparent, and Blanche, daughter of St. Louis, king of France (1214-70, r. 1226), was celebrated on 30 November with all the pomp and circumstance befitting such an occasion. Unfortunately for Alfonso, the ceremony and accompanying festivities generated enormous expenses for the crown, which, when combined with his constant need for revenue to finance his imperial aspirations, ultimately forced him to increase taxes in an effort to cover the resulting budget deficit.[12]

Alfonso took the opportunity provided by the convergence of nobles, prelates, and members of the third estate to summon the cortes in Burgos, which met immediately following the wedding, on 1-18 December 1269.[13] The rebellious nobles, in turn, took advantage of the occasion to further their conspiratorial schemes, and such was the extent and recklessness of their enterprise that Nuño González even dared to believe that he might somehow persuade Alfonso's father-in-law, Jaime I of Aragon, to side with the rebels. Jaime adroitly evaded the issue, all the while cognizant of the very real dangers which loomed on Alfonso's political horizon.[14] In a further exhibition of their disdain for him, the nobles arranged the marriage of Lope Díaz de Haro to Alfonso's cousin, Juana, daughter of Alfonso de Molina, the king's uncle and a co-conspirator, apparently without the king's express permission.[15]

Alfonso was sufficiently concerned by the increasing threat of rebellion that he spent a number of days seeking the counsel and advice of his father-in-law, even accompanying him on his return journey to Aragon as far as Tarazona during the Christmas holidays, on 20-26 December 1269.[16] In the course of the trip an event of singular importance occurred. Jaime I remarks in his *Crònica* that Alfonso fell gravely ill in Fitero de Navarra a few days after leaving Tarazona on his way back to Castile. Jaime met him there with his own physician, Maestre Johan, and stayed with him several days until he was well enough to travel. According to Jaime, Alfonso "was gravely ill, laid up in bed by a blow from a horse which he had received in Burgos."[17] Antonio Ballesteros, without citing any supporting documents, reports that the king convalesced in Lo-

groño, where his own physician, Alonso Martínez, prescribed a period of absolute rest.[18] Chancery documents indicate that Alfonso was back in Burgos by the middle of February, where he would remain until the end of June 1270.[19]

What type of injury had Alfonso sustained that would have required the emergency services of his father-in-law's physician for a period of three or four days and, later, a convalescence of nearly a month and a half? I believe we may reasonably infer that Alfonso had been kicked in the face by a horse and that the resultant fracture led to chronic sinusitis, caused by an obstruction of the maxillary sinus ostium into the nasal cavity, or perhaps even by osteomyelitis of the maxillary bone. An injury of this kind is consistent with the subsequent development of a squamous-cell carcinoma of the maxillary antrum, as described by Maricel Presilla.[20] A sharp, powerful kick or blow to any part of the body other than the face or head would hardly have occasioned such a lengthy period of recovery.[21] Thus we may reasonably conjecture that the blow Alfonso received in December 1269 resulted in facial contusions, which may well have evolved over a period of years into a serious, disfiguring illness that would leave an indelible mark on both the king and the affairs of his realm.

On 25 September 1270 Alfonso arrived in Vitoria, capital city of the province of Alava, midway between Pamplona and Burgos, a vantage point from which he could better observe the activities of the rebel Lope Díaz de Haro in Vizcaya and the possible collusion of Henry of Champagne, acting governor of Navarre during the absence of his brother, King Thibault II, who was on crusade with St. Louis against the Moors of Tunis.[22] Henry was married to a niece of St. Louis's, Blanche, the daughter of Robert I of Artois, in an alliance that was to prove a major hindrance to future Castilian plans in that area. Alfonso had always had an abiding interest in the affairs of Navarre and now with even greater urgency, faced as he was with possible Navarrese support for the conspirators. Henry's ascension to the throne on the death of Thibault II in December 1270 could not help but exacerbate Alfonso's fears of potential Navarrese intervention and was quite likely a factor in his decision to remain in the area of Vitoria and Burgos for the rest of the year.

On 5 February 1271 Alfonso arrived in Murcia, where he would reside for the next sixteen months in pursuit of his policy of undermining Moorish influence there by repopulating the area with Christian settlers. His absence in Castile, however, was a signal for the first act of open rebellion on the part of the recalcitrant nobles, who now met publicly in Lerma to plot his overthrow. Historical sources name some seventeen conspirators, including the four principal instigators, whose connivance dates from 1267: Prince Felipe, Nuño González de Lara, Lope Díaz de Haro, and Esteban Fernández de Castro.[23] These were joined by two new conspirators related to Alfonso's brother Prince Fadrique: his son-in-law, Simón Ruiz de los Cameros, and his brother-in-law, Ferrán Ruiz de Castro.[24] The *Crónica of Alfonso X* relates that a decision was made to send Felipe as emissary to Henry of Navarre and that in lieu of Navarrese support for their cause the nobles would turn to the sultan of Granada, Alfonso's perennial opponent, who feared that the king's alliance with the *arráeces,* Muslim governors of Málaga and Guádix, might prove injurious to his hegemony.[25]

In the meantime, apprised of the meeting in Lerma to betray him, the king dispatched his trusted friend Ferrán Pérez, dean of the cathedral of Seville, to demand an explanation from his brother Prince Felipe, while sending his lord chamberlain, or "repostero mayor," Enrique Pérez de Harana, as special emissary to the rebels in Palenzuela.[26] Why was Alfonso reluctant to act against the nobles at this time? Several reasons suggest themselves. The king's primary interests during this period appear to have been his quest for the crown of the Holy Roman Empire and his continuing conflict with the sultan of Granada, both of which were, in his mind, of greater importance than domestic unrest. By transferring his locus of operations to the major Mediterranean port city of Murcia, Alfonso had strengthened his relationships with the northern Italian states opposed to Guelf rule and thus favorable to his cause while placing the sultan of Granada on warning with regard to his firm intentions to maintain an alliance with the *arráeces* of Málaga and Guádix.

In August 1271, while still in Murcia, the king celebrated the marriage of his second daughter, seventeen-year-old Princess Beatriz, to the marquess of Monferrat, a turncoat Guelf and powerful supporter of Alfonso's imperial pretensions. The nuptial alliance was timely, for on 1 September 1271 a new pope, Gregory X, was finally chosen following a three-year interregnum, and his policies were to be openly hostile to Alfonso's political aspirations.[27] Gregory, who was in Palestine on crusade at the time of his election, was unable to return to Europe before February 1272. In this same month of February, between the sixth and the fourteenth, Alfonso requested an urgent meeting with his father-in-law, Jaime I of Aragon, to discuss the apparent consummation of a long-feared alliance between the Moors and the rebellious nobles of Castile, León, and Aragon.[28]

On 26 February Prince Fadrique arrived in Murcia from Tunis, where he had taken refuge nearly four years earlier following the ill-fated Battle of Tagliacozzo (23 June 1268) in which his younger brother, Prince Enrique (1230-1303), had been captured and imprisoned by the forces of Charles of Anjou.[29] Alfonso welcomed him warmly in a futile effort to forestall what he foresaw must be Fadrique's inevitable alliance with the subversive nobles.[30] The death on 2 April 1272 of Richard of Cornwall, Alfonso's only serious contender for the imperial crown, gave renewed impetus to the Castilian monarch's exertions in this context—so much so that Alfonso was willing to accede to the demands of the rebellious nobles, who now had the temerity to insist that the king pay them their annual feudal services, ill-gotten gains which they immediately employed to further their own treacherous ambitions. Alfonso's imperial aspirations had blinded him to the realities of the insurrection at home and made him overly tolerant of a dangerous situation which could never be improved by his misguided policy of appeasement.[31]

Searching for support for the rebellion, Prince Felipe had already made three visits to King Henry of Navarre but without success. The wily Henry would offer the nobles his backing but only in exchange for the provinces of Alava and Guipúzcoa, an arrangement the rebels found entirely unacceptable. Despairing of external support for their cause, the insurgents made the fateful decision to turn to Alfonso's perennial foes, the sultan of Granada and the Marinid emir of Morocco, Abu Yusuf, who were ever ready to take advantage of any friction between the forces of Christianity to further the Muslim jihad. What could have driven the disaffected nobility to this extreme at a time when the church and many of Europe's crowned heads were either actively involved in or seriously contemplating a crusade against the enemies of Christendom? The magnitude of their perfidy defies description and can only be seen as an act of desperate men. Yet Alfonso's relentless taxation, his ruinous fiscal policies in pursuit of the imperial crown, which had nearly bankrupted the country, and his prolonged isolation in Murcia, in part because of the threat of war with the Muslims of Granada and Morocco and perhaps in part because the symptoms of his illness were intensifying, had drastically curtailed or even eliminated the opportunity for a peaceful resolution of the problem. The disaffected nobles, then, were not entirely to blame, and their outrageous overtures to the infidel, while difficult to rationalize, underscore a much more serious domestic crisis than Alfonso was either prepared to acknowledge or able to understand.

Informed by his son Fernando and his youngest brother, Prince Manuel, that the Moroccan troops of Abu Yusuf had disembarked on Spanish soil with an army to aid the sultan of Granada, Alfonso left Murcia on 16 June 1272.[32] By 27 August he had advanced as far as Roa, some 100 kilometers to the south of Burgos, where he learned that the rebellious nobles had openly declared their unwillingness to cease negotiations with Henry of Navarre, a proclamation tantamount to treason. Arriving in Burgos on 6 September 1272, Alfonso undertook serious talks with the insurgents, who demanded that he convoke the cortes as soon as possible to deal with their problems, and it was agreed that representatives of the three estates would meet in Burgos on 29 September, immediately following Michaelmas. In the meantime the king received the unsettling news from his legation to the papal curia that his petition to be crowned emperor had been rudely rebuffed by Gregory X on 16 September.[33] To add to his great dissatisfaction, the cortes of Burgos, which continued until 10 December 1272, was punctuated by diverse acts of disobedience and disrespect for the monarch on the part of various representatives of both the aristocracy and the church, an ominous sign of the depth and unusual intensity of social discontent. Alleging royal abuse of power and specific violations of the laws of the land, the rebels were nonetheless no match for the very sovereign who had authored the **Siete partidas** and was himself an expert in jurisprudence.[34] A majority of the three estates upheld the king, with the result that the rejected nobles took what must have seemed the only avenue open to them which would at the same time preserve their dignity: the renunciation of all feudal ties to the king of Castile and León.

Their departure was hastened by the knowledge that any possible alliance with Henry of Navarre had been thwarted once and for all by the betrothal of Henry's infant son, Thibault, to Violante, Alfonso's daughter, in September of that same year. At the end of November the rebels, recalling the Cid's exile from Castile over two centuries earlier, requested a period of forty-two days to enable them to prepare for their voluntary expatriation.[35] They would seek refuge with the sultan of Granada and, in a fit of pique, ravage the lands through which they passed on their way toward the Moorish frontier. Alfonso was obliged to set out precipitately from Burgos on 13 December in an attempt to curtail these aggressions by heading off the rebels in the area of Madrid.[36]

From Toledo, on 22 January 1273, Alfonso sent word to his son Fernando and brother Manuel of the recent troublesome events, warning them of the approaching insurgents. Then he sat down to pen his famous "cartas justicieras," a somber and dispiriting catalogue of sins directed individually to each of the leaders of the rebellion by a totally disillusioned monarch, carefully recounting all of the former favors he had showered upon these ungrateful friends and relatives, who had now chosen to bite the hand that for so long had fed them so well.[37] The plaintive tone of these communications recalls one of the greatest and most consistent disappointments Alfonso was to suffer during his entire

reign: the ingratitude and betrayal of his erstwhile supporters, colleagues, and family members alike, most of whom eventually forsook him.

Towards the end of January 1273, Fernando and Manuel attempted to enter into negotiations with the conspirators in the town of Sabiote, to the north of Ubeda, but with little success, in spite of the shameful concessions Alfonso had instructed them to offer, including Lope Díaz de Haro's condition that Alfonso surrender the city of Vitoria, which Fernando held in fief. Without recognizing the urgency Alfonso felt to meet with the pope and settle the pressing matter of his pretensions to the imperial throne, it is difficult to understand such an abject attitude of appeasement toward the rebels, who were emboldened by this unexpected conciliatory tactic to make ever more embarrassing stipulations. Alfonso had set his priorities, and the requirements dictated by the nobles were of secondary importance when faced with the crisis of the imperial crown. Alfonso's letter to the rebels, conceding all their demands, is a monument to the futility and degradation of his conciliatory policies, which even the nobles were apparently too proud to accept.[38]

In the same month of January 1273, the seventy-three-year-old ruler of Granada, Ibn al-Ahmar, died and was succeeded by his son, Muhammad II (1273-1302), though only with the help of the rebellious Castilian nobles, who supported the young sultan against the perennial threats of the provincial governors of Málaga and Guádix, staunch friends and allies of Alfonso. By the end of February 1273, the king had arranged for a meeting in Almagro to which he invited many of the principal political figures of the realm, and their deliberations were duly transmitted to the rebels and the sultan of Granada.[39] The latter quite unexpectedly proposed that both he and Alfonso enter into compliance with the terms of the Treaty of Alcalá de Benzayde, an armistice signed by Alfonso and the new sultan's father in August 1265, at the close of the previous conflict between them. The conspirators now found themselves in an uncomfortable position which threatened their very existence in Granada, where they had taken refuge by swearing fealty to the sultan. This new development would reconfirm a treaty which declared the ruler of Granada to be a vassal of King Alfonso and by its provisions would bring the rebels once again under the jurisdiction of their royal nemesis.[40]

Alfonso, however, was interested not in revenge but in a rapid cessation of hostilities, which would allow him to pursue his imperial ambitions, especially in light of Pope Gregory's call in April 1273 for a European council of prelates and sovereigns in Lyons to seek, among other things, a lasting solution to the crucial question of the Holy Roman Empire. The king knew he had to be present for this critical convocation, scheduled to commence in May of 1274, if his pretensions were ever to be realized. To this end he convoked an assembly of the representatives of the towns of León and Extremadura to be held in Avila on 24 April 1273. The Ayuntamiento of Almagro in February had served to severely reduce the credibility of the conspirators. The assembly of Avila would prove to be even more devastating to their cause with the sudden and unexpected defection from the conspiracy of Prince Felipe's brother-in-law, Ferrán Ruiz de Castro, and his followers. For the moment it seemed that Alfonso had successfully defused the insurrection.[41]

Alfonso left Avila for Segovia between the first and the eighteenth of June. From Segovia he sent a letter to his son Fernando, informing him of his illness in Avila during the assembly there. This is one of the first documented references we possess of Alfonso's chronic infirmity and its attendant symptoms. In the king's own words, "I was in Avila where I came to speak with the councils of León and Extremadura, which I convoked there, and I was sick with rheum and a little fever, and I was greatly distressed that this should happen to me at such a time."[42] The fever and watery discharge of the eyes and nose to which he refers were severe enough to cause the sovereign some concern and under the circumstances were most probably related to the worsening maxillary sinusitis and eventual squamous-cell carcinoma that would complicate his existence for the next decade. This would explain why he did not accompany his wife, Queen Violante, whom he had sent as royal emissary to yet another meeting with the rebels and his son Fernando in Córdoba during this same month of June.[43] Alfonso was convalescing and physically unable to meet with the conspirators. In any case, it was evident that the king had another agenda, which would take him southeast in the direction of Valencia.

By 24 June Alfonso had reached Guadalajara and by 18 July he was in Cuenca, where he received an urgent request from Violante and Fernando to join them in their talks with the insurgents in Córdoba.[44] Again, we must suppose that Alfonso was unable to attend these important negotiations either because of illness or because of the impending meeting with his father-in-law, Jaime I, in Requena. Certainly the sovereign's journey toward Valencia was painfully slow, and we have no documentary evidence of Alfonso's whereabouts during the month of August 1273. The *Crónica* tells us he met with Jaime in Requena, a small town approximately 60 kilometers due west of Valencia.[45] Ballesteros has deduced from Aragonese records documenting the presence of Jaime I that the meeting with Alfonso must have occurred between 22 and 28 August 1273.[46] The *Crónica* recounts that they met to discuss, among other matters, the contumacious aristocracy in

both their realms, the forthcoming papal council, and the possibility of an invasion by the emir of Morocco, Abu Yusuf. The *Crónica* also recalls that Jaime left the meeting to return to Valencia but that Alfonso stayed in Requena recovering from a "terciana" or tertian fever, recurring at forty-eight-hour intervals and indicating what was by now a chronic illness.[47] A lack of correspondence or any other documentary evidence for Alfonso during the month of August is suggestive of a disability serious enough to halt the normal correspondence that regularly flowed from the king's chancery. Not even the exigencies of the critical matters discussed by the king and his father-in-law were sufficient to produce the customary number of communications we usually observe in these circumstances, and we must conclude that the king's ailment had prevented him from undertaking his typical duties at this time.[48]

Faced with a deficit of historical documentation, we are fortunate to have the evidence provided by *Cantiga* 235, which informs us that "in Requena, this king became gravely ill / and just as they thought he would die, he recovered from that malady; / She [the Virgin Mary] worked this miracle for him" (st. 7bcd).[49] Clearly, the king was not afflicted with a simple tertian fever but was close to death; those attending him thought he would not recover. Nowhere else do we find testimony of the gravity of this particular episode, and from the information furnished by the *Cantiga* we are now able to reconfirm the suspicion that the king's illness, not his preoccupation with the imperial crown, prevented him from negotiating with the rebels in Córdoba. Furthermore, the fact that Alfonso was in Guadalajara, a distance of more than 200 kilometers from Requena, on 2 September 1273, scarcely four days after his meeting with Jaime I, offers a striking endorsement of the *Cantiga*'s claim for a miraculous recovery.[50]

By 15 September the king was in Brihuega, less than 25 kilometers from Guadalajara, and two weeks later, on 27 September, he had arrived in San Esteban de Gormaz, from where he traveled to Burgos, arriving there on 15 October. It was here and in these disquieting circumstances that he most likely received the distressing news of the German princes' election of Rudolf of Hapsburg to the imperial throne on 29 September. In spite of the great disappointment that this severe blow to his cherished ambitions must have entailed and in contrast to his somewhat protracted journey back to Castile months earlier, due in all likelihood to the lingering effects of his illness, Alfonso had resolutely set out for the southeast, reaching Cuenca by 9 November and from there arriving in Seville on 16 December 1273.[51] Scarcely one week later, on 24 December, we find the king again in Burgos, an amazing distance for a man in his condition to have traversed in so short a time. His stay in Seville had been auspicious, marked by an agreement with the rebellious nobles and a windfall of 250,000 maravedís in tribute from the reconciled sultan of Granada, who by this act of obeisance had come into faithful compliance with the 1265 treaty of Alcalá de Benzayde. Alfonso, fiercely determined in spite of Rudolf's recent election, still planned to use this substantial sum of money to finance his forthcoming trip to meet with the pope concerning the imperial crown.[52]

The king spent the first three months of 1274 in Burgos, where he summoned a session of the cortes during March.[53] It is interesting to note that the contemporary *Crónica de Alfonso X* entirely omits the year 1274, variously assigning the activities from this twelve-month span to 1273 or 1275.[54] From Burgos Alfonso traveled south during the month of April, passing through Palencia on the seventeenth and arriving in Valladolid on the twenty-sixth.

A few days later, on the first of May, Jaime I of Aragon arrived at the papal court in Lyons to attend the European council of prelates and princes to discuss, among other matters, a final resolution of the imperial question so dear to the king of Castile and León. Why had Alfonso chosen not to attend the council from its inception, given his overweening ambitions in this direction and the past sacrifices he had made to achieve this elusive goal? First, and perhaps most importantly, the king was fully aware of the pope's preference for Rudolf of Hapsburg, whose candidacy now seemed assured in light of his election to the imperial throne by the German princes a year earlier. Yet his incredible persistence, a foolish obstinacy, and an inability to see things in proper perspective had already determined the course of events. The financial outlay for such a journey was formidable, given the favorable impression the king hoped to make as a charitable and magnanimous ruler capable of meeting the lavish expenses incumbent upon an emperor of the Holy Roman Empire. In fact, Jaime I was obliged to pledge his royal crown as security to meet his own expenditures for the trip, though he would realize no immediate economic advantage in this endeavor.[55] Alfonso had received some 250,000 maravedís from the ruler of Granada in December 1273, money which he fully intended to utilize for the purpose of pursuing his political interests in Lyons. The rebellious nobles, during this same month in Seville, had been reconciled to some extent with their suzerain. In these apparently favorable circumstances, why had Alfonso opted to postpone his own pilgrimage to the papal court at the most propitious moment if ever there was to be one for his fast-fading imperial aspirations? Aside from the definitive role of finances, the king would also have to muster a strong show of internal support for his claims to the imperial crown, and neither the nobility nor the church had shown themselves to be supportive of this most

nebulous of enterprises. Clearly Alfonso felt he had first to convince his compatriots to champion his cause before he could hope to persuade the pope to favor such a scheme. But the strength and stamina necessary for a vigorous campaign of this nature were clearly lacking, a not surprising circumstance when we consider the evidence we now possess concerning the king's fragile physical condition. It is this contingency which in all likelihood became the determinative factor in his decision to postpone negotiations with the pope. The symptomatology of his illness, with its cycle of agonizing pain and abrupt remission, was simply not conducive to forceful and deliberate action but rather predisposed the monarch to bouts of depression, indecision, and frequently bizarre behavior.

Deferring his embassy to the pope, Alfonso convoked an assembly of nobles, jurists, and prelates in Zamora during June and July 1274.[56] However, on the twenty-second of July a further complication ensued: Henry of Navarre died, leaving his two-year-old daughter, Jeanne I (r. 1274-1305), to inherit the throne, since his infant son, Thibault, betrothed to Alfonso's daughter, Violante, had also died shortly before. Henry's widow, Blanche of Artois, was first cousin to Philip III of France, who had succeeded to the French crown at the death of his father, St. Louis, in 1270, and Philip was very much interested in consolidating and perpetuating French claims to Navarre through a marriage of his own son and heir, Louis, to the infant Jeanne.[57] Henry's untimely demise now set the stage for a power struggle in Pamplona between three political factions allied variously with Castile, France, and Aragon.[58] Alfonso, ever mindful of the overarching need for peninsular unity, advanced his own rather tenuous claims to the Navarrese throne on the grounds that King García IV Ramírez of Navarre (1134-50) had been a vassal of Alfonso VII.[59]

In the meantime, Pope Gregory X presided over the Council of Lyons with single-minded resolve. Called from a crusade in Palestine to head the church in 1271, Gregory had never abandoned his determination to unite all of Christendom against the Moors, and the Council of Lyons was the instrument he would use to achieve this goal. Gregory realized the importance of settling the imperial question once and for all and the absurdity of yielding to Alfonso's preposterous demands, yet he could not easily afford to ignore the claims of a powerful political figure around whom so many of the antipapal Ghibelline factions of northern Italy had now rallied. The pope was also aware of the need to enlist Alfonso's support in any preparations to embark upon a new crusade, and to that end he issued a papal bull on 24 July 1274 condemning the divisive stratagems of the recalcitrant nobles, who by their actions had thwarted Castilian efforts to subdue the infidel while inviting Muslim intervention in the south of Spain. At the same time, Gregory made Alfonso a most generous offer: to share with him fully one-tenth of all ecclesiastical revenues for six years if the Castilian monarch would desist from his imperial pretensions and devote his efforts to a new crusade. The extent to which Alfonso's obsession with the imperial crown had driven him may be measured by his refusal of this most magnanimous proposition, though he did not reject the idea of a crusade.[60]

In August 1274 political intrigue in Navarre had become so intense that the regent queen, Blanche of Artois, was forced to take refuge in France with her young daughter, Jeanne, seeking the protection of her cousin, Philip III the Bold.[61] Alfonso had no doubt foreseen this possibility some months earlier as King Henry's condition began to deteriorate. The matter of the Navarrese succession was yet another problem he had to face, together with an economic crisis, the rebellious nobles, and his own perilous health. The king proceeded to renounce his personal claims to the Navarrese throne in favor of his son, Fernando de la Cerda, who marched without delay towards Pamplona, laying siege to the town of Viana on 3 September 1274. When his efforts in this area were frustrated, Fernando changed venues, besieging Mendavia, which surrendered to him toward the middle of November 1274.[62]

Pope Gregory X was not pleased by this display of strife among Christian nations and tried to obstruct Alfonso's pretensions to the imperial throne by issuing papal confirmation of the election of Rudolf of Hapsburg as emperor of Germany on 26 September 1274. Alfonso, who had left Zamora toward the end of July at the close of the assembly there, was in Cuéllar on 3 August and in Alcalá de Henares by 28 August. He was probably in the area of Santo Domingo de Silos, where he had arrived on 28 September, when he learned of Rudolf's confirmation and must have reasoned at this point that any further delay in meeting with Gregory would surely and permanently jeopardize his imperial aspirations. A conference between prince and pope was deemed crucial at this juncture, and Alfonso hurriedly set about making plans for his journey to the papal court.[63]

By 16 October the Castilian monarch had arrived in Alicante and spent several weeks there provisioning ships which would proceed in advance to Marseilles and thence up the mouth of the Rhône to Lyons to await his arrival, while he traveled with his court by land along the Mediterranean coast. Alfonso probably reached Valencia about the middle of November 1274, leaving a few weeks later for Barcelona, where he arrived during the Christmas holidays.[64] The king's lingering apprehensions concerning a possible renewal of conspiratorial activities on the part of the rebellious nobles and his brother Felipe were no doubt eased somewhat by news of Felipe's death in late November.[65] Any remorse Alfonso may have felt was most likely erased by the magnitude and warmth of his reception in Barcelona. Aragonese records show that Jaime spared no expense to accommodate his royal son-in-law and that Alfonso remained in Barcelona until about 22 January, making his way from there with an escort through the kingdom of Aragon as far north as Perpignan and the French border about 7 March 1275, where he left the queen, their children, and many of his retainers.[66] Passing through Narbonne and Béziers, Alfonso reached Montpellier, birthplace and feudal domain of Jaime I, sometime around the beginning of April.[67]

In that city, famous for its schools of law and medicine, Alfonso spent some fifteen days,[68] and there he would return following his audience with the pope to recover from a critical relapse of his illness, no doubt attended by some of the finest physicians in Europe.[69] In Montpellier he received word from the pope on 3 May proposing an interview in Beaucaire, a small town on the Rhône some 50 kilometers distant and more easily accessible than Lyons, which would have required a journey more than five times as far.[70] Why had Gregory altered his itinerary? Perhaps because the Council of Lyons had now concluded its deliberations after a nearly year-long session, or perhaps, with greater justification, the change was made in papal deference to the king's ill health, which had once again reached crisis proportions. *Cantiga* 235 tells us that "when he left his land and went to see / the pope of that time, he fell so gravely ill / that they thought he would surely die" (st. 8bcd).[71] This sober information, entirely at variance with the lighthearted account of the contemporary Catalan chronicler Ramon Muntaner (1265-1336), who emphasizes the festive air surrounding the entire expedition, specifies that Alfonso had become desperately ill on the road to Lyons. The delay in his journey, several weeks in Montpellier, lends credence to this report. At the same time, it may not have been politically expedient for Gregory to meet with Alfonso in a city which owed allegiance to Jaime I of Aragon, and Beaucaire was on French soil.[72]

The pope was in Beaucaire on 14 May 1275, and we may suppose that Alfonso had arrived there at about the same time.[73] The papal audiences were to last nearly three months, until the end of July.[74] The last document signed by Alfonso in Beaucaire is dated 20 July 1275,[75] but Gregory would not depart from there until shortly after 3 September.[76] The interviews were inconclusive. The pope was obsessed with the idea of embarking upon a fresh expedition to the Holy Land with Alfonso's assistance and was furthermore entirely unyielding in his demands that the king renounce all claims to the Holy Roman Empire. Equally obdurate, Alfonso never repudiated his imperial assertions in writing, and, in fact, the *Crónica de Alfonso X* scarcely mentions Beaucaire or the events which took place there.[77]

To compound his frustration, Alfonso had received word sometime in late May or early June that the vanguard of a new Muslim invasion had disembarked in Tarifa on 13 May, prompted no doubt by the persistently divisive activities of the rebellious nobles.[78] The advance troops were soon followed by Abu Yusuf, Marinid emir of Morocco, and the main Moorish assault forces on 16 August. Faced with an intransigent pope and no doubt disappointed with the outcome of their talks, Alfonso probably returned to Montpellier sometime in late August 1275. It was probably at this juncture that he learned of the sudden and unexpected demise of his son and heir, Fernando de la Cerda, on 24-25 July.[79]

Cantiga 235 recalls the moment and asserts that Alfonso nearly died: "Then he arrived in Montpellier and became so seriously ill / that of all the physicians there each and every one firmly believed / that he was surely dead; but he was completely cured by / the Holy Virgin, faithful Lady that She is" (st. 9).[80] This unique information, found nowhere else, is of the utmost consequence for a full understanding of Alfonso's actions in the next few months, which constitute a pivotal period in the history of Castile. To add to his misfortunes in Montpellier, Alfonso had to bear the loss of his own daughter Leonor and the anguish of his youngest brother, Prince Manuel, whose son Alfonso had also met an untimely end during this same month.[81] Undoubtedly, Alfonso's stay in Montpellier this time was longer and more painful than it had been on the way to his audience with Pope Gregory four months earlier. How long did he remain in Montpellier? Royal records are absent from 20 July to 10 December 1275.[82] *Cantiga* 235 together with other historical sources, however, will allow us to reconstruct a reasonable, if hypothetical, itinerary for this period.

The king had suffered a serious relapse of his illness before the conference with Pope Gregory, but the malady had once again become life threatening on his return through Montpellier, where *Cantiga* 235 asserts he was at death's doorstep. At some point during his illness, however, when his doctors had given up all hope of recovery, he was miraculously restored to health by the Virgin in a few short days, apparently fit and able to resume his journey to Castile, where he would more fully convalesce. Fortunate enough in this crisis to have found himself in a city famed as a European center of the healing arts, we must suppose that Alfonso would have been prepared to spend any length of time there his physicians felt necessary to effect a lasting cure. *Cantiga* 235, however, affirms that the Virgin "caused him to be able to ride in a few days / and to go back to

his own land to recover there; / he passed through Catalonia, where he had to cover great distances each day as one does on a long journey" (st. 10).[83] Some event more important than his own recovery had taken place, and the *Cantiga* implies that the king felt a certain urgency to return to Castile as quickly as possible. The Muslim invasion of the peninsula had commenced on 13 May, though preparations had been under way since the beginning of April. On 7 September the invading army confronted the Castilians in Ecija under the command of one of the principal rebels, Nuño González de Lara, governor of the frontier. The Spaniards were thoroughly routed with the loss of their leader, Nuño.[84]

The news of the disastrous Battle of Ecija would have been more than sufficient reason to compel Alfonso to leave Montpellier, but he had only arrived there, and his perilous physical condition would not have permitted him to leave at that point. A month later, on 20 October, Alfonso's brother-in-law Sancho (c. 1244-75), archbishop of Toledo and primate of Spain, was captured during the Battle of Martos in the bishopric of Jaén, where he was beheaded the following day.[85] Two days later the invaders were encamped outside the gates of Seville, and it certainly must have seemed to the ailing monarch that the situation in the south was getting out of hand.[86] News of the battle and the preceding devastation of the countryside around Seville[87] would not have reached the king for at least ten days to two weeks, and had he made a forced march back toward Castile at that time, he could not have arrived on the other side of the Pyrenees before the middle of November 1275.

Fortunately, the records chronicling the life of Jaime I are more precise. We know that Alfonso's father-in-law was in Lérida on 24 October and again between 11-14 and 19-26 November.[88] Ballesteros suggests that the motive for his trips to that city was to meet with his son-in-law, daughter, and grandchildren as he had between 9 and 25 June, when he traveled to Perpignan to visit Violante and her family while Alfonso was in Beaucaire.[89] Just as it provided a description of the expedition to Montpellier, Muntaner's *Crònica* details Alfonso's return trip to Castile, pointing out that the king did not pass through Barcelona but traveled directly to Lérida, which would suggest that he took the shorter overland route through the Pyrenees between Perpignan and Urgel, a total distance from Perpignan to Lérida of some 250 kilometers.[90] In this case, we may speculate that he spent five or six days on the road, if he was making a forced march as the *Cantiga* relates, arriving in Lérida around the middle of November, in time to cross paths with his father-in-law, who was in that city from 11 to 14 November. The *Crónica de Alfonso X* states that on the return trip Alfonso traveled the full length of Catalonia to Valencia and from there west to Requena and then north to Alcalá de Henares.[91] This itinerary seems highly unlikely in view of the fact that the population of Valencia and the surrounding territories had taken advantage of the Moorish invasion to rise up against Aragonese rule, and the dangerous political situation in the region at the time was simply too hazardous for the king to have ventured so far south. We must also consider that the earliest royal document to chronicle Alfonso's presence in Castile after the last diploma signed by him in Beaucaire on 20 July is dated 10 December in Brihuega,[92] some 50 kilometers to the northeast of Alcalá de Henares, while the next royal document, dated 22 December, was issued in Alcalá itself,[93] a sure indication that the king was traveling south from Lérida and not north from Valencia, as the *Crónica de Alfonso X* would depict it.

In the interim, the main Moorish invasion forces had surrounded Seville but without heavy siege machinery were unable to breach the city walls. Stymied in their hopes for conquest and threatened with a naval blockade organized by Alfonso's seventeen-year-old son, Prince Sancho, that would eventually cut off their supplies, the invaders were content to pillage the countryside and retreat at leisure.[94] By the middle of November Abu Yusuf's troops had returned to Algeciras with enough booty from a devastated Andalusia to warrant the initiation of peace talks, which were duly concluded by the end of December with the active intervention of Prince Sancho, whose newly minted reputation as a skillful warrior and negotiator would henceforth warrant him as a serious contender for the throne.

Arriving in Alcalá de Henares sometime after the middle of December,[95] Alfonso must have spent a bleak Christmas there sobered by the deaths of his son and brother-in-law and the knowledge that Pope Gregory's 15 October 1275 proclamation to the princes of Europe announcing Alfonso's abdication of the Holy Roman crown had forever extinguished his cherished dreams of empire. Gregory died in December, precluding any further attempts by Alfonso to influence the papal decision. Disillusioned with his personal state of affairs, though perhaps buoyed somewhat by Prince Sancho's success, Alfonso was now poised on the brink of the most disastrous period of his life, during which he would find himself rejected and reviled by all those whom he had once trusted and esteemed.

By 4 January 1276 the king was in Toledo, where in the following weeks he would meet with Prince Sancho and Lope Díaz de Haro, lord of Vizcaya, to discuss the matter of the succession to the throne, an issue of paramount importance which would rapidly develop as a new source of unrest for the sick and weary sovereign. The demise of Fernando de la Cerda, the heir apparent, had created yet another dilemma for the beleaguered monarch. On his deathbed Fernando had reportedly sworn his faithful vassal Juan Núñez de Lara—son of the late Adelantado Mayor Nuño González, who had fallen in the Battle of Ecija on 7 September 1275—to protect and promote the cause of his firstborn son, Alfonso, as successor to the throne, thus placing the powerful house of Lara squarely behind the de la Cerdas.[96] At the same time, the *Crónica de Alfonso X* narrates that Lope Díaz de Haro had made a pact with Alfonso's second son, Sancho, to support his rival claim as the new heir apparent.[97]

The situation was further complicated by the fact that Alfonso de la Cerda's mother was the sister of the king of France, Philip III the Bold, who had every reason to believe that his young nephew would be proclaimed heir to the throne of Castile and León.[98] Any challenge to the de la Cerda claim would be hotly contested by the French monarch.[99] Furthermore, King Alfonso was in a legal quandary: he had previously ruled in the *Espéculo* (2.16.1, 3), promulgated in 1255, and the *Siete partidas* (2.15.2), published before 1265, that legal succession to the throne descended in a direct line from father to firstborn son to grandson.[100] On the one hand, he was bound de jure by his own legal pronouncements; on the other hand, he was faced with his own de facto illness, the strong probability of renewed Muslim invasions on the frontier, and the unyielding reality that Alfonso de la Cerda, a five-year-old child at the time of his father's death, would be unable to rule as monarch in his own right until his majority, while Sancho was already a battle-tested warrior who commanded the allegiance of many of the most powerful lords of the realm.

Still suffering from the effects of his illness and perhaps for this reason unable to take a firm and decisive stance in the matter, Alfonso set the issue aside, returning to the north and arriving in Valladolid on 25 February 1276. In the meantime the confusion surrounding the line of succession in Castile was compounded by a series of events related to the papacy. With the death of Pope Gregory X in December 1275, the apostolic see would witness the election and demise of yet two more popes during the year 1276, Innocent V (21 January-22 June) and Adrian V (11 July-18 August). On 8 September the college of cardinals elevated the Portuguese Pedro Juliano Rebello, known as Petrus Hispanus, to the papacy as John XXI, a pontiff who would be noticeably favorable to Alfonso el Sabio.[101] By 30 April Alfonso was back in Burgos, where he summoned the cortes between May and the end of July 1276. Unable to further postpone a decision on the succession to the throne, he duly appointed Sancho as his heir, securing the approval of the representative assembly sometime toward the beginning of July.[102]

In the interim, the civil war in Navarre, which had smoldered since the death of King Henry on 22 July 1274, now flared up again with renewed violence in May and June 1276. The question of the Navarrese succession had been complicated by the flight to France of the queen mother, Blanche of Artois, and her daughter and heiress, Jeanne, in August 1274, when the queen regent had sought and received the protection of her cousin Philip III the Bold. The French king had now become the de facto ruler of Navarre with the additional political advantage conferred by the Treaty of Orléans (May 1275), in which the marriage of Jeanne I and his second son, the seven-year-old Philip, later Philip IV the Fair, had been arranged. To make matters worse, King Jaime I of Aragon, Alfonso's father-in-law, had died on 27 July with the resultant collapse of the Aragonese faction in Navarre, whose members now quickly realigned with Castile against French rule.

Suspicious at Alfonso's failure to ratify the rights of his nephew to the throne of Castile during the cortes held from May through July and rightly sensing a defeat in Navarre if he did not act with firm resolve, Philip III decided to raise an army and invade the peninsula.[103] At the same time, he dispatched a detachment of troops under the command of Blanche's brother Robert, count of Artois, to defend French claims in Pamplona.[104] Alfonso reacted to protect Castilian interests in Navarre by sending his own forces under the command of his brother Prince Fadrique and the prince's son-in-law, Simón Ruiz de los Cameros.[105] The expected battle never materialized. Inexplicably, the Castilian army marched to Monreal, a few kilometers to the southeast of Pamplona, and remained there without making any effort to relieve the beleaguered Castilian partisans, who were subsequently defeated by the French.

The reasons for such inaction soon became clear: the rebellious nobles had once again conspired to thwart the king, and in the same month, September 1276, Juan Núñez de Lara and his brother, Núñez González, sons of Nuño González de Lara who had died in the defense of Ecija a year earlier, both cousins of the king,[106] were in Angoulême with other Castilian nobles, where they withdrew their allegiance from Alfonso, pledging homage to Philip III.[107] No doubt Alfonso's refusal to certify the rights of his grandson, Alfonso de la Cerda, during the cortes held in May through July had alienated Juan Núñez, a staunch supporter of the deceased Fernando, to whom he had made a deathbed promise to uphold the de la Cerda interests.

A year earlier, in the fall of 1275, according to *Cantiga* 235, Alfonso had returned to Castile to the general applause of his subjects: "When he entered Castile, they came to meet him / all the people of the land, and told him thus: / 'A very good day to you, Lord'" (st. 11),[108] a claim substantiated by the contemporary account of the Catalan chronicler Ramon Muntaner.[109] *Cantiga* 235 then narrates that soon after, treacherous factions arose to betray him most disgracefully: "However, later, believe you me, / King don Sancho in Portugal was never betrayed so vilely" (st. 11de).[110] In the following stanza, however, the poet assures us that "the greater part of the nobles conspired, as I / know, to throw him out of the kingdom so that it would belong to them / and they could divide it among themselves. However, they failed in their attempt / for God raised him to the summit and drove them down into the depths" (st. 12).[111] The poet, in all likelihood Alfonso himself, wrote with hindsight that he would be avenged.

By 5 September the king had taken up residence in Vitoria, where *Cantiga* 235 recalls that "Another time, when he dwelt in Vitoria for a year and a month, / while he lay gravely ill, the king of France / attacked him with a very large army. However, he later behaved more courteously, / for God dissolved his plan as water dissolves salt" (st. 13).[112] Philip was about to move upon him with an army that might easily have overwhelmed him. But the French forces never got beyond Sauveterre-de-Béarn, 50 kilometers east of Bayonne, where an unusually rainy fall and lack of supplies obliged them to abandon their campaign.[113] Truly, Alfonso could gloat in the conviction that he had been spared by the hand of God.

As the fall wore on and the end of October drew near, Philip thought it wise to sue for peace and sent his emissaries to Vitoria, where the two sides reached an understanding of sorts on 7 November 1276. The Treaty of Vitoria contained a number of features favorable to Alfonso: a truce was declared between Castile and Navarre until Jeanne's majority; Prince Sancho was required to forswear all allegiances and promises of support pledged to him by the rebellious nobles against the claims of the de la Cerda children; Alfonso agreed to convoke the cortes within a year and place before the three estates the question of succession, promising to abide by their decision; at the same time, the king would pardon Juan Núñez de Lara and those of his retinue who had lately sworn fealty to Philip III. Perhaps in view of the fact that the details of the treaty were so advantageous to Alfonso, Philip never ratified the agreement.[114]

The new year, 1277, found Alfonso still in Vitoria with scant respite from the problems that had confronted him the year before. At some time during the winter of 1276-77 he would suffer an excruciating recurrence of his illness, which yet another *cantiga,* number 209, recounts in detail, informing us that he was once again near death.[115] In the meantime, the king of France, frustrated in his bid to dominate Castilian and Navarrese politics by brute force, was actively supporting those clandestine factions in Castile hostile to Alfonso in an attempt to coerce a resolution favorable to his nephew, Alfonso de la Cerda. For his part, Prince Sancho and his allies were hard at work to consolidate his own claims to the throne.

Suddenly and apparently without warning, Prince Fadrique and his son-in-law, Simón Ruiz de los Cameros, were executed by order of the king sometime at the end of April or the beginning of May 1277. The cortes had convened in Burgos by 9 May, and while several documents after this date may indeed have been confirmed by these two individuals, the names of Fadrique and Simón do not appear on a royal privilege dated 7 July or at any time thereafter.[116] The *Crónica de Alfonso X,* though mistakenly assigning the incident to the year 1276, gives a fuller picture of these events and some suggestion of the rapidity with which they took place: "and because the king had learned of certain things concerning Prince Fadrique, his brother, and Simón Ruiz de los Cameros, the king ordered Prince Sancho to seize Simón Ruiz de los Cameros and then to have him killed. And Prince Sancho then left Burgos and went to Logroño and found Simón Ruiz there and seized him; and this same day in which he was seized, Diego Lopez de Salcedo seized Prince Fadrique in Burgos by order of the king. And Prince Sancho went to Treviño and ordered Simón Ruiz to be burned there at the stake; and the king ordered Prince Fadrique to be strangled."[117] We have no conclusive data concerning the circumstances surrounding these executions. The remarks by the author of the *Crónica* are puzzling and obscure. Alfonso found out certain things about Fadrique and Simón, matters so threatening that they compelled him to act with the greatest dispatch and secrecy. The background events are illuminating.

Alfonso had arrived in Vitoria on 5 September 1276. Several days earlier, a French detachment under Robert of Artois had reached Pamplona, determined to end civil disorder and rout the Castilian sympathizers. Meanwhile, the Castilian army under the command of Fadrique and Simón Ruiz had remained nearby in Monreal though they made no attempt whatsoever to intervene.[118] The consequences of such inaction were predictable: French forces easily triumphed over the remaining resistance, giving Philip III fresh prospects for the success of his own proximate invasion of Castile. The disintegration of the French army by the forces of nature in Sauveterre-de-Béarn in October 1276, however, obliged Philip to resort to other, more surreptitious avenues of aggression against Alfonso.

Given Fadrique's conspicuous penchant for intrigue[119] and, as the commander of the Castilian forces in Navarre, his capacity to act with some authority, it is quite possible that he entered into collusion with the French monarch to depose his brother and perhaps even to dispose of him permanently if necessary.[120] Following Alfonso's decision to ignore the laws of the *Espéculo* and the *Partidas* in favor of Sancho, Fadrique might well have reasoned that those same documents, especially the *Espéculo,*[121] could be supportive of his own ambitions and that by removing Alfonso, he himself, as the next eldest brother, would have legitimate access to the throne. What other motive could have prompted Alfonso to have summarily executed Fadrique without recourse to proper legal proceedings?

Cantiga 235, which comments in rigorous chronological order upon several relevant events in Alfonso's life during the decade of the 1270s, makes an oblique, but revealing, reference to the incident: "Later He cured him of many serious illnesses, / which he suffered in Castile, where the Son of God / granted him great vengeance on those who were His / enemies and hence the king's also. Just as a long candle burns, / so did the flesh burn of those who did not love women" (sts. 14-15a).[122] Alfonso, with divine assistance, wreaked royal vengeance upon those who had attempted to evict him from his own domain. Those of his enemies who did not love women,[123] a not-so-veiled allusion to the crime of sodomy, were burned at the stake, perhaps the most often prescribed punishment for this much-feared crime.[124] The implication would seem to be that Simón Ruiz and Fadrique were discovered flagrante delicto and summarily dispatched without benefit of trial. Simón was burned at the stake, and Fadrique was "afogado," strangled, most likely with a golden silk cord symbolic of both his royal rank and the right to die a more dignified death than an individual of inferior station.[125]

The mysterious circumstances surrounding the incident and the disinclination of the several contemporary chroniclers who report the event to elaborate,[126] other than to remark that Alfonso had discovered something sinister concerning Simón and Fadrique, would seem to indicate an attempt to conceal some sordid or shameful affair.[127] While a case may be made for treason on the part of the two relatives, this is not emphasized by contemporary accounts. The hint of sexual perversion is even more plausible when we consider the particular circumstances: that homosexuality during this period was most often linked with members of the church and the nobility;[128] that it was considered to be a particularly rampant vice among the Arabs;[129] that Fadrique had lived for years among the Moors in Tunis, where it may be supposed he had become infected with their immorality;[130] and that there was a marked tendency on the part of officialdom everywhere in Europe to equate sodomites with traitors and heretics.[131] Furthermore, these events took place at a time in history characterized by a dramatic rise in public aversion and intolerance toward homosexuality, a crime for which the cruelest of punishments were now meted out.[132]

Given the added historical dimension provided by *Cantiga* 235, it now seems reasonable to posit that the liberal-minded Alfonso could have been quite tolerant of a homosexual relationship between Fadrique and his son-in-law Simón Ruiz, supposing that this relationship had been going on for some time, but when faced with their traitorous support of the rebellious nobles and the very real threat that they might use the Castilian army stationed in Navarre to overthrow him, Alfonso seized upon the excuse of their unnatural liaison as an appropriate justification for fratricide. By executing Fadrique and Simón for the unmentionable crime of sodomy, Alfonso was at once vindicated for killing his own brother and relieved of any further explanation for his actions. Nevertheless, Sancho would publicly rebuke his father for the murder of Fadrique "without cause"[133] and, in an act which would seem to belie either the validity of the charge of homosexuality or the seriousness with which the crime was viewed in Castile, ordered the body of his uncle removed from "the filthy place in which Alfonso had him interred,"[134] giving him honorable burial in the Trinitarian monastery in Burgos.

A document signed on 9 May 1277 by the assembled nobles, prelates, and members of the third estate at the cortes in Burgos reveals that they were aware of a fresh offensive by the Moroccan army: "At this time with the king here in Burgos, news arrived from the frontier that a great force of Moors had arrived from across the sea, and that they are raiding the land, and that they are capturing many people, and they carried off many cattle and caused great damage, and this they do each day."[135] The main invasion forces under Abu Yusuf disembarked in Tarifa on 1 July to pursue a new and more vigorous jihad. To this period we may assign stanza 16 of *Cantiga* 235: "After leaving Castile, the king was eager / to go to the frontier; but the virtuous Lady / did not wish him to go there just then, until he recovered more fully; / therefore She gave him a general fever throughout his body."[136] Though the gravity of the situation would certainly seem to mandate the presence of the king on the frontier, he would be unable to make the journey south for fully another year. *Cantiga* 235 states that he was physically incapable of meeting the invading Moroccan army because of a "febre gêeral," a chronic, debilitating fever.

The cortes of Burgos ended sometime before Pentecost on 16 May,[137] and shortly thereafter the king lost a close ally, the Portuguese Pope John XXI, who died on 20 May. A few days earlier Lope Díaz de Haro was in Pamplona, where he had abandoned his allegiance to Alfonso, having signed a receipt on 16 May for monies advanced for feudal service to the king of France.[138] Soon after, Alfonso had to confront the defection of his cousin, Fernán Pérez Ponce, who likewise had become a vassal of Philip III, receiving an advance for services in July.[139] It was an incongruous alliance: the Haros, supporters of Sancho, and the Laras, champions of the de la Cerda cause, now found themselves united on the side of the French against their own monarch. The precipitate flight of the rebellious nobles to France at this time can only be explained by the same conspiracy which had cost Fadrique and Simón Ruiz their lives some two months earlier.[140]

By 3 August Abu Yusuf had arrived at the gates of Seville, where he met and defeated the Castilian forces under Alfonso Fernández. In rapid succession the Moroccans attacked Jerez on 15 September and Córdoba on 30 October.[141] The worsening situation was aggravated by the absence of many of the most powerful nobles in Castile and León together with their feudal retainers. The election of Pope Nicholas III on 25 November would signal yet another source of irritation for Alfonso, who, sick with fever and attacked by the French in the north and the Moroccans in the south, would now be importuned by a pope bent on a rapid reconciliation of the princes of Christendom.[142] Given his perilous physical condition, Alfonso would remain in Burgos for the remainder of 1277.

By 11 March 1278 Alfonso was still in Burgos. At this juncture the *Cantiga* recounts that the king's illness intensified to such an extent that he went straightway to Valladolid, where the Virgin brought him near the point of death: "When they thought he would die, he went this time / directly to Valladolid. . . . However, before She made him well, / She caused his condition to reach such severity that no judge / would have pronounced him alive and the Holy Empress / caused him to experience death" (sts. 15abc-16abc).[143] In fact Alfonso left Burgos for Valladolid, passing on the way through Peñafiel on 24 March[144] and arriving in Valladolid on Palm Sunday, 10 April 1278.[145] In the image of Christ, he would spend Holy Week in the agony of death, his physicians having abandoned all hope for his recovery.[146]

Then, on Easter Day, the *Cantiga* informs us, the Virgin suddenly and miraculously healed him: "However, on the happy day / of Easter she wished him to live" (st. 18cd).[147] Easter Day 1278 fell on 17 April, a week after the king's arrival in Valladolid. The effects of the miraculous healing must have been substantial, since Alfonso had sufficiently recovered by the middle of May to attend the cortes in Segovia, where he turned over many of his royal responsibilities to Sancho.[148] The burden of his cancerous affliction would grow ever more oppressive with time, however, and he would not feel well enough to realize his ambition to launch a new offensive against the invading Moroccan forces until fully a year later, when he reached Seville during summer 1279.[149]

When was *Cantiga* 235 written? Most likely at some time between April 1278, the date of the Easter miracle in Valladolid, and Sancho's declaration of rebellion in April 1282, heralding the triumphant return of the king's hostile relatives, the rebellious nobles, and others who, the poem tells us in tones of righteous indignation, had earlier been routed and overthrown (st. 12). The only period corresponding to these optimistic circumstances would seem to be that interval in 1278 immediately following the miracle in April and continuing through the middle of October, when Alfonso set out for the frontier. The cortes in Segovia from May to the end of July was supportive of both the king's petition to invest Sancho with greater responsibilities and his request for funds to launch an offensive against the Moors in Algeciras, though Abu Yusuf had by now returned to Morocco and no longer presented such a serious threat to Andalusia.[150] Furthermore, a document dated 26 September 1278 indicates that two of the principal conspirators, Lope Díaz de Haro and his brother, Diego López de Haro, had been reconciled with the king, probably through the good offices of Sancho, whose candidacy they had assiduously promoted.[151]

Not all was well, however, for Queen Violante, her grandchildren, Alfonso and Fernando de la Cerda, and their mother, Blanche, had abandoned the king in Segovia, fleeing to Aragon and the protection of the queen's brother Pedro III, sometime during the cortes in June 1278. Both the *Crónica de Alfonso X* and Bernat Desclot confirm that Sancho and his uncle had carefully hatched the scheme to promote their mutual interests: by sequestering the children in Aragon, Pedro would at once remove a major obstacle to Sancho's accession to the throne and secure a bargaining chip with which to thwart his old nemesis and former brother-in-law, Philip III of France, the children's uncle.[152] Isolated by his illness, Alfonso was apparently unaware of the deception and wholly confused by Violante's actions, which further undermined the monarch's dwindling prestige and authority.

In the meantime, a letter to Alfonso from Pope Nicholas III in Viterbo on 15 July, urging a meeting between the princes of Castile and France, recognized that Alfonso himself might not be able to attend, perhaps due to his illness.[153] Nevertheless, there was an air of auspicious expectation, which the king must have shared when the Castilian fleet arrived from Seville to besiege the port of Algeciras on 6 August 1278. During the fall of this year, then, Alfonso, believing himself helped by the Virgin Mary, would appear to have triumphed over both his infirmity and his detractors, and this is perhaps the

tone and spirit which most closely approximates the attitude and perspective reflected in *Cantiga* 235.

Alfonso, reviewing a decade of suffering and illness in *Cantiga* 235, attempted to establish a rational pattern for his infirmity by asserting that he had pleaded with the Virgin to allow him to die in her service. She, in turn, had answered his prayers by bringing him to the brink of death five times, saving him at the last moment by what seemed to the king and his contemporaries to be a miraculous healing. These episodes of critical illness and sudden remission indicate that the monarch's malady must have been a constant source of pain, misery, and apprehension. Furthermore, Alfonso may have suffered social rejection and personal embarrassment because of symptoms which mimicked the dreaded disease of leprosy, with its inevitable implications of moral and spiritual turpitude.[154] The numerous instances when Alfonso has been accused by his detractors of indecision, vacillation, or inaction quite likely coincide with his recurrent bouts of illness, when either his great physical suffering or his repulsive physical appearance effectively eliminated him from any useful or constructive role. It may not be purely coincidental that the rebellious nobles began to plot openly and in earnest, meeting in Lerma in February 1271, little more than a year after Alfonso's equestrian accident during the cortes of Burgos in December 1269, when the effects of this mishap began to incapacitate the king. The flight of the insurgents to the kingdom of Granada and the ensuing efforts by Fernando and Queen Violante to resolve the matter while urging Alfonso, without success, to enter the negotiations himself are not to be understood simply as a failure on Alfonso's part to cope with the rebellion. With the help of *Cantiga* 235 we realize that Alfonso very nearly died during his visit in Requena with Jaime I in August 1273. Similarly, the king's inability to attend the Council of Lyons or to meet personally with Gregory X to resolve the question of the Holy Roman Empire before the summer of 1275 is most assuredly a matter not only of his uncertain political position but also of his fragile physical condition, one which found him "jazendo mui doente" during the entire campaign directed against him by Philip III—from the summer of 1276 to the fateful spring of 1277, when he ordered the executions of Fadrique and Simón Ruiz de los Cameros. The terrible pain produced by the swelling tumor left no time for quiet reflection and meditation on the problems of the realm; rather it gave rise to increasingly irrational behavior. In these circumstances it is not at all surprising that the king would now seek an outlet for his creative energies in the private pursuit of science and research, where his ailment and physical appearance were less of an obstacle than in the public prosecution of the affairs of state. The interval dating from his accident in 1269 to the end of his life in April 1284 closely corresponds to the period of Alfonso's greatest scholarly activity.[155]

In spite of several notable remissions, which he attributed to miraculous intervention, Alfonso gradually and inevitably succumbed to the tumor. The inexorable march of his illness as described by *Cantiga* 235 and the debilitating symptoms it produced during the decade of 1269-78 are the backdrop against which we must now view and reevaluate the drama of Alfonso's actions during this fateful period, certainly the most tragic and devastating years of his learned, yet troubled, reign.[156]

Notes

The original version of this paper was presented in a series of invited lectures at the 1990 University of Kentucky NEH summer institute, "Alfonsine Contributions to Medieval Spanish Literature and Culture." I would like express my gratitude to John E. Keller, codirector of the institute, for proposing the topic and to Joseph F. O'Callaghan for reading a draft of the essay and making numerous helpful suggestions; any errors of commission or omission, of course, are mine.

1. All references to the *Cantigas de Santa María* are taken from Walter Mettmann, ed., 4 vols. (Coimbra, 1959-72).

2. See Maricel Presilla's fundamental study, "The Image of Death and Political Ideology in the *Cantigas de Santa María*," in *Studies on the Cantigas de Santa María: Art, Music and Poetry,* ed. Israel J. Katz, John E. Keller, et al. (Madison, Wis., 1987), pp. 403-57 (p. 435); Presilla bases her conclusions on examinations of Alfonso's remains in 1579 and 1948 as reported in José Alonso de Morgado, *Historia de Sevilla* (Seville, 1587), 4:108; and Juan Delgado Roig, "Examen médico legal de unos restos históricos: Los cadáveres de Alfonso X el Sabio y Doña Beatriz de Suabia," *Archivo hispalense* 9 (1948), 135-53. While Presilla believes the symptoms first began around 1277, the evidence points to a much earlier period, possibly as early as June 1273.

3. The *Crónica de Alfonso X* 74, ed. Cayetano Rosell, Biblioteca de Autores Españoles 66 (Madrid, 1875), p. 58, reports that in June 1280 "el rey don Alfonso ovo una dolencia de dolor que ovo en el ojo, de que le oviera á perder." Antonio Ballesteros-Beretta, *Alfonso X el Sabio* (1963; repr. Barcelona, 1984), pp. 851-52, remarks, "Del carácter de la enfermedad poco sabemos, pero quizá pueda relacionarse con una tradición recogida por Gestoso. . . . Esta enfermedad de los

ojos es posible se repitiera el año 1278. Claro está que la escena en Triana con la presencia del rey no se verificó hasta el año 1279." José Gestoso y Pérez, *Sevilla monumental y artística,* 3 vols. (Seville, 1889-92), 3:175-89, reproduces an inscription on the wall of the Church of Santa Ana de Triana, which states that it was built in 1276 at the behest of Alfonso X when he was healed by a miracle of the Virgin: "Este sobredicho rey D. Alfonso estando doliente de sus ojos de muy gran mal saltosele el ojo derecho del casco e prometio a Ntra. Sra. la Virgen Sta. Maria el hacer aquí una iglesia que le dixesen Santa Ana Madre de Ntra. Sra. Santa Maria e luego en una hora se le torno el ojo sano y en su lugar." Diego Ortiz de Zúñiga, *Anales eclesiásticos y seculares de la muy noble y muy leal ciudad de Sevilla* (Seville, 1677), ed. Antonio María Espinosa y Carzel, 2 vols. (Madrid, 1795), 1:317-18, also recalls this same illness but places it in 1280, the year construction of the church was completed. This particular episode, however, is quite likely the incident referred to in *Cantiga* 209, which occurred in Vitoria during the winter of 1276-77; see below, n. 115.

4. *Crónica de Alfonso X* 18, p. 13; see also Joseph F. O'Callaghan, "Paths to Ruin: The Economic and Financial Policies of Alfonso the Learned," in *The Worlds of Alfonso the Learned and James the Conqueror,* ed. Robert I. Burns (Princeton, 1985), pp. 41-67, and *A History of Medieval Spain* (Ithaca, N.Y., 1975), pp. 364-68; James T. Todesca, "The Monetary History of Castile-Leon (ca. 1100-1300) in Light of the Bourgey Hoard," *American Numismatic Society Museum Notes* 33 (1988), 129-203; Octavio Gil Farrés, *Historia de la moneda española,* 2nd ed. (Madrid, 1976), pp. 307-72; Evelyn S. Procter, *Curia and Cortes in León and Castile, 1072-1295,* Cambridge Iberian and Latin American Studies 1 (Cambridge, Eng., 1980), pp. 214-16; Ballesteros, *Alfonso X,* pp. 435-45.

5. Beatriz, daughter of Alfonso and his "barragana" or concubine, Doña Mayor Guillén de Guzmán, was born c. 1244 and married to Afonso III in 1253; she died on 8 July 1300 and is not to be confused with Beatriz, daughter of Alfonso and Violante, born in 1254 and married to the marquess of Monferrat in 1271.

6. See Sheila R. Ackerlind, *King Dinis of Portugal and the Alfonsine Heritage,* American University Studies 9/69 (New York, 1990).

7. While the *Crónica de Alfonso X* 16, p. 14, mistakenly assigns this incident to the year 1269, Ballesteros, *Alfonso X,* p. 427, places it in the fall

of 1267; O'Callaghan, *History*, pp. 368-69, states with greater accuracy that the visit more reasonably took place in 1266 with the promises made to Prince Dinis subsequently reconfirmed by the Treaty of Badajoz a few months later, on 16 February 1267, when Alfonso X conceded the Algarve to Portugal and annulled the feudal services pledged to him by Afonso III in 1264 during the *mudéjar* rebellion in Anadalusia. O'Callaghan's views are supported by Ortiz de Zúñiga, *Anales*, 1:273-74, who also places Dinis's visit to Seville in 1266.

8. Alfonso had ceded Castilian rights in the Algarve to the Portuguese crown in 1253 with the marriage of Beatriz and Afonso III, retaining usufruct of the region until such times as a son born to the couple might reach seven years of age; see *Crónica de Alfonso X* 7, p. 7; O'Callaghan, *History*, p. 360.

9. Felipe (c. 1231-74), according to the Marqués de Mondéjar, *Memorias históricas del Rei D. Alonso el Sabio* (Madrid, 1777), p. 507, was married to Leonor Ruiz de Castro, daughter of Rodrigo Fernández de Castro and Leonor González de Lara, sister of Nuño. Gil González Dávila, *Theatro eclesiástico de las iglesias de España*, 2 vols. (Madrid, 1647), 2:50, claims that Felipe's disaffection was due in large part to promises of money and titles which Alfonso had made to his younger brother in 1258 in order to induce him to renounce the archbishopric of Seville and marry Princess Christine of Norway, promises which were never kept; see J. Pérez de Guzmán, "La princesa Cristina de Noruega y el Infante Don Felipe, hermano de Don Alfonso el Sabio," *Boletín de la Real Academia de la Historia* 74 (1919), 39-65, and Bruce E. Gelsinger, "A Thirteenth-Century Norwegian-Castilian Alliance," *Medievalia et humanistica* 10 (1981), 55-80. However, the *Crónica de Alfonso X* 29, p. 24, relates that following the cortes of Burgos 1272 and the subsequent expatriation of the rebellious nobles Alfonso sent messages to the insurgents which leave no doubt that Felipe had abandoned the archbishopric and married Princess Christine of his own free will and with the clear implication that the prince's studies in Paris had somehow been responsible for his desire to leave the clergy. See also A. Hernández Perrales, "El infante Don Felipe primer arzobispo electo de Sevilla, después de la reconquista," *Archivo hispalense* 31 (1959), 195-204.

10. *Crónica de Alfonso X* 19, p. 15; Ballesteros, *Alfonso X*, pp. 425-34. Ortiz de Zúñiga, *Anales*, 1:274-76, also gives a list of the rebels headed by Felipe in the chapter corresponding to the year 1270.

11. Ballesteros, *Alfonso X*, p. 478, perhaps overly influenced by the conspiratorial tone of the *Crónica de Alfonso X*, purports to find evidence of the spreading complicity of the aristocracy in several debatable circumstances: the uprising of the town of Escalona in March and the confiscation of certain properties in Seville belonging to the king's brother Fadrique (1223-77), who Ballesteros assumes had joined the renegades. Joseph O'Callaghan, however, in a letter to me of 4 January 1991, believes that the Escalona uprising was due not to machinations by the nobles but to internal problems among the townspeople and that Fadrique's properties were confiscated sometime around 1265.

12. Though the *Crónica de Alfonso X* 18, p. 13, mistakenly dates the wedding in 1268, it accurately documents the extravagant largesse dispensed by the Castilian monarch to his guests, many of whom remained in Burgos "grand parte de aquel año"; see also Ballesteros, *Alfonso X*, pp. 484-88; and O'Callaghan, "Paths to Ruin," p. 58.

13. See Joseph F. O'Callaghan, *The Cortes of Castile-León (1188-1350)*, Middle Ages Series (Philadelphia, 1989), p. 23; Ballesteros, *Alfonso X*, pp. 489-92.

14. *Crònica de Jaume I* 496, ed. Ferrán Soldevila, in *Les quatre grans cròniques*, Biblioteca Perenne 26 (Barcelona, 1971), p. 172; Ballesteros, *Alfonso X*, pp. 490-91.

15. Ballesteros, *Alfonso X*, pp. 490-91.

16. *Crònica de Jaume I* 497-98, p. 173; Ballesteros, *Alfonso X*, p. 496.

17. *Crònica* 499, p. 173: "E ell eixí's de Tarassona, e anà-se'n a Fitero, e d'aquí venc-nos missatge que ell era fort malalte de la cama de un colp que un cavall li havia dat en Burgos. E nós anamhi tantost; e foren ab nós tro a quatre o cinc cavallers, e nostra companya, e veem-lo, e conhortamlo. E menam ab nós un nostre cirurgià qui havia nom maestre Johan, e llevam ab nós tot ço que mester hi havíem. E estiguem aquí ab ell tro a quatre o a cinc dies, e ell prega'ns molt carament que nos en tornàssem, que ell guarit era." Ballesteros, *Alfonso X*, pp. 496-97, cites the *Chronica o commentari del gloriosíssim e invictissim rey En Jaume I*, ed. Mariano Aguiló y Fúster (Barcelona, 1873), which does not accord with the text of Soldevila's edition, while his various allusions to the "Crónica de Don Jaime" (pp. 369, 492), the *Crónica catalana* (p. 492), the *Llibre dels feyts* (p. 493), and the *Chronica* (p. 1133) are often confusing. For a thorough discussion of the complex history of the *Crònica* see Martín de Riquer, *Historia de la literatura catalana: Part antiga*, 2nd rev. ed., 3 vols. (Barcelona, 1980), "El 'Libre dels feyts' de Jaume

I," 1:394-429. It should be noted that Ballesteros's monumental *Alfonso X,* left unfinished at his death in 1949 and edited and published posthumously, must be used with caution due to the frequent omission or confusion of essential bibliographic data, which I have attempted to include or clarify whenever possible.

18. Ballesteros, *Alfonso X,* p. 497.

19. Ballesteros, *Alfonso X,* voices a "vehemente sospecha de que los procuradores . . . volvieron a congregarse, apenas el rey volvió a Burgos" (p. 510), alluding to several significant details in this context (pp. 510-14). O'Callaghan, *Cortes of Castile-León,* however, does not record any convocation of cortes in either 1270 or 1271. Though it is tempting to conjecture that Alfonso's accident and subsequent illness may explain the lack of a cortes between December 1269 and September 1272, we must remember that the average time between these assemblies from 1250 to 1350 was 2.8 years and thus conclude that perhaps there was simply no business of such importance as to require them during this particular period; see O'Callaghan, *Cortes of Castile-León,* p. 65.

20. Presilla, "The Image of Death," p. 435. I am indebted for medical information to David S. Shimm, M.D., of the Department of Radiation Oncology and the Department of Internal Medicine, University of Arizona. Dr. Shimm states that "there is a body of literature implicating a variety of physical traumas in the etiology of some squamous cell carcinomas of the skin. In particular, these cancers have been found at sites of skin ulcers and fistulae due to chronic osteomyelitis. It is these last two conditions that provide the most likely connection between a blow to the face and a subsequent maxillary sinus cancer, since both of these conditions are characterized by cancer arising at the site of a chronic infection" (letter to the author of 23 June 1990).

21. In his well-known translation of the *Crònica,* John Forster, *Chronicle of James I,* 2 vols. (London, 1883), gratuitously adds that Alfonso was kicked "in the leg" (2:618-19), though the location of the blow is nowhere given in the original text; see above, n. 17.

22. The fourteenth-century Arabic historian Ibn Khaldun recalls in his *Histoire des Berbères,* trans. Baron de Slane, ed. Paul Casanova, 3rd ed., 4 vols. (1925-56; repr. Paris, 1978), 2:364, that Alfonso's mutinous brother Fadrique was at the court of the sultan of Tunis when St. Louis's fleet disembarked there on 22 July 1270.

23. *Crónica de Alfonso X* 20, pp. 15-17; Marqués de Mondéjar, *Memorias,* pp. 280-82; Ballesteros, *Alfonso X,* pp. 518-19.

24. Fadrique was related by marriage to Ferrán Ruiz de Castro, whose sister, Leonor, was married in 1269 to Fadrique's brother Felipe following the death of Felipe's first wife, Christine of Norway; Fadrique's marriage to the Infanta Malespina produced Beatriz Fadrique de Castilla, who became the second wife of Simón Ruiz de los Cameros; see José Pellicer de Ossau y Tovar, *Casa de Sarmiento* (Madrid, 1663), fol. 51r; Enrique Flórez, *Memorias de las reinas católicas de España* (1761; 4th ed., 2 vols., Madrid, 1964), 1:577; Mondéjar, *Memorias,* pp. 490 and 507; Ballesteros, *Alfonso X,* p. 519.

25. *Crònica de Alfonso X* 16, pp. 11-12.

26. *Crònica de Alfonso X* 20, p. 16; Ballesteros, *Alfonso X,* pp. 527, 531.

27. The feelings between prelate and monarch were apparently mutual, and a satirical poem by Alfonso, "Se me graça ffezesse este papa de Roma," is said to have been directed against Gregory; see *Cancioneiro da Biblioteca Nacional: Antigo Colocci-Brancuti,* ed. Elza Paxeco Machado and José Pedro Machado, 8 vols. (Lisbon, 1949-60), no. 405, 2:308-9; also in M. Rodrigues Lapa, *Cantigas d'escarnho e de mal dizer dos cancioneiros medievais galego-portugueses* (Coimbra, 1965), no. 33, pp. 62-63.

28. *Crònica de Jaume I* 505-7, pp. 174-75; Ballesteros, *Alfonso X,* p. 545.

29. Prince Enrique's imprisonment would last nearly twenty-four years, until July 1291, and it was clearly to Alfonso's advantage to forestall any attempts to free him, since Enrique had shown himself to be openly hostile toward the king as early as 1246, when he had refused to recognize Alfonso as successor to their father, Fernando III; see Ballesteros, *Alfonso X,* pp. 108-9, who publishes a letter from Alfonso to Jaime I (Barcelona, Archivo de la Corona de Aragón, Cartas de Jaime I, núm. 125) relating the incident. Alfonso also composed a "cantiga de escarnio" either on this occasion or shortly thereafter in which he condemns Rodrigo, Enrique's majordomo, whom he accuses of inciting Enrique against him; see *Cantigas d'escarnho e de mal dizer,* ed. M. Rodrigues Lapa, no. 34, p. 64. Enrique's armed rebellion against Alfonso and subsequent flight to Tunis in 1255 are reported by the *Crónica de Alfonso X* 8, pp. 7-8 (which mistakenly places these events in the year 1259). At that same time in 1255 Enrique was amorously linked with the widowed Jeanne de Ponthieu, Fernando III's second wife, in a satirical poem by Gonzalo Eanes do Vinhal; see José Joaquim Nunes, *Cantigas d'amor dos trovadores galego-portugueses,* 3 vols. (Coimbra, 1926-28), 2:132. The intense rivalry between Al-

fonso and his younger brother Enrique (b. 1230), fourth son of Fernando III and Beatrix of Swabia, is amply reflected in the satiric poetry of that period: see Martín de Riquer, *Obras completas del trovador Cerverí de Girona* (Barcelona, 1947), no. 36, pp. 102-5, for a fierce invective by Cerverí against Alfonso because he would not help liberate his brother from prison, a topic which Riquer says "halló un notable eco de protesta entre los trovadores" (p. 102), including Paulet de Marselha, Bertolome Zorzi, Folquet de Lunel, Austor de Segret, and others. Enrique's exploits in Italy are extensively documented by Giuseppe del Giudice, *Don Arrigo, Infante di Castiglia* (Naples, 1875).

30. Alfonso had good reason to suspect his younger brother: Fadrique had allied himself with Prince Enrique's rebellion in 1255, but his animosity toward the king dates back at least to 1240, when as a young man of seventeen he was sent to Rome by his father, Fernando III, to claim the rights to the lands and title of the duchy of Swabia, which his mother, Beatrix, had left him in her will five years earlier. When Fadrique's entreaties were ignored, Alfonso, as firstborn, asserted his own rights, receiving from Innocent IV in 1246 a promising indication that he would be awarded the title. According to Mondéjar, *Memorias*, p. 344, Fadrique's resentment toward Alfonso for usurping his maternal inheritance was lifelong; also see Ballesteros, *Alfonso X,* for a history of the controversy (pp. 164-65, 731, 820) and for Fadrique's bitter disappointment as a possible motive for his conspiratorial activities, which would lead ultimately to his execution by Alfonso's command (pp. 270, 820, 825).

31. The *Crónica de Alfonso X* 21, p. 17, while mistakenly ascribing these events to 1271, leaves no doubt concerning Alfonso's overly trusting nature.

32. *Crónica de Alfonso X* 22, p. 18; this chapter also contains the text of letters from Abu Yusuf to the principal conspirators, including Felipe, Nuño González de Lara, and Lope Díaz de Haro in which the sultan refers to Alfonso in the most disparaging terms: "Alfonso de los tuertos . . . don Alfonso, que vos demandó demandas tuertas é que vos asacó monedas falsas é que vos quebrantó el fuero bueno que usábades en antigüedad" (ibid.).

33. See Jean Guiraud and E. Cadier, *Les registres de Gregoire X (1272-76) et Jean XXI (1276-77),* Bibliothèque des Ecoles Françaises d'Athènes et de Rome, ser. 2, 12 (Paris, 1902), 1:65, no. 192; Ballesteros, *Alfonso X,* pp. 674-76.

34. O'Callaghan, *Cortes of Castile-León,* remarks, "The cortes of Burgos 1272 was, without question, the most important of Alfonso X's reign" (p. 118); even the normally hostile *Crónica de Alfonso X* concedes that on this occasion "mostró el Rey tan bien su razon, que todos los que estaban y entendieron que él tenía razon é derecho, é que don Felipe é aquellos ricos omes facian aquel alborozo muy sin razon" (25, p. 22).

35. The *Crónica de Alfonso X* 27, p. 13, says "le pidiesen plazo de treinta dias é de nueve dias é de tres dias á que pudiesen salir de los reinos"; a nine-day grace period was customary, as in the *Poema de Mio Cid,* vv. 306-7, and the legend of Bernardo del Carpio, *Primera crónica general,* ed. Ramón Menéndez Pidal (Madrid, 1955), p. 372a, l. 36.

36. *Crónica de Alfonso X* 27, p. 23; Ballesteros, *Alfonso X,* pp. 587-90.

37. The text of the letters is found in *Crónica de Alfonso X* 28-36, pp. 24-29; also cited by Ballesteros, *Alfonso X,* pp. 594-615.

38. Alfonso's abject letter of capitulation to the rebels is recorded in the *Crónica de Alfonso X* 49, p. 31.

39. The *Crónica de Alfonso X* calls it an "ayuntamiento" of "ricos omes é infanzones é caballeros fijosdalgo, é otros caballeros fijosdalgo de las cibdades é villas quel Rey mandó llamar para esto" (47, pp. 35-36); see also O'Callaghan, *Cortes of Castile-León,* pp. 24-25, 52, and Ballesteros, *Alfonso X,* pp. 637-46.

40. *Crónica de Alfonso X* 48, p. 36; Ballesteros, *Alfonso X,* pp. 631-43.

41. *Crónica de Alfonso X* 50, pp. 37-38; see also O'Callaghan, *Cortes of Castile-León,* p. 25, n. 27, for additional bibliography and documentation; and Ballesteros, *Alfonso X,* pp. 646-47, 676-77.

42. *Crónica de Alfonso X* 52, p. 38: "era in Avila, que venia y, por fablar con los concejos de tierra de Leon é de las Extremaduras, que fice y ayuntar, é ove enfermedad de romadizo, é de calentura poca é pesóme mucho porque in tal tiempo me acaesciera."

43. *Crónica de Alfonso X* 53, p. 41.

44. *Crónica de Alfonso X* 55, p. 43; Ballesteros, *Alfonso X,* p. 664.

45. *Crónica de Alfonso X* 57, pp. 45-46.

46. Ballesteros, *Alfonso X,* p. 670, states, "Las vistas tuvieron efecto en agosto de 1273, mes que concuerda con ambos Itinerarios de Don Alfonso y de

Don Jaime. . . . Del 22 al 28 no hay documento real y entre esos días viajó Don Jaime a Requena y se verificarían las vistas." See Joaquim Miret i Sans, *Itinerari de Jaume I, "el Conqueridor"* (Barcelona, 1918), p. 485.

47. *Crónica de Alfonso X* 57, p. 45: "E con esto se partió de las vistas, é el rey don Jaimes fuese para Valencia, é el rey don Alfonso adoleció in Requena de terciana." Ballesteros, *Alfonso X*, p. 671, cites, without identifying the document, "Una serie de curiosos datos de la chancillería del rey Don Jaime," which appears to refer to expenses for a "malatia" or illness during Jaime's sojourn in Requena: "Yten ordinamus per 30 que despesa en la malatia VII solidos medio II dineros."

48. Ballesteros, *Alfonso X*, pp. 677-78, reaches a similar conclusion: "El rey cayó enfermo in Requena de un mal de terciana. Su salud no era buena desde el accidente de Burgos. Su dolencia in Fitero y aquel mismo año el *romadizo* en Avila demostraban que el cuerpo se resentía de los trabajos del espíritu y no era pequeña ocasión de enfermedad las preocupaciones del gobierno y los continuos disgustos producidos por los rebeldes."

49. "en Requena este Rey mal enfermou, / u cuidavan que morresse, daquel mal ben o sãou; / fez por el este miragre." I have used here and elsewhere the English version of *Cantiga* 235 kindly provided by Kathleen Kulp-Hill from her unpublished translation of the entire *Cantigas de Santa María.*

50. Ballesteros does not mention *Cantiga* 235 in this instance, though he does remind us of the Requena episode in a subchapter dealing with another disabling attack in Montpellier (August 1275) on the king's return from his meeting with the pope in Beaucaire, "El regreso del rey" (pp. 769-79). Presilla, "Image of Death," overlooks the Requena episode in her chronology of Alfonso's illness, leading her to conclude that "the symptoms could have started at around 1277" (p. 436), when in reality they probably first occurred in early June 1273, intensifying by the last few weeks of August in Requena to a point where the king was entirely incapacitated.

51. *Crónica de Alfonso X* 57, p. 46; Ballesteros, *Alfonso X*, pp. 678-81.

52. *Crónica de Alfonso X* 58, pp. 46-47; Ballesteros, *Alfonso X*, p. 676.

53. O'Callaghan, *Cortes of Castile-León*: "The business of the cortes was three-fold: to establish Fernando de la Cerda as regent during his father's absence; to arrange for a retinue of knights who would accompany the king on his journey; and to

obtain the necessary financial aid" (p. 101). See also Ballesteros, *Alfonso X,* "Las Cortes de Burgos," pp. 683-87.

54. Ballesteros, *Alfonso X*, p. 683.

55. Ballesteros, *Alfonso X*, p. 699, mentions this episode without identifying the source; Bonifacio Palacios Martín, "Los símbolos de la soberanía en la edad media española: El simbolismo de la espada," in *VII centenario del Infante don Fernando de la Cerda: Jornadas de estudio, Ciudad Real, Abril, 1975* (Madrid, 1976), pp. 273-96, provides the missing data from Barcelona, Archivo de la Corona de Aragón, Reg. 19, fol. 125r, and Reg. 20, fols. 222v-223r, adding, "En 1274 Jaime el Conquistador se ve en la necesidad de obligar una espléndida corona, acaso la que Pedro II recibió de Inocencio III y que dejó depositada junto con las demás insignias en el monasterio de Sigena, al mercader Bandino Amanati, de Pistoya, por un préstamo de 30.000 sueldos torneses. La corona, junto con las demás joyas empeñadas, fueron entregadas en depósito al comendador Raimundo de Baró, quien en febrero del año siguiente las devuelve al rey" (p. 275). See also Odilo Engels, "El Rey Jaime I de Aragón, y la política internacional del siglo XIII," in *Jaime I y su época. X Congreso de Historia de la Corona de Aragón: Ponencias* (Zaragoza, 1979), pp. 213-40.

56. While Ballesteros, *Alfonso X*, pp. 693-97, asserts that this was yet another session of cortes, O'Callaghan, *Cortes of Castile-León*, p. 120, argues that the meeting was primarily for the purpose of formulating the *Ordenanza de Zamora* involving legal procedures which did not necessarily require the participation of all of the estates but only of those individuals specifically qualified to speak to the matter in a juridical sense. See also Aquilino Iglesia Ferreirós, "Las Cortes de Zamora de 1274 y los casos de corte," *Anuario de historia del derecho español* 41 (1971), 945-71.

57. Like his ill-fated uncle and namesake, the firstborn of King Louis IX, who had been betrothed to Alfonso's daughter and heir Berenguela, Louis, the son and heir of Philip III, died a child in 1276; see Henri Martin, *Histoire de France*, 4th ed., 17 vols. (Paris, 1857-60), 4:363. Philip had envisioned the permanent acquisition of Navarre when young Louis succeeded to the throne, but his plans were thwarted by Gregory X, who effectively blocked this arrangement in the Treaty of Orléans (May 1275) by authorizing the betrothal of Jeanne of Navarre to Philip's second son, who would be known as Philip IV the Fair; see Ch.-V. Langlois, *Le règne de Philippe III le Hardi* (Paris, 1887), p. 98.

58. The Aragonese faction was captained at this juncture by Jaime I's son, Pedro, who would succeed him as Pedro III in 1276. By that time, however, Pedro had renounced his Navarrese pretensions and reached a reconciliation with his former brother-in-law Philip III, whose first marriage in 1262 to Pedro's sister, Isabel, had ended with her tragic death in January 1271; see Langlois, *Philippe III,* pp. 51-52, 105.

59. See O'Callaghan, *History,* pp. 223, 361; Ballesteros, *Alfonso X,* pp. 694-700.

60. See Peter Linehan, *The Spanish Church and the Papacy in the Thirteenth Century,* Cambridge Studies in Medieval Life and Thought, 3rd. ser., 4 (Cambridge, Eng., 1971), pp. 188-221; Ballesteros, *Alfonso X,* pp. 709-14.

61. Her actions in this instance foreshadow the future flight of Queen Violante to Aragon with her daughter-in-law, Blanche, and the young Infantes de la Cerda in June 1278, following the decision of the cortes in Segovia to support the future Sancho IV's claims to the throne over those of his young nephew, Alfonso de la Cerda.

62. Ballesteros, *Alfonso X,* pp. 701-3, 705, 717, points out that José de Moret (1615-87), the Jesuit historian and official chronicler of Navarre, does not mention the fall of Mendavia in his *Anales del reino de Navarra,* 12 vols. (1684; repr. Tolosa, 1890-93), but that an unidentified "privilegio," whose provenance Ballesteros does not record, was signed by Fernando in Mendavia on 17 November 1274 (p. 717).

63. *Crónica de Alfonso X* 59, pp. 47-48; Ballesteros, *Alfonso X,* p. 715.

64. The entire trip from Valencia to Montpellier is described in detail in the *Crònica de Ramon Muntaner* 22-23, ed. Soldevila, in *Les quatre grans cròniques* (above, n. 14), which, while rich in details of persons and places, is often unreliable and notably deficient in its chronology.

65. The *Crónica de Alfonso X* does not record the death of Felipe, who is last mentioned in chap. 59, p. 47, corresponding to a period during the fall of 1274 when Alfonso made elaborate preparations to meet with the pope, which the *Crónica* erroneously refers to as 1275. Mondéjar, *Memorias,* p. 507, states only that Felipe "era muerto por Abril del año 1275." Ballesteros, *Alfonso X,* does not specify the date. Pérez de Guzmán, "Cristina de Noruega," p. 56, cites a communication to the Real Academia de la Historia from Pascual de Gayangos dated 16 May 1856 in which he affirms, with no supporting documentation, that Felipe died on 28 November 1274. The source is Francisco de Rades y Andrada, *Chronica de las tres ordenes de Sanctiago, Calatraua y Alcantara* (Toledo, 1572), fol. 35v, who copied the date from an inscription on Felipe's tomb in Villa Alcázar de Sirga; cited by Flórez, *Reinas,* 1:25.

66. Bernat Desclot, *Llibre del rei En Pere* 66, ed. Soldevila, in *Les quatre grans cròniques,* p. 454: "E quan hac aquí estat quaranta-tres jorns, anà-se'n a Perpinyá e aquí lleixà la reina sa muller, e ses filles e gran res de sa companya," a statement later supported by the *Crònica de Jaume I* 549, p. 186: "entram en Perpinyà per veer la regina de Castella nostra filla, qui havia aquí estat depuis lo rei de Castella eixí de nostra terra et anà al papa"; Miret i Sans, *Itinerari,* p. 519, records Jaime's arrival on 8 June.

67. Ballesteros, *Alfonso X,* pp. 716-28.

68. *Crònica de Muntaner* 23, p. 687: "los jocs e l'alegre qui foren a Montpestller, passarien a totes altres festes. E aquí estegren quinze jorns."

69. Given the woeful lack of medical knowledge in Castile during this period and the apparent emphasis placed on spiritual as opposed to scientific intervention, it is not surprising that Alfonso may have opted to extend his stay in Montpellier, whose faculty during this century could boast such celebrated physicians as Arnold of Villanova and Bernard de Gordon; see Luis García-Ballester, "Medical Science in Thirteenth-Century Castile: Problems and Prospects," *Bulletin of the History of Medicine* 61 (1987), 183-202. It is well known that physicians trained at Montpellier were prominently featured in Alfonso's court, and one longtime retainer, Maestre Nicolás, was, according to the *Crónica de Alfonso X* 77, p. 65, with the king in his last hours some nine years later. Ballesteros, *Alfonso X,* p. 1049, reports, "Sobre maestre Nicolás existen unas trovas burlescas que ponen en duda su ciencia de curar. Era hombre culto, aficionado a la poesía y a la música, condiciones recomendables para ser médico del Rey Sabio. Había estudiado en Monpellier." The poems here mentioned are by Afonso Eanes do Cotom (no. 42, pp. 75-76) and Pedro d'Ambroa (no. 332, pp. 494-95) in *Cantigas d'escarnho e de mal dizer,* ed. Rodrigues Lapa (above, n. 27); see Juan Torres Fontes, "Un médico alfonsí: Maestre Nicolás," *Murgetana* 6 (1954), 9-16. For an excellent account of medical knowledge at Montpellier during the thirteenth century with extensive bibliography, see Luke E. Demaitre, *Doctor Bernard de Gordon: Professor and Practitioner,* Studies and Texts 51 (Toronto, 1980).

70. See Guiraud and Cardier, *Les registres de Grégoire X et de Jean XXI* (above, n. 33), 1:301-2; reproduced in Ballesteros, *Alfonso X*, p. 729.

71. "quando da terra sayu e que foi veer / o Papa que enton era, foi tan mal adoecer / que o teveron por morto."

72. See Archibald R. Lewis, "James the Conqueror: Montpellier and Southern France," in *The Worlds of Alfonso the Learned and James the Conqueror*, ed. Robert I. Burns (Princeton, 1985), pp. 130-49.

73. See August Potthast, *Regesta pontificum Romanorum* (Berlin, 1874-75), 2:1697; Ballesteros, *Alfonso X*, p. 730, says the pope was there on 10 May but provides no documentation.

74. See Claude de Vic and Joseph Vaisette, *Histoire générale de Languedoc,* 15 vols. (Toulouse, 1872-92), 9:47-48, who report that Alfonso stayed with the pope in Beaucaire for about four months.

75. Ortiz de Zúñiga, *Anales,* 1:288, cites an injunction dated 9 July, while Mondéjar, *Memorias,* p. 328, claims the same directive was written on 20 July; Ballesteros, *Alfonso X*, p. 731, believes the later document may have been a duplicate order, a not infrequent practice of the Alfonsine chancery.

76. Potthast, *Regesta,* 2:1699, cites the pope's last communication from Beaucaire on 3 September and records he was in Orange five days later; Ballesteros, *Alfonso X*, p. 770, says 13 September.

77. *Crónica de Alfonso X* 66, p. 52: "De las cosas que el rey don Alfonso pasó en cuanto fué al Imperio, la estoria escusado se ha de las contar, por cuanto no se falló en cuál manera pasaron." Carlos de Ayala Martínez, "Alfonso X: Beaucaire y el fin de la pretensión imperial," *Hispania* 47/165 (1987), 5-31, reviews in detail the evidence for the five principal reasons Alfonso traveled to see the pope, according to Jerónimo Zurita, *Anales de la Corona de Aragón* 3.93, ed. Angel Canellas López, 9 vols. (Zaragoza, 1967), 1:736-46, adding to the list the king's support for Genova and the Lombard League and, perhaps most importantly, the propagandistic value of his trip, which Ayala perceptively views as an attempt to rally to his cause the various elements of Ghibelline persuasion in Aragon, Catalonia, the Midi, and northern Italy. In that case Alfonso would have made every effort to conceal the nature and extent of his illness, which may well account for the lack of official records alluding to his condition.

78. See 'Ali ibn 'Abd Allah Ibn Abi Zar' al-Fasi (d. 1310-20), *Roudh el-Kartas: Histoire des souverains du Maghreb (Espagne et Maroc) et an-*

nales de la ville de Fès, ed. Auguste Beaumier (Paris, 1860), translated into Spanish by Ambrosio Huici Miranda, *El Cartás: Noticia de los reyes del Mogreb e historia de la ciudad de Fez, por Aben Abi Zara* (Valencia, 1918), pp. 318-19. Ballesteros, *Alfonso X*, p. 746, depends heavily upon this source as do many contemporary historians: Charles-Emmanuel Dufourcq, *L'Espagne catalane et le Maghrib aux XIIIe et XIVe siècles* (Paris, 1966). See also Ibn Khaldun, *Histoire des Berbères,* 4:76.

79. Contemporary accounts give conflicting dates for this event. The *Crónica de Alfonso X* 64, p. 51, "De commo el infante don Fernando se venia á la frontera á la guerra de los moros, é commo murió in Villa Real, de dolencia," recalls that "estando el infante Don Fernando in aquella villa, adolescio de grand dolencia, e . . . fino en el mes de agosto." The *Anales toledanos III*, ed. Enrique Flórez in *España sagrada,* 56 vols. (Madrid, 1747-1957), 23:410-23, reports that Fernando died on St. James's day, 25 July: "Anno Domini M.CC.LXXV. = VIII. Kalendas Agusti obiit Dominus Fernandus, filius Regis Castellae, illustris domini Alfonsi filius" (p. 419). The *Chronicon de Cardeña,* in Flórez, *España sagrada,* 23:375, states, "Era de MCCCXII [1274!] años murió el Infant D. Ferrando." O'Callaghan, *History,* p. 375, supports the *Anales toledanos III* date of 25 July. Fernando's grandfather, Jaime I, reports in *Crònica* 552, p. 186, that "nós estant en Girona, haguem ardit que en Ferrando, fill primogènit del rei de Castella e nét nostre, era mort"; Miret i Sans, *Itinerari,* p. 522, affirms that Jaime I was in Gerona between 30 July and 18-19 August 1275, which must have been about the same time Alfonso received the news. Jofré de Loaisa, *Crónica de los reyes de Castilla,* ed. Agustín Ubieto Arteta, Textos Medievales 30 (Valencia, 1971), states, "dompnus Fernandus . . . decubuit . . . apud Villam Regalem . . . , quod nondum XXVI peregisset annum, . . . obiit era M^aCCC^aXIII^a, in vigilia sancti Jacobi apostoli" (p. 18), noting that Fernando (1255-75) was not yet twenty-six when he died. Evelyn Procter, *Alfonso X of Castile: Patron of Literature and Learning* (Oxford, 1961), p. 38, cites only Loaisa in support of the 24 July date of death. Ballesteros, *Alfonso X*, p. 765, without citing either the *Crònica de Jaume I* or Loaisa, rejects both the July and August dates, basing his arguments exclusively on the *Crónica de Alfonso X,* which states that Fernando had already learned of the deaths of Nuño and Archbishop Sancho, who had died in battle on 7 September and 21 October respectively; Ballestros argues that the sequence of events and Fernando's knowledge of

them as reported by the *Crónica* oblige us to place his death toward the end of November 1275. In the final analysis, the evidence provided by the grandfather, the *Anales toledanos III,* and Loaisa, who must have been about Fernando's age and was also the son of Jofré, Sr., "ayo" or tutor to both Queen Violante and Fernando, is compelling. Loaisa may be excused for confusing Fernando's chronological age but hardly his date of death, which coincided with the feast day of Spain's patron saint, Santiago, a coincidence which must have seemed portentous to many Spaniards.

80. "E pois a Monpisler vẽo e tan mal adoeceu / que quantos fisicos eran, cada hũu ben creeu / que sen duvida mort'era; mas ben o per guareceu / a Virgen Santa Maria, como Sennor mui leal."

81. Desclot, *Llibre del rei En Pere* 66, p. 454: "E en aquell viatge, mentre se'n tornava a Barcelona, morí un seu nebot, fill d'En Manuel son frare, e una sua filla, molt bella donzella, qui havia nom dona Lionor. Enaixí tornà-se'n en Castella molt irat e malaut"; *Anales toledanos III,* p. 419: "in regresu aput Montempesulanum decesit Alfonsus Emanuelis, nepos ejus, & filius Domini Emanuelis fratris Regis, & Donna Elianor filia Regis mortua est in via in regresu"; *Chronicon domini Johannis Emmanuelis,* in *Las crónicas latinas de la Reconquista: Estudios prácticos de Latín medieval,* ed. Ambrosio Huici Miranda, 2 vols. (Valencia, 1913), 1:96: "Et obiit donnus Alfonsus filius infantis donni Emmanuelis in Montepelussano." The deaths of Manuel's son and Alfonso's daughter most likely occurred in Perpignan, where Alfonso had left his wife and family while he went on to meet the pope, and not in Montpellier, though possibly the monarch first heard the news upon his arrival in Montpellier.

82. Procter, *Alfonso X of Castile,* p. 38, has observed, "The illnesses at Beaucaire and Montpellier which are recounted in the *Cantiga* thus help to account for the otherwise puzzling six months' gap between Alfonso's audience with Gregory X in May and his return to Castile in December 1275," adding, in a footnote, "He was at Beaucaire until 20 July (Ballesteros, *Alfonso X, Emperador (electo) de Alemania* [1918], p. 63)." Ballesteros, however, revised this estimate in *Alfonso X* (1963), p. 770: "cabe pensar que el castellano dejaría Beaucaire in agosto, quizás a fines de mes." The *Crónica de Alfonso X* 66, p. 52, claims that "el rey don Alfonso estando en Belcaire, . . . sopo commo pasaron Aben Yuzaf aquende la mar con grandes poderes de gentes, é que mataron al arzobispo don Sancho é á don Nuño. E otrosí supo de commo era muerto el infante don Fernando,"

implying he was in Beaucaire until several weeks after the death of Archbishop Sancho on 21 October. However, we may suppose that the anonymous chronicler equated Alfonso's absence from Castile with his presence in Beaucaire, unaware of the monarch's grave illness and forced layover in Montpellier and admitting that in regard to these matters his source "escusado se ha de las contar" (ibid.).

83. "E feze-ll' in poucos dias que podesse cavalgar / e que tornass' a ssa terra por in ela ben sãar; / a passou per Catalonna, in que ouve de fillar jornadas grandes no dia, como quen and'a jornal."

84. *Crónica de Alfonso X* 62, pp. 49-50; Ballesteros, *Alfonso X,* pp. 747-54.

85. *Crónica de Alfonso X* 63, pp. 50-51; Ballesteros, *Alfonso X,* pp. 755-65. Impulsive and headstrong, the young Sancho had plunged recklessly into battle without waiting for the reinforcements which might have saved his life; Ballesteros, *Alfonso X,* pp. 445-54, analyzes his character based on contemporary accounts.

86. The *Crónica de Alfonso X* 66, p. 52, emphasizes the magnitude of Alfonso's concern that the whole of Andalusia might soon be lost: "é bien cuidó que la tierra de la frontera era en condicion de se perder toda ó la mayor parte della, ca non cuidó que el infante don Sancho, su fijo, se trabajase de la defender, nin que avia y quien le ayudase á ello."

87. Details of the invasion mentioned in *Cantiga* 323 help us to date the Florentine codex of the *Cantigas,* Biblioteca Nazionale Centrale, MS II.1.213; see Procter, *Alfonso X of Castile,* p. 46.

88. Miret i Sans, *Itinerari,* pp. 524-26; Ballesteros, *Alfonso X,* p. 775.

89. *Crònica de Jaume I* 549, p. 186; Ballesteros, *Alfonso X,* p. 771.

90. *Crònica* 24, p. 688: "Mas no tornà per aquelles parts on era entrat, ans se'n tornà per Lleida e per Aragon"; Ballesteros, *Alfonso X,* p. 775.

91. *Crónica de Alfonso X* 67, p. 52; Ballesteros, *Alfonso X,* p. 775.

92. A letter to the "alcaldes y alguacil de Sevilla" from the "Archivo catedral de Sevilla. Recopilación de privilegios reales, fol. 30v y legajo 9, número 37," published in Ballesteros, *Sevilla en el siglo XIII* (Madrid, 1913), p. 208; see also *Alfonso X,* pp. 777-78, n. 56.

93. A letter to the city of Burgos from the Archivo Municipal de Burgos, CI, 2574, published by Emiliano González Díaz, *Colección diplomática*

del concejo de Burgos (884-1369) (Burgos, 1984), no. 44, pp. 129-30; see also Ballesteros, *Alfonso X,* p. 778, n. 57.

94. *Crónica de Alfonso X* 65, p. 52.

95. Juan Manuel del Estal, *Documentos inéditos de Alfonso X el Sabio y del infante su hijo Don Sancho* (Alicante, 1984), has published a letter by Alfonso to the Concejo de Orihuela which he dates 17 December 1276 (pp. 111-15), but the manuscript reproduction on p. 114 clearly says "mil-CCC-XIII" and not "XIIII." On 17 December 1276 Alfonso was in Vitoria; given the other two documents we possess which place Alfonso in Brihuega, less than 60 kilometers away, on 10 December, and in Alcalá on 22 December, we may fairly conclude that he had arrived in Alcalá by 17 December 1275.

96. *Crónica de Alfonso X* 64, p. 51.

97. *Crónica de Alfonso X* 65, p. 51.

98. Jerry R. Craddock, "La cronología de las obras legislativas de Alfonso X el Sabio," *Anuario de historia del derecho español* 51 (1981), 365-418, in the process of establishing the date of composition for the *Siete partidas,* makes an extremely strong case for the existence of a pact between Alfonso X and Louis IX of France prior to the marriage of Fernando de la Cerda and Blanche on 30 November 1269, granting the right of succession to Fernando's children (p. 401). However, Craddock's claim that the surest indication of the existence of an earlier agreement to this effect was Philip III's reaction to Sancho's recognition as heir by the cortes of Segovia 1278 is in error, based as it is on the belief that Sancho was not proclaimed successor to the throne until the summer of 1278. In fact, Philip responded to Alfonso's choice of Sancho in the spring of 1276 by launching an attack on Castile in September, two years before the 1278 cortes.

99. The fictional and historical ramifications of the controversy are explored by Jerry R. Craddock, "Dynasty in Dispute: Alfonso X el Sabio and the Succession to the Throne of Castile and Leon in History and Legend," *Viator* 17 (1986), 197-219.

100. See Craddock, "Cronología," pp. 400-417, for an account of Alfonso's predicament; see also Robert A. MacDonald, "Alfonso the Learned and Succession: A Father's Dilemma," *Speculum* 40 (1965), 647-53.

101. Ballesteros, *Alfonso X,* p. 842.

102. O'Callaghan, *Cortes of Castile-León,* pp. 83-84; Procter, *Curia and Cortes,* pp. 138-43. Ballesteros, *Alfonso X,* pp. 789-93 and 852-57, believes

that Sancho was not appointed heir until the cortes of Segovia in April 1278, though the documents he subsequently cites, a charter to the Galician monastery of Melón dated Puebla de Valdeorras, 14 November 1276, in which Sancho refers to himself as "fijo mayor et heredero" (p. 824), and Sancho's use of the same title in a document dated Vitoria, 3 March 1277, clearly indicate that Sancho must have been recognized during the cortes of Burgos 1276. The *Crónica de Alfonso X* 67, p. 53, asserts that Sancho was proclaimed successor during the cortes of Segovia 1276, correctly identifying the year though not the place, which became the venue of the cortes two years later. The Latin *Cronica* of Jofré de Loaisa, pp. 20-21, claims Sancho was recognized in 1276: "Hoc fuit era milesima CCCa XIIIIa"; this is confirmed by the *Anales toledanos III,* p. 419; and Desclot, *Llibre del rey En Pere* 66, p. 454, who reports that upon his return to Castile from France, Alfonso "féu jurar totes les gents del regne de Castella e de tota l'altra terra a son fill En Sanxo"; see also Procter, *Curia and Cortes,* p. 141. Craddock, "Cronología," p. 410, citing an interpolated version of *Partidas* 2.15.3 that required the establishment of a regency until the young king reached the age of twenty, an alteration he attributes to the period between November 1275 and May 1278, may well have provided us with a key to the solution of the problem: Alfonso could not easily reject the very laws of succession he himself had previously promulgated in the *Espéculo* and the *Partidas,* yet neither could he, in extremely ill health, reasonably appoint a five-year-old child his successor. By establishing a regency for the seventeen-year-old Sancho in the event of his own death, he could temporarily defuse a dangerous situation by placing the ultimate choice in the hands of a council of regents should be die or become incapacitated. While this subterfuge was immediately rejected by Philip III of France and those among the rebellious nobles who supported Alfonso de la Cerda, it apparently sufficed for a majority of Castilians until the summer of 1278, when Sancho reached the age of twenty and was duly recognized in full by the cortes of Segovia.

103. Langlois, *Philippe III,* p. 105, relying entirely on the rhymed chronicle of an eyewitness, Guillaume Anelier de Toulouse (*Histoire de la guerre de Navarre en 1276 et 1277,* ed. Francisque Michel, in *Collection de documents inédits sur l'histoire de France* [Paris, 1856]), v. 4795, "Segunt que audi dire, foro.CCC. millers," declares that Philip assembled an army "qui comptait, selon les on-dit, trois cent mille hommes," a highly inflated figure repeated in Ballesteros, *Alfonso X,* p. 800.

104. Carlos, príncipe de Viana (1421-61), the son of Juan II of Castile and author of the *Crónica de los reyes de Navarra* 10, ed. José Yanguas y Miranda, Textos Medievales 27 (Pamplona, 1843; repr. Valencia, 1971), p. 149, claims, "el conde de Artois, con grant cura de complir la voluntat del Rey, llevó consigo toda la dicha gente, en que había cerca de diez mil de a caballo, e veinte mil peones"; a footnote to this same figure states, "cien mil, dicen tres códices." Moret, *Anales,* 5:63, who usually follows Carlos, here cites the chronicle of William de Nangis: "Veinte mil combatientes entre infantes y caballos dice que le dió el rey Guillermo Nangio, que al tiempo escribía." Langlois, *Philippe III,* p. 103, mentions the same figures with the remark "dit-on"; and Ballesteros, *Alfonso X,* p. 796, also repeats them. Anelier's rhymed chronicle, v. 4305, reports that the troops arrived in Pamplona on 3 September.

105. Carlos, principe de Viana, *Crónica* 11, p. 148: "el rey de Castilla invió el socorro de quatro mil de a caballo e quarenta mil peones." Moret, *Anales,* 5:66-67, however, while citing Carlos, argues that these figures represent a "suma poco creíble, si la infantería no se componía en mucha parte de milicias concejiles arrebatadamente sacadas; porque la guerra de Andalucía aún no había del todo cesado."

106. Juan Núñez and Núñez González, his older brother, were the sons of Nuño González de Lara and Teresa Alfonso, illegitimate daughter of Alfonso IX of León, and half sister of San Fernando; see Ballesteros, *Alfonso X,* pp. 801-4.

107. See Georges Daumet, *Mémoire sur les relations de la France et de la Castille de 1255 à 1230* (Paris, 1913), pp. 157-58; Ballesteros, *Alfonso X,* p. 803, cites Daumet but not the *Cartulario de Don Felipe III, rey de Francia,* ed. Mariano Arigita y Lasa (Madrid, 1913), which contains a substantial number of documents sent by Philip III to his administrators in Navarre indicating that not only the Laras but perhaps even the Haros were involved with the French monarch at this time; cf. no. 25, "Del mismo rey D. Felipe al gobernador de Navarra, para que prohiba la estancia en Navarra a Lope Díez [sic], su hermano y sus compañeros," dated Paris, 20 September 1276: "Et si nos arequis le deuent dit Lop Die, que nos le sofre sains ademorer en reaume de Nauarre par.VII. mois, mes nos ne leur auon pas volu otroler" (p. 21).

108. "E pois entrou in Castela, vëeron todos aly, / todalas gentes da terra, que lle dizian assy: / 'Sennor, tan bon dia vosco.'"

109. *Crònica* 24, p. 688: "E així ell fo tornat en Castella ab la reina e sos infants, on hagren gran plaer e gran goig los seus sotsmeses con lo hagren cobrat."

110. "Mas depois, creed' a my, / nunca assy foi vendudo Rey Don Sanch' en Portugal." Alfonso's reference here is to Sancho II of Portugal (1223-48), who was deposed at the Council of Lyons on 24 July 1245 by Pope Innocent IV in a papal bull commanding the Portuguese people to pay homage to Sancho's brother, Afonso, count of Boulogne. The parallels which Alfonso X drew between the defection of many of the Portuguese nobility who traveled to Paris in the fall of 1245 to swear allegiance to Afonso and the desertion of the Castilian nobility to Philip III thirty years later must have seemed particularly ominous since Alfonso was related to Sancho II, a first cousin of his father, Fernando III, and had witnessed at first hand the tragedy of his royal relative, who was to end his days in exile in Toledo in January 1248; see *Crónica de Alfonso X* 7, p. 7; O'Callaghan, *History,* pp. 349-51; Edward M. Peters, "*Rex inutilis*: Sancho II of Portugal and Thirteenth-Century Deposition Theory," *Studia Gratiana* 14 [= *Collectanea Stephan Kuttner* 4] (1967), 255-305. Also, Doña Mencía de Haro, Sancho's widow and sister of Diego López de Haro, lord of Vizcaya, was a favorite of Alfonso's and, according to the *Crónica de Alfonso X* 29, p. 25, was Fernando de la Cerda's godmother; Ballesteros, *Alfonso X,* pp. 146-47.

111. "Ca os mais dos ricos omes se juraron, per com' eu / sei, por deitaren do reyno et que ficasse por seu, / que xo entre ssi partissen; mas de fazer lles foi greu; / ca Deus lo alçou na cima et eles baixou no val."

112. "E depois, quand' en Bitoira morou un an' e un mes, / jazendo mui mal doente, contra el o Rey frances / se moveu con mui gran gente; mas depois foi mais cortes / ca Deus desfez o seu feito, com' agua desfaz o sal." The statement "a year and a month," falling as it does at the end of a verse, is a prime example of poetic license corresponding more accurately to the demands of the rhyme scheme in *-es* rather than to any attempt at chronological precision, since the king was demonstrably in Vitoria by 5 September 1276, leaving there for Burgos in May 1277, some nine months later, to attend the cortes. In this same context, however, we might also consider the geographical proximity of Burgos to Vitoria, a little more than 100 kilometers to the northeast, a

distance which could be traversed fairly quickly, leading us to generalize that Alfonso was in the area of Vitoria for a year and a month.

113. See *Anonymum Sancti Martialis Chronicon* in *Recueil des historiens des Gauls et de la France,* 21:802, and the *Chronicon* of Gerard de Auvergne, in *Recueil des historiens,* 21:212-19 and MGH SS, 26:592-95; see also Langlois, *Philippe III,* pp. 105-7, and Ballesteros, *Alfonso X,* pp. 800-801.

114. The treaty itself is extant in Paris, Archives nationales, J 599, no. 14. See Daumet, *Mémoire,* pp. 40-47; Langlois, *Philippe III,* pp. 107-8; Ballesteros, *Alfonso X,* pp. 804-6. The disastrous campaigns against Castile and later Aragon (1284-85) led by the son of Louis IX are recalled with scorn in a contemporary rhymed chronicle, the *Chroniques de Saint Magloire* (c. 1300), ed. Etienne Barbazan, in *Fabliaux et contes des poètes français,* 4 vols. (Paris, 1808; repr. Geneva, 1976), 2:221-35: "Et en Espaingne et en Sauveterre / Ala ses fiuz folie querre" (vv. 118-19).

115. In *Cantiga* 209 Alfonso recounts, "I lay in Vitoria, so ill that all believed I should die there and did not expect me to recover. For such a pain afflicted me that I believed it to be mortal" (sts. 3-4). Rejecting his physicians' advice to apply hot towels, the king sent for a copy of the *Cantigas:* "They put it on me and immediately I lay in peace" (st. 5). Though the nature of the infirmity is nowhere disclosed in the *cantiga,* whose accompanying miniature depicts Alfonso with an open book on his chest, the monarch's rapid recovery is consistent with the gradual accumulation and sudden release of pressure characteristic of a squamous-cell carcinoma; see John E. Keller and R. P. Kinkade, "Iconography and Literature: Alfonso Himself in *Cantiga* 209," *Hispania* 66 (1983), 348-52.

116. Ballesteros, *Alfonso X,* p. 823, believes they were executed "casi con seguridad, a fines de abril o comienzos de mayo" and that the prime motive was their complicity in a plot to overthrow Alfonso and place Sancho on the throne.

117. *Crónica* 68, p. 53.

118. Carlos, príncipe de Viana, writing nearly two hundred years later, recalls in his *Crónica,* "E dende, a poco tiempo, el rey de Castilla mató al dicho D. Jimen Ruiz de los Cameros, por que mas presto non socorrió a los de la Navarrería, e por que tanto estobieron en los dichos montes de Reniega. . . . E ansí acontesció la destrucción de la Navarrería; e fue en el año de 1276" (10, p. 151); Moret, *Anales,* 5:77, follows the prince in stating that Alfonso "tuvo tan gran dolor de que no fuese socorrida la Navarrería, que mantenida servía para ese fin, que dentro de poco tiempo que se perdió hizo degollar en Treviño a D. Jimeno Ruiz, General de sus armas en Navarra y Señor de los Cameros, . . . acriminándole el no haberla socorrido."

119. Born in Palencia in 1223, the second son of Fernando III and Beatrix of Swabia spent five years (1240-45) at the court of the emperor Frederick II, one of the most cunning of medieval monarchs, who predicted Fadrique would meet an evil end: see Jean Louis Alphonse Huillard-Bréholls, *Historia diplomatica Friderici Secundi,* 6 vols. (Paris, 1852-61), 6:340-42. Fadrique played an important role in the conquest of Seville (1248) and is mentioned disparagingly by Jaime I, *Crònica* 369, p. 138, in the context of the expulsion of the Moors from Valencia in 1254. In 1260 we find him in the service of the sultan of Tunis following his exile from Castile, most probably for complicity in the revolt led by his younger brother Enrique against the king in 1255; see Ballesteros, *Alfonso X,* pp. 270-73. By the end of 1266 Fadrique was with Enrique at the court of their cousin Charles of Anjou in Naples, where both cast their lot with the papal Guelfs against the Ghibellines, supporters of their brother Alfonso in the matter of the imperial crown. Soon, however, Fadrique would switch his allegiance and support the Ghibellines and their titular head, his cousin, fourteen-year-old Conradin, grandson of Frederick II. Following Conradin's defeat at the Battle of Tagliacozzo (23 August 1268) and Enrique's capture by the forces of Charles of Anjou, Fadrique managed to escape to Tunis, where he remained until his return to Murcia in February 1272. See del Giudice, *Don Arrigo* (above, n. 29), pp. 169-73, for passages from the texts of contemporary chronicles which mention Fadrique's activities in Italy; see also Ballesteros, *Alfonso X,* pp. 465-75, 537, 546-47.

120. Ballesteros, *Alfonso X,* pp. 818-27, cites Zurita, *Anales,* 1:229-30; Juan de Mariana, *Historia general de España* 14.3, in Biblioteca de Autores Españoles 30, 31 (Madrid, 1912), 2:404; and the Marqués de Mondéjar, *Memorias,* p. 343, all of whom refer specifically to the fact that Alfonso sought vengeance against those who had aided Queen Violante in her flight to Aragon with the de la Cerda children. Based on this information, Ballesteros concludes, "Tanto Zurita como Mariana opinan que las víctimas estaban complicadas en una conjura a favor de los infantes de la Cerda" (p. 820), though neither Zurita, Mariana, nor

Mondéjar specifically mentions a conspiracy. Furthermore, Ballesteros presumes that neither Fadrique nor Simón had backed Philip III but that their deaths were most likely linked with a coup to remove Alfonso and place Sancho on the throne. Zurita, *Anales* 4.3, p. 216, suggests Alfonso may have killed Fadrique because of an astrological prediction that a member of his own family would overthrow him, citing as his source "un autor antiguo portugués," a story which Ballesteros, *Alfonso X*, p. 820, repeats; Craddock, "Dynasty in Dispute," p. 206, identifies the source, Pedro Afonso, *Crónica geral de 1344,* from his own reading of the unedited portions of the work extant in Madrid, Biblioteca Nacional, MS 10815.

121. *Espéculo* 2.16.3: "Pero ssi ffijo o ffija o njeto o njeta o heredero non oviere y que desçende de la linna derecha que herede el rregno, tomen por ssennor al hermano mayor del Rey" (cited by Craddock, "Cronología," p. 406).

122. "E depois de muitos maes o sãou, grandes e greus, / que ouve pois in Castela, u quis o Fillo de Deus / que fillasse gran vingança daqueles que eran seus / ẽemigos e pois dele. E ben com' ard estadal // Ardeu a carne daqueles que non querian moller."

123. It is notable in this context that Fadrique in 1253 had patronized the Castilian translation from the Arabic of the *Libro de los engaños et los assayamientos de las mugeres,* the most misogynistic of all the early works of Spanish literature, related to the Syriac and Greek versions of the narrative tradition known variously as the *Sendebar, Historia septem sapientum,* and *Dolopathos;* see *El libro de los engaños,* ed. John E. Keller (Valencia and Chapel Hill, 1959), and Emilio Vuolo, *Libro de los engaños e los asayamientos de las mugeres: Edizione critica con un'appendice di brani dalle altre versioni spagnole del Libro de Sindibâd* (Naples, 1980).

124. See Jerry R. Craddock, "The Legislative Works of Alfonso el Sabio," in *Emperor of Culture: Alfonso X the Learned of Castile and His Thirteenth-Century Renaissance,* ed. Robert I. Burns, Middle Ages Series (Philadelphia, 1990), pp. 182-97, who cites the Fuero de Alarcón: "todo aquel omne que fuere fallado fodiendo a otro omne, sea quemado" (p. 186). *Siete partidas* 7.21.2, in *Códigos españoles,* 4 vols. (Madrid, 1848), 4:424, "De los que fazen pecado de luxuria contra natura," decrees capital punishment for sodomites, though not the manner of execution; *Fuero real* 4.9.2, in *Opúsculos legales del Rey don Alfonso el Sabio,* 2 vols. (Madrid, 1836), 2:1-169, written by Alfon-

so's jurists between 1252 and 1255, is more specific: "Maguer nos agrauia de fablar en cosa que es muy sin guisa de cuydar, e muy mas sin guisa de facer: pero porque mal pecado alguna vez aviene que un ome cobdicia a otro por pecar con él contra natura, mandamos que cualesquier que sean que tal pecado fagan, que luego que fuer sabido, que amos a dos sean castrados ante todo el pueblo, e despues al tercer dia que sean colgados por las piernas fasta que mueran, e nunca dende sean tollidos" (2:134). Michael Goodich, *The Unmentionable Vice: Homosexuality in the Later Medieval Period* (Santa Barbara, Calif., 1979), cites the anonymous French *Etablissements* (c. 1273), spuriously attributed to St. Louis, and the anonymous English legal manual *Fleta* (1290-1300), both of which prescribe death by fire for sodomites, who must suffer the same way in which Sodom and Gomorrah were punished by God (pp. 77, 83). James Brundage, *Law, Sex and Christian Society in Medieval Europe* (Chicago, 1987), p. 473, recounts that "The Bologna statutes of 1288 replaced the earlier fine levied for homosexual offenses with death by burning"; also, "legislators in the Crusader kingdom in the Levant . . . decreed that men guilty of sodomy should be burnt to death" (p. 213). Recently, Jesús Montoya Martínez, "La 'gran vingança' de Dios y de Alfonso X," *Bulletin of the Cantigueiros de Santa María* 3 (1990), 53-59, has theorized that the words "no querian moller" indicate the two were Catharist heretics, whose punishment was typically death by burning.

125. *Siete partidas* 7.31.8 requires that a judge consider the rank of a criminal before determining how he shall be executed: "que maguer el fidalgo . . . fiziesse cosa porque ouiesse a morir, non lo deuen matar tan abildamente como a los otros, assi como arrastrandolo, o enforcandolo, o quemandolo, o echandolo a las bestias brauas; mas deuenlo mandar matar en otra manera, assi como faziendolo sangrar, o afogandolo" (4:470-71). A chronicle from the second half of the fourteenth century recently discovered in the monastery of Silos by Derek W. Lomax, "Una crónica inédita de Silos," in *Homenaje a Fray Justo Pérez de Urbel,* 2 vols., Studia Silensia 4 (Silos, 1976), 1:323-37, fancifully recounts of Fadrique that the king "mandole meter en el castiello e meterlo en vna arca que estaua llena de fierros agudos, e alli murio" (p. 332).

126. *Crónica de Alfonso X* 68, p. 53: "De commo . . . el rey don Alfonso . . . mató á su hermano don Fadrique"; *Anales toledanos III,* 1:370, cited by

Ballesteros, *Alfonso X,* p. 819; Jofré de Loaisa, *Cronica,* p. 21: "fecit prefatum dompnum Fredericum in castro Burgensi suffocari; . . . era M*ª*C-CC*ª*XV*ª*."

127. Ballesteros, *Alfonso X,* citing Mondéjar's *Memorias,* alludes to the dissolute life led by Fadrique and Enrique at the court of the sultan of Tunis, seeming to hint at some hidden depravity: "Habituados ambos hermanos con el continuo trato y comercio con infieles a sus costumbres, y casi olvidados de la religión cristiana, se diferenciaban muy poco de los musulmanes en sus vidas escandalosas. Son apreciaciones de Mondéjar. Las mismas violencias y desaciertos cometieron en Roma y Sicilia. El marqués lo toma de Ughelo (tomo IX de su *Italia Sacra*) que a su vez la copió de un autor anónimo que escribió los sucesos y acciones del emperador Federico Barbarroja" (p. 819). Ballesteros, however, while quoting Mondéjar, apparently did not check the latter's primary source, Ferdinando Ughelli (1595-1670), *Italia sacra,* 10 vols. (Venice, 1717-22; repr. Bologna, 1972-74), 10:561-654, "Anonymus. De rebus Frederici Imperatoris, Conradi & Manfredi Regum ejus filiorum." This brief treatise deals not with Frederick Barbarossa but with his grandson Frederick II and the latter's son, Manfred (d. 1266), and grandson, Conradin (d. 1268). Strongly biased against the Hohenstaufens, it was probably written by a Guelf supporter of Charles of Anjou and the papacy and clearly links the downfall of Conradin to the support he sought and received from the morally iniquitous brothers Fadrique and Enrique of Castile and their Saracen allies: "Hi sane fratres Hispani pro Saracenorum conversatione diutina actibus Agarenorum imbuti, & ferè Christianae Religionis obliti à Saracenis ipsius vita parum & moribus differebant" (p. 650c). While we must read this extremely prejudiced account with some skepticism, there remains a kernel of truth to these accusations which cannot be ignored.

128. See Goodich, *The Unmentionable Vice,* p. 87.

129. Jacques de Vitry (c. 1160/70-1240), *Historia Hierosolymitana* 5, ed. Jacques Bongars (Hanover, 1611), 1:1055-56, flatly declared that Mohammed had introduced Arabs to the sin of sodomy; see also Brundage, *Law, Sex and Christian Society,* p. 399; and John Boswell, *Christianity, Social Tolerance, and Homosexuality: Gay People in Western Europe from the Beginning of the Christian Era to the Fourteenth Century* (Chicago, 1980), pp. 279-81.

130. Boswell, *Christianity,* states that "Crusaders who remained in the Holy Land were accused by Western propagandists of adopting the 'effeminate' ways of the Muslims, and those who returned were rumored to have brought back with them the filthy customs of the pagans" (p. 281). Fadrique had spent nearly ten years at the court of the sultan of Tunis, 1260-66 and again 1268-72, ample time to have acquired an unsavory reputation for Arabic vice.

131. Boswell, *Christianity*: "It became a commonplace of official terminology to mention 'traitors, heretics, and sodomites' as if they constituted a single association of some sort" (p. 284); Goodich, *The Unmentionable Vice*: "charges of sexual immorality were linked with political nonconformity" (pp. 84-85); see also Brundage, *Law, Sex and Christian Society,* p. 473.

132. Brundage, *Law, Sex and Christian Society,* p. 472: "The second half of the thirteenth century witnessed a sharp growth of legislation about homosexual relationships. Municipal statutes during this period prescribed far more savage penalties for deviant sexual behavior than appear earlier. The new hostility toward homosexuals may have stemmed in part from fear that their presence might trigger a salvo of divine wrath against the whole community."

133. In October or November 1283 Alfonso disinherited Sancho, citing among other things in his decree that the young rebel had accused him of murdering Fadrique "sin causa"; see a translation of the Latin text published by Jerónimo Zurita, *Indices de las gestas de los reyes de Aragón,* ed. Angel Canellas López, 2 vols. (Zaragoza, 1984), 1:264; reproduced by Ballesteros, *Alfonso X,* p. 994. The *Crónica de Alfonso X* 76, p. 62, also cites the murder of Fadrique as one of the principal causes of the rebellion.

134. *Crónica de Alfonso X* 76, p. 61: "E falló que el infante don Fadrique, su tio, que matára el rey don Alfonso, su hermano, que yacia enterrado en un lixoso lugar do el rey don Alfonso lo mandó enterrar, é tirólo dende, é enterrólo en una sepoltura mucho honrada que él fizo en el monesterio de los monjes de la Trinidad, y, en Búrgos."

135. J. M. Escudero de la Peña, "Súplica hecha al Papa Juan XXI para que absolviese al Rey de Castilla D. Alfonso X del juramento de no acuñar otra moneda que los dineros prietos," *Revista de archivos, bibliotecas y museos* 2 (1872), 58-59; Ballesteros, *Alfonso X,* pp. 836-37.

136. "E pois sayr de Castela, el Rey con mui gran sabor / ouve d'ir aa fronteira; mas a mui bõa Sennor / non quis que enton y fosse, se non säasse mellor; / porend' en todo o corpo lle deu febre gẽeral."

137. O'Callaghan, *Cortes of Castile-León,* states, "The most popular period for convocation was the Easter season, from the beginning of Lent until Pentecost, when the cortes met nineteen times," including the cortes of Burgos 1277 (p. 67 and n. 17); Easter that year was celebrated on 28 March so that Pentecost, seven weeks later, must have fallen on 16 May. Ballesteros, *Alfonso X,* p. 841, claims with no evidence that the cortes of Burgos lasted until the end of the year.

138. See Daumet, *Mémoire,* pp. 33-34; Ballesteros, *Alfonso X,* pp. 821-22.

139. See M. Arigita y Lasa, *Cartulario de Don Felipe III,* no. 28, Fontainebleau, July 1277 (pp. 23-24), and no. 115, 20 September 1277 (p. 81), where Philip assigns 3,000 *tournois* to Fernando Pérez de Ponce for forty days' service per year; the Laras also renewed the allegiance they had pledged a year earlier to the French king: see no. 116, Angoulême, September 1277, where Philip promises payment to Nuño González, "nostrum militem," for his services and those of 106 soldiers for three months (pp. 82-83).

140. Ballesteros, *Alfonso X,* pp. 823-24.

141. Although the invasion of 1277 is not recorded by the *Crónica de Alfonso X,* it is fully described by Ibn Abi Zarᶜ, *Roudh el-Kartas,* who is cited extensively by Ballesteros, *Alfonso X,* pp. 827-35.

142. See Linehan, *The Spanish Church,* pp. 217-20; Ballesteros, *Alfonso X,* pp. 841-48.

143. "e u cuidavan que morto era, foi-sse dessa vez / dereit' a Valedolide . . . Mas ante quis que en tal // Ponto vēess' a seu feito, que non ouvess' y joyz / que de vida o julgasse, e a Sant' Anperadriz / lle fez ben sentir a morte."

144. Ballesteros, *Alfonso X,* pp. 850, 1113; on this date Alfonso sent a letter from Peñafiel to the bishop and chapter of Córdoba (Córdoba, Archivo de la Catedral de Córdoba, Libro de las Tablas, fol. 30v) in which he expressed his desire to go to the frontier: "Et agora sere yo ayna alla en la tierra, si Dios quiere" (Ballesteros, *Alfonso X,* p. 867), a wish that corresponds exactly to the sentiment expressed in *Cantiga* 235, st. 16ab: "E pois sayr de Castela, el Rey con mui gran sabor / ouve d'ir aa fronteira."

145. Ballesteros, *Alfonso X,* p. 850, states only that "En abril ya está en Valladolid," though the first document signed by the king in Valladolid (ibid., p. 1113, doc. 1099) is dated 10 April, which was Palm Sunday; see Jacinto Agustí y Casanovas, Pedro Voltes Bou, and José Vives, *Manual de cronología española y universal,* Consejo Superior de Investigaciones Científicas, Escuela de Estudios Medievales 25 (Madrid, 1942), p. 190. We should not, in the case of such a profoundly pious individual as Alfonso, discount the symbolic significance of arriving in Valladolid on Palm Sunday, there to begin a bout of suffering during Holy Week, the most solemn period in the Christian calendar, which would parallel the sufferings of Jesus and eventually lead up to the central focus of *Cantiga* 235, the miraculous healing on Easter Day coinciding with the Resurrection of Christ.

146. Ballesteros, *Alfonso X,* in a subchapter entitled "La enfermedad del rey," pp. 787-89, inexplicably assigns the Valladolid episode, with the king's illness, recovery, and desire to return to Andalusia, to the year 1276; Procter, *Alfonso X of Castile,* pp. 39-40, accurately attributes the Valladolid miracle to Easter 1278.

147. "mais eno dia fiiz / de Pasqua quis que vivesse."

148. The confusion introduced by the *Crónica de Alfonso X* concerning the time and place of the cortes in which Sancho was designated heir to the throne is dispelled, in part, by our understanding of the degree to which Alfonso's disease must have dictated his actions. Both *Cantigas* 209 and 235 clearly state that the king had suffered major bouts of illness immediately prior to the cortes of Burgos 1276 and Segovia 1278, having been miraculously cured by the Virgin on both occasions. Given the extent and gravity of these episodes, when it was thought he would die, Alfonso must have necessarily given serious consideration to the matter of succession, and Sancho, though he was only eighteen in 1276, was certainly the most logical choice. O'Callaghan, *Cortes of Castile-León,* p. 25, remarks, "In order to be able to direct his undivided attention to the frontier, the king apparently entrusted Sancho with primary responsibility for the affairs of Castile and León in the cortes of Segovia in May 1278" (p. 25); he later concludes, "Perhaps this decision was taken because he turned twenty years old in May, thereby reaching his majority according to the *Partidas* (II.15.3), and if his father died, he could have reigned without a regency" (p. 84). Alfonso very nearly expired during Holy Week 1278, as *Cantiga* 235 confirms, and turning over much of his power to Sancho in the cortes later that spring must have been seen as the act of a prudent man; Procter, *Curia and Cortes,* p. 143, also underscores the importance of Alfonso's illness in the designation of Sancho in 1278 and cites a declaration by Sancho's tutor, Juan Gil de Zamora, that in this year Sancho "incipit coregnare" (*Liber de preco-*

niis Hispanie, ed. Fidel Fita, *Boletín de la Real Academia de la Historia* 5 [1884], 146).

149. Ballesteros, *Alfonso X,* p. 887, states without reference that "Ya del día 28 de junio ha llegado a Sevilla y expide un privilegio rodado al prior y a la Universidad de los clérigos parroquiales de la ciudad de Córdoba"; on p. 1117, however, he also catalogs a grant given by Alfonso in Seville on 28 July 1279 (doc. 1181).

150. O'Callaghan, *Cortes of Castile-León,* pp. 25, 84, et passim.

151. Ballesteros, *Alfonso X,* p. 855, cites without reference a "privilegio rodado que la chancillería expide a favor de la ciudad de Segovia" signed by Lope Díaz and Diego López de Haro.

152. *Crónica* 71, p. 55: "E en el tratamiento de la venida de la Reina, los mandaderos del infante don Sancho fablaron con el rey don Pedro de Aragon que desque la reina doña Violante fuese venida á Castilla, que el rey de Aragon mandase poner en prision á don Alfonso é á don Ferrando, porque non fuesen levados á Francia nin le viniese por ellos ningun estorbo." See also *Llibre del rei En Pere* 76, pp. 465-66; Ballesteros, *Alfonso X,* p. 862.

153. *Les registres de Nicholas III (1277-1280),* ed. Jules Gay, Bibliothèque des Ecoles Françaises d'Athènes et de Rome, ser. 2, 14 (Paris, 1898-1938), 1:98, no. 262: "Et quia non sine amaritudine paterne compassionis audivimus te infirmitate gravari, cupientes hujusmodi negotio in omnem eventum prout possumus providere, iterate adicimus exhortationis et persuasionis instantiam ut si te forsan in hujusmodi nuntiis destinandis impediri contingat, dilectus filius nobilis vir Sanctius natus tuus ipsos in forma simili studeat destinare"; see also Ballesteros, *Alfonso X,* p. 844.

154. We should remember that in his last days Alfonso cursed his son for, among other things, having referred to his father as a leper: "Don Sancho, en las oraciones, con que incitaba contra nos a los pueblos, prorrumpió en varias partes en muchas palabras feas, diciendo entre otras, mui a menudo, assi el, como sus sequaces 'El rey esta loco e leproso'" (trans. from the Latin by Zurita, *Indices,* 1:264). Presilla, "The Image of Death," has described the symptoms of squamous-cell carcinoma, including "purulent discharges through the nose at a fairly early stage and great deformities in the face in the more advanced stages" (pp. 435-36), traits which mirror precisely the manifestations of leprosy; see Saul N. Brody, *The Disease of the Soul: Leprosy in Medieval Literature*

(Ithaca, N.Y., 1974), pp. 25-35. Ballesteros, *Alfonso X,* pp. 994-95, believes the epithet "leproso" refers to an attack of dropsy or edema the king suffered subsequent to the June 1280 episode in Seville, when he nearly lost his eye (see above, n. 3). The incident is recounted by *Cantiga* 367, "How Holy Mary of the Port cured the King don Alfonso of a great sickness which caused his legs to swell so much that they would not fit inside his shoes." *Cantiga* 367 was probably composed at the same time a grateful Alfonso granted an enthusiastic privilege to Puerto de Santa María on 16 December 1281 (Ballesteros, *Alfonso X,* p. 955); it is quite graphic in its description of the king's distress: "While the king was traveling by sea, both his legs swelled so alarmingly and became so inflamed that all thought he would be long in recovering from that ailment. They had swollen to such an extent that they no longer fit into his boots, and, what is more, the skin on them split and yellow fluid came out" (sts. 8-9).

155. See Gonzalo Menéndez Pidal, "Cómo trabajaron las escuelas alfonsíes," *Nueva revista de filología hispánica* 5 (1951), 363-80: "Sin duda el rasgo principal de este segundo período alfonsí es su carácter creador. Ya no se conforma Alfonso con patrocinar y dirigir traducciones sino que se empeña en una labor sincrética total. . . . En este segundo períodó es cuando se escriben las obras más originales y personales" (p. 369).

156. An article by Francisco Torres González, "Rasgos médico-psicológicos de Alfonso el Sabio," in *Alfonso X y Cuidad Real: Conferencias pronunciadas con motivo del VII centenario de la muerte del Rey Sabio (1284-1984),* ed. Manuel Espadas Burgos (Ciudad Real, 1986), pp. 107-40, came to my attention while the current article was in press; while it presents an interesting and intelligent psychological portrait of Alfonso written by a psychiatrist, it is based primarily on Ballesteros, *Alfonso X,* and does not take into account Presilla, "Image of Death," or the critical episodes related by *Cantiga* 235.

George D. Greenia (essay date summer 1993)

SOURCE: Greenia, George D. "The Politics of Piety: Manuscript Illumination and Narration in the *Cantigas de Santa Maria.*" *Hispanic Review* 61, no. 3 (summer 1993): 325-44.

[*In the following essay, Greenia contends that it is the illustrations of the* Cantigas *that carry the linear storyline, while the lyrics are nonsequential.*]

Analyzing narrative technique in medieval manuscript miniatures and their accompanying texts and achieving some sort of synoptic vision of the two was thought unproblematic only a few years ago. Despite strong contributions toward a theory of narratology in medieval studies,[1] many researchers are no longer sure that we can believe in the stability of narrative in either text or images, let alone hope to make the two genuinely congruent. My own attempt here to justify a joint reading of the supposedly linear verbal narratives in the *Cantigas* of Alfonso X (1221-84) with the manuscript miniatures he commissioned and supervised is meant to suggest the possibility of a match-up, at least in this case, for somewhat curious reasons. Against expectations, it is the narrative discourse in the miniatures of the *códice rico* copy of the *Cantigas* that is apparently progressive and linear, while the lyrics with which the images are teamed loop back on themselves in a non-linear way.[2]

Just to lay out my conclusions at the outset, I think first that the patron in this case was intimately involved in his book painting, just as much as we know he was in the narrative and lyrical songs he personally contributed or ordered composed for this collection, and that he left instructions for decoding his royal intentions in the page design, color and style of the illuminations. This decoding I am going to call "parsing" for our purposes and for reasons that I will detail below. Second, I also suspect that song and painting, intriguingly, exchange their accustomed traits for this book—the linear narrative storyline is ostensibly in the miniatures, while the song lyrics, which should bear the brunt of the legend, deliberately obstruct their own sequential flow. Finally, I suspect that the songs and miniatures are likely aimed at different audiences, overlapping ones to be sure, but audiences susceptible to differing messages.

There are boundaries that we need to test here, not only in drafting a grammar of motives for the patron, but also in sifting metacriticism among the arts. This is actually the more familiar, and at the same time more challenging, territory for medievalists. Although most students of the Middle Ages are trained to some extent in the analysis of literary texts, we interpret "literary" more broadly than do our colleagues in other subfields of the history of discourse, and we are more accustomed—rightly, I think—to examine the archeology of the texts we work with: how they are configured in a manuscript, how they were transmitted and shared, and if they were meant to be celebrated under certain circumstances. We also draw upon information from forms of textual archeology (applications of paleography, diplomatics, historical linguistics and codicology) on the one hand, and cultural archeology (philosophy, theology, architecture, sculpture, art history, numismatics, material history, climatology and demographics) on the other.[3]

The challenge for those who practice our synoptic discipline comes from overfamiliarity with these procedures. We are so used to examining data from neighboring realms that we may casually presume that most forms of high culture can be read in the same way as linguistic discourse. To speak directly of the *Cantigas de Santa Maria,* one distinguished critic actually proposed an examination of the illuminations according to what he called the "nine classical elements" of "narrative design": "plot, conflict, setting, characterization, theme, style, effect, point of view and mood or tone."[4] While these might have some usefulness for a literary critic, they are factors alien to the analysis of the plastic arts, even when the art work is paired with a narrative text and meant to complement it. Representations can be sequenced, as they are in fact in the *Cantigas* panels, but they are bound by space, and not by the supposed linearity of discourse.[5] Representational miniatures may reflect incidents of plot and setting, but they always literalize detail, form, mass, and color that are unexpressed—and inexpressible—in any accompanying text, and they cannot communicate other things (such as verbal associations, combinations of meaning through position or phonetic equivalence, arousal of discursive generic expectations) that have to be encoded in words. One notable literary critic and philosopher of esthetics, W. J. Thomas Mitchell (author of *The Language of Images, Iconology,* and editor of *On Narrative*), has recently advised cultural historians to get out of the business of trying to do inter-art criticism altogether because it almost invariably falsifies the arts (most commonly verbal and graphic compositions) tossed together.[6]

Part of what I want to explore in this essay is, in fact, something like inter-art criticism, but I do so advisedly and because we have a special case with the *Cantigas* that allows for neither naïvely convergent nor repetitive narrative readings in these texts and images but for divergent and independent ones. They communicate according to different rules and, as I mentioned, perhaps for different audiences.

King Alfonso's multilayered role as patron of poetry and painting in the *Cantigas de Santa Maria* has been explored by Joseph Snow and by the art historian Ana Domínguez Rodríguez (see bibliography). Snow and Domínguez, in prudently independent examinations of the texts of the poems and the manuscript illuminations respectively, concur that Alfonso gave himself a unique representation both as king and artist.

Ana Domínguez in particular underscores for us how Alfonso signals his responsibility for all of his royal scriptorium manuscripts through their iconography. Presentation miniatures habitually show him dictating the works that were compiled and calligraphed for him. He is almost never shown merely receiving a finished work from a scribe. His pointing finger is that of an authority, directing a work in progress. In the first of two presentation miniatures in the *códice rico* manuscript (4ᵛ) he holds a scroll with the words written in while his attentive scribes still clutch blanks. Even when being presented with a finished book, as in the presentation miniature in the now paradoxically incomplete *Libro de las formas e imágenes* (Escorial h.I.16, 1ʳ), he points to the open volume in a confirmatory gesture.

PARSING A MINIATURE

One of the more celebrated features of the *códice rico* manuscript, and perhaps the most distracting feature for the modern critic, is the book's fascination with the details of daily life.[7] Distributed among the **Cantigas** illustrations one finds hoes and harvest tools, and pots and pans in the kitchen; dozens of species of birds, and sheep being sheared and herded; the furniture of the home, the castle and the camp; the clothing of every class and condition, and even oddities within classes, such as saints as madmen in rags, the bourgeoisie in their best finery, and the well-to-do reduced to tatters. Individuals are depicted in the solemnity of the court, the grave deliberations of the highest cabinets, the snappish transactions of the market place, the coy pleasures of the salon, and the unblushing delights of the bed chamber. Taken together, the **Cantigas** miniatures provide the best graphic record we have of the life and society of thirteenth-century Europe. But in truth, all that only amounts to so much visual furniture.

The comprehensiveness of the visual catalogue in the **Cantigas** is gratuitously archeological perhaps, but not because its illuminators or its patron—or anyone in the Middle Ages for that matter—were committed cultural historians of their own moment, trying to provide a visual time capsule of medieval Spain. The inclusion of the implements and habits of everyday life is to some extent only so much scenery that does not explain the architecture of its meanings or purpose of the work itself. Sweeping the socio-historical details together into a grand whole by saying that the collection represents intuitively democratic sentiments (as has been occasionally done) is also wide of the mark. Alfonso, if anyone, was a dedicated monarchist. What this inclusion does tell us is that his artistic team was encouraged to be expansive, and that their graphic program was socially comprehensive, willingly spiritualizing (and even religiously sentimentalizing) much of the grist of daily life.[8]

Although the social detail we briefly catalogued is abundantly displayed in the miniatures for these miracle stories, it is not the message itself. It is merely intended to facilitate the story telling, serving to mark the register of the message, contextualizing the linear narrative that is encoded in words. Even though these sequenced images accompany a story, they can only allude to the (essentially verbal) story line because pictures are not truly linear: they are atemporal, since we can look at them all at once and let our eyes play back and forth across the images. Furthermore, our eyes are guided in directions that may reinforce the logical sequence of a story, manipulate our visual experience, or stop us in our tracks to dwell on a graphic element of unusual thematic weight.[9] There are also usually enough coded signals to direct our intuitions about the presence and configuration of intended associations. Our ability to interpret this artistic code is premised on our general skills in parsing sign systems. Rubinstein and Hersh, writing on the construction of conceptual models for computer interfaces, provide this example of parsing:

> [A]lmost everyone in this country has an internal model of how airport terminals are laid out, built up over time from various experiences. People confronted by unfamiliar airports usually can make good predictions about where to find ticket counters, food, gates, or their luggage. The details of a particular airport ([its directional] signs, [the] traffic flow [of vehicles and other passengers], corridors [their lighting and equipment along the walls], and so on) provide confirming information. In effect, people develop the skill of *parsing* airports. They use the information they receive [on-site] in conjunction with their conceptual [model of a standard airport] to navigate.
>
> (43)

Parsing a manuscript illumination shares many of these implicit cognitive functions. It is partially derived from conceptual models built on previous exposure to book paintings, calligraphy and book structures in general, partially communicated within the assembly of miniatures in an illuminated book, and partially self-explanatory from a given unique image (the page before the viewer as a self-contained construct with its own instructions for parsing). The more dense the illuminations within a given volume, the more complex the encoded semiotic system that the artists may have dreamt up, and the greater the opportunity for silently coaching the receiver of this visual discourse on how to parse it.[10]

This is precisely the situation we find in the **Cantigas** illuminations. Developed over a long span of time, at the height of the technical abilities of the royal team of artists, and after long intimacy with the patron who was in constant contact with the emerging work, these Marian songs and pictures show a communicative program that can be parsed with relative confidence. Alfonso undoubtedly instructed his craftsmen in precisely how he wanted the finished product to look, and is "author" of these paintings in the same sense that he is author of his songs and histories and laws.

In undertaking an analysis of the **Cantigas'** classic, full-page miniatures and miracle stories that dominate the collection, we can consider one distinguished but typical example. *Cantiga* 63 tells of the knight who had the pious custom of attending three masses of the Virgin every day. One day he was committed to fight with Count García against the Moorish warlord Almançor, but refused to abandon his devotions even if, as his squire warned him, they might bring him great shame. He misses the battle, but the Virgin assumes his form and armor, and triumphs against great odds. When the real warrior finally comes out to meet his feudal lord after the contest, he is inexplicably showered with praise for his valiant intervention in the fight, at which point he realizes and proclaims the miracle.[11]

The opening strophes of *Cantiga* 63 read as follows:

"Quen ben serv' a Madre do que quis morrer por nos, nunca pod' en vergonna caer."

Dest' un gran miragre vos quero contar
que Santa Maria fez, se Deus m' anpar,
por hun cavaliero a que foi guardar
de mui gran vergonna que cuidou prender.
Quen ben serv' a Madre do que quis morrer . . .

Este cavaliero, per quant' aprendi,
franqu'e ardid' era, que bẽes ali
u ele morava nen redor dessi
d'armas non podian outro tal saber.
Quen ben serv' a Madre do que quis morrer . . .

E de bõos costumes avia assaz
e nunca con mouros quiso aver paz;
porend' en Sant' Estevão de Gormaz
entrou, quand' Almançor a cuidou aver,
Quen ben serv' a Madre do que quis morrer . . .

Con el conde don Garcia, que enton
tĩya o logar en aquela sazon,
que era bon om' e d'atal coraçon
que aos mouros se fazia temer.
Quen ben serv' a Madre do que quis morrer . . .

Cantiga 63, no less than the other miracle stories that the **Cantigas** proclaim, could be retold in a fairly straight-forward, temporally sequenced way, but all the poems are strophic in organization and marked by a ponderative refrain that rouses the public to join in the praise of the Virgin. This chorus (*refram* or *estribilho*) was undoubtedly the most memorable part of the poem, and was perhaps meant as the chief vehicle for the poem's public message. The refrains are, after all, the

key units in the original indexes of the *cantigas* manuscripts, they are carefully rendered in the Castilian translations of the first twenty-five songs (Mundi and Sáiz), and their overt sentiments (as opposed to the messages that might be communicated in the miniautres) are unassailable. As for the narrative, the progression of the tale is effectively obstructed by this temporal pause during its recitation, a theme statement to which the performers and audience are constantly returned. What should be linear is constantly being clipped in midstream to return to the devotional leitmotif.

The syntactic cutoffs are sometimes shocking, as a line is disrupted in mid-syntagm—cleaving noun from adjective, a subject from its verb, divisions in the middle of a prepositional phrase, and even tmesis, the rupture of a single word—not completed until the following strophe after the refrain has been repeated.[12] *Cantiga* 63 shows examples of this sort of forced *encabalgamiento* between stanzas three and four (above) and again between stanzas nine and ten ("e outras duas [missas] que y foron dizer, / *Quen ben serv' a Madre do que quis morrer* . . . / Que da Reynna eran epirital."). In studying how the tale told in the strophes is frequently broken off to reprise the *estribillo*, John D. Cummins has pointed out what strikes him as the absurdity of supposing that this could have been how the texts were actually performed and prefers that some may not have been intended for musical rendition at all. Carlos Vega has probed other possible resolutions for this anomaly and suggests that either the copyists' habit of transcribing the refrain after every strophe was merely conventional, and that the real performance (or reading) in many cases was continuous from strophe to strophe, or that the repetition of the chorus was truly central to the art form and the "thematic cell" (141) or "seminal poetic capsule" (146) that inspired each piece. The stanzas that relate the story, for Vega, may be in a sense secondary glosses on the *punto de arranque poético*, in the tradition of the Castilian *villancico*. The boundaries between lyric and narrative poetry are always soft at best; an affirmation of a devotional (lyrical) rationale at the heart of these poems meshes with what we know of Alfonso's spiritual intentions and helps explain why providing a continuous narrative seems a decidedly second-order concern.

The miniatures by contrast can present themselves as naïvely linear, but because they are graphic images and not language this pretense should be understood as part of their art. The sequence of events in the paintings obediently echoes the major junctures of the story, while showing a preference for extra visual messages interpolated into the ostensibly naturalistic representational forms. In a sense, temporal considerations are arbitrary in both text and images, lyrical or emotional time determining the "fullness" of the moments chosen for presentation or depiction. For these illuminations the impact of the full decorated page is crucial because of the staggered "perceptual cycle" on which the artists (and their royal patron) rely. The initial recognition and adscription of meaning is followed, in Ernst Gombrich's schematization, by a certain puzzlement or enigmatic phase during which the viewer confronts the disparate elements and asks, why these features? Why this relation among them? In the final phase of silent integration, the viewer settles on an interpretation that harmonizes the clues in the concrete forms.

In terms of supra-representational graphic design, the full-page illumination for *Cantiga* 63—and for all the other *Cantigas* in the *códice rico*—is framed by a highly colored border in abstract patterns. The hinge points for every frame are icons for the royal houses of Castilla and León. These decorations are not directional: they refuted the linearity implicit in the story. Instead, they lead the eye in straight lines from one icon to the next, reinforcing their emblematic cargo and stamping the entire page surface with willful order. The viewer's experience of the book, even if he or she were illiterate, as many of this book's courtly admirers would have been, is one of royal mandate.

But there are two other repeating fields of crisp geometrics here in *Cantiga* 63, one colored and common to most of the *Cantigas* illuminations, the other unique to this page. The colored one is the image of the Virgin herself, taken as a unit with her altar which is always depicted as faced with glazed tiles or an embroidered altar hanging. Amid the highly kinetic drafting of the rest of the image, these non-representational compositions of short, tight lines and shapes form fields bristling with static energy that hold the eye and prevent it from moving on. They are resting places without rest, timeless but not powerless. On the contrary, they mark the enduring power bases of these compositions and their spirituality. A statue of Mary on her altar may be shown several times within any given miracle narrative but that unit is almost always the visual coda of the six-panel arrangements as well, the goal of the eye as well as of the story and the heart. That the Virgin is marked by the same color scheme and graphic design as the royal escutcheons with their colored bands is surely no accident.

The other repeating field of tight geometric patterns is, of course, the knight's armor. It is beautiful in itself, it helps the viewer single him out in the crowd, and it enhances the visual movement of the battle scene. In the middle two panels of the page there is a wonderful leap forward where the knight's horse, decked in the same livery as his master, charges from one frame into the next. In themselves transitional "leaps" (routinely a human figure striding from one room or space into

another) are fairly common in Western manuscript illuminations. What is unique here is that the leap telescopes and accelerates time and space. The figure of the knight is separated from the rest of the Christian troops in the third panel by a hieratically privileged blank field. His advancing flank is reverently pointed out by one of their bannered lances. In the fourth panel they have already caught up with the other half of his mounted form to reinforce his charge. The counterattacking Moors are crushed into the right border, one of their horses taking a delightfully executed nose-dive into the corner of the frame, framing by the same motion the knight's advance.[13]

The point of the story is, of course, that this is not the knight who is still attending Mass back in the second panel. It is the Virgin, exempt from the strictures of time and space, saving her devotee, and by extension all her Christian believers, from the forces of evil and nonbelief. The chromatically-charged and visually-assertive black-and-white design is really hers and not the knight's because the eye has already been trained by exposure to other *cantigas* to read fields of high-energy static as ontologically empowered. The "perceptual cycle" folds back on itself as the viewer rechecks pattern against pattern. The cross-referencing of military prowess, royal authority and divine approbation in one graphic motif makes for a composition of shrewd intentions, and it is an artistically ingenious way to promote Alfonso's self-designated role as spiritual as well as civic leader for his nation.

María and Alfonso in the Lyric Songs of Praise

If we consider the lyrical compositions which feature Alfonso most prominently, we can draw out some of the implications of his poetic status as it emerges from the text and illuminations.

In Joseph Snow's appraisal of the poetry, Alfonso meant to adopt a fictive "performing self" that was at least spiritually autobiographical. He projects himself as a devoted servant of the Virgin who expresses his veneration through his songs. Their creation and performance are a celebration of divine favor, an exposition of the economy of intercession and salvation, and expiatory as well, making amends for the troubadour's many sins. For Snow this devotion is sincere, not just an artifice of the genre. Alfonso avoids heavy-handed announcements of himself as king, preferring to maintain his mask of poet/troubadour throughout the *Cantigas* texts, even if he wears that mask lightly. He prefers to represent himself simply as the prime mover of the anthology. Occasionally the unnamed poet prays for his own well-being and simultaneously for that of León and Castile (*Cantigas* 180, 401), a sense of responsibility which, especially in this form, could only be ascribed to the reigning monarch himself.

The occasional displacement of the authority for these *Cantigas* to the historical reality of Alfonso the monarch is found particularly in the prologue *cantigas* to the various arrangements of this collection that explain Alfonso's patronage of the project. Other first person references may only be the residue of the voices of collaborating troubadours who submitted their individual compositions to their patron. Their songs, and casual first person references if any, are subsumed under the king's own voice and readily made over to the project as a whole, a sort of dubbing for a patron too lofty (or too circumspect) to employ his own utterances.

Snow correctly insists, however, that the **Cantigas** anthology does not provide any sort of secret autobiography that was meant to be deciphered and contemplated posthumously, say to forestall a harsh judgement by history or by Alfonso's combative countrymen; i.e., these poems are not psychologically confessional, defensive, or seeking justification in others' eyes, nor is there anything pleading for understanding, displaying hurt for being misunderstood, revealing a political or national vision that it will take the passage of another generation to comprehend, all frequent hallmarks of modern autobiography.[14]

Alfonso is highly circumspect in the poetic texts intended for public performance in the court and among the masses as well. He is hardly ever directly named in the *cantigas* of praise that we associate with him personally. By contrast, his point-blank emergence as king and choirmaster in their illuminations is a message meant for a different audience, those courtiers who alone got to see the miniatures and who needed to be subtly schooled in this new role for the king. This is the vital nexus of the political and the pious, and the suppression of this political message in the verbal text is, I suspect, the reason why the spaces left above each illuminated panel to explain its content were habitually left blank for the *cantigas de loor;* it would be as impolitic as it would have been unavoidable to specify just what the monarch was doing in these songs that make no verbal reference to him.[15]

As for the miniatures in the non-narrative compositions, the regular alternation of the *cantigas de loor* with the narrative miracle stories in all the manuscripts—one lyrical song of praise of the Virgin as the keystone between every nine narrations—provides a certain rhythm to the corpus and to the expectations for sequence and movement in the miniatures. We need to note in passing, at least, that besides his protagonist's role in the miniatures for most of the lyric pieces, Alfonso himself takes part in some of the miracle stories as a participant, witness, or direct beneficiary.[16]

In these lyrical *cantigas* which gravitate so strongly toward advertising their patron, the miniaturists dropped all pretense of being strictly sequential. Each scene is an iconic representation of pious sentiment that is reinforced by the presence of the other images even if it does not rely on them for its primary spiritual meaning. One crucial feature of their composition is Alfonso's stance between the Virgin and his people as their intermediary and teacher.[17] He is visually situated to be the poet of their praise, the prophet who guides their prayer. This is a stronger statement about the learned king's self image in these *cantigas* than is usually suggested by those who have studied the song texts, but one which is supported by the disposition of the figures in the illuminations.[18]

In the *cantigas* where the Virgin is the sole protagonist of the action, her typical stance is an intermediary one, frontal and hieratic, poised between her followers and God (*Cantigas* 1, 20, 160, 180), which concurs with orthodox Marian theology which entitles her to be Mediatrix of all Grace. But when Alfonso emerges as her troubadour in these lyrical compositions, he steps visually into her role, displacing her on center stage and functioning as the conduit between heaven and earth (*Cantigas* 80, 100, 110, 120, 130, 160). Their alternation in the same pictographic disposition, sometimes on the same illuminated page, is hard to ignore, and the two sovereign personages function in effect as co-protagonists of many of the *cantigas de loor*.[19] More than dramatic coefficients, the graphic conventions that pertain to Blessed Mary show us how to parse the appearances of Alfonso as well.

Whereas heavenly favors flow down from God through Mary, the prayers of the faithful are prompted upward, at least in their first phase (*Cantiga* 20a), by Alfonso acting as prophet, priest and poet of this secularized liturgy of praise. Sometimes he is shown speaking to the faithful, other times in dialogue with the Virgin (*Cantiga* 100). She teaches mankind about God and Alfonso will duplicate the scene by taking her place.

One additional iconographic feature that underscores this reading is the space in which it is played out, as in *Cantiga* 110. The illuminators normally made sure of distinctions in the naturalistically depicted narrative miracles between heaven and earth, and between the imagined space of the heavenly court in its blue stratosphere and mankind below. When events happen on earth they are assigned with deliberateness and with an astonishingly varied repertoire of indicators to land, sea and air, and to the borders between them. But the *códice rico* in its lyrical pieces employs a nonrepresentational space as well, an airy blank background space that is timeless, dimensionless, clearly supernal, and naturally the Virgin's alone. The only human who shares this symbolic space of human initiates into the divine is Alfonso, and, by extension, those who join in his songs.[20]

As all are beneficiaries of the miracles of the Virgin, all should recognize the king's natural place in communicating those divine benefits she dispenses to her devotees and in channeling their pious attention back toward her. He has appropriated for himself a pivotal role in this exchange, designated himself national broker in the economy of salvation, and all without impious grasping. It is perhaps because his devotion is so sincere that he has assumed responsibilities far beyond what most kings would lay on their own shoulders. His role is comprehensive, and he seemingly felt that he owed it to his people to serve them in facilitating their salvation, as well as his own, in the process. That it gives his political authority a resonance that carries into the realms of the spirit is no accident.

In terms of authorship, we can count it part of Alfonso's intent that he not only could not write or illumine every *cantiga* but that he perhaps preferred not to. Projecting his intentions to an ever-widening circle of cultivated minstrels and artisans enabled them to express the royal will through their own words and pictures. We can be confident that an anthology nursed along as vigilantly as Alfonso shepherded this one does not stray from what the king himself wished to say or see. In the best sense—and in a rather intimate one in this case—his coauthors knew the mind of the king and helped him to graphically project it. The wonderfully diverse ways of praising and painting the Virgin ostensibly narrate stories of her favors, but are really focused on a non-progressive and non-sequential piety, dwelling on her abiding care. As courtly product, they formed an ongoing project for the religious welfare of the masses, and as an unobtrusive educational tool as well as for the nobles who contemplated the miniatures.

Alfonso showed keen political savvy in promoting a monarchy which could fuse personal spiritual leadership with royal authority and remarkable subtlety in merging these recursive lyrics and images in the *Cantigas de Santa Maria.*

Notes

1. Narrative in the visual arts has been recently explored by Kemp and by Deremble and Manhes (two works insightfully reviewed by Caviness), and by Aronberg.

2. By "linear" I mean sequenced or presented according to the implicit temporal logic of the events themselves. This is the most obvious assumption for a row of illustrations. Verbal narratives always appeal to a straight linear sequence of events that readers immediately construct for themselves but, in fact, stories are usually told with flashbacks and flashforwards of events or reactions to them (Goodman). The purely linear arrangement of events according to the logic of real time sequences is of little interest to storytellers, who know that their readers or listeners will intuitively generate one for themselves as a second-order backdrop from which narrative realities will emerge.

3. A stimulating (if uneven and combative) update on the range of tasks implicit in current medieval studies is attempted in the January, 1990 issue of *Speculum* on "The New Philology." That phrase was apparently coined in Jonathan D. Evans' Introduction to a special issue of *Semiotica* on "Semiotica Mediaevalia"; his opening remarks and ensuing essay on "Medieval studies and semiotics: Perspectives on research" are instructive.

4. Keller and Kinkade, *Iconography in Medieval Spanish Literature* 16. Keller has sketched the same procedures in *Pious Brief Narrative in Medieval Castilian and Galician Verse* (1978, 108-09; trans. 1987) and in "The Art of . . ." The list of nine elements originates in Ashley. Keller has also supported the interpretation of the *Cantigas* miniatures as perhaps representative of real performances (*Alfonso X, el Sabio* 92), going so far as to call them "incipient opera" ("Drama, Ritual . . ."). Domínguez is willing to consider the same possibility but concludes more cautiously that "quizá pueda tratarse simplemente de un sistema de narración que siga literalmente los conceptos o ideas evocados" ("La miniatura . . ." 152). Perhaps the best case against supposing that the *cantigas* are playlets (let alone opera) is that the script (the lyrics of the songs) is not in dramatic dialogue but usually couched in a single voice and perpetually interrupted by a refrain. Berceo, after all, displays a great deal more alternation of voices among his characters than Alfonso in narrating the same miracle stories and the most that is commonly suggested for the *Milagros* of the poet of Rioja is solo oral performance. At most, the *cantigas* illustrations would point to a troupe of mimes; the variety of naturalistic settings in them, however, militates against the conventions of stagecraft common in the Middle Ages. Although their lyrics may be "dramatic" in that the stories convey emotional tension, to my knowledge there is no direct supporting evidence of any sort for dramatic performances of the sacred *cantigas* in the Alfonsine court and, in any case, conjecturing real stagings is unnecessary for reading the miniatures.

Francisco Nodar Manso has attempted to recreate a performance text from a patchwork combination of various of the *cantigas profanas* ascribed to Alfonso X ("El carácter drámatico-narrativo del escarnio y maldecir de Alfonso X"). The results are interesting but still only hypothetical.

5. Discursive narrative is only seemingly linear; the pretense of strict sequence may be important but subtle or gross departures from logical temporal sequence are the rule rather than the exception for most narrations. See the discussion by Barbara Herrnstein Smith in "Narrative Versions, Narrative Theories" and Seymour Chatman's rejoinder (258-65).

6. "Against Comparison: Teaching Literature and the Visual Arts"; the other essays in that volume display no hesitation about performing interart criticism in just the ways Mitchell is concerned about. There have been few contributions to interart criticism involving Spanish literature and painting, but see the classic (if *sui generis*) Roaten and Sánchez Escribano volume on the *comedia,* Parr's study on *Celestina* and Ayerbe-Chaux on the *Caballero Zifar.*

7. Keller ("Daily living . . ." *et passim*) has studied this field extensively, and others (e.g., Seniff) have followed. The best compilation is undoubtedly that of Gonzalo Menéndez Pidal.

8. Domínguez observes that "Lo más sorprendente no es únicamente la presencia del rey trovador sino el tipo de imágenes religiosas que acompaña . . . Algunas son del tipo llamado imágenes de devoción (*imago pietatis*) destinadas más a provocar el fervor de los fieles y su participación sensible que su fe. Se dirigen ante todo a la sensualidad y no al intelecto. Inauguran el tipo de fervor que va a caracterizar la Baja Edad Media, con un sentimentalismo derivado en parte de San Bernardo pero puesto al día por los franciscanos y sobre todo por los espirituales." ("La miniatura . . ." 153-54).

9. For a discussion on the atemporality of pictorial representation, see Goodman. Verbal narrative is sequence-bound (you have to read it in a certain order) but takes its own liberties in recounting real time events and even presents its own words in artfully arranged ways to sequence thoughts and sensory impressions for the listener / reader.

10. Parsing, then, is the decoding and manipulation of a specific operational scheme based on a general conceptual model derived from related experiences. Semiotics by contrast is a larger field more concerned with theoretical relations both within a system of arbitrary and/or natural signs, and between those signs and the community that employs them.

11. The short title preceding the song text in the manuscripts reads "Como Santa Maria sacou de vergonna a un cavaliero que ouver' seer ena lide en Sant' Estevan de Gormaz, de que non pod' y seer polas suas tres missas que oyu" (texts from Mettman edition). A color image of this *cantiga* is available in Keller and Kinkade (*Iconography in Medieval*), plate 15.

12. On the refrains of the *Cantigas* see Montoya ("'Razón,' 'refrán' . . .'"), Cummins ("The Practical . . ."), Clarke ("Alfonso X: . . ."), and especially Vega ("The *Refram* . . ."). I regret not having access to the unpublished dissertation of Anna Mary McGregor Chisman, "Enjambement in *Las Cantigas de Santa Maria* of Alfonso X el Sabio" (Toronto, 1974); synopses of her work are available in DAI 36 (1975-76): 1550-1A; Keller (*Pious Brief Narrative* 92-93); Snow (*The Poetry* 362); and, most thoroughly, in Vega.

13. For another example of telescoping time and space in a single miniature see Keller "The Art . . ." Domínguez has suggested that a special artist, a "Maestro del Bestiario," was employed to paint the fine animals (tortoise, crab, lion, etc.) in the *Lapidario* ("La miniatura . . ." 140). The "Master of the Menagerie" (my coinage) in the *códice rico* of the *Cantigas* is his fellow illuminator's superior in the realism of his drafting and in the range of his repertoire, for his animals are invariably far more than mere zodiacal icons.

14. The surprising truth is that Alfonso is capable of precisely this sort of admission of hurt and betrayal, most eloquently in his admonitory letter to his eldest son Fernando de la Cerda and in his two unusually revealing—and touching—testaments (Solalinde edition). Full autobiographism emerges in only one *cantiga,* number 410, the "*Cantiga de pitiçon* [*petición*]," which takes up the same themes as in the documents above, the need of a king to be careful of the counsel of advisors, and betrayal as the most personal of affronts against the royal person and against the divine will he represents.

15. In Escorial MS. T.I.1 there are thirteen *cantigas* which lack text in their *letreros* or *rótulos* above the panels, eight in the *cantigas de loor.* Three illuminated pages for the *cantigas de loor* have been lost from this manuscript, for *Cantigas* 40, 150 and 200; they may or may not have had writing in their caption boxes (see edition of Beltrán 21). There are also *cantigas* in which Alfonso ap-

pears as a witness, and again his *rótulos* are left blank: 29, 113, and 169.

16. Alfonso is the grateful recipient of the Virgin's miraculous favors in *Cantigas* 97 (identity only revealed in the illumination), 142 and 209; his mother finds favor before Mary in *Cantiga* 256, and with his infante sister 122, his father Fernando in *Cantiga* 221. The king testifies to the validity of reports of the miracles in *Cantigas* 29, 113, and, with James of Aragon, in 169.

17. This theme is more fully developed in Greenia "*The Court of Alfonso X . . .*" from Solomon from which I adapt these paragraphs.

18. For Snow ("Alfonso X . . ."), Alfonso the troubadour is modeled on San Ildefonso, his patron and namesake who also wrote a book in honor of the Virgin that was worthy of miraculous rewards. For Domínguez ("La miniatura . . .", "El 'Officium Salomonis' . . ."), the historical template is Salomon, presiding over the acquisition of hermetic knowledge.

19. Alfonso's orthodoxy in these illuminations is open to question, and not entirely safeguarded by the attitude expressed in the texts of the *cantigas*: see Peter Lineham; Ana Domínguez suspects that the illuminated pages for *Cantigas* 40, and 150 may have been excised from the *códice rico* because of their questionable spirituality. She is certainly correct in her observation that Alfonso seems to have no need to be assisted in his devotions by ecclesiastical figures whose presence is incessant in contemporary French miniatures ("La miniatura . . ." 155-56).

20. Shapiro sketches the nature of the prepared surface as a ground for representation. Hieratic distance from other figures was already suggested for the illumination of *Cantiga* 63c.

Works Cited

Alfonso el Sabio. *Antología de Alfonso X el Sabio.* Ed. Antonio G. Solalinde. Madrid: Espasa-Calpe, 1941. Rpt. in *Antología.* México: Porrúa, 1973.

———. *Cantigas de Santa María.* Ed. Walter Mettman. 3 vols. Madrid: Castalia, 1986-1989.

———. *Las cantigas de loor de Alfonso X el Sabio. Edición bilingüe.* Trad. Luis Beltrán. Madrid: Júcar, 1990.

Aronberg Lavin, M. *The Place of Narrative. Mural Decoration in Italian Churches 431-1600.* Chicago: U of Chicago P, 1990.

Ashley, R. N. *The History of the Short Story.* New York: Simon and Schuster, 1958.

Ayerbe-Chaux, Reinaldo. "Las *Islas Dotadas:* Texto y miniaturas del manuscrito de París, clave para su interpretación." In *Hispanic Studies in Honor of Alan D. Deyermond. A North American Tribute.* Ed. John S. Miletich. Madison, WI: Hispanic Seminary, 1986. 31-50.

Caviness, Madeline H. Review of Deremble and Kemp. *Speculum,* 65.4 (1990): 972-75.

Chatman, Seymour. "Reply to Barbara Herrnstein Smith." In *On Narrative.* Ed. W. J. T. Mitchell. Chicago: U of Chicago P, 1981. 258-65.

Clarke, Dorthy Clotelle. "Alfonso X: Questions of Poetics." *Bulletin of the Cantigueiros de Santa Maria,* 1.1 (1987): 11-15.

Cummins, John G. "The Practical Implications of Alfonso el Sabio's Peculiar Use of the Zéjel." *BHS* [*Bulletin of Hispanic Studies*] 47 (1970): 1-9.

Deremble, Jean-Paul, and Colette Manhes. *Les vitraux légendaires de Chartres: Des récits en images.* Paris: Desclée de Brouwer, 1988.

Domínguez Rodríguez, Ana. "La miniatura del 'scriptorium' alfonsí." In *Estudios alfonsíes: Lexicografía, lírica, estética y política de Alfonso el Sabio.* Granada: U de Granada, 1985. 127-61.

———. "El 'Officium Salomonis' de Carlos V en el Monasterio de El Escorial. Alfonso X y el planeta Sol. Absolutismo monárquico y hermetismo." *Reales Sitios* 83 (1985): 11-28.

———. "Poder, ciencia y religiosidad en la miniatura de Alfonso X el Sabio." *Fragmentos,* 2 (1984): 33-46.

———. "El testamento de Alfonso X y la Catedral de Toledo." *Reales Sitios* 82 (1984): 73-75.

———. "Imágenes de un rey trovador de Santa María (Alfonso X en las Cantigas)." *Il medio Oriente e l'Occidente nell'Arte del XIII secolo.* A cura di Hans Belting. In *Atti del XXIV Congresso Internazionale di Storia dell'Arte Bologna, September, 1979.* Bologna: Bologna, 1982. 229-39.

———. "Imágenes de presentación de la miniatura alfonsí." *Goya* 131 (1976): 287-91.

Evans, Jonathan D., ed. "Medieval Studies and Semiotics: Perspectives on Research." *Semiotica* 63.1/2 (1987): 13-32.

Gombrich, E. H. "Image and Code: Scope and Limits of Conventionalism in Pictorial Representation." In *Image and Code.* Ed. Wendy Steiner. Ann Arbor: U of Michigan, 1981. 10-42. Rpt. in *The Image and the Eye.* Ithaca: Cornell UP, 1982. 278-97.

Goodman, Nelson. "Twisted Tales; or, Story, Study, and Symphony." In *On Narrative.* Ed. W. J. T. Mitchell. Chicago: U of Chicago P, 1981. 99-115.

————. *Languages of Art: An Approach to a Theory of Symbols.* Indianapolis: Bobbs-Merrill, 1968.

Greenia, George D. "The Court of Alfonso X in Words and Pictures: The Cantigas." In *Courtly Literature: Culture and Context. Acts of the Fifth Triennial Congress of the International Courtly Literature Society. Dalfsen, The Netherlands, 9-16, 1986.* Amsterdam: Benjamins, 1990. 227-37.

Herrnstein Smith, Barbara. "Narrative Versions, Narrative Theories." In *On Narrative.* Ed. W. J. T. Mitchell. Chicago: U of Chicago P, 1981. 209-32.

Keller, John E. "Daily Living as Presented in the Canticles of Alfonso the Learned." *Speculum,* 33 (1958): 484-89.

————. *Alfonso X, el Sabio.* New York: Twayne, 1967.

————. *Pious Brief Narrative in Medieval Castilian and Galician Verse, From Berceo to Alfonso X.* Studies in Romance Languages 21. Lexington: U of Kentucky P, 1978. Rpt. as *Las narraciones breves piadosas versificadas en el castellano y gallego medieval.* Trad. y ed. Antonio A. Fernández-Vázquez. Madrid: Alcalá, 1987.

————. "The Art of Illumination in the Books of Alfonso X (Primarily in the Canticles of Holy Mary)." *Thought* 60. 239 (1985): 388-406.

————. "Drama, Ritual and Incipient Opera in Alfonso's *Cantigas.*" In *Emperor of Culture: Alfonso X, the Learned of Castile and His Thirteenth-Century Renaissance.* Robert I. Burns, S. J. Ed. Philadelphia: U of Pennsylvania P, 1990. 72-89.

Keller, John E., and R. P. Kinkade. "Iconography and Literature: Alfonso Himself in *Cantiga 209.*" *Hispania* 66 (1983): 348-52.

————. *Iconography in Medieval Spanish Literature.* Lexington, U of Kentucky P, 1984.

Kemp, Wolfgang. *Die Erzählung der mittelalterlichen Glasfenster.* Munich: Schirmer/Mosel, 1987.

Lineham, Peter. "The Spanish Church Revisited: the Episcopal *gravamina* of 1279." In *Authority and Power: Studies on Medieval Law and Government Presented to Walter Ullman on his 70th birthday.* Eds. B. Tierney and P. Lineham. Cambridge: Cambridge UP, 1980. 127-47.

Menéndez Pidal, Gonzalo. *La España del siglo* XIII *leída en imágenes.* Madrid: Real Academia de la Historia, 1986.

Mitchell, W. J. Thomas. "Against Comparison: Teaching Literature and the Visual Arts." In *Teaching Literature and Other Arts.* Ed. Jean-Pierre Barricelli, Joseph Gibaldi, and Estella Lauter. New York: MLA, 1990. 30-37.

————. *Iconology.* Chicago: U of Chicago P, 1986.

————, ed. *On Narrative.* Chicago: U of Chicago P, 1981.

————. *The Language of Images.* Chicago: U of Chicago P, 1980.

Montoya Martínez, Jesús. "'Razón,' 'refrán' y 'estribillo' en las *Cantigas de Santa Maria.*" *Bulletin of the Cantigueiros de Santa Maria* 1.1 (1987): 61-70.

Mundi Pedret, Francisco, and Anabel Sáiz Ripoll. *Las prosificaciones de las Cantigas de Alfonso X el Sabio.* Madrid: Promociones y Publicaciones Universitarias, 1987.

"Narration in Ancient Art: A Symposium." *American Journal of Archaeology* 61 (1957): 43-91.

Nodar Manso, Francisco. "El carácter dramático-narrativo del escarnio y maldecir de Alfonso X." *RCEH [Revista Canadieuse de Estudios Hispánicos]* 9.3 (1985): 405-21.

Parr, James A. "Correspondencias formales entre *La Celestina* y la pintura contemporánea." In *Estudios sobre el Siglo de Oro en homenaje a Raymond R. MacCurdy.* Eds. Ángel González, Tamara Holzapfel y Alfred Rodríguez. Madrid: U of New Mexico (Albuquerque) and Cátedra, 1983. 313-26.

Roaten, Darnell H., and F. Sánchez Escribano. *Wölfflin's Principles in Spanish Drama 1500-1700.* New York: Hispanic Institute, 1952.

Rubinstein, Richard, and Harry Hersh. *The Human Factor: Designing Computer Systems for People.* Burlington, MA: Digital P, 1984.

Seniff, Dennis P. "Letter from Doña J. Alfau de Solalinde to R. Menéndez Pidal on her Projected Study of the *Cantigas de Santa Maria.*" *Bulletin of the Cantigueiros de Santa Maria* 1.1 (1987): 23-31.

Snow, Joseph T. "Alfonso as Troubadour: The Fact and the Fiction." In *Emperor of Culture: Alfonso X, the Learned of Castile and His Thirteenth-Century Renaissance.* Ed. Robert I. Burns, S. J., Philadelphia: U of Pennsylvania P, (1990). 124-40.

————. "Alfonso X y en sus Cantigas." In *Estudios alfonsíes: Lexicografía, lírica, estética y política de Alfonso el Sabio.* Granada: U de Granada, (1985). 71-90.

————. "Alfonso X: Sus 'Cantigas . . .': Apuntes para su (auto)biografía literaria." In *Josep María Solá-Solé: Homage, homenaje, homenatge: Miscelánea de estudios de amigos y discípulos.* Eds. Antonio Torres-Alcalá, Victorio Aguera y Nathaniel Smith, Barcelona: Puvill, (1984). Vol. 1: 79-89.

————. "Self-Conscious References and the Organic Narrative Pattern of the Cantigas de Santa María of Alfonso X." In *Medieval, Renaissance and Folklore Studies In Honor of John Esten Keller.* Ed. Joseph R. Jones. Newark, DE: Juan de la Cuesta, (1980). 53-66.

———. "The Central Role of the Troubadour Persona of Alfonso X in the *Cantigas de Santa Maria.*" BHS 56 (1979): 305-15.

———. *The Poetry of Alfonso X, el Sabio.* London: Grant and Cutler, 1977.

Solalinde, Antonio G. "Intervención de Alfonso X en la redacción de sus obras." *RFE* [*Revista de Filologia Espanola*] 2 (1915): 283-88.

Vega, Carlos Alberto. "The *Refram* in the *Cantigas de Santa Maria.*" In *Alfonso X of Castile, the Learned King (1221-1284).* Eds. F. Márquez-Villanueva and Carlos Alberto Vega. Cambridge: Dept. of Romance Languages & Literatures of Harvard U, (1990). 132-58.

Joseph F. O'Callaghan (essay date 1998)

SOURCE: O'Callaghan, Joseph F. "A Poetic Biography." In *Alfonso X and the* Cantigas de Santa Maria, pp. 1-13. Leiden, The Netherlands: Brill, 1998.

[*In the following excerpt, O'Callaghan discusses biographical elements in the* Cantigas *and comments on the date of composition of the poems.*]

Among the extraordinary personages of thirteenth-century Europe, Alfonso X, king of Castile-León (1252-1284) stands out as a scholar and patron of scholars unrivaled by any of his fellow monarchs.[1] *El rey sabio,* that is, the wise or learned king, gathered to his court students of law, history, astronomy, and astrology, as well as poets and artists of varying origins and backgrounds. Together with them he collaborated in the production of an immense number of legal, historical, scientific, literary, and poetic works. Though he failed to win the crown of the Holy Roman Empire, his contribution to European civilization prompted Robert Burns to dub him the "Emperor of Culture" and to describe his reign as a thirteenth-century renaissance.[2]

THE CANTIGAS DE SANTA MARIA

In the **Cantigas de Santa Maria,** one of the most attractive works executed by the king and his collaborators, Alfonso X has left us a kind of poetic biography; one might even call it an autobiography. Before explaining what I mean by that, let me first speak about the **Cantigas.** The **Cantigas de Santa Maria** is a collection of more than four hundred poems recounting miracles worked through the intercession of the Virgin Mary or songs of praise in her honor.[3] The text of many is il-luminated in full-page miniatures.[4] The poems were written in the language of medieval Galicia and Portugal, the medium of expression preferred by the lyric poets of that day. The verse form known as *zéjel* with its characteristic rhyme scheme (aaab, cccb, dddb), derived from Arabic but comparable to the Provençal *virelai,* was employed most often. Each line usually consisted of eight syllables, though there are lines of as few as two and as many as seventeen syllables; a refrain preceded each stanza.[5] As numerous *cantigas* were provided with a musical accompaniment, contemporaries may well have sung them on the great feasts of Our Lady as the king directed in his last will.[6] Indeed today there are many recordings of the *cantigas* and modern scholars have written extensively about their literary qualities.[7]

Investigation reveals that a number of the *cantigas* relate to events that transpired during the reign of Alfonso X. The intervention of the Virgin Mary in the king's life is attested in poems written either in the first person by the king himself or in the third person at his evident command. That being the case, one can argue that the **Cantigas de Santa Maria,** besides being a tribute to the Virgin Mary, is a form of poetic biography, unique in the annals of medieval Europe.

Medievalists are familiar with hagiography, that brand of biography dealing with the lives of the saints, and with such royal biographies as Einhard's *Life of Charlemagne* and Joinville's *Life of St. Louis,* one of Alfonso X's contemporaries.[8] Less well known is the *Llibre dels feyts* or *Book of Deeds,* the autobiography of Alfonso X's father-in-law, Jaime I of Aragón, a narrative of his life from conception to death.[9] Although Alfonso X in the *Estoria de Espanna* compiled under his guidance related the deeds of his predecessors down to the death of his own father Fernando III, he did not dictate an account of his career as Jaime I did.[10] Nor does it appear that he authorized anyone to write his biography, although Fray Juan Gil de Zamora (d. 1318), a Franciscan friar who tutored the king's son Sancho, wrote a brief, incomplete biographical sketch of the king about 1278.[11]

The **Cantigas de Santa Maria** are not a royal biography in the usual sense because they do not provide a connected narrative of Alfonso X's career. Nevertheless, they narrate specific events in his life and that of his kingdom and they reveal something of his personality and his spirituality. One of the most perceptive students of the text, Joseph Snow, remarked that the **Cantigas** "may prove to contain important keys—even at this remove of time—to the kind of person he [Alfonso X] was or, better yet, the kind of person he wanted to be." The knowledge that the **Cantigas** represents the king's reflections and habits of thought is precisely what makes this collection unique among medieval royal biographical materials.[12] For that reason the *Cantigas de Santa Maria* takes on a special importance as an invaluable source for the study of his reign.

THE *CANTIGAS DE SANTA MARIA* AS AN
HISTORICAL SOURCE

Only recently, however, have the *Cantigas* been studied as sources concerning the personal history of Alfonso X and of his kingdom. The *Cantigas,* as Burns pointed out, are a mine of information concerning the social and religious history of medieval Castile.[13] John Keller and others have emphasized the importance of the *Cantigas* to our understanding of daily living in the thirteenth century.[14] Women's lives and activities as portrayed in the *Cantigas* have been studied by Connie Scarborough.[15] Maricel Presilla completed a major study (as yet unpublished) of attitudes toward death revealed in the *Cantigas.*[16] The collection also offers details concerning historical events and circumstances in thirteenth-century Castile. Keller observed, for example, that Alfonso X consciously tried to foster the cult of the Virgin of Villa Sirga to draw attention away from Santiago de Compostela; not surprisingly, at that time the king was quarreling with the archbishop, whom he forced into exile.[17] Jesús Montoya Martínez utilized the *Cantigas* to illustrate the development of Andalucia and more specifically of Cádiz.[18] Joseph Snow has also drawn attention to the poems concerning El Puerto de Santa María as the most personal in the collection.[19] I commented on two *cantigas* treating the royal touch and the Cortes held in Seville in 1281,[20] while Richard P. Kinkade reviewed the historical events of the critical period from 1269 to 1278 as related in *CSM* [*Cantigas de Santa Maria*] 235.[21] Scholars utilizing the *Cantigas de Santa Maria* in this way are very much aware that this is a work full of pious legends and miracle stories and not a narrative or documentary history. Nevertheless, many of the *cantigas* not only reflect the life and customs of thirteenth-century Spain but also disclose the beliefs and activities of King Alfonso himself during a long and troubled reign. The *Cantigas* inform us, for example, about the king's parentage, contemporary attitudes toward the Moors, the nature of warfare between Christians and Moors, the projected crusade into Morocco, the Moroccan invasion of Spain, and attempts to repopulate Cádiz and El Puerto de Santa María; but above all they reveal the king's feelings about treachery among his own nobility, his frequent illnesses, and his fear of hellfire and eternal damnation. The Virgin Mary appears throughout as his advocate, protector, and consoler. Through her wondrous actions the king believed that he would triumph over his enemies and the adversities that beset him both within and without his realms. While we need not share his belief in miracles or in the active role of the Virgin

Mary in his life and that of his kingdom, we can accept as authentic the core, and indeed many of the details, of the stories that he tells us.[22]

My purpose now is to explicate the historical circumstances concerning those *cantigas* that refer to the king, the members of his family or court, or occurrences in his reign. This exercise imparts many new insights into the history of Castile-León in the second-half of the thirteenth century and enables one to draw conclusions about royal policy and actions that would not have been evident from other, more prosaic sources.

THE AUTHORSHIP OF THE *CANTIGAS*

Older scholars tended to accept at face value the statement that Alfonso X was the author of each and every one of the variety of literary, legal, historical, and scientific works attributed to him. The evident impossibility of that has resulted in a more balanced assessment. Antonio Solalinde pointed to a passage in the *General Estoria* which neatly explained the king's role:

> The king makes a book, not because he writes it with his hands, but because he sets forth the reasons for it, and he amends and corrects and improves them and shows how they ought to be done; and although the one whom he commands may write them, we say, nevertheless, on this account that the king makes the book.[23]

In other words, the king functioned as a patron and general editor, as Evelyn Procter called him, outlining the type of book he had in mind, assigning the authors or compilers, and revising their work, sometimes even ordering them to do it over again.[24]

The authorship of the *Cantigas de Santa Maria* is now very much under discussion. Fray Juan Gil de Zamora, mentioned above, related that "in the manner of [King] David, for the praise of the glorious Virgin, [Alfonso X] composed many beautiful songs measured with pleasing sounds and musical proportions."[25] In fact quite a number of *cantigas* are based on miracle stories of the Virgin Mary compiled in Latin by Fray Juan Gil, who also wrote Latin hymns, and perhaps also employed his poetic talent in the *Cantigas.*[26] In any case his words would seem to imply royal authorship of the entire collection, but few today would hold that all 420 poems came from the king's own hand. There can be no doubt, however, that the inspiration for the work and the way in which it was presented was his, a point emphasized by Snow and Montoya Martinez.[27] Walter Mettmann, the editor of the modern critical edition, believes that three to six poets collaborated on the work, but most of the poems came from the pen of a single author, Airas Nunes. One may attribute directly to the king those poems in which he speaks in the first person of his activities and aspirations. The first instance of that is the *Pitiçon* or Petition (*CSM* 401) which was intended to conclude the initial collection of 100 *cantigas*. In Mettmann's view the king actually wrote only about ten poems distinguished by comparable style and themes. Some others obviously relating to events in his life and the development of his kingdom certainly were written with his knowledge and perhaps at his direction.[28] Noting that the king and members of his family and court are mentioned in twenty-eight poems, Procter commented:

> This personal element is a characteristic which has no parallel in other collections and which merits more attention than has been given it. Precise and circumstantial details are often given which enable the miraculous incident to be dated.[29]

With that in mind, I intend to look at these poems to determine what they can tell us about the history of the king and of his kingdom.

THE CODICES

Before embarking on that adventure, an overview of the four extant codices of the **Cantigas de Santa Maria** will be helpful to our understanding.[30] One is preserved in the Biblioteca Nacional in Madrid, two are in the library of the Escorial, and the fourth is in the Biblioteca Nazionale in Florence.[31]

The codex in the Biblioteca Nacional in Madrid bearing the signature 10069 is commonly identified as To or Tol. Kept at one time in the cathedral of Toledo, it passed to the Biblioteca Nacional in 1869. This codex contains a title (prologue A), prologue B, and a total of 127 poems. Both Prologue A and the *Pitiçon,* a very personal poem written by the king and seemingly intended to conclude the collection, stated the king's intention to write 100 poems. The initial nucleus of 100 poems is grouped in decades. Every tenth poem is a song of praise (*cantar de loor*) of the Virgin Mary, while the others tell of miracles effected through her intervention. Following these are the *Pitiçon,* ten additional poems commemorating five feasts of the Virgin and five of Jesus, and then a concluding sixteen other miracle poems. Unlike other codices the miracle stories are not depicted in illuminated miniatures. The Toledan codex, in the judgment of most scholars, represents a copy produced between 1270 and 1280 of the original collection of Marian songs, which in turn was probably produced between 1264 and 1276.[32]

The Escorial manuscript identified as T has the signature T.I.1. Brought to the Escorial from Seville by order of Philip II in the sixteenth century, it has an index, a title, and a prologue, and 193 poems out of an intended 200.[33] The text of the prologue and the *Pitiçon* were emended to eliminate any reference to a specific number of poems. Nearly all the 100 poems in the Toledan codex were copied into T, but not in the same order. Every tenth *cantiga* (up to *CSM* 175, and then *CSM* 187) was a lengthy one illustrated in two pages of miniatures telling the story in twelve panels rather than the six usually assigned to most of the miracle stories. There are almost two hundred full-page miniatures in this beautifully illuminated volume. Not without reason is it called the *códice rico*. It may have been written after 1271, perhaps in the early 1280s.[34]

There seems to be general agreement that codex T (Escorial T.I.1) and the codex preserved in the National Library in Florence, identified as F (signature Banco Rari 20), constitute two volumes of an intended deluxe edition of the **Cantigas**.[35] The Florentine codex, many of whose illuminations and musical notation are unfinished, contains 113 poems, only four of which are found in the Toledan codex, and none in Escorial T.[36] More than likely this volume was copied after 1279-1280, and perhaps after the king's death in 1284.[37] Montoya Martínez noted that the *cantigas* in the Florentine codex tend to be located in northern Spain and southern France and bear some connection with the king's itinerary as he made his way to visit the pope at Beaucaire in 1274-1275. Many of these *cantigas* treat themes relating to the personal history of the king and his family.[38]

Finally, the Escorial codex B.1.2, identified simply as E, was also transferred from Seville by Philip II. This partially illuminated codex bearing a title (prologue A) and prologue B contains 417 poems, seven of which are repeated. Although it contains the greatest number of *cantigas,* with music for nearly all, it does not include ten poems found in the Toledan codex cited above. Anglés described it as "the most important musical codex of courtly religious monody in medieval Europe" because of its perfect musical notation and its content. It probably was copied after 1282.[39]

As already noted, the king's original intention was to compile a collection of 100 poems. Nevertheless, new poems were added and the complete number of *cantigas* taken from the four codices and eliminating any repetitions is 420. The poems are grouped in decades of which the first nine are miracle stories and the tenth is a *cantar de loor* or song of praise. This system was carried out regularly until *CSM* 400. The remaining poems are of a miscellaneous character. The whole is preceded by two prologues. Prologue A, which contains the royal intitulation, announced that the king made this collection of "poems and songs delightful to sing, all on different themes, as you may discover:"

fezo cantares e sões,[40]
saborosos de cantar,

todos de sennas razões,
com' y podedes achar

(25-28).

Prologue B is a poetic reflection on the king's intention, as Mary's troubadour, to sing her praises.

The *Cantigas* can be divided into two groups. The first group of more than 150 poems drawn from Latin or French collections of miracles of the Virgin Mary are mainly associated with France, Italy, Germany, or Britain.[41] A second group gathered at a later stage in the development of the collection are mostly concerned with miracles that took place in the Iberian kingdoms of Aragón, Portugal, and Castile-León.[42] For the most part the later *cantigas* are derived from oral tradition rather than from any written sources; because they relate to peninsular events they are of the greatest interest to the present study. Unfortunately only a few of them are accompanied by miniatures illustrating the story.

Although it is possible that some of the *cantigas* were written early in the king's reign, the compilation of the Toledan codex, the earliest extant redaction of the original collection of 100 poems, should probably be placed after 1266. Whereas the intitulation "king of the Romans" came into use only after Alfonso X's imperial election in 1257, references to the conquest of Jerez, Vejer, and Medina Sidonia suggest the date 1266. Contrary to the general opinion which holds that those towns submitted in 1264, the evidence indicates that they did so two years later. Several *cantigas* narrate events that occurred between 1264 and 1282, such as the revolt of the Mudéjars (*CSM* 169, 345), the king's illnesses (*CSM* 209, 235), the invasion of the Benimerines (*CSM* 215, 223), the war against Granada, and the Cortes of Seville held in November 1281 (*CSM* 386). That being the case it seems reasonable to conclude that the poems were written in the 1270s and 1280s; some even may have been written as late as 1283. As Montoya Martínez remarked, "We find ourselves, therefore, with the curious and surprising fact that Alfonso X was still occupied with his Marian *cancionero* even at this advanced date, two years before his death."[43] Mettmann proposed that collection of the first 100 *cantigas* was completed between 1270-1274, the next 200 between 1274-1277, and the remainder between 1277 and 1282. The full edition of more than 400 poems contained in Escorial B.1.2 dates from after 1279;[44] as suggested above, the date was probably after 1282.

The high regard in which King Alfonso held the *Cantigas de Santa Maria,* the most personal production of his scriptorium, is manifested in his last will, dated 10 January 1284. He made this disposition of the *Cantigas de Santa Maria*:

We also command that all the books of the songs of praise of Holy Mary (*Cantares de loor de Sancta Maria*) should be kept in that church where our body will be interred, and that they should cause them to be sung on the feasts of Holy Mary. If the one who is our rightful heir wishes to have these books of the *Cantares de Sancta Maria,* we command him to make some benefaction to the church whence he takes them, so that he may have them freely and without sin.[45]

The seventeenth-century historian of Seville, Ortíz de Zúñiga, remarked that those books were deposited in the cathedral of Seville and remained there until they were removed to the Escorial by order of King Philip II. No one, however, has been able to identify the codex of which Alfonso X spoke nor is it clear to which codex Ortíz de Zúñiga referred.[46]

Notes

1. Joseph F. O'Callaghan, *The Learned King: The Reign of Alfonso X of Castile* (Philadelphia: University of Pennsylvania Press, 1993); Antonio Ballesteros, *Alfonso X* (Barcelona-Madrid, 1963; reprint Barcelona: El Albir, 1984); Manuel González Jiménez, *Alfonso X, 1252-1284* (Palencia: La Olmeda, 1993).

2. Robert I. Burns, S. J., ed., *Emperor of Culture. Alfonso X of Castile and his Thirteenth-Century Renaissance* (Philadelphia: University of Pennsylvania Press, 1990), especially his introductory essay, "Stupor Mundi: Alfonso X of Castile, the Learned," 1-13; Francisco Márquez-Villanueva, *El Concepto cultural alfonsí* (Madrid: MAPFRE, 1994).

3. My references will be to the edition by Walter Mettmann, *Cantigas de Santa Maria,* 2 vols. (Vigo: Edicións Xerais de Galicia, 1981; reprint of the four-volume edition, Coimbra: Universidade de Coimbra, 1959-1972). Mettmann reproduced this edition in *Cantigas de Santa Maria,* 3 vols. (Madrid: Clásicos Castalia, 1986-1989). There is an earlier edition by the Marquess of Valmar, *Las Cantigas de Santa Maria,* 2 vols. (Madrid: Real Academia Española, 1889).

4. José Guerrero Lovillo, *Las Cántigas: Estudio arqueológico de sus miniaturas* (Madrid: Consejo Superior de Investigaciones Científicas, 1949). Gonzalo Menéndez Pidal, "Los manuscritos de las Cantigas. Cómo se elaboró la miniatura alfonsí," *Boletín de la Real Academia de la Historia* 150 (1962): 23-51, suggested that at least six artists collaborated in the production of the work: Don Andrés, Pedro Lorenzo (*CSM* [*Cantigas de Santa Maria*] 377), Bonamic (*CSM* 375), Juan González, Martín Pérez de Maqueda, and Juan Pérez.

5. Dorothy Clotelle Clarke, "Versification in Alfonso el Sabio's *Cantigas,*" *Hispanic Review* 23 (1955):

83-98; John E. Keller, *Alfonso X, el Sabio* (New York: Twayne, 1967), 70-73, 78-83.

6. Manuel González Jiménez, *Diplomatario Andaluz de Alfonso X* (Seville: El Monte. Caja de Huelva y Sevilla, 1991), 560, no. 521 (10 January 1284); *MHE,* 2:126, no. 221; Georges Daumet, "Les testaments d'Alphonse X le Savant, roi de Castille," *Bibliothèque de l'École des Chartes* 67 (1906): 91; Higinio Anglés, *La música de las Cantigas de Santa Maria del Rey Don Alfonso el Sabio,* 3 vols. (Barcelona: Diputación Provincial de Barcelona, Biblioteca Central, 1943-1964); Julián Ribera, *La música de las Cantigas* (Madrid: Real Academia Española, 1922); Ismael Fernández de la Cuesta, "Alfonso X el Sabio y la música de las Cantigas," in José Mondéjar and Jesús Montoya, eds., *Estudios alfonsíes. Lexicografía, lírica, estética y política de Alfonso el Sabio* (Granada: Universidad de Granada, 1985), 119-126; Juan José Rey, "Alfonso X y la música de su época," in *Alfonso X. Toledo 1984* (Toledo: Ministerio de Cultura, 1984), 103-113.

7. Roger D. Tinnell, *An Annotated Discography of Music in Spain before 1650* (Madison: Hispanic Seminary of Medieval Studies, 1980), 1-8; Israel J. Katz and John E. Keller, eds., *Studies on the Cantigas de Santa Maria: Art, Music, and Poetry* (Madison: Hispanic Seminary of Medieval Studies, 1987).

8. *Einhard's Life of Charlemagne. The Latin Text,* ed. H. W. Garrod and R. B. Mowat (Oxford: Oxford University Press, 1925); Jean de Joinville, *La vie de Saint Louis: Le Témoignage de Jehan, seigneur de Joinville. Texte du XIVᵉ siècle,* ed. Noel Corbett (Sherbrooke, Canada: Naaman, c. 1977).

9. *Crònica de Jaume I,* ed. J. M. Casacuberta and Enric Bagüe, 9 vols. (Barcelona: Barcino, 1926-1962); Robert I. Burns, S. J., "The Spiritual Life of James the Conqueror, King of Arago-Catalonia, 1208-1276: Portrait and Self-Portrait," *The Catholic Historical Review* 62 (1976): 1-35.

10. Ramón Menéndez Pidal edited the *Estoria de Espanna* giving it a new title *Primera Crónica General,* 2 vols. (Madrid: Gredos, 1955). Diego Catalán, *La Estoria de España de Alfonso X. Creación y evolución* (Madrid: Universidad Complutense de Madrid, 1992); Charles Fraker, *The Scope of History. Studies in the Historiography of Alfonso el Sabio* (Ann Arbor: University of Michigan, 1996).

11. The biography of Alfonso X occupies nine printed pages and ends in 1270; much of it in fact concerns the history of the crusades, Italy, and Hungary. Copying from the history of Archbishop Rodrigo Jiménez de Rada, Fray Juan also wrote sketches of Alfonso IX, Fernando III, respectively the grandfather and father of Alfonso X. Fidel Fita, "Biografías de San Fernando y de Alfonso el Sabio por Gil de Zamora," *BRAH* 5 (1885): 308-328, and "Biografía inédita de Alfonso IX, rey de León, por Gil de Zamora," *BRAH* 13 (1888): 291-295.

12. Joseph T. Snow, "Alfonso as Troubadour: The Fact and the Fiction," in Burns, *Emperor of Culture,* 124.

13. Robert I. Burns, S. J., "The *Cantigas de Santa Maria* as a Research Opportunity in History," *Cantigueiros* 1 (1987): 17-22.

14. John E. Keller, "Daily Living as presented in the Canticles of Alfonso the Learned," *Speculum* 33 (1958): 484-489; Dennis P. Senniff, "Falconry, Venery, and Fishing in the *Cantigas de Santa Maria,*" in Katz and Keller, *Studies,* 459-474; Albert Bagby, "The Figure of the Jew in the *Cantigas* of Alfonso X," *ibid.,* 235-247, and "The Jew in the Cantigas of Alfonso X el Sabio," *Speculum* 46 (1971): 670-688; Vikki Hatton and Angus MacKay. "Anti-Semitism in the *Cantigas de Santa Maria,*" *Bulletin of Hispanic Studies* 61 (1983): 189-199. Keller and Annette Cash have completed a book-length study soon to be published on daily life as depicted in the miniatures of the *Cantigas.*

15. Connie L. Scarborough, *Women in Thirteenth-Century Spain as Portrayed in Alfonso X's Cantigas de Santa Maria* (Lewiston, N.Y.: Edwin Mellen Press, 1993); also María Isabel Pérez de Tudela y Velasco, "El tratamiento de la mujer en las Cantigas de Santa Maria," *La condición de la mujer en la Edad Media* (Madrid: Universidad Complutense, 1986), 51-73.

16. Maricel Presilla, *The Image of Death in the Cantigas de Santa Maria of Alfonso X (1252-84): The Politics of Death and Salvation,* Ph.D. dissertation, New York University, 1989; see also her "The Image of Death and Political Ideology in the *Cantigas de Santa Maria,*" in Katz and Keller, *Studies,* 403-458.

17. John E. Keller, "King Alfonso's Virgin of Villa-Sirga, Rival of St. James of Compostela," in Frederic E. Coenen, et al., eds., *Middle Ages-Reformation-Volkskunde: Festchrift for John G. Kunstmann* (Chapel Hill: University of North Carolina Press, 1959) 75-82, and "More on the Rivalry between Santa María and Santiago de Compostela," *Crítica Hispánica* 1 (1979): 37-43. Both articles are reprinted in Dennis Seniff, ed.,

Collectanea Hispanica: Folklore and Brief Narrative Studies by John Esten Keller (Newark, Delaware: Juan de la Cuesta, 1987), 61-76.

18. Jesús Montoya Martínez, "Historia de Andalucía en las Cantigas de Santa Maria," *Andalucía medieval. Actas del I Congreso de Historia de Andalucía, Córdoba, diciembre de 1976,* 2 vols. (Córdoba: Monte de Piedad y Caja de Ahorros, 1978), 1:259-269, and "Las Cantigas de Santa Maria: Fuente para la historia gaditana," *Cádiz en el siglo XIII. Actas de las jornadas conmemorativas del VIII Centenario de la muerte de Alfonso el Sabio* (Cádiz: Universidad de Cádiz, 1983), 173-181.

19. Joseph T. Snow, "A Chapter in Alfonso's Personal Narrative: The Puerto de Santa María Poems in the *CSM,*" *La Corónica* 3 (1979-80): 10-21. See also his "Poetic Self-Awareness in Alfonso X's *Cantiga* 110," *Kentucky Romance Quarterly* 26 (1979): 421-432.

20. Joseph F. O'Callaghan, "The *Cantigas de Santa Maria* as an Historical Source: Two Examples (nos. 321 and 386)," in Katz and Keller, *Studies,* 387-402.

21. Richard P. Kinkade, "Alfonso X, *Cantiga* 235, and the Events of 1269-1278," *Speculum* 67 (1992): 284-323.

22. Jesús García-Varela, "La función ejemplar de Alfonso X en las cantigas personales," *Cantigueiros* 4 (1992): 3-16.

23. *General Estoria. Primera parte,* ed. Antonio G. Solalinde (Madrid: Molina, 1930), 1:477b.

24. Evelyn Procter, *Alfonso X of Castile: Patron of Literature and Learning* (Oxford: Clarendon Press, 1951), ch. 6: "The King and his collaborators."

25. Fita, "Biografías de San Fernando y de Alfonso el Sabio por Gil de Zamora," 315: "*More quoque Davitico etiam [ad] preconium Virginis gloriose multas et perpulchras composuit cantinelas, sonis convenientibus et proportionibus musicis modulatas.*"

26. Fidel Fita, "Cincuenta leyendas por Gil de Zamora combinadas con las Cantigas de Alfonso el Sabio," *BRAH* 7 (1886): 54-144; "Leyenda de San Isidro por el diacono Juan," *BRAH* 9 (1886): 97-157; "Poesías inéditas de Gil de Zamora," *BRAH* 6 (1885): 379-409; "Treinta leyendas por Gil de Zamora," *BRAH* 13 (1888): 187-225; "Variantas de tres leyendas por Gil de Zamora," *BRAH* 6 (1885): 418-429. See also Fray Juan Gil de Zamora, O. F. M., *De preconiis Hispanie,* ed. Manuel de Castro y Castro (Madrid: Universidad de Madrid, 1955), lxxxi-lxxxiii.

27. Joseph Snow, "Alfonso X y/en sus Cantigas," in Mondéjar and Montoya, *Estudios alfonsíes,* 71-90, and "Self-Conscious References and the Organic Narrative Pattern of the *Cantigas de Santa Maria* of Alfonso X," in Joseph R. Jones, ed., *Medieval, Renaissance and Folklore Studies in Honor of John Esten Keller* (Newark, Del.: Juan de la Cuesta, 1980), 53-65; Jesús Montoya Martínez, "Algunas precisiones acerca de las Cantigas de Santa Maria," in Katz and Keller, *Studies,* 366-385, and "O Cancioneiro Marial de Alfonso X. El primer cancionero cortesano español," *O Cantar dos Trobadores* (Santiago de Compostela: Xunta de Galicia, 1993), 215-216.

28. Walter Mettmann, "Algunas observaciones sobre la génesis de la colección de las Cantigas de Santa Maria y sobre el problema del autor," in Katz and Keller, *Studies,* 355-366. The nine poems of which the king, speaking in the first person, appears to be the author are 169, 180, 200, 209, 279, 300, 360, 401, and 406. Montoya Martínez, "O Cancioneiro Marial de Alfonso X," 213 records the names of several chanters and poets who received privileges from the king and may have participated in the work of the *Cantigas.*

29. Procter, *Alfonso X,* 33.

30. Mettmann, in *CSM* 28-31, gives a synoptic table of the contents of the four codices. Two other codices are known. One belonged to Isabel la Católica, but its whereabouts, if it still exists, is not known. Another codex first in the possession of Alfonso Siliceo and then in that of the seventeenth-century bibliophile, Juan Lucas Cortés, is now believed to be identical with the Florentine codex. "Inventario de la Biblioteca de la Reina Doña Isabel," *Memorias de la Real Academia de la Historia* 6 (1821): 457; Diego Ortiz de Zúñiga, *Anales eclesiásticos y seculares de la muy noble y muy leal ciudad de Sevilla, Metropolí de la Andalucía,* ed. Antonio María Espinosa y Carzel, 6 vols. (Madrid: Imprenta real, 1795; reprint Sevilla: Guadalquivir, 1988), 1:336, utilized the codex belonging to Cortés.

31. Procter, *Alfonso X,* 24-26; Mettmann, "Algunas observaciones," 354-355; Keller, *Alfonso X,* 69-70; Stephen Parkinson, "The First Reorganization of the *Cantigas de Santa Maria,*" *Cantigueiros* 1 (1988): 91-98.

32. Procter, *Alfonso X,* 43-46; Manuel Pedro Ferrera, "The Stemma of the Marian *Cantigas:* Philological and Musical Evidence," *Cantigueiros* 6 (1994): 58-97, studies this codex in detail. Montoya Martínez, "O Cancioneiro Marial de Alfonso X," 210-212, proposed that the Toledan codex was composed between 1266-1269.

33. There are Castilian prose renderings or prosifications at the foot of *Cantigas* 2-25 in this codex. Donna M. Rogers, "*Cantigas de Santa Maria* 2-25 and their Castilian Versions" in Nicolás Toscano, *Estudios Alfonsinos y otros escritos* (New York: National Endowment for the Humanities and National Hispanic Foundation for the Humanities, 1991), 196-204, argued that they are not simply translations or summaries of the Galician texts, but that "at least in some instances, an independent Castilian miracle story already existed and was matched with or adapted to the *cantiga* that related the same miracle." Anthony J. Cárdenas, "A Study of Alfonso's Role in Selected *Cantigas* and the Castilian Prosifications of Escorial Codex T.I.1," in Katz and Keller, *Studies*, 253-268, suggests that the prosifications were not done at Alfonso X's command—he would have regarded them as defacement—but were written by someone familiar with the king's conception of the *Cantigas* and having access to the codex—perhaps Juan Manuel.

34. *Alfonso X el Sabio, Cantigas de Santa María. Edición facsímil del Códice T.I.1 de la Biblioteca de San Lorenzo el Real de El Escorial. Siglo XIII*, 2 vols. (Madrid: Edilan 1979); Ferrera, "The Stemma of the Marian *Cantigas*," 59-60, 71. Scarborough, *Women in Thirteenth-Century Spain*, 1-16; Kathleen Kulp-Hill, "The Captions to the Miniatures of the 'Códice Rico' of the *Cantigas de Santa Maria*, a Translation," *Cantigueiros* 7 (1995): 3-64.

35. Gonzalo Menéndez Pidal, *La España del Siglo XIII leída en imágenes* (Madrid: Gráficas Lormo, 1986), 23-26, and "Los manuscritos de las Cantigas. Cómo se elaboró la miniatura alfonsí," *Boletín de la Real Academia de la Historia* 150 (1962): 25-51; Mettmann, "Algunas observaciones," 356-358. Antonio García Solalinde, "El códice florentino de las Cantigas y su relación con los demás manuscritos," *Revista de Filología española* 5 (1918): 143-179, had a slightly different view. He believed that Tol (BN 10069) was the earliest edition; that Escorial T (T.I.1) and F (Banco Rari 20) formed two volumes of the second redaction; and that E (B.1.2) was the definitive edition. Guerrero Lovillo, *Las Cántigas*, 19-22, and *Miniatura Gótica Castellana. Siglos XIII y XIV* (Madrid: Consejo superior de Investigaciones Científicas, 1956), 14-23, followed his judgment.

36. *Alfonso X el Sabio. Cantigas de Santa María. Edición facsímil del códice B.R. 20 de la Biblioteca Centrale de Florencia, siglo XIII*, 2 vols. (Madrid: Edilán, 1989); Amparo García Cuadrado, *Las Cantigas. El Códice de Florencia* (Murcia: Universidad de Murcia, 1993), studies the miniatures of this codex in great detail.

37. Ferrera, "The Stemma of the Marian *Cantigas*," 60-62, 71.

38. Jesús Montoya Martínez, "El Códice de Florencia: Una nueva hipótesis de trabajo," *Romance Quarterly* 33 (1986): 323-329.

39. See Anglés, *La música de las Cantigas,* volume 1 for a black and white facsimile of this codex, and 1:1-3, for a description of it. He believes that it was copied in Seville around 1280-1283 by Juan González, but it is difficult to determine whether he copied both the text and the musical notation. Ferrera, "The Stemma of the Marian *Cantigas*," 62, 71.

40. The Toledan codex reads "*fez cẽ cantares e sões*"—"he made 100 songs."

41. Jesús Montoya Martínez, *Las colecciones de milagros de la Virgen en la Edad Media. El milagro literario* (Granada: Universidad de Granada, 1981), compares the Marian collections of Gautier de Coincy, Gonzalo de Berceo, and Alfonso X.

42. Walter Mettmann, "A Collection of Miracles from Italy as a Possible Source of the *CSM*," *Cantigueiros* 1 (1988): 75-82. There are miracles attributed to Mary's shrines at Salas in Aragón, Terena in Portugal, Montserrat in Catalonia, as well as Villasirga and El Puerto de Santa María in Castile-León. Pedro Aguado Bleye, *Santa María de Salas en el Siglo XIII* (Bilbao: Garmendía, 1916); Theodore Kassier, "The Salas Miracles of the *Cantigas de Santa Maria*: Folklore and Social Reality," *Cantigueiros* 3 (1990): 31-38.

43. Montoya Martínez, "Algunas precisiones," 374-378; Procter, *Alfonso X,* 43-46.

44. See also Walter Mettmann, ed., *Cantigas de Santa Maria,* 3 vols. (Madrid: *Clásicos Castalia,* 1986), 1:21-24. *CSM* 1-100 are found principally in codices E, T, and To. *CSM* 101-200 are mainly in E and T. *CSM* 201-300 are in E and F, and 301-400 are in E, with a few from F and T.

45. "*Otrosi mandamos que todos los libros de los Cantares de loor de Sancta Maria sean todos en aquella iglesia do nuestro cuerpo se enterrare, e que los fagan cantar en las fiestas de Sancta Maria. E si aquel que lo nuestro heredare con derecho e por nos quisiere haber estos libros de los Cantares de Sancta Maria, mandamos que faga por ende bien et algo a la iglesia onde los tomare porque los haya con merced e sin pecado.*" *DAAX,* 560, no. 521; *MHE,* 2:122, no. 229. The

Latin will speaks of the *Libri cantilenarum, miraculorum et laudum etiam Beate Mariae.* See Daumet, "Les testaments d'Alphonse X," 87-99.

46. Ortiz de Zúñiga, *Anales,* 1:342.

Abbreviations

AHDE: Anuario de Historia del Derecho Español.

BAE: Biblioteca de Autores Españoles. 203 vols. thus far. Madrid: Real Academia Española, 1846-.

BRAH: Boletín de la Real Academia de la Historia.

CAX: Crónica del rey don Alfonso X, BAE, 66:3-66.

CE: Manuel Rodríguez Lapa, *Cantigas d'escarnho e de maldecir dos cancioneiros galegoportugueses,* 2d ed. Coimbra: Galaixa, 1970.

CLC: Cortes de los antiguos reinos de León y Castilla, 5 vols. Madrid: Real Academia de la Historia, 1861-1903.

CSM: Walter Mettmann, *Cantigas de Santa Maria,* 4 vols., Coimbra: Universidade de Coimbra, 1959-1972; reprint 2 vols. Vigo: Edicions Xerais de Galicia, 1981.

DAAX: Manuel González Jiménez, *Diplomatario Andaluz de Alfonso X.* Seville: El Monte. Caja de Huelva y Sevilla, 1991.

MHE: Memorial Histórico Español, 49 vols. Madrid: Real Academia de la Historia, 1851-1948.

Katz and Keller, *Studies*: Israel J. Katz and John E. Keller, eds., *Studies on the Cantigas de Santa Maria: Art, Music, and Poetry.* Madison: Hispanic Seminary of Medieval Studies, 1987.

PCG: Primera Crónica General, ed. Ramón Menéndez Pidal, 2 vols. Madrid: Gredos, 1955.

RABM: Revista de Archivos, Bibliotecas y Museos.

Narrative Sources

Alfonso X. *Estoria de Espanna.* See Alfonso X, *Primera Crónica General.*

———. *Primera Crónica General.* Ed. Ramón Menéndez Pidal. 2 vols. Madrid: Gredos, 1955.

Anales Toledanos III. ES 23:411-424.

Benavides, Antonio, ed. *Memorias de D. Fernando IV de Castilla.* 2 vols. Madrid: José Rodríguez, 1860.

Bernat Desclot. *Crònica.* Ed. M. Coll i Alentorn. 5 vols. Barcelona: Barcino, 1949-1951.

Chronica Adefonsi Imperatoris. Ed. Luis Sánchez Belda. Madrid: Consejo Superior de Investigaciones Científicas, 1950.

Chronicle of Albelda. In Yves Bonnaz, ed. *Chroniques asturiennes (Fin IXe siècle).* Paris: CNRS, 1987.

Chrónicon de Cardeña. ES 23:371-381.

Continuación de la Crónica del Arzobispo Don Rodrigo Jiménez de Rada. In *Colección de documentos inéditos para la historia de España.* Ed. Martín Fernández de Navarrete et al., 112 vols. Madrid: Calera et al., 1841-1895. 105-106.

Cooper, Louis, and Franklin M. Waltman. *Text and Concordance of the* Gran Conquista de Ultramar. *Biblioteca Nacional MS 1187.* Madison: Hispanic Seminary of Medieval Studies, 1989.

Crònica de Jaume I. Ed. J. M. Casacuberta and Enric Bagüe. 9 vols. Barcelona: Barcino, 1926-1962.

Crónica del Rey Don Alfonso X. BAE 66:3-66.

Crónica del Rey Don Alfonso XI. BAE 66:173-392.

Crónica del rey don Fernando IV. BAE 66:93-170.

Crónica del rey don Sancho el bravo. BAE 66:69-90.

Crònica general de Pere III el Cerimoniós, dita comunament Crònica de Sant Joan de la Penya. Ed. A. J. Soberanas Lleó. Barcelona: Alpha, 1961.

Crónica general de Espanha de 1344. Ed. L. F. Lindley Cintra. 6 vols. Lisboa: Academia Portuguesa da História, 1951-1983.

Crónica latina de los reyes de Castilla. Ed. Luis Charlo Brea. Cádiz: Universidad de Cádiz, 1984.

Estoria del Fecho de los Godos. See *Continuacion de la Crónica del Arzobispo Don Rodrigo.*

Fita, Fidel, "Biografías de San Fernando y de Alfonso el Sabio por Gil de Zamora," *BRAH* 5 (1885): 308-328.

———. "Biografía inédita de Alfonso IX, rey de León, por Gil de Zamora," *BRAH* 13 (1888): 291-295.

Flórez, Enrique, et al. *España Sagrada,* 52 vols. Madrid: Marin, 1754-1918.

Gayangos, Pascual, ed. *La gran conquista de Ultramar que mandó escribir el Rey Don Alfonso el Sabio.* In *BAE* 44. Madrid: Real Academia Española, 1858; reprint 1951.

Guillaume de Nangis. *Gesta Philippi Tertii Francorum regis.* In *Recueil des Historiens des Gaules et de la France.* Ed. Martin Bouquet et al., 24 vols. Paris: Académie des Inscriptions et Belles Lettres, 1738-1904. 20:466-539.

Ibn Abī Zar'. *Rawd al-Qirtas.* 2 vols. Tr. Ambrosio Huici. Valencia: Anubar, 1964.

Ibn 'Idhārī, *al-Bayān al Mugrib fi Ijtisar Ajbār Muluk al-Andalus wa al-Magrib.* Tr. Ambrosio Huici Miranda. *Colección de crónicas árabes de la Reconquista.* 3 vols. Tetuán: Marroquí, 1952-1953. 2-3.

Ibn Khaldūn. *Histoire des Berbères et des dynasties musulmanes de l'Afrique septentrionale.* 4 vols. Tr. Baron de Slane. Paris: Paul Geutner, 1852-1856.

Isidore of Seville. *Historia Gothorum, Wandalorum et Suevorum.* In *Monumenta Germaniae Historica. Auctores Antiquissimi,* 11. *Chronica Minora,* 2:267-303.

Jofré de Loaysa. *Crónica de los reyes de Castilla, Fernando III, Alfonso X, Sancho IV y Fernando IV, 1248-1305.* Ed. and tr. Antonio García Martínez. Murcia, 1961. Reprint, Murcia: Academic Alfonso X el Sabio, 1982.

Juan Gil de Zamora. *Liber de preconiis Hispaniae.* Ed. Manuel de Castro y Castro. Madrid: Universidad de Madrid, 1955.

————. *Liber de preconiis civitatis numantine.* Ed. Fidel Fita. "Dos libros inéditos de Gil de Zamora." *BRAH* 5 (1884): 131-200.

Juan Manuel. *Chronicon.* In Benavides, *Memorias de D. Fernando IV de Castilla.* 1:675-680.

Lomax, Derek W. "Una crónica inédita de Silos." *Homenaje a Fray Justo Pérez de Urbel.* 2 vols. Silos: Abadía de Silos, 1976. 1:323-337.

López de Ayala, Pedro. *Crónica de Juan I. BAE* 68:65-159.

Lucas of Tuy. *Chronicon Mundi.* Ed. Andreas Schott. *Hispania Illustrata.* 4 vols. Frankfort: Claudius Marnius et Heredes Joannis Aubrii, 1603-1608. 4:1-116.

————. *Crónica de España.* Ed. Julio Puyol. Madrid: Revista de Archivos, Bibliotecas y Museos, 1926.

Ramon Muntaner. *Crònica.* Ed. Enric Bagüe. 2d ed. 9 vols. Barcelona: Barcino, 1927-1952.

Rodrigo Jiménez de Rada. *De rebus Hispaniae.* In *Opera.* Ed. Francisco de Lorenzana. Madrid, 1793. Reprint, Valencia: Anubar, 1968.

LITERARY SOURCES

Alfonso X. *Alfonso X el Sabio. Cantigas de Santa María. Edición facsímil del Códice T.I.1 de la Biblioteca de San Lorenzo el Real de El Escorial. Siglo XIII.* 2 vols. Madrid: Edilán 1979.

————. *Alfonso X el Sabio. Cantigas de Santa María. Edición facsímil del códice B.R. 20 de la Biblioteca Centrale de Florencia. Siglo XIII.* 2 vols. Madrid: Edilán, 1989.

————. *Cantigas de Santa Maria.* 4 vols. Ed. Walter Mettmann. Coimbra: Universidade de Coimbra, 1959-1974. Reprint, 2 vols. Vigo: Edicions Xerais de Galicia, 1981.

————. *Cantigas de Santa Maria. Cantigas 1 a 100.* 2 vols. Ed. Walter Mettmann. Madrid: *Clásicos Castalia,* 1986.

————. *Las Cantigas de Santa Maria.* 2 vols. Ed. Marquess of Valmar. Madrid: Real Academia Española, 1889.

————. *Setenario.* Ed. Kenneth Vanderford. Buenos Aires: 1945. Reprint, Barcelona: Crítica, 1984.

Alvar, Carlos. *Textos trovadorescos sobre España y Portugal.* Madrid: CUPSA, 1978.

Álvaro Pelayo. *Collirium adversus hereses novas.* Ed. Richard Scholz, *Unbekannte kirchenpolitische Streitschriften aus der Zeit Ludwigs des Bayern, 1327-1354,* 2 vols. Rome: Loescher, 1914.

————. *Speculum regum (Espelho dos Reis).* Ed. Miguel Pinto de Meneses. Lisbon: Universidade de Lisboa, 1955.

Arberry, A. J., tr., *The Koran Interpreted.* 2 vols. New York: George Unwin, 1955.

Blanco García, Vicente, and J. Campos, eds. *San Ildefonso de Toledo (Santos Padres Españoles,* 1). Madrid: Biblioteca de Autores Cristianos, 1971.

Cancioneiro da Ajuda. Ed. Carolina Michaëlis de Vasconcellos. 2 vols. Halle: Niemeyer, 1904.

Cancioneiro da Biblioteca antiga Colucci-Brancuti. 8 vols. Ed. Elza Paxeco Machado and José Pedro Machado. Lisbon: Revista de Portugal, 1949-1964.

Fita, Fidel. "Cincuenta leyendas por Gil de Zamora combinadas con las Cantigas de Alfonso el Sabio." *BRAH* 7 (1886): 54-144.

————. "Leyenda de San Isidro por el diacono Juan." *BRAH* 9 (1886): 97-157.

————. "Poesías inéditas de Gil de Zamora." *BRAH* 6 (1885): 379-409.

————. "Traslación e invención del cuerpo de San Ildefonso. Reseña histórica por Gil de Zamora." *BRAH* 6 (1885): 60-71.

————. "Treinta leyendas por Gil de Zamora." *BRAH* 13 (1888): 187-225.

————. "Variantes de tres leyendas por Gil de Zamora." *BRAH* 6 (1885): 418-429.

García Morencos, Pilar. *Libro de ajedrez, dados y tablas de Alfonso X el Sabio. Estudio.* Madrid: Patrimonio Nacional, 1977.

Gonzalo de Berceo. *Milagros de Nuestra Señora.* Ed. Antonio García Solalinde. Madrid: Clásicos Castellanos, 1958.

————. *Obras completas de Gonzalo de Berceo.* Logroño: Instituto de Estudios Riojanos, 1974.

————. *Obras completas.* Ed. Brian Dutton. 3 vols. London: Tamesis, 1975.

Ildefonsus of Toledo. *Liber de viris illustribus.* Ed. C. Codoñer Merino. Salamanca: Universidad de Salamanca, 1972.

John of Paris. *De potestate regia et papali.* Ed. Jean Leclercq. *Jean de Paris et l'ecclésiologie du XIIIᵉ siècle.* Paris: J. Vrin, 1942.

———. *On Royal and Papal Power.* Tr. John A. Watt. Toronto: Pontifical Institute of Medieval Studies, 1971.

Juan Manuel. *Libro de los estados.* Ed. R. B. Tate and I. R. Macpherson. New York: Oxford University Press, 1974.

———. *Tractado de las armas.* BAE 51:257-264.

Juan Ruiz, Arcipreste de Hita. *Libro de buen amor.* Ed. Jacques Joset. 2 vols. Madrid: Espasa-Calpe, 1974.

Libro de los engaños e asayamientos de las mugeres. Ed. John E. Keller. Chapel Hill: University of North Carolina, 1959.

Núñez, José Joaquín. *Cantigas d'amigo dos trovadores galegos-portugueses.* 2 vols. Coimbra, 1926. Reprint, New York: Kraus, 1971.

Paredes Núñez, Juan, ed. *Alfonso X el Sabio. Cantigas profanas.* Granada: Universidad de Granada, 1988.

Pedro Marín. *Miraculos romanzados.* Ed. Sebastián de Vergara. *Vida y milagros de Santo Domingo de Silos.* Madrid: Francisco del Hierro, 1736.

Poema de Fernán González. Ed. Alonso Zamora Vicente. Madrid: Espasa-Calpe, 1946.

Ramos, Epifanio, ed. *Las Cantigas de escárnio y maldecir de Alfonso X.* Lugo: Reprografia Alvarellos, 1973.

Rodríguez Lapa, Manuel. *Cantigas d'escarnho e de mal dezir dos Cancioneiros medievais galego-portugueses.* Coimbra: Galaixa, 1970.

Sancho IV. *Castigos e documentos para bien vivir.* Ed. Agapito Rey. Bloomington: Indiana University, 1952.

The Book of the Wiles of Women. Tr. John E. Keller. Chapel Hill: University of North Carolina, 1956.

LEGAL AND DOCUMENTARY SOURCES

Alfonso X. *Espéculo. Texto jurídico atribuído al Rey de Castilla Don Alfonso el Sabio.* Ed. Robert A. MacDonald. Madison: Hispanic Seminary, 1990.

———. *Espéculo.* Ed. Gonzalo Martínez Díez and José Manuel Ruiz Asencio. Ávila: Fundación Claudio Sánchez Albornoz, 1985.

———. *Fuero real.* Ed. Gonzalo Martínez Díez, José Manuel Ruiz Asencio, and C. Hernández Alonso. Ávila: Fundación Claudio Sánchez Albornoz, 1988.

———. *Opúsculos legales del Rey Don Alfonso el Sabio.* Ed. Real Academia de la Historia. 2 vols. Madrid: Imprenta Real, 1836.

———. *Primera Partida según el Manuscrito Add. 20787 del British Museum.* Ed. Juan Antonio Arias Bonet. Valladolid: Universidad de Valladolid, 1975.

———. *Las Siete Partidas del Rey Don Alfonso el Sabio.* Ed. Real Academia de la Historia. 3 vols. Madrid: Imprenta Real, 1801.

Bullarium Ordinis Militiae de Calatrava. Madrid: Antonio Marín, 1761.

Canivez, Joseph M. *Statuta capitulorum generalium Ordinis Cisterciensium.* 8 vols. Louvain: Bibliothèque de la Revue d'Histoire ecclésiastique, 1933-1941.

Castro Garrido, Araceli. *Documentación del monasterio de las Huelgas de Burgos (1307-1321).* Burgos: Garrido Garrido, 1987.

Cortes de los antiguos reinos de León y Castilla. 5 vols. Madrid: Real Academia de la Historia, 1861-1903.

Daumet, Georges. *Mémoire sur les relations de la France et de la Castille de 1255 à 1320.* Paris: Bibliothèque de l'École des Hautes Études, 1913.

———. "Les testaments d'Alphonse le Savant, roi de Castille," *Bibliothèque de l'Ecole des Chartes* 67 (1906): 70-99.

"Documentos de la época de Alfonso el Sabio," *MHE,* 1-2.

Escudero de la Peña, J. M. "Súplica hecha al Papa Juan XXI para que absolviese al Rey de Castilla, D. Alfonso X, del juramento de no acuñar otra moneda que los dineros prietos." *RABM* 2 (1872): 58-59.

Ferotin, Marius. *Recueil des chartes de l'Abbaye de Silos.* Paris: Imprimerie Nationale, 1897.

Gay, Jules. *Les Registres de Nicholas III (1277-1280).* Paris: Bibliothèque des Écoles françaises d'Athènes et de Rome, 1898-1938.

González, Julio. *Repartimiento de Sevilla.* 2 vols. Madrid: Consejo Superior de Investigaciones Científicas, 1951.

González, Tomás. *Colección de cédulas, cartas patentes, provisiones, reales ordenes y documentos concernientes a las provincias vascongadas,* 6 vols. Madrid: Imprenta Real, 1829-1833.

González Crespo, Esther. *Colección documental de Alfonso XI.* Madrid: Universidad Complutense, 1985.

González Jiménez, Manuel. *Diplomatario Andaluz de Alfonso X.* Seville: El Monte. Caja de Huelva y Sevilla, 1991.

———— and A. González Gómez. *El Libro del repartimiento de Ferez de la Frontera. Estudio y edición.* Cádiz: Instituto de Estudios Gaditanos, 1980.

Gross, Georg. "Las Cortes de 1252. Ordenamiento otorgado al concejo de Burgos en las cortes celebradas en Sevilla el 12 de octubre de 1252 (según el original)," *BRAH* 182 (1985): 95-114.

Iglesia Ferreirós, Aquilino. "El Privilegio general concedido a las Extremaduras en 1264 por Alfonso X. Edición del ejemplar enviado a Peñafiel en 15 de abril de 1264." *AHDE* 53 (1983): 456-521.

Lizoain Garrido, José Manuel. *Documentación del monasterio de las Huelgas de Burgos (1268-1283).* Burgos: Garrido Garrido, 1987.

Mansilla, Demetrio. *La documentación pontificia de Honorio III (1216-1227).* Rome: Instituto Español de Historia Eclesiástica, 1965.

Martin, François Olivier. *Les Registres de Martin IV (1281-1285).* Paris: Bibliothèque des Ecoles françaises d'Athènes et de Rome, 1901.

Memorial Histórico Español, 49 vols. Madrid: Real Academia de Historia, 1851-1948.

Quintana Prieto, Augusto. *Tumbo viejo de San Pedro de Montes.* León: Caja de Ahorros y Monte de Piedad, 1971.

Rymer, Thomas. *Foedera, conventiones, litterae et cuiuscunque acta publica inter reges Angliae et alios quovis imperatores, reges, pontifices, principes.* 3d ed. 10 vols. The Hague: Joannes Neaulme, 1739-1745.

Sánchez Albornoz, Claudio. "Un ceremonial inédito de coronación de los reyes de Castilla." *Estudios sobre las instituciones medievales españolas.* Mexico City: Universidad Nacional Autónoma de Mexico, 1965. 739-763.

Torres Fontes, Juan, ed. *Colección de documentos inéditos para la historia de Murcia,* 18 vols. thus far. Murcia: Academia Alfonso X el Sabio, 1963-1989.

————. *Repartimiento de Murcia.* Murcia: Academia Alfonso X el Sabio, 1960.

Secondary Works

Aguado Bleye, Pedro. *Santa María de Salas en el Siglo XIII.* Bilbao: Garmendía, 1916.

Aguiar, Manuel de. "Cantigas de escarnio e maldezir: uma galeria de caricaturas." *Portugalia Historica* 2 (1974): 65-89.

Alfonso X. Toledo 1984. Toledo: Ministerio de Cultura, 1984.

Alvar, Carlos. *La poesía trovadoresca en España y Portugal.* Barcelona: CUPSA, 1977.

Anglés, Higinio. *La música de las Cantigas de Santa Maria del Rey Don Alfonso el Sabio,* 3 vols. Barcelona: Diputación Provincial de Barcelona, Biblioteca Central, 1943-1964.

Arco, Ricardo del. *Sepulcros de la Casa Real de Castilla.* Madrid: Consejo Superior de Investigaciones Científicas, 1954.

Arié, Rachel. *L'Espagne musulmane au temps des Nasrides (1232-1492).* Paris: Boccard, 1973.

Ariés, Philippe. *The Hour of Our Death.* Tr. Helen Weaver. New York: Alfred Knopf, 1981.

Baer, Yitzhak. *A History of the Jews in Christian Spain.* 2 vols. Philadelphia: Jewish Publication Society, 1966.

Bagby, Albert. "Alfonso and the Virgin Unite Christian and Moor in the *CSM.*" *Cantigueiros* 1 (1988): 111-118.

————. "The Jew in the *Cantigas* of Alfonso X el Sabio." *Speculum* 46 (1971): 670-688.

————. "The Figure of the Jew in the *Cantigas* of Alfonso X." In Katz and Keller, *Studies,* 235-247.

————. "The Moslem in the *Cantigas* of Alfonso X, El Sabio." *Kentucky Romance Quarterly,* 20 (1973): 173-204.

Ballesteros Beretta, Antonio. *Alfonso X, el Sabio.* Barcelona: Espasa-Calpe, 1963. Reprint, Barcelona: El Albir, 1984.

————. *Historia de España y su influencia en la historia universal.* 8 vols. in 9. Barcelona: Salvat, 1918-1941.

————. *Sevilla en el siglo XIII.* Madrid: Juan Pérez Torres, 1913.

————. "La toma de Salé en tiempos de Alfonso X el Sabio." *Al-Andalus* 8 (1943): 89-128.

Barbour, Neville. "The Significance of the Word *Maurus* with its Derivatives *Moro* and *Moor* and of the Other Terms used by Medieval Writers in Latin to describe the Inhabitants of Muslim Spain." *Actas do IV Congresso de Estudos Arabes e Islámicos. Coimbra 1968.* Leiden: E. J. Brill, 1971. 253-266.

Barkai, Ron. *Cristianos y musulmanes en la España medieval (El enemigo en el espejo).* Madrid: Rialp, 1984.

Beltrán, Vicente. "Los Trovadores en la Corte de Castilla y León (II): Alfonso X, Guiraut Riquier y Pero da Ponte." *Romania* 107 (1986): 486-503.

Benito Ruano, Eloy. *La prelación ciudadana. Las disputas por la precedencia entre las ciudades de la Corona de Castilla.* Toledo: Centro Universitario de Toledo, 1972.

Benito-Vessels, Carmen. "The San Ildefonso Miracle in the Margins of the *Cantigas de Santa Maria* and in the *Estoria de España:* Two Forms of Narrative Discourse," *Cantigueiros* 3 (1990): 17-30.

Bloch, Marc. *Les rois thaumaturges.* Paris: Armand Colin, 1961.

———. *The Royal Touch: Sacred Monarchy and Scrofula in England and France.* Tr. J. E. Anderson. London: Routledge, Kegan Paul, 1973.

Braegelmann, Sister A. *The Life and Writings of St. Ildefonsus of Toledo.* Washington, D.C.: The Catholic University of America, 1942.

Brodman, James W. *Ransoming Captives in Crusader Spain: The Order of Merced on the Christian-Islamic Frontier.* Philadelphia: University of Pennsylvania, 1986.

———. "Charity and Captives on the Medieval Spanish Frontier." *Anuario Medieval* 1 (1989): 34-45.

———. "Municipal Ransoming Law on the Medieval Spanish Frontier." *Speculum* 60 (1985): 318-330.

Burns, Robert I., ed. *Emperor of Culture. Alfonso X the Learned of Castile and his Thirteenth-Century Renaissance.* Philadelphia: University of Pennsylvania, 1990.

———. Ed. *The Worlds of Alfonso the Learned and James the Conqueror. Intellect and Force in the Middle Ages.* Princeton: Princeton University, 1985.

———. "*Stupor Mundi:* Alfonso X of Castile, the Learned." In Burns, *Emperor of Culture,* 1-13.

———. "The *Cantigas de Santa Maria* as a Research Opportunity in History," *Cantigueiros* 1 (1987): 17-22.

———. "The Spiritual Life of James the Conqueror, King of Arago-Catalonia, 1208-1276: Portrait and Self-Portrait." *The Catholic Historical Review* 62 (1976): 1-35.

———. "Warrior Neighbors: Alfonso el Sabio and Crusader Valencia. An Archival Case Study in his International Relations." *Viator* 21 (1990): 147-202.

Cádiz en el siglo XIII. Actas de las jornadas conmemorativas del VIII Centenario de la muerte de Alfonso el Sabio. Cádiz: Universidad de Cádiz, 1983.

Cárdenas, Anthony J. "A Study of Alfonso's Role in Selected *Cantigas* and the Castilian Prosifications of Escorial Codex T.I.1." In Katz and Keller, *Studies,* 253-268.

Carpenter, Dwayne E. "Alfonso el Sabio y los moros: Algunas precisiones legales históricas y textuales con respecto a Siete Partidas 7.25." *Al-Qantara* 7 (1986): 229-253.

Castrillo Llamas, María de la Concepción. "Monarquía y nobleza en torno a la tenencia de fortalezas en Castilla durante los siglos XIII-XIV." *En la España medieval* 17 (1994): 95-112.

Castro, Americo. *La realidad historica de España.* Mexico City: Porrua, 1962.

Catalán, Diego. *La Estoria de España de Alfonso X. Creación y Evolución.* Madrid: Universidad Autónoma de Madrid, 1992.

Clarke, Dorothy Clotelle. "Versification in Alfonso el Sabio's *Cantigas.*" *Hispanic Review* 23 (1955): 83-98.

Cómez Ramos, Rafael. *Las empresas artísticas de Alfonso X el Sabio.* Sevilla: Diputación Provincial de Sevilla, 1979.

———. "El retrato de Alfonso X, el Sabio en la primera Cantiga de Santa Maria." In Katz and Keller, *Studies,* 35-52.

Craddock, Jerry R. "Dynasty in Dispute: Alfonso X el Sabio and the Succession to the Throne of Castile and León in History and Legend." *Viator* 17 (1986): 197-219.

Daniel, Norman. *Islam and the West. The Making of an Image.* Edinburgh: University of Edinburgh, 1960.

Delgado Roig, Juan. "Examen médico-legal de unos restos históricos: Los cadáveres de Alfonso X el Sabio y Doña Beatriz de Suabia." *Archivo Hispalense* 9 (1948): 135-153.

Domínguez Rodríguez, Ana. *Astrología y arte en el Lapidario de Alfonso X el Sabio.* Madrid: Edilán, 1982.

———. "La miniatura del 'Scriptorium' Alfonsí." In Mondéjar and Montoya, *Estudios Alfonsíes,* 127-164.

Dufourcq, Charles Emmanuel. "Un projet castillane du XIIIᵉ siecle: La croisade d'Afrique." *Revue d'histoire et du civilisation du Magreb,* 1 (1966): 26-51.

Fernández de la Cuesta, Ismael. "Alfonso X el Sabio y la música de las Cantigas." In Mondéjar and Montoya, *Estudios alfonsíes,* 119-126.

Fernández del Pulgar, Pedro. *Historia secular y eclesiástica de la ciudad de Palencia.* 4 vols. Madrid: F. Nieto, 1679-1680.

Ferrera, Manuel Pedro. "The Stemma of the Marian *Cantigas:* Philological and Musical Evidence." *Cantigueiros* 6 (1994): 58-97.

Fortescue, Adrian. *The Mass. A Study of the Roman Liturgy.* London: Longmans 1912.

Fraker, Charles. *The Scope of History. Studies in the Historiography of Alfonso el Sabio.* Ann Arbor: University of Michigan, 1996.

Franssen, Maarten. "Did King Alfonso of Castile Really Want to Advise God Against the Ptolemaic System?" *Studies in History and Philosophy of Science* 24 (1993): 313-325.

Gaibrois de Ballesteros, Mercedes. *Historia del reinado de Sancho IV de Castilla,* 3 vols. Madrid: Revista de Archivos, Bibliotecas y Museos, 1922.

García Cuadrado, Amparo. *Las Cantigas. El Códice de Florencia.* Murcia: Universidad de Murcia, 1993.

García-Varela, Jesús. "La función ejemplar de Alfonso X en las cantigas personales." *Cantigueiros* 4 (1992): 3-16.

Giménez Soler, Andrés. *Don Juan Manuel: Biografía y estudio crítico.* Madrid: Real Academia Española, 1932.

Gómez Moreno, María Elena. *La Catedral de León* (León: Everest, 1973).

Goñi Gaztambide, José. *Historia de la bula de la cruzada en España.* Vitoria: Editorial del Seminario, 1955.

González, Cristina. *La tercera Crónica de Alfonso X: La Gran Conquista de Ultramar.* London: Tamesis, 1992.

———. "El último sueño de Alfonso X: La Gran Conquista de Ultramar." *Exemplaria Hispanica* 1 (1991-1992): 97-117.

González, Julio. *Alfonso IX.* 2 vols. Madrid: Consejo Superior de Investigaciones Científicas, 1945.

———. *El reino de Castilla en la época de Alfonso VIII.* 3 vols. Madrid: Consejo Superior de Investigaciones Científicas, 1960.

———. *Regesta de Fernando II.* Madrid: Consejo Superior de Investigaciones Científicas, 1943.

———. *Reinado y diplomas de Fernando III.* 3 vols. Córdoba: Monte de Piedad y Caja de Ahorros de Córdoba, 1980-1986.

González Jiménez, Manuel. *Alfonso X, 1252-1284.* Palencia: La Olmeda, 1993.

———. *En torno a los origenes de Andalucía.* 2d ed. Seville: Universidad de Sevilla, 1988.

———. "'De al-Qanatir al Gran Puerto de Santa María.'" In *El Puerto de Santo María entre los Siglos XIII y XVI. Estudios en homenaje a Hipólito Sancho de Sopranis en el centenario de su nacimiento.* El Puerto de Santa María: Ayuntamiento de El Puerto de Santa María, 1995.

———. "El Puerto de Santa María en tiempos de Alfonso X el Sabio." In *Nuestros orígenes históricos como El Puerto de Santa María.* Eds. Manuel González

Jiménez, Alfonso Jiménez, Jesús Montoya, and José Luis Tejada. El Puerto de Santa María: Ayuntamiento de El Puerto de Santa María, 1989.

———. "Esclavos andaluces en el reino de Granada." *Actas del III Coloquio de historia medieval andaluza: La sociedad medieval andaluza: Grupos no privilegiados.* Jaén: Diputación Provincial de Jaén, 1984. 327-338.

———. "Osuna en el Siglo XIII." In *Osuna entre los tiempos medievales y modernos (siglos XIII-XVIII).* Sevilla: Universidad de Sevilla, 1995. 27-38.

Grassotti, Hilda. *Las instituciones feudo-vasallaticas de León y Castilla,* 2 vols. Spoleto: Centro italiano di studi sull'alto medioevo, 1969.

Gual López, José Miguel. "La política ferial alfonsí y el ordenamiento general de las ferias castellanas en su época." In Miguel Rodríguez, et al. *Alfonso X el Sabio.* 95-114.

Guerrero Lovillo, José. *Las Cantigas: Estudio arqueológico de sus miniaturas.* Madrid: Consejo Superior de Investigaciones Científicas, 1949.

———. *Miniatura Gótica Castellana. Siglos XIII y XIV.* Madrid: Consejo Superior de Investigaciones Científicas, 1956.

Hernández Serna, Joaquín. "La Orden de la Estrella, o de Santa María de España, en la Cantiga 78 del Códice de la Biblioteca Nacional de Florencia." *Miscelánea Medieval Murciana* 6 (1980): 147-168.

Huici Miranda, Ambrosio. *Las grandes batallas de la reconquista durante las invasiones africanas.* Madrid: Consejo Superior de Investigaciones Científicas, 1956.

———. "La toma de Salé por la esquadra de Alfonso X." *Hesperis* 39 (1952): 41-52.

Impey, Olga Tudorica. "'Del duello de los godos de Espanna': la retórica del llanto y su motivación." *Romance Quarterly* 33 (1986): 294-307.

Jedin, Hubert, and John Dolan, eds. *Handbook of Church History,* 10 vols. New York: Herder and Herder, 1968-1981.

Johnson, Elizabeth. "Marian Devotion in the Western Church." In Jill Raitt, ed. *Christian Spirituality: High Middle Ages and Reformation.* New York: Crossroad, 1988.

Kantorowicz, Ernst. *The King's Two Bodies. A Study in Medieval Political Theology.* Princeton: Princeton University Press, 1957.

Kassier, Theodore. "The Salas Miracles of the *Cantigas de Santa María:* Folklore and Social Reality." *Cantigueiros* 3 (1990): 31-38.

Katz, Israel, and John E. Keller, eds. *Studies on the Cantigas de Santa María. Art, Music and Poetry.* Madison: Hispanic Seminary, 1987.

Keller, John Esten. *Alfonso X, el Sabio.* New York: Twayne, 1967.

————. *Collectanea Hispanica: Folklore and Brief Narrative Studies by John Esten Keller.* Ed. Dennis Seniff. Newark, Delaware: Juan de la Cuesta, 1987. 61-76.

————. "Daily Living as presented in the Canticles of Alfonso the Learned." *Speculum* 33 (1958): 484-489.

————. "King Alfonso's Virgin of Villa-Sirga, Rival of St. James of Compostela." In Frederic E. Coenen, et al., eds. *Middle Ages-Reformation-Volkskunde: Festchrift for John G. Kunstmann.* Chapel Hill: University of North Carolina Press, 1959. 75-82.

————. "More on the Rivalry between Santa María and Santiago de Compostela." *Crítica Hispánica* 1 (1979): 37-43.

————. "The Threefold Impact of the *Cantigas de Santa María:* Visual, Verbal and Musical." In Katz and Keller, *Studies,* 7-33.

Keller, John E., and Richard P. Kinkade. *Iconography in Medieval Spanish Literature.* Lexington: University of Kentucky, 1983.

Kinkade, Richard P. "Alfonso X, *Cantiga* 235, and the Events of 1269-1278." *Speculum* 67 (1992): 284-323.

————. "Don Juan's Father, Infante Manuel, in the Cantigas de Santa Maria." *Cantigueiros* 8 (1996): 68-74.

————. "Violante of Aragón (1236?-1300?): An Historical Overview." *Exemplaria Hispanica* 2 (1992): 1-37.

Kulp-Hill, Kathleen. "The Captions to the Miniatures of the 'Códice Rico' of the *Cantigas de Santa María,* a Translation." *Cantigueiros* 7 (1995): 3-64.

————. "'Toda manera de alegría': Pastimes Portrayed in the *Cantigas de Santa Maria.*" *Cantigueiros* 6 (1994): 42-52.

Ladero Quesada, Miguel Ángel. *Niebla, de reino a condado. Noticias sobre el Algarbe andaluz en la Baja Edad Media.* Madrid: Real Academia de la Historia, 1992.

Laín, Milagro. "La poesía profana de Alfonso X." *Revista de Occidente* 43 (1984): 145-165.

Le Goff, Jacques. *The Birth of Purgatory.* Tr. Arthur Goldhammer. Chicago: University of Chicago Press, 1984.

Leclercq, Jean, François Vandenbroucke, and Louis Bouyer. *The Spirituality of the Middle Ages (A History of Christian Spirituality,* 2). Minneapolis: Seabury, n.d.

Lévi-Provençal, Évariste. *Histoire de l'Espagne musulmane.* 3 vols. Leiden: E. J. Brill, 1950.

Lewis, C. S. *The Allegory of Love.* New York: Oxford University Press, 1958.

Lewis, Archibald R., and Timothy J. Runyan. *European Naval and Maritime History, 300-1500.* Bloomington: Indiana University Press, 1990.

Linehan, Peter. *History and the Historians of Medieval Spain.* Oxford: Clarendon Press, 1993.

López Ferreiro, Antonio. *Historia de la santa a.m. iglesia de Santiago de Compostela.* 11 vols. Santiago: Imprenta del Seminario conciliar y central, 1898-1909.

Manzano Rodríguez, Miguel Ángel. *La intervención de los Benimerines en la Península ibérica.* Madrid: Consejo Superior de Investigaciones Científicas, 1992.

Martínez García, Luis. *El Hospital del Rey de Burgos. Un señorío medieval en la expansión y en la crísis (siglos XIII y XIV).* Burgos: J. M. Garrido Garrido, 1986.

Martínez Montavez, Pedro. "Relaciones de Alfonso X de Castilla con el sultan mameluco Baybars y sus sucesores." *Al-Andalus* 27 (1962): 343-376.

Márquez-Villanueva, Francisco. *El Concepto cultural alfonsí.* Madrid: MAPFRE, 1994.

———— and Carlos Alberto Vega, eds. *Alfonso X of Castile: The Learned King (1225-1284). An International Symposium, Harvard University, 17 November 1984.* Cambridge: Harvard University, 1990.

Menéndez Pidal, Gonzalo. *La España del Siglo XIII leída en imágenes.* Madrid: Gráficas Lormo, 1986.

————. "Los manuscritos de las Cantigas. Cómo se elaboró la miniatura alfonsí." *Boletín de la Real Academia de la Historia* 150 (1962): 25-51.

Mettmann, Walter. "A Collection of Miracles from Italy as a Possible Source of the *CSM.*" *Cantigueiros* 1 (1988): 75-82.

————. "Algunas observaciones sobre la genesis de la colección de las Cantigas de Santa Maria y sobre el problema del autor." In Katz and Keller, *Studies,* 355-366.

Miguel Rodríguez, Juan Carlos de, Angela Múñoz Fernández, and Cristina Segura Graiño, eds. *Alfonso X el Sabio. Vida, obra y época. Actas del Congreso internacional de estudios medievales conmemorativos del VII Centenario de la muerte de Alfonso el Sabio.* Madrid: Sociedad Española de Estudios Medievales, 1989.

Mingüella, Toribio. *Historia de la diócesis de Sigüenza.* 3 vols. Madrid: Revista de Archivos, Bibliotecas y Museos, 1900-1913.

Mondéjar, Gaspar Ibáñez de Segovia, Marqués de. *Memorias históricas del Rey D. Alonso el Sabio i observaciones a su chrónica.* Madrid: Joaquín Ibarra, 1777.

Mondéjar, José, and Jesús Montoya, eds. *Estudios alfonsíes. Lexicografía, lírica, estética y política de Alfonso el Sabio.* Granada: Universidad de Granada, 1985.

Montes Romero-Camacho, Isabel. *El paisaje rural sevillano en la baja edad media.* Sevilla: Diputación Provincial de Sevilla, 1989.

Montoto, Santiago. *La Catedral y el Alcázar de Sevilla.* Madrid: Editorial Plus Ultra, n.d.

Montoya Martínez, Jesús. *Las colecciones de milagros de la Virgen en la Edad Media. El milagro literario.* Granada: Universidad de Granada, 1981.

———. "Algunas precisiones acerca de las Cantigas de Santa Maria." In Katz and Keller, *Studies,* 366-385.

———. "El Códice de Florencia: Una nueva hipótesis de trabajo." *Romance Quarterly* 33 (1986): 323-329.

———. "Historia de Andalucía en las Cantigas de Santa Maria." *Andalucía medieval. Actas del I Congreso de Historia de Andalucía, Córdoba, diciembre de 1976.* 2 vols. Córdoba: Monte de Piedad y Caja de Ahorros, 1978. 1:259-269.

———. "Judíos y moros en las Cantigas de Santa Maria." *Historia del Derecho (Granada)* (1980): 69-90.

———. "La 'carta fundacional' del Puerto de Santa Maria y las Cantigas de Santa Maria." *Cantigueiros* 6 (1994): 99-115.

———. "La 'gran vingança de Dios y Alfonso X." *Cantigueiros* 3 (1990): 53-59.

———. "Las Cantigas de Santa Maria: Fuente para la historia gaditana." *Cádiz en el siglo XIII. Actas de las jornadas conmemorativas del VIII Centenario de la muerte de Alfonso el Sabio.* Cádiz: Universidad de Cádiz, 1983. 173-181.

———. "Los nombres del Profeta: "Mafomete cão/ Bafomete' en la tradición hispánica." *Homenaje al Profesor José María Fórneas Besteiro.* Granada: Universidad de Granada, 1994. 403-409.

———. "O Cancioneiro Marial de Alfonso X. El primer cancionero cortesano español." *O Cantar dos Trobadores. Actas do Congreso celebrado en Santiago de Compostela entre os dias 26 a 29 de abril de 1993.* Santiago de Compostela: Xunta de Galicia, 1993.

——— and Aurora Juárez Blanquer. *Andalucía en las Cantigas de Santa María.* Granada: Universidad de Granada, 1988.

Moxó, Salvador de. "La nobleza castellano-leonesa en la edad media," *Hispania* 30 (1970): 5-68.

Nieto Soria, José Manuel. *Fundamentos ideológicos del poder real en Castilla (Siglos XIII-XVI).* Madrid: Eudema, 1988.

———. "Imágenes religiosas del rey y del poder real en la Castilla del siglo XIII." *En la España medieval* 5.2 (1986): 709-729.

O'Callaghan, Joseph F. *A History of Medieval Spain.* Ithaca: Cornell University, 1975.

———. *The Cortes of Castile-León, 1188-1350.* Philadelphia: University of Pennsylvania, 1989.

———. *The Learned King: The Reign of Alfonso X of Castile.* Philadelphia: University of Pennsylvania, 1993.

———. *The Spanish Military Order of Calatrava and its Affiliates.* London: Variorum 1975.

———. "Don Fernán Pérez, un Maestre desconocido de la Orden de Calatrava, 1234-1235." *Hispania* 43 (1983): 433-439.

———. "*Hermandades* between the Military Orders of Calatrava and Santiago during the Castilian Reconquest, 1158-1252." In *The Spanish Military Order of Calatrava and its Affiliates.* No. 5.

———. "Paths to Ruin: The Economic and Financial Policies of Alfonso the Learned and Their Contribution to His Downfall." In Burns, *Worlds,* 41-67.

———. "The Affiliation of the Order of Calatrava with the Order of Cîteaux." In *The Spanish Military Order of Calatrava and its Affiliates.* No. 1.

———. "The *Cantigas de Santa Maria* as an Historical Source: Two Examples (nos. 321 and 386)." In Katz and Keller, *Studies,* 387-402.

———. "The Cortes and Royal Taxation during the Reign of Alfonso X of Castile." *Traditio* 27 (1971): 379-398.

———. "The Mudéjars of Castile and Portugal in the Twelfth and Thirteenth Centuries." In James M. Powell, ed. *Muslims under Latin Rule, 1110-1300.* Princeton: Princeton University, 1990. 11-56.

Ocasio, Rafael. "Ethnic Underclass Representation in the *Cantigas:* The Black Moro as a Hated Character." In Toscano, ed. *Estudios Alfonsinos.* 183-195.

Ortiz de Zúñiga, Diego. *Anales eclesiásticos y seculares de la muy noble y muy leal ciudad de Sevilla, Metropolí de la Andalucía.* Ed. Antonio María Espinosa y Carzel. 2 vols. Madrid: Imprenta real, 1795; reprint Sevilla: Guadalquivir, 1988.

Paredes Núñez, Juan. "Las Cantigas de Alfonso X como fuentes históricas: La Guerra de Granada." *Cuadernos de Estudios Medievales* 14-15 (1985-1987): 241-250.

Parkinson, Stephen. "The First Reorganization of the *Cantigas de Santa Maria*." *Cantigueiros* 1 (1988): 91-98.

Pelikan, Jaroslav. *The Growth of Medieval Theology (600-1300)* (*The Christian Tradition: A History of the Development of Doctrine,* 3). Chicago: University of Chicago, 1978.

Pérez de Tudela y Velasco, María Isabel. "El tratamiento de la mujer en las Cantigas de Santa Maria." *La condición de la mujer en la Edad Media.* Madrid: Universidad Complutense, 1986. 51-73.

——. "La imagen de la Virgen María en las Cantigas de Santa Maria." *En la España medieval* 15 (1992): 297-320.

Pérez Embid, Florentino. "La marina real castellana en el siglo XIII." *Anuario de Estudios Medievales* 6 (1969): 141-185.

Post, Gaines. *Studies in Medieval Legal Thought: Public Law and the State, 1100-1322.* Princeton: Princeton University, 1964.

Powers, James F. *A Society Organized for War. The Iberian Municipal Militias in the Central Middle Ages, 1000-1284.* Berkeley: University of California, 1988.

Presilla, Maricel. *The Image of Death in the Cantigas de Santa Maria of Alfonso X (1252-84): The Politics of Death and Salvation.* Ph.D. dissertation, New York University, 1989.

——. "The Image of Death and Political Ideology in the *Cantigas de Santa Maria*." In Katz and Keller, *Studies,* 403-458.

Procter, Evelyn. *Alfonso X of Castile. Patron of Literature and Learning.* Oxford: Clarendon, 1951.

——. *Curia and Cortes in León and Castile 1072-1295.* Cambridge: Cambridge University, 1980.

——. *The Judicial Use of Pesquisa (Inquisition) in León and Castile, 1157-1369. English Historical Review,* Supplement 2. London: Longmans, Green, 1966.

Rey, Juan José. "Alfonso X y la música de su época." In *Alfonso X. Toledo 1984.* 103-113.

——. "El trovador don Alfonso X." *Revista de Occidente* 43 (1984): 166-183.

Ribera, Julián. *La música de las Cantigas.* Madrid: Real Academia Española, 1922.

Rivera Recío, Juan Francisco. *San Ildefonso de Toledo. Biografía, época y posteridad.* Madrid: Biblioteca de Autores Cristianos, 1985.

Rodgers, Paula. "Alfonso X Writes to his Son: Reflections on the *Crónica de Alfonso X*." *Exemplaria Hispánica* 1 (1991-1992): 58-79

Rodríguez Díez, Matías. *Historia de la ciudad de Astorga.* 2d ed. Astorga: Porfirio López, 1909.

Rogers, Donna M. "*Cantigas de Santa Maria* 2-25 and their Castilian Versions." In Toscano, ed. *Estudios Alfonsinos.* 196-204.

Roth, Norman. "Two Jewish Courtiers of Alfonso X called Zag (Isaac)." *Sefarad,* 43 (1983): 75-85.

Ruiz, Teófilo. "Images of Power in the Seals of the Castilian Monarchy: 1135-1469." *Estudios en Homenaje a Don Claudio Sánchez Albornoz en sus 90 años* 4 (1986): 455-463.

——. "Une royauté sans sacre: La monarchie castillane du bas moyen âge." *Annales: Économies, Societés, Civilisations* 39 (1984): 429-453.

Runciman, Steven. *A History of the Crusades.* 3 vols. New York: Harper Torchbooks, 1964-1967.

Russell, Jeffrey Burton. *Lucifer. The Devil in the Middle Ages.* Ithaca: Cornell University Press, 1986.

Scarborough, Connie L. *Women in Thirteenth-Century Spain as Portrayed in Alfonso X's* Cantigas de Santa Maria. Lewiston, N.Y.: Edwin Mellen, 1993.

——. "Alfonso X: Monarch in Search of a Miracle." *Romance Quarterly* 33 (1986): 349-354.

Schramm, Percy Ernst. *Las insignias de la realeza en la edad media española.* Madrid: Instituto de Estudios Políticos, 1960.

——. *A History of the English Coronation.* Tr. E. L. Legg. Oxford: Oxford University Press, 1937.

Senniff, Dennis P. "Falconry, Venery, and Fishing in the *Cantigas de Santa Maria*." In Katz and Keller, *Studies,* 459-474.

Snow, Joseph. *The Poetry of Alfonso X el Sabio. A Critical Bibliography.* London: Grant and Cutler, 1977.

——. "A Chapter in Alfonso X's Personal Narrative: The Puerto de Santa María Poems in the Cantigas de Santa Maria." *La Corónica* 8 (1979): 10-21.

——. "Alfonso as Troubadour: The Fact and the Fiction." In Burns, *Emperor of Culture,* 124-140.

——. "Alfonso X como segundo protagonista en sus Cantigas: Ultimas Consideraciones." *Studia Hispánica Medievalia II. III Jornadas de Literatura Española.* Eds. Rosa E. Penna and Maria A. Rosarossa. Buenos Aires: Universidad Católica, 1992. 32-41.

——. "Alfonso X: sus 'Cantigas . . .' Apuntes para su (Auto)biografía literaria." *Joseph Maria Solà-Solé: Homage, Homenaje, Homenatge. Miscelánea de Estudios de Amigos y Discípulos.* Eds. Vitorio Aguera and Nathaniel B. Smith. Barcelona: Puvill, 1984. 79-89.

————. "Alfonso X y/en sus Cantigas," *Jornadas de estudios alfonsíes*. Granada: Universidad de Granada, 1985. 71-90.

————. "Alfonso X y la Cantiga 409: Un nexo posible con la tradición de la *Danza de la Muerte*." *Studies in Honor of Lloyd A. Kasten*. Madison: Hispanic Seminary of Medieval Studies, 1975. 261-273.

————. "Gonzalo de Berceo and the Miracle of Saint Ildefonso: Portrait of a Medieval Artist at Work." *Hispania* 65 (1982): 1-11.

————. "Lo que nos dice la Cantiga 300 de Alfonso X." *Studia Hispánica Medievalia. II Jornadas de Literatura Española*. Eds. L. Teresa Valdivieseo and Jorge H. Valdivieso. Buenos Aires: Universidad Católica, 1988. 99-110.

————. "'Macar poucos cantares acabei e con son': La firma de Alfonso X a sus Cantigas de Santa Maria." *Actas del III Congreso de la Asociación Hispánica de Literatura Medieval. (Salamanca 3-8 Octubre 1989)*. Ed. M. I. Toro Pascua. Salamanca: Biblioteca española del Siglo XV. Departamento de Literatura Española e Hispanoamericana, 1990. 3:1021-1030.

————. "Poetic Self-Awareness in Alfonso X's *Cantiga* 110." *Kentucky Romance Quarterly* 26 (1979): 421-432.

————. "Self-Conscious References and the Organic Narrative Pattern of the *Cantigas de Santa Maria* of Alfonso X." In Joseph R. Jones, ed. *Medieval, Renaissance and Folklore Studies in Honor of John Esten Keller*. Newark, Del.: Juan de la Cuesta, 1980. 53-65.

————. "The Central Role of the Troubadour Persona of Alfonso X in the *Cantigas de Santa Maria*," *Bulletin of Hispanic Studies* 56 (1979): 305-316.

————. "The Satirical Poetry of Alfonso X: A Look at its Relationship to the '*Cantigas de Santa Maria*'." In Márquez-Villanueva and Vega, eds. *Alfonso X of Castile*, 110-131.

Socarras, Cayetano. *Alfonso X of Castile: A Study on Imperialistic Frustration*. Barcelona: Ediciones Hispam, 1976.

Solalinde, Antonio García. "El códice florentino de las Cantigas y su relación con los demás manuscritos." *Revista de Filología española* 5 (1918): 143-179.

Tinnell, Roger D. *An Annotated Discography of Music in Spain before 1650*. Madison: Hispanic Seminary of Medieval Studies, 1980.

Torres Balbás, Leopoldo. "La mezquita de al-Qanatir y el santuario de Alfonso el Sabio en el Puerto de Santa María." *Al-Andalus* 8 (1942): 417-437. Reprint in *Obra Dispersa. Al-Andalus. Crónica de la España musulmana*. 2 vols. Madrid: Instituto de España, 1982. 2:149-171.

Torres Delgado, Cristóbal. *El antiguo reino nazarí de Granada (1232-1340)*. Granada: Anel, 1974.

Torres Fontes, Juan. "La Orden de Santa María de España." *Miscelánea Medieval Murciana* 3 (1977): 75-118.

Toscano, Nicolás, ed. *Estudios Alfonsinos y otros escritos*. New York: National Endowment for the Humanities and National Hispanic Foundation for the Humanities, 1991.

Trivison, Mary Louise. "A Pilgrim Poem of the Marqués de Santillana: Resumé of Medieval Marian Lyric." In Toscano, *Estudios Alfonsinos*, 246-253.

Ullmann, Walter. *Principles of Government and Politics in the Middle Ages*. New York: Barnes and Noble, 1966.

Walmisley-Santiago, Olga. "Alfonso el Sabio's Attitude towards Moors and Jews as Revealed in Two of his Works." *Cantigueiros* 6 (1994): 30-41.

Williams, John. *Early Spanish Manuscript Illumination*. New York: George Braziller, 1977.

————. *The Illustrated Beatus. A Corpus of Illustrations of the Commentary on the Apocalypse*, 5 vols. London: Harvey Miller, 1994-1996.

Joseph F. O'Callaghan (essay date 1998)

SOURCE: O'Callaghan, Joseph F. "The Idea of Kingship." In *Alfonso X and the* Cantigas de Santa Maria, pp. 59-83. Leiden, The Netherlands: Brill, 1998.

[*In the following excerpt, O'Callaghan explores Alfonso's ideas on kingship based on references in the* Cantigas.]

THE ROYAL INTITULATION

The ***Cantigas de Santa Maria*** offer important insights (both literary and visual) into Alfonso X's conception of his office as king that complement the ideas presented in the ***Espéculo*** and the ***Siete Partidas***.[1] Prologue A, which identifies the king and records his titles, provides us with the first evidence in this regard.[2] Each title prompts our reflection on the historical past of the Crown of Castile-León and King Alfonso's participation in it.

> *Don Affonso de Castela,*
> *de Toledo, de Leon*
> *Rey e ben des Conpostela*
> *ta o reyno d' Aragon,*
>
> *De Cordova, de Jahen,*
> *de Sevilla outrossi*
> *e de Murça, u gran ben*
> *lle fez Deus, com aprendi,*

*Do Algarve, que gãou
de mouros e nossa ffe
meteu y, e ar pobrou
Badallouz, que reyno é*

*Muit' antigu', e que tolleu
a mouros Nevl' e Xerez,
Beger, Medina prendeu
e Alcala d' outra vez,*

*E que dos Romãos Rey
é per dereit' e Sennor,
este livro, com'achei
fez a onrr' e a loor*

*Da Virgen Santa Maria,
que éste Madre de Deus,
en que ele muito fia.
Poren dos miragres seus*

*Fezo cantares e sões,
saborosos de cantar,
todos de sennas razões,
com' y podedes achar.*

Don Alfonso of Castile,
of Toledo and León,
King, indeed from Compostela
to the kingdom of Aragón,

Of Córdoba and Jaén
and of Seville also
and of Murcia where God did
him a great good, as I learned,

Of the Algarve, which he won
from the Moors and there
established our faith and
populated Badajoz,

Which is a most ancient
kingdom, and who took from
the Moors Niebla and Jerez;
and seized Vejer, Medina and
Alcalá another time,

And who is King and Lord
of the Romans by right;
he made this book, as I found,
to the honor and praise

Of the Virgin Holy Mary
who is the Mother of God
in whom he trusts greatly.
Wherefore of her miracles

he made canticles and songs
sweet to sing
all with their own themes
as you may discover.

This intitulation, reflecting the historical reality of the multiplicity of Alfonso X's dominions, underlines the fact that the unity of his realms was very difficult to

achieve. This was not a single, unified kingdom, but rather a collection of eight, namely, Castile, Toledo, León, Córdoba, Jaén, Seville, Murcia, and the Algarve. By listing them all King Alfonso was surely boasting a bit, as indeed he was when he emphasized that his realms stretched from Compostela in the north-west to the kingdom of Aragón in the northeast. The list also points up the fact that each of these kingdoms was conquered at a different time. The formula used is not precisely that of the royal charters, nor is it identical with the intitulation in other compilations from the royal *scriptorium*, but it does enable us to date the prologue within reasonable limits.[3]

The three most important kingdoms were Castile, Toledo and León. Castile and León were the old Christian kingdoms of the north, whose origin could be traced to Asturias, the birthplace of the reconquest. Toledo, famed as the seat of the Visigothic monarchy, emerged as a petty Islamic kingdom or *taifa* after the fall of the caliphate of Córdoba in 1031. Alfonso VI of León-Castile conquered it in 1085.[4] In his earliest charters Alfonso X used the same intitulation as his father, Fernando III, identifying himself as king of Castile, Toledo, León and Galicia.[5] This formula derived from two sources. Fernando III combined the titles employed by his grandfather Alfonso VIII, king of Castile and Toledo, and by his father Alfonso IX, king of León and Galicia.[6] The towns in the assembly of León in 1345 raised the issue of precedence in the royal intulation when they asked Alfonso XI (1312-1350) to place León before Toledo. He agreed that León should have precedence, save in charters issued to Toledo itself.[7]

Fernando III conquered the next three kingdoms in his intitulation, Córdoba, Jaén, and Seville, in 1236, 1246, and 1248 respectively.[8] He sent his son, the then Infante Alfonso, to receive the homage of the Moorish king of Murcia and to take possession there in 1243-1244. Thus Murcia was really Alfonso's conquest. Quite possibly the "great good" mentioned by the poet may not mean the initial submission of Murcia to Infante Alfonso but rather its reconquest by his father-in-law, Jaime I of Aragón, in January 1266 after the revolt of the Mudé-jars. If that be so, then Prologue A should be dated after that date.[9]

Next comes the Algarve "which he won from the Moors and where he established our faith." The Algarve did not appear in Fernando III's intitulation nor in that of Alfonso X until March 1261. Although the Algarve today refers to the southernmost province of Portugal, there was some ambiguity concerning its usage in the thirteenth century. I believe that Alfonso X intended it to mean the tributary kingdom ruled by Ibn Maḥfūt and centered at Niebla. In ***CSM*** [***Cantigas de Santa Maria***]

183, when relating a miracle that occurred at Faro in the Portuguese Algarve, the poet stated that Ibn Maḥfūt, a brave man in war and peace, held the kingdom there.[10] Soon after his accession Alfonso X challenged Portuguese claims to the Algarve. By a settlement concluded in 1253 Afonso III of Portugal (1248-1279) conceded usufruct of the Algarve to the king of Castile for life. In 1267 Alfonso X restored all his rights there to Portugal. Even so the Algarve continued to figure in the royal intitulation for the remainder of his reign.[11]

Prologue A also stated that Alfonso X populated the very ancient kingdom of Badajoz. This was one of the eleventh century *taifas* occupied by Alfonso IX of León in 1230. His death soon after made it impossible for him to settle the kingdom which seems to have been sparsely populated in the time of Fernando III.[12] Fear of Portuguese designs in the adjoining frontier region likely prompted Alfonso X to visit Badajoz in November 1252 and to initiate repopulation. His charter of 20 January 1253 reveals the existence of a municipal council which complained that the Jews of Badajoz refused to pay the tribute known as *oncenas.* Another royal charter addressed to the council and *alcaldes* of Badajoz on 18 January 1254 indicates that municipal government was already in place. At that time the king prohibited any ecclesiastical institution from acquiring lands there to the prejudice of royal rights. In the following year on 18 May he authorized Badajoz to hold a fair at Eastertime.[13] After defining the municipal district on 31 March 1255 he also caused the establishment of a bishopric there and facilitated the construction of a cathedral.[14]

Next Prologue A tells us that the king took Niebla, Jerez, Vejer, Medina, and Alcalá from the Moors.[15] The royal chronicle also affirms that Niebla, where Ibn Maḥfūt ruled in vassalage to Castile, was the chief seat of the Algarve. Besieged in 1261, Niebla surrendered in February 1262.[16] Jerez de la Frontera, Vejer de la Frontera, and Medina Sidonia had acknowledged Fernando III's sovereignty after the fall of Seville, but they rebelled against Alfonso X in 1264 and did not submit to him again until two years later in October 1266.[17] The royal chronicle makes no mention of Alcalá in this connection and it is not certain which Alcalá the author of the prologue had in mind. Alcalá de los Gazules, directly east of Medina Sidonia, was probably intended.

After listing all these kingdoms, the Prologue then tells us that Alfonso was by right "King and Lord of the Romans"—*"dos Romãos rey é per dereit' e Sennor."* One faction among the German princes had elected him to the Holy Roman Empire in 1257. According to German imperial custom, the one elected was called *rex Romanorum* or king of the Romans until he was

crowned by the pope; then he was entitled emperor of the Romans. As Alfonso X was never crowned by the pope, he never called himself emperor, nor did he use the title "king of the Romans" in his Castilian chancery documents; he only did so in his Latin correspondence with the pope and with his German and Italian supporters.[18] Aside from the mention of the title "king of the Romans" here, the *Cantigas* are sparing in their use of imperial terminology. Nor do they argue for the superiority of Rome and the Roman people. Indeed the only three Roman emperors mentioned by name are Octavian, also called Augustus, Nero, and Julian the Apostate; neither of the latter two enjoyed the esteem of Christian Europe.[19] *CSM* 5 tells the story of Beatriz, Empress of Rome, whose husband (the poet confesses that he does not know his name) went off on crusade to Jerusalem. During the emperor's absence of two and a half years in Acre, his brother vainly attempted to seduce the empress. One might be tempted to identify the emperor as Frederick Barbarossa who in 1156 married Beatrix, the heiress to Burgundy and Provence; however, he died in 1190 during the Third Crusade without ever reaching Acre. Beatrix became the mother of Philip of Swabia and so was the grandmother of Fernando III's Queen Beatriz.[20] The imperial title was used most often to describe Mary as Empress of heaven.[21]

Only in *CSM* 409 do we find any allusion suggestive of King Alfonso's imperial aspirations. Here kings and emperors are paired in their common obligation to praise Mary because through her they are lords of all the people—*"Reis e emperadores . . . ca per ela sennores son de toda a gente"* (36-42). This linkage of kings and emperors is similar to that of Alfonso X's great law code, the *Siete Partidas,* which was begun soon after his imperial election with the evident purpose of illustrating his new status as emperor-elect.[22] The *Partidas* (2,1,8) affirmed that "kings have the same [powers] in their kingdoms and even greater ones" than "all those powers that we listed above which the emperors have and ought to have over the people of their empire." Indeed the royal power was greater because it derived from his hereditary right whereas that of the emperor came through election.[23]

On the basis of the foregoing, I think one may date Prologue A after October 1266 when Alfonso X recovered possession of Jerez, Vejer, Medina Sidonia, and Alcalá de los Gazules. The compilation of the first one hundred *cantigas* can probably be placed after that date as well.[24]

IMAGES OF THE KING

Depictions of the king and of royal symbols in the miniatures of the *Cantigas* offer visual testimony to his conception of kingship.[25] In the **Siete Partidas** (2,5,5), Alfonso X commented on the need for the king to maintain a distinctive dress and appearance:

> Dress enables one to recognize men as nobles or non-nobles. The ancient wisemen established that kings should wear garments of silk with gold and precious stones, so that men might recognize them immediately when they see them and not have to ask for them. When they go riding, they ought also to wear spurs and saddles of gold and silver and precious stones. When they hold their cortes on great feast days they should wear crowns of gold with very noble and richly worked stones. . . . They ought to wear all these honorable adornments at appropriate times and ought to use them suitably.[26]

In the miniature illustrating Prologue B (fol. 5 r) of Escorial MS T.I.1, the clean-shaven king, with brown shoulder-length hair, is seated on a chair on a platform and is looking at a book on a desk to his left. Musicians and scribes surround him. With a golden crown on his head, he has a red cloak over his shoulders and wears a long blue tunic (with a gold border around the neck) reaching to the shoes on his feet; his stockings are red.[27] In Prologue A (fol. 5 v) of MS T.I.1, he is shown in much the same manner, holding a long scroll in his hand, while his scribes, with scrolls in their hands, are seated about him. *CSM* 169 (panel 2) portrays him as Infante, wearing a biretta or square cap divided into sections showing castles and lions, the symbols of Castile and León that also appear on the royal seals and coins.[28] Panel 4 depicts him as a crowned King, seated on a chair covered with a cloth in a similar pattern of castles and lions. The principal difference between him and Jaime I of Aragón who appears in the opposite panel is that the latter is shown as an older man with white hair and beard. In many of the *cantares de loor,* King Alfonso appears standing, wearing a blue robe with a mantle of red or blue and a golden crown on his head. In ten of fourteen portrayals of the king he is clean shaven; he wears a beard in only four. Cómez Ramos believes that an attempt was made in the **Cantigas** to establish an official portrait of a youthful king.[29]

The miniatures in the Florentine codex (Banco Rari 20) also reveal the king, again unbearded, wearing a golden crown encrusted with precious stones, and dressed in a long robe and mantle. In *CSM* 95 in the Florentine codex (Mettmann 209), one of the most famous *cantigas,* we see him lying in bed wearing his crown; a pattern of castles and lions appears on his pillow and the border of the bedsheet.[30]

In the **Libro de ajedrez** King Alfonso is also seated, wearing his crown and a long all-encompassing tunic patterned into castles and lions. Both the *Lapidario* and the *General Estoria* (fol. 2) portray him seated with a crown on his head and holding a book in his hands. In the latter illustration the chair is somewhat more elaborate and even resembles a sort of altar.[31]

The manuscript of the *Primera Partida* in the British Library (Add. MSS 20787, fol. 1) presents a slightly different view.[32] The king, bearded and crowned and wearing a long tunic and a cloak, is seated on a raised chair covered with a cloth. In his right hand he bears a sword and in his left a book, presumably a book of the laws. Behind his left shoulder are mitred bishops. Seated to his right and left are various figures who are probably magnates, clergy, and courtiers, while at his feet are seated many persons who probably represent the people of the realm. This royal pose is reminiscent of the Emperor Justinian's statement in the prologue to the *Institutes* that "imperial majesty ought to be adorned not only by arms but also by laws" in order to rule effectively.[33]

Portraits of the king in manuscripts not composed in the royal *scriptorium* offer some variations. In the *Tumbo de Tojos Outos* he and Queen Violante and their son are seated on chairs with curving arms; the king wears a crown and holds a sword in his hand. Tumbo A of the Cathedral of Santiago shows a bearded king mounted on horseback, wearing a crown and bearing a shield quartered with castles and lions, and with spurs on his feet, but without a sword or armor. This is comparable to the mounted and crowned figure of the king that appears on the great seal of Alfonso X from 1255. The king has a sword in one hand and bears a shield quartered with castles and lions; castles and lions also appear on the covering of his horse and on the obverse of the seal.[34]

In the votive statue in the *capilla mayor* of the cathedral of Toledo the king is standing, wearing a long tunic and cloak, with a crown on his head, a scepter mounted by an eagle in his right hand and a sword in his left hand. The statues of Alfonso X and Violante in the cloister of the cathedral of Burgos present him with a crown, and dressed in a tunic and a cloak. According to a description of the royal tombs in the cathedral of Seville written in 1345 the effigy of King Alfonso wore a golden crown set with precious stones; in his right hand was a silver scepter with an imperial eagle on top and in his left hand a golden apple or orb surmounted by a cross.[35]

Alfonso X's imperial ambitions are illustrated in the stained glass windows in the cathedral of León whose construction was initiated about 1255 and proceeded apace during his reign and under his patronage.[36] The windows in the north choir of the cathedral depict the king, crowned and mounted on horseback, with a globe in hand, while one of his knights bears a standard and a shield with the castles and lions of Castile and León.

Another knight carries a green and yellow standard and a shield with the eagle of Swabia. In the rose windows above one sees the shields of Castile and León and the eagle of Swabia as well as a lion rampant symbolizing León. In the lower level of the stained glass window in the central nave the bearded and crowned king, standing between Pope Gregory X and Bishop Martín Fernández (1254-1289), carries in his right hand a scepter with the imperial eagle and in his left a globe of the world topped by a cross. Wheels surrounding the castles of Castile cover his red mantle.[37]

THE SYMBOLS OF KINGSHIP

The symbols of kingship illustrated in the *Cantigas* and in the other miniatures, statues, and windows mentioned above include the crown, the throne, the sword of justice, the scepter of command, and the imperial eagle.[38] It is a great misfortune that scarcely any of the regalia of the medieval Castilian kings have survived.[39] Nevertheless Diego Ortiz de Zúñiga reported that in 1579 when the tomb of Alfonso X was opened "a sword, scepter, crown, and staff of emperor (*baculo de emperador*)" were found; nevertheless at some time thereafter these symbols of sovereignty seem to have been removed.[40]

In the portraits of the king derived from the royal *scriptorium* the most consistent symbol of royalty is his crown. The crown is ordinarily gold in color with floral decorations (usually four) rising from the circlet and is often set with precious stones.[41] Abandoned by his family and fellow monarchs, Alfonso X in 1282 gave his crown in pledge to the Benimerines of Morocco in return for a loan of 100,000 gold dinars. Ibn Khaldūn (d. 1406) reported that the crown was still in the royal palace in Marrakech, but it seems to have disappeared since then.[42] Alfonso X had other crowns as appears from his last will in which he bequeathed to his heir "the crowns with stones and with cameos and with jewels."[43] Just such a crown was found in the sepulcher of Sancho IV (1284-1295) in the cathedral of Toledo. It is composed of eight silver rectangular plaques, each surmounted by a castle; sapphires alternated with cameos in each of the plaques. The absence of lions symbolic of León suggests that this crown may have been used by Alfonso VIII of Castile.[44] Speaking of different types of crowns in his *Libro de los castigos*, Sancho IV commented that "the first crown of gold set with precious stones is called the crown of honor. And kings and emperors wear this on their heads."[45]

The royal throne that appears in several of the miniatures is a rather simple chair or bench, without a back, raised on a slight platform. One can scarcely dignify the chair by calling it a throne.[46] Indeed in *CSM* 169 the Moorish king of Murcia is seated on a more elaborate throne than either of the Christian monarchs of Castile or Aragón. The statue of Fernando III built over his tomb in the cathedral of Seville, according to *CSM* 292.58-59, was seated on a chair (*cadeira*) covered with silver rather than a throne and bore a sword in hand, the sword that struck down Muhammad—"*con que deu colbe a Mafomete mortal.*"

The sword, a symbol of the king's responsibility to maintain his people in justice, was usually carried before him as a sign of his authority. In the miniatures in the *Cantigas* King Alfonso appears most often holding a book in hand, and never a sword. Nevertheless, the British Library codex of the *Primera Partida* and the *Tumbo de Tojos Outos* (which was not composed in the royal *scriptorium*), the statue in the cathedral of Toledo, and the great seal show him with a sword in hand.[47]

The scepter topped by an imperial eagle which the king holds in his hand in the stained glass windows of León, in the Toledan statue, and in the royal sepulcher, as well the orb, globe, or apple symbolized Alfonso X's status as emperor-elect. Imperial eagles also appear on the king's mantle in *CSM* 90. Sancho IV compared to the staff of Moses "the scepters that kings and emperors hold in their right hands when they are crowned."[48]

The clothing in which the *Cantigas* portray King Alfonso seems simple in form, but clearly was richly made and decorated with the intent of emphasizing the difference between his royal condition and that of his people. Menéndez Pidal made the point that the garments depicted are identical with those found in royal entombments. For example, the king's dress in *CSM* 100 (panels 1-2)—a blue tunic and a mantle entirely divided into squares of castles and lions—is the same as that in which the body of Fernando III was buried. Similarly the mantle in which Alfonso X was interred, a vestment richly embroidered in gold, silver and silk, with a pattern of castles and lions, and the imperial eagle, matches several miniatures.[49]

In the *Libro de los castigos* Alfonso X's son and successor Sancho IV described the accoutrements of a king whom he said he had seen. That king wore a golden crown set with rubies, emeralds, and sapphires, each of which symbolized the royal virtues of fear of God, true belief, good habits, benignity, chastity, knowledge, and memory. Dressed in cloth of gold and silk set with jewels and precious stones, the king wore golden armlets, and sat on a seat covered with gold, silver and precious stones; a footstool was before him. In his right hand he held a sword "to display the justice in which [the king] ought to maintain his people." In his left hand was a golden apple surmounted by a cross symbolizing the kingdom. A servant stood before him with a book of laws to enable the king "to render to each one his law and his deserts." Another held a scepter which was used to punish the wicked. This is obviously an idealized picture of a medieval king and is not matched exactly by any of the portrayals of Alfonso X. Nevertheless it does suggest something of contemporary ideas of the most solemn ceremonial dress of a king.[50]

As anyone who has read the **Espéculo** and the **Siete Partidas** can testify, Alfonso X had an exalted sense of majesty, such as that presented in the *Libro de los castigos*.[51] Although the learned king occasionally is represented bearing sword, scepter, or shield, the various royal portrayals in the **Cantigas** reveal a simplicity that underscores the essentially secular nature of Castilian kingship.

THE SECULAR CHARACTER OF THE MONARCHY

When one speaks of the secular character of the Castilian monarchy, one does not mean that it was irreligious or hostile to religion or lacking a spiritual element. One has only to read the preambles to royal charters of the twelfth and thirteenth centuries and to take into account the numerous royal donations to bishoprics and monasteries and to read the *Primera* and the *Segunda Partidas* to understand that the kings of Castile-León— kings by the grace of God—believed that the promotion of true religion was one of their paramount obligations. Individual monarchs expressed their religious devotion in various ways: Alfonso VIII and Queen Leonor by the foundation of the monastery of Las Huelgas; Alfonso IX by undertaking the pilgrimage to Santiago de Compostela; Fernando III by dedicating his life to the religious war against Islam that eventually gained him the honors of sainthood; and Alfonso X by the **Cantigas de Santa Maria.** In sum the kings of Castile-León were no less devout in their religious life and practice than any of their contemporaries.[52]

Nevertheless, Castilian kingship did not have the sacramental or priestly character ascribed to monarchy in England and France as a consequence of anointing and coronation.[53] In the northern realms the coronation ceremony was patterned after the consecration of a bishop and the vials of oil used in the royal anointing were supposedly brought from heaven; by virtue of anointing kings were raised to priestly or near-priestly rank and were said to be endowed with the power to heal scrofula.[54]

By contrast the rites concerning the accession of the Castilian kings were quite simple, consisting essentially of acclamation by the assembled prelates, nobles, and people, and an oath of allegiance. One finds scattered references to the anointing of the kings of Asturias-León in the ninth, tenth, and early eleventh centuries, as

well as to the imperial self-coronation of Alfonso VII in 1135. Yet the custom of anointing did not survive into the late twelfth and thirteenth centuries.[55] Unlike the northern European rulers, neither Alfonso VIII of Castile, Fernando II (1157-1188) and Alfonso IX of León, Fernando III, nor Alfonso X were crowned and anointed with holy oil.[56] Also unlike the archbishops of Rheims and Canterbury who anointed and crowned the kings of France and England respectively, neither the archbishop of Toledo, the primate of Spain, nor the archbishop of Santiago, guardian of the tomb of the Apostle St. James, ever anointed or crowned any of the late twelfth- or thirteenth-century Castilian or Leonese rulers. At the end of the thirteenth century the French theologian, John of Paris, commented on this divergent custom by noting that the kings of Spain (that is, of Castile-León) were not anointed.[57]

Ballesteros and Mondéjar before him described in some detail the coronation of Alfonso X at Seville in 1252, but the documentary evidence does not bear them out.[58] We know only that he was raised to the kingship and that he assumed the status of knighthood when his father was buried in the cathedral there on 1 June 1252.[59] More than likely Alfonso X crowned himself two years later at Toledo, as the poet Gil Pérez Conde implied when he reminded the king of past services:

> *Ben sabedes, senhor Rei,*
> *des que fui vosso vassalo,*
> *que sempre vos aguardei*
> *quer a pee quer de cavalo,*
> *sen voss' aver e sen dõa;*
> *mais atanto vos errei:*
> *non foi vosco en ora bõa.*
>
> *E en terra de Campou*
> *vos servei e en Olmedo*
> *assi fiz en Badalhou*
> *e outrossi en Toledo*
> *quand' i filhastes corõa;*
> *mais atanto me mengou*
> *non fui vosco en ora bõa.*[60]

> Well you know, my Lord King
> ever since I was your vassal
> that I always defended you
> whether on foot or on horse
> without your pay or gift
> but I failed you in this:
> I was not with you in good hour.
>
> In Tierra de Campos
> I served you and in Olmedo.
> I did so too in Badajoz
> And also in Toledo
> when you took the crown there;
> but I failed in this
> I was not with you in good hour.

The instance cited by the poet "in Toledo, when you took the crown there" is undated, but I think the king may very well have taken advantage of the assembly of the Cortes in Toledo in March-April 1254 to crown himself.[61] That was the occasion of his first visit to his native city after his accession to the throne. The importance of Toledo in his thinking is emphasized by the fact that **CSM** 2 recounts how the Virgin Mary gave St. Ildefonsus, the seventh-century archbishop of Toledo whose name Alfonso X bore—"*primado foi d'Espanna e Affons'era chamado*"—a vestment brought from Paradise.[62] As the king himself stated in 1274, when transferring the remains of the Visigothic King Wamba (672-680) to the city on the Tagus, Toledo was also the *cabeza de España*, "where anciently the emperors were crowned;" that was a reference to the Visigothic ascendancy over all of Spain and the claims of their medieval heirs, the rulers of Asturias-León-Castile, to be emperors of Spain.[63] After the Visigothic kings accepted orthodox Christianity at the end of the sixth century, the custom of royal anointing came into use, but none of them employed the title of emperor. Alfonso VI, who conquered Toledo in 1085, described himself as *imperator toletanus*—emperor of Toledo—but there is no record that he was crowned there.[64]

The possibility that Alfonso X crowned himself in Toledo is also suggested by the fact that his son, Sancho IV, after being acclaimed at Avila, hastened to Toledo where he received the crown in late April or early May 1284. The *Royal Chronicle* related that he was crowned by the bishops of Burgos, Cuenca, Coria, and Badajoz.[65] According to Jofré de Loaysa, Sancho IV declared that all his successors should also receive the crown there.[66] Fernando IV (1295-1312) was acclaimed in the cathedral of Toledo in 1295 and may have received the crown at that time, in accordance with his father's wishes, but there is no explicit evidence to that effect.[67] Alfonso XI, on the other hand, crowned himself at Las Huelgas de Burgos in 1332. Of all these kings, he was the only one known to have been anointed, not by the primate of Toledo, but by the archbishop of Compostela.[68] Juan I who crowned himself and his wife at Las Huelgas in 1379, was the last medieval king of Castile whose coronation was recorded.[69] Not until Charles V is there any further mention of a king being anointed and crowned.

THE ROYAL TOUCH

The reluctance of the kings of Castile to imitate their fellows north of the Pyrenees by adopting some of the symbols and trappings of sacred monarchy is well illustrated in **CSM** 321.[70] This is the story of a young girl from Córdoba who was healed of a severe illness by Holy Mary. The refrain reminds us that "the Virgin in a short time will cure the person who may never, or only after a long time, be cured by medicine"—"*O que mui tarde ou nunca / se pode por meeza sãar, en mui pouco tempo / guarez' a Santa Reynna*" (3-4). Indeed whatever the physician orders the sick person to do to regain health takes a long time, but Holy Mary through her great power heals quickly.

The story has it that the Córdoban girl suffered for three years from an affliction in her throat, called *lanparones*, a tumor of some sort, or scrofula:

> *Esta de Cordova era natural, e padecia*
> *enfermedade mui forte que na garganta avia,*
> *a que chaman lanparões, que é maa maloutia;*
> *e passara ja tres anos que esta door tiinna*
>
> (10-13).

The poor girl's mother vainly sought for a physician who could cure her, but none was able to do so, nor was the medicine they gave her of any use. The mother, who had spent 500 *maravedís* or more, despaired of ever seeing her daughter whole again:

> *Sa madre con coita dela, en tal que lla ben guarissen,*
> *non catou de dar a meges todo quanto lle pedissen,*
> *nen a fisicos da terra, rogando-lles que a vissen,*
> *e maravedis quinentos ou mais lles deu a mesqa.*
>
> *Mais eles, por nulla cousa que lles desse, non poderon*
> *sãa-la, nen prol lles ouve quanta fisica fezeron;*
> *pero todo-los deiros que ela lles deu ouveron,*
> *assi que a moller bõa ficou en cona espynna*
>
> (15-24).

Here we come to the critical part of the story. Just as the mother found herself at wit's end, not knowing what to do, a good man advised her to take her daughter to the king and tell him her story:

> *A moller con esta coita non sabia que fezesse*
> *e do aver e da filla que consello y presesse;*
> *mas enton ũu ome bõo conssellou-lle que dissesse*
> *est' al Rei e lla levasse, ca pera el convũa*
>
> (25-28).

The man said to her:

> *Ai, moller bõa, se Nostro Sennor m'ajude,*
> *todo-los reis crischãos an aquesto por vertude*
> *que sol que pon[n]an sas mãos sobre tal door, saude an*
>
> (30-33).

Good woman, may Our Lord help me,
all Christian kings have the power to heal this
malady merely by placing their hands on it.

He urged her to set out the next day and promised to accompany her to explain the girl's situation to the king. He assured the mother that once the king heard the tale, he would hasten to help her:

E poren vos consello que sejades mannana
Ant' el Rey, e yrei logo vosco, se Deus me defenda
de mal, e de vossa filla lle contarei a fazenda;
e des que llo ouver dito ben sei logo sen contenda
que el Rei por sa mercee vos acorrerá agynna

(33-38).

The good man related the story to the king, who surprised them, however, by his reply:

Amigo,
a esto que me dizedes vos respond' assi e digo
que o que me consellades sol non val un mui mal figo,
pero que falades muito e toste com' andora.
Ca dizedes que vertude ei, dizedes neicidade

(40-45).

My friend, in response to what you tell me, I say
that what you advise me is not even worth a very bad
　fig;
but you talk a lot and chatter like a swallow.
When you say that I have this power, you are talking
　nonsense.

Telling the man to be quiet and to do what he was commanded, the king said that he would take the girl before the image of the Virgin Mary wrapped in a red mantle:

mais fazed' agora tanto eu direi, e vos calade,
e levarey a minynna ant' a bela Magestade
da Virgen que é envolta ena purpura sangua

(46-48).

Once mass was said they should wash the face and body of the image of the Virgin and her Son with pure water. The girl should drink that water from the chalice on the altar where God's blood was made from the wine of the vineyard:

E pois for a missa dita, lávena da agua mui crara
a ela e a seu Fillo todo o corp' e a cara,
e beva-o a menynna do calez que sobr' a ara
está, u se faz o sangui de Deus do vo da va

(50-53).

Giving instructions that the girl should drink from the chalice for five days, one for each letter of the name *María,* the king guaranteed that the little shepherdess would be fully healed by the fifth day:

E beva-a tantos dias quantas letras son achadas
eno nome de Maria escritas e feguradas;
e assi no dia quinto serán todas acabadas,
e desta enfermidade guarrá log' a pastora

(55-58).

Indeed on the fourth day the girl was healed in her arm and her throat and restored to full health, without, concludes the poet, having to drink syrup or to have a tub bath:

Esto foi feit'; e a moça a quatro dias guarida
foi do braç' e da garganta pola Sennor que dá vida
aos que aman seu Fillo, e tal saude conprida
ouve sen bever sarope nen aver ban[n]o de ta

(60-63).

This story is one of two instances that I know of in the history of medieval Castile concerning the phenomenon of the royal touch, the supposed ability of the king to cure the disease of scrofula simply by placing his hand upon it. In the story, the girl evidently had a type of tumor associated with tuberculosis in her throat or neck and another in her arm. Although the king was not identified, it seems obvious that he was Alfonso X. The distinguished French historian, Marc Bloch, in his study of the royal healing power pointed out that the idea that the king could heal the sick by his very touch first appeared in the tenth century with King Robert the Pious of France (996-1031). With his grandson Philip I (1060-1108), the royal healing power was specifically described as the power to cure scrofula, which came to be called "the king's evil." In England Henry I (1100-1135) was probably the first king to claim this power, though to give the claim greater authority, he attributed its origin to the saintly King Edward the Confessor (1042-1066).[71]

The healing power illustrated the sacred and quasi-priestly character of kingship, a character received when the king was anointed with holy oil by the archbishop of Rheims (France) or the archbishop of Canterbury (England). The attribution of such a power to the king exalted him above the ranks of ordinary mortals. The twelfth-century writer Peter of Blois made this clear when he said:

I would have you know that to attend upon the king is
(for a cleric) something sacred, for the king himself is
holy; he is the Anointed of the Lord; it is not in vain
that he has received the sacrament of royal unction,
whose efficacy—if someone should chance to be
ignorant of it or doubt it—would be amply proved by
the disappearance of that plague affecting the groin and
by the healing of scrofula.[72]

In *CSM* 321 we have the first mention of the royal healing power in the Iberian peninsula.[73] More than likely the intermarriages between the Castilian, French, and English royal houses as well as general improvements in communication with northern Europe helped to disseminate this idea in Spain. As we know, Leonor, the wife of Alfonso VIII of Castile was the daughter of King Henry II of England, who is reported to have exercised the royal touch. Alfonso VIII's daughter, Blanche of Castile, married King Louis VIII of France (1223-1226) and was the mother of St. Louis IX (1226-1270), Alfonso X's contemporary and first cousin once removed. Alfonso X's half sister, Leonor, in 1254 married the future King Edward I of England (1272-1307) and Alfonso's oldest son and heir, Fernando de la Cerda, married Louis IX's daughter Blanche in 1269. In view of all this it is hardly surprising that the royal healing power should be known in the Castilian court in the thirteenth century.[74] An early fourteenth century coronation *ordo* apparently drawn up for Alfonso XI also alludes to this power. Through anointing "kings receive such power that they live in God's service and work miracles during their lives of the so-called malady of kings . . . because God grants kings a more distinct favor than others." The text does not claim, however, that any Castilian king had exercised the healing power.[75]

What is surprising is that Alfonso X, when offered an opportunity to employ the healing power and thus impress his people with a miracle, refused to do so and dismissed as foolishness the very thought that a king could cure by his touch. To understand this, we have to emphasize that the Castilian monarchy of the twelfth and thirteenth centuries did not have the near-priestly character claimed by the French and English kings. As already mentioned, the kings of Castile-León, contrary to the northern rulers, were not crowned and anointed by a prelate. The accession of the Castilian monarch was celebrated by secular ceremonies and no claims to miraculous powers were put forward on his behalf.

Even so, Alfonso X was very much concerned about the attributes of kingship, as a careful reading of his *Espéculo* and *Siete Partidas* reveals.[76] There we are told that the king is the soul of the people who live through him; he is the head of his kingdom, and the bond of unity linking his people in one body (*Espéculo*, 2,1,1,4; *Partidas*, 2,1,5; 2,15,5). The king holds the place of God on earth in order to do justice in temporal matters and whoever assaults or lays hands upon him offends directly against God (*Espéculo*, 2,1,5-6; *Partidas*, 2,1,1). The king has no temporal superior, and like the emperor, he can make laws (*Espéculo*, 1,1,13). From these and other texts, it is clear that Alfonso X saw himself as having received his power from God, to whom he was responsible, but there was no authority on earth, neither that of the pope nor of the emperor, that was over him in temporal affairs.[77]

Alfonso X's repudiation of the healing power attributed to him and to all Christian kings reflects, I think, a natural scepticism. He was a learned man, very much interested in science, who, while he was willing in the *Cantigas* to recognize that many miracles were performed by the Virgin Mary, was not prepared to claim the healing power for himself, nor to acknowledge it in other monarchs whose human frailties he knew well. Furthermore, I think he had no desire to cloak the Castilian monarchy in theocratic or priestly garb, as was the case in France and England. The healing power,

like anointing and coronation, was symbolic of that. Rather than allow the superiority of ecclesiastical authority to be implied in the ceremony of anointing and coronation, the king stressed the direct dependence of his monarchy upon God himself, without the pope or archbishop as intermediary. Boasting that they had gained an empire by their own valor, the kings of Castile had no need of the church's sanction conveyed through the imposition of holy oil; nor had they need to claim the miraculous power of the royal touch.[78] Their very human accomplishments in subjugating such a vast territory as Muslim Spain within such a brief time were sufficient testimony to their extraordinary powers and something truly to be marveled at. By comparison, the healing touch must have seemed a minor miracle.

I also suspect that Alfonso X deliberately sought to denigrate the power of healing claimed by the king of France. In the course of the thirteenth century France under his cousin Louis IX, who was recognized as a saintly man in his own lifetime, was becoming the dominant power in western Europe. The marriage of Fernando de la Cerda and the French Princess Blanche suggests that the two kings were on reasonably good terms.[79] Nevertheless, France under the rulership of Philip III (1270-1285) became a real threat to Castile. Not only did King Philip demand recognition of the rights to the Castilian throne of his nephew, Alfonso de la Cerda, but he also thwarted Alfonso X's expectations of annexing Navarre. Indeed in the last decade of his reign King Alfonso had every reason to be annoyed by the overweening power of France.[80]

Just as Alfonso X sought to establish a parity between king and emperor in the matter of making laws and to assure everyone that he had no superior on earth, so also I think he endeavored to undercut the special quality of the French monarchy symbolized in the healing power. His repudiation of this gift in *CSM* 321 was likely a calculated action prompted by the intensification of his conflict with Philip III after 1275. More than likely *CSM* 321 was written sometime after that date.

I have found only one other reference to this power attributed to the kings of Castile in the Middle Ages. The early fourteenth-century canonist and later bishop of Silves, Álvaro Pelayo, who ridiculed the claims of the kings of France and England as "lies and dreams" bordering on heresy, nevertheless stated that the kings of Castile had just such a healing power. While still a child he claimed to have seen Sancho IV expel a demon from an afflicted woman, by placing his foot on her throat (as the demon insulted him) and by reading from a book, presumably the Gospels. This was not an example of the royal touch to heal scrofula, but an equally marvelous exorcism by a king who had been crowned by four bishops at Toledo.[81] Thereafter healing by the kings of Castile was not mentioned again until seventeenth-century royalist writers endeavored to establish that it was a traditional attribute of the monarchy.[82] I think we may conclude, therefore that in Spain the tradition of a secular monarchy persisted throughout the Middle Ages.

Notes

1. O'Callaghan, *The Learned King*, 22-30.

2. *CSM*, 1:101.

3. *PCG*, prologue, 1:4: "*E por end Nos don Alfonsso, por la gracia de Dios, rey de Castiella, de Toledo, de Leon, de Gallizia, de Seuilla, de Cordoua, de Murcia, de Jahen et dell Algarue . . .*" *Espéculo*, 1: "*E por ende nos don Alfonso, por la gracia de Dios, rey de Castiella, de Toledo, de Leon, de Gallizia, de Sevilla, de Cordova, de Murcia, de Jahen . . .*" *Fuero real*, ed. Gonzalo Martínez Díez, José Manuel Ruiz Asencio, and C. Hernández Alonso (Avila: Fundación Claudio Sánchez Albornoz, 1988), 6: "*Et por ende nos don Alfonso, por la gracia de Dios, rey de Castiella, de Toledo, de Leon, de Gallicia, de Sevilla, de Cordova, de Murcia, de Jahen, de Baeza, de Badaioz, e del Algarve . . .*" *Siete Partidas*, 3: "*Por ende Nos don Alffonso, fijo del muy noble rey don Ferrando e de la muy noble reyna donna Beatriz, regnando en Castiella, en Toledo, en Leon, en Gallizia, en Seuilla, en Cordoua, en Murcia, en Jahen e en el Algarue . . .*" *Setenario*, 7, ley 1: "*Castilla, de Toledo, de León, de Gallizia, de Seuilla, de Córdoua, de Murcia, de Jahén, e de Badaioz e del Algarbe.*"

4. *CSM* 318.11 refers to the *reino de Toledo* and *CSM* 332.1 to the *reino de Leon*. See Joseph F. O'Callaghan, *A History of Medieval Spain* (Ithaca: Cornell University Press, 1975), 98-100, 120-126, 134-136, 194-207.

5. The order of the kingdoms listed in Fernando III's intitulation on 18 May 1252 was Castile, Toledo, León, Galicia, Seville, Córdoba, Murcia, and Jaén; González, *Fernando III*, 3:438-439, no. 848. The same order appears on the epitaph on the king's sacrophagus; del Arco, *Sepulcros*, 230-231. *Setenario*, 15, ley 9 states that Fernando III inherited León, Galicia, and Asturias, as well as the kingdom of Badajoz from his father Alfonso IX, and Castile, Toledo, Extremadura, Álava and Guipúzcoa from his mother, Berenguela.

6. Fernando III's intitulation in 1250 was "*rey de Castilla et de Toledo, de Leon, et de Galizia, de Sevilla, de Cordoba, de Murcia et de Jahen.*" For examples see González, *Alfonso IX*, 2 vols.

(Madrid: CSIC, 1945), *El reino de Castilla en la época de Alfonso VIII*, 3 vols. (Madrid: CSIC, 1960), and *Reinado y diplomas de Fernando III*, 3 vols. (Córdoba: Monte de Piedad y Caja de Ahorros, 1980-1986).

7. *Cortes de los antiguos reinos de León y Castilla*, 5 vols. (Madrid: Real Academia de la Historia, 1861-1903), 1:629, 637, art. 5, 32. Eloy Benito Ruano, *La prelación ciudadana. Las disputas por la precedencia entre las ciudades de la Corona de Castilla* (Toledo: Centro Universitario de Toledo, 1972), 13-14.

8. *CSM* 318.12, *CSM* 325.19, *CSM* 344.11, and *CSM* 347.10 refer to the *reino de Sevilla*. See also *Setenario*, 15, ley 9; O'Callaghan, *A History of Medieval Spain*, 337-357.

9. *Setenario*, 15, ley 9: "*Por su linaie ganó el rregno de Murcia, e ssennaladamente por su fijo el mayor don Alfonso.*" In his will of 10 January 1284 the king provided for his burial in Murcia, "*que es cabeza de este reyno, el primero lugar que Dios quiso que ganassemos a servicio del e a honrra del Rey don Fernando e de nos et de nuestra tierra.*" *DAAX*, 558, no. 521; *MHE*, 2:124, no. 229; Daumet, "Les testaments d'Alphonse X," 88; O'Callaghan, *The Learned King*, 185-186.

10. *CSM* 183, 1:593. The *Setenario*, 15, ley 9, attributes to Infante Alfonso a role in the conquest of the kingdoms of Jaén and the Algarve and the city and kingdom of Seville: "*e ffizol auer el de Jahén e otrossi el del Algarbe et ayudól a ganar la cibdat de Sseuilla e lo más de todo el rregno.*" Julio González, *Repartimiento de Sevilla*, 2 vols. (Madrid: CSIC, 1951), 1:85-91, discusses the reconquest of the Algarve.

11. See O'Callaghan, *The Learned King*, 156-162, for fuller discussion.

12. *Setenario*, 15, ley 9, says that the kingdom of Badajoz "*ffue antiguamiente muy onrrada cosa.*" González, *Alfonso IX*, 1:210, and *Fernando III*, 1:398, 408, 421-425.

13. *MHE*, 1:4-5, 18, nos. 3 (20 January 1253), 9 (18 January 1254); Tomás González, *Colección de cédulas, cartas patentes, provisiones, reales ordenes y documentos concernientes a las provincias vascongadas*, 6 vols. (Madrid: Imprenta Real, 1829-1833), 6:112, no. 258 (18 May 1255); José Miguel Gual López, "La política ferial alfonsí y el ordenamiento general de las ferias castellanas en su época," in Juan Carlos de Miguel Rodríguez, Angela Muñoz Fernández and Cristina Segura Graiño, eds., *Alfonso X el Sabio, Vida, obra y época. Actas del Congreso internacional de estu-*

dios medievales conmemorativos del VII Centenario de la muerte de Alfonso el Sabio (Madrid: Sociedad Española de Estudios Medievales 1989), 95-113.

14. On 18 October 1255 Pope Alexander IV authorized his legate, Bishop Lope of Morocco, and Alfonso X to establish bishoprics in places recovered from the Moors, namely, Cartagena, Silves, and Badajoz. Fray Pedro was made bishop of Badajoz. *MHE*, 1:18, no. 9 (31 March 1255); O'Callaghan, *The Learned King*, 81-83, 87; Ballesteros, *Alfonso X*, 198. On the cathedral of Badajoz see Cómez Ramos, *Empresas artísticas*, 85-88.

15. One wonders whether Fray Juan Gil de Zamora, *De preconiis Hispaniae*, 118, Tr. 5.28, had the *CSM* in mind when he summarized the king's conquests in these words: *"Rex autem Aldefonsus filius prefati regis Fernandi dum adhuc esset Infans, regnum obtinuit Murcianum et postquam regni suscepit gubernaculum villam que Nebula dicitur occupavit. Similiter obtinuit Xerez, Metinam Celi, Alcala, Beger et alia loca multa."*

16. *CAX*, 5-6, ch. 4; O'Callaghan, *The Learned King*, 174-178.

17. *CAX*, 9-11, 25-26, ch. 10-12, 14, 30; O'Callaghan, *The Learned King*, 181-188.

18. O'Callaghan, *The Learned King*, 202-202.

19. *CSM* 306.15 remarks that the Lateran palace once belonged to Octavian, the first of the Roman emperors. Emperor Julian the Apostate is cited in *CSM* 15.17-18 (*"Juyão falss' e felon, / que os crischãos matar queria"*—"the false and felonious Julian who wished to kill the Christians") and *CSM* 27.65 (*"emperador cruel, / que a Santa Maria non foi fiel"*—"the cruel emperor who was not faithful to Holy Mary"). *CSM* 145.52 mentions Nero (*"enperador Nero quando queimou Roma e tornou carvões"*—"emperor Nero when Rome burned and turned to ashes"). *CSM* 17, 1:152-154 and *CSM* 309, 2:151-152 speak of an unidentified emperor of Rome. *CSM* 342, 2:236-237 refers to Manuel Comnenus, Emperor of Byzantium (1143-1180). The Byzantine Emperor Alexius and his wife Jordana mentioned in *CSM* 131.10-12 may be Alexius I Comnenus (1081-1118); but there was also Alexius II Comnenus (1180-1183), and Alexius III Angelus (1195-1203), and Alexius IV Angelus (1203-1204). In a story about St. John of Damascus, *CSM* 265, 2:44-48, speaks about the emperor of Persia.

20. *CSM* 5, 1:115-120. The story bears some similarity to the reported seduction of Eleanor of Aquitaine, the wife of Louis VII of France, by her cousin Raymond of Antioch. Otto of Freising, *The Deeds of Frederick Barbarossa*, tr. Charles C. Mierow (New York: Columbia University Press, 1953), 164-165. Beatrix was the daughter of Count Rainald who died in 1148. *CSM* 136.19 mentions Conrad IV son of Emperor Frederick II (1212-1250).

21. *CSM* 35.120 and 115.299: *"a emperadriz do Ceo"*—"the Empress of heaven;" *CSM* 146.10: *"Santa Emperadriz Madre de Deus Emanuel"*—"the Holy Empress, Mother of God, Emmanuel;" *CSM* 265.115 *"Santa Emperadriz"*; *CSM* 298.51 *"tu que dos ceos es Emperadriz"*—"you who are Empress of the heavens."

22. Gonzalo de Berceo, "De los signos que aparesçeran ante del juicio," in *Obras Completas*, 295, verse 41, also linked sinful kings and emperors—*"non perdonarán a reyes nin a emperadores, Avran tales servientes quales fueron sennores."*

23. *CSM* 409, 2:377-379; O'Callaghan, *The Learned King*, 23-24.

24. Procter, *Alfonso X*, 44-46.

25. Rafael Cómez Ramos, "El retrato de Alfonso X, el Sabio en la primera Cantiga de Santa María," Katz and Keller, *Studies*, 35-52, brings together eleven contemporary portraits of the king.

26. Rodrigo Jiménez de Rada, *De rebus Hispaniae*, 67, Bk. 3, ch. 20, remarked that in the tomb of King Rodrigo, *"ultimus rex Gothorum"* were found his royal vestments: *"corona, vestes et insignia et calciamenta auro et lapidibus adornata."*

27. A similar pair of red stockings belonging to Archbishop Rodrigo Jiménez de Rada is shown in *Alfonso X. Toledo 1984*, 150, fig. 96.

28. In *CSM* 142 the king, while hunting, wears a biretta. A biretta divided into squares of castles and lions and found in the tomb of Infante Fernando de la Cerda is illustrated in *Alfonso X. Toledo 1984*, 138, fig. 67. That and a similar biretta on the funerary effigy of Infante Felipe at Villasirga are portrayed in Menéndez Pidal, *La España del Siglo XIII*, 37, 39, 82.

29. Cómez Ramos, "El retrato de Alfonso X en la Primera *Cantiga*," 49; Ana Domínguez, "La miniatura del 'Scriptorium' Alfonsí," in Mondéjar and Montoya, *Estudios Alfonsíes*, 127-161.

30. A pillow from the tomb of Sancho IV decorated with lions, fleur-de-lis, stars, and an eagle is shown in *Alfonso X. Toledo 1984*, 137, fig. 62.

31. See plates 3, 4, 5, 11 in Cómez Ramos, "El retrato de Alfonso X en la Primera *Cantiga*," 40-42, 48; Ana Domínguez Rodríguez, *Astrología y arte en*

el Lapidario de Alfonso X el Sabio (Madrid: Edilán, 1982); Menéndez Pidal, *La España del Siglo XIII*, 38-48.

32. See Evelyn Procter, *Curia and Cortes in Leon and Castile, 1072-1295* (Cambridge: Cambridge University Press, 1980), frontispiece.

33. *Justinian's Institutes,* ed. tr. by Peter Birks and Grant McLeod (Ithaca: Cornell University Press, 1987), 35: "*Imperatoriam maiestatem non solum armis decoratam, sed etiam legibus oportet esse armatam, ut utrumque tempus et bellorum et pacis recte possit gubernari et princeps Romanus victor existat non solum in hostilibus proeliis, sed etiam per legitimos tramites calumniantium iniquitates expellens, et fiat tam iuris religiossisimus quam victis hostibus triumphator.*"

34. Teofilo Ruiz, "Images of Power in the Seals of the Castilian Monarchy: 1135-1469," *Estudios en Homenaje a Don Claudio Sánchez Albornoz en sus 90 años,* 4 (1986): 455-463, esp. 459-460; Menéndez Pidal, *La España del Siglo XIII,* 154 shows a seal of 1262.

35. See plates 2, 7, 8, 9 in Cómez Ramos, "El retrato de Alfonso X en la Primera *Cantiga,*" 37, 44-46, and *Empresas artísticas,* 171, fig. 32. The figures identified as Alfonso X and Violante in the cathedral of Burgos were once thought to represent the marriage of Fernando III and Beatriz of Swabia in that cathedral in 1219. He is a crowned king offering a ring to a woman who wears a headdress tied under her chin, but not a crown. When Alfonso X married Violante at Valladolid, not Burgos, in 1249 he was not yet king. See Percy Ernst Schramm, *Las insignias de la realeza en la edad media española* (Madrid: Instituto de Estudios Políticos, 1960), 54-55. For Hernán Pérez de Guzmán's description of the royal tombs see *Alfonso X. Toledo 1984,* 79-80.

36. Cómez Ramos, *Empresas artísticas,* 73-85.

37. For the description of these windows see Cómez Ramos, *Empresas artísticas,* 181-182 185-186, figs. 34-35. For illustrations see María Elena Gómez Moreno, *La Catedral de León* (León: Everest, 1973), figs. 24-26.

38. Most of these symbols derived from the ancient Roman Empire. The emperors used both a *baculus* or long staff and a *sceptrum* or short staff. King Alfonso's scepter is only about arm's length. None of the miniatures depicts him with an orb.

39. Schramm, *Las insignias de la realeza,* 35-40.

40. Ortiz de Zúñiga, *Anales,* 1:306-307, 4:95, 5:321. The tomb of Fernando III, opened at the same time, revealed his sword, standard, spurs, a

statuette of the Virgin Mary, and a glass drinking cup with golden metal bands and the inscription: "*Dominus meus, Dominus mihi adjutor, et non timebo quid faciat mihi homo et despiciam inimicos meos. Señor mio, el Señor sea en mi guarda, y no temeré lo que puede hacer contra mi el hombre, y despreciaré mis enemigos.*"

41. *CSM* 22 in the Florentine codex presents a crown worn by an emperor over a cloth cap or bonnet. García Cuadrado, *Las Cantigas,* 80-81. Alfonso XI was crowned with a crown of gold set with precious stones. *Cronica del Rey Don Alfonso XI, BAE* 66:235, ch. 100.

42. Ibn Khaldūn, *Histoire des Berbères et des dynasties musulmanes de l'Afrique septentrionale,* 4 vols., tr. Baron de Slane (Paris: Paul Geutner, 1852-1856), 4:104-106; O'Callaghan, *The Learned King,* 264.

43. *DAAX,* 559, no. 521; *MHE,* 2:126, no. 229; Daumet, "Les testaments d'Alphonse X," 91. A "*corona imperial de piedras*" was found in Alfonso X's tomb in 1579, but was not mentioned by Delgado Roig when he examined the remains in 1948. Ortiz de Zúñiga, *Anales,* 5:321.

44. Sancho IV's crown is illustrated in *Alfonso X. Toledo 1984,* 18, 135, fig. 59; Menéndez Pidal, *La España del Siglo XIII,* 40-41; García Cuadrado, *Las Cantigas: El Códice de Florencia,* 80-81. The crown of Queen Beatriz found in her tomb was stolen in 1873; there is an illustration in Antonio Ballesteros, *Historia de España y su influencia en la historia universal,* 8 vols. in 9 (Barcelona: Salvat, 1918-1941), 3:10. See the commentary of Schramm, *Las insignias de la realeza,* 41-55.

45. *Castigos e documentos para bien vivir ordenados por el Rey Don Sancho IV,* ed. Agapito Rey (Bloomington: Indiana University Press, 1952), 174, ch. 37; Peter Linehan, *History and the Historians of Medieval Spain* (Oxford: Clarendon Press, 1993), 444-447.

46. García Cuadrado, *Las Cantigas,* 240-241.

47. Several thirteenth-century swords are illustrated in *Alfonso X. Toledo 1984,* 114-115, 124, 136-138, figs. 1-3 (2-3 may be swords of Fernando III), 29-30, 61 (Sancho IV), 64 (Infante Fernando de la Cerda).

48. Menéndez Pidal, *La España del Siglo XIII,* 39, shows the king in *CSM* 90; *Castigos e documentos,* 104, ch. 17.

49. A fragment of Fernando III's mantle with red lions on white squares and gold castles on red ones is illustrated in *Alfonso X. Toledo 1984,* 117, fig. 9,

and Menéndez Pidal, *La España del Siglo XIII*, 38-39; the mantle, gloves, and alms purse buried with Alfonso X are shown on 40, 42. According to the *Crónica del Rey Don Sancho el Bravo, BAE* 66 (1953): 69, ch. 1, Sancho IV, on learning of the death of his father, dressed in mourning (*paños de margas*) but after the requiem mass he donned *paños de oro reales* and was hailed as king. García Cuadrado, *Las Cantigas,* 77-83 discusses royal clothing.

50. *Castigos e documentos,* 82-83, ch. 11. He also tells us that (37, ch. 1) the devil dressed as a king ("*vestido de pannos de peso e con corona de oro en la cabeças e calças de oro e con alegre cara*") appeared to St. Martin.

51. O'Callaghan, *The Learned King,* 9-10.

52. José Manuel Nieto Soria, *Fundamentos ideológicos del poder real en Castilla (Siglos XIII-XVI)* (Madrid: Eudema, 1988), and "Imágenes religiosas del rey y del poder real en la Castilla del siglo XIII," *En la España medieval* 5.2 (1986): 709-729.

53. Teófilo Ruiz, "Une royauté sans Sacre: La monarchie castillane du bas moyen age," *Annales: Economies, Societés, Civilisations* 39 (1984): 429-453; Joseph F. O'Callaghan, "The *Cantigas de Santa Maria* as an Historical Source: Two Examples (nos. 321 and 386)," in Katz and Keller, *Studies,* 387-393; O'Callaghan, *The Learned King,* 24-25.

54. Percy Ernst Schramm, *A History of the English Coronation,* tr. E. L. Legg (Oxford: Oxford University Press, 1937); Ernst Kantorowicz, *The King's Two Bodies. A Study in Medieval Political Theology* (Princeton: Princeton University Press, 1957); Walter Ullmann, *Principles of Government and Politics in the Middle Ages* (New York: Barnes and Noble, 1966).

55. The British Library manuscript of the *Primera Partida* (1,4,13) speaks of the anointing of Old Testament kings and those of the Christian era, and concludes that anointing should be done as "related in the second book," but there is no further reference to royal anointing in the *Siete Partidas.* See *Primera Partida según el Manuscrito Add. 20787 del British Museum,* ed. Juan Antonio Arias Bonet (Valladolid: Universidad de Valladolid, 1975). The *Setenario,* 155, ley 39, after speaking of the anointing of Jesus as true temporal king, continues: "*Et antiguamente todos aquellos que eran llamados para sseer rreyes avyan a sser untados.*"

56. See Julio González, *Regesta de Fernando II* (Madrid: CSIC, 1943), 21-22, and *Alfonso IX,*

1:44-46, and *Alfonso VIII,* 1:150, 180, and *Fernando III,* 1:232-239, 255-263. The troubadour Raimon Vidal de Bezaudon commented that whereas Alfonso VIII "was neither anointed nor consecrated, he was nevertheless crowned with honor"—"*qu·el non era onhs ni sagratz, / mas de pretz era coronat.*" Alvar, *Textos trovadorescos,* 259.

57. John of Paris, *On Royal and Papal Power,* tr. John A. Watt (Toronto: Pontifical Institute of Medieval Studies, 1971), 190; Jean Leclercq, *Jean de Paris et l'ecclésiologie du XIIIᵉ siècle* (Paris: J. Vrin, 1942), 229.

58. Gaspar Ibáñez de Segovia, Marqués de Mondéjar, *Memorias históricas del Rey D. Alonso el Sabio i observaciones a su chrónica* (Madrid: Joaquín Ibarra, 1777); Ballesteros, *Alfonso X,* 54-55. See the critique of Mondéjar, Ballesteros, and Nieto Soria by Linehan, *History and the Historians of Medieval Spain,* 426-430, 439-445.

59. See the letter of Jofré de Loaysa to Jaime I of Aragón in Andrés Giménez Soler, *Don Juan Manuel: Biografia y estudio crítico* (Madrid: Real Academia Española, 1932), 221, no. 1; O'Callaghan, *The Learned King,* 4-8.

60. The last verse of this poem reads: "*Fostes mui ben aguardado / de min sempre u vos andastes, / e nunca foi escusado / nen vos nunca me escusastes / de servir per mia pessõa; / mais en tanto foi errado: non fui vosco en ora bõa.*" See Rodriguez Lapa, *Cantigas d'escarnho e de mal dezir,* 261, no. 167.

61. Linehan, *History and the Historians of Medieval Spain,* 447, n. 114, while admitting that "a poet's recollections are no worse historical evidence than any other," believes that "what was being remembered was not a coronation but a crown-wearing." With reference to crown-wearings he cites *Partidas* 2,5,5: "*et aun en las grandes fiestas quando facien sus cortes trayesen [los reyes] coronas de oro con piedras muy nobles et ricamente obradas.*" The arguments that I have adduced in the text lead me to believe that the poet was not simply referring to a crown-wearing but to a coronation.

62. *CSM,* 1:107-108. See above, 18.

63. See the text dated 13 April 1274 in Diego Catalán, *La Estoria de España de Alfonso X. Creación y Evolución* (Madrid: Universidad Autónoma de Madrid, 1992), 124-125; Pedro Fernández del Pulgar, *Historia secular y eclesiástica de la ciudad de Palencia,* 4 vols. (Madrid: F. Nieto, 1679-1680), 2:344-345; O'Callaghan, *The Learned King,*

147-150; Ballesteros, *Alfonso X*, 688-690; Linehan, *History and the Historians of Medieval Spain*, 455-460.

64. Bernard F. Reilly, *The Kingdom of León-Castilla under King Alfonso VI, 1065-1109* (Princeton: Princeton University Press, 1988).

65. *Crónica del Rey Don Sancho el Bravo, BAE*, 66:69, ch. 1: "*E luego que fuese para Toledo e fizose coronar a el e a la reina dona Maria, su mujer; e coronaronlo cuatro obispos.*" He had been acclaimed in Ávila on 5 April.

66. Jofré de Loaysa, *Crónica de los reyes de Castilla, Fernando III, Alfonso X, Sancho IV y Fernando IV*, ed. Antonio García Martínez (Murcia: Diputación Provincial de Murcia, 1961), 110, ch. 221: "*Nobilis rex Sancius . . . in regem in civitatem Abule sublimatus, qui postmodum in ecclesia sancte Marie toletane multum honorabiiter coronatus. Statuit ibidem et preffate ecclesie privilegium inde dedit ut omnes futuri reges successores ipsius coronarentur seu coronam reciperent in ecclesia memorata.*" See Linehan, *History and the Historians of Medieval Spain*, 446-448.

67. *Crónica del rey don Fernando IV, BAE* 66:93, ch. 1.

68. *Crónica del rey don Alfonso XI, BAE*, 66:233-235, ch. 99-101. Addressing the king, Álvaro Pelayo, *Speculum regum (Espelho dos reis)*, ed. Miguel Pinto de Meneses (Lisbon: Universidade de Lisboa, 1955), 2:138, made the point: "*Hoc officium te ungendi, coronandi et gladium tibi dandi in regno tuo iuste et digne praecipue competit archiflamini Compostellae, uicario almi apostoli Iacobi, regni tui precipuo protectori.*" Claudio Sánchez Albornoz, "Un ceremonial inédito de coronación de los reyes de Castilla," *Estudios sobre las instituciones medievales españolas* (Mexico City: Universidad Nacional Autónoma de Mexico, 1965), 739-763, published a fourteenth-century coronation *ordo* perhaps prepared for Alfonso XI by Bishop Ramón of Coimbra. The text presumed that the ceremony would take place at Compostela, that one of the bishops would anoint the king, who would then be knighted as a *cavallero de Santiago*, and finally crowned with the *corona imperii* by the bishop saying the mass.

69. Pedro López de Ayala, *Crónica del rey don Juan I, BAE*, 68:65, Año 1, ch. 1.

70. *CSM* 321, 2:183-185.

71. Marc Bloch, *Les rois thaumaturges* (Paris: Armand Colin, 1961), and *The Royal Touch: Sacred Monarchy and Scrofula in England and France*, tr. J. E. Anderson (London: Routledge, Kegan Paul, 1973).

72. *Epistolae*, 150, in Jacques Paul Migne, *Patrologia latina*, 222 vols. (Paris: J. P. Migne, 1842-1905), 207:440-442, cited by Bloch, *The Royal Touch*, 22.

73. Procter, *Alfonso X*, 33-34, drew my attention to *CSM* 321.

74. On these marriages see González, *Alfonso VIII*, 1:185-188, 206-207; Georges Daumet, *Mémoire sur les relations de la France et de la Castille de 1255 à 1320* (Paris: Bibliothèque de l'École des Hautes Études, 1913).

75. Sánchez Albornoz, "Un ceremonial inédito de coronación de los reyes de Castilla," 739-763: "*Et desta reciben los reyes tal virtud, que se uiuen a seruicio de Dios et faran miraglos en sus uidas. De las dolencias que llaman de los reyes como acaescio et acaesce de cada dia a muchos, ca muy mas apartada merced faze Dios a los reyes que a los otros, porque an de mantener la fe por justicia et por defendimiento de sancta yglesia et de la clerecia.*"

76. O'Callaghan, *The Learned King*, 17-30.

77. See also Lucas of Túy, *Crónica de España*, ed. Julio Puyol (Madrid: Real Academia de la Historia, 1926), 9; Vincentius Hispanus, cited by Gaines Post, *Studies in Medieval Legal Thought: Public Law and the State, 1100-1322* (Princeton: Princeton University Press, 1964), 490; Juan Gil de Zamora, *De preconiis Hispaniae*, 183, Bk. 7, ch. 3; Álvaro Pelayo, *Speculum regum*, 1:258; Juan Manuel, *Libro de los estados*, ed. R. B. Tate and I. R. Macpherson (New York: Oxford University Press, 1974), 258, Bk. 2, ch. 36.

78. See the references in the previous note. Américo Castro, *La realidad historica de España*, 370-371, said that Alfonso X rejected the idea because it failed to maintain the distinction between God and man that was evident to the adherents of the three religions in Spain. He concluded: "*Los reyes de España no se arrogaron poderes divinos; actuaban en virtud de la gracia que Dios les confería.*" Cayetano Socarras, *Alfonso X of Castile: A Study on Imperialistic Frustration* (Barcelona: Ediciones Hispam, 1976), 66, made the point that the Castilian monarchy did not acquire a charismatic value.

79. O'Callaghan, *The Learned King*, 237.

80. O'Callaghan, *The Learned King*, 231, 236-251, and *A History of Medieval Spain*, 358-381. Shortly after Alfonso X died, the French king led a crusade into Aragón (in 1285) to claim the throne for his second son, Charles of Valois, after King Pedro III (1276-1285) had been deposed by the pope.

81. Álvaro Pelayo, *Speculum regum*, 2:54: "*Reges etiam Franciae et Angliae habere dicuntur uirtutem, et reges deuoti Hispaniae, a quibus descendis, habere dicuntur uirtutem super energumenos et super quibusdam aegritudinibus laborantes, sicut uidi cum essem puer in auo tuo inclito domino rege Sancio, qui me nutriebat, quod a muliere daemoniata ipsum uituperante tenentem pedem super guttur eius et legentem in quodam libello ab ea daemonem expulsit et curatam reliquit.*" In his *Collirium adversus hereses novas*, ed. Richard Scholz, *Unbekannte kirchenpolitische Streitschriften aus der Zeit Ludwigs des Bayern, 1327-1354*, 2 vols. (Rome: Loescher, 1914), 2:509, he remarked: "*Ne dicat hereticus quod reges Francie et Anglie gratiam curationis habere consueverant quia hoc apocrifum enim vel sompnium.*" Schramm, *Las insignias de la realeza*, 59.

82. Bloch, *The Royal Touch*, 87-90.

Abbreviations

AHDE: Anuario de Historia del Derecho Español.

BAE: Biblioteca de Autores Españoles. 203 vols. thus far. Madrid: Real Academia Española, 1846-.

BRAH: Boletín de la Real Academia de la Historia.

CAX: Crónica del rey don Alfonso X, BAE, 66:3-66.

CE: Manuel Rodríguez Lapa, *Cantigas d'escarnho e de maldecir dos cancioneiros galegoportugueses,* 2d ed. Coimbra: Galaixa, 1970.

CLC: Cortes de los antiguos reinos de León y Castilla, 5 vols. Madrid: Real Academia de la Historia, 1861-1903.

CSM: Walter Mettmann, *Cantigas de Santa Maria,* 4 vols., Coimbra: Universidade de Coimbra, 1959-1972; reprint 2 vols. Vigo: Edicions Xerais de Galicia, 1981.

DAAX: Manuel González Jiménez, *Diplomatario Andaluz de Alfonso X.* Seville: El Monte. Caja de Huelva y Sevilla, 1991.

MHE: Memorial Histórico Español, 49 vols. Madrid: Real Academia de la Historia, 1851-1948.

Katz and Keller, *Studies:* Israel J. Katz and John E. Keller, eds., *Studies on the Cantigas de Santa Maria: Art, Music, and Poetry.* Madison: Hispanic Seminary of Medieval Studies, 1987.

PCG: Primera Crónica General, ed. Ramón Menéndez Pidal, 2 vols. Madrid: Gredos, 1955.

RABM: Revista de Archivos, Bibliotecas y Museos.

NARRATIVE SOURCES

Alfonso X. *Estoria de Espanna.* See Alfonso X, *Primera Crónica General.*

———. *Primera Crónica General.* Ed. Ramón Menéndez Pidal. 2 vols. Madrid: Gredos, 1955.

Anales Toledanos III. ES 23:411-424.

Benavides, Antonio, ed. *Memorias de D. Fernando IV de Castilla.* 2 vols. Madrid: José Rodríguez, 1860.

Bernat Desclot. *Crònica.* Ed. M. Coll i Alentorn. 5 vols. Barcelona: Barcino, 1949-1951.

Chronica Adefonsi Imperatoris. Ed. Luis Sánchez Belda. Madrid: Consejo Superior de Investigaciones Científicas, 1950.

Chronicle of Albelda. In Yves Bonnaz, ed. *Chroniques asturiennes (Fin IXe siècle).* Paris: CNRS, 1987.

Chrónicon de Cardeña. ES 23:371-381.

Continuación de la Crónica del Arzobispo Don Rodrigo Jiménez de Rada. In *Colección de documentos inéditos para la historia de España.* Ed. Martín Fernández de Navarrete et al., 112 vols. Madrid: Calera et al., 1841-1895. 105-106.

Cooper, Louis, and Franklin M. Waltman. *Text and Concordance of the* Gran Conquista de Ultramar. *Biblioteca Nacional MS 1187.* Madison: Hispanic Seminary of Medieval Studies, 1989.

Crònica de Jaume I. Ed. J. M. Casacuberta and Enric Bagüe. 9 vols. Barcelona: Barcino, 1926-1962.

Crònica del Rey Don Alfonso X. BAE 66:3-66.

Crónica del Rey Don Alfonso XI. BAE 66:173-392.

Crónica del rey don Fernando IV. BAE 66:93-170.

Crónica del rey don Sancho el bravo. BAE 66:69-90.

Crònica general de Pere III el Cerimoniós, dita comunament Crònica de Sant Joan de la Penya. Ed. A. J. Soberanas Lleó. Barcelona: Alpha, 1961.

Crónica general de Espanha de 1344. Ed. L. F. Lindley Cintra. 6 vols. Lisboa: Academia Portuguesa da História, 1951-1983.

Crónica latina de los reyes de Castilla. Ed. Luis Charlo Brea. Cádiz: Universidad de Cádiz, 1984.

Estoria del Fecho de los Godos. See *Continuacion de la Crónica del Arzobispo Don Rodrigo.*

Fita, Fidel, "Biografías de San Fernando y de Alfonso el Sabio por Gil de Zamora," *BRAH* 5 (1885): 308-328.

———. "Biografía inédita de Alfonso IX, rey de León, por Gil de Zamora," *BRAH* 13 (1888): 291-295.

Flórez, Enrique, et al. *España Sagrada,* 52 vols. Madrid: Marin, 1754-1918.

Gayangos, Pascual, ed. *La gran conquista de Ultramar que mandó escribir el Rey Don Alfonso el Sabio.* In *BAE* 44. Madrid: Real Academia Española, 1858; reprint 1951.

Guillaume de Nangis. *Gesta Philippi Tertii Francorum regis.* In *Recueil des Historiens des Gaules et de la France.* Ed. Martin Bouquet et al., 24 vols. Paris: Académie des Inscriptions et Belles Lettres, 1738-1904. 20:466-539.

Ibn Abī Zar'. *Rawd al-Qirtas.* 2 vols. Tr. Ambrosio Huici. Valencia: Anubar, 1964.

Ibn 'Idhārī, *al-Bayān al Mugrib fi Ijtisar Ajbār Muluk al-Andalus wa al-Magrib.* Tr. Ambrosio Huici Miranda. *Colección de crónicas árabes de la Reconquista.* 3 vols. Tetuán: Marroquí, 1952-1953. 2-3.

Ibn Khaldūn. *Histoire des Berbères et des dynasties musulmanes de l'Afrique septentrionale.* 4 vols. Tr. Baron de Slane. Paris: Paul Geutner, 1852-1856.

Isidore of Seville. *Historia Gothorum, Wandalorum et Suevorum.* In *Monumenta Germaniae Historica. Auctores Antiquissimi, 11. Chronica Minora,* 2:267-303.

Jofré de Loaysa. *Crónica de los reyes de Castilla, Fernando III, Alfonso X, Sancho IV y Fernando IV, 1248-1305.* Ed. and tr. Antonio García Martínez. Murcia, 1961. Reprint, Murcia: Academic Alfonso X el Sabio, 1982.

Juan Gil de Zamora. *Liber de preconiis Hispaniae.* Ed. Manuel de Castro y Castro. Madrid: Universidad de Madrid, 1955.

—————. *Liber de preconiis civitatis numantine.* Ed. Fidel Fita. "Dos libros inéditos de Gil de Zamora." *BRAH* 5 (1884): 131-200.

Juan Manuel. *Chronicon.* In Benavides, *Memorias de D. Fernando IV de Castilla.* 1:675-680.

Lomax, Derek W. "Una crónica inédita de Silos." *Homenaje a Fray Justo Pérez de Urbel.* 2 vols. Silos: Abadía de Silos, 1976. 1:323-337.

López de Ayala, Pedro. *Crónica de Juan I. BAE* 68:65-159.

Lucas of Tuy. *Chronicon Mundi.* Ed. Andreas Schott. *Hispania Illustrata.* 4 vols. Frankfort: Claudius Marnius et Heredes Joannis Aubrii, 1603-1608. 4:1-116.

—————. *Crónica de España.* Ed. Julio Puyol. Madrid: Revista de Archivos, Bibliotecas y Museos, 1926.

Ramon Muntaner. *Crònica.* Ed. Enric Bagüe. 2d ed. 9 vols. Barcelona: Barcino, 1927-1952.

Rodrigo Jiménez de Rada. *De rebus Hispaniae.* In *Opera.* Ed. Francisco de Lorenzana. Madrid, 1793. Reprint, Valencia: Anubar, 1968.

Literary Sources

Alfonso X. *Alfonso X el Sabio. Cantigas de Santa María. Edición facsímil del Códice T.I.1 de la Biblioteca de San Lorenzo el Real de El Escorial. Siglo XIII.* 2 vols. Madrid: Edilán 1979.

—————. *Alfonso X el Sabio. Cantigas de Santa María. Edición facsímil del códice B.R. 20 de la Biblioteca Centrale de Florencia. Siglo XIII.* 2 vols. Madrid: Edilán, 1989.

—————. *Cantigas de Santa Maria.* 4 vols. Ed. Walter Mettmann. Coimbra: Universidade de Coimbra, 1959-1974. Reprint, 2 vols. Vigo: Edicions Xerais de Galicia, 1981.

—————. *Cantigas de Santa Maria. Cantigas 1 a 100.* 2 vols. Ed. Walter Mettmann. Madrid: *Clásicos Castalia,* 1986.

—————. *Las Cantigas de Santa Maria.* 2 vols. Ed. Marquess of Valmar. Madrid: Real Academia Española, 1889.

—————. *Setenario.* Ed. Kenneth Vanderford. Buenos Aires: 1945. Reprint, Barcelona: Crítica, 1984.

Alvar, Carlos. *Textos trovadorescos sobre España y Portugal.* Madrid: CUPSA, 1978.

Álvaro Pelayo. *Collirium adversus hereses novas.* Ed. Richard Scholz, *Unbekannte kirchenpolitische Streitschriften aus der Zeit Ludwigs des Bayern, 1327-1354,* 2 vols. Rome: Loescher, 1914.

—————. *Speculum regum (Espelho dos Reis).* Ed. Miguel Pinto de Meneses. Lisbon: Universidade de Lisboa, 1955.

Arberry, A. J., tr., *The Koran Interpreted.* 2 vols. New York: George Unwin, 1955.

Blanco García, Vicente, and J. Campos, eds. *San Ildefonso de Toledo (Santos Padres Españoles,* 1). Madrid: Biblioteca de Autores Cristianos, 1971.

Cancioneiro da Ajuda. Ed. Carolina Michaëlis de Vasconcellos. 2 vols. Halle: Niemeyer, 1904.

Cancioneiro da Biblioteca antiga Colucci-Brancuti. 8 vols. Ed. Elza Paxeco Machado and José Pedro Machado. Lisbon: Revista de Portugal, 1949-1964.

Fita, Fidel. "Cincuenta leyendas por Gil de Zamora combinadas con las Cantigas de Alfonso el Sabio." *BRAH* 7 (1886): 54-144.

—————. "Leyenda de San Isidro por el diacono Juan." *BRAH* 9 (1886): 97-157.

—————. "Poesías inéditas de Gil de Zamora." *BRAH* 6 (1885): 379-409.

—————. "Traslación e invención del cuerpo de San Ildefonso. Reseña histórica por Gil de Zamora." *BRAH* 6 (1885): 60-71.

—————. "Treinta leyendas por Gil de Zamora." *BRAH* 13 (1888): 187-225.

————. "Variantes de tres leyendas por Gil de Zamora." *BRAH* 6 (1885): 418-429.

García Morencos, Pilar. *Libro de ajedrez, dados y tablas de Alfonso X el Sabio. Estudio.* Madrid: Patrimonio Nacional, 1977.

Gonzalo de Berceo. *Milagros de Nuestra Señora.* Ed. Antonio García Solalinde. Madrid: Clásicos Castellanos, 1958.

————. *Obras completas de Gonzalo de Berceo.* Logroño: Instituto de Estudios Riojanos, 1974.

————. *Obras completas.* Ed. Brian Dutton. 3 vols. London: Tamesis, 1975.

Ildefonsus of Toledo. *Liber de viris illustribus.* Ed. C. Codoñer Merino. Salamanca: Universidad de Salamanca, 1972.

John of Paris. *De potestate regia et papali.* Ed. Jean Leclercq. *Jean de Paris et l'ecclésiologie du XIIIᵉ siècle.* Paris: J. Vrin, 1942.

————. *On Royal and Papal Power.* Tr. John A. Watt. Toronto: Pontifical Institute of Medieval Studies, 1971.

Juan Manuel. *Libro de los estados.* Ed. R. B. Tate and I. R. Macpherson. New York: Oxford University Press, 1974.

————. *Tractado de las armas.* BAE 51:257-264.

Juan Ruiz, Arcipreste de Hita. *Libro de buen amor.* Ed. Jacques Joset. 2 vols. Madrid: Espasa-Calpe, 1974.

Libro de los engaños e asayamientos de las mugeres. Ed. John E. Keller. Chapel Hill: University of North Carolina, 1959.

Núñez, José Joaquín. *Cantigas d'amigo dos trovadores galegos-portugueses.* 2 vols. Coimbra, 1926. Reprint, New York: Kraus, 1971.

Paredes Núñez, Juan, ed. *Alfonso X el Sabio. Cantigas profanas.* Granada: Universidad de Granada, 1988.

Pedro Marín. *Miraculos romanzados.* Ed. Sebastián de Vergara. *Vida y milagros de Santo Domingo de Silos.* Madrid: Francisco del Hierro, 1736.

Poema de Fernán González. Ed. Alonso Zamora Vicente. Madrid: Espasa-Calpe, 1946.

Ramos, Epifanio, ed. *Las Cantigas de escárnio y maldecir de Alfonso X.* Lugo: Reprografia Alvarellos, 1973.

Rodríguez Lapa, Manuel. *Cantigas d'escarnho e de mal dezir dos Cancioneiros medievais galego-portugueses.* Coimbra: Galaixa, 1970.

Sancho IV. *Castigos e documentos para bien vivir.* Ed. Agapito Rey. Bloomington: Indiana University, 1952.

The Book of the Wiles of Women. Tr. John E. Keller. Chapel Hill: University of North Carolina, 1956.

LEGAL AND DOCUMENTARY SOURCES

Alfonso X. *Espéculo. Texto jurídico atribuído al Rey de Castilla Don Alfonso el Sabio.* Ed. Robert A. MacDonald. Madison: Hispanic Seminary, 1990.

————. *Espéculo.* Ed. Gonzalo Martínez Díez and José Manuel Ruiz Asencio. Ávila: Fundación Claudio Sánchez Albornoz, 1985.

————. *Fuero real.* Ed. Gonzalo Martínez Díez, José Manuel Ruiz Asencio, and C. Hernández Alonso. Ávila: Fundación Claudio Sánchez Albornoz, 1988.

————. *Opúsculos legales del Rey Don Alfonso el Sabio.* Ed. Real Academia de la Historia. 2 vols. Madrid: Imprenta Real, 1836.

————. *Primera Partida según el Manuscrito Add. 20787 del British Museum.* Ed. Juan Antonio Arias Bonet. Valladolid: Universidad de Valladolid, 1975.

————. *Las Siete Partidas del Rey Don Alfonso el Sabio.* Ed. Real Academia de la Historia. 3 vols. Madrid: Imprenta Real, 1801.

Bullarium Ordinis Militiae de Calatrava. Madrid: Antonio Marín, 1761.

Canivez, Joseph M. *Statuta capitulorum generalium Ordinis Cisterciensium.* 8 vols. Louvain: Bibliothèque de la Revue d'Histoire ecclésiastique, 1933-1941.

Castro Garrido, Araceli. *Documentación del monasterio de las Huelgas de Burgos (1307-1321).* Burgos: Garrido Garrido, 1987.

Cortes de los antiguos reinos de León y Castilla. 5 vols. Madrid: Real Academia de la Historia, 1861-1903.

Daumet, Georges. *Mémoire sur les relations de la France et de la Castille de 1255 à 1320.* Paris: Bibliothèque de l'École des Hautes Études, 1913.

————. "Les testaments d'Alphonse le Savant, roi de Castille," *Bibliothèque de l'Ecole des Chartes* 67 (1906): 70-99.

"Documentos de la época de Alfonso el Sabio," *MHE,* 1-2.

Escudero de la Peña, J. M. "Súplica hecha al Papa Juan XXI para que absolviese al Rey de Castilla, D. Alfonso X, del juramento de no acuñar otra moneda que los dineros prietos." *RABM* 2 (1872): 58-59.

Ferotin, Marius. *Recueil des chartes de l'Abbaye de Silos.* Paris: Imprimerie Nationale, 1897.

Gay, Jules. *Les Registres de Nicholas III (1277-1280).* Paris: Bibliothéque des Écoles françaises d'Athènes et de Rome, 1898-1938.

González, Julio. *Repartimiento de Sevilla.* 2 vols. Madrid: Consejo Superior de Investigaciones Científicas, 1951.

González, Tomás. *Colección de cédulas, cartas patentes, provisiones, reales ordenes y documentos concernientes a las provincias vascongadas,* 6 vols. Madrid: Imprenta Real, 1829-1833.

González Crespo, Esther. *Colección documental de Alfonso XI.* Madrid: Universidad Complutense, 1985.

González Jiménez, Manuel. *Diplomatario Andaluz de Alfonso X.* Seville: El Monte. Caja de Huelva y Sevilla, 1991.

———— and A. González Gómez. *El Libro del repartimiento de Ferez de la Frontera. Estudio y edición.* Cádiz: Instituto de Estudios Gaditanos, 1980.

Gross, Georg. "Las Cortes de 1252. Ordenamiento otorgado al concejo de Burgos en las cortes celebradas en Sevilla el 12 de octubre de 1252 (según el original)," *BRAH* 182 (1985): 95-114.

Iglesia Ferreirós, Aquilino. "El Privilegio general concedido a las Extremaduras en 1264 por Alfonso X. Edición del ejemplar enviado a Peñafiel en 15 de abril de 1264." *AHDE* 53 (1983): 456-521.

Lizoain Garrido, José Manuel. *Documentación del monasterio de las Huelgas de Burgos (1268-1283).* Burgos: Garrido Garrido, 1987.

Mansilla, Demetrio. *La documentación pontificia de Honorio III (1216-1227).* Rome: Instituto Español de Historia Eclesiástica, 1965.

Martin, François Olivier. *Les Registres de Martin IV (1281-1285).* Paris: Bibliothèque des Ecoles françaises d'Athènes et de Rome, 1901.

Memorial Histórico Español, 49 vols. Madrid: Real Academia de Historia, 1851-1948.

Quintana Prieto, Augusto. *Tumbo viejo de San Pedro de Montes.* León: Caja de Ahorros y Monte de Piedad, 1971.

Rymer, Thomas. *Foedera, conventiones, litterae et cuiuscunque acta publica inter reges Angliae et alios quovis imperatores, reges, pontifices, principes.* 3d ed. 10 vols. The Hague: Joannes Neaulme, 1739-1745.

Sánchez Albornoz, Claudio. "Un ceremonial inédito de coronación de los reyes de Castilla." *Estudios sobre las instituciones medievales españolas.* Mexico City: Universidad Nacional Autónoma de Mexico, 1965. 739-763.

Torres Fontes, Juan, ed. *Colección de documentos inéditos para la historia de Murcia,* 18 vols. thus far. Murcia: Academia Alfonso X el Sabio, 1963-1989.

————. *Repartimiento de Murcia.* Murcia: Academia Alfonso X el Sabio, 1960.

Secondary Works

Aguado Bleye, Pedro. *Santa María de Salas en el Siglo XIII.* Bilbao: Garmendía, 1916.

Aguiar, Manuel de. "Cantigas de escarnio e maldezir: uma galeria de caricaturas." *Portugalia Historica* 2 (1974): 65-89.

Alfonso X. Toledo 1984. Toledo: Ministerio de Cultura, 1984.

Alvar, Carlos. *La poesía trovadoresca en España y Portugal.* Barcelona: CUPSA, 1977.

Anglés, Higinio. *La música de las Cantigas de Santa Maria del Rey Don Alfonso el Sabio,* 3 vols. Barcelona: Diputación Provincial de Barcelona, Biblioteca Central, 1943-1964.

Arco, Ricardo del. *Sepulcros de la Casa Real de Castilla.* Madrid: Consejo Superior de Investigaciones Científicas, 1954.

Arié, Rachel. *L'Espagne musulmane au temps des Nasrides (1232-1492).* Paris: Boccard, 1973.

Ariés, Philippe. *The Hour of Our Death.* Tr. Helen Weaver. New York: Alfred Knopf, 1981.

Baer, Yitzhak. *A History of the Jews in Christian Spain.* 2 vols. Philadelphia: Jewish Publication Society, 1966.

Bagby, Albert. "Alfonso and the Virgin Unite Christian and Moor in the *CSM.*" *Cantigueiros* 1 (1988): 111-118.

————. "The Jew in the *Cantigas* of Alfonso X el Sabio." *Speculum* 46 (1971): 670-688.

————. "The Figure of the Jew in the *Cantigas* of Alfonso X." In Katz and Keller, *Studies,* 235-247.

————. "The Moslem in the *Cantigas* of Alfonso X, El Sabio." *Kentucky Romance Quarterly,* 20 (1973): 173-204.

Ballesteros Beretta, Antonio. *Alfonso X, el Sabio.* Barcelona: Espasa-Calpe, 1963. Reprint, Barcelona: El Albir, 1984.

————. *Historia de España y su influencia en la historia universal.* 8 vols. in 9. Barcelona: Salvat, 1918-1941.

————. *Sevilla en el siglo XIII.* Madrid: Juan Pérez Torres, 1913.

————. "La toma de Salé en tiempos de Alfonso X el Sabio." *Al-Andalus* 8 (1943): 89-128.

Barbour, Neville. "The Significance of the Word *Maurus* with its Derivatives *Moro* and *Moor* and of the Other Terms used by Medieval Writers in Latin to describe the Inhabitants of Muslim Spain." *Actas do IV Congresso de Estudos Arabes e Islámicos. Coimbra 1968.* Leiden: E. J. Brill, 1971. 253-266.

Barkai, Ron. *Cristianos y musulmanes en la España medieval (El enemigo en el espejo).* Madrid: Rialp, 1984.

Beltrán, Vicente. "Los Trovadores en la Corte de Castilla y León (II): Alfonso X, Guiraut Riquier y Pero da Ponte." *Romania* 107 (1986): 486-503.

Benito Ruano, Eloy. *La prelación ciudadana. Las disputas por la precedencia entre las ciudades de la Corona de Castilla.* Toledo: Centro Universitario de Toledo, 1972.

Benito-Vessels, Carmen. "The San Ildefonso Miracle in the Margins of the *Cantigas de Santa Maria* and in the *Estoria de España:* Two Forms of Narrative Discourse," *Cantigueiros* 3 (1990): 17-30.

Bloch, Marc. *Les rois thaumaturges.* Paris: Armand Colin, 1961.

———. *The Royal Touch: Sacred Monarchy and Scrofula in England and France.* Tr. J. E. Anderson. London: Routledge, Kegan Paul, 1973.

Braegelmann, Sister A. *The Life and Writings of St. Ildefonsus of Toledo.* Washington, D.C.: The Catholic University of America, 1942.

Brodman, James W. *Ransoming Captives in Crusader Spain: The Order of Merced on the Christian-Islamic Frontier.* Philadelphia: University of Pennsylvania, 1986.

———. "Charity and Captives on the Medieval Spanish Frontier." *Anuario Medieval* 1 (1989): 34-45.

———. "Municipal Ransoming Law on the Medieval Spanish Frontier." *Speculum* 60 (1985): 318-330.

Burns, Robert I., ed. *Emperor of Culture. Alfonso X the Learned of Castile and his Thirteenth-Century Renaissance.* Philadelphia: University of Pennsylvania, 1990.

———. Ed. *The Worlds of Alfonso the Learned and James the Conqueror. Intellect and Force in the Middle Ages.* Princeton: Princeton University, 1985.

———. "*Stupor Mundi:* Alfonso X of Castile, the Learned." In Burns, *Emperor of Culture,* 1-13.

———. "The *Cantigas de Santa Maria* as a Research Opportunity in History," *Cantigueiros* 1 (1987): 17-22.

———. "The Spiritual Life of James the Conqueror, King of Arago-Catalonia, 1208-1276: Portrait and Self-Portrait." *The Catholic Historical Review* 62 (1976): 1-35.

———. "Warrior Neighbors: Alfonso el Sabio and Crusader Valencia. An Archival Case Study in his International Relations." *Viator* 21 (1990): 147-202.

Cádiz en el siglo XIII. Actas de las jornadas conmemorativas del VIII Centenario de la muerte de Alfonso el Sabio. Cádiz: Universidad de Cádiz, 1983.

Cárdenas, Anthony J. "A Study of Alfonso's Role in Selected *Cantigas* and the Castilian Prosifications of Escorial Codex T.I.1." In Katz and Keller, *Studies,* 253-268.

Carpenter, Dwayne E. "Alfonso el Sabio y los moros: Algunas precisiones legales históricas y textuales con respecto a Siete Partidas 7.25." *Al-Qantara* 7 (1986): 229-253.

Castrillo Llamas, María de la Concepción. "Monarquía y nobleza en torno a la tenencia de fortalezas en Castilla durante los siglos XIII-XIV." *En la España medieval* 17 (1994): 95-112.

Castro, Americo. *La realidad historica de España.* Mexico City: Porrua, 1962.

Catalán, Diego. *La Estoria de España de Alfonso X. Creación y Evolución.* Madrid: Universidad Autónoma de Madrid, 1992.

Clarke, Dorothy Clotelle. "Versification in Alfonso el Sabio's *Cantigas.*" *Hispanic Review* 23 (1955): 83-98.

Cómez Ramos, Rafael. *Las empresas artísticas de Alfonso X el Sabio.* Sevilla: Diputación Provincial de Sevilla, 1979.

———. "El retrato de Alfonso X, el Sabio en la primera Cantiga de Santa Maria." In Katz and Keller, *Studies,* 35-52.

Craddock, Jerry R. "Dynasty in Dispute: Alfonso X el Sabio and the Succession to the Throne of Castile and León in History and Legend." *Viator* 17 (1986): 197-219.

Daniel, Norman. *Islam and the West. The Making of an Image.* Edinburgh: University of Edinburgh, 1960.

Delgado Roig, Juan. "Examen médico-legal de unos restos históricos: Los cadáveres de Alfonso X el Sabio y Doña Beatriz de Suabia." *Archivo Hispalense* 9 (1948): 135-153.

Domínguez Rodríguez, Ana. *Astrología y arte en el Lapidario de Alfonso X el Sabio.* Madrid: Edilán, 1982.

———. "La miniatura del 'Scriptorium' Alfonsí." In Mondéjar and Montoya, *Estudios Alfonsíes,* 127-164.

Dufourcq, Charles Emmanuel. "Un projet castillane du XIIIe siecle: La croisade d'Afrique." *Revue d'histoire et du civilisation du Magreb,* 1 (1966): 26-51.

Fernández de la Cuesta, Ismael. "Alfonso X el Sabio y la música de las Cantigas." In Mondéjar and Montoya, *Estudios alfonsíes,* 119-126.

Fernández del Pulgar, Pedro. *Historia secular y eclesiástica de la ciudad de Palencia.* 4 vols. Madrid: F. Nieto, 1679-1680.

Ferrera, Manuel Pedro. "The Stemma of the Marian *Cantigas:* Philological and Musical Evidence." *Cantigueiros* 6 (1994): 58-97.

Fortescue, Adrian. *The Mass. A Study of the Roman Liturgy.* London: Longmans 1912.

Fraker, Charles. *The Scope of History. Studies in the Historiography of Alfonso el Sabio.* Ann Arbor: University of Michigan, 1996.

Franssen, Maarten. "Did King Alfonso of Castile Really Want to Advise God Against the Ptolemaic System?" *Studies in History and Philosophy of Science* 24 (1993): 313-325.

Gaibrois de Ballesteros, Mercedes. *Historia del reinado de Sancho IV de Castilla,* 3 vols. Madrid: Revista de Archivos, Bibliotecas y Museos, 1922.

García Cuadrado, Amparo. *Las Cantigas. El Códice de Florencia.* Murcia: Universidad de Murcia, 1993.

García-Varela, Jesús. "La función ejemplar de Alfonso X en las cantigas personales." *Cantigueiros* 4 (1992): 3-16.

Giménez Soler, Andrés. *Don Juan Manuel: Biografía y estudio crítico.* Madrid: Real Academia Española, 1932.

Gómez Moreno, María Elena. *La Catedral de León* (León: Everest, 1973).

Goñi Gaztambide, José. *Historia de la bula de la cruzada en España.* Vitoria: Editorial del Seminario, 1955.

González, Cristina. *La tercera Crónica de Alfonso X: La Gran Conquista de Ultramar.* London: Tamesis, 1992.

———. "El último sueño de Alfonso X: La Gran Conquista de Ultramar." *Exemplaria Hispanica* 1 (1991-1992): 97-117.

González, Julio. *Alfonso IX.* 2 vols. Madrid: Consejo Superior de Investigaciones Científicas, 1945.

———. *El reino de Castilla en la época de Alfonso VIII.* 3 vols. Madrid: Consejo Superior de Investigaciones Científicas, 1960.

———. *Regesta de Fernando II.* Madrid: Consejo Superior de Investigaciones Científicas, 1943.

———. *Reinado y diplomas de Fernando III.* 3 vols. Córdoba: Monte de Piedad y Caja de Ahorros de Córdoba, 1980-1986.

González Jiménez, Manuel. *Alfonso X, 1252-1284.* Palencia: La Olmeda, 1993.

———. *En torno a los orígenes de Andalucía.* 2d ed. Seville: Universidad de Sevilla, 1988.

———. "'De al-Qanatir al Gran Puerto de Santa María.'" In *El Puerto de Santo María entre los Siglos XIII y XVI. Estudios en homenaje a Hipólito Sancho de Sopranis en el centenario de su nacimiento.* El Puerto de Santa María: Ayuntamiento de El Puerto de Santa María, 1995.

———. "El Puerto de Santa María en tiempos de Alfonso X el Sabio." In *Nuestros orígenes históricos como El Puerto de Santa María.* Eds. Manuel González Jiménez, Alfonso Jiménez, Jesús Montoya, and José Luis Tejada. El Puerto de Santa María: Ayuntamiento de El Puerto de Santa María, 1989.

———. "Esclavos andaluces en el reino de Granada." *Actas del III Coloquio de historia medieval andaluza: La sociedad medieval andaluza: Grupos no privilegiados.* Jaén: Diputación Provincial de Jaén, 1984. 327-338.

———. "Osuna en el Siglo XIII." In *Osuna entre los tiempos medievales y modernos (siglos XIII-XVIII).* Sevilla: Universidad de Sevilla, 1995. 27-38.

Grassotti, Hilda. *Las instituciones feudo-vasallaticas de León y Castilla,* 2 vols. Spoleto: Centro italiano di studi sull'alto medioevo, 1969.

Gual López, José Miguel. "La política ferial alfonsí y el ordenamiento general de las ferias castellanas en su época." In Miguel Rodríguez, et al. *Alfonso X el Sabio.* 95-114.

Guerrero Lovillo, José. *Las Cantigas: Estudio arqueológico de sus miniaturas.* Madrid: Consejo Superior de Investigaciones Científicas, 1949.

———. *Miniatura Gótica Castellana. Siglos XIII y XIV.* Madrid: Consejo Superior de Investigaciones Científicas, 1956.

Hernández Serna, Joaquín. "La Orden de la Estrella, o de Santa María de España, en la Cantiga 78 del Códice de la Biblioteca Nacional de Florencia." *Miscelánea Medieval Murciana* 6 (1980): 147-168.

Huici Miranda, Ambrosio. *Las grandes batallas de la reconquista durante las invasiones africanas.* Madrid: Consejo Superior de Investigaciones Científicas, 1956.

———. "La toma de Salé por la esquadra de Alfonso X." *Hesperis* 39 (1952): 41-52.

Impey, Olga Tudorica. "'Del duello de los godos de Espanna': la retórica del llanto y su motivación." *Romance Quarterly* 33 (1986): 294-307.

Jedin, Hubert, and John Dolan, eds. *Handbook of Church History,* 10 vols. New York: Herder and Herder, 1968-1981.

Johnson, Elizabeth. "Marian Devotion in the Western Church." In Jill Raitt, ed. *Christian Spirituality: High Middle Ages and Reformation*. New York: Crossroad, 1988.

Kantorowicz, Ernst. *The King's Two Bodies. A Study in Medieval Political Theology*. Princeton: Princeton University Press, 1957.

Kassier, Theodore. "The Salas Miracles of the *Cantigas de Santa María*: Folklore and Social Reality." *Cantigueiros* 3 (1990): 31-38.

Katz, Israel, and John E. Keller, eds. *Studies on the Cantigas de Santa María. Art, Music and Poetry*. Madison: Hispanic Seminary, 1987.

Keller, John Esten. *Alfonso X, el Sabio*. New York: Twayne, 1967.

———. *Collectanea Hispanica: Folklore and Brief Narrative Studies by John Esten Keller*. Ed. Dennis Seniff. Newark, Delaware: Juan de la Cuesta, 1987. 61-76.

———. "Daily Living as presented in the Canticles of Alfonso the Learned." *Speculum* 33 (1958): 484-489.

———. "King Alfonso's Virgin of Villa-Sirga, Rival of St. James of Compostela." In Frederic E. Coenen, et al., eds. *Middle Ages-Reformation-Volkskunde: Festchrift for John G. Kunstmann*. Chapel Hill: University of North Carolina Press, 1959. 75-82.

———. "More on the Rivalry between Santa María and Santiago de Compostela." *Crítica Hispánica* 1 (1979): 37-43.

———. "The Threefold Impact of the *Cantigas de Santa María*: Visual, Verbal and Musical." In Katz and Keller, *Studies*, 7-33.

Keller, John E., and Richard P. Kinkade. *Iconography in Medieval Spanish Literature*. Lexington: University of Kentucky, 1983.

Kinkade, Richard P. "Alfonso X, *Cantiga* 235, and the Events of 1269-1278." *Speculum* 67 (1992): 284-323.

———. "Don Juan's Father, Infante Manuel, in the Cantigas de Santa Maria." *Cantigueiros* 8 (1996): 68-74.

———. "Violante of Aragón (1236?-1300?): An Historical Overview." *Exemplaria Hispanica* 2 (1992): 1-37.

Kulp-Hill, Kathleen. "The Captions to the Miniatures of the 'Códice Rico' of the *Cantigas de Santa María*, a Translation." *Cantigueiros* 7 (1995): 3-64.

———. "'Toda manera de alegría': Pastimes Portrayed in the *Cantigas de Santa Maria*." *Cantigueiros* 6 (1994): 42-52.

Ladero Quesada, Miguel Ángel. *Niebla, de reino a condado. Noticias sobre el Algarbe andaluz en la Baja Edad Media*. Madrid: Real Academia de la Historia, 1992.

Laín, Milagro. "La poesía profana de Alfonso X." *Revista de Occidente* 43 (1984): 145-165.

Le Goff, Jacques. *The Birth of Purgatory*. Tr. Arthur Goldhammer. Chicago: University of Chicago Press, 1984.

Leclercq, Jean, François Vandenbroucke, and Louis Bouyer. *The Spirituality of the Middle Ages (A History of Christian Spirituality,* 2). Minneapolis: Seabury, n.d.

Lévi-Provençal, Évariste. *Histoire de l'Espagne musulmane*. 3 vols. Leiden: E. J. Brill, 1950.

Lewis, C. S. *The Allegory of Love*. New York: Oxford University Press, 1958.

Lewis, Archibald R., and Timothy J. Runyan. *European Naval and Maritime History, 300-1500*. Bloomington: Indiana University Press, 1990.

Linehan, Peter. *History and the Historians of Medieval Spain*. Oxford: Clarendon Press, 1993.

López Ferreiro, Antonio. *Historia de la santa a.m. iglesia de Santiago de Compostela*. 11 vols. Santiago: Imprenta del Seminario conciliar y central, 1898-1909.

Manzano Rodríguez, Miguel Ángel. *La intervención de los Benimerines en la Península ibérica*. Madrid: Consejo Superior de Investigaciones Científicas, 1992.

Martínez García, Luis. *El Hospital del Rey de Burgos. Un señorio medieval en la expansión y en la crísis (siglos XIII y XIV)*. Burgos: J. M. Garrido Garrido, 1986.

Martínez Montavez, Pedro. "Relaciones de Alfonso X de Castilla con el sultan mameluco Baybars y sus sucesores." *Al-Andalus* 27 (1962): 343-376.

Márquez-Villanueva, Francisco. *El Concepto cultural alfonsí*. Madrid: MAPFRE, 1994.

——— and Carlos Alberto Vega, eds. *Alfonso X of Castile: The Learned King (1225-1284). An International Symposium, Harvard University, 17 November 1984*. Cambridge: Harvard University, 1990.

Menéndez Pidal, Gonzalo. *La España del Siglo XIII leída en imágenes*. Madrid: Gráficas Lormo, 1986.

———. "Los manuscritos de las Cantigas. Cómo se elaboró la miniatura alfonsí." *Boletín de la Real Academia de la Historia* 150 (1962): 25-51.

Mettmann, Walter. "A Collection of Miracles from Italy as a Possible Source of the *CSM*." *Cantigueiros* 1 (1988): 75-82.

————. "Algunas observaciones sobre la genesis de la colección de las Cantigas de Santa Maria y sobre el problema del autor." In Katz and Keller, *Studies,* 355-366.

Miguel Rodríguez, Juan Carlos de, Angela Múñoz Fernández, and Cristina Segura Graiño, eds. *Alfonso X el Sabio. Vida, obra y época. Actas del Congreso internacional de estudios medievales conmemorativos del VII Centenario de la muerte de Alfonso el Sabio.* Madrid: Sociedad Española de Estudios Medievales, 1989.

Mingüella, Toribio. *Historia de la diócesis de Sigüenza.* 3 vols. Madrid: Revista de Archivos, Bibliotecas y Museos, 1900-1913.

Mondéjar, Gaspar Ibáñez de Segovia, Marqués de. *Memorias históricas del Rey D. Alonso el Sabio i observaciones a su chrónica.* Madrid: Joaquín Ibarra, 1777.

Mondéjar, José, and Jesús Montoya, eds. *Estudios alfonsíes. Lexicografía, lírica, estética y política de Alfonso el Sabio.* Granada: Universidad de Granada, 1985.

Montes Romero-Camacho, Isabel. *El paisaje rural sevillano en la baja edad media.* Sevilla: Diputación Provincial de Sevilla, 1989.

Montoto, Santiago. *La Catedral y el Alcázar de Sevilla.* Madrid: Editorial Plus Ultra, n.d.

Montoya Martínez, Jesús. *Las colecciones de milagros de la Virgen en la Edad Media. El milagro literario.* Granada: Universidad de Granada, 1981.

————. "Algunas precisiones acerca de las Cantigas de Santa Maria." In Katz and Keller, *Studies,* 366-385.

————. "El Códice de Florencia: Una nueva hipótesis de trabajo." *Romance Quarterly* 33 (1986): 323-329.

————. "Historia de Andalucía en las Cantigas de Santa Maria." *Andalucía medieval. Actas del I Congreso de Historia de Andalucía, Córdoba, diciembre de 1976.* 2 vols. Córdoba: Monte de Piedad y Caja de Ahorros, 1978. 1:259-269.

————. "Judíos y moros en las Cantigas de Santa Maria." *Historia del Derecho (Granada)* (1980): 69-90.

————. "La 'carta fundacional' del Puerto de Santa Maria y las Cantigas de Santa Maria." *Cantigueiros* 6 (1994): 99-115.

————. "La 'gran vingança de Dios y Alfonso X." *Cantigueiros* 3 (1990): 53-59.

————. "Las Cantigas de Santa Maria: Fuente para la historia gaditana." *Cádiz en el siglo XIII. Actas de las jornadas conmemorativas del VIII Centenario de la muerte de Alfonso el Sabio.* Cádiz: Universidad de Cádiz, 1983. 173-181.

————. "Los nombres del Profeta: "Mafomete cão/Bafomete' en la tradición hispánica." *Homenaje al Profesor José María Fórneas Besteiro.* Granada: Universidad de Granada, 1994. 403-409.

————. "O Cancioneiro Marial de Alfonso X. El primer cancionero cortesano español." *O Cantar dos Trobadores. Actas do Congreso celebrado en Santiago de Compostela entre os dias 26 a 29 de abril de 1993.* Santiago de Compostela: Xunta de Galicia, 1993.

———— and Aurora Juárez Blanquer. *Andalucía en las Cantigas de Santa María.* Granada: Universidad de Granada, 1988.

Moxó, Salvador de. "La nobleza castellano-leonesa en la edad media," *Hispania* 30 (1970): 5-68.

Nieto Soria, José Manuel. *Fundamentos ideológicos del poder real en Castilla (Siglos XIII-XVI).* Madrid: Eudema, 1988.

————. "Imágenes religiosas del rey y del poder real en la Castilla del siglo XIII." *En la España medieval* 5.2 (1986): 709-729.

O'Callaghan, Joseph F. *A History of Medieval Spain.* Ithaca: Cornell University, 1975.

————. *The Cortes of Castile-León, 1188-1350.* Philadelphia: University of Pennsylvania, 1989.

————. *The Learned King: The Reign of Alfonso X of Castile.* Philadelphia: University of Pennsylvania, 1993.

————. *The Spanish Military Order of Calatrava and its Affiliates.* London: Variorum 1975.

————. "Don Fernán Pérez, un Maestre desconocido de la Orden de Calatrava, 1234-1235." *Hispania* 43 (1983): 433-439.

————. "*Hermandades* between the Military Orders of Calatrava and Santiago during the Castilian Reconquest, 1158-1252." In *The Spanish Military Order of Calatrava and its Affiliates.* No. 5.

————. "Paths to Ruin: The Economic and Financial Policies of Alfonso the Learned and Their Contribution to His Downfall." In Burns, *Worlds,* 41-67.

————. "The Affiliation of the Order of Calatrava with the Order of Cîteaux." In *The Spanish Military Order of Calatrava and its Affiliates.* No. 1.

————. "The *Cantigas de Santa Maria* as an Historical Source: Two Examples (nos. 321 and 386)." In Katz and Keller, *Studies,* 387-402.

————. "The Cortes and Royal Taxation during the Reign of Alfonso X of Castile." *Traditio* 27 (1971): 379-398.

————. "The Mudéjars of Castile and Portugal in the Twelfth and Thirteenth Centuries." In James M. Powell, ed. *Muslims under Latin Rule, 1110-1300.* Princeton: Princeton University, 1990. 11-56.

Ocasio, Rafael. "Ethnic Underclass Representation in the *Cantigas:* The Black Moro as a Hated Character." In Toscano, ed. *Estudios Alfonsinos.* 183-195.

Ortiz de Zúñiga, Diego. *Anales eclesiásticos y seculares de la muy noble y muy leal ciudad de Sevilla, Metropolí de la Andalucía.* Ed. Antonio María Espinosa y Carzel. 2 vols. Madrid: Imprenta real, 1795; reprint Sevilla: Guadalquivir, 1988.

Paredes Núñez, Juan. "Las Cantigas de Alfonso X como fuentes históricas: La Guerra de Granada." *Cuadernos de Estudios Medievales* 14-15 (1985-1987): 241-250.

Parkinson, Stephen. "The First Reorganization of the *Cantigas de Santa Maria.*" *Cantigueiros* 1 (1988): 91-98.

Pelikan, Jaroslav. *The Growth of Medieval Theology (600-1300) (The Christian Tradition: A History of the Development of Doctrine, 3).* Chicago: University of Chicago, 1978.

Pérez de Tudela y Velasco, María Isabel. "El tratamiento de la mujer en las Cantigas de Santa Maria." *La condición de la mujer en la Edad Media.* Madrid: Universidad Complutense, 1986. 51-73.

————. "La imagen de la Virgen María en las Cantigas de Santa Maria." *En la España medieval* 15 (1992): 297-320.

Pérez Embid, Florentino. "La marina real castellana en el siglo XIII." *Anuario de Estudios Medievales* 6 (1969): 141-185.

Post, Gaines. *Studies in Medieval Legal Thought: Public Law and the State, 1100-1322.* Princeton: Princeton University, 1964.

Powers, James F. *A Society Organized for War. The Iberian Municipal Militias in the Central Middle Ages, 1000-1284.* Berkeley: University of California, 1988.

Presilla, Maricel. *The Image of Death in the Cantigas de Santa Maria of Alfonso X (1252-84): The Politics of Death and Salvation.* Ph.D. dissertation, New York University, 1989.

————. "The Image of Death and Political Ideology in the *Cantigas de Santa Maria.*" In Katz and Keller, *Studies,* 403-458.

Procter, Evelyn. *Alfonso X of Castile. Patron of Literature and Learning.* Oxford: Clarendon, 1951.

————. *Curia and Cortes in León and Castile 1072-1295.* Cambridge: Cambridge University, 1980.

————. *The Judicial Use of Pesquisa (Inquisition) in León and Castile, 1157-1369. English Historical Review,* Supplement 2. London: Longmans, Green, 1966.

Rey, Juan José. "Alfonso X y la música de su época." In *Alfonso X. Toledo 1984.* 103-113.

————. "El trovador don Alfonso X." *Revista de Occidente* 43 (1984): 166-183.

Ribera, Julián. *La música de las Cantigas.* Madrid: Real Academia Española, 1922.

Rivera Recío, Juan Francisco. *San Ildefonso de Toledo. Biografia, época y posteridad.* Madrid: Biblioteca de Autores Cristianos, 1985.

Rodgers, Paula. "Alfonso X Writes to his Son: Reflections on the *Crónica de Alfonso X.*" *Exemplaria Hispánica* 1 (1991-1992): 58-79

Rodríguez Díez, Matías. *Historia de la ciudad de Astorga.* 2d ed. Astorga: Porfirio López, 1909.

Rogers, Donna M. "*Cantigas de Santa Maria* 2-25 and their Castilian Versions." In Toscano, ed. *Estudios Alfonsinos.* 196-204.

Roth, Norman. "Two Jewish Courtiers of Alfonso X called Zag (Isaac)." *Sefarad,* 43 (1983): 75-85.

Ruiz, Teófilo. "Images of Power in the Seals of the Castilian Monarchy: 1135-1469." *Estudios en Homenaje a Don Claudio Sánchez Albornoz en sus 90 años* 4 (1986): 455-463.

————. "Une royauté sans sacre: La monarchie castillane du bas moyen âge." *Annales: Économies, Societés, Civilisations* 39 (1984): 429-453.

Runciman, Steven. *A History of the Crusades.* 3 vols. New York: Harper Torchbooks, 1964-1967.

Russell, Jeffrey Burton. *Lucifer. The Devil in the Middle Ages.* Ithaca: Cornell University Press, 1986.

Scarborough, Connie L. *Women in Thirteenth-Century Spain as Portrayed in Alfonso X's* Cantigas de Santa Maria. Lewiston, N.Y.: Edwin Mellen, 1993.

————. "Alfonso X: Monarch in Search of a Miracle." *Romance Quarterly* 33 (1986): 349-354.

Schramm, Percy Ernst. *Las insignias de la realeza en la edad media española.* Madrid: Instituto de Estudios Políticos, 1960.

————. *A History of the English Coronation.* Tr. E. L. Legg. Oxford: Oxford University Press, 1937.

Senniff, Dennis P. "Falconry, Venery, and Fishing in the *Cantigas de Santa Maria.*" In Katz and Keller, *Studies,* 459-474.

Snow, Joseph. *The Poetry of Alfonso X el Sabio. A Critical Bibliography.* London: Grant and Cutler, 1977.

————. "A Chapter in Alfonso X's Personal Narrative: The Puerto de Santa María Poems in the Cantigas de Santa Maria." *La Corónica* 8 (1979): 10-21.

————. "Alfonso as Troubadour: The Fact and the Fiction." In Burns, *Emperor of Culture,* 124-140.

————. "Alfonso X como segundo protagonista en sus Cantigas: Ultimas Consideraciones." *Studia Hispánica Medievalia II. III Jornadas de Literatura Española.* Eds. Rosa E. Penna and Maria A. Rosarossa. Buenos Aires: Universidad Católica, 1992. 32-41.

————. "Alfonso X: sus 'Cantigas . . .' Apuntes para su (Auto)biografía literaria." *Joseph Maria Solà-Solé: Homage, Homenaje, Homenatge. Miscelánea de Estudios de Amigos y Discípulos.* Eds. Vitorio Aguera and Nathaniel B. Smith. Barcelona: Puvill, 1984. 79-89.

————. "Alfonso X y/en sus Cantigas," *Jornadas de estudios alfonsíes.* Granada: Universidad de Granada, 1985. 71-90.

————. "Alfonso X y la Cantiga 409: Un nexo posible con la tradición de la *Danza de la Muerte.*" *Studies in Honor of Lloyd A. Kasten.* Madison: Hispanic Seminary of Medieval Studies, 1975. 261-273.

————. "Gonzalo de Berceo and the Miracle of Saint Ildefonso: Portrait of a Medieval Artist at Work." *Hispania* 65 (1982): 1-11.

————. "Lo que nos dice la Cantiga 300 de Alfonso X." *Studia Hispánica Medievalia. II Jornadas de Literatura Española.* Eds. L. Teresa Valdivieseo and Jorge H. Valdivieso. Buenos Aires: Universidad Católica, 1988. 99-110.

————. "'Macar poucos cantares acabei e con son': La firma de Alfonso X a sus Cantigas de Santa Maria." *Actas del III Congreso de la Asociación Hispánica de Literatura Medieval. (Salamanca 3-8 Octubre 1989).* Ed. M. I. Toro Pascua. Salamanca: Biblioteca española del Siglo XV. Departamento de Literatura Española e Hispanoamericana, 1990. 3:1021-1030.

————. "Poetic Self-Awareness in Alfonso X's *Cantiga* 110." *Kentucky Romance Quarterly* 26 (1979): 421-432.

————. "Self-Conscious References and the Organic Narrative Pattern of the *Cantigas de Santa Maria* of Alfonso X." In Joseph R. Jones, ed. *Medieval, Renaissance and Folklore Studies in Honor of John Esten Keller.* Newark, Del.: Juan de la Cuesta, 1980. 53-65.

————. "The Central Role of the Troubadour Persona of Alfonso X in the *Cantigas de Santa Maria,*" *Bulletin of Hispanic Studies* 56 (1979): 305-316.

————. "The Satirical Poetry of Alfonso X: A Look at its Relationship to the '*Cantigas de Santa Maria*'." In Márquez-Villanueva and Vega, eds. *Alfonso X of Castile,* 110-131.

Socarras, Cayetano. *Alfonso X of Castile: A Study on Imperialistic Frustration.* Barcelona: Ediciones Hispam, 1976.

Solalinde, Antonio García. "El códice florentino de las Cantigas y su relación con los demás manuscritos." *Revista de Filología española* 5 (1918): 143-179.

Tinnell, Roger D. *An Annotated Discography of Music in Spain before 1650.* Madison: Hispanic Seminary of Medieval Studies, 1980.

Torres Balbás, Leopoldo. "La mezquita de al-Qanatir y el santuario de Alfonso el Sabio en el Puerto de Santa María." *Al-Andalus* 8 (1942): 417-437. Reprint in *Obra Dispersa. Al-Andalus. Crónica de la España musulmana.* 2 vols. Madrid: Instituto de España, 1982. 2:149-171.

Torres Delgado, Cristóbal. *El antiguo reino nazarí de Granada (1232-1340).* Granada: Anel, 1974.

Torres Fontes, Juan. "La Orden de Santa María de España." *Miscelánea Medieval Murciana* 3 (1977): 75-118.

Toscano, Nicolás, ed. *Estudios Alfonsinos y otros escritos.* New York: National Endowment for the Humanities and National Hispanic Foundation for the Humanities, 1991.

Trivison, Mary Louise. "A Pilgrim Poem of the Marqués de Santillana: Resumé of Medieval Marian Lyric." In Toscano, *Estudios Alfonsinos,* 246-253.

Ullmann, Walter. *Principles of Government and Politics in the Middle Ages.* New York: Barnes and Noble, 1966.

Walmisley-Santiago, Olga. "Alfonso el Sabio's Attitude towards Moors and Jews as Revealed in Two of his Works." *Cantigueiros* 6 (1994): 30-41.

Williams, John. *Early Spanish Manuscript Illumination.* New York: George Braziller, 1977.

————. *The Illustrated Beatus. A Corpus of Illustrations of the Commentary on the Apocalypse,* 5 vols. London: Harvey Miller, 1994-1996.

Dwayne E. Carpenter (essay date 1998)

SOURCE: Carpenter, Dwayne E. "The Portrayal of the Jew in Alfonso the Learned's *Cantigas de Santa Maria.*" In *In Iberia and beyond: Hispanic Jews between Cultures—Proceedings of a Symposium to Mark the 500th Anniversary of the Expulsion of Spanish Jewry.* Edited by Bernard Dov Cooperman, pp. 15-42. Newark, N.J.: University of Delaware Press, 1998.

[*In the following essay, Carpenter analyzes instances of anti-Semitism in the* Cantigas.]

The *Cantigas de Santa Maria* (*Songs in Praise of Holy Mary*) is arguably the most sumptuous literary artifact of thirteenth-century Iberia. Although none of the four extant manuscripts is complete, together they comprise 420 poetic compositions, most of which recount the Virgin's miraculous intervention in a wide array of human affairs.[1] Each of the lavishly executed manuscripts contains, in addition to the text, either musical notation or illuminations, or both.[2] This multifaceted compendium, ascribed to Alfonso X, the Learned (1252-1284), is composed in Galician-Portuguese, with the exception of twenty-four prosified accounts in Castilian, which were later added to Escorial MS T.I.1.[3] Despite the traditional attribution of the *Cantigas* to Alfonso, he assuredly did not author the entire text, nor did he compose all of the accompanying music or produce the hundreds of superbly crafted miniatures. The inventory of hagiographic and Marian sources consulted by Alfonso and his collaborators is as varied as Gautier de Coinci's *Miracles de la Sainte Vierge,* Caesarius of Heisterbach's *Dialogus miraculorum,* Vincent de Beauvais's *Speculum historiale,* and Juan Gil de Zamora's *Liber Mariae,* to cite only a few of the best known collections.[4] Many of the *Cantiga* narratives are of Spanish provenance, and some clearly originated with Alfonso. As is the case with other works credited to the Learned King, it is likely that he supplied the overall design and, on occasion, authored portions of the text.[5] Whatever the extent of his involvement in the composition of the *Cantigas,* Alfonso clearly considered the collection to be a personal expression of his devotion to the Virgin—he often calls himself her troubadour—and, according to *cantiga* 209, a copy of the *Cantigas* even helped to restore the infirm monarch to health.[6]

In a collection of this size and pan-European pedigree, it is not surprising to discover a multitude of themes, all unified by the presence of the Virgin, both as consummate activist and as object of adoration.[7] The *Cantigas* is replete with stories of healings, resurrections—human and animal—deliverance from prison, wars, temptations, chastisements, and conversions. The cast of characters is equally diverse, including pious priests and wayward nuns, arrogant bishops, demons and demoniacs, besotted gamblers, Muslims and Jews. Within this thematic and dramatic miscellany, Alfonso adroitly casts the Virgin in a variety of roles. Always a compassionate mother toward her well-intentioned but errant children, and a merciful advocate before the stern celestial Judge, she at times threatens both Christians and infidels with death if they dare oppose her wishes or menace her devotees.

These diverse traits are evident in the Virgin's dealings with members of the two main religious minorities of medieval Spain: the Muslims and the Jews. The former appear in fifty-one *cantigas,* where their treatment ranges from ancillary allusions to detailed narratives.[8] Explicit mention of Jews, aside from references to the Old Testament, is found in forty *cantigas,* or approximately nine percent of the *cantigas* contained in Walter Mettmann's critical edition.[9] Within this corpus, I have identified the following five thematic groups: 1) Jewish culpability for the death of Jesus, 2) Jewish disparagement of the Virgin, Jesus, or Christianity, 3) Jews as allies of the Devil, 4) Jews as avaricious, and 5) the rescue and salvation of Jews. In addition, there are a number of miscellaneous references to Jews.[10]

There is no lack of scholarship on the depiction of the Jew in the *Cantigas.* Albert I. Bagby, Jr., Anita Benaim de Lasry, José Fradejas Lebrero, Vikki Hatton and Angus Mackay, John E. Keller, Jesús Montoya Martínez, B. N. Teensma, and Mary Louise Trivison have all devoted their efforts to this topic.[11] Their analyses vary considerably regarding objectives, thoroughness, and insight, but their conclusions fall into two broad categories: either the *Cantigas*—and by extension Alfonso—reflect hostility toward Jews, or they evince varying degrees of tolerance. In a number of largely repetitive studies, for example, Bagby claims that the *Cantigas* portrays Alfonso as personally antipathetic toward Jews.[12] Indeed, he claims that only three narratives, each ending with the conversion of the Jewish protagonist, depict Jews in a positive light.[13] Hatton and Mackay, on the other hand, discern a more ambivalent Alfonso. The essence of their argument is that hostile references to Jews are often incidental to the narrative, that such passages "may be balanced, or even outweighed, by more favourable aspects of the same story," that extremely hostile expressions of anti-Semitic themes are absent, and that not all themes are treated equally.[14]

Scholars concerned with the figure of the Jew in the *Cantigas* have focused their attention on one or more of the eleven *cantigas* with Jewish protagonists (4, 6, 12, 25, 27, 34, 85, 89, 107, 108, 286), while almost no mention has been made of the ostensibly incidental references to Jews, except to argue that they are, in fact, incidental. Bagby, for instance, despite his broad treatment of Jewish themes in the *Cantigas,* relegates such references to scanty footnotes.[15] For their part, Hatton and Mackay cursorily discuss the incidental nature of many passages in their effort to show that Alfonso is not as hostile toward Jews as has been alleged.[16] Yet, no scholar has indicated why certain references should be accorded more critical attention—though less moral significance—than others. The implicit assumption seems to be that the length of the passage determines its importance. It is not at all obvious to me, however, that the relatively detailed narratives are in fact intrinsically more significant than are the incidental references, and, as a result, that the extended accounts should be considered more indicative of pro- or anti-Jewish sentiment than should the so-called incidental passages.

In a similar vein, some scholars have claimed that Alfonso's reliance upon long-standing and widespread Jewish stereotypes reflects less hostility precisely because of the descriptions' traditional and pan-European character, and that such reliance ostensibly attenuates any hostility that Alfonso might have expressed toward Jews within the context of the *Cantigas*.[17] It is further argued that "eight of the thirty compositions [dealing with Jews] were widely-circulated accounts whose outline and content are clearly established and over which Alfonso (or his collaborators) had no control."[18] While there has indeed been a failure to appreciate the broad European background of many of the *cantigas* with Jewish themes, it does not follow that convention mitigates, or much less justifies, the blatantly dispective portrayals of Jews. There are many instances in which Alfonso injects disparaging and wholly gratuitous comments concerning Jews into narratives otherwise lacking Jewish characters or themes. In *cantiga* 5.140, for example, Alfonso describes the passengers on a ship as "good people; there were neither Jews nor Muslims."[19] And at times Alfonso refers to the Jews as *encreus*, "unbelievers" (419.56; 425.22). Clearly, the Alfonsine literary and pictorial representations are not *uniquely* hostile, since they belong to a well-established tradition of medieval anti-Semitism. But to argue that the severity of hostile references is diminished because they are commonplaces is to reduce the moral weight of a canard simply because of its widespread publicity.

These considerations are critical, since by far the largest single category of references to Jews in the *Cantigas,* eleven in all, repeats the traditional Christian claim of Jewish culpability for the death of Jesus, and these are, for the most part, the very references that scholars have deemed incidental. In all but one instance, Alfonso intercalates the accusation of deicide, usually expressed matter-of-factly in a line or two, into the broader narrative. The following example, taken from a story whose protagonist is a blaspheming Jewish gambler, is representative:

> The cursed one refused to see how God became flesh of the Virgin and was later killed by the Jews, but he determined with all his heart and mind to vilify Holy Mary, by whom God became flesh.[20]

The incidental placement of the accusation, and its resultant tangency to both the doctrinal issue and the narrative thread, should not lead us to underestimate the importance of the charge. Its recurrence in medieval literature in general and in Alfonso's works in particular, rather than evincing nonchalance, indicates that Jewish guilt for the death of Jesus was a given for medieval Christians, an item so common in the repertoire of anti-Semitic sentiments that within the *Cantigas* it required

neither elaboration nor emphasis.[21] While such gratuitous references may indeed be incidental to the narrative thread, they are not necessarily less malevolent than more fully developed and openly hostile stories. Entrenched disparagement is hardly less injurious than overt hostility; in fact, it may be more insidious precisely because of its parenthetical casting. The destruction of Jewish communities by the crusaders, rallying around the charge that the Jews had crucified Jesus, gives the lie to the argument that the charge of deicide was incidental either to the thinking or to the actions of medieval Christians.[22]

One *cantiga,* no. 12, deals at some length with a crucifixion, in this instance a mock crucifixion. During the celebration of the mass, according to the account, the archbishop of Toledo and his congregants hear a voice complaining that the Jews killed Jesus and that they still continue to torment Him. The parishioners hasten to the Jewish quarter, and there discover the Jews preparing to crucify a waxen image of Jesus. Seized with righteous indignation, the Christians slaughter all the Jews (fig. 3).[23]

The charge that Jews crucified images was common in European literature and law, and the appearance of a reference to that effect in a collection of hundreds of miracle stories would not be unexpected.[24] We might nonetheless justifiably inquire why this narrative recounting the crucifixion of a waxen image should be granted such prominent attention. The relevant legislation in the *Siete Partidas,* Alfonso's massive juridical compendium, may shed some light on the concern with waxen images. The treatise entitled "Concerning the Jews" states the following:

> Jews ought to conduct themselves meekly and without disorder among Christians, observing their own law and not speaking ill of the faith of Our Lord Jesus Christ, which Christians observe. Furthermore, they must take great care not to preach or convert any Christian, praising their own law and maligning ours. And whoever does contrary to this, shall die as a result and lose all that he has. And because we heard that in some places the Jews reenacted derisively—and continue to do so—on Good Friday the Passion of Our Lord Jesus Christ, stealing children and placing them on a cross, or forming waxen images and crucifying them when children are unavailable, we order that if we discover from this time forward that such a thing has occurred in any part of our kingdom, and if it can be determined, then all those involved shall be seized, arrested, and brought before the king. And as soon as he has determined the truth of the matter, he shall order the guilty parties to be mercilessly put to death. In addition, we order that on Good Friday no Jew shall dare to leave his quarter; rather, the Jews shall remain there behind closed doors until Saturday morning. And if they do otherwise, we decree that they shall have no claim to reparations for any damage or dishonor done them by Christians.[25]

As I have argued elsewhere, Alfonso's prohibition of ritual murder is notable in that he dilutes the impact of the charge with the vague announcement that "we heard that in some places the Jews reenacted derisively—and continue to do so—on Good Friday the Passion of Our Lord Jesus Christ."[26] The description thus appears to be founded largely on hearsay, and may even be based on non-Hispanic accounts. Even more important, the central concern of this entire law is blasphemy and the resultant disparagement of Christianity.[27] I contend that this same concern is evident in *cantiga* 12. It is not a case of ritual murder, since there are no children involved, the waxen image is of Jesus, and the incident allegedly occurs in August during the feast of the Virgin. Rather, *cantiga* 12 is primarily an indictment of Jewish blasphemy and insolence.[28]

This concern with the defamation of Christianity in general and of the Virgin in particular can be seen in a number of other narratives. In *cantiga* 2, for example, Alfonso lauds the seventh-century archbishop of Toledo, Ildefonsus, who, in the face of disparaging Jews and heretics, defended the doctrine of the virginity of Mary.[29] In *cantiga* 6, a Jewish gambler murders a Christian child because the latter sings the Virgin's praises. [30] *Cantiga* 34 tells of the demise of a Jew who dishonors an image of the Virgin.[31] In *cantiga* 108, Merlin prays that a Jewish baby be born with his head facing backwards as punishment for his father's obdurate unbelief in the Incarnation.[32] Alfonso also records Mary's fear that the Jews had abducted the young Jesus:

> The second [sorrow] was when
> your Son was lost
> for three days, and fearing
> that the Jews had hidden
> Him . . .
>
> (403.18-22)[33]

Not only do Jews overtly disparage Jesus and the Virgin, but when two Jews ridicule a Christian, Alfonso interprets the deed as a vicarious deprecation of Mary:

> But he [the Christian] said to Holy Mary: "Oh, Lord, grant me justice, if it please you, over these Jews, who are your enemies, for they killed your Son, who was man and God, and they mock you through me, as you can see."
>
> (286.30-34)[34]

Indeed, the hostility of the Jews toward the Virgin is so great that she fears they will destroy her body:

> "And as I [Mary] have heard, these evil Jews,
> who killed my Son like false unbelievers,
> threaten to burn my flesh and my bones . . ."
>
> (419.55-58)[35]

In this passage, and elsewhere, the charge of blasphemy is linked to Jewish unbelief.[36] Although such references are deceptively concise, and appear almost incidentally,

it is essential to realize that they were by no means incidental to a medieval audience for whom the single word *encreus*, "unbelievers," could conjure up a host of hateful sentiments.

Joshua Trachtenberg has amply demonstrated that a basic component of medieval anti-Semitism is the association of the Jews with the Devil.[37] Not surprisingly, this element appears in the *Cantigas*, although neither as frequently nor as viciously as one might expect.[38] Furthermore, the Devil-human being relationship is not limited to Jews, since at least on one occasion a cleric conjures demons (125). When Merlin and a Jew appear together, it is Merlin who is called "son of Satan" (*fillo de Sathanas* [108.73]). Of the four references to the Devil and the Jews, three occupy but a few lines, and even the well-known account of Theophilus contains but a brief mention of the Devil-Jew relationship.[39] Only *cantiga* 109, the story of a man freed from five demons, enlarges upon the diabolical connection. When asked why they do not seek the Jews, one of the demons responds that since the Jews already belong to him, the demons devote their efforts only to seducing those protected by the sign of baptism.[40] This same notion is expressed in *cantiga* 34, where a devil kills a Jew who possesses an image of the Virgin.[41] While it is undoubtedly true that Alfonso could have presented the Jews in a more hostile manner, the Devil-Jew connection alone places the Jews in a negative light. And the illustrations accompanying the Theophilus account, showing a horde of repugnant devils around the Jew, hardly suggest a benign portrayal. Hatton and Mackay's assertion that Alfonso's depiction of Jews could have been even less favorable seems to me a weak argument in favor of relative tolerance. The only factor mitigating the negative Devil-Jew relationship is the infrequent appearance of the theme in the *Cantigas*.

The common stereotype of Jews as avaricious appears in several *cantigas*. In one instance, a statue of the Virgin testifies that "the falseness of the Jews is great," when called upon to defend a Christian who has been defrauded by a Jew.[42] On another occasion, the Jews seek to recover a synagogue they have sold to the Apostles. When an image of the Virgin miraculously appears on the altar, the Jews forsake the premises (27). Another account tells of a Jew who steals an image of the Virgin, hides it, and then is killed by a devil (34). At one point, Alfonso condemns the count of Poitou for economically squeezing his enemy, "like Jews,"[43] and later refers to Jews as usurers.[44] He also devotes several verses to an account of Jewish treasure discovered by a king in Granada.[45] These *cantigas* depict Jewish greed, duplicity, and theft, thus perpetuating several negative stereotypes of Jews within an economic context.

Aside from the specific thematic issues raised in the *Cantigas* relative to the Jews, numerous additional references also appear, often of a theological nature, such as the coming of the Messiah (25.180-84; 71.16-18), the Jewish-Christian debate over the Incarnation (108.30-36), the characterization of Jews as unbelievers (419.55-58; 425.21-23), the location of the Nativity star in "the land of the Jews" (424.30), and the identity of Jesus as "Lord of the Jews and of the Law" (424.37).[46]

Critics have focused a great deal of attention on the various miracles describing conversions of Jews to Christianity. Bagby cites *cantigas* 89, 107, and, inexplicably, 133 as "positive characterization[s]" of Jews, and Hatton and Mackay refer to *cantigas* 85, 89, 107, and 108 as illustrative of "peaceful methods of conversion." Neither list, however, is complete, since *cantigas* 4 and 25 also deal with the conversion of Jews. Of the six *cantigas* containing the motif of Jewish conversion, the protagonists in four are either women or children. In *cantiga* 4, a young boy, Abel, is baptized after the Virgin protects him from the fire into which he has been cast by his irate father. *Cantiga* 89 recounts how Mary saved a pregnant Jewess who was near death because she was unable to deliver and, despite the taunts of other Jews, she and two children were baptized. In *cantiga* 107, Mary provides a soft landing for a Jewess who has been cast from a mountain, evidently after having been convicted of adultery.[47] And *cantiga* 108 tells how a Jewish boy was born facing backwards, just as Merlin had predicted, as punishment for his father's unbelief and blasphemy. Other Jews convert when they witness the miracle.[48]

In the first of the two *cantigas* involving Jewish men, a statue of the Virgin speaks on behalf of a Christian who has been defrauded by a Jew. The Jew collapses, believes in the Virgin and her Son, and accepts the Christian faith.[49] In the second case, Mary first allows a Jew to fall into the hands of thieves, who maltreat him, and then she comes to his rescue. The Jew does not convert, however, until he is shown how the devils inflict infernal tortures on Jews. The theme of Jewish stubbornness, even after heavenly succor, is thus woven into the narrative (85).

It is difficult to accept the assertion that the conversion miracles are positive portrayals of Jews, or that they portray Jews "like Christian sinners, as souls to be saved for Christ, rather than as infidels to be fought in his name."[50] Infidels are assisted or saved by their *relative* attention to the Virgin. Thus, Alfonso occasionally exhibits a pro-Muslim stance because of the Muslim belief in Mary, a posture particularly attractive given the Marian thread of the *Cantigas.*[51] Furthermore, the Virgin sometimes assists Muslims even though they do not subsequently convert, while Jews always either die or convert. The conversion of Jews takes place at the close of the narratives, and in some instances results only after there is pressure to convert.

We have seen that the literary depiction of Jews in the *Cantigas* is consistently negative, an unflattering presentation that accords well with traditional medieval stereotypes. With regard to the Jews, the overriding issues in the *Cantigas* are the charges of deicide, disparagement, and avarice. Despite the prevalence in European literature and art of the Devil-Jew theme, Alfonso does not emphasize it in the *Cantigas.* Finally, to argue that the conversion narratives constitute an exception to this negative portrayal because Jews are capable of conversion, and therefore not irredeemably evil, is salvation with faint praise.

The preceding analysis of the portrayal of the Jew in Alfonso X's *Cantigas de Santa Maria* has provoked once again the question of the degree of anti-Semitism or tolerance in the work. Ironically, this concern of the modern humanist was probably far from the mind of the Learned King as he orchestrated his poetic magnum opus. With regard to Alfonso's attitude toward Jews and Judaism, it is fair, I believe, to state that Alfonso does not go out of his way to malign Jews, especially in the widely diffused stories involving Jews, but neither does he provide positive portrayals. On numerous occasions, in fact, he incorporates gratuitous, disparaging comments into the narrative. From a literary standpoint, most of the references to Jewish culpability for the death of Jesus are incidental to the narrative, but they are central to the issue of medieval anti-Semitism. I think it difficult, if not impossible, to distinguish between expressions of traditional, institutionalized anti-Semitism and evidence of personal hostility, especially since the latter usually draws upon the former. Alfonso exemplifies within the *Cantigas* the precedent of theological and literary antipathy toward the Jews.[52] The *Cantigas* is a personal, didactic, and, to some extent, conventional work, in which Alfonso's reliance upon a Christian theological tradition, including a heritage of anti-Semitism, is everywhere present. Alfonso is not an anamoly in this regard, and we distort history and the man if we attempt to discover a tolerance that is inherently absent. . . .[53]

Notes

1. The total of 420 *cantigas* follows Walter Mettmann, *Cantigas de Santa Maria,* 2 vols. (Vigo: Xerais de Galicia, 1981), I, p. 31. For other calculations, see Francisco Mundi Pedret and Anabel Sáiz Ripoll, *Las prosificaciones de las "Cantigas" de Alfonso X el Sabio* (Barcelona: Promociones y Publicaciones Universitarias, 1987), p. 31, n. 1.

2. Walter Mettmann provides a paleographic description of the four manuscripts, along with references to earlier descriptions, in his four-volume critical edition and glossary (Coimbra: Acta Universitatis Conimbrigensis, 1959-72), I, pp. vii-xxiv; reprinted in two volumes (Vigo: Xerais de Galicia,

1981). An updated, three-volume edition by Mettmann has recently appeared (Madrid: Castalia,
1986-89). Matilde López Serrano also describes
the four manuscripts in the volume accompanying
the opulent facsimile edition of Escorial MS T.I.1
(Madrid: Edilán, 1979), pp. 19-32. The commentary contains useful historical background, a
transcription of Esc. MS T.I.1, and a Spanish prose
translation and commentary by José Filgueira Valverde (33-264), a linguistic study by Ramón
Lorenzo Vázquez (265-68), a comprehensive
analysis of the illuminations by José Guerrero
Lovillo (269-320), and musical transcriptions and
commentary by José María Lloréns Cisteró (321-
96). A useful bibliography, arranged thematically,
completes the work (397-406). Filgueira Valverde's commentary and translation are conveniently
reproduced in his *"Cantigas de Santa María":
Códice Rico de El Escorial, Ms. escurialense T.I.1*
(Madrid: Castalia, "Odres Nuevos," 1985). An
indispensable guide to work on the *Cantigas* and
on Alfonso's secular poetry is Joseph Snow, *The
Poetry of Alfonso X, el Sabio: A Critical Bibliography,* Research Bibliographies & Checklists No.
19 (London: Grant & Cutler, 1977). A supplement
is in preparation.

3. James R. Chatham, "A Paleographic Edition of
the Alfonsine Collection of Prose Miracles of the
Virgin," in *Oelschläger Festschrift, Hispanófila* 36
(Chapel Hill: Castalia, 1976), pp. 73-111. See the
monographic analysis of the prose miracles by
Mundi Pedret and Sáiz Ripoll, *Las prosificaciones
de las Cantigas;* as well as the useful study by
Anthony Cárdenas, "A Study of Alfonso's Role in
Selected *Cantigas* and the Castilian Prosifications
of Escorial Codex T.I.1," in Israel J. Katz et al.,
eds., *Studies on the "Cantigas de Santa Maria":
Art, Music, and Poetry. Proceedings of the
International Symposium on the "Cantigas de
Santa Maria" of Alfonso X, el Sabio (1221-1284)
in Commemoration of Its 700th Anniversary
Year—1981 (New York, November 19-21)*
(Madison: Hispanic Seminary of Medieval Studies, 1987), pp. 253-68. Finally, note the most
recent response to the provocative suggestion that
Juan Manuel, Alfonso X's nephew, composed the
prose miracles (Reinaldo Ayerbe-Chaux, "Las
prosificaciones castellanas de las *Cantigas de
Santa María*: ¿una obra perdida de don Juan Manuel?" *Bulletin of the Cantigueiros de Santa Maria*
3 [1990], pp. 39-52).

4. A useful list of sources is found in Mettmann,
Cantigas (Castalia), I, pp. 10-12; Filgueira Valverde, *Cantigas,* pp. xlviii-lvi; and John Esten
Keller, *Alfonso X, el Sabio* (New York: Twayne,
1967), pp. 73-77.

5. The problem of authorship is addressed by Mettmann, *Cantigas* (Castalia), I, pp. 17-20; and

Filgueira Valverde, *Cantigas,* pp. xxvii-xxxiv.
Joseph Snow discusses various aspects of Alfon-
so's participation in the *Cantigas* ("The Central
Role of the Troubadour *Persona* of Alfonso X in
the *Cantigas de Santa Maria," Bulletin of Hispanic
Studies* 56 [1979], pp. 305-16).

6. *E os fisicos mandavan-me põer / panos caentes,
mas nono quix fazer, / mas mandei o Livro dela
aduzer; / e poseron-mio, e logo jouv' en paz, /
Muito faz grand' erro, e en torto jaz . . . / Que
non braadei nen senti nulla ren / da door, mas
senti-me logo mui ben* (209.27-33). All citations
from the *Cantigas* are from Mettmann's two-
volume edition (1981). For a study of *cantiga* 209,
see John E. Keller and Richard P. Kinkade,
"Iconography and Literature: Alfonso Himself in
Cantiga 209," *Hispania* 66 (1983), pp. 348-52.

7. Filgueira Valverde, *Cantigas,* pp. lx-lxiii; and
Jesús Montoya Martínez, "Criterio agrupador de
las *Cantigas de Santa María,"* in *Estudios liter-
arios dedicados al profesor Mariano Baquero
Goyanes* (Murcia: Univ. de Murcia, 1974), pp.
285-96.

8. The total of 51 references is according to Mercedes García-Arenal, "Los moros en las *Cantigas*
de Alfonso X el Sabio," *Al-Qantara* 6 (1985), pp.
133-51, at 137, to date the best treatment of the
subject. Jesús Montoya Martínez, "Judíos y moros
en las *Cantigas de Santa Maria," Historia del
Derecho* (Granada, 1980), pp. 69-90, at 69, identifies 31 references to "moros," while Albert I.
Bagby, Jr., initially discovers 44 references to
Moors ("Some Characterizations of the Moor in
Alfonso X's *Cántigas," The South Central Bulletin* 30 [1970], pp. 164-67, at 164); and later finds
42 references ("The Moslem in the *Cantigas* of
Alfonso X, el Sabio," *Kentucky Romance Quarterly* 20 [1973], pp. 173-207, at 173). See also
Bagby's "Alfonso X, el Sabio compara moros y
judíos," *Romanische Forschungen* 82 (1970), pp.
578-83; and "Further Notes on the Moslems under
Alfonso X," *Kentucky Romance Quarterly* 24
(1977), pp. 3-13.

9. Considerable work remains to be done on *cantigas* patterned after Biblical accounts and on references to Old Testament personages. Albert I.
Bagby, Jr. claims that 30 *cantigas* contain references to Jews ("The Jew in the *Cántigas* of Alfonso X, el Sabio," *Speculum* 46 [1971], pp. 670-
88, at 674-75); while Montoya Martínez asserts
that there are 15 *cantigas* that have Jewish
protagonists, although he enumerates only 12
("Judíos y moros en las *Cantigas,"* 69, n. 1). Hatton and Mackay ("Anti-Semitism in the *Cantigas
de Santa Maria," Bulletin of Hispanic Studies* 61
[1983], pp. 189-99) discuss almost exclusively the
extended narratives featuring Jewish protagonists.

My tally of 40 *cantigas* containing references to Jews includes so-called incidental references.

10. Bagby classifies the references to Jews as follows: 1) the Jew as an archenemy of Christianity, 2) the Jew as the devil's disciple, 3) the Jew as a symbol of avarice, 4) the Jew as a traitor, and 5) the Jew as a Christian convert ("The Jew in the *Cántigas* of Alfonso X," p. 675; and "The Figure of the Jew in the *Cantigas*," *Studies on the Cantigas*, pp. 235-45, at 238-43).

11. Albert I. Bagby, Jr., "Alfonso X, el Sabio compara moros y judíos," *Romanische Forschungen* 82 (1970), pp. 578-83; "The Jew in the *Cántigas* of Alfonso X, el Sabio," *Speculum* 46 (1971), pp. 670-88; "Dos preconceitos de Afonso X, o Sábio," *Veritas* 96 (1979), pp. 449-70; and "The Figure of the Jew in the *Cantigas* of Alfonso X," *Studies on the "Cantigas,"* pp. 235-45; Anita Benaim de Lasry, "Marisaltos: Artificial Purification in Alfonso el Sabio's *Cantiga 107*," *Studies on the "Cantigas,"* pp. 299-311; José Fradejas Lebrero, "La *Cantiga* CVII o de Mari Saltos," *Fragmentos* 2 (1984), pp. 20-32; Vikki Hatton and Angus Mackay, "Anti-Semitism in the *Cantigas de Santa Maria*," *Bulletin of Hispanic Studies* 61 (1983), pp. 189-99; John E. Keller, "Miracle of the Jewess Thrown from a High Cliff: No. 107 of the *Cantigas de Santa Maria*," *Xavier Review* 2 (1982), pp. 63-67; Jesús Montoya Martínez, "Judíos y moros en las *Cantigas de Santa Maria*," *Historia del Derecho* (Granada: 1980), pp. 69-90; B. N. Teensma, "Os Judeus na Espanha do século XIII, segundo as *Cantigas de Santa Maria* de Afonso X o Sábio," *Ocidente* 79 (1970), pp. 85-102; Mary Louise Trivison, "Prayer and Prejudice in the *CSM*," *Bulletin of the Cantigueiros de Santa Maria* 1 (1988), p. 119-27.

12. "Alfonso X, el Sabio compara moros y judíos," *Romanische Forschungen* 82 (1970), pp. 578-83; "The Jew in the *Cántigas* of Alfonso X, el Sabio," *Speculum* 46 (1971), pp. 670-88; and "The Figure of the Jew in the *Cantigas* of Alfonso X," *Studies on the "Cantigas,"* pp. 235-45. Montoya Martínez ("Judíos y moros en las *Cantigas*," p. 77), and Teensma ("Os Judeus na Espanha do século XIII," 89, 102), likewise claim that the *Cantigas* evince Alfonso's personal hostility toward the Jews.

13. Nos. 89, 107, 133 ("The Jew in the *Cántigas* of Alfonso X," pp. 686-87; and "The Figure of the Jew in the *Cantigas*," p. 242).

14. "Anti-Semitism in the *Cantigas*," pp. 189-91.

15. "The other eleven *cántigas* which illustrate this category [the Jew as an archenemy of Christian-

ity] make only brief mention of Jews, so they will not be discussed here" ("The Jew in the *Cántigas* of Alfonso X," p. 678).

16. "Anti-Semitism in the *Cantigas*," p. 189.

17. Hatton and Mackay, "Anti-Semitism in the *Cantigas*," pp. 189-91. Snow takes Bagby, Teensma, and Montoya Martínez to task for not devoting sufficient attention to traditional anti-Semitism in the *Cantigas* (*The Poetry of Alfonso X*, pp. 95, 100, 102, 105; and in a forthcoming supplement generously supplied by the author).

18. Snow, *The Poetry of Alfonso X*, p. 103.

19.   [V]*yu vīir hūa nave preto de si, chẽa de romeus,*
      de bõa gente, que non avia y mouros nen judeus.

                         (5.139-40)

20.   *Non quis catar o maldito | como prendeu carne Deus*
      na Virgen e pois prendeu | por el morte dos judeos,
      mais o coraçon proposo | e todos los sisos seus
      en viltar Santa Maria, | de que Deus carne fillou.

                         (238.20-23)

21. See, in this regard, Joël Saugnieux, *Berceo y las culturas del siglo XIII* (Logroño: Servicio de Cultura de la Excma. Diputación Provincial, 1982) pp. 73-102.

22. A classic text in this regard is Shlomo Eidelberg, ed., *The Jews and the Crusaders: The Hebrew Chronicles of the First and Second Crusades* (Madison: Univ. of Wisconsin, 1977).

23. The final two verses of *cantiga* 12 provide an ironic twist to a passage found at the end of the book of Esther describing the victory of the Jews over their enemies:

    E por est' ouveron todos de morrer,
    e tornou-xe-lles en doo seu solaz.

                         (12.33-34)

(And for this reason, all of them [the Jews] had to die, and their pleasure was turned to grief.)

Cf. "As the days wherein the Jews rested from their enemies, and the month which was turned unto them from sorrow to joy, and from mourning unto a good day" (Esther 9.22).

24.

In accounts which portray Jewish maltreatment of waxen figures of Jesus, the actions of the Jews were construed as a renewal of the ancient antipathy toward the Christian messiah. In addition, the prevalence of stories about sanguineous crucifixes supports the idea that the populace believed that Jesus was present in images, just as He was present in the wine and wafer of the Eucharist.

Dwayne E. Carpenter, *Alfonso X and the Jews: An Edition of and Commentary on "Siete Partidas" 7.24 "De los judíos,"* Publications in Modern Philology, no. 115 (Berkeley: Univ. of California, 1986), p. 115. See, as well, Jacob R. Marcus, *The Jew in the Medieval World: A Source Book: 315-1791* (Philadelphia, 1938; repr. New York: Atheneum, 1979), pp. 155-58; and Joshua Trachtenberg, *The Devil and the Jews: The Medieval Conception of the Jew and its Relation to Modern Antisemitism* (New Haven: Yale Univ. Press, 1943; repr., with introduction by Marc Saperstein, Philadelphia: The Jewish Publication Society of America, 1983), pp. 109 ff.

25. Carpenter, *Alfonso X and the Jews*, p. 29.

26. Ibid., pp. 63-66.

27. The issue of blasphemy, both by Christians and non-Christians, forms an important part of medieval gambling legislation. In this regard, see my "Fickle Fortune: Gambling in Medieval Spain," *Studies in Philology* 85 (1988), pp. 267-78. Note, also, the frequent appearance of blaspheming gamblers in the *Cantigas*: nos. 6, 38, 72, 136, 154, 163, 174, 238, 294.

28. Hatton and Mackay's conclusion that "the one instance in which a group of Jews combine in an anti-Christian act, in *Cantiga* 12, appears fairly innocuous" ("Anti-Semitism in the *Cantigas*," p. 191) clearly is not shared by the Christians in the account, who find the action sufficiently disturbing to call for the death of all the Jews involved in the mock crucifixion.

29. *Ben enpregou el seus ditos, / com' achamos en verdade, / e os seus bõos escritos / que fez da virgiĩdade / daquesta Sennor mui santa, / per que sa loor tornada / foi en Espanna de quanta / a end' avian deytada / judeus e a eregia"* (2.17-25). Interestingly, Jews are not mentioned in the prose version of *cantiga* 2. In *cantiga* 91.10-11 Alfonso declares that neither Jews nor heretics can gainsay the Virgin's miracles: . . . *que non poden contradizer judeus / nen ereges, pero queiran dizer al.*

30.

> *No que o moço cantava | o judeu meteu mentes,*
> *e levó-o a ssa casa, | pois se foron as gentes;*
> *e deu-lle tal dũa acha, | que ben atro enos dentes*
> *o fendeu bẽes assi, | ben como quen lenna fende.*
>
> (6.42-45)

31. *Esta é como Santa Maria fillou dereito do judeu pola desonrra que fezera a sua omagen* (34.1-2).

32. *Poren te quero pregar / que, com' eu de certo sei / que o teu foi sen dultar, / que o que te rogarey / queras agora mostrar / a este da falssa ley / que*

anda con folia, / Dereit' é de ss' end' achar . . . / Que ssa moller enprennar / foi; o que lle nacer en / queras tu assi guisar / que com' outr' o rostro ten / adeante por catar, / tenna atras, e des en / and' assi todavia." (108.46-60)

33. *O segundo foi quando / seu Fill' ouve perdudo / tres dias, e cuidando / que judeus ascondudo / llo tĩan . . .* (403.18-22). Note, also, Alfonso's claim that the Virgin and Jesus fled to Egypt for fear of the Jews:

> . . . *e con pavor dos judeus*
> *fugiu con el a Egipto, | terra de rey Faraon.*
>
> (14.8-9)

34.

> *Mas diss' a Santa Maria: | "Ai, Sennor, destes judeus*
> *me dá, se te praz, dereito, | ca son ẽemigos teus*
> *que mataron a teu Fillo, | que era ome e Deus,*
> *e por ti me escarnecen, | como tu podes vẽer."*
>
> (286.30-34)

35.

> *E com' eu ei oydo, | estes maos judeus,*
> *que mataron meu Fillo | como falsos encreus,*
> *meaçan de queimaren | a carn' e estes meus*
> *ossos . . .*
>
> (419.55-58)

36. *Grand' alegria nos deu Deus / quando con pavor os judeus / do angeo, esses encreus, / cada un deles caya* (425.20-23).

37. *The Devil and the Jews.*

38. This feature has also been observed by Hatton and Mackay, "Anti-Semitism in the *Cantigas*," pp. 189-90, 192.

39. Nos. 3.19-23; 34.18-21; 109.35-45; 264.33. *Pois ar fez perdon aver / a Theophilo, un seu / servo, que fora fazer / per conssello dun judeu / carta por gãar poder / cono demo, e lla deu; / e fez-ll' en Deus descreer, / des i a ela negar* (3.16-23).

40. *Un judeu os conjurou por Deus / que dissessen porque os judeus / non fillavan. Diss' un demo: "Ca meus / sodes e punnades de me servir. / Razon an [os] diabos de fogir . . . / Por esto non vos fazemos mal, / ca sodes todos nossos sen al; / mai-los que do batismo o sinal / tragen, aqueles ymos percodir"* (109.35-43).

41. . . . *E poi-la levou sso ssa capa furtada, / en ssa cas' a foi deitar na camara privada, / des i assentou-ss' aly e fez gran falimento; / mas o demo o matou, e foi a perdimento. / Gran dereit'*

é que fill' o demo por escarmento . . . / Pois que o judeu assi foi mort' e cofondudo, / e o demo o levou que nunc' apareçudo / foi . . . (34.15-22).

42. *A falssidade dos judeus / é grand' . . .* (25.169-70). Curiously, Hatton and Mackay claim that the Jew is presented in a favorable light, since he is willing to loan money to a Christian ("Anti-Semitism in the *Cantigas*," p. 190).

43.

> *E desto vos contar quero | hũa mui gran demostrança*
> *que mostrou Santa Maria | en terra d'Orlens en França*
> *al Con de Peiteus,*
> *que un castelo cercara*
> *e come judeus*
> *a gent' en fillar cuidara.*
> *A Madre de Deus . . .*
> *Este castel' aquel conde | por al fillar non queria*
> *senon pola gran requeza | que eno logar avia.*
>
>   (51.7-15)

44.

> *Ca muit' é cousa sen guisa | de fazeren avolezas*
> *os que creen ena Virgen, | que é Sennor de nobrezas,*
> *que mais ama limpidõe | que avarento requezas,*
> *e piadad' e mercee | ca judeu dar [a] usura.*
>
>   (312.5-8)

45.

> *E mostrou-lle d'outra parte | a Virgen grandes tesouros*
> *Ben parte Santa Maria | sas graças e seus tesouros*
> *. . .*
> *De prata, d'our' e de pedras | mui ricas e mui preçadas,*
> *e panos muitos de seda | e çitaras ben lavradas*
> *e outras dõas mui nobres | de prata, todas douradas,*
> *dos judeos, seus ẽemigos, | a que quer peor ca mouros.*
>
>   (348.43-48)

46. Other miscellaneous references include 39.22-23; 91.6-11; 117.21-24; 187.9-12; 264.31-34; 305.67; 333.18; 404.52.

47. The *cantiga* is translated and the miniatures are reproduced in John E. Keller and Richard P. Kinkade, *Iconography in Medieval Spanish Literature* (Lexington: Univ. of Kentucky Press, 1984) pp. 38-39 and plate 38.

48. In both *cantigas* 4 and 108, the father of the Jewish child seeks to kill his offspring. In the first instance, the child is saved by his mother, and in the second Merlin protects him.

49. *Quand' est' o judeu entendeu, / bẽes ali logo de chão / en Santa Maria creu / e en seu Fill', e foi crischão* (25.176-79).

50. Hatton and Mackay, "Anti-Semitism in the *Cantigas*," p. 193; also, Bagby, "The Figure of the Jew," p. 686.

51. See, for instance, the following affirmation:

> *O soldan diss' ao mouro: | 'Eno Alcoran achey*
> *que Santa Maria virgen | foi sempr' . . .'*
>
>   (165.65-66)

52. On the other hand, when Alfonso includes the charge of deicide within the *Siete Partidas*, it is to justify the Jews' servile condition. As a legist, Alfonso seeks to protect Jews on the religious and economic front, not because of charitable feelings toward them, but because he desires to protect a valuable resource.

53. I would like to register my sincere appreciation to Alan D. Deyermond, Ann Kahn, M. Jean Sconza, and Joseph Snow for their assistance in the preparation of this study. My thanks go also to Boston College, the American Council of Learned Societies, Westfield College, London, and the Institute for Advanced Study, Princeton, for their material support of my research.

Appendix

REFERENCES TO JEWS IN THE *CANTIGAS*

2.17-25: Jews and heretics disparage the virginity of Mary.

3.16-23: A Jew counsels Theophilus to make a pact with the Devil.

4: A Jewish lad is saved by the Virgin after his father casts him into an oven. The father is then thrown into the same oven.

5.139-40: The passengers on a ship are good people—*i.e.* neither Muslims nor Jews.

6: A Jewish gambler murders a child who had sung praises to the Virgin. When captured by the Christians, he is burned and other Jews are put to the sword.

12: Jews attempt to crucify a waxen image of Jesus. All are killed by Christians.

14.8-9: The Virgin flees with Jesus to Egypt for fear of the Jews.

22.18: Charge of deicide.

25: A statue of the Virgin speaks on behalf of a Christian who has been defrauded by a Jew.

27: Mary miraculously enables a synagogue to be converted into a church.

34: A Jew who steals an image of the Virgin is killed by a devil.

39.22-23: Allusion to the Virgin's protection of the Jewish lad in *cantiga* 4.

51.7-12: The count of Poitou squeezes people economically, "like Jews."

71.16-18: The Jews await the Messiah, while the Christians already have him.

85: Mary rescues a Jew who has been beaten by robbers and, after he is shown how Jews suffer in Hell, decides to convert.

89: Mary saves a pregnant Jewess who is near death because she is unable to deliver. She and two children are baptized.

91.6-11: Neither Jews nor heretics can gainsay the Virgin's miracles.

107: Mary saves a Jewess who is cast from a mountain. The woman then converts.

108: Merlin requests that a Jewish child be born facing backwards, as punishment for his father's unbelief and blasphemy.

109.35-43: A Jew conjures devils to inquire why they do not bother Jews.

117.21-24: Jews and Christians are witnesses to the suffering of a woman punished for working on the Sabbath.

133.8: Charge of deicide.

135.36-37: Charge of deicide.

149.44-46: Jews and pagans are accused of deicide.

187.9-12: A monastery is built on the site of a former synagogue.

238.21: Charge of deicide.

264.31-34: An image of the Virgin is made in order to destroy the Jews.

286: A doorway falls on two Jews who ridicule a good man. The Jews are the Virgin's enemies because they killed Jesus.

305.67: General reference to Christians, Jews, and Muslims.

312.7-8: Jews are linked to usury.

333.18: Christians, Jews, and Muslims all witness an infirm man.

348.45-48: The Virgin hates the Jews, who possess much silver and gold, more than she does the Muslims.

390.22: Charge of deicide.

403.18-25: The Virgin fears that the Jews have abducted the young Jesus.

404.52-53: Neither Jews nor Christians are able to heal an infirm cleric.

415.22: Charge of deicide.

419.55-58: Charge of deicide. There is a report that the Jews, unbelievers, sought to burn the Virgin's body.

424.29-30, 37: The Nativity star is found in "the land of the Jews." Jesus is "Lord of the Jews and of the Law."

425.20-23: The Jews, unbelievers, fall to the ground at Jesus's resurrection.

426.7-8, 33, 43: Charge of deicide. The sermon on the Mt. of Olives is preached to "the Hebrews." The Pharisees do not believe in the resurrection.

FURTHER READING

Bibliography

Cárdenas, Anthony J. "In Search of a King: An Alfonsic Bibliology." In *Emperor of Culture: Alfonso X the Learned of Castile and His Thirteenth-Century Renaissance,* edited by Robert I. Burns, pp. 198-208. Philadelphia, Penn.: University of Pennsylvania Press, 1990.

> Discusses the abundance of Alfonsine studies generated in the 1980s, including journals, anthologies, conferences, audiovisual packages, monographs, bibliographies, and facsimile editions.

Biography

O'Callaghan, Joseph F. *The Learned King: The Reign of Alfonso X of Castile.* Philadelphia, Penn.: University of Pennsylvania Press, 1993, 388 p.

> Comprehensive work that includes chapters on Alfonso's impact on religious minorities, the economy, and literature.

Criticism

Anderson, Robert R. "Alfonso X El Sabio and the Renaissance in Spain." *Hispania* 44, no. 3 (September 1961): 448-53.

> Discusses how Alfonso's contributions to the arts, sciences, and law fostered conditions that eventually culminated in the Spanish Renaissance.

Callcott, Frank. "Alfonso El Sabio as King and Scholar." In *The Supernatural in Early Spanish Literature: Studied in the Works of the Court of Alfonso X, El Sabio,* pp. 15-26. New York, N.Y.: Instituto de las Españas, 1923.

Contends that affairs of state limited the amount of time and attention Alfonso could devote to his work as an editor.

Carpenter, Dwayne E. "Historical Introduction." In *Alfonso X and the Jews: An Edition of and Commentary on* Siete Partidas *7.24, "De los judíos,"* pp. 3-5. Berkeley: University of California Press, 1986.

Provides an overview of the legal status of Spanish Jews over the centuries and describes Alfonso's position in the matter as "one of restrained tolerance."

Costa Fontes, Manuel da. "On Alfonso X's 'Interrupted' Encounter with a *soldadeira*." In *Folklore and Literature: Studies in the Portuguese, Brazilian, Sephardic, and Hispanic Oral Traditions*, pp. 27-34. Albany: State University of New York Press, 2000.

Speculates that a pornographic and sacrilegious poem by Alfonso was considered a joke by his contemporaries.

Craddock, Jerry R. "Dynasty in Dispute: Alfonso X el Sabio and the Succession to the Throne of Castile and Leon in History and Legend." *Viator* 17 (1986): 197-219.

Documents instances of medieval chroniclers rewriting history involving Alfonso.

Franssen, Maarten. "Did King Alfonso of Castile Really Want to Advise God against the Ptolemaic System?: The Legend in History." *Studies in History and Philosophy of Science* 24, no. 3 (1993): 313-25.

Argues that it is unlikely that a blasphemous statement attributed to Alfonso was actually made by him, but was instead the product of parties seeking to discredit his reputation.

Hartman, Steven Lee. "Alfonso El Sabio and the Varieties of Verb Grammar." *Hispania* 57, no. 1 (March 1974): 48-55.

Analysis of inconsistent and conflicting verb forms in Alfonso's works.

Keller, John E. and Richard P. Kinkade. "Iconography and Literature: Alfonso Himself in *Cantiga* 209." *Hispania* 66, no. 3 (September 1983): 348-52.

A discussion of *Cantiga* 209, contending that it is especially autobiographical in nature.

O'Callaghan, Joseph F. "Alfonso X and the Castilian Church." In *Alfonso X, the Cortes, and Government in Medieval Spain*, pp. 417-29. Aldershot, Eng.: Ashgate Publishing Limited, 1998.

Analyzes the issues that caused the Castilian church to be hostile to Alfonso.

Procter, Evelyn S. *Alfonso X of Castile: Patron of Literature and Learning.* London: Oxford University Press, 1951, 149 p.

Focuses on Alfonso's translations, the *Cantigas*, legal treatises, and historical works.

Scarborough, Connie L. Introduction to *Songs of Holy Mary of Alfonso X, the Wise: A Translation of the* Cantigas de Santa Maria, translated by Kathleen Kulp-Hill, pp. xix-xxvi. Tempe, Ariz.: Arizona Center for Medieval and Renaissance Studies, 2000.

Explains the literary and historical importance of Alfonso's collection of religious hymns to the Virgin Mary.

Hrabanus Maurus
c. 776-856

(Full name Magentius Hrabanus Maurus. Also known as Raban, Rabanus, and Rhabanus) German theologian, nonfiction prose writer, and poet.

INTRODUCTION

Known as *Praeceptor Germaniae* (Germany's teacher), Hrabanus was one of the most prominent representatives of the Carolingian renaissance, a movement initiated by the Frankish emperor Charlemagne (ruled from 800 to 814) to spread learning, Christianity, and Latin culture throughout western Europe. Hrabanus's contemporaries, including his royal patrons, esteemed him for his prodigious literary output, which included biblical commentaries, hagiographies (lives of saints), religious poetry, theological treatises, and reference works. The quintessential churchman, Hrabanus, as scholars have observed, used his erudition to offer a systematic interpretation of the Scriptures. As a historian, he strove to attain a comprehensive view of Catholic tradition; as a defender of Catholic orthodoxy, he fought against heresies such as Adoptionism (the belief that the divine Christ is the natural son of God, while the human Christ is the adopted son of God), which threatened the spiritual unity of early medieval Christendom.

BIOGRAPHICAL INFORMATION

Born in Mainz, probably into an aristocratic family, Hrabanus received his earliest education in the monastery of Fulda, founded by St. Boniface around 750. In 802, a year after he was ordained deacon, he was sent to Tours to continue his education with Alcuin of York, the great English teacher and religious writer. When he returned to Fulda in 803 he was appointed head of the monastic school, eventually turning Fulda into a great center of learning. Ordained in 814, he became Abbot of Fulda in 822, retiring in 842, having led the monastery to material and spiritual prosperity. During a critical time for the Frankish Empire, when Charlemagne's three grandsons vied for power, Hrabanus supported Lothar, but found himself in a difficult situation in 840 when Louis the German defeated Lothar. However, Hrabanus's worries were unfounded: in 847 he was appointed Archbishop of Mainz, where he energetically addressed issues such as heresy and church

discipline in general. He remained at Mainz until his death. Hrabanus was buried in Mainz, in the monastery of St. Albans, but his relics were transferred to Halle. In Germany he is venerated as a doctor of the Church (the title is unofficial) and *beatus* (blessed), but the General Roman Calendar does not acknowledge his feast day (February 4th).

MAJOR WORKS

The dates of composition for most of Hrabanus's works are not known, but his literary career exemplifies the keen interest in writing typical of the Carolingian era. Following an idea expressed in the Old Testament, he "sets forth that writing is already sacred by virtue of the fact that God used it when he wrote the tables of the law," as Ernst Robert Curtius points out (see Further Reading). Because of this, Hrabanus insisted, writing is far superior to painting. Nevertheless, he combines these two arts in his *De laudibus sanctae crucis* (c. 819), consisting of twenty-eight figure poems that combine colors and configurations of characters to suggest such symbols as the cross. In these figure poems Hrabanus suggestively blends two art forms to create a work of extraordinary symbolic power.

De naturis rerum (before 856), also known as *De universo,* is regarded as one of the great medieval encyclopedias. As scholars have remarked, Hrabanus's model is Isidore of Seville (c. 560-636), whose encyclopedic work, *Etymologiae,* is a key link between antiquity and medieval learning. Expressing the spirit of the time, Hrabanus pays considerable attention to number symbolism, as evidenced by his use of such sacred numbers as three and seven in his works (there are three times seven poems in *De laudibus sanctae crucis*). *De naturis rerum* comprises twenty-two books reflecting the twenty-two letters of the Hebrew alphabet. While emulating Isidore's work, Hrabanus attempts to present a synoptic view of all knowledge, sacred and secular, of his time.

For centuries, Hrabanus was known as the author of the Pentecostal hymn "Veni Creator," but scholars now agree that this is a misattribution. However, scholars do not doubt Hrabanus's authorship of the long hymn "De fide catholica." Incorporating a portion of an Irish hymn from the sixth century, Hrabanus offers an apology for his faith, expressing his passionate dedication to Christianity in competently crafted verse.

CRITICAL RECEPTION

While some of Hrabanus's detractors ridiculed him as pedantic and unoriginal, such was not the general opinion of his contemporaries. He was known as one of the most learned scholars of his time. This admiration is crystallized in Dante Alighieri's *Paradiso,* where Hrabanus appears in Canto XII as one of the twelve greatest theologians. The idea of Hrabanus's lack of originality has persisted despite the fact that, as scholars point out, the modern concept of originality in art and literature was unknown in the Middle Ages. Curtius shifted this critical trend when he presented a more balanced view, approaching Hrabanus as a literary scholar and teacher and revealing Hrabanus's versatility and deep erudition. Later scholars have focused on particular aspects of Hrabanus's work. For example, in 1982, two years after an international conference devoted to Hrabanus, E. Ann Matter suggested a political interpretation of Hrabanus's biblical commentaries. Matter and other writers, including Mayke De Jong, have studied Hrabanus's biblical writings as political messages to Carolingian royalty who needed to be reminded of the fragility of power. De Jong draws parallels between the struggle for religious unity described in Hrabanus's Old Testament commentaries and Emperor Lothar's efforts to safeguard his politically volatile Christian realm. In her discussion of *De laudibus sanctae crucis,* Celia Chazelle identifies the theological and political symbolism of Hrabanus's poems, concluding that Hrabanus lauds not only spiritual, but also temporal power, as embodied by Louis the German.

PRINCIPAL WORKS

De institutione clericorum (handbook) 819

De laudibus sanctae crucis [*In honorem sanctae crucis*] (poems) c. 819

"De fide catholica" (hymn) before 856

De inventione linguarum (treatise) before 856

De naturis rerum [*De universo*] (encyclopedia) before 856

De vita Beatae Mariae Magdalenae et sororis ejus Sanctae Marthae naturis (hagiography) before 856

Principal English Translations

*Medieval Latin Lyrics (translated by Helen Waddell) 1929

†*Poetry of the Carolingian Renaissance* (edited by Peter Godman) 1985

The Life of Saint Mary Magdalen and of Her Sister Saint Martha (translated by David Mycoff) 1989

*This work includes translations of Hrabanus's poems by Helen Waddell.

†This work includes translations of Hrabanus's poems by Peter Godman.

CRITICISM

John M. McCulloh (essay date 1973)

SOURCE: McCulloh, John M. "The *Passio Mauri Afri* and Hrabanus Maurus's *Martyrology.*" *Analecta Bollandiana: Revue Critique d'Hagiographie* 91, nos. 3-4 (1973): 391-413.

[*In the following essay, McCulloh argues that Hrabanus may have relied on other written sources when he included the legend of Maurus, an African martyr who died in Rome during the reign of Emperor Numerianus (283-84 A.D.), in his* Martyrology.]

Maurus, an African monk who was martyred at Rome under the Emperor Numerianus, is the subject of a number of Latin Passions[1]. All of these texts relate similar legends regarding the saint, but they name different places—Parenzo, Fleury, Fondi, or Lavello[2]—as the site of his burial. Two scholars have made noteworthy, non-partisan attempts to solve some of the problems surrounding the identity of Maurus and the textual tradition of his Passions. Hippolyte Delehaye[3] concerns himself primarily with the identity of St. Maurus of Parenzo, and he establishes beyond any reasonable doubt that this Maurus was not an African martyred at Rome. He was instead a bishop and martyr of Parenzo to whom the legend of a homonymous Roman martyr, the African monk, came to be applied. Francesco Lanzoni[4] accepts Delehaye's distinction between the two Mauri and proceeds to try to discover the origin of the legend of Maurus of Rome. He suggests that Maurus, the African monk, is merely a legendary development of Maurus, son of the Tribune Claudius, who appears in the *Passio Chrysanthi et Dariae*[5]. In support of this view he cites the fact that in the *Passio Chrysanthi et Dariae* and in the *Passio Mauri* the names of the martyr and his persecutors are identical. Maurus, the Emperor Numerianus, and the Prefect Celerinus all appear in both texts. The transformation of Maurus the Roman into Maurus the African would, Lanzoni argues, present no difficulties since the fictional identification of the African's homeland could be based on the etymology of his name.

With regard to the textual tradition of the *Passio Mauri*, Delehaye and Lanzoni present similar views. Both scholars believe that the earliest form of the legend was a *Passio Romana*[6]. This text was, in their opinion, adapted and interpolated to create the *Passio Parentina*[7] honoring Maurus of Parenzo, and all the other Latin Passions of Maurus were ultimately derived from one or the other of these two forms of the legend[8]. The work of Delehaye and Lanzoni has resolved a number of problems regarding the Maurus tradition, but one form of the Passion deserves more careful consideration than either of these scholars has given it. This is the basis of the whole tradition, the *Passio Romana* itself.

The belief in the existence of a *Passio Romana* is based primarily on the notice for St. Maurus in Hrabanus Maurus' **Martyrology** no 21 November[9]. In Delehaye's view this notice represents the earliest form of the *Passio Mauri* which Hrabanus incorporated into his **Martyrology** either in its entirety or in an epitomized form[10]. I believe this assumption is unjustified. In this paper I intend to consider two major questions regarding the Maurus tradition: 1) Does Hrabanus' notice represent the earliest form of the *Passio Mauri?*; 2) What evidence is there, outside of Hrabanus' **Martyrology,** for the existence of a *Passio Romana* which could have formed the basis of the Maurus legend?

The importance which has been attributed to Hrabanus' notice is based on both the similarities and differences between it and the *Passio Parentina*. The verbal relationship between these two is so close that almost every word of Hrabanus' notice appears in the *Passio*. The *Passio* does, however, differ from Hrabanus' notice in several ways. The most important difference occurs at the end of the two texts. According to Hrabanus, a group of African sailors loaded Maurus' corpse onto their ship, and the Prefect Celerinus, hearing of their action, commanded that the ship be burned at sea. Hrabanus ends his notice with the words: *sed gubernante Domino martyrem suum, ubi Christus voluit, ad portum salutis perduxit.* The *Passio Parentina* describes these events word for word and then identifies the safe port which Hrabanus had left unnamed: *hoc est juxta litus Hystriae civitatis Pharentinae, ubi corpus martyris requiescil usque in hodiernum diem.* Hrabanus' failure to identify the *portus salutis* has led to the conclusion that his notice represents a form of the *Passio Mauri* which is earlier than the *Passio Parentina*.

Considering the similarities between the notice and the *Passio* this judgement is not surprising, but it is not the only possible conclusion. Hrabanus' notice and the *Passio Parentina* are verbally so close to one another that

the relationship between them can only be accounted for in one of three ways: either 1) the *Passio* is an expansion of Hrabanus' notice; or 2) both the *Passio* and the notice are based on a common source; or 3) Hrabanus' notice is an abbreviation of the *Passio Parentina.*

The first possibility, that the notice provided the basis of the *Passio Parentina,* is unlikely, and it can be dispensed with fairly quickly when we compare the text of Hrabanus' notice with the *Passio*[11]. The following is the text of the notice with the words which are common to the *Passio* printed in italics:

> *xi kl. Dec.*[12] Natale *Mauri* martyris, qui ab infantia Christianus fuit, *orationibusque et ieiuniis Christum Dominum deprecabatur, elimosinis viduis et egenis frequenter impensis non minuebat. Cumque hoc per omnes dies vitae sue perageret, nutu Dei Spiritus Sanctus inmisit in sensum eius ut monasterium ingrederetur. Cum ergo non multo tempore ibidem habitaret, ita caepit ab universis fratribus diligi ut veluti patrem eum omnes venerarentur. Cumque conplesset annos xviii agens vitam monachorum, introivit in sensum eius desiderium ut sancti Petri apostoli* sedem ad*visitaret, et proficiscens Deo auxiliante Romam pervenit; et cum didicisset omnia mysteria vel regulam ecclesiae, multo magis in urbe Roma coepit Christianis et aegenis consueta prebere solatia. Cum vero illic demoraretur annis tribus, eodem tempore quo imperium obtinuit Numerianus inpiissimus et cępit per civitates vel provincias sua praecepta urguenter dirigere, ut si quis Christianus inventus fuisset et non diis immolaret, diversis suppliciis maceratus morti traderetur. Ipso namque in tempore cum prefecturam Romae promeruisset Celerinus, et ipse idolis deditus diu requisisset per omnes civitates vel loca, ut sicubi Christiani reperirentur, diversis generibus tormentorum affecti deficerent,* hic beatum Maurum multiplicibus tormentis afflixit, hoc est *iussit eum primum fustibus nodosis cedi,* deinde *plumbatis maxillas eius contundi,* postea *in eguleo suspens*um *ungulis radi et lampades ardentes lateribus eius applicari,* ad extremum vero *caput eius amputa*ri. Cuius *corpus nocte nautae* A*ffricani cognoscentes eum ex sua patria ortum rapuerunt, et volventes eum linteaminibus mundis cum aromatibus* posuerunt in *sarcofagum. Scripserunt ad caput eius dicentes: Dei et Christi Iesu famulus Maurus, hunc seculum pro Christi fide relinquens, vitam aeternam adquisivit. Post aliquantos dies occulte eundem sarcofagum suam in navem omnes nautae uno animo levaverunt. Quo facto pervenit ad praefecti Celerini notitiam, et iratus iussit omnes nautas conprehendere. Quo audito omnes fugerunt et nullus eorum in ventus est. Videns haec Celerinus praefectus consilio diabuli ar matus iussit eandem navem, in quo martyris corpus erat, sarmentis impleri et igne subposito in medio mari conburi, sed gubernante Domino martyrem suum, ubi Christus voluit, ad portum salutis perduxit.*

The very close relationship between Hrabanus' notice and the *Passio Parentina* is obvious, but there are a few

Illustration from a 1265 Spanish manuscript of Maurus's De Universo *depicting heretics and Jews unable to hear the word of God.*

passages which are unique to Hrabanus' text. Of special interest are the phrase *qui ab infantia Christianus fuit,* the statement *Hic beatum Maurum multiplicibus tormentis afflixit, hoc est,* and the words *primum . . . deinde . . . postea . . . ad extremum,* which establish the chronological sequence of Maurus' sufferings. These passages are of particular importance because they are all common features in Hrabanus' **Martyrology.**

Hrabanus' construction *qui ab infantia* appears not only in his notice for Maurus but in five other notices as well[13] In each case the relative clause occurs very near the beginning of the notice and describes the pious youth of the saint in question. The words *qui ab infantia* are obviously a standardized formula which Hrabanus used to introduce a brief description of the earliest phase of a saint's life. The second important passage in Hrabanus' notice which has no parallel in the *Passio Parentina* is the general statement regarding Maurus' sufferings which precedes the enumeration of the specific tortures he endured. Such general statements of

torments, with or without specific details, are common in Hrabanus' notices for martyrs, and constructions which exactly parallel the Maurus notice (general statement + *hoc est* + specific tortures) are by no means rare. There are, in fact, nine other notices which exhibit this same pattern[14]. The last significant portion of Hrabanus' notice which does not occur in the *Passio* is the series, *primum . . . deinde . . . postea . . . ad extremum,* which emphasizes the order in which Maurus suffered various torments. This concern with the chronological sequence of sufferings is also typical of Hrabanus' **Martyrology.** The series of four words in the notice for Maurus is relatively long, but Hrabanus has seven other notices which contain similar series of equal or greater length[15]. The phrase *ad extremum,* with which Hrabanus prefaces Maurus' actual martyrdom, is particularly characteristic of his work. He uses these same words to prepare his reader for the death of a saint twenty-one times[16].

In each of these cases the passage which is unique to Hrabanus' text is typical of the author's personal style of composition. Two of these, the general statement of Maurus' tortures and the adverbial series, have no paral lel in the *Passio,* but the clause *qui ab infantia Christianus fuit* does correspond very closely to one sentence in the longer text. In the *Passio* (Num. 4)[17] the Prefect Celerinus asks Maurus whether he is a Christian or a pagan, and Maurus replies: *Christianus sum ab infantia.* These two passages are verbally very similar, but their positions in their respective texts are quite different. Hrabanus placed his clause at the beginning of his notice, while the author of the *Passio* inserted his sentence near the middle of his text. If the author of the *Passio* had used the notice as the basis for his composition, it would not be surprising to find that he had reworked the materials he took over from Hrabanus. The two texts do exhibit a number of minor variations of word order, but the *ab infantia* passages provide the only example of similar statements appearing in widely separated positions. If the author of the *Passio* did use Hrabanus' notice as his source, it is striking that he should make only one significant alteration in the order of his source text and that this alteration should involve one of the passages which is particularly characteristic of Hrabanus' style. If we were to argue that Hrabanus' notice is the source of the *Passio Parentina,* we would be compelled to make a farfetched assumption. We would have to assume that the author of the *Passio* was so well acquainted with Hrabanus' **Martyrology** that he could recognize the characteristic traits of Hrabanus' style. Furthermore, we would have to argue that the author having recognized these characteristic passages consciously and systematically omitted or altered them—and only them—while copying the rest of Hrabanus' text essentially verbatim. Such a situation is almost unthinkable.

If Hrabanus' notice is not the source of the *Passio Parentina,* then the close relationship between the notice and the *Passio* must be the result of both authors' having used a common source or of Hrabanus' having copied from the *Passio.* There is no way either to prove or to disprove conclusively the existence of a common source. This is particularly unfortunate since Delehave suggests this as a distinct possibility[18], and Lanzoni seems to treat it as established fact[19]. Nevertheless, there is evidence that Hrabanus did use the *Passio Parentina.* Thus, while we cannot absolutely reject the possibility of a common source, we are, I think, justified in dismissing it as unnecessary and unlikely.

There are two points which support the conclusion that Hrabanus employed the *Passio Parentina*: 1) given Hrabanus' normal method of composition, the *Passio Parentina* could be the source of his Maurus notice; and 2) Hrabanus had at his disposal a passionary which

contained this *Passio.* In order to determine whether the *Passio Parentina* could be the source of Hrabanus' notice we need to return to the comparison of the two texts. There are two major differences between the *Passio* and Hrabanus' notice. First, the *Passio* is longer: it contains a significant amount of material which Hrabanus does not include. Second, the *Passio* identifies the port to which Maurus' body was carried as Parenzo: Hrabanus leaves the port unnamed. Are these differences sufficient to show that the *Passio* is not the source of Hrabanus' notice?

The difference in the length is primarily due to the fact that the *Passio* contains a single, large block of material (Numm. 3-5) which is almost entirely missing from Hrabanus' notice. The narrative in this portion of the *Passio* is concerned with two series of events during the persecution in which Maurus died. In the first of these (Num. 3)[20] the saint, hearing of Celerinus' persecution, leaves Rome and takes up residence in a cave. After three months he has a dream in which he is commanded to return to the city. On his return he is recognized, captured, and brought before the prefect. None of this appears in Hrabanus' notice. The second series of events (Numm. 4-5) includes Maurus' interrogation and tortures, his final statement of faith and defiance, and his execution. Hrabanus describes the tortures and execution but nothing else. Except for the story of Maurus' withdrawal from and return to Rome, almost all of the material which is missing from Hrabanus' version of the story consists of verbal exchanges between Maurus and his persecutor Celerinus. The dialogue form of these passages is significant. Verbal duels of this sort between martyrs and their persecutors are a common feature of fictional passions[21], but despite the widespread use of dialogue in hagiographical writings, direct speech of any sort is very rare in Hrabanus' **Martyrology**[22], and dialogue is even rarer. Only three of Hrabanus notices contain any dialogue at all. In the notice for Torpes (iv kl. Apr.) there is conversation between Torpes and Antony, and in the notice for Victor of Le Mans (kl. Sept.) there is a dialogue between Victor and St. Martin of Tours. The notice for Nicholas (viii id. Dec.) contains two series of verbal exchanges, one between Nicholas and the Emperor Constantine and the other between the saint and the Prefect Ablabius. In both cases Nicholas demands the release of three *magistri militum* who have been unjustly imprisoned. These are the only examples of dialogue in Hrabanus' Martyrology, and not one of them is in the classic style of a debate between a martyr and his tormentor[23]. Thus, the fact that Hrabanus' notice for Maurus bears no trace of this portion of the Passion is no bar to arguing that he could have used the *Passio Parentina* as the basis of his notice. Indeed, omitting this part of the *Passio* would be typical of Hrabanus' method of composition.

The same argument cannot be made regarding the incident of Maurus' withdrawal from and return to Rome. This passage defies classification as one of Hrabanus' « standard omissions ». Nevertheless, Hrabanus was composing an historical martyrology and not a passionary. When he used Passions and Lives of the saints as sources for his notices he did not transcribe them in full: he epitomized them[24]. Hrabanus' notice for Maurus is one of the longest in his *Martyrology,* but there is nothing unusual about the fact that he did not include in it all the episodes related in the *Passio.*

The difference in length between the *Passio Parentina* and the notice in the *Martyrology* can be accounted for on the basis of Hrabanus' desire to abbreviate his sources, but this difference is relatively insignificant by comparison with the fact that Hrabanus does not mention the name of the safe port to which Maurus' corpse was miraculously translated. Nevertheless, Hrabanus' lack of concern with geographical precision is not limited to his notice for Maurus. A total of twenty-eight of his historical notices contain no direct indication of where the events he describes took place. This makes it difficult to see any particular significance in his failure to mention a given place-name. The omission of the name of the safe port might appear to be a special case, since the author mentions a specific place but refuses to name it. But even this situation is not unique in Hrabanus' *Martyrology.* In his notice for Menas (iii id. Nov.) and again in that for Nicholas (viii id. Dec.). Hrabanus mentions a city (*civitas*) without naming it. In each case the source he used[25] identifies the city in question. It is true that these Passions differ from the *Passio Parentina* in that they do not name the cities in immediate proximity to the passages which Hrabanus borrowed, but here, as in the notice for Maurus, we see Hrabanus referring to a specific place without identifying it.

Another interesting point about the Maurus notice is the fact that we are clearly told that he suffered martyrdom in Rome while his final resting place is left unnamed. Hrabanus sometimes provides information about the burial places of the saints he describes[26], but this is not always true even when we would most expect it. Hrabanus copied from Bede an historical notice for SS. Marcellinus and Peter (iv non. Iun.). In 827 Einhard

had ceremoniously translated the relics of these saints to his monastery at Seligenstadt[27]. In his youth Einhard had studied at Fulda, and Hrabanus spent twenty years of his life (822-842) as abbot of that house. Furthermore, Hrabanus was composing his *Martyrology* at the request of Ratleik, Einhard's successor as abbot of Seligenstadt[28]. Despite these points of connection between Hrabanus and Fulda on the one hand and Seligenstadt on the other, the author simply copies his notice for Marcellinus and Peter from Bede. He says nothing to indicate that the relics of these saints adorned an East Frankish monastery[29].

We encounter a similar silence when we look at saints whose bodies—or portions thereof—lay at Fulda. During his term as abbot Hrabanus was an eager collector of relics. Between the years 835 and 838 he received at least four shipments of holy remains[30]. Most of these saints appear in Hrabanus' *Martyrology,* but none of the notices contains any reference to Fulda[31]. Even more striking is Hrabanus' notice for St. Boniface (non. Iun.). Boniface, the martyred apostle of the Germans, had been the founder of Fulda, and his body was buried there, but Hrabanus' notice is a simple transcription of the notice in Bede's Martyrology[32]. It speaks only of Boniface's passion and makes no reference to the transfer of his corpse to Fulda.

Hrabanus' failure to mention Fulda in any of these notices would seem to suggest that he consciously avoided drawing attention to his own monastery. In his letters Hrabanus almost never mentions his own ecclesiastical rank[33], and this is normally considered to be evidence of his humility. It might be argued that Hrabanus' notices regarding saints buried at Fulda reveal a similar unwillingness to glorify his own house, but this is not the case. Three of his commemorations contain specific mention of Fulda. Two of these record the anniversaries of church dedications. On xvii kl. Feb. Hrabanus notes the dedication of the church of St. Michael in the cemetery at Fulda in 822[34], and on kl. Nov. he includes the dedication of the abbey church of St. Boniface and the translation of the saint's body which took place in 819[35]. The third reference to the abbey appears in the notice for Leoba (iv kl. Oct.), and in this case Hrabanus states specifically that the saint was buried at Fulda:

> Non solum multa miracula vivens fecit, immo post obitum in Bochonia silva, hoc est in monasterio Fulda, iuxta decretum sancti Bonifatii sepulta non paucis miraculis sanctitatem suam declaravit.

This precise reference to Fulda contrasts sharply with the more generalized nature of some of the other geographical data in this notice. Hrabanus says that Leoba was born in *Brittania insula*[36] and that at the request of St. Boniface she came *in Germaniam.* In this case I think Hrabanus' specific mention of Fulda can be explained by the fact that Leoba had been buried there at the express desire of St. Boniface[37], but whatever the reason for the individual references to Fulda, these examples clearly indicate that Hrabanus did not omit mentioning his own monastery on the basis of some general principle.

This review of the geographical information in some of Hrabanus' historical notices shows that the author is not entirely consistent in the way he deals with material of this sort. Sometimes he includes precise geographical data in his notices, but at other times his references are vague or nonexistent. Moreover, in a number of cases Hrabanus fails to include such information when it was clearly available to him. This characteristic of Hrabanus' *Martyrology* is important in considering the relationship between his notice for Maurus and the *Passio Parentina.* The *Passio* mentions Parenzo, and Hrabanus does not, but this is no basis on which to argue that Hrabanus used some text other than the *Passio Parentina* as the source of his notice.

Compared with Hrabanus' notice the *Passio Parentina* has, as we have seen, three unique features. One is the story of Maurus' withdrawal from and return to Rome, the second is the description of his interrogation and death at the hands of Celerinus—of which only the tortures and execution appear in the notice—and the third is the statement that the safe port where the ship carrying Maurus' body landed was Parenzo. One of these, the interrogation, is typical of the sort of material Hrabanus omitted in composing his notices. The other two would not qualify to be called «standard omissions», but they are the sort of materials which might very well appear in Hrabanus' source text without being taken over into his *Martyrology.* Clearly Hrabanus could have copied his notice from the *Passio Parentina,* or rather—since the evidence is essentially negative—there is no reason to say he could not have done so.

There is also evidence of a positive nature which suggests that Hrabanus actually did use the *Passio Parentina.* Henri Quentin noted that, in compiling his *Martyrology,* Hrabanus employed a passionary similar to that used by Ado of Vienne for the same purpose[38]. The most comprehensive copy of this collection was preserved in a Chartres manuscript of the tenth century[39], and this passionary contains a large number of texts

which served as bases for Hrabanus' historical notices. Hrabanus also took large amounts of material from Bede's Martyrology, the *Martyrologium Hieronymianum* (MH)[40], and the *Liber Pontificalis,* but all of these source collections and the passionary combined can only account for a maximum of 208 out of Hrabanus' 318 historical notices. Of the remaining notices forty-one correspond to materials contained in the hagiographical collection known as the *Passionarium maius* of St. Gall.

This passionary exists in Zurich, Zentralbibliothek Cod. C 10 i which was copied at St. Gall by a number of scribes in the mid-ninth century[41]. The contents of the manuscript have been described by Dom Emmanuel Munding[42]. The hagiographical documents in this passionary show a high degree of correspondence with the contents of Hrabanus' *Martyrology.* In the following comparison of these two collections I have indicated the saints whose Lives or Passions appear in the St. Gall passionary in the left-hand column[43]. The right-hand column contains the dates of the notices for these saints in Hrabanus' *Martyrology.* In those instances where I have been able to determine that Hrabanus' notice is based on a source other than the text in the passionary, I have identified Hrabanus' source in parentheses.

Turic. C 10 i	*Martyrologium*
1. Areleffi	kl. Iul.
2. Eustasii	
3. Burgundaforae	
3a. Bertolfi et al.	
3b. (De aliis monachis Bobiensibus)	
4. Theodosiae	iii non. Apr.
4a. (Ambrosii)	ii non. Apr.
5. Chyoniae, Hyrenis et Agapae	kl. Apr.; non. Apr[44]. (Bede)
6. Taraci et al.	
7. Quiriaci Iudae	kl. Mai.
8. [Inventio s. crucis][45]	[v non. Mai. (MH)]
9. Beati	vii id. Mai.
10. Faltonis Piniani et al.	vi id. Mai.
11. Floriani[46]	iv non. Mai.
12. Mariani et Iacobi	ii non. Mai.
13. Frontoni mon.	xviii kl. Mai.
14. Servatii	iii id. Mai.
15. Victoris et Coronae	ii id. Mai. (Bede)
16. Babilae et al.	ix kl. Feb.
17. Felicis et Regulae[47]	
18. Photini et al.	
19. Canti, Cantiani et Cantianillae	ii kl. Iun.
20. Medardi	vi id. Iun.
21. Rufini et Valerii	xviii kl. Iul. (MH)
22. Aviti	xv kl. Iul.
23. Donatiani et Rogatiani	ix kl. Iun. (MH)

Turic. C 10 i	*Martyrologium*
24. Anastasiae	viii kl. Ian. (Bede)
25. Germani ep. Paris.	vi kl. Iun.
26. Sisinnii	iv kl. Iun.
27* [Nazarii, Gervasii, Protasii, et Celsi][48]	
27. Marinae	xiv kl. Iul.
28. Paulinus ep. Nol.	x kl. Iul. (Greg. Mag., *Dial.*) ([Gregorius Magnus, *Dialog-orum Libri iv*])
29. Luceiae	vii kl. Iul. (MH)
30. Fusciani, Victorici et Gentiani	v kl. Iul.
31. Quintini	ii kl. Nov. (Bede)
32. Septem dormientium	v kl. Iul
33. Trium virginum	
34. Cirilli	vii id. Iul.
35. Procopii	viii id. Iul. (Bede)
36. Christinae	ix kl. Aug.
37. Arnulfi	xv kl. Aug. .
38. Victoris (Massil.)	xii kl. Aug.
39. Apollinaris	x kl. Aug. (Bede)
40. Christofori	viii kl. Aug.
41. Pantaleonis[49]	xii kl. Mar.
42. Lupi	iv kl. Aug. (Bede)
43. Abdon et Sennes	iii kl. Aug. (Bede)
44. Germani (ep. Autis.)[50]	ii kl. Aug. (Bede)
45. Felicis (m. Gerund.)	
46. Stephani ep. Rom.	iv non. Aug. (Bede)
47. Theodotae cum filiis suis	iv non. Aug.[51] (Bede)
48. Stephani, Nicodemi et Gamalielis de revela-tione corporum[52]	iii non. Aug. (MH)
49. Xisti	viii id. Aug. (Bede)
50. Memei	non. Aug.
51. Afrae	non. Aug.
52. Laurentii	iv id. Aug. (Bede)
53. Gaugerici	iii id. Aug.
54. Yppoliti	id. Aug. (Bede)
55. Radegundis	id. Aug. (MH)
56. Isaac et Maximiani	
57. Timothei et Apol-lenaris	
58. Claudii, Asterii, et Neonis	x kl. Sept.
59. Genesii (mimi Rom.)	viii kl. Sept. (*BHL* 3320)[53]
60. Iusti et Pastoris	
61. Genesii (notarii Arelat.)[54]	
62. Iuliani	
63. Victoris ep. (Cenom.)	kl. Sept.
64. Iusti ep. Lugd.	iv non. Sept.
65. Marcelli	ii non. Sept.
66. Evortii	vii id. Sept.
67. Cypriani Cartag. ep.	xviii kl. Oct. (Bede)
68. Mauricii cum sociis suis	x kl. Oct. (Bede)
69. Iohannis Baptistae revelatio quemadmo-dum caput	viii kl. Oct. (Bede)[55]

Turic. C 10 i	*Martyrologium*
70. Solemnis	viii kl. Oct.
71. Cosmae et Damiani	v kl. Oct. (Bede)
72. Frontonis ep.	kl. Oct.
73. Domnini	vii id. Oct.
74. Philippi ep. Adrian.	xi kl. Nov.
75. Crispini et Crispiniani	viii kl. Nov.
76. Symonis Chananei et Iudae Zelotis app.	v kl. Nov. (Bede)
77. Eustachii	
78. Benigni	kl. Nov. (Bede)
79. Aniani ep. Aurel.	xv kl. Dec. (MH)
80. Romani mon.	xiv kl. Dec.
81. Mauri	xi kl. Dec.
82. Caeciliae	x kl. Dec. (Bede)
83. Longini	x kl. Dec.[56]
84. Clementis	ix kl. Dec. (Bede)
85. Marculi	vii kl. Dec.
86. Crisogoni	viii kl. Dec. (Bede)
87. Saturnini	iii kl. Dec. (*BHL* 7501)
88. Landeberti	xv kl. Oct.
89. Andreae ap.	ii kl. Dec. (*Breviarium app.*) [*Breviarium apos-tolorum*]

90. Eligii (*BHL* 2474)
91. Eligii (*BHL* 2477)[57]

The St. Gall passionary contains texts which com-memorate ninety-three saints or groups of saints. Hra-banus' **Martyrology** has notices which correspond to seventy-seven of these. In other words, slightly over 80% of the texts in this collection correspond to notices in Hrabanus' work. The percentage of correspondence is even higher if we eliminate from the total contents of the passionary the four texts (N[os]. 2-3b) which deal with disciples of St. Columban and monks of Bobbio. Considering the historic connections between Bobbio and St. Gall, it is possible that these *Vitae* were added to the collection at St. Gall and were not included in the form of this passionary which was available to Hra-banus[58].

In addition to the general correspondence of the contents of the passionary and the **Martyrology,** there are other parallels between them. In a number of cases Hrabanus actually used as sources for his historical notices hagio-graphical texts like or very similar to ones contained in this manuscript[59]. One of these Lives (No. 1.) is of particular interest. Both Hrabanus and the passionary give the name of St. Carilef as *Arelef(f)us.* This form, which lacks the initial *C* or *K*, is rare[60].

These parallels between the St. Gall *Passionarium maius* and Hrabanus' work reveal another important source collection which the author exploited in compiling his **Martyrology,** but of particular interest is the fact that this passionary contains a copy of the *Passio Mauri Parentina* (No. 81). This version of the *Passio* is particularly closely related to Hrabanus' notice, as we can see when we compare a few lines from the first section of the text in the *Passionarium maius* with that published in *Catal. Lat. Brux.* The words in italics are those which also appear in Hrabanus' notice[61].

TURIC. [*Codex Turicensis*] C 10 i, fol. 222[v].

[Maurus] cottidie in Dei *orationibus et ieiuniis Christum Dominum depraecabatur, elemosinis viduis et egenis frequenter inpensis non minuebat. Cumque hoc per omnes dies vitae suae perageret, nutu Dei Spiritus Sanctus inmisit in sensum eius ut monasterium ingrederetur. Cum ergo non multo tempore ibidem habitaret* . . .

BRUX. 9289 (CATAL. LAT. BRUX., II, 297).

[Maurus] quotidie in *orationibus Dominum* precabatur, *jejuniis* corpus macerabat, *elemosinis viduis,* orphanis *et egenis frequenter impensis non* minuebatur. *Cumque hoc* omnibus diebus *vitae suae* incessanter *perageret, nutu Dei Spiritus sanctus immisit in sensum ejus ut monasterium ingrederetur. Cum ergo* ibi *habitarel* . . .

This passage provides a typical example of the relationship among the three texts in question. The two copies of the *Passio* are closely related to one another, but the version in the Brussels catalogue is slightly longer. This difference in length is due to what appear to be additions in the Brussels version. The variations in the Brussels text, such as *corpus macerabal, orphanis,* and *incessanter* in the passage above, serve to augment information in the shorter version: they do not constitute substantive additions to the narrative. Hrabanus' text normally agrees with the St. Gall version when there is a difference between that and the Brussels *Passio,* and this is always true when the difference is due to an addition in the Brussels text.

The comparison of Hrabanus' notice with the *Passio Parentina* has shown that Hrabanus could have used the *Passio* and the presence of this text in the *Passionarium maius* of St. Gall makes it extremely likely that he actually did so. The effect of these conclusions is to remove the most important piece of evidence for the existence of a *Passio Romana* in the textual tradition of the *Passio Mauri Afri.* Nevertheless, it seems unwise to reject out of hand the possibility that some such document might have provided the basis for the extant forms of the *Passio Mauri.* Earlier writers have not given much serious consideration to the evidence outside of that provided by Hrabanus' **Martyrology** for the existence of a *Passio Romana.* This is understandable, since it was assumed that no further proof of the existence of such a text was needed, but the reassessment of the significance of Hrabanus' notice demands a reconsideration of the other evidence available.

Besides Hrabanus' notice there is one other possible textual witness to the existence of a *Passio Romana.* This is the epitome of the *Passio Mauri* in Vincent of

Beauvais' *Speculum historiale*[62]. The late date of this document and the fact that it is clearly an abridgment of some earlier Passion limit its value as evidence for the existence of a *Passio Romana.* Nevertheless, this text is of interest because it omits any reference to a translation of Maurus to some place other than Rome. In fact, Vincent's version of the Passion ends with Maurus' death. He says nothing about the African sailors and the loading of the saint's corpse onto a ship.

Another point which deserves attention is Lanzoni's theory regarding the origins of the Maurus legend. Lanzoni argues that the Maurus of these Passions is the same Maurus who appears in the *Passio Chrysanthi et Dariae*[63]. In support of this hypothesis he cites the fact that Maurus, the Emperor Numerianus, and the Prefect Celerinus all occur in both texts. This argument is appealing and seems to be even more significant than Lanzoni himself recognized. Celerinus appears in these two Passions and nowhere else[64]. This adds weight to Lanzoni's suggestion that the occurrence of the same three characters in these two works is not mere coincidence. There is still another point in favor of this theory of the origins of the Maurus legend which apparently escaped Lanzoni. This is the date of Maurus' martyrdom. Lanzoni suggests[65] that the commemoration of Maurus on 22 November was based on the fact that the *Martyrologium Hieronymianum* places the martyrs of the Passion of Chrysanthus and Daria on 12 August and on 29 and 30 November. According to the *Passio Chrysanthi et Dariae,* Maurus suffered martyrdom before the saints of the title. Thus the date of 22 November was picked—apparently at random—to place the passion of Maurus before that of Chrysanthus and Daria. This explanation could be correct, but there is also another possibility which has the dual advantage of providing additional support for Lanzoni's general theory of the origins of the Maurus legend and of showing that the date 22 November was not simply chosen at random. The Maurus of the *Passio Chrysanthi et Dariae* has no historical connection with the martyrs of the title. He came to be associated with these saints because they were all buried in the cemetery of Thraso in the Via Salaria nova[66]. This Maurus appears in the *Martyrologium Hieronymianum* several times in the company of saints of that cemetery[67], but his true *dies natalis* is apparently 10 December[68]. Again the parallel between the two Mauri is striking. Maurus of the Via Salaria was honored on *dies X. Decembris,* and Maurus After suffered martyrdom on *X. kl. Decembris.* Thus the different anniversaries of the two saints can be easily explained on the basis of a scribal error. Once Maurus' passion came to be celebrated on 22 November, it would be a simple matter for him to be displaced again to 21 November, the date of Hrabanus' notice.

Returning to Lanzoni's theory of the derivation of Maurus Afer from the Maurus of the *Passio Chrysanthi et Dariae,* it is clear that there is more evidence in favor of this hypothesis than Lanzoni himself realized. The Maurus of the *Passio Chrysanthi* is based on the Maurus of the Via Salaria, and taken together these two Mauri have an impressive number of things in common with Maurus Afer. Maurus of the Via Salaria and Maurus Afer were venerated on dates which could be very easily interchanged. The *Passio Mauri Afri* and the *Passio Chrysanthi et Dariae* both include three characters with identical names, Maurus, the Emperor Numerianus, and the Prefect Celerinus. Furthermore, Celerinus is unique to these two works. It is almost inconceivable that all of these parallels could be the result of pure chance, and Lanzoni's theory that the *Passio Mauri Afri* is ultimately based on the *Passio Chrysanthi et Dariae* offers a very reasonable explanation of these common characteristics.

The basic question regarding the existence of a *Passio Mauri Romana* must be viewed in the light of this evidence for the origin of the Maurus legend. There is no known text of a *Passio Romana* prior to the thirteenth century and no unabridged text of any date. The earliest extant form of Maurus' Passion is the *Passio Parentina,* but all of the evidence in that text suggests that the body of the legend originated in Rome rather than Parenzo. Indeed if we were to reject the existence of a *Passio Romana,* we would almost be forced to conclude that the author of the *Passio Parentina* took the name, date, and persecutors of Maurus of Rome, created the legend of Maurus Afer, and then applied it to Maurus of Parenzo by means of a translation. If the *Passio Parentina* were in its entirety a Parenzo creation, it would make much more sense for the author to have placed the saint's passion as well as his burial in that city.

Since all of the evidence seems to favor the existence of a *Passio Romana,* it is worth considering what that text may have been like. Up to now all attempts to consider the *Passio Romana* have been distorted by the belief that this text was actually contained in Hrabanus' **Martyrology.** Since it is now clear that Hrabanus' text has no definite claim to priority, it is possible to consider it more dispassionately. We must admit that a Passion having the form of Hrabanus' notice for Maurus would be a curious one. Hrabanus describes a translation without mentioning the name of the city where the saint's body was laid to rest. A number of different places claimed to be the *portus salutis* to which the corpse was carried, but if Hrabanus' notice represented the original form of the *Passio Romana,* it would be surprising that more localities had not laid claim to that honor. To do so a clerk would only have had to insert the name of his own city or church at the end of the

Passio, as Delehaye would have us believe the author of the *Passio Parentina* did. It seems far more likely that the form of the *Passio Romana* had more in common with Vincent of Beauvais' epitome than with any of the extant full-length Passions. Vincent's text, as we noted earlier, ends with Maurus' death, and this could well have been true of the *Passio Romana* as well. If this Passion contained any information in addition to that contained in Vincent's epitome, it was probably a reference to Maurus' burial somewhere in the area of Rome—presumably in the Via Salaria. If this speculation on the form of the *Passio Romana* is correct, then the contribution of the author of the *Passio Parentina* is somewhat greater than has previously been thought. If the *Passio Romana* ended with Maurus' death or his burial at Rome, then the whole episode of the African sailors and the translation of the corpse is the creation of the author of the *Passio Parentina*[69]

This consideration of the form of the *Passio Romana* is of necessity speculative, but the materials we have examined do seem to justify certain conclusions regarding the tradition of the *Passio Mauri.* There is clearly no basis for viewing Hrabanus' notice for Maurus as representative of some form of the Passion which is earlier than the *Passio Parentina.* Instead the evidence points to the conclusion that Hrabanus actually used the *Passio Parentina* as the source of his notice. This means that there is no really reliable textual witness to the existence of the *Passio Romana* which Delehaye and Lanzoni both assumed formed the cornerstone of the Maurus tradition. Nevertheless, the Maurus legend has its roots in Rome, and the form in which this legend has come down to us is best explained on the assumption that there was indeed a *Passio Romana.*

Notes

1. *BHL [Bibliotheca hagiographica Latina]* 5786-5791f. I would like to express my thanks to the Rev. Guy Philippart for his advice and assistance in the preparation of this study.

2. The Fleury (*BHL* 5789-5790) and Lavello (*BHL* 5791f) Passions are both relatively late developments of the Maurus tradition, see H. DELEHAYE, *Saints d'Istrie et de Dalmatie,* in *Anal. Boll.,* t. 18 (1899), pp. 371-376. They will not be considered in this paper.

3. *Ibid.,* pp. 370-381.

4. *Le diocesi d'Italia dalle origini al principio del secolo* VII (Faenza, 1927), especially pp. 158-162.

5. *BHL* 1787; *Le diocesi,* pp. 160-161.

6. *BHL* 5786. Neither Delehaye nor Lanzoni employs the expression *Passio Romana.* The name seems justified since it refers to a form of the legend

which describes Maurus' passion at Rome without specifying his place of burial. I have used the term for convenience and to avoid the inherent ambiguity of the designation *Passio prima* which Lanzoni favors.

7. *BHL* 5787.

8. DELEHAYE, *Saints d'Istrie*, pp. 371-376; LANZONI, *Le diocesi*, pp. 160-162.

9. *Martyrologium Rhabani Mauri*, xi kl. Dec. (*PL* [*Patrologia latina*], t. 110, col. 1179-1180; and [McCulloh, John M. "The *Passio Mauri Afri* and Hrabanus Maurus's *Martyrology*." *Analectica Bollandiana: Revue Critique D'Hagiographie* 91, nos. 3-4 (1973): 391-413] 391-393) = *BHL* 5786. Except for the notice for Maurus, which is printed below, all further references to Hrabanus' *Martyrology* are to the edition in *PL*, t. 110, col. 1121-1188.

10. *Saints d'Istrie*, p. 371.

11. The *Passio Parentina* has been published numerous times, but I have based this comparison on the unpublished text contained in Zurich, Zentralbibliothek, Cod. C 10i, fol. 222v-223v. On the particularly close relationship between this version of the *Passio* and the text of Hrabanus' notice, see [McCulloh], pp. 408-409. I would like to thank Dr. A. Schönherr of the Zentralbibliothek, Zurich, who sent me photocopies of the *Passio*.

12. The text of the notice is from the earliest extant ms. of Hrabanus' Martyrology, [*Codex sangallensis*] 457, which, in the opinion of Prof. Bernhard Bischoff, was written in Hrabanus' circle at Mainz (*i.e.* 817-856).

13. Arelefus (kl. Iul.), *qui ab infantia Deo deditus;* Goar (ii non. Iul.), *qui . . . ab i. verus Dei cultor fuit;* Arnulfus (xv kl. Aug.), *q. ab i. ad Dei servitium aptus fuit;* Landebertus (xv kl. Oct.), *q. ab i. Dei servitio mancipatus fuit;* Solemnis (viii kl. Oct.), *q. ab i. Dei servitio devotus fuit.*

14. *E.g.* Macharius et Eugenius (x kl. Feb.), *mutta tormenta passi sunt, hoc est;* Theodosia (iii non. Apr.), *ei adhibita sunt varia tormenta, hoc est;* Victor (viii id. Mai.), *imperator iussit . . . Victorem . . . muttis modis cruciari, hoc est.* Parallel passages appear in the notices for Margaretha (iii id. Iul.), Christina (ix kl. Aug.), Mammes (xvi kl. Sept.), Genesius (viii kl. Sept.), Philippus, Severus, etc. (xi kl. Nov.), and Savinus (vii id. Dec.).

15. Iulianus et Basilissa (id. Ian.), Pantaleon (xii kl. Mar.), Eleutherius (xiv kl. Mai.), Primus et Felicianus (v id. Iun.), Reparata (viii id. Oct.), Mennas (iii id. Nov.), and Gregorius (x kl. Ian.). This

concern with the chronological sequence of tortures is not unique to Hrabanus' work. It is also evident in Bede's Martyrology: *e.g.* Cyriacus (xvii kl. Apr.), Victor et Corona (ii id. Mai.), Ferreolus et Ferrutio (xvi kl. Iul.). Hrabanus reproduces all of these in his own text, and he may well have used Bede as a pattern for this practice.

16. Hrabanus also uses similar constructions for the same purpose: *novissime* seventeen times and *ad ultimum* twice. The phrase *ad ultimum* is used in the same way eight more times in Hrabanus' work, but these are all verbatim borrowings, seven from Bede and one, Bartholomeus (ix kl. Sept.), from the *Breviarium Apostolorum* (*Act. SS.*, [*Acta Sanctorum*] Nov. t. II 2, p. 4). The three occurrences of the word *tandem* in a similar position are also from Bede: Agatha (non. Feb.), Felix Tubzoc. ep. (iv kl. Sept.; in Bede on iii kl. Sept.), and Andochius, Thyrsus, etc. (viii kl. Oct.).

17. All references to specific sections of the *Passio Parentina* are based on the divisions in the text as published in *Catal. Lat. Brux.*, [*Catalogus Latinus Bruxellensis*] t. 2, pp. 297-299.

18. *Saints d'Istrie*, p. 371.

19. Lanzoni never mentions Hrabanus, but some of his statements regarding the *Passio Romana*—or *Passio prima*, as he calls it—clearly show that he is not talking about Hrabanus' notice *per se*. For example, he argues (*Le diocesi*, p. 161) that the *Passio Parentina* and the *Passio Fundana* (*BHL* 5791, 5791b) are independently derived from the *Passio Romana*. The Parenzo and Fondi Passions contain verbally similar stories of Maurus' retirement to a cave for three months. This episode is not in Hrabanus' notice.

20. This account actually begins in the last two lines of Num. 2.

21. H. DELEHAYE, *Les passions des martyrs et les genres littéraires* (Brussels 1921), pp. 251-273, (2^d ed., 1966, pp. 183-197). The *Passio Mauri* in its known forms certainly has no claim to historicity, see Delehaye, *Saints d'Istrie*, p. 321.

22. Hrabanus has 318 historical notices of which only seventeen contain « direct quotations. » Three of these seventeen are from Bede: Almachius (kl. Ian.), Sebastianus (xiii kl. Feb.), and Marcus evangelista (vii kl. Mai.).

23. The closest approximation to this sort of exchange appears in the notice for Iulianus et Basilissa (id. Ian.). Here Hrabanus includes several speeches in which Iulianus argues with his parents who are urging him to marry. This is not a true dialogue, however. Iulianus is the only person quoted.

24. In the prologue to his Martyrology Hrabanus states: *. . . et cuiuscumque sancti obitum sive martyrium, qualiter praesentem vilam finierint, legi, breviter, prout polui notavi* (*MGH, Epistolae,* t. 5, p. 503). Cf. B. DE GAIFFIER, *De l'usage et de la lecture du martyrologe. Témoignages antérieurs au XIe siècle,* in *Anal. Boll.,* t. 79 (1961), p. 56.

25. These notices are based on the *Passio Mennae* (*BHL* 5921), ed. B. MOMBRITIUS, *Sanctuarium,* 11², 286-289; and the *Acta Nicolai* (*BHL* 6119), ed. K. MEISEN, *Nikolauskult und Nikolausbrauch im Abendlande* (Düsseldorf, 1931), pp. 527-530.

26. In the notice for Avitus (xv kl. Iul.) the question of where the saint should be laid to rest and the events which took place after his death account for more than half of the entire text. Two historical notices for Zeno of Verona (ii id. Apr. and vi id. Dec.) are devoted to a miracle at the church where he was buried; cf. Gregory the Great, *Dial.,* III, 19. Other notices in which Hrabanus describes a saint's burial place include those for Fursey (xvii kl. Feb.) and Antony (xvi kl. Feb.).

27. EINHARD, *Translatio et miracula SS. Marcellini et Petri* (*BHL* 5233), *MGH,* [*Monumenta Germaniae historica*] *Scriptores,* t. 15, I, pp. 238-264.

28. Hrabanus mentions this request in the dedicatory letter to Ratleik which appears as a prologue to his Martyrology: *Quia rogasti me, frater amantissime, ut martyrologium . . . tibi conscriberem . . . ,* Ep. 48, ed. E. DÜMMLER, *MGH, Epis tolae,* t. 5, p. 502.

29. The translation was certainly known at Fulda. Both Einhard and Hrabanus purchased relics from the same « dealer », Deusdona, a Roman deacon. On the career of Deusdona see J. GUIRAUD, *Le commerce des reliques au commencement du IXe siècle,* in *Mélanges G. B. De Rossi* (Paris, 1892), pp. 81-95.

30. RUDOLF OF FULDA, *Miracula Sanctorum in Fuldenses Ecclesias translatorum,* cc. 3-4, 9 (*MGH, Scriptores,* t. 15, I, pp. 332-333, 336); cf. H. DELEHAYE, *Cinq leçons sur la méthode hagiographique* (Brussels, 1934), pp. 87-89; K. LÜBECK, *Die Reliquienerwerbung des Abtes Rabanus Maurus,* in *Fuldaer Studien,* t. 2 (Fulda 1950), pp. 113-132; and above p. 400, n. 4.

31. The case of St. Emmeram is similar. He is mentioned in one of Hrabanus' *tituli* for the abbey church at Fulda (Carm. 41, xii, ed. E. DÜMMLER, *MGH, Poetae,* t. 2, p. 208), and his relics were a gift to Fulda from Bishop Baturich of Regensburg (*MGH, Epistolae,* t. 5, p. 518) who had spent some time at Fulda and to whom Hrabanus probably dedicated an early form of his *De institutione clericorum* (B. BISCHOFF, *Literarisches und künsllerisches Leben in St. Emmeram* [*Regensburg*] *während des frühen und hohen Mittelalters,* in *Mittelalteriche Studien,* t. 2, Stuttgart, 1967, pp. 77-78). Nevertheless, in his notice for Emmeram (x kl. Oct.) Hrabanus makes no mention of Fulda or even of Regensburg.

32. Hrabanus' notice corresponds to the first class of Bede mss., cf. Henri QUENTIN, *Les martyrologes historiques du moyen age* (Paris, 1908), p. 51. The Boniface notice was, of course, not composed by Bede himself, but it was present in the archetype of all the extant mss., *ibid.,* p. 115.

33. This presents problems for establishing the chronology of Hrabanus' works; see E. DÜMMLER, *Hrabanstudien,* in *Sitzungsberichte der königlich preussischen Akademie der Wissenschaften zu Berlin,* t. 54 (1898), III, pp. 33-34.

34. Cf. E. DÜMMLER, *MGH, Poetae,* t. 2, p. 209.

35. Cf. *ibid.,* p. 205. This notice of the *translatio* is the only reference in the Martyrology to the presence of Boniface's body at Fulda.

36. This phrase also appears in Rudolf of Fulda's *Vita Leobae* (*BHL* 4845, c. 2: *MGH, Scriptores,* t. 15, I, p. 123), and it is one of the few verbal parallels between the *Vita* and Hrabanus' notice. In his prologue (*ibid.,* p. 122). Rudolf states that he wrote the *Vita* at Hrabanus' command, and even if Hrabanus did not actually use this Life as a source for his Martyrology, his knowledge of the places with which Leoba was associated must have been greater than his notice for her reveals.

37. Hrabanus does not mention that Leoba was not buried exactly as Boniface had desired. Boniface had asked that they both be laid to rest in the same tomb, but this request was not carried out; see Rudolf, *Vita Leobae,* c. 21 (*ibid.,* p. 130).

38. *Mart. hist.,* p. 649, n. 1.

39. This ms., *Carnotensis* 506 (al. 144), was destroyed in 1944, but its contents are described in *Anal. Boll.,* t. 8 (1889), pp. 125-137; cf. QUENTIN, *Mart. hist.* pp. 645-648. The hagiographical collection of which the Chartres ms. was one representative is the subject of a forthcoming study by G. Philippart, cf. *Anal. Boll.,* [*Analecta Bollandiana*] t. 88 (1970), p. 201.

40. In addition to a text of the class MH H, Hrabanus made extensive use of the *Martyrologium Hieronymianum Cambrense,* ed. 11. Delehaye, *Anal. Boll.,* t. 32 (1913), p. 369-407.

41. Albert BRUCKNER, *Scriptoria Medii Aevi Helvetica,* t. 3 (Geneva, 1938), p. 123. Earlier writers sug-

gested a variety of dates: saec. x. ex., B. KRUSCH, *Ionae Vitae SS. Columbani, Vedastis, Iohannis* (Hanover and Leipzig, 1905), p. 66; saec. x. in., W. LEVISON, *Conspectus Codicum Hagiographicorum*, in *MGH, Scriptores Rerum Merovingicarum*, t. 7 (Hanover and Leipzig, 1920), p. 691; and saec. IX., L. C. MOHLBERG, *Katalog der Hss. der Zentralbibliothek Zürich*, t 1 (Zurich, 1951), p. 18. E. MUNDING, *Das Verzeichnis der St. Galler Heiligenleben und ihrer Handschriften in Cod. sangall. No. 566* (Leipzig, 1918), p. 44, believes that the ms. consists of a mixture of materials written in the ninth and tenth centuries at both St. Gall and Reichenau.

42. *Ibid.*, pp. 45-56. For more specific information on the recensions of texts in the ms. which have been edited in the *MGH* see LEVISON, *Conspectus Codd.*, p. 691.

43. I have given the names as they appear in the *lemmata* of the texts as printed by Munding.

44. Hrabanus' notice for Agape and Chionia (kl. Apr.) is entirely from Bede. His notice for Hyrenes (non. Apr.) consists of two parts: the first is directly from Bede, and the second (*quae a praedicto praefecto—spiritum reddiderunt*) appears to be paraphrased from Bede's notice for Agape and Chionia.

45. This text is not included in the ms., but it is mentioned in the original table of contents (MUNDING, p. 47).

46. The *Passio Floriani* is edited in W. NEUMÜLLER, *Der heilige Florian und seine 'Passio'*, in *Sankt Florian, Erbe und Vermächtnis. Festschrift zur 900-Jahr-Feier* (Linz, 1971 = *Mitteilungen des oberösterreichischen Landesarchivs*, t. 10), pp. 29-35. On the Zurich ms., see *ibid.*, p. 28.

47. The *Passio Felicis et Regulae* is edited in I. MÜLLER, *Die frühkarolingische Passio der Zürcher Heiligen*, in *Zeitschrift für schweizerische Kirchengeschichte*, t. 65 (1971), pp. 135-144. On the text in the Zurich ms., see *ibid.*, p. 133.

48. This text is also mentioned in the table of contents but omitted in the passionary itself (MUNDING, p. 49). Hrabanus' notice for Gervasius and Protasius (xiii kl. Iul.) is copied in part from Bede. The rest is excerpted from a Passion. A *Passio Vitalis, Gervasii et Protasii* appears in the Chartres collection, cf. *Anal. Boll.*, t. 8 (1899), p. 127, 17°.

49. There is also a *Passio Pantaleonis* in the Chartres collection, cf. *ibid.*, p. 130, 43°.

50. The *Vita Germani* is edited with a French translation in CONSTANCE DE LYON, *Vie de Saint Germain d'Auxerre*, ed. René BORIUS (Paris, 1965 = *Sourt*

ces chrétiennes, 112). On the text in the Zurich ms. and its relation to other early mss. of the *Vita*, see *ibid.*, pp. 51-52, 57-59.

51. Henricus Canisius, the first editor of Hrabanus' Martyrology (*Lectiones Antiquae*, t. 6, Ingolstadt, 1604 pp. 687-758), gave the name as *Theodorae*, and this has been reproduced in all the later editions. The mss. give *Theodotae*.

52. On the relationship of the Zurich ms. to other copies of this text, see E. VANDERLINDEN, *Revelatio Sancti Stephani*, in *Revue des études byzantines*, V. 1 (1946), p. 182, n. 10, and p. 185.

53. Hrabanus used this *Passio* which appears in the Chartres collection (*Anal. Boll.*, t. 8, 1889, p. 131, 53°) and not the brief text contained in the St. Gall passionary. The latter is printed by MUNDING, pp. 171-172.

54. On xvii kl. Ian. Hrabanus includes the notice, *Arelato dedicatio basilicae et altaris s. Genesii m.* (= MH), but there is no obvious connection between this notice and the *Passio* which is dated v kl. Sept.

55. Hrabanus' notice, *Conceptio Iohannis Baptistae*, is from Bede, and the date corresponds to that assigned to the *Revelatio* in the St. Gall passionary. Bede's Martyrology also contains the *Inventio capitis Praecursoris* (vi kl. Mar.) which Hrabanus did not include.

56. This notice is based on the *Passio* (*BHL* 4965) which occurs in both the St. Gall and Chartres collections (cf. *Anal. Boll.*, t. 8, 1889, p. 134, 77°). Hrabanus' other historical notice for Longinus (id. Mar.) appears to be a paraphrase of the November notice and, thus, only indirectly derived from the *Passio*.

57. This text is fragmentary, and Munding (p. 56) believes that the ms. is lacking at least one quaternio gathering.

58. The *Passio Felicis et Regulae* (No. 17), martyrs of Zurich, which has no parallel in Hrabanus' work, could also be a St. Gall addition.

59. Hrabanus' use of some of the materials contained in this ms. has already been noted. On the Lives of Memmius (No. 50) and Sollemnis (No. 70) see W. LEVISON, in *MGH, Scriptores Rerum Merovingicarum*, t. 5, p. 363; t. 7, p. 306; on the Lives of Florianus (No. 11), Avitus (No. 22), and Carilef (No. 1) see B. KRUSCH, *ibid.*, t. 3, p. 66, 381, 387. [In the case of Landebertus (No. 88). Krusch (*ibid.*, t. 6, p. 303) argues that Hrabanus used a form of the *Vita* different from that in this ms.]. On Hrabanus' use of the Lives of Avitus and Carilef see

also A. PONCELET, *Les saints de Micy,* in *Anal. Boll.,* t. 24 (1905), pp. 17, 37; and on the Life of Victor of Le Mans (No. 63) see W. GOFFART, *The Le Mans Forgeries* (Cambridge, Mass., 1966), p. 56. It was Prof. Goffart who first called my attention to the similarities between this *Passionarium* and Hrabanus' Martyrology.

60. To my knowledge *Arelef(f)us* appears only in these two texts, in MH, cod. B, and in *Cod. Brux.* 7984 (See *Catal. Lat. Brux.,* t. 2, p. 181, 26°; cf. GOF-FART, *Forgeries,* p. 77, n. 135). The Zurich and Brussels mss. both contain the *Vita BHL* 1568. The spelling *Harelepphus* appears in one ms. of *BHL* 1569, Naples, Bibl. Nat., [Bibliothèque Nationale] Cod. *VI. D. 40* (See *Anal. Boll.,* t. 30, 1911, p. 141).

61. See [McCulloh] pp. 393-394.

62. L. XII, c. 121.

63. *BHL* 1787.

64. B. BOSSUE, in *Act. SS.,* Oct. t. 11, p. 442.

65. *Le diocesi,* p. 161.

66. H. DELEHAYE, *Étude sur le légendier romain* (Brussels, 1936), p. 25.

67. 12 Aug. and 29 Nov., ef. *Comm. martyr. hieron.,* [*Commentarius perpetaus in Martyrologium Hieronymianum*] pp. 437-438, 626-627.

68. *Ibid.,* pp. 641-642.

69. If this is true, then Lanzoni's view (*Le diocesi,* p. 161) that the *Passio Fundana* is derived from the *Passio Romana* is incorrect. The *Passio Fundana* contains a translation story very similar to that in the *Passio Parentina* (See the excerpts from the *Passio Fundana* in DELEHAYE, *Saints d'Istrie,* pp. 372-373). This suggests that the *Passio Parentina* is the source of the *Passio Fundana.*

E. Ann Matter (essay date 1982)

SOURCE: Matter, E. Ann. "The Lamentations Commentaries of Hrabanus Maurus and Paschasius Radbertus." *Traditio: Studies in Ancient and Medieval History, Thought, and Religion* 38 (1982): 137-63.

[*In the essay below, Matter suggests that Hrabanus's reading of Lamentations, which she compares favorably to that of Paschasius, is addressed to contemporary rulers in order to remind them of the fragility of power.*]

In the study of Carolingian Christianity, biblical commentaries are a vast and largely untapped resource.[1] Exegesis, whether for teaching or homiletical purposes, dominated the ninth-century school tradition; in this world, nearly all theologians were primarily expositors of the Bible. It is one of the ironies of historical inquiry that the non-exegetical treatises of such figures as Hrabanus Maurus and Paschasius Radbertus have been studied to the exclusion of their biblical commentaries. Although this situation is beginning to change, much remains to be done, beginning with the crucial work on the texts.[2] Meanwhile, in the absence of critical editions of any of the major works of the Carolingian exegetical tradition, all scholarship in the field is a mere suggestion as to what might be discovered when the primary materials have been better presented. This study is no exception. The two treatises discussed here have received practically no attention from modern historians, and are printed only in the uncritical editions of the *Patrologia Latina.* It is my hope that this analysis will encourage further inquiry into Carolingian exegesis by showing some ways in which two commentaries, the first in the Latin tradition on the book of Lamentations, reveal the theological and pastoral concerns, and the exegetical methods, of two generations of ninth-century monastic authors.

LAMENTATIONS EXEGESIS BEFORE
THE NINTH CENTURY

The Lamentations are a series of five remarkably intense and beautiful poems mourning the Babylonian conquest of Jerusalem and the destruction of the Temple in 587 BCE. Although they are appended to the book of the prophet Jeremiah, the poems date from the century after the conquest, and are written by a hand, or hands, other than Jeremiah's.[3] The Lamentations contrast the former pomp of the city to the desolation so evident to the author or authors and offer a moral of purification through suffering.

In Hebrew, the first four poems (chapters 1-4) have an acrostic form.[4] No effort was made to maintain the acrostic in the Latin translations known to the medieval world, but in both Greek and Latin Bible versions, the Hebrew letters beginning each verse were preserved as verse headings.[5] Like the Psalms bearing Hebrew alphabetical titles, the five poems of Lamentations seem to have been originally intended as communal laments. In their final form, they have long been used for public recitation on the Ninth of Ab, the Jewish day of mourning and fasting in commemoration of the disaster of 587.[6]

Considering the highly emotional and recollective use of the poems in the Jewish liturgical tradition, it is not surprising that they found a place in the Christian commemoration of the suffering and death of Jesus as ritually re-enacted in the Holy Week liturgy. In the Roman Breviary, selections from all five books of Lamentations make up the lessons for the first nocturn of matins on Maundy Thursday, Good Friday, and Holy Saturday.[7] In this liturgical setting, the poems provide a highly emotional accompaniment to the solemn extinguishing of lights known as the Tenebrae. Although the origins of this ritual are cloudy, we know that it was native to the Gallican liturgy, and was probably fully developed by the seventh century.[8] This liturgical use later give rise to musical settings of Lamentations of exceptional number and beauty.

The impact of the Frankish liturgical tradition on the Lamentations commentaries of Hrabanus Maurus and Paschasius Radbertus will be considered below. At the outset, it seems that liturgical usage may well have inspired exegetical treatment of Lamentations, at least in the Latin church. It is a surprising fact that no Latin commentaries on Lamentations antedate the merging of Gallican and Roman liturgies which took place in ninth-century Frankland.

In the Greek patristic milieu, one Lamentations interpretation is known to have existed: Eusebius relates that Origen included the poems in his commentary on Jeremiah.[9] Origen's interpretation of the Jeremiah corpus was known in the Byzantine world, but is extremely elusive as a treatise, surviving only in patristic *catenae.*[10] The work was very little known in the Latin Middle Ages, partly because the Latin translation of Eusebius omits Lamentations from the list of biblical books interpreted by Origen.[11]

There is some evidence, on the other hand, that Origen's interpretation of Lamentations was known to Jerome.[12] But the father of Latin biblical studies seems not to have used Origen's treatise in his own exegesis, primarily because he never addressed himself directly to Lamentations. Jerome's lengthy commentary on the book of Jeremiah is an unfinished work which draws upon Origen in several places.[13] It has been suggested that Jerome meant to continue this work to include Lamentations, but was distracted by disciplinary problems in his monastery at Bethlehem.[14] Had Jerome finished the task, Origen's Lamentations treatise would probably have been his major source. It is possible that Jerome might even have translated Origen on Lamentations into Latin as a companion piece to his translation of Origen's homilies on Jeremiah.[15] Either possibility, had it come to pass, could have significantly changed the course of Latin exegesis of Lamentations.

Instead, as if by default, a letter of Jerome to Paula, which mentions Lamentations among several biblical texts using the Hebrew alphabet, became a standard resource for Latin interpretations of the five poems.[16] The critical passage here, which will be seen in both of the Carolingian Lamentations commentaries, is a discus-

sion of the allegorical meaning of each of the Hebrew letters and a number of consecutive readings of these letters.[17] The meaning assigned to the Hebrew letter at the head of each verse, rather than the meaning of the series of poems themselves, was Jerome's contribution to the medieval Latin understanding of Lamentations.[18]

Jerome's relative indifference is a hint of the lack of importance accorded Lamentations by patristic authors in general. Only occasional quotations from this book appear in authors of the first three centuries of Christianity exclusive of Origen; and in these allusions, there is a heavy concentration on two verses, 3.34 and 4.20, both of which bear a strong christological message.[19] But even though Lamentations was not in the mainstream of the developing Latin exegetical tradition, commentary on this book benefited directly from the methods and tools which evolved in the time of Jerome and Augustine, especially the system known as four-fold exegesis.

The *locus classicus* of the four-fold system of scriptural interpretation is the *Collationes* of the monastic author John Cassian, a contemporary of Augustine.[20] Cassian's explanation of the four senses of scripture, the historical, allegorical, anagogical, and tropological, culminates in the famous example of Jerusalem, which can be understood historically as the city of the Jews, allegorically as the Church of Christ, anagogically as the celestial city, 'the mother of us all' (Gal. 4.26), and tropologically or morally as the human soul.[21] Lamentations is not cited directly in this passage, but Cassian's example brings Jerusalem so greatly into exegetical prominence as to make it extremely influential for later expositors of Lamentations.

The most influential Latin author of the patristic age to quote extensively from Lamentations was Gregory the Great, who drew on the text in several of his works, but especially in the famous *Moralia* on the book of Job.[22] There are at least seventeen references to Lamentations in the *Moralia,* all with lengthy expositions of the cited verse.[23] In general, Gregory follows the exegetical tradition of Origen, in which the historical meaning of the text is enriched by christological and/or moral understandings, the senses termed by Cassian the allegorical and tropological. Thus, he sometimes interprets the adversities of Jerusalem as the tribulations which have from time to time afflicted the Church.[24] But, predictably, Gregory's favored method of exegesis is through the tropological sense. In keeping with the overall interpretive scheme of the *Moralia,* this is sometimes shown to rest visibly on the historical experience of the city of the Jews.[25] Although Gregory shows no methodological awareness of Cassian's scheme, it is worth noting that anagogical explications of Lamentations texts also predominate at some points.[26] Gregory was never led to write a full commentary on Lamentations, but these quotations clearly constitute the first Latin exegetical treatment of the book. Since the *Moralia* was one of the most widely read books of the Carolingian age, the influence of Gregory the Great was a major catalyst for the Lamentations interpretations of Hrabanus Maurus and Paschasius Radbertus.

THE CAROLINGIAN COMMENTARIES ON
LAMENTATIONS: HRABANUS MAURUS

For several years after the death of Louis the Pious in 840, the Carolingian Empire was torn by dissension and fratricidal strife. One of the most politically influential ecclesiastics of this age was Hrabanus Maurus, the venerable abbot of Fulda.[27] Hrabanus was the most erudite and successful of Alcuin's native Frankish students. He inherited from his teacher a concern for biblical teaching and an unshakable loyalty to the royal family. Hrabanus supported Louis the Pious during his abdication and, after the Emperor's death, gave his considerably weighty backing to the imperial plan of Lothar. The failure of Lothar's empire was evident by the spring of 842, at which time Hrabanus was forced to resign his abbacy. Already over the age of sixty, Hrabanus must have felt that such gloomy events marked the end of his influence with the rulers of the Empire. In fact this was not so, but the treatises written by Hrabanus between 840 and 842 reflect in a number of ways his disappointment and worry over the future of his world.[28]

To this traumatic period is dated Hrabanus' *Expositionis super Jeremiam prophetam libri viginti,* the last three books of which constitute the first Latin exposition of the whole text of Lamentations.[29] The preface, which dedicates the entire commentary 'Ad Lotharium Imperatorem,' explains that Hrabanus turned his hand to this book 'finally,' after commenting on the entire corpus of Old Testament historical books and some of the Wisdom books also.[30] Later in the introduction, Hrabanus notes that his work on the commentary had begun during the reign of Louis the Pious, but that the finished work was especially for Lothar, whose attitude toward the Empire was as benevolent and pious as that of his celebrated father.[31] There is an element of wishful thinking here; the end of the prologue, a long quotation from Jerome's translation of Origen's homilies on Jeremiah, spells out the catastrophes which were visited on ungodly realms in biblical times.[32]

For all the political warnings delivered by this dedication, the teacher, Hrabanus' favorite role, is also evident. Immediately after listing his own exegetical works, Hrabanus describes the patristic treatments of Jeremiah available to him in order to explain his purpose clearly. These sources are just what we might expect: Hrabanus

was able to find a commentary by Jerome (but only of the first half of the text),[33] Jerome's Latin translations of fourteen of the forty-four homilies of Origen mentioned by Cassiodorus,[34] and numerous references in the works of Gregory the Great.[35] Hrabanus discusses his use of Gregory at some length and explains that he had, at a previous time, brought together these quotations into one volume, not out of presumption, but in order to facilitate the studies of those who came after him.[36]

Of these admitted sources, only Gregory the Great is of any value for an interpretation of the text of Lamentations. Consequently, at the beginning of Book 18, where his commentary on the five poems begins, Hrabanus finds himself constrained to stop and consider the changed nature of his exegetical task.

The prologue to Book 18 is concerned first of all with the question whether Lamentations is a part of the book of Jeremiah. On the authority of Jerome, Hrabanus says that they must be understood as one coherent book in order that the total of the Old Testament books should equal twenty-four, the number of the elders of the Apocalypse.[37] To explain the form of the five poems, Hrabanus repeats Jerome's discussion of the meanings of the Hebrew alphabet.[38]

In his interpretation of Lamentations, Hrabanus uses the few patristic resources available. Like Gregory, he professes an exegetical method which begins by distinguishing the historical meaning of the text from mystical meaning(s) intended by the Holy Spirit.[39] Also like Gregory, he further divides the mystical sense, at least in theory, into allegorical and moral meanings, and, in practice, sometimes allows the moral sense to slip into an allegorical interpretation.[40] In fact, Hrabanus' use of the terms 'mystical,' 'allegorical,' 'moral,' and 'spiritual' are far from consistent, and his concern for the historical meaning is very slight. Hrabanus collapses the historical sense of the five poems in order to let other interpretations shine through; it is clear that he considers the destruction of Jerusalem to be only the beginning of the meaning of Lamentations. As his dedication to Lothar suggests, Hrabanus reads Lamentations as a cautionary tale for all realms and rulers, and each individual Christian soul.

Consequently, his quotations from Gregory's works are not limited to the passages where Lamentations is cited directly, but are worked in through numerous references to that definitive story of human suffering, the book of Job.[41] Through a sensitivity to biblical resonances, Hrabanus is able to introduce into his discussion allusions to other biblical books which also give him logical patristic commentaries ripe for the plunder, in particular, the commentary on the Psalms of Cassidorus.[42] Gregory and Cassiodorus, plus a number of references to Jerome's exegesis of other books, and one reference each to Eusebius and Augustine, are all the sources Hrabanus could find for his exposition of this biblical book.[43]

But these sources by no means cover the bulk of the text of Lamentations. To an extent unprecedented in his previous exegetical forays, the author found himself on his own in this 'last part of the prophet Jeremiah.' And here Hrabanus, generally considered the least original of the Carolingian scholars, rises to the occasion admirably. The greater part of Hrabanus' exposition of Lamentations, in direct contrast to the preceeding Jeremiah exegesis, comes from his own pen. In the first place, this is evident from the edition of the *Patrologia Latina,* where many passages are marked 'Maurus.'[44] Further, the history of manuscript dissemination shows that the later medieval students were also aware of the originality of this interpretation: one of the two extant pre-twelfth-century copies of Hrabanus on Lamentations places his interpretation directly following Jerome on Jeremiah, rather than as the concluding three books of Hrabanus on that prophet.[45]

Structurally, Hrabanus' commentary on Lamentations also takes bold and unprecedented steps. He divides the five poems into three books according to their format: Book 18 covers chapters 1-2, the first two acrostic poems;[46] Book 19 is wholly dedicated to the third chapter, the poem in triple acrostic, and carries at its head the appropriate passage from Jerome's discussion in Epistle 30;[47] Book 20 concludes by commenting on chapters 4 and 5 of Lamentations, again with a short recapitulation of Jerome's structural analysis.[48] This format brings the third chapter of Lamentations into special prominence and allows Hrabanus to show his basic three-fold exegetical approach in some detail.[49]

But in the lengthy conclusion following Hrabanus' treatment of the last verse of Lamentations, it is the moral understanding which has the last word. The city of Jerusalem, he says here, is the eternal city, the soul; the story of Lamentations is the fight of the soul against sin. Sobered by the knowledge of the end, assisted by the divine grace of the Incarnation available through the sacraments, the city of the soul can resist the ravages of sin. And so Hrabanus Maurus ends his commentary on the Lamentations with a hymn of praise.[50]

PASCHASIUS RADBERTUS

The second Carolingian commentary on Lamentations was also the product of a time of personal turbulence. From his childhood, Paschasius Radbertus had been closely associated with the influential abbey of Corbie; he entered this house in his early twenties and became abbot in 844.[51] Sometime around 849, Radbertus abdicated and left Corbie for the nearby monastery of

Saint-Riquier (Centula) where he lived in voluntary exile for some years. He later returned to Corbie, where he died, ca. 860.[52]

This self-imposed demotion and exile seems to have been motivated by factional disputes within the community, perhaps a result of misunderstandings between the younger monks and their abbot.[53] Radbertus' *Expositio in Lamentationes Jeremiae* was written either during his time at Saint-Riquier or after his return to Corbie, and is dedicated to Odilmannus, an old friend at his native house.[54] This is an interpretation of Lamentations alone, as a scriptural and theological unit independent of the rest of the Jeremiah corpus. It is the first such work in the Latin exegetical tradition.

In the dedication, even more gloomy than Hrabanus' epistle to Lothar, Radbertus states explicitly that his personal calamities were the impetus for his exposition of Lamentations.[55] The preface is an excursus on the theological significance of mourning. Of all the biblical laments, Radbertus says, Lamentations is the ultimate example, just as the Song of Songs is the most perfect song of praise.[56] The Song of Songs is often quoted in this treatise, and plays a crucial part in the overall expository scheme. For Radbertus, the Song of Songs and Lamentations describe contradictory spiritual states; the former tells of the joy of God's mystical embrace, the later describes the desolation of God's absence.[57]

This is a tantalizing glimpse of Radbertus' exegetical presuppositions, based on a theory of multiple uses of scripture. Near the end of the introduction, these are laid out more clearly than were Hrabanus' senses, when Radbertus explains that Lamentations relates to the past, present, and future, telling of at least three types of desolation: that of the city, that of the church, and that of the soul.[58] Curiously, this explanation comes at the end of a discussion of the symbolic importance of the four chapters headed by Hebrew alphabets, which take their significance from such cosmic groups of four as the elements and the cardinal directions.[59]

In fact, as de Lubac has pointed out, Radbertus is following a four-fold scheme in this work, offering interpretations along the lines of historical, allegorical, anagogical, and tropological or moral senses.[60] His pattern of exegesis is, however, consistently set out in groups of three. For each verse, he begins with an historical explanation, ends with the tropological meaning, and places in between a consideration with regard to the Church, either on earth (allegory) or at the end of time (anagogy).[61] Radbertus is flexible in his use of terms and freely substitutes the words 'spiritual' or 'moral' for the allegorical interpretations.[62] He also seems to be somewhat inconsistent in his conception of anagogy: at points, this term clearly means the time at the end of time, but in other places the anagogical interpretation is not distinguishable from the allegorical.[63]

Perhaps this uneasy alliance between the three-fold and four-fold systems of exegesis reflects the extent to which Radbertus was influenced by his major source, the ***Lamentations commentary*** of Hrabanus Maurus. In the first, second, and fourth books, Radbertus follows Hrabanus loosely, giving some of the same biblical quotations,[64] the same versions of passages of Gregory and other sources,[65] and occasional word-for-word citations from Hrabanus' own interpretations.[66] Two of these passages are so close that they deserve to be reproduced in full:

LAMENTATIONS 1.18

Hrabanus Maurus (PL 111.1195B-C)

(Lc 15) Unde in Evangelio ille qui ovem perditam requisivit, seu mulier quae drachmam perditam invenit, convocant amicas et vicinas, ut testes assistant et gaudii eorum participes fiant. Quod ergo juvenes et virgines abire in captivitatem deplorat, ostendit se inde maxime dolere, quod spem status sui vidit subito corruisse. Quando enim sobolem suam subito interire conspexit, spem futurae generationis amisit.

Paschasius Radbertus (PL 120.1095D-96A)

Unde ille in Evangelio (Lc 15), qui ovem perditam requisivit, vel mulier quae drachmam adinvenit, convocant amicos et vicinos volentes habere comparticipes gaudii sui, et consortes laetitiae. Quanto magis anima debet convocare omnes, quae suos non audet oculos erigere, pudore confusionis suae oppressa ad Deum, quem malis suis ad iracundiam conduxerat, et apud clementem judicem intercessores, per compassionem doloris et amoris, existant? Quod autem juvenes ejus et virgines captivantur, ostendit se magis inde dolere dum viderit robustiores cordis ejus affectus, vel virgineas cogitationes, in confusionem ire miserae captivitatis, spem uteri sui ab hostibus violari. Profecto, quia quando quisque viderit sobolem deperire suam, certus est spem futurae generationis suae amisisse.

LAMENTATIONS 2.11

Videns propheta nimiam contritionem gentis suae templumque incensum et civitatem devastatam, nullique sexui, vel aetati hostes in nece parcere, ingenti dolore turbatus, fletu maximo deplorat, ita et oculi prae lacrymis deficiant, et omnis jucunditas desiderii vertatur in anxietatem cordis. Quid enim majus dolendum fuit, quam quod natio antiqua, et semen patriarcharum atque amicorum Dei, divinis legibus erudita, et prophetarum oraculis saepius confortata, in tantam apostasiam venerit, ut Dei sui oblita propter immanitatem scelerum traderetur in manus hostium Dei nomen blasphemantium.

Paschasius Radbertus (PL 120.1125C)

Nec dubium, quin videns propheta contritionem populi, nullique sexui vel aetati hostes in nece parcere, ingenti dolore turbatus, fletu maximo deplorat, ita et oculi prae lacrymis deficerent, et omnis jucunditas delectamenti vertatur in anxietatem cordis. Quid enim magis dolendum, quam quod natio antiqua semen patriarcharum atque amicorum Dei, divinis legibus erudita, et prophetarum oraculis saepius confortata, in tantam apostasiam venerit, ut Dei sui oblita, propter immanitatem scelerum, traderetur in manus hostium?

Radbertus' heavy dependence on a contemporary author is not as surprising as it may seem at first glance. Hrabanus' exegesis of Lamentations was, of course, the most complete source available in the late ninth century. Although it predates Radbertus' Lamentations commentary by only a decade, it would have been accepted as an authority without any hesitation. The respect commanded by Hrabanus as a direct heir of Alcuin and the most imposing exegete of the age allowed Radbertus, among other monastic authors of his generation, to cite him as an authority of almost the same stature as Bede and the patristic authors.[67]

It is true that Radbertus nowhere acknowledges Hrabanus as a source for his Lamentations commentary, but this is a characteristic of his scholarly procedure in general. Even patristic authors are given the barest acknowledgment in Radbertus' works; this anonymous interweaving of a contemporary source is just what might be expected of an exegete whose interest in his sources is limited to their usefulness in the seamless web of his narrative exposition. In short, these quotations can be seen as an indirect testimony to the originality of Hrabanus' Lamentations commentary.

The other sources used by Radbertus here are easily summarized. Like Hrabanus, Radbertus relies on Jerome's Epistle 30 for an understanding of the structure of the book and the meaning of the Hebrew letters. References to this epistle are found in the general preface, and at the beginnings of books 2 and 5.[68] Unlike Hrabanus, however, Radbertus barely mentions Jerome as the originator of this scheme and subjects the allegorical meanings of the Hebrew letters to extensive explanations of his own.[69] Rather than simply repeating Jerome's meanings of the Hebrew letters at the beginning of his treatise, Radbertus sprinkles the definitions throughout his commentary, often using them as an entrée to the connection between the historical and allegorical interpretations.[70] Besides Jerome, Radbertus quotes one time each from the *Aeneid* of Vergil, and the *Liber apotheosis* of Prudentius (without mentioning either author by name),[71] and from Augustine's *De doctrina Christiana,* a quotation probably taken from Bede but cited only as a reference to the rules of Tyconius.[72] These, plus the repetition of Hrabanus' quotations from Gregory and Eusebius, represent the bulk of Radbertus' patristic and classical sources.

But another source is evident in every passage of the treatise: the Bible. Radbertus set about explicating Lamentations by a system of resonances to other biblical passages. Predictably, he favored the biblical books closest to the liturgical round of the monastic life: the Psalms most of all, the Gospels (especially Matthew and Luke), the epistles of Paul, the Apocalypse (mostly in Book 4), and, as we have already seen, the Song of Songs. The Song of Songs is also a favorite text for Radbertus' mariological works,[73] but here it appears in the more common interpretation of a love song between Christ and the soul, and, especially, Christ and the Church.[74]

The tight interweaving of sources in Radbertus' commentary is essential to the purpose of his exegesis. In moving from verse to verse, Radbertus often lets his ideas run ahead of the text and uses the meanings of the Hebrew letters to lead into the next verse. In this way, he is able to tell one coherent story—a warning of the evil which worldly and unholy priests and monks can bring upon the Church. His disillusionment with the politics of Corbie and his fears for the future of the Empire are evident throughout.

Structurally, Radbertus' commentary departs significantly from the example of Hrabanus Maurus. Each of the five chapters of Lamentations is given a separate book of this interpretation. Books 1, 2, and 4 (comprising the sections of the commentary which follow Hrabanus Maurus most closely) are of almost the same length.[75] But the third and fifth chapters of Lamentations receive rather different treatment at Radbertus' hand.

Whereas Hrabanus Maurus was inspired by the triple acrostic of chapter 3 to make it the central focus of his Lamentations commentary, Radbertus instead attempts to compress the discussion and make it equal in length to that of the other books. Inevitably, any exegetical treatment of Lamentations 3 is longer than that of chapters 1, 2, and 4; but in this case, the difference is not as great as one might expect.[76] Only in dealing with Lamentations 3.1-6 (that is, the verses headed by aleph and beth) does Radbertus maintain the triple acrostic in his commentary. Thereafter, with one exception, he deals with this chapter by commenting on three verses at a time. Thus, verses 7-9 are taken altogether under the single heading of gimel.[77] Of course, this is in itself an exegetical decision, an assumption that three verses speak as one. In the prologue to Book 3, Radbertus explains that this seemingly triple scheme is intended to bring out one profound meaning: the passion of Christ.[78] It is in the context of this understanding of Lamentations 3 that Radbertus refers to the Tyconian rule of Christ and his body.[79]

The non-acrostic nature of the final chapter of Lamentations also elicits a comment from Radbertus. He opines that chapter 5 is structured differently because, according to the rules of rhetoric, the conclusion must bring together the ideas developed throughout a work into one brief summary.[80] That chapter 5 begins with an invocation of God's mercy is for Radbertus a reminder that the lament over sin must end in judgment, and that it is only through sorrow and penance for sins that sin itself will finally be overcome.[81] For both Radbertus and Hrabanus Maurus, the end of Lamentations is the place where the anagogical sense is the clearest. Radbertus, however, is able to work this message into his exegesis instead of appending it to the end of his commentary; furthermore, his delivery, in conformity to the rules of rhetoric, is short and pungent.[82]

One other observation about Radbertus' Lamentations commentary must be made before moving to a conclusion: the Bible text used for this work is not Alcuin's Vulgate. This is evident on a large scale in several places where the order of the Hebrew letters and/or the texts of several verses are unlike that of the official Frankish Vulgate. Lamentations 2.16-17 and 4.16-17 are quoted by Radbertus with the titles reversed: phe becomes ain and vice versa. It will be recalled that a peculiarity of the acrostic structure of Lamentations, in Hebrew, Greek, and Latin versions, is that after the first chapter the normal progression ain—phe is turned around.[83] This inversion is found in the text followed by Hrabanus Maurus,[84] but Radbertus is using a Bible which reversed these letters, perhaps to make them agree with the normative order of the Hebrew alphabet. Even more striking is Radbertus' citation of Lamentations 3.46-51, the phe—ain triplets. Here, not only the Hebrew letters, but indeed the entire sections are reversed, so that verses 49-51 appear directly after verse 45, while 46-48 follow verse 51.[85] In this case, it seems that the correcting hand was not content merely to change the order of the Hebrew letters, but also moved the texts which those letters introduce.

Recent studies in the history of the Vulgate have provided the means to analyze these variants. The critical editions of the Vulgate show that these large structural differences in the Lamentations text do not come from Radbertus himself, but reflect the influence of a biblical version centered in early medieval Spain.[86] In the details of Radbertus' Lamentations text, however, this influence is not as clear. Variant readings from the Spanish tradition appear in some of Radbertus' quotations from Lamentations, but the majority of these are found in Hrabanus' text as well.[87] Furthermore, other significant variants of the Spanish text are not given by Radbertus, and at least two different readings in Radbertus' Lamentations text cannot be explained by what we currently know about this Spanish connection.[88]

It appears, therefore, that neither of these Carolingian exegetes used a Lamentations text completely uncontaminated by the Spanish, perhaps the Theodulfan, tradition. Yet Radbertus' text is, in its 'correction' of the phe—ain sequence of chapters 2, 3, and 4, a testimony to a Bible version available in late ninth-century Frankland which was connected to the Spanish Bibles in ways that are not yet clear. This may be evidence that Radbertus' Lamentations commentary was written in exile rather than after his return to Corbie, since, in contrast to those of Corbie, the Bibles of Saint-Riquier are thought to show a marked Spanish influence.[89]

CONCLUSIONS

Analysis of the Lamentations commentaries of Hrabanus Maurus and Paschasius Radbertus does not provide an easy answer to the most intriguing question raised by the existence of these texts: why were they written? It would seem plausible that the use of Lamentations in the matins of Holy Week provided a rationale for exegesis of biblical books which do not have a place in the lectionary, yet these commentaries give very little evidence of liturgical influence. In fact, only one passage in Radbertus can be read as a possible reference to the Paschal liturgy. In commenting on Lamentations 1.12, 'O vos omnes qui transitis per viam, attendite et videte si est dolor sicut dolor meus,' Radbertus perhaps uses the destruction of the Temple as a subtle allusion to the stripping of the altar on Maundy Thursday; a bit further on, he relates this verse directly to the passion of Christ.[90] This may resonate with the use of Lamentations 1.12 in the matins of Maundy Thursday, but it must be admitted that the allusion is vague. There is no overt reference to the Holy Week ceremonies in the Lamentations commentary of Hrabanus Maurus.

Of course, both interpretations have, at least as a part of their message, implicit allusions to the theology behind the Holy Week liturgy, but it cannot be said that the mechanics of these ceremonies and the place of Lamentations therein is predominant in these works. Instead, both commentaries give a rather personal and pastoral effect. Allusions to the proper (and improper) behavior of monks and clerics abound,[91] and, as we have seen, the personal woes of the authors are conscious filters through which the biblical text is perceived. Recognizing this, we can turn to the overall exegetical output of Hrabanus and Radbertus, and to their respective places in the evolving genre of exegesis, to see how these commentaries came to be.

In the case of Hrabanus Maurus, the motivating impulse for the exegesis of Lamentations may well have been a desire for completeness. Coming as it does at the end of a commentary on Jeremiah, Hrabanus' treatment of Lamentations is only a small part of a series on the major prophets intended for imperial perusal and meditation.[92] Although Lamentations did not appear directly after Jeremiah in all medieval Latin Bibles, it is evident that Hrabanus' Bible put the five poems in this place.[93] So, in moving through Jeremiah for the edification of Lothar, Hrabanus had to contend with this 'last part of the prophet Jeremiah,' even though, as he recognizes, there are few landmarks to guide him through this relatively unfamiliar territory. The fact that Hrabanus would not consider avoiding a problematic text thrown in the way of a quite distinct task shows his educational plan. Hrabanus meant to provide guides to the scriptures, as he found them, for those who are in need of divine guidance, whether for personal or political reasons. The thoroughness demonstrated is only to be expected of an exegete who commented on all but a few of the books of the Bible.[94]

For Radbertus, the catalyst was more immediate. His Lamentations commentary is the product of a time of disillusionment in which the message of purification through suffering was gladly received. The manuscript tradition of the commentary testifies that his personal outcry against harsh political reality touched spirits in later centuries: of the nineteen surviving manuscripts (over three times the number of extant copies of Hrabanus on Lamentations) at least fourteen are dated to the twelfth or thirteenth centuries, and five of these are associated with Cistercian monasteries.[95] It appears that the followers of Saint Bernard shared Radbertus' gloomy view of the world they mourned and prayed to save.

The fact that Radbertus' commentary is on Lamentations alone shows that he *chose* the text, rather than simply finding it. Such a choice is congruent with Radbertus' general approach to exegesis; he commented on biblical texts because of their theological interest, and worked out doctrinal issues first in the context of interpretation.[96] Unlike the exegetical corpus of Hrabanus Maurus, however, Radbertus' commentaries show no concern for a systematic program of biblical education.

In this, we see one important intellectual change between the early and the late Carolingian schools. Radbertus made ready use of the work of the learned abbot of Fulda, but from this source he created a commentary of great passion, a convincing reading of the intensely moving text of Lamentations. This was clearly his intention, just as the goal of Hrabanus had been to provide the basic tools for such an interpretation. The strength, beauty, even the continuing popularity of Radbertus' treatise speak well for the success of Hrabanus' efforts at biblical education in Carolingian Frankland.

Notes

1. This paper has grown out of a study of Lamentations exegesis and the Carolingian liturgy presented at the International Congress on Medieval Studies, Kalamazoo, Michigan, in May of 1980. A grant from the American Philosophical Society allowed me to examine important manuscripts in Karlsruhe and Munich.

2. The first critical edition of a major Carolingian biblical commentary is currently in preparation: Beda Paulus, O.S.B. is engaged in an edition of the *In Matthaeum* of Paschasius Radbertus for the Corpus Christianorum series. This is a logical first text to receive such honored treatment; the *In Matthaeum* has clear links to Radbertus' eucharistic writings, and has long been admired for its sophisticated christology.

3. For a thorough study of the form and theology of Lamentations, see N. K. Gottwald, *Studies in the Book of Lamentations* (London 1954). Gottwald believes (21) that all five poems were written, by someone other than Jeremiah, between 587 and 538 BCE. On p. 20, n. 2, he gives a list of the most useful modern commentaries on the book. For the history of the Jeremiah corpus, see P. M. Bogaert, 'La tradition des oracles et du livre de Jérémie, des origines au moyen âge,' *Revue théologique de Louvain* 8 (1977) 305-28.

4. The first poem follows the standard order of the Hebrew alphabet in 22 verses, the first beginning with aleph, the last beginning with tau. In the second, third, and fourth chapters, the letters ain (no. 16) and phe (no. 17) are reversed; the third poem has a further variant in that each letter appears three times, for a total of 66 verses. Chapter 5 is a non-acrostic poem. These formal differences have led to the suggestion that the poems were written by a variety of authors. Concerning this, Gottwald states (21) that the first four poems 'are the work of a single poet [but] with respect to the concluding poem it is impossible to be dogmatic.'

5. The best study of the Latin texts of Lamentations is in the introduction to the *Biblia sacra iuxta Latinam Vulgatam versionem* by the monks of the Pontifical Abbey of Saint Jerome (Rome 1972). The Lamentations text of this edition is exactly that of R. Weber's Vulgate edition (Stuttgart 1969). Both of these editions were consulted for the discussion of textual variants on pp. 158-59 below.

6. This tradition is discussed by E. Levine, *The Aramaic Version of Lamentations* (New York 1976) 13. Its power is especially evident in the fact (*ibid.* 9, 13) that the Aramaic Lamentations text printed by Levine mentions the fall of the *second* Temple in 70 CE, and was probably written as a response to this calamity, also celebrated on the Ninth of Ab.

7. On Maundy Thursday, the three lessons of the first nocturn of matins are Lamentations 1.1-14; on Good Friday, Lamentations 2.8-15 and 3.1-9 are read; on Holy Saturday, the readings are Lamentations 3.22-30, 4.1-6, and 5.1-11. For a standard modern edition of this ancient liturgical tradition, see *The Hours of the Divine Office in English and Latin* (Collegeville, Minnesota 1963) II 1106-9 (Thursday), 1133-35 (Friday), and 1156-59 (Saturday). This is the order dictated by a tenth-century liturgical codex from Saint-Martial, Limoges, Paris, B.N. lat. 740, fols. 175^v-179^r, the oldest manuscript testimony I have found.

8. E. Bishop reviews the evidence for the Gallican invention of Tenebrae in his classic discussion of the so-called Ordo of Saint-Amand, *Liturgica Historica* (Oxford 1918) 159; see also L. Duchesne, *Christian Worship: Its Origin and Evolution* (2nd ed., tr. M. L. McClure; London 1903) 248-49 for a discussion of the Gallican origin of the chant used in the Holy Week liturgies, and 452 n. 1 for a linking of the lections in the Office to the developing Gallican liturgy of the seventh century. The custom was certainly not of Roman origin; the Carolingian allegorist Amalarius was surprised to find that the clergy at the Lateran knew nothing of Tenebrae: *Libro de ordine antiphonarii* 44, ed. J. M. Hanssens, *Amalarii Episcopi opera liturgica omnia* III (Studi e Testi 140; Vatican City 1950) 79-81. In the *Liber officialis*, Amalarius discusses the symbolic importance of the nine prophetic lessons which begin matins on the last three days of Holy Week, but mentions neither Jeremiah nor Lamentations specifically: ed. Hanssens, II (Studi e Testi 139; Vatican City 1948) 470. On the origin of Tenebrae, Hanssens proposes a *terminus ante quem non* of the fifth century, because of the importance of Cassian in the development of Matins from the office of Vespers: *Nature et genèse de l'Office des Matins* (Analecta Gregoriana 57; Rome 1952) 45.

9. Eusebius, Εχχληοιαστιχὴς ἱστορίας VI.24.2, and VI.25.2 (ed. E. Schwartz, GCS, *Eusebius Werke* II² [Leipzig 1908] 572, 574). The second reference states explicitly: 'Ιερε μίας σὺν Θρήνοις χαὶ τη 'Επιστολη ἐν ἑνί, 'Ιερεμία,' but see nn. 10 and 11 below.

10. 'Klagelieder Kommentar,' ed. E. Klostermann, GCS, *Origenes Werke* III (Leipzig 1901). This text, extant only in Greek, is taken from *catenae*

on the Prophets and the Ochtateuch found in four manuscripts of the tenth and eleventh centuries: *ibid.* xxxix. It was first studied by Michaele Ghisleri, a Roman Theatine, whose *In Jeremiam prophetam commentarii* (Lyon 1623) III is taken from one Vatican MS and considerably corrected by Klostermann. For Ghisleri, see the article of B. Mas, *Dictionnaire de Spiritualité* (Paris 1967) VI 350-51. Ghisleri's edition is printed in PG 13.606-62, under the title 'Ex Origine Selecta in Threnos'; see F. Stegmüller, *Repertorium Biblicum Medii Aevi* (Madrid 1954) no. 6207.

Migne claims that Origen's Lamentations commentary was known to Nicephorus, the Byzantine historian: 'monitum,' PG [*Patrologia graeca*] 13.605-6. However, Nicephorus' list of Origen's works is so highly dependent on Eusebius that it is impossible to know for certain whether the text was actually available in thirteenth-century Constantinople. Compare Nicephorus' description: Ἰερεμίας σὺν Θρήνοις χαὶ τη ἐπιστολη ἐν Ἰερεμία,' PG 145.1101A, to Eusebius, n. 9 above. See also G. Gentz, *Die Kirchengeschichte des Nicephorus Callistus Xanthopulus und ihre Quellen* (Texte und Untersuchungen zur Geschichte der altchristlichen Literatur 98; Berlin 1966) 64. I am grateful to Brian Daley, of the Weston School of Theology, for his help with the Origen materials.

11. See the edition of Schwartz for Rufinus' translation of Eusebius' history. The reference to Lamentations in 6.24.2 is part of a paragraph omitted by the translator (573), and the Latin version (575) of the list in 6.25.2 renders Ἰερεμίας σὺν Θρήνοις . . .' as simply 'Hieremias.' No knowledge of the text was therefore available to the West through Eusebius.

12. In a long list of Origen's works written for his friend Paula, Jerome mentions 'In Lamentationes Hierem iaetomos V': Epistle 33.4 (ed. I. Hilberg, CSEL [*Corpus scriptorum ecclesiasticorum latinorum*] 54 [Vienna 1910] 250).

13. Ed. S. Reiter, CCL 74 (Turnhout 1960). Origen's homilles on Jeremiah and the *Lexicon nominum Hebraicorum* are cited: see the index, 376. The Lamentations do not figure prominently in this interpretation.

14. J. N. D. Kelly, *Jerome: His Life, Writings, and Controversies* (New York 1975) 327 n. 16, referring to the prologue of Jerome's commentary on Ezekiel (ed. F. Glorie, CCL [*Cologne Cathedral Library*] 75 [Turnhout 1964] 4), where the following reference is made to Lamentations: 'Quod opus si per Domini misericordiam ad calcem usque perduxero, transibo ad Hieremiam, qui in Lamentationibus suis sub typo Hierusalem quattuor plagas mundi quadruplici plangit alphabeto.' Kelly's assertion, based on this one sentence, is a bit tenuous.

15. Origen's homilies on Jeremiah are edited by P. Nautin, *Sources Chrétiennes* 232 (Paris 1976); Jerome's translation is found in *PL* [*Patrologia Latina*] 25.583-692. The translation is extant in a number of ninth-century manuscripts: see Nautin 34-35, and W. A. Baehrens, *Überlieferung und Textgeschichte der lateinisch erhalten Origenes Homilien zum Allen Testament* (Texte und Untersuchungen 42.1; Leipzig 1916) 207ff. For a thoughtful comparison of the translation with the original, see G. Lomiento, 'Note sulla traduzione geronimiana delle omelie sur Geremie di Origene,' *Vetera Christianorum* 10 (1973) 243-62. The translation was known to Cassiodorus, *De institutione divinarum litterarum* 3, *PL* 70.1114c, and, through him, to Hrabanus Maurus, *PL* 111.793.

16. Epistle 30, ed. I. Hilberg (*CSEL* 54; Vienna 1910) 243-49, from several manuscripts which might have been available to Hrabanus Maurus. Jerome says about Lamentations: 'habes et in Lamentationibus Hieremiae quattuor alfabeta, e quibus duo prima quasi Saffico metro scripta sunt, quia tres uersiculos, qui sibi conexi sunt et ab una tantum littera incipiunt, heroici comma concludit; tertium uero alfabetum trimetro scriptum est et a ternis litteris, sed eisdem, terni uersus incipiunt; quartum alfabetum simile est primo et secundo' 3.245. It is worth noting that the theology of Lamentations does not enter into this account.

17. Sections 5-12, ed. Hilberg, 246-47. For example, aleph means 'doctrina,' beth 'domus,' gimel 'plenitudo,' deleth 'tabularum,' and he 'ista'; therefore, 'Prima conexio est "doctrina domus plenitudo tabularum ista," quo uidelicet doctrina ecclesiae, quae domus dei est, in librorum repperiatur plenitudine diuinorum': 6.246.

18. This was unacceptable to the later compiler of the pseudo-Jerome 'In Lamentationes Jeremiae,' *PL* 25.787-92, a treatise which gives an ecclesiological interpretation of the first chapter of Lamentations and begins each verse with Jerome's definition of the meaning of the Hebrew letters. Migne, *Admonitio* says that this compilation 'certe videri Bedae,' but the three late manuscripts listed by Stegmüller (no. 3423) suggest that it was a product of the twelfth century. At any rate, it was not used as a source by either of the Carolingian exegetes of Lamentations.

19. Lamentations 3.34: 'Lamed. ut conteveret sub pedibus suis omnes vinctos terrae,' is a favorite

text of Methodius, who quotes it seven times: see *Biblia Patristica. Index des citations et allusions bibliques dans la littérature patristique*. II, *Le troisième siècle Origène exceptè* (edd. J. Allenbach et al.; Paris 1977) 210. Aside from this verse, there are only nine references to Lamentations (and none of more than three verses) in the writings of this group of authors.

Lamentations 4.20 (Res. Spiritus oris nostri christus dominus captus est in peccatis nostris cui diximus in umbra tua vivemus in gentibus) is quoted by Clement of Alexandria, Justin Martyr, Irenaeus (twice), and Tertullian (three times): see *Biblia Patristica* I, *Des origines à Clément d'Alexandrie et Tertullien* (edd. J. Allenbach et al.; Paris 1975) 210-11.

Jerome's contemporary, Augustine, cites Lamentations only once in his famous *De civitate Dei*, 18.33.14; this is again a christological reading of 4.20. It is curious that *De civitate Dei*, a work which shares the sorrow and dread of Lamentations, does not make further use of the poems.

20. *Collationes* XIV.viii (ed. E. Pichery; *Sources chrétiennes* 54; Paris 1958) 189-93.

21. 'Hierusalem quadrifarie possit intellegi: secundum historiam ciuitas Iudaeorum, secundum allegoriam ecclesia Christi, secundum anagogen ciuitas dei illa caelestis, quae est mater omnium nostrum, secundum tropologiam anima hominis . . .': ed. Pichery, 190. This is Cassian's order of the famous four senses of scripture, which in the medieval tradition usually appear in the order: historical, allegorical, moral/tropological, anagogical. In the words of Beryl Smalley, this example 'caught the imagination of the middle ages and became classical': *The Study of the Bible in the Middle Ages* (Notre Dame, Indiana 1964; from the second Oxford edition 1954) 28. For a discussion of Cassian's four senses in the context of patristic allegory, see H. de Lubac, *Exégèse médiévale*, I¹ (Lyon 1959) 190-93.

22. The first two volumes of the critical edition of M. Adriaen (CCL 143, 143A; Turnhout 1979) contain books I-XXII; a third volume, containing books XXIII-XXV, is forthcoming.

23. The number seventeen is taken from the continuation of the *Liber de expositione veteris et novi testamenti* of Gregory's chancellor, Paterius (*PL* 79.976-82), a series of biblical extracts from Gregory's writings arranged in the order of the canon. As A. Wilmart has demonstrated, only the first volume of this work can be attributed to Paterius; the second part of the Old Testament compi-

lation (which includes Lamentations) and the New Testament volume are thought to date from the twelfth century: 'Le recueil Grégorien de Paterius et les fragments wisigothiques de Paris,' *Revue bénédictine* 29 (1927) 81-101. But perhaps an earlier compilation of Gregory's citations of Lamentations was done by Hrabanus Maurus: n. 35 below. In the absence of the final volume (and indices) of Adriaen's edition, Paterius and the Paterius continuation is still the only source for the biblical citations of the *Moralia*.

24. 'Maxilla quippe Ecclesiae sancti praedicatores sunt, sicut sub Judiae specie per Jeremiam dicitur: "Plorans ploravit in nocte, et lacrimae ejus in maxillis ejus" [Lamentations 1.2]; quia adversitate Ecclesiae illi amplius plangunt qui vitam carnalium confringere praedicando noverunt': *Moralia* 13.12.15 (ed. Adriaen; CCL 143A677).

25. For example, *Moralia* 5.31.55: 'Vnde sub Judaeae specie per prophetam torpens otio anima defletur, cum dicitur: "Viderunt eam hostes, et deriserunt sabbata eius" [Lamentations 1.7]. Praecepto etenim legis ab exteriori opere in sabbato cessatur. Hostes ergo sabbata videntes irrident, cum maligni spiritus ipsa vacationis otia ad cogitationes illicitas pertrahunt; ut unaquaeque anima quo remota ab externis actionibus Deo servire creditur, eo magis eorum tirannidi illicita cogitando famuletur' (ed. Adriaen; CCL 143.257).

26. 'Hine Jeremias luctum cordis sui considerari deposcens ait: "O vos omnes qui transitis per viam, attendite, et videte si est dolor sicut dolor meus" [Lamentations 1.12]. Qui enim praesentem vitam non quasi viam transeunt, sed quasi patriam attendunt, luctum cordis electorum considerare nesciunt. Illos ergo ut dolorem suum considerent exquirit quos in hoc mundo contigit animum non fixisse': *Moralia* 15.57.68 (ed. Adriaen, CCL 143A793). See also *Moralia* 32.22.46 (*PL* 76.663A), and 33.28.49 (*PL* 76.705c). The logical consequence of a 'moral' reading of scripture is, of course, the final redemption of the just, a subtlety of which both Origen and Gregory were surely aware. For a brief but sensitive discussion of Gregory's exegetical methodology and its impact on later authors, see de Lubac I¹ 187-90.

27. This synopsis follows the excellent biography of Hrabanus found in the introduction of J. McCulloh's edition of the *Martyrologium* (CCL, cont. med. 44 [Turnhout, 1979] xi-xxiv). Additional bibliography on Hrabanus' involvement in the political turmoil of this period is found in McCulloh's extensive footnotes.

28. McCulloh says, 'Psychologically he was faced with having supported a lost cause, and his writ-

ings during this period reveal discouragement with the chaos of the political situation in general' (xviii), with a note referring to several letters of 841-842. By 843, however, Hrabanus had yielded to the conciliatory overtures of Louis the German. In 847, with Louis the German's support, Hrabanus was ordained the Archbishop of Metz, which position he held until his death in 856. See McCulloh, xix-xxiv.

29. *PL* 111.793-1272, from the 1534 Basel edition of H. Petri. Lamentations is covered by Books 18-20, *PL* 111.1181D-1272. The prologue is also edited by E. Dümmler, *MGH* Ep. [*Monumenta Germaniae historica, Epistolae*] V (1893) 443-44.

30. 'Post Commentariolos quos mea parvitas in Heptateuchum, et in libros Regum, atque in Paralipomenon edidit; post explanatiunculas historiarum Esther, Judith, et Machabaeorum, nec non et voluminis Sapientiae atque Ecclesiastici, aliorumque opusculorum meorum labores, ad extremum in Jeremiam manum misi, ut collectis undique sanctorum Patrum sententiis, hujus quoque prophetae sensus aliquantulum avido lectori aperirem': *PL* 111.793A.

31. '. . . modo praesens opus expositionis videlicet Jeremiae prophetae, quod bonae memoriae genitori vestro Ludovico Augusto adhuc vivente inchoaveram, et post obitum ejus consummaveram, vestrae devotioni simul et auctoritate committo, ut habeatis illud legatisque, et ad bonum studium nostrum exercendum cum nostris eo utamini': *PL* 111.795A. At the end of the next expansive sentence, Hrabanus is even more explicit about Lothar's virtues as a ruler: '. . . sanctissime atque augustissime imperator Lothari, cujus mentem divina sapientia illustrans, non permittit fraude invidorum corrumpi, nec versutia perversorum seduci: sed in aequitatis et justitiae regula conservans, per viam veritatis sedulo deducit': *PL* 111.795B.

32. *PL* 111.795-798A.

33. '. . . beati Hieronymi explanationes in hunc prophetam nusquam ad integrum reperire potui, sed tantum primos sex libros, qui pertingunt pene usque ad medietatem voluminis prophetici': *PL* 111.793B. This is, of course, the sum of Jerome's finished commentary on Jeremiah, see nn. 13 and 14 above. Hrabanus' sources from chapter 33 of Jeremiah through the end of Lamentations have been studied by J. B. Hablitzel, 'Kleine Mitteilungen der Jeremias-Kommentar des Hrabanus Maurus,' *Studien und Mitteilungen zur Geschichte des Benediktiner-Ordens und seiner Zweige* 40 (1919-1920) 243-51.

34. 'Nam fertur Origenis quadraginta quinque homiliis praesentem prophetam Attico sermone exposuisse. Ex quibus quatuordecim tantum translatas inveni, quae me in hoc opere non parum adjuvabant': *PL* 111.793C. Hrabanus quoted directly here from Cassiodorus, for whom see n. 15 above.

35. 'Sic et beatus papa Gregorius non parum nobis in dictando profuit, qui in diversis opusculis suis, more suo, divinorum librorum sententias exponendo, istius quoque prophetae plurima testimonia enodavit': *PL* 111.795C-D.

36. 'His ergo omnibus consideratis, unum opusculum condere disposui, quod tamen in viginti libros dispartire decrevi, ne longitudo librorum fastidium lectori faceret, imo brevitas ad singula discutienda acutiorem redderet. Nec me praesumptuosum aut superfluum quisquam in conditione hujus operis debet dicere . . . nec jam sibi laborare necesse esse inquirendo, ubi aliorum labore quieti suae invenerit consultum': *PL* 111.795D-96A. Further study may show this to be the collection of Gregory's Jeremiah quotations included in the extant *Liber de expositione* attributed to Paterius: see n. 22 above. However, the selections from Lamentations published in *PL* 79 are not all included in Hrabanus' commentary, which gives other passages from Gregory not included in the compilation. This suggests that Hrabanus' collection, a more complete version than that of the text attributed to Paterius, is no longer extant in its original form.

37. '. . . ipsa pars in unum librum cum caetera prophetia Jeremiae conjungitur, apud quosdam vero sequestratim ponitur, et per se libri nomen habere censetur . . . ut priscae legis libri apud Hebraeos viginti quatuor esse demonstrentur: quo sub numero viginti quatuor seniores Apocalypsis Joannis inducit . . .': *PL* 111.1181D.

38. *PL* 111.1182D-84A, where Jerome's Epistle 30 is described as addressed 'ad Marcellam,' rather than 'ad Paulam.' In both this detail and many variant readings, Hrabanus' text of the epistle agrees with Hilberg's manuscripts *II* ('Turicensis Augiensis 49 s. IX') and D ('Vaticanus lat. 355 + 356 saec. IX-x'). It is only logical that Hrabanus used a form of this letter known at Tours, where he studied with Alcuin.

39. '. . . quo ipse propheta locutus est nos illustrare voluerit, secundum historiam et secundum mysticum sensum exposituri': *PL* 111.1181C.

40. Hrabanus says that all of Lamentations 'ad Christi et Ecclesiae pertinere sacramenta,' and, since the soul is the temple of God, it also deals with the

struggle of good against evil: *PL* 111.1184A and 1184C-85A. The anagogical sense is most clearly evident in the final summary, wedged between his discussion of the allegorical and moral interpretations: 'Sed quoniam finis libri ejus in Lamentationibus propheticis consummatur, nostri quoque opusculi libet finem querimoniis et fletibus terminare, quem propria miseria, et mei similium terrent facinora, futuraeque poenae horrorem incutiunt supplicia, cui jam mundi defectus gravitudinem ingerit, et metus futuri examinis lacrymarum flumina per maxillam producit, ut deprecatio nostrae humilitatis ad indulgentiam provocet elementiam superni judicis. Metuo enim diem judicii, metuo tenebrarum diem, diem tubae diem amarum, diem durum et tristem': *PL* 111.1268D.

41. Cf. *PL* 111.1216D, where Gregory's treatment of Job 30 follows Lamentations 3.2. Similar examples are found in PL 111.1217-18, and *passim.* Twenty quotations from the *Moralia,* two from Gregory's Homily 39, and one each from Gregory's Homily 2, Homily 33, and the *Regula Pastoralis* are listed by Hablitzel, 248-49.

42. Of course, the Psalms were always prominent in the mind of such a dedicated monk as Hrabanus. Five references to Cassiodorus on the Psalms are given by Hablitzel, 248-49.

43. Hablitzel lists (248-49) four references to Jerome's commentary on Isaiah, and one each from Epistle 132, and the commentaries on Ezekiel and Malachi. At *PL* 111.1185B, Hrabanus refers to Eusebius' description of the conquest of Jerusalem by the Romans (*Ecclesiasticae Historiae* 3.1-10). He quotes Augustine on Psalm 63 (from the *Enarrationes*) at *PL* 111.1214C. Hablitzel (245-47) did not mention Eusebius, but found traces of the *Antiquities* of Josephus in Hrabanus' exegesis. These can probably be traced to Eusebius, who quotes extensively from Josephus in *Ecclesiasticae Historiae* 3.6-8.

44. *PL* 111.1209D, 1214B, 1217B, 1218B, 1221A,C, 1222D, 1228D. 1230A, 1232A, 1235B, 1239C, 1240B, 1241D, 1244B,D, 1246C, 1248B, 1254B, 1255C, 1256C, 1259B, 1261A, 1262A,C, and 1266C. Critical study of the five manuscripts of this commentary listed by Stegmüller (no. 7054) will help to determine how many other passages are original to this interpretation. Hablitzel is loath to admit that such a large part of the Lamentations commentary came from the hand of Hrabanus. He writes (249): 'Wenn man diese Inhaltsangabe überblickt, so findet man sehr oft eine selbständige Erklärung Hrabans. Bei den Klageliedern habe ich statt Hraban unbekannte Quelle gesetzt, denn es

ist schlechterdings nicht immer möglich, festzustellen, ob die Auslegung nicht doch aus einem patristischen Autor genommen ist . . . .' However, in view of the scant resources for earlier commentaries on Lamentations, there is little reason to deny Hrabanus credit for what cannot be shown *not* to be his own work.

45. Vatican, Vat. lat. 520, saec. XI, Italy, where Hrabanus' commentary on Lamentations (fols. 172^r-187^v) follows *Jerome's* exposition of Jeremiah (fols. 119^v-173^r). That this juxtaposition was purposeful is apparent from the fact that the book numbers of the two treatises have not been brought into accord. Although the beginning of Book 18 is missing (fol. 173^r begins 'Habes in lamentationibus Hieremie quattuor alfabeta'; *PL* 111.1183), Book 19 is clearly rubricated on fol. 179^r, Book 20 on 183^v, even though the last part of Jerome's commentary ends 'EXPLICIT LIBER VI' (fol. 172^v). Fol. 187^v has the rubric 'EXPLICIT EXPOSITIO BEATI HIERONIMI PRESBYTERI. IN LAMENTATIONIBUS HIEREMIE, PROPHETE,' which suggests that the composite may have been copied from an earlier exemplar. This manuscript was acquired (fol. 198^v) for the Roman monastery of Sancta Croce in Gerusalemme by 'Dominus Damianus.' Its exemplar is unknown; the only earlier manuscript of Hrabanus on Lamentations is Sankt Gallen 282 (saec. IX), a copy of Books 13-20 of Hrabanus' text.

46. *PL* 111.1181-1216B.

47. *PL* 111.1215C-48B; 1215C quotes from Jerome's Epistle 30.3, ed. Hilberg 245.

48. *PL* 111.1247C-68C, where the conclusion begins.

49. Hrabanus says the three-fold format of this chapter shows 'hoc in primis volentes sciri quod haec pars primum calamitatem gentis Judaeae, seu potius humani generis deflendo pronuntiat, deinde sacramentum Dominicae incarnationis ac passionis manifeste exprimit, ubi Judaeorum persecutio innocentis Christi poena ac mors describitur': *PL* 111.1215C.

50. This conclusion begins at 1268D with a brief discussion of allegorical and anagogical understandings of Lamentations. On 1269A, Hrbanus discusses the plight of 'civitas nostra interna' through interwoven quotations taken in order from the first two chapters of Lamentations. This section is a short commentary in the tropological mode which ends at 1271B. The final surge of gratitude for the saving grace of the Incarnation carries a veiled reference to the liturgy (1271C): 'Scrutemur ergo vias nostras, et "revertamur ad Dominum," elevemusque corda nostra cum mani-

bus in coelum ad Deum.' The words in quotation marks paraphrase Lamentations 5.21; the following phrase is, of course, from the Roman Canon of the Mass. The commentary ends (1272c) with a reference to the opening of Augustine's *Confessiones*: 'Tui sumus, Domine, ad te pertinemus, et tu nobis miserando consulis, in aeternum coram te vivemus. Fiat, Domino, super nos semper tua misericordia, ut laudem tuam annuntiemus.'

51. The details of Radbertus' early life are reported in a laudatory poem written by Engelmodus of Soissons, 'Ad Ratbertum Abbatem': *MGH, PLAC [Poetae Latini aevi Carolini]* II 62-66. According to this account, Radbertus was left as an infant at the door of the monastery of Sancta Maria in Soissons, where Theodrada, a cousin of Charlemagne, was abbess. Theodrada's brothers, Adalard and Wala, served as abbots of Corbie in the first decades of the ninth century. Radbertus' monastic career is clearly tied to his family, as his biographies of Adalard (*Vita Adalardi, PL* 120.1507-56) and Wala (*Epitaphium Arsenii, PL* 120.1557-1650; also ed. E. Dümmler, Berlin 1900) show. For further information, see H. Peltier, *Paschase Radbert* (Amiens 1938) and G. Mathon, 'Paschase Radbert et l'évolution de l'humanisme carolingien,' in *Corbie, abbaye royale* (Lille 1963) 135-46.

52. Very few of the dates in Radbertus' personal chronology have been determined absolutely. We know that he attended the Council of Quierzy-sur-Oise in 849 as abbot of Corbie, but his successor, Odo, filled this function at the Council of Soissons in 853: P. Grierson, 'Eudes, Ier Évêque de Beauvais,' *Le Moyen Âge* 6 (1935) 161-98; Peltier, 80-81. The estimations of Radbertus' death-date range from 859 to 865.

53. Two letters of Lupus of Ferrières (nos. 56 and 57; *PL* 119.521-22) speak of the difficulties Radbertus had with a younger monk named Ivo, who wished to leave Corbie but was forced by Radbertus to stay and do penance. Peltier suggests (78-79) that a simple generation gap is to blame. There is no evidence that Radbertus' disputes with Ratramnus over the eucharist and the virginity of Mary had a major part in this decision to leave Corbie, inviting as this theory might seem.

54. *PL* 120.1059-1236D; 'Prologus ad Odilmannum Severum,' *PL* 120.1059c-62A. Odilmannus, under the name of Severus, appears as one of the interlocutors of the *Epitaphium Arsenii*. The prologue to Book 2 of the *Epitaphium* indicates that it was written, at least in part, after Radbertus' retirement from active life: PL 120.1605/06D-

1607A. Since Lamentations is quoted extensively here, it seems likely that the Lamentations commentary dates from the same period, ca. 852. Peltier (82-83) suggests that the commentary was written some five years later, after Radbertus' return to Corbie. His reason for this is a reference in Book 4 to the burning of Paris by 'piratae': *PL* 120.1220c. Peltier sees this as an acknowledgment of the Norman sack of that city in 857, described by the chronicler Prudentius of Troyes as the work of 'Piratae Danorum': *Prudentii Trescensis Annales* (ed. G. H. Pertz; MGH Script [*Scriptores*] I [Hannover 1826] 450). Pertz gives the passage from Radbertus in n. 47, showing that he also links the two events. However, Prudentius of Troyes also mentions (441) a Norman invasion of Paris in 845 after which the barbarians were engaged in battle by Frankish troops led by Charles the Bald. A similar description of 'paganorum et hostium incursiones' is found in *Epitaphium Arsenii* II.7 (*PL* 120.1615A), which shows that Radbertus was aware of earlier ravages of the Northmen.

55. 'Multo cogor longoque confectus vitae taedio, tristes lacrymarum inire modos. Gemebunda jam quia profecto meis praegravata malis inopinate senectus non vocata venit. Quam dum inspicio, specie deformatus, aliena perhorresco, eo quod me subito animo non mutatus, quod fui non invenio, evadere tamen nequeo, illa decipiente, quae amisi. Unde congelatus usu longiori durior effectus, nullis jam emolliri queo fletibus, quamvis multis miseriarum mearum intus forisve premar doloribus. Quibus quotidie saltem ad suspiria propulsus Jeremiae prophetae inter discrimina ultimae vitae, Threnus explanare decrevi': *PL* 120.1059c-60c.

56. 'Sicut in divinis Litteris diversa leguntur cantica, ita et Spiritu sancto reserante lamentationes diversae: et sicut proprie appellatur liber Salomonis Cantica Canticorum, ita et appellari queunt Threni Jeremiae Lamentationes lamentationum': *PL* 120.1061A.

57. '. . . quia sicut omnino praecellunt illa, in quibus sponsus ac sponsa dulcibus fruuntur amplexibus, ita et lamentationes istae vincunt omnia Scripturarum lamenta, in quibus abscessus sponsi ab sponsa; magnis cum fletibus vehementius deploratur: ex quo sola civitas sedere, ac domina gentium quasi vidua, amarissime satis plangitur. In illis quippe canticis, diversae introducuntur ad gaudia nuptiarum personae, in istis vero deversae planguntur': *PL* 120.1061b.

58. 'Quibus profecto verbis ostenditur, quod non solum ad praesentia et futura, verumetiam et ad praeterita lamentatio haec superextenditur. . . .

Propterea et nos non minus super ejusdem civitatis ruinam, quam et super Ecclesiae damna, super-
que animarum discrimina, decrevimus easdem tri-
pliciter exponere lamentationes, et prout oportuerit
ad eadem tria tempora sensus dirigere': *PL*
120.1063B-64A.

59. 'Ideoque quadruplici Threnos totius lamenti, ut
aestimo, contextuit alphabeto: quia tam nos quam
et hic mundus quatuor constat conditus elementis,
igne videlicet et aqua, aere et terra: ut qui quatuor
consistimus existentiis, sub quatuor recte planga-
mur litterarum alphabetis . . . ut sub quadrato coeli cardine praesentis saeculi delicta quadrato
lugeat alphabeto, et ad lamenta omnia invitet': *PL*
120.1063A-B.

60. 'Dans son commentaire des *Lamentations*, Paschase Radbert est constamment fidèle à cet [i.e.,
de Lubac's second] ordre; pour désigner le deuxième terme, aussitôt après l'histoire, il parle tantôt
d'allégorie, tantôt d'anagogie, tantôt de sens
mystique, etc., sans que cette diversité de vocables
trouble jamais la régularité du schéma': de Lubac
I[1] 148.

61. Thus, it is difficult to see why de Lubac claims
that Radbertus belongs to the group which followed the 'second formula' of four-fold exegesis,
consisting of the order historical, allegorical,
tropological, anagogical. Although Radbertus does
consistently place allegorical interpretations before
the moral, he never ends a passage with the anagogical meaning of a verse.

62. For example, in Lamentations 1.1, Radbertus calls
this sense 'spiritualiter' (*PL* 120.1064D); in 1.2,
the term is 'juxta allegoriam' (*PL* 120.1066D); 1.5
simply mentions the Church (*PL* 120.1073B); 1.6
uses 'mystice' for the ecclesiological sense (*PL*
120.1074D). For more examples, see de Lubac I[1],
148 n. 14. 1.3 and 1.4 have anagogical explanations in this place: see n. 63 below.

63. The anagogical interpretation of 1.4 speaks of the
'viae supernae Sion ac portae' (*PL* 120.1071A-B),
whereas the 'juxta anagogen' of 1.3 is concerned
with the trials of the Church on earth (*PL*
120.1069D-70B).

64. For example, the quotations from Deuteronomy
31 and Acts 7 (Hrabanus, *PL* 111.1184C; Radbertus, *PL* 120.1064C-D), Daniel 3 (Hrabanus; *PL*
111.1193B; Radbertus, *PL* 120.1090D), Isaiah 63
and Psalm 11 (Hrabanus, *PL* 111.1193C-D; Radbertus, *PL* 120.1091D), Psalm 70 (Hrabanus, *PL*
111.1197C; Radbertus, *PL* 120.1099D, 1 John 2
(Hrabanus, *PL* 111.1196A; Radbertus, *PL* 120.
1096C), 1 Peter 2 (Hrabanus, *PL* 111.1200D; Rad-

bertus, *PL* 120.1109D), Psalm 73 (Hrabanus, *PL*
111.1201B, Radbertus, *PL* 120.111D), and 1 Corinthians 3 (Hrabanus, *PL* 111.1251C; Radbertus *PL*
120.1207B), all cited in similar expositions of the
same verses.

65. For example, *Moralia* 5.31, quoted in the explication of Lamentations 1.7 (Hrabanus *PL* 111.1189C;
Radbertus, *PL* 120.1077A—a shorter quotation
with other material interjected), *Moralia* 25.23.49,
used in 1.11 (Hrabanus, *PL* 111.1191C; Radbertus,
PL 120.1084B), *Moralia* 3.32.62 used in 1.20
(Hrabanus, *PL* 111.1197A; Radbertus, *PL* 120.
1098C), and the conflation of *Regula pastoralis*
2.7 and *Moralia* 50.27.43 and *Moralia* 50.34.15
for 4.1 (Hrabanus, *PL* 111.1248C, with interpolated
material from Matthew 7; Radbertus, *PL* 120.
1199B). Hrabanus' references to Eusebius are also
echoed by Radbertus; both mention Chaldeans,
Vespasian, and Titus in their discussions of
Lamentations 1.1 (Hrabanus, *PL* 111.1185B; Radbertus, *PL* 120.1063C), and Josephus at Lamentations 1.11 (Hrabanus, *PL* 111.1191B; Radbertus,
PL 120.1083C). Both authors also give the same
etymology for Edom at 4.21 (Hrabanus, *PL* 111.
1261B-C; Radbertus, *PL* 1233D-34B).

66. Compare the discussions of 1.4 (Hrabanus, *PL*
111.1187A-B; Radbertus, *PL* 120.1071B-D), 1.6
(Hrabanus, *PL* 111.1188C-D; Radbertus *PL* 120.
1074D-75B), which bear some word-for-word correspondences, and the similar analysis of 3.11
(Hrabanus, *PL* 111.1218D; Radbertus, *PL*
120.1155A).

67. Angelomus of Luxeuil, a contemporary of Rad-
bertus, used the Old Testament commentaries of
Hrabanus extensively in his exegesis; see J. B.
Hablitzel, 'Angelom von Luxeuil und Hrabanus
Maurus,' *Biblische Zeitschrift* 19 (1931) 215-27,
and M. L. W. Laistner, 'Some Early Medieval
Commentaries on the Old Testament,' *Harvard
Theological Review* 46 (1943) 27-46, repr. *The
Intellectual Heritage of the Early Middle Ages*
(ed. C. G. Starr; Ithaca, New York 1957) 181-201.
In his analysis of this literary dependence, Laistner suggests a redefinition of Angelomus' phrase
'moderno tempore.' These conclusions are equally
apt for Radbertus, who unselfconsciously drew
upon Alcuin in several other works.

68. The Prologue (*PL* 120.1063A-64B) loosely follows
Jerome, Epistle 30.3, ed. Hilberg 245. Book 2 (*PL*
120.1104C-1106A) repeats and interprets the seven
combinations of letters given by Jerome in Epistle
30.6-12, ed. Hilberg 246-47. The prologue to Book
4 (*PL* 120.1197B-98B) also echoes paragraph 3 of

Jerome's letter, but gives an entirely original interpretation (based on the significance of the number four) of the importance of the alphabet in this chapter.

69. The only direct mention of Jerome (*PL* 120.1064A) is in the general prologue: 'Neque silendum putavimus quod propheta sanctus, sicut divinae legis interpres Hieronymus testatur, Threnos tanti lamenti lege metri condiderit.' The extensive discussions of Jerome's seven combinations of letters at the beginning of Book 2 are laced with references to other biblical passages illustrating the *meaning* of such phrases as 'doctrina domus plenitudo tabularum.' These analyses are consistently along moral and christological lines. It should be noted that there is nothing in Radbertus' use of Jerome which he could not have taken from Hrabanus rather than directly from the source.

70. Even the undistinguished letter tau, which Jerome defined as 'et,' is woven by Radbertus into the interpretation of a verse: see his commentary on Lamentations 1.6, *PL* 120.1074C.

71. The Vergil quotation is a paraphrase of *Aeneid* 6.730: 'Hinc metuunt cupiuntque dolent gaudentque,' for which Radbertus reads 'Hi metuunt, cupiunt, gaudentque, dolentque': *PL* 120.1153A. The verse is used by Radbertus in commenting on Lamentations 3.9, 'Conclusit vias meas lapidibus quadris,' in which Radbertus interprets the stumbling-blocks as sin and wickedness crafted by our own hands and by the hands of heretics wishing to trip the Church (*PL* 120.1153B). The passage in Vergil describes the thousand-year-long cleansing process necessary before souls take on new bodies, a concept of uncertain origin: see H. E. Butler, *The Sixth Book of the Aeneid* (Oxford 1920) 223-35. Radbertus' idea of sins' creating their own punishments is similar, but he does not mention purgatory or the underworld. I am indebted to the late William C. McDermott, of the University of Pennsylvania, for his wise and generous advice on this matter.

Prudentius is quoted in the interpretation of Lamentations 1.4: 'Unde et a quodam poetarum, prima credendi via Abraham appellatur' (*PL* 120.1071B), from *Liber apotheosis,* 372-75 (ed. M. Cunningham; CCL 126 [Turnhout 1966] 90). Prudentius is a favorite poet of Radbertus and is quoted frequently in his other works.

72. Prologue to Book 3: 'Sed ut haec quae ad caput pertinent, quaeve ad corpus melius discernantur, commemoranda est illa regula, quam Tichonius unam de septem esse voluit, ex quibus etiam eru-

ditissimi ad intelligendas Scripturas plurimum adjuvantur. Quarum prima est ipsa de Christo et ejus corpore, quando a capite sine permutatione personae ad corpus, vel a corpore transitur ad caput, vel quando ipsa eademque sententia non minus capiti, quam et corpori congruere videtur: nec tamen ab una eademque persona receditur, sicuti in quamplurimis locis Scripturarum recte probatur, sed et in hac lamentatione interdum invenitur, ut est': *PL* 120.1141B-C. The reference is to *De doctrina Christiana* 3.31.44 (ed. J. Martin; CCL 32 [Turnhout 1962] 104), but C. Maus points out that the quotation comes almost verbatim from the preface of Bede's commentary on the Apocalypse (*PL* 93.131B-C): *A Phenomenology of Revelation: Paschasius Radbert's Way of Interpreting Scripture* (Pontificium Athenaeum Antonianum, Facultas Theologica, Theses ad Lauream 180; Dayton, Ohio 1970) 63 n. 4. Maus tries to show that Radbertus' overall hermeneutic was based on the principle of species and genus taken from the Tyconian tradition.

73. That is, the *Cogitis me* (ed. A. Ripberger, Spicilegium Friburgense 9; 1962), the *De partu Virginis* (ed. J. M. Canal, *Marianum* 30 [1968] 53-160, new ed. by E. A. Matter forthcoming in CL), and the *Expositio in Psalmum 44* (*PL* 120.993-1060). Maus (83-104) discusses the application of the genus/species rule in the Song of Songs quotations in these last two works and the *Expositio in Matthaeum* (*PL* 120.31-994).

74. See n. 57 above for tropological readings of the Song of Songs. A striking example of the christological/ecclesiological understanding is found in Radbertus' exegesis of Lamentations 5.16: 'Cecidit corona capitis nostri vae nobis quia peccavimus,' which quotes Song of Songs 4.8 and 3.11, and ends 'Quam sane coronam Ecclesia, quae vere sponsa Christi est, perdit, quando decorem fidei, et integritatem operum ejus amittit in his qui summi videntur in membris Christi. Aut certe corona capitis nostri tunc ruit, quando hi qui videbantur ad decorem et gloriam insigniri, pro diademate in Christo, qui caput est totius Ecclesiae, in perfidiam, vel in scelera, vel flagitia cadunt. Cadit quippe corona capitis nostri, cum hi defluunt, qui in Christo ornamentum videbantur esse decoris: sed tunc vae imminet, cum et hi per diversa coruunt, qui videntur summi: deinde vulgus lasciviens, in peccata et flagitia venit. Hinc est quod propheta simul cum populo, imo pro eo plangit: "Vae nobis, quia peccavimus"': *PL* 120.1251B-C.

75. Book 1 is found in *PL* 120.1061A-1104B, Book 2 in *PL* 120.1103C-42A, Book 4 in *PL* 120.1197C-

1238B. Each of these chapters of Lamentations is discussed in approximately forty columns.

76. Book 3 is in *PL* 120.1141B-98A, where it occupies fifty-seven columns.

77. *PL* 120.1151B-53D. The exception is samech (Lamentations 3.43-45), treated in *PL* 120.1177C-79D. Although all three verses are quoted at the beginning of this section, verse 44 ('Opposuisti nubem tibi . . .') is repeated under a second samech title at *PL* 120.1178D. This may be simply a scribal error in the unidentified MS behind this edition, since the discussion in both sections includes all three verses headed by samech.

78. 'Unde et tertium alphabetum quasi ad quosdam decrevi calentes prophetae fontes, quia excelsiora sunt sub alterius genere metri, ea quae aptantur trimetro, promulgata profundius manum mittere. In quo nimirum opere terni versus una eademque incipiunt littera, quod non ita in tribus Sapphicis constat alphabetis. Sed quia quaedam de Ecclesia sunt, et multa ibi quae de passione Christi altius aperiuntur, altior est sensus requirendus, licet non inveniri posse credam sine fletibus': *PL* 120.1139D-42A.

79. See n. 72 above.

80. 'Quintus igitur liber non eadem lege est editus, qua praemissi quatuor: sed eorum conclusio in hoc uno recapitulatur, lege rhetorum, qui sub epilogo in fine concludunt et determinant ac dinumerant singulas res breviter, quas attigerant': 'Prologus Libri Quinti,' *PL* 120.1235D.

81. 'Lamentantes ergo sunt, qui pietatis intuitu celsa mente deflent civitatum ruinas, excidia patriae, depopulationes et vastitates, nec non et interitum suorum civium, inter quae connumerant quae jam passi aut certe passuri sunt variis cruciatibus, et contumeliis innumeris. Unde monet Apostolus, charitatem proximi persuadens, gaudere cum gaudentibus, flere cum flentibus. Et quia hic est fratrum amator, teste angelo, qui multum orat pro populo et pro civitate sancta Dei Jerusalem, merito lamentationibus suis vincit omnium lamentationum lamenta: et suis fletibus provocat omnes, ut simul defleant totius saeculi ruinas et peccata': 'Prologus Libri Quinti,' *PL* 120.1238A-B.

82. Book 5 (found in *PL* 120.1237B-56B, in nineteen columns) is roughly half as long as the commentary on Lamentations 1, 2, and 4.

83. See n. 4 above. Radbertus shows a generally critical approach to his Bible text: see his discussion of the variants of Symmachus and Theodotion for Lamentations 2.14, *PL* 120. 1131B-C.

84. Compare the citations of Lamentations 2.16-17 (Hrabanus, *PL* 111.1209D; Radbertus, *PL* 120.1133B-D), and Lamentations 4.16-17 (Hrabanus, *PL* 111.1256C-58B; Radbertus, *PL* 120.1224B-26B).

85. *PL* 120.1180A-1182C; compare Hrabanus' treatment of 3:46-51, *PL* 111.1235C-40D.

86. The 1969 and 1972 Vulgate editions (for which see n. 5 above) attribute these variants to a textual tradition represented in the *stemma codicum* by Λᴸ (Codex Gothicus Legionensis, Léon, San Isidoro, written ca. 960). For a discussion of this codex, see B. Fischer, *Vetus Latina* 2 (Freiburg im Breisgau 1951) p. 1* (no. 91).

87. Lamentations 1.20 interficit for interfecit (*PL* 120.1098B; also Hrabanus, *PL* 111.1196B), 2.1 caelo + in (*PL* 120.1106B; also Hrabanus, *PL* 111.1199D), 2.1 est recordatus for recordatus est (*PL* 120.1107B; also Hrabanus, *PL* 111.1199D), 2.18 omit per² (*PL* 120.1135C), 2.19 aquam for aqua (*PL* 120.1136D; also Hrabanus, *PL* 111. 1212C), 2.20 occiditur for occidetur (*PL* 120. 1138D; also Hrabanus, *PL* 111.1214B), 3.14 in derisum for in derisu (*PL* 120.1157B; also Hrabanus, *PL* 111.1221A), 5.11 humiliauerunt + et (*PL* 120.1246D).

88. Among the variants which do not appear in Radbertus' Lamentations commentary are 1.10 omit in after intrarent (*PL* 120.1082A), 1.11 factus for facta (*PL* 120.1084B), 3.15 omit me² (*PL* 120.1157B), 3.17 est + a pace (*PL* 120.1159A), 3.41 ad Deum for ad Dominum *PL* 120.1176A). Hrabanus Maurus has the variant of this last verse (*PL* 111.1233B), but this could easily be the result of a common scribal error, as the abbreviations for Deus and Dominus are virtually indistinguishable.

In his commentary on Lamentations 4.13-14, Radbertus has a changed order for both text and title, placing nun. 'Erraverunt . . .' before mem. 'Propter peccata . . . ,' *PL* 120.1221B-C. In what should be verse 14 (nun) Radbertus omits the word 'sunt' between 'polluti' and 'sanguine,' whereas the text reads 'polluti sunt *in* sanguine,' and Hrabanus (*PL* 111.1255C-56B) gives the standard Vulgate text. There is no parallel to Radbertus' text in the *apparatus criticus* of either the 1969 or the 1972 Vulgate editions. Of course, the question of how Hebrew letters are represented in the manuscripts of Latin Lamentations commentaries is an important aspect of this problem. One of the two oldest copies, Karlsruhe, Aug. Perg. CXLVI (a tenth-century copy from Corbie's daughter house, Corvey) notes the Hebrew letters in the margins in brown ink, rather than placing them in the body of the text, or in rubrication. If this was the norm rather than the exception, such differences as the mem-nun reversal of 4.13-14 could happen very easily and not necessarily reflect a variant of the biblical text.

89. In discussing the Corbie Bibles, S. Berger summarizes: 'En somme, le texte de la bible de Corbie n'est nullement un text espagnol. Le peu qu'il a d'éléments espagnols lui vient du dehors, et les soudres s'en voient encore. C'est par là que les textes de Corbie se distinguent de ceux de Saint-Denis et Saint-Riquier': *Histoire de la Vulgate pendant les premiers siècles du moyen âge* (Paris 1893) 108. For the Spanish influences on the Saint-Riquier Bibles (although with no mention of Lamentations) see Berger, 93-100.

The 822 Bible of Saint-Riquier (Paris, B.N. lat. 11504 and 11505) is mentioned by B. Fischer as an Old Latin version of the 'Spanischer Toletanustyp' ('Bibeltext und Bibelreform unter Karl dem Grossen,' *Karl der Grosse* II, *Das geistige Leben* [ed. B. Bischoff; Düsseldorf 1965] 184), but it has not been thoroughly studied. I have not examined these manuscripts.

90. *PL* 120.1084c-87b. '. . . psalterium eorum humiliatur, hymnus conticuit, et exsultatio tota dissolvitur, lumen candelabri exstinguitur . . . et vasa quaeque pretiosissima transferuntur ad exteros' (*PL* 120.1085a) may apply equally to the destruction of the Temple and the extinguishing of the altar rituals from Thursday night until midnight of the Easter Vigil. On the subject of those who pass by on the road, Radbertus says: 'Ad paschales namque vocati dapes, paschalia celebrantes vota, agnum, ut jussum est ex lege, festinantes comedunt': *PL* 120.1085d. This attention to the sufferings of Christ diverts Radbertus to another favorite theme, the sufferings of the Virgin Mary.

91. The best example in Hrabanus Maurus is *PL* 111.1227b-28a, where, in commenting on Lamentations 3.28, he includes a long discussion (with resonances of the prologue to the *Regula Benedicti*) of the types of the monastic life. Radbertus, addressing a fellow-monk rather than an emperor, makes greater use of this theme; for example, 'Dicuntur ergo genae Ecclesiae . . . Dicuntur et sicut areolae aromatum quae consitae sunt a pigmentariis [Song of Songs 5.13], etiam ut eos insinuet qui theoricam sectantur vitam, et orationibus die noctuque deserviunt, in quibus vere est pulchritudo ecclesiarum et virtutum odor': *PL* 120.1067c. See also *PL* 120.1074d, 1077a, 1082c-d, 1109c-d, 1123c-d, 1152b-c, 1171a, 1207c, 1213a-14a (an especially interesting complaint

against contemporary mores), 1218b-c, 1222b-c, 1226c, and many other places, with the concern for a direct relation to the monastic life becoming more prominent toward the end of the work.

92. Besides the Jeremiah commentary, Hrabanus' commentary on Ezekiel (*PL* 110.493-1084, prologue ed. E. Dümmler, MGH Ep. 5.475) was intended for Lothar. The unpublished Daniel commentary (prologue ed. E. Dümmler, MGH Ep. 5.467) is dedicated to Louis the German. The Isaiah commentary, also unpublished, was written 'quorundam amicorum peticioni consentiens' (prologue ed. E. Dümmler, MGH Ep. 5.501), but is dated after 842, that is, about the time of the treatise on Daniel; it may have also been read by Louis the German.

93. At least as early as the third century BCE, two Hebrew versions of the Jeremiah corpus were in circulation. One of these was adapted to look more like Isaiah and Ezekiel by the placement of the oracular material of the book in the middle: see Bogaert's description, 316-23. In the Septuagint tradition, the book of Baruch, a pseudepigraphon dated between 63 and 70 BCE, was also conflated with Jeremiah-Lamentations, usually in the order Jeremiah—Baruch 1-5—Lamentations—Baruch 6. This order in found in the Spanish Vulgate manuscripts Δ^{LM} (León, Capit. Cath. 6, dated 920, and Madrid, Academ. Hist. 20, ca. 900) and Λ^{L} (León, San Isidoro, dated 960).

The Theodulfan Bibles (the Θ tradition, including $\Theta^{E \cdot}$ Paris B.N. lat. 11553, a ninth-century copy from Corbie) place Baruch between Jeremiah and Lamentations. Jerome, following the Masoretic text, rejected the canonicity of Baruch. Alcuinian Bibles followed suit, although at least one extant copy from this tradition (T = Paris, B.N. [Bibliothéque Nationale] nouv. acq. lat. 1586, ca. 780, from Tours) places the major prophets in the order Isaiah—Jeremiah—La-mentations—Ezekiel. As Baruch is used liturgically at Easter and Pentecost, there was a gradual reintegration of this book into the Vulgate text; by the thirteenth century it appears in almost all Bible copies, although often written in by a second hand, and no longer separated by Lamentations. For this history, see Bogaert, 324-27 and the notes to the 1972 Rome edition of the Vulgate.

The significance of this history for Lamentations commentaries lies in the changing position of the five poems within the canon. We have very few Latin Bibles written prior to the ninth century, and so cannot be sure of how aware Hrabanus and Radbertus were of these changes. But I expect that both were using Vulgate texts in which Lamentations was cut loose from the Baruch material, and that this relatively new textual circumstance influenced at least Radbertus' decision to write on the book. The difficult problem of identifying Radbertus' Spanish-influenced Bible remains.

94. Besides the commentaries on the major prophets, Hrabanus wrote on all the Old Testament historical books, Judith and Esther, Wisdom and Ecclesiastes, Maccabees, the Gospels of Matthew and John, the Acts of the Apostles, and the Pauline Epistles: cf. Stegmüller, nos. 7021-77.

95. See Stegmüller, no. 6262 for a list of the MSS, to which should be added Berlin, Sammlung Hilton (1960) 48^1, Charleville 15, and Brussels 1375, 1376, and 1377. The Cistercian MSS are: Dijon 68 (49) saec. XII, Cîteaux; Troyes 448 and 558, saec. XII-XIII, Clairvaux; Brussels 1375 (II.2564) saec. XII, Sancta Maria de Balerna (near Besançon); Charleville 159, saec. XII, Sancta Maria Signiaci, in the Ardennes.

96. I would contend that Radbertus' theological writings come out of his exegetical endeavors. The context of each major exegetical work is quite specific: after teaching Matthew to novices at Corbie, he wrote a commentary (*PL* 120.31-994, see the prologues to Book 1, *PL* 120.31B; Book 5, *PL* 120.333A; and Book 9, *PL* 120.643B); this interest led to the famous *De corpore et sanguine Domini,* written in the middle of his long-term work on Matthew. In a similar fashion, at the request of his friends at Soissons, Radbertus wrote the *Cogitis me,* an explanation of the Assumption, which sparked the exposition of Psalm 44 (*PL* 120.993-1060), which was, in turn, instrumental in the *De partu Virginis.* The possibility that Radbertus also wrote a commentary on the Song of Songs is intriguing. The case of the *De benedictionibus patriarcharum* (found in only one manuscript, Portsmouth Cathedral, Vertue and Cahill Library 8473, saec. XII, for which see P. Grierson, 'Un traité *De benedictionibus patriarcharum* de Paschase Radbert,' *Revue bénédictine* 28 [1911] 425-32) is more problematic, since nothing is known of its context.

Matti Kilpiö (essay date 1987)

SOURCE: Kilpiö, Matti. "Hrabanus's *De Laudibus Sanctae Crucis* and *The Dream of the Rood.*" *Neophilologica Fennica* 45 (1987): 177-91.

[*In the following essay, Kilpiö maintains that the Old English* The Dream of the Rood *may have influenced Hrabanus's* De laudibus sanctae crucis.]

Hrabanus Maurus, the famous Frankish scholar and a pupil of Alcuin, started his literary career with *De laudibus sanctae crucis* in c. 810.[1] The work consists of twenty-eight poems (*figurae*) written in hexameter, each accompanied by an explanation in prose (*declaratio figurae*) (Book 1) and prose paraphrases of the poems (Book 2).[2] The poems are called *figurae* as in each of them there is a cruciform figure superimposed on the poem.[3] Thus, for instance, in F 3 the words *crux* and *salus* are placed over the poem [in the shape of a cross].

The letters inside the figures form words and sentences mostly independent of the poem. As **"F 3"** [**"Figura"**] deals with the nine orders of angels, each of the nine letters contains the name of one of the orders; for instance, the letter L contains the word *throni* 'thrones' . . . .

The pictorial elements in the figures range from near-naturalistic representations of e.g. Christ and the author to letters and geometrical shapes, the unifying feature being the cruciform arrangement.

The main purpose of this article is to suggest the possibility that *De laudibus* may have prompted some of the imagery of *The Dream of the Rood.*[4] Parallels between the two works have been pointed out before,[5] but to my knowledge *De laudibus* has never been suggested as a possible source for the *Dream.*

I

I first discuss three passages in *The Dream of the Rood* where the imagery may draw on both the pictorial elements and the language of *De laudibus.*

> (1) Þuhte me þæt ic gesawe   syllicre treow
>   on lyft lædan,   leohte bewunden,
>   beama beorhtost.   Eall þæt beacen wæs
>   begoten mid golde.   Gimmas stodon
>   fægere æt foldan sceatum,   swylce þær fife wæron
>   uppe on þam eaxlegespanne.   Beheoldon þær engel dryhtnes ealle,
>   fægere þurh forðgesceaft. Ne wæs ðær huru fracodes gealga,
>   ac hine þær beheoldon   halige gastas,
>   men ofer moldan,   ond eall þeos mære gesceaft.
>
>   (4-12)

"F 3" in *De laudibus* was already referred to above. In **"DF 3"** [**"Declaratio Figurae"**] Hrabanus quotes God speaking through Ezekiel to the first angel, Lucifer:[6]

> (2) Omnis lapis pretiosus operimentum tuum, sardius, topazius, et jaspis, chrysolithus, onyx, et beryllus, saphirus, carbunculus, et smaragdus.
>
>   (161C)

and continues with the following comment:

> (3) Ecce novem dixit nomina lapidum, quia profecto novem sunt ordines angelorum. . . . Tenet ergo haec species sanctae crucis in inferiori sua parte, duos ordines, id est, angelos et archangelos; in brachio dextro duos, hoc est, virtutes et potestates; in brachio sinistro item duos, id est, principatus et dominationes; in medio unum, id est, thronos;
>
> (161D)

Here the nine orders of angels are thus compared to the nine kinds of gems said to be the covering of the first angel.[7] It could be imagined that the *Dream* poet took "**F 3**" and the equation between the orders of angels and gems as his starting point on ll. "7-9"; *gimmas stodon . . . on þam eaxlegespanne*. The two letters in "**F 3**" at the bottom, V and X, standing for archangels and angels, could be referred to by *gimmas stodon fægere æt foldan sceatum*, while *Dream* "7-8" *swylce þær fife wæron on þam eaxlegespanne* could refer to the five letters, S A L V S, on the horizontal beam of the cross. From the point of view of Old English this interpretation presupposes the meaning 'by' or 'near' for *æt* and 'the horizontal beam of a cross' for the hapax legomenon *eaxlegespann*.[8]

This would be the contribution of the pictorial elements of "**F 3**" to *Dream* "4-12." But there are also verbal analogues. The following sentence is a famous crux which has called forth a number of interpretations and textual emendations:[9]

> Beheoldon þær engel dryhtnes ealle
> fægere þurh forðgesceaft.
>
> (9-10)

A theme presented by Hrabanus in "**F 3**" and developed in "**DF 3**" as well as in "**PP 3**" ["**Prose Paraphrase**"] is that angels point forward to Christ. The following quotation may suffice:

> (4) Credendum ergo nobis est quod facta angelorum quae Vetus Testamentum narrat, adventum et gloriam significent redemptoris nostri, cum Novum Testamentum statim in primordio nativitatis ejus, ejus gloriam in excelso, Deo magno tripudio cecinisse, et pacem hominibus adoptasse describat.
>
> (268C)

If the Anglo-Saxon poet indeed knew *De laudibus* and made use of it, it would be logical for him to utilize the themes of "**F 3**": after mentioning the gems (= angels) and their position on the cross he would point to their prophetic task. The reading of Dickins and Ross, *engeldryhte* 'hosts or orders of angels' for MS *engel dryhtnes ealle* would make excellent sense in this context: 'The orders of angels looked, beautiful, through the future'.

So far, only "**F 3**," "**DF 3**" and "**PP 3**" have been suggested as possible sources for *Dream* "4-12." But there are further analogues.

First, there are parallels between *Dream* 4-6 *syllicre treow . . . beama beorhtost* and a number of passages in *De laudibus*. The unique quality of the cross-tree comes out well from the following passages:

> (5) "**PP 2**": O sancta crux Christi, quae potestate tibi collata excellis super omnia!
>
> (267A)

> (6) "**PP 5**": O inclyta crux Domini, aulae Christi pretiosum fundamentum!
> tu es pulchrior florifera specie omnium germinum: . . .
>
> (270C)

> (7) "**F 13**": Arbor odore potens . . .
> Omnes excedens altas gravitudine sylvas.
>
> (199A)

> (8) "**F 13**": O tu, crux speciosa, o pinus pulchrior, omnia
> Quae vincis nemora, . . .
>
> (200A)[10]

The analogy between the absolute comparatives *syllicre* and *pulchrior* (Ex. (8)) is noteworthy as the superlative is the degree that would be expected in a context like this.

The idea of brightness in *leohte bewunden* and *beama beorhtost* has also parallels in *De laudibus*:[11]

> (9) "**F 2**" Pulchra nites cultu, te visu gloria cingit
>
> (156A)
>
> and
>
> "**PP 2**" Pulchra nites ornatu, teque cernentibus gloriosa appares.
>
> (267C)

> (10) "**PP 8**": . . . notemus hos radios quos diffundit haec sanctae crucis species
> (273B) and
> O sacrum germen, quod clara luce fidei et sapientiae corda hominum in
> tenebris infidelitatis posita illuminas: tu es videlicet crux sancta,
> miraculis coruscans.
>
> (274B)

> (11) "**F 9**": Crux quae est vester honor, stabilis lux, pacifer ordo,
> Laus, probitas, series, per cuncta et saecula lumen: . . .
>
> (183A)
>
> and
> Tu sacra stirps quae clara die ornas cuncta tenebris,

Crux, quoque sancta micas . . .

(184A)

(12) **"F 13"** [the text inside the uppermost cross]
Forma sacrata crucis
venerando fulget amictu
"PP 13": ex sanguine Christi purpureo fulgore
nites

(278A)

Further examples are found in **"PP 13," "F 21," "PP 21"** and **"PP 26."**

Ne wæs ðær huru fracodes gealga, . . .

Dream 10

has an analogue in **"PP 4"**:

(13) Conditor utique et rex noster, qui pro nobis in alta
crucis confixus est stipite, quam magis decet thronum
imperialem vocari quam servile tormentum, . . .

(269C)

and the immediate continuation

ac hine þær beheoldon   halige gastas,
men ofer moldan,   ond eall þeos mære gesceaft.

Dream 11-12

has, in spite of the difference in meaning between *be-healdan* and the verbs *venerare* and *colere,* a close counterpart in **"DF 18"**:

(14) Merito ergo crux ipsa sancta sanctorum dici potest,
quae ab omnibus sanctis in terra veneratur et colitur,
nec non ab ipsis sanctis spiritibus angelicis, qui de re-
demptione nostra gratulantur, omni honore (ut
credimus) digna deputatur, qui recordantur Christum
propter obedientiam crucis exaltatum, et traditum illi
nomen, quod est super omne nomen, ut in nomine
Hiesu omne genu flectatur coelestium, terrestrium et
infernorum.

(222C)

Here the parallelism between *halige gastas* and *sanctis spiritibus angelicis* is especially striking. Another paral-lel is found in **"PP 2"**:

(15) Nam multiplices laudes Deo in sanctis angelorum
coetibus excitas, et simili ratione ad glorificandum
Deum devotos reddis terrarum incolas. Te generaliter
totus orbis, aer, mare et ignea coelorum sidera sanctifi-
cant, ac specialiter unaquaeque species creaturae ex
quatuor mundi partibus magna devotione celebrat.

(267A)

where the hosts of angels, the inhabitants of the earth and the whole universe praise and adore the cross.

The second passage that could possibly show the combined influence of the pictorial elements and the language of **De laudibus** on *The Dream of the Rood* is at ll. 18-20:

(16) Hwæðre ic þurh þæt gold   ongytan meahte
earmra ærgewin,   þæt hit ærest ongan
swætan on þa swiðran healfe.

"F 11" of **De laudibus** has five squares, representing the five books of Moses, superimposed on the poem. Genesis is placed at the top, Deuteronomy at the foot, Exodus on the right[12] and Numbers on the left arm,[12] with Leviticus being placed in the centre. The portion of **"F 11"** dealing with Exodus mentions miracles con-nected with water; two of them are especially relevant here:

(17) At veterem hoc lignum legis dulcavit abyssum:
Bis petram excutit, vivam produxit et undam
. . .

(192A)

The same miracles are again referred to in **"PP 11"**:

(18) Hinc plebs Israelitarum . . . pervenit ad fontem
Marat, qui per lignum mysticum dulcatus est.

(276B)

(19) Denique veteris legis abyssum sancta crux im-
missa dulcavit, et petram solidissimam excidens fontem
viventis aquae produxit.

(276C)

The first of these two miracles is the event, mentioned in Ex 15, 23-5, where Moses made the water of Marah sweet by throwing into it a log shown him by God. The second one is told in Ex 17. 1-6: Moses struck the rock in Horeb with a staff so that water poured out of it. Ex. (19) above shows that both pieces of wood are seen as a type for the cross: 'Finally the holy cross made sweet the abyss of the Old Law, being thrown into it, and cut-ting the most solid of rocks drew forth a fountain of living water'.

If the *Dream* poet drew on the imagery of **"F 11"** at ll. 18-20, *earmra ærgewin* could possibly be seen as refer-ring to the hardships of the Jewish people on their long journey from Egypt to the promised land. The exact spatial reference of the tree sweating on the right side could in this context refer to the place of the book of Exodus in **"F 11"** and the sweating itself to the miracles connected with water. It is noteworthy in this connec-tion that the early church believed that Christ on the cross bled on the right side.[13] Within the framework of the present hypothesis there would thus be a double reason for making the spatial reference.

What is the meaning of *ærest* in this context? In the light of the typological interpretation of the two pieces of wood used by Moses as types for the cross, *ærest* could conceivably imply that the first connection of the cross with moisture occurred in the miracles told in

Exodus and again when Christ suffered on the cross, when it became moist (*roscida* 'dewy, wet') with Christ's blood, cf. **"F 13"**

> (20) Purpureo regis sub tactu roscida fulges.
>
> (199A)

There is a parallelism between the suggested relationships linking **De laudibus** and *Dream* 7-10 and 18-20: they show an impressionistic mixture of exact spatial references and typological exegesis. Although the interpretations are complex and contain disparate elements, they are in harmony with what Swanton recognizes as one of the characteristics of the *Dream*, the combination of visual and doctrinal motifs.[14]

The third passage where the *Dream* poet could have been influenced by both the pictorial elements and the wording of **De laudibus** is

> (21) Gebæd ic me þa to þan beame   bliðe mode,
> elne mycle,   þær ic ana wæs
> mæte werede.   Wæs modsefa
> afysed on forðwege,   feala ealra gebad
> langunghwila.   Is me nu lifes hyht
> þæt ic þone sigebeam   secan mote
> ana oftor   þonne ealle men,
> well weorþian.   Me is willa to ðam
> mycel on mode,   ond min mundbyrd is
> geriht to þære rode.
>
> (122-31)

"F 28," the last *figura* in **De laudibus,** has a picture of Hrabanus kneeling at the foot of the cross. The text of the poem contains the following passage in which the author addresses both Christ and the cross:

> (22) Namque ego te Dominum pronus et laetus adoro,
> Atque cruci demisse tuae hinc dico salutans:
> Spem oro te ramus aram ara sumar, et oro hinc,
> Hoc meus est ardor clarus, hoc ignis amoris,
> Hoc mea mens poscit primum, hoc famen et ora,
> Hoc sitis est animi, mandendi magna cupido:
> Ut me tu pie suscipias, bone Christe, per aram
> Oblatum famulum, quod victima sim tua, Hiesus.
>
> (262A)

"PP 28" expresses the same ideas in more or less similar words:

> (23) te Dominum verum supplex et laetus odoro, atque cruci tuae submisse et humiliter salutans dico: O lignum vitale et ara salutifera, te adoro, spem vitae aeternae deprecans, ut per te structuram sanctissimam hostia grata Deo oblatus existam. Hoc meum est desiderium, hoc validus amoris fervor, hoc tota intentio mentis et famina linguae exorant, hoc esuries cordis et sitis est animae, ut per passionis tuae gratiam me tibi oblatum famulum suscipias, . . .
>
> (293B)

The basic situation in both *Dream* 122—31 and **F 28** is exactly the same: the poet is seen praying and adoring the cross. The exceptionally concrete picture in **F 28**—the only comparable ones in this respect are **"Figurae 1, 4 and 15"**—could have suggested to the Anglo-Saxon poet the idea of solitude: the kneeling poet is the only person in the picture, he is *ana* and *mæte werede*. The expression *laetus adoro* (both **"F 28"** and **"PP 28"**) could be reflected in *Gebæd ic . . . bliðe mode*. In addition to the theme of adoration there is another theme common to Ex. (21) and the Latin passages in Exx. (22) and (23). In a climactic series of clauses introduced by *hoc* Hrabanus expresses his fervent hope of being received by Christ; the same hope of heaven is met in *Dream* 124-5 *Wæs modsefa afysed on forðwege*. There could also be further verbal echoes from **"F 28"** and **"PP 28"** in Ex. (21). The phrases *ardor clarus* (**"F 28"**) and *validus amoris fervor* (**"PP 28"**) could be reflected in *elne mycle,* and there is a striking correspondence between *spem vitae aeternae* (**"PP 28"**) and *lifes hyht* (126), although, unlike the OE collocation here, the former specifically refers to the cross. Note also that earlier in PP 28, in a long address to God and Christ there is the phrase *tu pius protector tuarum ovium* and *Dream* 130 uses the noun *mundbyrd* for the cross as a 'spiritual patron'.[15]

II

There are a number of further, purely verbal, parallels between **De laudibus** and the *Dream*. They will be discussed here in the order in which they appear in the OE poem.

> (24)   Geseah ic wuldres treow,
> wædum geweorðode   wynnum scinan, . . .
>
> (14-5)

For the idea of the cross shining there are parallels from **De laudibus** already quoted above [Exx. (9)-(12)]. The phrase *wædum geweorðode* might be an echo of *venerando . . . amictu* 'with a venerable garment' in Ex. (12).

> (25)   geseah ic þæt fuse beacen
> wendan wædum ond bleom;
>
> (21-2)

Here there is an obvious parallel between *wendan wædum ond bleom* and *varios colores* in **"F 13"**:

> (26) Arbor sola tenens varios virtute colores,
> Purpureo regis sub tactu roscida fulgens
>
> (199A)

also noted by Swanton.[16]

For

> (27)   Gestah he on gealgan heanne,

modig on manigra gesyhðe,   þa he wolde mancyn lysan.

(40-1)

there are parallels in "**F 8**" and, with almost the same
wording, in "**PP 8**":

> (28) Christus rex dominus divinus munere summus
> Scandens alta crucis en robora, funditus in hoc
> Istam tunc speciem plantando pandere caelos
> tradidit et voluit gratos conquirier illic:

(180A)

> (29) Christus ergo rex summus et coelestia tribuens
> Dominus, munere divino
> scandens alta crucis robora, mani-
> feste innotuit, hanc speciem
> formando, per hanc se pandere coelos mundo, et
> vult ut sequentes ejus
> vestigia, vitae per hanc reperiamus introitum.

(273C)

There is a counterpart for *Dream* 40 in *Scandens alta
crucis en robora* and for *þa he wolde mancyn lysan* in
"**F 8**" *voluit . . . illic* and "**PP 8**" *vult ut . . . reperiamus introitum.*

> (30)   Is nu sæl cumen
> þæt me weorðiað   wide ond side
> menn ofer moldan,   ond eall þeos mære
> gesceaft,
> gebiddað him   to þyssum beacne.

(80-3)

can be compared with Ex. (15) and also with the following passage in "**PP 3**":

> (31) Te totus orbis beatificat, the coelorum agmina col-
> laudant. Per te in nomine Jesu . . . omne genu sive
> voluntate sive vi flectitur, coelestium videlicet, ter-
> restrium et infernorum.

(268A)

The next passage to be considered is *Dream* 87-9, for
which I am willing to see a parallel in "**F 12**" and "**PP
12**":

> (32) Iu ic wæs geworden   wita heardost,
> leodum laðost,   ærþan ic him lifes weg
> rihtne gerymde,   reordberendum.

Superimposed on "**F 12**" is the name of Adam, and
both "**F 12**" and "**PP 12**" dwell on the theological
contrast between the first Adam and Christ, the second
Adam. "**PP 12**" contrasts the tree of transgression in
paradise, bringing death to all the earth, with Christ's
cross, through which death is made captive, and through
which Christ opened the entrance to life for all:

> (33) Denique sicut per lignum praevaricationis mors in-
> troivit in totum orbem terrarum, et in infernum omnes
> descenderunt, etiam ipsi electi, ita et per lignum Do-

minicae passionis mors captivata est, et multi evaserunt
ex ea, etiam peccatis obnoxii. Universo scilicet orbi
Christus per crucem aditum vitae aperuit, . . .

(277B)[17]

Of the two trees in paradise, the tree of life has a
straightforward typological correspondence to the cross,
cf. "**PP 11**" *statim in ligno vitae, quod est in medio
paradisi, vitale lignum sanctae crucis praefigurabatur*
(267A), but also the *lignum scientiae* has been connected with the cross. R.E. Kaske refers to a piece of
the shaft from a stone churchyard cross in the south
porch of the church at Newent (Glos. [Gloucestershire]),
variously assigned to the eight or ninth century and
generally thought to show either Northumbrian or Mer-
cian characteristics. On one face of this piece 'is the
lignum scientiae, flanked by Adam and Eve and
entwined about by the serpent; from its top spring two
circling tendrils, and from the end of the right tendril
extends a small upright cross.'[18] Although the relationship between the tree of knowledge of good and evil
and the cross is half-antithetical and half-causative,[19]
there is still reason enough for considering the former
tree as a type for the cross.[20]

With this in mind, it is tempting to think that the *Dream*
poet first lets the cross speak as the *lignum scientiae*
(87-88a) and then as Christ's cross (87b-88), by first
referring to its hateful role in paradise and then to its
role as the opener of the way to life. This interpretation
would make the temporal contrast expressed by *Iu* and
ærþan understandable. If, on the other hand, we think
that *ic* refers to the cross all through *Dream* 87-9, it is
more difficult to account for the two stages of time, unless we assume that the first *ic* refers generically to the
cross as a type of punishment and the second *ic* specifically to Christ's cross.

There is a clear parallel for *ic him lifes weg rihtne
gerymde* at the end of Ex. (33). Further analogues can
be found in "**PP 17**" (*Crux quoque Christi via est jus-
torum, ascensus ad coelum, . . .* 282C), "**PP 21**"
(*Denique sancta atque magnifica crux . . . seque viam
atque ducem ad perpetuam vitam nobis esse demonstrat*
286B) and "**PP 28**" (*tu sancte Salvator . . . es . . . via
recta* 293B). In the last example, in which Christ is addressed, there is the collocation *via recta,* which
provides an analogue for *rihtne* modifying *weg.*

The following group of examples shows striking verbal
correspondences:

> (34) Nu ic þe hate,   hæleð min se leofa,
> þæt ðu þas gesyhðe   secge mannum,
> onwreoh wordum   þæt hit is wuldres beam,
> se ðe ælmihtig god   on þrowode
> for manycynnes   manegum synnum
> ond Adomes   ealdgewyrhtum.

(95-100)

To this may be compared the following passage from "F 8"

(35) Hinc decet ut genus humanum et luminis exul
    Noret hos radios: quos erigit haec benedicta
    Crux salvans, et reddens quem jam primus habe-
bat
    Exortum lucis, nocuus quo abscesserat Adam.

(179A)

and its prose paraphrase:

(36) Quapropter congruit ut nos terrigenae et paradisi exules notemus hos radios quos diffundit haec sanctae crucis species, per quam Christus nos salvat et reddit splendorem luminis quem protoplastus peccans olim jam amiserat.

(273B)

Both the Latin versions contain the same basic idea: it is fitting that mankind should know the rays of the blessed cross through which Christ saves us and restores the light that Adam, sinning, once lost. *Dream* 95-100 contains roughly the same elements as Exx. (35) and (36); the only major difference is that the cross is the speaker in the OE passage.

Dream 101-2 has a fairly close parallel in "PP 19":

(37) Deað he þær byrigde,   hwæðere eft dryhten aras
    mid his miclan mihte   mannum to helpe.

(38) et in cruce degustans mortem, ipsum mortis de-vicit auctorem. Huc omnes convenite aegroti, et aegri-tudinis vestrae ne vos pudeat illi molestias conqueri.

(283D)

The closest parallel is between *Deað he þær byrigde* 'he tasted death there' (= on the cross) and *in cruce de-gustans mortem* 'tasting death on the cross', but also *hwæðere eft dryhten aras* 'yet the Lord rose again' and *ipsum mortis devicit auctorem* 'he defeated the origina-tor of death himself' can be said to deal with the same theme; the same kind of free relationship can be seen between *mannum to helpe* 'as a help for men' and the sentence beginning with *Huc*: 'All you who are ill, come to him, and do not feel ashamed to bewail to him the troubles of your illness'.

The almost immediate sequel in *The Dream of the Rood*,

(39)   Hider eft fundaþ
    on þysne middangeard   mancynn secan
    on domdæge   dryhten sylfa,
    ælmihtig god,   ond his englas mid,
    þæt he þonne wile deman,   se ah domes
geweald,
    anra gehwylcum   swa he him ærur her
    on þyssum lænum   life geearnaþ.

(103-9)

contains one of the closest and most sustained parallels with *De laudibus*, cf. "PP 22":

(40) quatenus in secundo suo adventu, cum advenerit in gloria Patris sui, cum angelis suis reddere unicuique secundum opera sua, tales inveniat quibus propter merita bona aeterna reddat et praemia.

(287B)

Here there are parallels for the Latin through the whole sentence: the Lord will return to the earth with his angels in order to recompense everyone according to his deeds.

In the following group of examples the parallelism is not complete, but there is the image of the cross, as a psychopomp, taking the author away, either from the avenging flames or this transitory life. The image is striking but based on tradition.[21]

(41) "DF 28": Tum rogo me eripiat flammis ultricibus ipsa (sc. crux):

(263)

(42) obsecro ut tunc a flammis ultricibus sancta crux me eripiat, . . .

(294A)

(43) ond ic wene me

    daga gehwylce   hwænne me dryhtnes rod,
    þe ic her on eorðan   ær sceawode,
    on þysson lænan   life gefetige

(135-8)

Ex. (42) is from "PP 28". The same chapter provides close parallels for

(44) ond me þonne gebringe   þær is blis mycel,
    dream on heofonum,   þær is dryhtnes folc
    geseted to symle,   þær is singal blis,
    ond me þonne asette   þær ic syþþan mot
    wunian on wuldre,   well mid þam halgum
    dreames brucan.

(139-44)

This can be compared with

(45) Et nunc, bone Salvator, deprecor ut des mihi requiem illam quam fidelibus tuis promiseras te datu-rum in arce polorum, ubi vere populus tuus sabbatizat, sabbato perenni fruens.

(294B)

and

(46) Praesta ut in te gaudens tecum permaneam in aeterna laetitia.

(294C)

The joys of heaven are described in rather similar terms: Christ's people enjoy eternal Sabbath there (Latin) or sit at a feast (OE); the 'eternal joy' (*aeterna laetitia*) of the Latin has parallels in the near-synonymous *blis* and *dream* and an exact counterpart in the collocation *singal blis*.

The Harrowing of Hell, referred to by *Dream* 150-4, is a theme also met in **De laudibus**. The following passage from **"PP 21"** is particularly interesting as it combines Christ's redeeming passion and the Harrowing of Hell in one and the same sentence, cf. the reference to Christ's passion and the redemption at *Dream* 145-7:

> (47) Omnia namque peccata mundi Christus in passionis suae ardore consumpsit, quando ex parte carnis in ipsa mortem gustavit, ac per potentiam divinitatis suae electos suos ab inferni carcere liberavit, . . .
>
> (286D)

Immediately before this sentence **"PP 21"** has the following piece of numerological argumentation:

> (48) Octonarius namque numerus et novenarius, in se multiplicati, septuagenarium et binarium creant, quorum octonarius ad resurrectionis tempus, novenarius vero ad novem ordines angelorum respectat; sicque catholica fides tenet quod in fine mundi, hoc est in octava aetate saeculi, sancti resurgentes in societatem transeant angelorum,
>
> (286C)

The end of the passage is relevant to the present discussion: the holy ones, rising at the end of the world, will join the company of angels: a parallel to *Dream* 153.

Further references to the Harrowing of Hell are found in **"F 1"** (152A), **"PP 1"** (266 A), **"PP 10"** (275A), **"F 15"** (207A), **"PP 15"** (280A) and **"F 18"** (220A).

III

How probable is it that **De laudibus** could have been a source for all or some of the *Dream* passages quoted above? In attempting to answer this question, we must have a look at two chronological questions: the early circulation of **De laudibus** and the chronological problems connected with the *Dream*. After that, the evidence presented above must be evaluated.

According to Müller, the remarkable number of still extant 9th century manuscripts of **De laudibus** is evidence for the vivid interest the contemporaries of Hrabanus showed in this work. He also points out that the work arrived in England at an early date: this is shown by Codex Cambridge B.16.3, a 10th century MS.[22] This MS—which incidentally represents the second phase of development, to be placed at c. 834/44,

in the history of **De laudibus**,[23]—is not the first MS of this work in England, if it was produced in Canterbury. **De laudibus** may have come to England as early as the 9th century, though it is impossible to prove this.

How does this fit in with the chronology of *The Dream of the Rood*? Here a complicating factor is the date of the runic inscriptions on the Ruthwell Cross and their relation to the Vercelli version.

If the Ruthwell inscriptions are as old as the cross itself, they antedate **De laudibus sanctae crucis** by about a century.[24] Swanton sees three possible relationships between the Ruthwell text and the *Dream*: 'It may be that an original inscription on the cross, partly poetic in form, inspired the composition of a much fuller poem. Or the sculptor may have chosen and modified appropriate extracts from an already extant poetic text. This in turn may either have been in a form approximating the Vercelli text as we have it, or an earlier version of it'.[25] Swanton does not believe in the first alternative but thinks that the sculptor quoted from a longer poem. If that poem indeed approximated to the Vercelli text, the influence from **De laudibus** would have to be excluded. According to Swanton, however, this longer poem need not necessarily be in the form preserved in the Vercelli book.[26]

In order for the hypothesis of the influence from **De laudibus** to be possible at all, it must be assumed that the poem paraphrased by the Ruthwell sculptor was considerably shorter than *The Dream of the Rood* in the Vercelli book. The parallels between **De laudibus** and the *Dream* discussed above are basically restricted to ll. 1-27 (The introduction) and to ll. 78-156 (The cross's homily, the author's monologue and the final homiletic section from 1. 147 onwards). They do not concern the earlier part of the prosopopoeia section, with the exception of ll. 40-1 *Gestah he on gealgan heanne, / modig on manigra gesyhðe, þa he wolde mancyn lysan.* This is a passage for which there a partial parallel in the Ruthwell Cross inscriptions:[27]

> þa he walde on gal gu gisti ga
> [m]odig f[○ ○ ○ ○ ○ ○ ○] men

In my opinion, the existence of a partial parallel for *Dream* 40-1 in RC does not, however, present an obstacle to the hypothesis presented in this article. The parallelism between *heanne* and *alta* as well as that between þa he wolde mancyn lysan and Exx. (28) and (29) discussed above can well be attributed to the familiarity of a later reviser with **De laudibus**: for the idea of Christ climbing the gallows, present in the Ruthwell lines, there are parallels e.g. in early Latin hymns.[28]

If the influence of **De laudibus** is accepted it follows that most, or at least some part, of *Dream* 28-77 represents an earlier stage in the history of the poem.

This section is characterised by a large number of hypermetric lines and, at the level of subject matter, by narrative rather than contemplation or theological argumentation. A striking feature is the initial position of the finite verb in many of the sentences: *Genaman,* . . . *geworhton* . . . , *heton* . . . , *Bæron* . . . , *gefæstnodon* . . . etc.

Would this earlier prosopopoeia section make a satisfactory whole in itself? A 'proto-*Dream*' could very well start with the beginning of the prosopopoeia section, but it must be admitted that the short allusion to the Invention of the Cross at ll. 75-7 does not provide a convincing ending for an entire poem so intensely dedicated to the depiction of the crucifixion scene. On the other hand it has been suggested that the poem seems to divide at l. 78: the rest of the poem from this line onwards does not afford any metrical or linguistic evidence necessitating the assumption of an early date, and is stylistically inferior.[29]

It seems to me that even if a composite origin for the Vercelli *Dream* is accepted, it will be impossible to reconstruct the earlier version with any accuracy,[30] simply because there are too many unknown factors involved; nor is it necessary for the hypothesis presented here. The essential point here is that the chronological problems caused by the existence of the Ruthwell Cross inscriptions can be overcome, as the parallels between *De laudibus* and the *Dream* need not concern the Ruthwell Cross portions of the poem.

If this is accepted, is the evidence presented in parts I and II of this article convincing enough to suggest **De laudibus** as a source for parts of the *Dream*? A major complicating factor in any attempt to find sources and analogues for the *Dream* lies in the topic itself, central to Christian teaching. No wonder possible sources have been detected in e.g. the liturgy, hymns, patristic sources and Christian art. Still Swanton, in 1970, is compelled to make the following statement: 'And it has not proved possible to identify a convincing source for any large part of its material. While the poet of the *Dream* shows himself familiar with both contemporary liturgy and current exegetics, this amounts to little more than common phraseology or allusion; . . . The remoteness of apparent analogues to any part merely confirms the originality of the poet. We are obliged to consider the poem entirely in its own terms as an easy and natural development out of the religious concerns of its day'.[31]

The large number of possible sources for the *Dream* serves as a useful warning against jumping into conclusions concerning **De laudibus**. Yet there are, to my mind, several arguments in favour of the possibility that **De laudibus** was a source for the *Dream*:

1. Well-known in its own time, **De laudibus** is a work which, like the *Dream*, deals intensively with the cross. It provides a quarry of material dealing with various theological topics in a curious mixture of encyclopedic erudition, warm devotional feeling and a strongly attractive visual form. Its multilayered nature, hiding as it does words and whole sentences formed from the letters of the poems proper, must have appealed to the Anglo-Saxon mind, which delighted in riddles, double meaning and allusion.

2. The hypothesis presented here, if accepted, gives a coherence to the imagery of *Dream* 4-12 that is not otherwise attained. It also provides a possible explanation for the imagery at ll. 18-20, one that accounts for the spatial and temporal references.

3. The sheer wealth of the analogies, impressive though it is, is inconclusive in itself because of the large number of other possible sources. But many of the analogies show striking verbal correspondences between the two works; also, a few of the correspondences are of a more sustained nature.

I cannot claim that I have been able to prove **De laudibus** to be a source for *The Dream of the Rood*, but I hope that I have made a fairly strong case for regarding this as a possibility. It is fascinating to think that Hrabanus, himself an inheritor of the Northumbrian renaissance through the teaching of Alcuin, could have contributed to the imagery of one of the greatest Old English poems and one that is so intimately connected with the golden age of Northumbria.[32]

Notes

1. See Hans-Georg Müller, *Hrabanus Maurus, De laudibus sanctae crucis. Studien zur Überlieferung und Geistesgeschichte mit dem Textabdruck aus Codex Reg. lat. 124 der vatikanischen Bibliothek. Mittellateinisches Jahrbuch, Beiheft 11*, 1973, p. 3.

2. The following abbreviations will be used below: F = *figura*, DF = *declaratio figurae* and PP = prose paraphrase. Thus, for instance, *Figura* 3, its *declaratio figurae* and prose paraphrase will be referred to by "F 3," "DF 3" and "PP 3."

3. Hrabanus follows here a long tradition of 'figure poems' (*Figurengedichte*); the conspicuous rise in the popularity of these in the Carolingian period may be due to the influence of the Anglo-Saxons, Bede and Alcuin among others: see Müller pp. 121-34.

4. The former work is quoted, by column, from Migne's *Patrologia latina* [PL] 107, cols. 153-294, the latter from G.P. Krapp (ed.), *The Vercelli Book, The Anglo-Saxon Poetic Records*, vol. II (Baltimore, 1932).

5. See Michael Swanton (ed.), *The Dream of the Rood* (Manchester, 1970), p. 49, p. 51, fn. 2, p. 106, note to 1. 15 and p. 111, note to 1. 22.

6. Literally speaking, the words (Ez 28, 13) are addressed to the King of Tyre; the interpretation in *De laudibus* is also met in Jerome's Commentary on Ezekiel, *PL* 25, cols. 270A, 272A and 273B.

7. Cf. Jerome's Commentary on Ezekiel, *PL* 25, col. 272C, where the equation between angels and stones is also made.

8. For the interpretation of *gimmas* as the jewels on a 'crux gemmata' representing the wounds of Christ see Swanton, p. 101.

9. See Swanton, pp. 103-4, Bruce Dickins and Alan S.C. Ross (eds.), *The Dream of the Rood* (London, 1967), pp. 21-2 and F.G. Cassidy and Richard N. Ringler, *Bright's Old English Grammar and Reader* (New York, 1971), p. 311.

10. For examples (7) and (8) there are parallels in PP 13, cols. 277-8.

11. Swanton, p. 101, points out that the brilliance of the cross is a familiar feature of the Constantinian tradition.

12. From the point of view of the person on the cross, not from that of the spectator. In DF 11 Hrabanus gives his reasons for placing Exodus on the right: 'Exodus vero bene in dextra ponitur, in quo exitus filiorum Israel de Aegypto conscribitur, et ibidem plura a Domino facta miracula narrantur, juxta illud Psalmistae: Dextera Domini fecit virtutem. Et item: Qui percussit Aegyptum cum primogenitis eorum, et eduxit Israel de medio ejus, in manu forti et brachio excelso.' (194B)

13. See Swanton, p. 109, where reference is made to a passage in Bede's *De Templo Salomonis Liber.*

14. Swanton, p. v.

15. Swanton, note to 1. 130, p. 133.

16. Note to 1. 22, p. 111.—Swanton, in his comment on *Dream* 15 *wœdum*, p. 106, also refers to the second line in Ex. (26) when discussing the possibility that *wœdum geweorðode* could be an image based on the royal *vexillum*. He quotes the line in Hrabanus as a parallel to *Arbor decora et fulgida ornata regis purpura* in 'Vexilla regis' by Fortunatus.

17. For the same contrast, see also PP 21, col. 268A, the sentence beginning *Nam quia per lignum vetitum. . . .*

18. "A Poem of the Cross in the Exeter Book: 'Riddle 60' and 'The Husband's Message", *Traditio* 23 (1967), p. 66.

19. See the quotation from an article by Gerhardt Ladner in Kaske, p. 65.

20. See also Swanton, p. 46.

21. See Swanton, p. 78, fn. 1.

22. Müller, p. 144. See also Helmut Gneuss, "A preliminary list of manuscripts written or owned in England up to 1100", *ASE* 9 (1981), p. 14, where Gneuss gives the date of the MS as the middle of the 10th century ('x med.') and suggests Canterbury as a possible place for the origin and provenance of the MS.

23. Müller, p. 86.

24. For a dating of the cross to the early 8th century see Elisabeth Okasha, *Handlist of Anglo-Saxon Non-Runic Inscriptions* (Cambridge, 1971), p. 109 and Kristine Edmonson Haney, "The Christ and the beasts panel on the Ruthwell Cross", *ASE* 14 (1985), p. 221 and fn. 32.

25. Swanton, p. 39.

26. *Ibid.,* p. 41.

27. Quoted from Dickins and Ross, p. 25.

28. Swanton, note to 1. 40, p. 114.

29. Dickins and Ross, p. 18.

30. D.R. Howlett's reconstruction of the Ruthwell 'crucifixion poem' does not offer any solution to this problem, as it only gives a slightly expanded version of the Ruthwell inscriptions, not a reconstruction of that poem which Howlett assumes to have been the source of the Ruthwell and Vercelli versions; see D.R. Howlett, "A Reconstruction of the Ruthwell Crucifixion Poem", *Studia Neophilologica* 48 (1976), pp. 54-8.

31. Swanton, p. 62.

32. My thanks are due to Professors Norman F. Blake and Matti Rissanen, as well as Dr Paavo Rissanen and Mr Jyrki Knuutila for their valuable comments on an earlier version of this article.

Michel Banniard (essay date 1991)

SOURCE: Banniard, Michel. "Rhabanus Maurus and the Vernacular Languages." In *Latin and the Romance Languages in the Early Middle Ages,* edited by Roger Wright, pp. 164-74. London, United Kingdom: Routledge, 1991.

[*In the following essay, Banniard discusses Hrabanus's scholarly interest in the Germanic vernacular, suggesting that he may deliberately have used the vernacular in an effort to reach ordinary parishioners who did not understand Latin.*]

Linguistic Consciousness: Latin, Germanic, and Romance

Carolingian Europe aimed to be Christian, Latin, and Imperial. Languages and cultures that played no direct role in this tripartite intention rarely came to the conscious attention of the intellectuals of the time, and only gradually came to play a part in their activities (Wolff 1982). As a result, the eventual surfacing of the Romance languages and cultures happened along very complex paths. The study of the phenomena that led to this evolution (or revolution) has progressed significantly over the last thirty years or so. The holding of the ICHL [International Conference on Historical Linguistics] workshop serves to show simultaneously the novelty of the recent methods used to explore these centuries of sociolinguistic change, the success that has come from the development of new theoretical approaches, and the gaps which our present state of knowledge still faces the challenge of filling.

The characteristic property of this period, in which the Middle Ages were born, is that it offers us parallel fields of research that are different in the different cultural areas, according to whether we are considering the Germanic-speaking or Latin-speaking world. It has seemed valuable, for the present volume, to highlight some points of comparison and reference from the other half of the Frankish political and cultural world. The three connected problems of the birth of a new language, the realization of the existence of this previously unknown entity, and the consecration of this change via the elaboration of a *scripta* that breaks with traditional modes of writing, can be posed in much simpler terms when we consider the Germanic languages than when we consider the Romance languages. In this case the second and third aspects of the change are the relevant ones. In other words, since it was already clear that a different language existed, the next step was for the intellectuals to give some kind of status to this language that was neither Latin nor sacred (cp. Borst 1961) in the heart of Latin culture, before they confirmed their acceptance of its status by working out a written form.

I would argue here that, given the cultural, religious, and intellectual unity that characterized the start of 'Europe' (Banniard 1989), studying the sociolinguistic situation there was across the Rhine can help us understand better the initial stages of the development of the written Romance languages in general, and of the 'langue d'oil' in particular. In my view, political fragmentation raises no obstacle to there being reciprocal influences between the Germanic and Romance worlds. Anglo-Saxon was the first western language that was neither sacred nor Latin to be given (by Bede) its cultural consecration and intellectual status (see

Manitius 1965: 74). Three centuries later, Otfrid of Weissenburg was to do the same for Old High German, which he promoted, in practice but also especially in theory, to the rank of a literary language (Haubrichs 1982: 188).

Between these two dates are placed the official birth of the Romance languages, proclaimed, as everyone knows, to have happened at Tours in 813, and the appearance of the first texts prepared in a Romance *scripta,* at Strasbourg in 842. Broadly speaking, it is in this first half of the ninth century that the intellectual developments occur which lead to the development of the vernacular *scriptas,* the first manifestations of Romance literature, and also the first texts of Germanic literature. The first great strictly Germanic learned figure of the age was Rhabanus Maurus, the *praeceptor Germaniae* (Brünholzl 1982), who was intellectually active during this period of maturation, to which he contributed directly, for important documentary evidence of his teaching in *lingua theotisca* has survived (Manitius 1965: 301). His choices of language seem, therefore, to be quite different from those made a little earlier by his teacher, Alcuin, who expresses almost no interest in the vernacular languages he is aware of, neither his native language nor his adopted one (Banniard 1990: Ch. 6). Neither of them, however, show the creative courage of Otfrid. They correspond to the earlier phase, when the French *scripta* was being developed within the scriptoria, and more particularly within people's minds, of which we have no evidence.

Can we learn something useful to our purpose by looking at Rhabanus? I think we can, if we consider his personality as a whole. To put it another way, does his written work (which was, of course, in Latin) include any indications, even if only indirect, to suggest that his mental furniture was in the process of changing, relative to that of his teacher, as regards the status of the vernacular languages? This is equivalent to asking whether his attitude, as a *litteratus,* and his sociolinguistic practice were in harmony.

Tendencies to Linguistic Isolationism?

Alcuin's intellectual legacy, characterized by the desire for forced marches back to a *norma rectitudinis* in every area of Christian teaching, plays such a dominant role in Rhabanus' thoughts that we cannot help being tempted to conclude that his frame of mind must have impelled him to cut himself off entirely from the linguistic realities of his people and time. In general, the Abbot of Fulda has been criticized for a total lack of innovative spirit and for having been no more than a compiler of the works of others; according to this view, his pastoral activities would have been entirely like this (Knöpfler 1900, followed by Manitius 1965; Bisanti

1985, however, disagrees), and in his **De clericorum institutione** (819) he would have been merely following in the wake of Augustine, Cassiodorus, and (in particular) Isidore, offering no new ideas of his own.

And yet he continually praises a discipline which the Fathers of the Church had effectively deposed from any position of intellectual importance, that is, *grammatica*. Echoing Alcuin, Rhabanus responds across the centuries to the comments of Gregory the Great, when he says that 'inculpabiliter enim, immo laudabiliter hanc artem discit' (**De cler. inst.** [**De clericorum institutione**] 3.19). He even praises the art of classical metrics (in the same paragraph), despite the fact that Augustine had abandoned it in his desire to communicate to the uneducated. And then he sings the praises of venerable masters such as Varro (ibid., 3.24). His admiration is not merely theoretical, either, since he composed a lengthy **Excerptio de arte grammatica Prisciani,** where I would go so far as to say that the key point is a detailed account of classical metrics, in which he had himself composed many poems (now in *MGH*, PAC, [*Monumenta Germaniae historica, Poetae Latini aevi Carolini*] vol. II). Priscian was the most learned, the most demanding, and the most complicated of the Latin grammarians, and a reliable inspiration for high-minded linguistic purism.

This conclusion is reinforced by the comments that Rhabanus adds to his appraisal of the texts where Augustine prescribes the manner in which a preacher ought to express himself when addressing his congregations. Modern scholars have, indeed, noticed that Rhabanus does not follow his mentor all the way here; indeed, his requirement of the preacher is the very opposite of Augustine's, that he should express himself in the most perfect Latin that he can (Blumenkranz 1951). Any idea of compromising with a level of Latinity approximating the *sermo humilis*, and above all the *rusticus*, is hereby banished from his own teaching. Was Rhabanus then, in his turn, engaging in oral communication through a kind of linguistic isolationism?

We can also, on the other hand, find in his work special praise of *rusticitas* ('Sancta rusticitas solum sibi prodest', **De cler. inst.**, 3.27). This seems here to be a moral quality rather than a stylistic one, but its implications (which are confirmed by the accompanying commentaries) are close to being stylistic. In any case, he has read carefully Augustine's recommendations that the preacher should adapt his language to the ability of his public to understand (**De cler. inst.**, 3.30; *De [disciplina ecclesiastica]*, 1, **De sacris ordinibus**, in *PL* 112, c. 1193-6). Altogether, the reorganization and rewriting that he gives to his sources show that he was actively thinking himself about the problems discussed.

This is corroborated by another of Rhabanus' great works of synthesis, his **De rerum naturis** (also called **De uniuerso**): far from merely being the servile follower of Isidore and the Encyclopedists, here he reshapes the fabric of what he inherited to come up with a new pattern; similarly, instead of beginning in the traditional way with an account of the *artes liberales,* he starts his work with theological matters (Heyze 1969). It has also proved possible to show that, in an area that was essentially a sideline of his pastoral activity, Church Law, Rhabanus was able to choose, from within the traditions of Church Law, the regulations that were relevant to the needs of his own time (Kottje 1982).

In these circumstances it would be much too simple a solution to explain the contradictions, or failures to adapt, that we think we can find in his work, merely as the result of intellectual inertia. They are really the result of an inappropriate level of reading on our part; it is precisely the combination of this apparent lack of adaptation with Rhabanus' own creative abilities that can lead us to detect in him a new mental attitude, both caused by and giving rise to new cultural structures.

ONE CULTURE, FACING TWO WAYS

We can resolve this difficulty if we accept that this attested dichotomy corresponds in reality to a deep mental division between the two aspects of a new Christian culture, one of which looks back to the legacy of the Latin tradition, and the other forward to the first signs of a vernacular literature. Rhabanus is aware of the need to adapt himself to modern times. Significantly, even the word, *modernus,* has a place in his vocabulary. He does not aim for this characteristic in cases where it is important to underline the antiquity of an edifying work (**De vita b. M.** [**Beatae Mariae**] **Magdalenae,** *PL* [*Patrologia Latina*] 112, Prologue, c. 1573); but on the other hand he does consider this important when he addresses to Lothar a treatise on the art of war, inspired by Vegetius, but recast specifically 'ne forte ea scribere uiderer quae tempore moderno in usu non sunt' (**Tract.** [**Tractatus**] **de anima, Praef.** [**Praefatio**], *PL* 110, c. 1109). When he is addressing his king, he replaces the traditional terms *imperium* and *regnum* with the contemporary word *Europa*, thereby consecrating a new geopolitical perspective (**De uniuerso, Praef.**).

As well as his search for an erudite Latinity, Rhabanus also finds room for a certain curiosity concerning less elevated cultural concerns. He is happy to give house room to the word *paganus*, of the spoken vernacular (**De cler. inst.**, 1.27; **De uniuerso, Praef. altera, Ad Haymonem**), rather than using the classical terms *rustici, gentiles*, because, in his own words, 'pagi <sunt> conuenticula rusticorum' (**Excerptio,** *PL* 111, c. 668). With the aim of making his pastoral instructions clearer, he replaces terms that are slightly technical with their 'vulgar' equivalent: 'Magi sunt qui uulgo malefici . . . nuncupantur' (*De magicis art.*, [*artibus*] *PL* 110, c. 1097); 'hi sunt qui uulgo mathematici dicuntur' (ibid., c. 1098). This fondness for *realia* also breaks through into his Encyclopedic work (*De rerum naturis*: 'Burgos uulgo uocant', 16.2; 'hunc uulgus aureum solidum uocat', 18.1). The meaning of the word *uulgus* in Rhabanus is clear; it means the whole mass of the people without any distinctions; 'Vulgus est passim inhabitans multitudo' (16.4). That means that, occasionally, he was happy to give a cultural 'safe-conduct' pass to the popular spoken language.

Naturally, Rhabanus, like all the *potentes* of his time, can only have had ambivalent feelings towards the masses. He also happened to hear a sign of irritation let slip by his king: Lothar described himself as 'uulgari tumultu caesis auribus circumseptus' in 842 (*Comm. in Ezec.*, [*Commentarius in Ezechielem*] *PL* 110, c. 493). But his serious-minded awareness of his apostolic mission, which led him to direct the programmes of the various councils that he convened as Archbishop of Mainz (Hartmann 1982) towards a more reforming approach, gave him the intellectual abilities needed to overcome this prejudice. When he came to analyse in due course the origins at Babel of the linguistic fragmentation of the human world (*De cler. inst.*, 3.8: *De uniuerso*, 16.1), Rhabanus drew out the evangelical consequences of this divine punishment, insisting on the obligation to make the words of salvation accessible to those of other tongues ('Linguis omnium gentium loquerentur <discipuli>, ut nulla illis gens extera, nulla lingua barbaris inaccessa uel inuia uideretur', *De cler. inst.*, 2.56). So he took a close interest in the practical conditions of Christian communication, and described in detail the necessity of translation, 'ut ex his unaquaeque gens et natio propriae linguae adminiculo intellectum sibi salubrem adtraheret, interpretando ac colloquendo sensum eundem canonicum propriis uerbis' (*De cler. inst.*, 3.8). The insistence on the words *propria lingua, propriis uerbis* (even if Rhabanus is following here Augustine and Isidore) is particularly noticeable.

Indeed, these are the very words used, in Anglo-Saxon or Germanic-speaking areas from the eighth century on, by synods and councils requiring preachers to teach the illiterate faithful (Lentner 1963). Now, we have every reason to believe that when the Abbot of Fulda writes these words he usually has in mind the vernacular of the eastern part of the Empire, since he happens to add in his remark an unexpectedly specific comment based on the existence of the language in which he himself and his addressees expressed themselves: 'omnes nobiscum linguae Latinae homines' (*De cler. inst.*, 2.8). Even when copying word for word the *De doctrina christiana*, where Augustine used the phrase *lingua nostra*

(opposed to Hebrew and to Greek), Rhabanus clarifies it with the words 'id est latina' (ibid., 3.9). This modest addition means that the writer is aware of the ninth-century context, despite following a fourth-century source: for the monks and clerics of Germania *lingua nostra* would here have meant *lingua theotisca*. Both as abbot and as archbishop, Rhabanus never forgets the unique cultural circumstances of his own area. Even when he is preparing his *De catechizandis rudibus*, he stresses in the dedicatory letter addressed to Bishop Reginbald that his flock was still held back in a way of life that was profoundly pagan (*De eccl. disc.*, [*eccleseastica disciplina*] *Praef.*, *PL* 112, c. 1191).

We are now in a position to collect together these scattered data. The reason why Rhabanus feels justified in praising a purified type of Latinity is that in his own circumstances there is no need for his own Latinity to be at all formally constrained by any need to use it to teach the illiterate. When Rhabanus considers the illiterate, he knows that they represent an imperfectly Christianized mass whose language and whose culture still have no place within written norms or Christian precepts. So he has decided to make the necessary linguistic compromises by using the *propria lingua* of the *uulgus*. That means that he has as a result to leave the areas of prescribed language and plunge into the problematic thickets of other types of speech; but that is precisely what he read Augustine encouraging him to do, taking up his well-known instructions to express himself *uulgi more* and give up the *integritas locutionis*, so that the mass of the faithful can take in and understand the evangelizing message (*De cler. inst.*, 3.30). It is the 'barbarous' language of the Germanic speakers that Rhabanus refers to with such urgency, because this has no other name than *theotisca*, that is, 'popular' (Baesecke 1943; Weisberger 1941).

THEORY AND PRACTICE OF THE NEW *SCRIPTA*

The transition of the 'popular' language towards norms that would eventually include it within the traditions of civilization is helped by being compared to the Hebrew language. On one hand, Rhabanus usually insists on the sacred nature of Hebrew, on the usefulness of knowing it, and on the benefits that have accrued to Christian learning from the work of the translators (*De inst. cler.*, 3.10). On the other hand, when teaching grammar, he puts Hebrew, when he comes to teach about syllabic quantity, in the same category as the 'Barbarian' languages: 'In *el* productam barbara,' ut hic Daniel, Michael, Gabriel. . . . In *ar* correptam Latina et Graeca et barbara masculini et neutri generis, ut hic Caesar, hic bostar, hoc nectar, hoc calcar' (*Excerptio, PL* 111, c. 636-7). That does not prevent him from recalling, in a brief survey of literary history, that the Jews had a taste for poetry and song before the pagans did (he means before the Greeks), even if the latter took on ametrical forms in their case (*Excerptio,* c. 666).

It follows that for a scholar like Rhabanus, Hebrew was a 'Barbarian' language, but that even so, thanks to its role in the history of the texts of salvation, it had the right to the status of written language, and even a language of art. Since the learned abbot had already come to a similar conclusion as regards the 'Barbarian' language of the people in charge of whose souls he found himself, it is understandable that—by a kind of implicit comparison between the different elements of these two cultural and linguistic domains, separated in time but also closely allied in Christian pastoral logic— Rhabanus had the intellectual abilities that allowed him to give Germanic the status of a written language, even of a literary language.

This final stage is implied in several anticipatory hints in Rhabanus' works. He often used the word *cantilena* (*De [ecclesiasticis officiis]*, 2.48; 3.24), whose contemporary associations are well known, both in the Germanic and the Romance fields (Delbouille 1972a: 39; 1972b: 559). In these cases the close connection between Rhabanus' implicit theoretical approach and his practical creativity becomes clear. He promoted the 'popular' language (and we must insist that this is the meaning of *theotisca*) to the level of a poetic language that he incorporated into both the biblical tradition of hymnody and the classical tradition of Alexandrine poetry; this becomes clear in his own poetry, where very often, in fact, in the notes written in classical metres that he used to send to his colleagues, he comments on the meaning of the Germanic personal names included there, and praises them on the basis of their names' etymology (*Carmen* **11,** lines 40-2; 17, 21; 19, 5; 32, 4-9, **Ad Isanbertum presbyterum**: 'Nomen, quo clarus dignus honore fias: // ferrum te fortem, clarum uirtute decorum // signant'). In this way the vernacular language gains a firm foothold within the realms of civilization, that is, within *grammatica.*

I feel able now to go so far as to say that Rhabanus reflected a great deal on the problems of raising the popular language to the level of being inserted into *grammatica.* He ran into the awkward problem of the translation into Germanic of certain key words in Hebrew: 'Quae duo uerba, amen et alleluia nec graecis, nec latinis, nec barbaris licet in suam linguam omnino transferre, uel alia lingua annuntiare' (*De uniu.,* 5.9). He appreciated from experience how difficult it is to establish all the rules of a language, having grappled with the complexity of the data (*Excerptio,* c. 627; c. 663); it is worth recalling that Charles himself had been unable to get a grammar of Frankish established (Banniard 1990: Ch. 6). He understood very clearly the basic distinction between grapheme and phoneme

(*Excerptio,* c. 617). Indeed, rather than leaving them on one side as having no value for the study of Latin grammar (and, as we have seen, he is entirely capable of making this kind of distinction), he became closely interested in the sounds and letters that were exclusive to Greek (*Excerptio,* c. 617). Some of these phonemes, particularly the chi and the spirantized *d* and *t,* are features of Old High German, and some of the written letters also turned up in its alphabet ('Item si fuerit *t* praeposita aspirationi pro Θ ponitur', *Excerptio,* c. 617).

It is logical, then, to conclude that it was as a result of the active influence of its abbot that the scriptorium of Fulda became, in the ninth century, a veritable experimental laboratory, in which they tried out the new written symbols that led to the elaboration first of a *scripta* and then of a *grammatica* of their vernacular language (Bischoff 1985: 107). In my view, the brief work that Rhabanus composed on the invention of alphabets is certainly not a minor appendix due only to encyclopedic curiosity and bereft of any practical purpose. In his famous passage on the invention of runes (*De inuentione litterarum*), Rhabanus recalls that the language family that includes the one that is represented in the runic alphabet is related to the *lingua theotisca* that his own compatriots speak, before he deplores the pagan state in which the speakers of the latter live (Derolez 1954: 354).

He did not confine himself, then, to the difficult but somewhat detached role of grammarian and scholar. On the contrary, his oral teaching within his monastery left traces and evidence (in the form of long lists of glosses where Latin was translated into Germanic) of his own personal investment in the task of pinning down and promoting the popular language.

THEOTISCA AND VULGARIS LINGUA

It was rather too soon, without doubt, for Rhabanus to be able to raise the popular language of Germania to the level of a literary language comparable to that which devised the *Artes liberales;* he was the initiator, or, if you prefer, the mediator between two cultural stages (Fleckenstein 1982), and that is why I believe, contrary to the established view (Haubrichs 1982: 192) that the Archbishop of Mainz, within his own context, was no less responsible than Otfrid for the emergence of Germanic culture.

Taking all things into account, it is legitimate to claim that there is a harmony between Rhabanus' linguistic practice and his intellectual outlook. At the very least, even if no trace had survived of his work in the vernacular, it would have been legitimate to postulate that, faithfully following Augustine's principles, he devoted himself to addressing the illiterate masses; and this, both at Fulda and Mainz, meant using Germanic.

His thoughts developed further than it might seem at first sight, in that the *lingua theotisca* is given sufficient status in his mind that gradually it becomes able to acquire a rank equal to that of the other languages of culture. The intellectual structures, within which the appearance of Germanic literature came to be possible and welcomed, were prepared in advance in people's minds. Furthermore, the general increase in the intellectual level of clerics and monks made something possible which would hardly have been possible a century earlier; the creation and edition of a 'Germanic Donatus'.

Consequently, I suggest, the reciprocal influences that existed between the Eastern and the Western Franks inevitably encouraged the intellectuals in the western area to go further themselves in accepting the culture, working out a *scripta* and grammar, and promoting the literature of their own *lingua vulgaris*.[1]

Notes

1. The second canon of the Council of Mainz of 847, held as soon as Rhabanus became archbishop, repeated the famous Canon 17 of the Council of Tours of 813 concerning the need to consider how best to 'transferre' sermons into 'rusticam Romanam linguam aut in Thiotiscam' so that it was easier for all to understand what was being said.

Bibliography

Baesecke, G. (1943) 'Das Nationalbewusstein der Deutschen des Karolingerreiches nach den Zeitgenössigen Benennungen ihrer Sprache', in T. Mayer (ed.), *Der Vertrag von Verdun 843*, Leipzig, 116-36.

Banniard, M. (1989) *Genèse culturelle de l'Europe (Ve-VIIIe siècle)*, Paris: Eds Du Seuil.

——. (1990) *Viva Voce: Communication écrite et communication orale du IVe au IXe siècle en Occident Latin*, Paris: Etudes Augustiniennes.

Bisanti, A. (1985) 'Struttura compositiva e tecnica compilatoria nel libro III del *De inst. cler.* di Rabano Mauro', *Schede Medievali* 8: 5-17.

Bischoff, B. (1985) *Paléographie de l'Antiquité romaine et du Moyen Age Occidental*, Paris: Picard (German original, 1979).

Blumenkranz, B. (1951) 'Raban Maur et Saint Augustin: compilation ou adaptation? A propos du latin biblique', *Revue du Moyen Age Latin* 7: 97-110.

Borst, A. (1961) *Der Turmbau von Babel. Geschichte der Meinungen über Ursprung und Vielfalt der Sprachen und Völker*, vol. II, Stuttgart: Hiersemann.

Brunhölzl, F. (1982) 'Zur geistigen Bedeutung des Hrabanus Maurus', in R. Kottje and H. Zimmermann (eds), *Hrabanus Maurus, Lehrer, Abt und Bischoff*, Wiesbaden: Steiner, 1-17.

Delbouille, M. (1972a) 'Tradition latine et naissance des littératures romanes', in M. Delbouille (ed.) *Grundriss der romanischen Literaturen des Mittelalters*, vol. I: *Généralités*, Heidelberg: Winter, 4-56.

——. (1972b) 'Les Plus Anciens Textes et la formation des langues littéraires', in M. Delbouille (ed.), *Grundriss der romanischen Literaturen des Mittelalters*, vol. I: *Généralités*, Heidelberg: Winter, 559-621.

Derolez, R. (1954) *Runica manuscripta. The English Tradition*, Bruges: De Tempel.

Fleckenstein, J. (1982) 'Hrabanus Maurus. Diener seiner Zeit und Vermittler zwischen den Zeiten', in R. Kottje and H. Zimmermann (eds), *Hrabanus Maurus, Lehrer, Abt und Bischoff*, Wiesbaden: Steiner, 194-208.

Hartmann, W. (1982) 'Die Mainzer Synoden des Hrabanus Maurus', in R. Kottje and H. Zimmermann (eds), *Hrabanus Maurus, Lehrer, Abt und Bischoff*, Wiesbaden: Steiner, 130-44.

Haubrichs, W. (1982), 'Althochdeutsch in Fulda und Weissenburg—Hrabanus Maurus und Ottfried von Weissenburg', in R. Kottje and H. Zimmermann (eds), *Hrabanus Maurus, Lehrer, Abt und Bischoff*, Wiesbaden: Steiner, 182-93.

Heyze, E. (1969) *Hrabanus Maurus Enzyklopädie 'De rerum naturis'. Untersuchungen zu den Quellen und zur Methode der Kompilation*, Munich: Münchener Beiträge zur Mediävistik und Renaissancen Forschung, 4.

Knöpfler, A. (ed.) (1901) *Rabani Mauri De institutione clericorum libri tres*, Munich: Ludwig-Maximilians Universität.

Kottje, R. (1982) 'Hrabanus und das Recht', in R. Kottje and H. Zimmermann (eds), *Hrabanus Maurus, Lehrer, Abt und Bischoff*, Wiesbaden: Steiner, 118-29.

Lentner, L. (1963) *Volkssprache und Sakralsprache. Geschichte einer Lebensfrage bis zum Ende des Konzils von Trient*, Vienna: Herder.

Manitius, M. (1965) *Geschichte der lateinischen Literatur des Mittelalters*, vol. I, 2nd edn, Munich: Beck.

MGH, PAC = *Monumenta Germaniae Historica, Poetae Latini Aevi Carolini*, ed. E. Dümmler, Berlin: Weidmann, 1884 (Rhabanus Maurus' poems are in vol. II).

PL = *Patrologia Latina*, ed. J. P. Migne, Paris: Teubner (Rhabanus Maurus' works are in vols 107-12, 1864-78).

Steinmeyer, E. (1879) *Die althochdeutsche Glossen*, vol. I, Berlin: Weidmann.

Weisberger, L. (1941) *Die Entdeckung der Muttersprache im europäischen Denken*, Lunebourg: Heliand.

Wolff, P. (1982) *Les Origines linguistiques de l'Europe Occidentale,* 2nd edn, Toulouse: Privat.

Mayke De Jong (essay date 2000)

SOURCE: De Jong, Mayke. "The Empire as *Ecclesia*: Hrabanus Maurus and Biblical *Historia* for Rulers." In *The Uses of the Past in the Early Middle Ages,* edited by Yitzhak Hen and Matthew Innes, pp. 191-226. Cambridge, United Kingdom: Cambridge University Press, 2000.

[*In the following essay, De Jong analyzes Hrabanus's commentaries on several Old Testament narratives, pointing out that Hrabanus drew didactic parallels between the struggle for religious unity in ancient Israel and Emperor Lothar's (ruled 840-55) efforts to save his Christian empire from discord.*]

Shortly before his death in 855, the Emperor Lothar I, Charlemagne's grandson, wrote to Hrabanus Maurus, monk, reknowned theologian and at this date archbishop of Mainz. He commissioned a liturgical compendium for use on his travels, containing the readings for mass all year round, each accompanied by its own explanatory homily (*expositio et omiliaticus sermo*). The homilies were to be read aloud to the emperor during meals, to sustain his *homo interior* with the infinite riches of spiritual food while he sat down at the imperial table.[1] Apparently earlier efforts to gather suitable homilies for the annual liturgical cycle had failed in the face of an overwhelming and impenetrable amount of patristic commentary. Lothar's requirements were specific. Not only did the emperor need homilies for ordinary Sundays and feast days, but also for a host of special masses: on fast days or rogations, against invading armies, famine and poverty, against winter floods, barren earth and failing harvest; for a multitude of saints' days, for Ember Days, for the commemoration of the dead and for ceremonies of consecration—and there would be other masses of which Hrabanus could easily think if he put his mind to it. Furthermore, Jacob's blessings for his sons should be added, along with the benedictions Moses pronounced over the people of Israel on the eve of his death, as well as sermons for All Souls and the Invention of the Holy Cross. Initially Lothar demanded that all this be contained in one volume, but towards the end of the letter he relented, conceding that two volumes or even three might be needed to do justice to the scope of the undertaking, but no more. This was indeed the amount of room Hrabanus needed to comply with the emperor's wishes. Two volumes were written and duly dispatched to Lothar, with promises of a third to follow soon. Word of Lothar's death probably reached Hrabanus before he completed his task; there is no sign that the third volume was ever written.

Interesting as this homiliary—or *lectionarium,* as Lothar called it—may be in itself, it is an earlier passage from Lothar's letter which concerns me here. Explaining why he needed a handy volume, the emperor wrote:

> Indeed it is well known to you, father, that on all my military campaigns I cannot always take and carry with me the entire wealth of commentaries, historical and allegorical, in which the aforesaid readings are embedded, when it is often difficult enough to have merely the *bibliotheca historiarum* at hand.[2]

What was this 'library of histories', which apparently had absolute priority among books to take along on military and other expeditions, even if it was too much trouble to bring the 'entire wealth of commentaries' (*omnis copia commentariorum*)? Scripture was often referred to as *sacra/divina historia* or, shortly, *bibliotheca.*[3] The latter might be further specified to be 'the library of the Old and New Testament', but there was no need for this: *bibliotheca* sufficed. At first sight Lothar's *bibliotheca historiarum* therefore appears to be a large and cumbersome full (most likely Turonian) bible.[4] This interpretation is problematic, however, and not merely because it overestimates the logistics of transporting a hefty codex. The expression *historia* for Scripture without any further specification ('sacred', 'divine', 'of the Old and New Testament') is already very rare, and I have found no instances of the plural *historiae* designating Scripture. In combination with *bibliotheca* it may have assumed this meaning, but there are equally good reasons for arguing that Lothar had something more specific in mind. Given the importance of this *bibliotheca historiarum* to Lothar it seems safe to assume that the core of these 'histories' was indeed biblical, but not all of Scripture necessarily qualified as *historiae.* Lothar's letter itself indicates as much, for it envisaged the fathers having gathered suitable *lectiones* from the 'evangelical sentences' pertaining to 'various sacred histories', thus creating a distinction between the gospel on the one hand and 'historical' parts of Scripture on the other. Lothar's letter also mentions special masses when the epistle had to be substituted by a 'reading from some history' (*lectio ex quaquam historia*). Usually such an alternative first reading was taken from the Old Testament. I am therefore still inclined to think that Lothar's *bibliotheca historiarum* must have been a collection of Old Testament texts, possibly embedded in commentary. After all, Lothar complained of the difficulties of taking along the *omnis copia commentariorum,* 'the entire wealth of commentary' going with the annual readings, on 'all his expeditions'; this suggests that a section of this 'wealth of commentaries' was singled out to accompany the emperor on his travels, as an integral part of the *historiae.*

Although the precise contents of Lothar's *bibliotheca historiarum* remain elusive, this intriguing expression makes one wonder about the uses of Old Testament *historia* and Hrabanus' commentary for Carolingian kings and queens. Given the lack of critical editions of Hrabanus' vast exegetical production, or in some cases, of any edition at all, answers to this question can only be tentative.[5] Yet enough of his work is accessible to enable a provisional inquiry into royal interest in Hrabanus' commentary.[6] It is particularly the historical books of the Old Testament which interest me here, for it was to this part of Scripture that Hrabanus Maurus devoted most of his vast exegetical *oeuvre*, including the commentaries he wrote at the request of emperors, kings and queens, or dedicated to them of his own accord. Almost all these 'royal' commentaries were concerned with those parts of Scripture that Hrabanus unambiguously classified as *historia*: the four Books of Kings for Louis the Pious, Chronicles and Maccabees for Louis the German, Joshua for Lothar, and Judith and Esther for the Empress Judith; the commentary on Esther he later also dedicated to Lothar's wife, the Empress Irmingard.

Hrabanus was neither the first, nor the only, biblical commentator to dedicate his work to Carolingian kings.[7] His prefatory letters, however, provide an exceptional wealth of information concerning the 'utility' of biblical history for his royal patrons which has not yet been sufficiently tapped. These letters form the basis for the following exploration, together with three commentaries on biblical *historiae* for which Hrabanus had no patristic model: those on Esther, Judith and Maccabees. Here Hrabanus was forced to rely more than normally on his own devices; these commentaries are also special because two of them (Judith and Maccabees) dealt with apocryphal books, and those on Judith and Esther were dedicated to empresses.

Hrabanus could rely on a sophisticated royal audience, able to understand the restricted code of allegory and typology, assisted by *lectores* who were part of the retinue of rulers. The king acted as the final judge: to him, exegetical writing was sent *ad legendum et ad probandum,* but he was surrounded by *peritissimi lectores* who might find fault as well.[8] Hrabanus expected these 'readers' to discuss and criticize his work while reading it, as becomes clear from one of his dedicatory letters to Emperor Lothar:

> Order this to be read in your presence, and if you discover something that is not correctly explained because of the weakness of my understanding, or distorted by scribal errors, make your learned readers correct it, and thus you will be rewarded forever with your just reward in Heaven by Christ, the lord of all, for your noble struggle and for having corrected me.[9]

This passage nicely shows which intermediaries intervened between the author of biblical exegesis and its royal recipient: not only scribes but also *lectores*

helped to convey the message. This was a court culture in which rulers had Latin texts read to them by professional readers, pondering and censuring what they heard while the reading session progressed.[10] Biblical commentary for kings was not just a matter of image-building: a *rex sapientissimus* was expected to be familiar with the intricacies of biblical exegesis. Lothar's two extant letters to Hrabanus are revealing, for the emperor's requests for commentary were highly specific, evoking a ruler completing a collection of commentaries and taking a lively interest in them too.[11] Hrabanus also discussed the problems of exegesis with Louis the German, and worried about the criticism his work might receive in courtly circles—not entirely without reason, judging by his occasional mortification.[12]

It was not merely biblical *historia* itself that kings were interested in: they wanted exegesis. Sometimes this could be 'literal' or 'historical', but more often this exegesis would be 'allegorical', *spiritalis* or *mystice,* as Hrabanus expressed it. This was the kind of commentary he considered fit for kings and queens. He was not the only one who deemed a real, and therefore spiritual, understanding of biblical history an asset indispensable to a true ruler. Thegan celebrated Louis the Pious's learning, not only praising his fluency in Latin, but also his ability to grasp spiritual exegesis; accordingly, Louis had forsworn the *poetica carmina gentilia* he learned in his youth, refusing to read, hear or teach them.[13] At Louis the Pious's court 'stories gave way to histories',[14] but it was not an interest in contemporary record-keeping with which Thegan credited his ruler. He depicted a kind of *conversio:* from a young man liking 'gentile songs' Louis turned into a king who was an expert in understanding the spiritual, moral and anagogical meaning of Scripture. This was not the image of a king exchanging 'oral history' for its written counterpart, but of one who preferred the intricacies of Latin exegesis to the performance of secular—but not necessarily pagan—*carmina.*[15] Only a *rex sapientissimus* capable of fathoming the many-layered meaning of Scripture could be a true *rector* of his Christian people.[16] Judging by Hrabanus' correspondence with rulers, such kings were not a mere figment of Thegan's imagination. Thegan was anxious, however, to project this image of a scripturally based royal *conversatio* backwards, to include Charlemagne. Not only did he hail the son as an expert in allegorical exegesis, but he also radically redrew Einhard's portrayal of the father's preparations for death. According to Thegan, the old emperor had devoted the end of his life to prayer, almsgiving and assiduously correcting sacred texts, particularly the four gospels.[17]

Against this background of royal interest in biblical *historia,* including its spiritual meaning, secular history pales into insignificance. It has been maintained that the genre of *historia,* that is, narrative and moralistic historiography as opposed to mere record-keeping, catered to the needs of kings looking to their historians to unravel the confusing myriad of events they were faced with in this world. In other words, the secular *historia* of the early Middle Ages, including those histories dealing with contemporary events, should be viewed as a continuation of its Old Testament model; like biblical commentators, historians were to explain God's intentions to rulers.[18] The influence of biblical—and especially Old Testament—models on early medieval historical narrative was indeed ubiquitous.[19] Yet it is one thing to say that Carolingian historians lived in a biblical universe which left a deep imprint on their work, but quite another to credit them with a role similar to that of biblical commentators, revealing God's hand in history for the benefit of kings.[20] Augustine had drawn a sharp line between sacred and secular history: only sacred history could be subjected to an *expositio,* an interpretation of its deeper layers of meaning, for only in sacred history had God revealed himself to humanity.[21] Carolingian authors were well aware of this distinction, and it was perhaps the most important reason why Carolingian kings and queens were more interested in biblical history and its commentary than in historiography of contemporary events. It may have been 'the most ancient practice, customary for kings from then to now, to have deeds written down in annals for posterity to learn about',[22] yet there is little evidence of kings actually requesting contemporary historiography: a teleological perspective was not easily combined with an intelligent approach to contemporary events.[23] The chronicle written by Hrabanus' friend Freculph, bishop of Lisieux, was an ambitious work running from the creation up to the seventh century and two highly symbolic events: the consecration of the Pantheon to the Virgin Mary and all the martyrs, and the establishment of papal primacy.[24] It consisted of two coherent parts, of which the first was dedicated to Arch-chaplain Helisachar, the second to the Empress Judith, for the education of her son Charles the Bald.[25] This work was certainly destined for the court, but it was not concerned with the confusing turmoil of the present needing to be sorted out by an exegetically minded historian. The central theme of Freculph's sophisticated Augustinian narrative, recently uncovered by Nikolaus Staubach, was the victory of the 'right cult', by which the universal *ecclesia* distinguished itself from older cultic unities narrowly identified with peoples and states.[26] Although Freculph did not engage in full-blown *expositio,* his kind of historiography bordered on biblical commentary, not least because his instructions from Helisachar included taking the historical level of exegesis into account when dealing with Old Testament history;[27] Freculph's central concerns—the *ecclesia* and the cor-

rect cult—had much in common with the truths Hrabanus Maurus expounded over and over again in his exegesis for rulers. Freculph's work seems to confirm that royal taste ran more to salvation history than to contemporary *historia.* The one significant exception was Nithard's *Historiae,* written at Charles the Bald's behest. This indeed was *historia* proper, a moralizing narrative of contemporary history by a historian writing for his ruler and trying to make sense of the confusing experiences of his own time. But with Nithard we are far removed from confident historical exegesis at the service of kings. His was the tale of an increasingly demoralized courtier and warrior, who looked backwards with nostalgia to times when aristocratic loyalty still reigned supreme, but none the less shared in the general confusion of his day and age.[28] Charles the Bald may even have been disappointed with Nithard's deeply pessimistic historical account; certainly it did not offer the sure-footed exposition of truth a learned king might expect from biblical exegesis.

This is not to say that there was no such thing as court historiography in this period. On the contrary, history writing in the ninth century was overwhelmingly court-oriented, and, as Janet L. Nelson expressed it, the court was a 'frame of mind' encompassing episcopal sees and monasteries.[29] Yet when it came to kings expressing an active interest, biblical history and its commentary took precedence over secular historiography. Royal sensitivity to the implied criticism in some narratives about contemporary events may have played a role in this, but is only a partial explanation at best.[30] It was the self-assigned role of Carolingian rulers as the guardians of the correct interpretation of God's law and the correct cult which made them the recipients and connoisseurs *par excellence* of biblical commentary. Although the contours of a ruler safeguarding the unity and correctness of the *cultus divinus* are already in evidence in the *Concilium Germanicum* (743) and the capitularies of Pippin III, this image was only fully elaborated in Charlemagne's *Admonitio Generalis* (789): 'For we read in the *Books of Kings* (II Reg. 22-23) how the holy Josiah, by visitation, correction and admonition, strove to recall the kingdom which God had given him to the worship of the true God . . .'[31] King Josiah, who had reinstated the Temple, eradicated idolatry, found and imposed God's law, renewed the pact between God and his people and reorganized the priesthood, was the ruler with whom Charlemagne emphatically, though humbly, compared himself; like that of his biblical predecessor, Charlemagne's return to the *cultum veri Dei* was to be founded upon the 'words of the book of the law'. All this is well known, but it has taken modern historians a long time to realize the implications of this vision for 'political' history. As John Contreni observed recently:

The Bible and the Middle Ages are so interwoven for us, that it is difficult to appreciate the boldness—and the idealism—of Charlemagne's initiative. No secular leader before him—no Constantine, no Theodosius, no Clovis—had so dramatically privileged the sacred text. The history of the Bible and of biblical exegesis during the Carolingian period must begin with the realization of the Bible's significance in Carolingian culture broadly speaking, in religion and spirituality, to be sure, but also in political culture and in every thinking person's notion of the right ordering of Frankish society.[32]

In this biblically centred political culture exegesis was relevant to rulers,[33] and Hrabanus became their most important supplier. Flattering him into compiling a concise liturgical travel-companion, Lothar paid homage to Hrabanus' exceptional position as a *magister orthodoxus*. The bountiful Lord had provided his predecessors with the likes of Jerome, Augustine, Gregory and Ambrose, but he—Lothar—had been equally blessed with Hrabanus.[34] In 854-5, when he made his request, the emperor was looking back on decades of Hrabanus' scholarly service. Lothar himself was getting on for sixty, Hrabanus was almost seventy-five years old. For both men death was to come soon.[35] The old emperor appreciated Hrabanus' work more than later generations of scholars, who accused him of having done nothing except copying the Fathers. Those who now tend to evaluate his work on his own terms still feel the need to defend him against the taint of 'lack of originality'.[36] Even during his own lifetime Hrabanus came in for nasty criticism from 'know-alls' (*scioli*) maintaining that he never wrote anything he had thought of himself. Mortally offended, he asked Lothar what on earth was wrong with inserting excerpts from the writings of the Fathers if he duly indicated them as such, rather than passing them off as his own work; proper humility had compelled him to give pride of place to the exegesis of the Fathers instead of his own.[37] Making patristic commentary available to his contemporaries was indeed his paramount goal. Much of his exegetical work operated according to the principle of the *florilegium;* gathering flowers—or wholesome food—in the works of the *patres* is a recurrent image in Hrabanus' prefatory letters.[38] In this respect he did precisely what those commissioning his commentary asked for. They wanted brevity *and* their Fathers, relying on Hrabanus either to supply patristic exegesis if they lacked it, or to provide a handy compendium when they had so much of it they got lost in it. When Freculph of Lisieux asked Hrabanus for a commentary on the Pentateuch he complained that in his new bishopric 'on the Western shores of the Ocean' he did not even have all the biblical books at his disposal, let alone the relevant commentary. He craved spiritual food from Hrabanus, 'so that our regard will be turned eastward, Judea will border us in the West, and our Breton neighbours will become

Israelites'.[39] Hrabanus swiftly complied, producing five books of commentary at a time (822-9) when he was already the extremely busy abbot of Fulda. He explained to Freculph that he had distinguished patristic commentary from his own by marking his own additions with '*nota agnominis mei*',[40] a principle he was to stick to in later work, duly identifying his own commentary in the margin with an 'M'.[41] Already in his exegetical debut, a commentary on Matthew offered in 821-2 to Archbishop Haistulph of Mainz, Hrabanus was adamant that the layout of the text, including the colour of the ink and the size of the script, would not only help the reader to tell the biblical text apart from its commentary, but also make the commentary quickly accessible.[42] This in itself shows that his own voice was also heard, but in his prefatory letters he consciously projected the image of someone who, like his master Alcuin, wished to do nothing but follow in the footsteps of the Fathers.[43] His concern with the layout of his commentary served the same purpose as his faithful adherence to the *vestigia maiorum:* he considered it his principal duty to make the *sententiae patrum* accessible to his contemporaries. The indefatigable energy with which he devoted himself to this task helped to provide the groundwork upon which later critics of Hrabanus' exegetical methods depended: the *scioli* who spoke ill of him in the 840s, claiming that the commentator merely copied the work of others, could do so because they enjoyed the benefits of two decades of Hrabanus' biblical scholarship.[44]

Hrabanus' emphasis on the *vestigia maiorum* was in keeping with the demands of his patrons and with the spirit of his age;[45] it was also reinforced by his monastic background. In the epitaph he wrote for himself, Hrabanus defined himself as a monk, first and foremost: born in Mainz, and reborn through baptism, he became acquainted with Holy Scripture in Fulda, where as a monk he obeyed the orders of his superiors and the Rule became the guideline of his life.[46] For Hrabanus himself these were the essential data about his life, and it was as a monk that he wished to be remembered. This is not surprising for someone who entered Fulda as a child oblate in 788, when he was eight years old at most, but probably younger.[47] Hrabanus bore the early imprint of the cloister for the rest of his life; as Hincmar was to say later, he had been brought up on milk from the breasts of the Church.[48] But already at an early stage the court began to impinge upon his life,[49] and it would continue to do so throughout his career as teacher and abbot of Fulda and archbishop of Mainz.[50] Most of his numerous biblical commentaries were written during his busy years as abbot of Fulda. Lothar called him the *magister orthodoxus,* but Hrabanus only gradually acquired this position of authority. His first 'royal' commentary, the one on Kings, was initially (829) dedicated to Archchaplain Hilduin. Judging by the accompanying letter Hrabanus carefully tested the waters, securing Hilduin's approval before he dared to offer his work to the one who should really understand Israel's royal history: Louis the Pious. Apparently Hilduin had asked him for a specimen of his exegesis, without being specific in his demands; Hrabanus humbly referred to the rich library Hilduin had at his disposal at the palace, and wondered whether this 'little work of ours' composed for Fulda's monks would be good enough for the great man.[51] Apparently it was, for Hrabanus later proudly recounted to King Louis the German how his commentary on Kings had been written at Hilduin's request (*Hilduini rogatu*); moreover, the work had been presented to Louis's father when he had been 'personally present in our monastery'—a reference to the emperor's visit to Fulda in 832.[52]

Was there a gift more suitable to a Christian ruler visiting a royal monastery than a commentary on the Books of Kings? When in 834 or shortly thereafter Hrabanus sent his commentary on Chronicles to Louis the German, he wrote:

> It used to be the custom that a most Christian king, much occupied with divine precepts, was offered the history of the kings of Judah, that is, of the confessors, with some explanation of its spiritual meaning. Because your noble prudence rules over a Christian people [*populus ecclesiasticus*] redeemed by the precious blood of God's son and most accustomed to profess God's name, it suits a pious prince, that is to say, the *rector* of the members of the true king Christ, God's only son, to have and practice the right form of government which is in accordance with Scripture . . .'[53]

This neatly summarizes Hrabanus' views on the uses of biblical commentary for rulers. It should be a practical guide to Christian kings who were *rectores,* first and foremost, ruling a people defined by the fact that it was '*ecclesiasticus*'. Yet it was not merely biblical history itself, but above all its spiritual commentary which was harnessed to this cause. 'Accept this history of earlier kings [*regum priorum historia*] and love most in it everything concerning its spiritual meaning, which pertains to the grace of Christ.' The reference to David's key (Apoc. 3:7) was another allusion to the ability of kings to fathom the spiritual meaning of Scripture.[54] Hrabanus was adamant that his exegesis was, above all, meant to be useful, but this 'practicality' operated primarily at an allegorical level: it was to aid the royal understanding of the deeper and truly Christian meaning of the 'history of prior kings'. After his usual protestations about following the *vestigia patrum* and doing so with the required brevity, Hrabanus clearly stated his intentions: instead of presenting long flowery treatises, 'I have decided to write commentaries on divine histories, of which the function is to pass over the obvious, and to explicate the obscure'.[55]

It was in this spirit that Hrabanus wrote biblical commentary for Carolingian rulers and their spouses. His royal recipients perceived his work as *munera*, gifts, a view shared by the author himself;[56] in this respect, exegetical production was part of the circuit of gift-exchange between royal *fideles* and the ruler. Presentations of work or royal requests for commentary were instrumental in creating, maintaining or restoring good relations, yet this was more than an offering intended to curry royal favour. Hrabanus bestowed biblical exegesis upon the ruler both as a gesture of loyalty and as an acknowledgement of royal legitimacy. As his authority and renown grew, Hrabanus' 'gifts' became something like a hallmark of legitimacy. It was the legitimate ruler who deserved biblical commentary, for only he (or she) would possess the *sapientia* needed for a true spiritual understanding.

This particular function of exegesis emerged quite clearly once strife became endemic in the royal family, and Carolingian magnates—including Hrabanus—had a hard time identifying their legitimate monarch. Throughout the troubles of 830-4 Fulda and its abbot remained a bastion of loyalty to Louis the Pious.[57] Hrabanus' first gift of biblical commentary—the Books of Kings!—signalled his unwavering fidelity to the emperor, and in 832 can have been no less than an explicit gesture of support. It was Hrabanus who voiced the sentiments of the loyalists in a treatise which his pupil Rudolf called an *epistola consolatoria*,[58] but which was in fact a compilation of biblical texts on the obedience which sons owed to their fathers and subjects to their kings; once restored to power, the emperor requested a more extensive work on the *honor parentum* and the duties of the various *ordines* in the *ecclesia Dei,* that is, the realm.[59] The commentaries on Esther and Judith destined for the Express Judith also belonged to this veritable avalanche of loyal support during and after the tribulations of 833; the abbot of Fulda referred to the enemies Judith had conquered, and would go on conquering as long as she followed the biblical models of her namesake, and her predecessor Queen Esther.[60] Hrabanus stressed the empress's legitimacy by calling himself 'a particle of the people committed to you by God', and reminded her of his daily prayers for the royal family.[61] In a prefatory *carmen figuratum* a crowned Judith is depicted at the centre of a square field of letters, under the blessing hand of God.[62] Concern for the unity of the realm may also have inspired the commentary on Chronicles for Louis the German. Did it serve as a gesture of gratitude to the young Louis, who had been instrumental in restoring his father to the throne? Hrabanus praised the king's *cultum pietatis,* of which he had long heard, but which he had now personally experienced, and invited him to scrutinize Scripture in order to govern legitimately, according to the example of 'preceding fathers' (*patres praecedentes*).[63] It looks as if Hrabanus had both biblical and contemporary fathers in mind: Louis the Pious hovers in the background, for it was in this letter that Hrabanus recalled how 'some years ago' he had presented the emperor with his commentary on the Books of Kings.[64] Like his father earlier, the loyal son now received the *divina historia* of his Old Testament predecessors.

When discord flared up again in 838, Hrabanus remained staunchly at the emperor's side, but in 840 the old emperor died, and the moment of truth had arrived. In a letter to Humbert of Würzburg Hrabanus complained not only of physical illness, but also of anxiety about the 'common peril which threatens us greatly at this time', expressing a fear of failure in the face of impending difficulties.[65] He could have written these words anywhere between 838 and 842, but they best fit the period after Louis's death, when minds had to be made up in an uncertain situation. Lothar seems to have taken the initiative in ensuring Hrabanus' loyalty and approval, requesting a 'mystical and moral' commentary on the part of Ezekiel not yet covered by Gregory the Great. Hrabanus pleaded an illness ('not that I ever amounted to much, but nowadays I feel much different from what I used to be: I lie in bed more often, oppressed by serious illness, than I sit in my study to write or read'),[66] but also complained of the 'difficulties of Ezekiel'.[67] This complicated book of visionary prophecy must indeed have presented problems without a reliable patristic guide; apart from this, there was its vitriolic denunciation of Jerusalem as a perfidious whore (Ez. 16:1-43), and its soaring vision of the New Israel and the restoration of the Temple (Ez. 40-8). The precarious political situation of 840 can hardly have facilitated a 'mystical and moral' commentary on such themes. Ezekiel's diatribes were too harsh, his prophecy of renewed unity too lofty. Instead, Hrabanus offered Lothar a commentary on Jeremiah which he had already started when 'your late father, the Emperor Louis' was still alive, and which he had finished after Louis's death.[68] Jeremiah was a meaningful gift in troubled times; again Hrabanus used biblical commentary to convey the message that Lothar was Louis's legitimate successor by explicitly linking the father and the son in his prefatory letter. Work on Jeremiah had started during Louis's life, and was now formally presented to the son and heir. 'And because the wills of many run in various directions, dispositions differ, and opinons waver and purposes vacillate, it pleases me to appeal to you as the one and only benevolent and most wise judge, saintliest and most august Emperor Lothar . . .'[69] Hrabanus' assertion that Lothar was the only one capable of judging the commentary's 'purity' had a clear implication: Lothar was the rightful emperor. Hence, Hrabanus ended his letter with a solemn pledge of life-long fidelity and a prayer asking God to protect Lothar from his earthly enemies and to grant him an eternal reign in heaven.

But things turned out differently. In the spring of 842 Louis the German occupied the region and claimed the royal abbey of Fulda. Hrabanus fled to Lothar, albeit only for a few days; when he returned, the monks had elected his friend Hatto to the abbacy.[70] Hrabanus retired to the Petersberg, a small monastic establishment a few kilometres from Fulda with a church 'eminently visible' (*valde conspicua*) on the mountain, which he had founded himself in 836 and consecrated 'in honour of the sainted apostles, patriarchs, prophets, martyrs, confessors, virgins and all the heavenly saintly spirits'.[71] His reasons for giving up the abbacy were complex: not only his loyalty to Lothar counted, but also longstanding tensions in the community since Abbot Ratger's conflict-ridden reign, and then there was his advanced age.[72] When his old pupil Lupus commented on his master having 'relinquished all care and toil to our Hatto', he made it sound like a straightforward retirement, though he may have been suspicious, for he asked for a full account.[73] Whatever the case, Hrabanus withdrew with good grace, keeping excellent relations with Fulda and its new abbot Hatto, 'the dearest of men and the most solicitous keeper of God's flock', as he wrote shortly after retiring.[74] If there was any real estrangement between Hrabanus and King Louis it did not last long, for in 845 at the latest, but possibly as early as 843,[75] the king called him to Rasdorf, a *cella* of Fulda, where the two men discussed Scripture and the king commissioned an allegorical commentary on the Canticles for Matins.[76] Again a royal request for biblical commentary served as a way to cement or restore good relations, with Hrabanus hastening to express his faithful *servitium*. Significantly, he called Louis a *sapientissimus rex, in omnibus bene eruditus*—his hallmark of legitimacy—and vowed to pray for the king's salvation and the stability of his realm.[77] Hrabanus was no longer the abbot of a great royal monastery, but, as he subtly reminded the king, the power of his monastic prayer was still indispensable to political order.[78] More exegetical work for King Louis was to follow in those years when he was not burdened by the duties of high office. Contrasting busy monastic life with that of 'those who are well versed in reading books and meditating on Sacred Scripture, and have the leisure to read and write what they want',[79] he may have had himself in mind, and his obligation to make good use of his time. He sent the king a commentary on Daniel, and, one year later, the *expositio* on Maccabees he had written 'some years ago, at the request of friends', that is, for Gerolt, an archdeacon of Louis the Pious: a seasonal gift, offered between the first Sundays of November and December, 'when the Apostolic See has decreed the Books of Maccabees to be read in church'.[80] Louis asked for more: 'Recently, when I [Hrabanus] was in your presence, you said you heard I wrote a new work on the properties of language and the mystical significance of things, and you asked me to send it.' This was **De Rerum Naturis,** a gigantic undertaking made possible by Hrabanus' retirement to the Petersberg. Predictably, his dedicatory letter was full of allusions to royal *sapientia* and Solomon. It opened with praise for a king whose good repute had reached 'all of Gaul and Germany, and almost all parts of Europe'; Hrabanus said he could not write on Scripture without sharing his work with Louis. In this new work *de sermonum proprietate et mystica rerum significatione* the king could find *historia* as well as *allegoria;* like the Old Testament itself, it was divided into twenty-two books. In other words, to Hrabanus himself his 'encyclopedia' was above all another work of exegesis.[81]

Meanwhile Emperor Lothar also remained an eager recipient of Hrabanus' commentary. He sent his former *fidelis* two letters, 'one of which is to read, the other to read and append as a preface to your work',[82] making some very specific demands: a literal commentary on the beginning of Genesis, a spiritual exposition of those parts of the exhortations (*sermones*) of Jeremiah on which he lacked Jerome's commentary, and the anagogical commentary on the part of Ezekiel which had not been covered by Gregory the Great, for which he had asked earlier. Even the 'official' letter, written in Lothar's customary flowery prose, breathes the spirit of old friendship: the emperor alluded to their involuntary separation, and added some words of consolation about Hrabanus' rural exile, which surely was better suited to the *homo interior* than the beauty of royal cities.[83] Obviously political circumstances did not prevent excellent and frequent relations between the emperor and *Hrabanus noster,* for the letter makes it clear that a messenger had recently brought Lothar a copy of Hrabanus' commentary on Joshua, and promises of more (*de divinis aliis libris expositio*).[84] Hrabanus set to work, complying with the emperor's wishes but according to his own views. For a literal commentary on Genesis, Lothar had to turn to Augustine; Hrabanus was not going to improve on *De Genesi ad litteram.*[85] He did send Lothar a commentary on the beginning of Genesis, but this also included allegory. Hrabanus also reminded Lothar of the fact that he had already sent him his exegesis of Jeremiah. Is this a case of imperial loss of memory or loss of commentary? As for Ezekiel, Hrabanus outdid himself: he treated not only the last part Lothar had asked for twice, but the entire Ezekiel, following Gregory's *vestigia* as well as the footsteps of others, with *nota nominorum eorum* in the margin, and adding the occasional commentary of his own. Hrabanus was somewhat apologetic about the length of the work, but assured Lothar he had left out a great deal that might have been included, for its 'utility' to the reader remained his first concern.[86] Lothar's wife, the

Empress Irmingard, also became the recipient of biblical exegesis, for to her Hrabanus re-dedicated his commentary on Esther. He reminded her of her kindness towards him when he met the imperial couple in Mainz in August 841,[87] perhaps an indication that the commentary was offered not too long afterwards; his dedicatory poem emphasized Irmingard's imperial position, and the mantle of Judith having fallen onto her shoulders.

Judging by the letter of 840 in which he swore eternal fidelity to Lothar, Hrabanus' exegesis for rulers was part of a larger programme: 'After having written little commentaries on the Heptateuch, Kings and Chronicles, and after my little explanations [*explanatiunculae*] of the *historiae* of Esther, Judith and Maccabees, not to mention my work on books of Wisdom and Jesus Sirach and my other writings, I now put my hand to Jeremiah . . .'[88] It is to the three commentaries explicitly defined as *historia* that I will now finally turn.

What made these texts suitable for dedication to a king and two queens? Hrabanus was well aware that two of these texts were apocryphal according to the Hebrew canon, but the Apostolic See had given Maccabees a fixed place in the liturgy,[89] he assured Louis the German, and the Church 'of modern times' treated Maccabees and Judith as a part of Scripture.[90] All the same, Hrabanus' commentaries represented an important stage in their canonization.[91] Esther was the last book to be included in the Jewish canon, and by a narrow margin. Hrabanus considered Esther to be a historical tradition *par excellence,* explaining to the Empress Judith that the 'interpreter of sacred history', Jerome, had translated the book of Esther word by word, 'from the archives of the Jews' (*de archivis Ebreorum*), and that its history derived 'from Jewish sources' (*ex Ebreorum fonte*).[92] Unable to follow his cherished *vestigia patrum,* he had to rely on what he called, with dutiful humility but not without pride, his own 'feeble intellect' (*nostri ingenioli*).[93]

This is not to say that Esther, Judith and Maccabees were the only books to be classified as 'history'. Surveying his work he distinguished between the *libri hystorici* he had already commented upon, and the *libri prophetici,* on which he was now about to embark seriously, except this order had been upset because 'friends' (read: kings) had begged him for exegesis of Ezekiel, Jeremiah and Daniel.[94] Here he considered all the biblical books he worked on prior to the prophets to be 'historical', including the Pentateuch. There was nothing revolutionary about this: after all, Isidore of Seville deemed Moses to be the very first historian,[95] and Augustine had classified all Old Testament books from Genesis to Ruth as *historia,* because they adhered to a chronological sequence with the exception of Job, Tobias, Esther, Judith, Maccabees and Ezra which should have continued where Chronicles left off.[96] Hrabanus' definition of biblical 'history' varied. It was deeply influenced by the exegetical meaning of *historia,* that of the 'historical' level of exegesis as opposed to its counterpart which was 'spiritual' or *mystice.* This duality, which pervades Hrabanus' work, could of course apply to both Testaments, but the principle of prefiguration tended to turn the Old Testament into the part of Scripture which was by definition 'historical': what the Old Testament narrated in a historical way, the New Testament demonstrated spiritually.[97] The Old Testament remained 'history' as long as it had not yet been explicated by means of allegory; hence, Hrabanus referred to the spiritual meaning of Genesis as the *sacramentum historiae.*[98] Yet biblical *historia* also had a more restricted and simple meaning for Hrabanus: that of a chronologically ordered narrative of past events.[99] Thus he opposed prophetical to historical parts of the Old Testament: whereas prophetical narrative spoke about the future and should therefore not be expected to be chronologically accurate, one might search historical books for references to factual queries.[100]

Esther, Judith and Maccabees qualified on both counts: as historical truth to be unveiled through spiritual exegesis, and as exciting stories of historical events. In different ways, these three books tell the story of the people of Israel faced with persecution and possible extinction, but ultimately gaining victory with God's help. Hrabanus' commentaries were written at a time of great political upheaval in the Carolingian Empire, and dedicated to rulers who, in the midst of turmoil, must have perceived some similarities between the plight of the Old Israel and that of its Frankish successor. The tale about Esther is set in the Persian Empire, where King Assuerus rejects his wife Vashti and chooses as a new wife Esther, the ward and niece of one of the Jews in exile, Mordecai. The latter earns the king's good favour by uncovering a plot against him, but incurs the wrath of the second man in the empire, Haman, who decides to exterminate not only Mordecai, but the entire Jewish people. This dire fate is prevented by Esther, who manages to turn the tables on Haman. He finds his death on the gallows he prepared for Mordecai, who now takes Haman's place; instead of being slaughtered themselves, the Jews are allowed to exterminate their enemies. Judith's story also features a female saviour of her people. Here it is 'Nebuchadnezzar, king of the Assyrians', who, together with his general Holofernes, threatens the Jews, just settled down after returning from exile. The Ammonite Achior tries to dissuade Holofernes from attacking the Jews, but the latter besieges Betulia. Judith, a rich and beautiful widow from Betulia, manages to gain access to Holofernes; she gets him drunk during dinner, and cuts off his head when he lies down in a drunken stupor. Here as well distress turns into triumph: Achior converts, and the fleeing Assyrians are now beleaguered by the Jews.

Unlike the narratives about Esther and Judith, which have no verifiable basis in history, Maccabees presents itself as the historical record of the revolt started in 167 BC by the priest Mattathias against the Seleucid king Antiochus IV Epiphanes (175-164 BC), who had robbed and desecrated the Temple. Mattathias' son Judas Maccabeus continued the revolt, purifying and newly consecrating the Temple (164 BC); his brothers Jonathan and Simeon eventually succeeded in procuring an independent status for Israel, with Simeon being chosen as 'king' by his people. The central theme of the first book of Maccabees is that faithful and tenacious adherence to God's law will pay off in the end. Whereas the first book mostly features human heroics and the perfidy of Israel's foreign enemies, the second book—which recaps large parts of the first—stresses God's help and vengeance, the expiating effects of martyrdom, and Israel's own guilt as the main cause of its suffering.

These biblical histories about a people overcoming deep distress to reach ultimate victory served as a source of inspiration in different times and circumstances,[101] but their special appeal to Carolingian rulers in the troubled 830s and 840s is obvious. The image of victorious Judith and Esther, saviours of their people, was intended to please an empress who had repeatedly weathered revolt and captivity.[102] Similarly, Maccabees with its central narrative about the cultic unity of a people was offered to Louis the German, a king recovering from the wars of 840-3 and busily reorganizing his realm. Hrabanus' treatment of these texts was not a simple comparison between Israel and the Franks, however, not only because he worked within an exegetical tradition with its own restricted code, but also because he was acutely aware of the Jews as a people of the past, whose history was claimed by both Jews and Christians in the present. Writing about the fate of the biblical Israel in distress inevitably led to the vexed question of the relation between the Old and the New Israel.[103] Above all, Hrabanus intended to make it crystal clear that the history of Israel was 'ours' instead of 'theirs'. The drama of Esther's *historia* and its allegorical exegesis reach their joint culmination when the king prefers Mordecai over Haman:

> What else is the fact that King Assuerus gave the house of Haman, the adversary of the Jews, to Queen Esther, if not that our true king and lord has given every dignity and every honour which the earlier people [*prior populus*] used to have because of their knowledge of the law and the prophets, and their pious cult—but which it spurned after the incarnation of the mediator between God and man, not wishing to accept his Gospel—to the holy Church for its full use, so that it may possess all spiritual riches and may become the most upright guardian of all virtues?[104]

Likewise, the golden sword given to Judas the Macca-bee by Jeremiah (II Macc. 15:15-16) had been passed on to the *doctores,* who would use this gift—Scripture and its spiritual meaning—to defend the Church.[105] His own sword in this particular battle was allegory, but this rested on historical foundations he tried to make as sound as possible, according to Augustine's instruc-tions: 'History narrates facts faithfully and usefully.'[106] Many histories, also those of the *gentes,* could be help-ful in understanding the sacred books.

Hrabanus' prefatory letter to Gerolt clearly expressed his views on the various types of history he had dealt with in his commentary on Maccabees:

> For the rest I also want your Saintliness to know that I have fashioned this work partly from divine history, partly from the tradition of Josephus the historian of the Jews, and partly from the history of other peoples, for in this book not only the people of the Jews and their princes, but also those of other peoples [*aliarum gentium*] are mentioned, so the truth of sacred history will appear through the combination of many books and the meaning of its narration may become more clear to the reader.[107]

It was the truth of biblical history and the spiritual meaning of its narrative (*sensum narrationis*) which mattered most. None the less, the royal recipients of Hrabanus' commentary had to cope with long historical digressions, for which the key sources were Justinus' *Epitome* of Pompeius Trogus, Sulpicius Severus' *Chronicon,* Eusebius' *Ecclesiastical History* in Rufinus' translation, the *Chronicon* of Eusebius/Jerome, Bede's *Chronicon* and, above all, Flavius Josephus' *Antiqui-tates Iudaeorum.*[108] Hrabanus heavily leaned on Jose-phus in his historical exegesis of Maccabees as a substitute of Jerome, the *sacra historiae interpres* who was his usual model for historical commentary, but his work on Esther and Judith also opens with an extensive historical background drawn from secular historiogra-phy. Given the shaky factual basis of these books, he predictably ran into trouble. Some might ask, he said, at which time and under which kings the *historia Iudith* had been written, all the more since the two kings mentioned in Judith—Arphaxad of the Medes and Neb-uchadnezzar of the Assyrians—were nowhere to be found in the lists of rulers of these peoples.[109] This led him into a potted version of the history of ancient peoples in order to uncover the 'historical truth' for his reader, but also into a chronological quagmire: an As-syrian king who should be a Babylonian. Eusebius had offered a way out by suggesting that the Persian king Cambyses had been called a second Nebuchadnezzar by the Jews, but this still left Hrabanus with sacred history saying that he was an Assyrian king conquering a Mede, which ran against all his notions of ancient chronology. Possibly there had been a time when the realms of the

Assyrians and the Persians had been united, with Cam-byses gaining victory over a Medan king Arphaxad—but 'to this opinion I do not want to lead anyone against their will. Let everyone select from this what seems useful as long as it does not contradict the spiritual meaning of biblical truth.'[110] He faced similar problems when it came to identifying King Assuerus. Was he Cyrus, as Josephus suggested, or Artaxerxes, as Euse-bius had it? Hrabanus settled for Eusebius' explanation, all the more because Ezra never mentioned the story of Esther.[111]

While grappling with biblical chronology, Hrabanus did not exclude Scripture from a measure of historical criti-cism and analytical scrutiny. Of course he ultimately believed that the Evangelical Truth was the author of the two Testaments,[112] but he also actively engaged in a running debate with the *scriptor historiae,* the author of the biblical book he was commenting on, explaining why 'he' wrote as he did and why he might possibly be somewhat confused in his rendering of sacred history. His constant analysis of the way in which 'the writer of this history' had structured his narrative could even to the Acts of the Apostles,[113] but it occurs most frequently in the commentary on Old Testament books.[114] At times he was simply dissatisfied with biblical narrative, concluding that important facts were omitted, or that the author of Maccabees called Alexander 'the first king' or Judas Maccabeus the 'tenth priest' for no good reason whatsoever.[115] Sacred history of course had its own laws. The beginning of the first book of Macca-bees was incongruous, for it started with '*Et factum est*', which was not a real beginning: one would expect something in front of this conjunctive sentence (*sermo coniunctionis*). Hrabanus compared this with Ezekiel, which had a similar opening, and concluded that prophets and authors of divine history viewed things from the perspective of spiritual meaning and therefore perceived 'presence' where human ignorance could only see 'absence'.[116] On the other hand his analysis of the relation between the first and second book of Macca-bees much resembles scholarly (and literary) criticism. The second book is shorter and has a different begin-ning, Hrabanus explained, but this does not destroy the *historica veritas,* for although it contains much of what is mentioned in the first book, it also adds new informa-tion left out earlier because of the 'haste of the narrator'.[117]

It is in this patently historical narrative about the Mac-cabees that Hrabanus relied most heavily on Flavius Jo-sephus, to the extent that he inserted entire or abbrevi-ated sections from the *Antiquitates,* and constantly compared Josephus' narrative and that of the *historiae gentium,* with that of the *scriptor praesentis historiae,* the author of his biblical text.[118] 'The author of the earlier book of this history' and 'Josephus in the twelfth book of his Jewish Antiquity' sometimes seem to be treated on a par, as two equally reliable sources supporting Hrabanus' explanation of II Maccabees.[119] Clearly Hrabanus had access to a copy of the *Antiquitates,* though he must also have encountered parts of this text in Jerome's work. Josephus held a privileged position, for he offered an alternative version of Jewish history which might throw light on biblical narrative. To Hrabanus, Josephus was the *historiographus Iudaeorum*[120] or *Hebraeorum doctissimus.*[121] In his commentary on Maccabees, Hrabanus introduced an extensive passage from the *Antiquitates* as follows:

> What Josephus has to say here does not seem unworthy to be inserted into this work; and it should not hinder the reader if the narrations from different histories are compared, for in combination they seem to enhance each other, to explain the chronological order of the matter and to uncover the truth at a historical level.[122]

In his historical exegesis Hrabanus operated much like a historian, comparing his sources, checking one against the other and being explicit about the problems he encountered. At this level the biblical text was just as much *historia* as Josephus, and therefore subject to criticism. All this was just the jumping board, however, for the actual aim of the operation: making 'sense' of the narrative, that is, spiritual sense. As Hrabanus wrote to the Empress Judith: 'We have explained what has come to us from the source of the Jews in an allegorical fashion.'[123] Hrabanus' typology was dominated by a set cast of characters.[124] The *ecclesia* and her *sponsus,* Jesus Christ, dominated the scene, aided by the ubiquitous *sancti doctores* and *praedicatores* guarding the salvation of the Christian people; on the other side stood the Old Enemy, supported by the Antichrist and a perfidious army of the *pagani, heretici, schismatici* and *Judaei,* who together formed the *persecutores ecclesiae.* This typology ran along predictable lines, but the casting was not always simple. If Esther was the *typus* of the *sancta ecclesia,* who else, within the limits of this biblical narrative, could then be her bridegroom but King Assuerus?[125] Hrabanus realized that some might object to associating Jesus Christ with a king devoted to food, drink and a large harem, so he took his time to explain that other *typi* of Christ (Moses, Aaron, David, Saul, Solomon, Hesekiah, St Peter) were not exactly free from shortcomings either.[126] *Mutatis mutandis,* a reprehensible king who none the less had some virtues could also serve as the figure of Christ. Once the two lead roles were firmly in place, the rest of the casting went according to plan: Queen Vashti banished from the presence of the king stood for the synagogue;[127] Mordechai for the *doctores gentium* and preachers of the gospel, particularly Paul;[128] the eunuch Egeus for the *pastorum ordo castissimus;*[129] the two other eunuchs for the Scribes and Pharisees, or, alternatively, for the heretics and schismatics;[130] Haman, of course, for the

Spiritual Enemy of the Christian people, leader of the persecutors of the Church,[131] but also for the arrogance of secular princes.[132]

A detailed analysis of Hrabanus' exegetical methods exceeds the scope of this article. None the less, I offer some preliminary comments on the possible contemporary resonance of his biblical scholarship to a ninth-century royal audience. Needless to say, Hrabanus stuck to the *vestigia maiorum:* the ubiquitous army of heretics and schismatics pervading his commentary was derived from an inherited typology. Moreover, there is nothing surprising about early medieval clerics being more intransigent about heretics, the perfidious insiders who should have known better, than about pagans or Jews. Yet Hrabanus' invective about perfidious *heretici* may have had a special resonance in the 830s, when these commentaries were written. Possibly Hrabanus' personal battle with one particular heretic had an impact as well: Gottschalk, the former child oblate who left Fulda in 829 under a cloud.[133] Hrabanus' typology of the *viri impii et iniqui ex Israel, et Alcimus dux eorum* as those who relapse into apostasy after having embraced the faith, led on by heretics,[134] need not have been too specific, but his vitriolic remark about 'those who nowadays refuse to accept ecclesiastical discipline, and abominate those who try to eliminate their evil, making accusations against them with the secular powers, in order to convert the latter to hatred of them and to incite them to persecution' sounds as if he had contemporary adversaries on his mind.[135] The shockwaves of the conflict with Gottschalk in 829 reached the highest circles, for Hrabanus appealed to Louis the Pious; after his departure from Fulda the rebellious monk went to Corbie and Reims, where he took part in a public theological debate in the presence of the emperor himself.[136] Before Eberhard of Friuli took him under his wing in the early 840s, there doubtless were other *saeculi potestates* who lent their ear to the brilliant and wayward theologian.[137] Some of Hrabanus' frustration about the success of his wayward former pupil may have ended up in his commentary on Maccabees. Yet personal controversy does not entirely account for his shrill insistence on the evils of heretics and schismatics. In his typology he developed the image of social cohesion and purity (the *ecclesia* and her *praedicatores*) besieged by the forces of disruption and rebellion (*heretici* and *schismatici*).[138] Onto this typological drama of good and evil contemporary anxieties about disorder in the realm could be projected. Once the enemy was known as a 'heretic' according to the *sensus narrationis* of sacred history, a strategy of *diffamatio* Could begin. The 'them' and 'us' of Old Testament history, translated into a clear-cut typology, empowered the classification and domination of seemingly uncontrollable forces of evil and disorder. Typology, with its unmistakable cast of saviours and antagonists, could thus serve as an immutable and fixed universe, in which the confusing events of the present could be located and subdued.

Hrabanus' contemporaries were capable of grasping implicit and specific meanings which have become elusive to the modern reader, for the commentator used the restricted code of allegory and typology. This allowed him to say the unspeakable by appealing to biblical associations which came readily to mind. Historians like Hincmar and the author of the Annals of Fulda did the same when they wrote about Charles the Bald's corpse stinking so badly that his army could no longer stand it. Those who knew their Maccabees thought 'Antiochus!', and those who knew Hrabanus' commentary on Maccabees thought 'Antichrist!'.[139] The ability to determine the *sensus narrationis*, the spiritual reading of Scripture, was a powerful weapon within an elite used to the language of typology. Hrabanus was well aware of this: Judas' sword (II Macc. 15:15-16) was given 'with divine Scripture glittering with spiritual meaning' to the *doctores*, to strengthen the Church and defend the people committed to them.[140] In fact, 'spiritual understanding' was one of the key issues of Hrabanus' exegesis of Maccabees: he deftly wielded the sword of allegory to defend the validity of this very method. The insistence on the superiority of spiritual over 'carnal' understanding of Scripture was as old as the very beginnings of allegorical exegesis, but the endurance of such themes does not necessarily detract from their actuality. The central notion that shaped Carolingian political ideology and identity, *correctio*, hinged upon two aspects: a correct (that is, spiritual) understanding of Scripture and a correct liturgy. Hence, biblical interpretation and the *cultus divinus* were politically loaded issues which Hrabanus did not skirt in his commentary written for a court audience.

It was the spiritual exegesis which turned the history of the Old Israel into that of the New, and that of the synagogue into that of the *ecclesia*. For this very reason Old Testament history could never be complete without its spiritual interpretation, which made 'their' history into 'ours'. The transforming power of allegory was highlighted in Hrabanus' exegesis of the request by Judas Maccabeus of a peaceful passing through enemy territory from the people of Efron.[141] He compared Judas with the 'saintly preachers' who said: 'Let us read the history of your books, so that through its allegorical meaning we may find our promised fatherland in heaven; and nobody will hurt you, because our passing will not be harmful to you.'[142] Not only Jews, but also heretics fell into the error of understanding 'carnally': in fact, this was the central defining characteristic of heresy. Those in Efron resisting Judas signified *haeretici* who followed the letter of the Old Testament, refusing access to a spiritual understanding of Scripture. Efron represented empty adherence to the law in times of

grace, and for those who, lost in darkness, opposed the preachers of the gospel with the weapon of historical tradition;[143] Judas stood for the *doctores sancti* who gave their audience the free road of intelligence into Scripture, allowing everyone access to truth according to their needs—be it tropological, allegorical or anagogical.[144] If like Judas we want to be in possession of God's law and its spoils (*spolia*), i.e. the different levels of understanding of Scripture, we should first get rid of the superficiality of literal interpretation, Hrabanus contended. This theme crops up time and again in his commentary on Maccabees, obviously within a Pauline frame of reference,[145] but also with a vehemence suggesting that Hrabanus was involved in a contemporary debate.

Ultimately, two interconnected issues were at stake: the spiritual understanding of Scripture and the proper *cultus divinus*. Both underpinned the social order, as is clear from Hrabanus' diatribe against gentile philosophers and Christian heretics and schismatics attacking the 'truth of Christ's Law' (*veritas legis Christi*), and to whom the 'divine cult and Christian religion' were an affront. The more they attempted to lead others into error, the more they induced them to discord, for they were incapable of concord themselves.[146] Just as Assuerus could be the 'type' of Christ, Antiochus' letter ordering all in his realm to follow the same law (I Macc. 1:41-2) could have a positive meaning. After all, uniformity was something Hrabanus was strongly in favour of when it came to Frankish law;[147] he deftly managed to turn this biblical text about hostile unification into a diatribe against discord. Given the Carolingian ideology of *concordia*—and its concomitant horror of strife (*discordia*)—these words have an unmistakable resonance extending to the political and social domain. Yet there was more at stake: 'correct liturgy' itself defined the boundaries of the truly Christian society. The decrees of the Antichrist, Antiochus IV, ordered the Jews to follow the *leges gentium* in cultic matters, 'and therefore these [laws] also defined the holocausts and sacrifices and *placationes* to be made in the Temple of the Lord'; Hrabanus again read this passage in terms of the dichotomy between carnal and spiritual, explaining that the 'pagans and heretics' were out to keep the faithful from the offer (*holocaustum*) of love in the secrecy of their heart, from the mystical sacrifice of the body and blood of the Lord sustained by prayer and good works, and from the Sabbath, that is, future eternal rest in the celestial kingdom.[148] Antiochus' onslaught on the Temple was that of all those attacking the cult of the one God (*cultus unius Dei*), and God's house, the *sancta ecclesia*.[149]

The notion of the *cultus unius Dei* or *cultus divinus* under threat is as much part of the language of Carolingian capitularies and conciliar decrees as of the rhetoric of biblical commentary.[150] The restoration of the Temple and all it entailed—including reform of the clergy—was central to the Carolingian reform programme. In this biblically inspired re-ordering of the realm the king operated as the protector of the cult, safeguarding its unity and correctness—which is precisely what Carolingian rulers from Pippin III onwards set out to do. This meant that political boundaries were also cultic boundaries. Wherever the limits of this Christian polity were reached, the *confusio* of heresy, paganism, idolatry and Judaism began.

The empire as the *ecclesia,* and vice versa—this was the framework of Hrabanus' exegesis. The concomitant sacralization of political unity might lead to uproar over any subsequent *divisio imperii,* as happened in 833, but it also had the potential of transcending incidental division and strife. Within this vision of a united *ecclesia* clerical leadership inevitably took centre stage, as did the *sancti praedicatores/doctores* in Hrabanus' commentary. Yet the image of King Josiah who found the law and corrected his people was still a valid one in the 830s, certainly to loyal Hrabanus. The cooperation between King Demetrius and Jonathan (I Macc. 11: 41) elicited a clear comment on how the Carolingian *ecclesia* should function. The 'saintly doctors' and the 'rulers of the *gentes*' were mutually dependent: neither order could perform its ministry without the aid of the other. In other words, no preaching of the faith was possible without rulers dominating those to be converted, and no hope of eternal salvation could be held out by rulers to their subjects without proper instruction by *magistri.*[151] This might be read as a statement about the tactics of mission, but also as a programme for collaboration of rulers and clergy within the realm itself: kings should discipline their peoples and promise them salvation, but they were helpless without assistance from their ecclesiastical *fideles.*

The precariousness of a realm held together by, and defined in terms of the 'divine cult' was also the topic of Hrabanus' exegesis of the *historia* of Maccabees, and, albeit to a lesser extent, of his interpretation of the *historiae* of Judith and Esther. For this very reason his work was eminently relevant to its royal recipients: Hrabanus showed how sacred history about the cultic unity of the past prefigured the contemporary *ecclesia*—that is, Carolingian Christendom. To the diligent and well-trained reader, the perils of the 'prior people' signified and illuminated the hazards of the present. This was the *sensus narrationis* he wished his royal patrons to grasp.

Notes

1. Hrabanus Maurus, *Epistolae,* 49, ed. E. Dümmler, *MGH Epp.* [*Monumenta Germaniae Historica, Epistolae*] 5 (Berlin, 1899), p. 503. About the lec-

tionary for Emperor Lothar, see R. Etaix, 'L'homéliaire composé par Raban Maur pour l'empereur Lothaire', *Recherches Augustiniennes* 19 (1984) pp. 211-40. Hrabanus' letters have been preserved mostly as prefatory letters to his writings, or as separate treatises: see Hrabanus, *Epistolae,* pp. 381-516. The abbey of Fulda's collection of letters is now lost, but it was used by Flacius Illyricus and his collaborators when in 1559-74 they produced the first comprehensive Lutheran church history; see H. Scheible, *Die Entstehung der Magdeburger Zenturien* (Gütersloh, 1966). Their quotations from the letter collection were added by E. Dümmler as an appendix to his edition of Hrabanus' letters: *Epistolarum Fuldensium fragmenta ex octava nona et decima centuriis ecclesiasticae historiae, MGH Epp.* 5, pp. 517-33. Hrabanus' work was edited by G. Colvenerius, *Hrabani Mauri opera quae reperiri potuerant omnia. Collecta J. Pamelii. Nunc vero in lucem emissa Antonii de Henen, Episcopo Iprensis, ac studia et opera Georgii Colvenerii* (2 vols., Cologne, 1627). This edition has been followed by most of Migne *PL* [*Patrologia cursus completus, series Latina*] 107-112.

2. Hrabanus, *Epistolae,* 49, p. 503, ll. 38-41: 'Siquidem bene novit vestra paternitas omnem nos commentariorum copiam, in quibus iuxta gestarum rerum ordinem et expositionem prefate continentur lectiones, in cunctis expedicionibus non posse semper gerere et habere, cum sola historiarum bibliotheca difficile possit etiam haberi plerumque.'

3. M. Duchet-Suchaux and Y. Lefèvre, 'Les noms de la Bible', in P. Riché and G. Lobrichon (eds.), *Le Moyen Age et la Bible* (Paris, 1984), pp. 13-23.

4. I expressed my doubts about this interpretation in M. De Jong, 'The Emperor Lothar and his *Bibliotheca Historiarum*', in R. H. A. Nip, H. van Dijk, E. M. C. van Harts, C. H. Kneepkens and G. A. A. Kortekaas (eds.), *Media Latininas. A Collection of Essays to Mark the Retirement of L. J. Engels.* Instrumenta patristica 28 (Turnhout, 1996), pp. 229-35. J. P. Gumbert, arguing that both *historia* and *bibliotheca* could designate Scripture (I could not agree more, and said so in my article), countered that 'we should no doubt assume that this book, which should be taken everywhere, although with great difficulty, was simply the book which might also be referred to as 'bibliotheca' or 'historia': a (probably Turonian) Bible in one volume' (trans. by the present author): J. P. Gumbert, 'Egberts geschenken aan Egmond', in G. N. M. Vis (ed.), *In het spoor van Egbert. Aartsbisschop Egbert van Trier, de bibliotheek en geschied-*

schrijving van het klooster Egmond (Hilversum, 1997), p. 39. Gumbert's conclusion bypasses the issue I raised, i.e. whether the highly unusual combination of *bibliotheca* and *historiae* (plural!) might have a more specific meaning. As far as I can see Hrabanus did not use the expression *bibliotheca* for Scripture, but quite regularly for 'library' or 'collection of books'. Cf. Hrabanus, *Commentaria in libros IV Regum,* II, c. 1, PL 109, col. 72B; Hrabanus, *De Rerum Naturis,* c. 4, PL 111, cols. 121C, 405A.

5. For a basic, but very incomplete list of manuscripts of Hrabanus' biblical commentary, see F. Stegmüller, *Repertorium Biblicum Medii Aevi* 5 (Madrid, 1955), pp. 7-37 (nos. 7019-87); see also H. Spelsberg, *Hrabanus Maurus Bibliographie,* Veröffentlichungen der Hessischen Landesbibliothek Fulda, 4 (Fulda, 1984), for a list of works and editions. A substantial part of Hrabanus' exegetical work remains unedited: see R. Kottje, 'Hrabanus Maurus', *Die deutsche Literatur des Mittelalters. Verfasserlexikon* 4 (1983), cols. 173-4. Burton Edwards's unpublished bibliography of Carolingian exegesis (an ongoing project, now accessible on the Internet) lists more than 280 manuscripts for Hrabanus; Kottje, 'Hrabanus Maurus', col. 167 mentions a total of more than 1200 manuscripts (until the sixteenth century) for Hrabanus' entire *œuvre;* however, Professor Kottje kindly informed me that he now estimates this number to be closer to 1500. For Hrabanus' commentary on Kings, Jeremiah, Matthew and Romans alone, his list of manuscripts contains 124 items (letter of 4 March 1998). An excellent example of the technical kind of research still to be undertaken for Hrabanus' biblical commentary is that of M. Gorman on various Carolingian biblical commentators; see, *inter alia,* M. Gorman, 'The encyclopedic commentary on Genesis prepared for Charlemagne by Wigbod', *Recherches Augustiniennes* 17 (1982), pp. 173-201; 'Wigbod and biblical studies under Charlemagne', *Revue Bénédictine* 107 (1997), pp. 40-76; 'The commentary on Genesis of Claudius of Turin and biblical studies under Louis the Pious', *Speculum* 72 (1997), pp. 279-329. An exemplary treatment of biblical commentary in relation to political thought is provided by G. E. Caspary, *Politics and Exegesis. Origin and the Two Swords* (Berkeley, Los Angeles and London, 1979). This model has inspired P. Buc, who combines manuscript work and historical analysis in *L'Ambiguïté du Livre. Princes, pouvoirs et peuple dans les commentaires de la Bible au Moyen Age,* Théologie historique 95 (Paris, 1994), which treats the period from 1150 to 1350; see also P. Buc, 'David's adultery with Bathseba

and the healing powers of Capetian kings', *Viator* 23 (1993), pp. 101-20.

6. Hrabanus' biblical commentary has none the less attracted a lot of interest: J. Hablitzel, 'Hrabanus Maurus. Ein Beitrag zur Geschichte der mittelalterlichen Exegese', *Biblische Studien* 11/3 (1906), pp. 1-105; B. Blumenkranz, 'Raban Maur et Saint Augustin. Compilation ou adaptation? A propos du Latin Biblique', *Revue du Moyen Age Latin* 7 (1951), pp. 97-110; H. Butzmann, 'Der Ezechiel-Kommentar des Hrabanus Maurus und seine älteste Handschrift', *Bibliothek und Wissenschaft* 1 (1964), pp. 1-22; H. Reinelt, 'Hraban als Exeget', in W. Böhne (ed.), *Hrabanus und seine Schule* (Fulda, 1980), pp. 64-76; E. A. Matter, 'The lamentations commentaries of Hrabanus Maurus and Paschasius Radbertus', *Traditio* 38 (1982), pp. 137-63; F. Brunhölzl, 'Zur geistigen Bedeutung des Hrabanus Maurus', in R. Kottje and H. Zimmermann (eds.), *Hrabanus Maurus. Lehrer, Abt und Bischof* (Mainz, 1982), pp.1-17; Philippe Le Maitre, 'Les méthodes exégétiques de Raban Maur', in M. Sot (ed.), *Haut Moyen-Age. Culture, éducation et société. Etudes offertes à Pierre Riché* (Paris, 1990), pp. 343-52; R. Savigni, 'L'interpretazione dei libri sapienziali in Rabano Mauro: tradizione patristica e "moderna tempora"', *Annali di storia dell'esegesi* 9 (1992), pp. 557-87; R. Savigni, 'Instanze ermeneutiche e redifinizione del canone in Rabano Mauro: il commentario ai Libri dei *Maccabei*', *Annali di storia dell'esegesi* 11 (1994), pp. 571-604; M. De Jong, 'Old law and new-found power: Hrabanus Maurus and the Old Testament', in J. W. Drijvers and A. A. MacDonald (eds.), *Centres of Learning. Learning and Location in Pre-Modern Europe and the Near East* (Leiden, New York and Cologne, 1995), pp. 161-76; D. Appleby, 'Rudolf, Abbot Hrabanus and the Ark of the Covenant Reliquary', *The American Benedictine Review* 46 (1995), pp. 419-43; M.-A. Aris, *'Nostrum est citare testes.* Anmerkungen zum Wissenschaftsverständniss des Hrabanus Maurus', in G. Schrimpf (ed.), *Kloster Fulda in der Welt der Karolinger und Ottonen,* Fuldaer Studien 7 (Frankfurt, 1996), pp. 437-64.

7. See above, n. 5; for an introduction to Carolingian biblical studies, see R. E. McNally, *The Bible in the Early Middle Ages* (Westminster, 1959); P. Riché, 'Divina pagina, ratio et auctoritas dans la théologie Carolingienne', in *Settimane* 27 (1981), pp. 719-58; J. J. Contreni, 'Carolingian biblical studies', in U.-R. Blumbenthal (ed.), *Carolingian Essays: Andrew W. Mellon Lectures in Early Christian Studies* (Washington, DC, 1983), pp. 71-98 [reprinted in J. J. Contreni, *Carolingian*

Learning, Masters and Manuscripts (Aldershot, 1992), ch. 5]; J. J. Contreni, 'Carolingian biblical culture', in G. van Riel, C. Steel and J. McEvoy (eds.), *Iohannes Scottus Eriugena. The Bible and Hermeneutics. Proceedings of the Ninth International Colloquium of the Society for the Promotion of Eriugenian Studies,* Ancient and Medieval Philosophy, De Wulf-Mansion Centre, series 1/20 (Louvain, 1996), pp. 1-23.

8. Hrabanus, *Epistolae,* 34, p. 468 (to Louis the German, *c.* 842-6); see also another letter from this period to the same king, ibid., 37, pp. 472-3, ll. 41-2: 'et si aliquid in eo dignum emendatione repertum fuerit, cum vestris sagacissimis lectoribus, prout ratio dicat, illud emendare curetis'.

9. Ibid., p. 505, ll. 35-9: 'Iubete illud coram vobis legi et si quid in eo propter tenuitatem sensus mei non rite prolatum vel scriptorum vitio depravatum conspexeritis, per vestros eruditos lectores facite illud corrigi, et sic vobis merces condigna pro vestro bono certamine et nostra simul correctione a Christo omnium domino perpetualiter recompensabitur in caelis.' See J. Fleckenstein, 'Über Hrabanus Maurus. Marginalien zum Verhältnis von Gelehrsamkeit und Tradition im 9. Jahrhundert', in N. Kamp and J. Wollasch (eds.), *Tradition als historische Kraft. Interdisziplinäre Forschungen zur Geschichte des früheren Mittelalters* (Berlin and New York, 1989) pp. 204-13, esp. p. 212; De Jong, 'Old law', pp. 164-6.

10. This also explains why Hrabanus was worried that the *lector* might leave out essential information, such as the names of authoritative authors that he had dutifully marked in the margin; if the *lector* did so, Hrabanus warned, the listener (*auditor*) might get confused; cf. Hrabanus, *Epistolae,* 23, p. 429 (to Lupus of Ferrières).

11. Ibid, 38 and 49, pp. 469-70 and 503.

12. Ibid., 39, p. 477; De Jong, 'Old law', pp. 173-4.

13. Thegan, *Vita Hludowici,* c. 19, ed. E. Tremp, *Thegan, Die Taten Kaiser Ludwigs, MGH SRG* [*Scriptores rerum Germanicarum*] 64 (Hanover, 1995), p. 200: 'Sensum vero in omnibus scripturis spiritalem et moralem, nec non anagogen optime novererat. Poetica carmina gentilia quae in iuventute didicerat, respuit, nec legere, nec audire, nec docere voluit.'

14. J. L. Nelson, 'History-writing at the courts of Louis the Pious and Charles the Bald', in A. Scharer and G. Scheibelreiter (eds.), *Historiographie im frühen Mittelalter,* Veröffentlichungen des Instituts für Österreichische Geschichtsforschung 32 (Vienna, 1994), pp. 435-42, at p. 435.

15. See M. Innes's contribution to this volume, chapter 10. The opposition between biblical exegesis and *poetica carmina gentilia* suggests equally biblical overtones in the expression '*gentilis*', in the sense of *gentes* which are not yet part of a Christian *conversatio*. Thegan's most recent editor, Ernst Tremp, does translate the passage as 'pagan songs', but suggests (p. 201, n. 101) that it might also mean 'germanische Heldenlieder', comparing this expression with Alcuin's renunciation of pagan classical texts (*Vita Alcuini,* c. 16, ed. W. Arndt, *MGH* 15/1 (Hanover, 1887), p. 193), and with Alcuin's celebrated pronouncement: 'Verbi Dei legantur in sacerdotali convivio. Ibi decet lectorem audiri, non citharistam; sermones patrum, non carmina gentilium. Quid Hieneldus cum Christo?' (Alcuin, *Epistolae,* 124, ed. E. Dümmler, *MGH Epp.* 4 (Berlin, 1895), p. 183). The latter passage also points to a concern with Christian *conversatio* at the court, which should be oriented towards sacred texts rather than towards more traditional forms of conviviality.

16. About the Carolingian image of the *rex sapiens* and its consequences for royal involvement in theological debates, see N. Staubach, *Rex christianus. Hofkultur und Herrschaftspropaganda im Reich Karls des Kahlen, II: Die Grundlegung der 'religion royale',* Pictura et poesis 2 (Cologne, Weimar and Vienna, 1993), pp. 21-104 (and p. 12, n. 45, about biblical commentary for rulers and royal preference for allegory).

17. Thegan, *Vita Hludowici,* c. 7, pp. 184-6: 'Postquam divisi fuerant [i.e. Charlemagne and Louis], domnus imperator nihil coepit agere, nisi in orationibus et elemosinis vacare, et libros corrigere; et quattuor evangelia Christi, quae praetitulantur nomine Mathei, Marci, in ultimo ante obitus sui diem cum Grecis et Siris optime correxerat.'

18. K. F. Werner, 'Gott, Herrscher und Historiograph. Der Geschichtsschreiber als Interpret des Wirken Gottes in der Welt und Ratgeber der Könige (4. bis 12. Jahrhundert)', in E.-H. Diehl, H. Seibert and F. Staab (eds.), *Deus qui mutat tempora. Menschen und Institutionen im Wandel des Mittelalters* (Sigmaringen, 1987), pp. 1-31; K. F. Werner, 'L'historia et les rois', in D. Iognia-Prat and J.-C. Picard (eds.), *Religion et culture autour de l'An Mil* (Paris, 1990), pp. 135-42. Also H.-W. Goetz, *Das Geschichtsbild Ottos von Freising,* Beihefte zum Archiv für Kulturgeschichte 19 (Cologne and Vienna, 1984), pp. 78-86; H.-W. Goetz, 'Die "Geschichte" im Wissenschaftssystem des Mittelalters', in F.-J. Schmale, *Funktion und Formen mittelalterlicher Geschichtsschreibung* (Darmstadt, 1985), pp. 165-213. About medieval

notions of *historia,* see A. Seifert, 'Historia im Mittelalter', *Archiv für Begriffsgeschichte* 21 (1977), pp. 226-84; J. Knape, *'Historie' im Mittelalter und früher Neuzeit. Begriffs- und gattungsgeschichtliche Untersuchungen im interdisziplinären Kontext,* Saecula spiritalia 10 (Baden-Baden, 1984); H.-W. Goetz, 'Die Gegenwart der Vergangenheit im früh- und hochmittelalterlichen Geschichtsbewusstsein', *Historische Zeitschrift* 255 (1992), pp. 61-97.

19. On this topic, see M. Heinzelmann, *Gregor von Tours (538-594): 'Zehn Bücher Geschichte'. Historiographie und Gesellschaftskonzept im 6. Jahrhundert* (Darmstadt, 1994), pp. 32-83.

20. In a similar vein: N. Staubach, 'Christiana tempora. Augustin und das Ende der alten Geschichte in der Weltchronik Frechulfs von Lisieux', *Frühmittelalterliche Studien* 29 (1996), pp. 167-206, at p. 196, n. 112; M. Innes and R. McKitterick, 'The writing of history', in R. McKitterick (ed.), *Carolingian Culture: Emulation and Innovation* (Cambridge, 1994), pp. 193-220, at pp. 215-16.

21. R. A. Markus, *Saeculum: History and Society in the Theology of St Augustine* (Cambridge, 1970), pp. 1-21.

22. Ardo Smaragdus, *Vita Benedicti abbatis Anianensis,* prol., ed. O. Holder-Egger, *MGH* [*Scriptores*] 15, 2 (Hanover, 1887), p. 201; trans. Nelson, 'History-writing', p. 435.

23. Innes and McKitterick, 'The writing of history', p. 215.

24. Staubach, 'Christiana tempora', pp. 177-8.

25. Freculph of Lisieux, *Chronicon, PL* 106, cols. 917-1258, at cols. 907-8, 1115-16.

26. Staubach, 'Christiana tempora', *passim.*

27. Freculph, Preface to Helisachar, ed. E. Dümmler, *Epistolae variorum* 13, *MGH Epp.* 5, ll. 19-20 (also *PL* 106, col. 917): 'iussisti ut perscrutando diligenter volumina antiquorum seu agiographorum sive etiam gentilium scriptorum, quaeque pertinent ad historiae veritatem, breviter ac ludice colligere desudarem, a conditione quidem primi hominis usque ad Christi nativitatem domini: eo scilicet modo, ut quicquid de primo saeculo, quod ante generalem fuerat cataclismum, sive de secundo, quod fit post diluvium usque ad nativitatem Abrahae, et regis Assyriorum Nini regnum, nostri sive gentiles senserunt scriptores, pandere diligentius curarem. Quaestiones etiam difficiles, quae per haec tempora in scriptis habentur legislatoris, enodare non negligere, quantum attinet ad historiae veritatem.'

28. J. L. Nelson, 'Public histories and private history in the work of Nithard', *Speculum* 60 (1985), pp. 251-93 [reprinted in J. L. Nelson, *Politics and Ritual in Early Medieval Europe* (London, 1986), pp. 195-237]. Nelson later criticized her own use of the public/private opposition, arguing that history might be court-oriented without necessarily being official: Nelson, 'History-writing', pp. 439-42.

29. Cf. Nelson, 'History-writing', p. 439. Also R. McKitterick, 'Constructing the past in the early Middle Ages: the case of the Royal Frankish Annals', *Transactions of the Royal Historical Society* 7 (1997), pp. 101-29.

30. For a discussion of possible royal tolerance of criticism, revising her earlier view on this matter, see Nelson, 'History-writing', pp. 438-42; for an illuminating discussion of a royal and aristocratic interest in biblically inspired *sapientia* on the one hand and a dearth of contemporary court historiography on the other, see J. L. Nelson, 'Charles le Chauve et les utilisations du savoir', in D. Iogna-Prat, C. Jeudy and G. Lobrichon, *L'Ecole Carolingienne d'Auxerre de Muretach à Rémi, 830-908. Entretiens d'Auxerre 1989* (Paris, 1991), pp. 37-54. Nelson stresses that during the reign of Charles the Bald this royal and aristocratic *sapientia utilis* was expressed in capitularies rather than in historiography.

31. *Admonitio Generalis,* Prologue, *MGH Cap* [*Capitularia regum Francoram*] 1, ed. A. Boretius (Hanover, 1883), p. 54, ll. 2-4: 'Nam legimus in regnorum libri, quomodo sanctus Iosias regnum sibi a Deo datum circumeundo, corrigendo, ammonendo ad cultum veri Dei studuit revocare . . .'

32. Contreni, 'Carolingian biblical culture', p. 3.

33. Charlemagne already appreciated for allegorical commentary, his son Louis the Pious and his grandsons had a preference for it, a development culminating in Charles the Bald's predilection for John Scotus Eriguena; see Staubach, *Rex christianus,* p. 12, n. 45 and pp. 41-104; Gorman, 'Wigbod and biblical studies', pp. 74-6.

34. Hrabanus, *Epistolae,* 49, p. 504: 'Nam si illis Hieronimum, Augustinum, Gregorium Ambrosiumque et ceteros plurimos prebuit, et nobis idem opifex eiusdem meriti et scientiae contulit Rhabanum Maurum.' For a variation on this theme, see Notker Balbulus, *Gesta Karoli Magni* I, c. 9, ed. H. F. Haefele, *MGH SRG* n.s. 12 (Berlin, 1959), p. 12.

35. For Hrabanus' biography, see M. Sandmann, 'Hraban als Mönch, Abt und Erzbischof', *Fuldaer Geschichtsblätter* 56 (1980), pp. 133-80; furthermore,

R. Kottje, 'Hrabanus Maurus', *Die deutsche Literatur des Mittelalters. Verfasserlexikon* 4 (1983), pp. 166-96, and the excellent introduction to Hrabanus Maurus, *Martyriologium, De Computo,* ed. J. McCulloh, CCCM [*Corpus Christianorum continuatio Medievalis*] 44 (Turnhout, 1979), pp. ii-xxiv, both with extensive references to older literature. Shortly before his death in 855 Lothar entered the monastery of Prüm: J. F. Böhmer and E. Mühlbacher, *Regesta Imperii I. Die Regesten des Kaiserreiches unter den Karolingern, 751-918* (Innsbruck, 1908), p. 481, no. 1177a.

36. Aris, '*Nostrum est citare testis*', p. 437.

37. Hrabanus, *Epistolae,* 39, p. 477, ll. 21-4: 'Nec enim illud silendum arbitror, quod quibusdam narrantibus comperi, quosdam sciolos me in hoc vituperasse, quod excerptionem faciens de sanctorum patrum scriptis, eorum nomina praenotarem, sive quod aliorum sententiis magis innisus esse, quam propria conderem . . .'

38. For an analysis of Hrabanus' methods as expounded in his prefatory letters, see Le Maitre, 'Les méthodes exégétiques'; De Jong, 'Old law'; Aris, '*Nostrum est citare testes*'.

39. Hrabanus, *Epistolae,* 7, p. 392, ll. 22-4: 'vertetur occasus noster in orientem, et regio contigua axi occiduo fiet Iudea, nostrique Brittonum vicini erunt Israhelitae'.

40. *Ibid.*, 8, p. 394, ll. 4-7: 'Si quid vero gratia divina indigno mihi elucidare dignata est, in locis necessariis simul cum nota agnominis mei interposui, quatinus sciret lector, que ex patrum traditione haberet, et que ex parvitate nostra, licet sermone rustico, tamen ut credo sensu catholico exposita inveniret.'

41. *Ibid.*, 14, p. 403; 23, pp. 429-30.

42. *Ibid.*, 5, p. 390.

43. The tone is set in the prefatory letter of 819 dedicating *De Institutione Clericorum* to Bishop Haistulph of Mainz. *Ibid.*, 3, p. 386: 'Confido tamen omnipotentis Dei gratiae, quod fidem et sensum catholicum in omnibus tenerem, nec per me quasi ex me ea protuli, sed auctoritati innitens maiorum, per omnia illorum vestigia sum secutus.' See also *ibid.*, 11, p. 398, ll. 14-15; 18, p. 423, l. 24; 19, p. 424, ll. 23-4. About the expression *vestigia patrum* in Alcuin's work, see Aris, '*Nostrum est citare testes*', p. 443. Hrabanus accurately summed up his method in a letter to King Louis the German, *Epistolae,* 34, pp. 467-8, ll. 31-2: 'Unde etiam ego non de propria scientia, sed de salvatoris nostri misericordia confidens, temptavi

iuxta maiorum dicta vel sensum aliqua interponere, ubi vel minus ludice explanata, vel poenitus omissa repperi, ut si non aliorum, tamen nostrorum paupertati consulerem, qui nec multos libros habent nec diversorum auctorum codices.' About the tension between Hrabanus' wish to follow the *patres* and his need to speak out for himself, see De Jong, 'Old law', pp. 170-3.

44. Aris, '*Nostrum est citare testes*', p. 461.

45. Contreni, 'Carolingian biblical studies', pp. 85-9.

46. Hrabanus Maurus, *Carmina,* 97, ed. E. Dümmler, *MGH PLAC* [*Poetae Latini aevi Carolini*] 2 (Hanover, 1884), p. 244.

47. M. De Jong, *In Samuel's Image. Child Oblation in the Early Medieval West* (Leiden, New York and Cologne, 1996), pp. 73-7; E. Freise, *Die Anfänge der Geschichtsschreibung im Kloster Fulda,* Inaugural-Dissertation (Münster, 1979), pp. 80-4, and p. 202, n. 770.

48. Hincmar, *Ad reclusos et simplices,* ed. W. Gundlach, *Zeitschrift für Kirchengeschichte* 10 (1889), p. 262: 'Rhabanum . . . ab orthodoxo et magno doctore Alchuino in sanctae ecclesiae utilitatibus uberibus ipsius catholico lacte nutritum.'

49. D. Schaller, 'Der junge "Rabe" am Hof Karls des Grossen (Theodulf Carm. 27)', in J. Autenrieth and F. Brunhölzl (eds.), *Festschrift Bernhard Bischoff zu sienem 65. Geburtstag* (Stuttgart, 1971), pp. 123-41.

50. M. Sandmann, 'Die Folge der Äbte', in K. Schmid (ed.), *Die Klostergemeinschaft von Fulda im früheren Mittelalter,* 1, Münstersche Mittelalter-Schriften 8/1 (Munich, 1978), p. 185, with a list of Hrabanus' visits to various kings and emperors.

51. Hrabanus, *Epistolae,* 14, p. 402.

52. *Ibid.*, 18, p. 423, ll. 30-3: 'Ante annos enim aliquot rogatu Hilduini abbatis in Regum libros secundum sensum catholicorum patrum quattuor commentariorum libros edidi, quos et sacratissimo genitori vestro Hludowico imperatori presentialiter in nostro monasterio tradidi . . .' About this visit: H. P. Wehlt, *Reichsabtei und König, dargestellt am Beispiel der Abtei Lorsch, mit Ausblicken auf Hersfeld, Stablo und Fulda,* Veröffentlichungen des Max-Planck-Instituts für Geschichte 28 (Göttingen, 1970), p. 236.

53. Hrabanus, *Epistolae,* 18, p. 423, ll. 1-8: 'Fas enim erat, ut regi christianissimo et in divinis preceptis studiosissimo historia regum Iuda, hoc est confitentium cum spiritali sensu aliquantulum explanata offeretur. Nam quia populum ecclesiasticum

filii Dei pretioso sanguine redemptum et in confessione nominis Dei assuetissimum, vestra nobilis ad servitium Dei regit prudentia, ideo bene convenit piissimo principi, hoc est rectori membrorum veri regis Christi, unigeniti videlicet Dei, ritum regiminis secundum divinam scripturam habere et agere, maximentissime cum sapientia, quae in ipsis litteris maxime elucet, ammonens dicat: "Per me reges regnant et conditores legum iusta decernunt" (Prov. 8:15).'

54. Ibid., ll. 11-15: 'Accipe ergo regum priorum historiam et sensum spiritalem ad gratiam Christi pertinentem super omnia in illa amate. Lex enim Dei spiritalis est, et revelatione opus est, ut intellegatur, ac revelata facie gloriam Dei contemplemur. Unde in Apocalipsin liber septem signaculis signatus ostenditur, quem nemo aperit, nisi ille resereat qui habet clavem David, qui aperit, et nemo claudit; claudit et nemo aperit.' Cf. Apoc. 3:7: 'Those are the words of the holy one, the true one who holds the keys of David; when he opens none may shut, when he shuts none may open'.

55. Ibid., ll. 27-9: 'Non enim longos florentesque tractatus, in quibus plausibilis ludit oratio, sed commentarios in divinas historias scribere decrevi, quorum officium est preterire manifesta, obscura disserere.'

56. Ibid., ll. 37-9: 35, p. 469; ibid., 38, ll 23-6, p. 475.

57. B.-S. Albert, 'Raban Maur, l'unité de l'empire et ses relations avec les Carolingiens', *Revue d'histoire ecclésiastique* 86 (1991), pp. 5-44 (esp. pp. 9-11); E. Boshof, *Ludwig der Fromme* (Darmstadt, 1996), p. 204. It was Fulda which served as a prison for the scapegoat of the rebellion of 833, Archbishop Ebo of Reims; P. R. McKeon, 'Archbishop Ebbo of Reims: a study in the Carolingian Empire and Church', *Church History* 43 (1974), pp. 437-47, at p. 443; Boshof, *Ludwig der Fromme*, p. 211.

58. Rudolf of Fulda, *Miracula Sanctorum in Fuldenses Ecclesias Translatorum*, c. 15, ed. G. Waitz, *MGH SS* [*Scriptores*] 15/1 (Hanover, 1887), p. 341.

59. Hrabanus, *Epistolae*, 15 and 16, pp. 403-20.

60. Hrabanus, *Epistolae*, 17a, p. 421, ll. 3-8: 'Quae quidem ob insigne meritum virtutis tam viris quam etiam feminis sunt imitabiles, eo quod spiritales hostes animi vigore, et corporales consilii maturitate vicerunt. Sic et vestra nunc laudibilis prudentia, quae iam hostes suos non parva ex parte vicit, si in bono cepto perseverare atque semetipsam semper meliorare contenderit, cunctos adversarios suos feliciter superabit.' About Judith: E. Ward,

'Caesar's wife: the career of the Empress Judith, 819-829', in P. Godman and R. Collins (eds.), *Charlemagne's Heir. New Perspectives on the Reign of Louis the Pious (814-840)* (Oxford, 1990), pp. 205-37; G. Bührer-Thierry, 'La reine adultère', *Cahiers de civilisation médiévale* 35 (1992), pp. 299-312.

61. Hrabanus, *Epistolae*, 17a, p. 420, ll. 28-9: 'nos etiam quantulacumque pars plebis a Deo vobis commissae sub pietate vestra degentes . . .'

62. E. Sears, 'Louis the Pious as *Miles Christi*: the dedicatory image in Hrabanus Maurus's *De Laudibus Sancti Crucis*', in Godman and Collins (eds.), *Charlemagne's Heir*, pp. 605-28, at p. 620; M. Perrin, 'La représentation figurée de César-Louis le Pieux chez Raban Maur en 835: religion et idéologie', *Francia* 24 (1997), pp. 61-4; P. Delogu, '"Consors regni": un problema carolingo', *Bulletino dell'Instituto Storico per il Medioveo e Archivo Muratoriano* 76 (1964), pp. 85-98. I owe this last reference to Cristina La Rocca.

63. Hrabanus, *Epistolae*, 18, p. 422, ll. 30-7.

64. Ibid., p. 423, ll. 35-7.

65. Ibid., 27, pp. 441-2, ll. 27-33: 'tu tantum nostram infirmitatem sacris orationibus et piis exortationibus releves, quia non solum proprie aegritudinis molestia, verum etiam communis periculi, quod instanti tempore valde inminet, anxietate pregravatus sum. Ac ideo vestra oratione atque omnipotentis Dei misericordia maxime indigeo, ne deficiam in tribulationibus, in necessitatibus, in periculis et in temptationibus diversis.'

66. Ibid., 28, p. 444, ll. 3-5: 'Qui licet aliquid magni numquam fuerit, tamen modo longe aliud me esse sentio quam fueram: qui gravi aegritudine pressus iam saepius in lectulo accumbo, quam ad scribendum vel ad legendum in meditatorio sedeo.'

67. Ibid., pp. 443-4.

68. Ibid., p. 444.

69. Ibid., ll. 20-9: 'Et quoniam plurimorum diverse sunt voluntates et differunt ingenia vacillantque sententie, placuit mihi te unum ac solum iudicem benevolum et sapientissimum expetere, sanctissime atque augustissime imperator Hludhari, cuius mentem divina sapientia illustrans non permittit fraude invidorum corrumpi nec versutia perversorum seduci, sed in equitatis et iustitie regula conservans per viam veritatis sedulo deducit. Tibi ergo equo iudici presens opus offero, ut tuo examine ad purum probetur, et tua auctoritate contra invidos aemulorum morsus tueatur. Cum enim habuerim te propitium et benignum iudicem, pro

nihilo aliorum opiniones falsas deputo, sed tui iuris amator ac tue sancte voluntatis devotus exscecutor, fidelis tibi, Christo tribuente, quamdiu vixero, perseverabo.'

70. O. G. Oexle, 'Memorialüberlieferung und Gebetsgedächtnis in Fulda vom 8. bis zum 11. Jahrhundert', in Schmid et al. (eds.), *Die Klostergemeinschaft von Fulda im früheren Mittelalter,* pp. 164-5.

71. Rudolf, *Miracula,* c. 14, p. 339.

72. Cf. Oexle, 'Memorialüberlieferung', p. 164, n. 163; Hrabanus, *Martyriologium,* ed. McCulloh, 'Introduction', pp. xviii xix. Yet Albert, 'Raban Maur', pp. 24-8 speaks of 'la disgrâce prologée de Raban', and even of a most severe punishment, i.e. 'un exile prolongé et une démission irréversible', rejecting out of hand all suggestions that Hrabanus might have stepped down of his own accord, or at least with a minimum of fuss. Albert offers no arguments to support her view, however, and ignores all evidence pointing in the opposite direction. Hrabanus' exile a few kilometres from Fulda, with excellent relations with his successor and soon again with the ruler who 'punished' him, caused him no particular anguish. Sandmann rightly pointed out that Hrabanus remained a monk and a member of the monastic community of Fulda ('Hraban als Mönch', pp. 152-3); as Kottje ('Hrabanus Maurus', col. 169) noted, his literary production was copied out in the Fulda scriptorium and brought to its recipients by Fulda monks, which surely would not have been possible without Abbot Hatto's consent. A letter in which Hrabanus contentedly described how he sat 'quietly, far from all worldly business, in my little cell', concentrating on the study of Scripture, was most likely written during this period: Hrabanus, *Epistolae,* 40, p. 478.

73. Lupus of Ferrières, *Epistolae,* 27, ed. L. Levillain, *Loup de Ferrières, Correspondance* 1 (Paris, 1927), pp. 128-30.

74. Hrabanus, *Epistolae,* 31, p. 455, ll. 14-15: 'carissime virorum et solertissime custos gregis Dei Bonose . . .'

75. Hrabanus, *Martyrologuim,* ed. McCulloh, 'Introduction', p. xix, n. 69.

76. Hrabanus, *Epistolae,* 33, p. 465: 'Nuper quando ad vos in cellula monasterii nostri, quae vocatur Ratestorph, vocatus veni, et sermo fuit inter nos de scripturis sacris, persuadere mihi dignati estis, ut cantica, quae in matutinais laudibus sancta psallit ecclesia, vobis allegorico sensu exponerem . . .' These Canticles for Matins were all taken from the Old Testament.

77. Ibid., p. 467, ll. 12-17.

78. Cf. M. De Jong, 'Carolingian monasticism: the power of prayer', in McKitterick (ed.), *The New Cambridge Medieval History II,* pp. 622-53.

79. Hrabanus, *Epistolae,* 34, p. 468, ll. 11-13.

80. Ibid., 35, ll. 11-13, p. 470: 'Praeterito siquidem anno transmisi vobis tractatum in Danielem prophetem, quem non solum ex dictis maiorum, quin et ex nostrae parvitas sensu feceram. Nunc vero quia tempus est illud, quod apostolica sedis constituit libros Machabeorum legi in ecclesia, eorundem librorum expositionem, quam ante annos aliquot rogantibus amicis sensu historico simul et allegorico dictaveram, excellentiae vestrae defero, ut, si aliquando sensum mysticum in eis dinoscere vos delectet, habeatis in promptu, quo illum explicitum invenire valeatis: non dico valde disserte et oratione rhetorica, sed lucido sermone et catholica fide.' Given that this commentary was dedicated to King Louis after the meeting in Rasdorf, and one year after Hrabanus offered Louis his work on Daniel, *c.* 845 seems a likely date. In the mid-830s Hrabanus had already dedicated his commentary on Maccabees to Gerolt, an archdeacon of Louis the Pious; cf. ibid., 19, pp. 424-5. This dedication took place when Hrabanus had already offered Chronicles (for which Gerolt had also asked) to the younger Louis, but promised the archdeacon to 'reserve' Maccabees for him. About Gerolt: P. Lehmann, 'Corveyer Studien', in P. Lehmann, *Erforschung des Mittelalters* 5 (Stuttgart, 1959; orig. 1909), pp. 105-6; J. Fleckenstein, *Die Hofkapelle der deutschen Könige* 1, Schriften der MGH 16 (Stuttgart, 1959), pp. 65, 85; also H. Keller, 'Machabaeorum pugnae. Zum Stellenwert eines biblischen Vorbildes in Widukinds Deutung der ottonischen Königsherrschaft', in H. Keller and N. Staubach, *Iconologia sacra. Mythos, Bildkunst und Dichtung in der Religions- und Sozialgeschichte Alteuropas. Festschrift für Karl Hauck,* Arbeiten zur Frühmittelalterforschung 23 (Berlin and New York, 1994), p. 422. Gerolt entered Corvey in 847, donating a great number of books to the monastery, which possibly included Hrabanus' commentary on Maccabees. Keller thinks the commentary was written *c.* 840; I would opt for an earlier date. It seems to belong to the work produced in or shortly after 834, in the aftermath of the revolt against Louis the Pious. A careful study of the manuscripts may shed more light on this matter.

81. Hrabanus, *Epistolae,* 37, p. 472, ll. 30-1. See M. Rissel, *Rezeption antiker und patristischer Wissenschaft bei Hrabanus Maurus,* Lateinische

Sprache und Literatur des Mittelalters 7 (Frankfurt, 1976); T. Burrows, 'Holy information: a new look at Raban Maur's De naturis rerum', *Parergon* 5 (1987), pp. 28-37.

82. Hrabanus, *Epistolae*, 38, p. 476, ll. 10-12: 'Duas tibi epistolas misi, quarum una tantum est legenda, haec vero altera et legenda et in libro operis tui anteponenda.'

83. Ibid., p. 476, ll. 1-2: 'Plus enim interiorem hominem rustica montium solitudo, quam regalis urbium pulcritudo delecteat . . .' Lothar had the needs of the *homo interior* on his mind; cf. ibid., 49, p. 503, ll. 3-2.

84. Ibid., 38, p. 475.

85. B. Van Name Edwards, 'The commentary on Genesis attributed to Walahfrid Strabo: a preliminary report from the manuscripts', *Proceedings of the PMR Conference* 15 (1990), pp. 71-89. Edwards suspects that 'Hrabanus Maurus himself was responsible for the abbreviated commentary on Genesis commonly attributed to Walahfrid', and that it was this text which he sent to his imperial patron.

86. Hrabanus, *Epistolae*, 39, pp. 476-8.

87. Ibid., 46, p. 500.

88. Ibid., 28, p. 443, ll. 3-6: 'Post commentariolos, quos mea parvitas in Eptaticum et in libros Regum atque in Paralipomenon edidit, postque explanatiunculas historiarum Hesther, Iudith et Machabaeorum, necnon et voluminis Sapientiae atque Ecclesiastici aliorumque opusculorum meorum labores ad extremum in Hieremiam manum misi . . .'

89. Ibid., 35, p. 470, ll. 3-4: 'Nunc vero quia tempus est illud, quo apostolica sedis constituit libros Machabeorum legi in ecclesia . . .' (From the first Sunday in October until the first Sunday in November). Hrabanus included 'the saints of the Maccabees, seven brothers and their mother, who suffered under Antiochus' (II Macc. 7) in his Martyrologium, to be celebrated on 1 August: Hrabanus, *Martyrologium*, p. 76.

90. Hrabanus, *Epistolae*, 20, p. 426, ll. 5-9 (prefatory letter to the commentary on Wisdom, to Otgar of Mainz): 'divinae legis interpres Hieronimus dicat eundem librum apud Hebreos nusquam haberi, sed Grecam magis redolere eloquentiam, nec inter canonicas scripturas apud antiquos recepi, ut Iudith et Tobi et Machabaeorum libros, quos et moderno tempore inter scripturas sacras sancta enumerat ecclesia legitque in publico sicut ceteris scripturas canonicas . . .' (= Hieronymus, *Prologus in Libris Salomonis*, ed. R. Weber, *Biblia Sacra de He-*

braeo Translatus Iuxta Vulgatam (Stuttgart, 1969), p. 957). See also Hrabanus, *De Institutione Clericorum*, III, c. 7, ed. A. Knöpfler, *Rabani Mauri de Institutione Clericorum Libri Tres*, Veröffentlichungen aus dem kirchenhistorischen Seminar München, 5 (Munich, 1900), p. 201 (= Augustine, *De Doctrina Christiana*, ed. J. Martin, *CCSL* [*Corpus Christianorum series Latina*] 32 (Turnhout, 1962), p. 39; repeated in Hrabanus, *De Rerum Naturis* V, c. 1, PL 111, col. 105C/D). The expression 'moderno tempore' is Hrabanus' own, however; the opposition between the exegesis of 'ancient' (= patristic) and modern times (from Bede onwards) is a recurrent theme in his letters (*Epistolae*, 8, p. 393; 14, p. 403; 18, p. 423); cf. Savigni, 'L'interpretazione dei libri sapienziali'; for the expression 'modern' in Carolingian exegesis, see M. Laistner, 'Some early medieval commentaries on the Old Testament', *Harvard Theological Review* 46 (1953), pp. 29-30. About perceptions of time in Carolingian historiography, with insights valid for biblical commentary, H.-W. Goetz, 'Historiographisches Zeitbewußtsein im frühen Mittelalter. Zum Umgang mit der Zeit in der karolingischen Geschichtsschreibung', in Scharer and Scheibelreiter (eds.), *Historiographie im frühen Mittelalter*, pp. 58-78.

91. Savigni, 'Instanze ermeneutiche e redifinizione del canone'.

92. Hrabanus, *Epistolae*, 17b, p. 422, ll. 1-2, 5. Hieronymus, *Prologus Hester, Biblia Sacra*, ed. Weber, p. 712, ll. 1-2.

93. Hrabanus, *Epistolae*, 12, p. 399, l. 14; cf. also 47, p. 502, l. 8 ('iuxta modulum ingenii mei'); Hrabanus, *Commentaria in Libros Machabaeorum*, II, c. 14, col. 1254A/B: 'allegoriae autem sensus juxta modum ingenioli mei de hac eadem re ibi expositus est . . .' By 'ibi' Hrabanus refers to his commentary on the first Book of Maccabees.

94. Hrabanus, *Epistolae*, 47, p. 502, ll. 3-5. Given that at this stage he had finished the commentaries on these prophets this letter seems to date from the mid 840s or later.

95. Isidore, *Etymologiae*, I, c. 42.1, ed. W. M. Lindsay (Oxford, 1911), vol. 1: 'Historiam autem apud nos primus Moyses de intitio mundi conscripsit. Apud gentiles vero primus Dares Phrygius de Graecis et Troianis historiam edidit, quam in foliis palmarum ab eo conscriptam esse ferunt.'

96. Augustine, *De Doctrina Christiana*, II, c 8, *CCSL* 32, p. 39, ll. 28-34: 'Haec est historia, quae sibimet annexa tempora continet atque ordinem rerum; sunt aliae tamquam ex diverso ordine, quae

neque huic ordini neque inter se connectuntur, si-cut est Iob et Tobias et Esther et Iudith et Macha-baeorum libri duo et Esdrae duo, qui magis subse-qui videntur ordinatam illam historiam usque ad Regnorum vel Paralipomenon terminatam . . .' Hrabanus did not incorporate this passage into *De Institutione Clericorum;* instead, he cited Isidore's (and Jerome's) division of the Old Testament into law, prophets and historiographers. Cf. Hrabanus, *De Institutione Clericorum,* III, c. 7, p. 199; Isi-dore, *Etymologiae,* VI, 1. Cf. also Hieronymus, *Prologus in Libris Regum, Biblia Sacra,* ed. We-ber, pp. 364-6.

97. Hrabanus, *Epistolae,* no. 12, p. 399, ll. 17-20: 'scilicet quod ita historialiter ordinentur vetera, ut spiritaliter omnia demonstrentur nova, et legis per figuram patefaciat littera, quae sacer evangelii tex-tus in se continet sacramenta'. About Hrabanus and the Old Testament (or certain parts thereof) as *vetus lex,* see De Jong, 'Old law'.

98. Hrabanus, *Commentaria in Genesim,* III, c 3, *PL* 107, col. 568C.

99. About the use of *historia* (including the *historia gentium*) as a chronological framework for exege-sis, Hrabanus, *De Institutione Clericorum,* III, c. 17, pp. 219-20, which consists of excerpts from Augustine, *De Doctrina Christiana,* II, cc. 27-8, *CCSL* 32, p. 62. Hrabanus left out a passage in which Augustine distinguished historical narrative *about* human institutions from history as an ir-reversible process instituted by God, and therefore not a human institution.

100. Hrabanus, *Commentaria in Ezechielem,* XI, c. 30, *PL* 110, col. 812 AB: 'Possumus autem hoc dicere quod et in prophetis nequaquam historiae ordo servetur, duntaxat non in omnibus, sed in quibus-dam locis. Neque enim narrant praeterita, sed fu-tura praenuntiant, prout voluntas Spiritus sancti fuerit. In historia vero ut sunt Moysi quinque libri et Jesu, et Judicum volumina, Ruth quoque Esther, Samuel et Malachim: Paralipomenon liber et Ezrae, juncto sibi pariter Noemia praeposteram narrationem nequaquam reperiri' (= Hieronymus, *Commentariorum in Ezechielem Libri xiv,* lib. 9, c. 30, ed. F. Glorie, *CCSL* 75 (Turnhout, 1964), p. 432, ll. 1456-64).

101. Cf. Keller, '*Machabaeorum Pugnae*'; J. Dunbabin, 'The Maccabees as exemplars in the tenth and eleventh centuries', in K. Walsh and D. Wood (eds.), *The Bible in the Medieval World. Essays in Memory of Beryl Smalley,* Studies in Church His-tory, Subsidia 4 (Oxford, 1985), pp. 31-41. A nice instance of ninth-century enthusiasm about the Maccabees to which Matthew Innes drew my at-

tention: *Annales Fuldenses* s.a. 868, ed. F. Kurze, *MGH SRG* 7 (Hanover, 1891), p. 66, where the author calls Robert the Strong an 'alter quoddam-modo nostris temporis Machabeus'.

102. See above, n. 60, and Hrabanus, *Epistolae,* 17b, p. 422, ll. 11-13, with an implicit comparison between the calamities of the past and the present, and the role of both queens: 'Deus omnipotens, qui illius regine mentem ad relevandas populi sui calamitates erexerat, te simili studio laborantem ad eterni regni gaudia perducere dignetur.'

103. Savigni, 'Instanze ermeneutiche e redifinizione del canone', pp 581-3.

104. Hrabanus, *Expositio in Librum Esther,* c. 11, col. 661A: 'Quid est quod rex Assuerus dedit Esther reginae domum Aman adversarii Judaeorum, nisi quod rex verus et Dominus noster omnem digni-tatem et omnem honorem quem prior populus ex scientia legis et prophetarum atque cultu piae reli-gionis habuit, postquam adventum mediatoris Dei et hominum in carne sprevit, atque ejus Evange-lium recipere noluit, totum ad santae Ecclesiae transtulit usum, ut ipsa possideret spirituales divi-tias, et custos fieret honestissima omnium virtutum.'

105. Hrabanus, *Commentaria in Libros Machabaeorum* II, c. 15, *PL* 109, col. 1256AB: 'Hic ergo dedit gladium aureum Judae cum divinam Scripturam sensu spiritali fulgentem ad munimentum totius Ecclesiae defensionemque populi sui concessit doctoribus, quatenus contra hostes universos ar-matura uterentur . . .'

106. Augustine, *De Doctrina Christiana,* II, 28 (44), p. 63; Hrabanus, *De Institutione Clericorum,* III, 17, p. 220: 'Historia facta narrat fideliter atque utiliter . . .' See also Hrabanus, *Commentaria in Gen-esim,* IV, c. 14, *PL* 107, cols. 654D-655A: 'Sed prius historiae fundamenta ponenda sunt, ut aptius allegoriae culmen priori structurae superponatur.'

107. Hrabanus, *Epistolae,* no. 19, pp. 424-5, ll. 30-2: 'De cetero quoque volo sanctitatem tuam scire, quod ipsum opus ideo partim de divina historia, partim de Iosephi Iudaeorum historici traditione, partim vero de aliarum gentium historiis contexui, ut quia non tantum gentis Iudeae ac principum eius, sed et aliarum gentium similiter in ipso libro mentio fit, ex multorum librorum conlatione veri-tas sacrae historiae pateat et sensus narrationis eius lectori lucidior fiat.'

108. R. McKitterick, 'The audience for Latin historiog-raphy in the early Middle Ages: text transmission and manuscript dissemination', in Scharer and Scheibelreiter (eds.), *Historiographie im frühen Mittelalter,* pp. 96-114.

109. Hrabanus, *Expositio in Librum Judith,* c. 1, *PL* 109, col. 541: 'Quidam quaerendum putant, historia Judith quo tempore, quibusve sub regibus edita fuerit; ob hoc maxime, quia ipsi reges in historia notati sunt, hoc est, Arphaxad et Nabuchodonosor, apud eos qui Assyriorum vel Medorum historias conscripsere, in ordine regum utriusque regni inserti non reperiuntur.'

110. Ibid., col. 543C.

111. Hrabanus, *Expositio in Librum Esther,* c. 1, *PL* 109, cols. 636C-637A.

112. Hrabanus, *Commentaria in Libros Machabaeorum,* I, c. 2, *PL* 109, col. 1147A.

113. Hrabanus, *Commentaria in Genesim,* IV, c. 9, *PL* 107, col. 646AB: 'sanctus Lucas, qui ipsius scriptor historiae est . . .' Cf. Hieronymus, *Hebraicae Questiones in Libro Geneseos,* ed. P. de Lagarde, *CCSL* 72 (Turnhout, 1959), p. 50: 'Non enim debuit sanctus Lucas, qui ipsius historiae scriptor est, in gentes actuum apostolorum uolumen emittens contrarium aliquid scribere aduersus eam scripturam, quae iam fuerat gentilibus diuulgata.'

114. Hrabanus, *Commentaria in Libros IV Regum,* I, c. 1, *PL* 109, col. 25A; c. 13, col. 40D; Hrabanus, *Commentaria in Libros II Paralipomenon,* I, c. 2, *PL* 109, col. 293B; c. 12, col. 333A; II, c. 16, col. 352D: IV, c. 20, col. 492B; c. 26, col. 510B; *Commentaria in Librum Sapientiae,* II, c. 3, *PL* 109, col. 700D; c. 12, col. 726A; *Commentaria in Ecclesiasticum,* VI, c. 3, *PL* 109, col. 944D; VIII, c. 8, col. 1025A; ibid., IX, c. 5, col. 1068A; X, c. 30, col. 1113D. Ubiquitous in the commentaries on Esther, Judith and Maccabees.

115. Hrabanus, *Commentaria in Macchabaeorum,* I, c. 1, *PL* 109, col. 1129A; II, c. 5, col. 1234C.

116. Ibid., I, c. 1, col. 1128A; see also above, n. 99.

117. Ibid., II, prol., col. 1223BC; c. 4, col. 1254AB: 'quae omnia in prioris libri historia continentur; licet aliqua quae ibi propter festinationem narrantis omissa sunt, in hujus narratione inserta reperiantur: allegoriae autem sensus juxta modum ingenioli mei de hac eadem re ibi expositus est, nec iterare operae pretium esse videtur'; see also ibid., c. 13, col. 1253A/B, where he added a brief summary of his earlier allegory (ibid., I, c. 6, cols. 1174-5) of the story of Eleazar being killed by one of Antiochus' elephants (I Macc. 6:41-6), and his failure to find confirmation for II Macc. 1 in any other biblical books (ibid., II, c. 2, cols. 1225D-1226A).

118. Ibid., I, c. 1, col. 1132D: 'sicut in historiis gentium copiosissime scriptum invenitur. Sed ex iis plurimis omissis scriptor praesentis historiae ad

Antiochum Epiphanem pervenit . . .' Schreckenberg came to the conclusion that Hrabanus' use of Josephus' *Antiquitates* was merely indirect, but obviously did so without taking all his work into account—and certainly not all his commentary on Maccabees. Schreckenberg based his conclusion on expressions like 'de Josephi historici traditione' in Hrabanus' letter to Gerolt (*Epistolae,* 19, p. 424), which does not necessarily imply an indirect use of this text. Cf. H. Schreckenberg, *Die Flavius-Josephus-Tradition in Antike und Mittelalter,* Arbeiten zur Literatur und Geschichte des hellenistischen Judentums 5 (Leiden, 1972), pp. 116-17. About Flavius Josephus' readership in the early Middle Ages, see McKitterick, 'The audience for Latin historiography', p. 105. Also, H. Schreckenberg and K. Schubert, *Jewish Historiography and Iconography in Early Medieval Christianity* (Assen, 1992), pp. 76-84.

119. Hrabanus, *Commentaria in Libros Machabaeorum,* II, c. 1, col. 1225B: 'liber prior historiae istius commemorat, et Josephus in historiarum Antiquitatis Judaicae libro duodecimo testatur dicens . . .'

120. Hrabanus, *Commentaria in Genesim,* II, *PL* 107, c. 2, col. 508D.

121. Hrabanus, *De Institutione Clericorum,* III, c. 22, p. 231.

122. Hrabanus, *Commentaria in Libros Machabaeorum,* I, 8, col. 1175D: 'Quid Josephus hinc referat non indignum videtur huic opero inserere; nec grave debet videri lectori si diversarum historiarum invicem conferuntur narrationes, quia alterutrum se juvare videntur ad explanandam rei rectitudinem historice retexere veritatem.'

123. Hrabanus, *Epistolae,* 17b, p. 422, ll. 5-6: 'Nos autem ea, quae ex Ebreorum fonte prolata sunt, allegorico sensu exposuimus.'

124. Cf. Isidore of Seville, *Allegoriae Quaedam Scripturae Sacrae, PL* 83, cols. 99-130, which along with Jerome's prefaces to biblical books served as a typological 'Who's who' in the Old and New Testament. See ibid., no. 122, col. 116A: 'Judith et Esther typum Ecclesiae gestant, hostes fidei puniunt, ac populum Dei ab interitu eruunt'; no. 129, col. 116BC: 'Machabaei septem, qui sub Antiocho acerbissima perpessi tormenta, gloriosissime coronati sunt, significant Ecclesiam septiformem, quae ab inimicis Christi multam martyrum stragem pertulit, et gloriae coelestis coronam accepit.'

125. Hrabanus, *Expositio in Librum Esther,* c. 1, col. 637D 638A: 'Quod autem Esther typum Ecclesiae teneat, nulli dubium est; nec ipsa alicujus sponsa

quam Christi ullo modo dicenda est. Unde refugere quilibet hanc interpretationem non debet, pro eo quod ille rex historicus perfidus erat, quasi propter hoc regis justi typum tenere nullo modo possit . . .'

126. Ibid., col. 638AB.

127. Ibid., c. 4, col. 649BC.

128. Ibid., c. 3, col. 646B.

129. Ibid., col. 646CD.

130. Ibid., c. 5, cols. 650D-651C.

131. Ibid., c. 9, col. 658B; c. 10, col. 659B.

132. Ibid., c. 6, col. 652B.

133. De Jong, *In Samuel's Image,* pp. 77-91, with references to older literature.

134. Hrabanus, *Commentaria in libros Machabaeorum,* I, c. 7, *PL* 109, col. 1177BC.

135. Ibid., c. 9, col. 1192BC, about I Macc. 11:21: 'sed sicut tunc quidam de his qui oderant gentem suam viri iniqui adierunt regem accusantes Jonatham, sic et nunc hi qui sibi iniquitatem suam auferre conantur, accusantes eos apud saeculi potestates, quatenus eos in odium illorum convertant et persecutionem eis insistant [suscitent]; sed non praevalent, quoniam Deus adjutor et protector eorum est, et ex omnibus tribulationibus corum liberavit eos'; cf. also ibid., II, c. 1213A: 'quales et istius temporis aetas nonnullos habet, qui, licet magistros non occidunt gladio, tamen invidia atque odiis persequi non cessant'.

136. C. Lambot (ed.), *North Italian Service Books of the Eleventh Century* (London, 1928), pp. 298-300; D. Ganz, 'Theology and the organisation of thought', in McKitterick (ed.), *The New Cambridge Medieval History,* p. 768.

137. D. Ganz, 'The debate on predestination', in M. Gibson and J. L. Nelson (eds.), *Charles the Bald. Court and Kingdom,* 2nd rev. edn (London, 1990), pp. 282-302; as Nelson noted, those who had sided with Ebo of Reims in 833 also tended to support Gottschalk; Hincmar linked the two issues: see his *De praedestinatione dissertatio posterior,* c. 36, *PL* 125, col. 386. See also J. L. Nelson, *Charles the Bald* (London, 1992), p. 168.

138. See N. Zeddies, 'Bonifatius und zwei nützliche Rebellen: die Häretiker Aldebert und Clemens', in M. T. Fögen, *Ordnung und Aufruhr. Historische und juristische Studien zur Rebellion,* Ius Commune, Sonderhefte 70 (Frankfurt a/M, 1995), pp. 217-63, for a perceptive analysis of early medieval definitions of social disorder in terms of 'heresy'. I owe this reference to Philippe Buc and Rob Meens.

139. *Annales Sancti Bertiniani,* s.a. 877, p. 254. I am grateful to Philippe Buc for alerting me to Hincmar's implicit reference to II Macc. 9:9.

140. Hrabanus, *Commentaria in Libros Machabaeorum,* II, c. 15, *PL* 109, col. 1256A.

141. 'Transeamus per terram vestram ut eamus in terram nostram et nemo vobis nocebit' (I Macc. 5:48).

142. Hrabanus, *Commentaria in Libros Machabaeorum,* I, c. 5, *PL* 109. col. 1170BC: 'Legamus librorum vestrorum historiam, ut ibi allegorico sensu promissam in coelis reperiamus nobis patriam; et nemo vobis nocebit, quia noster transitus innoxius vobis erit; tantum pedibus transibimus, quando gressu bonorum operum regnum supernum adire cupimus. Qui nolebant aperire, cum in tradita sibi lege nolebant cum Evangelii praedicatoribus communicare.'

143. Ibid., col. 1170A.

144. Ibid., col. 1170C.

145. Ibid., c. 9, cols. 1186D-1187A. See also c. 2, cols. 1145D and 1147A; c. 3, col. 1149D. Ubiquitous.

146. Ibid., c. 1, col. 1137B.

147. Hrabanus, *Liber de Oblatione Puerorum,* col. 432AB. After explaining that there was no reason for the Saxon Gottschalk not to accept Frankish testimony (after all, which people had been converted first?) Hrabanus argued that in the Persian and Roman empires all *gentes* had happily followed one law: 'Narrant enim historiae totam Asiam sub centum satrapis constitutam, legibus Persarum obedisse. Sic etiam Romanorum dominationi omnes gentes censu ac sensu secundum sancita imperatorem per diversas provincias suis temporibus subiectas esse, civemque Romanum ascribi pro magna dignitate ac veneratione apud omnes nationes haberi.'

148. Hrabanus, *Commentaria in Libros Machabaeorum,* I, c. 1, col. 1137C.

149. Ibid., cols. 1137CD and 1138D; II, c. 4, col. 1229D.

150. Cf. Staubach, 'Cultus divinus', esp. pp. 555-7; see also R. Kottje, 'Karl der Grosse und der Alte Bund', *Trierer theologische Zeitschrift* 76 (1967), pp. 15-31. Cf. *MGH Cap.* [*Capitularia regum Francorum*] 1, no. 85, p. 184; for other capitularies in this vein, see ibid., no. 87, p. 274, and particularly Louis the Pious's letter to Archbishop Hetti of Trier (ibid., no. 173, p. 356) where the emperor insists on the purity of the priesthood, with references to Leviticus and the consecration of Aaron.

151. Hrabanus, *Commentaria in Libros Machabaeorum*, c. 11, col. 1193: 'Quid est quod Jonathas a rege Demetrio petiit . . . nisi quod doctores sancti expetunt a gentium principibus et ab omni populo erroris et superbiae debellationem, et ipsi similiter a sanctis doctoribus postulant suffragium doctrinae et orationis ad superandos spiritales inimicos: neuter enim ordo sine alterius opitulatione effectum ministerii sui rite perficere valet, quia nec doctores sancti meritum lucrificandi sine conversione et oboedientia subditorum, nec ipsi subditi salutem promereri possunt sine documento et instructione magistrorum . . .' See also Hrabanus, *Expositio in Librum Iudith*, c. 12, col. 571A.

Abbreviations

CCCM: Corpus Christianorum continuatio medievalis

CCSL: Corpus Christianorum series latina

CDL: Codice Diplomatico Longobardo, 3 vols.: vols. I-II, ed. L. Schiaparelli; vol. III, ed. C. Brühl (Rome, 1929-73)

CSEL: Corpus Scriptorum Ecclesiasticorum Latinorum

MGH: Monumenta Germaniae Historica

AA: Auctores antiquissimi

Cap.: Capitularia regum Francorum

Epp.: Epistolae

LNG: Leges nationum Germanicarum

PLAC: Poetae Latini aevi Carolini

SRG: Scriptores rerum Germanicarum

SRL: Scriptores rerum Langobardicarum et Italicum

SRM: Scriptores rerum Merovingicarum

SS: Scriptores

PL: Patrologia cursus completus series latina, 234 vols., ed. J. P. Migne (Paris, 1844-55)

SC: Sources chrétiennes

Settimane: Settimane di Studio dell Centro Italiano di Studi sull'alto Medioevo (Spoleto, 1953-)

Celia Chazelle (essay date 2001)

SOURCE: Chazelle, Celia M. "The Crucified God in the Gellone Sacramentary and Hrabaus Maurus's *In Honorem Sanctae Crucis*." In *The Crucified God in the Carolingian Era: Theology and Art of Christ's Passion*, pp. 75-131. Cambridge, United Kingdom: Cambridge University Press, 2001.

[*In the following excerpt, Chazelle discusses the theological and political underpinnings of Hrabanus's defense of the cross as a valid symbol of both spiritual and temporal power, concluding that Hrabanus's meditations on the cross culminate in his apology to Louis the German—a true Christian emperor in the image of Constantine.*]

Among the surviving eighth- and early-ninth-century images of Christ from centers north of the Alps are a relatively few representations of the crucifixion, the vast majority if not all depicting him with stiffly erect body and open eyes.[1] The staring savior on the Werden Casket;[2] the enigmatic miniature in the Würzburg Pauline Epistles, where bands and dots of color fill the bodies of the living Christ and two thieves;[3] the solemn, crucified lord in the Durham gospel fragment;[4] the crucifixion watched by angels in the Gospels of St. Gall . . .;[5] the early-ninth-century ivory, attributed to the court, of Mary and John with the loincloth-clad, crucified Christ, who gazes impassively at the viewer as he bleeds from the wounds in his hands and side;[6] the ivory in the cathedral treasury of Narbonne, a work sometimes dated c. 810, depicting the crucifix surrounded by witnesses and scenes from the passion to the pentecost,[7] exemplify artists' efforts in early medieval northwestern Europe to create images that invite contemplation of Jesus' immortality even as he hung on the cross.

Innumerable depictions of the cross from the same period and region also offer reminders of Jesus' divine omnipotence: cross pages in manuscripts, a mode of decoration that reaches the peak of its popularity in the late eighth century; an increasing number of cross-decorated book covers from the same years, such as the late-eighth-century "first" cover of the Book of Lindau, where four busts of Christ mark the cross's center;[8] crosses decorating church furnishings and walls; gemmed altar and processional crosses such as the splendid one in Brescia, where Christ sits enthroned at the center.[9] Other eighth- and early-ninth-century productions in various media recall his power and kingship by portraying the *Majestas Domini* or lord of the apocalypse, his miracles, the ascension, the enthroned Mary holding her child. On the following page to the crucifixion miniature in the St. Gall Gospels, a bust of Christ holding a cross staff is watched by two angels blowing horns and the apostles, a scene that links the passion with his ascension, enthronement in heaven, and return at the end of time.[10] Several early Carolingian ivories have survived that show the lord treading on the beasts, a motif based on Psalm 90.13, a psalm used in the Roman Good Friday liturgy. . . .[11] Works of art where Christ himself is not represented, such as an ivory of St. Michael spearing the dragon,[12] the illumination of the fountain of life in the Godescalc Gospel Lectionary,[13] and Theodulf's mosaic of the Ark of the

Covenant at St.-Germigny-des-Prés . . ., commemorate in other ways his divine origins, heavenly governance, and victory against death and the devil.

Although it is important not to oversimplify the signification of these varied images, they all generally offer visual testimony to the strength of the cult of the conquering son of God reflected in so much of the early Carolingian literature investigated in the last chapter. In certain ways, the same claim can be made about the decoration of the two books that are my principal concern in the following pages: the Gellone Sacramentary (Paris, BNF, MS lat. 12048), and *In honorem sanctae crucis,* the treatise containing twenty-eight *carmina figurata* honoring the cross that Hrabanus Maurus completed in 813/814, while head of the school at his monastery, Fulda.[14] As I will try to show particularly by reference to their depictions of the crucified Christ, however, these works also provide evidence that their designers expressly sought iconographic means to convey the doctrine not only that Jesus is God, but that he unites two complete natures in his one person. . . .

. . . . .

In honorem sanctae crucis

With *In honorem sanctae crucis,* the Christ-centered deliberations of Charlemagne's scholars may be more distantly remembered than in the Gellone Sacramentary. The passion's Christology is more fully presented, however, partly since the combination of text with artistic design in the treatise's *carmina figurata* . . . allows for further exploration of this issue than do the miniatures of the sacramentary's initials. A dedicatory poem for a copy of *In honorem* sent to the monks of Tours notes that Hrabanus learned the "art of meter" from Alcuin while a student at the abbey, c. 803,[15] and the prologue alludes to the inspiration provided by Porphyry's figure poems for Constantine.[16] But despite some comparability with Porphyry's fourth-century collection and with poetry by other late antique and early medieval authors, including the poems that Alcuin, Joseph, and Theodulf gave Charlemagne, Hrabanus' treatise is unique among writings in this genre.[17] Not only is it longer than any extant series of figure poems since the one Porphyry presented to his emperor; the intricacy of most of its figures is unrivaled in ancient or medieval *carmina figurata.* Other Latin poets before Hrabanus—Porphyry, Venantius Fortunatus, Ansbert of Rouen, Boniface, Alcuin and his colleagues—usually created simple geometric "grid-poems," most often with cruciform figures.[18] A few of Porphyry's designs are more complex, but none matches the "image-poems" that Hrabanus produced for most of *In honorem sanctae crucis,* where the figures represent a variety of motifs and three of the original compositions, in addition to the Christ of Poem 1, incorporate human or animal forms.[19] Moreover, as Michele Ferrari has recently shown, *In honorem* is unusual as a collection of figure poetry for its internal coherence. Unlike Porphyry's series for Constantine and that offered to Charlemagne, each individual piece in Hrabanus' treatise was conceived as part of a carefully unified examination of a single set of themes.[20]

Hrabanus recognized the difficulties that even a skilled reader of his poems might encounter because of the need to decipher the words within each figure and the constraints the designs impose on the Latin of the poetry. To clarify the figures' signification, as both artistic forms and lines of verse, he set a prose *declaratio figurae* ("declaration of the figure") on the page opposite each composition; to ease understanding of the poem as a whole that frames each figure, he also provided a prose paraphrase in a second book, possibly written at a later stage.[21] The resulting anthology of verse, prose, and imagery communicates meaning on several levels at once: the immediate one of the poetical texts, Book 2, the crosses, and the other representational imagery of the figures, a less accessible level of figural symbolism, which is unveiled chiefly in the declarations; and a third level at which the figures, their coloring, and numerical and geometric relations suggested by them and the verses possess symbolic values not discussed in the poetry or prose, but which the attentive Carolingian reader might have discerned.[22] Such varied poetry and figures, the interplay between them, the prose analyses attributing to the poems a polyvalent symbolism, clearly displlay Hrabanus' mastery of a classical literary genre and the encyclopedic knowledge of biblical exegesis, sacred history, ancient secular and Christian literature that he already possessed in producing this, his first work. Its elaborate compendium of art and text was an achievement of which the poet was justifiably proud for the rest of his life, and it remained very popular in later centuries. Approximately eighty-one manuscripts and manuscript fragments of the treatise are extant;[23] numerous copies, some of which survive, are known to have been made under Hrabanus' own supervision at Fulda and later when he was archbishop of Mainz (847-856). Among the identified recipients are his friend Hatto, who evidently helped in the treatise's initial preparation, monasteries, and high-level personnages such as the previous archbishops of Mainz, Haistulf (d. 826) and his successor, Otgar (d. 847), Louis the Pious (d. 840), the abbeys of St.-Martin of Tours and St.-Denis, Archbishop Raoul of Bourges, Pope Gregory IV (who died before his copy reached him, in 844; it was received by his successor, Sergius II), and Count Eberhard of Friuli (d. c. 865).[24]

The first third of Hrabanus' Poem 1 . . ., the opening of Book 2 Chapter 1, and the figural verses formed by the crucified Christ's body hail the son of God's powerful victory against his enemies and his revelation of kingship. This is the eternal lord and "holy creator" come into the world to seize the prize from the deep, the God placed on the cross who bestowed the supernal crown.[25] The rest of the poem and Chapter 1 mainly consist of a list of Christ's names, beginning with those that pertain strictly to his divinity and membership in the Trinity, then moving to others more closely related to his assumption of humanity and incarnate existence. Despite references to his role as the sacrificial victim, though, his human nature is principally viewed from the perspective of the God who became man. "For our redemption" he received human nature "like a vestment for his divinity," a nature that hides the "splendor of his majesty from human sight and the rays of his brilliance from the eyes of the impious," even as "by shining miracles and thundering gospel he signifies that he is true God."[26] On the whole, Poem 1 more clearly balances praise of the divinity with remembrance of the incarnate humanity than does the *Opus Caroli regis,* yet dwells less than do the anti-Adoptionist tractates on Christ's experience of suffering and mortality. In line with the acclamations of his divinity and power, the figure, like the Gellone *Te igitur* miniature . . . , portrays the living crucified lord. Dressed in the perizoma, his head framed by a cruciform halo, Jesus stands erect with arms extended straight from his sides, his open eyes designated by two letter O's. In other respects, the depiction that Hrabanus envisioned for the poem—as far as we can judge from the figural verses defining its form in its varied copies—is somewhat closer to the Narbonne crucifixion tablet than to the Gellone painting.[27] Both the **In honorem** and Narbonne Christs wear the perizoma and have open eyes, erect bodies, and cruciform halos; both, too, unlike the Gellone Christ, have shoulder-length hair, navels that are visible above their loin-cloths (marked by an O in *In honorem*), splayed feet, and weight shifted at the hips so that the right leg is thrust very slightly in front of the left.

One detail clearly distinguishing the **In honorem** Christ from the Narbonne as well as the Gellone depictions, though, is the absence of a cross behind him.[28] In order to understand why he is thus shown, it is necessary to give some thought to the treatise's subsequent textual and visual contents. Throughout the following poems of *In honorem sanctae crucis,* the center of praise is the omnipotent deity who triumphed in the passion and resurrection and, more directly, his cross, the emblem of that conquest and his universal dominion.[29] The power displayed in the passion now radiates from the cross, which itself controls and orders the created universe and all sacred history. Each section of the treatise (poem, *declaratio figurae,* chapter of Book 2) advances some aspect of this theme by lauding the savior, the cross, and the passion and developing an

intricate exegesis, often structured around number symbolism, of a single sacred phenomenon or group of phenomena with roots in scripture.[30] The readers/viewers of the treatise are expected to contemplate how both figures and texts demonstrate that the Christian teachings set forth there conform to the cross's structure, the primary motif of each figure, and therefore reflect the divine ordering of the cosmos over which Christ reigns.

Yet while Poem 1 and the other *carmina figurata* repeatedly stress Christ's divinity and cosmic majesty, another refrain of their verses is the miracle of his incarnation. He is simultaneously the second person of the Trinity and the redeemer who possessed humanity capable of being fixed to a cross, in order to vanquish sin/death/ Satan and restore the universe to God. Poem 4, for example . . . , depicts an equal-armed cross flanked by two, six-winged seraphim above (so identified in the texts) and two, two-winged cherubim below.[31] The poem, *declaratio figurae,* and chapter announce that Isaiah's vision of seraphim, and the cherubim who stood next to the Ark of the Covenant in the tabernacle and Temple, foreshadowed the glory of the conquering cross, the "likeness of our redemption" that Christ the king wished to be visible even before his incarnation. The angelic creatures sing the praises of the cross, the "royal throne" and "conciliation of the world" to which the creator and heavenly king was fastened, the structure that the reader is asked to behold in the poem's figure. They hail, too, the lord who used the cross as his weapon in order to defeat the devil, the savior who rules in heaven and will return as judge. The seraphim prefigure the "image of Christ's cross" with their wings reaching up, down, and to their sides; their *Sanctus* hymn (Isaiah 6.1-3) is the threefold voice that exhorts the elect before and after the incarnation, since all are redeemed in Christ's one passion, by which he "conquered sadness," "burned up iniquity," and "put the evil powers to flight." The cherubim next to the Ark and propitiatorium—next to the cross in the poem's figure— foreshadow the propitiation that occurred in the incarnation, their wings forever extended to signify that the redemption brought in Christ's passion is for all time.[32]

Poem 15 . . . is decorated with the four evangelist symbols arranged around the lamb of God, suggesting the four arms of an equal-armed cross with the lamb at its center. The verses hail Christ, "born of the highest father," for his victory that "broke the fearsome weapons," and they laud the four gospel writers and symbols for their accounts of his incarnate humanity and divinity: John (the eagle) describes the son "forever with the father" who was the universe's creator yet assumed a human soul and body; Mark (the lion) recalls Christ's conquest, his priesthood and offering of himself as sacrifice; Luke (the calf) remembers that Jesus is both king and saving victim, the "admirable infant" born of Mary and the "ancient of days" who, although "suspended on the cross, sustained the stars"; Matthew describes his descent from David, the one from that line promised as the world's savior.[33] The *declaratio figurae* announces the "likeness" of the cross that the figure reveals in the apocalyptic vision of the four beasts around the lamb. While the lamb signifies the one who, fixed to the cross, "bore away the world's sins," the four beasts signify the evangelists, all of whom "agree in witnessing to the lord's passion and resurrection" and reveal different mysteries of his humanity and divinity along with other secrets pertaining to the number four.[34] Poem 23 . . . opens by referring to its figure of a cross, the ends formed of triangles composed of six squares each, as the "noble flower" here "painted" with the name of Christ the king. The words *Jesus* and *Christus* intersect at the S marking the figure's center.[35] The remaining verses, *declaratio figurae,* and chapter explore the mysteries of the numbers four and six, symbolic of the beauty of the universe that the omnipotent God created and then saved through the crucifixion. The numbers refer to the "perfection of Christ's passion and our redemption," since on the cross "the maker of all things provided a sign of his own consummation, when, having received the cup, he said, 'It is consummated'." They also signify the "concourse of people from the four regions of the world praying to their redeemer" for their salvation; the "twenty-four books" of the Old Testament; David's division of the tribe of Levi and the priesthood of the sons of Aaron, prefiguring the priesthood of Christ who was also the sacrifice; the twenty-four elders of the apocalypse, designating the church; and, ultimately, all the "perfected" works of God that point towards the perfect creator, "who made us and multiplied us, [and] freed us from the enemy's power by his own blood.[36]

The climax of these encomia of the incarnate, divine lord occurs in Poem 28 (fig. 15), where Hrabanus is depicted kneeling in veneration, beneath an equal-armed cross that floats above his head. The poem praises Christ as the high majesty, sabaoth, creator, and with other names that allude to his work of salvation. Everything written on the preceding pages, it is claimed, was directed to the honor of the savior whom the poet now adores. Hrabanus prostrates himself in order to "adore" his lord and, he adds in Book 2, the cross as well;[37] he prays that Jesus will receive him as a new sacrifice, and that the crucifixion will burn up all sinfulness in him, in preparation for the terrifying return on the last day. The *declaratio figurae* announces that twenty-eight poems are contained in the treatise because the number represents the perfection and consummation of all things,[38] and it confirms that the poet's adoration is directed to the "eternal and perpetual and inseparable God, Trinity and unity" who inspired and assisted him to prepare his work. The treatise is variously described

as honoring the cross, the passion, and Christ the redeemer and savior, who, "having been born the only begotten from [the father] before the ages, wished temporally to assume human flesh and soul and undergo the cross for the salvation of the human race."[39]

The prologue of **In honorem sanctae crucis** states that Hrabanus composed his treatise in order to honor God by fulfilling the injunction of Exodus 25.2 to bring to him the "first fruits," in this instance the author's first published work.[40] The reverence paid to the cross is indicated to be synonymous with worship of Christ and remembrance of his incarnation and saving passion.[41] The accomplishment of the Exodus command gave Hrabanus the opportunity to demonstrate his prowess as a poet, his familiarity with classical literary forms, his command of the large fund of biblical and patristic learning that provides the core of each poem and *declaratio figurae*. In a sense, the "first fruits" of Charlemagne's educational reforms are seen here, one of the earliest works of literature from the second generation of scholars who would dominate Carolingian intellectual and cultural activity during the first half of the ninth century: a son of Frankish aristocracy, educated at the court and Tours by the Anglo-Saxon, Alcuin. Thus the treatise implicitly pays respect not only to God but to Alcuin, dead only a decade when it was completed, with whom Hrabanus studied scripture and the church fathers and who taught him how to write *carmina figurata*. That Hrabanus believed the works a fitting memorial to his teacher is evident from the dedication poem composed for the copy sent to Tours, where Alcuin is imagined asking St. Martin to assure that God accepts this gift from the pupil.[42]

The size of **In honorem,** the large prose apparatus provided to assist the reader, and the sheer volume of information about sacred history and Christian dogma communicated by both literary and artistic means attest the educational function the treatise was also designed to fulfill, as was appropriate for a work by the master of the Fulda school. Hrabanus' didactic intentions may underlie, too, the decision to write in the form of the *carmen figuratum,* in spite of the difficulties the genre creates for reading his verse. At the simplest level, he perhaps thought, the intriguing integration of figures with texts would encourage readers to closer study of the meaning of both and the mysteries embedded in each poem, figure, and each poem plus figure. By such means, they would arrive at a better understanding of the doctrines communicated in the different sections of his treatise than if they were to meditate on images alone, concerning whose utility Hrabanus was hesitant, as will be discussed shortly, or simply on the written word.[43]

Furthermore, a series of *carmina figurata* may have seemed especially well suited to educating readers about, specifically, the cross's signification of divine majesty, the divinely ruled cosmos, and of God's work of salvation. While these are traditional themes of exegesis of the cross in early medieval literature, including other *carmina figurata,* Hrabanus develops them to unprecedented lengths, both textually and visually. A certain tension is apparent between the heavy load of ideas that the figures and texts of *In honorem* together teach and the relatively simple shape of the cross. In the *carmina figurata* by Alcuin, Joseph, and Theodulf and in earlier examples of such poetry, the usually geometric figures merge into the verses, so that the eye moves easily from one to the other and each poem can be studied as a single unit. In contrast, the more intricate designs of *In honorem sanctae crucis* present visual expressions of quite involved teachings that may require the reader to consult the prose *declarationes figurarum* on the opposite pages, or the chapters of Book 2—to turn away from text plus image and consult pure text—in order to grasp the full weight of this thought. Moreover, although each figure of *In honorem* purportedly represents the cross, most in fact consist of arrangements of quite different motifs that, in many cases, barely bring to mind the cross's appearance, or that suggest a cruciform design on the verge of disintegrating into individual components. According to the *declaratio figurae* of Poem 7, for example . . . , the figure designates the presence of the cross's form in the fourfold ordering of nature, yet what we actually see are four, separate circles that can be identified as "cruciform" only from what is said in poetry and prose.[44]

Nonetheless, regardless of these problems, *carmina figurata* honoring the cross quite possibly appeared to Hrabanus exceptionally acute demonstrations of its sanctity and Christ's majesty, precisely because of the nature of the literary genre. Three factors need here to be borne in mind. The first is the cross's special status, in its own right, as both representational form and written language, through its traditional association with the letter Tau or Tav and the first letter, symbol, and abbreviation of the name of the savior who, himself, is the word and image of God. For Hrabanus and contemporary readers, the poems of *In honorem,* like other cross-figure poetry, may have announced the cross's holiness by both depicting and also writing its "sign."[45] Second, the extant verses of another poem that Hrabanus wrote for his friend, Hatto, echoing ideas espoused in the *Opus Caroli regis* and earlier by Augustine and Isidor, declare that artistic representations are inferior to the written word. Images are "empty" (*vana in imagine forma*) and deceptive (*falsa colorum*), incapable of showing the "figures of things" (*rerum . . . figuras*) correctly or contributing beauty to the soul.[46] A passage in the *declaratio figurae* of Poem 11 of *In honorem* stresses the value of the "figure" (*figura*) in leading thoughts to sacred truth. The reference is to

Old Testament typology, but in Hrabanus' mind it was clearly applicable to his *carmina figurata,* as well. This should probably be read not as contradicting the verses for Hatto, but as an expression of essentially the same idea from another perspective. Artistic images do *not* show the "figures of things" correctly, and therefore do not convey holy teachings; the *carmen figuratum,* however, guides the viewer's thoughts to the spiritual realm, and hence to awareness of the glory of the savior and his cross, because it presents not images but indeed figures, by joining visual forms with words praising Christ.[47]

Third, as Giselle de Nie has observed, early medieval churchmen conceived of miracles as repetitions of patterns established in the Bible. The ability to recognize a miracle as such depends on knowledge of the scriptural paradigm. For the sixth-century bishop, Gregory of Tours, the effort is comparable to that needed in order to read scripture. Developing a doctrine of Augustine's, Gregory suggests that while heretics read or see the same texts as true believers, lack of faith impedes them from recognizing the marvel—the divine truth—contained there.[48] The supreme, biblical pattern for miracles was the creation and its corollary, the incarnation, the re-creation through Christ, and any extraordinary occurrence was regarded as, to some measure, a drawing out of the conjunction of nature and miracle in those two events.[49] Given these ideas, it is reasonable to ask whether Hrabanus and Carolingian readers of *In honorem sanctae crucis* might have considered its intersection of text and figure—words fashioning images and images fashioning words, despite their contradictory natures—as possessing a special value through its analogy to the miracle pattern of the incarnation. The cross's holiness is announced in the repeated union of word and image that honors and depicts its form. Thus these *carmina figurata* mirror, on a lower plane, the miraculous joining of divine and human in the second person of the Trinity—a renewal of creation echoing through the universe that, because it is divinely ordered, as Hrabanus' treatise demonstrates, conforms to the cross's shape.

Hrabanus probably knew the existence of the *Opus Caroli regis* when he composed his treatise, yet it is uncertain to what degree he would have been acquainted with its contents. Although he was associated with the court at the time of its preparation, he was most likely a boy less than ten years old. While he may have learned something about its argumentation from Alcuin, there is no direct allusion to the *Opus* in the writings of either scholar, just as there is no evidence of continued discussion of its teachings on images among Charlemagne's scholars after the council of Frankfurt in 794.[50] Still, by presenting views related to those of the *Opus Caroli regis,* as in some ways may be true of the decoration of the Gellone Sacramentary, *In honorem* provides additional evidence of how Theodulf's doctrines belonged to and possibly influenced the particular climate of thought about Christ and images that prevailed in the early Carolingian period. Hrabanus did not necessarily get any ideas directly from the *Opus*, but in certain respects his thinking moves in remarkably similar directions. One is his expressed antipathy towards artistic imagery, in the verses for Hatto. A second parallel with Theodulf's treatise, as should already be obvious, is the significance that *In honorem* attributes to the cross as the sacred instrument of the crucified Christ's conquest and eternal rule. Here, however, a divergence with the *Opus Caroli regis* should also be noted, for it is fairly clear that Hrabanus ascribes sacral significance not only to the true cross but to its manufactured images, in spite of his evident disinterest in other types of artistic depiction. As does not appear true of the *Opus*, *In honorem* seems to associate all manner of cross images with the praise rendered both the cross and the poems' figures. Any such representation, not merely the figure of a *carmen figuratum*, is implied to be rightly the subject of contemplation and of the worship the poet bestows in Poem 28 . . . Repeatedly, through figures and words, *In honorem* urges readers to meditate on the cross's form, to look at and study its structure in order to enter into the sacred mysteries manifested there. That these comments apply to other depictions of the cross besides the treatise's figures seems confirmed by the *declaratio figurae* of Poem 1, which remarks that "as often as we behold the/a cross," we should be brought to remember Christ's suffering and victory and increase our devotion to him.[51]

While *In honorem* is not overtly polemical, Hrabanus may have been partly encouraged to affirm the value of both the cross and crosses by interference from Abbot Ratgar with processions of crosses at Fulda, in the decade prior to Ratgar's deposition in 817.[52] Along with the remarks concerning crosses in Book 1 Chapter 19 of the *Opus Caroli regis*,[53] Ratgar's actions and those of Bishop Claudius of Turin (817-827), to be discussed below, imply that the practice of using such objects in Carolingian devotional practises did not meet unanimous approval. But although Hrabanus seems to believe that crosses are worthy objects of reverence, whereas Theodulf and Claudius evidently deny this, it is striking how closely the reasons for Hrabanus' acceptance of their holiness correspond to the definition of *res sacratae* in the *Opus Caroli regis*. Essentially, the criteria remain the same, yet they are found to be fulfilled in a type of object to which Theodulf would appear to deny their applicability. *In honorem* insists that the crucified Christ blessed not merely the cross but its form, a blessing proclaimed in the Bible, as the *Opus* asserts is the case for all sacred things. Apparently, therefore, a visible repetition of the form of the cross may be considered sacred.[54] A primary function of Poem 1 . . . is to identify Christ, the crucified savior and universal lord, as this blessing's source. That is why no cross appears behind him, as becomes apparent from the opening of the poem's *declaratio figurae*, where occurs the reference to beholding the/a cross noted above:

> Look, the image of our lord, by the position of his limbs, consecrates for us the most saving, sweetest, and most lovable form of the holy cross, in order that as we believe in his name and obey his mandates, we have hope of eternal life because of his passion. Hence as often as we behold the/a cross, we remember him who suffered on it for us in order to snatch us from the power of darkness, indeed abolishing death so that, now that he has departed into heaven with the angels and powers and virtues subjected to himself, we might be heirs to eternal life. Let us thus recognize that we are not redeemed by corruptible silver and gold, following the vanity of ancient tradition, but by Christ's precious blood, like that of a pure and spotless lamb, so that we may be holy [and] immaculate in his sight, in [his] love, and through this may become consorts of the divine nature, fleeing the corruption of worldly greed.[55]

The form of the cross and consequently any representation of its structure, it seems, mirror the position of Christ's body in the crucifixion. There is no cross in the poem's figure, since the purpose is not only to recall that he was crucified, but to teach viewers that the crucified humanity exemplified the cross's shape and thereby sanctified it. In Poem 1, Christ's body *is* the cross, the supreme manifestation of the glory that its form radiates because of his blessing, and that is depicted and lauded in the remaining poems of *In honorem sanctae crucis*. In gazing at a cross, the Christian is made mindful of the miracle of redemption that is the source of its consecration and revelation of sacred wisdom, as recorded in scripture. By this means, he or she is inspired to turn from this world, in which human flesh is imprisoned in sin, to the divinity that belongs to the same Christ and the divine secrets revealed in the cross's form.[56]

Finally, *In honorem sanctae crucis* is reminiscent of the *Opus Caroli regis* and, more generally, of the theological concerns of Charlemagne's court in the centrality of Christological doctrine to its teachings. Like the Gellone Sacramentary and several of Alcuin's writings that touch on Christological issues, Hrabanus' treatise did not overtly contribute to the inquiries regarding Adoptionism or Byzantine image worship. In its exploration of why the crucifixion is salvific and the cross holy, though, the treatise shows an attentiveness to the passion's role as proof of Christ's mediatorship that must reflect Hrabanus' years at the court or his closeness with Alcuin. The theme of the divine incarnation and the relation between divinity and humanity in

Christ regularly arises in the prose and poetical texts of *In honorem;* but it is especially Poem 1 and its *declaratio figurae* that show the two natures' union to be the basis of the passion's efficacy and its manifestation of the cross's role as the redeemed universe's sacred symbol: the poem through its list of Christ's names, where the humanity's union with divinity is clearly asserted but references to the former nature are permeated by reminders of the latter, the *declaratio figurae* through its explanation of the source of the cross's blessing. As these texts indicate, the incarnation provided a body that, for all its humanity, possessed the power to consecrate the form of the cross by the very position of its crucified limbs. It is because Christ is not only divine but God-made-man, with arms and legs indeed belonging to God, that he was able to establish the cross's visible form as a symbol of the whole creation governed in his invisible divinity. The *declaratio figurae* of Poem 1 develops this theme in the lines following the passage just quoted. Some of the names Christ listed in the verses designate the "substance of his divinity," it remarks, while others are drawn "from the assumed dispensation of the received humanity." Thus it is shown that "the same is the mediator of God and men, in deity consubstantial and coequal to the father, and in the received humanity co-similar and co-natural with the mother, since he assumed our entire nature perfectly, without sin."[57] Which names refer to the human and which to the divine nature is easily recognized through the use of reason. Christ is called anointed because he is both king and priest, Emmanuel because he is "God with us," since "born through the virgin he appeared to men as God in mortal flesh." He is God since one substance with the father, and figure, "since receiving the form of servant, through the likeness of works and virtues, he designated in himself the father's image and immense greatness."[58]

The conviction that Christ's mediatorship lies behind the passion's ability to redeem and the cross's holiness, though, is less forcefully announced in the texts of Poem 1 than it is visually. Once again, the interweaving of text and figure in the *carmen figuratum* was ideal for Hrabanus' purpose. Reaching over the length of the poem, with arms stretched to either side of the page to signify both his rule of the cosmos and his consecration of the cross's form, Christ embraces the entire list of divine and human names that runs through his body. His posture alone reveals that all these titles refer to the one figure, which literally contains the divinity as well as the humanity praised in the verses. The body imitated in the form of the cross, whose limbs, because perfectly human, could be covered with a "small garment," according to the verses in the perizoma, belongs to the God who "encloses the earth in his hand."[59] The absence of a cross, the cruciform halo marked by the *alpha,* "*M*" [for "middle"], and *omega,* the erect body, open

eyes, and lack of signs of suffering underscore Christ's divinity. Even more than the Gellone images of the crucified Jesus, this figure seems divorced from temporal considerations, whether the historical circumstances of the crucifixion or the return at the end of time. On the other hand, the depiction is of a human body. Although in a work that draws on a classical literary genre, Christ's loincloth was conceivably intended to recall a late antique crucifixion image like the fifth-century London ivory,[60] his semi-nudity was probably also understood to emphasize his true humanity. No single aspect of the figure in Poem 1, however, symbolizes the union of divine with human better than the three letters of the word *Deo* designating Jesus' nipples and navel, the last-named attribute one of the strongest imaginable proofs of his human birth.[61]

THE ADORATION OF THE CROSS

In their efforts to find artistic means to express the presence of two natures in one crucified person, both the Gellone Sacramentary and *In honorem sanctae crucis* are reminiscent of the crucifixion theologies articulated in the early Carolingian court's defenses of orthodox doctrine of Christ. Of the two works, the sacramentary, probably made between 790 and c. 804, was perhaps more directly affected by the doctrinal discussions of the 790s. While much of its painting likely serves other purposes, such as simply decoration, its iconographic references to the Virgin's power, prestige, and royalty, to the joining of divinity with humanity in the crucified body received in the eucharist and commemorated in Holy Week, and to Jesus' status as adopter seem to reveal a direct sensitivity to the Christology that took shape as Charlemagne's scholars attacked Greek and Hispanic teachings. The image (possibly) of *Ecclesia* opposite the *Te igitur* illumination and, possibly, Mary's identification with the church link catholic belief with ecclesiastical authority, further evidence that the church is the representative and defender of the true faith.

In honorem sanctae crucis, in which Hrabanus' poetry and prose shed greater light on the imagery's signification than do the sacramentary's texts, was completed a decade after Alcuin's death and after the court circle's discussions of Nicea II and Adoptionism had largely concluded. It is conceivable that Hrabanus was interested in the deliberations over the *filioque* at Aachen in 809, and in the challenge to Christ's full divinity that Greek opposition to this insertion to the creed supposedly presented.[62] There is no evidence that the *filioque* debate influenced *In honorem sanctae crucis,* though, or that this treatise has a polemical purpose, despite the possibility that one motivation for its composition came from the actions of Abbot Ratgar. Overall, *In honorem* is a didactic work whose encomia of the cross, the passion, and Christ provide a wide-reaching display of

Hrabanus' poetical talents and learning. Yet still, here as in the Gellone Sacramentary, the perception of the cross and the crucified Christ appears informed by concerns similar to those of the first generation of Carolingian theologians—possibly concerns over the function of images and the relative value of imagery and the written word, such as are discussed in the *Opus Caroli regis,* but also, again, over Christological belief. Perhaps inspired by Alcuin, Hrabanus used the genre of the *carmen figuratum*—a much more thorough amalgam of text and image than liturgical prayers made possible in the Gellone Sacramentary—to demonstrate through both media the conjunction of two natures in Christ, and to suggest their union's significance to the passion's saving power and to the sanctity of the cross and its form.

Given what has been said so far about **In honorem sanctae crucis,** it is helpful to give some attention to the Carolingian tracts of the 820s to 840s that defend the holiness of the cross and crosses and their worship, particularly their "adoration." Most of these writings were directed against Bishop Claudius of Turin or meant to respond to the iconoclastic quarrels that resurged in Byzantium in the first quarter of the ninth century. While certain differences between them and Hrabanus' treatise are obvious—that of literary genre, for one, and the more clearly polemical function of the majority of the later texts—an examination of their thought will assist in clarifying what is distinctive about his approach.

Probably soon after election to the see of Turin in 817, Claudius decided to remove crosses and artistic images from his diocesan churches because he disapproved of the reverence the public paid them.[63] Abbot Theutmir of Psalmody (Nîmes) had written to Claudius that complaints about the bishop's beliefs and actions were being heard "throughout the entirety of Gaul up to the borders of Spain."[64] Claudius' letter-book responding to Theutmir situates his attack on images alongside his opposition to worship and adoration of crosses, including possibly crucifixes, his campaign against pilgrimages to St. Peter's shrine in Rome, and his doubts about papal supremacy. Two treatises challenging Claudius have survived, one by Dungal, written before the bishop of Turin's death in 827 but probably after the synod of Paris (825), which Claudius evidently was asked but refused to attend,[65] the other by Jonas, Theodulf's successor at Orléans. Jonas abandoned his work in 827 but returned to it in the early 840s, because, its introduction claims, allies of the late bishop of Turin had emerged whom, together with Claudius, Jonas accuses of supporting Adoptionism, a heresy he links with Arianism. The charge, the bishop of Orléans asserts, is partly based on papers left among Claudius' affairs after his death;[66] it is apparently also connected with Claudius' earlier association with Felix of Urgel, and conceivably, too, with the rationale he offered for his opposition to

crosses as well as perhaps crucifixes. People "of false religion and superstition," he argues to Theutmir, wrongly justify the "worship, veneration, or adoration" of a cross (crucifix?) by declaring that the reverence is directed to Christ, in whose memory and honor the object is "depicted and imaged" (*ob recordationem salvatoris nostri crucem pictam atque in eius honore imaginatam*). What such persons actually honor is Christ's mortal humanity alone and, therefore, the "shame of [his] passion and ridicule of [his] death," the focus of Jews and pagans who deny the resurrection. They forget the words of St. Paul: "And if we have known Christ according to the flesh; but now we know him so no longer" (2 Cor. 5.16).[67] Claudius' comments might be read differently if we knew the larger context in which they were made; only fragments from his treatise are extant. But taken on their own they suggest a tendency, to which his followers may also have subscribed, to separate Christ's humanity radically from his divinity and to associate the passion solely with the former nature, as though the man was crucified without the God. Such a perspective on the crucifixion recalls some of the accusations made by Alcuin, Paulinus, and Benedict against Felix and Elipandus.

The bishop of Turin's ideas had most likely caused worry at Louis the Pious' court before he received a letter in November 824 from the Greek emperors, Michael II and Theophilus. This outlines the moderate form of iconoclasm the Byzantine government had reinstituted and expected the Carolingian emperor to support. The churchmen meeting at Paris in 825 to consider the eastern position were clearly concerned about Claudius, as well, even though their documents do not expressly mention him. Their opinions are outlined in a *libellus* prepared for Louis; from this, Jonas of Orléans and Jeremiah of Sens made an *epitome* for Pope Eugenius II, who had authorized the synod to examine the issues of the Greek controversy.[68]

Along with the documents of the council of Paris and the anti-Claudian treatises by Dungal and Jonas, several other Carolingian writings from the 820s to 840s also discuss artistic images and/or crosses. One is the *Liber officialis* of Amalarius of Metz, initially published in 823 and twice revised before 835; the chapter on the *Adoratio crucis* defends that ritual and possibly refers to the controversy Claudius stirred about crosses.[69] Further tracts to note are *De picturis et imaginibus* by Agobard of Lyons, probably written for or in reaction to the synod of 825;[70] Einhard's *Quaestio de adoranda cruce,* composed in spring 836 to answer a request from Lupus of Ferrières for an explanation of why the cross merits adoration;[71] and Walafrid Strabo's *De exordiis et incrementis,* dating to the decade before his death in 849, which contains a chapter on the role of images.[72] Like the *Opus Caroli regis,* the writings of this group that comment on artistic representations, by which I mean images other than crosses (therefore excluding Amalarius' *Liber officialis* and Einhard's letter to Lupus), present positions that their authors see as falling between the two "extremes" of iconoclasm and iconodulism; the latter error is defined as the bestowal on images of the adoration owed to God. Dungal, Jonas, Agobard, and the Paris synod mainly develop their arguments through pastiches of patristic texts; one of the sources they all cite is the correspondence of Gregory I.[73] Aside from Dungal's treatise, neither these writings nor Walafrid's discussion of images attributes to artistic productions a religious significance comparable to that which ninth-century Carolingian writings generally assign to crosses and relics, yet images are understood to perform certain important functions. Most often mentioned are decoration, the commemoration of past events and holy persons, the demonstration or encouragement of love for Christ and the saints, and the assistance of the ignorant or illiterate to knowledge of the persons and deeds depicted. Every Carolingian treatise on images mentioned except Claudius' tract opposes iconoclasm, though Agobard is so worried about the inappropriate worship of images that he suggests they should not be allowed in churches if such behavior occurs.[74] All of them reject the notion that images should receive the adoration God alone deserves; but certain of them, in particular the Paris synod's *libellus* and Walafrid's treatise, seem to leave open the possibility that some acts of reverence might be tolerable, and Dungal clearly accepts this viewpoint.

Lupus' request to Einhard, Einhard's reply, and Jonas' decision to complete his treatise in the early 840s suggest that worries about the worship or adoration of the cross and crosses, perhaps even outright attempts to halt acts of reverence, continued after Claudius' death in 827. Two basic teachings about the cross in these tracts and in the writings of Amalarius, Dungal, and the Paris synod show similarities to, though also significant differences from, the perspective in Hrabanus' work. In some ways, it can therefore be seen, *In honorem* represents a transition from the concerns of Charlemagne's court to those that predominated in the second quarter of the ninth century. The first doctrine has to do with cross worship. In line with the contrast drawn between bodily vision and true worship of God through the eyes of the soul, the *Opus Caroli regis* does not praise crosses or defend their veneration. Indeed, it has nothing explicitly positive to say about physical acts of worship performed toward any inanimate material things except relics, even other *res sacratae*.[75] A different attitude is suggested in Hrabanus' treatise; but although the cross and crosses are shown to deserve reverence as well as praise, especially in Poem 28, the precise liturgical contexts in which crosses should be revered, the conduct, and the nature of the reverence to

be accorded are not major issues. Moreover, the "crosses" of Hrabanus' poems, forms that float in a cosmic realm created of words, differ noticeably from the manufactured representations and relics worshiped in churches. In general, however, the later writings by Einhard, Jonas, and others on crosses and images show greater interest in distinguishing the possible modes of physical worship of visible things and the meanings of those acts, including the veneration given to relics of the saints, where they are discussed.[76] This effort to define the various types of worship corresponds to the relative openness some of the same ecclesiastics demonstrate (Dungal, the Paris synod, Walafrid) to the veneration of artistic representations. Given that multiple "degrees" of reverential practice exist, not all such behavior involving images is necessarily idolatrous.[77] Similarly, where Dungal, Jonas, the synod of Paris, Einhard, and Amalarius comment on the cross, many reasons for its greatness are proposed, but the basic consideration guiding the discussion is its place in the liturgy and the right of its relics and images to liturgical worship, especially adoration on Good Friday. As Hrabanus also implies in Poem 28 yet does not discuss as directly, both images and relics of the cross are to be worshiped or adored on these occasions not for their own sakes, but in memory and honor of the unseen, crucified savior and God.[78] According to Einhard and Amalarius commenting on Jerome—Jonas makes a similar remark—the worshiper prostrates himself before the cross or its relic, "as if he saw the lord hanging there."[79] Christ is the sight the worshiper most desires and who deserves this respect, yet the material, visible cross is an acceptable substitute.

Second, like Hrabanus in *In honorem sanctae crucis,* all these theologians accept that the cross is holy and, although the rationale for this belief is not clarified, that this sanctity is somehow reflected in or shared by its manufactured representations. Dungal, Jonas, the Paris synod, and to a lesser degree Amalarius uphold the concept that the crucified savior's blessing made the cross into the heavenly sign of his divine omnipotence and majesty, an idea to which Agobard also alludes.[80] In support, they quote and cite passages from scripture, poetry, liturgical texts, and patristic treatises that remember and praise the crucifixion, the cross, and the "sign" of the cross, describe the manifestations of its glory in visions, miracles worked through its relics, and the sign made by hand or worn inwardly, point to the use of signing in Christian devotion, and look forward to the cross's return with Christ at the end of time. Underlying these arguments, as is true with *In honorem sanctae crucis,* is the cult of the holy cross whose strength is evident from abundant eighth- and ninth-century sources, and the widely held doctrine of the passion as Christ's victory and revelation of divinity. The event that sanctified the cross was the conquest of sin/death/Satan by the son of God, the celestial lord.[81] Attacking Claudius' association of crosses with Jesus' torments and "shameful" death, Dungal stresses the power present even in the redeemer's humility, as revealed in the devil's defeat. For him, the crucifixion's glory is proven by Christ's command that the event be commemorated in the mass and by the disciples' imitation of his sufferings.[82] While Einhard does not discuss the origins of the cross's holiness in his *Quaestio de adoranda cruce,* he connected its glorification with Christ's conquest on his triumphal arch. . . .[83] This silver structure, which may have been originally surmounted by a cross, was decorated with images of warrior saints or *milites Christi,* two on horseback treading on serpents to symbolize the victory over evil. Above were depicted the annunciation and John the Baptist pointing to Christ as the lamb of God, evangelist portraits, and an enthroned Christ with the apostles. The arch's inscription refers to the cross relic, the "trophy of the eternal victory," contained either in it or in the reliquary cross it bore.[84]

Insofar as Hrabanus in his *In honorem,* Einhard, and the other scholars mentioned ascribe sanctity not only to the true cross but its representations and stress their value to Christian devotion, they reflect the new interest, among Carolingian ecclesiastics, in the role of corporeal sight in the exercise of faith.[85] The *Opus Caroli regis* defends the spirituality of true worship of God and sharply distinguishes this from contact with the material, visible world, in spite of the link the treatise posits between meditation on the divine and Bible study. In contrast, even though the crosses of *In honorem* are embedded in texts (perhaps reflecting the impact of discussions of art's function at Charlemagne's court) and the responses to Claudius and the Byzantine iconoclastic controversy reject the "excessive" veneration of artistic images, these treatises all recognize that religious devotion suitably involves the body's eyes. This idea is suggested by other features of Carolingian piety, too, that gain prominence in the ninth century, some of which I will return to in the following chapters: the expansion of the cult of relics, visible reminders of the departed saints; discussions of the liturgy's visual representation of holy events and their actors; the increase in vision literature; the debates over the relationship between what is seen in the eucharist (bread and wine) and the sacral reality it contains; the analyses of the final vision of God that occurred partly within the context of the quarrel over divine predestination. But most of the later Carolingian writings (by Einhard, Dungal, etc.) that defend crosses, their sanctity, and their worship do not place their arguments within a Christological framework of thought such as *In honorem sanctae crucis* presents. Despite their association of the cross and crosses with Christ's power and, on the other hand, occasional allusions to his suffering, they

do not give significant attention to the union between immortal divinity and mortal humanity as the basis of the holiness of the cross or crosses, or of the passion's ability to save. Only in Jonas' *De cultu imaginum* do similar issues clearly arise, as a result of his concern that Claudius and his followers showed Adoptionist and Arian tendencies. Evidently because Claudius seemed to divide the divine from the human in the crucified Christ, Jonas more noticeably than Dungal stresses their union, though the theme is not, by any means, as consistently or fully developed as in the anti-Adoptionist tracts or *In honorem sanctae crucis.* Jesus' death did not constitute a source of "shame" and the cross was no mere instrument of humiliation, Jonas declares, for then the crucifixion would not have been salvific. The passion's sufferings do not displease Christians as they do Claudius, since the faithful know them to have been redemptive and that death was followed by resurrection. The man who died is the same one who rose from the tomb. The cross's torments along with the victory, the crucifixion together with the resurrection are the foundation of the hope for redemption and of reverence for the cross.[86]

As will be discussed further in chapter 4, the emphasis on liturgical devotion and the cross's liturgical significance in the writings of the 820s to 840s is indicative of the Carolingian church's growing attentiveness, after Charlemagne's death, to the signification and proper conduct of ecclesiastical ritual. This is an important element of the background to the mid ninth-century quarrels over divine predestination and the nature of the eucharistic presence that will be investigated in chapters 5 and 6. The less interest that *In honorem s. crucis* shows in liturgical worship, and the far greater effort to establish a Christological basis for belief in the cross's sanctity, distinguish Hrabanus' treatise from the later tractates. In spite of the other characteristics of thought they share in common, these features, particularly the second-mentioned, tie *In honorem* instead to the intellectual preoccupations of Alcuin and Charlemagne's court. In its Christology as perhaps in the attitudes it implies towards the artistic image and the definition of a sacred thing, *In honorem sanctae crucis,* like the Gellone Sacramentary, testifies to the impact of the doctrines formulated against Nicea II and Adoptionism on Carolingian churchmen beyond the scholars involved in those affairs.

Nevertheless, during the 820s to 840s, Hrabanus' work was most likely regarded by him and fellow scholars as a major precedent for the efforts to defend the cross and manufactured crosses as legitimate subjects of praise, meditation, and liturgical reverence. Possibly this sheds light on some of the early copies of *In honorem,* since the first important period of its diffusion outside Fulda was the second quarter of the ninth century.[87] Four of its extant manuscripts were probably produced at Fulda while Hrabanus was abbot and two were completed under him at Mainz; others from the same period, now lost, are known from dedications.[88] The dedicatory verses do not mention the debates over artistic images, crosses, and their worship, and it is significant that these are the years in which Hrabanus had greatest access to the resources necessary for the production of copies; yet the energy put into the task was conceivably motivated by contemporary issues. That may be especially true with the presentation copy made for Louis the Pious. The dedication figure poem for Louis . . . , presented in subsequent copies as an integral part of the treatise,[89] depicts the emperor as a *miles Christi*. Dressed in armor, holding a shield and cross staff, he stands ready to fight his savior's battles on earth with both material and spiritual weapons, but above all the cross lauded in the remaining pages of *In honorem sanctae crucis*.[90] Like Charlemagne in the *carmina figurata* by Alcuin, Joseph, and Theodulf . . . , Louis is implicitly compared to Constantine, who was honored in the collection of figure poetry by Porphyry that influenced Hrabanus as well as, probably, Alcuin and Joseph. A clear parallel is also drawn with Christ, that is, between the victorious redeemer and the earthly ruler who conquers in his name. The cross is the sign of *imperium* by which the Frankish emperor defends Christianity in his lands, the weapon that allows justice to triumph in him, just as through the cross Christ, the heavenly king, overcame sin and death.[91] Christ's blessing and protection of Louis' rule are sought, assistance that is merited because of the latter's justice and propagation of the faith.[92] Michel Perrin has Louis at his coronation by Pope Stephen III in 816.[93] Whether written in 835 or earlier in the 830s, as Elizabeth Sears has proposed, the dedication poem may have reminded Louis that he deserved the imperial throne and reliquary crown because, like Charlemagne and Constantine before him but unlike the iconoclasts who in the 830s controlled the eastern empire, he defended orthodoxy, including true belief regarding the cross and artistic images.[94]

Notes

1. A possible exception in the Gellone Sacramentary is discussed below, this chapter. Generally on Carolingian crucifixion images, see Johannes Reil, *Christus am Kreuz in der Bildkunst der Karolingerzeit* (Leipzig, 1930).

2. Werden, Abbey Church; *799: Kunst und Kultur der Karolingerzeit, Karl der Grosse und Papst Leo III. in Paderborn: Katalog der Ausstellung Paderborn 799*, 2 vols., ed. C. Steigemann and M. Wemhoff (Mainz, 1999), 2. 479 VII.35; Victor H. Elbern, "Der fränkische Reliquienkasten und Tragaltar von Werden," in *Das erste Jahrtausend:*

Kultur und Kunst im werdenden Abendland an Rhein und Ruhr, 3 vols., ed. V. H. Elbern (Düsseldorf, 1962), 1.436-470 . . . .

3. Würzburg, Universitätsbibliothek, Mp. theol. fol. 69, fol. 7r; Ernst H. Zimmermann, *Vorkarolingische Miniaturen,* 4 vols. (Berlin, 1916), vol. 3, pl. 220 (a).

4. Durham, Cathedral Library, A.11.17, fol. 38 v; Zimmermann, *Vorkarolingische Miniaturen,* vol. 3, pl. 222 (a).

5. St. Gallen, Stiftsbibliothek, *Cod. Sang.* [*Codex sangallensis*] 51, p. 266; see Gertrud Schiller, *Iconography of Christian Art,* trans. J. Seligman (Greenwich, CT, 1972), vol. 2.102.

6. Formerly Berlin, Staatliche Museen No. 601; Adolph Goldschmidt, *Die Elfenbeinskulpturen aus der Zeit der Karolingischen und Sachsischen Kaiser, VIII.-IX. Jahrhundert,* vol. 1 (Berlin, 1914), no. 8.

7. Narbonne, Cathedral Treasury; Danielle Gaborit-Chopin, *Elfenbeinkunst im Mittelalter,* trans. Gisela Bloch and Roswitha Beyer (Berlin, 1978), 52 fig. 43, cat. 45, dating the ivory *c.* 810, but noting that it has also been assigned to the reign of Charles the Bald.

8. New York, Pierpont Morgan Library; Hubert et al., *L'Empire carolingien,* 211 fig. 192; Victor H. Elbern, "Liturgisches Gerät in edlen Materialen," in W. Braunfels, ed., *Karl der Grosse: Lebenswerk und Nachleben,* 4 vols., vol. 3: *Karolingische Kunst,* ed. Braunfels and H. Schnitzler (Düsseldorf, 1965), 115-167, at 154 fig. 26. See Bernhard Bischoff, "Kreuz und Buch im Frühmittelalter und in den ersten Jahrhunderten der spanischen Reconquista," *Mittelalterliche Studien: Ausgewählte Aufsätze zur Schriftkunde und Literaturgeschichte,* 3 vols., vol. 2 (Stuttgart, 1967), 284-303; Frauke Steenbock, "Kreuzförmige Typen frühmittelalterlicher Prachteinbände," in *Das erste Jahrtausend,* ed. Elbern, 1.495-513, esp. 498.

9. Brescia, Museo Cristiano; *799: Kunst und Kultur, Katalog* 1. xxxvi, pl. 1; Braunfels, ed., *Karl der Grosse,* 3, Color Plate 31. Cf. the manuscripts and other objects reproduced in *799: Kunst und Kultur: Katalog,* esp. vol. 2, e.g. 445 VII.12, 453 VII.15, 626 IX.12, 650 IX.32, 652 IX.33, 653 IX.34, 776 Pl. 3, 783 XI. 2, 798 XI.12.

10. St. Gall, Stiftsbibl., MS 51, pg. 267; Zimmermann, *Vorkarolingische Miniaturen,* 3, pl. 188 (a).

11. Oxford, Bodleian Library, MS Douce 176, ivory cover. Also, the Genoels-Elderen diptych in Brussels, Musées Royaux d'Art et d'Histoire, Nr. 1474; the Lorsch Gospels cover in the Vatican, Museo

Sacro, A. 62; *799: Kunst und Kultur: Katalog* 2.735 x.22b; Gaborit-Chopin, *Elfenbeinkunst,* cat. 37, 39, 40.

12. Leipzig, Museum des Kunsthandwerks (Nr. 5350); *799: Kunst und Kultur: Katalog* 2.748 x.30; Gaborit-Chopin, *Elfenbeinkunst,* 50 fig. 40, cat. 42.

13. Paris, BNF [Bibliothèque Nationale de France], nouv. acq. lat. 1203, fol. 3v; Hubert et al., *L'Empire carolingien,* 279 fig. 279; Percy Ernst Schramm, Hermann Fillitz, and Florentine Mütherich, *Denkmale der deutschen Könige und Kaiser,* 2 vols., vol. 1: Schramm and Mütherich, *Ein Beitrag zur Herrschergeschichte von Karl der Grossen bis Friedrich II. 768-1250* (Munich, 2nd expanded edn., 1981), 213 pl. 8.

14. *In honorem sanctae crucis, CCCM [Corpus Christianorum Continuatio Medievalis]* 100, ed. M. Perrin (Turnhout, 1997). Subsequent references to individual texts and figures in this edition indicate section (A, B, C, D) and line numbers. Reproductions are from Biblioteca Apostolica Vaticana, Reginensis Latinus 124; on this manuscript, see Perrin, ed., *In honorem s. crucis, CCCM* 100, esp. xxx, xxxiv-lv. French translation in idem, *Raban Maur, Louanges de la Sainte Croix* (Paris, 1988). On the treatise's date, Ferrari, *Liber s. crucis,* 12-13, and *passim* for an excellent study of the treatise, focusing on its place in the evolution of medieval poetry. See also Ernst, *Carmen figuratum,* 222-292; Herrad Spilling, *Opus Magnentii Hrabani Mauri in honorem sanctae crucis conditum: Hrabans Bezichung zu seinem Werk* (Frankfurt, 1992). Facsimile of a ninth-century copy in *Hrabanus Maurus. Liber de laudibus sanctae crucis. Codex Vindobonensis 652 der Österreichischen Nationalbibliothek, Wien. Vollständige Faksimile-Ausgabe* (Graz, 1972).

15. Ferrari, *Liber s. crucis,* 12. Perrin, *Louanges,* 17.

16. Hrabanus, *In honorem, CCCM [Corpus Christianorum, Continuatio medievalis]* 100, A7, lines 68-69; see Ferrari, *Liber s. crucis,* 59.

17. See Massin, *Letter and Image,* trans. Caroline Hillier and Vivienne Menkes (New York, 1970), 158-167, esp. 161-167.

18. Cf. chapter 2, nn. 1-3.

19. Hrabanus, *In honorem, CCCM* 100, B4 (two seraphim and two cherubim), B15 (four beasts of the Apocalypse around the lamb), B28 (Hrabanus kneeling beneath a cross). Compare Porphyry, *Carm.* 26, *Carmina* 1.103-105. See Ernst, *Carmen figuratum,* 98-108; Perrin, *Louanges,* 18-19, 25-29.

20. Ferrari, *Liber s. crucis,* 101-165.

21. Perrin, ed., *In honorem, CCCM* 100.xviii-xix. For the combination of verse with prose Hrabanus notes his debt to Prosper of Aquitaine and Sedulius, though here he particularly has in mind his treatise's second book, in which the "sense" of the poems is repeated in prose. He also refers to Horace's *Ars poetica: In honorem, CCCM* 100, D 0, esp. lines 6-7, 20-23. For the *declarationes figurarum,* he was probably influenced by the transcriptions and explications of the figural verses that Porphyry placed on the facing pages to the poems in his collection. See Ferrari, *Liber s. crucis,* 271-273; Perrin, *Louanges,* 18-20; Spilling, *Opus Magnentii Hrabani Mauri,* 12-14, 22.

22. Perrin, *Louanges,* 20-25.

23. Perrin, ed., *In honorem, CCCM* 100.xxx.

24. See Ferrari, *Liber s. crucis,* 24-29; Perrin, ed., *In honorem s. crucis, CCCM* 100.xii-xxvi.

25. Hrabanus, *In honorem, CCCM* 100, B 1, lines 11-14, C 1 lines 111-140, D 1 lines 4-22.

26. Ibid., *CCCM* 100, D 1 lines 37-43, see 44-62, B 1 lines 27-47.

27. See above, n. 7.

28. The wounds, too, are usually not depicted in copies of Hrabanus' poem, though the figural verse along Christ's left hand declares that he washes away sins by his blood; see Hrabanus, *In honorem, CCCM* 100, C 1 line 115. The lack of cross recalls the crucifixion scene on the fifth-century door of Sta. Sabina, Rome, an image that otherwise seems unrelated to the *In honorem* figure: see Wirth, *Image médiévale,* 124 . . . .

29. The theme is already introduced in Hrabanus, *In honorem, CCCM* 100, B 2 and C 2. The cosmic role attributed to the cross is stressed by Ferrari, *Liber s. crucis,* see esp. 132-135, 253.

30. See Burkhard Taeger, *Zahlensymbolik bei Hraban, bei Hincmar—und im "Heliand"? Studien zur Zahlensymbolik im Frühmittelalter* (Munich, 1970), 3-86.

31. Hrabanus, *In honorem, CCCM* 100, B 4, C 4, see esp. lines 18-64.

32. Ibid., *CCCM* 100, B 4, C 4.

33. Ibid., *CCCM* 100, B 15, D 15.

34. Ibid., *CCCM* 100, C 15, esp. lines 31-37.

35. Ibid., *CCCM* 100, B 23 lines 1-2. The *declaratio figurae* states that the cross's arms spread like the petals of a lily: C 23 lines 59-61.

36. Ibid., *CCCM* 100, B 23, C 23, D 23, esp. lines 41-44.

37. Ibid., *CCCM* 100, B 28 line 15, D 28 lines 22-26.

38. Ibid., *CCCM* 100, C 28 lines 67-69. See Ferrari, *Liber s. crucis*, 128-129; Perrin, *Louanges*, 20-23.

39. Hrabanus, *In honorem, CCCM* 100, C 28 lines 1-4.

40. Ibid., *CCCM* 100, A 7 lines 4-6, 9-10.

41. Ibid., *CCCM* 100, A 7 lines 17-28. Perhaps, as Herrad Spilling has proposed, the gift was meant to parallel the one Hrabanus would offer when celebrating his first mass as priest: Spilling, *Opus Magnentii Hrabani Mauri*, 10. See also Ferrari, *Liber s. crucis*, 27.

42. Hrabanus, *In honorem, CCCM* 100, A 2, see esp. lines 1-14. Perrin has suggested (*Louanges*, 25) that Hrabanus may have begun work on the treatise while still at Tours, under Alcuin's direction. As Ferrari notes, Hrabanus does not specifically mention the *carmina figurata* of Alcuin, Joseph, and Theodulf as models for his work: *Liber s. crucis*, 407.

43. See Ferrari, *Liber s. crucis*, 315-316. The comments of Giselle de Nie, Sabine MacCormack, and others who heard my paper on Hrabanus' treatise at Kalamazoo, May 1998, have helped me enormously to develop these ideas.

44. Hrabanus, *In honorem, CCCM* 100, B7, C7.

45. On the early history of this doctrine, F.J. Dölger, "Beiträge zur Geschichte des Kreuzzeichens, I-IX," *Jahrbuch für Antike und Christentum* 1-10 (1958-1967).

46. Hrabanus, *Carm.* 38, *MGH PLAC* [*Monumenta Germaniac Historica, Poetae Latini aevi Merovingcarum*] 2.196 lines 1-7. Cf. Ferrari, *Liber s. crucis*, 19-21.

47. Hrabanus, *In honorem, CCCM* 100, C 11 lines 1-13; cf. Ferrari, *Liber s. crucis*, 314-316, with a different interpretation. A poem by Hrabanus on an image of Christ in a chapel of Fulda implicitly distinguishes the artistic representation from the sacral realm to which Christ belongs: *Carm.* 61, *MGH PLAC* 2.222; see Herbert L. Kessler, "Real Absence: Early Medieval Art and the Metamorphosis of Vision," *Morfologie sociali e culturali in Europa fra tarda antichitàe alto medioevo*, Settimane di studio del Centro Italiano di Studi Sull'Alto Medioevo, 45 (Spoleto, 1998), 1157-1211, at 1195-1196.

48. Giselle de Nie, "Word, Image and Experience in the Early Medieval Miracle Story," in *Language and Beyond/Le langage et ses au-delà, Text: Studies in Comparative Literature* 17, ed. P. Joret and A. Remael (Amsterdam, 1998), 97-122, at 101. De Nie has explored this issue in several other important articles, as well, e.g. "Iconic Alchemy: Imaging Miracles in Late Sixth-Century Gaul," *Studia Patristica* 30 (Leuven, 1997), 158-166; and "Seeing and Believing in the Early Middle Ages: a Preliminary Investigation," in *Word and Image: the Pictured Word, Interactions* 2, ed. M. Heusser et al. (Amsterdam, 1998), 67-76. Pope Gregory I, too, implies a correspondence between the seeing of an artistic image and of a miracle, when he draws on Augustine's ideas about the latter activity in order to explain art's value to Serenus of Marseilles: see Chazelle, "Pictures, Books, and the Illiterate," 146-147.

49. Benedicta Ward, *Miracles and the Medieval Mind* (Philadelphia, rev. edn., 1987), 3-5.

50. Cf. Ferrari, *Liber s. crucis*, 314-319.

51. Hrabanus, *In honorem, CCCM* 100, C 1, esp. lines 5-7. (Latin text below, n. 101)

52. See Luke Wenger, "Hrabanus Maurus, Fulda, and Carolingian Spirituality" (Ph.D. diss., Harvard University, 1973), 228 and n. 5. The interference is reflected in a chapter of Fulda's *Supplex libellus,* presented to Charlemagne in 812 to win the emperor's support for the monks against their abbot: "Ut crucis gloriatio in singulis diebus dominicis fiat ante missam fratribus omnibus circa vicina quaeque loca monasterii crucem sequentibus hymnos et antiphonas cantantibus sicut apud maiores nostros usus erat in diebus dominicis passionis et resurrectionis domini gloriam celebrari. Et quod in diebus ieiuniorum ab episcopo decretis crucem portare et litanias facere liceat." *CCM* [*Corpus Consuetudinem Monasticarum*] 1.319-327, at 326. I mentioned the possibility of a connection with Hrabanus' treatise in my dissertation, "The Cross, the Image, and the Passion in Carolingian Thought and Art" (Ph.D. diss., Yale University, 1985), 192-193. This idea was expanded by Johannes Fried, "Fulda in der Bildungs- und Geistesgeschichte des früheren Mittelalters," in *Kloster Fulda in der Welt der Karolinger* (1996), 3-38, at 23-26; further discussion in Ferrari, *Liber s. crucis*, 386-388.

53. Theodulf, *Opus Caroli regis* 1.19.192-193. See chapter 2, at n. 128.

55. The doctrine is clearly influenced by the traditional belief that the crucified Christ's posture, and hence his cross's four arms, signify his universal dominion. It is also connected with the notion that the sign of the cross is holy, whether traced by hand, written as a sacred letter, or carried spiritu-

ally within the faithful soul. The verses of Sedulius' *Carmen paschale* praising the four-part cross as symbol of Christ's rule over the cosmos, for instance, are quoted in C 12, lines 21-26 (Sedulius, *Carmen paschale* 5, lines 190-195). Cf. Dölger, "Beiträge zur Geschichte des Kreuzzeichens, I-IX"; Ferrari, *Liber s. crucis,* 408-409. An interesting parallel to Hrabanus' doctrine is hinted in a letter of Pope Nicholas I, referring either to a cross or to a crucifix; see Jean-Marie Sansterre, "Entre *Koinè méditerranéenne,* influences byzantines et particularités locales: le culte des images et ses limites à Rome dans le haut Moyen Age," in *Europa medievale e mondo bizantino: contatti effettivi e possibilità di studi comparati,* ed. G. Arnaldi and G. Cavallo (Rome, 1997), 109-124, at 119.

55. Hrabanus, *In honorem, CCCM* 100, C 1 lines 1-15: "Ecce imago Saluatoris membrorum suorum positione consecrat nobis saluberrimam, dulcissimam et amantissimam sanctae crucis formam, ut in eius nomine credentes et eius mandatis oboedientes, per eius passionem spem uitae aeternae habeamus; ut quotiescumque crucem aspiciamus, ipsius recordemur, qui pro nobis in ea passus est, ut eriperet nos de potestate tenebrarum, 'deglutiens quidem mortem, ut uitae aeternae heredes efficeremur,' profectus in caelum subiectis sibi angelis et potestatibus et uirtutibus; utque recogitemus, 'quod non corruptibili argento uel auro redempti [sumus] de uana [nostra] conuersatione paternae traditionis, sed pretioso sanguine quasi agni incontaminati et inmaculati Christ,' ut simus sancti et inmaculati in conspectu eius, in caritate, ut per haec efficiamur diuinae consortes naturae, fugientes eius quae in mundo est concupiscentiae corruptionem." See 1 Peter 1.18, 3.22.

56. Cf. Hrabanus, *In honorem, CCCM* 100, A 7 lines 20-28.

57. Ibid., *CCCM* 100, C 1 lines 16-23.

58. Ibid. *CCCM* 100, C 1, esp. lines 24-26, 29, 35-38, 57-60.

59. Ibid., *CCCM* 100, B 1 lines 23, 28-29; D 1 lines 32-37.

60. See above . . . .

61. See Hrabanus, *In honorem, CCCM* 100, C 1 lines 135-136.

62. David Ganz, "Theology," [*The New Cambridge Medieval History,* volume 2: c. 700-c. 900]. 2.766.

63. See Wirth, *Image médiévale,* 155-162.

64. Claudius, *Ep.* [*Epistole*] 12, *MGH Epp.* 4. ed. E. Dümmler (Berlin, 1895), 610-613, at 610 lines 20-21. See Chazelle, "Memory, Instruction, Worship," 196-197; Ferrari, *Liber s. crucis,* 311-314. On the relationship between Claudius and Theutmir: Gorman, "Commentary on Genesis of Claudius of Turin," 282-283.

65. Dungal, *Ep.* 9, *MGH Epp.* 4.583-585, at 585 lines 17-18 (recalling that Claudius had referred to the synod as a "congregationem asinorum"). Dungal's full treatise, *Liber Adversus Claudium Taurinensem,* is published in *PL* 105.457-530, see 529A.

66. Jonas, *De cultu imaginum* 1, *PL* [*Patrologia cursus completus, Series Latina*] 106.305-388, see 307-311B. Cf. Dungal, *Adv. Claudium, PL* 105.466B/C.

67. Claudius, *Ep.* 12, *MGH Epp.* 4.611. If "omne lignum scemate crucis factum" should be adored because Christ was crucified, the bishop continues, then so should other objects representing things he did "through the flesh." To worship a cross is to crucify the son of God again and through the "execrable sacrileges of idols" to bring one's soul to everlasting damnation. Here the reference seems clearly to crosses. On Claudius' early years and education under Felix, see the clear overview by Joop van Banning, SJ, "Claudius von Turin als eine extreme Konsequenz des Konzils von Frankfurt," in *Das frankfurter Konzil von 794,* ed. Berndt, 2.731-749, esp. 733-734. I cannot accept, however, van Banning's assertion that the treatise *De picturis et imaginibus* attributed to Agobard (*CCCM* 52. 149-181) is actually by Claudius, for one reason that it implies that representations of the cross are holy and deserve respect, a position at odds with the disparaging comments in Claudius' letter. See below, n. 74.

68. *Libellus synodalis parisiensis, Concilium Parisiense A. 825, MGH Conc.* [*Concilia*] 2.480-532; *Epitome libelli synodalis parisiensis,* ibid. 535-551. See Hartmann, *Synoden,* 168-171.

69. Amalarius, *Liber officialis* 1.14, *ST* [*Studi e Testi*] 139.99-107, see esp. 104, cf. above, n. 68.

70. Agobard, *De picturis et imaginibus, CCCM* 52.149-181. Freeman, ed., *Opus Caroli regis,* 11-12 and n. 69, suggests that Agobard was reacting to the letter of Michael II to Louis' court that led to the Paris synod of 825.

71. Einhard, *Quaestio de adoranda cruce,* ed. K. Hampe, *MGH Epp.* 5 (Berlin, 1899), 146-149.

72. Walafrid, *De exordiis et incrementis quarundam in observationibus ecclesiasticis rerum* 8, *MGH Capit.* [*Capitularia*] 2, ed. V. Krause (Hanover, 1897), 473-516, at 482-484. Lucid translation with commentary in Alice Harting-Corrêa, *Walafrid*

Strabo's Libellus de exordiis et incrementis quarundam in observationibus ecclesiasticis rerum: a Translation and Liturgical Commentary (Leiden, 1996).

73. *Libellus* 11-14, *MGH Conc.* 2.487-489, 507-508, 527-528 (including the ps-Gregorian letter to Secundinus; see 489 n. 1); *Epitome* 12-13, ibid., 539-540, see 547; Jonas, *De cultu imaginum* 1, *PL* 106.310-311, see 332; Dungal, *Adv. Claudium, PL* 105.468-469; cf. Agobard, *De picturis* 22, *CCCM* 52.171-172. Gregory's correspondence is used to support different viewpoints, however. The teachings of these tractates and their relation to Gregory's own thought are discussed in Chazelle, "Memory, Instruction, Worship," see esp. 192-201.

74. Agobard, *De picturis* 33, *CCCM* 52.180.

75. Cf. chapter 2, at nn. 92, 127.

76. On saints and their relics, Jonas, *De cultu imaginum* 3, *PL* 106.365-388; Dungal, *Adv. Claudium,* esp. *PL* 105.496-518. Several of the treatises quote from Augustine's analysis of the different forms of worship in *De civitate Dei* 10.1: e.g. Dungal, *Adv. Claudium,* esp. *PL* 105.484-485; Jonas, *De cultu imaginum* 1, *PL* 106.319-320; *Libellus* 63, *MGH Conc.* 2.501-502. Cf. (not using Augustine) Walafrid, *De exord. et increment.* 8, *MGH* Capit. 2.482.

77. Their tolerance of such practices relative to what is found in the *Opus Caroli regis* may reflect the gradual increase of influence north of the Alps, during the Carolingian period, of attitudes earlier well established in the Italian peninsula. Not only the veneration/adoration of images but even stories of miracle-working images have been traced in Italy to before the ninth century. These have been the subjects of several careful studies by Jean-Marie Sansterre; see in particular, "La vénération des images à Ravenne dans le haut moyen âge: notes sur une forme de dévotion peu connue," *Revue Mabillon,* n.s. 7 (= t. 68) (1996), 5-21; idem, "L'image blessée, l'image souffrante: quelques récits de miracles entre Orient et Occident (vie-xiie siècle)," *Bulletin de l'Institut historique belge de Rome* 69 (1999), 113-130.

78. See Amalarius, *Liber officialis* 1.14, *ST* 139.101-102; *Libellus* 65-76, *MGH Conc.* 2.502-506, esp. 506, see *Epitome,* ibid., 549-551, where liturgical concerns are not paramount; Dungal, *Adv. Claudium, PL* 105.477-496, esp. 481-485, see 527D-528; Einhard, *Quaestio, MGH Epp.* 5.146-149; Jonas, *De cultu imaginum* 1, 2, *PL* 106.331-366, esp. 331-333, 342-343. Cf. Agobard, *De picturis*

19, *CCCM* 52.168. As Wenger noted, Hrabanus does not directly connect the choice of subject for *In honorem* with liturgical practice, despite the possible influence of Ratgar's objections to cross processions: Wenger, "Hrabanus Maurus," 228. Still, the figure as well as the verses of Poem 28 suggest that, in defending the cross and its form, he is mindful of the devotion Christians pay to it through ecclesiastical ritual: *In honorem, CCCM* 100, B 28, C 28, D 28.

79. Einhard, *Quaestio, MGH Epp.* 5.149; Amalarius, *Liber officialis* 1.14, *ST* 139.101 (Jerome, *Ep.* 108). See Jonas, *De cultu imaginum* 2, *Praef., PL* 106.342.

80. Agobard, *De picturis* 19, *CCCM* 52.168.

81. As Jonas, for example, explains, "nec tamen ideo crucem ut Dominum adoramus, sed magis eum qui per crucem mortis destruxit imperium, atque chyrographum peccati nostri affixit, pacificans in ea sanguine suo sive quae in terris, sive quae in coelis sunt": *De cultu imaginum,* 2, *Praef., PL* 106.342D. See Col. 2.14.

82. Dungal, *Adv. Claudium, PL* 105.478-479B.

83. Paris, BNF, cod. fr. 10440, fol. 45r.

84. See Lawrence Nees, "Art and Architecture," *NCMH* [*The New Cambridge Medieval History*] 2.834, with reference to earlier literature. David Ganz (oral communication, September 1999) suggested that it is not absolutely certain the arch was surmounted by a manufactured cross.

85. E.g. concerning relics of the saints and pilgrimages to their shrines, Jonas states, "Sane est etiam proprium humanae menti non adeo compungi ex auditis sicut ex visis": *De cultu imaginum* 3, *PL* 106.368C.

86. Jonas, *De cultu imaginum* 1, *PL* 106.334-336. Cf. Dungal, *Adv. Claudium, PL* 105.466, 528A.

87. Perrin, ed., *In honorem, CCCM* 100.xv-xvii, xx-xxvi; Ferrari, *Liber s. crucis,* 23-25.

88. Biblioteca Apostolica Vaticana, Reginensis Latinus 124 (Fulda, second quarter ninth century); Paris, BNF, lat. 2423 (Fuda, second quarter ninth century); Amiens, BM 223 (Fulda, second quarter ninth century); Turin, Biblioteca Nazionale Universitaria K. II. 20 (Fulda, second quarter ninth century); Paris, BNF, lat. 2422 (Mainz and Fulda, mid-ninth century); Vienna, Österreichische Nationalbibliothek 652 (Mainz and Fulda, mid-ninth century). See Perrin, ed., *In honorem, CCCM* 100. xx-xxvi, xxx-xxxii.

89. Ferrari, *Liber s. crucis,* 216; on the poem and its figure, see Sears, "Louis the Pious," in *Charlemagne's Heir,* ed. Godman and Collins, 605-628.

90. Hrabanus, *In honorem, CCCM* 100, A5. Ferrari, *Liber s. crucis*, 216-217, 338-339; Ernst, *Carmen figuratum*, 292-297; Sears, "Louis the Pious," 610-620.

91. Hrabanus, *In honorem, CCCM* 100, A5, lines 1-4, 8-10, 12, 31-35.

92. Ibid., *CCCM* 100, A 5, lines 9-23, 31-38.

93. "Tu, Hludouuicum, Criste, corona"; see ibid., *CCCM* 100, A 6 (*declaratio figurae*) lines 92-93; Perrin, ed., ibid., *CCCM* 100.xxii and n. 33. Perrin argues (xlviii-lv) that Biblioteca Apostolica Vaticana, Reginensis Latinus 124 was probably not the copy intended for Louis. Cf. Sears, "Louis the Pious," 624-627. On Constantine's crown given to Louis see Elbern, "Liturgisches Gerät," 137-138; Anatole Frolow, *La Relique de la vraie croix: recherches sur le développement d'un culte* (Paris, 1961), 217, no. 91; Ermoldus Nigellus, *In honorem Hludowici, MGH PLAC* 2.5-79, esp. 36-37, lines 425-426, 447-450.

94. The Synod of Paris convened at the behest of Louis and Lothar (*Libellus, MGH Conc.* 2.481 lines 1-6), and Dungal dedicated his treatise to the same rulers (*Ep.* 9, *MGH Epp.* 4.583 lines 20-23; *Adv. Claudium, PL* 105.465A). Jonas began his treatise for Louis but finished it for Charles the Bald: *De cultu imaginum, Praef., PL* 106.305-307.

Select Bibliography

PRIMARY SOURCES

The list is limited to printed editions of the principal Carolingian sources used.

Adrevald of Fleury, *De corpore et sanguine Domini contra ineptias Joannis Scoti, PL* 124.947-954.

Agobard, *Opera Omnia, CCCM* 52, edited by L. Van Acker, Turnhout, 1981.

Alcuin, *Adversus Elipandum libri IV, PL* 101.231-300.

———. *Adversus Felicem Urgellitanum Episcopum libri VII, PL* 101.119-230.

———. *Carmina, MGH PLAC* 1, edited by E. Dümmler, pp. 160-351, Berlin, 1881.

———. *Carmina rhythmica, MGH PLAC* 4.3, edited by K. Strecker, pp. 903-910, Berlin, 1923.

———. *Commentaria in S. Joannis Evangelium, PL* 100.737-1008.

———. *De baptismi caeremoniis, PL* 101.611-614.

———. *De fide sanctae et individuae Trinitatis, PL* 101.11-58.

———. *De virtutibus et vitiis ad Widonem comitem, PL* 101.613-638.

———. *Epistolae, MGH Epp.* 4, edited by E. Dümmler, pp. 1-481, Berlin, 1895.

———. *Expositio in epistolam Pauli Apostoli ad Hebraeos, PL* 100.1031-1084.

———. *Expositio pia ac brevis in psalmos poenitentiales, in psalmum CXVIII et graduales, PL* 100.569-638.

———. *Liber contra haeresim Felicis: Edition with an Introduction,* edited by G. B. Blumenshine, *ST* 285, Vatican City, 1980.

———. *Missae,* edited by J. Deshusses, "Les messes d'Alcuin," *Archiv für Liturgiewissenschaft* 14 (1972), 7-41.

———. *Versus de patribus, regibus et sanctis euboricensis ecclesiae,* edited and translated by P. Godman, *The Bishops, Kings, and Saints of York,* Oxford, 1982.

Amalarius, *Opera liturgica omnia,* 3 vol., *ST* 138-140, edited by J. M. Hanssens, Vatican City, 1948-1950.

Amolo of Lyons, *Opuscula* 1-2, *PL* 116.97-106.

Angilbert of St.-Riquier, *Carmina, MGH PLAC* 1, edited by E. Dümmler, pp. 355-366, Berlin, 1881.

———. *Institutio de Diversitate Officiorum, CCM* 1, edited by K. Hallinger, pp. 283-303, Siegburg, 1963.

Audradus Modicus, *Liber de fonte vitae, MGH PLAC* 3, edited by L. Traube, pp. 73-84, Berlin, 1896.

———. *Carminum supplementum, MGH PLAC* 3, edited by L. Traube, pp. 739-745, Berlin, 1896.

Benedict of Aniane, *Opuscula* 1-2, *PL* 103.1381-1411.

Bernowin, *Carmina, MGH PLAC* 1, edited by E. Dümmler, pp. 413-425, Berlin, 1881.

Candidus, *Opusculum de passione Domini, PL* 106.57-104.

Carmina Centulensia, MGH PLAC 3, edited by L. Traube, pp. 265-368, Berlin, 1896.

Christian of Stavelot, *Expositio in Matthaeum evangelistam, PL* 106.1261-1504.

Claudius of Turin, *Apologeticum atque rescriptum adversus Theutmirum abbatem, MGH Epp.* 4, edited by E. Dümmler, pp. 610-613, Berlin, 1895.

———. *Enarratio in Epistolam D. Pauli ad Galatas, PL* 104.841-912.

Concilium Francofurtense A. 794, MGH Conc. 2.1, edited by A. Werminghoff, pp. 110-171, Hanover, 1906.

Concilium Parisiense A. 825, MGH Conc. 2.2, edited by A. Werminghoff, pp. 475-551, Hanover, 1908.

Concilium Parisiense A. 829, MGH Conc. 2.2, edited by A. Werminghoff, pp. 606-680, Hanover, 1908.

Corpus Consuetudinem Monasticarum, vol. 1; *Initia Consuetudinis Benedictinae,* edited by K. Hallinger, Siegburg, 1963.

De Conversione Saxonum Carmen, MGH PLAC 1, edited by E. Dümmler, pp. 380-381, Berlin, 1881.

Dicta Albini/Dicta Candidi, edited by J. Marenbon, *From the Circle of Alcuin to the School of Auxerre: Logic, Theology and Philosophy in the Early Middle Ages,* pp. 151-170, Cambridge, 1981.

Drogo-Sakramentar, Ms. Latin 9428, Bibliothèque nationale, Paris. Vollständige Faksimile-Ausgabe im Originalformat, 2 vols., edited by F. Mütherich, *Commentary* by W. Köhler, Graz, 1974.

Dungal the Scot, *Responsa contra perversas Claudii Taurinensis episcopi sententias, MGH Epp.* 4, edited by E. Dümmler, pp. 583-585, Berlin, 1895.

———. *Liber Adversus Claudium Taurinensem, PL* 105.457-530.

Einhard, *Quaestio de adoranda cruce, MGH Epp.* 5, edited by K. Hampe, pp. 146-149, Berlin, 1899.

Florus of Lyons, *Opuscula adversus Amalarium 1-3, PL* 119.71-96. *Opusculum* 1 also edited by E. Dümmler, *MGH Epp.* 5, pp. 267-273, Berlin, 1899.

———. *Opusculum de expositione missae, PL* 119.15-72.

———. (Pseudo-Remigius), *De tribus epistolis liber, PL* 121.985-1068.

———. (Pseudo-Remigius), *Libellus de tendenda immobiliter scripturae veritate, PL* 121.1083-1134.

Gosbert, *Carmen acrostichum, MGH PLAC* 1, edited by E. Dümmler, pp. 620-622, Berlin, 1881.

Gottschalk of Orbais, *Die Gedichte des Gottschalk von Orbais,* edited by M.-L. Weber, Frankfurt am Main, 1992.

———. *Œuvres théologiques et grammaticales de Godescalc d'Orbais,* edited by D. C. Lambot, Louvain, 1945.

Haimo of Auxerre, *Divi Pauli epistolas expositio, PL* 117.361-938.

———. *Homiliae de tempore, PL* 118.11-746.

Heiric of Auxerre, *I Collectanea di Eirico di Auxerre,* edited by R. Quadri, Fribourg, 1966.

———. *Homiliae per circulum anni, CCCM* 116-116B, edited by R. Quadri, Turnhout, 1992-1994.

The Heliand: the Saxon Gospel, translated by G. Ronald Murphy, Oxford, 1992.

Hincmar of Rheims, *De regis persona et regio ministerio, PL* 125.833-856.

———. *De cavendis vitiis et virtutibus exercendis, MGH Quellen zur Geistesgeschichte des Mittelalters* 16, edited by D. Nachtmann, Munich, 1998.

———. *Carmina, MGH PLAC* 3, edited by L. Traube, pp. 406-420, Berlin, 1896.

———. *Explanatio in ferculum Salomonis, PL* 125.817-834.

———. *De praedestinatione Dei et libero arbitrio, PL* 125.65-474.

———. *Epistolae, MGH Epp.* 8.1, Berlin, 1939.

———. *Ad simplices,* edited by W. Gundlach, "Zwei Schriften des Erzbischofs Hinkmar von Reims, 11," *Zeitschrift für Kirchengeschichte* 10 (1889), 258-310.

Hrabanus Maurus, *Carmina, MGH PLAC* 2, edited by E. Dümmler, pp. 154-258, Berlin, 1884.

———. *Commentariorium in Matthaeum, PL* 107.727-1156.

———. *De institutione clericorum libri tres,* edited by A. Knoepfler, Munich, 1900/1901.

———. *De videndo Deum, de puritate cordis et modo poenitentiae, PL* 112.1261-1332.

———. *Epistolae,* edited by E. Dümmler, *MGH Epp.* 5, pp. 379-516, Berlin, 1899.

———. *Homiliae de festis praecipuis, item de virtutibus, PL* 110.9-134.

———. *In honorem sanctae crucis, CCCM* 100, edited by M. Perrin, Turnhout, 1997. Translated into French by M. Perrin, *Raban Maur, Louanges de la Sainte Croix,* Paris, 1988. Facsimile edition in *Hrabanus Maurus. Liber de laudibus sanctae crucis. Codex Vindobonensis 652 der Österreichischen Nationalbibliothek, Wien. Vollständige Faksimile-Ausgabe.* Graz, 1972.

Liber de sacris ordinibus, PL 112.1165-1192.

John Scottus Eriugena, *Eriugenae Carmina,* edited and translated by M. W. Herren, Scriptores Latini Hiberniae 12, Dublin, 1993.

———. *De praedestinatione, CCCM* 50, edited by G. Madec, Turnhout, 1978.

———. *Periphyseon,* Books 1-3, *CCCM* 161-163, edited by E. Jeauneau, Turnhout, 1996-1999. *Periphyseon (De diuisione naturae) Liber* 4, edited by E. Jeauneau with the assistance of Mark Zier, translated by J. J. O'Meara and I. P. Sheldon-Williams, Scriptores Latini Hiberniae 13, Dublin, 1995. The full treatise (Books 1-5) is published in *PL* 122. Translation of the entirety by I. P. Sheldon-Williams, revised by John J. O'Meara, *Eriugena, Periphyseon (Division of Nature)* (Montreal, 1987).

————. *Commentaire sur l'évangile de Jean (In Iohannis Evangelium)*, *SC* 180, edited and translated into French by E. Jeauneau, Paris, 1972.

————. *Expositiones in Ierarchiam Coelestem*, *CCCM* 31, edited by J. Barbet, Turnhout, 1975.

Jonas of Orléans, *De cultu imaginum*, *PL* 106.305-388.

————. *Le métier du roi (De institutione regia)*, *SC* 407, edited and translated into French by A. Dubreucq, Paris, 1995.

Joseph the Scot, *Carmina*, *MGH PLAC* 1, edited by E. Dümmler, pp. 149-159, Berlin, 1881.

Leidrad of Lyons, *Liber de sacramento baptismi*, *PL* 99.853-872.

Liber Sacramentorum Gellonensis, *CCSL* 159-159A, edited by A. Dumas, Turnhout, 1981.

Lupus of Ferrières, *Liber de tribus quaestionibus*, *PL* 119.619-648.

Magnus of Sens, *Libellus de mysterio baptismatis*, *PL* 102.981-984.

Milo of St.-Amand, *Carmina figurata*, *MGH PLAC* 3, edited by L. Traube, pp. 561-565, Berlin, 1896.

Odilbert of Mainz, *Erzbischof Odilbert von Mailand über die Taufe*, edited by F. Wiegand. Aalen, 1972, reprint of Leipzig, 1899 edition.

Ordines Romani. Les ordines romani du haut moyen âge, 5 vols., edited by M. Andrieu, Louvain, 1931-1961.

Otfrid of Weissenburg, *Otfrids Evangelienbuch*, edited by O. Erdmann, 4th edition, Tübingen, 1962.

Pascasius Radbertus, *De corpore et sanguine Domini cum appendice epistola ad Fredugardum*, *CCCM* 16, edited by B. Paulus, Turnhout, 1969.

————. *De partu Virginis*, edited by E. A. Matter, *CCCM* 56C, pp. 5-96, Turnhout, 1985.

————. *Epistola ad Paulam et Eustochium de Assumptione Sanctae Mariae Virginis*, edited by A. Ripberger, *CCCM* 56C, pp. 97-172, Turnhout, 1985.

————. *Expositio in Matheo Libri XII*, *CCCM* 56-56B, edited by B. Paulus, Turnhout, 1984.

Paul the Deacon, *Die Gedichte des Paulus Diaconus: kritische und erklärende Ausgabe*, edited by K. Neff, Munich, 1908.

————. "Homéliaire de Paul Diacre," edited by R. Grégoire, *Les Homéliaires du Moyen Age: inventaire et analyse des manuscrits*, pp. 71-114, Rome, 1966.

Paulinus of Aquileia, *Contra Felicem libri tres*, *CCCM* 95, edited by D. Norberg, Turnhout, 1990.

————. *L'Œuvre poétique de Paulin d'Aquilée*, edited by D. Norberg, Stockholm, 1979.

————. *Liber exhortationis*, *PL* 99.197-282.

Precum libelli quattuor aevi karolini, edited by A. Wilmart, Rome, 1940.

Prudentius of Troyes, *Epistola tractoria*, *PL* 115.1365-1368.

De praedestinatione, *PL* 115.1009-1366.

Quierzy (Frühjahr 853), *MGH Conc.* 3, edited by W. Hartmann, pp. 294-297, Hanover, 1984.

Ratramnus of Corbie, *De corpore et sanguine Domini*, edited by J. N. Bakhuizen Van Den Brink, 2nd edition, Amsterdam, 1974.

————. *De praedestinatione Dei*, *PL* 121.11-80.

Remigius of Auxerre, *Expositio missae*, (Pseudo-Alcuin) *Liber de divinis officiis* 40, *PL* 101.1246-1271.

Sacramentaire grégorien, 3 vols., edited by J. Deshusses, Fribourg, 1971-1982.

Sedulius Scottus, *Collectanea in omnes beati Pauli epistolas*, *PL* 103.9-270.

Theodulf of Orléans, *Carmina*, *MGH PLAC* 1, edited by E. Dümmler, pp. 437-578, Berlin, 1881.

————. *Opus Caroli regis contra synodum (Libri Carolini)*, *MGH Leges* 4, *Conc.* 2, *Supplementum* 1, edited by A. Freeman in collaboration with P. Meyvaert, Hanover, 1998.

————. *De ordine baptismi*, *PL* 105.223-240.

Tusey (22. Oktober-7. November 860), *MGH Conc.* 4, edited by W. Hartmann, pp. 12-42, Hanover, 1998.

Utrecht-Psalter: vollständige Faksimile-Ausgabe im Originalformat der Handschrift 32, Utrecht-Psalter, aus dem Besitz der Bibliotheek der Rijksuniversiteit te Utrecht, 2 vols., *Commentary* by K. van der Horst and J. A. Engelbregt, Graz, 1984.

Valence (8. Januar 855), *MGH Conc.* 3, edited by W. Hartmann, pp. 347-365, Hanover, 1984.

Walafrid Strabo, *Libellus de exordiis et incrementis quarundam in observationibus ecclesiasticis rerum*, edited by V. Krause, *MGH Capit.* 2, pp. 473-516. Hanover, 1897. Translated by A. Harting-Corrêa, *Walafrid Strabo's Libellus de exordiis et incrementis quarundam in observationibus ecclesiasticis rerum: a Translation and Liturgical Commentary*, Leiden, 1996.

SECONDARY SOURCES

Belting, Hans, "Der Einhardsbogen," *Zeitschrift für Kunstgeschichte* 36 (1973), 93-121. *Likeness and Presence: a History of the Image before the Era of Art,* translated from the German by E. Jephcott, Chicago, 1994.

Belting, Hans, and Christa Belting-Ihm, "Das Kreuzbild im *Hodegos* des Anastasios Sinaites: ein Beitrag zur Frage nach der ältesten Darstellung des toten Crucifixus," in *Tortulae: Studien zu altchristlichen und byzantinischen Monumenten,* edited by W.N. Schumacher, pp. 30-39, Rome, 1966.

Berndt, Rainer, ed., *Das frankfurter Konzil von 794: Kristallisationspunkt karolingischer Kultur,* 2 vols., Mainz, 1997.

Bischoff, Bernhard, "Kreuz und Buch im frühmittelalter und in den ersten Jahrhunderten der spanischen Reconquista," *Mittelalterliche Studien: ausgewähle Aufsätze zur Schriftkunde und Literaturgeschichte,* 3 vols., vol. 2, pp. 284-303, Stuttgart, 1967.

Braunfels, Wolfgang, ed., *Karl der Grosse: Lebenswerk und Nachleben,* 4 vols., Düsseldorf, 1965-1967.

———. *Die Welt der Karolinger und ihre Kunst,* Munich, 1968.

Bullough, Donald, "Alcuin's Cultural Influence: the Evidence of the Manuscripts," in *Alcuin of York: Scholar at the Carolingian Court,* edited by L. A. J. R. Houwen and A. A. MacDonald, pp. 1-26, Groningen, 1995.

———. *Carolingian Renewal: Sources and Heritage,* Manchester, 1991.

"The Carolingian Liturgical Experience," *Studies in Church History* 35 (1999), 29-64.

Chazelle, Celia, "Archbishops Ebo and Hincmar of Reims and the Utrecht Psalter," *Speculum* (1997), 1055-1077. Reprinted in *Approaches to Early-Medieval Art,* edited by Lawrence Nees, pp. 97-119, Cambridge, MA, 1998.

———. "Figure, Character, and the Glorified Body in the Carolingian Eucharistic Controversy," *Traditio* 47 (1992), 1-36.

———. "Images, Scripture, the Church, and the *Libri Carolini,*" *Proceedings of the Patristic, Medieval, and Renaissance Studies Conference* 16/17 (1993), 53-76.

———. "Matter, Spirit, and Image in the *Libri Carolini,*" *Recherches augustiniennes* 21 (1986), 163-184.

———. "Memory, Instruction, Worship: 'Gregory's' Influence on Early Medieval Doctrines of the Artistic Image," in *Gregory the Great: a Symposium,* edited by J. C. Cavadini, pp. 181-215, Notre Dame, 1996.

———. "'Not in Painting but in Writing': Augustine and the Supremacy of the Word in the *Libri Carolini,*" in *Reading and Wisdom: the De doctrina Christiana of Augustine in the Middle Ages,* edited by E. D. English, pp. 1-22, Notre Dame, 1995.

———. "Pictures, Books, and the Illiterate: Pope Gregory I's Letters to Serenus of Marseilles," *Word & Image* 6 (1990), 138-153.

Corrigan, Kathleen, "Text and Image on an Icon of the Crucifixion at Mount Sinai," in *The Sacred Image East and West,* edited by R. Ousterhout and L. Brubaker, pp. 45-62, Urbana, 1995.

———. *Visual Polemics in the Ninth-Century Byzantine Psalters,* Cambridge, 1992.

de Nie, Giselle, "Iconic Alchemy: Imaging Miracles in Late Sixth-Century Gaul," *Studia Patristica* 30, pp. 158-166, Louvain, 1997.

———. "Seeing and Believing in the Early Middle Ages: a Preliminary Investigation," in *Word and Image: the Pictured Word, Interactions* 2, edited by Martin Heusser et al., pp. 67-76, Amsterdam, 1998.

———. "Word, Image and Experience in the Early Medieval Miracle Story," in *Language and Beyond/Le Langage et ses au-delà, Text: Studies in Comparative Literature* 17, edited by P. Joret and A. Remael, pp. 97-122, Amsterdam, 1998.

Dölger, F. J., "Beiträge zur Geschichte des Kreuzzeichens, I-IX," *Jahrbuch für Antike und Christentum* 1-10 (1958-1967).

Elbern, Victor H., "Der fränkische Reliquienkasten und Tragaltar von Werden," in *Das erste Jahrtausend: Kultur und Kunst im werdenden Abendland an Rhein und Ruhr,* vol. 1, edited by V. H. Elbern, pp. 436-470, Düsseldorf, 1962.

Ernst, Ulrich, *Carmen figuratum: Geschichte des Figurengedichts von den antiken Ursprüngen bis zum Ausgang des Mittelalters,* Cologne, 1991.

Ferrari, Michele, "*Hrabanica.* Hrabans *De laudibus sanctae crucis* im Spiegel der neueren Forschung," in *Kloster Fulda in der Welt der Karolinger und Ottonen,* edited by G. Schrimpf, pp. 493-526, Frankfurt, 1996.

———. *Il "Liber sanctae crucis" di Rabano Mauro: testo-immagine-contesto,* Bern, 1999.

Flint, Valerie, *The Rise of Magic in Early Medieval Europe,* Princeton, 1991.

Fried, Johannes, "Fulda in der Bildungs-und Geistesgeschichte des früheren Mittelalters," in *Kloster Fulda in der Welt der Karolinger und Ottonen,* edited by G. Schrimpf, pp. 3-38, Frankfurt, 1996.

Frolow, A, *La relique de la vraie croix: recherches sur le développement d'un culte,* Paris, 1961.

Gaborit-Chopin, Danielle, *Elfenbeinkunst im Mittelalter,* translated from the French by G. Bloch and R. Beyer, Berlin, 1978.

Ganz, David, *Corbie in the Carolingian Renaissance,* Sigmaringen, 1990.

————. "The Debate on Predestination," in *Charles the Bald: Court and Kingdom,* edited by M. T. Gibson and J. L. Nelson, revised edition, pp. 281-302, Aldershot, 1990.

————. "Theology and the Organisation of Thought," in *NCMH* 2, edited by R. McKitterick, pp. 758-785, Cambridge, 1995.

Goldschmidt, Adolph, *Die Elfenbeinskulpturen aus der Zeit der karolingischen und sächischen Kaiser, VIII-IX. Jahrhundert,* vol. 1, Berlin, 1914.

Gorman, Michael, "The Commentary on Genesis of Claudius of Turin and Biblical Studies under Louis the Pious," *Speculum* 72 (1997), 279-329.

Hartmann, Wilfried, *Die Synoden der Karolingerzeit im Frankenreich und in Italien* Paderborn, 1989.

Hubert, Jean, J. Porcher, and W. F. Volbach, *L'Empire carolingien,* Paris, 1968.

Kartsonis, Anna, *Anastasis: the Making of an Image,* Princeton, 1986.

Kessler, Herbert L., "*Facies bibliothecae revelata:* Carolingian Art as Spiritual Seeing," in *Testo e immagine nell'alto medioevo,* Settimane di studio del Centro Italiano di Studi Sull'Alto Medioevo, 41, pp. 533-594, Spoleto, 1994.

————. "Real Absence: Early Medieval Art and the Metamorphosis of Vision," in *Morfologie sociali e culturali in Europa fra tarda antichità e alto medioevo,* Settimane di studio del Centro Italiano di Studi Sull'Alto Medioevo, 45, pp. 1157-1211, Spoleto, 1998.

Kornbluth, Genevra, *Engraved Gems of the Carolingian Empire,* University Park, PA, 1995.

Lewis, Suzanne, "A Byzantine *Virgo Militans* at Charlemagne's Court," *Viator* 11 (1980), 71-93.

McKitterick, Rosamond, ed., *The New Cambridge Medieval History,* vol. 2: *c. 700-c. 900.* Cambridge, 1995.

————, ed., *Carolingian Culture: Emulation and Innovation,* Cambridge, 1994. *The Carolingians and the Written Word,* Cambridge, 1989.

————. "Charles the Bald (823-877) and His Library: the Patronage of Learning," *English Historical Review* 95 (1980), 28-47.

————. *The Frankish Church and the Carolingian Reforms, 789-895,* London, 1977.

————. *The Frankish Kingdoms Under the Carolingians, 751-987,* London, 1983.

————, ed., *The Uses of Literary in Early Medieval Europe,* Cambridge, 1990.

Nees, Lawrence, "Art and Architecture," in *NCMH* 2, edited by R. McKitterick, pp. 809-844, Cambridge, 1995.

————. *A Tainted Mantle: Hercules and the Classical Tradition at the Carolingian Court,* Philadelphia, 1991.

————. "Theodulf's Mythical Silver Hercules Vase, *Poetica vanitas,* and the Augustinian Critique of the Roman Heritage," *Dumbarton Oaks Papers* 41 (1987), 443-451.

Nordhagen, Per Jonas, *The Frescoes of John VII (A.D. 705-707) in Santa Maria Antiqua in Rome,* Rome, 1968.

Reil, Johannes, *Christus am Kreuz in der Bildkunst der Karolingerzeit,* Leipzig, 1930. *Die frühchristlichen Darstellung der Kreuzigung Christi,* Leipzig, 1904.

Sansterre, Jean-Marie, "Entre *koinè méditerraneene,* influences byzantines et particularités locales: le culte des images et ses limites á Rome dans le haut moyen âge," in *Europa medievale e mondo bizantino: contatti effettivi e possibilità di studi comparati,* edited by G. Arnaldi and G. Cavallo, pp. 109-124, Rome, 1997.

————. "L'image blessée, l'image souffrante: quelques récits de miracles entre Orient et Occident (VIE-XIIE siècle)," *Bulletin de l'Institut historique belge da Rome* 69 (1999), 113-130.

Schiller, Gertrud, *Iconography of Christian Art,* vol. 2, translated by J. Seligman, Greenwich, CT, 1972.

Schramm, Percy Ernst, Hermann Filitz, and Florentine Mütherich, *Denkmale der deutschen Könige und Kaiser,* 2 vols., vol. 1: Schramm and Mütherich, *Ein Beitrag zur Herrscergeschichte von Karl dem Grossen bis Friedrich II, 768-1250,* 2nd expanded edn., Munich, 1981.

Sears, Elizabeth, "Louis the Pious as *Miles Christi:* the Dedicatory Image in Hrabanus Maurus' *De laudibus sanctae crucis,*" in *Charlemagne's Heir: New Perspectives on the Reign of Louis the Pious,* edited by P. Godman and R. Collins, pp. 605-628, Oxford, 1990.

Spilling, Herrad, *Opus Magnentii Hrabani Mauri honorem sanclae crucis conditum, Hrabanus Beziehung zu seinem Werk,* Frankfurt, 1992.

Steenbock, Frauke, "Kreuzförmige Typen frühmittelalterlicher Prachteinbände," in *Das erste Johrtausend: Kultur und Kunst im werdenden Abendland an Rhein und Ruhr,* vol. 1, edited by V. H. Elbern, pp. 495-513, Düsseldorf, 1962.

Steigemann, Christoph, and Matthias Wemhoff, eds., *799: Kunst und Kultur der Karolingerzeit, Karl der Grosse und Papst Leo III. in Paderborn: Katalog der Ausstellung Paderborn 799,* 2 vols. and *Beiträge,* Mainz, 1999.

Suntrup, Rudolf, "Präfigurationen des Messopfers in Text und Bild," *Frühmittelalterliche Studien* 18 (1994), 468-528.

————. *"Te igitur*-Initialen und Kanonbilder in mittelalterlichen Sakramentarhandschriften" in *Text und Bild: Aspekte des Zusammenwirkens zweier Künste im Mittelalter und früher Neuzeit,* edited by C. Meier and U. Ruberg, pp. 278-382, Wiesbaden, 1980.

Taeger, Burkhard, ed., *Der Heliand: Studienausgabe in Auswahl,* Tübingen, 1984.

————. *Zahlensymbolik bei Hraban, bei Hincmar- und im "Heliand"?: Studien zur Zahlensymbolik im Frühmittelalter,* Munich, 1970.

Weitzmann, Kurt, *The Monastery of Saint Catherine at Mount Sinae: the Icons,* vol. 1: *From the Sixth to the Tenth Century,* Princeton, 1976.

Wenger, Luke, "Hrabanus Maurus, Fulda, and Carolingian Spirituality," Ph.D. dissertation, Harvard University, 1973.

Wirth, Jean, *L'Image médiévale: naissance et développements (VIe-XVe siècle),* Paris, 1989.

Abbreviations

BNF: Bibliothèque Nationale de France

CCCM: Corpus Christianorum, Continuatio Mediaevalis

CCM: Corpus Consuetudinem Monasticarum

CCSL: Corpus Christianorum, Series Latina

CSEL: Corpus Scriptorum Ecclesiasticorum Latinorum

MGH: Monumenta Germaniae Historica

Capit.: Capitularia

Conc.: Concilia

Epp.: Epistolae

PLAC: Poetae latini aevi Carolini

SRM: Scriptorum rerum Merovingicarum

SS: Scriptores

NCMH2: The New Cambridge Medieval History, volume 2: *c. 700-c. 900*

PL: Patrologia cursus completus, series latina

SC: Sources chrétiennes

ST: Studi e Testi

FURTHER READING

Criticism

Curtius, Ernst Robert. *European Literature and the Latin Middle Ages,* translated by Willard R. Trask. Princeton, N.J.: Princeton University Press, 1953, 662 p.
  Includes analyses of various facets Hrabanus's work in the historical context of early medieval literature. This work was originally published in 1948.

De Jong, Mayke. "Old Law and New-Found Power: Hrabanus Maurus and the Old Testament." In *Centres of Learning: Learning and Location in Pre-Modern Europe and the Near East,* edited by Jan Willem Drijvers and A. A. MacDonald, pp. 161-76. Leiden, The Netherlands: E. J. Brill, 1995.
  Discusses Hrabanus's Old Testament commentaries, explaining that he regarded divine law as the foundation of social stability.

Laistner, M. L. W. *Thoughts and Letters in Western Europe* A.D. *500-900.* London, United Kingdom: Methuen, 1931, 354 p.
  Includes a discussion of Hrabanus's writings on biblical and ecclesiastical subjects within the context of Carolingian theology.

Le Berrurier, Diane. *The Pictorial Sources of Mythological and Scientific Illustrations in Hrabanus Maurus's De rerum naturis.* New York: Garland, 1978, 285 p.
  An art historian's view of Hrabanus's richly illustrated encyclopedia that includes analyses of various facets of his work in the historical context of early medieval literature.

McKitterick, Rosamond. *Books, Scribes, and Learning in the Frankish Kingdom 6th-9th Centuries.* Variorum, England: Aldershot, 1994, 340 p.
  Provides intellectual background of Hrabanus' work as a writer and educator.

Raby, F. J. E. *A History of Christian-Latin Poetry.* Oxford, United Kingdom: Clarendon Press, 1953, 494 p.
  Includes a discussion of Hrabanus's Christian didactic poetry.

Sears, Elizabeth. "Louis the Pious as *Miles Christi:* The Dedicatory Image in Hrabanus Maurus's *De laudibus sanctae crucis.*" In *Charlemagne's Heir: Perspectives on the Reign of Louis the Pious,* edited by P. Godman and R. Collins, pp. 605-28. Oxford, United Kingdom: Oxford University Press, 1990.

Discusses the powerful symbolism of Hrabanus's tribute to Louis, whom he describes as the authentic Christian monarch.

Additional coverage of Hrabanus's life and career is contained in the following sources published by Thomson Gale: *Dictionary of Literary Biography,* **Vol. 148; and** *Literature Resource Center.*

Prudentius
348-c. 410-15

(Full name Aurelius Clemens Prudentius) Spanish-born Latin poet.

INTRODUCTION

Widely considered the greatest of the early Christian poets, Prudentius composed the *Psychomachia* (c. 405), which represents the first extended use of personification allegory, pitting Vice and Virtue in a battle for the soul of mankind. Its popularity brought forth a host of imitators well into the Middle Ages. Prudentius is also invaluable to historians and literary scholars studying the advent of Christianity in Rome because he was a poet loyal to both. He believed that the state and classical, pagan models of literature could be used as tools for the spread of Christianity. Prudentius was one of the earliest hymnists, as represented by two volumes, the *Liber Cathemerinon* (c. 405) and the *Liber Peristephanon* (c. 405).

BIOGRAPHICAL INFORMATION

Virtually all that is known of Prudentius's life is drawn from what he himself states in the forty-five verses of the *Praefatio* (c. 405), or preface, to a collection he made of his works. Prudentius was born in northern Spain, probably in Saragossa (Caesaraugusta), presumably to moderately wealthy Christian parents. He was well educated in rhetoric and literature and had a career as a lawyer, and later as governor of two cities, until he was called to serve the emperor. He spent most of his life in the area of his birthplace, but he traveled to Rome one or two times. Although it has sometimes been claimed that Prudentius began writing in 405, at age fifty-seven, evidence indicates that he may actually have started as far back as the 380s, and almost certainly by the 390s. His date of death is unknown, but probably fell between 410 and 415.

MAJOR WORKS

The *Liber Peristephanon* contains fourteen hymns or tributes to martyrs, most of whom were Spanish. Scholar Jill Harries advances the idea that Prudentius may have started this work in the 380s. The *Contra Orationem Symmachi* is comprised of two volumes, the first probably written between 394 and 395, the second from 402. Here Prudentius argues against some of the positions taken by a pagan senator, Symmachus. Prudentius's most celebrated work is the *Psychomachia*, in which seven virtues—Fides (faith), Pudicitia (chastity), Patientia (patience), Mens Humilis (humility), Sobriety (soberness), Operatio (good works), and Concordia (concord)—represented by Christian characters, wage battle against seven vices—Veterum Cultura Deorum (worship of old gods), Sodomita Libido (lust of the sodomite), Ira (anger), Superbia (pride), Luxuria (indulgence), Avaritia (avarice), and Discordia (discord)—represented by pagans. The vices are vanquished by the soldiers of virtue. The *Praefatio,* also known as the *Prooemium,* lays out Prudentius's statement of Christian poetics. Composed in about 405, the *Apotheosis* defends the orthodox doctrine of the Trinity and the *Hamartigenia* (c. 405) attacks the Gnostic dualism that sought to separate the God of the Old and New Testaments. The *Liber Cathemerinon* (c. 405) consists of twelve hymns, including songs for morning, mealtime, bedtime, fasting, burial, and Christmas. Five of the poems are part of the Roman Breviary. The *Tituli Historiarum* (c. 405), also known as the *Dittochaeon,* consists of forty-nine quatrains describing Bible scenes represented on murals in a church. Prudentius's complete works total approximately 11,000 lines.

CRITICAL RECEPTION

Although in general the textual tradition of Prudentius elicits few serious disagreements, Maurice P. Cunningham discusses several problems related to the questionable inclusion of some lines. Cunningham rejects suggestions of deliberate mischief, blaming instead human error, but expresses disappointment with scholars who have been too quick to change a word or phrase they deem incorrect. Charles Witke focuses on the *Praefatio* and the *Epilogue,* in which the poet explains his sense of Christian poetics. Witke credits Prudentius with taking a new direction that mediates the tension between the Latin tradition and the advent of Christianity. Robert W. Gaston discusses how Prudentius was used in the sixteenth century by scholars of early church history. Gaston notes that the choice had merit: "Throughout the Middle Ages Prudentius had been the most widely read Christian Latin poet of the Roman period. His popularity from the fifth to the fourteenth century is evident not only in the several hundred surviving manuscripts of his works, but also in the number of references to him and quotations from his poems in medieval books." John P. Hermann discusses the *Psychomachia*'s influence in his study of an Old English poem. In Macklin Smith's introduction to his book examining the *Psychomachia,* the author explores how Prudentius may have conceived such a work and what conditions may have prepared an audience for it. Smith analyzes Prudentius's use of personification allegory, notes that "its skillful imitation of Vergil is anti-Vergilian," and also summarizes some of the critical responses to the volume. Smith asserts that Prudentius was the best Latin poet between the Augustan Age and the twelfth century. Alison Goddard Elliott contends that the *Peristephanon* more closely resembles medieval epic than classical epic and explores its possible influence on Old French *chansons de geste.* Jill Harries looks at various passages of Prudentius, including ones that refer to Theodosius I and his son Honorius, which can be used to date some of the poet's works. She concludes that the two books of the *Contra Orationem Symmachi* were written some seven years apart. William J. McCarthy explores how Prudentius "Christianized" Lucretius's theory of atomism. McCarthy, who calls Prudentius's poetry "occasionally masterful," examines his use of Lucretius's *De rerum natura.* Martha A. Malamud provides an exposition of the *Psychomachia* and compares and contrasts Prudentius's work with Claudian's *In Rufinum.* Robert Levine explores the question of Prudentius's literary excesses. Levine remarks on Prudentius's portrayal of the martyrs, who "endure pain and death not merely with conventional Stoic fortitude, but with joy, a sense of play, and in several instances, among which *Peristephanon* X is the most elaborate, with a loquacity that is simultaneously stunning and disturbing." Eva Kimminich uses the *Psychomachia* to help determine medieval views regarding spiritual welfare. Kimminich finds that Prudentius broke somewhat with the prevailing Augustinian theology that emphasized grace, and instead adopted Origen's, which emphasized a vigorous free will. Joseph Pucci uses examples from the *Praefatio* and the *Cathemerinon* to demonstrate Prudentius's skill in using both the classical (as exemplified by Horace) and the Christian traditions in his poetry. Jill Ross's study of the *Peristephanon* centers on "the redemptive power of the written word" as practiced by Prudentius, and his complex use of imagery and metaphor in describing the spiritual strength of martyrs." Ross contends that he made "bloody texts" of the martyrs' bodies "so that they can mimic Christ's redemptive role in the function of their wounded bodies as instruments of salvation."

PRINCIPAL WORKS

Contra Orationem Symmachi. 2 vols. (poetry) 394 or 395; 402
Apotheosis (poetry) c. 405
Epilogus (poetry) c. 405
Hamartigenia (poetry) c. 405
Liber Cathemerinon (poetry) c. 405
Liber Peristephanon (poetry) c. 405
Praefatio [*Prooemium*] (poetry) c. 405
Psychomachia (poetry) c. 405
Tituli Historiarum [*Dittochaeon*] (poetry) c. 405
Aurelii Prudentii Clementis Carmina (poetry) 1967

Principal English Translations

Prudentius. 2 vols. (edited by H. J. Thomson) 1949-53

CRITICISM

Maurice P. Cunningham (essay date 1968)

SOURCE: Cunningham, Maurice P. "The Problem of Interpolation in the Textual Tradition of Prudentius." *Transactions and Proceedings of the American Philological Association* 99 (1968): 119-41.

[*In the following essay, Cunningham defends the manuscripts of Prudentius against charges that they have been altered with deliberate insertions of text written by others.*]

The matter of real, apparent, or alleged interpolations in the textual tradition of Prudentius raises a number of problems both on a practical and a theoretical level, which I wish to discuss in some detail since they seem to have application to the general theory of the transmission of Latin texts from antiquity to the earlier middle ages.[1]

In my edition of Prudentius (p. xxii) I said that in general in classical texts some intrusive elements occur as the result of human frailty, others are deliberate attempts by someone to foist upon readers words other than those of an author as the author's own. I use the word "deliberate" here in the sense of the legal term "with malice aforethought" (*dolo malo*). I say that I do not recall an instance of this second kind of interpolation in the primary manuscripts of Prudentius. This statement has not gone unchallenged. Dom Paul Antin cites Gnilka's paper of 1965 on *S.* [*Symmachum*]

2.423-27 and *Ham.* [*Hamartigenia*] 887-91. Gnilka also, in a review of Herzog's monograph, objects to and deplores my sterile approach.

In this paper I address myself particularly to Dr. Gnilka and those whom he has persuaded, in order to try to convince them that his position is not well founded in fact. I do not deny that, from time to time, one finds in manuscripts of Prudentius lines which do not belong there or do not belong where we find them. But I believe that their presence can be accounted for by simpler hypotheses than that of deliberate interpolation. The commonest source of intrusive elements of a line or more in length I take to be parallel passages written in the margin, that is, quotations of some other line or lines of verse which seemed in some way to the person who put them there in the first place to illustrate or exemplify a point raised by the text. Some possibilities are: a line which illustrates either similar or contrasting prosody, possible imitations where Prudentius may be imitator or imitated, a passage illustrating similar or contrasting treatment of a topic, and so on. I presume that we are all familiar with this sort of thing. A slightly different sort of addition is the line added at the end of the *Apotheosis* in A by a medieval hand in pseudo-rustic capitals:

> superna regna monstrando nos illuc cupit adire.

This line is also found in CD and Einsiedeln 312. In those manuscripts one might call it an interpolation; but it is just a "tag line." I do not think it was intended to deceive anyone.

Let us now examine in detail the passages which are said by Gnilka to be deliberate interpolations.

Contra Symmachum 2.423-27

> Displicet hic subito status et bis quina creantur
> summorum procerum fastigia, quos duodeni
> circumstant fasces simul et sua quemque securis.
> Rursus se geminis reddit ductoribus omnis
> publica res et consulibus dat condere fastos.

This passage occurs in the section of the poem in which Prudentius discusses Symmachus' (*Rel.* 3.8) statement: "ut animae nascentibus ita populis fatales genii diuiduntur." Prudentius first objects that the concept of *genius* is vague, and in any case it does not support Symmachus' parallel between men and peoples or cities. Granting that there was such a *genius,* when did it first enter the body of Rome (393-94)? He invites us (403) to laugh at some of the answers. Then, taking the notion more seriously for the moment, he asks why can it not act like a man with free will in the matter of religion and be capable of conversion. Rome made a number of changes in her form of government until she finally

achieved the best form in the empire: why should she not accept the true religion now that she knows at last what the true religion is (436-40)?

The specific passage Gnilka discusses occurs in Prudentius' development of the topic that Rome's *geniusue animusue publicus* drifted along for about 700 years without quite knowing what form of government it really wanted. It may come as a shock to us to learn that Prudentius assumes that the empire is the natural and right form of government for his world, but there is no doubt that he says that it is (430-31):

> tandem deprendere rectum
> doctus iter caput augustum diademate cinxit. . . .

Previous to that time Rome's *genius* was constantly in doubt about what would be the best form of government for it (414 *semper dubitans*). The Romans demonstrated this doubt by changing the form. First (416 *exortam*) came the kings, who ruled with the cooperation of the senate. Next (418 *mox*) came the rule of nobles (*proceres*) of the senatorial class. Then (419 *inde*) the *plebs* achieved a mixed constitution, and this lasted for a long time (*diu*). The strength of the nobles lay in the consul (422); the *plebs* placed their trust in the tribune. Suddenly (423 *subito*) they abolished the mixed constitution for the decemvirate. And then (426 *rursus*) they went back to consuls. Finally (428 *ultima*) came the triumvirs.[2] Only after all these vicissitudes did Rome achieve the natural stability of the imperial office.

Gnilka takes the passage as a whole about as I do, though he says little about Prudentius' stress on Rome's vacillation about her proper form of government. But he wishes to exclude lines 423-27 on the decemvirate as an interpolation, inserted by someone who wished to expand the argument.

His reasons for regarding the passage as an interpolation fall under three heads. First, he believes that it has already been established that there is a good deal of interpolation of this sort in the text of Prudentius. Second, he believes that there is manuscript evidence for some tampering at this spot. And, third, he tries to show that the lines in question are so out of place in relation to their context that it is impossible to believe that Prudentius himself is responsible for them. So far as language goes, the lines are thoroughly Prudentian, but that only demonstrates the skill of the interpolator (Gnilka 246, note 3).

Each of these points requires careful study and consideration, for allegations of interpolation usually rest upon more than one of them. If an answer is given in terms of one point only, recourse will be had to one of the others. One might remark incidentally that the matter of language is used unfairly. If the lines appeared in any way un-Prudentian, that would be used as an argument against them. But the fact that they do sound like Prudentius cannot also be used as evidence that they are spurious.

Let us take up the matter of context first. A good test of any suggestion that lines in a tradition are intrusive (for any reason) is to assume that the suggested reading is in fact traditional and to see how it fits.

According to Gnilka, then, Prudentius says (404), "Let us assume the existence of something through which the Roman *res publica* got its destiny (*fatum*) and existence (*animetur*). . . . For 700 years it was in constant doubt about the proper form of government." Then (416) we would have a detailed illustration of this topic sentence, listing monarchy, aristocracy, mixed constitution, triumvirate, and empire. Does this orderly sequence really bear out the topic announced in the words *semper dubitans* and the rest of 413-15? I do not believe that it does. Prudentius' topic is not orderly progression but doubt and vacillation. Surely, Prudentius would have strengthened his case by some reference to the consular tribunes or to the decemvirate as modifications of the republican form. The institution of consular tribunes, however, is regularly regarded as involving only a modification of the consulate, not of the mixed constitution itself. But Livy (3.33) describes the decemvirate as a major constitutional change:

> anno trecentensimo altero quam condita Roma erat, iterum mutatur forma ciuitatis, ab consulibus ad decemuiros, quem ad modum ab regibus ante ad consules uenerat, translato imperio. minus insignis quia non diuturna mutatio fuit.

The same ideas are found in the received text of Prudentius. The terms *subito* and *rursus* reinforce the idea of *semper dubitans*. *Displicet* in 423 picks up *placeret* in 414. *Diu* in 421 may be an echo of Livy's *diuturna*.

Gnilka agrees that lines 423-27 are based on Livy, but he denies that Prudentius could have written them. The key word for him in this passage is (421) *diu*. On it he says every attempt to reconcile the various statements of the received text must founder (p.249, "An dem Wörtchen *diu* muss jeder Harmonisierungsversuch endgültig scheitern"). With the received text he claims that the mixed constitution is restricted to the period from the introduction of the tribunate to the decemvirate and that Prudentius knew too much Roman history to use the word *diu* of this period, especially since he presently mentions the long period from the decemvirate to the triumvirate. To support this view he must take (p. 250, note 2) 423 *displicet* as marking an item

in Prudentius' list on a par with 418 *mox*, 419 *inde*, and 428 *ultima*. One would like a parallel for the verbal pattern involved; the *Thesaurus* lists no examples of anything comparable under *inde* or *mox*. His is not the most natural way of understanding the word nor the passage in question, which says practically the same thing about the decemvirate that Livy does. It involved a major constitutional change, but, since it did not last, it was in effect a mere temporary interruption of the republican form or mixed constitution.

Gnilka does have a difficulty, and it lies in the word *diu*. But he seems to ask the wrong question. The real question, which remains even after his deletion, is: What do the word *diu* and its meaning have to do with Prudentius' thesis? This is the only constitutional development for which Prudentius furnishes an indication of a time span. Why? Does *diu* support Prudentius' thesis? No. In part, it may form an objection to that thesis if a single earlier constitutional form lasted for over four centuries. Thus, the train of thought goes something like this: "Although the mixed constitution lasted for a long time, it too was not without interruption."

Nor does leaving out lines 423-27 solve the problem which the word *diu* poses. The mixed constitution lasted for a long time and Prudentius says it did. However, his thesis is not that there was an orderly progression in Rome's constitutional history, but rather that things drifted along from one thing to another and sometimes back again until Rome finally learned to take the right course and achieved her proper form of government. In the repetition of *errauit* (413 and 430) together with the extended nautical metaphor one may see a sort of subliminal allusion to the wanderings of Aeneas. Prudentius' thesis, expressed succinctly in the words *semper dubitans*, is strongly supported by lines 423-27, which are admittedly Prudentian in their form of expression. Gnilka's argument neglects to give proper consideration to the first sentence of this section (413-15):

> Sic septingentis errauit circiter annis
> lubricaque et semper dubitans quae forma placeret
> imperii, quae regnandi foret aequa potestas.

One should note the words *errauit*, *lubrica*, and *semper dubitans*. The same theme is stressed once more in the conclusion of this section (436-40):

> Quod si tot rerum gradibus totiens uariatis
> consiliis. . . .

One can go further. Because of the necessary implications of the word *diu* in 421, if lines 423-27 were by some chance missing from the tradition, we ought to be able to recognize a lacuna between either 421 or 422 and 428. Far from supporting Gnilka's thesis, internal evidence in fact confirms the received text.

By way of summary I offer a rough translation of *S.* 2.413-40:

Just so Rome's ghost or soul drifted about for roughly 700 years, slipping around and constantly in doubt about what was her proper form of government, what type of rule was most fitting. Monarchy controlled the city at its beginning although elders also shared governmental functions. Next, we see that nobles of the senatorial class managed the helm of policy. After that, the plebeians were united with the patricians on a basis of equality and both ruled together for a long time in managing affairs in war and peace. The nobility was strong through the consulship; the *plebs* depended upon the tribunate. This arrangement was suddenly voted out, and ten chief magistrates were elected from the nobility, each with a full set of twelve *fasces* and accompanying axe; but the whole community turned back to two magistrates and let consuls function again. At the end, bloody triumvirs threw the world into turmoil. Once upon a time, the Roman people's fate or genius or spirit drifted as these waves carried it. Finally, it learned to set its right course, circled its imperial head with a diadem, calling him *Pater Patriae,* helmsman of people and senate, determined that he should be its leader in war, and likewise its chief magistrate, good censor, master of morals, guardian of wealth, punisher of crimes, and dispenser of honors.

But, if only after so many constitutional steps, so many changes of mind, did it with difficulty finally arrive at a system that it could approve and which the people's respect by a solemn undertaking could preserve, why does it hesitate to acknowledge divine rights it did not know before but which have at last been revealed?

Gnilka also claims that the assumption of an interpolation is supported by external evidence in the manuscript tradition. He cites Bergman's note that line 422 is found after 427 in CPEO and that 423-27 are omitted by the first hand in D, where they are supplied by a second hand with an indication that 422 is to follow 427. Gnilka stresses this omission in D, which he believes is a major witness to an independent textual tradition with the authority and prestige of the Puteanus (A) behind it (p. 248). But there is no such textual tradition in the *Contra Symmachum.* There is no evidence that the Puteanus ever contained that work, and there is some positive evidence that it did not at the time that the tradition represented by C and D was accessible to readings of A.

Among Bergman's manuscripts, C, D, and P belong to the tradition I call Δ, which is now represented in its purest form by E. At some time, presumably in the early ninth century, and probably in Northern France, readings deriving directly or indirectly from A are introduced into the E tradition. In E itself this process occurs most frequently in the form of a marginal note "alii libri habent" or "alii habent," followed by the reading of A. The same thing happens in C, D, and P,

except that in them the A reading sometimes appears in the text; the E reading then becomes the marginal variant. In E this phenomenon continues to occur down to *Pe.* [*Peristephanon*] 5.99-100. A breaks off at *Pe.* 5.142, and, unless I have made a mistake, there are no instances of *alii libri habent* or the like in E except in those portions of the work of Prudentius which are now extant in A. The same holds true so far as I have checked the matter in the case of other manuscripts of this group (C, D, P, G, F, q, and a).

Gnilka is obviously influenced by Klingner's[3] attempt to better Bergman's interpretation of his manuscripts in terms of Bergman's own apparatus. I hope that my treatment of the manuscripts of the *Cathemerinon, Apotheosis,* and *Hamartigenia* will now appear more acceptable, since it is based upon fuller evidence. Although I have not published a separate discussion of the recension of the manuscripts in the other works, I believe that sufficient information for our purpose is presented in my edition. The evidence shows that A influences C and consequently D in *Peristephanon* 1 to 5.142. After that point, where A breaks off, CD present a text which combines elements of the tradition of E with that of the tradition of S and its fellows, with no indication of a third independent line. The same combination of these two traditions is found in CD in the *Contra Symmachum.* Though D is considerably later than C in this section,[4] they belong together. The following readings are illustrative.

S. 1 ante 42	CD share the *inscriptiones* here and elsewhere with S
S. 1.350	cernuaque S CD
S. 1 post 366	extra verse added in C; added post 367 in S
S. 1 post 480	verse added S CD
S. 2.448-49	om. St D
S. 2.386	membrorum E CD
S. 2.814	sordida sus E CD

This should be enough to give one an idea. My study of D specifically has been fairly cursory; it is based upon Bergman's apparatus and his almost complete photographs of the manuscript. I feel safe in saying that D represents a somewhat later stage of the tradition represented by C.

In summary, the omission of *S.* 2.423-27 in D is easily accounted for by mechanical factors. As Gnilka himself points out, there are other purely mechanical omissions in this part of D (see his p. 248, note 2). The evidence of this manuscript here is of no special importance for the constitution of the text.

Gnilka, however, betrays a point of view in his note on the omissions in D which should not go unnoticed. He says specifically that D omits some lines which are indispensable in their contexts. One must protest that indispensability in this sense is not nearly so common in verse as might be assumed (*Ad Herennium* 2.34 supplies a refreshing corrective).

Granted that the lines in question fit their context and that the manuscript evidence does not help to prove them spurious, a person seeking possible interpolations has a third resource. Relying on a good deal of published work he may claim, as Gnilka does (p. 246), that the textual tradition is an interpolated one and that it has already been established that deliberate interpolations do occur in the textual tradition and that it has even been possible to formulate with some precision the motives for such interpolations. When I said that I did not recall seeing any such interpolations in the major witnesses to the textual tradition of Prudentius, Gnilka seemed shocked and frankly incredulous. Obviously my only hope of convincing him and others who feel as he does is to discuss at least some of the other passages where they are convinced we have to do with deliberate interpolation.

Hamartigenia 887-91

> Vna animas semper facies habet et color unus
> aëris, ut cuique est meritorum summa, sinistri
> seu dextri. Alternas nec commutabile tempus
> conuertit uariatque uices; longum atque perenne est
> quidquid id est, unus uoluit sua saecula cursus.

Ham. 887-91 is the second of the two passages discussed by Gnilka in the paper we have been studying.[5]

The passage occurs in a section devoted to a vivid and imaginative realization of the implications of the scene between Lazarus and the Rich Man in Luke 16:24. After a mention of this scene, Prudentius says:

> (863) Do not be surprised that this can happen. Between Heaven and Hell sight operates both as vision, the art of the eye of the one who sees (865 *conspicuos uisus*), and as visibility, i.e. that which makes it possible for the fate which each type of soul has earned to be seen and recognized (*notari*). (867) It is a mistake to judge the powers of the eye of the soul by those of our bodily eyes. The eyes of the soul are free of the inhibiting factors that apply to the eyes of the body. Soul's eyes are keen (874 *uiua acies*) and they can see right through to Hell (882). (883) Bodily eyes can see neither color nor shape at night or on an occasion when illumination is absent (884 *caeco tempore*). (885-86) But do the eyes of the soul free of the body lose the ability to recognize distinguishing marks or do they make mistakes? (887) No; because here we are dealing with a situation where soul sees soul, and at this point each soul has a permanently fixed *facies* and *color*, which for each is the final balance of his moral condition (*ut cuique est meritorum summa*), Left or Right. (889-90) In other

words, souls have one *facies* and one *color aeris,* which corresponds to the total of their deserts, that is, it is the *aer* of either Right or Left. Time causes changes; but there is no time here to modify or vary them from one condition to another. Lasting and forever is whatever that condition is. One course carries them along through all its ages, that is, whatever each one gets, lasts.

Then, after illustrating the soul's ability to see by analogies, first from dreams, and then from the vision of the Apocalypse (1:9-10), Prudentius concludes that it is a sure belief that those in Hell are to be seen by those in Heaven, and likewise those in Heaven by those in Hell.

Gnilka objects (p. 258, note 1) that 887-91 apply only to the Blessed seeing the Damned in darkness, since the Blessed are bright and the soul's vision knows no obstacles. But this is niggling. The point of these lines is that both the Blessed and the Damned have permanent recognizable features (*facies* and *color*) by which each can see that the other has his just desserts. This point is made again clearly in the last line of the section (930):

> inque uicem meritorum mutua cernunt.

The key point at issue in the interpretation of this passage is, as Gnilka clearly sees (p. 257), lines 885-86:

> Numquid et exuti membris ac uiscere perdunt
> agnitione notas rerum uel gressibus errant?

He says that these lines can be taken in two senses: (1) *notas rerum non uident,* or (2) *notas rerum ipsi non habent.* The first he says is certainly what Prudentius meant; the second is the way it was understood by the person who added 887-91. But this is not quite right. Gnilka, along with most of the translators, does not seem to give any proper force to the word *agnitione* (886).

To understand this word and its context better we should review the passage as a whole in terms of the theory of vision Prudentius is using. That theory recognizes two elements in the process of vision: (1) the active power of the seeing organ, and (2) the visibility of the object seen (865). I believe that Gnilka leaves this second point out entirely in his discussion of the context. As for the active power, it is a mistake to think that the power of sight in the soul is restricted by internal or external obstacles as that of the body is (877-82). But there is another point (883 *nempe*); the visibility of the very objects of bodily vision, color and shape (883 *colores,* 884 *formae*), are subject to vicissitudes of light and darkness. They perish (883 *pereunt*) at times. Do those persons also who are free of limbs and the flesh (*exuti* etc.) in the matter of recognition (*agnitione*) lose the ability to perceive the distinguishing marks of things (*numquid . . . perdunt . . . notas rerum?*) or are they subject to uncertainty (*uel gressibus errant?*)? For the next two lines, containing Prudentius' answer to these questions, I am quite in agreement with Gnilka on how to take the Latin. He paraphrases: "animae una sunt semper facie, uno colore," and adds "*Facies* und *color* bezeichnen Qualitäten der Seele selbst!" But, instead of regarding this as irrelevant, I regard it as an answer to Prudentius' own question. He implies a negative answer by explaining why. In fact, if the text broke off at 886 and the next thing we heard was 892, that is, if 887-91 were absent from the tradition, surely one would mark a lacuna here.

The whole train of thought demands something very like what we do in fact have here. Souls can be seen because they possess the qualities essential for visibility (887), *facies* (cf. 884 *formae*) and *color* (cf. 883 *colores*), and these qualities remain constant depending only upon *meritorum summa*. Left or Right, Damned or Blessed. There is no variation (889-91) and thus no margin for error; this latter part is in answer to the question: *uel gressibus errant?* The question that remains to be answered at the end of 886 is not one about the ability of the eye of the soul to see, but one about the visibility of the objects to be seen: the objects of its vision, souls in the other place. Lines 883-84 deal with the fact that objects are sometimes not visible to our ordinary eyes, because the very objects of vision, shapes and colors, are lost (*pereunt*). The next two lines ask a similar question about the eyes of the soul; in the matter of recognition do they lose *notas rerum*? The answer, like the question, deals not with the vision of the seeing soul but with the visibility of the one to be seen. That is the sense in which Prudentius answers it. If he did not do so, there would be no proper foundation laid for the conclusion in lines 922-30, where one should note especially that he says that the furnaces of Hell and the rewards of Heaven are both visible from the other place (925 *expositos* and 927 *ostendi*).

From our review of *Ham.* 887-91 and their context I believe we can conclude that Gnilka's thesis is not well founded. It fails the first test; for he must somehow show that the lines are out of place in their context. But they are far from being out of place; in fact, without them the topic announced in the word *notari* in 867 would remain undeveloped until it is repeated in the concluding lines of this section (922-25): "caminos . . . oculis longum per inane remoti / pauperis expositos," and (925-27): "aurea dona . . . eminus ostendi poenarum carcere mersis."

CONTRA SYMMACHUM 2.325-26 AND 325-27

In his discussion of the notion of deliberate interpolation in the text of Prudentius, Gnilka depends heavily on a paper by W. Schmid published in 1953. The thesis of this paper must now receive careful consideration.

The facts are quite simple. In **Contra Symmachum** 2, Prudentius, following a suggestion in Ambrose, *Epist.* 18.27, draws a parallel between the successive stages of a man's life (*uita hominis*) and those of the human race (*genus humanum*). Man passes through infancy, childhood, adolescence, maturity, and old age. Similar stages are found in the life of the race. Corresponding to *infantia repit* (318) is 325-26:

> sic hebes inter
> primitias mersumque solo ceu quadrupes egit.

This is the reading of all but one group of manuscripts (i.e. of TSQ). In the group represented by E we find 325-27:

> sic hebes inter
> primitias mersumque solo titubauit et instar
> quadrupedis pueri lactantia uiscera traxit.

(quadrupedis *E^c*, -dos *E*).

If we had had such a simple statement of the facts to begin with, I doubt that anyone would have seen much of a problem here. It seems fairly obvious that in E the unit *titubauit . . . traxit* has replaced the expression *ceu . . . egit*. One notes further that the reading of E is quite out of place in this context. The notion expressed in *lactantia uiscera traxit* has nothing to do with what Prudentius is talking about, and *titubauit* would be pointedly misleading, since he uses this word in 319 above of childhood, not of infancy. What the reading of E does do is to provide a parallel for the use of *quadrupes* of the human child in the crawling stage. I see in it nothing more than a marginal note of a parallel passage which has been taken by a copyist as a correction and copied into the text. We can see a paradigm of the whole process at work in the Bongarsianus, U. (The following information is based upon autopsy.) The second version above is written in the text; then the same scribe, U[1], deletes *titubauit et instar* by putting a dot under each letter; he also puts a symbol in the form of two acute accents close together (") before *titubauit* with a similar symbol in the margin followed by the words of the first version (" *ceu quadrupes egit*). He also places a symbol consisting of a diagonal line and two dots (%) in the margin right before 327; I take this to be a mark of deletion, since 327 is meaningless when 326 has been corrected.

Professor Schmid in his very learned and interesting article sees in this passage an instance of Doppelfassung. He says nothing about the diplomatic evidence for the two variants, presumably believing that both had about equal authority in the tradition. But he sees the second version as a deliberate but misguided attempt to make Prudentius say something other than what he did say.

To answer Schmid properly one must recognize that there are two separate problems here. What needs to be explained? And what is required of an explanation of a textual variation for it to be adequate?

As for the first question, Schmid apparently inferred reasonably enough, as I have said, that the authority for the two readings was about the same. But, now that he knows that we have to do merely with a variant in one line out of the three or four in the tradition, perhaps he will see this variant in much the same light as E's *tantum studium* for *tantus amor* in *S.* 2.335. *Tantum studium* is excluded from serious consideration by metrics, just as the second version of our lines is excluded by sense. In one instance, the text has been displaced by a gloss, in the other it has been replaced by a marginal parallel. But in both instances the corruption is in essence a purely mechanical one.

The second point has to do with the adequacy of explanations of textual variants. When a simple hypothesis and a complex one compete for our acceptance, surely one should in general prefer the simple one, unless there is some fact which it fails to explain. Hypotheses are not to be multiplied beyond necessity.

Here I think Professor Schmid believed that there was an additional fact to be explained, namely, the occurrence in the text of Prudentius of a fairly large number of doublets with roughly equal authority. We will not really have answered Schmid's argument until we take up at least some of these other instances of textual variation.

Contra Symmachum 2.143 and 142a-b

The very first one of these to demand our attention is a passage which Schmid discusses in this same paper, namely, **Contra Symmachum** 2.143 and 142a-b.

The problem here can be presented most compendiously if I simply copy my text and the relevant part of the apparatus and then give Thomson's Loeb translation of the alternatives. *S.* 2.141-43:

> Atque aeuum statui sub quo generosa probarem
> pectora, ne torpens et non exercita uirtus
> robur eneruatum gereret sine laude palaestrae.

post 142 *uersu* 143 *omisso praebet* E:

142a eneruare suum corrupta per otia robur

142b posset et in nullo luctamine pigra iaceret.

Hi uersus absunt a TStQ. Locus similis est. Post 142 *sua linea praebet* t: ignauiam trahere uitam.

Thomson: and I have set a period in which to prove noble hearts, lest their goodness being dormant and unexercised should wield a strength that was nerveless, winning no credit in the training-school.

(142a-b): might unman its strength in degenerate idleness and lie inactive, engaging in no struggle.

Schmid agrees with Bergman that lines 142a-b explain and simplify what is said in line 143. He says nothing of Arévalo's suggestion that someone rewrote 143 so as to preserve the long quantity of the first vowel in *eneruare*.

These are accounts of the facts; but what is the simplest explanation of them? Lines 142a-b stood in the margin of an ancestor of E next to line 143. A copyist took them as a correction of that line and substituted them for it.

This suggestion is not mere guesswork. In fact, what I suggest happened there is comparable to what did happen in U, where (according to my notes taken while looking at the manuscript) 142a-b stand between 142 and 143, but with a mark by the first hand that seems to indicate that they should be deleted. That things do get into the text from the margin is clear from the reading of t (though I hold no brief for its Latinity). Why were 142a-b written in the margin? I do not know. But reasonable conjectures are not hard to make. A reader with access to writing materials observed a similarity of diction and subject matter between Prudentius and a passage of another poet, and he made a note of the fact; or he wanted to cite an example of the more normal prosody of *eneruare;* or he noted a passage which Prudentius adapted or which adapted Prudentius; or perhaps more than one of these factors may have operated simultaneously; and so on. None of these hypotheses require us to believe that the person responsible in the first instance for the presence of these lines somewhere in some manuscript wished to expunge what Prudentius had written and to substitute something of his own composition or choosing instead. But these are reasonable hypotheses. Consequently, this passage cannot be relied upon as a certain example of a place where someone deliberately substituted other words for those of Prudentius.

The suggestion that this item has something to do with prosody is supported by *S.* 1.367-68:

> Cum subnixa sedet solio, Plutonia coniunx
> imperitat Furiis et dictat iura Megaerae.

After 367 in S we find:

> cum rapitur furia est et torui Plutonis uxor.

This line seems to be an illustration of an alternative quantity for the *o* in *Plutonia*. After the line gets into the tradition, one sees that an attempt was made to provide a readable text in C, which puts this line before 367. But that is another story. C is not a direct witness to one of the main ancient lines of the tradition.

Now I want to glance briefly at some other notorious instances of alleged deliberate interpolation in the text of Prudentius, but at the same time I want also to notice other factors which lead to corruption that may superficially resemble the results of deliberate interpolation.

> *C.* 1.26: est forma mortis perpetis.
> mortis imago est perpetis *A*

I explain the reading of A as the result of a gloss *imago est* above the line. This gloss then is copied into the text; but something has to give. The full version would have been: *est forma mortis imago est perpetis,* but enough of the first part of the line is omitted to yield something like proper metre: *mortis imago est perpetis.*

In *C.* [*Contra Symmachum*] 3.100, I see a similar process at work. I take it that the text read:

> flauit et indidit ore animam.

I assume a gloss *dedit* for *indidit,* and *ex proprio* as a gloss on *ore.* If all this was copied, we would get:

> flauit et indidit ore animam dedit ex proprio.

With the same technique of dropping words at the beginning of the line which we observe in *C.* 1.26, we would get the actual reading of A:

> ore animam dedit ex proprio.

Theology has nothing to do with the variant readings here. The thought of either version is paralleled by *Ham.* 829, "flatu ex proprio."

C. 6.6 seems to be a somewhat similar case. Let us assume that the non-A reading stood in a text with a gloss, *potestas,* and a mark to introduce it above *uis,* thus:

> .(potestas
> VISVNALVMENVNVM

I suggest one possible form of the symbol for gloss which can be misread as AC. No easy omission from the first part of the line gives anything even resembling proper metre. It seems likely that apparently superfluous words were in this instance omitted from the end of the line, giving the reading of A:

> VISACPOTESTASVNA

This line is not metrical either; but at least it has the right number of syllables and it seems possible.

Some of the other passages to which Gnilka refers are not really relevant to the point at issue between us. My statement was that deliberate interpolations do not so far as I recall occur in the primary manuscripts of Prudentius. He cites *Apoth.* [*Apotheosis*] 937a, which is absent from ATES; *Ham.* pr. 43a, which is also absent from ATESt; and *Ham.* 69, which is absent from ATESt.

However, it will be helpful to discuss each of these items briefly.

Apoth. 937a, "quid peccatorum prosapia corpore in illo," is not an alternative to anything in the text; it is a parallel to line 938:

> Quid Christi in membris peccati saeua satelles
> poena ageret?

Ham. pr. 43a, "qui caduci rem laboris offerens" (S[2]), seems to be a parallel to illustrate the word *caducus* in line 43:

> Hic se caduco dedicans mysterio.

The reading of U (*Hic qui*) seems to involve a correction *metri causa.*

Ham. 69, "imperitare uagis mundi per inania formis," seems to be what is left of an illustration or a parallel passage. I suspect that the point was that some other poet said the same thing somewhat differently. We must remember that the works of Prudentius were used as a schoolbook in the ninth century and probably before. We can expect to find here and there in the text or margins of our manuscripts variants that would naturally result from such a use of the books themselves.

To these passages Gnilka has most recently added *Ham.* 858a-f, which is a group of six lines found in some manuscripts after *Ham.* 858. I am not sure quite what point Gnilka attempts to make in connection with them. They do not illustrate interpolation in the primary manuscripts, for they are not found written in the text by the first hand in those manuscripts. Presumably for him they illustrate the process of deliberate interpolation at work. In any case, Gnilka deplores the fact that I classify them under the general heading of a parallel passage. But, beyond remarking that they appear to be hopelessly corrupt, what can one say about them in the absence of any indication of author, date, or original context, except that they seem to be a description of the damned and thus they are on more or less the same subject as *Ham.* 859-62 (or possibly 824-38).

What is really at stake in the problems we are discussing is not merely a few textual problems in a poet whom a great many Latinists do not read anyway. These points are at issue; and they are important. But more important perhaps for us all is the relation between these problems and the underlying theory which has helped to make the problems.

This theory is what I call the "Bad Guys Theory" of textual corruption. Enough errors and other confusions occur not only in manuscripts but in printed books through what I call human frailty that there is no great need to see malevolence and deliberate deceit lurking behind textual variants at every turn. For the moment I resist the temptation to develop this *locus communis.*

But one point must be stressed. The allegation of deliberate interpolation, as the concept is employed by Schmid and Gnilka among others, involves two theses which must both be proved before the allegation can be said to be well founded. First, they must of course prove that the lines they suspect are in fact foreign to their context and impossible to attribute to their author; otherwise they may merely be in the wrong place. But, granted that they prove that lines in one or more manuscripts of an author, for example Prudentius, are out of place and not by him, they must still prove that only deliberate interpolation and no other rational explanation of the occurrence of the lines accounts for their presence. For, if deliberate interpolation is only one of a number of possible or likely explanations, the case for it must surely be regarded as not proven. And frequently the allegation of deliberate interpolation is unnecessary, gratuitous, and irrelevant. If lines are intrusive for whatever reason, the sensible thing to do is to demonstrate the fact, remove them, and to get on with the job of interpreting our author.

At this point I would like to call attention to a different set of facts which the normal seeker after interpolations rather tends to neglect. Let us note rather the number of omissions consisting of a line or more in our primary manuscripts of Prudentius.

As textual traditions go, this is a very good one for a Latin author. Prudentius in fact is the only Latin author for whom we have both a rustic capital manuscript and one in uncials. Both are of the sixth century and probably of the first half. Both contain a very substantial portion of his text. Thus they are to be dated roughly within a century and a half of the first appearance of his works. This would be like having a manuscript of Vergil or Horace from the time of Hadrian. In addition, there are a large number of ninth century manuscripts, from which we can with reasonable confidence reconstruct three other traditions going back to the sixth century.

One plain fact about these traditions is that they all omit passages consisting of a line or more from time to time. For example, I calculate that the sixth century rustic capital manuscript, the Puteanus (A), has an omission of a line or more on the average of once every 440 verses. Total lines omitted average out to one for every 220 verses of text. Many of these omissions are made good by a correcting hand; but this hand seems definitely to belong to another scriptorium, since its letter-forms are different. From that fact I conclude that A as corrected offers traces of another tradition, but one which we are quite unable to recover fully. The Ambrosianus (B) in uncials has considerably fewer omissions on the average, but it and the other manuscript traditions all have their share of omitted lines. This is not the place to give details. I wish merely to say that in general in a tradition that we know is characterized by omissions, but where additions are rare or doubtful, we might be better advised to worry more about accidental lacunae and less about deliberate interpolation. I mean this suggestion very seriously, because it depends upon using evidence which is clear, uncontrovertible, and plain for all to see.

I am not trying to start a new hunt for lacunae as a substitute for the traditional hunt for interpolations. In fact, in my text I do not mark any lacunae, because I have the impression that we have enough different independent lines of tradition that what is missing through inadvertence in one or more of them is to be found preserved in one or more of the remaining lines.

On the other hand, I feel a deep suspicion of those allegations of deliberate interpolation in Prudentius that I have seen, because they appear to be founded upon a fundamental misconception of the professional standards, competence, and integrity of the scribes who produced the primary manuscripts and those from which the primary manuscripts are derived. And I firmly believe that one must make an independent assessment of the professional standards of book production exhibited in a manuscript tradition before basing conclusions upon guesses about those professional standards.

In summary, the main points I am trying to make are as follows. The following facts are certain. In some manuscripts of Prudentius from time to time there occur apparent additions to the text consisting of one or more complete lines of verse. Diplomatic and other external evidence is sufficient to show that in at least some of these instances the lines in question are truly later additions to Prudentius' text.

Two hypotheses are offered to account for these additions: (1) Since some of these additions are clearly the result of glosses, parallel passages, and the like written in manuscripts outside the text, the simplest explanation of all of them is that they arise from such sources. None of the additions require any further hypotheses to account for their presence; hence, no further hypotheses are in order. (2) On the assumption that some of the additions to the text of Prudentius have been demonstrated to be deliberate interpolations, the hypothesis of more such interpolations is to be entertained.

The question then resolves itself into fairly simple terms: Has the existence of deliberate interpolations in the text of Prudentius been established for the main lines of the tradition, ΑΒΓΔΘ? I believe that the answer to this question is negative. Thus the first hypothesis above seems adequate, since it is simpler.

Let us recall that the theory of deliberate interpolation assumes the existence of a specific person at a particular time and place with access to some specific manuscript; it assumes a certain set of abilities on the part of that person and a certain set of intentions, and assumes that he carried out those intentions in a particular way. In other words, the theory of deliberate interpolation relies on a fairly large number of assumptions, which can rarely be subject to verification, especially since other activities can give rise to results which are often in and of themselves indistinguishable from the results of deliberate interpolation. Thus, although such deliberate interpolation may from time to time be suspected, it would require some special set of circumstances to permit exclusion of other equally acceptable explanations.

But poor logic is just one of the effects of the hunt for interpolations. Another more important one, as we have seen, is the tendency this activity has to discourage close analysis of the received text to see what it really does mean. The passages discussed in detail above illustrate the evil effect of this tendency. In each of these passages, the attractiveness of "interpolation" as a cure-all for a supposed difficulty led excellent scholars to abandon the analysis of a line of thought too soon.

APPENDIX: CORRIGENDA IN EDITION OF PRUDENTIUS[6]

Some reviewers, notably A. Hudson-Williams (*CR* n.s. 17 [1967] 293-96) and P. Frassinetti (*Paideia* 22 [1967] 175-76) have gently called attention to a number of details in my edition that should be corrected. To their collections I add some items of my own.

IN EDITIONE MEA (1966) HAEC UITIA SIUE PRELI
SIUE EDITORIS CORRIGENDA SUNT:

IN TEXTU:

p. 125 *Ham.* 254 cumulos (*pro* cumulus)

p. 171 *Psych.* 599 frusta (*pro* frustra)

p. 192 *S.* 1.181 celebrarent (*pro* celebarent)

S. 1.193; (*i.e.* Tullus; *pro* Tullus.)

p. 206 *S.* 1.587 Christe (*pro* Christi)

p. 281 *Pe.* 3.92 diuide (*pro* duiuide)

p. 340 *Pe.* 10.305 edentularum (*pro* eduntularum)

p. 358 *Pe.* 10.820 quod (*pro* quid)

p. 370 *Pe.* 11.23 peruersi (*pro* preruersi)

IN APPARATU:

p. 8, ad *C.* 2.57 *seriore*

p. 53, ad 9-16, lin. 13 *duos libros,* lin. 23 *priore*

p. 73, "*De ornamentis . . . ,*" lin. 4 "*in E*" . . . *maiore*

p. 147, ad *Ham.* 931 *maiore*

p. 170, ad *Psych.* 575-94 *amissae*

p. 175, ad *Psych.* 726/729, lin. 4: *ix* (i.e. saeculi noni) et in 727 (ibidem, lin. 6) postquam (*pro* postquem), lin. 14: late *in* 732 (*pro: late in* 731)

p. 181, ad *Psych.* 907 *seriore*

p. 195, ad *S.* 1.282 adde: regione *B*

p. 285, ad *Pe.* 3.211-15 *excepto*

p. 297, ad *Pe.* 5.100, lin. 2 *qui* (*additur*), lin. 4 *margine*

p. 329, Subscr. ad *Pe.* 9 *seriore*

p. 390, Inscr. ad libr. lin. 2 *priore;* De inscriptionibus, lin. 3 *numeri, quos editores*

p. 429, Index s.v. similitudo, lin. 1 ceu

IN PRAEFATIONE:

p. XI (§6) lin. 14 qui, 17 qui, 19 Hi; (§7) lin. 24 primi, 25 qui; (§8) lin. 31 primi, 33 ceteri; (§9) lin. 39 idem; 43 esset.

p. XII (§10) lin. 5 careat, 6 praebeat; (§13) lin. 23 amissi; (§16) lin. 39 posteriore . . . priore, 42 scribam priorem, 43 sciret, 44 perrexisse.

p. XIII (§18) lin. 4-*S.* 1.336 (337-560); (§22) lin. 19 diiudices.

p. XIV (§26) lin. 6 maiore; (§27) lin. 13 qui; (§30) lin. 29 amisso; (§31) lin. 36 crassiore, 37 priore.

p. XV (§36) lin. 22 Ernest, 25 margine superiore.

p. XVIII (§50) lin. 10 *dele* quosdam (*i.e.* uersus quos); (§54) lin. 41 integro.

p. XX (§65) lin. 16 alii, quos, eos, 17 praetermittendos.

p. xxiii (§80) lin. 26 conlati.

p. xxiv (§83) lin. 4 quam traditionem; (§87) lin. 29 maiore, 33 maiore; (§88) lin. 39 quas.

p. xxvi (§100) lin. 14 est; (§102) lin. 22 constructiones; (§105) lin. 44 quendam (*dele* homo).

p. xxvii (§108) lin. 9 quam.

p. xxix (§121) lin. 33 alia.

p. xxxv (§126) lin. 39 accommodatae, 46 uiderer.

p. xxxviii (§131) lin. 41 nostras.

p. xxxix (§134) lin. 12 Hae, 20 potuerim.

p. xlvii (§151) lin. 12 attulerim.

p. l, lin. 11 duae; 12 scriba qui se ipse corrigit.

Notes

1. Familiarity with the following items is assumed throughout this paper. When one of them is cited in my text, page number reference is given when appropriate.

   Aurelii Prudentii Clementis Carmina, ed. M. P. Cunningham, Turnholti 1966 (Corpus Christianorum, Series latina, vol. 126); I take advantage of this opportunity to provide in an appendix a list of corrigenda for this volume. M. P. Cunningham, "A Preliminary Recension of the Older Manuscripts of the *Cathemerinon, Apotheosis,* and *Hamartigenia* of Prudentius," *Sacris Erudiri* 13 (1962) 5-59. The earlier standard text of Prudentius is that of J. Bergman, Vienna 1926 (*CSEL* [*Corpus scriptorum ecclesiasticorum Latinorum*] 61).

   On the definition of deliberate interpolation, see Paul Maas, *Textkritik*[3] (Leipzig 1957) 12.

   On alleged interpolations in Prudentius, see Paul Antin, (review of my edition) *Révue belge de philologie et d'histoire* 45 (1967) 990. Christian Gnilka, "Zwei Textprobleme bei Prudentius," *Philologus* 109 (1965) 246-58; and his review of R. Herzog, *Die allegorische Dichtkunst* etc., in *Gnomon* 40 (1968) esp. 361-62. Wolfgang Schmid, "Die Darstellung der Menschheitsstufen bei Prudentius und das Problem seiner doppelten Redaktion," *Vigiliae Christianae* 7 (1953) 171-86.

   Dr. Gnilka and I have attempted to clarify by correspondence matters on which we disagree. (I quote below from his letter of October 10, 1968). He understood me to say (1) that the existence of interpolations dating from earlier than the medieval period had not been demonstrated ("dass Ihres Erachtens antike Interpolamente im Prudentiustext nicht nachgewiesen seien"); and (2) that I regard "malice aforethought" (*dolus malus*) as the motive for the origin of an interpolation ("dolus malus ist also in Ihren Augen das Motiv für die Entstehung einer Interpolation"). The first point is disproved by my note on *Cath.* 5.161-64. As for the second, I distinguish between interpolations which are the result of human frailty and those which are deliberate. The latter I define as "dolo malo factas." Even so, I do not say that none occur in the tradition, but only that I do not believe I have found any in the primary manuscripts.

   Another major source of disagreement is that Gnilka gives more allegiance to Jachmann's theories than I am prepared to.

2. One should note also that the reference in 428 *triumuir* is solely to what we now call the second triumvirate of young Caesar, Antonius, and Lepidus.

3. F. Klingner, review of Bergman's edition, *Gnomon* 6 (1930) 39-52.

4. R. A. B. Mynors, *Durham Cathedral Manuscripts* (Oxford 1939) pp. 26-27.

5. Lavarenne removes these lines from the text here and places them after line 930. See M. Lavarenne, "Note sur un passage de l'Hamartigénie de Prudence," *REL* [*Revue des études latines*] 19 (1941) 76-78.

6. See above, note 1.

Charles Witke (essay date 1968)

SOURCE: Witke, Charles. "Prudentius and the Tradition of Latin Poetry." *Transactions and Proceedings of the American Philological Association* 99 (1968): 509-25.

[*In the following essay, Witke examines Prudentius as a Christian poet.*]

The voluminous *opera* of Aurelius Prudentius Clemens[1] were at some point during their author's life gathered together. He prefaces and situates the collected work with a prologue, which perhaps more than the works themselves, or their epilogue, is of basic interest in formulating Christian poetics.[2] It explains what Prudentius wanted his audience to think about his body of poetry, and it provides a convenient place to begin evaluating his rôle as Christian poet. If Christian here is taken as an adjective meaning "of a distinctive culture" as well as "of a particular religion, i.e. not pagan," Prudentius as Christian poet will display certain traits not found in, say, Paulinus of Nola, who only intermittently synthesized his religion and his verse but who is often called a Christian poet.

This **Prooemium** or **Praefatio**—the MSS vary; Prudentius used Greek titles—may be considered a poem in which Prudentius introduces himself, and sets in motion certain of his preoccupations. If viewed not as a Christian document but as a literary text, the **Prooemium** is highly instructive.

> Per quinquennia iam decem,
> ni fallor, fuimus; septimus insuper
> annum cardo rotat, dum fruimur sole volubili.
>
> Instat terminus et diem
> vicinum senio iam deus adplicat:
> quid nos utile tanti spatio temporis egimus?
>
> (1-6)

The first strophe provides a historical datum and a literary comparison: the poet at age 57.[3] The tone is dignified; the imagery of *cardo rotat* and *sole volubili* is one of flowing time, time in nature moving in steady recurrence. A classical borrowing is Lucan 7.381, *extremi cardinis annos,* where Pompey foretells a life of shame in his old age if he does not conquer. The whole passage reads: "ultima fata / deprecor ac turpes extremi cardinis annos, / ne discam servire senex." This reminiscence with its coloring of tragic grandeur and speculation about old age is highly appropriate, and strengthens the classically trained reader's sense of tension, which the second strophe specifically sets forth. Here the flow of time is blocked: *instat terminus,* vividly set against *sole volubili* spinning a never-ending course. *Terminus* is ambiguous here. It means both goal of life and end of living, and draws heavily upon circus-imagery. The heavenly turning of stars was associated with the circus, in whose confines racers move on fixed courses. The actual circus itself was more than a place of entertainment or a garden circus. It was assigned a sacred function in view of its close association with "running the race of life," as Paul put it.[4] Both pagans and Christians assigned religious symbolism to the circus.[5] Prudentius here builds on an architectural and iconographic as well as literary convention.

The question of the second strophe presumes a Roman ethic in *quid utile,* and in the review of life which follows:

> Aetas prima crepantibus
> flevit sub ferulis, mox docuit toga
> infectum vitiis falsa loqui non sine crimine.

> Tum lasciva protervitas
> et luxus petulans—heu pudet ac piget!—
> foedavit iuvenem nequitiae sordibus et luto.
>
> Exim iurgia turbidos
> armarunt animos et male pertinax
> vincendi studium subiacuit casibus asperis.
>
> (7-15)

The three strophes pass from school and manhood (lines 7-9) to the consequences of physical maturity (10-12) and to the career in law-courts (13-15). Each ends with words which signify the drawbacks or bad features now seen in the perspective of the poet's present view. Line 9, *falsa loqui,* is one of the activities of cultural life avoided and stigmatized by the Christian man of letters, like Paulinus of Nola, poem 22.12-13, ed. Hartel. *Lasciva protervitas* (line 10) seems related to Horace, *Carm.* 1.19.3, where the poet says Venus and Bacchus and "lasciva Licentia" order him "finitis animum reddere amoribus"—an ode of erotic sensibility. As for line 14, *male pertinax,* Horace *Carm.* 1.9.24 is relevant. The outdoor scene of night movement in the warm city ends reflections on time's passing, leaving man stranded at the end of his non-cyclic movement from greenness to whiteness, but bringing cyclic rebirth to nature. "Pignusque dereptum lacertis / aut digito male pertinaci." Here the girl's resistance is ineffectual; very likely the classical association should be carried over into Prudentius. He may not have had a drive for winning, but ran risks for his career by not resisting.

The career went forward, in the civil service, as the strophes to which it is hard to assign precise meanings show:

> Bis legum moderamine
> frenos nobilium reximus urbium:
> ius civile bonis reddimus, terruimus reos.
>
> Tandem militiae gradu
> evectum pietas principis extulit
> adsumptum proprius stare iubens ordine proximo.
>
> (16-21)

These strophes are not unlike a Roman funeral-inscription, particularly in the self-characterization in line 18. Prudentius is objectively setting forth his life's work in answer to one set of possible responses to the question *quid utile?* So far his measured response has been no more unclassical than any careerist's; even the modest disassociation from and gentle castigation of youth's excesses, the *concessa Venus* of Horace ("heu pudet ac piget") is not far from Pliny himself commenting on his *nugae,* a standard pose.

However, the next movement of this poem is unusual in that it brings forward a personal insight stated in lyrical terms into an official context of career-summary.

Haec dum vita volans agit,
inrepsit subito canities seni
oblitum veteris me Saliae consulis arguens,

sub quo prima dies mihi
quam multas hiemes volverit et rosas
pratis post glaciem reddiderit, nix capitis probat.

(22-27)

Here the movement looks back to the first and second strophes. *Vita volans* is checked, confronted with *inrepsit subito canities seni; terminus* and *deus* of lines 4 and 5 have changed into the realistic effects of age, as *senio* (5) and *seni* (23) suggest. There is a distinct Horatian imagery at work here too, drawn in large part from *Carm.* 1.9, whence *male pertinax* came to inhabit Prudentius' preface. Horace, in this ode as elsewhere,[6] contrasts the green of nature and the white hair of age. Soracte's snow will melt; spring will come to nature but not to a white-crowned man: "Donec virenti canities abest / morosa," *Carm.* 1.9.17-18.[7]

Prudentius makes explicit Horace's implied connection between *nive candidum Soracte* and *canities: nix capitis probat*. Horatian also are the *rosas pratis post glaciem,* e.g. *Carm.* 2.3.13 ff., 1.4.1 ff., especially 9 ff., etc. But what in Horace was allusive, evocative, and suggestive use of language has become in Prudentius explicit and unmistakably unambiguous: symbolism has become one-for-one equivalence. There is more basis of a Christian style in *nix capitis probat* of line 27 here than in the yards of lines written about the crucifixion as if it were an event in Aeneas' epic adventure. The lyric line ends in referential significance.

What is important is that the lyric line is there in the first place. Prudentius is here neither embellishing his work with poetic imagery nor revealing his powers as poet in the books that lie ahead. His poems nowhere exhibit gratuitous or fortuitous strivings after metaphor. Rather, Prudentius characterizes his view of his life and life in general by using specific concrete terms like roses brought back to meadows after winter's cold and ice. He expects us to respond emotionally and sympathetically.

This deliberately evoked warm feeling about being alive is undercut in the next strophe:

Numquid talia proderunt
carnis post obitum vel bona vel mala,
cum iam, quidquid id est, quod fueram, mors aboleverit?

(28-30)

After the roses and snow, the vacantness and lack of concreteness of this strophe's language are a signal of death itself, abstract and colorless. This passage from life to death is explicit, reminiscent of classical Latin poetry (e.g. Catullus 1) in its preparation and execution and language, specifically its non-committal *quidquid id est, quod fueram.* But the sentiment, as the succeeding strophe shows, is Christian. Here there is more than classical form purveying Christian content. There is no separating content from form in poetry, and here there is no exception. Both are Roman; men did not stop being Romans when they became Christians. The possibility of the one being the other at all itself precludes such abandonment of an identity. Likewise, a poet could be a Christian poet if he was first a Roman, then a Latin poet, presenting his life and its movements as they were lived, interpreted literally and not doctrinally. Prudentius is a better poet than Ausonius or Paulinus of Nola on purely poetical grounds. He is a Christian poet as Paulinus is not, because Prudentius lived as a whole man (a Christian) writing poetry. Intellectual content is almost beside the point. Lucretius' handling of the Magna Mater procession is what makes him an epic poet, not his intellectual viewpoint or didactic function. Horace's treatment of roses makes him lyric whether he praised or blamed their shortness of life. So too, Prudentius is a Christian poet because of his ability to write within a culture which was for him Christian. His relationship with God is his outlook. He does not teach or justify. He writes, and writes conventionally, out of the possibilities set up by this outlook. The conventions adhere in the Latin language's resources, in the world of poems written before Prudentius, and in Prudentius' own practice. He is a Christian poet because he is not trying to be anything except a Latin poet, writing out of energized commitment to life in the Latin Empire of the late fourth century.

To return to the preface: at the far side of the brink of death, Prudentius represents the necessity of his declaring an obvious truth.

Dicendum mihi: "quisquis es,
mundum quem coluit, mens tua perdidit;
non sunt illa dei, quae studuit, cuius habeberis."

(31-33)[8]

The *quisquis* of the spirit looks back to the *quidquid* of the flesh in the preceding line. Like Hadrian, Prudentius addresses his soul, but after death, as a rational entity rather than as a butterfly, *animula vagula*, at the moment of departing this life. Again the career, as it were, here proleptically anticipated, reveals itself. Certain orderings, certain patternings of time and consequence, certain obvious and ascertainable but ignored aspects of life's implications must be set forth by Prudentius, just as by Horace or Persius or any other "life-poet." Prudentius again is fully de-personified. It is the poet as a particular man, undergoing death and addressing himself at that point, not a didactic teacher speaking from an institutionalized or codified authority, that stands behind *dicendum mihi.* Common life experience, rather than shared religious views, binds him and his audience into an act of speaking and hearing.

In a way reminiscent of the Vergil whom he read with such profit, Prudentius initiates a response to the situation which he has depicted. But whereas Vergil at the end of his *Bucolica* suggests the genres in which he worked without revealing inner drives to write as he did, Prudentius reveals himself as writing out of a total awareness of the existential as he perceives it; there is much courage as well as public belief in poetry's efficacy in his *atqui:*

> Atqui fine sub ultimo
> peccatrix anima stultitiam exuat;
> saltem voce deum concelebret, si meritis nequit.
>
> (34-36)

Characteristically for ancient society, the response is literary: *voce* rather than *meritis.*[9] Art is brought closer to the fabric of a total, all-embracing view of life than it had before in the historical Mediterranean world. Classical Latin poets' art was more than craft, admittedly. But it was not an unfiltered response to an all-embracing life-view where art, poetry, was equated with transcribing without particularizing the categories or modes of experience. Prudentius' creation of the concept of life as song is not far from Francis of Assisi and his Hymn to the Sun, which presents likewise a cosmos energized from a single, and hence divine, source. Here Prudentius makes a departure from the tradition of Latin poetry, or, better, an extension of it.

If the end of writing were single, the hymning of God, the genres were thought capable of specification according to broad headings. Prudentius concludes:

> Hymnis continuet dies
> nec nox ulla vacet, quin dominum canat;
> pugnet contra hereses, catholicam discutiat fidem:
>
> conculcet sacra gentium,
> labem, Roma, tuis inferat idolis;
> carmen martyribus devoveat, laudet apostolos.
>
> Haec dum scribo vel eloquor,
> vinclis o utinam corporis emicem
> liber, quo tulerit lingua sono mobilis ultimo!
>
> (37-45)

As is well known, the first strophe refers to the **Liber cathemerinon,** the **Liber apotheosis,** and to the **Hamartigenia** (and **Psychomachia** too no doubt). The next strophe implies the **Libri duos contra Symmachum** and the **Peristephanon.**

Prudentius does not represent himself as performing these actions, though he introduces himself (fully in accord with the tradition of preface statements) at the end.

Out of the continuous praise of God grow the putting down of error and teaching truth, overthrowing superstition and idols, and issuing panegyrics of the faith's heroes. The direct address of Rome is basically sympathetic. Elsewhere we see that Prudentius esteemed Rome as both civilization (he knew no other) and as a city with palpable fabric. A poet, he could respond in his poetry to sensible elements in his environment.

The last strophe moves toward the conventional apotheosis of the poet, as Horace, *Carm.* 1.1.36, 3.30, 2.20.35 ff., where elevation implies approaching the divine. In contrast, Prudentius does not point to his poems to justify or anticipate his flight to heaven. He expresses a wish, and points not to poem but to process: the efficacious act itself. "Haec dum scribo vel eloquor." His art is the scene of his flight to heaven just like poets of the Latin tradition. But by poising the act of moving "quo tulerit lingua sono mobilis ultimo" in the context of continuous service to the divine in poetry, Prudentius puts the creative act into a personal light. It is no longer the effect, a publicly accessible monument, the text, that liberates from this world's limits, but rather liberation may come (and is implored to come) in the midst of poetic endeavor privately and individually going forward in the praise of God. Prudentius integrates art into a total seamless continuum of life, and literature thus reasserted as the significance of Prudentius' existence comes to characterize it exclusively.

The **Liber cathemerinon** reflects this aspect of unceasing praise. The poems are grouped in such a way that the early ones follow the hours of the day, from cockcrow to sleep, and go on to cover other aspects of a Christian life; fasting, funerals, the Nativity and Epiphany find a place in these hymns. The most important result is the consecration of daily aspects of living in poetry of high order. Daily life is the context of the unceasing praise of God in Prudentius' life and in his poetry, which he makes coterminous with life. The accidentals of fifty-seven years of age, the private and public career, a sudden intimation of old age stealing upon an unexamined life and a realization of death's implications: out of these historically conditioned events grows the whole corpus. In all fairness to Latin literature, many poems of Prudentius are less than first-rate. But likewise, in fairness to Prudentius, many more poems are adornments of the Latin tradition. In Prudentius, Christian poetry can be seen as an entity distinguished from its Latin forebears. Prudentius' jettisoning the classical persona enables him conventionally to connect his *opera* with literally himself in the **Prooemium** and likewise with himself in the **Epilogue**: "omne vas fit utile / quod est ad usum congruens herilem."

The **Cathemerinon** has already been characterized briefly above. Its twelve hymns implicitly and explicitly assign poetry a high function, and use the conventional

An artistic rendition of the vice of Anger, by Pieter Brueghel the Elder (c. 1515-69).

signs of poetry, such as the muse and the exalted *vates,* in the traditional ways. A good example is 3, a *Hymnus ante cibum,* written in dactylic trimeter hypercatalectic, in 41 strophes or 205 lines. As a reflective consecration of a portion of one's time spent in the daily activity of feeding oneself, it is effective in referring even this banality to heavenly concern. Since it is so long, analysis will be made of only a few of the opening strophes. They give a good idea of the poetry of the **Cathemerinon,** and at one place Prudentius explicitly confronts poetry of the Latin tradition.

> O crucifer bone, lucisator,
> omniparens pie, verbigena,
> edite corpore virgineo,
> sed prius in genitore potens,
> astra, solum, mare quam fierent!
>
> (1-5)

The poet here invokes the divinity, characterized at the outset as in the old type of formal hymn addressed to a god. The parallel vocatives in lines 1 and 2 are examples of the symmetry upon which Prudentius sometimes builds, as discussion will shortly show. The stately punctuated movement of the first two lines is succeeded by the third, fourth, and fifth lines, ending with the succession of heaven, firmament, and sea, which form the groundwork and base line in time for Christ's efficacy, before incarnation and before creation itself.

> Huc nitido, precor, intuitu
> flecte salutiferam faciem
> fronte serenus et inradia,
> nominis ut sub honore tui
> has epulas liceat capere!
>
> (6-10)

This strophe builds on the first. The poet, having specified and characterized the divinity, now implores Him to attend the specific situation, *has epulas,* in a manner prescribed by the poet. So far, except for the nature of the qualifications given to God, the hymn follows pretty carefully the ancient form. The next strophe introduces a new note, deliberately in tension with the old form.

Te sine dulce nihil, domine,
nec iuvat ore quid adpetere,
pocula ni prius atque cibos,
Christe, tuus favor inbuerit
omnia sanctificante fide.

(11-15)

Here the divine figure is no longer merely the traditional benevolent participator in the *epulae* or its generous provider or even enhancer. Christ, the poet asserts, changes the substantial and personal response to the wine and food: "te sine dulce nihil, domine." This inward-looking, this shift of attention away from the broader significance of the meal to the substance ingested, is novel. Subjective response of this sort is, I submit, a new thing. Even the romantic Latin elegists did not say that the beloved made wine taste sweeter. Wine tasted like wine in the ancient world; friendship, love, a divinity, enhanced the event of drinking wine, not the substance itself. Christian sacramentalism has its inception in valuing mundane things as things in themselves and simultaneously as things set apart, conveying the divine in some way. Prudentius does not indulge here in metaphor of Christ's body and blood. He is talking about real, ordinary, daily food and drink. But God has so invaded and penetrated his world that his personal reaction to everyday things is filtered through this continuous awareness.

The next strophe makes this even more explicit:

Fercula nostra deum sapiant,
Christus et influat in pateras,
seria, ludicra, verba, iocos,
denique, quod sumus aut agimus,
trina superne regat pietas.

(16-20)[10]

This needs little comment; the divine care permeates all aspects of living. Prudentius continues:

Hic mihi nulla rosae spolia,
nullus aromate fraglat odor.
sed liquor influit ambrosius
nectareamque fidem redolet
fusus ab usque patris gremio.

(21-25)

This assertion follows the jussive subjunctives. The traditional accompaniments of feasting give way to abstractions which come from God and reveal God. The rejection is not of the roses and unguents themselves,[11] but of their effects: the perfume of faith, of God's origin, brings its own sweetness. Thus Prudentius does not go outside the fabric of his poem to set himself and *epulae* apart from those conventionally occurring in this kind of hymn. Rather, by remaining within the surface shell of hymn of praise, by avoiding rending his

textured work here, with an energetic disclaimer of what he will disavow he puts what is not present ("nulla rosae spolia, nullus . . . odor") in service of what he asserts is present. What the *liquor* stands in place of characterizes the *liquor:* itself abstract, vehicle for intellectualized (or perhaps better hypostatized) quality, access to it and understanding of it are provided by suggesting what conventional element of banqueting it replaces.

The same economy is at work in the next strophe, perhaps the most significant for this brief study:

Sperne, camena, leves hederas,
cingere tempora quis solita es,
sertaque mystica dactylico
texere docta liga strofio
laude dei redimita comes!

(26-30)

Poetry is a traditional element in a feast of elaborate quality, and it is often enough love-poetry. In a hymn presenting God permeating all nature and sanctifying it, the poetry is assigned the task of praising God's works. The frivolous ivy is replaced with *mystica serta.* The image in this strophe again is instructive in its specific application: the muse is *docta,* as everywhere; she is not ejected from the feast. Rather, her learning is put to serve the praise undertaken in this hymn. She is told to give up one function or convention ("leves hederas, / cingere tempora quis solita es"), reminded of innate capacities ("sertaque mystica dactylico / texere docta . . . strofio") and commanded ("liga . . . / laude dei, redimita comas"). The figure of the dactylic muse binds her hair to praise God in the shorter meter of dactylic trimeter; the person of the interested muse reflects the kind of poetry written.[12]

The figure of Camena here typifies Prudentius' use of classical poetry in general. Using the conventions provided by Camena, he writes a new poetry without casting off the old. This smooth incorporation, this capability of liberating convention for a new purposeful expression, marks Prudentius as a Christian poet of stature and maturity. He does not disavow the old only to bring it surreptitiously through the back door, nor does he ignore a commitment to the new faith and its attendant artistic implications. Rather, Prudentius creates a new poetry through the old conventions recharged with a function and an energy derived from the liveliness of his mind's engagement with the new life-system offered by Christianity. Christianity called for a new set of responses beyond fusion of Judaic and Classical motifs and techniques.

This hymn's succeeding strophes hold much of interest:

Quod generosa potest anima,

lucis et aetheris indigena,
solvere dignius obsequium,
quam data munera si recinet
artificem modulata suum?

(31-35)

Here the closed world of God and the poetry-singing soul stands forth in all its simplicity. The shape of art reveals the presence and shape of the divine.

The conceits which follow are very much in the tradition of Hellenistic poetry; Prudentius' catalogue of the edibles provided for man by God is comprehensive and ingeniously written. His description of cheese is worth quoting:

Spumea mulctra gerunt niveos
ubere de gemino latices
perque coagula densa liquor
in solidum coit et fragili
lac tenerum premitur calatho.

(66-70)

A sensitivity for picture and detail can easily be seen at work here.

Prudentius refers once more to ancient poetry, specifically epic and lyric, but not to dispraise them. He introduces these genres in comparison with the task of praising God, in order to show the great magnitude of the latter (rather as he had used the rose to show what sweetness faith brought, lines 21-22):

Quae veterum tuba quaeve lyra
flatibus inclyta vel fidibus
divitis omnipotentis opus,
quaeque fruenda patent homini,
laudibus aequiperare queat?

(81-85)[13]

Prudentius' next strophe but one provides a useful comparison with a passage of Paulinus of Nola.

Quod calet halitus interior,
corde quod abdita vena tremit,
pulsat et incita quod resonam
lingua sub ore latens caveam,
laus superi patris esto mihi.

(91-95)

Here Prudentius builds up the conceit of the poet as a musical (or praise-giving) instrument himself. His approach is not the literal one of Paulinus[14] which gradually lifts into a sublime metaphor. Rather, Prudentius, self-restrained and unecstatic as always, controls and shapes the strophe from the inside out, from *halitus interior* to *laus superi patris,* from the lowly heart to God above. His strophic form, as distinguished from Paulinus' continuous hexameters, encourages this kind

of careful shaping.[15] There is no one-for-one correspondence of idea to external referent here. Prudentius is both more concrete and more allusive. The poet's rhythm of life, his breath, his heart, are grounds for God's praise. Paulinus, in his effort to constrict poetry of any value extraneous to Christ, made the latter *musicus auctor;* Prudentius, re-addressing the situation, makes the poet *musicus,* and once more reasserts the efficacy of art, but art as service of praise. This Judaeo-Christian concept is given a habitat in Latin poetry which both suits it and sustainingly nourishes it with the Latin tradition of art's transcendence.

When God is invoked, it is to protect and to defend the poet's household, as lines 166 ff. of this hymn show:

Tu mihi, Christe, columba potens,
sanguine pasta cui cedit avis,
tu niveus per ovile tuum
agnus hiare lupum prohibes
subiuga tigridis ora premens.

Da, locuples deus, hoc famulis
rite precantibus, ut tenui
membra cibo recreata levent
neu piger inmodicis dapibus
viscera tenta gravet stomachus.

Haustus amarus abesto procul . . .

(166-76)

The vision is less exalted than the passage of Paulinus of Nola just referred to, but the artistic fabric is more controlled, the poet is in sure command, and conveys a sense of order (mirrored in the arrangement of words into strophes). There is less grasping after concepts and more measured living after precepts in these poems of the *Cathemerinon.*

Prudentius elsewhere uses the conventional apparatus of poetical composition in *Liber Cathemerinon.* For instance, 9.1 ff., a *Hymnus omnis horae* in trochaic tetrameter catalectic:

Da, puer, plectrum, choraeis ut canam fidelibus
dulce carmen et melodum, gesta Christi insignia!
hunc camena nostra solum pangat, hunc laudet lyra.

(1-3)

This mode of initiating discourse of an elevated style is familiar from poetry of the classical period; its availability and appropriateness in Prudentius' eyes is remarkable. He does not set his *camena* packing, but uses her for a basically traditional purpose: to praise a hero's deeds. In the same way he builds useful lines of previous poems into his own, e.g. *Cath.* 3.11, "te sine dulce nihil, domine," which has behind it *Aen.* 12.882, "quidquam mihi dulce meorum te sine, frater, erit"

(Juturna to Turnus), and Claudian, *In Rufinum* 2.268, "te sine dulce nihil" (the rebuked army to Stilicho). Neither of these contexts edifies Prudentius' address to Christ.

Prudentius makes these points about poetry in another way in his **Epilogue,** which uses the imagery of different kinds of utensils from "Paul" in the second letter to Timothy, 2:20; cf. *Romans* 9:21. Since Prudentius has no *sanctitas* and no money to give the poor, he gives God his iambs and trochees:[16] talent is conserved and dedicated to God, who approves the *pedestre carmen,* line 12. Here the adjective *pedestre* no longer refers to the *genera dicendi* of rhetoric, high, medium, and low. It refers to the poet himself, who is so at one with his verse that his lowliness as a creature of God comes to be the lowliness of the poem itself in God's universe: hence the point of the *vasa parata ligno:* poet and poem are *vas,* to be used in that great heavenly household, *paternum atrium,* line 25. The *munus fictile* has its use there.[17]

In his self-appraisal in the **Epilogue,** Prudentius follows the Latin tradition, but the identification of the humanity of the poet, to be judged by God with the poetry, is extraneous to that tradition. In a real way, the classical poets are their poems, and the immortality which they arrogate to themselves is the immortality of Rome and of Latin literature. But the poet as one man subject to personal cosmic regulation nowhere appears; it is Horace's common humanity of birth and life leading to death that he writes of in some of his poems, not his individuated sense of this, his apprehension or private coming to terms with it. Personal quittance with heaven does not enter into the Latin tradition. Prudentius systematically expands this theme, deepens it, and makes literature more a part of the individual's separate existence, which in the **Epilogue** he links only to the poems on the one side, and his God on the other. Even Persius, that apologist for a backward-looking but not society-rejecting version of Stoicism, does not compromise his poetic stance by confusing it with his humanity and its problems and seasons. Prudentius in his **Epilogue,** as well as in his other poems, makes his persona coincide as closely as possible with his Christian soul, his religious life of the mind. The satirists Horace, Persius, and to a degree Juvenal inculcated the interior life; Augustine wrote his Confessions within its territory; but Prudentius was the first to make literary talent and practice an equivalent for the "dona conscientiae / quibus beata mens abundat intus," **Epil. [Epilogue]** 3-4. Writing in Prudentius is a way of seeing God; Catullus perhaps could have understood if the terms had been changed to mean his kind of love. If the poet offers himself in his poems, their subject as well is the God to

whom the poet makes offerings; "iuvabit ore personasse Christum," **Epil.** 34. The act itself has merit and is sweet, "quidquid illud accidit," **Epil.** 33.

Prudentius is no foe of poetry of the Latin tradition. His use of classical lines for important sacred events shows as much, as does his careful use of meter and his sense of symmetry in strophic composition. Almost every aspect of his poetry is classical in basis. Though other poets could be adduced, Prudentius, in his metrical variety, consciously invites comparison with Horace. He also links himself to Horace specifically in the **Prooemium** by saying that he writes in his fifty-seventh year, which Horace just failed to attain. His meter there is one not used by Horace, but a combination of Horatian meters. Prudentius' rather lengthy detailed texts elsewhere, his relish for grotesque injury in the **Peristephanon,** and his Christian subjects themselves have put off critical judgment. Contrast with a classical Latin poet like Silius Italicus is instructive in showing how little excellence depends on subject. Prudentius is a Latin poet of considerable ability, and one who does not write only in the traditional way. He goes beyond his tradition and in this liberation he is at his most original and important.

The form which this new direction in Latin poetry takes is conventional. Prudentius invents no new genres, he shatters no metrical, lexical, or grammatical norms (though he innovates in metrical combination), and he is formally a Latin Christian poet. In one important way, he was never successfully imitated: once the way had been found by Prudentius, no other poet followed (or perhaps had scope for following; Prudentius like Catullus and Horace leaves few if any possibilities inherent in his artistic stance unexplored.) Fortunatus was to write his mystic hymns out of a refulgency of personal imagination illuminated by learning, and Corippus' epic was to show how naturally and comfortably Christian poetry could use that form. But Prudentius' inner landscape of offering was not penetrated again until much later, by the Latin and vernacular poets of love, both sacred and profane, of the eleventh and twelfth centuries. Prudentius saw that what we call antiquity offered the possibility for a range of expression new to the world, and he took the opportunity which the new Christian subculture afforded him with its stable life-system. Others saw less, and accordingly were more confined in their habits of representing Christian event (whether Christ or daily life) in the forms of the Latin tradition without mediating the tensions between them or inhabiting the new ground which this confrontation implied.

Notes

1. M. P. Cunningham ed., Vol. 126, *Corpus Christianorum, Series Latina* (Turnhout 1966).

2. Kl. Thraede, *Studien zu Sprache und Stil des Pru-dentius = Hypomnemata* 13 (Göttingen 1965) 21 ff., tries to show that this is an epilogue. M. Cunningham, *CW* [*Classical World*] 60 (1966) 76-77, gives the essential caveat. For a discussion of allegorical *praefatio* in Prudentius and Claudian, see R. Herzog, *Die allegorische Dichtkunst des Prudentius = Zetemata* 42 (1966) 119-35.

3. The birthday that Horace just failed to attain; see below, p. 524.

4. *I Corinthians* 9:24.

5. See A. Frazer, "The Iconography of the Emperor Maxentius' Buildings in the Via Appia," *Art Bulletin* 48 (1966) 385-92; G. Gatti, "Una Basilica di età costantiniana recentemente riconosciuta presso la Via Prenestina," *Capitolium* 35 (1960) 3-8; also G. Gatti, "Scoperta di una Basilica christiana presso S. Lorenzo f. l. m.," *Capitolium* 32 (1957) 16-20.

6. Ch. Witke, "Questions and Answers in Horace *Odes* 2.3," *CP* [*Classical Philology*] 61 (1966) 250-52, and the literature there cited. Other classical poets, conventions, and topoi were used by Prudentius. I single out Horace here and elsewhere without implying anything about other poets.

7. See also Horace, *Carm.* 4.13.12, *capitis nives,* not locked into nature imagery, but used to characterize aspects of aging unpleasant to a woman.

8. I take *mihi* as dative of agent; the passage seems to refer to the Particular Judgment after death.

9. Professor E. A. Havelock has kindly suggested to me that the Hebrew tradition of vocal praise of God also lies behind *voce* here.

10. See Chr. Gnilka, *Gnomon* 40 (1968) 366. It appeared after my work was written.

11. Christ was tendered the latter by the anonymous woman who upset his dinner-companions: Matthew 36:17; cf. Mark 14:8; John 12:3.

12. See e.g. Ovid, *Amores* 1.1.

13. See also Isidoro Rodriguez-Herrera, *Poeta Christianus: Prudentius' Auffassung vom Wesen und von der Aufgabe des christlichen Dichters* (Inaugural-Diss. Speyer 1936) 38.

14. Poem 20, lines 32-55, W. von Hartel ed., *CSEL* [*Corpus scriptorum ecclesiasticorum Latinorum*] 30 (Vienna 1894).

15. Rodriguez (above, note 13) 28 says in gross but suggestive exaggeration that Prudentius becomes like a lyre himself.

16. See Thraede (above, note 2); Rodriguez advanced the ideas of "Dichtung als Opfer" and "Dichter als die Opfergabe," (above, note 13) 14 and 28-46. He is much concerned with Prudentius' inner motivation.

17. Thraede (above, note 2) 51 ff., seeks to assimilate the *pedestre carmen* to epistolary style. See also 71-73 for a particularizing of the *iuncturae* here.

Robert W. Gaston (essay date 1973)

SOURCE: Gaston, Robert W. "Prudentius and Sixteenth-Century Antiquarian Scholarship." *Medievalia et Humanistica: Studies in Medieval and Renaissance Culture* n.s. no. 4 (1973): 161-76.

[*In the following essay, Gaston discusses how Prudentius, after a period of neglect during the Renaissance, was rediscovered by Christian historicists.*]

During the sixteenth century the study of the early Church was established as one of the primary fields of historical scholarship.[1] The present essay is concerned with one aspect of this development: the use of literary sources for the clarification of archaeological evidence. Our focus will be the scholarly use made of the writings of Aurelius Prudentius (348-c. 405 A.D.). The Spanish born poet, who visited Rome towards the end of the fourth century, is one of the few ancient witnesses to leave us descriptions of catacombs and the cults of the martyrs buried in them.

The choice of Prudentius is not an arbitrary one. The first published account of the cemetery of the Giordani after its discovery in 1578 gave an eloquent appraisal of the poet's significance for the study of the catacombs. Cardinal Cesare Baronio, in the second volume of the monumental *Annales ecclesiastici,* printed in 1593, vividly recalled his impressions of entering the catacomb twelve years previously. He concluded with the observation that scholars like himself who had read about the catacombs in manuscripts of Prudentius and Jerome, or had seen the parts of the ancient cemeteries still exposed to view, were able immediately to understand what they could now see with their own eyes.[2]

Throughout the Middle Ages Prudentius had been the most widely read Christian Latin poet of the Roman period. His popularity from the fifth to the fourteenth century is evident not only in the several hundred surviving manuscripts of his works, but also in the number of references to him and quotations from his poems in medieval books. We still lack a satisfactory account of the reading of Prudentius in the Middle Ages.

The philologists have been predominantly interested in the verbal imitation of Prudentius by later authors.[3] Also, philologists and art historians have understandably been preoccupied with the *psychomachia* theme,[4] which had an immensely fruitful afterlife in the art and literature of most European countries. Haskins and others have drawn attention to the use of Prudentius in medieval school curricula,[5] where he played a rather minor role in the study of grammar. Prudentius appeared quite frequently in the *libri manuales* and *florilegia*[6] from the Carolingian period onwards; however, he was clearly not regarded as an indispensable author for Christian education, as were Vergil, Ovid, and Statius.

But what happened to Prudentius during the Renaissance? Did he maintain his pre-eminence among the Christian poets, or did he fall by the wayside, a victim of changing tastes and priorities in literature? The humanist scholars of the fourteenth and early fifteenth centuries showed little enthusiasm for Prudentius or the other early Christian poets, Arator, Juvencus, Sedulius, and Paulinus of Nola. Sabbadini[7] demonstrated that the libraries of the leading humanists were nearly always stocked with patristic manuscripts as well as classical ones, though the Christian poets did not fare as well as the prose writers, the preference being for Augustine, Ambrose, Jerome, Lanctantius, and Gregory, and more rarely Tertullian, Salvian, Cyprian, and Orosius. Among the Greek fathers, Basil, John Chrysostom, Gregory Nazianzen, Gregory of Nyssa, and Eusebius were the most commonly read.[8] Although Petrarch owned a manuscript containing several works by Prudentius, he had scant interest in its contents.[9] Boccaccio admitted to an appreciation of Prudentius, Sedulius, Arator, and Juvencus, particularly because the first two had revealed sacred truth *sub tegumento*.[10]

In Prudentius' case the stumbling-block was his style. While it was granted that he was *lyrico insignis carmine,*[11] it was altogether exceptional in these years for his style to be called elegant.[12] This stylistic obstacle was to prove most embarrassing for the Christian humanists of the Renaissance. They were keen to disseminate the pedogogic content of Prudentius' religious poetry, but as scholars of grammar nourished on a diet of classical literature they were acutely aware of the anti-classical tendencies of Prudentius' Latin. Erasmus, for example, oscillated between two extremes in his attitude to Prudentius. It is unlikely that he had become acquainted with the poet while at school in Deventer, since he was there more than a decade before an edition of Prudentius was printed there (see below). After 1484 he moved to Steyn, where he entered the monastery of the Augustinian canons and remained until 1492. Béné proposes that Erasmus' renewed friendship in the monastery with his schoolfriend from Deventer, Corne-

lius Gerard, was the key event in his initial acceptance of Prudentius.[13] However, we still lack the proof. In any case, there is the prefatory letter to Erasmus' 1497 edition of the poems of Guillaume Hermans, in which he attacked the "modern versifiers" who chose as models Catullus, Tibullus, Propertius and Ovid, rather than St. Augustine, Paulinus of Nola, Prudentius, Juvencus, and even rather than David and Solomon, "as if they were ashamed of being Christians."[14] However, by 1519 Erasmus had modified his position. Now he disagreed with Latomus' recommendations that the obscene pagan poets be ousted by the early Christian poets. His reasons were clear enough: "as if one could profit any from Juvencus in the formation of one's style; or from Paulinus, who wrote only one or two poems; as if Prudentius could be read by anyone other than a theologian!"[15] Yet by 1528, when Froben printed Erasmus' *Ciceronianus* at Basel, the master was at least prepared to concede that he would much prefer one hymn by Prudentius to three books of Sannazaro.[16] Erasmus' change of heart had been signalled four years earlier in his edition of Ovid's *Elegies,* dedicated to the two children of Thomas More and including for their benefit two hymns by Prudentius on the Nativity and the Epiphany.[17]

In prescribing Prudentius for the religious edification of More's children, Erasmus had fallen into stride with a number of Christian educators in England and on the Continent. Dean Colet of St. Paul's had recommended Prudentius, along with Sedulius, Juvencus, Baptista Mantuanus, and Lactantius, for his school's Latin course as early as 1512, as examples of "good auctors suych as have the veray Romayne eliquence joyned withe wisdome."[18] This development had its beginnings around the turn of the century and is bound up with the printing of the first complete editions of Prudentius' works. We are much in need of a detailed study of the early editions of Prudentius; the existing catalogues of early editions of the poet are incomplete and tend to give a distorted picture of the geographical distribution of his works. Identifying even the *editio princeps* remains problematical since the contenders for this honour do not bear dates of publication. However, it is likely that the first collected edition is among the group of undated exemplars prepared by Rodolphus Langius and printed by Richard Paffroet at Deventer, all of which predate April 1498. They have been variously dated 1490-97.[19] There is no evidence for the existence of a Deventer edition of 1472.[20] The Deventer group were published without commentaries,[21] so we have little in the way of direct information about their origins.

We do know more, however, about Paffroet and the contemporary scene at Deventer. Rudolph of Langen, (died 1519) was a student of the Brethren of the Common Life at Deventer and eventually became provost of the house at Munster. A number of the early editors and commentators of Prudentius who were born north of the Alps—the list includes Langius, Agricola, Wimpfeling, Reuchlin, Celtis, and Erasmus—had either been schooled at Deventer or had some degree of contact with the Brethren of the Common Life and the Devotio Moderna.[22] The press managed by Paffroet and Jacobus de Breda at Deventer between 1477 and 1500 had the largest output among the Dutch and Belgian presses. The establishment had intimate connections with the Brethren, whose school seems to have been the major consumer of the predominantly theological and edificatory works chosen for printing.[23] It is probable that Prudentius was here first used as a schoolbook in printed form.

I

The intentions of the Christian humanists in "rediscovering" the early Christian poets are clearly expressed in the preface to Aldo Manuzio's collected edition of Prudentius (along with Prosper of Aquitaine and John Damascene) published at Venice in 1501.[24] Aldo mentions that his manuscript had come to him from Britain, "where it had remained hidden for eleven centuries." He had published the Christian poets as a substitute "for the lies and the books of the ancients," for the benefit of youth, "and to distinguish the true from the false," putting youth in touch with orthodox teaching and the virtues. "My intention was," he wrote, "to see these works in our schools, where the tender spirits of our youth are instructed, and brought into contact with pious men." He added to the volume a life of Prudentius, a brief but original study which became appended to most sixteenth-century editions of the complete works.[25]

If the humanist printer's claims to have brought Prudentius to light after a thousand years of darkness seem to us mere hyperbole, then we are in danger of overlooking the fact that genuine discoveries were made during these years in connection with Prudentius manuscripts. Not every Quattrocento library possessed manuscripts of Prudentius.[26] Professor Kristeller's meticulous survey of Quattrocento library holdings has shown, on the other hand, that there may have been more copying of the poet's manuscripts in fifteenth-century Italy than one would have expected.[27] There are occasional hints of a lively interest in Prudentius manuscripts in the 1490's. In 1493 Matteo Bossi of Verona sent to Angelo Poliziano in Florence a manuscript in a pre-Caroline script which contained works by Ausonius and Prudentius. Later in the decade exploratory visits to the library at Bobbio and to libraries of the Milanese monasteries by Merula and Galbiate, and after them by Aulo Parrasio, uncovered other Prudentius manuscripts whose identity today is difficult to establish.[28] The discovery of new and supposedly better

manuscripts of Prudentius continued throughout the sixteenth century, and nearly all of the subsequent editors in the North were able to amend the Aldine text (for better or for worse) with the help of a *codex antiquissimus*.[29]

It was in the North, and particularly in Germany during the first three decades of the sixteenth century, that a genuine learned enthusiasm for Prudentius came to the fore. There is evidence that Prudentius was introduced into university curricula in Germany. Jacob Wimpfeling began his summer course of 1498 at the University of Heidelberg, where he was professor of rhetoric and poetry, with lectures on St. Jerome's letters and the poetry of Prudentius.[30] Petrus Mosellanus, in his jocular book, *Paedologia* (1518), completed an account of the coming semester's course at the University of Leipzig in these words:

> Lastly, a few books of Virgil's poems will be expounded, doubtless in order that this fine poet, as Augustine says, fixed in youthful minds, may remain throughout all life. In addition to these things, since it is not fitting that Christians should be all wrapped up in pagan books in these days when we are celebrating feasts, we should also hear the most splendid and solemn hymns of Aurelius Prudentius, that grave and saintly man, or if they are not satisfactory, the *Enchiridion militis Christiani* of Erasmus Roterdamus studiously commented on.[31]

Here was a thinly-veiled hint that Prudentius' style could be rather too turgid for a university literature course.

At Leipzig in 1499 Jacob Thanner printed a separate edition of the *Liber historiarum* which ran to two more editions in 1503 and 1505. Johannes Murmellius edited Prudentius' hymn on St. Romanus at Cologne in 1507, and in 1508 the hymn on St. Cassian was published there too. An edition of the **Cathemerinon,** prefaced with a letter from Petrus Mosellanus to Matthew Meyner on the educational merits of Prudentius, appeared at Leipzig in 1522. A decade later, from the same press of Nicolaus Faber, came the curious little book of poems by Prudentius and Virgil set to music (*Melodiae Prudentianae et in Virgilium magna ex parte nuper natae,* Lipsiae 1532 or 1533?). Presses at Augsburg, Erfurt, and Schlettstadt also printed Prudentius during these years, and there is a single edition of the **Hamartigenia** in folio which appeared at Nuremberg as early as 1475.[32]

Austrian and Swiss humanists also contributed their talents. Johann Cuspinian's earliest work was an edition of the **Cathemerinon** (Vienna 1494?);[33] another, including a preface by Agricola, was printed in 1515. A number of editions appeared at Basel after Sichard's of 1527. In the Low Countries we find a single printing of the *Psychomachia* at Zwolle of c. 1500, and several editions of the *opera* at Antwerp from the 1530's onward.[34] In France, the main centres of interest in Prudentius were Lyon, Paris, Poitiers, and Avignon.[35] In Spain, Antonio of Nebrija published editions at Logroño and Salamanca,[36] and his commentaries became integrated to later editions in the North. The *Peristephanon* was printed by Mathias Scharffenberg at Cracow in 1526.

Italy alone seems to have remained satisfied with the Aldine edition of 1501. Goldschmidt was right in suggesting that "the humanist tendencies of the Italian schoolmasters" were opposed to experiments introducing the post-classical poets to school curricula. Judging by his preface to Prudentius in the *Poetae Christiani,* Aldo Manuzio's pedagogic ideals were not far removed from those of the Northern humanists who championed Prudentius. In October 1502, Manuzio wrote to Johannes Reuchlin, sending him, among other books from his own press, "Prudentius the Christian poet, with some others written in Greek, and also Sedulius, with Juvencus and Arator . . ."[37] Reuchlin's Germany was to prove a more fertile soil.

Space will not permit further investigation of the widespread interest in Prudentius shown by Northern humanists and printers. I have noted additional material of importance in the writings of Joachim Vadian, Thomas Murner, Nikolaus Mameranus, the two Pirckheimers, Konrad Celtis, Amerbach, Aventinus, Theodore Poelman, Victor Ghisselinck, Laevinus Torrentius, and Petrus Nannius.[38]

II

Concern for the historical information afforded by Prudentius' poems lagged far behind the textual developments. The humanist antiquarians of the fifteenth century had not been entirely unaware of the value (and limitations) of patristic writings in dealing with the intricacies of Roman monumental remains. Biondo Flavio produced a dazzling array of patristic texts in his disputes with Bartolomeo of Sassoferrato and Giacomo Tolomeo regarding the placement of the statues of SS. Peter and Paul along the new access-stairs to the Vatican basilica.[39] Cyriac of Ancona had sought out literary sources from the early Church to clarify the details of his journeys in the eastern Mediterranean.[40] But on the whole, the fifteenth-century scholars did not pause to gather the scattered passages in the fathers dealing with Roman topography and monuments[41] in order to substantiate or test the more familiar evidence in the classical authors. Cyriac of Ancona carefully wove into his narrative couplets from the classical poets bearing on topographical matters: where else could one find historical evidence expressed in such succinct and

artistic form? Yet we will search in vain throughout the treatises of the fifteenth-century antiquarians—and even those writing directly on the monuments of the early Church in Rome—for a similar use of Prudentius.

The *Catalogus* of Trithemius provided scholars in the early sixteenth century with a moderately detailed biographical survey of the fathers of the Church. Trithemius' medieval predecessors had rarely devoted more than a sentence or two to Prudentius and the other Christian poets; nor were their brief notices always correct.[42] The first comprehensive, chronologically systematic history of the Church (at least of the first thirteen centuries) to be produced during the Reformation was the Magdeburg *Centuries.* Published between 1559 and 1574 at Basel and researched by a team of Lutheran scholars, the *Centuries* worked laboriously through the historical-biographical details of the developing Church, seizing upon Roman "errors" at every turn and propagating a Protestant viewpoint on major issues. There are few references to Prudentius in the seven folio volumes of the *Centuries.* The Roman martyr Lawrence is mentioned in *Cap.* XII of the third century: the authors quote Prudentius' hymn on the saint in its entirety. In *Cap.* X of the fourth century we find a brief sketch of Prudentius' life and works which includes selections from his poems on dogmatic issues, on the cult of the martyrs, and on the struggles against heretics. There is a note on the meaning of the *Dittochaeum* which acknowledges Aldo's 1501 edition as the source of information.[43] Here, then, Prudentius is examined primarily for the needs of the dogmatic historian, and Trithemius' bare account has been fleshed out to this end.

The most important antiquarian studies of the early sixteenth century do not use Prudentius as an historical witness. Andrea Fulvio (*Antiquitates Urbis,* 1527) and Giovanni Marliano (*Urbus Romae topographia,* 1534) do not mention him, although both use a range of patristic authors, and Fulvio has a brief chapter on the Roman cemeteries. Prudentius is also mysteriously absent from the writings of Conradus Brunus, one of the stalwarts of German Catholicism during these years. Prudentius does not appear either in his *De caeremoniis* (in which part of Lib. IV dealt with Christian burial customs) or in his *De imaginibus,* in which he cited Athanasius, Nilus, Eusebius, Gregory of Nyssa, John Chrysostom, and Basil.[44] Martin Luther himself was attracted to some of Prudentius' hymns, and included one in his *Christliche Geseng leteinisch und deutsch zum Begrebnis,* printed at Wittemberg in 1542.[45]

III

Prudentius enters the main stream of antiquarian scholarship in the works of Onofrio Panvinio. Panvinio, who had devoted his early studies to Roman imperial history, was the first scholar to compose a separate treatise on the Roman cemeteries. While his acquaintance with the Roman catacombs was limited to the few accessible sites, his research into the literary evidence had the flavour of originality. In the *De ritu sepeliendi mortuos apud veteres christianos* of 1568, Panvinio used Cyprian, Ambrose, Eusebius, Augustine, Sozomen, Gregory, Gregory Nazianzen, Gregory of Tours, Tertullian, Origen, Chrysostom, Epiphanius, Basil, Jerome, Socrates, Damasus, Ignatius, John Damascene, Isidore, Rufinus, Gregory of Nyssa, and a range of Carolingian and later medieval writings touching on the subject. Three times he quoted Prudentius at length to illustrate early Christian burial customs. A decade earlier, in his *De civitate Romana,* Panvinio had drawn attention to Prudentius' valuable account of the Vestal Virgins' role in late-Roman state religions.[46]

In 1568 Johannes Molanus, theologian at the University of Louvain, published a revised edition of the ninth-century *Martyrologium* of Usuardus. In his text Usuardus had made four references to Prudentius in connection with the feasts of SS. Agnes, Vincent, and Hippolytus, three of the many saints and martyrs honoured with poems in the *Peristephanon*. Bede may have been the first to include Prudentius as a witness in a *martyrologium*. He was followed in this respect by Rabanus Maurus, and the short notices found their way into Usuardus' version. Molanus did not augment Prudentius' role in his edition of the text. However, two years later, in his *De picturis et imaginibus sacris,* Molanus demonstrated an easy familiarity with both Prudentius and Paulinus of Nola, quoting or citing Prudentius on the use of the sign of the cross on the forehead, on the existence of pictures of SS. Cassian and Hippolytus in the early Church, on the use of lamps in churches, and on the Magi.[47]

Molanus' *De picturis* had a profound impact on Cardinal Gabriele Paleotti, archbishop of Bologna, who addressed himself to the issue of sacred images in a lengthy discourse published in 1582. An original attempt to set out the Church's teaching on images for the benefit of his own diocese, Paleotti's *Discorso intorno alle imagini* was fully documented with patristic sources. Prudentius figured in two significant entries, one on the virtues and vices, and another where the source is not specified. This is in a discussion of decorum *(onestà)* in sacred art where Paleotti considers "Pitture fiere et orrende." He argues (Lib. II, cap. XXXV) that one of the rare cases in which gross cruelty is justified in religious painting is when the subject depicts the patient sufferings of the Christian martyrs:

> . . . daily we see the dreadful torments of the saints represented and, expressed in detail, the wheels, razors, iron hooks, fiery ovens, gridirons, racks, crosses and an infinite range of the cruellest tortures.

This catalogue of tortures betrays Paleotti's acquaintance with the *Peristephanon* of Prudentius.[48] Paolo Prodi has added another dimension to our understanding of this section of the *Discorso* in demonstrating Paleotti's close dependence on the ideas of the classicist and scientist Ulisse Aldrovandi. The Bolognese scholar maintained that the skilled painter should familiarize himself with the classifications of natural and manmade objects in consultation with experts like himself. While Paleotti's *Discorso* was in press, Aldrovandi composed a treatise for the archbishop on this subject, observing that:

> . . . the painter should converse with the most excellent anatomists and study carefully all the sections of the human body, both internal and external, so that he can know how to represent the heart, the liver, the spleen, the intestines, the stomach, the throat, the brain; so that when he happens to paint a martyrdom like that of S. Erasmus and others like it . . . he will be able to depict it in a natural manner.[49]

It would be surprising if Paleotti, his learned friends, and perhaps even the artists in the diocese who took commissions depicting scenes of early martyrdoms, were not aware of Prudentius' brutally realistic accounts of torn, burned, and broken bodies in the *Peristephanon*. Further research into the genesis of late sixteenth-century paintings depicting the deaths of martyrs to whom Prudentius dedicated hymns in the *Peristephanon* may throw light upon the origins, literary and otherwise, of the visceral, almost obscene realism which characterizes much of the religious painting of those years.

In 1588 Pompeo Ugonio published at Rome his *Historia delle Stationi di Roma,* dedicated to Sixtus V. In this work we encounter the first attempt to use fully Prudentius' information about the Roman churches of his day. Some examples will indicate the importance of Ugonio's contribution. In his discussion of the tribune of S. Sabina, Ugonio dealt with the numerous meanings of the term *tribunal* in antiquity, using Prudentius' *Perist.* [*Peristephanon*] XI, 225-26 to demonstrate how *tribunal* could mean a raised pulpit in an early Christian basilica.[50] In topographical matters Ugonio could use Prudentius to give his interpretations an aura of preciseness which, for the most part, eluded his predecessors. Here is his account of the exact location of the martyrdom of St. Lawrence:

> Those who have composed books on the antiquities of Rome, like Fulvio, Pomponio Leto, Biondo, Marliano and others, put the Baths of Olympiadis in this part of the Viminal hill. Having said this, following the writers of the Martyrdom of S. Lorenzo, they say that he was martyred in the aforesaid baths. This is then the place where the most illustrious and glorious saint was crowned in martyrdom . . . The Christian poet Pruden-

tius indicated this place when naming the different parts of Rome where the holy Martyrs were massacred, and named there the Suburra, which as I have said, stood in this part of the Viminal hill, and he doubtless alludes to the martyrdom of S. Lorenzo.[51]

No scholar before Ugonio thought of comparing Prudentius' topographical notices on martyrdom with those preserved in the *Acts* of the Roman martyrs. Moreover, Ugonio seems to have been the first to adduce Prudentius' evidence on the location of the Suburra.[52] Ugonio's most brilliant application of Prudentius was in his description of the interior decoration of S. Paolo fuori le mura. Here, quoting *Perist.* XII, 49 ff., he used the text to elucidate two features of the decoration whose early date and character could only be explained by reference to Prudentius:[53]

> In the arches which span from one column to another in the central nave, and on the bottom and outside, the most beautiful foliage is worked in stucco on a green background, and perhaps that of which Prudentius spoke in the following verses: "Then [the emperor] covered the curves of the arches with splendid glass of different hues, like meadows that are bright with flowers in the spring."

> In some places the walls show signs of having had inlaid marble tablets. But the soffit was already covered with gold plate, as Prudentius also shows, when he says: "He laid plates on the beams so as to make all the light within golden like the sun's radiance at its rising."[54]

In the same year, 1588, Baronio published two works of astounding erudition: the first volume of the *Annales* and his revision of Molanus' edition of the *Martyrologium Romanum.* In their treatment of Prudentius' evidence, both works call for comparison with their earlier rivals, the Magdeburg *Centuries* and the 1568 *Martyrologium.* Baronio's works were immeasurably more systematic and thorough in their exploration of the patristic evidence. In the *Annales* the early Christian poets, especially Gregory Nazianzen and Prudentius, were used on a scale never before envisaged in historical research. In Tom. I alone, Baronio extracted a wider range of information from Prudentius than any previous writer. The poet was cited or quoted at length on the following issues: the types of animals present at the Nativity; the star of the Magi; the anointing of martyrs' bodies; the use of chrism in administering sacraments; exorcism; the effects of image prohibition in fourth-century Spain; paintings of martyrs Cassian and Hippolytus; the frequency of feasts for the saints; the use of musical instruments to accompany the singing of hymns; the martyrdom dates of SS. Peter and Paul; the place of Peter's crucifixion; Peter's inverted cross; Peter's burial in the Vatican area; prodigies in Nero's reign; the odious habits of Jews; the locations of martyrdoms under Domitian.[55] We may smile at Bar-

onio's historical *naïveté* in reinforcing the New Testament accounts with evidence from fourth-century poets. We can be more in sympathy with his occasional forays into mature source-criticism, as in his demonstration (in Tom. II, Anno 229) that Prudentius had confused three separate men, each named Hippolytus, in his poetic tale of the martyr's death (*Perist.* XI).[56] In the first six tomes of the *Annales,* Baronio consistently used Prudentius to substantiate arguments that he first proposed on the basis of other literary evidence. However, in the *Martyrologium* the poetic evidence of Prudentius was given a more autonomous role. Baronio ransacked Prudentius for passages bearing on the Roman calendar of martyrs, blending this evidence with selections from Damasus, Paulinus of Nola, Venantius Fortunatus and material from the prose writers, to produce a closely-woven tapestry of documentation.[57] In this rather specialized context, Prudentius and the other hagiographic poets came into their own as witnesses of Roman *consuetudo.*

Cardinal Baronio's researches constituted a watershed in patristic studies in the last years of the sixteenth century. In the field of Christian archaeology, activities were confined to the collection and examination of the evidence in the catacombs; a substantial summary of that evidence would only appear in print in Bosio's book of 1632-34. In the meantime, Antonio Gallonio published two studies at Rome in 1591 which gave Prudentius his due as leading witness to the hideous deaths of the early Christian martyrs. In his *Historia delle Sante Vergini Romane,* and particularly in the *Trattato degli instrumenti di martirio e delle varie maniere di martoriore,* Gallonio exploited Prudentius' evidence to the fullest extent, and in the latter work illustrated the text with a series of engravings showing the types of deaths suffered by the martyrs.[58] The engravings literally depict many of the episodes so vividly recounted by Prudentius, and it was fitting that they were chosen in the nineteenth century to accompany the Migne text of Prudentius' *opera.*

The culminating point of the developing interest in Prudentius among sixteenth-century antiquarians actually lay in Bosio's posthumous *Roma sotterranea.* Although Bosio's use of Prudentius deserves a lengthy study in itself, a few brief comments are appropriate here. First it must be pointed out that the editor, Giovanni Severano, considerably reduced the documentation of the manuscript for publication. Bosio had worked from a massive compilation of patristic evidence (now four folios in the Bibl. Vallicelliana) which, in De Rossi's words, contained all that was shown to Bosio's age for the study of the catacombs and their decoration. In the *Roma sotterranea* Prudentius was quoted repeatedly as an unimpeachable observer of the cult of the martyrs in its heyday. It would be difficult to find a passage in Prudentius touching on the martyrs, burial customs, and the cemeterial topography of Rome that was not quoted and assessed by Bosio in the light of other evidence.[59]

Prudentius was now firmly enshrined as a source for early Christian antiquarian studies. In Bosio's book and in the less-distinguished Latin translation by Aringhi (*Roma subterranea novissima,* 1651), the preliminary reports on the catacombs were carried all over Europe to scholars of all denominations. During the next three centuries the findings and conclusions of Bosio and his contemporaries would often be subjected to scrutiny and, in some cases, would be rejected in favour of new interpretations as archeological method became more scientific. Today we recognize Prudentius as one of the primary and indispensable sources for the study of early Christian archeology. It remains one of the major achievements of the sixteenth-century pioneers of Christian archeology to have searched deeply into the literature of the early Church and to have drawn out authors like Prudentius, who might otherwise have remained unfashionable curiosities.[60]

Notes

1. See the following studies on aspects of patrology in the Renaissance: C. Dejob, *De l'influence du Concile de Trente sur la littérature et les beaux-arts chez les peuples catholiques,* Paris 1884. P. O. Kristeller, "Augustine and the Early Renaissance," *Review of Religion,* VIII (1944), pp. 339-58. E. Wind, "The Revival of Origen," *Studies in Art and Literature for Belle da Costa Greene,* Princeton 1954, pp. 412-24. D. P. Walker, "Origène en France au début du XVIe siècle," *Courants religieux et humanisme à la fin du XVe et au début du XVIe siècle,* Paris 1959, pp. 101-19. S. L. Greenslade, *The English Reformers and the Fathers of the Church,* Oxford 1960. P. Fraenkel, *Testimonia Patrum. The Function of the Patristic Argument in the Theology of Philip Melanchthon* (Travaux d' Humanisme et Renaissance, XLVI) Geneva 1961. R. Peters, "The Use of the Fathers in the Reformation Handbook *Unio Dissidentium,*" *Studia Patristica,* IX (Berlin 1966) pp. 570-77. Natalie Davis, "Gregory Nazianzen in the Service of Humanist Social Reform," *Renaissance Quarterly,* XX (1967) pp. 455-64. P. Petitmengen, "Le Codes Veronensis de saint Cyprien," *Revue des Etudes Latines,* XLVI (1968) pp. 330-78. A. Hufstader, "Lefèvre d'Etaples and the Magdalen," *Studies in the Renaissance,* XVI (1969) pp. 31-60.

2. *Annales ecclesiastici,* II, Rome 1594, p. 81; in the Lucca edition of 1738, pp. 117-18: further references are to this edition.

3. Still indispensable are the indices of M. Manitius, *Geschichte der lateinischen Literatur des Mittelalters,* I-III. Munich 1911-31. Also, E. B. Vest, *Pru-*

dentius in the Middle Ages, (unpubl. Ph.D.) Harvard 1932, using Manitius' references but almost entirely concerned with *loci similes.* For the manuscripts, see J. Bergman, "De codicum Prudentianorum generibus et virtute," *Sitzungsberichte der Phil.—hist. Klasse der kaiserl. Akad. der Wiss. in Wien,* 157 (1908) Heft 5; M. Lavarenne, *Prudence* (Coll. Guillaume Budé) 1, Paris 1951, Introduction. H. Silvestre, "Aperçu sur les commentaires carolingiens de Prudence," *Sacris Erudiri,* 9 (1957) pp. 50-75; A. Kurfess, s.v. "Prudentius," Pauly-Wissowa, *Realencyclopädie der klassischen Altertumswissenschaft,* XXIII, 1, 1957, esp. cols. 1068-70 on Prudentius' influence; recently, the edition of the *Carmina* by M. P. Cunningham, (Corpus Christianorum, Ser. Lat. 126) Turnholt 1966, with an up-to-date bibliography.

4. See C. Gnilka, *Studien zur Psychomachie des Prudentius* (Klassisch-Philologische Studien, 27) Wiesbaden 1963.

5. C. H. Haskins, *The Renaissance of the Twelfth Century,* Cambridge, Mass. 1927, pp. 82, 113, 116. In Ruotger's Life of Bruno, archbishop of Cologne (late 10th-early 11th cent.), we hear that Bruno began his education in grammar with Prudentius (*M.G.H. SS.* IV, p. 256). E. Garin notes that Prudentius' so-called *Dittochaeum* (identified in the Middle Ages by the incipit *Eva columba*) was included in some collections of instruction texts in the scholastic period (*L'educatione in Europa 1400-1600,* Bari 1957, p. 72, note 45).

6. See Eva M. Sanford, "Classical Latin Authors in the Libri Manuales," *Transactions of the American Philological Association,* LV (1924) pp. 190-248. Prudentius appears 29 times in the 414 manuscripts described, but Sanford's list is neither detailed enough in the entries nor wide enough in scope to give a clear idea of Prudentius' role. Cf. also B. L. Ullman, "Tibullus in the mediaeval Florilegia," *Classical Philology,* XXIII (1928) pp. 128-74; G. Billanovich, "'Veterum vestigia vatum' nei carmi dei preumanisti padovani," *Italia medioevale e umanistica,* 1 (1958) pp. 155-243, esp. 160. Among the highpoints in the scholarly use of Prudentius which require further attention are Bede's inclusion of him in his *De arte metrica,* perhaps his earliest appearance in a schoolbook; in the seventh century, Julian of Toledo's peculiar interest in Prudentius' *Dittochaeum,* then read as allegorical excerpts from Scripture; in the ninth century, Dungalus' application of proof-texts culled from superlative manuscripts of Prudentius and Paulinus of Nola, in his *Responsa* to bishop Claudius of Turin, an important episode in the western side of the iconoclastic controversy; and

in the twelfth century, Prudentius' role in the *Libelli de lite,* whose polemically-slanted use of patristic proof-texts significantly prefigured the Reformation debates on *consuetudo.*

7. *Le scoperte dei codici latini e greci ne'secoli XIV e XV,* Florence 1905, and *Nuove ricerche col riassunto filologico dei due volumi,* Florence 1914.

8. See the illuminating study by E. F. Jacob, "Christian Humanism," in *Europe in the Late Middle Ages,* ed. J. R. Hale *et al.,* London 1965, pp. 437-65. The memoirs of Vespasiano da Bisticci indicate the continued and lively interest of his princely clients in patristic literature that was either rare or not easily accessible. The rediscovered writings of the fathers were given a new significance in religious education by scholars like Lefèvre d'Etaples. See E. F. Rice Jr., "The Humanist Idea of Christian Antiquity: Lefèvre d'Etaples and his Circle," *Studies in the Renaissance,* IX (1962) pp. 126-60.

9. P. de Nolhac, *Petrarque et l'humanisme,* Paris 1907, p. 103 on the manuscript, now Paris, Bibl. Nat. fonds lat. no. 8500; cf. pp. 210-11. On the Paris manuscript and related codices, see R. Weiss, "Ausonius in the Fourteenth Century," in *Classical Influences on European Culture A.D. 500-1500,* ed. R. R. Bolgar, Cambridge 1971, pp. 67-72.

10. *Genealogia deorum gentilium,* Lib. XIV, cap. XXII. (Ed. G. Ricci, Naples 1965, pp. 1056-58). The passage was quoted in Giovanni Dominici's *Lucula Noctis* of 1404; see Sabbadini, *Nuove ricerche,* p. 177. See also Salutati's letter to Dominici, in F. Novati, *Epistolario di Colluccio Salutati* (Fonti per la Storia d'Italia, Epist., Sec. XIV) Rome 1905, p. 232. Giovanni Colonna (born c. 1265) knew the *Psychomachia* and *Dittochaeum* (Sabbadini, *ibid.,* p. 55); Amplonius Ratinck (born c. 1365) owned a Prudentius codex, along with Sedulius and Prosper (*ibid.,* pp. 15-16).

11. As he was described by Nicola de Clemangis (born c. 1360); cited by Sabbadini, *ibid.,* p. 80.

12. Domenico de' Bandini (1335-1418) named only Prudentius as a Christian poet: (Sabbadini, *ibid.,* p. 185, note 36). Du Pin wrote at the end of the seventeenth century: *Prudentius is no very good poet, he often useth harsh Expressions not reconcilable to the Purity of Augustus's* Age (*Nouvelle bibliothèque des auteurs ecclésiastiques du premier au 17ᵉ siècle,* Paris 1690-1723, cited from the London translation of 1693, III, p. 5).

13. Ch. Béné, *Erasme et saint Augustin* (Travaux d'Humanisme et Renaissance, CIII) Geneva 1969,

p. 47. Cf. C. Reedijk, *The Poems of Desiderius Erasmus,* Leiden 1956, p. 100.

14. See A. Renaudet, *Préreforme et humanisme à Paris pendant les premières guerres d'Italie 1494-1517,* Paris 1916, p. 278; the phrase "comme s'ils rougissaient d'être chrétiens" probably came to Erasmus from his reading of Gregory Nazianzen's *Discourses,* where the emperor Julian is described in similar terms.

15. Béné, *op. cit.,* p. 319.

16. A. Gambaro, *Desiderio Erasmo da Rotterdam, Il Ciceroniano,* Brescia 1965, pp. 278-79.

17. E. E. Reynolds, *Thomas More and Erasmus,* London 1965, p. 137.

18. Quotation from E. W. Hunt, *Dean Colet and his Theology,* London 1956, p. 3; see A. M. Stowe, *English Grammar Schools in the Reign of Queen Elizabeth,* New York 1908, p. 109. Prudentius was prescribed as late as 1583 at Saint Bees school (p. 111).

19. The following provide incomplete lists of early editions: F. Didbin, *An Introduction to the Knowledge of Rare and Valuable Editions of the Greek and Latin Classics,* Vol. 2, 3rd ed., London 1808, pp. 180-83; A. Dressel, *Aurelii Prudentii . . . Carmina,* Leipzig 1860, p. XXV ff.; A. Palau y Dulcet, *Manual de librero Hispanoamericano,* XIV, Oxford/Barcelona 1962, pp. 237-40; E. P. Goldschmidt, *Medieval Texts and Their First Appearance in Print,* London 1943, p. 43. On the dating, see M. F. A. G. Campbell, *Annales de la typographie neérlandaise au XVᵉ siècle,* The Hague 1874 ff., no. 1456; L. Polain, *Catalogue des livres imprimés au quinzième siècle des bibliothèques de Belgique,* III, Brussels 1932, no. 3263; A. Thurston and C. F. Bühler, *Check List of Fifteenth Century Printing in the Pierpont Morgan Library,* New York 1939, no. 13432; F. R. Goff, *Incunabula in American Libraries,* New York 1964, p. 509 ff. The only detailed study of the Deventer press known to the author does not consider the dating of the Prudentius editions: L. A. Sheppard, "Printing at Deventer in the Fifteenth Century," *The Library,* 4th Ser., XXIV (1944) pp. 101-19.

20. See J. A. Fabricius, *Bibliotheca Latina,* II, Venice 1728, p. 288, and the rebuttals of Dibdin and Dressel (*loc. cit.*); J.-C. Margolin, *Erasme, Declamatio de pueris statim ac liberaliter instituendis,* Geneva 1966, p. 349, note 434, refers to such an edition.

21. In May 1493 Paffroet published the *Liber Cathemerinon* with an *Interpretatio* by Antonius Liber;

see *Short-Title Catalogue of Books Printed in the Netherlands and Belgium . . . in the British Museum,* London 1965, p. 173.

22. However, one must acknowledge the tenuous nature of the evidence for the influence of the Brethren and the *Devotio* on these scholars. R. R. Post argues that of this group only Erasmus had "any contact of importance with the Devotio Moderna . . . Agricola, Wimpfeling and Mutian may also have absorbed a little influence from a distance" (*The Devotio Moderna,* Leiden 1968, pp. 10-12). On Langius, see Jöcher, *Allgemeines Gelehrten-Lexicon,* Leipzig 1750, *s.v.* Lange.

23. On the printing activities of the Brethren themselves, see E. F. Jacob, "The Brethren of the Common Life," in *Essays in the Conciliar Epoch,* 3rd rev. ed. Manchester 1963, pp. 121-38.

24. See A. Firmin-Didot, *Alde Manuce et l'hellénisme à Venise,* Paris 1875, p. 186 ff.; cf. P. Renouard, *Bibliographie des impressions et des oeuvres de Josse Badius Ascensius, Imprimeur et Humaniste, 1462-1535,* II, Paris 1908, p. 507, for comments by Badius Ascensius.

25. Sixteenth-Century scholars frequently used the account of Prudentius' works in the *Catalogus Scriptorum Ecclesiasticorum* of Johannes Trithemius, printed in 1494 and often reprinted (*Opera Historica,* Frankfurt 1601, p. 210 ff.); following Gennadius, Trithemius wrongly attributed to Prudentius a work *In hexameron lib. 6,* and even "epistolas . . . non paucas." Prudentius won a brief mention in G. I. Vossius' *De historicis latinis,* Lyon 1527, p. 190.

26. Prudentius does not appear in the 1411 inventory of the papal library at Avignon; however, only 648 of the 882 codices are actually described in the document. See Anneliese Maier, "Der Katalog der päpstlichen Bibliothek in Avignon vom Jahr 1411," *Archivum Historiae Pontificiae,* 1 (1963) pp. 97-178. Yet the catalogue of the same library for 1379 does list a manuscript containing Terence, Prudentius and Macrobius; see F. Simone, *Il rinascimento francese,* 2nd ed., Turin 1965, p. 17. Nor does Prudentius figure in the fifteenth century inventories of the Vatican Library; see E. Müntz and P. Fabre, *La bibliothèque du Vatican au XVᵉ siècle d'après des documents inédits,* Paris 1887. Prudentius does appear in the catalogue of a private library in Cremona: G. Mainardi, "Due biblioteche private cremonesi del secolo XV," *Italia medioevale e umanistica,* 2 (1959) p. 450. He was listed in the 1470 inventory of Hieronymus Münzer's personal library (E. P. Goldschmidt, *Hieronymus Münzer und seine Bibliothek,* London

1938, p. 134); and later, to cite one of many examples, in both manuscript and printed form (the Aldine edition) in Fulvio Orsini's library (P. de Nolhac, *La bibliothèque de Fulvio Orsini,* Paris 1887, pp. 368, 388).

27. P. O. Kristeller, *Iter Italicum,* I, London/Leiden 1965, pp. 73, 157, 272, 412; Vol. II, 1967, pp. 128, 129, 197, 318, 326, 395, 490, 558. Also, Johannes Murmellius listed the following commentaries: "In Prudentiam Rudolphus Agricola, Hermannus Buschius Hadrianus Barlandus, Johannes Murmellius" (A. Bömer, *Des münsterischen Humanisten Johannes Murmellius De magistri et discipulorum officiis Epigrammatum liber,* Münster 1892, Heft V, p. 144).

28. Sabbadini, *Le scoperte dei codici,* p. 154, 159-60, 170; Weiss, *art. cit.,* pp. 69-70; G. Soranzo, *L'umanista canonico regolare lateranense Matteo Bossi di Verona (1472-1502),* Padua 1965, p. 188.

29. See, for example, P. Lehmann's comments on Sichard's 1527 edition of Prudentius' *Opera,* in which he emended the Aldine text using a Strassburg manuscript, and derived his scholia "ex codicibus vetustioribus" (*Iohannes Sichardus und die von ihm benutzten Bibliotheken und Handschriften,* Munich 1911, p. 48ff. and 184).

30. See P. Adam, *L'humanisme à Selestat,* Schlettstadt 1962, p. 39; O. Herding, *Jacob Wimpfelings Adolescentia,* Munich 1965, pp. 71-72, 89, 314.

31. R. F. Seybolt, *Renaissance Student Life: The Paedologia of Petrus Mosellanus,* Chicago 1927, Dialogue 9, p. 29; the preceding part of the curriculum included Cicero, Quintilian and Terence.

32. For the German editions see Dressel, pp. XXVII-XXX; Palau y Dulcet, pp. 237-40; G. Bauch, *Geschichte der leipziger Frühhumanismus,* Leipzig 1889, p. 71 ff.; D. Reichling, *Johannes Murmellius,* Freiburg i. Br. 1880, pp. 64-65, 142-44. On the Augsburg *Psychomachia* printed by Oeglin in 1506, see Dressel, p. XXVII; Palau y Dulcet, p. 238. Goldschmidt, *Medieval Texts,* p. 43, notes the existence of a "single title" edition at Erfurt, but I have not seen another reference to one. On the Schlettstadt *Cathemerinon* published by Spiegel in 1520, see A. Horawitz and K. Hartfelder, *Briefwechsel des Beatus Rhenanus,* Leipzig 1886, pp. 221-22; cf. also on Prudentius pp. 18, 235, 607-8; E. König, *Konrad Peutingers Briefwechsel,* Munich 1923, pp. 214, 447. The Nuremberg edition is noted in W. A. Copinger, *Supplement to Hain's Repertorium Bibliographicum,* I, London 1895, no. 13437; Palau y Dulcet, p. 238; Goff, *op. cit.,* p. 510, for American copies.

33. H. Ankwicz von Kleehoven, *Documenta Cuspiniana,* Vienna 1957, pp. 90-91, for the dating 1494. On the Basel editions see Lehmann, *op. cit.,* p. 49; Dressel, pp. XXX-XXXI.

34. Palau y Dulcet, p. 237, lists editions of 1536, 1540, 1545, 1546, 1564, 1594.

35. See J. Baudrier, *Bibliographie Lyonnaise,* 7 Ser. Lyon/Paris 1908, pp. 8-9; 11 Ser. 1914, p. 487; Palau y Dulcet, pp. 237-38.

36. Dressel, pp. XXVIII-XIX; C. Haebler, *Bibliografia Iberica del Siglo XV,* New York 1903 ff., no. 599; J. Lycell, *Early Book Illumination in Spain,* London 1926, p. 286. On the influence of this edition in Spain, see D. W. McPheeters, *El Humanista español Alonso de Proaza,* Valencia 1961, p. 117 ff. On patristic studies in early 16th century Spain, and notes on the poets, see F. Rubio, "Don Juan de Castilla y el movimento humanistico de su reinado," *La Ciudad de Dios,* CLXVIII (1955) pp. 55-100; M. de Riquer, *L'humanisme Català (1388-1494),* Barcelona 1934, esp. pp. 14, 47, 57; C. Lynn, *A College Professor of the Renaissance. Lucio Marineo among the Spanish Humanists,* Chicago 1937, esp. pp. 178, 181 on Sedulius; Palau y Dulcet, p. 238.

37. See C. Dionisotti, "Aldo Manuzio umanista," *Lettere italiane,* 12 (1960) pp. 375-400, esp. 383; E. K. Quaranta, "La formazione culturale di Aldo Manuzio ed il suo criterio nella scelta dei testi," *Studi Bibliografici: Atti del Convegno dedicato alla storia del Libro Italiano nel V Centenario dell'introduzione dell'arte tipografico in Italia,* Florence 1967, pp. 147-58; also Firmin-Didot, *op. cit.,* p. 235.

38. See W: Naf, *Vadian und seine Stadt St. Gallen,* St. Gall 1944, pp. 208, 285; P. Lehmann, *Mittelalterliche Bibliothekskataloge Deutschlands und der Schweiz,* I, Munich 1918, p. 59 ff. P. Scherrer, *Thomas Murners Verhältnis zum Humanismus,* Basel 1929, p. 5. N. Didier, *Nikolaus Mameranus,* Freiburg 1915, pp. 213-14. A. Reimann, *Die alteren Pirckheimer,* Leipzig 1944, p. 117; J. Pfanner, *Briefe von, an und über Caritas Pirckheimer (aus den Jahren 1498-1530),* Landshut 1966, p. 78. H. Rupprich, *Der Briefwechsel des Konrad Celtis,* Munich 1934, pp. 121, 527; Celtis owned a Prudentius manuscript and lent it to his friends: it is now Cod. Vind. 247, and is described by H. J. Hermann, *Die deutschen-romanischen Handschriften,* VIII, II Teil, Leipzig 1926, p. 33. Celtis signed the manuscript in 1507. A. Hartmann, *Die Amerbachkorrespondenz,* II (1514-1524) Basel 1943, no. 956, p. 469. J. Turmair, *Aventinus, kleinere historische und philologische Schriften,* Bd.

I, Munich 1881, pp. 521, 545-49; Bd. VI, p. 79. On Poelman, see H. de Vocht, *Cornelii Valerii ab Auwater, Epistolae et Carmina,* Louvain 1957, p. 402. On Ghisselinck, see *ibid.,* p. 488, and H. de Vocht, *Literae virorum eruditorum ad Franciscum Craneveldum, 1522-1528,* Louvain 1928, pp. 543, 600-01. Marie Delcourt and J. Hoyoux, *Laevinus Torrentius Correspondance,* III, Paris 1954, p. 263. A. Polet, *Une gloire de l'Humanisme belge. Petrus Nannius (1500-1557),* Louvain 1936, pp. 177-78.

39. B. Nogara, *Scritti inediti e rari di Biondo Flavio* (Studi e Testi, 48) Rome 1927, pp. 202-07; for patristic sources, see pp. 109, 153, 162, 167, 178 ff. In the *De Roma triumphante,* posthumously published at Basel, 1559, Biondo uses Augustine, Eusebius, Jerome, Ambrose, Cassiodorus and Chrysostom, but seems not to have known Prudentius' important evidence on the *vestales,* in the *Contra Symmachum.* R. Weiss noticed that Biondo "was too sharp to overlook the fact that Christian and medieval writers had also something to contribute." (*The Renaissance Discovery of Classical Antiquity,* Oxford 1969, p. 67).

40. *Kyriaci Anconitani Itinerarium,* Florence 1742, esp. pp. 3-4, 55, 66.

41. There are a few flashes of interest in the patristic evidence. Giovanni Cavallini used Lactantius and Isidore in his *Polhistoria de virtutibus et dotibus Romanorum* (R. Valentini and G. Zucchetti, *Codice topografico della città di Roma,* IV, Rome 1953, pp. 29-30, 43, 46, 54). In his *Descriptio urbis Romae* of 1430 Nicolo Signorili listed his sources, among them the two Christians Augustine and Orosius (*ibid.,* pp. 162-63). Cola di Rienzo appears to have been in some doubt as to whether the fifth crown for his coronation as Cavaliere should be of olive as Prudentius intimated (Ore columba refert ramum viriditatis olive/in gaudium pacis date), or of laurel, as Isidore (and the *Graphia aureae urbis*) had it; see A. Gabrelli, *Epistolario di Cola di Rienzo,* Rome 1890, p. 247; cf. Valentini-Zucchetti, III, p. 99.

42. See, for example, Ekhard's *Chronicon universale*: Anno 399. Huius tempore Claudianus et Prudentius poetae insignis habentur (*M.G.H. SS.,* VI, p. 134). Sigebert's *Chronica*: Anno 393. In Hispania Prudentius lyricus poeta claret. Anno 407. Prudentius quoque poeta luculento metrici operis libello blasphemias Simmachi refellit. . . . Conrad of Hirschau used Gennadius' account in his *Didascalon;* see Manitius, III, pp. 317-18; further examples in *M.G.H. SS.,* XXIII, p. 512; XXI, p. 128. John of God mistakenly speaks of "Prudencius Equitanensis," in his *Cronica: M.G.H. SS.,* XXI, p. 310.

43. On the genesis and method of the *Centuries,* see E. Feuter, *Geschichte der neueren Historiographie,* Munich/Berlin 1911, pp. 249-53. For Prudentius in the *Centuries,* see Cent. III, pp. 297-301, Cent. IV, pp. 1180, 1186-87.

44. *D. Conradi Bruni . . . De Caeremoniis Libri Sex,* in *D. Conradi Bruni . . . Opera Tria nunc primum aedita,* Mainz 1548, pp. 97-105. Nor does *Lib.* V, *cap.* II on church singing mention Prudentius.

45. See *Works of Martin Luther . . . The Philadelphia Edition,* 6, Philadelphia 1932, pp. 280-81; cf. *Table Talk* (same ed., 54, 1967, p. 147); also *D. Martin Luthers Werke, Kritische Gesamtausgabe* (Weimarer Ausgabe), 54, p. 34; cf. G. Sixt, "Eine Prudentiusübersetzung Adam Reissners (1471-1563)," *Blätter für Hymnologie,* VII (1889) pp. 170-73.

46. On Panvinio, see G. Ferretto, *Note storico-bibliografiche di archeologia cristiana,* Vatican City 1942, pp. 91-99. The *De ritu sepeliendi* was first printed at Cologne 1568; edited by G. Jogh, Frankfurt/Leipzig 1717 (this ed. cited here); see pp. 14-15, 16-17, 18. *Onuphrii Panvinii Civitas Romana,* Venice 1558, in J. G. Graevius, *Thesaurus antiquitatum romanarum,* Leiden 1694-99, I, cols. 230-31. Cf. also Panvinio's *De ecclesiis Christianorum, cap.* III, in Mai *Specilegium Romanum,* IX, Rome 1843, pp. 147-48, 150, 179; and the *De rebus antiquis . . . Basilicae Sancti Petri, Lib.* II (ibid., esp. pp. 226-27).

47. *Usuardi Martyrologium quo Romano Ecclesia ac permultae aliae utuntur . . . et Annotationibus,* Louvain 1568; see under Jan. 22, Feb. 30, Dec. 17. *De picturis et imaginibus sacris, liber unus,* Louvain 1570, pp. 23, 29, 63-4, 88; Molanus also used Paulinus of Nola extensively; a 2nd rev. ed. appeared in 1594. See esp. P. Prodi, "Richerche sulla teorica delle arti figurative nella Riforma cattolica," *Archivio italiano per la Storia della Pietà,* 4 (1962) pp. 121-212, esp. 139-40.

48. See Paola Barocchi, *Trattati d'arte del Cinquecento fra Manierismo e Controriforma,* II, Bari 1961, pp. 417, 460. Cf. Prudentius' *Perist.* I, 55-57; III, 116-20, 144-50; IV, 137-38; V, 109-12, 206-08, 217-20; VI, 33; X, 108-10, 756-59.

49. See Prodi, p. 166 ff.

50. *Historia delle Stationi,* p. 8ᵛ.

51. *Ibid.,* p. 75ʳ.

52. For recent opinion on the ancient location of the Suburra see A. von Gerkan, "Zum Suburaproblem," *Rheinisches Museum für Philologie,* 96 (1953) p. 69 ff. Fifteenth century opinion is indexed in Valentini-Zucchetti, IV, p. 600.

53. See L. Martinez Fazio, "Un discutido testimonio de Prudencio sobre le ornamentación de la basilica ostiense en tiempos de Innocencio I," *Archivum Historiae Pontificiae,* 2 (1964) pp. 45-72.

54. Cf. also pp. 73ʳ, 88ʳ⁻ᵛ on the burial places of Peter and Paul, 174ʳ⁻ᵛ on the Temple of Roma on the Via Sacra, 227ᵛ-228ʳ, 229ʳ⁻ᵛ, 233ᵛ, 236ʳ all on St. Paul and his church.

55. Lucca ed. 1738: I, pp. 2, 12, 218, 228-29, 408, 458-59, 525, 575, 629-30, 635-37, 639, 676, 747; II, pp. 117-18, 125, 286, 474, 481; III, pp. 12, 93, 127, 147, 370, 455, 506 ff., 523, 524-25, 527, 532; IV, pp. 57, 67, 187; V, pp. 36, 48, 357-58, 553, 570, 577, 607-08; VI, pp. 49, 52, 92-93, 143, 149, 176, 180-81, 272, 435. In Tom. I Baronio also cited Paulinus of Nola on the dress of John the Baptist (p. 68), Juvencus on Judas' death (p. 141), Arator on Peter's miracles (p. 208), etc. He obviously thought the poets were close enough in time to the events to be cogent witnesses.

56. II, p. 481.

57. *Martyrologium Romanum ad Novam Kalendarii Rationem, et ecclesiasticae historiae veritatem restitutum;* a 3rd ed. appeared at Antwerp in 1589, and I cite the latter: on Prudentius, pp. 2, 4, 22, 37, 40, 42, 43, 54, 59, 104, 128, 136, 169, 196, 223, 250, 287, 328, 339, 347, 357, 378, 487, 510, 541.

58. See the *Historia,* p. 24, and the *Trattato,* pp. 34, 36, 37, 38, 45, 47, 62, 63, 83, 107.

59. See Bosio, *Roma sotterranea,* Pref., where Severano outlines his editorial approach; cf. G. B. De Rossi, *Roma sotterranea cristiana,* I, Rome 1864, p. 31 ff. De Rossi calls the Vallicelliana manuscript "questo stupendo tesoro di testi illustrare la sacra antichità." However, none of the patristic sources was as important to Bosio as the inscriptions from the catacombs which he discovered in his explorations. On Prudentius, see Bosio pp. 4, 6, 7-8, 10-14, 15-19, 22-23, 27, 45, 297, 398-99, 417, 477, 547, 601, 613, 629, 655.

60. I wish to thank Professor Charles Mitchell for his valuable criticism.

John P. Hermann (essay date 1976)

SOURCE: Hermann, John P. "The Pater Noster Battle Sequence in *Solomon and Saturn* and the *Psychomachia* of Prudentius." *Neuphilologische Mitteilungen: Bulletin of the Modern Language Society* 77, no. 2 (1976): 206-10.

[*In the following essay, Hermann demonstrates that certain elements of* Solomon and Saturn, *an Old English poem, were patterned after combat descriptions in Prudentius's* Psychomachia.]

In the introduction to his edition of *Solomon and Saturn*, Robert J. Menner wrote that "the personifications of the letters and the detailed descriptions of battles are an extraordinary feature of the poem to which it is hard to find an exact parallel. The battles are vaguely reminiscent of those in the **Psychomachia** of Prudentius."[1] A comparison of the battles of the **Psychomachia** with those in *Solomon and Saturn* will show that there are several parallel elements to the poem of Prudentius in the battle descriptions of the Old English poem, and that the vague reminiscences of the Latin work which Menner noted might be more accurately termed conscious artistic manipulations of its materials.

The battle sequence is couched within Solomon's long speech in praise of the Pater Noster that begins at line sixty-three of the first part of the poem, and ends with the insertion of the prose fragment after line one hundred sixty-nine of MS. 422 of Corpus Christi College, Cambridge. Solomon's encomium on the efficacy of the prayer is quite fervent:

> And se ðe wile geornlice   ðone godes cwide
> singan soðlice,   and hine siemle wile
> lufian butan leahtrum,   he mæg ðone laðan gæst,
> feohtende feond,   fleonde gebrengan
>
> (84-7) . . .

Whenever such conditions are present, the letters of the Pater Noster will fight against the devil. Most of the letters of the Lord's Prayer are then presented by means of the rhetorical figure of prosopopoeia, first in the runic alphabet, then in their standard forms, apparently with the intention that each letter would appear only once, although of the nineteen letters which make up the prayer, only sixteen are actually used, some are not accompanied by their runic equivalents, and their sequence is scrambled in places. The letters are personified as powerful warriors against the devil, and their great spiritual potency is indicated by means of vivid battle descriptions. These battle descriptions are elaborate for certain letters and truncated for others.

Certain of the letters are described in a manner which suggests the influence of scenes from the Christian allegorical epic of Prudentius, an allegory of a rather different mode which has as its subject the battle of the virtues and vices within the soul:

> · ↑ T· hine teswað   and hine on ða tungan sticað,
> wræsteð him ðæt woddor   and him ða wongan
> brieceð
>
> (94-5).

This description is tripartite: the letter T stabs the grim fiend's tongue, twists his throat, and breaks his jaws. The first element of the description finds an exact parallel in Prudentius' poem. After *Fides* listens to the vaunting speech of *Discordia/Heresis,* she drives the point of her javelin through the vice's tongue:

> Non tulit ulterius capti blasfemia monstri
> uirtutum regina Fides, sed uerba loquentis
> inpedit et uocis claudit spiramina pilo
> pollutam rigida transfigens cuspide linguam
>
> (715-18).

Such imagery is particularly appropriate for a figure such as *Discordia/Heresis,* whose heretical teachings can only be defeated by the power of faith. I have been unable to find imagery of pierced tongues in any of the other works which might be supposed to have influenced the Old English poet, lending further support to the argument that the *Solomon and Saturn* poet was recalling the vivid description from Prudentius.[2] The other two elements of the description are paralleled by the *Operatio-Avaritia* encounter in the **Psychomachia**:

> Inuadit trepidam Virtus fortissima duris
> ulnarum nodis obliso et gutture frangit
> exsanguem siccamque gulam; conpressa ligantur
> uincla lacertorum sub mentum et faucibus artis
> extorquent animam, nullo quae uulnere rapta
> palpitat atque aditu spiraminis intercepto
> inclusam patitur uenarum carcere mortem
>
> (589-95).

The second element of the T-rune description, the twisting of the fiend's throat, is present in this passage from Prudentius, and the breaking of the jaws of the devil was probably suggested by the powerful grip of *Operatio*'s arms beneath the chin of *Avaritia.*

The S-rune is given fuller treatment than the T-rune:

> Ðonne · N · S· cymeð,   engla geræswa,
> wuldores stæf,   wraðne gegripeð
> feond be ðam fotum,   læteð foreweard hleor
> on strangne stan,   stregdað toðas
> geond helle heap.   Hydeð hine æghwylc
> æfter sceades sciman;   sceaða bið gebisigod,
> Satanes ðegn   swiðe gestilled
>
> (111-17).

This description is fourfold: the letter S seizes the fiend by his feet, pounds his cheek upon a stone, which results in his teeth being scattered throughout the throng in hell, and causes each of the fiends to hide himself throughout the shadowy gloom. The parallel passage in the **Psychomachia** occurs when *Sobrietas* attacks *Luxuria*:

> Addit Sobrietas uulnus letale iacenti
> coniciens silicem rupis de parte molarem,
> hunc unexilliferae quoniam fors obtulit ictum
> spicula nulla manu sed belli insigne gerenti.

Casus agit saxum, medii spiramen ut oris
frangeret et recauo misceret labra palato.
Dentibus introrsum resolutis lingua resectam
dilaniata gulam frustis cum sanguinis inplet

(417-24).

The first element of the S-rune description, the seizure of the fiend by his feet, is not present in this passage. I shall discuss the significance of this omission presently. Furthermore, there is some slight variation in the manner in which the imagery of the **Psychomachia** is employed, although the sequence and basic materials are identical. *Sobrietas'* smashing of the stone against the face of the fiend is answered in the Old English poem by the description of the S-rune's smashing the face of the fiend against the stone. The strange image of the scattering of the fiend's teeth is a more graphic description than that of the Latin poem, in which the teeth are spewed forth from *Luxuria's* mouth: *Insolitis dapibus crudescit guttur et ossa/conliquefacta uorans reuomit quas hauserat offas* (425-6). Finally, the behavior of the lesser fiends who hide themselves after the slaughter of their leader (115b-117) furnishes an exact parallel to the behavior of *Luxuria's* retinue of vices: *Caede ducis dispersa fugit trepidante pauore/ nugatrix acies* (432-3).

But what is to be made of the absence of the seizure of the fiend by his feet in the parallel which has been adduced? Furthermore, what of the descriptions in *Solomon and Saturn* which do not precisely duplicate scenes from the **Psychomachia**? Examples of the latter include the R-rune's shaking the fiend by his hair, and the devil's great consternation at such rough treatment, the whips of the N and O-runes, the spears and arrows of the F, M, Q and U-runes, and the fire which the F and M-runes set upon the fiend's hair. It seems to me that these apparently unparalleled events, when examined more closely, argue rather for the influence of the **Psychomachia** upon the Old English poem than otherwise, and it is to a consideration of the nature of the creative process at work in the poem that we shall now turn.

On a reliquary from Troyes Cathedral completed around the end of the twelfth century, *Largitas/Operatio* is shown piercing the eye of her traditional opponent *Avaritia* with a spear, and holding the vice upside-down while her hand clenches the vice's ankle.[3] Any possibility of the influence of this piece of work upon the S-rune description is, of course, out of the question; furthermore, one could hardly argue cogently the opposite line of influence. Yet the very fact that this work, which is certainly derived from the illustrated **Psychomachia** manuscript tradition, was executed by its artisan in a manner which does not find a precise counterpart in that poem, points up the malleability of the basic

motifs of Prudentius' poem. The process of artistic creation in the Middle Ages, whether in the fine arts or otherwise, did not always involve exact duplication of a source, although this now and then occurs. In constructing his allegory of spiritual battle, the Old English poet recalled images from the first great Christian allegory of spiritual battle, and employed them freely, not slavishly, although his debt to Prudentius for certain of his descriptions is unmistakable. Prudentius' poem is one of those happy triumphs of poetic art, like the later medieval development of the pilgrimage theme, which admits to as many permutations of the basic materials as the individual artist had the wherewithal to construct. While the T and S-rune descriptions correspond rather closely to scenes in the Latin poem, the other battles in *Solomon and Saturn* are more freewheeling adaptations of what is nevertheless Prudentian material. For example, *Superbia* is seized by her hair in **Ps.** [*Psychomachia*] 280-1, a whip appears as one of the accountrements of *Discordia* in **Ps.** 685, and spears and arrows are put to many diverse uses throughout the poem.[4] One should not neglect the possible influence of the illustrated **Psychomachia** manuscripts upon the Old English poet, such as in the matter of the placing of fire on the fiend's hair in *Solomon and Saturn* 129-30, which is paralleled by portrayals of flame-haired vices in certain of the illustrated manuscripts.[5] The battle of the letters of the Lord's Prayer in *Solomon and Saturn* shows in certain clearly parallel images, as well as in an overall design which incorporates elements which are present in the Prudentian poem, the influence of the **Psychomachia**.

Notes

1. Robert J. Menner, ed., *The Poetical Dialogues of Solomon and Saturn* (New York, 1941), p. 42. All quotations from the Old English poem are from the edition of E. V. K. Dobbie, *The Anglo-Saxon Minor Poems* (New York, 1942), *The Anglo-Saxon Poetic Records*, Vol. VI. Quotations from the *Psychomachia* are from M. P. Cunningham, ed., *Aurelii Prudentii Clementis Carmina* (Turnholt, 1966), *Corpus Christianorum, Series Latina*, Vol. CXXVI.

2. I have been unable to discover such imagery in the Bible, or in the works of Vergil, Statius, Juvencus, Avitus, Cyprianus Gallus, Arator, or Aldhelm. A different sort of image, in which a weapon completely severs the tongue, occurs quite frequently, but it will be observed that such imagery is at one remove from that under consideration.

3. Adolf Katzenellenbogen includes an illustration of the Troyes reliquary in his *Allegories of the Virtues and Vices in Medieval Art* (New York, 1964), Fig. 21.

4. See *Ps.* 25, 47, 111, 115, 129, 130, 133, 135, 136, 161, 204, 324, 332, 436, 488, 509, 533, 677.

5. Of the sixteen illustrated *Psychomachia* manuscripts which survive to the present day, discounting minor fragments, four originated in England: CCCC MS. 23, BM Add. MS. 24199, Cotton MS. Cleopatra C. viii, and Cotton MS. Titus D. XVI. All the illustrated *Psychomachia* manuscripts are reproduced in Richard Stettiner, *Die illustrierten Prudentius-Handschriften, Tafelband* (Berlin, 1905).

Macklin Smith (essay date 1976)

SOURCE: Smith, Macklin. "Critical Introduction." In *Prudentius's* Psychomachia: *A Reexamination,* pp. 3-28. Princeton, N.J.: Princeton University Press, 1976.

[*In the following excerpt, Smith explains the importance of placing Prudentius in proper historical context, regarding him as situated between the ancient and the medieval traditions.*]

Literary historians know Prudentius' *Psychomachia*[1] (c. 405) as the first sustained personification allegory, one notable for its powerful influence upon medieval and Renaissance culture; they have viewed it as a poetic representation of animated virtues and vices who fight for dominion over the mind of a Christian everyman.[2] The action of the allegory is simple: despite near reversals, the Christian virtues led by Faith win a series of epic combats over the vices, after which the victorious army constructs a holy city (in the mind) on whose citadel stands a glorious temple dedicated to Wisdom.

The meaning of this psychic narrative is more complex than it initially seems, however, because the poet relates his personification allegory to scriptural and ecclesiastical history. His prefatory narration of the career of Abraham, interspersed with scriptural emblems and contemporary allusions, indicates that the allegory participates in universal salvation-history. And inspired as it is—or so the poet claims—by Christ, this allegory is meant to aid in the salvation of its Christian audience. Thus the poem, its scriptural and liturgical context, and its effect on others' souls all exist in one continuum of spiritual reality. Scanning its entire range of spirituality, we observe that the *Psychomachia* is no simple narrative, but a sophisticated version of Christian history operative in several moral senses.

In order to do full justice to the complexity of the *Psychomachia,* another large context must be considered in addition to Christian history—the entire Roman literary tradition, that is, the epic tradition, and particularly its paragon Vergil. Prudentius has obviously absorbed, imitated, and—not to exaggerate—mastered this tradition. He follows Roman, not scriptural, models when he employs dactylic hexameter as the vehicle for a narrative of arms and civilization-building. He imitates certain features of Vergilian prosody to achieve epic effects. And he borrows half-lines and phrases from the *Aeneid,* weaving them into his own narrative. Such practices have been explained as stemming from a profound Christian humanism, from the desire to incorporate the cultural excellences of pagan Rome into the new Christian civilization. This thesis I find unsound. It is quite probable that Prudentius' audience was aristocratic and senatorial, therefore imbued with the Roman tradition and expectant of its imitation. But to posit this sociology for the work is not to restrict questions of literary criticism, and we must therefore ask how the poet responds to the expectations of his audience. Is the quotation of Vergil in the *Psychomachia* merely a pleasant embellishment upon the Christian allegory? Is the *imitatio* straightforward? I hope to demonstrate convincingly that such is not the case, that Prudentius' stance towards his Roman literary tradition is fundamentally ironic.

If my reading of the *Psychomachia* is correct, there exists a range of correspondence—from typological to parodic, from sacramental to ironic—between the personification allegory and the rival testaments of sacred and profane culture. Charles Witke, commenting on the literature that Prudentius brought to bear on his poetic production, offers this formulation: "His own private synthesis is between the Bible and Vergil, between his God and his culture."[3] My agreement with the basic elements here identified does not extend to the analysis of the compound. It seems to me that no "synthesis" occurs precisely because the poet cannot conceive his culture apart from his God, that his cultural orientation is exclusively Christian. For clarification's sake I anticipate my findings: By simultaneous use of different linguistic modes, Prudentius relates his allegory of soul-struggle to divinely revealed salvation-history and to the pagan distortion of history as embodied in Vergil's *Aeneid*. This concomitant struggle of historical analogies is not statically expressed; rather, evolving interpretations of sacred and profane literature accompany the progress of the personification allegory, and these interpretations are completed when the allegorical struggle is resolved in holy peace. As the scriptural illumination of the allegory brightens, Vergil's old heroic monument to Augustan Rome is cast in ever darkening moral shadow. Thus, out of this one Christian Latin text emerges a contrast of opposing visions, and this contrast places the microcosmic personification allegory in the perspective of macrocosmic struggle. The warfare in everyman's soul implies the war of the Church against the forces of Satan, a war indeed being fought in literary circles c. 405. The allegorical process, ending in a return to the arena of the putative reader's mind, is intended to have a moral effect on his sense of duty to embrace the Word of God and to reject the false pleasures and teachings discovered from the masterwork of Roman literature.

The complexity of Prudentian allegory has gone unnoticed for want of determined analysis, the reason probably being that few literary historians specialize in late antiquity, and thus classicists, medievalists, and general readers tend to neglect this period. Considered merely as personification allegory, the *Psychomachia* is manifestly original; and, it is revolutionary in its impact, being the major source of a rich allegorical tradition extending through the Middle Ages and into the eighteenth century. Therefore, many modern scholars have been able to remark on its importance in literary history and in the history of art; but few have investigated its poetic workings, and fewer still have appreciated its intrinsic worth. There are three problems with the pigeonhole "medieval personification allegory": it hides the document, discouraging analysis; it misclassifies historically; and it oversimplifies generic classification. Perhaps our uncertainties about the Early Christian Period or about "the nature of allegory" have more strongly impelled us to pigeonhole the *Psychomachia.* Clearly the very feature—allegory—that has guaranteed it a place in literary history has retarded literary criticism and, in turn, appreciative reading. The allegorical mode, unpopular for two centuries, still confounds our critical senses—and our historical senses as well. In truth, Prudentius' place in literary history has been poorly defined. To categorize the *Psychomachia* as the first personification allegory is not to explain the conditions that gave rise to it. What poetic mentality could conceive the *Psychomachia*? What historical conditions at the beginning of the fifth century prepared an audience to receive it?

Such areas of inquiry, largely unexplored, have determined in part the organizational logic of my study. Chapter divisions follow the assumption that an appreciation of the personification allegory itself and of its special complexities requires prior knowledge of motivating historical forces. The poet's will is one such force, and the social conditions affecting him another. So Chapter I treats the poet in his times, analyzing Prudentius' sense of poetic purpose from the evidence of his *opera,* and describing in some detail two major threats, heresy and paganism, which were subjectively recognized by the poet and objectively faced by the Church at the close of the fourth century. Chapter II, a general consideration of the allegory, treats the nature of the personifications and the Christian metaphors by which these personifications are animated to perform their moral roles in the basic plot of spiritual conver-

sion. Discussions of scriptural and Vergilian elements fill the concluding chapters, III and IV, respectively. These discussions are complementary excursions from Chapter II, but insofar as the anti-Vergilian irony is significant mainly as an adjunct to the scriptural imagery and structure, Chapter IV may truly be said to follow and depend on Chapter III. It will be evident that my treatment is not exhaustive in terms of either historical or literary analysis: The complete story of Prudentius' times cannot be told adequately by treating the Church's struggle against paganism and heresy; many interesting elements in the *Psychomachia,* such as metrics, vocabulary, and non-Vergilian allusions, are not dealt with here, and while these particular topics have received some critical attention, others, such as the relation of sound to meaning, have not. I do believe, however, that the topics I discuss are of sufficient weight to yield a satisfying reading of the *Psychomachia,* and at the same time suggest further lines of inquiry.

Before taking up these topics, I should like to comment on two vexed issues: Prudentius' historical period and the nature of his allegory.

Aurelius Prudentius Clemens (348-c. 410) wrote in troubled times. In all probability he died in the very year that Alaric's Visigothic army sacked Rome, till then the *urbs aeterna,* afterwards of problematic destiny. All of Prudentius' verse is the product of these late and last years (c. 392 and after), a period of political and economic uncertainty in his native Spain as well as in the Roman metropolis so important (biographically and symbolically) to his poetic culture. Under the weak and divided rule of Honorius and Arcadius, the Western and Eastern empires were politically unstable and subjected to a series of intriguing regents, generals, and ministers. War against the Visigoths and Huns was an almost yearly occurrence. The hazards of travel, the stagnation of commerce, the deterioration of city life, the flight into the countryside to avoid taxation—these are the well-known features of late Roman life.[4]

Within this unstable environment, Prudentius composed for a cultivated audience whose social class at least approached his own—that is, for the aristocracy and for the high administrators of Empire and Church.[5] This class had no solid ideological unity. It was torn by the Christian-pagan struggle, to some extent by heresy within the Christian group, and it was troubled by uncertainty of its social destiny. Indeed, its very existence as a class was being undermined by changes, including barbarian invasions, which were to cause the collapse of the Roman order. That our lay poet and many of his contemporaries in the Church hierarchy could share firm hope in the legacy of the powerful Emperor Theodosius—one universal Christian Empire— confirms the transitoriness of this class's subjective outlook. Documentation of the subjective change can be found in St. Augustine's *City of God.* Although *Romanitas* persisted through later centuries, no longer (at least till the time of Charlemagne) was this ideal reflective of political institutions.[6]

It may seem paradoxical that in this brief period of flux would flourish the most traditionally Latin poet—formally speaking—of the entire three centuries' span conventionally known as the Early Christian Period. Prudentius did not write (as St. Ambrose wrote his hymns) as a representative of a Church office, but surely his work was in some way guided or overseen by the Church. Unfortunately, Prudentius' status as layman has encouraged the attribution of special qualities in his works to individual genius per se, and this has of course been accompanied by a minimizing of historical considerations. Granted that Prudentius' formal classicism is atypical, a transitory phenomenon in the tradition of Early Christian poetry, it can be explained as resulting not only from a personal engagement with literary ancestors, but from a timely responsiveness to his audience's desperate need for stability.

In any case, the uniqueness of Prudentius underscores the real brevity of his proper period. Time soon passed him by: not that his reputation was anything but strong and enduring, but his full achievement could not be understood. In response to the drastic fifth-century shift in the politico-economic order,[7] there occurred a comparable shift in Christian spirituality. The socially organized asceticism of the monastic movement soon could satisfy men's psychological (and material) needs better than an illusory hope for a Church triumphant in this world. Therefore much of the topicality—ecclesiastical as well as political—of Prudentius' works became obscure. Another change affected understanding of his use of classical models and allusions. With the dissolution of the Roman bureaucracy, the homogeneous Roman educational system and the class of *rhetores* ceased to exist. Education became Church-sponsored (except in senatorial families), and in monastic and ecclesiastical centers the favorite subjects of the antique schools of rhetoric received considerably less attention than before. A few decades after the composition of the **Psychomachia,** the intensive literary knowledge required for its full appreciation (especially vis-à-vis the use of Vergil) had become practically unattainable.[8] Interpretation of the allegory was then limited to exposition of ascetic psychology, and this narrow appreciation of the **Psychomachia** persisted, in the main, throughout the medieval period.

Two early notices of Prudentius show that by the second half of the fifth century his works were being appreciated according to divergent standards, neither of which adequately captured the range of meaning intended by the poet. The first notice is that of Sidonius Apollinaris. In one of his elegant epistles, Sidonius describes a delightful sojourn [*tempus voluptuosissimum*] on the estates of sympathetic hosts. Here to be enjoyed, along with the pleasures of gaming and country dining, is a library worthy of comparison to the Athenaeum. "The arrangement was such that the manuscripts near the ladies' seats were of a devotional type, while those among the gentlemen's benches were works distinguished by the grandeur of Latin eloquence; the latter, however, included certain writings of particular authors which preserve a similarity of style though their doctrines are different [*in causis disparibus dicendi parilitatem*]; for it was a frequent practice to read writers whose artistry was of a similar kind—here Augustine, there Varro, here Horace, there Prudentius."[9]

By writing of authors *in causis disparibus dicendi parilitatem,* Sidonius anticipated the modern commonplace of Prudentius scholarship: Christian content in classical form. There can be no denying that Prudentius uses classical forms and presents a Christian message, yet the observation of these elements does not explain *how* or *why* Prudentius chose to emulate the eloquence of traditional Latin poetry. Sidonius is not interested in such considerations, and perhaps he has no way of knowing that only some decades before him the juxtaposition of classical form and Christian content could signify something in addition to, or other than, identification with the Roman literary tradition. It should be noted that his library classification system is based primarily on levels of style. The *stilus religiosus* is for women; while the women are denied all the pagan authors, only certain Christian works of quality (and hence of generic distinction) are deemed fit for the men. Whatever the sociological basis of this reading arrangement, Sidonius' aesthetic assumptions are clear enough. With a certain wit, the bishop asserts the effeminacy of "merely Christian" writings while recognizing the vigor of certain exceptionally eloquent Christian writings—this from the standpoint of proper literary taste based on a typically Roman sense of literary history. His standards of judgment for Christian literature are thus literary rather than religious.

Our other fifth-century notice of Prudentius hints at a different critical standpoint. Avitus of Vienne also observes in Prudentius the coexistence of great artistry and Christian doctrine, but his priorities of importance reverse those of Sidonius. Here the context is monastic. Prudentius in this case is recommended for a female reader's moral instruction (which involves no relegation of the poet to a lower order). The following lines occur in Avitus' verse epistle *De Virginitate,* addressed to one sister Fuscina, and are in praise of the **Psychomachia**:

Hae virtutis opes, haec sunt solatia belli,
Quis dubium adversus mentis cum corpore bellum
Ipsa suos armat clamantis buccina Pauli,
Quae prudenti olim cecinit Prudentius ore.

[These are the strengths of virtue, these the reliefs of
war, by means of which the very trumpet of Paul cry-
ing forth arms its own forces for the uncertain war of
mind against body—these Prudentius with prudent lips
once sang.][10]

A composer of a biblical epic himself, Avitus could not
fail to recognize that the **Psychomachia** is imitative of
the *Aeneid* and that it is scattered through with Vergilian quotations and themes. But he chooses not to make
the comparison. Given his totally different treatment of
epic mode in the *De Mosaicae Historiae Gestis*, Avitus
may not have fully understood Prudentius' use of Vergil.
Certainly he would have been better attuned to Prudentius' use of scriptural allegory. With the reference to the
Apostle Paul, he links Prudentius to the biblical rather
than the classical tradition. Avitus' concern is less with
the style—the rhetorical nicety of the pun on the poet's
name notwithstanding—than with the moral reality
(*solatia belli*) of the **Psychomachia** in terms of religious
experience. Rather than a discrete fictional or rhetorical
construct, he finds the **Psychomachia** a version of
Christian truth.

Both fifth-century ecclesiastics have judged Prudentius
from a standpoint external to the age of Prudentius: Sidonius from that of the Roman literary tradition emanat-
ing from the Augustan Age, Avitus from that of a
monastic Christian morality detached from immediate
temporal and literary issues. Both have contributed correct observations, but these observations cannot
constitute a total interpretation because they ignore the
poet's historical situation, especially his role in the
Church's task c. 400 of defining the position of pagan
literature versus Scripture. Not that Sidonius and Avitus
should be faulted for failing to be historical critics; the
necessary historical relativism was outside the ken of
fifth-century Christendom and would remain so until
modern times.[11]

Nor should modern commentators be blamed for having
acquired standpoints external to Prudentius' times.
Scholarship has suffered from a factor largely beyond
the control of literary scholars: Prudentius straddles the
boundary between two historical periods of which he
was entirely ignorant, the ancient and medieval periods.
No matter how useful this periodization is generally, it
has proved a culprit or at least a nuisance in our
particular area of study.

Ever since the great Bentley (following Sidonius?)
called Prudentius "the Horace and Vergil of the Christians,"[12] classicists have tended to investigate the **Psy-**
chomachia in terms of its Roman ancestry. Their
contributions have been extremely useful in the matter
of specific data. Having known that Prudentius was
totally familiar with Augustan literature, classicists have
identified Horatian and Vergilian elements—vocabulary,
meter, *topoi,* allusions, quotations—in his works.[13] But
interpretation of these elements has floundered. Is Prudentius Horatian because he uses the meters and
language of Horace, or is he Vergilian because he quotes
Vergil and employs an epic mode in the **Psychoma-**
chia? Such reductive conclusions have continually been
drawn.[14] Even Charles Witke, who has written with fine
sensitivity on Prudentius' lyrics and who is deeply
informed about the history of Christian hexameters,
vastly misjudges Prudentius' classicism: thus Prudentius "is a Christian poet because of his ability to write
within a culture which was for him Christian. His
relationship with God is his outlook. He does not teach
or justify. He writes, and writes conventionally, out of
the possibilities set up by this outlook. The conventions
adhere in the Latin language's resources, in the world
of poems written before Prudentius, and in Prudentius'
own practice. He is a Christian poet because he is not
trying to be anything except a Latin poet. . . ."[15] And
again: "Prudentius is no foe of poetry in the Latin tradition. His use of classical lines for important sacred
events shows as much, as does his careful use of meter
and sense of symmetry in strophic composition. Almost
every aspect of his poetry is classical in basis."[16] Such
an interpretation precludes the possibility of mere
formal appropriation, of a cynical Christian use of classical elements. The classical bias is present also in an
otherwise admirable monograph, Klaus Thraede's *Stu-*
dien zu Sprache und Stil des Prudentius. For example,
Thraede devotes great attention to the classical *topos* of
false modesty which he discerns in the *Epilogus,* but
meanwhile he passes over the New Testament concept
of humility.[17] Thraede also treats Prudentius' conception
of poetry as an offering to God, so he is not unaware of
its essentially religious nature; yet he misjudges the
spirituality of the modesty *topos.* With Witke, Thraede
tends to overstress the positive meaningfulness of the
classical form at the expense of the Christian content.[18]

Oriented in the other direction, medievalists have tended
to study the **Psychomachia** in terms of its iconographic
or generic offspring. Their orientation also is not without
basis in literary history. Just as classical scholars point
to Prudentius' proficiency in traditional Latin forms of
poetry, so medievalists point to his inventiveness and
originality. So Prudentius justly joins Ambrose and Hilary as an inventor of the Christian hymn. His
Peristephanon Liber is the first collection (discounting
Pope Damasus' inscriptions) of poetic celebrations of
the Christian martyrs. And the doctrinal anti-pagan and
anti-heretical hexameter compositions are original in
several respects. But for the medievalists, of course, the

Psychomachia is Prudentius' major achievement because of its influence. Raby's *Christian Latin Poetry* (1927) summarizes a strain of scholarly opinion on the *Psychomachia*: "[It] has been described . . . as aesthetically the weakest, but the most important from the literary and historical standpoint. For it presents the first poetical Christian allegory, an original creation, which caught the fancy of the Middle Ages and inspired many imitations."[19] Even today, the majority of readers approach the *Psychomachia* because of an interest in medieval allegory and theory of allegory: What did this distant ancestor of the *Roman de la Rose* look like?[20] Given this and other oblique paths toward the *Psychomachia,* it is surprising that some of the best criticism of the poem is embedded in treatments of much later literature.[21]

But the dangers in this outside orientation should be recognized. Experience with later Christian literature does not necessarily guarantee an understanding of early Christian literature. The social basis of poetry in the High Middle Ages, the period of Dante, Jean de Meun, Chaucer, is different enough even from that of the early medieval period of monastic poetry; and Prudentius almost antedates, and in temperament is totally removed from, the age of monasticism. He has not witnessed the fall of Rome, and he believes deeply, despite his orientation toward the afterlife, in his citizenship in a Roman Christian Empire, which after centuries of misbelief now follows Christ. Clearly an interpretation of Prudentius according to monastic or later medieval conventions must be shunned. If classicists have much to learn from medievalists in the area of early patristic materials, medievalists have much to learn from classicists specializing in late antiquity in the matter of Prudentius' historical context.

What then is Prudentius' period? The units of periodization smaller than "classical" and "medieval" have their drawbacks: "late classical" (*spätantike*) invariably evokes the idea of decadence; "early Christian" evokes ideas of naiveté, immaturity, undevelopment. Although such sub-periods bring us closer to the object of study, still the question remains: if within the sub-period there exist heterogeneous religious and cultural forces, what does the sub-periodization contribute to our understanding of their relationship? Prudentius and Claudian both called themselves Christians and both were first-rate poets. Whence their differences? Even more striking are the differences between Prudentius and the Christian hexameter poets from Juvencus to Arator. A symptom of the problem of periodizing early Christian poetry is seen in Charles Witke's great contribution to the literary history of these times, *Numen Litterarum,* where Prudentius is discussed in one chapter and the history of Christian hexameter poets from Juvencus onward in another. There is of course a generic distinction at work

between scriptural paraphrase and original composition based on classical models. But if Prudentius cannot be treated in critical terms applicable to his fellow poets and fellow Christians, of what use is the sub-period that unites them? Perhaps none.

The excursus on "Early Christian Poetry" in Ernst Robert Curtius' *European Literature and the Latin Middle Ages* further illustrates these difficulties. Curtius discerns "two directions" possible in that poetry between Constantine's reign and A.D. 600 which was not cult poetry but was "conceived as literature." "On the one hand, the Christian poet could treat the matter of Christian piety (sanctification of daily work, cult of martyrs) and of Christian dogma and ethics (doctrine of the Trinity, the origin of sin, apologetics, battle of the vices and virtues). It was Prudentius' great accomplishment that he followed this path. With full command of classical literary style he opened up great new realms to poetry. High gifts and intense experience were the springs of his creation. The rich flood of his poetry is independent of the system of the antique genres and hence is not forced to come to terms with antique literary theory. He is the most important and most original of the early Christian poets. But he is also a solitary phenomenon. The majority of the early Christian poets followed another path: that of keeping to the antique genres and filling them with Christian matter."[22] Of the two paths said to be open during this 300-year period, the one was chosen just once, by Prudentius, the other by all the other poets. We must ask: since Prudentius was unique in having chosen the path of "independence from antique genres"[23] (a path described tautologically in terms of his *opera*), in what sense can this path have existed for the other poets? If Prudentius was indeed a solitary phenomenon, it seems rather more likely that the path in question was open for only a short period during the 300-year span. If so, then perhaps the other Christian poets did not have a choice and, conversely, perhaps when Prudentius lived the path of biblical epic, which Curtius proceeds to describe, was closed. It is hard to avoid suspecting that even the sub-period of Early Christian Poetry is too broad a category to apply to Prudentius. This suggests that the works of Prudentius should be examined in relation to contemporary texts and events, to a really quite brief period of time.

The value of a restricted historical scope is further confirmed by Curtius' discussion of biblical epic before and after Prudentius. The major figures, Juvencus and Sedulius, are contrasted without mention of the fact that no writers of biblical epic flourish alongside of Prudentius, a fact that suggests that this tradition is discontinuous. (Only scattered hexameters on biblical themes survive from the end of the fourth century; these are all brief, with little narrative movement.) Curtius describes Juvencus' admiration for antique poetry and his desire to create its Christian counterpart, to build up "literature of Christian content in antique form." He next contrasts Sedulius "to Juvencus' smooth, clear poetic language, elevated by Virgilian echoes, to Prudentius' ringing Christian Classicism. . . ." Sedulius does not mention the names of Vergil and Homer, as Juvencus does, but instead proclaims that he will sing in the manner of David. "These statements," Curtius concludes, "are significant. They contain the germ of a Christian theory of literature (sacred subjects should be treated after the model of the Biblical bard). But they also announce a rigoristic rejection of antique poetry and the antique pantheon. This is the sign of a new period."[24] Thus the Early Christian Period of 300 years is split in half, Prudentius with his "ringing Christian Classicism" joining Juvencus, Sedulius launching a sub-sub-period. Yet the very signs of this new period are evident in Prudentius: rejection of the antique pantheon, emulation of the biblical bard, conspicuous refraining from mention of Vergil. This does not mean that Prudentius launches a new period himself, but that his works display radical differences from those of poets on either side of him.

My working hypothesis is that two significant shifts in poetic outlook bracket the career of Prudentius, giving late fourth-century Christian literature certain characteristics of its own. The first shift, separating Prudentius from Juvencus, is marked by a sharp ideological break with Roman liberalism by the Church and by Theodosius and his successors. This break with Roman liberalism included an attack not only against the pagan ritual long sheltered by it, but against its characteristic philosophical eclecticism and secular historical outlook. The polemical nature of much of Prudentius' verse should be seen in this anti-liberal context. His anti-Vergilianism responds to a quiet but firm aristocratic movement gathering all the grand old—and by now outlawed—pagan traditions under the cultural aegis of Vergil. To a degree, the Church-State coalition under Theodosius and his heirs anticipated Alaric's sacking of the pagan temples in Rome. Not all the outlawed pagan idols were placed in art museums as the Theodosian edicts had instructed: the cultural program of the Church opposed not only the religious observances of paganism but, in part, the art and literature associated with them.[25] Prudentius, I shall attempt to show, was a willing participant in the activity against pagan culture—not perhaps as a hammer-wielding iconoclast, but as a cultivated, sophisticated man of letters.

The second shift in poetic outlook takes place after Prudentius' death, and is signaled by rejection of Theodosian political piety in favor of other-worldly Christian asceticism.[26] This second shift will not concern us much, for it falls beyond the object of our inquiry; but certain features of Prudentius' poetry may be partly explicable—for example, his interest in the immediate worldly relevance of scriptural typology—by the fact that the broad social impact of monastic values had not yet been felt.

Prudentius' own concept of periodization is that he lives in the era of the New Law, of fulfilled prophecy, of the Church founded by Christ for the salvation of souls. He sees his own existence within the Church, which moves on the advancing stream of time between the Incarnation and the Last Judgment. He understands the moral significance of his life (including the writing of poems) in relation to the contemporary Church and, beyond this, in relation to these supreme events—the cardinal and the last—of sacred history. The poet's response to literature and language is therefore first and foremost a response to Scripture, where the New Law is supremely revealed. The present study will show that the major themes of the *Psychomachia* are scriptural; it will consider how the manifold presence of scriptural allusions and language operates upon these themes. The writings of the Church Fathers are ancillary in defining the meaning of the *Psychomachia*; if (as the *Psychomachia*'s poet also claims) inspired by God's grace, these writings are nevertheless inferior to the unique Word of God.[27] In relation to both Scripture and patristic writings, however, literature produced by pagans is outside the fold of truth. Insofar as Prudentius conceives the *Psychomachia* as an expression of orthodox Christian faith, his allusions to pagan literature must be qualitatively different from allusions to scriptural or patristic writings. The Latin literary heritages available to the poet are thus not only varied but conflicting. When joined together they are able to create strong crosscurrents, literary turbulence. Why this turbulence was created at the close of the fourth century will be a topic of historical investigation in the first chapter; afterwards the actual presence of scriptural, patristic, and pagan literary elements in the text of the *Psychomachia* will be treated.

If the *Psychomachia* is such a battle between literatures, between the Word of God and the words of Satan's followers, then the definition of its literary genre vis-à-vis the scriptural and classical traditions becomes crucially important. Take the genre classification often used: "allegorical epic." In what sense "allegorical" and in what sense an "epic"? Do these terms refer to the Roman literary tradition, in which case the *Psychomachia* is at least recognizable by its classical form? Or is the *Psychomachia* instead a poem of a new type, allegorical and epic in ways beyond and outside of the classical tradition, in imitation of Scripture? Or—and this is my understanding—does the *Psychomachia* refer to both profane and sacred traditions in radically different ways?

C. S. Lewis, in his influential *The Allegory of Love*, has termed *Psychomachia* "the fully-fledged allegorical poem."[28] He refers to the significant presence of abstract personifications who move within a consistent world defined by their existence, a fictional space-time continuum. The origin of allegory he explains this way: ". . . you can start with an immaterial fact, such as the passions which you actually experience, and can then invent *visibilia* to express them. If you are hesitating between an angry retort and a soft answer, you can express your state of mind by inventing a person called *Ira* with a torch and letting her contend with another invented person called *Patientia*. This is allegory. . . ."[29] Elsewhere Lewis remarks that allegory is "simile seen from the other end,"[30] a representation rather than a mode of expression. According to this viewpoint, allegory achieves the embodiment of immaterial experience only at the cost of abstracting, of distancing, of making less real the psychological reality of the mind. Given this basis, allegory will be either good or bad depending upon the extent to which it captures the fundamental equivalence between experience and the abstraction of experience.[31]

Lewis's characterization of the *Psychomachia*'s personification allegory encapsulates nineteenth-century charges of artificiality—and lends them theoretical sophistication. Over the past decade and a half, however, Lewis's views have been challenged theoretically by the view that ancient and medieval allegory, far from being an abstracting representation, is a mode of expression equally or perhaps more "real" (to its audience) than quotidian experience. And Lewis's views have been challenged practically by investigation in the *Psychomachia* of another sort of "allegory" besides personification allegory, that is, scriptural allegory. St. Paul allegorized events and persons of the Old Testament in terms of their fulfillment in the events and persons—especially Christ—of the Gospels. This figural relationship St. Paul in turn applied to contemporary moral problems. An intelligible pattern of scriptural history was thus capable of fulfillment in the life of the individual Christian. It goes without saying that this sort of "allegory" is unlike that described by C. S. Lewis, for it in no way permits a lessening of the reality of events in the moral scheme of things. We shall deal with the scriptural allegory of the *Psychomachia* in later pages; here it will suffice to indicate recent advances in understanding the figural relationship of the *Psychomachia* to Scripture.

Scholars have for some time noticed and commented briefly on the existence of biblical characters and symbols in the poem, but these elements have been considered merely "allusions," rhetorical flourishes meant to decorate the personification allegory.[32] Little effort was made to understand the relation between scriptural allegory and personification allegory until Henri de Lubac, in his monumental *Exégèse médiévale: les quatre sens de l'Écriture,* pointed to the Old Testa-

ment characters Judith, Job, David, and Samuel "solemnly drawn" beneath the figures of Pudicitia, Patientia, Sobrietas: this was biblical typology grafted onto Vergilian language.[33] Laura Cotogni had suggested some twenty years prior to Lubac that the *Psychomachia* was "a poetic elaboration of allegorical exegesis" and had pointed to its typological "Praefatio" by way of evidence—but Cotogni's suggestion was not followed by others until recently.[34] Contemporaneously with Lubac, Hans Robert Jauss echoed Cotogni: the poet's intention was to expound typological exegesis of Scripture in the epic mode.[35] Since Lubac and Jauss, it has become a critical commonplace to speak of the typology or scriptural allegory or exegetical structure of the *Psychomachia.* This positive development has changed our conception of the allegory and our appreciation of its sophisticated structure. Yet scriptural allegory in Prudentius requires much more attention. Even the recent treatments of this matter have been hasty and superficial, the monograph of Gnilka being the only exception.[36] Too often the presence of typology in the *Psychomachia* has been treated as structural framework, as mere form, rather than as an impulse behind the moral content of the poem. And the influence of the Epistles upon the allegory has not been appreciated. Specifically, the Old Testament themes of warfare and temple-building, interpreted by Pauline exegesis, should be seen as the major Christian metaphors animating the *Psychomachia*; of equal impact is Paul's interpretation of Abraham, the father of Israel, the spiritual type of all Christian faithful. The mere presence of the Old Testament characters mentioned by Lubac is secondary in relation to this dynamic Christian typology. Finally, the anagogic pull of the Apocalypse of John is strong indeed; while a number of scholars have pointed to allusions to this book of future history, they have not explored the relation of such to scriptural allegory. Chapters II and III of this study treat such matters in order to gain a general understanding of how Prudentius employs Scripture in the *Psychomachia.*

After discussion of personification allegory and scriptural allegory, there remains the problem of the poem's epic form and mode. Given the vital scriptural presence in the *Psychomachia,* to what degree is depiction of heroic conventions contingent upon scriptural themes? Does Prudentius intend to ennoble his scriptural allegory by means of the epic mode as he borrows it from the Roman literary tradition? Or rather, does he intend the scriptural allegory to generate a revised conception of the heroic in the minds of his readers? Such questions have never been seriously addressed, possibly on account of an entrenched belief that Prudentius is the preeminent poet of Christian humanism, the poet who could join the best features of Roman civilization and Christian spirituality. E. K. Rand writes:

"I look with sympathy on the attempt of the Church to guard its peculiar treasure with zeal, but to treasure no less devoutly its heritage in the culture of the past."[37] By culture is meant, of course, Roman culture, but did Prudentius, a poet of the Church, treasure this culture? History suggests, and Prudentius' text proves, that he did not. My concluding topic is the status of Vergil at the close of the fourth century and of Vergil in the works of Prudentius. Although several detailed studies have been published on Prudentius' use of Vergil, these have not evidenced a critical understanding of the poet's reaction against the late fourth-century cult of Vergil.[38] Prudentius' use of Vergil has been treated either as a purely rhetorical device, or as thematically important only very locally in the context of this or that passage. My intention is to uncover the deeper anti-Vergilian ironies contained in the epic mode generally and in the Vergilian quotations specifically.

To reveal the scriptural and Vergilian presences in the **Psychomachia** as essentially antagonistic is to challenge the view of Prudentius as humanist. The poet is in fact fervently anti-pagan because he connects the salvation of his own soul with the preservation of his embattled Church. He writes on behalf of both. Possessing great poetic gifts and a complete grasp of the literary tradition in which he has been trained, Prudentius is most willing to use these gifts and this literary tradition against the culture in which he was raised and on behalf of that culture which, for him, is alone worthy: the culture of souls in the Church.

Notes

1. Text used is *Prudentius* (Loeb Classical Library), ed. and trans. H. J. Thomson, 2 vols. (London, 1961). Citations will be by title and line numbers in parentheses. The Loeb edition has been chosen as the most accessible and as the most convenient for readers with inadequate Latin. Thomson's translation is probably the best in any modern language: it captures the literal meaning of the original without claiming for itself high literary value, and it is especially good in its sensitivity to Prudentius' figural use of Scripture and exegetical vocabulary. No important scholarly obstacles prevent our using the Loeb edition. The textual tradition of Prudentius is sound in comparison with that of most classical authors; interpolations are not a problem; variant readings are for the most part inconsequential for our interpretation. But readers may wish to consult the authoritative Latin edition of Ioannes Bergman, *Aurelii Prudentii Clementis Carmina*, CSEL, [*Corpus Scriptorum Ecclesiasticorum Latinorum*] Vol. 61 (Vienna, 1926). The edition of Arevalo (1788) reprinted in *Patrolgia Latina*, ed. Migne, Vols. 59, 60 (Paris,

1847), has been superseded yet retains a certain usefulness because of its apparatus of early Latin and German glosses. That of Maurice P. Cunningham, *Corpus Christianorum*, Series Latina, 126 (Turhout, 1966), is in my view the best, but it remains controversial—see, e.g., Christian Gnilka, review of R. Herzog, *Die allegorische Dichtkunst bei Prudentius*, in *Gnomon*, 40 (1968), n. 2; and see Cunningham's defense and corrigenda of his edition in "The Problem of Interpolation in the Textual Tradition of Prudentius," *Transactions and Proceedings of the American Philological Association*, 99 (1968), 119-141. A modern language edition comparable to Thomson's is that of Maurice Lavarenne, *Prudence*, 4 vols. (Paris: Budé, 1943-1951). The *Psychomachia* has been edited separately by Lavarenne (Paris, 1933). Other editions exist. Bibliographical notes follow, but readers should consult the full bibliography in Cunningham's edition.

2. For the idea of animated personifications, I am indebted to Morton W. Bloomfield, "A Grammatical Approach to Personification Allegory," *Modern Philology*, 60 (1962-1963), 161-171.

3. Charles Witke, *Numen Litterarum: The Old and the New in Latin Poetry from Constantine to Gregory the Great* (Leiden, 1971), p. 105.

4. For a survey of these times, see, e.g., A.H.M. Jones, *The Later Roman Empire, 284-602* (Oxford, 1964), and Henry Chadwick, *The Early Church*, Pelican History of the Church, Vol. 1 (London, 1967); also the highly detailed study of Alan Cameron, *Claudian: Poetry and Propaganda at the Court of Honorius* (Oxford, 1970), with bibliography; the fuller bibliography in François Paschoud, *Roma Aeterna: Études sur le patriotisme romain dans l'occident latin à l'époque des grandes invasions*, Bibliotheca Helvetica Romana, Vol. 7 (1967); Lynn White, ed., *The Transformation of the Roman World: Gibbon's Problem After Two Centuries* (Los Angeles, 1966); and A. Momigliano, ed., *The Conflict between Paganism and Christianity in the Fourth Century* (Oxford, 1963).

5. With Sidonius' testimony (below, nn. 8, 9) may be placed the hard evidence of the Rustic Capital script—that script usually reserved for Vergil—in the earliest Prudentius manuscript.

6. The Roman senatorial aristocracy, however, persisted intact into the sixth century; see P.R.L. Brown, "Aspects of the Christianization of the Roman Aristocracy," *Journal of Roman Studies*, 51 (1961), 1-11, and Paschoud, cited above n. 4. My general point is that despite the continuity of the "Romans of Rome," urban life changed drasti-

cally throughout the Empire in the fifth century. For internal transformation of the Roman aristocracy, see especially Herbert Bloch, "The Pagan Revival in the West at the End of the Fourth Century," in Momigliano (cited n. 4), pp. 193-218.

7. The intolerability of fifth-century life is well pictured in the *De Gubernatione Dei* by Salvian the Presbyter.

8. Boethius is the exception to the decline of learning, because the senatorial aristocracy to which he belonged was the social exception. The erudition of Sidonius should be noted as well, but his frozen panegyrics signal a dying culture rather than a vital literary tradition. Alan Cameron, *Claudian* (cited n. 4), p. 318, calls Sidonius' verse "precious and monotonous in the extreme."

9. Letter II, 9. Trans. from *Sidonius: Poems and Letters* (Loeb Classical Library), ed. W. B. Anderson, 2 vols. (London, 1936-1965), Vol. 1, pp. 453-455.

10. Text from Arevalo's *Prolegomena in Editionem Prudentii, Patrologia Latina,* Vol. 59, col. 752; trans. mine. In *Oeuvres complètes de Saint Avit,* ed. Ulysse Chevalier (Lyon, 1890), line 3 of our passage is excised as an interpolation.

11. A convenient introduction to this method of literary analysis is D. W. Robertson, Jr., "Historical Criticism," *English Institute Essays: 1950,* ed. Alan S. Downer (New York, 1951), pp. 3-31.

12. *Christianorum Maro et Flaccus*—Richard Bentley, *Horatius Flaccus* (Cambridge, 1711), on *Carm.* II. 2. 15.

13. For Horace in Prudentius, see Herrmann Breidt, *De Aurelio Prudentio Clemente Horatii Imitatione* (Diss., Heidelberg, 1887); L. Strezelecki, *De Horatio Rei Metricae Prudentianae Auctore* (Krakow, 1935). For Vergil in Prudentius, see Christian Schwen, *Vergil bei Prudentius* (Diss., Leipzig, 1937); Albertus Mahoney, *Virgil in the Works of Prudentius* [Diss.], The Catholic University of America Patristic Studies, Vol. 39 (Washington, D.C., 1934). Similarly, Marie L. Ewald, *Ovid in the Contra Orationem Symmachi of Prudentius* [Diss.], The Catholic University of America Patristic Studies, Vol. 66 (Washington, D.C., 1942); Stella Marie [Hanley], "Prudentius and Juvenal," *Phoenix,* 16 (1962), 41-52. The editions of Bergman, Lavarenne, and Cunningham all contain useful *indices auctorum*.

14. But for a denial of the Horatian character of Prudentius, see Ilona Opelt, "Prudentius und Horaz," *Forschungen zur römischen Literatur: Festschrift Karl Büchner* (Wiesbaden, 1970), pp. 206-213.

15. Charles Witke, "Prudentius and the Tradition of Latin Poetry," *Transactions and Proceedings of the American Philological Association,* 99 (1968), 513-514.

16. Witke, "Prudentius and the Tradition of Latin Poetry," 524. This language, and that of the preceding quotation, is repeated almost verbatim in *Numen Litterarum* (cited n. 3), pp. 110, 143-144. Other moderns have shown a "humanist" appreciation of Prudentius. See Gaston Boissier, *La fin de paganisme,* 2 vols. (Paris, 1891), Vol. 2, p. 175; and H. J. Thomson's *Prudentius* (Loeb Classical Library), pp. xiii-ix: "He regards the pagan literature and art not as things to be rejected but as part of the inheritance into which Christian Rome enters. . . . It is as a poet in whom is embodied a reconciliation between the new faith and the old culture, and in whom Christian thought claims rank in the world of letters, that Prudentius is historically important."

17. Klaus Thraede, *Studien zu Sprache und Stil des Prudentius,* Hypomnemata, 13 (Göttingen, 1965), pp. 48-72 *passim.*

18. Witke and Thraede are members of a new movement appreciative of Prudentius. The earlier French scholars have valued the poet mainly as an interesting example of decadence. So Aimé Puech, *Prudence: Étude sur la poésie latine chrétienne au IVᵉ siècle* (Paris, 1888); P. de Labriolle, *Histoire de la littérature latine chrétienne,* 3rd ed. (Paris, 1947); and, in large measure, the editor Lavarenne.

19. F.J.E. Raby, *Christian Latin Poetry* (Oxford, 1927), p. 61.

20. The most comprehensive treatment of the influence of the *Psychomachia* up to the fourteenth century is the unpublished dissertation of Eugene B. Vest, "Prudentius in the Middle Ages" (Harvard University, 1932).

21. Thus Hans Robert Jauss, "Form und Auffassung der Allegorie in der Tradition der *Psychomachia,*" *Medium Aevum Vivum: Festschrift für Walther Bulst,* ed. Jauss and Schaller (Heidelberg, 1960), pp. 179-206; Jauss, "La transformation de la forme allégorique entre 1180 et 1240: d'Alain de Lille à Guillaume de Lorris," *L'humanisme médiéval dans les littératures romanes du XIIᵉ au XIVᵉ siècle,* Actes et Colloques du Centre de Philologie et de Littératures romanes de l'Université de Strasbourg, Fasc. 3 (Paris, 1964), pp. 107-146; Marc-René Jung, *Études sur le poème allégorique en France au moyen âge,* Romanica Helvetica, series linguistica, Vol. 82 (Berne, 1971), pp. 25-34.

       CLASSICAL AND MEDIEVAL LITERATURE CRITICISM, Vol. 78

22. Ernst Robert Curtius, *European Literature and the Latin Middle Ages,* trans. Willard R. Trask, Bollingen Series 36 (New York, 1953), pp. 458-459.

23. But Charles Witke, *Numen Litterarum,* p. 144, claims: "Prudentius invents no new genres." I discuss Prudentius' genres in Chapter I.

24. *European Literature and the Latin Middle Ages,* pp. 459-462. Boethius' *De Consolatione Philosophiae* is the last major work of late antiquity produced outside the Church's secular and regular organizations.

25. Only in part. Examples of the tolerance of pagan culture are given in Chadwick (cited n. 4), pp. 171-173; see also Brown (cited n. 6) for pagan culture in the fifth century and generally for the Church's liberalism (e.g., towards mixed marriages) as a means of gradually converting the Roman aristocracy. If the late dating of Macrobius' *Saturnalia* is correct, we have a certainly pagan work produced by a certainly pagan high official c. 430; and the sixth-century historian Zosimus is a pagan who attempts to demonstrate that the fall of Rome resulted from abandonment of the old religion. At the end of the fourth century, the aged Ausonius and the young Claudian were, whatever their professed belief, not more than lukewarm Christians, at least in their verse. But if the break with liberalism may be said to have hardly affected a poet like Claudian, perhaps his special role as Stilicho's propagandist (involving a narrowness of poetic task, of audience) disqualifies him from being considered representative of his period; on this matter, and on the more basic question of whether Christian-pagan cultural relations are to be characterized by struggle or peaceful coexistence, I disagree with Alan Cameron (cited n. 4). Further discussion in notes below.

26. Christian asceticism was still considered a rather exotic, Egyptian phenomenon in late fourth-century Rome. It had Roman adherents, as witnesses the correspondence of Jerome; and see D. Gordini, "Origine e sviluppo del monachesimo a Roma," *Gregorianum,* 37 (1956), 220-260. Augustine himself records the conversion of two centurions upon reading the *Life of St. Anthony*—see *Confessions* VIII; but the ascetic movement was new, radical, atypical.

27. The excellent recent article of P. F. Beatrice, "L'allegoria nella *Psychomachia* di Prudenzio," *Studia Patavina,* 18 (1971), 25-73, is unfortunately marred by its overemphasis on the influence of patristic writers—in this case, problematically, of Origen—on Prudentius; yet many of the key scriptural references are provided in footnotes.

28. C. S. Lewis, *The Allegory of Love* (Oxford, 1936), p. 66. Likewise Raby, see n. 19.

29. Lewis, pp. 44-45.

30. Lewis, p. 125.

31. Lewis's conviction that the *Psychomachia* does not capture this fundamental equivalence is evident from his commentary on pp. 68-69. Lewis's deprecation of Prudentian allegory and, by extension, much medieval allegory, has been unfortunately influential. It ends with this treatment of a "mechanical defect in the pitched battle": "that fighting is an activity that is not proper to most of the virtues. Courage can fight, and perhaps we can make a shift with Faith. But how is Patience to rage in battle? How is Mercy to strike down her foes, or Humility to triumph over them when fallen? Prudentius is almost everywhere embarrassed by this difficulty, and his attempts to solve it are failures because they betray his deficiency in humour."

32. Such is the attitude of Lavarenne. Even Auerbach, amazingly, errs: "Prudentius [in the *Psychomachia*] does not seem to recognize figural interpretation."—"Figura," trans. Ralph Manheim, in *Scenes from the Drama of European Literature* (New York, 1959), n. 36. In the same footnote the *Dittochaeon* of Prudentius is mentioned as an exception. Auerbach finds only personification allegory in the *Psychomachia.* He attaches the footnote to general remarks: "Most of the allegories we find in literature or art represent a virtue (e.g. wisdom), or a passion (jealousy), an institution (justice), or at most a very general synthesis of historical phenomena (peace, the fatherland)—almost never a definite event in its full historicity. Such are the allegories of late antiquity and the Middle Ages, extending roughly from the *Psychomachia* of Prudentius to Alain de Lille and the *Roman de la Rose*" ("Figura," p. 54).

33. Henri de Lubac, *Exégèse médiévale: les quatre sens de l'Écriture,* 2 Parts [2 vols. in each] (Paris, 1959-1964), Part 2, Vol. 2, p. 214.

34. Laura Cotogni, "Sovrapposizione di visioni e di allegorie nella *Psychomachia* de Prudenzio," *Rendiconti della R. Accademia Nazionale dei Lincei, classe di scienze morali, storiche e filologiche,* Serie 6, Vol. 12 (1936), 441.

35. Jauss, "Form und Auffassung der Allegorie in der Tradition der *Psychomachia*" (cited n. 21), p. 188.

36. Christian Gnilka, *Studien zur Psychomachie des Prudentius,* Klassisch-Philologische Studien, 27 (Wiesbaden, 1963).

37. E. K. Rand, "Prudentius and Christian Humanism," *Transactions and Proceedings of the American Philological Association*, 51 (1920), 72.

38. For bibliographical discussion of Vergil in the works of Prudentius, see Chapter IV.

Alison Goddard Elliott (essay date 1978)

SOURCE: Elliott, Alison Goddard. "The Martyr as Epic Hero: Prudentius's *Peristephanon* and the Old French *Chanson de Geste*." *Proceedings of the PMR Conference* 3 (1978): 119-35.

[*In the following essay, Elliott discusses the similarity of specific hymns by Prudentius to medieval epic.*]

I

The search for the literary antecedents of the Old French *chanson de geste* has been largely unsuccessful. Heroes such as Roland or Guillaume do not bear much resemblance to Aeneas, for example, in spite of energetic attempts to point to similarities.[1] Those scholars still desirous of demonstrating Latin or, more generally, clerical antecedents for vernacular epic, note that the earliest Gallo-Romance manuscripts are hagiographic and argue for the direct influence of the religious poems on the secular. Concentrating largely on verbal similarities, they have concluded that clerics either wrote our epic texts or significantly influenced those who did.[2] But although more widely accepted than the conclusions of proponents of Vergilian influence, the hypotheses of this school are also vulnerable to attack. While the priority of the religious manuscripts is undeniable, there is considerable evidence that epic poems were in circulation before any extant manuscript was copied.[3] Consequently the counterclaim that the secular poems may have influenced the religious in matters of diction and style cannot be dismissed out of hand.[4]

More substantial arguments against hagiographic influence have focused on genre. Italo Siciliano, for instance, concedes that a poem such as the Hildesheim version of the *Vie de saint Alexis* may permit us to see the origins of some of the literary techniques of the *chansons de geste,* but he cautions against wholesale identification of the two genres: "Identifier l'hagiographie avec l'épopée c'est risquer de vider celle-ci de tout sens."[5] For Siciliano the ethos of each genre differs significantly. Paul Zumthor grants that "l'étroite parenté originelle de ces deux formes poétiques est probable sinon certaine"; nevertheless, he considers that the differences between the two genres outweigh similarities: "On pourrait dire que le thème général et commun des chansons de geste, par opposition aux chansons de saint, est l'héroïsme." Zumthor characterizes "epic" heroism as "L'émerveillement suscité dans la communauté humaine par la reconnaisance de son pouvoir d'agir: pouvoir qui ne procède plus de quelque dynamisme externe, magique ou divin, mais d'une source où se reflète l'image même de l'homme."[6]

Zumthor and Siciliano are not alone in their objections to seeing too close a connection between epic and hagiography. In his essay, "The Concept of the Hero in the Early Middle Ages," Bernard Huppé, discussing Old English texts, gives voice to widely held opinions. His argument merits extensive quotation:

> . . . The art of the homily and of the saints' lives is not the art of the epic, of the heroic. . . . Saints are heroic but they are not heroes; they are examples, models of perfect living and perfect dying. The clash of swords, the bang of shields are missing, and the loss is essential. The medieval hero must do battle as did Aeneas, one obvious prototype for the medieval hero.

> . . . But such a hero [for example, Aeneas] is not simply driven; he must himself act, and act heroically. It is only through his actions, and beyond his actions, that we may perceive the playing out of the divine plan of things. The saint, on the other hand, too clearly embodies divine providence as an actual example of its operations. The saint's life is a miracle and is punctuated by miracles which are in fact the invisible hand of God made visible. . . .[7]

For many hagiographic accounts the *vitae* of the worthy bishops very popular in Carolingian hagiography, for example—the strictures of Zumthor and Huppé are valid. But the heroes of early Christianity, the martyrs, were men and women sanctified by a specific act of personal courage.[8] Not all *passiones,* however, deserve the epithet "epic." In the earliest *Acta* (those called "historic," or *acta sincera),* the narration is sober and restrained, little more than a courtroom deposition.[9] If the martyr did suffer heroically, these accounts devote little attention to this aspect of the story. For some of the later passions Zumthor's and Huppé's objections are also well-taken. Here the drama testifies to divine, not human, power. A *passio* such as that of St. George is so laden with miracles that the only sense in which we might employ the word "epic" is that of the Hollywood press agent. In order for St. George to endure all the torments designed for him, he has miraculously to be brought back to life three times; his passion extends over seven years.[10]

The inclusion of the miraculous, however, does not of itself suffice to render an account automatically "non-epic." As far as hagiography is concerned, miracles are common, indeed almost required, elements of the narrative. But in many passions (such as that of St. Vincent of Sarogossa), the miracles occur after the saint's death and constitute the outward confirmation of his holiness. While such phenomena have major religious significance, they tell us little about the relative heroism of the saint's life. During the scenes preceding death, the martyr may be depicted as a courageous hero who, in the case of Vincent, is comforted by an angel,[11] but who is not enabled to perform miraculous deeds nor miraculously to come unscathed through terrible torments. Furthermore, if the traditional hero is not a miracle-worker, he is one for whom miracles are worked. In poems admitted by all to be epics—the *Iliad,* the *Aeneid,* and the *Chanson de Roland* are convenient examples—"miraculous" intervention plays a necessary role in motivating and directing the action. Near the beginning of the *Iliad,* Athena intervenes to stay the hero's hand from premature murder, and near the end his goddess-mother brings him miraculous armor. Divine action preserves Hector's body from corruption after death.[12] In the *Aeneid* a miraculous cloud permits the hero to enter Carthage unobserved; later, at Jupiter's behest, Mercury must stir Aeneas to leave Carthage and pursue his divinely-appointed task, the founding of Rome. In the *Roland* the delaying of the sun's course enables Charlemagne to defeat his enemies and avenge the fallen hero; to accomplish this victory, moreover, the faltering monarch must be exhorted to presevere by the angel "who is accustomed to speak to him" ("ki od lui soelt parler," 2452).[13] The question, then, is one of function and quantity. If the miraculous, for whatever reason, obscures the role of human action, of human courage, then the text under consideration is not truly epic. If, however, their role is to demonstrate god's majesty and the sanctity of the hero—who remains the active agent in his drama—miracles alone do not place a given work outside the epic genre.

In addition to objecting to miracles, Huppé considered that the lack of emphasis on martial deeds disbarred hagiographic accounts from participation in the epic mode. While it is true that most traditional epic heroes are warriors, ancient and medieval theoreticians defined the genre less narrowly than do modern critics. Aristotle stated that epic, like tragedy, was an imitation of serious matters (μίμησις σπουδαίων).[14] Gaius Marius Victorinus (4th C. A.D.), a Neoplatonist and Christian convert, divided metrical poetry into four genres of which epic was the first: *epos* concerned itself with a mixture of divine and human affairs, and especially with the deeds of heroes ("vel maxima heroum facta").[15] Isidore of Seville's definition of heroic poetry is equally applicable to accounts of saints or secular heroes, for it narrates the actions of brave men ("virorum fortium res et facta narrantur"). Heroes, furthermore, are those men deemed worthy of heaven because of wisdom and bravery ("caelo digni propter sapientiam et fortitudinem").[16] Much medieval hagiographic poetry does

not fit the definitions of Victorinus and Isidore, but some does. A number of early Latin accounts of the martyrs—those men and women who earned immediate entry into heaven through their courageous actions—display marked epic tendencies. Aeneas is not the only hero to emerge from the Latin tradition. Warfare is a convenient metaphor,[17] but qualities other than spear-rattling may define the hero in any age, and battles may be fought on more than one plain.

Revering saintly rather than secular heroes did not in itself constitute a total rejection of the classical past, although differences may be as marked as similarities. Isidore distinguished heroes as those worthy of heaven "propter sapientiam et fortitudinem." In his discussion of the nature of sanctity, Festugière has shown the extent to which two traits essential to the Greek conception of heroism were necessary to the Christian as well. For the Greeks, the "holy" (αγνός) life was defined by two qualities—right action and wisdom.[18] A life denied the power of action was αβίωτος 'unlivable.' All heroes, then, must act, but wisely. The martyr is a man or woman singled out by a specific wise act.

II

Certain of Prudentius' hymns in honor of the martyrs, the **Peristephanon,** display qualities which deserve the epithet "epic." While they share some features with classical epics such as the *Aeneid,* they have far more in common with medieval epic.

When, around 405 A.D., Prudentius came to write of the martyrs, the conflict between pagan and Christian was still immediate and relevant, the danger of apostasy still a present danger.[19] Prudentius was thirteen when Julian offered pagan Rome one final, if unsuccessful, chance to reassert herself. Macrobius' *Saturnalia* bears witness to the liveliness of the intellectual struggle between the two cultures as late as 430.[20] But when Prudentius turned to celebrate the Christian heroes, he deemed the precedent set by Macrobius' much-admired Vergil inappropriate, reserving the hexameter for explicit didactic poetry.[21] For the martyrs, Prudentius turned instead to lyric and hymnal meters—to the forms traditionally identified with a more personal poetic statement Previous poems in honor of the martyrs had been comparatively short, unpretentious works—the hymns of St. Ambrose (32 lines of iambic dimeter), and the still briefer epigrams of Pope Damasus. In the **Peristephanon [Per.],** Prudentius transformed such accounts into dynamic and detailed narratives of triumphant heroism. But if his heroes were new heroes for Christianity, were they epic heroes?

Hippolyte Delehaye has labeled epic many of the passions written around the time of Prudentius.[22] In these passions he distinguishes a new emphasis on the miraculous, although miracles play a far less important role than they do in romanesque passions such as that of St. George. More important, however, is a new recognition that the martyr is indeed a hero: "L'hagiographe fait comprendre que, pour le chrétien le martry est ce que sont pour les peuples les héros qui, au prix de leur vie, ont fondé la nationalité."[23]

In common with all epics, the martyr's *passio* depicts the values of an entire society.[24] In a national epic such as Vergil's *Aeneid* or Lucan's *Pharsalia,* the hero's struggle is a paradigm of the struggle of the Roman people. Anchises' long, prophetic speech in Book VI of the *Aeneid* contains a warning, not for Aeneas, but for Rome. Athough martyrdom constitutes an individual act of heroism, its purpose is not an affirmation of the individual *per se* but a rejection of membership in an imperfect society in order to join a more perfect one. The conflict portrayed in the *passio* is universal; the martyr's personal *imitatio Christi* provides an example for *all* Christians to follow, whether literally or metaphorically.

In spite of some similarities, however, accounts of the martyrs such as the **Peristephanon** more closely resemble medieval than classical epic. First, both medieval *epic* and martyr's *passio* depict a society in which values are unambiguous and morally polarized. The *Aeneid* ends on a somber note as Aeneas gives way to overmastering anger ("furiis accensus et ira terribi-lis," XII, 946-947) and slays Turnus. A modern reader, carefully conditioned throughout the epic to reject as-sociations with *impius furor,* may feel that Aeneas' final, irrational action controverts the rationality which he has represented throughout the poem. For a medieval reader, I suggest, no such ambiguity existed (the *Roman d'Enéas* ends on a note of triumph, not tragedy). By medieval epic standards, Aeneas' violent anger towards an enemy, provoked by the desire to avenge the death of his young friend Pallas, would not have seemed reprehensible. Right and wrong were polar opposites and there was no middle ground. In a recent study Charles Altman has analyzed the plot structures of ha-giographic accounts. He writes: "The passiones, . . . like the medieval epic, operate according to the principles of diametrical opposition."[25] The *passio,* in Altman's view, is a unified narrative depicting a single, heroic action; it opens with a confrontation between saint and tyrant during which the latter tries to convince the former to recant. The purpose of this scene is to identify the values represented in the *passio* not with the particular individuals portrayed but with the groups and religions which they represent. Virtue and vice are exemplified through the opposition of the two parties and are absolute values—"Paien unt tort e chrestïens unt dreit," as the *Chanson de Roland* (1015) confidently proclaims.

The following discussion will ignore the most obvi-ously epic feature of the **Peristephanon** (one whose importance, however, is underlined by criteria such as Huppé's), that is, Prudentius' careful exploitation of the Pauline metaphor of *militia Christi* conspicuous, for example, in *Per.* I, a celebration of two obscure soldier-saints, or in *Per.* II, in which St. Lawrence is explicitly described as the successor to the military heroes of old Rome, Cossus, Camillus, Caesar.[26] I shall turn instead to the treatment of two non-military saints, Vincent of Sa-ragossa (*Per.* V) and Eulalia of Mérida (*Per.* III), to consider the ways in which these hymns manifest epic tendencies.

III

The *Acta* of St. Vincent published by the Bollandists[27] are a good example of the epic passion. The miracles, however, are confined to the end of the account, and most of them involve the tyrant's frustrated attempts to dispose of Vincent's body. The saint's heroic nature is defined by verbal rather than literal battles with the enemy, a confrontation which forms the most dynamic section of Prudentius' poem. In the few historically ac-curate passions extant,[28] the interrogation of the saint is a relatively straightforward affair. The saint identifies himself and makes a brief profession of faith; the magistrate then tries, often with apparent sympathy, to persuade him to recant. In the *Acta* of Vincent, however, the saint responds to the Roman governor's questions with long, defiant sermons. The governor, Dacian, is transformed into an inhuman monster—"furore caecus," "prae ira extra se positus,' "fervens insania"[29]—a melodramatic stereotype which Prudentius not only retained but expanded.

In general, Prudentius followed the *Acta* closely, but he made a number of informative alterations and omis-sions. Most notably, he chose to free his hero from all personal and local associations. For instance, in the previous hymn, *Per.* IV, in honor of the eighteen martyrs of Saragossa, Prudentius made much of St. Vincent's local connections. In the fifth hymn, however, he does not mention the saint's origins; there are, in fact, no geographical references at all in *Per.* V. This omission alone is somewhat surprising, given Prudentius' deserved reputation for patriotic Hispanicity and the spirit of local fervor which frequently permeates ha-giography. For Prudentius, moreover, Vincent would have been a local hero, having been born at Osca (Huesca), and educated at Caesaraugusta (Saragossa), where he served as archdeacon, although actually mar-tyred at Valentia (Valencia). But in this poem Pruden-tius deemed all such geographic references undesirable. He also ignored the saint's family, omitting the names of Vincent's parents, contained in the *Acta,* as well as the tradition that Vincent was the nephew of St. Lawrence (the hero of *Per.* II).

Prudentius isolated Vincent's passion in time and space. Avoiding all extraneous details and minor characters, he has built his narrative around the interactions of four mortals—Vincent, Dacian, a single jailor (omitting the throng of guards who witness the Angel's appearance in prison), and the soldier charged with the disposal of the saint's body—together with the Angel who appears dramatically at the center of the poem. Consequently the lines of Prudentius' account stand out in stark relief. Unlike ordinary men, Vincent is superior to private and personal concerns, and his drama is thereby universalized. Vincent becomes a hero for all Christendom, not merely for Spain or for Saragossa. *Per.* IV exalts a group of martyrs for their local associations, as does *Per.* VI, dedicated to the martyrs of nearby Tarragona. Placed between these two expressions of local piety, the fifth hymn celebrates one of Saragossa's martyrs in universal terms.

By removing specific geographic and personal references from his poem, Prudentius has given the hymn almost epic proportions. The conflict is not the confrontation between two individuals named Vincent and Dacian; it is a figuration of the cosmic conflict between good and evil, new and old.[30] The action occurs not in early fourth-century Caesaraugusta or Valentia but anywhere and everywhere. This is the correct interpretation of a hagiographic text. The passion of the martyr is not only an individual *imitatio Christi,* but it is also an example for all Christians to follow even after the days of literal martyrdom have come to an end, for it is an image of the fight between good and evil which is fought by Christians everywhere.

After a brief, hymnal proem, Prudentius plunges into his drama. He omits the first act, to which the *Acta* devoted an entire chapter, the arrest of Vincent's immediate superior, Bishop Valerius, and the subsequent exile of the bishop. His poem begins abruptly with Dacian's first speech interrogating the saint after Valerius' exile. Dacian summarily orders Vincent to obey Roman law and sacrifice. In the *Acta* the martyr's refusal is preceded by a long profession of faith; Prudentius retains this speech but reduces it to its essentials in order to highlight more dramatically the diametrical opposition between pagan and Christian.

> "Tibi ista praesint numina,
> tu saxa, tu lignum colas,
> tu mortuorum mortuus
> fias deorum pontifex;
>
> "nos lucis auctorem patrem
> eiusque Christum filium
> qui solus ac uerus deus,
> Datiane, confitebimur."[31]

(33-40)

["Let these be your masters; you may worship stones and wood and become the dead priest of dead gods. We shall confess the Father, the author of light, and Christ His Son, who is the only and true God, O Dacian."]

The balanced structure of the strophes reflects the binary opposition as the first, with its triple anaphora, stresses the pagan's error; the second, whose first word is "nos" and whose last is "confitebimur," states the Christian position.

In the *Acta* Vincent's refusal to sacrifice throws Dacian into a rage, and he immediately orders the infliction of the severest punishments upon the martyr. For Prudentius, however, the confrontation between saint and tyrant is the high point of the drama, so he prolongs the scene. Dacian orders Vincent to sacrifice or die. Vincent replies with a thirty-nine line speech of excited defiance, continuing to attach pagan religion (54-93). It is in this scene that the absolute opposition between Christian and pagan is most clearly stated, as both antagonists remain inflexible. Then physical violence replaces verbal, as Dacian hands Vincent over to the torturers. To Dacian's utter frustration, Vincent only smiles at the torments and threatens the pagan governor of Tarragona with hellfire.

> "Exemplar hoc, serpens, tuum est,
> fuligo quem mox sulpuris
> bitumen et mixtum pice
> imo inplicabunt tartaro."
>
> His persecutor saucius
> pallet rubescit aestuat
> insana torquens lumina,
> spumasque frendens egerit.

(197-204)

["This is your example, serpent, whom one day soon sulphurous soot and bitumen and pitch will envelop deep in hell." Wounded by these words, the persecutor turns first pale, then red, and in the heat of his passion rolls his maddened eyes, gnashing his teeth and foaming at the mouth.]

With this depiction of Dacian as an insane beast, the first section of the hymn concludes. It has been characterized by the unyielding opposition between the representatives of good and evil; neither side will give an inch. The more terribly the tyrant rages, the more defiant and scornful the martyr becomes. More than three-quarters of this dramatic scene has consisted of *oratio recta* as the martyr confesses his faith and challenges the beliefs of his adversary.[32] Now actions replace words. The baptism by blood begins.

The transition between the first and second sections stresses the binary opposition between good and evil.

spes certat et crudelitas,
luctamen anceps conserunt
hinc martyr illinc carnifex.

(214-216)

[Hope and Cruelty do battle, and martyr on one side,
torturer on the other, they join in the crucial struggle.]

Vincent's tortures are described in minute and painful
detail for eight lines (225-232) to emphasize the
martyr's heroic indifference to them: "Haec inter inmotus manet / tamquam dolorum nescius" (233-234).[33]
Finally, as a previously unheard-of torment, the saint is
thrust into a totally dark dungeon and there made to
rest his battered body on the sharp edges of broken
potsherds. In prison he is comforted by a band of angels,
one of whom addresses him. Prudentius has structured
his poem so that Angel's speech occurs at the very
center of the 576-line poem (lines 285-305).

"Exsurge, martyr inclyte,
exsurge securus tui,
exsurge et almis coetibus
noster sodalis addere!"

(285-288)

["Arise, illustrious martyr, arise, confident of yourself,
arise, and as our companion join the propitious
throng!"]

This is the only speech in the middle section of the
poem (209-368), in contrast to the first section where
direct address accounted for the majority of the narrative. Portions which in the *Acta* had been in *oratio
recta*—for example, the order to inflict on the saint the
punishment of imprisonment in total darkness—have
been shifted to *oratio obliqua*. As a result the Angel's
speech rings out in dramatic contrast to the surrounding
descriptive passages. The invitation to join the band of
Angels prior to the Last Judgment is the specific reward
for martyrdom, a doctrinal point which the structure of
the poem throws into high relief.

Out of a number of familiar elements Prudentius has in
Per. V created a poem of considerable originality.[34] The
meter is the Ambrosian, iambic dimeter, but in spite of
the metrical simplicity, the poem is dramatic and
rhetorically sophisticated. Prudentius has elegantly
varied his narrative techniques to avoid tedium and to
underline certain didactic points. The confrontation
scene, in which the uncompromising opposition between
pagan and Christian was established, consisted largely
of direct speech, the most lively and dramatic means of
recreating an event. In **Per.** V, however, unlike some of
the hymns (II or X, for example), the speeches never
metamorphose into sermons.[35] The poem remains a narrative, its didactic message conveyed in dramatic terms.

Prudentius was indeed radically innovative. He has
adopted a lyric meter (one therefore "uncontaminated'
by classical epic) for a narrative which is primarily

concerned with polarized action. He has limited his cast
of characters to active agents, eliminating those (the
saint's parents and Bishop Valerius) who did not play
definitive roles in the action. Medieval theoreticians, as
we saw, defined heroic song as poems about deeds,
facta heroum. What Prudentius has done is to take the
less sharply polarized account contained in the prose
Acta, a combination of biography and history, and
convert it into a triumphant narrative of binary opposition—into medieval epic.

It was natural to see in the martyr the ideal epic hero,
the *miles Christi* unflinching in pursuit of a goal which
was not only his own personal goal of salvation but
also that of his society as a whole. Through his personal
sacrifice and subsequent intercession for his fellows,
members of his society can also hope to be saved.

A poem like **Per.** V does not present an allegorical battle
as does the **Psychomachia,** but the hero is a warrior
("miles Dei," 117; "miles inuictissime," 293). The
conflict, nevertheless, is not limited in significance to
the struggle between two human beings named Vincent
and Dacian. It is fought between *Spes* and *Crudelitas*
(214), between the angel and the serpent. In the Garden
of Eden the serpent triumphed momentarily; in the
serpent Dacian's prison, the harrowing of hell is
symbolically re-enacted—a re-enactment which is both
a reflection of the first harrowing and a prophecy of the
last. The conflict is therefore universal and epic.

IV

If **Per.** V resembles medieval epic in terms of its
organization by diametrical opposition, the celebration
of another Spanish martyr calls to mind the characterization of the medieval epic hero. Vincent was portrayed
as a hero for all Christendom, his passion generalized
in time and space. But saints were also local heroes, the
places associated with their suffering ennobled by the
holy blood which had been shed there. For our purposes,
the most interesting hymn to a local saint is the third in
honor of St. Eulalia.[36] Martyred at the age of twelve,
Eulalia was a resident of the populous and important
Lusitanian city of Emerita Augusta (Mérida). The hymn
opens with an evocation of the glory which the martyr
has conferred upon her native city; Emerita is great,
Eulalia has made it greater (1-10). Throughout the
poem, Prudentius stresses the local nature of Eulalia's
cult. The hymn closes with a description of the church
built in the saint's honor; its natural setting is pictured,
and local place names figure prominently.

Nunc locus Emerita est tumulo
clara colonia Vettoniae,
quam memorabilis amnis Ana
praeterit et uiridante rapax
gurgite moenia pulchra lauit.

(186-190)

[Now her tomb is at Emerita, the famous town in Vettonia, which the well-known river Ana passes and greedily washes the lovely walls with its green flood.]

Prudentius' hymn has been much admired, especially for the evocative descriptive writing,[37] but earlier critics have found themselves distressed by certain features, thereby missing a crucial point. They have rightly praised the lovely conclusion of the poem, but the behavior of Prudentius' "torua puellula" (103), as she spits in the eye of the Roman praetor while he is trying to reason with her, smashing the sacrificial offerings to the ground and kicking the pagan idols, does not conform to their romantic notions of appropriate feminine conduct. T. R. Glover called Eulalia a "sadly precocious child."[38] Francesco Arnaldi preferred to hasten by this section of the poem ("Tralasceremo le parti più sconcertanti—lo sputo in faccia al tiranno, per esempio . . .").[39] E. K. Rand, more positive but still sentimental, considered her a "plucky little girl."[40] Eulalia's actions, however, cannot be glossed over or ignored, nor should they be lamented. They are the key to Prudentius' heroic conception of the martyr. In a sermon in her honor, St. Augustine celebrated Eulalia as a "sancta et fortis femina, quae per affectum vicit sexum."[41] Prudentius has made the girl into an uncompromising epic heroine, although she has more in common with her medieval descendants than she does with her classical ancestors.

Prudentius has organized his depiction of the young martyr around the figure of oxymoron. A common topos of hagiographic encomium is the *puer-senex;*[42] the hagiographer describes the childhood of his hero, pointing to the stern decorum with which the youthful saint conducted his childhood years, spurning toys and other frivolities. But Prudentius' development of the topos in *Per.* III is more than the expression of a commonplace; contradiction of expectation is thematic throughout the poem. Eulalia was indeed a model "puella-senex":

ipsa crepundia reppulerat
ludere nescia pusiola.

Spernere sucina, flere rosas,
fulua monilia respuere,
ore seuera, modesta gradu,
moribus et nimium teneris
canitiem meditata senum.

(19-25)

[. . . for even as a little girl she had rejected toys and was ignorant of play. She scorned amber beads, lamented the existence of roses, spurned golden necklaces; she was grave of face, modest in her gait, and, although very young, she imitated hoary age.]

All Eulalia's actions contradict expectations based on the behavior of ordinary people. One who is so young should be delicate (*tenera,* compare line 24); Eulalia, however, is *aspera.*

terruit aspera carnifices
supplicium sibi dulce rata.

(14-15)

[. . . harsh, she terrified her executioners, thinking her punishment a pleasure for herself.]

The frightening torturers are themselves frightened; their cruel torments seem sweet to the delicate girl.

Eulalia is characterized by a cluster of violent words and actions. A woman, she challenges the weapons of men (compare St. Augustine's remark, "per affectum vicit sexum"). She is fierce (*fera,* 38). To her are applied words such as *infremuit* and *ferox,* seemingly more appropriate to a savage tyrant than to a twelve-year old girl.[43]

infremuit sacer Eulaliae
spiritus ingeniique ferox
turbida frangere bella parat,
et rude pectus anhela Deo
femina prouocat arma uirum.

(31-35)

[The holy spirit of Eulalia roared, and, fierce in nature, she prepared to shatter the violent onslaught; with the heart in her young breast panting for God, a woman she challenged the weapons of men.]

Martyr ad ista nihil; sed enim
infremit inque tyranni oculos
sputa iacit, simulcra dehinc
dissipat inpositamque molam
turibulis pede prosubigit.[44]

(126-130)

[The martyr makes no reply, but she roars and spits into the tyrant's eyes and then scatters the images and with her foot kicks over the meal placed on the censers.]

Classically *infremere* had negative connotations. Vergil used it to describe a wild boar, Silius Italicus the roar of a lion.[45] *Ferox* is morally somewhat more neutral; connoting "war-like," as well as "fierce," it is applicable to the warrior as well as the martyr although surprising, perhaps, when used of a child.

In all her actions Eulalia displays *ferocitas.* She is impetuous and intolerant of any delay (42), seeking out the tribunal of her own accord. She is proud (*superba,* 64), as she imperiously challenges the Roman magistrate instead of waiting to be questioned. Atypically, she, not the tyrant, is the first to speak (66). In everything Eulalia seizes the initiative and attacks. The praetor's characterization of her, "torua puellula," sums up her oxymoronic nature, as her harshness (cf. "torua") contrasts with the usually affectionate diminutive, "puellula." Evaluations of the saint such as Glover's "sadly precocious child," or Rand's "plucky little girl," place the Spanish martyr in a context in which she does not belong. She should not be viewed as an example—good or bad—of childhood or womanhood, romantically defined. She is a martyr and as such is better viewed in the company of other medieval heroes.

Prudentius has characterized Eulalia as *ferox* ("ingeniique ferox / turbida frangere bella parat," 32-33). In his article, "*Orgueil* and *Fierté* in Twelfth-Century French," Glyn S. Burgess has pointed out that from an examination of the *Chanson de Roland,* "it immediately becomes clear that *fierté* is, for the most part, an epic virtue."[46] According to Burgess, *fierté* is essentially a military quality, "a combination of pride and ferocity." Medieval poets, moreover, "[do] not allow us to forget the etymological meaning of the term *fier* (< FERUS, but with probable semantic contact with FEROX)" (p. 105). To give only one example, the hero Guillaume is described as an excellent knight; he is also as *fiers* as a hungry leopard:

> Li cuens Guillelmes fu molt bons chevaliers:
> Vers orgoillos se faiseit molt tres fiers,
> Come leiparz qui gent deie mangier.[47]
>
> (*Couronnement de Louis,* 1931-1933)

Eulalia's militant *ferocitas* towards her adversaries links her with medieval epic heroes such as Guillaume.

Humility is one of the central virtues of Christianity, but it is not one for which any of Prudentius' martyr-heroes (or medieval epic heroes) are particularly noteworthy. If Eulalia is the most physically violent, the distinction is one of degree, not of kind. All the martyrs display *ferocitas* and *superbia*. Another young virgin martyr, Agnes, is described by Prudentius as a "fortis puella" (XIV, 2) who faces the threats of her persecutors unafraid, "feroci robore pertinax" (18). In a sermon on St. Agnes, St. Augustine drew attention to the etymology of her name: "Agnes latine agnam significat; graece castam. Erat quod vocabatur: merito coronabatur."[48] Prudentius, on the other hand, avoided any lamb-like associations in his depiction of the *fortis puella*. Yet a third virgin martyr, Encratis, one of the eighteen martyrs of Saragossa, is celebrated as a "uiolenta uirgo" (IV, III).

The fierce pride of both Prudentius' martyrs and the heroes of medieval epic has upon occasion given critics pause (witness the comments on Eulalia cited above and discussions of Roland's seeming "desmesure"[49]). In evaluating either group of heroes, we must be careful to avoid "contamination" from critical biases based on Aristotelian norms. Neither epic nor hagiography are tragedy, nor was the influence of the *Poetics* significant before the Renaissance.[50] Both martyr and hero were

those who, in Delehaye's words, "au prix de leur vie, ont fondé la nationalité." As such their *ferocitas* is only praiseworthy.

Prudentius' heroes do not have much in common with *pius Aeneas*. They are new heroes for a new society. Their true descendants are found on the battlefields of the *chansons de geste,* warriors once again diametrically opposed to pagan superstition,[51] and prepared to die for their beliefs, assured that if they should perish, they would receive the reward of martyrdom, immediate entry into heaven prior to the last judgment. While the ethos of the *Chanson de Roland,* for example, is not to be explained by a wholesale evocation of Christian values, Roland does die a Christian martyr. Before the battle at Rencesvals, Archbishop Turpin exhorted the soldiers to confess and pray for God's mercy; those who died would, he promised, be holy martyrs (1134-1135). After Roland's death, the poem shows the hero receiving the specific reward for martyrdom as the cherubim and the archangels escort his soul to paradise (2393-2396).[52] His death is a vindication, not a tragic defeat.[53]

It was inevitable, given the treatment of his death in the *Chanson de Roland,* that a cult of St. Roland should emerge. In the church of St. Romanus at Blaye the sarcophagus of the hero, together with those of Olivier, Turpin, and the others, was displayed and venerated. The twelfth-century pilgrim's guide to the Camino de Santiago which forms the fifth book of the *Codex Calixtinus* describes the burial place of Roland and his companions, making reference to the body of "beati Rotolandi martyris."[54] In the *Pseudo-Turpin Chronicle* (Book IV of the *Codex Calixtinus*), Roland is called "Xristi martyr."[55]

There are other possible parallels between the martyr's *passio* and the Old French epic.[56] In the *Couronnement de Louis,* prior to Guillaume's first battle against the Saracens, the hero engages in a heated theological debate with his opponent, Corsolt, which is entirely reminiscent of the confrontation between saint and tyrant. Neither champion will yield to the other. Their opposition is total; Corsolt exclaims, "Chrestiienté est *toz* foleiemenz!" (844).[57] Significantly this theological argument prefaces the series of combats which punctuate the epic, just as the confrontation in the *passio* prefaces the ensuing drama in hagiographic accounts. In the epic, of course, the hero wins a victory of a different nature, life instead of death. Had he died, however, Guillaume had been promised the crown of martyrdom (426-430). The *Pseudo-Turpin Chronicle* depicts two similar theological debates prior to battles, between Charlemagne and Agolant and between Roland and the giant Ferragut. To give a final example, the Saracens, unlike the Romans, did not in fact worship idols, but in the epic *Fierabras* the Christian heroes imitate Eulalia's action, kicking the pagan statues.

That men in the Middle Ages should see a similarity between martyrs and epic heroes is not surprising. Both were diametrically opposed to pagan superstition; both were willing to die for those beliefs. The days of literal martyrdom largely came to an end with the Peace of Constantine, but the conflict between Christianity and Islam gave new meaning and vitality to the ideal of martyrdom. "Paien unt tort e chrestïens unt dreit."

One final point remains. Prudentius' hymns are sophisticated poems, written in polished and correct Latin. The Old French *chansons de geste* are mainly popular works. One need not, however, posit direct or written lines of influence. Hagiography is a popular genre, the accounts retold many times by poet and preacher alike.[58] Indeed, Old French literature may be said to "begin" around the year 881 with a narrative poem celebrating the heroine of *Per.* III, the *Séquence de sainte Eulalie.*[59] Many of the **Peristephanon** were incorporated into the Mozarabic liturgy, including III and V.[60] Thus in Spain at least these hymns remained accessible to those whose Latin or whose literary tastes might preclude the reading of extended passages of Vergil or Lucan. In this respect, therefore, it is highly likely that the attractive models offered by *passiones* such as those of Vincent and Eulalia were available, however indirectly, to the jongleurs who sang the deeds of Roland and Guillaume.

Notes

1. For a discussion, and ultimate rejection, of Vergilian influence, see Joseph J. Duggan, "Virgilian Inspiration in the *Roman d'Enéas* and the *Chanson de Roland*," in *Medieval Epic to the Epic Theater of Brecht*, ed. Rosario P. Amato and John M. Spalek, University of Southern California Studies in Comparative Literature, 1 (Los Angeles, 1968), 9 -23.

2. Considerations of space preclude a complete biobliography of this topic: for a convenient survey, see Mario Pei, *French Precursors of the Chanson de Roland* (New York: Columbia University Press, 1948). Among more recent proponents of the thesis are Cesare Segre, "Problemi di tradizioni de testi romanzi: Dai poemetti agiografici alle 'chansons de geste,'" in *Concetto, storia, miti e immagini del medio evo*, ed. Vittore Branca (Sansoni, 1973), pp. 339-351; J. W. B. Zaal," *A Lei Francesca (Sainte Foy, v. 20): Etude sur les chansons de saints gallo-romaines du XIᵉ siècle* (Leiden: Brill, 1962).

3. Rita Lejeune, "La Naissance du couple littéraire 'Roland et Olivier,'" *Mélanges Henri Grégoire*, II, *Annuaire de l'Institut de Philologie et d'Histoire*

Orientales et Slaves, X (1950), 371-401. See also Georges Zink, "Chansons de geste et épopées allemandes," *Etudes germaniques,* 17 (1962), 125-126.

4. Rudolf Baehr, "Das Alexiuslied als Vortragsdictung," *Serta Romanica* (Festschrift Rohlfs), (Tübingen, 1968), pp. 174-188; Timothy D. Hemming, "La forme de la laisse épique et le problème des origines," Société Rencesvals, *Actes du VIᵉ Congrès International* (1974), pp. 223-239.

5. Italo Siciliano, *Les Chansons de geste et l'épopée: Mythes, histoires, poèmes,* Biblioteca di Studi Francesi, 3 (Torino: Società editrice internazionale, 1968), p. 323.

6. Paul Zumthor, *Essai du poétique médiévale* (Paris: Editions du Seuil, 1972), pp. 323-324.

7. In *Concepts of the Hero in the Middle Ages and the Renaissance,* ed. Norman T. Burns and Christopher J. Reagan (Albany: State University of New York Press, 1975), p. 2.

8. "The key-word that distinguishes the saint is 'heroism.' The saint is the man or woman who gives himself, herself, to God *heroically";* Donald Attwater, *A Dictionary of Saints* (1965; rpt. Harmonsworth: Penguin Books, 1976), pp. 10-11 (author's emphasis).

9. Adolf Harnack offers an interesting collection of texts in *Militia Christi: Der christliche Religion und der Soldatenstand in der ersten drei Jahrhunderten* (Tübingen: J. C. B. Mohr, 1905).

10. Hippolyte Delehaye, *Les Légendes grecques des saints militaires* (Paris: A. Picard, 1909). St. George, however, is a special case, an example of a near-eastern divinity "reduced" to the role of saint and hero; see H. S. Haddad, "'Georgic' Cults and Saints of the Levant," *Numen,* 16 (1969), 21-39.

11. The appearance of a divine messenger, whether sent to comfort or to exhort, is a standard feature of secularly inspired epic as well as hagiography; for a discussion of the motif, see Thomas M. Greene, *The Descent from Heaven: A Study in Epic Continuity* (1963; rpt. New Haven: Yale University Press, 1975). Greene, however, jumps from Statius to Ariosto, with only a few pages on the *Chanson de Roland,* so his work sheds little *direct* light on the issue under discussion.

12. It may be objected that some of the Homeric parallels are not "miracles" but metaphors or techniques of externalizing inner conflicts, a way to depict states of mind for which the oral poet has no other means at his command to portray; see, for ex-

ample, the excellent article of Joseph Russo and Bennett Simon, "Homeric Psychology and the Oral Epic Tradition," *Journal of the History of Ideas,* 29 (1968), esp. p. 488. While the "miracles" do *function* as Russo and Simon describe, they remain "miracles" in terms of the narrative.

13. All citations of *Roland* are from the edition of F. Whitehead, *La Chanson de Roland* (Oxford: Basil Blackwell, 1975). Other *chansons de geste* contain miracles; God's intervention is necessary for a happy outcome in *Le Pèlerinage de Charlemagne* and *Le Moniage Guillaume* (an epic which contains considerable parody of hagiographic motif). For a discussion of the death and "resurrection" of Vivien in *La Chançun de Willame* as a genuine miracle, see Barbara Levy Silver, "The Death of Vivien in *La Chançun de Willame,*" *Neuphilologisches Mitteilungen,* 7 (1970), 306-311, and John D. Niles, "Narrative Anomalies in *La Chançun de Willame,*" *Viator,* 9 (1978), 251-264, esp. 258 ff.

14. *Poetics* 1449b10, in Gerald P. Else, *Aristotle's Poetics: The Argument* (Cambridge, Mass.: Harvard University Press, 1967), p. 203.

15. Keil, *Grammatici Latini,* Vol. II, "Scriptores Artis Metricae," (1857; rpt. Hildesheim: Teubner, 1961), 50. Victorinus, however, goes on to quote Horace that epic, following in Homer's footsteps, narrates "res gestae regumque ducumque et tristia bella" (*Ars Poetica,* 73-74).

16. Etym. I, xxxix, 9, in *Isidori Hispalensis Episcopi Etymologiarum sive Originum Libri XX,* ed. W. M. Lindsey (1911; rpt. Oxford: Oxford University Press, 1971), Vol. I.

17. The *Psychomachia* is the most obvious example of the exploitation of this metaphor. *Apropos* of the *Psychomachia* and epic, Emanuel J. Mickel, Jr., sees "a striking similarity" between this poem and the *Roland;* "Parallels in Prudentius' *Psychomachia* and *La Chanson de Roland,*" *SP,* 67 (1970), 439-452. Mickel, however, does not posit direct influence. Another example of the metaphor of *Militia Christia* (one among many) occurs in the *Te Deum:* "Te martyrum candidatus laudat exercitus."

18. A. J. Festugière, *La Sainteté* (Paris: Presses Universitaires, 1942), ch. II. Of the martyr Festugière writes (p. 25): "Le martyr est, par excellence, un héros, il est *le* héros du christianisme antique."

19. Herbert Bloch, "The Pagan Revival in the West at the End of the Fourth Century," in *The Conflict between Paganism and Christianity in the Fourth Century,* ed. Arnaldo Momigliano: (Oxford: Clarendon Press, 1963), p. 199.

20. Alan Cameron, "The Date and Identity of Macrobius," *Journal of Roman Studies,* 56 (1966), 25-38.

21. The most recent discussion of Prudentius' attitude towards Vergil is Macklin Smith, *Prudentius' Psychomachia: A Reexamination* (Princeton: Princeton University Press, 1976).

22. *Les Passions des martyrs et les genres littéraires,* Subsidia Hagiographica, 20 (1966), 171 ff.

23. *Les Passions,* p. 172.

24. Paul Zumthor writes: "L'épopée élève l'histoire du group social à la dignité de l'universel" (*Langue et technique poétiques à l'époque romane [XIᵉ - XIIIᵉ siècles]* [Paris: C. Klincksieck, 1963], p. 13).

25. *Medievalia et Humanistica,* 6 (1975), 1-12.

26. *Per.* II, 14. At the end of the poem (555), the hero is depicted wearing the civic crown, the wreath of oak-leaves awarded to a Roman soldier for saving the life of another soldier in battle.

27. *Acta Sanctorum,* Vol. II, 22 January.

28. As a result of the last great persecution during which Diocletian ordered the destruction of Church records, there are perhaps no more than 70 authentic *Acta* extant; see Ferdinand Lot, *The End of the Ancient World and the Beginning of the Middle Ages* (1931; rpt. New York/Evanston: Harper Torchbooks, 1961), p. 162.

29. *Acta Vincenti, AASS,* [*Acta Sanctorum*] II, 7-8. For a study of Dacian as the typical tyrant (a role he owes to his association with the passion of St. Vincent), see B. de Gaiffier, S. J., "Sub Daciano Praeside: A Study of Some Spanish *Passios,*" *Classical Folia,* 21 (1967), 3-21.

30. For a discussion of this general theme in Prudentius, see Smith, *Prudentius' Psychomachia,* p. 237.

31. All citations of Prudentius are from the edition of Maurice P. Cunningham, *Aurelii Prudentii Clementis Carmina,* Corpus Christianorum, Series Latina, 126 (Turnhout: Brepols, 1966).

32. There are ten speeches in the 188 lines; the longest, Vincent's attack on pagan religion, is thirty-nine lines.

33. Some see "inmotus manet" as a Vergilian echo, citing *Georg.* II, 294, *Aen.* IV, 449, *etc.;* see Isidoro Rodriguez Herrera and José Guillén, *Obras completas de Aurelio Prudencio* (Madrid: Editorial Catolica, 1950), p. 785. A more immediate parallel is to be found in the description of *Patientia* in the *Psychomachia,* who stands "inmota" (110) before the attack of *Ira. Ira* is described in the same terms as the traditional tyrant of the *passiones.*

34. Of Prudentius' originality, Cunningham writes: "Not only do the poems of Prudentius, for the most part, lack direct filiation in the classical Latin tradition; a good many of them in fact represent striking innovations even in terms of contemporary practice so far as we know it"; Maurice P. Cunningham, "Contexts of Prudentius' Poems," *CP,* [*Classical Philology*] 71 (1976), 61.

35. There is nothing comparable to St. Lawrence's sermon, *Per.* II, 186-312.

36. Prudentius' hymn is our only detailed account of this martyr, popular throughout Spain and Africa; see Rodriguez and Guillén, *Obras completas,* p. 522.

37. For example, Michele Pellegrino, "Structure et inspiration des 'Peristephanon' de Prudence," *Bulletin de la Faculté des Lettres de Strasbourg,* 39 (1960-1961), 437-450.

38. *Life and Letters in the Fourth Century* (Cambridge: Cambridge University Press, 1901), p. 262.

39. "Cristianismo e sensibilità moderna nell'arte di Prudenzio," *Atene e Roma,* N. S. 5 (1924), 92.

40. *Founders of the Middle Ages* (Cambridge, Mass.: Harvard University Press, 1928), p. 192.

41. This sermon was first identified and published by Dom. G. Morin, O.S.B., "Une page inédite de saint Augustin," *Revue Bénédictine,* 8 (1891), 418.

42. E. R. Curtius, *European Literature and the Latin Middle Ages,* trans. Willard R. Trask (1953; rpt. New York/Evanston: Harper Torchbooks, 1963), pp. 98-101.

43. Cf. Sulpicius Severus, *Vita sancti Martini* 4, 4, "tyrannus infremuit"; Fortunatus, *De vita sancti Martini,* I, 71, "fremuit Julianus in iras."

44. Cf. Vergil, *Georg.* III, 256, "et pede prosubigit terram"; the phrase is here used of a wild boar, an animal associated in patristic literature with *ira.* See the discussion by Marianne Cramer Vos, "Aspects démoniques de quelques protagonistes rolandiens," *Charlemagne et l'épopée romaine, Actes du VII⁰ Congrès International de la Société Rencesvals,* II (Liège: Congrès et Colloques de l'Université de Liège, 76, 1978), 579.

45. Vergil, *Aen.* X, 711, "substitit infremuitque ferox"; Silius Italicus, II, 45, "immane sub ira infremuit leo."

46. *Zeitschrift für romanische Philologie,* 89 (1973), 104.

47. All citations are from the edition of Ernest Langlois (2nd ed.; Paris, 1968).

48. *PL* [*Patrologia curus completus, series latina*] 38, 1250.

49. For example, Alfred Foulet, "Is Roland Guilty of Desmesure?" *Romance Philology,* 10 (1956-57), 145-148; Larry S. Crist, "A propos de la *desmesure* dans la *Chanson de Roland*: quelques paroles (démesurés?)," *Olifant,* 1 (1974), 10-20.

50. William W. Ryding, *Structure in Medieval Narrative* (The Hague: Mouton, 1971), p. 10.

51. See Pierre van Nuffel, "Probleme de sémiotique interprétive: L'épopée," *Lettres Romanes,* 27 (1973), 150-152; Larry S. Crist, "Deep Structures in the chansons de geste: Hypotheses for a Taxonomy," *Olifant,* 3 (1975), 3-35.

52. In *La Chançun de Willame* Vivien exhorts his men, saying that St. Stephen and the other martyrs are no better than those who will die "for God" in the ensuing battle at Archamp (544-47).

53. It is, however, a defeat in the clerical *Pseudo-Turpin Chronicle,* where the disaster is viewed as a punishment for the Franks' immoral behavior. In *Le Motif du repentir dans la littérature française mediévale* (Geneva: Droz, 1967), p. 103, Jean-Charles Payen signals a change in attitude towards the "defeat" from the 11th to the 12th century: "Le désastre de Roncevaus est une epreuve providentielle mais ce n'est pas un châtiment, et l'on ne saurait trop déplorer qu'il soit si vite apparé tel au public du XII⁰ siècle."

54. Quoted by André Burger, "La légende de Roncevaux avant la *Chanson de Roland,*" *Romania,* 70 (1948-49), 437 (I do not subscribe to Burger's hypothesis that a Latin poetic *Passio beati Rotolandi* lies behind the *Chanson de Roland.*)

55. Burger, p. 438.

56. Gerard J. Brault maintains that the representation of death in the *Roland* is indebted to hagiographic traditions; "Le Thème de la mort dans la *Chanson de Roland,*" *Actes du IV⁰ Congrès International de la Société Rencesvals* (Heidelberg), *Studia Romanica,* 14 (1969), 220-237.

57. Of this scene Jean Frappier remarks, "Corsolt avait engagé la controverse en théologien" (*Les Chansons de geste du cycle de Guillaume d'Orange,* II [Paris: Société d'édition d'enseignement supérieur, 1967], 126). There are, as Frappier notes, other scenes of theological debate in the epics (for example, *La Chanson de Guillaume* [ed. Wathalet-Willem], 2111-24, and *Aliscans* [ed. Weinbeck], 1223-28). These confrontations, however, conform less closely to the pattern of the *passio;* they are brief and do not serve, as it were, as introductions

to the ensuing dramas. The scene in the *Couronnement* functions in the way Altman *(vide supra)* defines; the scene identifies the concerned parties with the ideologies they represent. Thus they are "champions," not private citizens. I discuss this subject at greater length in an essay, "The Power of Discourse: Martyr's *Passio* and Old French Epic."

58. For a recent discussion of the popular nature of hagiography, see Bruce A. Beatie, "Saint Katharine of Alexandria: Traditional Themes and the Development of Medieval German Hagiographic Narrative," *Speculum,* 52 (1977), 785-800.

59. For this view, see Peter Dronke, *Poetic Individuality in the Middle Ages* (Oxford: Clarendon Press, 1970), pp. 2-3. Dronke is here arguing (rightly) against the double claim of E. R. Curtius that French literature "begins" with the *Vie de saint Alexis,* and that "Latin loosed the tongue of French" *(European Literature and the Latin Middle Ages,* p. 384). While the vernacular *Séquence de sainte Eulalie* owes no apparent debt to Prudentius (the modes of death differ), it is a narrative poem, and the confrontation scene with the Roman official occupies eight of the poem's twenty-nine lines.

60. Bernard M. Peebles, *The Poet Prudentius,* Boston College Candlemas Lectures on Christian Literature, 2 (New York: McMullen Books, 1951), p. 156. Peebles points out that at least nine of the *Peristephanon* attained some liturgical use in Spain (including both III and V). Maurice P. Cunningham, "The Nature and Purpose of the *Peristephanon* of Prudentius," *Sacris Erudiri,* 14 (1963), 44, maintains that all of the *Peristephanon,* with the exception of VIII and X (and I would question XI, a verse epistle) were originally intended for liturgical use.

Jill Harries (essay date 1984)

SOURCE: Harries, Jill. "Prudentius and Theodosius." *Latomus: Revue d'Études Latines* 43 (1984): 69-84.

[*In the following essay, Harries uses historical evidence concerning Theodosius I to date some of Prudentius's writings and discusses how the politics of his time inform Prudentius's work.*]

The aim of what follows is to reconsider the political contexts and inspiration of the poems of Prudentius which treat of Theodosius I and (to a lesser extent) his son Honorius. Although Prudentius supplies few clues as to dating. I shall suggest from his manner of referring to emperors that much of the *Peristephanon* and the first book **Contra orationem Symmachi** may date from late in the reign of Theodosius. Some of the arguments offered will be based on the assumption that Prudentius, although the most innovative of Christian Latin poets, also conformed to, and was bound by, contemporary poetic conventions.

I

Aurelius Prudentius Clemens, a Christian and a Spaniard, could not fail to be influenced, as were many others, by his imperial compatriot Theodosius. Born in 349[1], the poet would have been forty-five when Theodosius died on January 17, 395: the bulk of the poet's official career as advocate and 'twice governor of noble cities'[2] was presumably behind him. It is tempting to place that career in the context of those westerners who served in Theodosius' court at Constantinople, or who flocked to him when he first visited the West (388-91)[3]. However, unlike other notable Theodosians, Prudentius has no certain links with the East. The one such indication, some brief topographical references in his **Tituli Historiarum (Dittochaeon)**[4] to Eastern Holy Places, the oak of Abraham at Mamre and Sarah's cave tomb, could be personal recollection but are more likely to be derived from pilgrims' reports of the sites disseminated in the West (and according with the *Genesis* accounts). Prudentius' public service may have been only western.

Finally, *tandem militiae gradu / euectum pietas principis extulit / adsumptum propius stare iubens ordine proximo*[5]. The **Praefatio** (either to a single work or to a 'collected edition') is dated to 404/5[6] but there is no agreement as to which *princeps* is meant, Theodosius or Honorius. Emperors in Prudentius, unlike saints, are never named but their identities, living or dead, are usually apparent from their context. On Julian, for example, Prudentius recalls him as a boyhood memory who was a valiant soldier, a lawgiver, eloquent, skilled and patriotic—but a foe of religion[7]. Even without the *me puero* clue, the apostate emperor is unmistakable from the religious reference alone, which is then elaborated into the standard story of the spoiled sacrifice. Likewise, the second book against Symmachus has unnamed *duces armorum dominos uernantes flore iuuentae, / inter castra patris genitos*[8] addressed by the *orator catus,* Symmachus; in the immediate aftermath of the Roman victory at Pollentia, near Turin, won over Alaric and a host of invading Visigoths, the reader of 402 needed no prompting to recognise Arcadius and Honorius, the sons of Theodosius. Later in the same poem they are the 'brother leaders'[9], *principes*[10], *clari duces, generosa propago/principis inuicti*[11], where their father Theodosius is obviously the *princeps,* but the title later reverts to Honorius, *sit (Roma) deuota Deo, sit tanto principe digna*[12].

It happens that Prudentius himself supplies the historical context for his unnamed *duces* or *princeps* and their father in the **Contra orationem Symmachi** II. Even without it, however, it is legitimate to infer that Prudentius, when he uses an imperial title without qualification, refers to '*the* emperor', that is, the *living* emperor. If this is right, the *pietas principis* which elevated Prudentius was that of Honorius.

This argument has important consequences for the interpretation of the Theodosian references in the **Peristephanon.** The second of Prudentius' fourteen poems on saints is devoted to St Laurence who, while on the gridiron, has a prophetic vision of a 'future emperor', a *seruus Dei,* who will forbid Rome to pay service to foul sacred rites and will bolt and bar the temples[13]. There is no reference here to Theodosius' military victory over Eugenius and Arbogast at the Frigidus (September 6, 394) but the omission is not significant. Praise of Theodosius' laws could be independent of his victories in the field and, as the favourable treatment of the emperor in Augustine's *De Ciuitate Dei* of 415 and in Orosius two years later shows[14], the fascination of the Theodosian theme outlived its immediate historical context. In theory, then, Prudentius could have inserted his prophecy in honour of a dead emperor who, although unnamed, was uniquely associated with the destruction of pagan rites. Yet it is as plausible that the *futurum principem* was still alive at the time of writing and that his insertion into the Laurence story was a graceful compliment to his recent achievement.

Whatever its date, the St Laurence poem is early. In it, Prudentius writes of Roman saints as if they were far away across the ranges of the Cottian Alps and the Pyrenees[15] and that the Vascones on the Ebro had barely heard how full Rome was of saints[16]. This and the absence of the visual and topographical descriptions dear to the poet and included elsewhere wherever possible support the view that the poem predates Prudentius' visit, the date of which is itself uncertain.

The poems on St Cassian of Imola[17], however, St Hippolytus and the Apostles Peter and Paul[18] with their vivid descriptions of the shrines, churches and religious celebrations witnessed by the poet clearly derive from a Roman journey. It was a mission in which doubt and perhaps danger were present, and the poet implores the help of Cassian for his mission, which appears to have been both a personal and a public one[19]. One of the objects certainly was to report on Roman festivals. The closing lines of the Peter and Paul poem take the form of advice from a stranger to the poet to go home and remember to celebrate the *diem bifestum* as he has seen it in Rome[20]. And in the Hippolytus poem, he asks his Spanish bishop to add the festival of Hippolytus to

those of Cyprian, Chelidonius (with Emeterius, the main saint of Calagurris) and Eulalia (of Emerita), saints celebrated in other poems of the **Peristephanon,** which may also have been composed before the visit[21].

A Theodosian allusion in the Peter and Paul poem may have important implications for the date of the visit. Referring to the dedication of San Paolo fuori le mura in 391, the poet reports, *regia pompa loci est: princeps bonus has sacrauit arces / lusitque magnis ambitum talentis*[22]. Here again is Theodosius, the *princeps bonus,* whose *praefectus urbi* made the dedication in, ironically, the consulship of the pagan Symmachus. Here, surely, the unnamed *princeps* must be the living emperor. The objection that the identity of the *princeps* was sufficiently obvious from the fact of the dedication has less weight in this case. The dedication of San Paolo, although a conspicuous act of Christian munificence, hardly ranked with the anti-pagan legislation or victory over usurpers for which Theodosius was most widely celebrated. A Roman audience might have been expected to be familiar with the dedication but Prudentius was not concerned with them alone (if at all) but with the Spanish readership whom he was supposed to inform on Roman saints. For the Vascones on the Ebro the *bonus princeps,* Theodosius, was bound to be the living emperor[23].

Therefore, Prudentius' visit to Rome, the first but not perhaps the only one[24], took place sometime after 391 and before Theodosius' death early in 395. Three poems on saints were the result of it, to be added to others, including that on St Laurence, probably composed before. But the reasons for Prudentius' interest in saints should not be tied too closely to the emperor. The poems on the Spanish saints[25] show a strong liturgical inspiration as well as extensive acquaintance with *passiones* and shrines, the outcome of local and first-hand knowledge. More speculatively, behind the celebration of the Roman saints Laurence and Agnes[26] may be detected the hand of Pope Damasus (died, 384) who saw and exploited the potential in the poetic promotion of saints. Damasus may have translated the relics of the martyr Quirinus of Siscia to Rome (although this is uncertain): if he did, the occasion may have been marked by Prudentius' poetic *passio* of the saint[27], the inclusion of whom in the **Peristephanon** is otherwise hard to explain. In which case, the inception of Prudentius' poetic activity should be pushed back well into the 380s, a more plausible hypothesis than that his poetic talent emerged suddenly and fully-fledged into the reign of Honorius.

II

The achievement of Theodosius is most fully dealt with in the first book **Contra orationem Symmachi,** which sandwiches a general attack on the pagan gods[28] of a type familiar in anti-pagan polemic between an opening section on Theodosius the Christian leader whose laws are 'now' threatened by a pagan revival and an extensive laudation of Theodosius' outlawing of paganism after his victory at the Frigidus in September 394. The association of the Theodosian Book I with the second book, which is unambiguously dated to soon after Honorius' and Stilicho's victory at Pollentia in April 402 (but before that of Verona in the summer of 402 or possibly 403)[29], has led scholars almost unanimously to conclude that the whole work was written in 402, soon after the appearance of Claudian's *De Bello Getico*. Although, as M. P. Cunningham pointed out, 'the classical tradition offers no parallel for a composition of this form'[30], the generally accepted view is that expressed by T. D. Barnes, that the poem 'was conceived and clearly composed as a unity'[31].

The issue of a separate date of composition for Book I in late 394 or early 395 is not, however, so easily shelved. A. Faguet, who in 1883 first raised the question of a separate date of 394 for Book I, based his views on the present tenses of the opening lines, which place the reader firmly in the context and atmosphere of the early 390s, when Christian hopes raised by Theodosius' laws of 391 and 392 were threatened by the spectre of a pagan revival, *renouata lues*[32]:

> Credebam uitiis aegram gentilibus urbem
> iam satis antiqui pepulisse pericula morbi
> nec quidquam restare mali, postquam medicina
> principis immodicos sedarat in arce dolores.
> sed quoniam renouata lues turbare salutem
> temptat Romulidum, patris inploranda medella est
> . . .[33]

Faguet might have added that the failure to name the *princeps*, Theodosius the lawgiver, is evidence that the poem is written in the lifetime of the *princeps*. However, J. Bergman in 1926[34] rejected *medella est* and other present tenses cited by Faguet as historic presents and drew attention to the imperfect *credebam* in the first line of the poem and to the fact that the conversion of Rome is described as having already taken place by lines 506ff[35]. Neither set of arguments is conclusive. The present tenses of the opening lines are designed to evoke an atmosphere of doubt, but the threat has been overcome by the end of the book, with Theodosius' victory and the 'conversion' of the Senate. *Credebam*, however, looks back to the laws of Theodosius of 391 and 392 which were threatened by the limited restoration of pagan cult under Eugenius spear-headed by Nicomachus Flavianus and his connections[36] and is therefore 'past' in terms of 394. And the conversion of Rome and the Senate, described as past, is closely associated with the reaction of the senators to the *sententia principis*, when they show their enthusiasm for Christianity in the present tense by crossing the floor of

the Senate-house freely to vote in its favour in huge numbers[37]. The constant shifting between past and present shows Prudentius' sense of dramatic occasion and his versatility in the manipulation of time but supplies no conclusive evidence as to the date of the whole poem.

Faguet's idea can, however, be supported on other grounds. While *sub specie aeternitatis* it may matter little whether Prudentius' Theodosian inspiration was the immediate result of the Frigidus in 394 or the outcome of seven years' reflection after the event, the case for the separate composition and at least limited circulation (for example into the hands of Claudian) of Book I is worth stating. For, if composed separately, its amalgamation with Book II may teach us something of Prudentius' poetic technique and, if the result of Theodosius' victory and perhaps the poet's own visit to Rome in the mid-390s, it will bring Prudentius himself into sharper focus as a poet of the Theodosian era.

The key point in the argument is that, if the two books appeared together as we have them in 402, complete with their two prefaces, the poem as a whole would almost certainly have caused offence at the imperial court. The first book celebrates a wide range of Theodosian achievements, but his fathering of Arcadius and Honorius, reigning emperors in 402, is not among them, directly or by the slightest implication. In so sensitive an area as the treatment of emperors, not to mention the reigning *principes* at all before the opening of Book II was an error of tact surely to be avoided by even the most unconventional of poets. Moreover, in this sphere, Prudentius was not unconventional. He was not a writer of panegyric in the sense that Claudian was, but his approach to Arcadius and Honorius is that of the panegyricist and is consistent with their 'official' image. Thus the poet exaggerates their martial qualities (questionable at the best of times), introducing them at the outset of Book II as the *armorum dominos*, whose reponse to Symmachus' first specious argument for the Altar of Victory is that wars were to be won by the strength and martial prowess which they, by implication, represent[38]. The uniting of the two emperors in victory was not a reflection of actual events—the two never met in person again after their separation to rule their sections of the Empire in 395—but of the imperial propaganda which maintained the appearance of unity despite the dissensions of imperial ministers[39]. The two were represented together in the official art of the period; a column of Arcadius erected in Constantinople in 402 portrays the two emperors as consuls together with right hands raised, receiving the *aurum oblaticium* from the senates of Rome and Constantinople[40]. Prudentius was therefore in accord with imperial imagery.

His playing up of the victory at Pollentia on Easter Day (April 6), 402, is also characteristic of the panegyricist.

Verbal echoes from Claudian indicate that he had the *De Bello Getico* before him[41], and his description of Stilicho as the *comes* and *parens* of Honorius[42] suggests that he had also absorbed the Stilichonian view of that minister's guardianship of the young emperors, argued for also in Ambrose's funeral oration for Theodosius in 395[43]. Stilicho was in fact the main victor but Prudentius invariably associates the emperor with him as the superior, *dux agminis imperiique / christipotens nobis iuuenis fuit*[44], with Stilicho following in second place, and it is the emperor in his triumphal chariot whom Rome is to welcome[45]. The two, says the poet, sacrifice on a Christian altar[46] after a victory over an enemy greater than Hannibal. Two years later, Claudian was to admit that Alaric had escaped with his cavalry intact, but in the immediate euphoria of spring 402 Prudentius, had he known such details, could safely have ignored them[47].

However, Prudentius' exaggeration of the importance of Pollentia (although he may himself have been deceived) was also necessary for his argument for Christian *uictoria* and this Christian dimension might make him appear superficially less of a panegyricist than Claudian. But contemporary art again portrayed that most unmilitary of figures, Honorius, as a soldier of Christ and successor of Constantine: the consular diptych of Fl. Anicius Petronius Probus, western consul in 406, shows Honorius in full armour, flanked by a globe and Victory on one side and, on the other, a military standard bearing the words *in nomine Christi uincas*[48]. In this context, concepts of Christian *uictoria* could not be separated from imperial image-building.

Prudentius, therefore, is consistent with contemporary conventions in his treatment of emperors in Book II. Of course, the work as a whole is more than a celebration of emperors and much even of Book II is devoted to refutation of the arguments of Symmachus point by point, initially by the emperors but later, by a subtle shift, by the poet himself. Nevertheless, the different emphasis of his poem would not have absolved him from following rules of courtesy where emperors were concerned. In view of his success in reflecting the tone of imperial propaganda, and his sophistication in the use of chronology already remarked, it is surely impossible that he would have totally ignored the living emperors throughout his first book *Contra orationem Symmachi,* if both had been composed and appeared together in 402.

It is therefore possible that the *Contra orationem Symmachi* was a serial composition, in which the two books were written seven years apart, the first being a response to the events of late 394, as is established by the opening lines (excluding the Preface) already discussed, the second a reaction to events of 402.

A further anomaly is that, if the Prefaces are excluded, neither Symmachus nor his *oratio* make any appearance until the very end of Book I (line 622). This conflicts with Prudentius' practice elsewhere of clearly heralding his subject-matter: the **Hamartigenia** opens with the story of Cain and Abel (interestingly, not the Fall); the first lines of the **Psychomachia** ask how the *mens* is armed to resist sin; and the **Apotheosis** begins with an assertion of the orthodox doctrine of the Trinity, which is to be upheld in the rest of the poem. As Prudentius' contemporaries, such as Claudian or Paulinus of Nola, were also straightforward in their introduction of their main theme, be it St Felix of Nola, Stilicho, Rufinus or Honorius[49], it is the more peculiar that Prudentius should appear to set not just the opening but the whole of the first book of a poem written in 402 in the context, and the reign of the emperor, of late 394.

However, the Prefaces cannot be omitted from the discussion. Although some have believed that the Prefaces were, or could have been, added later as they are independent of the main structure, they are nevertheless part of the poem as we have it. The choice of stories about Paul and Peter, the Apostolic equivalents of Romulus and Remus as founders of the new Christian Rome, brings out a theme common to the two books, that both are about the triumph of Christianity at Rome, and thus obscures the fact that, historically, the subject-matter of the two books is divergent.

The story of Paul, the Preface to Book I, is of his coming ashore after a storm, lighting a fire and being then bitten by a viper, which he shakes off into the fire and is then miraculously healed of the wound. Prudentius then translates the story into his own terms: Paul's ship becomes the ship of (Christian) Wisdom *sub sacricolis territa regibus*[50], which has barely reached safe harbour when it is attacked by the serpent, Symmachus, whose poisonous eloquence is turned aside before it can take effect[51]. The reader then moves effortlessly into the opening lines of Book I itself, to find there the belief that Rome had rid herself of paganism newly challenged by the *renouata lues,* which he will assume to be the *oratio* of Symmachus. However, the poetic context of Book I, as a whole, makes it quite clear that the *lues* is a revival of paganism; Symmachus' sole function in Book I is to conduct a rearguard action alone against Theodosius' final outlawing of pagan cult after his victory over Eugenius[52]. The Preface to Book I is therefore, on the surface, misleading: we will not meet the eloquence of Symmachus, but what it represents.

The Preface to Book II is built round St Peter's uncertain attempts to walk on the water at the command of Christ; the poet doubts his ability to pass across the stormy waters of Symmachus' eloquence without divine aid. The reader therefore expects the refutation of the *oratio, Relatio* III, which duly follows. But there is one oddity. Prudentius talks about his project as a departure from the 'safety of silence', *sic me tuta silentia / egressum dubiis loquax / infert lingua periculis*[53]. This could hardly apply if Prudentius had already spent a book attacking the *oratio* and reinforces the idea that only the second book was designed to be against the oration of Symmachus and that the first was written at a different time and for a different, though related, purpose.

Therefore, I would suggest that Prudentius' **Contra orationem Symmachi** was originally two separate books, the first a response to Theodosius' victory in 394 and the second an attack on Symmachus partly motivated by the recent victory of the Christian emperor Honorius at Pollentia. How, when and why the two books were united as we have them is open to speculation: they were perhaps put together and the Prefaces added a little after the battle of Verona in summer 402 or 403, when the excitement of Pollentia had died down and the effect of that battle had been diminished both by a second victory and perhaps a more general realisation of the indecisiveness of a victory that allowed Alaric to return so quickly. However, these areas of uncertainly do not affect the grounds for separate composition of the two books offered above: the lack of overlap between Books I and II; the slight incompatibility of the first Preface with the subject of the first book; and, most important, the discourtesy to the emperor entailed by his total omission from Book I which, had it first appeared in 402, could not but have caused considerable and unnecessary offence.

III

Finally, we should consider the historical inspiration of the two books. The background for Prudentius' treatment of Theodosius is the *medicina principis,* his laws, and his victory over two usurpers, the pagan-supported Eugenius and the in fact very Christian Maximus, who are associated in wickedness as *tyranni* by Prudentius as they were by Ambrose in his funeral sermon for Theodosius in winter 395[54]. The bulk of the main Theodosian section of Book I is taken up with an address to Rome by that emperor as he views her *pulchra moenia* and seven hills[55]. Few now believe that Theodosius paid a second visit to Rome in late 394 after his victory[56]. Certainly, Prudentius is no evidence for it. The emperor's speech is directed to the helmeted female figure of Rome familiar in poetic representation and in such illustrations as those of the *Notitia Dignitatum* and need be no more than a literary device[57]. To juxtapose Theodosius and Rome was analogous to bringing Arcadius and Honorius together in Northern Italy and it had important poetic justification. To associate Theodosius with Rome was to underline the parallel with Constantine[58], whose victory at the Milvian Bridge had been won under the very walls of Rome. The parallels were legion: conquest of usurpers; victory under the labarum; and, most important for Prudentius' purpose, the freeing of the Senate by a Christian emperor. There were reasons enough, then, for Theodosius to be pictured as addressing Rome, even though he did not in fact go there.

But is the debate in the Senate described by Prudentius[59] also fictitious? The existence of such an occasion, followed by a vote in which the pagans were defeated, does not depend on the historicity of Theodosius' visit to Rome; his message could have been delivered by letter to the Senate and debated in his absence[60]. Zosimus, following the unreliable Eunapius, has Theodosius visit Rome in person and order the cancellation of subsidies for pagan cults[61]. The pagans object on the grounds that state cults should be celebrated publicly and at public expense, the standard recipe for ensuring the safety of the state. Despite their opposition, the motion was carried and it was for this reason, complained the pagan historian, that the western empire was overrun by barbarians. But although Zosimus' account contains obvious similarities to Prudentius' imperial *sententia,* debate and vote, it is not, in isolation, evidence that can be relied on.

Such a debate could, however, have taken place. Eugenius, although cautious about making concessions to the vociferous pagan element among his supporters, had in the end agreed to supply money from his own funds to certain prominent pagans, which they could use to finance the renewing of pagan ceremonies[62]. Although this stopped short of restoring public subsidies, for many observers it could have amounted to the same thing. Theodosius was therefore bound to stop all funding of pagan cult as part of his annulment of Eugenius' acts as a whole and, although the laws in the Theodosian Code on the subject date from the reign of his sons, there can be little doubt that he did so[63]. Opposition to Theodosius' religious policy could well have been expressed in the Senate, only to be over-ridden. Indeed, Symmachus, had he participated, would have been in a good position, politically, to do so, having been otherwise occupied and preserved a low profile during the usurpation[64]. However, whether Symmachus was personally involved or not, if Prudentius did set pen to paper in late 394 or early 395, perhaps in Rome itself on the occasion of the visit suggested above, the annulment of pagan subsidies may have provided the incentive for a poem that was both a general attack *contra paganos* and a vindication of Theodosius' specific achievement.

Book II raises further questions as to historical background and inspiration. The victory at Pollentia supplies a congenial context for the celebration of

Christian *uictoria* but does not entirely explain why the form of the second book is an attack on the *Relatio* III on the Altar of Victory, by now nearly twenty years old. Part of the reason may lie in the status of the *Relatio* as a classic pagan manifesto, which had outlived its immediate context and was still the most effective statement of the pagan position on Prudentius' prime interest in the poem, *uictoria*.

This may be sufficient explanation, but this has not deterred scholars from advancing other hypotheses. The idea has recently[65] been revived that Prudentius was goaded into action by an embassy of Symmachus to Honorius early in 402, interpreted as yet another attempt by the pagans to have restored some form of subsidy for, or recognition of, pagan cult. Given the threat of Alaric then looming over Italy, the pagan element in the Senate, along with some waverers perhaps, may have felt more acutely the need for some form of divine assurance.

However, the little that is known of this last embassy of Symmachus tells against this theory. Although Symmachus was not noticeably reticent on religious matters, his six surviving letters from early 402 supply no hint of a religious purpose for his mission. More important, one of the six letters is addressed to Stilicho himself, and states[66] that the Senate had charged the writer with a mission to Stilicho as well as to the emperor, that Stilicho must read the copies of the Senate's petition enclosed, and that everything depended on his decision; *de censurae enim tuae pendet arbitrio spes communis officii.* In another letter to his son[67] soon after his arrival at Milan and audience with the emperor, Symmachus again stresses the need for Stilicho's presence.

Why Stilicho? Perhaps Honorius was so inept that even on pagan subsidies which were the emperor's responsibility, he could make no decision without his minister. But Stilicho was less noted for his interest in pagan cult than for his military experience and his dealings with barbarians. The Senate would have remembered his dealings with them in 398, when he requested recruits off the senatorial estates to furnish troops to fight Gildo in Africa. The senators offered money but troops were not forthcoming. After the revolt was crushed, Stilicho had granted the Senate the doubtful privilege of trying minor supporters of Gildo, perhaps their own colleagues. Relations had been strained but neither party desired a long feud and matters had been patched up[68].

In early 402 attention would have been concentrated on the material risk posed by Alaric. Subsidies for pagan cult or the restoration of the Altar of Victory could have been seen, on one level, as effective countermeasures, but Stilicho was not the man to supply them; Honorius alone was enough. The necessity for the ailing Symma-chus to await Stilicho's return from subduing Vandals in Raetia indicates that the Senate's petition, perhaps a request for some decision on the military defences of Italy (and the senatorial estates therein), concerned Alaric, not paganism.

Symmachus' letters come to an end after his embassy and it is assumed that the winter journey was too much for him and that he died soon after. If this was so, his death may have provided the stimulus for the Symma-chean form of Prudentius' poem. A possible parallel is the reaction accorded to the death of Vettius Agorius Praetextatus late in 384: his passing brought about a period of public mourning but the laudations of the official obituary in Symmachus' *Relationes* XI and XII were counteracted on the Christian side by a diatribe from Jerome[69]. Similarly the death of Symmachus may have prompted Prudentius to write a poem which, while a response to Symmachus' death, was also a reminder of Ambrose's victory in the Altar of Victory controversy, where his arguments, reused and expanded by Prudentius, had prevailed, and a celebration of the Christian victory at Pollentia.

Although Prudentius was himself reticent about his life and background, more can be inferred from the fact that he was a man of his time who shared the preoccupations of his day with contemporaries whom he may have influenced or who influenced him: Claudian, for example, if the first book 'against Symmachus' was written and circulated (perhaps not under that title) in or soon after 394/5, could have known the work[70]. As we have seen, it was because Prudentius was subject to contemporary conventions that he could not have produced the two books **Contra orationem Symmachi** together in 402 as a new work. His experiments with panegyric in a Christian guise place him alongside those other Christians who praised Theodosius in 395, Ambrose and (in a lost work) Paulinus of Nola (who could have known Prudentius in his stay in NE Spain from 389 to mid-395). The prominence of the conversion of the Senate in the writings on Laurence and Theodosius indicates close ties with Christian senators, perhaps as patrons of his work. But in his celebration of emperors, Prudentius was not only a Christian but a former office-holder who owed (or was to owe) his elevation to the *pietas principis.* As such, perhaps as a fringe member of Theodosius' pious Spanish coterie, he was subject to the conventions binding on courtiers, and to the ephemeral hopes and delusions to which followers of emperors were always prone[71].

Notes

1. PRUDENTIUS, *Praef.*, 24-5, *oblitum ueteris me Saliae consulis arguens / sub quo prima dies mihi* . . .

2. *Ibid.,* 16-18.

3. On some of them, see J. Matthews, *Gallic Supporters of Theodosius,* in *Latomus,* 30 (1971), p. 1073-99.

4. *Tit. Hist.,* 4 and 5; cf. *Genesis,* XVIII.4 and XXIII.9-20.

5. *Praef.,* 19-21.

6. From *Praef.,* 1-3, *Per quinquennia iam decem, / ni fallor fuimus; septimus insuper / annum cardo rotat . . .* with the date of birth of 349, n. 1 above. For the question of the 'collected edition' and the separate publication of Prudentius' poems as they appeared, see A. Cameron, *Claudian. Poetry and Propaganda at the Court of Honorius,* Oxford, 1970, p. 470-1.

7. Prudentius, *Apoth.,* 449-53, *principibus tamen e cunctis non defuit unus / me puero ut memini, ductor fortissimus armis / conditor et legum, celeberrimus ore manuque, / consultor patriae, sed non consultor habendae / religionis.*

8. *Contra Symm.,* II, 6-9.

9. *Ibid.,* 17-8.

10. *Ibid.,* 67 and 644.

11. *Ibid.,* 655-6.

12. *Ibid.,* 1130.

13. *Perist.,* II, 473-80.

14. Augustine, *De Ciu. Dei,* V, 25 and Orosius, *Historia aduersus paganos,* VII, 35. To these add praise of Theodosius at the time or soon after, in the lost panegyric of Paulinus of Nola (395) and Rufinus of Aquileia's continuation of Eusebius, IX.33.

15. *Perist.,* II, 537-40.

16. *Ibid.,* 541-4.

17. *Perist.,* IX, in which Prudentius describes a picture of the martyrdom of Cassian seen by him on his journey to Rome.

18. *Perist.,* XI and XII.

19. *Perist.,* IX, 101-4, *tunc arcana mei percenseo cuncta laboris, / tunc quod petebam, quod timebam murmuro, / et post terga domum dubia sub sorte relictam / et spem futuri forte nutantem boni.*

20. *Perist.,* XII, 65-6, *tu domum reuersus / diem bifestum sic colas memento.*

21. *Perist.,* XI, 237-8, *inter solemnes Cypriani uel Chelidoni / Eulaliaeque dies currat et iste tibi.*

22. *Perist.,* XII, 47-8.

23. The *princeps* cannot be Honorius who completed but did not dedicate the church. For its successive stages, see A. Chastagnol, *Sur quelques documents relatifs à la basilique de Saint-Paul hors-les-murs,* in *Mel. Piganiol,* Paris, 1966, p. 421-37.

24. *Perist.,* I (Emeterius and Chelidonius of Calagurris), III (Eulalia of Emerita), IV (the Eighteen of Caesaraugusta), V (St. Vincent of Caesaraugusta), VI (Fructuosus, Augurius and Eulogius of Tarraco).

25. Despite his *Epil.,* 10 (*nec ad leuamen pauperum potentes*), he presumably had the means as well as the leisure to travel from Spain. *Contra Symm.,* II is Rome-centred enough to be the result of a second visit (if the first is admitted) in 402.

26. *Perist.,* XIV (Agnes) has no evidence of first-hand knowledge of her places of martyrdom and cult. She shared a church with SS Vincent and Eulalia in SW France in 450 (*CIL,* XII, 4311), and may have been popular in the region earlier.

27. *Perist.,* VII, a bald account of the martyrdom. For the possible *translatio,* A. Ferrua, *Epigrammata Damasiana,* Rome, 1942, no. 64, p. 235f.

28. *Contra Symm.,* I, 42-407.

29. The previously accepted date of summer 402 was queried by T. D. Barnes, *The Historical Setting of Prudentius' Contra Symmachum,* in *AJP,* 97 (1976), p. 373-86.

30. M. P. Cunningham, *Contexts of Prudentius' poems,* in *CPh.* [*Classiques de Philosophie*] 71 (1976), p. 56-66, esp. p. 59.

31. Barnes, *art. cit.,* p. 373.

32. A. Faguet, *De Aurelii Prudentii Clementis carminibus lyricis,* Bordeaux, 1883, p. 24-6. My thanks to Professor Cameron for this reference.

33. *Contra Symm.,* I, 1-6.

34. Bergman (ed.), *Prudentii carmina, CSEL,* 61, 1926, p. xv-xvi.

35. *Contra Symm.,* I, 506-8, *talibus edictis urbs informata refugit / errores ueteres et turbida ab ore uieto / nubila discussit . . .*

36. See J. Matthews, *Western Aristocracies and Imperial Court, A.D. 364-425,* Oxford, 1975, p. 238-47.

37. *Contra Symm.,* I, 608-12.

38. *Contra Symm.,* II, 20-66.

39. See esp. Cameron, *op. cit.,* chs. IV and VI.

40. For the official context, see S. MacCormack, *On the Imperial Ceremonial of adventus,* in *Historia,* 21 (1972), esp. p. 740f.

41. The echoes are cited by Cameron, *op. cit.,* p. 473: *Contra Symm.,* II, 75 echoes *Get.,* 103; II, 697 parallels *Get.,* 81; II, 715 parallels *Get.,* 633; II, 719 parallels *Get.,* 423; II, 763 parallels *Get.,* 88.

42. *Contra Symm.*, II, 710-11, *et comes eius / atque parens Stilicho* . . . But Stilicho was also related to Honorius by marriage twice over: he had married Theodosius' niece Serena and in 398 his daughter Maria was married to Honorius himself.

43. AMBROSE, *De Ob. Theod.*, 5.

44. *Contra Symm.*, II, 709-10.

45. *Ibid.*, 731-2.

46. *Ibid.*, 712-3 and, on Hannibal, *ibid.*, 738-49. This anticipates the triumphal entry Honorius could be expected to make as consul early in 404.

47. CLAUDIAN, *VI Cons. Hon.*, 285.

48. For the inscription, *ILS*, 8991 = *ILCV*, 1626. There is a very good and accessible photograph in T. CORNELL and J. MATTHEWS, *Atlas of the Roman World*, Oxford, 1982, p. 210.

49. Cf. the practice of Claudian, on his main subjects e.g.: the Anician consuls of 395 (*Prob. et Olyb. coss.*, 8); Rufinus (*Ruf.*, I, 20) and with Stilicho (*Ruf.*, II, 4, 6); Gildo (*Gild.*, I, 10); Mallius Theodorus consul in 399 (*Theod.*, 14); Eutropius as *eunucho consule* (*Eutr.*, I, 8) and by name (I, 23 and II, 21); Stilicho as consul in 400 (*Stil.*, I, 9) and as victor at Pollentia (*Get.*, 14); Serena (*Ser.*, 2); and Honorius as consul in 398 (*IV Cons. Hon.*, 4) and in the context of his *aduentus* at Rome in 404 as *princeps uenerande* (*VI Cons. Hon.*, 53).

50. *Contra Symm.*, I, *Praef.*, 47. The story of Paul comes from *Acts*, XXVII, 14-XXVIII, 6.

51. *Ibid.*, 74-7, *seps insueta subit serpere flexibus / et uibrare sagax eloquii caput: / sed dextra impatiens uulneris inritos / oris rhetorici depulit halitus* . . .

52. *Contra Symm.*, I, 622-31. Symmachus is reminded that Theodosius made him consul in 391, *cuius religio tibi displicet, o pereuntum / adsertor diuum, solus qui restituendos / Vulcani Martisque dolos Venerisque peroras.*

53. *Contra Symm.*, II, *Praef.*, 44-6.

54. *Contra Symm.*, I, 462-3. Cf. AMBROSE, *De Ob. Theod.*, 39, *Contra autem Maximus et Eugenius in inferno quosi "nos nocti indicat scientiam", docentes exemplo miserabili quam durum sit arma suis principibus inrogare.* For the *ad hoc* measures of *tyranni* against paganism, PRUDENTIUS, *Contra Symm.*, I, 22-4.

55. *Contra Symm.*, I, 410ff.

56. For arguments against the visit, see W. ENSSLIN, *War Kaiser Theodosius I zweimal im Rom?*, in *Hermes*, 81 (1953), p. 500ff.

57. *Contra Symm.*, I, 416-22.

58. *Ibid.*, 467-95, *hoc signo inuictus tramsmissis Alpibus ultor* . . . The picture of Maxentius is that of Constantinian propaganda; see EUSEBIUS, *Hist. Eccles.*, VIII. 14, 1-6 (Maxentius' pursuit of wives of senators and murders of senators for their money); LACTANTIUS, *De Mort. Pers.*, 8.4 (rich senators falsely accused of aiming at imperial power); EUTROPIUS, *Breu.*, X, 4, 3.

59. *Contra Symm.*, I, 608ff. On the debate, briefly, see P. BROWN, *Religion and Society in the Age of St. Augustine,* London, 1972, p. 163-4; 'this explanation by Prudentius is a poetic fiction; the exercise of his authority in so blunt a manner by a Christian Emperor could never, in itself, explain the religious transformation of Rome'.

60. Cf. SYMMACHUS, *Ep.*, I, 95 on the delivery of an imperial *oratio* to him to communicate to the Senate, *cum mihi a principibus aeternis legenda in conciliis patrum delegaretur oratio.* On senatorial procedure in response to *orationes,* see F. MILLAR, *The Emperor in the Roman World,* London, 1977, p. 277 and 341ff.

61. ZOSIMUS, *Historia Noua*, IV, 59, 1-3.

62. AMBROSE, *Ep.*, 57.

63. *CTh.*: [*Classical Theology*] XV, 14, 9-12, esp. 11 with reference to Eugenius' reign to be made 'as if it had not been'. Cf. the annulment of the acts of Maximus, *ibid.*, 6, 7, and 8 (of September 388 to January 389).

64. He was concerned with his son's quaestorian games and corresponded with Eugenius, Flavianus and Arbogast on neutral topics. For convincing refutation of the theory that Symmachus' correspondence was edited and compromising letters removed, see B. CROKE, *The Editing of Symmachus Letters to Eugenius and Arbogast,* in *Latomus,* 35 (1976), p. 533-49.

65. T. D. BARNES, *art. cit.* (see above, note 29).

66. SYMMACHUS, *Ep.*, IV, 9, *Cum sublimi excellentia tua legationem mihi amplissimus ordo mandauit, ad quam suscipiendam me et necessitas impulit patriae et tui culminis prouocauit auxilium. peruectus igitur ad comitatum domini et principis nostri Honorii in notitiam magnificentiae tuae deferre non distuli aduentus mei causam, de censurae* . . .

67. *Ibid.*, VII, 14, *in praesentiam uiri cuncta praecelsi comitis agenda produco; quem mox deo iuuante adfore nuntiorum confirmat adsertio.*

68. CAMERON, *op. cit.*, 231-7.

69. JEROME, *Ep.*, 23, 3.

70. *Contra Symm.*, I, 15 echoed in CLAUDIAN, *Eutr.*, II, 15; perhaps *Contra Symm.*, I, 153 echoed in *Theod.*, 334, *subnixus in aeuum.* Both Claudian poems date from 399.

71. I am grateful to Professor Alan Cameron for much encouragement and many helpful suggestions on this subject six years ago, and to Dr John Matthews and Dr John Richardson for their help and salutary criticism since. The errors that remain are my responsibility.

William J. McCarthy (essay date 1986)

SOURCE: McCarthy, William J. "*Resurrectio particulatim*: Atomism and *Consolatio* in Prudentius's *Apotheosis.*" In *Diakonia: Studies in Honor of Robert T. Meyer.* Edited by Thomas Halton and Joseph P. Williman, pp. 87-100. Washington, D.C.: Catholic University of America Press, 1986.

[*In the following essay, McCarthy discusses why Prudentius rejected Lucretius's theory of atomism and examines the Christian atomism that he fashioned in its place.*]

Prudentius' well-crafted and occasionally masterful poetry, a confluence of elements Christian and non-Christian, is just beginning to attract the sort of literary interest which was formerly reserved for the more traditional classics. Of the methods by which these works are interpreted, that which meticulously attends to the contexts from which words or phrases are drawn and into which they are set often may reveal much of the skill and purpose of an author. Not unreasonably may we anticipate that the Christian poet, thoroughly familiar with the tradition in which he is working, is also capable of subtle allusion in the service of his own themes.[1]

Nearly a century ago A. Puech noted that Prudentius modeled his **Apotheosis** on Lucretius' *De rerum natura*, the prototypical didactic (and polemic) poem of Latin literature.[2] Strangely, while agreeing that these poems share a general similarity of genre and tone, succeeding scholars have discerned but few ringing verbal echoes and have scrutinized the literary implications of none of these.[3] The purpose, then, of the present brief contribution, one offered in praise of and gratitude to the *honorandus,* is to demonstrate that within the ambient irony of a Christian poem which is both "Lucretian" and anti-Epicurean there is at least one specific borrowing (*particulatim* [1077]) which is quite pointed. Because the **Apotheosis** defends not only the divinity and human-

ity of Christ but also the "divinization" of the human body, a doctrine which is, of course, thoroughly un-Epicurean,[4] the astute borrowing of this atomistic term in the closing lines, where the poet expresses his hope and confidence in the resurrection, enhances our appreciation both of the irony implicit in the choice of poetic model and of the drama of the concluding *consolatio* addressed by the soul to the body.

A simplified version of Rank's organization of the poem provides us an adequate overview of its contents:[5]

proem (on the Trinity)	12 lines
preface:	
The difficulty of discerning the *recta fides* amidst false teachings.	56 lines
I. The majesty of God the Father:	
God is invisible, formless, impassible; the Son is the form by which He appears.	1-177
II. The fatherhood of God:	
God is a true Father and is distinct from the Son, not to admit which is to destroy both Father and Son.	178-320
III. The Jews:	
Their failure to see Christ as true God, true Temple; their fate as a consequence.	321-551
IV. The mystery of Christ:	
Christ was born of a virgin, truly a man and truly God.	552-781
V. The nature of the soul:	
The soul is not divine, but a divine creation. It is susceptible to sin through its union with the body. Christ's incarnation, suffering, and death have saved it.	782-951
VI. The Manichaean error:	
Christ, who is God, has a real body whose resurrection is the hope of man's own.	952-1084

While Rank recognizes the apotheosis of man himself as a "theme that is interwoven through the entire poem" (p. 27), he overlooks how skill-fully Prudentius moves toward the climactic profession of confidence in the resurrection with which the poem concludes. We may note that the structure of the latter half (552-1084) follows an interesting pattern: Christ is not only human but also divine (IV), not only divine but also human (VI [952-1018 = 67 lines]); the human soul is not divine but has a divine origin, and has been saved through Christ's incarnation (V), and the human body, also God's creation, has been given a divine destiny through Christ's incarnation and resurrection (VI [1019-1084 = 66 lines]). The two major themes, one of the union of the two different natures in Christ and the other of the difference between man's two natures, are carefully interwoven, and thereupon resolved in the final lines. The ultimate "reconciliation" between soul and body in the general resurrection, that which is prefigured in Christ's, constitutes the crowning of the reconciliation between God and man. Pertinent to the resolution of these themes, and apropos of the poem's Lucretian model, is the subtle implication of an "atomistic" resurrection in the conclusion. But before we turn to the closing lines, let us first consider an echo of Lucretius in the opening lines of its sixth and final section.

The refutation of the docetist assault on the concrete reality of Christ's body begins with the ascription of a wryly phantasmal savior to the Manichaeans:

> est operae pretium nebulosi dogmatis umbram
> prodere, quam tenues atomi conpage minuta
> instituunt, sed cassa cadit ventoque liquescit
> (955) adsimilis fluxu nec se sustentat inani.
> aërium Manicheus ait sine corpore vero
> pervolitasse Deum, mendax fantasma cavamque
> corporis effigiem nil contrectabile habentem.[6]

[It is worthwhile to produce the shadow of a mistry doctrine—a shadow which fine atoms in a very closely fitted structure comprise. But hollow it descends (sc. to the earth) and begins to disintegrate liquidly into the wind, very like the hemorrhaging of a weakened frame, nor does it hold itself together in the void. The Manichaean says that an insubstantial God without a true body flitted through this form, a God possessed of a false image and a hollow figure of a body which contained nothing tangible.]

(952-958)

The body of this Christ is, as we ought to expect of the Manichaean savior, insubstantial, some sort of a phantom;[7] yet, the description of it is paradoxical. Or rather, perverse. Prudentius' intention in introducing the heretical doctrine is not to explain it accurately or fairly but to seek to lay the groundwork for a refutation. Thus, he deliberately confuses *dogma* with *umbra* (both are "misty"—part of the satirical treatment[8]—so that we should not presume to dismiss the phrase *nebulosi dogmatis umbram* as hypallage) and immediately signals a less than earnest effort to explain the nature of the phantom. The pun of *umbram prodere* (the verb apparently also intending the sense of "project") is elaborated into the scathingly ludicrous notion of a divine savior, supposedly a being of light, who possesses a body which is a frail and sickly shadow (see note 10). The absurdity is compounded by the emphasis on the "airy" quality of the Manichaean Christ and, in consequence, that of man.[9] Most significantly, however, the very terms in which the composition of the unstable shadow is defined are at odds with the fundamental docetism of Manichaean soteriology because they are distinctly Epicurean (hence, ironically, the most materialist which ancient philosophy could offer), viz., *atomi* and *inane*.[10] Nonetheless, if the initial wit and sarcasm make the major points of the no less sarcastic and vituperative arguments to follow, it is important to bear in mind that atomism itself has been neither mocked nor rejected.

While the introduction to the Manichaean Christ provides an undeniable general reminiscence of Lucretius, we should be careful to note that, of the key terms *atomi* and *inane*, the former does not occur in the *De rerum natura*. Of course, Prudentius' fondness for Greek words may account for this substitution. For his part though, Lucretius, in avoiding the word, seems to have completely overcome the *patrii sermonis egestas* of which he complains (see 1.136-139, 830-833, and 3.258-260), for he meticulously shapes a range of equivalents or near-equivalents: *primordia, corpora, corpuscula, semina, elementa, figurae, materies* (or *materia*), and *particulae*.[11] Prudentius, then, whether or not he was much aware of the fine shades of meaning which apparently distinguish these terms, at any event clearly had all at his disposal. If, in reference to the phantom savior, the Greek term (more exotic?) is preferred, the Latin *particula* plays an important role in his expression of belief in the resurrection and proves to be of special philological note to us. In the first place, it alone has an adverbial form, *particulatim*, which Lucretius uses (and only once). The word occurs in that section of the poem which argues against the survival of the soul after the body's death (3.417-829):[12]

> (540) quin etiam si iam libeat concedere falsum
> et dare posse animam glomerari in corpore
> eorum,
>   lumina qui linqunt moribundi particulatim,
>   mortalem tamen esse animam fateare necesse,
>   nec refert utrum pereat dispersa per auras
> (545) an contracta suis e partibus obbrutescat,
>   quando hominem totum magis ac magis undique
> sensus
>   deficit et vitae minus et minus undique restat.[13]

[(Body and soul are observed to die gradually, and there is no concentration of soul within the dying body.) And indeed, even if it should be possible to concede that which is false and thus grant that the soul of those who are leaving the light, dying atom by atom, can be gathered together in their body, even so you would have to confess that the soul is mortal, nor does it matter whether it perishes by scattering through the air, or becomes stupified after it has withdrawn from its proper parts, since sensation wanes ever more swiftly everywhere throughout the whole person, and throughout less and less of life remains.]

(3.540-547)

Regarded strictly as the adverbial form of *particula* (and not of either *pars* [= *partim*] or *membrum* [= *membratim*], each of which adverbs is to be found in Lucretius), *particulatim* should refer here to the mortal decay of the body "atom by atom" rather than "part by part" or "limb by limb."[14] This atomistic interpretation is buttressed by our observation that the process of a slow bodily degeneration which is described here appears to be paired with a correspondingly gradual "clumping together" (*glomerari* implies the dense packing of many elements [= atoms]) of the soul. According to the theory rejected by Lucretius, then, as the body loses its soul (and the accompanying *sensus* and *vita*) *particula* by *particula*, its abandoned parts die. In this way we arrive at a neatly atomistic scheme which, even if Lucretius rejects the theory of the concentration of soul, takes much better account of his terminology.

Also philologically noteworthy is the infrequency of *particulatim:* despite the fact that it is not a great rarity in Latin prose, save for its occurrence in the above cited passage of the *De rerum natura,* the adverb is not found in poetry.[15] Thus, the recurrence at the end of the *Apotheosis,* in the same metrical position as in Lucretius' poem, should scarcely be counted as adventitious, especially if we take into account that this is arguably the Christian poet's most "Lucretian" poem. Let us then consider the new context.

To conclude his dismissal of the insubstantial Christ, Prudentius asserts God's love of man, body and soul (*tantus amor terrae, tanta est dilectio nostri* [1027]),[16] and then expressly recognizes his own self in Christ:[17]

> Christus nostra caro est; mihi solvitur et mihi surgit;
> solvor morte mea, Christi virtute resurgo.
> cum moritur Christus, cum flebiliter tumulatur,
> me video; e tumulo cum iam remeabilis adstat,
> (1050) cerno Deum. si membrorum fantasma meorum est,
> et fantasma Dei est . . .

[Christ is our flesh. For me he (or perhaps more specifically "his flesh") is dissolved and for me he rises. By my death I am dissolved, by Christ's power I rise again. When Christ dies, when tearfully he is buried, I see myself. And now when he emerges from the tomb and stands upright, I see God. If he is a ghostly image of my body, so too is he a ghostly image of God.]

(1046-1051)

Moreover, the future resurrection of the poet's own body (*nosco meum in Christo corpus consurgere* [see 1062ff.]) will be a complete restoration,

> debet enim mors victa fidem, ne fraude sepulchri
> (1075) reddat curtum aliquid, quamvis iam curta vorarit
> corpora; debilitas tamen et violentia morbi
> virtus mortis erat; reddet quod particulatim
> sorbuerat quocumque modo, ne mortuus omnis
> non redeat, si quod pleno de corpore desit.

[for conquered Death[18] must keep faith lest, by the deceit of the grave, he return something imperfect even though he now devours imperfect bodies; yet, feebleness and wracking disease were the peculiar strengths of Death. He shall return that which atom by atom he took away, however he took it away, lest the whole of the dead man not return if he should be lacking some portion of a whole body.]

(1074-1079)

In view of the already discussed infrequency of the word among the Latin poets, this recurrence of *particulatim* may be deemed a learned borrowing from Lucretius. We may also import its atomistic sense into the new context. By seeing himself in Christ, that is, his own resurrected body in Christ's, the poet leaves no doubt of an essential identity between the two. Neither is a phantom (note the echo of *fantasma* from 957 at 1051-1052), neither is anything less than true flesh. That the stuff of this flesh be atoms is both an idea not unwelcome in a poem of recognized "Lucretian" tone and a clever structural feature which ironically contrasts the skewered atomistic portrait of the Manichaean Christ at the opening of the final section with the gloriously imagined resurrection of the poet's own body at the end—where the now "Christianized" atomism inverts (inevitably) a basic Epicurean doctrine.

The views of the two poets on the condition of the soul vis-à-vis that of the body dying "atom by atom" differ radically. For Prudentius, the soul neither "clumps together" in the body (the view which Lucretius rejects) nor helplessly dissipates in the atmosphere as it departs (the accepted view). If in this case the manner of its departure is left unclear,[19] clear nonetheless is the fact that in the concluding lines the poet's "voice" is that of the soul addressing the body:

> (1080) pellite corde metum, mea membra, et credite vosmet
> cum Christo reditura Deo; nam vos gerit ille
> et secum revocat. morbos ridete minaces,
> inflictos casus contemnite, taetra sepulchra
> dispuite; exsurgens quo Christus provocat, ite.

[Banish fear from your hear, O parts of my body, (see note 22) and you yourself believe as well that you shall return with Christ who is God. For he puts you on and summons you back with himself. Laugh at the diseases which threaten you, scorn the disasters which befall you, spit with contempt on the vile tomb. Go forth to where Christ at his rising summons you.]

(1080-1084)

In general, because Prudentius deliberately discards the classical persona and thus is able "conventionally to begin his *opera* with literally himself in the *Proemium* and [to] end likewise with himself in the Epilogue,"[20] each of his poems is "personal" in a distinctly Christian manner. For him poetry is inextricably an expression of his soul's desire to attain heaven and the presence of God. His aspiration, then, is radically different from that of his classical models—the longing for imperishable *fama* among men.[21] At the conclusion of the *Apotheosis* this "personal" aspect assumes a particularly dramatic form in the address of the poet's soul to his moribund *membra.*

For Lucretius, the obvious mortality of the body provides a key sign from which to infer that of the soul.

If the body, constituted of matter, dies, then the soul, material as well (though the stuff be very fine) is also mortal and it dies when does its proper vessel, the body. As a consequence of this conclusion, the Epicurean *consolatio,* whose cold eloquence concludes Book 3 (830-1094) of Lucretius' poem, must seek to remove the fear of death by promising that the results of the dissolution of body and soul are the absence of all sensation and complete oblivion.

Prudentius, on the other hand, assumes the immortality of the finely structured (see 868-869) soul, sprung from God's breath and God-like. The body, in its turn, was created by God's hand and then later, because man had fallen into sin, was lovingly taken on (with the soul) by Christ. Such has he elevated the dignity of the formerly mortal body that ultimately all bodies will become the eternal partners of their proper souls, just as Christ's body is already the eternal partner of his divinity. The preeminent proof and guaranty of this divinization is, of course, the resurrection. In order to emphasize the real corporeality of Christ, Prudentius refutes the docetist/ Manichaean view with an absurd "atomism," while at the conclusion of the poem, through his careful borrowing from Lucretius, he suggests a sort of Christian atomism, a *resurrectio particulatim* of the body which completely negates its *mors particulatim,* in order to underscore the completeness of that ultimate and eternal restoration.

If we infer that, because no part of it is to be lost to death, the body will come together again, just as it first will have perished, "atom by atom," "in atoms," then *mea membra*—better rendered *"parts* of my body" rather than simply "my body"—in line 1080 should be regarded as having a broad, atomistic sense. That is, *membra* refers to the body as the vast and presently ever-fracturing confederacy of atoms which is the soul's "brother" (see 827ff.).[22] Thus interpreted, Prudentius' self-consolation takes on an appropriately cosmic character in which the eternal reconciliation of human and divine in Christ is dramatically manifest in man (note that the body itself is "personified"). When, albeit previously dissolved, the *membra* are fully reconstituted on the Last Day, by following Christ to an eternal home with the soul, and God, among the stars,[23] this body will have realized for the hopeful soul the apotheosis which Christ prefigures. Furthermore, because sensation is restored to the absence of oblivion (i.e., the body to the soul) in that blessed state, Prudentius' closing *consolatio* subverts, deliberately we may argue, the message of Lucretius' *consolatio* (and diatribe against the fear of death), and in particular the intended meaning of the well-known *sententia* of Epicurus with which he begins the final section of *De rerum natura* 3:[24]

> nil igitur mors est ad nos neque pertinet hilum.

> [Death, then, is nothing to us and has not a whit of relevance.]

(3.830)

Through the voice of the immortal soul to its mortal (but only for a time) body the *topos* of the nothingness of death "to us" takes on a completely Christian coloring. Weak and contemptible, Death, in effect, no longer exists, and in that sense it is "nothing to us," soul and body.

Notes

1. Thus, this paper proceeds from the assumption that Prudentius, certainly one of the better students of the classics of Latin literature (in which all the later poets and rhetoricians were schooled as a matter of course), carefully exploits the received tradition in an effort to reformulate Roman culture as Christian culture.

2. *Prudence, Étude sur la poésie latine chrétienne au IVe siècle* (Paris, 1888), pp. 159-188, 219. Compare the similar (and equally general) observations of Puech's contemporary, G. Boissier, in *La fin du paganisme* (Paris, 1891), vol. 2, pp. 151ff. (= pp. 133ff. in the 1913 edition).

3. C. Brakman ("Quae ratio intercedat inter Lucretium et Prudentium," *Mnemosyne,* n.s., 48 [1920], pp. 434-448), having cited a number of echoes and "coloristic" reminiscences of the one poet in the other (but only slightly supplementing the *index imitationum* of the *Apotheosis* [Cunningham's *CCSL* edition records none, Bergman's *CSEL* but one, and the *BAC* of Guillen and Rodriguez two]), concludes (p. 448) that "dubitare non possumus quin postremus poeta didacticus . . . studiosissime legerit et diligentissime pervolitaverit de Rerum Natura." G. B. A. Fletcher ("Imitationes vel loci similes in poetis latinis," *Mnemosyne,* n.s., 1 [1933-1934], pp. 202-203) also assembled a small group of unimposing reminiscences. Efforts to appreciate and to make good sense of the "Lucretian" properties of this Christian poem have been made by E. Rapisarda, "Influssi lucreziani in Prudenzio, un suo poema lucreziano e antiepicureo," *Vigiliae Christianae* 4 (1950), pp. 46-60; K. Smolak, "Die dreifache Zusammenklang (Prud. *Apoth.* 147-154)," *Wiener Studien,* n.s., 5 (1971), pp. 180-194 (esp. 182-185, 190-193); J. Fontaine, *Naissance de la poésie dans l'occident chrétien* (Paris, 1981), pp. 197-199.

4. The *locus classicus* of the Epicurean (as well as the Stoic) rejection of the resurrection is Acts 17:16ff. For its part, Christian polemic against

Epicureanism, tending to draw on the arguments of the Stoa and the Middle Academy, condemns the philosophy for amorality, its perversely asocial character, its lack of scientificness, and, most of all, atheism (see W. Schmid, art. "Epikuros," *RAC* 5 (1962), cols. 792-799). Certainly the theme of life out of death in the *Apotheosis,* when set over against the chillingly atheistic atomism (according to which the only real life, the only true *amor,* is atomic) of the *De rerum natura,* obviates the irony of the latter serving as a model for the former. In this connection J. Fontaine (*Naissance,* p. 199) aptly remarks: "Ce mot [*apotheosis*] apparemment inquiétant résume donc, en réalité, l'essentiel de sa christologie qui fait l'objet du poème. On n'en comprendra bien le sens que dans la profession de foi finale du poète en sa propre résurrection. Cette profession contraste absolument avec le triomphe de la mort qui couronne le poeme lucrétien, et non moins avec la divinisation poétique d'Épicure."

5. R. G. Rank, "The *Apotheosis* of Prudentius: A Structural Analysis," *Classical Folia* 20 (1966), pp. 18-31.

6. In arriving at his interpretation of the final section of the *Apotheosis,* the author has been careful to compare the more recent but much maligned (see, for example, the scathing review by K. Thraede in *Gnomon* 40 [1968], pp. 681-691) edition of Cunningham (*CCSL* 126 [1966]) with those of Lavarenne (Les Belles Lettres, 1945), and Bergman (*CSEL* 61 [1926]). Although there are some minor differences in spelling and punctuation, these editors are, fortunately, in essential harmony with respect to the text of lines 952ff. Thus, citations of Prudentius in this paper contain no significant problematic readings, and are punctuated as deemed appropriate.

7. Because even the *editores antiquissimi* used the section titles we find in the *Apotheosis* (see Cunningham, p. xxiv), that of the final section is noteworthy: "Adversum fantasmaticos qui Christum negant verum corpus habuisse." This would indicate that here we are dealing with a very broadly defined "Manichaeism." Indeed, for Prudentius, as commonly during this period, the name of the heresy was "the *terminus technicus* for any form of dualism . . . [because it] was the most prominent and outspoken protagonist of a radically dualistic concept of universe and man" (J. P. Asmussen, "Manichaeism," in *Historia Religionum,* vol. I, ed. C. Bleeker and G. Widengren [Leiden, 1961], p. 607). Nonetheless, it is clear that the vitriolic satire of the poem's final section is directed toward the fundamental (if scarcely

unique) Manichaean revulsion from the material. As E. Rose (*Die manichäische Christologie* [Wiesbaden, 1979], p. 121) observes of the attitude of this heresy toward Christ, "Für die Manichäer war der blosse Gedanke, der göttliche Erlöser habe sich mit dem befleckten Fleisch verbunden, eine massive Schändung ihres Jesusbild, weshalb bei ihnen von einer Fleischwerdung der Logos keine Rede sein konnte."

8. A. H. Weston ("Latin Satirical Writing Subsequent to Juvenal" [Ph.D. diss., Yale, 1915], pp. 43-56) has long since made the case for Prudentius' skills as a satirist (for examples from the *Apotheosis,* see pp. 44-45), declaring in summary (p. 56): "He may be characterized . . . as the principal satirist of Christian Latin poetry, and rivalled only by Claudian of the other poets subsequent to Juvenal." A detailed exploration of the influence of satire on Prudentius was provided by S. M. Hanley in her dissertation ("Classical Sources of Prudentius" [Cornell, 1959], pp. 110-157), from which she subsequently developed the article "Prudentius and Juvenal," *Phoenix* 16 (1962), pp. 41-52.

9. Note that, having described the Manichaean Christ as *nebulosus* and *aërius* in his introduction of the heresy, Prudentius pursues this image and idea to absurd limits, and reaches the conclusion (1010-1018) that, if Christ deceived mankind *ventosa arte* (962), his phantom body (a kind of garment = *omne, quod est gestum* [Lavarenne: "toute notre enveloppe corporelle" (1017)] which the *tenues aurae* scatter) implies that the bodies of men are also not real (a point emphasized by the polyptoton of 1011ff.: *aërios . . . aërium . . . aëria . . . aëria*), that *sit fabula quod sumus omnes* ("all of us may be but a fiction").

10. Inasmuch as the *umbra* is without question made up of atoms, an allusion to its disintegration "in the void" as a result of instability would neatly round off this thumbnail "atomistic" parody of the (typically Gnostic) descent (= *cadit*) of a supermundane entity. However, the construe of *inani* as the locative of the Lucretian term *inane* involves a reevaluation of the syntax and meaning of *fluxu.* First, so that *inani* may stand alone, we must reckon the principal caesura of line 955 to fall after *fluxu* (as it does more naturally) rather than after *adsimilis,* where Lavarenne and other editors place a comma (to indicate the caesura there) because they wish to take *adsimilis* with *ventoque* in line 954. While their maneuver is not unreasonable, it does force *fluxu* into the clause introduced by *nec,* a conjunction which normally takes first position. With the caesura after *fluxu,* we may

take that noun as a poetical dative with *adsimilis,* and *ventoque* with *liquescit.* An appropriately pathological interpretation of the *fluxus* which the *umbra* suffers guides this construe. The noun, just as the verb *fluo* and the adjective *fluxus,* really ought never to be deprived of the fundamental sense of a "flowing" of some sort. In connection with the body, such "flowing" may pertain to one of its fluids (often menstrual blood or "seed"); and, in a sometimes related but more metaphorical sense, the "flowing" condition of the body indicates its enfeeblement, i.e., either its infirmity (due to disease, deprivation, adverse climate) or its slackness (brought on by luxury and indulgence). We see that the Manichaean shadow-body "flows" because it is an enfeebled structure of *tenues atomi.* Further, we interpret that, upon descending, "it begins to disintegrate liquidly (thus fully exploiting both the image and the inchoative suffix of the verb) into the wind" (= the dative of direction [see M. Lavarenne, *Étude sur la langue du poète Prudence* (Paris, 1933), p. 140]). Proceeding from these points, we may conclude that Prudentius, having already confused the *umbra* with its *dogma,* pursues his satiric treatment by describing its demise as a hemorrhaging (note that *fluxus* is used in this sense in the Latin Bible at Matthew 9:20) of its *tenues atomi* into the wind. *Adsimilis fluxu,* then, has been translated "very like the hemorrhaging of a weakened frame" in order that account be taken of the poet's apparent intention to apply to the *umbra* the literal and metaphorical senses which *fluxus* has in connection with the human body.

11. Concerning all these terms and their distinctions, see Katherine Reiley, *Studies in the Philosophical Terminology of Lucretius and Cicero* (New York, 1909), pp. 35-66 (on *particula* = ἄτομος [4.776, and possibly 3.708 and 4.261], see p. 59). More recent scholars have demonstrated the great precision with which Lucretius fashions and distinguishes his renderings of the term. For example, R. Keen ("Notes on Epicurean Terminology and Lucretius," *Apeiron* 13 [1979], pp. 63-69) astutely observes in connection with the translation *primordia* (pp. 63-64) that, because Epicurus (in the *Letter to Herodotus*) uses ἄτομος as an adjective (neuter [understood with σῶμα] or feminine [understood with φύσις]), the Latin term "does not represent 'atom' . . . but . . . the indivisible quality of those bodies." See also P. Grimal, "*Elementa, primordia, principia* dans le poème de Lucrèce," in *Mélanges P. Boyancé* (Rome, 1974), pp. 357-366, in which Lucretius' strict distinction between *primordia* (the "atoms") and *principia* (the "elements") is explored.

12. The structure of the third book may be sketched as follows:

    A. Introduction: praise of Epicurus; a syllabus of the elements of this book's topic, the fear of death (1-93)

    B. The nature and structure of the soul (94-416)

    C. The proofs of the soul's mortality (417-829)

    D. The folly of the fear of death (830-1094)

13. Here and throughout the Latin text is cited from the edition by C. Bailey (*Oxford Classical Texts*).

14. Adverbs which terminate in *-im* returned into vogue in later antiquity following their fall into desuetude in the classical period. A. Funck ("Die lateinischen Adverbia auf *-im,* ihre Bildung und ihre Geschichte," *Archiv für lateinische Lexikographie und Grammatik* VIII [Leipzig, 1893], pp. 77-114) discussed at length the history and semantics of such forms, and furnished an extensive list (pp. 111-114). Brakman ("Quae ratio," pp. 445-446), for his part, took general note of the Lucretian *similitudo* which such adverbial forms (along with the infinitives in *-ier* and the use of Greek words) lend certain poems of Prudentius. The archaizing adverbs in *-im* are, however, not all that uncommon in Prudentius (see Lavarenne, *Étude,* pp. 422-423). Nonetheless, for our purposes the form *particulatim* is to be regarded as quite significant because it is unique (in Latin poetry) to Lucretius and Prudentius (see the following note), and it is a Lucretian term for "atom."

In addition, important to the point at hand is the question of how we are to understand *particulatim.* To this end the author, through a private communication, solicited the expertise of R. Newman, who is presently at work on the *particulatim* article for the *Thesaurus Linguae Latinae.* Prof. Newman was kind enough to disclose his (at this stage) preliminary findings concerning the semantic range of the adverb: of the two major divisions of the meaning, a distributive and a kind of limiting sense, the former "sometimes had a temporal notion attached (both Prudentius and Lucretius fall under this category)." Thus, we should understand *particulatim* (as an atomistic term) not in the sense of "atomwise" (or better, "as concerns atoms," if it should seem best to avoid a trend of modern colloquial English [compare "lengthwise," "leastwise," "moneywise," etc.]), but in that of "atom by atom," on the analogy of *guttatim* ("drop by drop," "in drops").

15. First found in Varro (e.g., *De lingua latina* 5.32), it is also absent from the works of Tertullian, whose *Adversus Praxean* is sometimes mentioned

as a possible source for the *Apotheosis*. R. Newman (see the previous note) has assured the author, who himself had already failed to discover other occurrences of the adverb among all of the major (Lucretius, Vergil, Horace, Ovid, and Juvenal) and most of the minor poets from whom Prudentius borrows, that the Christian and the Epicurean "are the only two poets who use *particulatim;* it is otherwise strictly prosaic."

16. The first half of this line is that of Vergil, *Georgics* 2.301, where, if its precise meaning is not uncontested (see W. Richter's commentary [Munich, 1957], p. 227), the agricultural context at least is certain. In borrowing the hemistich, Prudentius clearly has made it refer to the deep affection of the lofty for the lowly, and apparently means to have it combine the idea of God as the molder of man's clay with that of Christ as the one "planted" in it (compare God's mingling of Christ with *incorruptum solum* at 1038ff.). *Dilectio nostri,* then, is best taken to mean that love which God/Christ, human and divine, bears for "us," his lesser physical and spiritual creations.

17. The notion of Christ as a kind of mirror in which Prudentius sees himself (*me video . . . cerno deum*) contrasts, perhaps intentionally, with the figurative *speculum* of the past (3.972-975) offered the frightened and dying old man addressed by *Natura* at *De rerum natura* 3.931-977. There, as we might anticipate, the universal oblivion and mortality reflected in that mirror bears the image of both present and future. See T. Stork, *NIL IGITUR MORS EST AD NOS: Der Schlussteil des dritten Lukrezbuches und sein Verhältnis zur Konsolationsliteratur* (Bonn, 1970), p. 104.

18. Here (with Lavarenne ["La Mort, vaincue, doit avoir l'honnêteté de ne pas rendre . . ."]) we should regard death, already addressed at line 767, as a personified figure.

19. As a poet, Prudentius apparently felt free to embroider the manner in which this event takes place. Probably the most splendid vision is that of the death of Eulalia (*Peristephanon* 3.161ff.), whose soul departs her body in the form of a pure white dove making for the stars (*astra sequi*).

20. C. Witke, *Numen Litterarum: The Old and the New in Latin Poetry from Constantine to Gregory the Great* (Mittellateinische Studien und Texte 5; Leiden, 1971), p. 113.

21. Nowhere is this difference better expressed than in the closing lines of the "programmatic" *Praefatio*:

> haec dum scribo vel eloquor,

> vinclis o utinam corporis emicem
> liber, quo tulerit lingua sono mobilis ultimo!

> [While I write or recite my poems, O would that I might flash forth, free from the bonds of my body, to where my tongue, stirred by its final utterance, shall go!]

43-45

22. Although Lucretius does not use *membra* in the sense of *atomi,* his thoroughly atomistic thinking about all bodies always at least implies a regard for *membra* (human or otherwise) as an accident of atoms. See, for example, 3.967-969 (*Natura* is speaking [see note 17]):

> materies opus est ut crescant postera saecla;
> quae tamen omnia te vita perfuncta sequentur;
> nec minus ergo ante haec quam tu cecidere cadentque.

> [There must be material (one of Lucretius' terms for *atomi*) so that future ages may grow, yet all that will follow you when life comes to an end. Like you, these things have passed away before and shall pass away no less again.]

It is especially apt for Prudentius to have an "atomic" body in mind at the conclusion of the *Apotheosis*. If, for Lucretius, the *membra* of the human body are real and permanent only at the atomic level, for Prudentius the complete restoration of *membra* in the resurrection proves that the sum of the "parts," the body which is the "brother" of the soul, is absolutely real and, in the end, eternal.

23. Belief, both popular and intellectual, in the aetherial or astral destiny of the soul recurs throughout antiquity. (See R. Lattimore, *Themes in Greek and Latin Epitaphs* [Urbana, 1962], pp. 31ff., for a very useful diachronic overview.) Christians, and certainly Prudentius, add what pagans characteristically regarded with shock and scorn—an "astral destiny" of the body as well. Although at the end of the *Apotheosis* the poet is not explicit about where Christ will lead the newly resurrected body, we may compare *Cathemerinon* 3.196ff.:

> credo equidem (neque vana fides)
> corpora vivere more animae;
> nam modo corporeum memini
> de Flegetonte gradu facili
> ad superos remeasse Deum.

> spes eadem mea membra manet,
> quae redolentia funereo
> iussa quiescere sarcophago
> dux parili redivivus humo
> ignea Christus ad astra vocat.

> [And indeed I believe—nor is it an empty faith—that bodies live in the manner of the soul; for even now I call to mind that a God with a body

returned from Phlegethon to the heavens with an easy step. The same hope awaits my flesh which, smelling of its burial spices and bidden to rest quietly in the tomb, Christ, its leader, risen from the very same earth, summons to the fiery stars.]

See K. Thraede ("'Auferstehung der Toten' im hymnus ante cibum des Prudentius [*Cath.* 3.186-205]," in *Jenseitsvorstellungen in Antike und Christentum: Gedenkschrift für A. Stuiber* [*JbAC* Ergänzungsband 9 (1982)], pp. 68-78) for an appreciation of Prudentius' reworking of traditional themes, especially the Vergilian *descensus* in *Aeneid* 6, in the closing strophes of this poem.

24. This grim *sententia* (ὁ θάνατος οὐθ'εν πρὸς ἡμᾶς [Κύριαι Δόξαι 2, at Diogenes Laertius 10.139; *Epistula ad Menoeceum* 125 = von der Muehll, p. 45, line 19]) is attributed to the sophist Prodicus at *Axiochus* 369b; however, Epicurus, who likely drew, in part at least, on Platonic ideas put forth most explicitly at the conclusion of the *Apology* and in the *Phaedo,* may rightly be judged its originator. (See J. P. Hershbell, *Pseudo-Plato, Axiochus* [Ann Arbor, 1981], pp. 14ff.) In any event, regardless of the true originator, Lucretius almost certainly intended the *sententia* to be taken as one of his master's. We may note that it rather abruptly introduces the third book's final section, a compelling combination of *consolatio* (see T. Stork, *NIL IGITUR* [pp. 25-42 on the dictum]) and diatribe (see B. Wallach, *Lucretius and the Diatribe against the Fear of Death* [Amsterdam, 1976], pp. 11-109 [pp. 11-20 on the dictum]) in which the preceding scientific arguments against the soul's survival give way to the more dramatic rhetorical devices (prosopopeia, for example). The fact that Lucretius' purpose in this section, to prosecute a more emotional disuasion of his audience from the fear of death, nicely parallels the purpose of the brief but empassioned self-consolation which concludes the *Apotheosis* suggests that here again, as in the use of *particulatim,* Prudentius had his eye on the third book of the *De rerum natura.*

The *consolatio* genre, the modern pioneer in whose study was C. Buresch (*Consolationum a Graecis Romanisque scriptorum historia critica* [Leipziger Studien zur klassischen Philologie 9.1; Leipzig, 1886]), has been conveniently reviewed recently by R. C. Gregg in *Consolation Philosophy: Greek and Christian Paideia in Basil and the Two Gregories* (Patristic Monograph Series 3; Cambridge, Mass., 1975), pp. 1-50.

Abbreviations

Titles of classical Greek works are abbreviated as in H. G. Liddell, R. Scott, and H. S. Jones, *A Greek-English Lexicon* (Oxford); titles of patristic Greek works as in G. W. H. Lampe, *A Patristic Greek Lexicon* (Oxford); titles of Latin works as in the *Thesaurus Linguae Latinae* (Leipzig).

BAC: Biblioteca de Autores Cristianos, Madrid

CCSL: Corpus Christianorum, Series Latina, Turnhout

CSEL: Corpus Scriptorum Ecclesiasticorum Latinorum, Vienna

JbAC: Jahrbuch für Antike und Christentum, Münster

RAC: Reallexikon für Antike und Christentum, Stuttgart

Martha A. Malamud (essay date 1989)

SOURCE: Malamud, Martha A. "Words at War." In *A Poetics of Transformation: Prudentius and Classical Mythology,* pp. 47-78. Ithaca, N.Y.: Cornell University Press, 1989.

[*In the following excerpt, Malamud compares and contrasts Prudentius's* Psychomachia *with the works of Claudian.*]

Prudentius' younger contemporary Claudian appears superficially to have been everything Prudentius was not. They were from different parts of the empire—Prudentius from Spain, Claudian from Alexandria. Prudentius was a Latin speaker from a province with a proud literary heritage; Claudian was not a native Latin speaker and composed a number of poems in Greek. Prudentius wrote poetry on Christian subjects, Claudian on traditional pagan themes, such as his unfinished short epic, *De raptu Proserpinae.* Claudian's poetry relies heavily on the traditional apparatus of mythology, while Prudentius (not surprisingly for a poet who writes on Christian themes) eliminated the pagan gods as active participants in the action of his poems. But perhaps the greatest difference is that Claudian was an overtly political poet—much of his poetry was based on contemporary political events—while Prudentius concentrated on metaphysical and theological subjects that seem to have little bearing on the politics of his day.

And yet despite the apparently radical differences between the two men, the relationship between them deserves, as Alan Cameron has suggested, closer study.[1] Not only is there ample evidence of allusions to Claudian in Prudentius' poetry (and, as Cameron suggests, evidence of borrowings from Prudentius in Claudian's), but it can be shown that the two men shared basic thematic preoccupations. Although Prudentius maps the metaphysical realm and Claudian the historical and political, there is a strange congruence in their poetic techniques and in the unstable and often frightening worlds they describe. This similarity goes beyond shared themes and imagery to the way both poets manipulate the classical poetic tradition and to their use of language. In this chapter I begin with a look at how Claudian treats a traditional topos—the *sparagmos,* or dismemberment—and uses it as an emblem for civil strife. I then examine Prudentius' use of the same motif and his development of ideas present in the Claudian passage in the climactic scene of his **Psychomachia.** This scene, the final battle of the war between the personified Virtues and Vices, contains many of the same thematic preoccupations with *discordia* and with thresholds and boundary violations as the **Peristephanon** poems discussed in the next chapters. We also find in both works a persistent tension between imagery of binding and weaving on the one hand and dismemberment and dissolution on the other. An elucidation of Prudentius' sources and his manipulation of language in this scene are a useful introduction to the more complicated and subtle poems of the **Peristephanon.** I focus here on Concord and Discord in the **Psychomachia,** figures with their own genealogy in epic poetry, and conclude by considering the philosophic and political implications of Prudentius' use of the duel between these two figures to end the battle within the soul which forms the subject of the poem.

THE DEATH OF RUFINUS

In Rufinum is Claudian's often surrealistic caricature of the career of Rufinus, the man the Western imperial court loved to hate.[2] Rufinus was the praetorian prefect of the Eastern empire who dominated the ineffectual young emperor Arcadius. The second book of the poem, written not long after Rufinus' dramatic death in 395, has as its climax Rufinus' gruesome assassination at the hands of the army, which took place before the eyes of Arcadius himself. Rufinus is literally torn to pieces by a mob of furious soldiers; in Claudian's version of the story, when the people of Constantinople hear the news, they pour out of the city gates to join in the dismemberment.[3]

Claudian surrounds his account of Rufinus' death with imagery that is both haunting and significant. The actual dismemberment, as we shall see, conjures up predictable allusions to Pentheus (dismembered by a band of Bacchants led by his own mother) and the unfortunate hunter Actaeon (ripped to pieces by his own dogs). Before the actual death, however, Claudian sets the stage for it in a simile comparing Rufinus to a beast doomed to die in the arena:

ut fera, quae nuper montes amisit avitos
altorumque exul nemorum damnatur harenae
muneribus, commota ruit; vir murmure contra

hortatur nixusque genu venabula tendit;
illa pavet strepitus cuneosque erecta theatri
respicit et tanti miratur sibila vulgi.

(*In Ruf.* 2.396-399)

Like a beast who has just been exiled from the mountains where her fathers roamed, banished from the high forests, she is doomed to the games in the arena. She runs in terror; encouraged by the noise, the man kneels to set his net. She is afraid, and standing erect, she looks back at the uproar in the stands of the theater and marvels at the hissing of the huge mob.

This simile does not work, as one might expect it to, as another demonstration of Rufinus' bestiality. Instead, the poet rather subtly emphasizes the human characteristics of the doomed animal in the arena. Once free to wander in the mountains and woods, she is now in exile from her native land and condemned to take part in the gladiatorial games which, as the Roman poets never tired of pointing out, were originally a form of human sacrifice. The beast, through her role in the *muneribus,* acquires the characteristics of a human being: she is endowed with ancestors and a homeland (*avitos montes*); she suffers from emotion (*commota, pavet*); finally, when she hears the crowd and sees the theater, she stands erect (*erecta*) and marvels (*respicit, miratur*) at the animal-like hissings of the mob. The last detail alludes to a philosophic commonplace, that humans alone of all the animals stand erect and look at the heavens and so are inspired to reason. The beast of the simile is thus, at the moment of death, made human by the atrocity she is about to suffer. In the same way, Rufinus, though an entirely unsympathetic and grotesque character throughout the poem, becomes almost human in light of the gruesome death he is about to suffer.

The image suggests another curious reversal of roles as well. Claudian, a pagan poet with little sympathy for Christian conservatism, has nevertheless appropriated one of the archetypal images of Christian martyrdom: death in the arena.[4] The image of the martyr as the athlete of God, winning victory through death in combat, reaches back to the earliest days of the church. But whereas the Christians went unarmed against the wild beasts of the arena, Claudian shows us the more sporting form of gladiatorial combat, with an armed man facing a beast—in this case, a curiously human, defenseless beast. This inversion of the Christian trope is, perhaps, ironic—Claudian may have particularly enjoyed casting Rufinus in the role of "martyred" beast, for he was known for his aggressive persecution of pagans and heretics and for his particular devotion to the cult of the martyrs. He even had a martyrium built at his home in Chalcedon which contained the relics of Saints Peter and Paul (acquired in Rome in 389) and imported a community of monks from Egypt to conduct services.[5]

This reversal of roles extends, as we shall see, beyond the simile to the murder of Rufinus, which one would expect, from the tone of the poem up to this point, to result in the purging of evil from the body politic. Claudian has certainly made no bones about casting Rufinus as the embodiment of evil, but his death does not, in fact, perform this cleansing function. Instead of ending the savagery Rufinus epitomizes, his death, ironically, spreads murderous violence throughout the army and the civilian population. Claudian prefigures the dehumanizing effect of violence on those who commit it in this striking passage, which has the ring of science fiction in its eerie metamorphosis:

> huc ultrix acies ornatu lucida Martis
> explicuit cuneos. pedites in parte sinistra
> consistunt. equites illinc poscentia cursum
> ora reluctantur pressis sedere lupatis;
> hinc alii saevum cristato vertice nutant
> et tremulos umeris gaudent vibrare colores.
> quos operit formatque chalybs; coniuncta per artem
> flexilis inductis animatur lamina membris
> horribiles visu; credas simulacra moveri
> ferrea cognatoque viros spirare metallo.

(In Ruf. 2.351-360)

Now the avenging army, glittering in the spoils of war, deployed its ranks. Foot soldiers stand together on the left; near them horsemen saw at the reins, fighting to restrain their beasts, who yearn to gallop. Over here other men savagely shake their crested heads, making the trembling colors dance along their armored shoulders. Hard iron shrouds and shapes them: artfully joined, link by link, the supple steel breathes life from the flesh inside. It's a horrible sight—you'd think they were moving metal statues, or that men in metal casings could breathe.

The crowd in the arena simile, massed in ranks, *cuneos,* like the soldiers in this passage, become like wild beasts in their anticipation of the bloody games about to take place. The soldiers here, waiting to take part in the murder of Rufinus, undergo a more sinister transformation. In the lines that describe the soldiers and their armor (357-360), the distinction between the animate and the inanimate begins to blur: the armor is alive and seems to draw energy from the men hidden inside it. Claudian emphasizes this strange symbiosis with an anagrammatic wordplay: there is ANIMA, spirit or breath, in the LAMINA, the armor that wraps itself around the limbs of the soldiers; moreover, when read backwards, the word for armor reveals what it is becoming: ANIMAL. This metamorphosis moves both ways, for as the lifeless metal becomes a living thing, the living soldiers become moving statues. These soldiers, hovering between the animate and the inanimate, form a fitting escort for Rufinus as he sets off to his death, for they are *liminal* figures and Rufinus, too, though unwittingly, is poised on the threshold between life and death.

In the actual death scene, we find once more the implication that violence transforms the aggressor into something less than human:

> hi vultus avidos et adhuc spirantia vellunt
> lumina, truncatos alii rapuere lacertos.
> amputat ille pedes, umerum quatit ille solutis
> nexibus; hic fracti reserat curvamina dorsi;
> hic iecur, hic cordis fibras, hic pandit anhelas
> pulmonis latebras. spatium non invenit ira
> nec locus est odiis. consumpto funere vix tum
> deseritur sparsumque perit per tela cadaver.
> sic mons Aonius rubuit, cum Penthea ferrent
> Maenades aut subito mutatum Actaeona cornu
> traderet insanis Latonia visa Molossis.

(In Ruf. 2.410-420)

Some tear at his greedy face and his eyes, still flashing with life; others tear his arms out by the roots and carry them off. One man cuts off a foot, another shakes a shoulder free from its disintegrating joints. One unhinges the curved ribs from his broken spine; one lays bare his liver; someone else explores the gasping caverns of his lungs. Rage can find no space, there is no room for hatred. But even when his death was more than certain, they could hardly leave him, and so they carried his ruined body home on their spears. It was like this when the Aonian mountain turned red with blood when the Maenads slaughtered Pentheus, and when Diana, suddenly discovered, betrayed Actaeon—now a stag, not a man—to his Molossian hounds.

As the attackers dismember Rufinus' body, the crowd becomes fragmented, losing its unanimity and becoming not a group but a collection of individuals, each bent on his own gory task, as *hi . . . alii* gives way in the text to *ille . . . ille . . . hic . . . hic . . . hic,* each man tearing his own piece from the battered body. The men are compared to the Bacchae, who roam the mountains, free of the bonds that hold society together, and to the hounds of Actaeon, who turn on their no longer human master.

Claudian has led us through a series of reversals: Rufinus, through the beast simile, loses his savagery and becomes, for a moment, a human victim, while the soldiers and the people of Constantinople are transformed from Rufinus' long-suffering victims to savage predators. Claudian has used similes, wordplay, and striking imagery to reiterate a theme that the Roman poets, steeped in Rome's bitter heritage of civil strife, return to again and again: that violence is infectious and that you can defeat an enemy only by taking his place—by becoming, that is, what you have fought against. It is this stark vision that prevents *In Rufinum* from falling into the category of sheer personal abuse, for Claudian's concern is more than the simple condemnation of a fallen political enemy. He analyzes the spread of violence, from the top down, through society as a whole.

The Battlefield of Semantics

This concern with the spread of violence and with the uncertain boundaries between friend and foe, victim and victor, is shared by Prudentius and expressed most clearly and dramatically in the *Psychomachia,* his allegorical epic of the inner space of the soul.[6] In a sense, the *Psychomachia* proceeds logically from the groundwork established by Claudian. In the dismemberment scene quoted above, Claudian moves his characters out of the world of the city for the climactic scene of dismemberment. As Rufinus, the soldiers, and finally the citizens of Constantinople leave the civic space enclosed by the city walls, Claudian marks this transition by similes that place the characters in the world of myth. Rufinus' death is described in paradigmatic, mythic terms—he is Pentheus and Actaeon—rather than as a historic incident. And as Rufinus takes on mythic dimensions at the end of the poem, the danger he represents is shown to be something more than the appalling behavior of a single human being. His anger and hatred infect the mob of citizens and soldiers to such an extent that they cannot be contained even after Rufinus is completely disintegrated (*spatium non invenit ira nec locus est odiis,* lines 416-417).

In the *Psychomachia,* Prudentius shows us anger and hatred raging on in battle although his poem takes place in no definable time or space. The locus is not history or even myth, but the timeless world of the psyche, and as the setting is eliminated, so, in a way, are the characters. Instead of using political figures, as Claudian does, or characters from myth, as was the usual epic practice, Prudentius takes the radical step of peopling the blank world of his poem with abstractions—mere words.[7] Prudentius, of course, was not the first writer to introduce personified abstractions as characters in his work. The technique goes back at least as far as the figures on the shield of Achilles in *Iliad* 18, in which Strife, Uproar, and Fate are shown participating in a battle scene. More elaborately, Xenophon shows Heracles forced to choose between Pleasure and Virtue, two abstractions personified as women,[8] and Euripides has Lyssa, the personification of madness, appear as a character in his *Heracles Mainomenos.* Vergil, too, uses personified abstractions in the *Aeneid,* as in this passage describing the gates of Hell:

> vestibulum ante ipsum primusque in faucibus Orci
> Luctus et ultrices posuere cubilia Curae,
> pallantesque habitant Morbi tristisque Senectus,
> et metus et malesuada Fames ac turpis Egestas,
> terribilis visu formae, Letumque Labosque,
> tum consanguineus Letis Sopor et mala mentis
> Gaudia, mortiferumque adversum in limine Bellum,
> ferreique Eumenidum thalami et Discordia demens
> vipereumque crinem vittis innexa cruentis.
>
> (*Aen.* 6.273-281)

Before the very entrance, just inside the jaws of Orcus, Grief and the vengeful Cares have set their couches. There live the pale and trembling Diseases and sad Old Age, Fear and evil-counseling Hunger, and squalid Poverty—shapes horrible to see. And Death is there, and Toil; Death's brother Sleep and the evil Pleasures of the mind. Facing these on the threshold are deadly War, the iron chambers of the Furies, and mad Discord, her hair bound with sacred ribbons stained with blood.

Vergil, however, seldom shows us his abstractions interacting with his other characters. They are there to form allegorical set pieces, and they remain outside the main action of the epic. This is not true in the strange and chaotic world of Statius' *Thebaid,* in which gods, humans, and personified abstractions mix indiscriminately, and any action carried out at one level of the narrative reverberates through the whole. Prudentius, in the *Psychomachia,* carries Statius' technique to its logical extreme—he eliminates the human characters entirely, except for occasional Old Testament figures in the background. (One could argue that he sees these as allegorical as well—figural types who foreshadow New Testament personages and symbolize the state of the individual soul.) Only the abstractions remain.[9]

In Prudentius' poem, the words themselves do battle, carrying out their struggle on the field of semantics. As the personified abstractions move through their series of combats, it becomes evident that puns, etymological wordplays, allusions to classical and biblical texts, and similes are more than elaborate ornaments decorating the surface of the text. Rather, they control the action and shape of the poem. The function of Prudentius' allegory is not simply to tell a story—the *Psychomachia* has very little plot, and what there is is entirely predictable—but also to force the reader to become a player in Prudentius' poetic game. Like the player of the *ostomachia,* the reader of the *Psychomachia* is free to manipulate the poetic "bones" into whatever semblance of reality he chooses (with helpful hints provided by the poet).

In the *Psychomachia* Prudentius appears to have created a new genre of poetry, and in so doing, he has laid his poetic cards on the table. His choice of the sustained personification allegory directs the reader's attenton to his treatment of characters not as people or as symbols whose meaning is always fixed, but as signs whose meaning is variable and inconstant. The paradox of Prudentius' technique is that by creating iconographically clear allegorical figures out of words, and giving them the ability to act, he endows his abstractions with all the inconsistencies and ambiguities of human characters.

Concordia and Discordia

The *Psychomachia,* in a sense, has a false ending. The poem consists of seven battles, each between one or more of the Virtues, who are professed Christians, and the Vices, who, in addition to being vicious, are pagans as well. Like the simile in Claudian's *In Rufinum* which we examined above, the battles here suggest the arena rather than the battlefield as their setting. In most cases, the fighting in the poem is done in single combat. But despite the gladiatorial atmosphere, the Virtues in the poem are by no means martyrs. They do not submit to death and claim it as a form of victory, but rather they participate in combat ferociously and inflict gruesome wounds and hideous deaths upon their enemies. A number of critics have noticed the paradox of this unchristian blood-thirstiness in the Virtues, but they generally have ascribed it to Prudentius' and his era's lack of good taste or to his Spanish blood.[10] In the analysis of the battle between Concordia and Discordia which follows I suggest an alternative explanation for the Virtues' puzzling behavior, for the outcome of their combat, which seems to end forever the battle in the soul, is not as decisive a victory for the Virtues as it appears to be.

After the Virtues seem to have defeated their enemies conclusively in six major battles, Concordia appears on the scene, leading the victorious army into the walls of their camp. The army, however, has been infiltrated: Concordia's opposite, Discordia, has thrown off the whip and torn robe that emblematize her disruptive power and assumed the dress, the pacific olive wreath, and the joyful expression of the Virtues. Thus disguised, she gets close enough to Concordia to attack her with a concealed weapon. She is unable to kill the Virtue, but she does manage to inflict a flesh wound, the only casualty the Virtues suffer in the war.

The infuriated Virtues instantly surround Discordia and demand to know her name, her allegiance, and who sent her. She replies with a disjointed but disdainful speech, announcing that she is Discord, also known as Heresy, and that the god she worships is ever changing and inconstant. Her short speech so angers and alarms Fides that she transfixes Discordia's tongue with a javelin (one of several instances of mutilated tongues in Prudentius' poetry).[11] Once Discordia's tongue has been pinned, the rest of the Virtues descend upon her and tear her limb from limb, just as the vengeful soldiers tore apart the wretched Rufinus. The remains of her dismembered body are hurled to the beasts of the earth, sea, and sky. This scene recalls not only the death of Rufinus but also the brutal dismemberment of the classical hero Hippolytus, as we shall see in the next chapter.

Throughout the episode, Prudentius puts a particular emphasis on thresholds, stressing the liminality of the scene. When Discordia makes her appearance, for example, the Virtues are just about to cross the double-doored entrance to their camp. Prudentius packs his

verses with words that mean door, threshold, entrance, hinge, and so on:

> ventum erat ad fauces portae castrensis, ubi artum
> liminis introitum bifori dant cardine claustra.
> nascitur hic inopina Mali lacrimabilis astu
> tempestas, placidae turbatrix invida Pacis
> quae tantum subita vexaret clade triumphum.

(*Ps.* [*Psychomachia*] 665-669)

They had come to the mouth of the camp gate, where the bolts hung on the hinge of the double doors opened a narrow entry to the threshold. Here a sudden cyclone springs up: born of the cunning of that lamentable Evil, the jealous one who shatters placid Peace, it would whirl the great triumph into sudden slaughter.

The description of the entrance is unusually elaborate; the threshold, with its well-defended gates, marks the boundary between the Virtues' camp and the battlefield. Discordia, by her very nature, is best suited to functioning in just such an ambiguous area, for it is characteristic of her to be neither one thing nor another. She is a master of disguise, and it is her ability to be indistinguishable from the Virtues that makes her the most dangerous of all the Vices. Prudentius' description of her disguise, particularly by his allusion to classical texts, reinforces this aspect of her nature:

> nam pulsa Culparum acie Discordia nostros
> intrarat cuneos sociam mentita figuram,
> scissa procul palla structum et serpente flagellum
> multiplici media camporum in strage iacebant.
> ipsa redimitos olea frondente capillos
> ostentans festis respondet laeta choraeis.

(*Ps.* 683-688)

For when the army of the Faults had been beaten back, Discordia entered our ranks as an ally, her shape transformed. Her torn robe and whip of twisted snakes were lying far away at the center of the battlefield's web of slaughter. Holding high her head, she happily joins the victory song.

Discordia's snaky whip is an obvious allusion to the Furies; interestingly enough, the disguise she wears links her to the Furies as much as her normal costume does. Prudentius has modeled his scene on *Aeneid* 7, in which the Fury Allecto appears in disguise to incite Turnus to war:

> Allecto torvam faciem et furalia membra
> exuit in vultus sese transformat anilis
> et frontam obscenam rugis arat, induit albos
> cum vitta crinis, tum ramum innectit olivae.

(*Aen.* 7.415-418)

Allecto shed her twisted frown and her Fury's form and changed herself into the shape of an old woman, tracing furrows on her obscene brow. She put on white hair and a sacred headband woven with an olive branch.

In this passage Allecto appears to the sleeping Turnus disguised as Calybe ("Veiled One"), a priestess of Juno. Like Discordia, she transforms her features and wears a wreath of deceptively peaceful olive in her snowy hair. Her mission is to bring Turnus and the Latins to war with the Trojans by driving Turnus mad with jealousy and battle lust; she is thus the immediate catalyst for the war that breaks out between the two races who would one day found Rome. In a similar scene from the *Thebaid,* the ghost of Oedipus' father Laius appears to his grandson Eteocles; his purpose, like Allecto's, is to provide the immediate impulse for war, this time between the feuding sons of Oedipus, Eteocles and his twin brother Polyneices. Laius' ghost, like Allecto and Discordia, assumes a false appearance for his mission: he puts on the form of Tiresias, the blind seer, and his hair, too, is bound with a deceptive olive wreath.[12] By adopting this topos, Prudentius makes ambiguity and false appearance as much a part of Discordia's nature as strife and violence. Discordia's ability to assimilate herself to her opponents is remarkable, and Prudentius subtly emphasizes this by his verse. As soon as the olive wreath is twined into the Vice's now neatly bound hair, there is a perfect golden line (a five-word hexameter line with a symmetrical arrangement of nouns and adjectives around a central verb). As Discordia's normal attributes are cloaked by her peaceful disguise, the verse achieves apparent harmony in a line that shows her singing in concert with the army of Virtues: *ostentans festis respondet laeta choreis.*

Concordia, who bears the brunt of Discordia's sneak attack, is also distinguished by a significant costume. She is clad in a remarkable suit of bristling armor, which Prudentius describes in verses that themselves bristle with densely packed *c, t, x,* and *s* sounds:

> inter confertos cuneos Concordia forte
> dum stipata pedem iam tutis moenibus infert,
> excipit occultum Vitii latitantis ab ictu
> mucronem laevo in latere, squalentia quamvis
> texta catenato ferri subtegmine corpus
> ambirent sutis et acumen vulneris hamis
> respuerent, rigidis nec fila tenacia nodis
> impactum sinerent penetrare in viscera telum.
> rara tamen chalybem tenui transmittere puncto
> commissura dedit, qua sese extrema politae
> squama ligat tunicae, sinus et sibi conserit oras.

> (*Ps.* 670-680)

Concordia by chance was coming through the congregated companies of men, surrounded by a crowd, ready to set foot at last inside the safety of the walls. Suddenly her left side felt a hidden blade, the blow of the lurking Vice, though a scaly fabric woven from chains of steel wound about her body, repelling wounding weapons with woven hooks, and the tenacious threads, tied in rigid knots, would not allow a weapon's thrust to penetrate her heart. But just on the edge where the outer links of the bright tunic joined with the breast-piece, a fine blade slipped through the boundary between the pieces.

Concordia is characterized by language and imagery that strongly suggest restraint and enclosure—so strongly, indeed, that one might say she is caricatured rather than characterized. She appears surrounded by a crowd of massed soldiers (*confertos cuneos*), and her movement is toward the inside of the massively fortified camp. Not only do her circumstances and her movements suggest enclosure, but the description of her armor abounds with images of binding and restraint. The armor is woven from chain mail (*squalentia . . . texta catenato ferri*); its stiff threads are tied together in rigid knots (*rigidis . . . fila tenacia nodis*). The only chink in her armor is, significantly, at the boundary between two of its parts, the liminal area that belongs by rights to Discordia, whose own disintegrating dress is the exact opposite of Concordia's tightly woven chain mail.

DISCORDIA DISMEMBERED

Discordia, as we have seen, represents not only physical disintegration and dismemberment, but also disguise and deceit. Her speech after her capture reveals her essential personality and raises serious questions about the nature of language in the poem:

> circumstat propere strictis mucronibus omnis
> Virtutum legio exquirens fervente tumultu
> et genus et nomen, patriam sectamque, deumque
> quem colat et missu cuiatis venerit. illa
> exsanguis turbante metu: "Discordia dicor,
> cognomento Heresis; Deus est mihi discolor," inquit,
> "nunc minor aut maior, modo duplex et modo simplex,
> cum placet, aerius et de phantasmate visus,
> aut innata anima est quotiens volo ludere numen;
> praeceptor Belia mihi, domus et plaga mundus.

> (*Ps.* 705-714)

Instantly the whole army of Virtues surrounds her, swords drawn, demanding through the seething confusion her family, her name, her country, and her sect, which God she worshipped, and who had sent her. White with whirling fear, she says: "I am called Discord. My other name is Heresy. My God is variable—sometimes small, sometimes huge; sometimes two, sometimes one. When I wish, he seems like an airy phantom; or when I want to play tricks with divine power, he is the inborn soul. Belial is my teacher, the world is my territory and my home."

Despite her fear, Discordia is able to identify herself in a series of soundplays on her name, linking the concept of *discordia* with language and the shifting world of false appearances. The punning echoes of her own name in the series *Discordia dicor . . . Deus est mihi discolor* suggest, through the repetition of rhyming syllables, that the act of speech itself (*dicor*) is a form of *discordia*—the unreliable sounds that shift their meaning according to context in a Lucretian manner seem to demonstrate the impossibility of finding stable signs to represent true meanings. The use of the adjective *discolor*, "of variable color," appears motivated by its sound, allowing Prudentius, through the similarity of the words, to establish a connection with the world of shifting appearances on etymological grounds. *Discolor* is a relatively unusual adjective; perhaps the best known use of it is in *Aeneid* 6, in which it describes the strange appearance of the golden bough, the mysterious token that allows Aeneas to make the transition from the world of the living to the world below.[13] If this echo is deliberate, it reminds us once again that Discordia is constantly associated with liminal areas.

Discordia calls attention to her own facility with wordplay when she boasts of her different definitions of God—she calls this playing (*ludere*) with his divinity (*numen*). In fact, she has just finished reeling off a series of plays on her own *nomen*. By including *deus* in the series of words playing off the sounds of *discordia*, she has attempted to confine God, the master binder himself, in her disintegrating web of words. For although her webs disintegrate as quickly as she weaves them, Discordia is a weaver of sorts as well, as the language of the passage indicates. The repetition of *plex* in *simplex* and *duplex* recalls the *multiplici . . . strage* (line 686), "manifold slaughter," of the battlefield, where she hid her torn robe and whip before assuming her deceptive disguise. The repetition of the *plic* root hints at her connection with the dangerous side of weaving imagery, the cunning snare and the net, instruments of complicated deceit.

Discordia's speech reveals an underlying dynamic of the ***Psychomachia***. From one point of view, the speech violates the sense of the narrative—it is difficult to accept that Discordia, whose very nature is to be ambiguous and deceptive, would deliver such a straightforward and honest description of herself, and yet she does. Her speech is not deceptive, but it is nevertheless characteristic of her nature. Instead of trying to maintain her disguise, Discordia chooses an even more radical and unsettling move: she tries to undermine language by revealing its arbitrary nature. It is no wonder that Fides, the leader of the Virtues and the one most concerned with the language of truth, is unable to endure Discordia's speech and tries to stop her appropriation of language by transfixing her tongue, the instrument of ambiguity, with her spear:

> non tulit ulterius capti blasphemia monstri
> Virtutum regina Fides, sed verba loquentis

> impedit et vocis claudit spiramina pilo,
> pollutam rigida transfigens cuspide linguam.

> (*Ps.* 715-718)

> Unable to endure the captive monster's blasphemies any longer, Faith, queen of the Virtues, cut off Discordia's words as she spoke, closing off her vocal chords with a javelin and then transfixing her polluted tongue with a rigid spear.

By stopping Discordia's tongue, Fides attempts to prevent her polysemous punning and her dissemination of ambiguity.[14] The verse echoes this effort to achieve clarity in another golden line (718), this one with the pattern adjective, adjective, verb, noun, noun, but the effort is in vain. The Virtues kill Discordia, to be sure, but instead of enclosing her and containing her dangerous force, they, in their fury, rip her body to pieces and disseminate it through each of the three realms: earth, air, and sea. Discordia's death echoes Claudian's description of the death of Rufinus, and as in that passage, there is a reversal of roles at the moment of death. The Virtues, imbued with their opponent's divisive nature, become agents of dismemberment and dissolution.

This is not a random echo on Prudentius' part. Discordia's death is the climax of the ***Psychomachia*** and thus carries great thematic significance. Furthermore, it is unlikely that any of Prudentius' contemporaries would have missed an allusion to a recent event as important and as well publicized as Rufinus' spectacular assassination. There is at the very least a heavy irony in Prudentius' decision to use Rufinus' death as the model for the death of Discordia *cognomento Heresis*, and it is an irony that saps the foundations of any "straight" interpretation of the ***Psychomachia***. For Rufinus, whatever his other character defects may have been, was, as we have noted, a pious orthodox Christian well known for his persecution of heretics. To find him the model for the personification of Heresy, and at the very climax of Prudentius' poem, calls for some explanation.

But indeed the unexpected allusion to Rufinus and the strange reversal of roles between Virtues and Vice at the moment of Discordia's death are part of a pattern that runs throughout the ***Psychomachia***. The relationship between the Virtues and the Vices is consistently problematic. As Georgia Nugent remarks, "Just as on the narrative level the poem unmasks from time to time the myth that *virtus* and *vitium* are neat polarities, so linguistically *virtus* is not irrevocably fixed as one stable term in a polar opposition but can mediate between virtue and vice, expressing the powers of either."[15] Throughout the poem Prudentius makes it clear that the Virtues and the Vices have at least one thing in common: *vis*, or "force." *Virtus*, in one of its more general meanings (strength or force) is used to describe both the Virtues and the Vices, and this common name shows their fundamental similarity. They are not so much opposing moral categories as opposing *forces*. Though the battles maintain the fiction of ending consistently in decisive victory for the Virtues, one finds on closer inspection that Vice and Virtue exchange roles. To conquer a given Vice, the opposing Virtue must adopt some of her characteristics. One example serves particularly well. When Superbia (Pride) has fallen into a trap, her opponent, Mens Humilis (Humility), stands by the pit, smiling modestly and assuming a friendly expression hardly (as has been pointed out) appropriate to the occasion: *os quoque parce erigit et comi moderatur gaudia vultu*. She appears content to watch her enemy writhing at the bottom of the pit with a broken leg until Spes (Hope) comes forward to urge her on to the kill. Spes brings with her a sword—and something else:

> cunctanti Spes fida comes succurrit et offert
> ultorem gladium laudisque inspirat amorem.

> (*Ps.* 278-279)

> As she hesitates, her faithful companion Hope runs up to help, and offers her a sword of vengeance, breathing into her the love of glory.

Laudis amor, the fatal desire for glory that brings so many Vergilian heroes to their deaths, is an attribute that surely belongs by rights to Superbia, not her humble opponent. It is not until she has absorbed this dangerous desire that Mens Humilis can bring herself to cut off her opponent's head.

Thus, though the two armies oppose each other, they are not polar opposites. There is a middle ground of ambiguity where Vices and Virtues meet and are difficult to distinguish, expressed in the text by such puzzling events as the Vices claiming to possess *virtus,* and Mens Humilis propelled into violent action by the lust for fame. The same sort of opposition, in which the identities of the opponents are partially merged even though one is annihilated, is operating in the battle between Concordia and Discordia. This final battle is fought out on a topological middle ground. It takes place on the threshold of the camp, somewhere between the inside, the realm of Concordia, and the unlimited outside, the realm of Discordia, who knows no limits. That the enemies have something in common is emphasized by a point embedded in the most literal level of the text. If we strip both Concordia and Discordia of their prefixes and suffixes, we find the same root at the center of their names: COR, "heart." Concordia and Discordia, in their ambivalent relationship to one another, epitomize the battle in the heart that is the ***Psychomachia***'s subject. In the tradition of Latin epic, which finds all civil wars ultimately self-destructive, we

find in the desperate struggle of the Virtues to overcome the Vices a peculiar exchange of attributes between victor and vanquished. Just as Rufinus' attackers descended to the level of animals as a result of their vicious hatred of him, so the Virtues assimilate the disintegrating force of Discordia which they have been fighting against. Thus the stage is set for yet another cycle of this brutal war.

The poem ends in apparent harmony, with the establishment of a temple to Christ. Yet the possibility for further conflict is there. Discordia's disguise, so much like the disguises of Allecto and Laius, points to that possibility. Allecto and Laius are catalysts of wars that spin out of control, ominous precedents for this battle. Furthermore, the allusion to Rufinus removes the battle between orthodoxy and heresy from the realm of the purely abstract to the issues of Prudentius' own day, anchoring the poem for the first time in contemporary history. To find Rufinus the model for political discord is not surprising, but to find him the model for heresy is paradoxical, and it is this paradox that points to one of the deeper issues of the poem.

Prudentius and Claudian seem to interpret the death of Rufinus in similar ways. Claudian appreciates the irony of the persecutor persecuted, as we see from his beast-in-the-arena simile, and condemns Rufinus even in death for spreading violence throughout society. Prudentius uses Rufinus as his model for Heresy to point to the same issues. We must remember that persecution of heretic Christians was a new development in the late fourth century, and one that was not greeted with enthusiasm by all Christians, orthodox or otherwise. Many saw it as a policy that was tearing the church apart—Martin of Tours, a man of impeccable orthodoxy, tried to intervene on behalf of Priscillian and his followers in one of the earliest cases of government suppression of heresy. It is at least conceivable that Prudentius, by modeling Discordia on Rufinus and recalling his physical dismemberment at the hands of a mob of angry soldiers, was implicitly criticizing not only Rufinus, but also the government policy of religious intolerance Rufinus worked so hard to implement for Theodosius. For Prudentius, though a Christian, was not an intolerant one: he even made a plea to Honorius to allow pagan statues and temples to stand unharmed and used the dead Theodosius as his mouthpiece.

Thus the final battle of the ***Psychomachia*** ends in a Pyrrhic victory for the Virtues. Discordia, though she appears to end the conflict by her defeat in the seventh and apparently conclusive battle of the poem, nevertheless takes her place beside Allecto and the ghost of Laius as a catalyst, spreading violence and disruption into the army of the Virtues. The stage is set for the battle in the soul to continue at a new level of intensity—and as we shall see in the next section, the battle in the soul is only a small-scale model of chaos and confusion on the larger levels of the state and the cosmos.

CIVIL DISCORD

Prudentius' Discordia is not entirely his own invention. The personification of Discordia is something of a to-pos in Latin epic poetry, and the imagery of binding and weaving which Prudentius associates so strongly with both Concordia and Discordia has a clearly traceable origin in Stoic philosophy and poetry. We will look first at Discordia as she appears in the *Aeneid* and in Petronius' *Bellum civile,* where she is an emblem of civil strife, and then we will consider the Stoic image of the binding of the cosmos, which was adopted and reversed by Lucan, Manilius, and Prudentius himself.

Despite Prudentius' decision to locate the ***Psychomachia*** in a world outside of history, his poem is not without political overtones, as we have seen. The allusion to Rufinus' death, which must have been an extremely dramatic political event, anchors the poem in time and suggests that Prudentius' model of civil war in the soul reflected the civil and religious strife that was straining the resources of the empire to the breaking point in Prudentius' day. Discordia, though certainly associated with Heresy in the ***Psychomachia,*** is above all else a *political* figure in earlier epics. In the *Aeneid* she appears as one of the figures from Roman history which adorn Aeneas' shield:

> . . . saevit medio in certamine Mavors
> caelatus ferro, tristesque ex aethere Dirae,
> et scissa gaudens vadit Discordia palla,
> quam cum sanguineo sequitur Bellona flagello.

(Aen. 8.700-703)

In the middle of the battle rages the war god Mars, carved in steel, and sorrow-making Dirae from heaven, and Discord in her torn robes strides along rejoicing, while Bellona follows with her bloody whip.

Discordia and her companions—the Dirae, Mars, and Bellona—are at the center of Vulcan's depiction of Actium, the final battle of Rome's bloody civil war. She has the torn cloak, which she discards in favor of a disguise in Prudentius' poem, but the whip she carries belongs here to Bellona, who follows her into battle.

Discordia is given a larger role, with a speaking part, in Petronius' *Bellum civile,* which appears to be a parody of Lucan's *Pharsalia.*[16] The poem, which describes the Roman civil war, is going to be a *proper* epic, as its narrator carefully explains beforehand, with *ambages* (digressions) and plenty of divine machinery (unlike Lucan's poem, which does have digressions, but which

lacks gods). Discordia is only one of a number of personified figures and interfering deities in the poem, which features appearances by Dis, Mars, Fors, and Fama, among others. Petronius gives a far more elaborate description of the goddess' appearance than Vergil does:

> Intremuere tubae ac scissa Discordia crine
> extulit ad superos Stygium caput. Huius in ore
> concretus sanguis, contusaque lumina flebant,
> stabant aerati scabra rubigine dentes,
> tabo lingua fluens, obsessa draconibus ora,
> atque inter torto laceratam pectore vestem
> sanguineam tremula quatiebat lampada dextra.

(B.C. 271-277)

The trumpets wavered. Discord, her hair all torn, raised her hellish head to the heavens. Blood was scabbed on her face; her bruised eyes oozed with tears; her brassy teeth stood covered in scaly rust. Her tongue drooled rot; her face was besieged by snakes. A torn and bloody garment covered her twisted breast, and her trembling hand brandished a torch.

Her mission, like that of Allecto in *Aeneid* 7, is to stir Italy into civil war, and she barks out orders to the chief political figures of the day, including Caesar, Curio, and Pompey:

> "Tu legem, Marcelle, tene. Tu concute plebem,
> Curio. Tu fortem, ne supprime, Lentule, Martem.
> Quid porro tu, dive, tuis cunctaris in armis,
> non frangis portas, non muris oppida solvis
> thesaurosque rapis? Nescis tu, Magne, tueri
> Romanos arces? Epidamnia moenia quaere
> Thessalicosque sinus humano sanguine tingue."
> Factum est in terris quicquid Discordia iussit.

(B.C. 288-295)

"Cling to your legalities, Marcellus; Curio, strike at the common people. Lentulus, don't try to suppress the war god's force. And you, divine one, why are you holding back your weapons? Why don't you break down the gates, shatter the town walls, and carry away the spoils? And you, great Pompey, have you forgotten how to defend the Roman citadel? Then go to the walls of Epidamnus and dye Thessalian harbors red with human blood." And all that Discord ordered was done on earth.

This Discordia is a ludicrously overdrawn figure, with her bruised and weeping eyes, blood-smeared face, and rusty teeth, but her role in the parody as the instigator of civil strife shows that her image as an icon of civil war was so common as to be a cliché. Prudentius has borrowed this highly politicized figure from the earlier poets and used her to represent strife on the microcosmic level of the soul. But by her very appearance, and by the similarity of her death to that of the once powerful politician Rufinus, he reminds us that Rome could not, in his day, shed the divisive legacy of civil war. The strife between brothers which marked Rome's birth still plagued the empire more than a thousand years later.

COSMIC DISCORD

The final battle of the **Psychomachia** is connected, through poetic allusions and elaborate imagery, not only to the political theme of civil war, but also to philosophic speculations about the destruction of the cosmos. Concordia's armor and Discordia's dress form an iconographic representation of a metaphor that pervades Prudentius' poetry and was widespread in later Latin literature. This is the metaphor of cosmic binding, which Michael Lapidge has traced from the Stoic philosopher Chrysippus through Cicero, Manilius, and Lucan, to the church fathers and the poets of Late Antiquity.[17]

According to Chrysippus, the matter that makes up the cosmos is permeated by a fiery substance (*pneuma*, breath), which, by its movement in the mass of matter, creates a "pneumatic tension" (*pneumatikos tonos*) that holds the universe together and keeps the elements from disintegrating. He called this tension a bond (*desmos*). Cicero, recapitulating his theory in *De natura deorum,* translates *desmos* as *vinculum* (chain).[18] The Latin poets adopted the metaphor of the bond or chain as an image of cosmic harmony. Lucan shifts his emphasis from the bonds that maintain the universe to the universal destruction that arises when the bonds are broken. In this evocative passage from *Pharsalia* 1, he imagines the catastrophic Roman civil war as an event that loosens the bonds of the cosmos and plunges the entire physical universe into chaos:

> invida fatorum series summisque negatum
> stare diu nimioque graves sub pondere lapsus
> nec se Roma ferens. sic, cum compage soluta
> saecula tot mundi suprema coegerit hora,
> antiquum repetens iterum chaos, omnia mixtis
> sidera sideribus concurrent ignea pontum
> astra petent, tellus extendere littora nolet
> excutietque fretum, fratri contraria Phoebe
> ibit et obliquum bigas agitare per orbem
> indignata diem poscet sibi, totaque discors
> machina divolsi turbabit foedera mundi.
> in se magna ruunt: laetis hunc nomina rebus
> crescendi posuere modum.

> (*Phars.* 1.70-82)

It was a thread spun by the jealous fates; a fall from the heights where no one stands for long; a terrible collapse under an impossible weight: it was Rome, unable to bear the burden of herself. So, when the fabric of the universe is dissolved and the world's last hour puts an end to the ages, the constellations will collide, star upon star, seeking to drown their fires in the sea. The earth will roll up her flat shores and shake off the waters of the sea; the moon, shamed by her chariot's oblique path, will defy her brother and demand the day for herself; and the whole disheartened, disjointed machine of the shattered universe will turn upon its own laws and break them. Great things are ruined from within— the gods have put a limit on success.

For Lucan, the dissolution of the microcosmic bond of human society is the first break in the chain, the beginning of an unstoppable plunge into universal chaos and confusion.[19]

The idea of the bond that maintains universal harmony was congenial to Christian writers as well as to Stoics. The Christians adopt the notion that God maintains order through the bond of *philia*, love, and they accept Philo's notion that the name of the Lord (*despotes*) is derived from *desmos,* bond, because it is God who binds the universe together and keeps it in harmony. Prudentius, in another of his poems, the **Hamartigenia,** or "Origin of Sin," takes up the motif of cosmic bonding at length in a passage that strongly recalls Lucan's picture of universal dissolution:

> ipsa quoque oppositum destructo foedere certo
> transcendunt elementa modum rapiuntque ruuntque
> omnia legirupis quassantia viribus orbem.
> frangunt umbriferos aquilonum proelia lucos,
> et cadit immodicis silva exstirpata procellis. . . .
> nec tamen his tantam rabiem nascentibus ipse
> conditor instituit, sed laxa licentia rerum
> turbavit placidas rupto moderamine leges.
> nec mirum si membra orbis concussa rotantur,
> si vitiis agitata suis mundana laborat
> machina, si terras luis incentiva fatigat.
> exemplum dat vita hominum, quo cetera peccent.

> (**Ham.** [*Hamartigenia*] 236-240, 244-250)

Once the alliance is shattered, the elements themselves exceed their limits. All things hurtle into ruin; the energy released from the broken laws shakes the universe. The battling winds snap the shady trees of the forest, and the whole wood comes crashing down, uprooted by the limitless power of the storm. . . . But the Creator himself planted no such wrath in the world at its birth. Freedom, too much freedom threw the peaceful laws into turmoil and shattered all restraint. No wonder the stunned planet is sent spinning; no wonder the great machine of the universe, driven from within by its own flaws, staggers and strains, and a burning wave of corruption beats upon the lands! It is man who sets the pattern for the world's sins.

Here the elements break their bonds and shake the universe, causing a universal tempest. Prudentius' description of the forest uprooted by the blasts of storm winds is a metaphor for the destruction of the universe, a metaphor based on etymology, for *silva*, the word for forest, is a translation of the Greek *hule,* which means both "wood" (or "forest") and "matter." Servius, commenting on *Aeneid* 1.314, says:

> quam Graeci hulen vocant, poetae nominant silvam, id est elementorum congeriem unde cuncta procreantur.

What the Greeks call *hule,* the poets call *silva* (wood), that is, the gathering of elements from which all things are created.

MASTER BINDERS: GOD AND THE POET

The collapsing bonds of the universe are mirrored in the apparent disintegration of Prudentius' own verse in the passage just quoted from the *Hamartigenia.* Immediately before the passage, Prudentius placed the line *pabula lascivis dederit sincera capellis.* This is a perfect golden line, with the symmetrical arrangement noun, adjective, verb, adjective, noun. In the verses that follow, describing the chaos of the universe, he repeatedly uses five-word lines, but he never quite manages to come up with another that has a verb in the middle balancing a pair of words on either side in symmetrical arrangement. For example, in line 246, *turbavit placidas rupto moderamine leges,* the verb *turbavit* is at the beginning of the line instead of the middle and thus disturbs the orderly progress of the verse as much as its subject, *laxa licentia rerum,* disturbs the peaceful laws of the universe. The obvious parallel between the collapse of the universe and the collapse of the poet's verse suggests a parallel between the two creators, God and poet. The metaphor of binding which Prudentius applies to God is also his metaphor for poetic creation. In *Cathemerinon* 3, for example, he speaks of his poems as a wreath or crown:

> sperne, Camena, leves hederas,
> cingere tempora quis solita es,
> sertaque mystica dactylico
> texere docta liga strophio,
> laude Dei redimita comas.

> **(Cath. [Cathemerinon] 3.26-30)**

Muse, put away the light ivy you use to crown your brow. Learn to weave mystic garlands and bind them with a ribbon of dactyls; decorate your hair with praise of God.

Here Prudentius picks up an ancient topos, one that goes back at least as far as Pindar's *Odes.* The poet wins a double crown: the first is in token of his mastery of the art of weaving verses, and the second is the verse itself, thought of as a woven crown of flowers that will never fade. The notion of the poet as master of the power of binding and weaving was an essential part of Prudentius' poetic persona and is a dominant motif in his *Peristephanon* ("On the Crowns").

Yet despite its associations with divine creation and the production of poetry, weaving and binding imagery is not uniformly benign in Prudentius' poetry. In his *Preface,* for example, Prudentius uses the metaphor of cosmic binding to describe God's creative powers, but the harmony of the universe does not necessarily bode well for the poet:

> per quinquennia iam decem
>   ni fallor, fuimus; septimus insuper
>   annum cardo rotat, dum fruimur sole volubili.

> instat terminus, et diem
>   vicinum senio iam Deus adplicat.

> **(Praef. 1-5)**

I have lived, if I'm not deceived, for five decades now. On top of that, the turning world spins a seventh year, while I enjoy the swift sun. The end presses upon me, and the day God weaves now is close to old age.

The beginning of the poem is about time. Prudentius describes the spinning of the sun and the turning of the vault of the sky in words that suggest the inevitable turning of the Fates' spindle. After the turning and spinning imagery, we find God at work weaving the fabric of space and time—but, significantly, what he weaves for the poet is old age and death. Spinning and weaving, though creative, are at the same time binding forces, and Prudentius longs for release and freedom. He closes the poem with this wish:

> haec dum scribo vel eloquor
>   vinclis o utinam corporis emicem
>   liber, quo tulerit lingua sono mobilis ultimo.

> **(Praef. 43-45)**

As I write and speak these things, I wish I could flash forth, free of the chains of the flesh, to where my mobile tongue would guide me with its final note.

In this final verse, Prudentius' poetry becomes the potential instrument of his liberation. He would follow his tongue and transcend the bonds that restrain him: the poetic book, *liber,* which this preface introduces, will make him *liber,* free.[20]

Returning now to the *Psychomachia,* we can better understand the paradoxical force of the binding and weaving imagery in the poem's final battle. Concordia's armor, as closely woven as a garment can be, marks her as a representative of the powerful force shared by God and the poet himself, who hopes to use the power of binding as an instrument of release. Concordia's strangely martial appearance (one would expect her to be the most peaceful of the Virtues) and the bristling, unpleasant sound of the verses that describe her armor, alert us to the ambiguity of this force, which can be either harmonious and creative or violent and repressive. Discordia represents the equally powerful force of dissolution and disintegration, a negative force in the context of the *Psychomachia,* but with its positive side as well, for it can be a means of liberation and release from bondage. The tension between the two forces, and between the conflicting values that can be ascribed to each, is dramatically played out in the final battle of the *Psychomachia.* But the reversal of roles between Virtues and Vices, the association of Discordia with figures who begin rather than end epic cycles of violence, and the disintegration of language we witness in the final battle lead us to question the apparently peaceful resolution of conflict at the end of the poem. In the chapters that follow, we shall see how Prudentius develops some of the themes suggested in this discussion. Binding and dismemberment are important images in his portrayal of the Christian Saint Hippolytus, whose death by dismemberment is based in part on the death of Rufinus and on Prudentius' own description of the death of Discordia. Tracing this imagery through the poems about Hippolytus, Cyprian, and Agnes will enable us to learn much about Prudentius' poetic technique and will shed some light upon his manipulation of myth, history, and the poetic tradition.

Notes

1. Alan Cameron, *Claudian: Poetry and Propaganda at the Court of Honorius* (Oxford, 1970), app. B.

2. Cameron, *Claudian*, pp. 63-92, discusses Rufinus' career and some of the political reasons for Claudian's savage treatment of him in the poem. For more about Rufinus, see also the introduction to Harry Levy's edition of *In Rufinum* (New York, 1935).

3. Cameron, *Claudian*, pp. 63-66, 90-92.

4. Cf. Tertullian *De spectaculis* 29, a passage that anticipates the psychic battles of the *Psychomachia*:

   > haec voluptates, haec spectacula Christianorum sancta perpetua gratuita; in his tibi circenses ludos interpretare, cursus saeculi intuere, tempora labentia, spatia peracta dinumera, metas consummationis exspecta, societates ecclesiarum defende, ad signum dei suscitare, ad tubam angeli erigere, ad martyrum palmas gloriare. . . . Vis et pugilatus et luctatus? praesto sunt, non parva et multa. Aspice impudicitiam deiectam a castitate, perfidiam caesam a fide, saevitiam a misericordia contusam, petulantium a modestia adumbratum, et tales sunt apud nos agones, in quibus ipsi coronamur.

   These are the pleasures and the spectacles of the Christians: holy, eternal, and free of charge. In these recognize your circus games; watch the race of time and the gliding seasons; count the laps that have been driven; wait for the finish of the final testing; defend the teams of the churches; jump up when you see the banner of god; stand up straight when you hear the angel's horn; rejoice in the victories of the martyrs. . . . You want boxing and wrestling matches? Here they are, and there are many and important ones. Look at shamelessness thrown to the ground by chastity; faithlessness by faith; cruelty stunned by mercy; wantonness overshadowed by modesty. Such are the contests among us, in which we ourselves win crowns.

5. John Matthews, *Western Aristocracies and the Imperial Court: A.D. 364-425* (Oxford, 1975), pp. 134-136.

6. For other interpretations of the *Psychomachia,* see Macklin Smith, *Prudentius' "Psychomachia": A Reexamination* (Princeton, N.J., 1976); S. Georgia Nugent, *Allegory and Poetics: The Structure and Imagery of Prudentius' "Psychomachia"* (Frankfurt, 1974); Christian Gnilka, *Studien zur "Psychomachie" des Prudentius* (Wiesbaden, 1963); Klaus Thraede, *Studien zu Sprache und Stil des Prudentius* (Gottingen, 1965); C. S. Lewis, *The Allegory of Love,* rev. ed. (Oxford, 1963); Kenneth R. Haworth, *Deified Virtues, Demonic Vices, and Descriptive Allegory in Prudentius' "Psychomachia"* (Amsterdam, 1980); E. Rapisarda, *Psychomachia: testo con introduzione e traduzione* (Catania, 1962); Reinhart Herzog, *Die allegorische Dichtkunst des Prudentius, Zetemata* vol. 42 (Munich, 1966). For a general discussion of theories of allegory in the classical and late antique periods, see Robert Lamberton, *Homer the Theologian: Neoplatonist Allegorical Reading and the Growth of the Epic Tradition* (Berkeley, Calif., 1986).

7. Haworth, *Deified Virtues,* demonstrates that a number of the Virtues mentioned in the *Psychomachia* were personified forces actually worshipped in the ancient world, a point worth emphasizing. The cult of personified virtues may well have influenced Prudentius' descriptions of the Virtues' appearance and costumes, but my emphasis here is on Prudentius' fascination with the nature of language and the idea of verbal abstractions.

8. *Iliad* 18.53off.; Xenophon *Memorabilia* 2.1.

9. There are hints of this sort of allegorical treatment of personified abstractions in other early Christian sources—for example, the Tertullian passage cited above in this chapter and Methodius' *Symp.* 8.172, in which the world appears as a stage and mankind is faced with demonic adversaries.

10. For example, Lavarenne in his introduction to Prudentius' collected works says (my translation from the French): "Unfortunately, there are also gross defects in his work which seem to stem both from the times in which he lived and from his Spanish origin" (p. xii); and, "he is notable, finally, for a predilection for horrible details, a predilection which Prudentius shares with his compatriots, Seneca and Lucan" (p. xiii). Prudentius, *Oeuvres* vol. 1, ed. Maurice Lavarenne (Paris, 1955).

11. See my discussion in Chapter 5 of Cyprian's tongue in *Peristephanon* 13 and compare

Peristephanon 10.895-925, in which the martyr Romanus loses his tongue but is miraculously able to deliver a *long* and impassioned speech without it.

12. Statius *Theb.* 2.94-100: "tunc senior quae iussus agit, neu falsa videri / noctis imago queat, longaevi vatis opacos / Tiresiae vultus vocemque et vellera nota / induitur. mansere comae compexaque mento / canities pallorque suus, sed falsa cucurrit / infula per crines, glaucaeque innexus olivae / vittarum provenit honos" (Then the old man does what he is ordered, and lest he should seem to be a false image of the night, he puts on the shadowy features, the voice, and the familiar fillets of the long-lived seer Tiresias. His hair, the white beard combed over his chin, and his own pallor remained, but a false headband ran through his hair and an ornament woven of grey-green olive was clearly visible.)

13. *Aen.* 6.201-204: "inde ubi venere ad fauces grave olentis Averni, / tollunt se celeres liquidumque per aera lapsae / sedibus optatis gemina super arbore sidunt, / discolor unde auri per ramos aura refulsit" (Then, when they had come to the jaws of Avernus with its heavy vapors, they swiftly rise and, gliding through the clear air, they rest in their chosen perches above the double-natured tree, from which a strange-colored aura of gold shone through the branches). Vergil's choice of adjective for the golden bough is, as so often, motivated by wordplay. Pluto, lord of the underworld, gets his name (wealth) from the gold and other precious stones and metals that lie beneath the earth. One of Pluto's other names is *Dis;* the bough, which is made of gold, is thus Dis's color.

14. There is, perhaps—if we can agree with Frederick Ahl's contention that double letters, though separately pronounced, can be resolved into a single letter for the purpose of anagrammatic wordplays—another bilingual pun operating here. Discordia's tongue is *pollutam,* polluted, because she cannot stick to one meaning, as if *pollutam* were derived from Greek *polu,* "many." See Ahl, *Metaformations: Soundplay and Wordplay in Ovid and Other Classical Poets* (Ithaca, N.Y., 1985), pp. 56-57.

15. Nugent, "Vice and Virtue in Allegory," p. 71.

16. See F. Baldwin's edition of the *Bellum civile* (New York, 1911); P. Grimal, *La guerre civile de Petrone dans ses rapports avec la pharsale* (Paris, 1977).

17. Michael Lapidge, "A Stoic Metaphor in Late Latin Poetry: The Binding of the Cosmos," *Latomus* 39 (1980):817-837. Much of what follows is a summary of Lapidge's article.

18. Cicero *De natura deorum* 2.115: *quasi quodam vinculo circumdato colligantur* (they are bound together as if surrounded by a kind of chain).

19. Frederick M. Ahl, *Lucan: An Introduction* (Ithaca, N.Y., 1976), p. 242, discusses this passage briefly.

20. For a similar play on *l'iber* and *līber,* see Ovid *Tristia* 1. 1.

Selected Bibliography

This bibliography contains only works cited in the text and is not comprehensive.

Ahl, Frederick M. *Lucan: An Introduction.* Ithaca, N.Y.: Cornell University Press, 1976.

————. *Metaformations: Soundplay and Wordplay in Ovid and Other Classical Poets.* Ithaca, N.Y.: Cornell University Press, 1985.

Cameron, Alan. *Claudian: Poetry and Propaganda at the Court of Honorius.* Oxford: Clarendon Press, 1970.

Cicero. *De Natura Deorum.* Edited by Wilhelm Ax. Leipzig: Teubner, 1961.

Gnilka, Christian. *Studien zur "Psychomachie" des Prudentius.* Wiesbaden: Otto Harrassowitz, 1963.

Grimal, Pierre. *La guerre civile de Petrone dans ses rapports avec la Pharsale.* Paris: Les Belles Lettres, 1977.

Haworth, Kenneth R. *Deified Virtues, Demonic Vices, and Descriptive Allegory in Prudentius' "Psychomachia."* Amsterdam: Adolf M. Hakkert, 1980.

Herzog, Reinhart. *Die allegorische Dichtkunst des Prudentius.* Zetemata vol. 42. Munich: Beck, 1966.

Lamberton, Robert. *Homer the Theologian: Neoplatonist Allegorical Reading and the Growth of the Epic Tradition.* Berkeley: University of California Press, 1986.

Lapidge, Michael. "A Stoic Metaphor in Late Latin Poetry: The Binding of the Cosmos." *Latomus* 39 (1980):817-837.

Lewis, C. S. *The Allegory of Love.* Rev. ed. Oxford: Clarendon Press, 1973.

Matthews, John. *Western Aristocracies and the Imperial Court:* A.D. *364-425.* Oxford: Clarendon Press, 1975.

Methodius. *Le Banquet.* Edited by Herbert Musurillo. Translation and Notes by Victor-Henry Debidour. Paris: Éditions du Cerf, 1963.

Nugent, S. Georgia. *Allegory and Poetics: The Structure and Imagery of Prudentius' "Psychomachia."* Studien zur klassischen Philologie 14. Frankfurt: Lang, 1985.

———. "Vice and Virtue in Allegory: Reading Prudentius' *Psychomachia*." Diss., Cornell University, 1980.

Ovid. *Tristia*. Edited by Georg Luck. Heidelberg: Winter, 1967.

Prudentius. *Aurelii Prudentii Clementis Carmina*. Edited by Maurice Cunningham. Corpus Christianorum Series Latina, vol. 126. Turnholt: Brepols, 1966.

———. *Hamartigenia*. Edited with translation and commentary by Roberto Palla. Pisa: Giardini Editori e Stampatori, 1981.

———. *Prudence: Oeuvres*. Edited and translated by Maurice Lavarenne. 4 vols. 2d ed. Paris: Les Belles Lettres, 1955.

———. *Prudentius*. Edited and translated by H. J. Thomson. 2 vols. Cambridge: Harvard University Press, Loeb Classical Library, 1962.

———. *Psychomachia: testo con introduzione e traduzione*. Edited by Emmanuele Rapisarda. Catania: Centro di Studi sull' Antico Cristianesimo, 1962.

Smith, Macklin. *Prudentius' "Psychomachia:" A Reexamination*. Princeton, N.J.: Princeton University Press, 1976.

Statius. *Thebais*. Edited by Alfredus Klotz. Leipzig: Teubner, 1973.

Thraede, Klaus. *Studien zu Sprache und Stil des Prudentius*. Hypomnemata 13. Gottingen: Vandenhoeck & Ruprecht, 1965.

Robert Levine (essay date winter 1991)

SOURCE: Levine, Robert. "Prudentius's Romanus: The Rhetorician as Hero, Martyr, Satirist, and Saint." *Rhetorica: A Journal of the History of Rhetoric* 9, no. 1 (winter 1991): 5-38.

[*In the following essay, Levine explains how some of the martyrs depicted by Prudentius used rhetoric as a weapon against their torturers.*]

Although almost all readers of Prudentius agree that he is the major poet produced by early Christianity, some have been disturbed by what seems to them his bad taste.[1] They find his use of violence excessive, his mixing of genres anti-classical, and his shifts of tone generally troublesome.

Typical of this group of readers, Pierre LaBriolle finds the "failings of taste" in the *Peristephanon* even more intolerable than those in the *Cathemerinon*. His greatest objections are to the "grandiloquent verse in the mouths of the martyrs," and to the "interminable harangues" they deliver to their tormentors.[2] He particularly objects to the rhetorical abilities Prudentius bestows upon Romanus:

> One (martyr) "under examination" utters no fewer than six tirades—the two last of 32 and 93 lines—after his tongue has been cut out! Prudentius does not know how to keep himself within limits.

He attributes Prudentius' lack of self-control to "the natural bent of his Spanish temperament nourished on Roman rhetoric."

Among those who have been less eager to attribute Prudentius' peculiar qualities to Iberia, two groups have formed to argue about whether he is working in a classical or anti-classical tradition. Klaus Thraede and Charles Witke argue that Prudentius is essentially a classical poet.[3] On the other hand, Macklin Smith, proceeding from a reading of Curtius' excursus on "Early Christian Poetry," argues that, "The rich flood of his poetry is independent of the system of the antique genres and hence is not forced to come to terms with antique literary theory."[4] The basis for his opposition to Thraede, as well as to Charles Witke, is the fear[5] that Prudentius' Christian intentions may be overlooked: "With Witke, Thraede tends to overstress the positive meaningfulness of the classical form at the expense of the Christian content."[6] One faction, then, is primarily interested in dogma, the other in poetry.[7]

Part of what gives rise to the controversy is the range of Prudentius' imagination, which, as Filippo Ermini remarks, not only combines "l'orrido, l'atroce e il comico," but is also remarkably elastic: "Sovente il tropo è anche più ardito e più lontana è l'analogia con la realtà."[8] These distinctive qualities are what compel Jacques Fontaine to borrow Curtius' use of the term "mannerism"[9] to characterize Prudentius' poetry. The Mannerist, Fontaine says, displays an interest in irrationality, instability, excess, affective violence, as well as a taste for display, a pleasure in ambiguity, constructive imbalance, structure and ornament that do not match, and broken unity.[10] Fontaine invokes another term from art history when he suggests that the choice of lyric measures instead of hexameters freed Prudentius to indulge in "baroque" excess.[11] In addition, he finds Prudentius' performance in the *Peristephanon* naive and folkloric, offering, as the extreme case, as well as "le plus exemplaire" of these qualities, the poem devoted to the martyrdom of Romanus.[12]

Hippolyte Delehaye also finds *Peristephanon* X exemplary, but of a whole genre, and not merely of Prudentius' individual style: "La longue histoire du martyre de S. Romain pourrait être donnée comme spécimen du genre tout entièr."[13]

The genre to which it belongs, however, is compounded out of other genres, and the strange mixture has contributed to the critical disagreement about exactly what Prudentius produced. Walther Ludwig, for example, points out that Prudentius introduces bucolic in a hymn, and satire in a learned epic.[14] In his remarks on *Peristephanon* X, Walther argues that Prudentius attempts to produce a Christian tragedy, in which Romanus plays the part of "ein beredter Bekenner des christlichen Glaubens." Although Walther correctly points out that the meter is that of Senecan tragedy, it is also that of Plautine and Terentian comedy. Furthermore, as Walther himself remarks, Prudentius' decision to compose *Peristephanon* IX in the verse form Horace used to describe his journey to Brundisium seems to be a conscious allusion to comedy.[15] Prosody alone, then, does not reveal Prudentius' intentions.

Other readers have resorted to compounding genres in their attempts to describe Prudentius' accomplishments. In his discussion of the *Peristephanon,* Raby found in Prudentius' text "a combination of the epic and lyric which can almost be described as a ballad."[16] Another Prudentian text in lyric measures, the *Cathemerinon* XII, provoked Jean-Louis Charlet to speak of the mixture of lyric, allegorical, epic, tragic, and idyllic elements, producing what he calls, borrowing Brozek's term, a Pindaric quality.[17]

The mixture of genres, however, would be merely academic were it not for the sensational, violent subject matter, which is by definition unendurable. Herbert Musurillo expresses a general discomfort when he tries to deal with the accusation that martyrdom is a psychotic state: ". . . surely it is to go to excess to speak of the 'martyr psychosis' and the masochistic phenomenon of early Christianity."[18] Fantasies involving mutilation, pain, sadism, and death penetrate the poems, as martyr after martyr endures unbearable torture. Avid for specific detail, Prudentius expresses his regret, in the opening poem of the *Peristephanon,* that truly bloody details are unavailable for the *carmen triumphalis* of Hilarius:[19]

> haec loquentes obruuntur mille poenis martyres;
> nexibus manus utrasque flexus involvit rigor,
> et chalybs adtrita colla gravibus ambit circulis.
>
> o vetustatis silentis obsoleta oblivio!
> invidentur ista nobis fama et ipsa extinguitur.
> chartulas blasphemus olim nam satelles abstulit,
> ne tenacibus libellis erudita saecula
> ordinem, tempus modumque passionis proditum
> dulcibus linguis per aures posterorum spargerent.
>
> (Lns. 70-78)

At these words the martyrs are overwhelmed with a thousand tortures. Stiff fetters curve round their two hands and clasp them in their grip, and heavy rings of iron surround and chafe their necks. Alas for what is forgotten and lost to knowledge in the silence of the old time! We are denied the facts about these matters, the very tradition is destroyed, for long ago a reviling soldier of the guard took away the records, lest generations taught by documents that held the memory fast should make public the details, the time and manner of their martyrdom, and spread them abroad in sweet speech for posterity to hear.

However, Prudentius' martyrs endure pain and death not merely with conventional Stoic fortitude,[20] but with joy, a sense of play, and in several instances, among which *Peristephanon* X is the most elaborate, with a loquacity that is simultaneously stunning and disturbing.

For them, torture is sport and pain is pleasure. They deliver speeches of great length, while parts of their bodies are cut, burned, whipped, and amputated, in scenes that seem designed to illustrate Wordsworth's contention that verse is a kind of *pharmakon,* enabling readers or listeners to endure what they could not bear to see or hear in the real world.[21]

In *Peristephanon* V, for example, Vincent grows *laetior* (l. 125) as he is torn to pieces:

> Ridebat haec miles dei
> manus cruentas increpans
> quod fixa non profundius
> intraret artus ungula.

But the soldier of God laughed at these commands, rebuking the blood-stained hands because the claw thrust into him did not enter more deeply into his body.

When he is taken from the pit, his followers wander with their kisses over the double rows made in his body by the claws, joyfully licking the purple gore:

> ille ungularum duplices
> sulcos pererrat osculis,
> hic purpurantem corporis
> gaudet cruorem lambere.
>
> (Lns. 337-40)

One covers with kisses the double cuts made by the claws, another eagerly licks the red gore on the body.

In *Peristephanon* XI, Prudentius varies the representation of dismemberment by describing a painting[22] that depicts Hippolytus' death, with a catalogue of bodily parts, and the martyr's fellow Christians soaking up the blood from the sand:

> Ille caput niveum conplectitur ac reverandam
>   canitiem molli confovet in gremio;
> hic umeros truncasque manus et bracchia et ulnas
>   et genua et crurum fragmina nuda legit.
> Palliolis etiam bibulae siccantur harenae,

ne quis in infecto pulvere ros maneat.
Si quis et in sudibus recalenti aspergine sanguis
    insidet, hunc omnem spongia pressa rapit.

(Lns. 137-44)

One clasps the snowy head, cherishing the venerable
white hair on his loving breast, while another picks up
the shoulders, the severed hands, arms, elbows, knees,
bare fragments of legs. With their garments also they
wipe dry the soaking sand, so that no drop shall remain
to dye the dust; and wherever blood adheres to the
spikes on which its warm spray fell, they press a sponge
on it and carry it all away.

When the executioner approaches Agnes, in *Peristephanon* XIV, she greets him as a savage lover, more welcome than a delicate, perfumed young man; she promises to respond eagerly to the full, vigorous thrust of his sword between her breasts:

exulto, talis quod potius venit
vaesanus atrox turbidus armiger,
quam si veniret languidus ac tener
mollisque ephebus tinctus aromate,
qui me pudoris funere perderet.
hic, hic amator iam, fateor, placet:
ibo inruentis gressibus obviam,
nec demorabor vota calentia;
ferrum in papillas omne recepero
pectusque ad imum vim gladii traham.

(Lns. 69-78)

"I rejoice that there comes a man like this, a savage, cruel, wild man-at-arms, rather than a listless, soft, womanish youth bathed in perfume, coming to destroy me with the death of my honour. This lover, this one at last, I confess it, pleases me. I shall meet his eager steps half-way and not put off his hot desires. I shall welcome the whole length of his blade into my bosom, drawing the sword-blow to the depths of my breast."

This is the kind of detail that provoked Fontaine and others to invoke the term "Mannerism." The art of rhetoric, however, rather than the plastic arts, may account for more of what goes on in Prudentius' verse.

When panegyrists claimed saints' lives as their material, Delehaye points out, "l'éloquence s'empare d'un thème nouveau."[23] For Christian poets, then, saints' lives offer a new subject for an ancient discipline—Graeco-Roman rhetoric—as Walther implies when he describes Romanus as "ein beredter Bekenner des christlichen Glaubens." Prudentius shows none of the guilt about using classical rhetoric that penetrates the texts of Jerome and Augustine, perhaps because he sees literary ramifications in the Eusebian proposition of "the empire as a providential preparation for the unity of mankind in Christ."[24] By exploiting pagan rhetoric, then, he may adapt it to Christian uses, and he may also surpass it.

On the basis of this hypothesis, violence, for example, becomes more appropriate and comprehensible. Certainly Virgil's description of the death of Priam should

satisfy most appetites for *Grausamkeit*.[25] Fascination with the horrible had characterized the Roman declamatory tradition, and the poems of Lucan, and the plays of Seneca reflect that tradition.[26] Four centuries later, Prudentius' use of violence is not necessarily a violation of classical decorum, as Miceislaus Brozek suggests when he points out that several passages in Quintilian might have served as models for Prudentius' use of gruesome detail.[27] According to the statistics compiled by Henderson, only twenty percent of the lines in the *Peristephanon* qualify as in some sense violent.[28] More important, he suggests, is the rhetorical, thematic function of the violence: "Prudentius' intention is clear; the greater the mortification of the flesh in all its terrifying details, the greater the triumph of the spirit."[29] The violence, then, is not necessarily a sign of a Spanish fondness for "excess," which for some readers is a word synonymous with "rhetorical."[30] Instead, Prudentius' rhetorical excess is part of a deliberate, even programmatic attempt to provide his subject matter with what Milton, in a similar predicament, called "answerable style."

Traditionally, the defense of literary excess relies on matching words either to subject matter, or to feelings. For example, Roland Barthes defends the stylistic excesses of late eighteenth-century writers by insisting that their words matched the events themselves. In addition, he insists upon the difficulty of later times perceiving the function of rhetorical amplification:

The Revolution was in the highest degree one of those great occassions when truth, through the bloodshed that it costs, becomes so weighty that its expression demands the very forms of historical amplification. Revolutionary writing was the one and only grand gesture commensurate with the daily presence of the guillotine. What today seems turgid was then no more than life-size.[31]

On the other hand, Henri Peyre defends the inflationary tendencies of Romantic rhetoric on the basis of the need to express an excess of feeling:

Even when they resorted to inflated language or to exclamatory rhetoric to convey an experience they deemed unique, they were trying to render passionately and exaltedly what they had experienced ardently.[32]

Prudentius' poems offer an opportunity for both defenses; the poet attempts to fabricate a style analogous both to the divine nature of the events related, and to the poet's feelings about his subject matter.[33]

Even his prosody shows signs of deliberate excess. The number and variety of metrical forms he uses is at least remarkable, if not excessive; the *Praefationes,* for example, offer alternating iambic trimeter and dimeter, iambic trimeter, and aeolian verse (aesclepedians and glyconics). The *Cathemerinon* offers hypercatalectic dactylic trimeter, Phalaceans, asclepedians, catalectic diambs, iambic trimeter, sapphics, catalectic trochees, and catalectic anapestic dimeters. The variety among the fourteen poems that make up the *Peristephanon* is equally impressive.

Prudentius' prosodic self-consciousness also asserts itself in a cadenza on Saint Vincent, inserted into *Peristephanon* IV, where he exceeds the number of syllables permissible in a sapphic line, in order to introduce the name of Saturn.[34] In the process of violating the rules, he fastidiously calls attention to his transgression, and claims that his subject matter is sufficient excuse for what otherwise would be blameworthy and, in effect, in bad taste:

> quattuor posthinc superest virorum
> nomen extolli renuente metro,
> quos Saturninos memorat vocatos
>   prisca vetustas.
> carminis leges amor aureorum
> nominum parvi facit, et loquendi
> cura de sanctis vitiosa non est
>   nec rudis umquam.

> (Lns. 161-68)

It still remains to exalt the names of four though my meter refuses. Old times of long ago tell that they were each called Saturninus. Love of their golden names makes light of the rules of verse, and concern to speak of the saints is never incorrect nor barbarous.

By divine literary standards, Prudentius insists that his measure is "full," or "complete," and appropriate for the heavenly book, to be explicated at the right moment:

> plenus est artis modus adnotatas
> nominum formas recitare Christo,
> quas tenet caeli liber explicandus
>   tempore justo.

> (Lns. 169-72)

The measure of art is full if we recite to Christ the forms of the names as they are written down and contained in the book of heaven which shall be opened at the due time.

Prudentius' self-conscious use of images of the book is one of several ways in which he implies that his achievements will be judged in terms of, rather than in spite of, his rhetorical propensities. In several poems of the *Peristephanon,* rhetoric itself becomes not merely a tool, but the central subject matter.[35] In addition to Romanus, at least three other Prudentian martyrs provide examples of self-conscious, even heroic, rhetorical competence. In *Peristephanon* III, for example, composed in hypercatalectic dactylic trimeters, Saint Eulalia's major use of language is to provoke her tormentors. When they respond by tearing her sides, she triumphantly calls the torn flesh "God's writing."[36]

> Nec mora, carnifices gemini
> iuncea pectora dilacerant
> et latus ungula virgineum
> pulsat utrimque et ad ossa secat
> Eulalia numerante notas.
> "Scriberis ecce mihi, domine.
> Quam iuvat hos apices legere,
> qui tua, Christe, tropaea notant.
> Nomen et ipsa sacrum loquitur
> purpura sanguinis eliciti."

> (Lns. 131-40)

In a moment, two executioners are tearing her slim breast, the claw striking her girlish sides and cutting to the bone, while Eulalia counts the marks. "See, Lord," she says, "thy name is being written on me. How I love to read these letters, for they record thy victories, O Christ, and the very scarlet of the blood that is drawn speaks the holy name."

Even more self-consciously involved with images drawn from books and writing, although more involved with literal elements, *Peristephanon* IX, composed in alternating dactylic hexameters and iambic senarii, depicts the martyrdom of Saint Cassian, the *magister litterarum* of Imola. The poem begins with Prudentius praying at the saint's tomb, looking at a picture of Cassian's martyrdom:

> Erexi ad caelum faciem, stetit obvia contra
>   fucis colorum picta imago martyris
> plagas mille gerens, totos lacerata per artus,
>   ruptam minutis praeferens punctis cutem.
> innumeri circum pueri, miserabile visu,
>   confossa parvis membra figebant stilis,
> unde pugillares soliti percurrere ceras
>   scholare murmur adnotantes scripserant.

> (Lns. 10-16)

I lifted my face towards heaven, and there stood confronting me a picture of the martyr painted in colours, bearing a thousand wounds, all his parts torn, and showing his skin broken with tiny pricks. Countless boys round about (a pitiful sight!) were stabbing and piercing his body with the little styles with which they used to run over their wax tablets, writing down the droning lessons in school.

Since the children and their weapons are small, the wounds they make are small, but sufficient in number to bring about the death of Cassian.

A verger who happens to be present proceeds to relate the story to the grateful poet, assuring him that the event represented in the picture has been *tradita libris,* in good faith, and is no *inanis aut anilis fabula.* Cassian's skill was not in composing poetry or prose, but in the physical, necessarily tedious act of writing:

> praefuerat studiis puerilibus et grege multo
>   saeptus magister litterarum sederat,

verba notis brevibus conprendere cuncta peritus,
raptimque punctis dicta praepetibus sequi.

(Lns. 21-24)

He had been in charge of a school for boys and sat as a teacher of reading and writing with a great throng around him, and he was skilled in putting every word in short signs and following speech quickly with swift pricks on the wax.

When Cassian refused to worship pagan gods, he was taken from the classroom, and then handed over to those whom he used to beat, *donetur ipsis verberator parvulis* (ln. 38). With the roles reversed, he now becomes the object of sport to his pupils:

ut libet inludant, lacerent inpune manusque
tinguant magistri feriatas sanguine.
ludum discipulis volupe est ut praebeat ipse
doctor severus quos nimis coercuit.

(Lns. 39-42)

"Let them make sport of him as they please, give them leave to mangle him at will, let them give their hands a holiday and dip them in their master's blood. It is a pleasant thought that the strict teacher should himself furnish sport to the pupils he has too much held down."

His former pupils hurl writing instruments at him, and as he heroically encourages them to redouble their efforts, they ironically describe themselves as paying him back in kind:

non potes irasci quod scribimus; ipse iubebas
numquam quietum dextera ut ferret stylum. . . .

(Lns. 73-74)

Exerce imperium, ius est tibi plectere culpam,
si quis tuorum te notavit segnius.
Talia ludebant pueri per membra magistra . . .

(Lns. 81-83)

"You cannot be angry with us for writing; it was you who bade us never let our hand carry away an idle style . . . Use your authority; you have power to punish a fault, if any of your pupils has written carelessly on you."

Cassian, however, is not the most satisfying rhetorical hero, since the pupils, not the martyr, get to "play," and they also get the last word in the exchange.

Saint Lawrence offers a better model for the *rhetor* as hero; in the iambic dimeters of **Peristephanon** II, play, dogma, and literary self-consciousness combine to produce a martyr with an unusual sensibility. At one point in the poem, in response to a lengthy harangue against materialism that Lawrence has just delivered, and which the saint has supported by an allegorical reading of a group of beggars, the angry prefect exclaims that he is being mocked.

"ridemur," exclamat fremens (furens A)
praefectus, "ac miris modis
per tot figuras ludimur:
et vivit insanum caput!
    inpune tantas, furcifer,

strofas cavillo mimico
te nexuisse existimas,
dum scurra saltas fabulam?
Concinna visa urbanitas
tractare nosmet ludicris?
egon cachinnis venditus
acroma festivum fui?

(Lns. 313-24)

"He is mocking us," cries the prefect, mad with rage, "making wonderful sport of us with all this allegory. And yet the madman lives! Think you, rascal, to get off with contriving such trickeries with your comedian's quibbling and theatrical buffoonery? Do you think it neat pleasantry to make a butt of me? Have you made your guffaws out of me and turned me into a merry piece of entertainment?"

That he is laughing at his tormentor becomes theatrically clear when, on the gridiron, Lawrence makes jokes well enough to serve as Curtius' example of medieval kitchen humor:[37]

"converte partem corporis
satis crematum iugiter,
et fac periclum, quid tuus
Vulcanus ardens egerit."

praefectus inverti iubet.
tunc ille: "coctum est, devora,
et experimentum cape
sit crudum an assum suavius.

(Lns. 401-408)

"This part of my body has been burned long enough; turn it round and try what your hot god of fire has done." So the prefect orders him to be turned about, and then, "It is done," says Lawrence; "eat it up, try whether it is nicer raw or roasted."

Lawrence's sense of humor in this poem is one of the items that offended Pierre de LaBriolle:[38] "St. Lawrence draws an almost ludicrous parallel between physical ills and the ills of the soul." The pun that Lawrence makes in the following passage, referring to *morbus regius* (jaundice) as the illness from which his judge suffers, is what particularly offended LaBriolle:

tute ipsis, qui Romam regis,
contemptor aeterni Dei,
dum daemonum sordes colis,
morbo laboras regio.

(Lns. 261-64)

You yourself who rule over Rome, who despise the everlasting God, worship foul devils, are suffering from the ruler's sickness.

The ludic element appears again, though only briefly, in the iambic dimeters of **Peristephanon** V, when Saint Vincent speaks of dying as a Christian sport:

> tormenta carcer ungulae
> stridensque flammis lammina
> atque ipsa poenarum ultima
> mors christianis ludus est.

(Lns. 61-64)

Torture, imprisonment, the claws, the hissing red-hot plate, even to the final suffering of death, are all mere sport to Christians.

His persecutor picks up the motif:

> inpune ne nostris sibi
> dis destruendis luserit.

(Lns. 101-104)

He shall not get off with pulling down our gods for his amusement.

Both the torture and the tortured, then, describe their common activity as "play."

Prudentius' tendency to attribute a ludic quality to elaborately amplified scenes of pain and violence is responsible for producing most of the disapproval which LaBriolle and others, particularly those primarily interested in Christian dogma, have expressed. However, piety and play are not necessarily exclusive categories, as the work of Huizinga, Rahner, Suchomski, and others has demonstrated.[39]

In the poems of Prudentius, the sense of play embraces several elements, including athletic contest, rhetorical contest, and laughter. Saints are traditionally represented as God's athletes, and, in his description of Romanus, John Chrysostom compares the martyr's efforts to those of the Olympic athlete.[40] Jacques Fontaine's richly evocative comment that the struggle of Jacob with the angel, "vaut aussi pour toutes les formes de l'imaginaire dans la poésie de Prudence," may have even wider implications than Fontaine intended.[41] Brozek also likes the analogy, and uses it to support his argument for Prudentius as the Christian Pindar.[42]

The sense of rhetorical contest is more complex. The primary contest in **Peristephanon** X is the extensive attack on pagan religion Romanus delivers in three lengthy speeches to his tormentor Aesclepiades.[43] At the same time, Prudentius engages in a contest with the predominantly pagan texts and traditions from which he derives his skill and authority, but whose beliefs he as a Christian poet must oppose. Neither contest can be won by the strength and competence of an individual human being, since each is designed to demonstrate the superior efficacy and truth of Christianity.[44]

The ludic elements also fit the doctrinal purpose. Play involving laughter as well as competition was part of Roman declamatory training, as S. F. Bonner suggests,[45] but laughter was also interpreted as an imitation of God's divine play, in the texts of Gregory of Nazianus, Philo, Clement of Alexandria, and Augustine.[46] According to Gregory, God the Word plays with the world:

> παίζει γὰρ λόγος αἰπὺς ἐν εἴδεσι παντοδαποισι
> χίρνας ὡς ἐθυλει χόσμον ὅλον ἔνθα χαὶ ἔνθα.

The Holy Word plays; with colored pictures he decorates the whole world.

In his attempt to explicate Gen. 26:8, Philo composes an elaborate Platonic allegory on Abimelech's discovery of the true nature of the relationship between Isaac and Rebecca:

> χατὰ γοῦν τὸν ἱερώτατον Μωυσ῀ην τελος ἐστί
> σοφίας παιδιὰ χαὶ γελως, ἀλλ' οὐχ ἃ τοῖς νηπίοις
> ἄνευ φρονήσεως π῀ασι μελετ῀αται, ἀλλ' ἃ τοῖς
> ἤδη πολιοῖς οὐ χρόνῳ μόνον ἀλλὰ χαὶ βουλαις
> ἀγαθαῖς γεγονόσιν οὐχ ὁρᾷς ὅτι τὸν αὐτηχόου
> χαὶ αὐτομαθουνς χαὶ αντουργοῦ τησς ἐπιστήμης
> ἀρυσάμενον οὐ μετέχοντα γέλωτος, ἀλλ' αὐτὸν
> γέλωτα εἰναί φησιν; οὗτός ἐστιν Ισαάχ, ὃς
> ἑρμηνεύεται γέλως, ω παίζειν μετὰ τῆς ὑπομονῆς,
> ἥν Ρεβέχχαν Εβραῖοι χαλοῦσιν, ἁρμόττει. XLI.
> τὴν δὲ | θείαν παιδιὰν τῆς ψυχῆς ἰδιώτῃ μὲν οὐ
> θέμις ἰδεῖν, βασιλεῖ δὲ ἔξεστιν, ὤ πάμπολυν χρόνον
> παρώχησεν, ει, χαὶ μὴ πάντ ἐνωχησε τον αἰῶνα,
> σοφία. προσαγορεύεται οὗτος' Αβιμέλεχ, ὅς
> διαχύψας τή θυρίδι, τῶ διοιχθέντι χαὶ φωσφόρῳ
> τῆς διανοίας ὄμματι, τὸν Ισαὰχ εἰδε παίζοντα μετὰ
> 'Ρεβέχας τῆς γυναιχος αυτού

> τί γὰρ ἄλλο ἐμπεπ῾ες ἔργον σοφῷ ἤ τὸ παίζειν
> χαὶ γανουσθαι χαὶ συνευφραίνεσθαι τη τὼν χαλ῀ων
> ὑπομονη;

Moses, at all events, holiest of men, shows us that sport and merriment is the height of wisdom, not the sport which children of all sorts indulge in, paying no heed to good sense, but such as is seen in those who are now becoming grey-headed not only in respect of age but of thoughtfulness. Do you not observe that when he is speaking of the man who drew directly from the well of knowledge, listening to no other, learning through no other, resorting to no agency whatever, he does not say that he had a part in laughter, but that he was laughter itself? I am speaking of Isaac, whose name means "laughter," and whom it well befits to sport with "patient waiting," who is called in Hebrew "Rebecca."[47]

The transaction among Isaac, Rebecca, and Abimelech provoked Clement of Alexander to compose verses in which the allegorical, or at least figural, potential of laughter and play is Christianized:

> ὤ τ῀ης φρονίμου παιδι῀ας.
> γέλως δι' ὑπομον῀ης βοηθούμενος

χαὶ ἔφορος ὁ βασιλεύς.
ἀγαλλιᾶται τὸ πνεῦμα
τῶν ἐν Χριστω παίδίων
ἐν ὑπομονῇ πολιτευομένων
χαὶ αὕτη ἢ θεία παιδιά.

Oh, what wise child's-play. It is laughter supported by patience, and the king is the onlooker. Happy is the spirit of those who are patient children in Christ. That is holy play.

The paradoxical combination of youth and wisdom articulated by Clement seems analogous with the rhetorical *topos, puer senex,* to which Curtius devotes considerable attention, and which reappears vividly in the portrayal of the infant martyr in **Peristephanon** X.[48]

Prudentius participates in this sense of divine laughter, which clearly has little to do with what we normally mean by a sense of humor. For the Christian rhetorician, engaged in a battle against the forces of darkness, laughter expresses power, not pleasure, and therefore becomes both a weapon and a sign of victory. Prudentius is also capable of turning comic material to serious purposes. For example, if Jean-Louis Charlet is correct in locating the source for the phrase *cantilenae suaserint* (**Peristephanon** X. 351), then Prudentius turned a phrase Ausonius used for the mildest kind of humor into part of Romanus' diatribe against pagan religion.[49] For the Christian rhetorician, as Peter von Moos has suggested, "everything written is exploitable."[50]

However, to demonstrate the full range of Prudentius' abilities to combine play, contest, violence, poetry, and Christian doctrine, one must turn to the longest of the poems in the **Peristephanon,** the 1,140 iambic septenarii devoted to Romanus, whom Eusebius[51] lists among those martyred by Galerius at Antioch in A.D. 303. A combination of hagiography, polemic, diatribe, and lyric, **Peristephanon** X has generated the most exasperation and disapproval among its professional readers.[52] "It is a strange mixture of a poem, extended beyond reason, with anti-climactic results, the clearest case in the **Peristephanon** that Prudentius could fail to see that the half may be better than the whole."[53] Charles Witke, perhaps the most tolerant of Prudentius' American readers, suggests that the length and detail of some of the texts, as well as "his relish for grotesque injury in the **Peristephanon,**" account for the difficulties readers have experienced.[54] Prudentius' excess, then, is the problem.

The answer to the problem lies in the subject matter and the poet's relationship to it, as Prudentius indicates at the beginning of **Peristephanon** X. Anticipating the major miracle in the poem—Romanus' ability to continue speaking even after his tongue has been cut off—Prudentius offers an initial declaration of incompetence, which also provides the first example in the poem of the poet's ability to make a conventional *topos* into an integral part of the poem's theme:

Romane, Christi fortis adsertor Dei,
elinguis oris organum fautor move,
largire comptum carmen infantissimo,
fac ut tuarum mira laudum concinam.
nam scis et ipse posse mutos eloqui.

(Lns. 1-5)

Romanus, stout defender of the divine Christ, grant thy favour and stir up the tongue within my speechless mouth, bountifully bestow graceful song on the mutest of men and enable me to sing the wonders of thy glory; for thou knowest, thyself too, that the dumb can speak.

Prudentius now extends and complexifies the inability-topos by combining it with what will become the motif of milkiness, *spiritali lacte,* to reinforce the image, begun in line three by *infantissimo,* of the poet as baby, a figure that combines both innocence and incompetence:

sic noster haerens sermo lingua debili
balbutit et modis laborat absonis,
sed si superno rore respergas iecur
et spiritali lacte pectus iniges,
vox inpeditos rauca laxabit sonos.

(Lns. 11-15)

So my speech sticks and stammers with feeble tongue and labours in inharmonious measures; but if thou sprinkle my heart with the dew from on high and flood my breast with the milk of the spirit, my hoarse voice will unloose the sounds which are now obstructed.

For the powerless, of course, Christ, *potens facundiae,* is the solution; therefore Prudentius declares Christ to be his tongue:[55]

evangelista scripsit ipsum talia
praecepta Messian dedisse apostolis:
"nolite verba, cum sacramentum meum
erit canendum, providenter quaerere;
ego inparatis quae loquantur suggeram."
sum mutus ipse, sed potens facundiae
mea lingua Christus luculente disserent.

(Lns. 16-22)

The Evangelist has written that the Messiah himself instructed the apostles in this wise: "Seek not with forethought for words when my mystic doctrine is to be proclaimed. I shall furnish the unready with what they shall say." In myself I am dumb, but Christ is master of eloquence; he will be my tongue and discourse excellently.

Here Prudentius turns part of Matt. 10:18-19 into verse, without giving the full message, which is made explicit in Matt. 10:20: "Nos enim vos estis qui loquimini, sed Spiritus Patris vestri qui loquitur in vobis."

The enemy in the perpetual contest is represented now by the image of a wounded snake, suggested by the recollection of the devil in the process of being defeated by Christ:

Sic vulneratus anguis ictu spiculi
ferrum remordet et dolore saevior
quassando pressis immoratur dentibus,
hastile fixum sed manet profundius
nec cassa sentit morsuum pericula.

(Lns. 26-30)

Just so a serpent wounded by stroke of spear-point
bites back at the steel and keeps on shaking it in the
grip of its teeth, growing more savage with the pain,
but the lance has pierced too deeply and stays fast,
unconscious of the futile danger of the bites.

Perhaps no figure is more familiar in Christian doxolo-
gies than that of the evil snake; however, Prudentius'
use of the figure, in connection with the mouth, both in
this poem and in the *Hamartigenia,* has a special
significance. It provides a negative, perverse mirror image for the creative power of the Logos.[56] In the *Hamartigenia,* the image is accompanied by what Prudentius
represents as a perverse sexual union by the vipers,
whose oral method of impregnation destroys the three-
tongued male of the species:

Si licet ex ethicis quidquam praesumere vel si
de physicis exempli aliquid, sic vipera, ut aiunt,
dentibus emoritur fusae per viscera prolis,
mater morte sua, non sexu fertilis aut de
concubitu distenta uterum, sed cum calet igni
percita femineo, moriturum obscena maritum
ore sitit patulo. Caput inserit ille trilingue
coniugis in fauces atque oscula fervidus intrat
insinuans oris coitu genitale venenum.

(Lns. 581-89)

If we may draw on the moralists for anything or take
an instance from natural history, it is thus, they say,
that the viper perishes by the teeth of the progeny that
is brought forth through her flesh. She becomes a
mother by her own death; she does not bear her young
by an organ of sex, nor does her womb swell from
intercourse, but when she burns with the excitement of
the female's heat the lewd beast opens her mouth wide
in thirst for a mate that is doomed. He puts his three-
tongued head into his spouse's jaws, eagerly entering
her alluring mouth and inserting his baneful seed by an
oral union.

At the moment of highest passion, the female decapitates
the male:

Nupta voluptatis vi saucia mordicus haustum
frangit amatoris blanda inter foedera guttur
infusaque bibit caro pereunte salivas.

(Lns. 190-92)

The bride, smitten with the strong pleasure, takes her
lover's head between her teeth and breaks his neck
with a bite in the middle of the fond compact, drinking
in the injected slaver while her dear one dies.

The female, however, does not last long, but dies in the
act of giving birth, as her children tear her belly apart

to escape from her body. Prudentius continues the
simile, describing the soul imbibing evil from the devil,
thereby producing countless sins.

No such graphic scenes of copulation and birth occur in
Peristephanon X, but the matrix of serpents, sexuality,
and procreation recurs several times.[57] The image of the
serpent reappears a few lines later, applied to Galerius
persecuting Christians with his "royal mouth":

haec ille serpens ore dictat regio . . .

(Ln. 36)

It was the serpent that uttered these words by the imperial lips . . .

Opposed to the royal mouth, however, Romanus defends
himself against Asclepiades, *ore libero* (ln. 96), provoking the king's representative to torture him. Because of
Romanus' rank, the rack cannot be used; instead, he is
lashed. Romanus takes the event as material for an *ex
tempore* rhetorical display, in this case on the nature of
nobility of blood: "generosa Christi secta nobilitat vi-
ros" ("It is Christ's noble teaching that enobles men")
(ln. 125). Furthermore, Romanus asserts that the root of
true nobility begins, genealogically, *Dei ab ore,* from
God's mouth, and he urges his tormentor to continue
the torture, to ennoble the victim: "incumbe membris,
tortor, ut sim nobilis" (ln. 138). Romanus continues to
develop the topic,[58] insisting that all symbols of earthly
nobility pass away:

Nonne cursim transeunt
fasces secures sella praetexta et toga
licta tribunal et trecenta insignia
quibus tumetis, moxque detumescitis?

(Lns. 142-46)

Do not they pass away quickly, the rods, the axes, the
chair of state, the bordered robe, the lictor, the
judgement-seat, and all the thousand badges of honour
on the strength of which you swell with pride, and then
fall flat?

At this point, Romanus begins attacking pagan religion
as ludicrous, not in the sense of holy play, but as vulgar
and absurd. The Lupercal, for example, where each
celebrant runs naked, like a slave, "puellas verbere ictas
ludicro" (ln. 165),[59] is *vilissimum.*

The sequence of nudity and women at least partially
generates the next part of Romanus' speech, an attack
on the sexual profligacy of pagan gods, their base
progeny, and the deceptions they practice on their
deluded wives:

lubes, relictis patris et Christi sacris
ut tecum adorem feminas mille ac mares,
deas deosque deque sexu duplici,

natos nepotes abnepotes editos
et tot stuprorum sordidam prosapiam.

Nubunt puellae, saepe luduntur dolis,
amasionum conprimuntur fraudibus,
incesta feruent, furta moechorum calent,
fallit maritus, odit uxor paelicem,
deos catenae colligant adulteros.

(Lns. 176-85)

You bid me abandon the worship of the Father and
Christ, and along with you venerate a thousand males
and females, goddesses and gods and children, grandchildren, great-great-grandchildren of both sexes born
to them, and the base progeny of their many unchasti-
ties. The girls marry, or often they are made the sport
of trickery and violated by dishonest lovers, lewdness
and stratagems of paramours go briskly on, a husband
is unfaithful and a wife hates a mistress, chains bind
adulterous gods.

Plato, of course, had voiced the same misgivings about
the behavior of the Homeric gods, but Prudentius' Romanus goes to much greater lengths, with much more
specific detail. He attacks the homosexuality of Apollo,
who corrupted the young while they were at play:

Delphosne pergam? set vetat
corrupta ephebi fama, quem vester deus
effeminavit gymnadis licentia.

(Lns. 189-90)

Shall I go to Delphi? No, I am forbidden by the spoiled
of the lad on the exercise-ground, whom your god dis-
honoured, taking advantage of the freedom of the
wrestling-bout.

At this point Romanus also recalls that Apollo's lover
Hyacinth was accidentally killed while at play, "oc-
cisum gravi / disco" (lns. 191-92).

Moving from homosexuality to castration—a topic to
which he returns towards the end of the poem, significantly, after his tongue has been cut out—Romanus
cites the emasculation of Attis (lns. 196ff.) as another
abhorrent pagan myth:

an ad Cybebes ibo lucum pineum?
puer sed obstat gallus ob libidinem
per triste vulnus perque sectum dedecus
ab impudicae tutus amplexu deae,
per multa Matri sacra plorandus spado.

(Lns. 196-200)

Or shall I go to Cybebe's pinegrove? No, for there
stands in my way the lad who emasculated himself
because of her lust, and by a grievous wound cutting
the parts of shame saved himself from the unchaste
goddess's embrace.

From the sexual nightmare that anticipates his own
sacrificial act, Romanus turns to the ludicrous, adulterous activities of Jupiter. In the theater, Romanus asserts,
Jupiter's actions are a source of laughter that has nothing to do with what is sacred:

cygnus stuprator peccat inter pulpita,
saltat Tonantem tauricornem ludius;
spectator horum pontifex summus sedet
ridesque et ipse, nec negando diluis
cum fama tanti polluatur numinis.

(Lns. 221-25)

The ravisher swan does his evil deed on the stage, a
player dances the part of the Thunderer with the bull's
horns, while you, the high priest, sit and watch these
things and laugh at them yourself, and never discredit
them by denying their truth, though the good name of
this great deity is soiled.

The Roman stage offers Venus as a *meretrix* (ln. 228),
lustfully mourning for Adonis, Ganymede as a symbol
of Jove's perversity, Ceres searching for the daughter
raped by a divinity, and Hercules made into a *ludibrium*
(ln. 240) by his passion.[60]

Faunus, Priapus, nymphs at the bottom of frog-ponds,
"divinitatis ius in algis vilibus" (1. 245), all make
laughter a necessity:

nonne pulmonem movet
derisus istas intuens ineptias,
quas vinolentae somniis fingunt anus?

(Lns. 248-50)

Does not derisive laughter shake your sides at the
contemplation of these absurdities, the phantasies of
tipsy old wives' dreams?

Romanus continues his diatribe, attacking the absurd
worship of animals (lns. 256-58) and vegetables (lns.
259-60), as well as the practice of worshipping statues.
Developing the biblical injunction against worshipping
statues, Romanus attacks pagan gods, because they are
made of metal utensils, "broken and melted":

Non eruescis, stulte, pago dedite,
te tanta semper perdisse obsonia,
quae dis ineptus obtulisti talibus,
quos trulla pelvis cantharus sartagines
fracta et liquata contulerunt vascula?

(Lns. 296-300)

Do you not blush, foolish man, devoted to pagan worship, to think that you have always wasted all those
victuals that you have absurdly offered to gods like
these, made out of an assemblage of ladles, basins,
tankards, frying-pans, broken vessels melted down?

Here he goes beyond Commodian, the "black sun"[61] of
early Christian poetry, who had reworked the biblical
injunction into unscannable verse:

Nolite, inquid, adorare deos inanes
De manibus vestris factos ex ligno vel auro.[62]

Romanus now turns from ridiculing pagan religion to
deliver a sermon of almost one hundred lines on the
nature of true Christian belief. In response to Romanus'

tirade and doxology, Asclepiades delivers a thirty-line declaration of outrage, accusing Romanus of upholding a new-fangled religion and of simultaneously violating political and religious authority, "ore foedans impio" (ln. 400).

When Aesclepiades threatens to make him pay with his blood for refusing to honor the ancient gods, Romanus refuses, and the soldiers plow lines in the saint's body until the white bones show:

> Scindunt utrumque milites taeterrimi
> mucrone hiulco pensilis latus viri,
> sulcant per artus longa tractim vulnera,
> obliqua rectis, recta transversis secant
> et iam retectis pectus albet ossibus.
>
> (Lns. 451-55)

The foul soldiers cut both his sides with gashing sword as he hangs, ploughing wounds in long lines over his body and making criss-cross cuts, till his breast shows white where the bones are laid bare.

Claiming to fell no pain, Romanus continues to defy his tormentors, arguing that what he feels is less than the pain felt by those with fever, arthritis, gout, as well as less painful than that inflicted by doctors in their attempts to cure physical ills. He describes in detail his own torture and the medical practice of lancing, to prepare for a kind of Socratic paradox by means of which the torturer is the healer:

> Putate ferrum triste chirurgos meis
> inferre costis, quod secat salubriter.
> Non est amarum quo reformatur salus.
> Videntur isti carpere artus tabidos,
> sed dant medellam rebus intus vividis.
>
> (Lns. 501-505)

Fancy that the surgeons are putting the grim knife to my ribs and it is cutting me for the good of my health; that by which health is restored is not vexatious. These men appear to be rending my wasting limbs, but they give healing to the living substance within.

Romanus now modulates to an attack on the flesh and its pleasures, appealing to the *carnifex* to "heal" him by leaving nothing for the devil to cut off: "quod tyrannus amputet" (ln. 520), continuing the motif of amputation.[63] Drawing from Isa. 24:4, and Rev. 6:13-14, his vision of the end of all things includes the vision of the book: "quandoque caelum ceu liber plicabitur" (ln. 536). In recognition of his opponent's rhetorical superiority, Asclepiades becomes so angry that he wants to cut into Romanus' very words:

> verbositatis ipse rumpatur locus,
> scaturrientes perdat ut loquacitas
> sermonis auras perforatis follibus,
> quibus sonandi nulla lex ponit modum;
> ipsa et loquentis verba torqueri volo.
>
> (Lns. 551-55)

"Shatter the seat of his verbosity, puncture the bellows so that his loquacity may lose the gushing winds of words, since no law puts a stop to their sounding. I will have the very words tortured even as he speaks."

After his face has been slashed, anticipating the remarks Shakespeare's Antony makes at Caesar's funeral, Romanus asserts that the results are in his favor, since the multiple wounds give him multiple mouths:

> grates tibi, o praefecte, magnas debeo,
> quod multa pandens ora iam Christum loquor.
> artabat ampli nominis praeconium
> meatus unus, inpar ad laudes Dei.
>
> (Lns. 562-65)

"Much thanks I owe to you, sir, because now I open many mouths to speak of Christ. The single passage used to restrict the publishing of his mighty name; it was too little for the praises of God."

Romanus' supreme rhetorical ability to make something good out of everything bad continues, when the increasingly furious Asclepiades decides to burn his victim, to humiliate him, as Christ was humiliated on the cross. Romanus takes the cue, and argues that Christ's humiliation was a symbolic act of sublimity; rather than new-fangled, it is eternal.

To prove the strength of his position, Romanus now asks to examine a child, to hear from the harmless infant's "milky mouth" the truth of Christianity:

> ardens experiri innoxiam
> lactantis oris indolem.
>
> (Lns. 666-67)

Asclepiades agrees, and orders a child ("nec olim lacte depulsum") brought forth to be examined.[64] Paradigmatically pious, the child gives the answers which Prudentius tells us were imbibed at his mother's twin fountains:

> ego, ut gemellis uberum de fontibus
> lac parvus hausi, Christum et hausi credere.
>
> (Lns. 684-85)

And I in drinking as a babe the milk from the twin founts of her breasts drank in also the belief in Christ.

Infuriated once again, Asclepiades orders that the child be beaten; when the child cries out with thirst, he is castigated by his mother, in whose speech the motif of milk reappears, now mingled with blood and honey, in a passage that recalls, both for the child and for the readers of the poem, the Massacre of the Innocents:

> Hic hic bibendus, nate, nunc tibi est calix,
> mille in Bethleem quem biberunt parvuli;
> oblita lactis et papillarum immemor

aetas amaris, mox deinde dulcibus
refecta poclis mella sumpsit sanguinis.

(Lns. 736-40)

This, this, my son, is the cup you now must drink. A thousand little ones in Bethlehem drank of it; forgetting their milk, with no thought of the breast, their life was restored by bitter cups that turned to sweet, partaking of blood that was changed into honey.

Addressing him now as *fortis puer,* she reminds him that he has also received *sapientia,* as she weaves the ludic motif together with the idea of sacrifice, reminding the child that his play was learning Christian doctrine. In the Bible, she reminds him, Isaac stretching his neck at the altar, prepared by his father is the major model for infant sacrifice:

Scis, saepe dixi, cum docenti adluderes
et garrulorum signa verborum dares,
Isaac fuisse parvulum patri unicum,
qui, cum immolandus aram et ensem cerneret,
ultro sacranti colla praebuerit seni.

(Lns. 746-50)

You know, for I have often told you, when you used to turn my lessons into play and prattle sounds that stood for words, that Isaac was a little boy, his father's only child, and how, when he was to be sacrificed and saw the altar and the sword, of his own will he stretched out his neck to the old man who was making the offering.

Her next biblical illustration is taken from 2 Macc. 7, where children again died before their mother's eyes.[65] Like a typical Prudentian speaker, she provides specific, graphic detail for the "contest" ("certamen") (ln. 753), which she paraphrases:

Comam cutemque verticis revulserat
a fronte tortor, nuda testa ut tegmine
cervicem adusque dehonestaret caput. . . .

(Lns. 761-63)

The torturer tore away the hair and skin of the head from the brow backwards, so that the bare skull uncovered down to the neck should dishonour it.

Anticipating Romanus' own fate, the child's mother describes the amputation of the tongue of one of the biblical martyrs, allowing the Maccabean mother to compose an encomiastic series of apostrophes to the tongue, culminating in addressing the tongue as "redemptrix prima membrorum omnium," an analogue for Christ himself:

Linguam tyrannus amputari iusserat
uni ex ephebis; mater aiebat: "Satis
iam parta nobis gloria est, pars optima
deo immolatur ecce nostri corporis,
digna est fidelis lingua, quae sit hostia.

Interpres animi, enuntiatrix sensuum,
cordis ministra, praeco operti pectoris,
prima offeratur in sacramentum necis
et sit redemptrix prima membrorum omnium."

(Lns. 765-74)

The oppressor commanded the tongue of one of the young lads to be cut out, and his mother said: "Now we have won glory enough, for lo, the best part of our body is being sacrificed to God. The faithful tongue is worthy to be an offering. The mind's spokesman, which declares our sentiments, the heart's servant, which proclaims the silent thoughts of our breast, let it be offered first for the celebration of the mystery of death, and be the first to redeem all the members."

Responsive to his mother's exhortation, *laetus,* the child laughs at the blows that fall upon him, provoking Asclepiades to torture and decapitate him. As the executioner strikes her baby's neck, the blood pours over his ecstatic mother, and the *docta mulier* sings Ps. 115:6-7 (116:15-16 AV), then catches the blood (lns. 841-45) and "palpantis oris exciperet globum" (ln. 844). In an ironic reworking of the motif of milk, then, the maternal flow undergoes a grim reversal, and the "pectoris nectar" (ln. 783) is returned as a flood of blood.[66] The child, then, is the ultimate *puer senex,* a Christ-like martyr, whose mother, like Mary, is left with the remains of her son; unlike Mary, however, she is left not with the body, but with the blood of her son.

The death of the child may also be an example of the contest with pagan texts in which Prudentius imagined himself to be engaged, if the scene is regarded as an attempt to "correct" a scene in Statius' *Thebaid.* Mourning the death of the infant Opheltes, killed by a snake, Hypsipyle describes her milk as a barren, unfortunate rain falling from her breasts upon the child's wounds, and she attributes the calamity to the gods:

sic equidem luctus solabar et ubera parvo
iam materna dabam, cui nunc venit inritus orbae
lactis et infelix in vulnera liquitur imber.
nosco Deos . . .

(V.617-20).

For so indeed did I console my griefs, and gave the babe a mother's breasts, where now in my bereavement the milk flows in vain and falls in barren drops upon thy wounds. "'Tis the gods' work I see . . ."[67]

Where Hypsipyle blames the gods, Prudentius' Christian mother thanks the one God, in an example of intertextuality that anticipates Dante's use of Rifeo to correct Vergil's "diis aliter visum."[68]

Prudentius now returns to Romanus' predicament. When the pyre being prepared for him is extinguished by rain, Asclepiades becomes enraged that his victim seems to be turning punishment into play:

"Quousque tandem summus hic nobis magus
inludet," inquit, "Thessalorum carmine
poenam peritus vertere in ludibrium?"

(Lns. 868-70)

"How long," he asked, "is this great sorcerer to make
game of us through his skill in turning punishment to
mockery with a Thessalian spell?"

If "quousque tandem" is intended to invoke the opening
of the first oration against Catiline, then Cicero is both
invoked and defeated in this passage, since Asclepiades
in the analogy is parallel to the most famous Roman
orator. If the suggestion that Romanus is parallel to
Catiline weakens the impulse to draw the parallel,
however, the saint's ability to speak after his tongue is
cut out may rekindle the enthusiasm. Since Cicero, in
the process of being assassinated, said nothing after losing his tongue, the comparison with Romanus' tongue-
less performance suggests that the Christian speaker is
superior.

Prudentius continues to ring the changes on the motif
of dismemberment; Asclepiades now expresses the
desire to kill Romanus as many times as his victim has
members. To carry out his wishes in a responsible,
professional manner, he summons a *medicus,* who
undertakes, as his first assignment, the task of amputat-
ing Romanus' tongue. Prudentius focuses sharply on
the extended tongue, on the scalpel as it cuts, on the tis-
sue being torn, and on Romanus' Stoic ability to resist
clenching his teeth or swallowing the blood:

Linguam deinde longe ab ore protrahens
scalpellum in usque guttur insertans agit.
Illo secante fila sensim singula
numquam momordit martyr aut os dentibus
conpressit artis nec cruorem sorbuit.

(Lns. 901-905)

Then drawing the tongue far out from the mouth he
puts his lancet inside, right down to the gullet. While
he was gradually cutting the filaments one by one, the
martyr never bit nor let his teeth meet to close his
mouth, nor swallowed blood.

The amputated tongue was a hagiographical commonplace,[69] which Prudentius also uses in the recollection of 2 Macc. 7 that occurs in **Peristephanon** V:

Num Maccabei martyris
linguam tyrannus erutam
raptamve pellem verticis
avibus cruentis obtulit.

(Lns. 533-36)

Did the oppressor offer the Maccabean martyr's tongue
to bloodthirsty birds after it was plucked out, or the
skin of the head after it was torn out?

However, the amputated tongue was also a commonplace in the literature of pagan philosopher-martyrs.
Zeno of Elia mutilates his inquisitor, the tyrant

Nearchus, by biting off either his ear or his nose, then
biting off his own tongue and spitting it at his tormentor, in return for which he is pounded to death in a
mortar. Diogenes Laertius tells roughly the same story
about Anaxarchus.[70]

Since the pagan martyrs with whom Romanus, in a
sense, is competing, cut out their own tongues, and
since Romanus denounces self-mutilators twice in the
poem, another correction of a pagan notion may be taking place here also.[71]

Romanus, however, kingly in the purple of his own
blood, without a tongue in his head, speaks on (lns.
926ff.), explaining that this miraculous speech is a gift
of the creator, who can change the laws of nature, since
he who established them may violate them at will.
Furthermore, Romanus' ability to speak after his own
tongue has been cut out reinforces the validity of the
miracles Christ performed in biblical times:

Habet usitatum munus hoc divinitas,
quae vera nobis colitur in Christo et patre,
mutis loquellam, percitum claudis gradum,
surdis fruendam reddere audientiam,
donare caecis lucis insuetae diem.

Haec si quis amens fabulosa existimat,
vel ipse tute si parum fidelia
rebare pridem, vera cognoscas licet.
Habes loquentem, cuius amputaveras
linguam. Probatis cede iam miraculis.

(Lns. 951-60)

It is a familiar power of the true divine nature which
we worship in Christ and the Father, to restore speech
to the dumb, a quick step to the lame, the benefit of
hearing to the deaf, and give to the blind the unwonted
light of day. If any man is fool enough to think these
things are fabulous, or if you yourself formerly judged
them unworthy of belief, you may learn that they are
real: you have here a man speaking after you have cut
his tongue out. Yield now to miracles you have proved.

Cede infuriates Asclepiades yet once more; instead of
yielding, however, he attacks the incompetence of the
doctor who performed the mutilation. The doctor replies
that Asclepiades should look for himself, and asks for a
test pig upon whom to perform a repetition of the operation. When Asclepiades asks whether the blood that he
saw was truly that of Romanus, the saint insists that the
blood is his own ("Meus iste sanguis verus est, non
bubulus") (ln. 1007). Blood now becomes a topic to be
amplified, and he proceeds to compose an attack on
pagan blood-letting rites of initiation.

First he attacks the *taurobolium,* with a graphic description of the slaughtered ox and the priest who stands
below the bleeding animal, bathing in the blood and
drinking the dark gore as it rains upon his tongue:

Quin os supinat, obvias offert genas,
supponit aures, labra nares obicit,
oculos et ipsos perluit liquoribus,
nec iam palato parcit et linguam rigat,
donec cruorem totus atrum conbibat.

(Lns. 1036-1040)

Laying his head back he even puts his cheeks in the
way, placing his ears under it, exposing lips and
nostrils, bathing his very eyes in the stream, not even
keeping his mouth from it but wetting his tongue, until
the whole of him drinks in the dark gore.

Prudentius' Romanus scornfully describes the blood-
smeared priest standing before the devotees of Mithras
and the Magna Mater, an absurd object of worship
("visu horridus") (ln. 1043), and then proceeds to attack
hecatombs ("centena ferro cum cadunt animalia") when
so many animals are slaughtered that the worshippers
seem in danger of drowning in blood:

vix ut cruentis augures natatibus
possint meare per profundum sanguinis.

(Lns. 1054-55)

So that the augurs almost have to swim to make their
way through the sea of blood?

Modulating from this sardonic attack on mutilating
animals, Romanus turns to self-mutilation, attacking the
pagan practice of castration, extending his earlier
diatribe against the ritual (lns. 196ff.) with a routine on
the indeterminancy of the resultant sexuality:

ast hic metenda dedicat genitalia,
numen reciso mitigans ab inguine
offert pudendum semivir domum deae;
illam revulsa masculini germinis
vena effluenti pascit auctam sanguine.

uterque sexus sanctitati displicet,
medium retentat inter alternum genus,
mas esse cessat ille, nec fit femina.
felix deorum mater inberbes sibi
parat ministros levibus novaculis.

(Lns. 1066-75)

Another makes the sacrifice of his genitals; appeasing
the goddess by mutilating his loins, he unmans himself
and offers her a shameful gift; the source of the man's
seed is torn away to give her food and increase through
the flow of blood. Both sexes are displeasing to her
holiness, so he keeps a middle gender between the two,
ceasing to be a man without becoming a woman. The
Mother of the Gods has the happiness of getting herself
beardless minsters with a well-ground razor!

Now almost at the end of his final diatribe, Romanus
attacks the practice of branding the body with burning
needles, a lesser form of self-mutilation, but one whose
absurdity permits Romanus to return to the ludic motif,
in this case offering the practice as evidence of demonic
delusion:

Has ferre poenas cogitur genitilitas,
hac di coercent lege cultores suos.
Sic daemon ipse ludit hos quos ceperit,
docet execrandas ferre contumelias,
tormenta inuri mandat infelicibus.

(Lns. 1086-90)

Such are the sufferings pagans are compelled to bear,
such the law their gods impose on their worshippers;
this is how the devil himself makes sport of those
whom he has taken captive, teaching them to suffer accursed indignities and ordaining that marks of torture
be branded on his luckless victims.

Asclepiades now orders him to prison, giving specific
instructions to strangle Romanus by breaking his
windpipe:

Aliter silere nescit oris garruli
vox inquieta quam turba si fregero.

(Lns. 1104-05)

"The restless voice in your chattering mouth can only
be silenced if I break its pipe."

As the poem moves towards its conclusion, images of
books return; Prudentius asserts that Asclepiades sent
written documents ("chartulis vivacibus") as a report of
his proceedings against Romanus to the emperor, but
time has decayed them; Christ's page, however, is immortal, and Romanus' martyrdom is recorded forever
"in regestis . . . caelestibus."

At the end of the poem, as he had at the beginning of
the poem, Prudentius calls upon Romanus for assistance, in a version of the humility-topos, this time
not to aid him to speak, but to become an analogue for
the the Word itself. He says that Romanus' prayer could
change him from a goat to a lamb, from the abhorrent
animal, the pagan "scapegoat," to the sacred Christian
animal, the "agnus Dei," i.e., the Logos:[72]

Vellem sinister inter haedorum greges
ut sum futurus, eminus dinoscerer
atque hoc precante diceret rex optimus:
"Romanus orat, transfer hunc haedum mihi;
sit dexter agnus, induatur vellere.

(Lns. 1136-40)

Would that I, standing as I shall be on the left among
the flocks of goats, might be picked out from afar and
at Romanus' petition the King most excellent might
say: "Romanus prays for him. Bring this goat over to
me; let him stand on my right hand as a lamb and be
clothed in a fleece."

Thus Prudentius provides a hero whose *fortitudo* and
sapientia are fused. Polemic dominates the poem; like
the **Psychomachia,** and the **Contra orationem Symmachi, Peristephanon** X represents a battle, in which the
hero's only weapon is speech, winning an argument his

only task. Romanus wins the encounters with his torturer-antagonist by drawing his arguments both from Christian doctrine, and, giving the impression that he is performing *ex tempore,* from his opponent's own words. Stripped of his only weapon, his tongue, he manages nevertheless to perform the ultimate rhetorical accomplishment for a Christian poet: He defeats the religion of the culture that produced the very skill in which he is supreme.[73]

The result, a poem compounded out of hagiography, polemic, diatribe, and lyric, offers a rare combination of ideology and literary technique[74] that reflects what Charles Witke described as "an inner landscape of offering . . . not penetrated again until much later, by the Latin and vernacular poets of love, both sacred and profane, of the eleventh and twelfth centuries."[75]

Notes

1. Macklin Smith gives a useful summary of critical responses to Prudentius in *Prudentius' Psychomachia: A Reexamination* (Princeton: Princeton Univ. Press, 1976), 3-28. W.J. Henderson gives a survey of responses to a particularly disturbing aspect of Prudentius' style in "Violence in Prudentius' *Peristephanon,*" *Akroterion* 28 (1983): 84-92.

2. *History and Literature of Christianity,* trans. H. Wilson (New York, 1968), 450. Maurice Lavarenne, a major contributor to Prudentius scholarship, attributes to his subject a bizarre taste for the horrible, in *Etude sur la langue du poète Prudence* (Paris, 1933), chap. 3.

3. Klaus Thraede, *Studien zu Sprache und Stil Prudentius* (Göttingen, 1965), 48-72; Charles Witke, "Prudentius and the Tradition of Latin Poetry," *Transactions of the American Philological Society* 99 (1968): 524: "Almost every aspect of his poetry is classical in basis."

4. *Op. cit.,* 18.

5. A fear that is not unique to him, as Kenneth R. Haworth points out when he speaks of "the disposition to over-emphasize Prudentius' Christianity" among readers of Prudentius, in *Deified Virtues, Demonic Vices and Descriptive Allegory in Prudentius' Psychomachia* (Amsterdam, 1980), 112-13. Haworth proposes instead, "He was more a Roman than a Christian."

6. See Thraede, *op. cit.,* 16. In fact, Witke does nothing of the sort; he concentrates on Prudentius' abilities as a Roman, Latin poet in order to demonstrate his effectiveness as a Christian poet.

7. Maurice Cunningham, in his edition of the poems (Turnholt, 1966), xxxv, offers as his contribution to the discussion:

Non est igitur Christianus Maro vel Flaccus, ne Pindarus quidem Latinus.

Prudentius est poeta Christianus; nomen utrum meruit.

8. Filippo Ermi, *Peristephanon* (Rome, 1914), 160-61, 210. Jacques Fontaine speaks of "la puissance de l'imagination visuelle, qui est peut-être la faculté poétique majeure de Prudence," in *Naissance de la poésie dans l'occident chrétien* (Paris, 1981), 188.

9. In spite of Fridolf Kudlein's respectful request that the term be laid aside when speaking of Prudentius, in "Krankheitsmetaphorik in Laurentiushymnus des Prudentius," *Hermes* 90 (1962): 104-15.

10. Jacques Fontaine, "Le mélange des genres dans la poésie de Prudence," in *Forma Futuri: studi in onore del Cardinale Michele Pellegrino* (Torino, 1975), 757. The opposition of classical to some other decorum may remind some readers of the polarity between "classical" aesthetics and "grotesque realism" conceived and promulgated by Mikhail Bakhtin, in *Rabelais and His World* (Cambridge, 1968).

11. *Op. cit.,* 771.

12. *Ibid,* p. 772.

13. H. Delehaye, *Les passions des martyres et les genres littéraires* (Brussels, 1921).

14. Walther Ludwig, "Die Christliche Dichtung des Prudentius und die Transformation der Klassischen Gattung," in *Christianisme et formes littéraires de l'antiquité tardive en occident,* ed. Manfred Fuhrmann, (Geneva: Fondations Hardt, 1976), 305. On mixed genres, see also E. R. Curtius, *European Literature and the Latin Middle Ages* (New York, 1963), 424.

15. *Op. cit.,* 335ff, 338.

16. F. J. E. Raby, *A History of Christian-Latin Poetry from the Beginning to the Close of the Middle Ages,* 2d ed. (Oxford, 1953), 50.

17. Jean-Louis Charlet, *La création poétique dans le Cathemerinon de Prudence* (Paris, 1982), 187.

18. Herbert Musurillo, *Acts of the Pagan Martyrs* (Oxford, 1954), 236, n. 1.

19. All quotations from Prudentius' poems are from Maurice P. Cunningham's edition, *Carmina* (Turnholt, 1966). Translations are from the Loeb Classical edition of Prudentius, edited by H. J. Thomson (Cambridge, 1949).

20. For Stoic indifference to death, combined with extraordinary rhetorical competence, see Musurillo, *op. cit.,* 237.

21. Lactantius' interest in the details of suffering offers a useful contrast, since he devotes lavish attention to the sufferings of those who refuse to accept Christianity, producing what J. L. Creed describes as "an uncharitable delight . . . in the sufferings of the discomfited persecutors," in *De Mortibus Persecutorum* (Oxford, 1984). The detailed, graphic description of Maximilian Galerius' illness, 50 ff., is probably as disgusting as any produced in this particular branch of Christian diatribe. For more on this topic, see Arnaldo Momigliano, "Pagan and Christian Historiography in the Fourth Century A.D.," in *The Conflict between Paganism and Christianity in the Fourth Century* (Oxford, 1963), 79.

22. A technique he also uses in *Peristephanon* IX for the death of Cassian.

23. *Op. cit.,* 184.

24. M. A. Wes's formulation, in a review article in *Vigiliae Christianae* 25 (1971), 234.

25. *Aeneid* 3.618 and 4.64 supply grotesque images of feeding, as well as gory sacrifice, that may have provoked Prudentius' competitive impulses.

26. S. F. Bonner, *Roman Declamation in the Late Republic and Empire* (Liverpool, 1969), 59-60, 165. Bonner also gives momentary consideration to the influence of Iberia: "The love of gruesome detail, in which Seneca is only equalled by his nephew Lucan, may perhaps be partly a Spanish characteristic, but probably owes something to the declaimers" (165). See also G. Sixt, "Des Prudentius Abhängigkeit von Seneca und Lucan," *Philologus* 51 (1982): 501-506.

27. "De Prudentio—Pindaro Latino," in *Eos* 49 (1957): 140. He also remarks: "Nam rhetoricam videmus Prudentio fuisse generis dicendi magistram praecipuam, rhetores autem scimus alumnos ita loquendi arte exercuisse, ut multas variasque possent res et copiose tractare et accuratissime describere."

28. *Op. cit,* 84.

29. *Ibid.,* 91. See also R. Henke, *Studien zum Romanushymnus der Prudentius* (Bern, 1983), 88 ff., for the arguments that the graphic representation of horror is a means of emphasizing the supernatural powers granted to the martyrs by God.

30. In the Loeb Classical edition of Prudentius, the editor, H. J. Thomson, finds "an excess of rhetoric" in the *Peristephanon* (Cambridge, 1949), xiii.

Such judgments characterize much of the criticism of early Latin Christian poetry; see, for example, Dag Norberg's response to Sedulius' description of the martyrdom of the Innocents in *Au Seuil du Moyen Age* (Padua, 1974), 148-49.

31. Roland Barthes, *Writing Degree Zero* (New York, 1968), 21.

32. Henri Peyre, *Literature and Sincerity* (New Haven, 1963), 134.

33. A process clearly antithetical to the process described and labelled "Augustinian" by Erich Auerbach in *Literary Language and its Public in Late Latin Antiquity and in the Middle Ages* (New York, 1965), pp. 37 ff. Auerbach does remark that although Prudentius cannot be wholly identified with the *sermo humilis,* he nevertheless has much in common with it. See also remarks below on *Peristephanon* XII.

34. For an analysis of *Peristephanon* IV, with considerable emphasis on the significance of speech, see Alison Goddard Elliot, *Roads to Paradise* (Hanover, 1987), 27-33.

35. Henke, *op. cit.,* establishes the precedents, with an emphasis on Christian texts, for some of what Prudentius does. As a result, however, two elements in Prudentius' poem, which contribute to its unique (and for some, its unbearable) quality, are left unaccounted for: his use of Roman rhetorical strategies to attack ancient Roman religion, and a related element, the ludic motif that runs through the hymn to Romanus, as well as through several of the other poems in the *Peristephanon.*

36. See Curtius, *op. cit.,* 311-12, for comments on Prudentius' self-consciousness about language, particularly in his use of images of the book and writing.

37. Curtius, *op. cit.,* 425-26.

38. *History and Literature of Christianity* (London, 1924), 454. See below for Romanus' use of medical material.

39. For discussion of the relationship between play and Christian doctrine, see Johann Huizinga, *Homo Ludens* (New York, 1970); Hugo Rahner, "Der spielende Mensch," *Eranos-Jahrbuch* 16 (1949), and his article, "Eutrapélie," in *Dictionnaire de spiritualité* 4.2 (Paris, 1960): 1728; Jean Charles Payen, "Le comique de l'énormité," *L'esprit créature* 16 (1976): 46-60; Joachim Suchomski, *Delectatio und utilitas* (Bern, 1975), 55-61; and R. Levine, "Wolfram von Eschenbach: Dialectical *Homo Ludens,*" *Viator* 13 (1982): 177-201.

40. PGL 50.606.

41. Fontaine, *Naissance*, 189.

42. *Op. cit.*, 146.

43. See Thraede, *op. cit.*, 132, for an attempt to deal with the charge that these speeches do not develop from the situation, but are, in effect, left over from the tirade against Symmachus. A century before Prudentius, Arnobius, whom LaBriolle called a "pitiless satirist" (197), had compiled the *Adversus Nationes*, "the most intense and most sustained of all extant counterattacks upon the contemporary pagan cults" (George E. McCracken, *Arnobius of Sicca: The Case against the Pagans* [New York, 1949], 4). For a concise description of the satiric traditions upon which early Christian apologists drew, see David Wiesen, *Saint Jerome as a Satirist* (Ithaca, 1964), 1-19: "The fourth century after Christ . . . witnessed the sudden reawakening of interest in the classical writers of satire" (3).

44. In addition, a pagan revival was going on in Rome; see H. Bloch, "The Pagan Revival in the West at the End of the Fourth Century," in Momigliano, *op. cit.*, 200.

45. *Op. cit.*, 49.

46. Play may also have negative connotations. Firmicus Maternus, for example, in the midst of attacks on pagan religion that resemble those Prudentius makes, calls the devil *ludibriosus hostis;* see Ilona Opelt, "Schimpfwörter in der Apologie De error profanarum religionum des Firmicus Maternus," *Glotta* 52 (1974): 114-26.

47. F. H. Colson and G. H. Whitaker, eds., *Philo* 3 (London, 1954): 301.

48. See below. For *puer senex* among the Jews, see H. W. Surkan, *Martyrien in jüdische und frühchristlicher Zeit* (Göttingen, 1938).

49. Jean-Louis Charlet, *L'influence d'Ausone sur la poésie de Prudence* (Aix-en-Provence, 1980), 70-71.

50. Peter Von Moos, "The Use of *Exempla* in the *Policraticus* of John of Salisbury," in *The World of John of Salisbury,* ed. Michael Wilks (Oxford, 1984), 247.

51. *PG:* [*Patrologia Graeca*] 20.1464-67. For graphic descriptions of torture and martyrdom nearly equal to those Prudentius provides, see also the events of A.D. 177 as Eusebius describes them in the *Ecclesiastical History,* V.I; see also W. H. C. Frend, *Martyrdom and Persecution in the Early Church* (Oxford, 1965).

52. Charles Witke, *Numen Litterarum* (Leiden, 1971), 128, finds that the opening strophes of *Pe* X offers a "rather curious congruence." Thraede, *op. cit.*

53. Bernard M. Peebles, *The Poet Prudentius* (New York, 1951), 91.

54. *Transactions,* 524.

55. A figure he may have borrowed from Chrysostom (PGL 614).

56. See F. Zambon, "Vipreus liquor," in *Cultura neolatina* XL (1980): 1-15, for the "generation of vipers," with sources in Herodotus, Pliny, Hermetic literature, various patristic writings, and Ambrose particularly, since his influence on Prudentius is significant. According to Zambon, Prudentius transcends Ambrose in his use of this *incubo teologico* (15).

57. For a convincing reading of *Peristephanon* XIII, emphasizing the sexual perverseness of Cyprian, as well as drawing parallels between Cyprian's tongue and Romanus' tongue, see Martha Malamud, *A Poetics of Transformation* (Ithaca, 1989), 115-48.

58. For some of the sources for the topic of "natural nobility," see Henke, *op. cit.*, 155-70. For a comprehensive catalogue see G. M. Vogt, "Gleanings for the History of Sentiment: *Generositas Virtus non Sanquis,*" *JEGP* [*Journal of English and Germanic Philology*] 24 (1925): 102-23.

59. In *Contra Symmachus* II.862, Prudentius also attacks this ritual, but does not use "game," and no specific mention of women is made.

60. See *Contra Orationem Symmachi* I. 103ff. for attack on Priapus, Hercules' homosexual inclinations, and the perverse sexuality of ancient Roman religion.

61. Fontaine's phrase, in *Naissance,* 39.

62. *Instructiones* 1.2.2-4, ed. Joseph Martin, *Commodiani Carmina* (Turnhold, 1960), 3.

63. Torture that cures occurs in Eusebius' description of the martyrdom of Sanctus V.i.24.

64. See Henke, *op, cit.*, 136-51, on the use of children as a means of argument in ancient literature.

65. Prudentius also uses the incident in *Peristephanon* V.523ff.

66. The mother grateful to God for her child's death is a commonplace of the genre, according to Delehaye, *op. cit.*, 228.

67. Text and translation from *Statius,* ed. J. H. Mozley, (Cambridge, 1957).

122, points out the anomaly of a martyr at Antioch in a list of Spanish martyrs, and gives some attempt at answers.

68. *Paradiso* XX.

69. See Delehaye *op. cit.*, 281.

70. Diogenes Laertius, *Lives of Eminent Philosophers,* trans. R. D. Hicks (Cambridge, 1965), II, 436-37, 472-73. Plutarch says that Zeno bit his tongue off to prevent himself from revealing anything; see *de garrulitate* 505 D, in *Moralia,* trans. W. C. Helmbold (Cambridge, 1939), VI, 414-15. See also Woldemar Görler, "From Athens to Tusculum," *Rhetorica* 6 (1988): 230-33, on the philosophical martyr.

71. Since both fabliaux and saints' lives draw upon popular traditions, R. Howard Bloch's proposal of a connection between mutilation and linguistic competition may have some relevance in a discussion of this commonplace: "False castration casts the fabliaux in the mold of narrative competition between various protagonists, a competition that, once again, mirrors the rivalry between jongleurs" (*The Scandal of the Fabliaux,* [Chicago, 1986]; 98). Bloch connects castration with the "desire for narrative," speaks of the poet as trickster, makes a parallel between bodily dismemberment and linguistic disruption, and points out that under these conditions absences speak (101-102). That the connection between sex and speech may have psychoanalytic significance does not exclude the fact that such a connection was part of the rhetorician's stock-in-trade.

72. As Wolf Steidle has remarked, for Prudentius the Logos made flesh was more significant as a factor in man's salvation than the death on the cross; see "Das Dichterische Konzeption des Prudentius umd das Gedicht contra Symmachum," *Vigiliae Christianae* 25 (1971): 247.

73. Anne-Marie Palmer offers an example of such competition when she speaks of Prudentius "out-satirizing" Juvenal (in *Peristephanon* X.269-95) in *Prudentius on the Martyrs* (Oxford, 1989), 182.

74. See Gian Biagio Conte, *The Rhetoric of Imitation* (Cornell, 1986), 97, for the conventional split.

75. *Transactions* 525.

Eva Kimminich (essay date spring 1991)

SOURCE: Kimminich, Eva. "The Way of Vice and Virtue: A Medieval Psychology." *Comparative Drama* 25, no. 1 (spring 1991): 77-86.

[*In the following essay, Kimminich considers the influence of the* Psychomachia *on the medieval public's understanding of vice and virtue.*]

The principal concern of medieval thinking was man's spiritual welfare. It was deeply rooted in the dichotomy of the generally negatively defined body and the positively evaluated soul with the redemption of the soul—and also the body—as the main aim. This central idea runs throughout the thought and imagery of the Christian Middle Ages.

In iconography, literature, and drama we can take note of increasing differentiation with regard to the presentation of the vices, which are treated with much greater specificity in the later Middle Ages than had been the case in late antiquity or the early medieval periods[1]— e.g., in the time of Aurelius Prudentius (c.348-405), whose **Psychomachia**[2] is a seminal text with regard to our study. The increasing sensitivity with which the symbols and their attributes were handled must be considered the result of more acute psychological observation and analysis of human conduct and the motivations behind the way people behave or misbehave.

Sinfulness was initially often connected with the influence of demonic powers or with planetary influences. The association between the planets and behavior in particular was based on the pre-Christian and Neo-Platonic worldviews of late antiquity, which in many cases tended to see the human being's physical and moral condition as dominated by planetary deities. Such deities were believed to implant positive or negative qualities in the soul on its descent through the celestial spheres down to earth—views which subsequently continued to receive attention in Christian theology. For instance, Martin, Archbishop of Braga (c.520-80), in his *De Correctione Rusticorum* represented the planetary deities as malign: Jupiter as a magician and adulterer, Venus as a whore, and so forth.[3] In his view these qualities were indicative of the lapsarian state of man, whose natural tendencies toward sin were thus displayed.

The Church Fathers—for example, St. Augustine (354-430)—had allocated responsibility for a human being's spiritual welfare to the person himself. Not surprisingly, differing interpretations were developed.[4] While St. Augustine did not deny the influence of the stars, he nevertheless stressed free will and grace as stronger forces in the psychological battle of man against vice.[5] In Augustine's view, sin is the renunciation of God caused by man's pride, while self-love is the result of surrender to one's sensual desires, the various kinds of concupiscence which negate his better self and lead him to become guilty. He argued that only active sinfulness will turn Original Sin, which is inherited along with the human condition, into personal guilt that cannot be set aside by any human action and, unless grace intercedes, may result in eternal damnation. Accordingly, as is well known, he differentiated between a temporal city devoted to selfishness and a heavenly community devoted to good, between the earthly city (*civitas terrena*) and city of God (*civitas Dei*). In the former—the synonymous name of which, *civitas diaboli,* points to the end which the unregenerate, whose devotion is to this city, will endure—two alternative ways of life are open to the human being so that he himself would be responsible for the fate of his soul. A colored woodcut in the edition of St. Augustine's *De Civitatis Dei* printed at Freiburg in 1494 illustrates the author writing down his ideas; at his right, the people of Zion are shown in the heavenly Jerusalem, while at his left is Babylon, founded by Cain, with the devil on its pinnacles.[6] The virtuous life and the vicious life are symbolized by the narrow and arduous path on the one hand, and the broad and comfortable avenue on the other. For Augustine, the choice was between these two paths, one the way of temptation and the other leading away from such surrender of oneself to the world. The efforts of the individual Christian therefore had to be directed toward recognizing the direct connection between his conduct in his earthly life and the reward or punishment awaiting him in the next world.

A more optimistic tradition has been traced to Origen.[7] The defense of this more moderate view can be seen particularly in the poetry of Prudentius, who vehemently opposed the fatalism which characterized the thinking of the Gnostics. His insistence on an absolutely free will[8] stands in contrast with Augustine's theology and hence sets aside the insistence found in his contemporary's thought on the overpowering necessity of grace for salvation. While Augustine became the dominant figure philosophically and theologically, Prudentius' *Psychomachia,* which depicts a symbolic battle of an army of virtues against a troupe of sinful desires, nevertheless presented exciting and long-lasting ideas for pictorial representation.[9] Indeed, the illustrations of manuscripts of the *Psychomachia* reflect a sensitive characterization of human behavior as well as a compelling story of the downfall of vice. These illustrations, for example, show Superbia, the only vice depicted on horseback, thundering proudly along and falling into the snare of Fraud[10]—a vivid depiction of the way in which the vices destroy each other. All attack with weapons except Luxuria, who instead substitutes flowers,[11] which symbolize the seductive aspect of temptation. She will be put down by her opposite, the virtue designated as Sobrietas, who by holding up the cross makes the horses of her opponent's chariot become frightened so that she loses control; she then kills her with a millstone,[12] normally a symbol of earthly restlessness and greed. In the end Luxuria is choked by her own tongue,[13] defined as an organ of sinfulness[14]—i.e., she is destroyed by her own desires.

The optimistic and the pessimistic views outlined above were both traceable in the various ways of depicting the world in the visual arts. The latter view was shown above all in the demonic figures on the capitals of cathedrals and churches and in the drastic torments in hell displayed in the depictions of the Last Judgment. The optimistic battle imagery introduced by Prudentius' *Psychomachia* and ultimately derived in part from St. Paul's admonition to Christians to arm themselves in preparation for warfare against evil (see *1 Thessalonians* 5.8 and *Romans* 6.12), on the other hand, prompted representations of virtue triumphant, as on the thirteenth-century western portal of Strasbourg Cathedral and the portal at Aulnay that both show the personified virtues standing upon the defeated vices, which also display human faces.[15] Active resistance to evil necessarily had consequences with regard to man's ultimate spiritual welfare—consequences that can be traced in iconography in such examples as the famous tympanum of the second quarter of the twelfth century at the Abbey Church of Ste.-Foy at Conques.[16] Here there is a striking scene of Christ in Majesty along with the weighing of souls by St. Michael—the general Judgment at which the effects of human actions are determined. The deeds of men are weighed to discover whether they are to be admitted to paradise or to the place of everlasting damnation. The *psychostasis,* a motif perhaps with its origin in ancient Egypt,[17] had already appeared in the writings of Augustine[18] and in manuscript illuminations, but became a motif in three-dimensional art—i.e., in capitals, tympana, etc.—in the eleventh and twelfth centuries.[19]

If the individual held responsibility for specific deeds which might be judged at the particular Judgment following the moment of death and again at the Last Judgment at the end of history, the rigidly binary next world, which knew only good and evil, heaven and hell, reward or punishment, required enlargement. Developments in this regard may be demonstrated especially in visionary literature which included reports based on purported personal experience for the purpose of moral instruction and demonstration of the theological and moral definitions of sin as well as its differentiation according to its seriousness. Ultimately the concept of the next world was altered to allow for the description of an intermediate place between heaven and hell where sins could be cleansed. The vagueness of the Church Fathers about a place of expiation, proposed as early as Clement of Alexandria, was thus replaced by a very specific belief in purgatory. This place, having become necessary in consequence of the distinction between venial and deadly sins[20] and through repentance in this life offering rescue from everlasting damnation by means of penance in the next, led to extended arguments between theologians. So only in the thirteenth century did purgatory come to be officially defined as a Church doctrine.

This development[21] went hand in hand with the development of a taxonomy which distinguished gradations of the various vicious deeds.

The development of the category of venial sins thus antedates a fully articulated belief in purgatory, for individually adjusted punishments could be assigned according to the seriousness, intensity, and frequency of such sins. The establishment of such categories also influenced the ways in which the *psychostasis* was visualized in the visual arts—a motif which hardly appears by accident in tympana and frescoes or wall paintings at the same time that purgatory was officially being proclaimed as a doctrine.

At that time, gradations also came to be more clearly followed in depictions of the punishments in hell. From biblical literature it had been determined that hell was a place of fire and brimstone and a pit, often in art transformed into a cauldron with a fire under it where souls were punished. After the twelfth century, the date of the *Hortus Deliciarum* of Herrad of Landsberg (c.1195) who provided specific torments for sins, artists often likewise attempted to fit the punishment to the sin.[22]

Fully developed and especially clear are the hierarchies of punishments in representations that came into being in the fourteenth century after Dante's *Divine Comedy,* which summed up the medieval view of the next world and lastingly influenced the visual imagination, especially in Southern Europe. In the cycle of frescoes by Taddeo di Bartolo in San Gimignano (1396), for instance, the proud man has his head sawn off, the miser has his wealth poured into his body as in Herrad's hell, and the envious has his intestines torn out. Such scenes of punishment, adjusted to specific types of misbehavior which appear under the rubrics of the Seven Deadly Sins, also were illustrated in the popular Shepherds' Calendars—e.g., the *Kalendrier et compost des Bergiers* published by Nicolas le Rouge at Troyes in 1496.[23] Here the proud are punished on wheels, which serve as an apt punishment for those who have effected too exalted a posture. Similar punishment was meted out to the proud in the later representation of this motif in the Last Judgment frescoes at Albi of the end of the fifteenth century.[24]

The tendency to differentiate more and more clearly between individual virtues and vices was a result, then, of the understanding of purgatory and hell as hierarchical—a direct consequence of the differing levels of sin, venal and deadly, in which one had participated in this earthly life. Ullrich von Lilienfeld, for example, in his *Concordantia caritatis* (1349-51) assigned to each vice an animal, a tree, a devil, and a historical personality.[25] In the case of Taddeo di Bartolo's fresco, cited above, the designation of parts of the body—the head to *superbia,* the intestines to *invidia*—will explain why their punishments would have been felt to be appropriate. Such assignment of a person's punishment to an organ felt to be associated with his specific deadly sin had already appeared, however, in Patristic literature.[26]

Characteristic actions of virtues and vices are depicted in Giotto's cycle in the Arena Chapel at Padua (1305-06), where Despair is shown as a hanged woman while Injustice is illustrated by the atrocities ordered by a hard-hearted nobleman. In Cecco d'Ascoli's work of 1337 Luxuria lifts her hem temptingly, and Libido is consumed by her lustful desires, symbolized by her burning skirts.[27] Accordingly, the figures of the triumphant virtues were also treated in greater detail. While the twisting vices had not been differentiated on the Strasbourg portal, a later illustration, a fourteenth-century miniature by Nicola da Bologna, showed them as historical personalities; here Justitia stands on Nero, Fortitudo on Holofernes, Temperantia on Epicurus, and so forth.[28] Finally, a cycle of frescoes at Brixon of approximately 1420 shows concrete patterns of behavior—e.g., the gesture of generosity or greediness.[29] The evidence of the visual arts suggests that the representations of the vices in particular—representations that had their basis originally in demonic creatures or planetary influences—came increasingly to be utilized as a means by which human conduct might be analyzed and presented.

This evidence is also corroborated by developments in literature and in dramatic performances. For example, journeys of the soul, becoming popular in the thirteenth century, join psychology and iconography.[30] In the fourteenth century, Guillaume de Deguileville's *Pèlerinage de la Vie Humaine* presented a pilgrim who meets a beautiful female figure named God's Grace.[31] She baptizes him, teaches him to achieve self-control, and explains various theological principles which appear as personifications. Among others, Penance and Confession are introduced to him. Afterward he is supplied with weapons which are to protect him against danger on his travels. He receives a pilgrim's satchel, Faith, and a pilgrim's staff, Hope. The four cardinal virtues are given to him as armor, though he will find this protection too heavy to continue to wear (he will take it off). God's Grace feels obliged to have him accompanied by Memory. Reason explains to him that he consists of body and soul and that he must understand his greatest enemy to be his own lustful desires; to allow him to experience the weakness of the body alone without the sustenance of the soul's strength, she temporarily makes him soulless—a very illustrative elucidation of the body-soul principle. As soon as he has started on his way, the thoughtless pilgrim is led into a false direction by Idleness, and immediately the

Seven Deadly Sins appear. Laziness binds his feet to prevent him from going to confession. Pride is characterized by a white cloak called Hypocrisy which, it is explained, will cover her disgusting features and suggest intellectual abilities that in fact are lacking. Such an endeavor to disguise the truly ugly appearance of this figure is the result of the *deformitas carnalis* characterizing the vices which had been discussed already by Augustine.

In Prudentius' **Psychomachia** and subsequent works of literature—e.g., the *Anticlaudianus* of Alan de Insulis or the *Songe d'enfer* of Raoul de Hudenc—the conflicting virtues and vices were fighting over the soul of the human being outside of his body, but in Deguileville's work the contest moves to the individual himself, who is identified in the text as "ego." A decisive innovation appears, however, in Huon de Mery's *Tornoiemenz Antecrit* (1234-35) for the first time:[32] Man is now an autonomous being, an opponent of and equal fighter against the vices. He has become an acting subject. It is he himself who decides success or disaster. By his laziness, symbolized by the rejection of his armor, he is thrown into the chaos of his own weakness. Thereby it is made quite clear that the vices are no longer identified with demonic beings but are human wishes and desires. The cloak of Pride, which as we have seen is Hypocrisy, shows how reluctant man is to admit to himself that he is essentially feeble and hence unable of his own unaided strength to make himself better. The example of laziness who keeps the pilgrim from going to confession makes him aware of his own idleness in an amusing but very clear way.

The approach described above, rather than being indicative of the quality of abstraction often attributed to allegory, instead allows the human being to become an acting, self-reliant subject. As such, he was also brought onto the stage. Hence in *Mankind*,[33] an English morality of c.1470, the principal champion of evil robs the protagonist of his spade to keep him from a life of industrious piety. Here Mankind is attacked not with weapons and roses as in Deguileville's work, but rather by robbing him of those things which he needs to go about his business; thus circumstances are used as an excuse for not turning away from evil. The devil Titivillus who steals the spade is only a pretext not to overcome one's own laziness or sloth, which to be sure is one of the Seven Deadly Sins. This evasion is clearly unmasked by the change of names used as a cover-up for vicious conduct in other plays such as Henry Medwall's *Nature*,[34] written at the end of the fifteenth century. In this play, Deadly Sins approach the representative of humankind using assumed names rather than disguises—e.g., Wrath claims to be Manhode (l. 738), Pryde to be Worshyp (ll. 836-37), and Glotony to be Good Felyshyp (l. 759). Through these name changes

the negative character of the qualities would seem on the surface to be transformed into positive ones, but the cleverness only hides their true nature. To the warning against the vices is added another caution: to avoid self-deception.

As I have attempted to demonstrate, medieval iconography and psychology can be drawn upon to sketch not only the way in which the person was made responsible for his misbehaviors or sins but also the manner in which he was forced to realize that his own weaknesses were his enemies. Furthermore, he was shown how to recognize his failures—failures which are commonly denied through various mental processes of rationalization.

The symbols and metaphors which surrounded the person in the Middle Ages and early Renaissance hence actually stimulated a critical look at the self and at the coherence of the Christian conception of the world. The symbols and metaphors would frighten, admonish, but also strengthen him. By the fifteenth century, the formerly abstract allegorical figures representing the vices became exact character studies which referred the human being to his own responsibility for his actions. It is for this reason that this philosophical and symbolic system can be called a medieval psychology which allows the study of the development of human consciousness and the recognition of each individual's individuality. This development is a crucial one for drama at the end of the Middle Ages and thereafter.

Notes

1. The present study grows out of work on the influence of medieval representations of vices on popular festivals; already published is Eva Kimminich, *Des Teufels Werber: Mittelalterliche Lastergestaltung und Gestaltungsformen der Fastnacht,* Artes Populares, 11 (Frankfort: Petter Lang, 1986). See also Jacques Le Goff, "Métier et profession d'après les manuels de confesseurs au Moyen Age," in *Beiträge zum Berufsbewusstsein des mittelalterlichen Menschen,* ed. Paul Wilpert, Miscellanea Mediaevalia, 3 (1964), pp. 44-60; Siegfried Wenzel, "The Seven Deadly Sins: Some Problems of Research," *Speculum,* 43 (1968), 1-22; Lester K. Little, "Pride Goes before Avarice: Social Change and the Vices in Latin Christendom," *Historical Review,* 76 (1971), 16-49.

2. Prudentius, *Die Psychomachie,* ed. and trans. Ursmar Engelmann (Basel, Freiburg, and Vienna: Herder, 1959).

3. *Martini Episcopi Bracarensis Opera Omnia,* ed. Claude W. Barlow, Papers and Monographs of the American Academy in Rome, 12 (New Haven:

Yale Univ. Press, 1950), pp. 159-203; see also *Martin von Bracaras Schrift "De correctione rusticorum"* (Christiania, 1883), pp. 7-9.

4. See Jean Seznec, *The Survival of the Pagan Gods,* trans. Barbara F. Sessions (1953; rpt. New York: Harper and Row, 1961), pp. 42-56.

5. See ibid., p. 44, and Augustine, *De Civitatis Dei* V.7.

6. Appenzell, Library of the Capuchin monastery.

7. Georg Teichtweier, *Die Sündenlehre des Origenes* (Regensburg: Pustet, 1958), p. 348.

8. Prudentius, *Hamartingenia,* ed. and trans. Jan Stam (Amsterdam: H. J. Paris, 1960), ll. 531, 673, 769ff.

9. Prudentius, *Die Psychomachie, passim;* Richard Stettiner, *Die illustrierten Prudentius-Handschriften* (Berlin: Grote, 1895; Tafelband, 1905); Otto Homburger, *Die illustrierten Handschriften der Burgerbibliothek Bern: Die vorkarolingischen und die karolingischen Handschriften* (Bern: Selbstverlag der Burgerbibliothek, 1962), pp. 136-58.

10. See *Die Psychomachie,* ll. 257-58.

11. See ibid., ll. 326-27.

12. Ibid., ll. 407-09; with regard to the stone used for this act, cf. ll. 417ff.

13. Ibid., ll. 425-26.

14. The sins assigned to the tongue are described in numerous theological works; see, for example, Peter Damian, *De vitio linguae, Patrologia latina,* CXLIV, 912.

15. Adolf Katzenellenbogen, *Allegories of the Virtues and Vices in Mediaeval Art,* trans. Alan J. P. Crick (London: Warburg Institute, 1939), pp. 19-20, fig. 19; and Émile Mâle, *L'Art religieux du XIIIe siècle en France* (Paris: Colin, 1925), p. 104, fig. 49. The artist of Aulnay illustrated the same pairs of vices and virtues that had been introduced by Prudentius.

16. Émile Mâle, *Religious Art in France: The Twelfth Century,* trans. Marthiel Mathews (Princeton: Princeton Univ. Press, 1978), pp. 413-15, fig. 288, and Don Denny, "The Date of the Conques Last Judgment and Its Compositional Analogues," *Art Bulletin,* 66 (1984), 7-14.

17. Mâle, *Religious Art in France: The Twelfth Century,* p. 415. See also Pamela Sheingorn, "'For God is such a Doomsman: Origins and Development of the Theme of Last Judgment," in *Homo,*

Memento Finis: The Iconography of Just Judgment in Medieval Art and Drama, Early Drama, Art, and Music, Monograph Ser., 6 (Kalamazoo: Medieval Institute Publications, 1985), pp. 40-46; and Beat Brenk, *Tradition und Neuerung in der christlichen Kunst des ersten Jahrtausends: Studien zur Geschichte des Weltgerichtsbildes,* Wiener byzantinische Studien, 3 (Vienna: Böllau in Komm., 1966), p. 20.

18. Augustine, *Sermones,* Sermo I in VI Pentecost, xvi.

19. Mâle, *Religious Art in France: The Twelfth Century,* pp. 413-15; an early representation also appears in the mosaics at Torcello; see Leopold Kretzenbacher, *Die Seelenwaage: Zur religiösen Idee vom Jenseitsgericht und der Schicksalswaage in Hochreligion, Bild, Kunst und Volksglaube* (Klagenfurt: Verlag des Landesmuseums für Kärnten, 1958), pp. 100-01.

20. See Augustine, *Enchiridion,* cx, in *Patrologia latina,* XL, 283; for differentiation between *peccata minima* and *peccata maiora,* see the *Prognosticon S. Julianii,* in *Patrologia latina,* XCVI, 483-84. On the spread of such conceptions through sermons, see W. Stoke, "Tidings of Doomsday," *Revue Celtique,* 4 (1879-80), 245-57, and Marie Gotheim, "Die Todsünden," *Archiv für Religionswissenschaft,* 10 (1907), 458-60.

21. See Jacques Le Goff, *La naissance du purgatoire* (Paris: Gallimard, 1981), *passim,* and Gaby and Michel Vovelle, *Vision de la mort et de l'audelà en Provence d'après les autels des âmes du purgatoire XVe-XXe siècles,* Cahiers des Annales, 29 (Paris: Colin, 1970), pp. 12-17.

22. Herrad of Hohenbourg, *Hortus Deliciarum,* ed. Rosalie Green *et al.,* Warburg Institute Studies, 36 (London: Warburg Institute, 1979), *passim.*

23. These woodcuts are conveniently reprinted by Ernst Lehner and Johanna Lehner, *Devils, Demons, Death and Damnation* (New York: Dover, 1971), pp. 42-48; see also Victor Champier, *Les anciens almanachs illustrés: Histoire du calendrier depuis les temps anciens jusqu' à nos jours* (1886; rpt. Osnabrück: Illmer, 1976), pp. 36-40.

24. Mâle points out that these frescoes are copies of the *Kalendrier des Bergiers* (*L'Art Religieux de la Fin du Moyen Age en France* [Paris: Colin, 1908], pp. 503, 517-18).

25. Stift Lilienfeld, Cod. 151, fols. 225v, 256r.

26. For instance, Isidore of Seville speaks of the abdomen as the location of sin (*Sententiarum,* II.xlii, in *Patrologia latina,* LXXXIII, 648). In his *Moralia*

in Job, Gregory the Great explains that punishment is executed on the organ responsible for the sin; see *Patrologia latina,* LXXV, 913; elsewhere he points out that the penalty is adapted to the type of sin, the extent to the intensity; see Gregory the Great, *Dialogi,* 2nd ed., ed. Umberto Moricca (Rome, 1926), pp. 284-85, 303. Also, Peter Comestor in his *Historia Scholastica* shows how punishment was differentiated in accordance with the various deeds and intentions of the damned; see *Patrologia latina,* CXCVIII, 1613. Detailed information about the types of punishment is given in the *Purgatory of St. Patrick;* see *Patrologia latina,* CLXXX, 995-96.

27. Cecco d'Ascoli, *L'Acerba* (Florence: Biblioteca Laurenziana, Cod. Plut. 40.52, fols. 24-31); reproduced in Kimminich, *Des Teufels Werber,* figs. 25-31.

28. Milan, Biblioteca Ambrosiana, Cod. 3 M.S. B. 42 nf, fol. 1; the miniature is reproduced in *Dante: I Grandi di tutti i Tempi,* ed. Arnoldo Mondadori (Milan, 1976), pp. 12-13.

29. See C. E. Keyser, *A List of Buildings in Great Britain and Ireland Having Mural and Other Painted Decorations* (London: Eyre and Spottiswood, 1883), p. 397, for a list of six wall paintings showing the Seven Deadly Sins contrasted to the Acts of Charity.

30. See also Kimminich, *Des Teufels Weber,* pp. 35-54, and Clifford Davidson, *Visualizing the Moral Life: Medieval Iconography and the Macro Morality Plays* (New York: AMS Press, 1989), *passim.*

31. *The Pilgrimage of the Life of Man,* trans. John Lydgate, ed. F. J. Furnivall and A. W. Pollard, EETS, e.s. 77, 83, 92 (1899-1904; rpt. New York: Kraus, 1978).

32. *Tournoiemenz Antecrit,* ed. Georg Wimmer, Ausgaben und Abhandlungen aus dem Gebiet der romanischen Philologie, 76 (Marburg, 1888); for comment on widespread knowledge of this work and its numerous manuscripts, see *ibid.,* p. 9.

33. For text and introduction, see *The Macro Plays,* ed. Mark Eccles, EETS, 262 (London, 1969); see also Davidson, *Visualizing the Moral Life,* pp. 15-47.

34. For text and commentary, see Henry Medwall, *The Plays,* ed. Alan H. Nelson (Cambridge: D. S. Brewer, 1980); cf. Alois Brandl, ed., *Quellen des weltlichen Dramas in England vor Shakespeare: Ein Ergänzungsband zu Dodsley's Old English Plays* (Strassburg, 1898), pp. 73-158.

Joseph Pucci (essay date July-September 1991)

SOURCE: Pucci, Joseph. "Prudentius's Readings of Horace in the *Cathemerinon.*" *Latomus: Revue d'Etudes Latines* 1, no. 3 (July-September 1991): 677-90.

[*In the following essay, Pucci discusses how Prudentius made use of Horace's poetry in the* Cathemerinon.]

This essay[1] is a study in the ways the Christian Latin poet Prudentius[2] (fl. AD 400), makes use of the *Odes* and *Epodes* of Horace[3] in his Christian hymn-book, the **Cathemerinon.** Elsewhere Prudentius has been studied as a poet of the Christian tradition[4]. Here, I am interested in uncovering some of the ways in which he was a poet of both the Christian and the classical tradition[5], viewing his writing and the culture in which he wrote less as a product of the so-called "conflict" between paganism and Christianity than is usually the case in studies of his verse[6]. I bring to this project the idea of mediation, viewing Prudentius a mediator, and categorizing (at least implicitly) the various poetic stances he takes as mediatory. Such an approach has its limits, of course, but it is useful to the extent that it allows Prudentius to be seen as a poet who mediated two contradictory and opposing traditions. In many ways, of course, all poets are mediators, between their thought and the language they use, or between language and symbol. But some poets must mediate not only between thought and language, or language and symbol, but also between competing modes of thought, language, or symbol, both of which embody a legitimate, accepted repertoire of poetic expression.

Prudentius was, I suggest, such a poet. He, of course, is not alone in this characterization, for much of the history of the Christian Latin poetry written in the early Middle Ages is a history of the competition between classical and Christian modes of expression. But poetic stances vary from poet to poet as to the way they mediate between those competing modes. Arguably, the history of the Latin poetry of Prudentius' age and beyond is a history also of the dialectic of poetic conflit and synthesis, as different poets made different uses of the modes of expression at their disposal.

Where Prudentius seems to stand apart from his contemporaries is precisely on the question of "conflict". The issue of choice and predilection in selecting a mode of expression (Christian or pagan) seems never to have been cast in terms of "conflict" for Prudentius, especially when we view his verse in the light of, say, Avitus[7], who always seems in his poetry to want to replace the classical tradition with a Christian tradition of equal vigor and beauty. One cannot easily view Prudentius as such a poet: he makes wide and constant use of both repertoires of expression and does so with varying degrees of intensity. He could be sensitive to classical images—for my purposes, Horace's images—but he could be at the same time ironic or corrective in his attitude toward Horace. Yet, as I also hope to demonstrate, Prudentius made use of the classical literary tradition to help him better fashion a Christian tradition, then the much younger of the competing modes of expression. Prudentius seems never to have held the idea that the classical tradition was somehow evil or contaminated[8], and he seems never to have held the view that the classical tradition was a treasure equal to his Christian faith[9]. Prudentius was, rather, a "middle-man", a mediator, who most likely never conceived of himself as such, and so without self-consciousness took a stance that opened for him a vast poetic repertoire, his use of which enables modern readers to understand him to be the master of both the Christian and the classical traditions in the early medieval period.

1. *Odes* 1.9 and 1.19 in the *Praefatio*.

—A poem can profit from a borrowed image (an allusion) in many ways. It can profit by the vivid and unique rhetorical qualities that comprise it, or an image can be borrowed with the intent to be understood in the specific context of the older poem, that is to say, with the intent that the older meaning, often a unique or special meaning, be understood in the new poem. In such a borrowing, it is no longer the rhetoric nor even the image alone that matters as much as a precise meaning embodied in the rhetoric or image.

The **Praefatio** to Prudentius' **Cathemerinon** is especially fertile in this regard and can be read profitably in the light the specific meaning some of its words take on in the context of particular Horatian odes. In fact, of any poem of Prudentius', the preface to his collected works is the most Horatian, in its meter, tone, style, and above all in those qualities of self-judgment, self-assessment, and simple charm that so commend Horace to modern readers. That Horace was on Prudentius' mind in more than a general way is evidenced as well by the three Horatian borrowings found in the Preface, two of which concern me presently. The first example I want to consider might best be understood through a reading of the Preface up to the point where the borrowing appears:

Cath. [Cathemerinon] Praef. [Praefatio] 1-12

Per quinquennia iam decem,
ni fallor, fuimus; septimus insuper
annum cardo rotat, dum fruimur sole uolubili.
Instat terminus, et diem
uicinum senio iam Deus adplicat.
Quid nos utile tanti spatio temporis egimus?
Aetas prima crepantibus
fleuit sub ferulis. Mox docuit toga

infectum uitiis falsa loqui, non sine crimine.
Tum lasciua proteruitas
et luxus petulans (heu pudet ac piget!)
foedauit iuuenem nequitiae sordibus ac luto.

Odes 1.19.3-7

Mater saeua Cupidinum
Thebanaeque iubet me Semelae puer
et lasciua Licentia
finitis animum reddere amoribus.
Vrit me Glycerae nitor,
splendentis Pario marmore purius;
urit grata proteruitas
et uoltus nimium lubricus aspici.

The progressive and recapitulative nature of Prudentius' poem is exemplary. The poem is comprised of natural blocks of material which correspond to blocks of Prudentius' life and the recapitulation of each block of material is colored by specific meanings and images. In lines 1-3, the image of time is fundamental: Prudentius states his age in an affected, poetical way by referring to the rotation of the earth and sun. Lines 4-6 are different: they take on a wholly moral and internal color. Having set the external scene (the aging poet in the world), now Prudentius reckons the implications of the life lived in that world. He is old, his end is near: *quid nos utile tanti spatio temporis egimus*? Here the contrast of a finite life rendered in the cycle and flow of the universe could not be starker or more deftly emotional. As Horace often does, Prudentius has drawn a picture of the world for us and made us see him (and so ourselves) in it.

The fundamental point of the **Praefatio** is to answer the question *quid utile*? Prudentius begins to answer it at once by grouping his life into the abovementioned blocks of material. Lines 7-9 are Prudentius' memories of his childhood, weeping under the schoolmaster's rod and infected by the toga, representing the (false) rhetoric taught in the schools. In the subsequent block of material, lines 10-12, the lines I want to discuss presently, Prudentius writes that a *luxus petulans* and a *lasciua proteruitas foedauit [me] sordibus ac luto;* that a lewd sauciness and wanton indulgence marred him[10].

The terms *lasciua* and *proteruitas* are of first importance here. The terms are not joined in Horace's 1.19, but both words appear in prominent positions in the ode, which is concerned with the topic of love. Horace, who perhaps gave up on love or lost a lover, is ordered by, among others, *lasciua Licentia, animum reddere amoribus.* Glycera, the object of Horace's love, could not overwhelm Horace more. *Lasciua Licentia* has so ordered this love to manifest itself. It is not simply Glycera's beauty that bewitches him, but also *grata proteruitas* that burns in Horace. He can write of nothing except her and orders his slaves to make a sacrifice to Venus and Licentia to lessen the insatiable carnal and sexual yearning of which he is possessed.

In the **Praefatio,** there can be little doubt that Prudentius means line 10-12 to refer to the consequences of physical maturity, to erotic love. Hence, an Horatian poem about sexual desire informs the sexual block of material in the **Praefatio.** But what is important here is that Prudentius has used a word, *lasciua,* in this block of material that always has an erotic sense in Horace's poetry, and clearly does so in *Ode* 1.19, in order to render a specific context to this physical maturity, this erotic love[11].

The specific context of that maturity, already erotic in nature, is clearer if we return to *Ode* 1.19 and analyze the deployment of the term *proteruitas* by Horace. *Grata proteruitas* is an oxymoron: "the grace or beauty of her forwardness", might be a proper rendering[12]. But the oxymoron points to the irrationality, the insatiable yearning of Horace for Glycera, and points to a frenetic and maddened state in Horace, where even Glycera's less appealing characteristics seem beautiful to him. This is precisely the kind of eroticism that envelops adolescents: passionate, irrational, uncontrollable. It is this meaning that Prudentius seems to want to emphasize in connecting *lasciua,* a word of eroticism in Horace's *Odes,* with *proteruitas,* a word in this ode that conjures up a special kind of eroticism, embodied in Horace's love for Glycera. In his linkage to Horace's text, Prudentius is better able to specify the idea of erotic frenzy and youthful lust within the very narrow confines of poetry, not through the addition of verses, but by suggesting a semantic context to the deployment of words, grouping in this instance in line 10 two central words from Horace's *Ode* 1.19, and by implication grouping his own line together with Horace's meaning.

Thomson has rendered *lasciua proteruitas* to mean "a lewd sauciness", but I do not think this does justice to the sense intimated by an understanding of the relevant passages in Horace. In Thomson's translation there is a suggestion of sexual promiscuity but the tone of the translation is noncommittal. Lavarenne's French edition of the **Cathemerinon,** however, makes what is only intimated in Thomson a stated fact: "Puis une folie de passion, une dissipation effrontée (quelle honte et quel remords!) souilla ma jeunesse de l'ordure, de la boue de la débauche"[13]. Lavarenne's phrase "folie de passion" seems right on the mark; he has read nothing into the Latin that is not there, based on the semantic history of the words *lasciua* and *proteruitas* in *Ode* 1.19.

After the block of material recounting his own youthful eroticism, Prudentius moves to a psychological aspect of his development, his passion for victory. He says:

Cath. Praef. 13-15

Exim iurgia turbidos
   armarunt animos, et male pertinax
   uincendi studium subiacuit casibus asperis.

Odes 1.9.22-24

. . . Gratus puellae risus ab angulo
pignusque dereptum lacertis
   aut digito male pertinaci.

Horace's ode embodies the *carpe diem* motif. *Permitte diuis cetera,* Horace says, *. . . quid sit futurum cras, fuge quaerere et / quem Fors dierum cumque dabit lucro / adpone* (1.9.9 and 13-15). But such casualness about fate is meant to be carried over to a personal, sexual level, for this is also an ode about sexual pleasure and coyness. The scene set by Horace moves from the panoramic view of the mountain, where winter abounds, to a room, where the hearth is piled high and made warm, and where wine aged just so is drunk. The action is then focused even more: Horace moves us to a corner in the room where a laugh "but heard" and the ring or bracelet snatched from the finger or the arm only feigning resistance captures our view entirely. Our vision in the end narrows to a maiden's arm or finger and to one especial aspect of it: its feigned resistance.

In returning to the **Praefatio,** several implications of Horace's presence become clearer. The most important linkage centers on a grammatical point: how does one construe *pertinax.* In the **Praefatio,** it has traditionally been seen to be nominative, modifying *studium,* whereas *male* has been traditionally adverbial, meaning, as Thomson translates it, "perversely"[14]. In Horace's *Ode* 1.9, however, *male pertinaci,* in a different grammatical construct, means something like "that but feigns resistance"[15]. My interest is not with *pertinax* as much as with *male,* for if Prudentius meant *male* to be construed along grammatical lines established in Horace, as a negative, then this changes the meaning of the **Praefatio**[16]. Instead of: ". . . and a perversely stubborn passion for victory laid itself open to cruel falls", we would read: ". . . and a passion that but feigns resistance (or pretends stubbornness) laid itself open to cruel falls". The only grounds I have for pursuing such a reading are Prudentius's reliance upon semantic linkages of this sort at other points in the **Cathemerinon,** and a suggestive sentence of Charles Witke in his comments on the **Preface,** which discusses the possibility of Horatian reverberation in noting that Prudentius may "not have had a drive for winning but ran risks by not resisting"[17].

Such a reading makes for interesting poetry. It of course gives us a glimpse into the psychology of Prudentius as a youth, and as an old man reflecting on that youth and viewing his submission to social pressure in a light only old age can afford. But such a reading can be seen to highlight at this point in Prudentius's life a particular aspect of his own harsh judgment of himself. In such a reading, Prudentius is really condemning himself twice, for he is not only condemning the profession of rhetor, as we would expect, telling us it was an immoral practice to pursue. More than this, by drawing upon an image of absolute pretense and duplicity found in Horace, he exposes the utter pretense and duplicity of his own character at this stage of his life. This is to say, he is not simply condemning his activity at this stage of his life; he is also suggesting his shallowness and sinfulness by saying he really had no desire to pursue such rhetorical activity in the law courts but did not have the courage to not do it: he ran risks, in Witke's words, by not being as stubborn as he had been trained to. In fact, in the light of the succeeding lines in the **Praefatio,** I think the reading I have suggested makes better sense, for while a "perversely stubborn' passion for victory can be understood to have prepared Prudentius for "cruel falls", clearly a passion for victory that was feigned, only half-hearted, would have made Prudentius more vulnerable to such falls.

2. Praefatio and Cath. 10.

An image may be deployed on account of its rhetoric, or it may be deployed—as in the previous section— with a special, older, meaning intended to be understood in the new poem. But the context of an older image may also be used as a foil in a new poem, whereby the original meaning of an image, carried over into a new poem, is corrected, altered, or in the end, completed. This stance, essentially an ironic one on the part of the new poet toward the old, is taken by Prudentius at two points in the **Cathemerinon,** the first of which occurs in the **Preface,** by which we may conveniently conclude our progression through its lines.

When we left the preface a moment ago, Prudentius had just finished reviewing the second stage of his life, the rhetor's stage. After offering two more blocks of material which constitute phases of his life in which he served as consul and in the service of the Emperor, Prudentius then moves his readers forward again into the present:

Cath. Praef. 22-27

Haec dum uita uolans agit,
  inrepsit subito canities seni,
    oblitum ueteris me Saliae consulis arguens,
  sub quo prima dies mihi
    quam multas hiemes uoluerit, et rosas
  pratis post glaciem reddiderit, nix capitis probat.

Odes 4.13.9-12

Importunus enim transuolat aridas
quercus, et refugit te, quia luridi
  dentes te, quia rugae
  turpant et capitis niues.

Nix capitis is a fundamental image for Prudentius. Having recalled that old age crept in upon him, Prudentius reflects in a deeply emotional way, by contrasting the snows and roses of the meadows, through which he may count his years, to the snow atop his own head, the former subject only to the eternal ebb and flow of nature's cycle, the latter subject to the inevitable approach of death. At this point in the **Praefatio,** a shadow of sadness envelops the progress of Prudentius' story. A question parallel to *quid utile* occurs to him: will the deeds of his life, good or bad, mean anything when he is dead; does not death wipe away everything that a person was[18]?

In *Odes* 4.13, the picture of old age is drawn in much the same terms as in the **Preface.** Here, Lyce is aged, with yellow teeth and wrinkles, and with *niues capitis,* snowy locks, all of which are, in Horace's eyes, disfigurements. The beautiful youth whom Cupid once watched, the beauty who stole me, Horace says, "from myself", is gone. Horace tells us in a chilling picture of old age that Lyce is allowed to live now so those full of youth can see the "torch fallen to ashes". Lyce still desires after youth, attempts to look as she once did, and still goes through the rituals she once performed so gracefully in her now disfigured way. But Lyce's fate is to have lived too long, whereby nothing can make her beautiful again. Lyce, like Prudentius, is old.

Prudentius has relied upon Horace's image of snowy locks in his preface, and he has also tried, undoubtedly, to conjure up the emotional response we feel for Lyce at this point in his own poem (successfully, I think). Horace well understood old age and was able to express its characteristics from different angles, both as a man watching his former lover, and as a man himself aged and approaching death. As Fraenkel notes, what is described in this ode is "our common lot", including Horace's lot[19]. Horace has well expressed an image and context, that of old age, and Prudentius has carried that image and context forward into his own poem. *Nix capitis* in either poem is an image of irretrievable youth, and immutable old age.

But such an image, fixed in Horace's ode, is introduced in Prudentius' **Preface** only to be denied the last word. Having deployed Horace's image in its original context, Prudentius now progresses in the **Preface** to reflect upon the ultimate meaning of life in Christian terms. The question that occurs to him, as I have noted (*talia* *proderunt, uel bona uel mala, post obitum carnis*), is a sad question because Prudentius had not told us yet that things of the world, *uel bona uel mala, quae studuit, non sunt Dei, cuius habeberis* (**Praef.** 29-33). Until he tells us this, we have every right to view him as Lyce, pathetically, as a victim of time and of death. Once Prudentius makes his Christian context clear, however, Horace's image, even though it has aided Prudentius in forming a powerful and dynamic image, is challenged and its meaning, in effect, is completed. In its new context, Prudentius' old age is absolutely the opposite of Lyce's, for Prudentius, as a Christian, can look forward to an eternal life. In this instance, then, Prudentius has drawn upon a Horatian image and, as it were, made it stand as a metaphor that points in its starkness to a sure Christian truth[20].

A further instance of this phenomenon, again, concerning death, is evidenced in Hymn 10 of the **Cathemerinon,** the hymn for the burial of the dead. Here, as in our most recent example, an Horatian image is called into use in its original context, only to be completed in a Christian context.

Cath. 10.57-60

Hoc prouida Christicolarum
pietas studet, utpote credens
fore protinus omnia uiua,
quae nunc gelidus sopor urget.

Odes 1.24.5-6

Ergo Quintilium perpetuus sopor
urget?

The phrase *sopor urget* in Prudentius' hymn is borrowed from Horace *Odes* 1.24, the dirge for Quintilius. Prudentius seemingly has lifted a passage from Horace's poem about death to use in his own hymn about death. To be sure, both poems are about death, but they are also poems about dealing with death, that is, about consolation. As Plessis says, "cette ode est moins une lamentation sur la mort de Quintilius Varus qu'une consolation adressée à Virgile, qui ne pouvait se résigner à la perte de son ami"[21]. And Horace's message is clear; against the irreparable and immutable force of death, one ought to appeal to a unique remedy, resignation. *Patientia fit leuius, quicquid corrigere est nefas.* Time heals all; this is our consolation.

Of course, for Prudentius, the notion that time heals all is trite, for his answer to Virgil would in any case be supra-temporal. As Prudentius tells us, death is not for Christians a time of mourning. Grief, while it may be felt, is unnecessary. Unnecessary, too, is this question of Horace's: *quis desiderio sit pudor aut modus / tam cari capitis? Praecipe lugubres / cantus, Melpomene*

(1.24.1-3), for Prudentius orders mothers to suspend their tears, and silence their sad lamentations: *more haec reparatio uitae est* (**Cath.** 10.120). This is the key point for Prudentius. The Horatian image of death drawn upon by Prudentius is but one side of the picture, and whereas the image of death is final in Horace, in Prudentius it is the final image of one phase of Christian life for, precisely, *mors est reparatio uitae.* By drawing on an older image, therefore, an image that renders to his new poem a specific color and texture, Prudentius was better able to contrast and to make stark the meaning embodied in that older image. Further, he was able to embody an ultimate and essential Christian truth and in a sense point to the Christian discovery of the "ultimate" truth in so doing.

A further aspect of this kind of usage is evident here also, for Horace's advice to Virgil is not by any means "happy" advice; it is the advice of a Stoic. There is nothing Virgil can do, Horace seems to say, except wait, for waiting makes lighter what is impossible to change. Of course, this fatalism is not the answer Prudentius has in mind either. Death, naturally, is inevitable, as it is the result of original sin; the body must become infirm and die. But the very fact that Virgil is sad is unthinkable in Prudentius' context. We care for graves, bury our dead, and even grieve, but we have no real reason to be sad. The life that is immutably consumed in Horace is, in fact, renewable in Prudentius' hymn, a *reparatio* the hymn itself metaphorically brings about through its very reading/singing.

3. CATHEMERINON 4 AND EPODE 2.

Cath. 4.58-59

Cernit forte procul dapes inemptas
quas messoribus Ambacum profeta . . .

Epodes 2.39-48

Quod si pudica mulier in partem iuuet
   domum atque dulcis liberos,
Sabina qualis aut perusta solibus
   pernicis uxor Apuli,
sacrum uetustis exstruat lignis focum
   lassi sub aduentum uiri,
claudensque textis cratibus laetum pecus
   distenta siccet ubera,
et horna dulci uina promens dolio
   dapes inemptas apparet . . .

When Prudentius wrote his hymn after the meal, whose occasion he took to talk about nourishment, his mind seems to have fled to Christ, the Old Testament, and Horace. He extols the spiritual nourishment of Christ, as one might expect, but he takes from Horace's *Epode* 2 the exact phrase by which to render a central metaphor of the hymn, the deployment of which is an example of another kind of poetic stance (mediation, if you will) on Prudentius' part. In this stance, an Horatian image is called upon by Prudentius to render specific qualities and characteristics to sacred scripture.

Prudentius' hymn after the meal begins on a moral and almost an indignant note: we have fled our flesh, as its *imbecilla lex* requires us to do. Now let us praise the Father, for he is food for our souls²². At once, a duality of nourishment, paralleling the duality of body and soul is established, and henceforward there is no doubt as to which kind of nourishment Prudentius is most concerned to teach us about. Such a superiority is evidenced in the terms used to describe God, the source of the soul's nourishment. Prudentius seems intent from the start, in fact, to establish in precise ways the divinity, royalty, and the incomparability of God, and to stress the originality and the primality of God: he is *rerum conditor, repertor orbis, fons uitae, infusor fidei, sator pudoris, mortis perdomitor, salutis auctor,* and he is all of these in the course of four lines (***Cath.*** 4.9-12).

The primal activity of God is paramount here: God's incomparability is due to his position as founder of all things and creator of a world in which all things dwell. He is the source of life, flowing from heaven, and he is the author of salvation because he is the tamer of death. God is, above all, a concerned God, a God active in the world, a God whose incomparability does not make him intangible. Indeed, the whole point of this hymn is to teach Christians that God does touch them in potent and unique ways, and that the incomparable *fons uitae* is also an active force in their own lives.

God's intangibility is evidenced, for example, in the nourishment he gives to our souls. Daniel is an example of this. By means of God's intervention with food, understood to be both a real meal and spiritual nourishment, by God's proffering what Prudentius calls *dapes inemptas,* Daniel was saved from the jaws of hungry lions. That Daniel's story is a metaphor for spiritual nourishment in Prudentius' view there can be little doubt. But such a metaphor is deployed by him not in biblical language, nor in an exclusively Christian language, but rather through a phrase—*dapes inemptas*—drawn from *Epode* 2.

There are special qualities to be associated with this usage founded initially in a comparison of other words used by Prudentius to mean "meal". Why, for example, does Prudentius use the word *dapes* when the three other words he employs in Hymn 4 to mean "food", "meal", or "feast", might have done as well in line 58²³? A look to Horace at once is instructive. Traditionally, *dapes* means a religious feast, a sacrificial feast, or a feast offered at a religious ceremony, and at least the religious aspect certainly is in Prudentius' mind, though

in a Christian way. But Horace invariably uses *dapes* to mean a feast that is itself incomparable, superlative, magnificent, using it when he refers to Jove or the very highest of the Roman gods²⁴. It is a superlative for "food", then, in Horace's poetry and Prudentius seems to have remembered this and carried it over to his own poetry: *dapes* is food fit for or food made by gods. *Dapes,* in other words, is no ordinary meal.

But why *dapes inemptas,* a meal that is "unbought"? This is a special kind of special food. Prudentius may be using the phrase to stress over again the incomparability of the meal: it is unbought because no one could ever buy it, since in one sense, the most important sense, it is not a meal to be eaten at all, but a food to be given by God. But in Horace's *Epode* 2 there is a special sense to the word "unbought" also, and Prudentius seems to have thought of this meaning when he rendered into his own terms the idea of spiritual nourishment.

The idea of Horace's poem is rather clear. The joys of country life are extolled there, and the reader is enjoined to follow those joys. Horace's image of nature is one of perfection and ideal: nature's poplar trees and autumn's fruits are flatteringly compared to the woes of business life. The grapes of the vine and the pears and other fruits of the trees are seen as nature's bounty, over and against the rather worthless bounty of *negotium.* Happy is he who, far away from the cares of business, works his ancestral lands like *prisca gens.* In so working his lands, a man is purer, cleaner, spiritually better, and all the more so when he is listening to nature's sounds and comprehending her glories. By far the greatest pleasure for Horace and his character Alfius, whom he has enjoined to the country life, is to have a *pudica mulier* tending to the fire, enclosing the flock, milking the cows, that is to say, gathering nature's bounty in order to prepare an unbought meal, a meal taken over and made from nature.

In this context, *inemptas* represents the purity, the absolute uniqueness, in Horace's view, of nature's bounty, for what can be purer, more unique, than that which purity itself gives forth? I think we can agree with Fraenkel when he says that "leaving aside for the moment Horace's mocking conclusion, we may see in this poem a fundamentally true expression of Horace's ideal vision of the country", a vision embodied in qualitative distinctions made between the urban world of *negotium* and the country life, and a vision also very much embodied in the language of *dapes inemptas*²⁵. Plessis says, regarding the term *inemptas,* that "il est question de distribution gratuite"²⁶, and he is correct. There is a special and gratuitous sense to the deployment of this word in Horace, whose meaning is dependent upon the context of the poem itself for clarification. Precisely, this poem is an ideal vision of nature, and the fruits of that nature must be seen in the same light.

The linkage from Horace to Prudentius is clearer in the light of the meanings of *dapes* and *inemptas* in *Epode* 2. Prudentius seems to have remembered Horace's turn of phrase because the context of the poem plays upon the ideas of supremacy and uniqueness. Prudentius wants to recall the image of the incomparability of nature's meal and apply it to God's bounty in his hymn after the meal. In employing Horace's terms to render Daniel's feast, Prudentius gives a specific character to what the *Old Testament* calls simply a mixture of boiled stew and bread: he has embellished this sacred image of God's nourishment. He does not conceive of spiritual nourishment as the Jews did, in very dry dreams, nor yet does he conceive of it in Christian terms. When Prudentius, at least in this instance, thought about a Jewish text as a Christian, he distilled his thought through classical literature. In so doing, he rendered to the simple language of the *Old Testament* a turn of phrase of Roman literature, thereby rendering the Christian image he was after, the image of spiritual nourishment.

There is something special and exciting in this moment in Christian poetry. Embodying the ideas of supremacy drawn out for him by Horace, Prudentius is able to blend classical and Christian language to give shape— meaning—to his own reading of sacred scripture. Here Horace serves the needs of the Christian poet, without losing any integrity as regards his own meaning or vision. The blend is perfect, and the result impressive. Thomson has translated *dapes inemptas* as "home-grown meal", but I do not think this is strong enough. I prefer Lavarenne's rendering, which is precisely how the Latin reads: "des mets non achetés"[27] literally, "foods un-bought". This is exactly what Prudentius had on his mind, given the Horatian context he seems to have used.

When he has been studied, Prudentius has often been cast as a poet embodying a core of belief, his Christian faith, and has been seen as a poet of the Christian tradition. But allied closely to that Christian tradition are the formative characteristics of the classical tradition which were synthesized, modified, rejected, or borrowed by Christian writers of the early medieval period. The larger purpose of this paper has been to underline this process of selection, adaptation, and creation within this period by viewing various stances Prudentius took in relation to the poetry of Horace. In the light of such stances, I think we can better see Prudentius as both a Christian believer and a classical *littérateur*, who formed a particular *corpus* of Christian poetry by embracing classical culture and making use of it in specific ways.

Based on his stance toward Horace, I think it may be said that Prudentius, at least in the ***Cathemerinon,*** made use of classical culture not only because it was a "given" for him, but also because he was first and foremost a poet. Prudentius wrote less as a Christian polemicist, or as a Christian apologist, or *ex cathedra,* than simply through the guise of poetry, as a poet. Indeed, Prudentius was a Christian poet because he was first and foremost simply a poet, and this is most strongly evidenced in his response, understanding, and appreciation of the varied qualities of Horace's language, and in his deployment of that language within the framework of his own vision and voice.

An old view of Prudentius made prominent by E. K. Rand holds that Prudentius loved his Christian faith in equal measure to his classical cultural inheritance. I think, however, that a more apt summary of Prudentius' poetic stance might be to say that he was equally fond of his Christian faith and his vocation as a poet. Such an equality, in any event, is suggested by Prudentius's use of Horace in the ***Cathemerinon.*** His poetry there gives us evidence that he understood language and expression to be seamless and essentially neutral in character, available for deployment in new contexts and in support of new systems of belief. The power of language, his poetry suggests to us, lies in its ability to devour what is foreign, and so make what was once foreign familiar. So it is in the end that Prudentius can be viewed accurately not as the first Christian who happened to do poetry very well, but as the first truly great poet who happened to be Christian.

Notes

1. The basic source for evidence (still) is H. BREIDT, *De Aurelio Prudentio Clemente Horatii Imitatore,* Heidelberg, 1887, p. 49-51. Breidt gives an exhaustive listing of Horatian "echoes" in the works of Prudentius. He lists 60 borrowings in the *Cathemerinon* alone.

2. My edition of Prudentius is M. P. CUNNINGHAM (ed.), *Aurelii Prudentii Clementis Carmina,* Turnhout, 1966, p. 1-72, hereafter referred to as *Cath.*

3. My edition of Horace is E. C. WICKHAM (ed.), *Q. Horati Flacci Opera,* Oxford, 1901, hereafter referred to as *Odes.* I have made an occasional change in punctuation.

4. By, for example, M. LAVARENNE, *Étude sur la langue du poète Prudence,* Paris, 1933, whose argument is well summarized in this regard by Ch. WITKE, *Numen Litterarum: The Old and the New in Christian Poetry from Constantine to Gregory the Great,* Leiden-Köln, 1971, p. 103 and n. 4, 7.

5. As I. RODRIGUEZ-HERRERA has seen him in *Poeta Christianus: Prudentius' Auffassung vom Wesen*

und von der Aufgube des christlichen Dichters, Speyer, 1936; and so WITKE, *Numen Litterarum,* p. 102-144 and in his article *Prudentius and the Tradition of Latin Poetry* in *Transactions of the American Philological Association* 99, 1968, p. 509-535; and to a lesser extent E. K. RAND, *Prudentius and Christian Humanism* in *Transactions of the American Philological Association* 51, 1920, p. 71-83, and in his book, *Founders of the Middle Ages,* New York, 1957, especially p. 184, 192-193, 207-213, and 216-217.

6. On this in general see A. CAMERON, *Paganism and Literature in the Late Fourth Century* in *Christianisme et formes littéraires de l'Antiquité tardive en Occident,* Geneva, 1976, p. 1-30.

7. As, for example, in his *Libri Poematum V* dealing with the Genesis and Exodus accounts. Cf. F. J. E. RABY, *A History of Christian Latin Poetry from the Beginning to the close of the Middle Ages,* Oxford, 1927 [1953], p. 77-79.

8. See, for example, M. SMITH, *Prudentius' Psychomachia: A Re-examination,* Princeton, 1976, esp. p. 1-38. The point of Smith's book is to say that Prudentius' stance toward Virgil in the *Psychomachia* was ironic and essentially hostile, and to say that Prudentius was exclusively a Christian. A new and provocative reading of Prudentius along contextual and thematic lines (though not of the *Cathemerinon* itself), is M. MALAMUD, *A Poetics of Transformation: Prudentius and Roman Mythology,* Cornell, 1989.

9. See, for example, E. K. RAND, *Prudentius and Christian Humanism,* p. 80-83.

10. This is H. J. Thomson's translation in *Prudentius,* London, 1961, vol. I, p. 2.

11. I owe the history of *lasciua* in Horace's poetry to R. G. M. NISBET and M. HUBBARD, *A Commentary on Horace: Odes I,* Oxford, 1970.

12. *Ibid.,* p. 240. The translation is that of C. E. BENNETT (ed. and transl.), *Horace: The Odes and Epodes,* London, 1914 [1918], p. 59.

13. Thomson's translation is in *Prudentius,* p. 3. Cf. M. LAVARENNE [ed. and transl.], *Prudence: Cathemerinon Liber, Livre d'Heures,* vol. I, Paris, 1943, p. 1.

14. THOMSON, *Prudentius,* p. 3.

15. This is Bennett's translation in *Odes,* p. 29.

16. Cf. NISBET and HUBBARD, *A Commentary on Horace,* p. 125, and the instructive note to be found in Fr. PLESSIS et al. [ed.], *Odes, Épodes et Chant Séculaire* (Paris, 1924 [1966]), p. 32-33, where it is interestingly suggested that *male* can be interpreted in two ways, though he supports the traditional view that it negates *pertinaci.*

17. WITKE, *Numen Litterarum,* p. 107-8.

18. *Cath. Praef.* 28-31.

19. E. FRAENKEL, *Horace,* Oxford, 1957, p. 414.

20. Witke has discussed the *nix capitis* imagery with reference to other Horatian odes as an image of nature, not aging. He sees the stanza comprised of lines 25-27 as deliberately evoking a warm feeling about being alive, to make stark the next three lines, which represent death. See *Numen Litterarum,* p. 108-109, and his *Questions and Answers in Horace, Ode 2.3* in *Classical Philology* 61, 1966, p. 250-252.

21. PLESSIS, *Odes, Épodes et Chant Séculaire,* p. 69.

22. Cf. *Cath.* 4.1-3.

23. E.G., *pastus* (v. 35), *esca* (v. 87), or *cibus* (v. 92).

24. Cf. *Epode* 9.1; *Odes* 1.32.13; 1.37.4; 4.4.12; *Epode* 5.33; 17.66. I owe this evidence to L. COOPER [ed. and comp.]. *A Concordance to the Words of Horace,* Washington, D.C., 1916, p. 108.

25. FRAENKEL, *Horace,* p. 60.

26. PLESSIS, *Odes, Épodes et Chant Séculaire,* p. 335.

27. Thomson's translation is in *Prudentius,* p. 35; Lavarenne's is in *Prudence,* p. 22.

Jill Ross (essay date fall 1995)

SOURCE: Ross, Jill. "Dynamic Writing and Martyrs' Bodies in Prudentius's *Peristephanon.*"[1] *Journal of Early Christian Studies* 3, no. 3 (fall 1995): 325-55.

[*In the following essay, Ross examines Prudentius's use of the extended metaphor of the martyr's body as divine text.*]

The **Peristephanon,** written by the Hispano-Roman poet Prudentius in the late fourth century, is the product of a highly literate late antique Christian culture in which both oral and written forms of discourse were cultivated in a masterly and sophisticated manner.[2] In the **Peristephanon,** a series of poems dedicated to the martyrs of the early Christian Church, death and writing become one in the transformation of the bodies of the martyrs into texts inscribed with bloody letters. Prudentius raises up writing from the dead by making the textualization of the martyrs' bodies into a redemptive affirmation of a writing that is remarkably fertile and dynamic.

In the Roman world, attitudes towards writing were quite complex and often contradictory. As Françoise Desbordes has recently shown, writing was considered to be both an arbitrary, external and imperfect representation of speech and a powerful tool of logic and abstraction that enables the human mind to master the world.[3] Unlike his contemporary St. Augustine who shares this profound ambivalence toward the act of writing,[4] Prudentius himself embraces and participates fully in the highly developed literary aesthetic of late antique culture. Prudentius' graphic descriptions in the **Peristephanon** of the blood and gore of martyrdom and his emphasis on the miraculous evince "an enthusiasm for the weird and wonderful" typical of fourth-century literary tastes.[5] Prudentius often dresses his striking subject matter in language notable for its rich visual and semantic patterning, the hallmarks of what Michael Roberts has termed the jeweled style of late antique poetics.[6] Prudentius participates in an already established tradition of reading and writing where images, intertextual allusions, and etymological wordplay convey more meaning than plot and narrative. The location of meaning in the poet's manipulation of language allows the reader a much greater role in the construction of this meaning. Prudentius' linguistic playfulness (both literal and semantic) manifests itself in the use of etymology, wordplay, and anagrams which all invite the reader to engender meaning, to participate in the dynamism of literary discourse.[7] The vitality of Prudentius' poetic text is mirrored by his conception of the act of writing as a dynamic force capable of achieving the redemption of both Christian souls and discourse.

Prudentius' **Peristephanon** [**Pe**] is an eloquent witness to the redemptive power of the written word. The poet declares himself to be painfully aware of the mediatory power of the poems he offers to the martyrs:

> . . . O Christi decus,
> audi poetam rusticum
> cordis fatentem crimina
> et facta prodentem sua.
>
> Indignus, agnosco et scio
> quem Christus ipse exaudiat,
> sed per patronos martyras
> potest medellam consequi.[8]

. . . Oh glory of Christ, listen to an unsophisticated poet as he confesses the sins of his heart and puts his deeds in writing. I am unworthy, I know and own, that Christ himself should hear me; but through the intercession of the martyrs, a cure may be attained.

Prudentius, although referring to his poetic activity, attributes conventional qualities of orality to his poems ("audi," "exaudiat"), and thereby betrays an attitude that views writing as a kind of indirect speech that will reach the ears of Christ.[9] Prudentius hopes that his poetic text will enable him to communicate with the martyrs, who will then themselves assume a textual role in that they will instantaneously relay his words to God: "audiunt statimque ad aurem regis aeterni ferunt" ("they listen to our prayer and straightway carry it to the ear of the eternal King,' **Pe** I.18). Prudentius, then, is writing a poem free from the deformative temporal gap that severs author from text. His belief in and reliance upon the efficacy of writing poetry in order to gain a hearing before God, and hopefully to be granted salvation, is manifested most clearly by his metaphorization of the martyrs' salvific bodies as written texts and by the transformation of the experience of martyrdom into an act of writing. The martyrs' role as intercessors between human beings and Christ is effectively concretized by their textualization.[10]

The metaphor of the body as text in the *opera* of Prudentius has received very little critical attention. Most of the critics who have dealt with the **Peristephanon** have directed their efforts more towards determining Prudentius' sources and the classical influences upon him than to the study of his poetic imagery.[11] The first critic to comment on Prudentius' use of textual metaphors was Ernst Robert Curtius who viewed him as one of the links in the chain of the literary continuity of the "metaphorics of the book" extending from antiquity through the Renaissance.[12] However, Curtius was not interested in the function which the image of the body as book has within the **Peristephanon,** nor in the importance of this metaphor for an understanding of the poet's views about written language in general, and the poetic Christian text in particular. More recently, Klaus Thraede has meticulously traced Prudentius' sources of "Schreibmatephern" from their Greek roots, through their elaboration in rhetorical, patristic and literary texts.[13] His treatment, although highly nuanced, makes no attempt to analyze Prudentius' use of the metaphorics of writing as a self-reflexive means of considering the nature of writing and authorship. Most recently, Michael Roberts has discussed the textualization of the martyrs' bodies in the **Peristephanon,** but his interest lies more in the "sacred poetics" of martyrdom created by Prudentius, than in the linguistic and textual implications of this metaphor.[14]

Prudentius is, perhaps, the first writer to use the image of the martyr's body as a written text in order to formulate a specifically Christian conception of writing. For him, writing acquires a divine corporeality that physically engenders more language, be it in the form of more spoken words or human poetic texts. Prudentius revels in the corporeality of writing and redeems it by literally transforming it into an agent of bodily punishment and death capable of conferring salvation upon those who receive its marks. By transmuting martyrs into texts, Prudentius sanctifies writing, presenting it as divine discourse which is not just a shadow of the fullness of the spoken Word, but which retains its dynamism even if it is several times removed from its sacred source.

The martyrs are not merely dead texts severed from their author or vivifying principle. Rather, they have the textual advantage of fixity or permanence in that they cannot by erased or expunged from heaven, ensuring their connection with their divine Author. Yet, precisely because they are written texts independent from the mind (i.e., God's) which gave birth to them, they retain an immortal life of their own and are capable of seeing to it that salvation be bestowed on others. The most striking aspect of Christian writing as embodied by the martyrs is its dynamic fertility which is manifested figuratively by the production of spiritual fruit in the form of more believers and salvation, and literally, by the engendering of more discourse in the form of textual offspring.[15] In this essay, I would like to examine the configuration of the martyr-text, the ways in which Prudentius exploits its revivifying qualities, and the relationship he sets up between his own written text, the *Peristephanon,* and the Christian writing of the martyrs' bodies.

Textual Elements of Martyrdom

In the *Peristephanon* the connection between martyrdom and writing is established from the outset. The first lines Prudentius writes contain the inscription of the martyrs' names in the book of heaven:

> Scripta sunt caelo duorum martyrum uocabula,
> aureis quae Christus illic adnotauit litteris,
> sanguinis notis eadem scripta terris tradidit.
>
> (*Pe* I.1-3)
>
> Written in heaven are the names of two martyrs; Christ has made note of them there in letters of gold, while on earth he has recorded them in characters of blood.

By opening the poem with a textualization of martyrdom, Prudentius is hinting that his conception of martyrdom is inseparable from a poetic, or literary experience: it occurs along with an act of inscription. Also, the martyrs come to be associated with books in which they are textually apotheosized. The martyrs' names written into the book of heaven (*Pe* IV.169-172) are, metonymically speaking, the embodiment of the martyrs themselves. This conception of martyrdom can also be found in artistic representations of martyrs nearly contemporaneous with Prudentius. In the Chapel of St. Victor in the Church of St. Ambrose in Milan, there is a mosaic dating from the early fifth century which depicts the martyr Victor holding an open book in front of him on whose pages the name "Victor" is written.[16] Since Prudentius spent many years serving in

the imperial court in Milan,[17] he would likely have been familiar with this artistic convention of equating a martyr with a written text.

Martyrdom was also described as a process of becoming intelligible. St. Ignatius of Antioch, in a letter written before his martyrdom in 117, terms his imminent execution a conversion from "*phone,*" an inarticulate, empty voice into "*logos,*" a meaningful, intelligible word of God.[18] Although St. Ignatius employs terms that are from an oral register to describe his experience, what is at issue here is martyrdom's ability to give meaning to language. Like St. Ignatius' conversion from *phone* to *logos,* martyrdom for Prudentius is a process whereby the dumb, animal flesh is transformed into a divine text.[19] In effect, textualization is a form of ascetic discipline which enables the inscribed object to transcend the carnal and to pass on to a realm of pure reason and spirit.[20] By repeatedly referring to the martyrs' torn bodies as texts, Prudentius is emphasizing that the martyrs are dead to the fleshly world, and, as written texts, they rise above the chaotic cacophony of the carnal to abide eternally in the spiritual world of silent, organized, rational, intelligible discourse where everything is pregnant with God's meaning.

The extended metaphor of the martyr's body as text is a characteristic feature of Prudentius' poetic vocabulary. The poems dedicated to Eulalia and Cassian (*Pe* III and IX) are ones in which the image of the martyr's body as text is particularly strong and, interestingly enough, these are the poems for which Prudentius has no known literary source.[21] There are, however, some earlier isolated instances in which a martyr's wounded body is described as a written text. Lactantius, for example, referred to martyrs as bearing letters impressed on their tortured bodies:

> quis cum uideat laterum suorum cicatrices, non magis oderit deos, propter quos aeterna poenarum insignia et impressas uisceribus suis notas gestet?[22]
>
> Who when he sees the scars on the sides of his body will not hate the gods even more, on whose account he bears eternal marks of torment and letters engraved onto his flesh?

In Prudentius, this textual metaphor is far more explicit and highly developed than in any earlier Christian writer. Romanus is called "inscripta Christo pagina" ("a page inscribed by Christ," *Pe* X.1119), and Cassian is a page wet with red ink ("umens pagina," *Pe* IX.50). Eulalia observes that God's name is written on her body: "scriberis ecce mihi, domine" (*Pe* III.136), thereby attesting to her transformation into an immortal text.

The martyr's unbroken body which is a blank and receptive page or parchment is only part of the configuration of the body-text. The marks or letters recorded in the text are the wounds inflicted on the martyr's body. The angel who takes notes on Romanus' passion includes the wounds on his body as part of the discourse that is being recorded:

> Excepit adstans angelus coram deo
> et quae locutus martyr et quae pertulit;
> nec uerba solum disserentis condidit,
> sed ipsa pingens uulnera expressit stilo
> laterum genarum pectorisque et faucium.
>
> (*Pe* X.1121-1125)

An angel standing in the presence of God took down all that the martyr said and all that he bore, and not only recorded the words of his discourse but with his pen drew exact pictures of the wounds on his sides, cheeks, breast and throat.

Romanus' wounds are treated in exactly the same way as his words by the recording angel, thus cementing the equivalence of wounds and words. In *Peristephanon* I it is stated that God wrote the names of the martyrs in letters of blood on earth (*Pe* I.2-3). The bloody letters etched into the martyrs' bodies do not always signify their names. In the case of Eulalia, the holy name of God is written on her body:

> Nomen et ipsa sacrum loquitur
> purpura sanguinis eliciti.
>
> (*Pe* III.139-140)

the very scarlet of the blood that is drawn speaks the holy name.

The holy text inscribed upon Eulalia is a perfectly legible one since she says that she is able to read the letters which signify God's victory for her (*Pe* III.137-138).

The marks scored into the bodies of the martyrs come from the pen of God. Eulalia addresses God directly while she is being written upon (*Pe* III.136), and it is Christ's pen that produces the letter-wounds upon the earthly bodies of Emeterius and Chelidonius (*Pe* I.2-3). Since it is God who writes on the martyr, the resulting text must possess unique qualities. God imbues Romanus with immortality when he becomes a divine, eternal text inscribed by the powerful pen of Christ: "inscripta Christo pagina inmortalis est" (*Pe* X.1119). The torturer who tears Romanus' face is, in reality, God who is creating an indelible and indestructible text:

> *Charaxat* ambas ungulis scribentibus
> genas cruentis et secat faciem notis,
>
> (*Pe* X.557-558)

He engraves both cheeks with marks written by the claws and he cuts bloody letters into his face

The word "charaxat" refers to a divine kind of writing. The only contemporary attestation of this verb which was borrowed from the Greek occurs in a Pseudo-

Augustinian text where it is used to describe the etching of the Decalogue by God.[23] The etymologically related word *character* appears in the Vulgate, but only in the Apocalypse of John (13.16; 13.17; 14.9; 14.11; 16.2; 19.20; 20.4), and is used to refer to the mark impressed on the foreheads and right hands of the damned by the beast of the Apocalypse. Here, the *character* is also akin to writing whose origin is supernatural or divine. Prudentius, in his use of the uncommon verb *charaxare*, is emphasizing the divine source of the martyrs' wounds and is indirectly comparing them to the awesomely powerful and durable text miraculously engraved on tablets of stone by the finger of God.

The martyr-text is a transcendent text copied by God from the earthly body of the martyr into the book of heaven (*Pe* I.1-3). The immortal and indelible nature of the heavenly martyr-text is underlined by the contrasting ephemeral nature of texts written by men. Earthly texts are subject to deterioration and destruction, whereas Christ's writing can never fade:

> Illas sed aetas conficit diutina,
> fuligo fuscat, puluis obducit situ,
> carpit senectus aut ruinis obruit.
> Inscripta Christo pagina inmortalis est
> nec obsolescit ullus in caelis apex.
>
> (*Pe* X.1116-1120)

But those records the long passage of time destroys, grime blackens them, dust covers them in neglect, old age tatters them or buries them under ruins; whereas the page written upon by Christ is immortal, and not even one little stroke fades away in heaven.

Earthly texts can be deliberately manipulated or suppressed by those who want to control the flow of information, in contrast to the divine text of the martyrs which, since it is inscribed in the heavens, is eternally accessible to all those who would read and believe.[24] The pagan soldier may attempt to prevent the fame of the martyrs from spreading by destroying the written account of their suffering (*Pe* I.73-78), but he cannot expunge the sparkling letters of gold which spell out their names in Heaven (*Pe* I.1-2).[25]

Like Christ, whose body was racked and torn so that he would be able to defeat death and thereby redeem humanity, the martyrs' bodies too become bloody texts so that they can mimic Christ's redemptive role in the function of their wounded bodies as instruments of salvation. Their wounds are the gateways to heaven: "nobilis per uulnus amplum porta iustis panditur" ("through the wide wound a glorious gateway opens to the righteous," *Pe* I.29). However, since the wounds are also letters (*Pe* I.3), the reading of these bloody marks can also result in the attainment of salvation. It is not enough that the martyrs' bodies bear redemptive wounds, since what is required is a participation in their suffering made possible by the transformation of their bodies into texts. To share actively in their martyrdom one must read the marks on their bodies before salvation can be conferred.

In addition to facilitating salvation, the transformation of a martyr's body into a written text can have other, more mundane consequences. The inscription of a body reflects a desire to objectify and control: the letters are markers of possession. By turning a martyr-text into a repository of the holy, Prudentius is also, in effect, turning it into a commodity subject to exchange, a kind of currency bearing the signs of its maker.[26] It is interesting to note that it was in the fourth century, the period of Prudentius' poetic production, that martyrs' bodies began to be treated like commodities.[27] Bodies were transferred from one tomb to another, or they were fragmented into relics which were dispersed and traded, and became the currency of spiritual power. Prudentius could very well have been witness to the commercialization of martyrs' bodies, since Ambrose, in the year 390, transported the remains of several martyrs found in Milan and Bologna to a Milanese basilica[28] at which time Prudentius may have been in Milan. The metaphor of the martyr's body as a written text is, perhaps, Prudentius' own interpretation of the logic of the commodification of the martyrs. By turning their martyred bodies into poems, Prudentius can ensure that they will circulate from reader to reader, and like relics, impart spiritual power to those with whom they come into contact.[29]

As Peter Brown has shown,[30] the Church hierarchy was attempting, in the fourth century, to counter the trend towards "privatized" access to the holy whereby wealthy Christian patrons would obtain martyrs' bodies and place them in family tombs. Churchmen such as Ambrose were dedicated to breaking down the social hierarchization evident in such a monopoly of holiness by democratically rendering the martyrs accessible to the whole community.[31] However, even the development of a martyr's cult that was open to all imposed certain limitations on the availability of the saint's *praesentia*. Martyrs' cults were usually local and thus the holiness of the martyr's body was accessible only to those who were physically present at that place. Even if the faithful were to seek close proximity to the holy by going on pilgrimages to martyrs' shrines, they still could only achieve partial and limited access to relics, given the tendency of such shrines to hide or block the view of the holy.[32] What is novel and daring in Prudentius' transformation of martyrs' bodies into texts is the true democritization of the holy. Prudentius makes possible full disclosure and possession of the holy by turning martyrs into texts that can potentially reach many faithful.[33] By touching *and* reading the text, Christians can

experience the holiness and glory of martyrdom more fully than by going on pilgrimage.[34]

FERTILE WRITING AND MARTYRS' BODIES

The most remarkable aspect of the martyr-text is its fertility. Prudentius combines in complex ways a series of images which he uses to emphasize the renewal and rebirth that the martyrs' intercession entails. Prudentius draws upon Ambrose's characterization of Christ as a fertile seed and extends the comparison to the martyrs, who are the imitators of Christ's passion. Christ, the Logos, died and was planted and reborn in order to bring the fruit of salvation:

> ut enim Dominus noster Iesus Christus sicut
> granum cecidit in terram et mortuus est, ut
> multum fructum afferret.[35]

> for our lord Jesus Christ fell into the earth like a seed
> and died, so that he would bring forth much fruit.

Augustine brings out the linguistic implications of the fertility of Christ by speaking of the sowing of Christ as the implanting of a name:

> Mortuus est; et non periit nomen eius,
> sed seminatum est nomen eius:
> mortuus est; sed granum fuit, quo mortificato
> seges continuo exsurgeret.[36]

> He died [i.e., Christ]; and his name did not perish, but
> rather his name was sown: he died; but he was a seed
> by whose mortification a crop immediately would arise.

The bodies of the martyrs may also bear Christ's name written on them (for example, Eulalia), and thus they too are potentially fertile.

In the early Church the martyr was conceived of as an extension of the bloody sacrifice of Christ, and thereby as a participant in the redemptive fertility of the blood spilled by Christ.[37] Christ embodies the fertile Word of God, whereas Prudentius' martyr-texts become fertile written texts. The fecundity of the blood spilled by Christian martyrs was considered to consist of its ability to attract more believers to the Christian faith. Tertullian, in his *Apologeticum,* tells his persecutors that Christian blood is fertile and will result in a harvest of more Christians[38] whereas in the liturgy the Apostles are celebrated as those who planted the Church by their blood.[39] Augustine, in *Sermo* CCLXXX, "In natali martyrum Perpetuae et Felicitatis" (*PL* [*Patrologia curus completus, series latina*] 38.1283) explicitly describes martyrdom as a fertile sowing whose fruits are the faithful:

> Sicut ille unus animam suam pro nobis posuit: ita et
> imitati sunt martyres, et animas suas pro fratribus posu-
> erunt, atque ut ista populorum tanquam germinum co-
> piosissima fertilitas surgeret, terram suo sanguine irri-
> gaverunt. Fructus laboris ergo illorum etiam nos sumus.

Just as he alone gave up his soul for us, so the martyrs imitated him and gave up their souls for their brothers, and they watered the earth with their blood so that this great fertile abundance of people or, as it were, seeds, should spring up. We are the fruits of their labour.

Prudentius extends the metaphor of the blood of Christian martyrs as fertile seeds which result in the production of more offspring for the Church in the form of more believers, by metaphorizing the martyrs' bodies themselves as fields made fertile by the ploughing of the instruments of torture.[40] An essential element of Prudentius' Christian anthropology is the association of human bodies with the earth from which God originally formed them.[41] This link between human bodies and earth takes on a heightened significance in light of the language Prudentius uses to speak of the martyrs. Cassian is closely related to the ground which he consecrates with his body. When the character "Prudentius" arrives at Cassian's tomb in Imola, he bows down to the ground before it:

> Stratus humi tumulo advolvebar, quem sacer ornat
> martyr dicato Cassianus corpore.

> *(Pe* IX.5-6)

In front of the tomb I fell prostrate upon the earth which the holy martyr Cassian honors with his consecrated body.

The word "humus" which denotes "soil, earth, ground," evokes the fertility of the soil, and is commonly used when referring to sowing as in Ovid's *Metamorphoses* 5.647: "semina spargere humo" ("to sow seeds in the earth"). The earth and the neighbouring tomb of Cassian are made holy by the proximity of his body, which, as it were, fertilized the surrounding earth.

The mutilation of Cassian's body by the vengeful schoolboys who tear it or write upon it with their *stili* is likened to the ploughing of a field. His body is like a wax tablet furrowed by writing: "aratis cera sulcis scribitur" ("The wax is marked by the ploughing of furrows," *Pe* IX.52). The students refer to their writing on Cassian's body as an interweaving of furrows: "Pangere puncta libet sulcisque intexere sulcos," ("We like making pricks and interlacing furrows with other furrows," *Pe* IX.77).[42] When the judge of the martyr Vincent speaks of reopening the martyr's wounds in order to cause him more pain, he directs the torturers to re-plough, to refurrow Vincent's body:

> "Praesicca rursus ulcera,
> dum se cicatrix colligit
> refrigerati sanguinis,
> manus resulcans diruet."

> *(Pe* V.141-144)

When the wounds are quite dry and the congealed blood is gathering in a scar, your hand will plough them up again and tear them open.

Agricultural language is also used to describe the wounds or letters on Romanus' body which an angel transcribes into the book of heaven:

> Omnis notata est sanguinis dimensio,
> ut quamque plagam sulcus exarauerit

> *(Pe* X.1126-1127)

The measure of blood from each was noted, and how the ploughing furrowed each wound.

The repeated use by Prudentius of the word *sulcus* to refer to the wounds on the martyrs' bodies clearly brings out the idea that they are fertile fields whose lines or furrows of writing are opened up so that something can be implanted by God, the result of which will be the yielding of a marvelous fruit, the fruit of salvation.

In the case of some martyrs, the fruit springing from their fecund bodies is metaphorized as flowers. The martyrs were sometimes visualized in heaven bearing bouquets of flowers.[43] The bodies of female saints seem especially susceptible to this kind of figurative language, since it amounts to a translation or redirection of the fertility associated with a woman's body. Prudentius' account of the martyrdom of St. Eulalia and its aftermath is structured around the metaphorical transformation of Eulalia's body into a fertile field in which flowers bloom. When Eulalia first goes before the judge, she impresses him by her extreme youth. He calls her a "flos . . . tener" ("tender flower," *Pe* III.109) when referring to her tender age and virginal body. This is an ironic foreshadowing of her actual transformation into a flower since she will not only become a flower in the Church's garland of martyrs,[44] but the wounds her body receives will undergo a miraculous metamorphosis and will reappear as blood-red flowers.

In a brilliant series of metonymies, Prudentius moves from Eulalia's wounds, to the floor of her tomb, and then to the flowers springing up around the tomb. The sacred text of Eulalia's body is described in vivid color:

> Nomen et ipsa sacrum loquitur
> purpura sanguinis eliciti.

> *(Pe* III.139-140)

the very scarlet of the blood that is drawn speaks the holy name.

When Eulalia's martyred body is enshrined in the earth the holy wounds she bore are transferred to and imprinted upon the floor of her tomb, which, like her maiden's body is a virginal meadow:

> saxaque caesa solum uariant,
> floribus ut rosulenta putes
> prata rubescere multimodis.

> *(Pe* III.198-200)

Cut stones color the floor so that it seems like a rose-covered meadow blushing with varied blooms.

The flowers which appear to be blooming on the stone floor of the martyr's tomb are concretized, in reality, in the living flowers growing in the earth outside the tomb, whose floor, instead of remaining only a metaphorically intact meadow that contains the virginally fertile body of Eulalia, becomes a fertile field or body that yields real flowers:

> Carpite purpureas uiolas
> sanguineosque crocos metite!
> Non caret his genialis hiems,
> laxat et arua tepens glacies,
> floribus ut cumulet calathos.
>
> (*Pe* III.201-205)

Pluck the purple violets, gather the blood-red crocuses. Joyful winter has no lack of them; the cold is tempered and frees the fields to load our baskets with flowers.

The blood-red crocuses and scarlet ("purpureas") violets are the metamorphosized bloody letter-wounds which Eulalia's body bore. The flowering of the martyr's body in the earth which was fertilized by her body and blood attests to the redemptive power of Eulalia whose body has force sufficient to change the laws of nature and cause the earth to yield flowers in the midst of winter.[45]

There is a remarkable representation of the transformation of a female martyr into a flower in early Christian art. The picture in question is a fresco from an anonymous martyrium at Abu Girge (near Alexandria) dating from the fifth or sixth centuries. In it a saint is depicted who appears to be sprouting in a field like a flower. The martyr is surrounded by other flowers, some of which bear the symbol of the cross, suggesting that their martyred bodies have become flowers in paradise.[46] Eulalia too has assuredly become a flower in paradise, but she, through the fertility of her martyred body has strewn the earth with salvific fruit.

The image of Eulalia's body as a fertile field has very strong sexual associations. In ancient Greek literature, to call a woman's body a field, was, in effect, to establish a metaphorical connection between the field and the woman's sexual organs.[47] The flowering of Eulalia is, paradoxically, the fruit of a chaste marriage, by means of which she preserves her virginity and allows herself to be made fertile. Eulalia resists being ploughed or inscribed by a human husband by defying both parental and civic authority, and remaining firm in her desire to maintain her virginity:

> Iam dederat prius indicium
> tendere se patris ad solium
> nec sua membra dicata toro;
>
> (*Pe* III.16-18)

Already she had given an early sign that she sought the Father's throne, and that her body was not destined for marriage.

Eulalia will give in to no man as her body is preserved only for that husband with whom she will be united spiritually.

The judge urges Eulalia to reconsider her foolish opposition and tries to dissuade her from her course of action by reminding her of the joys she will lose if she dies before she reaches the married state:

> respice gaudia quanta metas,
> quae tibi fert genialis honor!
>
> (*Pe* III.104-105)

consider how many joys you are cutting off which the honor of marriage offers you.

He evokes the sorrow she will cause her family by bringing an untimely death upon herself:

> ingemit anxia nobilitas
> flore quod occidis in tenero
> proxima dotibus et thalamo.
>
> (*Pe* III.108-110)

Your noble stock mourns over you in distress because you are dying in the bloom of youth when you are just reaching the age of dowry and wedlock.

Eulalia, however, rejects physical union with any man. As soon as the judge finishes haranguing her, she spits in his face, and this act sets in motion the instruments of torture. Her body receives the imprint of Christ as it is broken open or ploughed by her torturers, thereby implying that she is being wedded to Christ. Although this marriage will not result in the production of children, Eulalia's marriage to God is still a fertile one, since her body blooms with colorful flowers.[48]

The rending of Eulalia's body is not described in terms of sexual union. The joining of the martyr with Christ is sexualized to the extent that it is portrayed as a substitute for marriage to a man, and that it involves the opening up of Eulalia's formerly integral body. Prudentius, in his narration of the martyrdom of Agnes, another young virgin saint, fills in this metaphorical gap. When Agnes refuses to give offerings to pagan gods, the judge condemns her to prostitution since he knows of her desire to preserve her virginity for Christ. God, of course, thwarting the judge's cruel intentions, protects Agnes from all defilement. Mad for revenge, the judge orders his soldier to draw his sword to kill Agnes, who, upon seeing the naked weapon, welcomes it like a lover who is soon to consummate her marriage:

> vt uidit Agnes stare trucem uirum
> mucrone nudo, laetior haec ait:

"Exulto, talis quod potius uenit
uaesanus atrox turbidus armiger,
quam si ueniret languidus ac tener
mollisque ephebus tinctus aromate,
qui me pudoris funere perderet.
Hic, hic amator iam, fateor, placet.
Ibo inruentis gressibus obuiam
nec demorabor uota calentia;
ferrum in papillas omne recepero
pectusque ad imum uim gladii traham.

(*Pe* XIV.67-78)

When Agnes saw the fierce man standing there with his naked sword her gladness increased and she said: "I rejoice that such a man comes, a savage, cruel, wild man-at-arms rather than a listless, soft, womanish youth bathed in perfume, coming to destroy me with the death of my modesty. This one, this lover at last, I confess pleases me. I shall meet his eager steps half-way and not put off his hot desires. I shall welcome the whole length of his blade into my bosom, drawing the sword-blow to the depths of my breast.

This striking passage leaves no doubt that Agnes views her union with Christ like the physical consummation of an earthly marriage. However, although the metaphorical sexual penetration envisioned by Agnes takes the form of decapitation rather than the more sexually charged stabbing, Agnes' death redirects her fertile female sexuality to a more spiritual plane and enables her to produce offspring or "fruit" that takes the form of heavenly splendour radiating from her martyr's crown:[49]

Cingit coronis interea deus
frontem duabus martyris innubae;
unam decemplex edita sexies
merces perenni lumine conficit,
centenus extat *fructus* in altera.

(*Pe* XIV.119-123)

Meanwhile God encircles the unwedded martyr's brow with two crowns.

Recompense issuing sixty-fold makes the one out of eternal light, and fruit, a hundredfold, appears in the other.

Like Eulalia, Agnes too is a virgin field, ploughed by Christ and made fertile. This passage recalls Matthew 13.23 where the parable of the sower is explained: "qui vero in terra bona seminatus est hic est qui audit verbum et intellegit et fructum adfert et facit aliud quidem centum aliud autem sexaginta porro aliud triginta" ("And the seed sown in rich soil is someone who hears the word and understands it; this is the one who yields a harvest and produces now a hundredfold, now sixty, now thirty). Thus, Agnes is not only made fertile by the grisly marking of martyrdom, but she herself, as martyr, as witness to and upholder of God's word, becomes the seed which will miraculously result in a superabundance of offspring.

In the case of Eulalia, the tearing of her body is at the same time an inscription which carries with it resonances of sexual violence.[50] The blood-red letters carved into her body are evocative of the scarlet thread used by Procne in Ovid's *Metamorphoses* to narrate the story of her rape by Tereus: "purpureasque notas filis intexuit albis" ("She wove purple letters on a white background," *Met.* VI.577).[51] Eulalia, too, bears red letters on a background of white parchment or flesh, and it can even be said to have been embroidered:

Dirus abest dolor ex animo
membraque picta cruore nouo
fonte cutem recalente lauant.

(*Pe* III.143-145)

The dreadful pain did not reach her spirit while the fresh blood painted [or embroidered] her body and washed her skin in its warm stream.

The verb *pingo* can refer to pictorial representation produced both by a pencil and a needle. Thus, Eulalia's body is painted or decorated by Christ's pen as well as being embroidered by his needle. The echoes of rape and violence embodied in this metaphor of Eulalia's body as a white garment sexually violated by the sword, pen and needle of her tormentor are disturbing since it is Christ himself who is inscribing and possessing her. However, in order for Eulalia to become a martyr, she must suffer a violent death. Thus, her "rape" by Christ via the sword of her persecutor is a necessary element in the economy of Christian salvation. Just as Christ had to die in order to defeat death, in the same way, Eulalia must die a sexually violent death so as to transcend both her carnality and her mortality.[52]

The bloody text written on the body of the martyr can also be replicated on the earth, which is itself often assimilated to the martyr's body in Prudentius' imagistic system. If the earth yields the offspring of the martyrs' bodies, it too can be the metaphorical recipient of the bloody letters marked on the latter. The land of Spain is marked or written upon by the divine pen whose bloody ink dripped from the martyrs' bodies to the soil of Calagurris:

Hic calentes hausit undas caede tinctus duplici,
inlitas cruore sancto nunc harenas incolae
confrequentant obsecrantes uoce uotis munere.

(*Pe* I.7-9)

Here it drank in the warm streams when it was wetted by the slaughter of the two, and now its people throng to the ground that was stained with their holy blood, making petitions with voice and heart and gifts.

The martyrs have turned Spain into a holy text whose letters or markers of sanctity are their bones (*Pe* I.5). The faithful who follow the holy text by visiting *mar-*

tyria internalize and appropriate for themselves the passion and sacrifice of the martyrs in a pilgrimage that is analogous to an act of reading.

The image of the earth as a text stained by the blood of martyrs and subsequently read by other Christians is most clearly expressed in the narration of Hippolytus' martyrdom.[53] Prudentius, when in Rome, reads a visual narrative on Hippolytus' tomb which represents the horrible passion of the martyr who was torn apart by horses:

> picta super tumulum species liquidis uiget umbris
>   effigians tracti membra cruenta uiri.
> Rorantes saxorum apices uidi, optime papa,
>   purpureasque notas uepribus inpositas.
>
> (*Pe* XI.125-128)

> Depicted above the tomb, the spectacle comes to life in flowing images, actively portraying the drawn man's bleeding body parts. I saw the tips of the rocks dripping, most excellent father, and scarlet marks imprinted on the briars.

The word "notas" is used by Prudentius to describe the letter-wounds inscribed upon the martyrs' bodies,[54] and the tips of the rocks ("apices saxorum") are like *stili* that write their bloody text on the briars. (The immortal text etched on Romanus' body consisted of "apices" which would never fade away in heaven.[55]) The letters or wounds inflicted upon Hippolytus' body are rewritten on the rocky earth since his body is so destroyed that it has become illegible.

As Hippolytus' loving disciples gather up the pieces of his body they must follow a gory trail of body parts and of blood-soaked rock and earth:

> Maerore attoniti atque *oculis rimantibus* ibant
>   inplebantque sinus uisceribus laceris.
> Ille caput niueum conplectitur ac reuerendam
>   canitiem molli confouet in gremio;
> hic umeros truncasque manus et bracchia et ulnas
>   et genua et crurum fragmina nuda *legit*.
>
> (*Pe* XI.135-140)

> Stunned with grief they went seeking with their eyes, and gathering the mangled flesh in their bosoms. One clasps the snowy head, cherishing the venerable white hair on his loving breast, while another collects the shoulders, the severed hands, arms, elbows, knees, and bare fragments of legs.

Hippolytus' followers, by collecting his remains, also read the text his body left on the earth, as is evinced by the two-fold meaning of the verb *lego* ("to read; to gather"). Such a *collatio* is not unlike the process of memory as described in the Ciceronian rhetorical tradition whereby material to be remembered is impressed onto the mind in a highly structured and organized man-

ner. The re-membering of Hippolytus by his followers will serve as well as a kind of mnemonic of violence of the sort recommended by the *Rhetorica ad Herennium*. In this pseudo-Ciceronian rhetorical manual, the author counsels the formation of striking or bloody *imagines agentes* as a means of facilitating the retention of material in the memory.[56] The action of collecting Hippolytus' body parts and blood (XI.135-144) suggests that the martyr will live on in a very vivid way in the hearts and memories of his faithful disciples and of those who read Prudentius' poem.

The "oculis rimantibus" also suggests the action of reading in which the eyes seek out the words and letters which are then introduced into the mind.[57] The use of the verb *rimor* to designate the act of reading posits a fascinating link between textuality and sowing. *Rimor*, in addition to meaning "to seek," is also an agricultural term for tearing up or ploughing the ground. The disciples of Hippolytus who collect his body and who read his bloody text are also ploughing or fertilizing this sacred text which will enable him to be a more fertile text, i.e., one which will result in the springing up of more spiritual offspring who will accrue to the Church. Hippolytus' scattered body parts are like letters or seeds.[58] The ancient Greek myth of Kadmos posits an essential connection between writing and sowing. Kadmos killed the dragon guarding the city of Kadmeia and then sowed the beast's teeth in the earth whence sprung the Spartoi, the ancestors of the Thebans. Kadmos was also credited with the introduction of the alphabet and writing into the Greek world:

> The alphabet, marks carved into stone, bronze, wax or wood, is, like seed, disseminated over a blank, receptive surface. The invention of writing is metaphorically equivalent to the sowing of the dragon's seed; the autochthonous Spartoi are reproduced like letters on a blank tablet.[59]

The martyrs' bodies that are written upon are ploughed and receive the seeds of Christ from which grow flowers or more Christian believers. The bodies of martyrs ploughed and furrowed by torture[60] become tombstones furrowed by writing:

> Nos pio fletu, date, perluamus
> marmorum sulcos. . . .
>
> (*Pe* IV.193-194)

> Come, let us with pious tears wash the furrows of letters cut into the marble slabs. . . .

The fertile tombstone-texts jutting out from the earth like teeth recall the sowing of the dragon's teeth. However, instead of Spartan warriors emerging from the earth, the redeemed bodies of the martyrs will arise and lead all believers to salvation:

Sterne te totam generosa sanctis
ciuitas mecum tumulis, deinde
mox resurgentes animas et artus
    tota sequeris.

(*Pe* IV.197-200)

Cast thyself down along with me, noble city, on the
holy graves, then when their souls and bodies rise
again, you and all your people will follow them.

PRUDENTIUS' POETIC TEXT AND THE DIVINE WRITING OF MARTYRDOM

The offspring of the fecund martyr-texts manifests itself
not only in the form of flowers, but also in the generation of new marks, of more discourse. If martyrdom,
for Prudentius, is coterminous with writing, then the
fertility of the martyr's body-text implies a concept of
language whose regenerative capacities are equal to that
of the martyr's body-field. Indeed, the flowers which
spring from Eulalia's body-field are related to discourse.
Palmer cites an Ovidian intertext for the "sanguineos
crocos" (*Pe* III.202) which are equivalent to Eulalia's
metamorphosed letter-wounds.[61] In Ovid's *Metamorphoses,* after Ajax is killed, his blood is absorbed by the
earth and is transformed into a purple flower whose petals are inscribed with letters:

expulit ipse cruor, rubefactaque sanguine tellus
purpureum viridi genuit de caespite florem,
qui prius Oebalio fuerat de vulnere natus;
littera communis mediis pueroque viroque
inscripta est foliis, haec nominis, illa querellae.

(*Met.* XIII.394-398)

the blood itself drove it out. The blood-stained ground
produced from the green sod a purple flower, which in
old time had sprung from Hyacinth's blood. The petals
are inscribed with letters, serving alike for hero and for
boy: this one a name, and that a cry of woe.

Prudentius is very aware of the textual nature of the
blood-red flowers growing out of Eulalia. The poet, unlike the girls and boys who pick the flowers around Eulalia's tomb and present them to her, weaves poetic
garlands of words in order to honor her:

Ista comantibus e foliis
munera, uirgo puerque, date!
Ast ego serta choro in medio
texta feram pede dactylico,
uilia marcida, festa tamen.

(*Pe* III.206-210)

Give her these gifts, girls and boys, from the luxuriant
leaves. But I, in the midst of your company will bring
garlands woven of dactylic measures, of little worth,
withered, but still joyous.

Prudentius offers a text to Eulalia woven from poetic
flowers which are the letter-wounds of the saint's body
which have, in turn, been converted back to letters by

the poet in order to reinscribe the text of Eulalia's
martyrdom. Those who gather the heavenly flower-
letters outside of the martyr's tomb can "read" and
inhale the odor of her wounds of sanctity in the same
way that the reader can appropriate the flowers of words
which reenact the inscribing (i.e., martyrdom) of Eulalia.

The fertility of Eulalia on a textual level is manifested
in the poem Prudentius writes for her, which is a
transcription of the holy text of the martyr's body. The
regenerative power of divine writing or speech has as
its paradigm the Word or Logos of God. Augustine
conceives of the Word of God as responsible for the
multiplication of earthly creatures[62] or as a "nomen"
which is planted and yields fruit.[63] The holy text on the
martyrs' bodies behaves in a similar fashion in that it is
a miraculously dynamic and fecund form of discourse.
Romanus' torturers plough furrows into his face so as
to stop his incessant speech:

. . . Vertat ictum carnifex
in os loquentis inque maxillas manum
sulcosque acutos et fidiculas transferat.

(*Pe* X.548-550)

Let the executioner turn the stroke to his speaking
mouth. Let him transfer his hand to the jaws and inflict
severe gashes and cords.

These furrows dug into the martyr's face are explicitly
termed divine writing by the poet:

Charaxat ambas ungulis *scribentibus*
genas cruentis et secat faciem *notis,*

(*Pe* X.557-558)

He engraves both cheeks with marks written by the
claws and he cuts bloody letters into his face.

The judge, however, cannot force sterility or silence
upon Romanus, since each of the wounds inflicted on
him only generates more discourse:

Rimas patentes inuenit uox edita
multisque fusa rictibus reddit sonos
hinc inde plures et profatur undique
Christi patrisque sempiternam gloriam.
Tot ecce laudant ora sunt uulnera."

(*Pe* X.566-570)

Now the voice I utter finds open fissures; issuing by
many a wide-open mouth, it delivers more sounds on
this side and on that, proclaiming from all sides the
everlasting glory of Christ and of the Father. For every
wound I have, you see a mouth uttering praise.

The irrepressible superabundance of verbal offspring issuing from the wound-furrows of Romanus is manifested by the astonishing length of the discourse which
he sustains and which is faithfully recorded by the pen
of Prudentius.[64]

The ability of the martyr-texts to engender more discourse is also reflected in a proliferation of narrative levels so that the martyr's text multiplies and is mirrored in many forms. The martyrdom of Cassian is first encountered by Prudentius in the form of a painting, a visual narrative. The visual text is then glossed by the commentary of the sacristan who recounts the event to the poet. Within the sacristan's narrative is the divine text of martyrdom written upon Cassian's body which lies at the heart of and is the rationale behind all the other levels of narrative. All these narrative layers or boxes are framed by the controlling poem written by Prudentius through which the other forms of discourse are filtered.

A similar technique is used in the poem about Hippolytus' martyrdom. Prudentius learns of Hippolytus by reading an epitaph dedicated to him (*Pe* XI.18-20), and this presumably intimates what manner of death he suffered, since the poet launches into an account of it. Then, the reader discovers that Prudentius is reading the bloody occurrence from a painting (*Pe* XI.123-126), itself a representation of the writing of a sacred, gory text upon the ground by means of Hippolytus' body and blood which is read by his disciples. The reader of Prudentius' poem reads about the character "Prudentius" who reads a painting in which Hippolytus' followers read the saint's holy text. The sacred text of the martyr's body is, again, at the centre of the narrative and radiates outward through various layers of narrative. The reader of Prudentius' poem can still discern the divine body-text which is the kernel of the narrative, but it is filtered through other levels of discourse and thus appears "per speculum in aenigmate" (I Cor. 13.12).

The most telling result of the fecundity of the martyrs and the texts inscribed upon them is the poetic production of Prudentius who thereby ensures the perpetuation of the martyrs' textual offspring. Prudentius, like God's angel who records the oral and written discourse of Romanus' martyrdom, is the transcriber of a divine text. The poet appeals to God to fill his mouth with eloquent words which he may then record in poetic form:

> Sum mutus ipse, sed potens facundiae
> mea lingua Christus luculente disseret.

> (*Pe* X.21-22)

> In myself I am dumb, but Christ is master of eloquence; he will be my tongue and discourse excellently.

In effect, Prudentius mimetically writes the same text as the angel by recreating in words the bloody text carved into Romanus' body and by recording the passionate words uttered by the saint during his trial. Prudentius' role as poet is also that of a disseminator of the holy martyr-texts. Since the martyrdom of St. Laurence occurred in far-away Rome, neither the poet nor his fellow Spaniards can see or read the holy text of Laurence's charred body. Thus, Prudentius looks to heaven in order to read the sacred text written by God, and transcribes the heavenly narrative into his own book:

> Sed qui caremus his bonis
> nec sanguinis uestigia
> uidere coram possumus,
> caelum intuemur eminus.

> (*Pe* II.545-548)

> Still though we lack these blessings and cannot see the traces of blood with our own eyes, we look up to heaven on high.

The recopying of the martyr-texts into Prudentius' book is his contribution to the preservation and exaltation of the martyrs' eternal glory.

The poems which recopy and reenact the sufferings of the martyrs are themselves, in a sense, metaphorical martyr-texts, since, as was pointed out above, the very act of writing embodies martyrdom. In the poem dedicated to Eulalia, Prudentius is, in effect, retextualizing the bloody letters or words which Christ had inscribed on her body. The verbal flowers (which are really Eulalia's metamorphosized wounds) which the poet interweaves to form a poetic text constitute an actualization of the martyrdom and an evocation of the holy body-text of the martyr herself. Prudentius' text is equivalent to Eulalia's body. Prudentius, through his transcription of the holy martyr-text, makes Eulalia's body present and accessible to all Christians. Only Eulalia and the eye-witnesses of the passion could read the bloody words written on her by Christ. Prudentius reinscribes the body so that all believers can read God's miraculous text and he also revivifies the saint's body so it can manifest its sanctity more easily in the world.[65]

The poetic garland of flowers woven by Prudentius for Eulalia is not only a mimetic representation of her martyred body, but is also a reflection of his ***Peristephanon,*** which consists of a series of poems, each of which embodies one or several martyrs. He has turned the martyrs into poems woven or strung together to form a garland or crown for the Church. By reading the ***Peristephanon,*** the reader can metaphorically wear the crown, and can thereby fleetingly participate in the drama of martyrdom. By assimilating his own poetic creation to the bodies of the martyrs, Prudentius is indirectly exalting his own poetry as well as the martyrs' body-texts, since his book is raised to the same level of imperishable and immortal textuality as are these holy texts.[66]

Indeed, Prudentius' attitude towards the power of the written text is manifested by his treatment of St. Cyprian's writings.[67] In Cyprian's case, his eloquent writings are the relics, not his body's bloody text of martyrdom:

> Incubat in Libya sanguis, sed ubique lingua pollet,
> sola superstes agit de corpore, sola obire nescit,
>
> (*Pe* XIII.4-5)

His blood rests in Africa, but his tongue is potent everywhere, it alone of all his body still survives in life, it alone cannot die.

Prudentius turns almost immediately from talking about Cyprian's body to his written texts and their reading:

> Dum liber ullus erit, dum scrinia sacra litterarum,
> te leget omnis amans Christum, tua, Cypriane, discet.
>
> (*Pe* XIII.7-8)

As long as there shall be any book, any collections of sacred writings, every lover of Christ will read you, Cyprian, and learn your teachings.

Cyprian's linguistic relics have the same power that is more normally associated with the body or body parts of a martyr:

> Desine flere bonum tantum, tenet ille regna caeli
> nec minus inuolitat terris nec ab hoc recedit orbe.
> Disserit eloquitur tractat docet instruit profetat.
>
> (*Pe* XIII.99-101)

Weep no more for this great blessing! He has attained to the realms of heaven, yet none the less he moves over the earth and does not leave this world: he still discourses, speaking out, expounding, teaching, instructing, prophesying.

Prudentius' poems, since they are simultaneously texts about *and* bodies of martyrs, ought to be able to have an impact both on earth and in heaven.

In choosing to fashion his poetry out of the corpus of martyrdom narrative and out of the *corpora* of the martyrs themselves, Prudentius has incorporated the most perfect *materia* into his poetic art. The recital to God of the names of the martyrs by an angel constitutes the highest form of poetry:

> Plenus est artis modus adnotatas
> nominum formas recitare Christo,
> quas tenet caeli liber explicandus
>   tempore iusto.
>
> (*Pe* IV.169-172)

The measure of the art is full if we read aloud to Christ the forms of the names as they are written down and contained in the book of heaven which will be opened at the due time.

The names of the martyrs are the only criterion for perfect poetry. They establish new poetic rules:

> Carminis leges amor aureorum
> nominum parui facit et loquendi
> cura de sanctis uitiosa non est
>   nec rudis umquam.
>
> (*Pe* IV.165-168)

Love of their golden names makes light of the rules of verse, and concern to speak of the saints is never sinful nor barbarous.

Thus, the martyrs are the perfect subject for the poet since they cannot but enhance his poetic art. Likewise, the martyrs' wounds are also the essence of poetic *materia* since they embody poetic meter. Wounds which are "longam" or "brevem" (*Pe* X.1128) can be likened to long or short vowels which are the metrical basis of poetry.

By writing a book of poetry which has the martyrdom of Christian bodies as its subject and form, Prudentius has shown himself to be a quintessentially Christian poet. His poems, which are mimetic reenactments and representations of martyred bodies, are a fitting attempt to gain the salvation he so desires. Just as the martyrs' bodies are redemptive texts which can intercede on behalf of the faithful, so Prudentius hopes his **Peristephanon** will be able to gain him a hearing with the holy martyrs who then will plead his case with Christ. Prudentius, in the **Praefatio** to his poetic works, clearly defines his conversion to a more Christian way of life as being embodied in his poetic vocation:

> Atqui fine sub ultimo
>   peccatrix anima stultitiam exuat;
>   saltem uoce deum concelebret, si meritis
>   nequit.
>
> (**Praef.** 34-36.)

Yet as my last end draws near, let my sinning soul put off her folly. With voice at least, let her honor God, if with good deeds she cannot.

Prudentius expresses the wish that he meet death while engaged in the act of writing poetry:

> Haec dum scribo uel eloquor,
>   uinclis o utinam corporis emicem
>   liber quo tulerit lingua sono mobilis ultimo!
>
> (**Praef.** 43-45)

And while I write or speak of these themes, O may I fly forth in freedom from the bonds of the body, to the place where my busy tongue's last word is born.

The poet sees the dedication of his life to the praising of God and his saints in poetry as a means of gaining personal salvation.[68]

By incorporating the inscribed martyr-texts into his own poetry and thus enabling the fertile language of God to proliferate, Prudentius is perhaps attempting to harness

the power of the martyrs on his own behalf.[69] Prudentius sees his own corpus of poetry as a transmuted form
of the martyrs' divine body-texts, and therefore as
capable of exercising the same mediatory function.
Martyrs mediate between man and Christ, whereas his
poems mediate between himself and the martyrs:

> Sic uenerarier ossa libet
> ossibus altar et inpositum,
> illa [Eulalia] dei sita sub pedibus
> prospicit haec populosque suos
> carmine propitiata fouet.
>
> (*Pe* III.211-215)

So ought her bones be venerated and an altar placed
above them, while she, set at the feet of God, views all
our doings, our song wins her favor, and she cherishes
her people.

Although Prudentius' poetry is only a pale reflection of
the divine writing on the martyrs' bodies, he is hopeful
that it retains and participates in some of the divine
fullness he has attempted to capture in his recreation of
the text of martyrdom.

The conception of language and writing developed by
Prudentius in the **Peristephanon** is one which makes
redemption possible. Christ, the Word who bestows
salvation, has written his name upon Eulalia, thereby
achieving a fusion of and harmonization between speech
and writing. The inscription of the martyrs' bodies is a
kind of writing in which there is no gap between the
immediacy of the spoken Word and the reflective,
shadowy quality of the written word. The metaphorical
transformation of the martyrs' bodies into divinely written texts redeems their bodies and souls as well as the
inscriptions they bear. By extension, Prudentius' body
of poems about the martyrs' body-texts is also a
redemptive text since it embodies the Logos' name
inscribed upon the martyrs. The salvific potential of the
written word explains why Prudentius' poetic vocation
was of such importance to him. It not only enabled him
to experience fully his Christianity, but it held out the
promise of salvation by virtue of his collaboration in
the embodiment of God's writing.

Notes

1. I would like to thank John Corbett, Patricia Eberle,
   Daniel Sheerin, Brian Stock, Eugene Vance, and
   the readers for *JECS* [*Journal of Early Christian
   Studies*] for their helpful comments on this essay
   during the various stages of its gestation.

2. Peter Brown, *The World of Late Antiquity: From
   Marcus Aurelius to Muhammad* (London: Thames
   and Hudson, 1971), 116-117; Henri I. Marrou, *A
   History of Education in Antiquity,* trans. George
   Lamb (New York: Sheed and Ward, 1956), 414-

416. William V. Harris points out on pp. 321-322
   of *Ancient Literacy* (Cambridge: Harvard University Press, 1989) that although the general level of
   literacy did decline in late antiquity, "there was an
   almost entirely new social location for the written
   word among the more professionally and enthusi-
   astically pious of the Christians."

3. Françoise Desbordes, *Idées romaines sur l'écriture*
   (Lille: Presses Universitaires de Lille, 1990), 99.

4. See Joseph Pucci, "The Dilemma of Writing: Augustine, *Confessiones* 4.6 and Horace, *Odes* 1.3,"
   Arethusa 24 (1991), pp. 257-279, for a textured
   account of "Augustine's sensitivity to the fundamental moral dilemma involved in writing" (pp.
   278-279). According to Pucci, for Augustine, to
   write is to engage in an act that is simultaneously
   "*audax*" vis-à-vis God, and paradoxically delightful (p. 278). Aside from Pucci's article, there is
   little published on attitudes towards and conceptions of the act of writing in late antique pagan
   and Christian writers (as opposed to late antique
   literary aesthetics or Christian attitudes toward
   literature). Brian Stock will soon be publishing an
   extensive study on writing in Augustine which
   should shed some light on this issue.

5. Anne-Marie Palmer, *Prudentius on the Martyrs*
   (Oxford: Clarendon Press, 1989), 43. See the
   chapter entitled "*Curiositas* and Credulity" for a
   good summary of fourth-century literary tastes.

6. See Michael Roberts, *The Jeweled Style: Poetry
   and Poetics in Late Antiquity* (Ithaca: Cornell
   University Press, 1989).

7. Martha Malamud, in *A Poetics of Transformation:
   Prudentius and Classical Mythology* (Ithaca: Cornell University Press, 1989) studies Prudentius'
   manipulation of language, classical mythology,
   and readers' participation in deciphering the
   cultural, literary, and linguistic codes embedded in
   his poetry. See especially Chapter Two, "Word
   Games," for a discussion of poets' manipulation
   of language and its intended effect upon readers.

8. *Peristephanon* II.573-580 (CCSL 126). All further
   references to the *Pe* will be to this edition. The
   translations are those of H. J. Thomson in vol. II
   of *Prudentius,* Loeb Classical Library (Cambridge:
   Harvard University Press, 1949) which I have
   sometimes modified slightly. The verb *prodo* in
   this passage may be taken to refer either to oral
   expression or to written production. See Lewis
   and Short, *A Latin Dictionary,* s.v., *prodo*.

9. Prudentius was of course well aware that his
   poems would not have been read silently. Orality
   was an integral part of the reading process in the

late antique world. See Paul Saenger, "Silent Reading: Its Impact on Late Medieval Script and Society," *Viator* 13 (1982), 370-373, for a good description of the oral nature of Roman reading practices.

10. The body, in early Christian thought, was sometimes considered as an intermediary. Methodius, in his *Symposium,* treats the bodies of virgins as the perfect mediators between heaven and earth. Such a logic of mediation may explain the easy passage from body to text since both fulfil a fundamentally mediatory function. See Peter Brown, *The Body and Society: Men, Women and Sexual Renunciation in Early Christianity,* Lectures on the History of Religions, New Series, vol. 13 (New York: Columbia University Press, 1988), 185. Prudentius' textualization of the martyrs' bodies is perfectly consistent with such a corporeal concept of mediation.

11. See for example, Antonio Salvatore, *Studi Prudenziani* (Naples: Libreria Scientifica Editrice, 1958). Even some of the most recent scholarship on Prudentius has the same tendency: see Anne Marie Palmer's *Prudentius on the Martyrs.*

12. Ernst Robert Curtius, *European Literature and The Latin Middle Ages,* trans. Willard Trask, Bollingen Series XXXVI (Princeton: Princeton University Press, 1953), 311. For Curtius' comments on Prudentius' use of the book metaphor, see pp. 311-312.

13. See the chapter entitled "Schreibmetaphern bei Prudentius: Vorgeschichte und literarische Funktion," pp. 79-140 of Klaus Thraede, *Studien zu Sprache und Stil des Prudentius* (Göttingen: Vandenhoeck & Ruprecht, 1965).

14. See Michael Roberts, *Poetry and the Cult of the Martyrs: The "Liber Peristephanon" of Prudentius* (Ann Arbor: University of Michigan Press, 1993). Roberts discusses the description of Cassian on pp. 141-145 and relates it to the "representation" of the martyrdom in Prudentius' text (p. 145). The textual nature of Hippolytus' bodily remains is also noted by Roberts (pp. 155-156) who views Prudentius' poem as repeating the original "reading" of Hippolytus' body.

15. The representation of martyrdom as the sowing of fertile words of torture recalls the Parable of the Sower in Luke 8.4-11. Here the seed that falls in good ground yields fruit a hundredfold (Lk 8.8). In verse 11, the explication of the Parable reveals that the seed is linguistic in nature: "Est autem haec parabola semen est verbum Dei."

16. André Grabar, *Martyrium: Recherches sur le culte des reliques et l'art chrétien antique* (Paris: Collège de France, 1946), vol. II, plate XXXVI.1.

17. Palmer, *Prudentius on the Martyrs,* ch. 1.

18. Ignatius of Antioch, "The Epistle to the Romans," 2:1 in *Ignatius of Antioch,* ed. Helmut Koester with commentary by William R. Schoedel (Philadelphia: Fortress Press, 1985). Quoted in Geoffrey Galt Harpham, "The Fertile Word: Augustine's Ascetics of Interpretation," *Criticism* 28 (1986): 252, note 2. J. B. Lightfoot in *The Apostolic Fathers,* Part II: *S. Ignatius, S. Polycarp* (London: Macmillan and Co., 1889) interprets this verse as follows: "His martyrdom alone would make his life an intelligible utterance; otherwise it was no better than the passionate cry of some irrational creature to whom life is pleasure or pain, and nothing more" (p. 200). The Latin translation of this letter of St. Ignatius mirrors the contrast between *logos* and *phone:* "si enim taceatis a me, ego verbum dei; si autem desideretis carnem meam, rursus factus sum vox." The Latin text is printed in *Patrum apostolicorum opera,* fasciculus II: *Ignatii et Polycarpi: Epistulae, Martyria, Fragmenta,* ed. Theodorus Zahn (Leipzig: J. C. Hinrichs, 1876).

19. John the Monk, writing in the late fourth century, comments on the Dopposition between *logos* and *phone* in St. Ignatius as being that between flesh and spirit: ". . . for every beast and bird together with cattle and creeping thing of the earth utter the voice only; but because man has in him a soul and is not like the rest of the other bodies, he uses the Word and the Voice. . . ." John's comments are cited on p. 199 in J. B. Lightfoot, *The Apostolic Fathers,* Part II: *S. Ignatius, S. Polycarp.*

20. Galt Harpham, "The Fertile Word," p. 239.

21. Palmer, *Prudentius on the Martyrs,* p. 174.

22. Lactantius, *Institutiones divinae* V, 13.9 (SC 204).

23. See the entry for *charaxo* in the *Thesaurus linguae latinae* [TLL]. The *TLL* cites the following passage from the Pseudo-Augustinian *Altercatio ecclesiae et sinagogae:* "cum primum Moyses in monte Sina charaxatas decalogo duplices tabulas accepisset."

24. This passage recalls Jesus' words in the Sermon on the Mount where he states that the law of the prophets is to remain intact and inviolate: "Amen quippe dico vobis donec transeat caelum et terra iota unum aut unus apex non praeteribit a lege donec omnia fiant" (Matt 5.18: "For truly I tell

you, until heaven and earth pass away, not one dot, not one stroke of a letter, will pass from the law until all is accomplished." See also Luke 16.17). Here, Prudentius seems to be suggesting an equivalence between a martyr's body and the law. Both are immortal, unchanging texts whose meaning must be respected and communicated to others as a precondition for entry into heaven (cf. Matt 5.19).

25. The function of the martyrs as divine, heavenly texts is also evident in the fourth-century *Passio Saturnini, Dativi et aliorum plurimorum martyrum in Africa*, in *Actas de los mártires*, ed. Daniel Ruiz Bueno (Madrid: Biblioteca de Autores Cristianos, 1968). The martyr Emeritus, when responding to the judge's question as to whether he possesses Scriptures, states that they are written in his heart ("In corde meo illas habeo," p. 984). Emeritus goes on to suggest that the martyrs' bodies are akin to walking divine books: "O martyrem Apostoli memorem, qui legem Domini conscriptam habuit, non atramento, sed Spiritu Dei uiui, non in tabulis lapideis, sed in tabulis cordis carnalibus" (XI, pp. 984-985: "Oh martyr mindful of the Apostle who had God's law written, not by means of ink but by the spirit of the living God, not on stone tablets, but on the carnal tablets of the heart.")

26. See p. 135 of Page DuBois' *Sowing the Body: Psychoanalysis and Ancient Representations of Women* (Chicago: University of Chicago Press, 1988), for a discussion of the objectification and commodification of the body through inscription or decoration.

27. André Grabar, *Martyrium*, I, p. 40; Nicole Hermann-Mascard, *Les reliques des saints: Formation coutumière d'un droit* (Paris: Klincksieck, 1975), 29, 35, 49.

28. Grabar, *Martyrium*, I, 40.

29. Michael Roberts also points out that Prudentius is aware that a martyr's presence is as fully present in the text of his/her passion as it is in the sacred place of the martyr's shrine. Therefore, Roberts also considers that "Prudentius himself extends the principle of the plenitude of relics to the text of the passion and therefore to his own poetic endeavour." See pp. 192-193 of *Poetry and the Cult of the Martyrs.*

30. See his *The Cult of the Saints: Its Rise and Function in Latin Christianity*, The Haskell Lectures on History of Religions, New Series, No. 2 (Chicago: University of Chicago Press, 1981).

31. Brown, *Cult of the Saints*, 34.

32. *Ibid.*, 86-87.

33. On the possible readers of Prudentius, see Anne-Marie Palmer, *Prudentius on the Martyrs*, 91-94.

34. Michael Roberts points out that Prudentius' martyrdom narratives share "the ability of the devotional moment itself to transcend temporal distinctions" (*Poetry and the Cult of the Martyrs*, 19).

35. Ambrose, *Enarrationes in duodecim psalmos davidicos* 43.38 (*PL* 14.1108).

36. Augustine, *Enarrationes in psalmos* 40.I (CCSL 38).

37. Michele Pellegrino, "Le Sens ecclésial du martyre," *Revue des sciences religieuses* 35 (1961), 152.

38. Tertullian, *Apologeticum* 50.13 (CCSL I, 171): "Nec quicquam tamen proficit exquisitior quaeque crudelitas uestra: illecebra est magis sectae. Etiam plures efficimur, quotiens metimur a uobis: semen est sanguis Christianorum!"

39. Michele Pellegrino, "Le Sens ecclésial du martyre," 156.

40. Klaus Thraede has traced the sources of the writing as sowing metaphor on pp. 79-113 of *Studien zu Sprache und Stil des Prudentius*. There are many other examples of the language of sowing applied to the suffering of martyrdom. For example, the *Passio Saturnini* VIII (p. 980 in Ruiz Blanco) describes the torture of martyrdom as follows: "geminata martyris dignitas iterato ungulis sulcantibus exaratur" ("again the two-fold dignity of the martyr is ploughed deeply by the claws that furrow him"). In another example, John Chrysostom in *De Sanctis Martyribus* refers to the torture of martyrs as the tilling of the earth: "They tied the martyrs to the rack; making deep furrows they pierced their sides as if they were tilling the earth with a plough, and not mutilating human bodies." (Cited on pp. 158-159 of Hippolyte Delehaye, *Les Passions des martyres et les genres littéraires* [Brussels: Société des Bollandistes, 1966]. For the Greek text, see *PG* [*Patrologia Graeca*] 50.708). Although images of sowing are common in the *passiones* of martyrs, Prudentius revivifies the metaphor by exploiting and directing its connotations of fertility and dynamism to the nature of martyrdom and the discourse in which it is expressed.

41. Joaquín Pascual Torro, *Antropología de Aurelio Prudencio* (Rome: Iglesia Nacional Española, 1974), 20.

42. For a fuller discussion of Prudentius' treatment of the inscription of Cassian, see Roberts, *Poetry and*

the Cult of the Martyrs, 132-148. See especially pp. 141-145 for the representation of Cassian in textual terms.

43. Pseudo-Ambrosius, *Sermo* 59B.5 (*PL* 17.726): "tunc venient in exsultatione portantes manipulos suos, cum in resurrectione receperint flores suos" ("then will they come in exultation bearing their trophies since, in their resurrection, they will have received their flowers"). Gregory the Great also spoke of martyrdom as a flowering: "Ecce iam mors martyrum floret in fide viventium" ("Behold, the death of the martyrs now blooms in the faith of the living"). *Homiliarum in Evangelia* II.38.5 (*PL* 76.1285).

44. Palmer, *Prudentius on the Martyrs*, p. 168.

45. It was common practice to refer to virgin-martyrs as "flowers." Once again, Prudentius breathes new life into what was, by his time, quite a dead metaphor. Michael Roberts points out that the motif of springtime in winter carries strong nuptial associations, and thus that the celebration of Eulalia's feast day is an ironic symbol of her rejection of physical marriage, and instead a joyous sign of her chaste, spiritual union with Christ. See *Poetry and the Cult of the Martyrs*, 98-100. Anne-Marie Palmer also notes this connection on pp. 168-169 of *Prudentius on the Martyrs*.

46. Grabar, *Martyrium*, II, Plate LX.3. There is no commentary in Grabar about the scene represented in the fresco. I am suggesting my own interpretation of the scene in question.

47. DuBois, *Sowing the Body*, p. 39.

48. John Petruccione in "The Portrait of St. Eulalia of Mérida in Prudentius' *Peristephanon 3*," *Analecta Bollandiana* 108 (1990), pp. 81-104, provides ample evidence that Eulalia's martyrdom should be read as an epithalamium. See especially pp. 98-102.

49. The ambivalent oscillation between the poles of chastity and sexuality that characterizes Agnes is discussed by Martha Malamud on pp. 78-82, and 83-84 of "Making a Virtue of Perversity: The Poetry of Prudentius," *Ramus* 19 (1990). Malamud on pp. 169-170 of *A Poetics of Transformation* views Agnes' wished-for penetration by the executioner's sword as explicitly sexual.

50. In a fascinating study of the interpenetration of the sexual and the textual in the martyrdom narrative of Eulalia, Martha Malamud points out that Eulalia becomes a text that "reads and interprets itself" and thus raises the question of the location of textual authority. See pp. 76-85 of "Making a Virtue of Perversity."

51. Although very little work has been done on Ovidian intertexts in the *Pe*, there is much evidence that points to a great familiarity of Prudentius with the work of Ovid. See W. Evenepoel, "La Présence d'Ovide dans l'oeuvre de Prudence," in *Colloque Présence d'Ovide*, ed. R. Chevallier, Collection Caesarodunum 17B (Paris: Les Belles Lettres, 1982): 165-176. See also Antonio Salvatore, "Ovidio cristiano," pp. 35-57 in his *Studi Prudenziani* (Napoli: Libreria Scientifica Editrice, premessa 1958).

52. Although Eulalia is consumed by fire, the sexually charged torture of her body that precedes her death is an equally integral element of her martyrdom.

53. Roberts on pp. 155-156 of *Poetry and the Cult of the Martyrs* also points out Prudentius' use of the language of writing in the Hippolytus martyrdom. He too views the collection of Hippolytus' body parts by his disciples as the deciphering of a text, analogous to the reading of an inscription that must be reconstructed in order to confer meaning.

54. For example, see *Pe* III.135.

55. *Pe* X.1119-1120:

inscripta Christo pagina inmortalis est,

nec obsolescit ullus in caelis apex.

56. *Rhetorica ad Herrenium,* ed. and trans. Harry Caplan (Cambridge: Harvard University Press, 1954), III.xxii.37: "We ought, then, to set up images of a kind that can adhere longest in the memory. And we shall do so if we establish likenesses as striking as possible; . . . if we somehow disfigure them, as by introducing one stained with blood or soiled by mud or smeared with red paint . . . that, too will ensure our remembering them more readily."

See also Mary Carruthers, *The Book of Memory: A Study of Memory in Medieval Culture,* Cambridge Series in Medieval Literature, vol. 10 (Cambridge: Cambridge University Press, 1990), 133-134, for an exposition of the development of this mnemonic of violence in the early fourteenth-century *ars memorativa* attributed to Thomas Bradwardine.

57. The verb *rimor,* although not a precise term for "reading" does have the sense of "searching for with the mind." Such a definition is consonant with the activity of reading which requires active cognitive participation on the part of the reader. A good example of this usage of the verb occurs in Aulius Gellius' *Noctes Atticae* 1.4.1: "scripta omnia antiquiora . . . spectabat et aut virtutes pensitabat aut vitia rimabatur." This example is taken from the *Oxford Latin Dictionary*.

58. See DuBois, *Sowing the Body,* p. 56, for an ancient precedent for the linking o the themes of writing and sowing in Theban legend.

59. DuBois, *Sowing the Body,* p. 55.

60. *Pe* IV.118-120:

> carnis et caesae spolium retentans
> taetra quam sulcos habeant amaros
> vulnera narras.

61. Palmer, *Prudentius on the Martyrs,* p. 174.

62. *Confessions* XIII.xx.27. See also Galt Harpham, "The Fertile Word," p. 249, for a discussion of the Word's fertility.

63. Augustine, *Enarr. in Psalm.* 40.I: "Mortuus est; et non periit nomen eius, sed seminatum est nomen eius:"

64. At 1,140 lines of verse, the narrative of Romanus' passion is by far the longest in the *Peristephanon.* For more on Romanus' rhetorical *copia,* see Robert Levine, "Prudentius' Romanus: The Rhetorician as Hero, Martyr, Satirist, and Saint," *Rhetorica* 9 (1991), pp. 5-38.

65. In early Christian practice, the reading aloud of a saint's passion on his or her feast day was a powerful means of evoking the presence of the saint, of making available the saint's *potentia.* The narrative recreation of the saint's suffering was a vital element in the diffusion of holy power. See p. 82 of Brown's *Cult of the Saints.* As a poet who fashions his text out of the tortured bodies of the martyrs, Prudentius surely must have been aware of his own participation in a literary process that was vital to both the recreation of the martyrs' physical presence and to the dissemination of their power. Prudentius, by linking his own poetic production directly to the martyrs' corporeal presence, arrogates to himself a privileged position for the control of the holy.

66. Martha Malamud has also noted Prudentius' audacious attempt "to reinscribe his relationship with the Christian God within a paradigm that promises the ultimate vindication of the artist." See pp. 84-86 of "Making a Virtue of Perversity."

67. Michael Roberts on pp. 123-125 of *Poetry and the Cult of the Martyrs* also uses Cyprian as the exemplification of "the status of Christian writing by attributing to it a power equivalent to that of martyrs after their death."

68. See Palmer, *Prudentius on the Martyrs,* pp. 15-16. See also Italo Lana, *Due Capitoli Prudenziani* (Rome: Editrice Studium, 1962), 84.

69. Haijo Westra makes the interesting suggestion that one of the reasons St. Augustine was silent about the work of Prudentius may have been due to Prudentius' exalted claims that his poetry and his own role as poet were a means of salvation. See p. 96 of Haijo J. Westra, "Augustine and Poetic Exegesis," in Hugo A. Meynell, ed. *Grace, Politics & Desire: Essays on Augustine* (Calgary: University of Calgary Press, 1990), 87-100.

FURTHER READING

Criticism

Burrus, Virginia. "Reading Agnes: The Rhetoric of Gender in Ambrose and Prudentius." *Journal of Early Christian Studies* 3, no. 1 (spring 1995): 25-46.

Contrasts two accounts of the Christian martyr Agnes and contends that Prudentius's version both accommodates and subverts orthodox Christian discourse.

Edwards, M. J. "Chrysostom, Prudentius, and the Fiends of *Paradise Lost.*" *Notes and Queries* n.s. 42, no. 4 (December 1995): 448-50.

Cites a few literary debts of Milton to Prudentius.

Harris, Duncan S. "The Paradox of Allegory: Being and Becoming in Spenser and Prudentius." *Wascana Review* 9, no. 1 (spring 1974): 66-74.

Compares and contrasts treatments of moral allegory by Spenser and Prudentius.

Haworth, Kenneth R. "Allegoria." In *Deified Virtues, Demonic Vices, and Descriptive Allegory in Prudentius's* Psychomachia, pp. 12-41. Amsterdam, The Netherlands: Adolf M. Hakkert, 1980.

Examines the history of allegory to demonstrate what allegory must have meant to Prudentius.

Jackson, M. J. "Psychomachia in Art from Prudentius to Proust." *British Journal of Aesthetics* 30, no. 2 (April 1990): 159-65.

Explores medieval artistic renditions of spiritual warfare, some of which are borrowed from Prudentius.

McCarthy, William. "Prudentius, *Peristephanon* 2: Vapor and the Martyrdom of Lawrence." *Vigiliae Christianae* 36, no. 3 (September 1982): 282-86.

Analyzes Prudentius's comparison of the physical heat of torture to the spiritual heat of sin.

Mickel Jr., Emanuel J. "Parallels in Prudentius's *Psychomachia* and *La Chanson de Roland*." *Studies in Philology* 67, no. 4 (October 1970): 439-52.

Describes numerous episodes in *Roland* that are similar to episodes in the *Psychomachia*.

Palmer, Anne-Marie. "The Form and Purpose of the *Peristephanon*." In *Prudentius on the Martyrs*, pp. 57-97. Oxford, England: Clarendon Press, 1989.

Argues that the *Peristephanon* consists not of hymns but rather a series of martyr-poems.

Petruccione, John. "The Portrait of St. Eulalia of Mérida in Prudentius's *Peristephanon 3*." *Analecta Bollandiana* 108 (1990): 81-104.

Argues that Prudentius's intention in the *Peristephanon* was not historical accuracy but religious instruction.

———. "Prudentius's Portrait of St. Cyprian: An Idealized Biography." *Revue des Etudes Augustiniennes* 36, no. 2 (1990): 225-41.

Defends Prudentius's account of Cyprian as a skillful portrait that emphasizes its subject's affinity to Saint Paul.

———. "The Persecutor's Envy and the Rise of the Martyr Cult: *Peristephanon* Hymns 1 and 4. *Vigiliae Christianae: A Review of Early Christian Life and Language* 45, no. 4 (December 1991): 327-46.

Details the method by which Prudentius showed the ineffectiveness of persecutors of Christians in their attempts to suppress the fame of martyrs.

———. "The Martyr Death as Sacrifice: Prudentius's *Peristephanon 4. 9-72*." *Vigiliae Christianae: A Review of Early Christian Life and Language* 49, no. 3 (August 1995): 245-57.

Discussion of the influence of Origen on Prudentius's views regarding the death of martyrs and salvation.

Roberts, Michael. "Poet and Pilgrim." In *Poetry and the Cult of the Martyrs: The* Liber Peristephanon *of Prudentius*, pp. 131-88. Ann Arbor: University of Michigan Press, 1993.

Analyzes poems 9, 11, and 12, in which "narrator and devotee are most completely fused."

Wieland, Gernot R. "Aldhelm's *De Octo Vitiis Principalibus* and Prudentius's *Psychomachia*." *Medium Ævum* 55, no. 1 (1986): 85-92.

Discusses connections between the Anglo-Saxon author Aldhelm (c. 640-710) and Prudentius.

———. "The Anglo-Saxon Manuscripts of Prudentius's *Psychomachia*." *Anglo-Saxon England* 16 (1987): 213-31.

Describes the ten extant Anglo-Saxon manuscripts of Prudentius's *Psychomachia* and concludes that they cannot be categorized into coherent groups.

———. "*Psychomachia* Manuscripts." *Old English Newsletter* 27, no. 1 (fall 1993): B16-9.

Further examination of the Anglo-Saxon *Psychomachia* manuscripts, focusing on their illustrations.

———. "The Origin and Development of the Anglo-Saxon *Psychomachia* Illustrations." *Anglo-Saxon England* 26 (1997): 169-86.

Detailed study of the manuscript illustrations.

Additional coverage of Prudentius's life and career is contained in the following sources published by Thomson Gale: *European Writers*, Vol. 1; *Literature Resource Center*; and *Reference Guide to World Literature*, Eds. 2, 3.

How to Use This Index

The main references

```
Calvino, Italo
   1923-1985 ....... CLC 5, 8, 11, 22, 33, 39,
                            73; SSC 3, 48
```

list all author entries in the following Gale Literary Criticism series:

AAL = Asian American Literature
BG = The Beat Generation: A Gale Critical Companion
BLC = Black Literature Criticism
BLCS = Black Literature Criticism Supplement
CLC = Contemporary Literary Criticism
CLR = Children's Literature Review
CMLC = Classical and Medieval Literature Criticism
DC = Drama Criticism
HLC = Hispanic Literature Criticism
HLCS = Hispanic Literature Criticism Supplement
HR = Harlem Renaissance: A Gale Critical Companion
LC = Literature Criticism from 1400 to 1800
NCLC = Nineteenth-Century Literature Criticism
NNAL = Native North American Literature
PC = Poetry Criticism
SSC = Short Story Criticism
TCLC = Twentieth-Century Literary Criticism
WLC = World Literature Criticism, 1500 to the Present
WLCS = World Literature Criticism Supplement

The cross-references

```
See also CA 85-88, 116; CANR 23, 61;
DAM NOV; DLB 196; EW 13; MTCW 1, 2;
RGSF 2; RGWL 2; SFW 4; SSFS 12
```

list all author entries in the following Gale biographical and literary sources:

AAYA = Authors & Artists for Young Adults
AFAW = African American Writers
AFW = African Writers
AITN = Authors in the News
AMW = American Writers
AMWR = American Writers Retrospective Supplement
AMWS = American Writers Supplement
ANW = American Nature Writers
AW = Ancient Writers
BEST = Bestsellers
BPFB = Beacham's Encyclopedia of Popular Fiction: Biography and Resources
BRW = British Writers
BRWS = British Writers Supplement
BW = Black Writers
BYA = Beacham's Guide to Literature for Young Adults
CA = Contemporary Authors
CAAS = Contemporary Authors Autobiography Series
CABS = Contemporary Authors Bibliographical Series
CAD = Contemporary American Dramatists
CANR = Contemporary Authors New Revision Series
CAP = Contemporary Authors Permanent Series
CBD = Contemporary British Dramatists
CCA = Contemporary Canadian Authors
CD = Contemporary Dramatists
CDALB = Concise Dictionary of American Literary Biography
CDALBS = Concise Dictionary of American Literary Biography Supplement
CDBLB = Concise Dictionary of British Literary Biography

CMW = *St. James Guide to Crime & Mystery Writers*
CN = *Contemporary Novelists*
CP = *Contemporary Poets*
CPW = *Contemporary Popular Writers*
CSW = *Contemporary Southern Writers*
CWD = *Contemporary Women Dramatists*
CWP = *Contemporary Women Poets*
CWRI = *St. James Guide to Children's Writers*
CWW = *Contemporary World Writers*
DA = *DISCovering Authors*
DA3 = *DISCovering Authors 3.0*
DAB = *DISCovering Authors: British Edition*
DAC = *DISCovering Authors: Canadian Edition*
DAM = *DISCovering Authors: Modules*
   DRAM: *Dramatists Module;* **MST:** *Most-studied Authors Module;*
   MULT: *Multicultural Authors Module;* **NOV:** *Novelists Module;*
   POET: *Poets Module;* **POP:** *Popular Fiction and Genre Authors Module*
DFS = *Drama for Students*
DLB = *Dictionary of Literary Biography*
DLBD = *Dictionary of Literary Biography Documentary Series*
DLBY = *Dictionary of Literary Biography Yearbook*
DNFS = *Literature of Developing Nations for Students*
EFS = *Epics for Students*
EXPN = *Exploring Novels*
EXPP = *Exploring Poetry*
EXPS = *Exploring Short Stories*
EW = *European Writers*
FANT = *St. James Guide to Fantasy Writers*
FW = *Feminist Writers*
GFL = *Guide to French Literature,* Beginnings to 1789, 1798 to the Present
GLL = *Gay and Lesbian Literature*
HGG = *St. James Guide to Horror, Ghost & Gothic Writers*
HW = *Hispanic Writers*
IDFW = *International Dictionary of Films and Filmmakers: Writers and Production Artists*
IDTP = *International Dictionary of Theatre: Playwrights*
LAIT = *Literature and Its Times*
LAW = *Latin American Writers*
JRDA = *Junior DISCovering Authors*
MAICYA = *Major Authors and Illustrators for Children and Young Adults*
MAICYAS = *Major Authors and Illustrators for Children and Young Adults Supplement*
MAWW = *Modern American Women Writers*
MJW = *Modern Japanese Writers*
MTCW = *Major 20th-Century Writers*
NCFS = *Nonfiction Classics for Students*
NFS = *Novels for Students*
PAB = *Poets: American and British*
PFS = *Poetry for Students*
RGAL = *Reference Guide to American Literature*
RGEL = *Reference Guide to English Literature*
RGSF = *Reference Guide to Short Fiction*
RGWL = *Reference Guide to World Literature*
RHW = *Twentieth-Century Romance and Historical Writers*
SAAS = *Something about the Author Autobiography Series*
SATA = *Something about the Author*
SFW = *St. James Guide to Science Fiction Writers*
SSFS = *Short Stories for Students*
TCWW = *Twentieth-Century Western Writers*
WLIT = *World Literature and Its Times*
WP = *World Poets*
YABC = *Yesterday's Authors of Books for Children*
YAW = *St. James Guide to Young Adult Writers*

Literary Criticism Series
Author Index

Agnon, S(hmuel) Y(osef Halevi)
1888-1970 .... **CLC 4, 8, 14; SSC 30; TCLC 151**
See also CA 17-18; 25-28R; CANR 60, 102; CAP 2; EWL 3; MTCW 1, 2; RGSF 2; RGWL 2, 3

Agrippa von Nettesheim, Henry Cornelius
1486-1535 .... **LC 27**

Aguilera Malta, Demetrio
1909-1981 .... **HLCS 1**
See also CA 111; 124; CANR 87; DAM MULT, NOV; DLB 145; EWL 3; HW 1; RGWL 3

Agustini, Delmira 1886-1914 .... **HLCS 1**
See also CA 166; DLB 290; HW 1, 2; LAW

Aherne, Owen
See Cassill, R(onald) V(erlin)

Ai 1947- .... **CLC 4, 14, 69**
See also CA 85-88; CAAS 13; CANR 70; DLB 120; PFS 16

Aickman, Robert (Fordyce)
1914-1981 .... **CLC 57**
See also CA 5-8R; CANR 3, 72, 100; DLB 261; HGG; SUFW 1, 2

Aidoo, (Christina) Ama Ata
1942- .... **BLCS; CLC 177**
See also AFW; BW 1; CA 101; CANR 62; CD 5; CDWLB 3; CN 7; CWD; CWP; DLB 117; DNFS 1, 2; EWL 3; FW; WLIT 2

Aiken, Conrad (Potter) 1889-1973 .... **CLC 1, 3, 5, 10, 52; PC 26; SSC 9**
See also AMW; CA 5-8R; 45-48; CANR 4, 60; CDALB 1929-1941; DAM NOV, POET; DLB 9, 45, 102; EWL 3; EXPS; HGG; MTCW 1, 2; RGAL 4; RGSF 2; SATA 3, 30; SSFS 8; TUS

Aiken, Joan (Delano) 1924-2004 ...... **CLC 35**
See also AAYA 1, 25; CA 9-12R, 182; 223; CAAE 182; CANR 4, 23, 34, 64, 121; CLR 1, 19, 90; DLB 161; FANT; HGG; JRDA; MAICYA 1, 2; MTCW 1; RHW; SAAS 1; SATA 2, 30, 73; SATA-Essay 109; SATA-Obit 152; SUFW 2; WYA; YAW

Ainsworth, William Harrison
1805-1882 .... **NCLC 13**
See also DLB 21; HGG; RGEL 2; SATA 24; SUFW 1

Aitmatov, Chingiz (Torekulovich)
1928- .... **CLC 71**
See Aytmatov, Chingiz
See also CA 103; CANR 38; CWW 2; DLB 302; MTCW 1; RGSF 2; SATA 56

Akers, Floyd
See Baum, L(yman) Frank

Akhmadulina, Bella Akhatovna
1937- .... **CLC 53; PC 43**
See also CA 65-68; CWP; CWW 2; DAM POET; EWL 3

Akhmatova, Anna 1888-1966 ..... **CLC 11, 25, 64, 126; PC 2, 55**
See also CA 19-20; 25-28R; CANR 35; CAP 1; DA3; DAM POET; DLB 295; EW 10; EWL 3; MTCW 1, 2; PFS 18; RGWL 2, 3

Aksakov, Sergei Timofeyvich
1791-1859 .... **NCLC 2**
See also DLB 198

Aksenov, Vasilii (Pavlovich)
See Aksyonov, Vassily (Pavlovich)
See also CWW 2

Aksenov, Vassily
See Aksyonov, Vassily (Pavlovich)

Akst, Daniel 1956- .... **CLC 109**
See also CA 161; CANR 110

Aksyonov, Vassily (Pavlovich)
1932- .... **CLC 22, 37, 101**
See Aksenov, Vasilii (Pavlovich)
See also CA 53-56; CANR 12, 48, 77; DLB 302; EWL 3

Akutagawa Ryunosuke 1892-1927 ... **SSC 44; TCLC 16**
See also CA 117; 154; DLB 180; EWL 3; MJW; RGSF 2; RGWL 2, 3

Alabaster, William 1568-1640 .... **LC 90**
See also DLB 132; RGEL 2

Alain 1868-1951 .... **TCLC 41**
See also CA 163; EWL 3; GFL 1789 to the Present

Alain de Lille c. 1116-c. 1203 .... **CMLC 53**
See also DLB 208

Alain-Fournier .... **TCLC 6**
See Fournier, Henri-Alban
See also DLB 65; EWL 3; GFL 1789 to the Present; RGWL 2, 3

Al-Amin, Jamil Abdullah 1943- .... **BLC 1**
See also BW 1, 3; CA 112; 125; CANR 82; DAM MULT

Alanus de Insluis
See Alain de Lille

Alarcon, Pedro Antonio de
1833-1891 .... **NCLC 1; SSC 64**

Alas (y Urena), Leopoldo (Enrique Garcia)
1852-1901 .... **TCLC 29**
See also CA 113; 131; HW 1; RGSF 2

Albee, Edward (Franklin) (III)
1928- .. **CLC 1, 2, 3, 5, 9, 11, 13, 25, 53, 86, 113; DC 11; WLC**
See also AAYA 51; AITN 1; AMW; CA 5-8R; CABS 3; CAD; CANR 8, 54, 74, 124; CD 5; CDALB 1941-1968; DA; DA3; DAB; DAC; DAM DRAM, MST; DFS 2, 3, 8, 10, 13, 14; DLB 7, 266; EWL 3; INT CANR-8; LAIT 4; LMFS 2; MTCW 1, 2; RGAL 4; TUS

Alberti (Merello), Rafael
See Alberti, Rafael
See also CWW 2

Alberti, Rafael 1902-1999 .... **CLC 7**
See Alberti (Merello), Rafael
See also CA 85-88; 185; CANR 81; DLB 108; EWL 3; HW 2; RGWL 2, 3

Albert the Great 1193(?)-1280 ...... **CMLC 16**
See also DLB 115

Alcaeus c. 620B.C.- .... **CMLC 65**
See also DLB 176

Alcala-Galiano, Juan Valera y
See Valera y Alcala-Galiano, Juan

Alcayaga, Lucila Godoy
See Godoy Alcayaga, Lucila

Alciato, Andrea 1492-1550 .... **LC 116**

Alcott, Amos Bronson 1799-1888 .... **NCLC 1**
See also DLB 1, 223

Alcott, Louisa May 1832-1888 . **NCLC 6, 58, 83; SSC 27; WLC**
See also AAYA 20; AMWS 1; BPFB 1; BYA 2; CDALB 1865-1917; CLR 1, 38; DA; DA3; DAB; DAC; DAM MST, NOV; DLB 1, 42, 79, 223, 239, 242; DLBD 14; FW; JRDA; LAIT 2; MAICYA 1, 2; NFS 12; RGAL 4; SATA 100; TUS; WCH; WYA; YABC 1; YAW

Alcuin c. 730-804 .... **CMLC 69**
See also DLB 148

Aldanov, M. A.
See Aldanov, Mark (Alexandrovich)

Aldanov, Mark (Alexandrovich)
1886(?)-1957 .... **TCLC 23**
See also CA 118; 181

Aldington, Richard 1892-1962 .... **CLC 49**
See also CA 85-88; CANR 45; DLB 20, 36, 100, 149; LMFS 2; RGEL 2

Aldiss, Brian W(ilson) 1925- . **CLC 5, 14, 40; SSC 36**
See also AAYA 42; CA 5-8R, 190; CAAE 190; CAAS 2; CANR 5, 28, 64, 121; CN 7; DAM NOV; DLB 14, 261, 271; MTCW 1, 2; SATA 34; SFW 4

Aldrich, Bess Streeter
1881-1954 .... **TCLC 125**
See also CLR 70

Alegria, Claribel
See Alegria, Claribel (Joy)
See also CWW 2; DLB 145, 283

Alegria, Claribel (Joy) 1924- .... **CLC 75; HLCS 1; PC 26**
See Alegria, Claribel
See also CA 131; CAAS 15; CANR 66, 94, 134; DAM MULT; EWL 3; HW 1; MTCW 1; PFS 21

Alegria, Fernando 1918- .... **CLC 57**
See also CA 9-12R; CANR 5, 32, 72; EWL 3; HW 1, 2

Aleichem, Sholom .... **SSC 33; TCLC 1, 35**
See Rabinovitch, Sholem
See also TWA

Aleixandre, Vicente 1898-1984 .... **HLCS 1; TCLC 113**
See also CANR 81; DLB 108; EWL 3; HW 2; RGWL 2, 3

Aleman, Mateo 1547-1615(?) .... **LC 81**

Alencar, José de 1829-1877 .... **NCLC 157**
See also DLB 307; LAW; WLIT 1

Alencon, Marguerite d'
See de Navarre, Marguerite

Alepoudelis, Odysseus
See Elytis, Odysseus
See also CWW 2

Aleshkovsky, Joseph 1929-
See Aleshkovsky, Yuz
See also CA 121; 128

Aleshkovsky, Yuz .... **CLC 44**
See Aleshkovsky, Joseph

Alexander, Lloyd (Chudley) 1924- ... **CLC 35**
See also AAYA 1, 27; BPFB 1; BYA 5, 6, 7, 9, 10, 11; CA 1-4R; CANR 1, 24, 38, 55, 113; CLR 1, 5, 48; CWRI 5; DLB 52; FANT; JRDA; MAICYA 1, 2; MAICYAS 1; MTCW 1; SAAS 19; SATA 3, 49, 81, 129, 135; SUFW; TUS; WYA; YAW

Alexander, Meena 1951- .... **CLC 121**
See also CA 115; CANR 38, 70; CP 7; CWP; FW

Alexander, Samuel 1859-1938 .... **TCLC 77**

Alexie, Sherman (Joseph, Jr.)
1966- .... **CLC 96, 154; NNAL; PC 53**
See also AAYA 28; BYA 15; CA 138; CANR 65, 95, 133; DA3; DAM MULT; DLB 175, 206, 278; LATS 1:2; MTCW 1; NFS 17; SSFS 18

al-Farabi 870(?)-950 .... **CMLC 58**
See also DLB 115

Alfau, Felipe 1902-1999 .... **CLC 66**
See also CA 137

Alfieri, Vittorio 1749-1803 .... **NCLC 101**
See also EW 4; RGWL 2, 3

Alfonso X 1221-1284 .... **CMLC 78**

Alfred, Jean Gaston
See Ponge, Francis

Alger, Horatio, Jr. 1832-1899 .... **NCLC 8, 83**
See also CLR 87; DLB 42; LAIT 2; RGAL 4; SATA 16; TUS

Al-Ghazali, Muhammad ibn Muhammad
1058-1111 .... **CMLC 50**
See also DLB 115

Algren, Nelson 1909-1981 ..... **CLC 4, 10, 33; SSC 33**
See also AMWS 9; BPFB 1; CA 13-16R; 103; CANR 20, 61; CDALB 1941-1968; DLB 9; DLBY 1981, 1982, 2000; EWL 3; MTCW 1, 2; RGAL 4; RGSF 2

al-Hariri, al-Qasim ibn 'Ali Abu Muhammad al-Basri 1054-1122 .... **CMLC 63**
See also RGWL 3

Ali, Ahmed 1908-1998 .... **CLC 69**
See also CA 25-28R; CANR 15, 34; EWL 3

Ali, Tariq 1943- .... **CLC 173**
See also CA 25-28R; CANR 10, 99

Alighieri, Dante
See Dante

Allan, John B.
See Westlake, Donald E(dwin)

Allan, Sidney
See Hartmann, Sadakichi

Allan, Sydney
See Hartmann, Sadakichi

Allard, Janet .... **CLC 59**

Allen, Edward 1948- .... **CLC 59**

Allen, Fred 1894-1956 .... **TCLC 87**

Allen, Paula Gunn 1939- .... **CLC 84, 202; NNAL**
See also AMWS 4; CA 112; 143; CANR 63, 130; CWP; DA3; DAM MULT; DLB 175; FW; MTCW 1; RGAL 4

Allen, Roland
See Ayckbourn, Alan

Allen, Sarah A.
See Hopkins, Pauline Elizabeth

Allen, Sidney H.
See Hartmann, Sadakichi

Allen, Woody 1935- .... **CLC 16, 52, 195**
See also AAYA 10, 51; CA 33-36R; CANR 27, 38, 63, 128; DAM POP; DLB 44; MTCW 1

Allende, Isabel 1942- ... **CLC 39, 57, 97, 170; HLC 1; SSC 65; WLCS**
See also AAYA 18; CA 125; 130; CANR 51, 74, 129; CLR 99; CWW 2; DA3; DAM MULT, NOV; DLB 145; DNFS 1; EWL 3; FW; HW 1, 2; INT CA-130; LAIT 5; LAWS 1; LMFS 2; MTCW 1, 2; NCFS 1; NFS 6, 18; RGSF 2; RGWL 2; SSFS 11, 16; WLIT 1

Alleyn, Ellen
See Rossetti, Christina (Georgina)

Alleyne, Carla D. .... **CLC 65**

Allingham, Margery (Louise) 1904-1966 .... **CLC 19**
See also CA 5-8R; 25-28R; CANR 4, 58; CMW 4; DLB 77; MSW; MTCW 1, 2

Allingham, William 1824-1889 ...... **NCLC 25**
See also DLB 35; RGEL 2

Allison, Dorothy E. 1949- .... **CLC 78, 153**
See also AAYA 53; CA 140; CANR 66, 107; CSW; DA3; FW; MTCW 1; NFS 11; RGAL 4

Alloula, Malek .... **CLC 65**

Allston, Washington 1779-1843 .... **NCLC 2**
See also DLB 1, 235

Almedingen, E. M. .... **CLC 12**
See Almedingen, Martha Edith von
See also SATA 3

Almedingen, Martha Edith von 1898-1971
See Almedingen, E. M.
See also CA 1-4R; CANR 1

Almodovar, Pedro 1949(?)- .... **CLC 114; HLCS 1**
See also CA 133; CANR 72; HW 2

Almqvist, Carl Jonas Love 1793-1866 .... **NCLC 42**

al-Mutanabbi, Ahmad ibn al-Husayn Abu al-Tayyib al-Jufi al-Kindi 915-965 .... **CMLC 66**
See also RGWL 3

Alonso, Damaso 1898-1990 .... **CLC 14**
See also CA 110; 131; 130; CANR 72; DLB 108; EWL 3; HW 1, 2

Alov
See Gogol, Nikolai (Vasilyevich)

al'Sadaawi, Nawal
See El Saadawi, Nawal
See also FW

Al Siddik
See Rolfe, Frederick (William Serafino Austin Lewis Mary)
See also GLL 1; RGEL 2

Alta 1942- .... **CLC 19**
See also CA 57-60

Alter, Robert B(ernard) 1935- .... **CLC 34**
See also CA 49-52; CANR 1, 47, 100

Alther, Lisa 1944- .... **CLC 7, 41**
See also BPFB 1; CA 65-68; CAAS 30; CANR 12, 30, 51; CN 7; CSW; GLL 2; MTCW 1

Althusser, L.
See Althusser, Louis

Althusser, Louis 1918-1990 .... **CLC 106**
See also CA 131; 132; CANR 102; DLB 242

Altman, Robert 1925- .... **CLC 16, 116**
See also CA 73-76; CANR 43

Alurista .... **HLCS 1**
See Urista (Heredia), Alberto (Baltazar)
See also DLB 82; LLW 1

Alvarez, A(lfred) 1929- .... **CLC 5, 13**
See also CA 1-4R; CANR 3, 33, 63, 101, 134; CN 7; CP 7; DLB 14, 40

Alvarez, Alejandro Rodriguez 1903-1965
See Casona, Alejandro
See also CA 131; 93-96; HW 1

Alvarez, Julia 1950- .... **CLC 93; HLCS 1**
See also AAYA 25; AMWS 7; CA 147; CANR 69, 101, 133; DA3; DLB 282; LATS 1:2; LLW 1; MTCW 1; NFS 5, 9; SATA 129; WLIT 1

Alvaro, Corrado 1896-1956 .... **TCLC 60**
See also CA 163; DLB 264; EWL 3

Amado, Jorge 1912-2001 ... **CLC 13, 40, 106; HLC 1**
See also CA 77-80; 201; CANR 35, 74; CWW 2; DAM MULT, NOV; DLB 113, 307; EWL 3; HW 2; LAW; LAWS 1; MTCW 1, 2; RGWL 2, 3; TWA; WLIT 1

Ambler, Eric 1909-1998 .... **CLC 4, 6, 9**
See also BRWS 4; CA 9-12R; 171; CANR 7, 38, 74; CMW 4; CN 7; DLB 77; MSW; MTCW 1, 2; TEA

Ambrose, Stephen E(dward) 1936-2002 .... **CLC 145**
See also AAYA 44; CA 1-4R; 209; CANR 3, 43, 57, 83, 105; NCFS 2; SATA 40, 138

Amichai, Yehuda 1924-2000 .. **CLC 9, 22, 57, 116; PC 38**
See also CA 85-88; 189; CANR 46, 60, 99, 132; CWW 2; EWL 3; MTCW 1

Amichai, Yehudah
See Amichai, Yehuda

Amiel, Henri Frederic 1821-1881 .... **NCLC 4**
See also DLB 217

Amis, Kingsley (William) 1922-1995 ...... **CLC 1, 2, 3, 5, 8, 13, 40, 44, 129**
See also AITN 2; BPFB 1; BRWS 2; CA 9-12R; 150; CANR 8, 28, 54; CDBLB 1945-1960; CN 7; CP 7; DA; DA3; DAB; DAC; DAM MST, NOV; DLB 15, 27, 100, 139; DLBY 1996; EWL 3; HGG; INT CANR-8; MTCW 1, 2; RGEL 2; RGSF 2; SFW 4

Amis, Martin (Louis) 1949- .... **CLC 4, 9, 38, 62, 101**
See also BEST 90:3; BRWS 4; CA 65-68; CANR 8, 27, 54, 73, 95, 132; CN 7; DA3; DLB 14, 194; EWL 3; INT CANR-27; MTCW 1

Ammianus Marcellinus c. 330-c. 395 .... **CMLC 60**
See also AW 2; DLB 211

Ammons, A(rchie) R(andolph) 1926-2001 ...... **CLC 2, 3, 5, 8, 9, 25, 57, 108; PC 16**
See also AITN 1; AMWS 7; CA 9-12R; 193; CANR 6, 36, 51, 73, 107; CP 7; CSW; DAM POET; DLB 5, 165; EWL 3; MTCW 1, 2; PFS 19; RGAL 4

Amo, Tauraatua i
See Adams, Henry (Brooks)

Amory, Thomas 1691(?)-1788 .... **LC 48**
See also DLB 39

Anand, Mulk Raj 1905-2004 ...... **CLC 23, 93**
See also CA 65-68; CANR 32, 64; CN 7; DAM NOV; EWL 3; MTCW 1, 2; RGSF 2

Anatol
See Schnitzler, Arthur

Anaximander c. 611B.C.-c. 546B.C. .... **CMLC 22**

Anaya, Rudolfo A(lfonso) 1937- ...... **CLC 23, 148; HLC 1**
See also AAYA 20; BYA 13; CA 45-48; CAAS 4; CANR 1, 32, 51, 124; CN 7; DAM MULT, NOV; DLB 82, 206, 278; HW 1; LAIT 4; LLW 1; MTCW 1, 2; NFS 12; RGAL 4; RGSF 2; WLIT 1

Andersen, Hans Christian 1805-1875 .... **NCLC 7, 79; SSC 6, 56; WLC**
See also AAYA 57; CLR 6; DA; DA3; DAB; DAC; DAM MST, POP; EW 6; MAICYA 1, 2; RGSF 2; RGWL 2, 3; SATA 100; TWA; WCH; YABC 1

Anderson, C. Farley
See Mencken, H(enry) L(ouis); Nathan, George Jean

Anderson, Jessica (Margaret) Queale 1916- .... **CLC 37**
See also CA 9-12R; CANR 4, 62; CN 7

Anderson, Jon (Victor) 1940- .... **CLC 9**
See also CA 25-28R; CANR 20; DAM POET

Anderson, Lindsay (Gordon) 1923-1994 .... **CLC 20**
See also CA 125; 128; 146; CANR 77

Anderson, Maxwell 1888-1959 .... **TCLC 2, 144**
See also CA 105; 152; DAM DRAM; DFS 16, 20; DLB 7, 228; MTCW 2; RGAL 4

Anderson, Poul (William) 1926-2001 .... **CLC 15**
See also AAYA 5, 34; BPFB 1; BYA 6, 8, 9; CA 1-4R; 181; 199; CAAE 181; CAAS 2; CANR 2, 15, 34, 64, 110; CLR 58; DLB 8; FANT; INT CANR-15; MTCW 1, 2; SATA 90; SATA-Brief 39; SATA-Essay 106; SCFW 2; SFW 4; SUFW 1, 2

Anderson, Robert (Woodruff) 1917- .... **CLC 23**
See also AITN 1; CA 21-24R; CANR 32; DAM DRAM; DLB 7; LAIT 5

Anderson, Roberta Joan
See Mitchell, Joni

Anderson, Sherwood 1876-1941 .. **SSC 1, 46; TCLC 1, 10, 24, 123; WLC**
See also AAYA 30; AMW; AMWC 2; BPFB 1; CA 104; 121; CANR 61; CDALB 1917-1929; DA; DA3; DAB; DAC; DAM MST, NOV; DLB 4, 9, 86; DLBD 1; EWL 3; EXPS; GLL 2; MTCW 1, 2; NFS 4; RGAL 4; RGSF 2; SSFS 4, 10, 11; TUS

Andier, Pierre
See Desnos, Robert

Andouard
See Giraudoux, Jean(-Hippolyte)

Armah, Ayi Kwei 1939- . **BLC 1; CLC 5, 33, 136**
See also AFW; BRWS 10; BW 1; CA 61-64; CANR 21, 64; CDWLB 3; CN 7; DAM MULT, POET; DLB 117; EWL 3; MTCW 1; WLIT 2

Armatrading, Joan 1950- .... **CLC 17**
See also CA 114; 186

Armitage, Frank
See Carpenter, John (Howard)

Armstrong, Jeannette (C.) 1948- .... **NNAL**
See also CA 149; CCA 1; CN 7; DAC; SATA 102

Arnette, Robert
See Silverberg, Robert

Arnim, Achim von (Ludwig Joachim von Arnim) 1781-1831 ..... **NCLC 5; SSC 29**
See also DLB 90

Arnim, Bettina von 1785-1859 ...... **NCLC 38, 123**
See also DLB 90; RGWL 2, 3

Arnold, Matthew 1822-1888 ..... **NCLC 6, 29, 89, 126; PC 5; WLC**
See also BRW 5; CDBLB 1832-1890; DA; DAB; DAC; DAM MST, POET; DLB 32, 57; EXPP; PAB; PFS 2; TEA; WP

Arnold, Thomas 1795-1842 .... **NCLC 18**
See also DLB 55

Arnow, Harriette (Louisa) Simpson 1908-1986 .... **CLC 2, 7, 18**
See also BPFB 1; CA 9-12R; 118; CANR 14; DLB 6; FW; MTCW 1, 2; RHW; SATA 42; SATA-Obit 47

Arouet, Francois-Marie
See Voltaire

Arp, Hans
See Arp, Jean

Arp, Jean 1887-1966 .... **CLC 5; TCLC 115**
See also CA 81-84; 25-28R; CANR 42, 77; EW 10

Arrabal
See Arrabal, Fernando

Arrabal, Fernando 1932- ... **CLC 2, 9, 18, 58**
See Arrabal (Teran), Fernando
See also CA 9-12R; CANR 15; EWL 3; LMFS 2

Arrabal (Teran), Fernando 1932-
See Arrabal, Fernando
See also CWW 2

Arreola, Juan Jose 1918-2001 .... **CLC 147; HLC 1; SSC 38**
See also CA 113; 131; 200; CANR 81; CWW 2; DAM MULT; DLB 113; DNFS 2; EWL 3; HW 1, 2; LAW; RGSF 2

Arrian c. 89(?)-c. 155(?) .... **CMLC 43**
See also DLB 176

Arrick, Fran .... **CLC 30**
See Gaberman, Judie Angell
See also BYA 6

Arrley, Richmond
See Delany, Samuel R(ay), Jr.

Artaud, Antonin (Marie Joseph) 1896-1948 .... **DC 14; TCLC 3, 36**
See also CA 104; 149; DA3; DAM DRAM; DLB 258; EW 11; EWL 3; GFL 1789 to the Present; MTCW 1; RGWL 2, 3

Arthur, Ruth M(abel) 1905-1979 ..... **CLC 12**
See also CA 9-12R; 85-88; CANR 4; CWRI 5; SATA 7, 26

Artsybashev, Mikhail (Petrovich) 1878-1927 .... **TCLC 31**
See also CA 170; DLB 295

Arundel, Honor (Morfydd) 1919-1973 .... **CLC 17**
See also CA 21-22; 41-44R; CAP 2; CLR 35; CWRI 5; SATA 4; SATA-Obit 24

Arzner, Dorothy 1900-1979 .... **CLC 98**

Asch, Sholem 1880-1957 .... **TCLC 3**
See also CA 105; EWL 3; GLL 2

Ascham, Roger 1516(?)-1568 .... **LC 101**
See also DLB 236

Ash, Shalom
See Asch, Sholem

Ashbery, John (Lawrence) 1927- .. **CLC 2, 3, 4, 6, 9, 13, 15, 25, 41, 77, 125; PC 26**
See Berry, Jonas
See also AMWS 3; CA 5-8R; CANR 9, 37, 66, 102, 132; CP 7; DA3; DAM POET; DLB 5, 165; DLBY 1981; EWL 3; INT CANR-9; MTCW 1, 2; PAB; PFS 11; RGAL 4; WP

Ashdown, Clifford
See Freeman, R(ichard) Austin

Ashe, Gordon
See Creasey, John

Ashton-Warner, Sylvia (Constance) 1908-1984 .... **CLC 19**
See also CA 69-72; 112; CANR 29; MTCW 1, 2

Asimov, Isaac 1920-1992 ..... **CLC 1, 3, 9, 19, 26, 76, 92**
See also AAYA 13; BEST 90:2; BPFB 1; BYA 4, 6, 7, 9; CA 1-4R; 137; CANR 2, 19, 36, 60, 125; CLR 12, 79; CMW 4; CPW; DA3; DAM POP; DLB 8; DLBY 1992; INT CANR-19; JRDA; LAIT 5; LMFS 2; MAICYA 1, 2; MTCW 1, 2; RGAL 4; SATA 1, 26, 74; SCFW 2; SFW 4; SSFS 17; TUS; YAW

Askew, Anne 1521(?)-1546 .... **LC 81**
See also DLB 136

Assis, Joaquim Maria Machado de
See Machado de Assis, Joaquim Maria

Astell, Mary 1666-1731 .... **LC 68**
See also DLB 252; FW

Astley, Thea (Beatrice May) 1925-2004 .... **CLC 41**
See also CA 65-68; 229; CANR 11, 43, 78; CN 7; DLB 289; EWL 3

Astley, William 1855-1911
See Warung, Price

Aston, James
See White, T(erence) H(anbury)

Asturias, Miguel Angel 1899-1974 .... **CLC 3, 8, 13; HLC 1**
See also CA 25-28; 49-52; CANR 32; CAP 2; CDWLB 3; DA3; DAM MULT, NOV; DLB 113, 290; EWL 3; HW 1; LAW; LMFS 2; MTCW 1, 2; RGWL 2, 3; WLIT 1

Atares, Carlos Saura
See Saura (Atares), Carlos

Athanasius c. 295-c. 373 .... **CMLC 48**

Atheling, William
See Pound, Ezra (Weston Loomis)

Atheling, William, Jr.
See Blish, James (Benjamin)

Atherton, Gertrude (Franklin Horn) 1857-1948 .... **TCLC 2**
See also CA 104; 155; DLB 9, 78, 186; HGG; RGAL 4; SUFW 1; TCWW 2

Atherton, Lucius
See Masters, Edgar Lee

Atkins, Jack
See Harris, Mark

Atkinson, Kate 1951- .... **CLC 99**
See also CA 166; CANR 101; DLB 267

Attaway, William (Alexander) 1911-1986 .... **BLC 1; CLC 92**
See also BW 2, 3; CA 143; CANR 82; DAM MULT; DLB 76

Atticus
See Fleming, Ian (Lancaster); Wilson, (Thomas) Woodrow

Atwood, Margaret (Eleanor) 1939- ... **CLC 2, 3, 4, 8, 13, 15, 25, 44, 84, 135; PC 8; SSC 2, 46; WLC**
See also AAYA 12, 47; AMWS 13; BEST 89:2; BPFB 1; CA 49-52; CANR 3, 24, 33, 59, 95, 133; CN 7; CP 7; CPW; CWP; DA; DA3; DAB; DAC; DAM MST, NOV, POET; DLB 53, 251; EWL 3; EXPN; FW; INT CANR-24; LAIT 5; MTCW 1, 2; NFS 4, 12, 13, 14, 19; PFS 7; RGSF 2; SATA 50; SSFS 3, 13; TWA; WWE 1; YAW

Aubigny, Pierre d'
See Mencken, H(enry) L(ouis)

Aubin, Penelope 1685-1731(?) .... **LC 9**
See also DLB 39

Auchincloss, Louis (Stanton) 1917- .. **CLC 4, 6, 9, 18, 45; SSC 22**
See also AMWS 4; CA 1-4R; CANR 6, 29, 55, 87, 130; CN 7; DAM NOV; DLB 2, 244; DLBY 1980; EWL 3; INT CANR-29; MTCW 1; RGAL 4

Auden, W(ystan) H(ugh) 1907-1973 . **CLC 1, 2, 3, 4, 6, 9, 11, 14, 43, 123; PC 1; WLC**
See also AAYA 18; AMWS 2; BRW 7; BRWR 1; CA 9-12R; 45-48; CANR 5, 61, 105; CDBLB 1914-1945; DA; DA3; DAB; DAC; DAM DRAM, MST, POET; DLB 10, 20; EWL 3; EXPP; MTCW 1, 2; PAB; PFS 1, 3, 4, 10; TUS; WP

Audiberti, Jacques 1899-1965 .... **CLC 38**
See also CA 25-28R; DAM DRAM; EWL 3

Audubon, John James 1785-1851 . **NCLC 47**
See also ANW; DLB 248

Auel, Jean M(arie) 1936- .... **CLC 31, 107**
See also AAYA 7, 51; BEST 90:4; BPFB 1; CA 103; CANR 21, 64, 115; CPW; DA3; DAM POP; INT CANR-21; NFS 11; RHW; SATA 91

Auerbach, Erich 1892-1957 .... **TCLC 43**
See also CA 118; 155; EWL 3

Augier, Emile 1820-1889 .... **NCLC 31**
See also DLB 192; GFL 1789 to the Present

August, John
See De Voto, Bernard (Augustine)

Augustine, St. 354-430 .... **CMLC 6; WLCS**
See also DA; DA3; DAB; DAC; DAM MST; DLB 115; EW 1; RGWL 2, 3

Aunt Belinda
See Braddon, Mary Elizabeth

Aunt Weedy
See Alcott, Louisa May

Aurelius
See Bourne, Randolph S(illiman)

Aurelius, Marcus 121-180 .... **CMLC 45**
See Marcus Aurelius
See also RGWL 2, 3

Aurobindo, Sri
See Ghose, Aurabinda

Aurobindo Ghose
See Ghose, Aurabinda

Austen, Jane 1775-1817 ...... **NCLC 1, 13, 19, 33, 51, 81, 95, 119, 150; WLC**
See also AAYA 19; BRW 4; BRWC 1; BRWR 2; BYA 3; CDBLB 1789-1832; DA; DA3; DAB; DAC; DAM MST, NOV; DLB 116; EXPN; LAIT 2; LATS 1:1; LMFS 1; NFS 1, 14, 18, 20; TEA; WLIT 3; WYAS 1

Auster, Paul 1947- .... **CLC 47, 131**
See also AMWS 12; CA 69-72; CANR 23, 52, 75, 129; CMW 4; CN 7; DA3; DLB 227; MTCW 1; SUFW 2

Austin, Frank
See Faust, Frederick (Schiller)
See also TCWW 2

Baraka, Amiri 1934- .... **BLC 1; CLC 1, 2, 3, 5, 10, 14, 33, 115; DC 6; PC 4; WLCS**
See Jones, LeRoi
See also AFAW 1, 2; AMWS 2; BW 2, 3; CA 21-24R; CABS 3; CAD; CANR 27, 38, 61, 133; CD 5; CDALB 1941-1968; CP 7; CPW; DA; DA3; DAC; DAM MST, MULT, POET, POP; DFS 3, 11, 16; DLB 5, 7, 16, 38; DLBD 8; EWL 3; MTCW 1, 2; PFS 9; RGAL 4; TUS; WP

Baratynsky, Evgenii Abramovich 1800-1844 .... **NCLC 103**
See also DLB 205

Barbauld, Anna Laetitia 1743-1825 .... **NCLC 50**
See also DLB 107, 109, 142, 158; RGEL 2

Barbellion, W. N. P. .... **TCLC 24**
See Cummings, Bruce F(rederick)

Barber, Benjamin R. 1939- .... **CLC 141**
See also CA 29-32R; CANR 12, 32, 64, 119

Barbera, Jack (Vincent) 1945- .... **CLC 44**
See also CA 110; CANR 45

Barbey d'Aurevilly, Jules-Amedee 1808-1889 .... **NCLC 1; SSC 17**
See also DLB 119; GFL 1789 to the Present

Barbour, John c. 1316-1395 .... **CMLC 33**
See also DLB 146

Barbusse, Henri 1873-1935 .... **TCLC 5**
See also CA 105; 154; DLB 65; EWL 3; RGWL 2, 3

Barclay, Alexander c. 1475-1552 .... **LC 109**
See also DLB 132

Barclay, Bill
See Moorcock, Michael (John)

Barclay, William Ewert
See Moorcock, Michael (John)

Barea, Arturo 1897-1957 .... **TCLC 14**
See also CA 111; 201

Barfoot, Joan 1946- .... **CLC 18**
See also CA 105

Barham, Richard Harris 1788-1845 .... **NCLC 77**
See also DLB 159

Baring, Maurice 1874-1945 .... **TCLC 8**
See also CA 105; 168; DLB 34; HGG

Baring-Gould, Sabine 1834-1924 ... **TCLC 88**
See also DLB 156, 190

Barker, Clive 1952- .... **CLC 52, 205; SSC 53**
See also AAYA 10, 54; BEST 90:3; BPFB 1; CA 121; 129; CANR 71, 111, 133; CPW; DA3; DAM POP; DLB 261; HGG; INT CA-129; MTCW 1, 2; SUFW 2

Barker, George Granville 1913-1991 .... **CLC 8, 48**
See also CA 9-12R; 135; CANR 7, 38; DAM POET; DLB 20; EWL 3; MTCW 1

Barker, Harley Granville
See Granville-Barker, Harley
See also DLB 10

Barker, Howard 1946- .... **CLC 37**
See also CA 102; CBD; CD 5; DLB 13, 233

Barker, Jane 1652-1732 .... **LC 42, 82**
See also DLB 39, 131

Barker, Pat(ricia) 1943- ...... **CLC 32, 94, 146**
See also BRWS 4; CA 117; 122; CANR 50, 101; CN 7; DLB 271; INT CA-122

Barlach, Ernst (Heinrich) 1870-1938 .... **TCLC 84**
See also CA 178; DLB 56, 118; EWL 3

Barlow, Joel 1754-1812 .... **NCLC 23**
See also AMWS 2; DLB 37; RGAL 4

Barnard, Mary (Ethel) 1909- .... **CLC 48**
See also CA 21-22; CAP 2

Barnes, Djuna 1892-1982 .... **CLC 3, 4, 8, 11, 29, 127; SSC 3**
See Steptoe, Lydia
See also AMWS 3; CA 9-12R; 107; CAD; CANR 16, 55; CWD; DLB 4, 9, 45; EWL 3; GLL 1; MTCW 1, 2; RGAL 4; TUS

Barnes, Jim 1933- .... **NNAL**
See also CA 108, 175; CAAE 175; CAAS 28; DLB 175

Barnes, Julian (Patrick) 1946- . **CLC 42, 141**
See also BRWS 4; CA 102; CANR 19, 54, 115; CN 7; DAB; DLB 194; DLBY 1993; EWL 3; MTCW 1

Barnes, Peter 1931-2004 .... **CLC 5, 56**
See also CA 65-68; CAAS 12; CANR 33, 34, 64, 113; CBD; CD 5; DFS 6; DLB 13, 233; MTCW 1

Barnes, William 1801-1886 .... **NCLC 75**
See also DLB 32

Baroja (y Nessi), Pio 1872-1956 .... **HLC 1; TCLC 8**
See also CA 104; EW 9

Baron, David
See Pinter, Harold

Baron Corvo
See Rolfe, Frederick (William Serafino Austin Lewis Mary)

Barondess, Sue K(aufman) 1926-1977 .... **CLC 8**
See Kaufman, Sue
See also CA 1-4R; 69-72; CANR 1

Baron de Teive
See Pessoa, Fernando (Antonio Nogueira)

Baroness Von S.
See Zangwill, Israel

Barres, (Auguste-)Maurice 1862-1923 .... **TCLC 47**
See also CA 164; DLB 123; GFL 1789 to the Present

Barreto, Afonso Henrique de Lima
See Lima Barreto, Afonso Henrique de

Barrett, Andrea 1954- .... **CLC 150**
See also CA 156; CANR 92

Barrett, Michele .... **CLC 65**

Barrett, (Roger) Syd 1946- .... **CLC 35**

Barrett, William (Christopher) 1913-1992 .... **CLC 27**
See also CA 13-16R; 139; CANR 11, 67; INT CANR-11

Barrett Browning, Elizabeth 1806-1861 ... **NCLC 1, 16, 61, 66; PC 6, 62; WLC**
See also BRW 4; CDBLB 1832-1890; DA; DA3; DAB; DAC; DAM MST, POET; DLB 32, 199; EXPP; PAB; PFS 2, 16; TEA; WLIT 4; WP

Barrie, J(ames) M(atthew) 1860-1937 .... **TCLC 2, 164**
See also BRWS 3; BYA 4, 5; CA 104; 136; CANR 77; CDBLB 1890-1914; CLR 16; CWRI 5; DA3; DAB; DAM DRAM; DFS 7; DLB 10, 141, 156; EWL 3; FANT; MAICYA 1, 2; MTCW 1; SATA 100; SUFW; WCH; WLIT 4; YABC 1

Barrington, Michael
See Moorcock, Michael (John)

Barrol, Grady
See Bograd, Larry

Barry, Mike
See Malzberg, Barry N(athaniel)

Barry, Philip 1896-1949 .... **TCLC 11**
See also CA 109; 199; DFS 9; DLB 7, 228; RGAL 4

Bart, Andre Schwarz
See Schwarz-Bart, Andre

Barth, John (Simmons) 1930- ... **CLC 1, 2, 3, 5, 7, 9, 10, 14, 27, 51, 89; SSC 10**
See also AITN 1, 2; AMW; BPFB 1; CA 1-4R; CABS 1; CANR 5, 23, 49, 64, 113; CN 7; DAM NOV; DLB 2, 227; EWL 3; FANT; MTCW 1; RGAL 4; RGSF 2; RHW; SSFS 6; TUS

Barthelme, Donald 1931-1989 ... **CLC 1, 2, 3, 5, 6, 8, 13, 23, 46, 59, 115; SSC 2, 55**
See also AMWS 4; BPFB 1; CA 21-24R; 129; CANR 20, 58; DA3; DAM NOV; DLB 2, 234; DLBY 1980, 1989; EWL 3; FANT; LMFS 2; MTCW 1, 2; RGAL 4; RGSF 2; SATA 7; SATA-Obit 62; SSFS 17

Barthelme, Frederick 1943- ...... **CLC 36, 117**
See also AMWS 11; CA 114; 122; CANR 77; CN 7; CSW; DLB 244; DLBY 1985; EWL 3; INT CA-122

Barthes, Roland (Gerard) 1915-1980 .... **CLC 24, 83; TCLC 135**
See also CA 130; 97-100; CANR 66; DLB 296; EW 13; EWL 3; GFL 1789 to the Present; MTCW 1, 2; TWA

Bartram, William 1739-1823 .... **NCLC 145**
See also ANW; DLB 37

Barzun, Jacques (Martin) 1907- ..... **CLC 51, 145**
See also CA 61-64; CANR 22, 95

Bashevis, Isaac
See Singer, Isaac Bashevis

Bashkirtseff, Marie 1859-1884 .... **NCLC 27**

Basho, Matsuo
See Matsuo Basho
See also PFS 18; RGWL 2, 3; WP

Basil of Caesaria c. 330-379 .... **CMLC 35**

Basket, Raney
See Edgerton, Clyde (Carlyle)

Bass, Kingsley B., Jr.
See Bullins, Ed

Bass, Rick 1958- .... **CLC 79, 143; SSC 60**
See also ANW; CA 126; CANR 53, 93; CSW; DLB 212, 275

Bassani, Giorgio 1916-2000 .... **CLC 9**
See also CA 65-68; 190; CANR 33; CWW 2; DLB 128, 177, 299; EWL 3; MTCW 1; RGWL 2, 3

Bastian, Ann .... **CLC 70**

Bastos, Augusto (Antonio) Roa
See Roa Bastos, Augusto (Antonio)

Bataille, Georges 1897-1962 .... **CLC 29; TCLC 155**
See also CA 101; 89-92; EWL 3

Bates, H(erbert) E(rnest) 1905-1974 .... **CLC 46; SSC 10**
See also CA 93-96; 45-48; CANR 34; DA3; DAB; DAM POP; DLB 162, 191; EWL 3; EXPS; MTCW 1, 2; RGSF 2; SSFS 7

Bauchart
See Camus, Albert

Baudelaire, Charles 1821-1867 . **NCLC 6, 29, 55, 155; PC 1; SSC 18; WLC**
See also DA; DA3; DAB; DAC; DAM MST, POET; DLB 217; EW 7; GFL 1789 to the Present; LMFS 2; PFS 21; RGWL 2, 3; TWA

Baudouin, Marcel
See Peguy, Charles (Pierre)

Baudouin, Pierre
See Peguy, Charles (Pierre)

Baudrillard, Jean 1929- .... **CLC 60**
See also DLB 296

Baum, L(yman) Frank 1856-1919 .. **TCLC 7, 132**
See also AAYA 46; BYA 16; CA 108; 133; CLR 15; CWRI 5; DLB 22; FANT; JRDA; MAICYA 1, 2; MTCW 1, 2; NFS 13; RGAL 4; SATA 18, 100; WCH

Benary-Isbert, Margot 1889-1979 .... **CLC 12**
See also CA 5-8R; 89-92; CANR 4, 72;
CLR 12; MAICYA 1, 2; SATA 2; SATA-
Obit 21

Benavente (y Martinez), Jacinto
1866-1954 .... **DC 26; HLCS 1; TCLC 3**
See also CA 106; 131; CANR 81; DAM
DRAM, MULT; EWL 3; GLL 2; HW 1,
2; MTCW 1, 2

Benchley, Peter (Bradford) 1940- .. **CLC 4, 8**
See also AAYA 14; AITN 2; BPFB 1; CA
17-20R; CANR 12, 35, 66, 115; CPW;
DAM NOV, POP; HGG; MTCW 1, 2;
SATA 3, 89

Benchley, Robert (Charles)
1889-1945 .... **TCLC 1, 55**
See also CA 105; 153; DLB 11; RGAL 4

Benda, Julien 1867-1956 .... **TCLC 60**
See also CA 120; 154; GFL 1789 to the
Present

Benedict, Ruth (Fulton)
1887-1948 .... **TCLC 60**
See also CA 158; DLB 246

Benedikt, Michael 1935- .... **CLC 4, 14**
See also CA 13-16R; CANR 7; CP 7; DLB
5

Benet, Juan 1927-1993 .... **CLC 28**
See also CA 143; EWL 3

Benet, Stephen Vincent 1898-1943 ..... **PC 64;**
SSC 10; TCLC 7
See also AMWS 11; CA 104; 152; DA3;
DAM POET; DLB 4, 48, 102, 249, 284;
DLBY 1997; EWL 3; HGG; MTCW 1;
RGAL 4; RGSF 2; SUFW; WP; YABC 1

Benet, William Rose 1886-1950 ..... **TCLC 28**
See also CA 118; 152; DAM POET; DLB
45; RGAL 4

Benford, Gregory (Albert) 1941- ..... **CLC 52**
See also BPFB 1; CA 69-72, 175; CAAE
175; CAAS 27; CANR 12, 24, 49, 95,
134; CSW; DLBY 1982; SCFW 2; SFW
4

Bengtsson, Frans (Gunnar)
1894-1954 .... **TCLC 48**
See also CA 170; EWL 3

Benjamin, David
See Slavitt, David R(ytman)

Benjamin, Lois
See Gould, Lois

Benjamin, Walter 1892-1940 .... **TCLC 39**
See also CA 164; DLB 242; EW 11; EWL
3

Ben Jelloun, Tahar 1944-
See Jelloun, Tahar ben
See also CA 135; CWW 2; EWL 3; RGWL
3; WLIT 2

Benn, Gottfried 1886-1956 .. **PC 35; TCLC 3**
See also CA 106; 153; DLB 56; EWL 3;
RGWL 2, 3

Bennett, Alan 1934- .... **CLC 45, 77**
See also BRWS 8; CA 103; CANR 35, 55,
106; CBD; CD 5; DAB; DAM MST;
MTCW 1, 2

Bennett, (Enoch) Arnold
1867-1931 .... **TCLC 5, 20**
See also BRW 6; CA 106; 155; CDBLB
1890-1914; DLB 10, 34, 98, 135; EWL 3;
MTCW 2

Bennett, Elizabeth
See Mitchell, Margaret (Munnerlyn)

Bennett, George Harold 1930-
See Bennett, Hal
See also BW 1; CA 97-100; CANR 87

Bennett, Gwendolyn B. 1902-1981 .... **HR 2**
See also BW 1; CA 125; DLB 51; WP

Bennett, Hal .... **CLC 5**
See Bennett, George Harold
See also DLB 33

Bennett, Jay 1912- .... **CLC 35**
See also AAYA 10; CA 69-72; CANR 11,
42, 79; JRDA; SAAS 4; SATA 41, 87;
SATA-Brief 27; WYA; YAW

Bennett, Louise (Simone) 1919- .... **BLC 1;**
CLC 28
See also BW 2, 3; CA 151; CDWLB 3; CP
7; DAM MULT; DLB 117; EWL 3

Benson, A. C. 1862-1925 .... **TCLC 123**
See also DLB 98

Benson, E(dward) F(rederic)
1867-1940 .... **TCLC 27**
See also CA 114; 157; DLB 135, 153;
HGG; SUFW 1

Benson, Jackson J. 1930- .... **CLC 34**
See also CA 25-28R; DLB 111

Benson, Sally 1900-1972 .... **CLC 17**
See also CA 19-20; 37-40R; CAP 1; SATA
1, 35; SATA-Obit 27

Benson, Stella 1892-1933 .... **TCLC 17**
See also CA 117; 154, 155; DLB 36, 162;
FANT; TEA

Bentham, Jeremy 1748-1832 .... **NCLC 38**
See also DLB 107, 158, 252

Bentley, E(dmund) C(lerihew)
1875-1956 .... **TCLC 12**
See also CA 108; DLB 70; MSW

Bentley, Eric (Russell) 1916- .... **CLC 24**
See also CA 5-8R; CAD; CANR 6, 67;
CBD; CD 5; INT CANR-6

ben Uzair, Salem
See Horne, Richard Henry Hengist

Beranger, Pierre Jean de
1780-1857 .... **NCLC 34**

Berdyaev, Nicolas
See Berdyaev, Nikolai (Aleksandrovich)

Berdyaev, Nikolai (Aleksandrovich)
1874-1948 .... **TCLC 67**
See also CA 120; 157

Berdyayev, Nikolai (Aleksandrovich)
See Berdyaev, Nikolai (Aleksandrovich)

Berendt, John (Lawrence) 1939- ...... **CLC 86**
See also CA 146; CANR 75, 93; DA3;
MTCW 1

Beresford, J(ohn) D(avys)
1873-1947 .... **TCLC 81**
See also CA 112; 155; DLB 162, 178, 197;
SFW 4; SUFW 1

Bergelson, David (Rafailovich)
1884-1952 .... **TCLC 81**
See Bergelson, Dovid
See also CA 220

Bergelson, Dovid
See Bergelson, David (Rafailovich)
See also EWL 3

Berger, Colonel
See Malraux, (Georges-)Andre

Berger, John (Peter) 1926- .... **CLC 2, 19**
See also BRWS 4; CA 81-84; CANR 51,
78, 117; CN 7; DLB 14, 207

Berger, Melvin H. 1927- .... **CLC 12**
See also CA 5-8R; CANR 4; CLR 32;
SAAS 2; SATA 5, 88; SATA-Essay 124

Berger, Thomas (Louis) 1924- .. **CLC 3, 5, 8,**
11, 18, 38
See also BPFB 1; CA 1-4R; CANR 5, 28,
51, 128; CN 7; DAM NOV; DLB 2;
DLBY 1980; EWL 3; FANT; INT CANR-
28; MTCW 1, 2; RHW; TCWW 2

Bergman, (Ernst) Ingmar 1918- ...... **CLC 16,**
72, 219
See also CA 81-84; CANR 33, 70; CWW
2; DLB 257; MTCW 2

Bergson, Henri(-Louis) 1859-1941 . **TCLC 32**
See also CA 164; EW 8; EWL 3; GFL 1789
to the Present

Bergstein, Eleanor 1938- .... **CLC 4**
See also CA 53-56; CANR 5

Berkeley, George 1685-1753 .... **LC 65**
See also DLB 31, 101, 252

Berkoff, Steven 1937- .... **CLC 56**
See also CA 104; CANR 72; CBD; CD 5

Berlin, Isaiah 1909-1997 .... **TCLC 105**
See also CA 85-88; 162

Bermant, Chaim (Icyk) 1929-1998 ... **CLC 40**
See also CA 57-60; CANR 6, 31, 57, 105;
CN 7

Bern, Victoria
See Fisher, M(ary) F(rances) K(ennedy)

Bernanos, (Paul Louis) Georges
1888-1948 .... **TCLC 3**
See also CA 104; 130; CANR 94; DLB 72;
EWL 3; GFL 1789 to the Present; RGWL
2, 3

Bernard, April 1956- .... **CLC 59**
See also CA 131

Bernard of Clairvaux 1090-1153 .. **CMLC 71**
See also DLB 208

Berne, Victoria
See Fisher, M(ary) F(rances) K(ennedy)

Bernhard, Thomas 1931-1989 ..... **CLC 3, 32,**
61; DC 14; TCLC 165
See also CA 85-88; 127; CANR 32, 57; CD-
WLB 2; DLB 85, 124; EWL 3; MTCW 1;
RGWL 2, 3

Bernhardt, Sarah (Henriette Rosine)
1844-1923 .... **TCLC 75**
See also CA 157

Bernstein, Charles 1950- .... **CLC 142,**
See also CA 129; CAAS 24; CANR 90; CP
7; DLB 169

Bernstein, Ingrid
See Kirsch, Sarah

Beroul fl. c. 1150- .... **CMLC 75**

Berriault, Gina 1926-1999 .... **CLC 54, 109;**
SSC 30
See also CA 116; 129; 185; CANR 66; DLB
130; SSFS 7,11

Berrigan, Daniel 1921- .... **CLC 4**
See also CA 33-36R, 187; CAAE 187;
CAAS 1; CANR 11, 43, 78; CP 7; DLB 5

Berrigan, Edmund Joseph Michael, Jr.
1934-1983
See Berrigan, Ted
See also CA 61-64; 110; CANR 14, 102

Berrigan, Ted .... **CLC 37**
See Berrigan, Edmund Joseph Michael, Jr.
See also DLB 5, 169; WP

Berry, Charles Edward Anderson 1931-
See Berry, Chuck
See also CA 115

Berry, Chuck .... **CLC 17**
See Berry, Charles Edward Anderson

Berry, Jonas
See Ashbery, John (Lawrence)
See also GLL 1

Berry, Wendell (Erdman) 1934- ... **CLC 4, 6,**
8, 27, 46; PC 28
See also AITN 1; AMWS 10; ANW; CA
73-76; CANR 50, 73, 101, 132; CP 7;
CSW; DAM POET; DLB 5, 6, 234, 275;
MTCW 1

Berryman, John 1914-1972 ... **CLC 1, 2, 3, 4,**
6, 8, 10, 13, 25, 62; PC 64
See also AMW; CA 13-16; 33-36R; CABS
2; CANR 35; CAP 1; CDALB 1941-1968;
DAM POET; DLB 48; EWL 3; MTCW 1,
2; PAB; RGAL 4; WP

Bertolucci, Bernardo 1940- ...... **CLC 16, 157**
See also CA 106; CANR 125

Berton, Pierre (Francis Demarigny)
1920-2004 .... **CLC 104**
See also CA 1-4R; CANR 2, 56; CPW;
DLB 68; SATA 99

Bertrand, Aloysius 1807-1841 .... **NCLC 31**
See Bertrand, Louis oAloysiusc

Blom, Jan
   See Breytenbach, Breyten
Bloom, Harold 1930- .... **CLC 24, 103**
   See also CA 13-16R; CANR 39, 75, 92,
   133; DLB 67; EWL 3; MTCW 1; RGAL
   4
Bloomfield, Aurelius
   See Bourne, Randolph S(illiman)
Bloomfield, Robert 1766-1823 ..... **NCLC 145**
   See also DLB 93
Blount, Roy (Alton), Jr. 1941- .... **CLC 38**
   See also CA 53-56; CANR 10, 28, 61, 125;
   CSW; INT CANR-28; MTCW 1, 2
Blowsnake, Sam 1875-(?) .... **NNAL**
Bloy, Leon 1846-1917 .... **TCLC 22**
   See also CA 121; 183; DLB 123; GFL 1789
   to the Present
Blue Cloud, Peter (Aroniawenrate)
   1933- .... **NNAL**
   See also CA 117; CANR 40; DAM MULT
Bluggage, Oranthy
   See Alcott, Louisa May
Blume, Judy (Sussman) 1938- .... **CLC 12, 30**
   See also AAYA 3, 26; BYA 1, 8, 12; CA 29-
   32R; CANR 13, 37, 66, 124; CLR 2, 15,
   69; CPW; DA3; DAM NOV, POP; DLB
   52; JRDA; MAICYA 1, 2; MAICYAS 1;
   MTCW 1, 2; SATA 2, 31, 79, 142; WYA;
   YAW
Blunden, Edmund (Charles)
   1896-1974 .... **CLC 2, 56; PC 66**
   See also BRW 6; CA 17-18; 45-48; CANR
   54; CAP 2; DLB 20, 100, 155; MTCW 1;
   PAB
Bly, Robert (Elwood) 1926- .... **CLC 1, 2, 5,
   10, 15, 38, 128; PC 39**
   See also AMWS 4; CA 5-8R; CANR 41,
   73, 125; CP 7; DA3; DAM POET; DLB
   5; EWL 3; MTCW 1, 2; PFS 6, 17; RGAL
   4
Boas, Franz 1858-1942 .... **TCLC 56**
   See also CA 115; 181
Bobette
   See Simenon, Georges (Jacques Christian)
Boccaccio, Giovanni 1313-1375 ... **CMLC 13,
   57; SSC 10**
   See also EW 2; RGSF 2; RGWL 2, 3; TWA
Bochco, Steven 1943- .... **CLC 35**
   See also AAYA 11; CA 124; 138
Bode, Sigmund
   See O'Doherty, Brian
Bodel, Jean 1167(?)-1210 .... **CMLC 28**
Bodenheim, Maxwell 1892-1954 .... **TCLC 44**
   See also CA 110; 187; DLB 9, 45; RGAL 4
Bodenheimer, Maxwell
   See Bodenheim, Maxwell
Bodker, Cecil 1927-
   See Bodker, Cecil
Bodker, Cecil 1927- .... **CLC 21**
   See also CA 73-76; CANR 13, 44, 111;
   CLR 23; MAICYA 1, 2; SATA 14, 133
Boell, Heinrich (Theodor)
   1917-1985 ..... **CLC 2, 3, 6, 9, 11, 15, 27,
   32, 72; SSC 23; WLC**
   See Boll, Heinrich
   See also CA 21-24R; 116; CANR 24; DA;
   DA3; DAB; DAC; DAM MST, NOV;
   DLB 69; DLBY 1985; MTCW 1, 2; SSFS
   20; TWA
Boerne, Alfred
   See Doeblin, Alfred
Boethius c. 480-c. 524 .... **CMLC 15**
   See also DLB 115; RGWL 2, 3
Boff, Leonardo (Genezio Darci)
   1938- .... **CLC 70; HLC 1**
   See also CA 150; DAM MULT; HW 2

Bogan, Louise 1897-1970 .... **CLC 4, 39, 46,
   93; PC 12**
   See also AMWS 3; CA 73-76; 25-28R;
   CANR 33, 82; DAM POET; DLB 45, 169;
   EWL 3; MAWW; MTCW 1, 2; PFS 21;
   RGAL 4
Bogarde, Dirk
   See Van Den Bogarde, Derek Jules Gaspard
   Ulric Niven
   See also DLB 14
Bogosian, Eric 1953- .... **CLC 45, 141**
   See also CA 138; CAD; CANR 102; CD 5
Bograd, Larry 1953- .... **CLC 35**
   See also CA 93-96; CANR 57; SAAS 21;
   SATA 33, 89; WYA
Boiardo, Matteo Maria 1441-1494 .... **LC 6**
Boileau-Despreaux, Nicolas 1636-1711 . **LC 3**
   See also DLB 268; EW 3; GFL Beginnings
   to 1789; RGWL 2, 3
Boissard, Maurice
   See Leautaud, Paul
Bojer, Johan 1872-1959 .... **TCLC 64**
   See also CA 189; EWL 3
Bok, Edward W(illiam)
   1863-1930 .... **TCLC 101**
   See also CA 217; DLB 91; DLBD 16
Boker, George Henry 1823-1890 . **NCLC 125**
   See also RGAL 4
Boland, Eavan (Aisling) 1944- .. **CLC 40, 67,
   113; PC 58**
   See also BRWS 5; CA 143, 207; CAAE
   207; CANR 61; CP 7; CWP; DAM POET;
   DLB 40; FW; MTCW 2; PFS 12
Boll, Heinrich
   See Boell, Heinrich (Theodor)
   See also BPFB 1; CDWLB 2; EW 13; EWL
   3; RGSF 2; RGWL 2, 3
Bolt, Lee
   See Faust, Frederick (Schiller)
Bolt, Robert (Oxton) 1924-1995 .... **CLC 14**
   See also CA 17-20R; 147; CANR 35, 67;
   CBD; DAM DRAM; DFS 2; DLB 13,
   233; EWL 3; LAIT 1; MTCW 1
Bombal, Maria Luisa 1910-1980 .... **HLCS 1;
   SSC 37**
   See also CA 127; CANR 72; EWL 3; HW
   1; LAW; RGSF 2
Bombet, Louis-Alexandre-Cesar
   See Stendhal
Bomkauf
   See Kaufman, Bob (Garnell)
Bonaventura .... **NCLC 35**
   See also DLB 90
Bond, Edward 1934- .... **CLC 4, 6, 13, 23**
   See also AAYA 50; BRWS 1; CA 25-28R;
   CANR 38, 67, 106; CBD; CD 5; DAM
   DRAM; DFS 3, 8; DLB 13; EWL 3;
   MTCW 1
Bonham, Frank 1914-1989 .... **CLC 12**
   See also AAYA 1; BYA 1, 3; CA 9-12R;
   CANR 4, 36; JRDA; MAICYA 1, 2;
   SAAS 3; SATA 1, 49; SATA-Obit 62;
   TCWW 2; YAW
Bonnefoy, Yves 1923- . **CLC 9, 15, 58; PC 58**
   See also CA 85-88; CANR 33, 75, 97;
   CWW 2; DAM MST, POET; DLB 258;
   EWL 3; GFL 1789 to the Present; MTCW
   1, 2
Bonner, Marita .... **HR 2**
   See Occomy, Marita (Odette) Bonner
Bonnin, Gertrude 1876-1938 .... **NNAL**
   See Zitkala-Sa
   See also CA 150; DAM MULT
Bontemps, Arna(ud Wendell)
   1902-1973 ..... **BLC 1; CLC 1, 18; HR 2**
   See also BW 1; CA 1-4R; 41-44R; CANR
   4, 35; CLR 6; CWRI 5; DA3; DAM
   MULT, NOV, POET; DLB 48, 51; JRDA;
   MAICYA 1, 2; MTCW 1, 2; SATA 2, 44;
   SATA-Obit 24; WCH; WP

Boot, William
   See Stoppard, Tom
Booth, Martin 1944-2004 .... **CLC 13**
   See also CA 93-96, 188; 223; CAAE 188;
   CAAS 2; CANR 92
Booth, Philip 1925- .... **CLC 23**
   See also CA 5-8R; CANR 5, 88; CP 7;
   DLBY 1982
Booth, Wayne C(layson) 1921- .... **CLC 24**
   See also CA 1-4R; CAAS 5; CANR 3, 43,
   117; DLB 67
Borchert, Wolfgang 1921-1947 .... **TCLC 5**
   See also CA 104; 188; DLB 69, 124; EWL
   3
Borel, Petrus 1809-1859 .... **NCLC 41**
   See also DLB 119; GFL 1789 to the Present
Borges, Jorge Luis 1899-1986 ... **CLC 1, 2, 3,
   4, 6, 8, 9, 10, 13, 19, 44, 48, 83; HLC 1;
   PC 22, 32; SSC 4, 41; TCLC 109;
   WLC**
   See also AAYA 26; BPFB 1; CA 21-24R;
   CANR 19, 33, 75, 105, 133; CDWLB 3;
   DA; DA3; DAB; DAC; DAM MST,
   MULT; DLB 113, 283; DLBY 1986;
   DNFS 1, 2; EWL 3; HW 1, 2; LAW;
   LMFS 2; MSW; MTCW 1, 2; RGSF 2;
   RGWL 2, 3; SFW 4; SSFS 17; TWA;
   WLIT 1
Borowski, Tadeusz 1922-1951 .... **SSC 48;
   TCLC 9**
   See also CA 106; 154; CDWLB 4; DLB
   215; EWL 3; RGSF 2; RGWL 3; SSFS
   13
Borrow, George (Henry)
   1803-1881 .... **NCLC 9**
   See also DLB 21, 55, 166
Bosch (Gavino), Juan 1909-2001 ..... **HLCS 1**
   See also CA 151; 204; DAM MST, MULT;
   DLB 145; HW 1, 2
Bosman, Herman Charles
   1905-1951 .... **TCLC 49**
   See Malan, Herman
   See also CA 160; DLB 225; RGSF 2
Bosschere, Jean de 1878(?)-1953 ... **TCLC 19**
   See also CA 115; 186
Boswell, James 1740-1795 ... **LC 4, 50; WLC**
   See also BRW 3; CDBLB 1660-1789; DA;
   DAB; DAC; DAM MST; DLB 104, 142;
   TEA; WLIT 3
Bottomley, Gordon 1874-1948 ..... **TCLC 107**
   See also CA 120; 192; DLB 10
Bottoms, David 1949- .... **CLC 53**
   See also CA 105; CANR 22; CSW; DLB
   120; DLBY 1983
Boucicault, Dion 1820-1890 .... **NCLC 41**
Boucolon, Maryse
   See Conde, Maryse
Bourdieu, Pierre 1930-2002 .... **CLC 198**
   See also CA 130; 204
Bourget, Paul (Charles Joseph)
   1852-1935 .... **TCLC 12**
   See also CA 107; 196; DLB 123; GFL 1789
   to the Present
Bourjaily, Vance (Nye) 1922- .... **CLC 8, 62**
   See also CA 1-4R; CAAS 1; CANR 2, 72;
   CN 7; DLB 2, 143
Bourne, Randolph S(illiman)
   1886-1918 .... **TCLC 16**
   See also AMW; CA 117; 155; DLB 63
Bova, Ben(jamin William) 1932- ...... **CLC 45**
   See also AAYA 16; CA 5-8R; CAAS 18;
   CANR 11, 56, 94, 111; CLR 3, 96; DLBY
   1981; INT CANR-11; MAICYA 1, 2;
   MTCW 1; SATA 6, 68, 133; SFW 4
Bowen, Elizabeth (Dorothea Cole)
   1899-1973 . **CLC 1, 3, 6, 11, 15, 22, 118;
   SSC 3, 28, 66; TCLC 148**
   See also BRWS 2; CA 17-18; 41-44R;
   CANR 35, 105; CAP 2; CDBLB 1945-

1960; DA3; DAM NOV; DLB 15, 162; EWL 3; EXPS; FW; HGG; MTCW 1, 2; NFS 13; RGSF 2; SSFS 5; SUFW 1; TEA; WLIT 4

Bowering, George 1935- .... **CLC 15, 47**
See also CA 21-24R; CAAS 16; CANR 10; CP 7; DLB 53

Bowering, Marilyn R(uthe) 1949- .... **CLC 32**
See also CA 101; CANR 49; CP 7; CWP

Bowers, Edgar 1924-2000 .... **CLC 9**
See also CA 5-8R; 188; CANR 24; CP 7; CSW; DLB 5

Bowers, Mrs. J. Milton 1842-1914
See Bierce, Ambrose (Gwinett)

Bowie, David .... **CLC 17**
See Jones, David Robert

Bowles, Jane (Sydney) 1917-1973 ..... **CLC 3, 68**
See Bowles, Jane Auer
See also CA 19-20; 41-44R; CAP 2

Bowles, Jane Auer
See Bowles, Jane (Sydney)
See also EWL 3

Bowles, Paul (Frederick) 1910-1999 . **CLC 1, 2, 19, 53; SSC 3**
See also AMWS 4; CA 1-4R; 186; CAAS 1; CANR 1, 19, 50, 75; CN 7; DA3; DLB 5, 6, 218; EWL 3; MTCW 1, 2; RGAL 4; SSFS 17

Bowles, William Lisle 1762-1850 . **NCLC 103**
See also DLB 93

Box, Edgar
See Vidal, (Eugene Luther) Gore
See also GLL 1

Boyd, James 1888-1944 .... **TCLC 115**
See also CA 186; DLB 9; DLBD 16; RGAL 4; RHW

Boyd, Nancy
See Millay, Edna St. Vincent
See also GLL 1

Boyd, Thomas (Alexander) 1898-1935 .... **TCLC 111**
See also CA 111; 183; DLB 9; DLBD 16

Boyd, William 1952- .... **CLC 28, 53, 70**
See also CA 114; 120; CANR 51, 71, 131; CN 7; DLB 231

Boyesen, Hjalmar Hjorth 1848-1895 .... **NCLC 135**
See also DLB 12, 71; DLBD 13; RGAL 4

Boyle, Kay 1902-1992 .... **CLC 1, 5, 19, 58, 121; SSC 5**
See also CA 13-16R; 140; CAAS 1; CANR 29, 61, 110; DLB 4, 9, 48, 86; DLBY 1993; EWL 3; MTCW 1, 2; RGAL 4; RGSF 2; SSFS 10, 13, 14

Boyle, Mark
See Kienzle, William X(avier)

Boyle, Patrick 1905-1982 .... **CLC 19**
See also CA 127

Boyle, T. C.
See Boyle, T(homas) Coraghessan
See also AMWS 8

Boyle, T(homas) Coraghessan 1948- .... **CLC 36, 55, 90; SSC 16**
See Boyle, T. C.
See also AAYA 47; BEST 90:4; BPFB 1; CA 120; CANR 44, 76, 89, 132; CN 7; CPW; DA3; DAM POP; DLB 218, 278; DLBY 1986; EWL 3; MTCW 2; SSFS 13, 19

Boz
See Dickens, Charles (John Huffam)

Brackenridge, Hugh Henry 1748-1816 .... **NCLC 7**
See also DLB 11, 37; RGAL 4

Bradbury, Edward P.
See Moorcock, Michael (John)
See also MTCW 2

Bradbury, Malcolm (Stanley) 1932-2000 .... **CLC 32, 61**
See also CA 1-4R; CANR 1, 33, 91, 98; CN 7; DA3; DAM NOV; DLB 14, 207; EWL 3; MTCW 1, 2

Bradbury, Ray (Douglas) 1920- .... **CLC 1, 3, 10, 15, 42, 98; SSC 29, 53; WLC**
See also AAYA 15; AITN 1, 2; AMWS 4; BPFB 1; BYA 4, 5, 11; CA 1-4R; CANR 2, 30, 75, 125; CDALB 1968-1988; CN 7; CPW; DA; DA3; DAB; DAC; DAM MST, NOV, POP; DLB 2, 8; EXPN; EXPS; HGG; LAIT 3, 5; LATS 1:2; LMFS 2; MTCW 1, 2; NFS 1; RGAL 4; RGSF 2; SATA 11, 64, 123; SCFW 2; SFW 4; SSFS 1, 20; SUFW 1, 2; TUS; YAW

Braddon, Mary Elizabeth 1837-1915 .... **TCLC 111**
See also BRWS 8; CA 108; 179; CMW 4; DLB 18, 70, 156; HGG

Bradfield, Scott (Michael) 1955- .... **SSC 65**
See also CA 147; CANR 90; HGG; SUFW 2

Bradford, Gamaliel 1863-1932 .... **TCLC 36**
See also CA 160; DLB 17

Bradford, William 1590-1657 .... **LC 64**
See also DLB 24, 30; RGAL 4

Bradley, David (Henry), Jr. 1950- .... **BLC 1; CLC 23, 118**
See also BW 1, 3; CA 104; CANR 26, 81; CN 7; DAM MULT; DLB 33

Bradley, John Ed(mund, Jr.) 1958- . **CLC 55**
See also CA 139; CANR 99; CN 7; CSW

Bradley, Marion Zimmer 1930-1999 .... **CLC 30**
See Chapman, Lee; Dexter, John; Gardner, Miriam; Ives, Morgan; Rivers, Elfrida
See also AAYA 40; BPFB 1; CA 57-60; 185; CAAS 10; CANR 7, 31, 51, 75, 107; CPW; DA3; DAM POP; DLB 8; FANT; FW; MTCW 1, 2; SATA 90, 139; SATA-Obit 116; SFW 4; SUFW 2; YAW

Bradshaw, John 1933- .... **CLC 70**
See also CA 138; CANR 61

Bradstreet, Anne 1612(?)-1672 ...... **LC 4, 30; PC 10**
See also AMWS 1; CDALB 1640-1865; DA; DA3; DAC; DAM MST, POET; DLB 24; EXPP; FW; PFS 6; RGAL 4; TUS; WP

Brady, Joan 1939- .... **CLC 86**
See also CA 141

Bragg, Melvyn 1939- .... **CLC 10**
See also BEST 89:3; CA 57-60; CANR 10, 48, 89; CN 7; DLB 14, 271; RHW

Brahe, Tycho 1546-1601 .... **LC 45**
See also DLB 300

Braine, John (Gerard) 1922-1986 . **CLC 1, 3, 41**
See also CA 1-4R; 120; CANR 1, 33; CD-BLB 1945-1960; DLB 15; DLBY 1986; EWL 3; MTCW 1

Braithwaite, William Stanley (Beaumont) 1878-1962 .... **BLC 1; HR 2; PC 52**
See also BW 1; CA 125; DAM MULT; DLB 50, 54

Bramah, Ernest 1868-1942 .... **TCLC 72**
See also CA 156; CMW 4; DLB 70; FANT

Brammer, William 1930(?)-1978 ...... **CLC 31**
See also CA 77-80

Brancati, Vitaliano 1907-1954 .... **TCLC 12**
See also CA 109; DLB 264; EWL 3

Brancato, Robin F(idler) 1936- .... **CLC 35**
See also AAYA 9; BYA 6; CA 69-72; CANR 11, 45; CLR 32; JRDA; MAICYA 2; MAICYAS 1; SAAS 9; SATA 97; WYA; YAW

Brand, Dionne 1953- .... **CLC 192**
See also BW 2; CA 143; CWP

Brand, Max
See Faust, Frederick (Schiller)
See also BPFB 1; TCWW 2

Brand, Millen 1906-1980 .... **CLC 7**
See also CA 21-24R; 97-100; CANR 72

Branden, Barbara .... **CLC 44**
See also CA 148

Brandes, Georg (Morris Cohen) 1842-1927 .... **TCLC 10**
See also CA 105; 189; DLB 300

Brandys, Kazimierz 1916-2000 .... **CLC 62**
See also EWL 3

Branley, Franklyn M(ansfield) 1915-2002 .... **CLC 21**
See also CA 33-36R; 207; CANR 14, 39; CLR 13; MAICYA 1, 2; SAAS 16; SATA 4, 68, 136

Brant, Beth (E.) 1941- .... **NNAL**
See also CA 144; FW

Brant, Sebastian 1457-1521 .... **LC 112**
See also DLB 179; RGWL 2, 3

Brathwaite, Edward Kamau 1930- .... **BLCS; CLC 11; PC 56**
See also BW 2, 3; CA 25-28R; CANR 11, 26, 47, 107; CDWLB 3; CP 7; DAM POET; DLB 125; EWL 3

Brathwaite, Kamau
See Brathwaite, Edward Kamau

Brautigan, Richard (Gary) 1935-1984 .... **CLC 1, 3, 5, 9, 12, 34, 42; TCLC 133**
See also BPFB 1; CA 53-56; 113; CANR 34; DA3; DAM NOV; DLB 2, 5, 206; DLBY 1980, 1984; FANT; MTCW 1; RGAL 4; SATA 56

Brave Bird, Mary .... **NNAL**
See Crow Dog, Mary (Ellen)

Braverman, Kate 1950- .... **CLC 67**
See also CA 89-92

Brecht, (Eugen) Bertolt (Friedrich) 1898-1956 ..... **DC 3; TCLC 1, 6, 13, 35; WLC**
See also CA 104; 133; CANR 62; CDWLB 2; DA; DA3; DAB; DAC; DAM DRAM, MST; DFS 4, 5, 9; DLB 56, 124; EW 11; EWL 3; IDTP; MTCW 1, 2; RGWL 2, 3; TWA

Brecht, Eugen Berthold Friedrich
See Brecht, (Eugen) Bertolt (Friedrich)

Bremer, Fredrika 1801-1865 .... **NCLC 11**
See also DLB 254

Brennan, Christopher John 1870-1932 .... **TCLC 17**
See also CA 117; 188; DLB 230; EWL 3

Brennan, Maeve 1917-1993 ... **CLC 5; TCLC 124**
See also CA 81-84; CANR 72, 100

Brent, Linda
See Jacobs, Harriet A(nn)

Brentano, Clemens (Maria) 1778-1842 .... **NCLC 1**
See also DLB 90; RGWL 2, 3

Brent of Bin Bin
See Franklin, (Stella Maria Sarah) Miles (Lampe)

Brenton, Howard 1942- .... **CLC 31**
See also CA 69-72; CANR 33, 67; CBD; CD 5; DLB 13; MTCW 1

Breslin, James 1930-
See Breslin, Jimmy
See also CA 73-76; CANR 31, 75; DAM NOV; MTCW 1, 2

Breslin, Jimmy .... **CLC 4, 43**
See Breslin, James
See also AITN 1; DLB 185; MTCW 2

Bresson, Robert 1901(?)-1999 .... **CLC 16**
See also CA 110; 187; CANR 49

Burroughs, William S(eward)
1914-1997 .. **CLC 1, 2, 5, 15, 22, 42, 75, 109; TCLC 121; WLC**
See Lee, William; Lee, Willy
See also AAYA 60; AITN 2; AMWS 3; BG 2; BPFB 1; CA 9-12R; 160; CANR 20, 52, 104; CN 7; CPW; DA; DA3; DAB; DAC; DAM MST, NOV, POP; DLB 2, 8, 16, 152, 237; DLBY 1981, 1997; EWL 3; HGG; LMFS 2; MTCW 1, 2; RGAL 4; SFW 4

Burton, Sir Richard F(rancis)
1821-1890 .... **NCLC 42**
See also DLB 55, 166, 184

Burton, Robert 1577-1640 .... **LC 74**
See also DLB 151; RGEL 2

Buruma, Ian 1951- .... **CLC 163**
See also CA 128; CANR 65

Busch, Frederick 1941- ... **CLC 7, 10, 18, 47, 166**
See also CA 33-36R; CAAS 1; CANR 45, 73, 92; CN 7; DLB 6, 218

Bush, Barney (Furman) 1946- .... **NNAL**
See also CA 145

Bush, Ronald 1946- .... **CLC 34**
See also CA 136

Bustos, F(rancisco)
See Borges, Jorge Luis

Bustos Domecq, H(onorio)
See Bioy Casares, Adolfo; Borges, Jorge Luis

Butler, Octavia E(stelle) 1947- .. **BLCS; CLC 38, 121**
See also AAYA 18, 48; AFAW 2; AMWS 13; BPFB 1; BW 2, 3; CA 73-76; CANR 12, 24, 38, 73; CLR 65; CPW; DA3; DAM MULT, POP; DLB 33; LATS 1:2; MTCW 1, 2; NFS 8; SATA 84; SCFW 2; SFW 4; SSFS 6; YAW

Butler, Robert Olen, (Jr.) 1945- ...... **CLC 81, 162**
See also AMWS 12; BPFB 1; CA 112; CANR 66; CSW; DAM POP; DLB 173; INT CA-112; MTCW 1; SSFS 11

Butler, Samuel 1612-1680 .... **LC 16, 43**
See also DLB 101, 126; RGEL 2

Butler, Samuel 1835-1902 .... **TCLC 1, 33; WLC**
See also BRWS 2; CA 143; CDBLB 1890-1914; DA; DA3; DAB; DAC; DAM MST, NOV; DLB 18, 57, 174; RGEL 2; SFW 4; TEA

Butler, Walter C.
See Faust, Frederick (Schiller)

Butor, Michel (Marie Francois)
1926- .... **CLC 1, 3, 8, 11, 15, 161**
See also CA 9-12R; CANR 33, 66; CWW 2; DLB 83; EW 13; EWL 3; GFL 1789 to the Present; MTCW 1, 2

Butts, Mary 1890(?)-1937 .... **TCLC 77**
See also CA 148; DLB 240

Buxton, Ralph
See Silverstein, Alvin; Silverstein, Virginia B(arbara Opshelor)

Buzo, Alex
See Buzo, Alexander (John)
See also DLB 289

Buzo, Alexander (John) 1944- .... **CLC 61**
See also CA 97-100; CANR 17, 39, 69; CD 5

Buzzati, Dino 1906-1972 .... **CLC 36**
See also CA 160; 33-36R; DLB 177; RGWL 2, 3; SFW 4

Byars, Betsy (Cromer) 1928- .... **CLC 35**
See also AAYA 19; BYA 3; CA 33-36R, 183; CAAE 183; CANR 18, 36, 57, 102; CLR 1, 16, 72; DLB 52; INT CANR-18; JRDA; MAICYA 1, 2; MAICYAS 1; MTCW 1; SAAS 1; SATA 4, 46, 80; SATA-Essay 108; WYA; YAW

Byatt, A(ntonia) S(usan Drabble)
1936- .... **CLC 19, 65, 136**
See also BPFB 1; BRWC 2; BRWS 4; CA 13-16R; CANR 13, 33, 50, 75, 96, 133; DA3; DAM NOV, POP; DLB 14, 194; EWL 3; MTCW 1, 2; RGSF 2; RHW; TEA

Byrd, Willam II 1674-1744 .... **LC 112**
See also DLB 24, 140; RGAL 4

Byrne, David 1952- .... **CLC 26**
See also CA 127

Byrne, John Keyes 1926-
See Leonard, Hugh
See also CA 102; CANR 78; INT CA-102

Byron, George Gordon (Noel)
1788-1824 ..... **DC 24; NCLC 2, 12, 109, 149; PC 16; WLC**
See also BRW 4; BRWC 2; CDBLB 1789-1832; DA; DA3; DAB; DAC; DAM MST, POET; DLB 96, 110; EXPP; LMFS 1; PAB; PFS 1, 14; RGEL 2; TEA; WLIT 3; WP

Byron, Robert 1905-1941 .... **TCLC 67**
See also CA 160; DLB 195

C. 3. 3.
See Wilde, Oscar (Fingal O'Flahertie Wills)

Caballero, Fernan 1796-1877 .... **NCLC 10**

Cabell, Branch
See Cabell, James Branch

Cabell, James Branch 1879-1958 .... **TCLC 6**
See also CA 105; 152; DLB 9, 78; FANT; MTCW 1; RGAL 4; SUFW 1

Cabeza de Vaca, Alvar Nunez
1490-1557(?) .... **LC 61**

Cable, George Washington
1844-1925 .... **SSC 4; TCLC 4**
See also CA 104; 155; DLB 12, 74; DLBD 13; RGAL 4; TUS

Cabral de Melo Neto, Joao
1920-1999 .... **CLC 76**
See Melo Neto, Joao Cabral de
See also CA 151; DAM MULT; DLB 307; LAW; LAWS 1

Cabrera Infante, G(uillermo) 1929- . **CLC 5, 25, 45, 120; HLC 1; SSC 39**
See also CA 85-88; CANR 29, 65, 110; CD-WLB 3; CWW 2; DA3; DAM MULT; DLB 113; EWL 3; HW 1, 2; LAW; LAWS 1; MTCW 1, 2; RGSF 2; WLIT 1

Cade, Toni
See Bambara, Toni Cade

Cadmus and Harmonia
See Buchan, John

Caedmon fl. 658-680 .... **CMLC 7**
See also DLB 146

Caeiro, Alberto
See Pessoa, Fernando (Antonio Nogueira)

Caesar, Julius .... **CMLC 47**
See Julius Caesar
See also AW 1; RGWL 2, 3

Cage, John (Milton, Jr.)
1912-1992 .... **CLC 41; PC 58**
See also CA 13-16R; 169; CANR 9, 78; DLB 193; INT CANR-9

Cahan, Abraham 1860-1951 .... **TCLC 71**
See also CA 108; 154; DLB 9, 25, 28; RGAL 4

Cain, G.
See Cabrera Infante, G(uillermo)

Cain, Guillermo
See Cabrera Infante, G(uillermo)

Cain, James M(allahan) 1892-1977 .. **CLC 3, 11, 28**
See also AITN 1; BPFB 1; CA 17-20R; 73-76; CANR 8, 34, 61; CMW 4; DLB 226; EWL 3; MSW; MTCW 1; RGAL 4

Caine, Hall 1853-1931 .... **TCLC 97**
See also RHW

Caine, Mark
See Raphael, Frederic (Michael)

Calasso, Roberto 1941- .... **CLC 81**
See also CA 143; CANR 89

Calderon de la Barca, Pedro
1600-1681 .... **DC 3; HLCS 1; LC 23**
See also EW 2; RGWL 2, 3; TWA

Caldwell, Erskine (Preston)
1903-1987 .... **CLC 1, 8, 14, 50, 60; SSC 19; TCLC 117**
See also AITN 1; AMW; BPFB 1; CA 1-4R; 121; CAAS 1; CANR 2, 33; DA3; DAM NOV; DLB 9, 86; EWL 3; MTCW 1, 2; RGAL 4; RGSF 2; TUS

Caldwell, (Janet Miriam) Taylor (Holland)
1900-1985 .... **CLC 2, 28, 39**
See also BPFB 1; CA 5-8R; 116; CANR 5; DA3; DAM NOV, POP; DLBD 17; RHW

Calhoun, John Caldwell
1782-1850 .... **NCLC 15**
See also DLB 3, 248

Calisher, Hortense 1911- ..... **CLC 2, 4, 8, 38, 134; SSC 15**
See also CA 1-4R; CANR 1, 22, 117; CN 7; DA3; DAM NOV; DLB 2, 218; INT CANR-22; MTCW 1, 2; RGAL 4; RGSF 2

Callaghan, Morley Edward
1903-1990 ..... **CLC 3, 14, 41, 65; TCLC 145**
See also CA 9-12R; 132; CANR 33, 73; DAC; DAM MST; DLB 68; EWL 3; MTCW 1, 2; RGEL 2; RGSF 2; SSFS 19

Callimachus c. 305B.C.-c. 240B.C. .... **CMLC 18**
See also AW 1; DLB 176; RGWL 2, 3

Calvin, Jean
See Calvin, John
See also GFL Beginnings to 1789

Calvin, John 1509-1564 .... **LC 37**
See Calvin, Jean

Calvino, Italo 1923-1985 .... **CLC 5, 8, 11, 22, 33, 39, 73; SSC 3, 48**
See also AAYA 58; CA 85-88; 116; CANR 23, 61, 132; DAM NOV; DLB 196; EW 13; EWL 3; MTCW 1, 2; RGSF 2; RGWL 2, 3; SFW 4; SSFS 12

Camara Laye
See Laye, Camara
See also EWL 3

Camden, William 1551-1623 .... **LC 77**
See also DLB 172

Cameron, Carey 1952- .... **CLC 59**
See also CA 135

Cameron, Peter 1959- .... **CLC 44**
See also AMWS 12; CA 125; CANR 50, 117; DLB 234; GLL 2

Camoens, Luis Vaz de 1524(?)-1580
See Camoes, Luis de
See also EW 2

Camoes, Luis de 1524(?)-1580 . **HLCS 1; LC 62; PC 31**
See Camoens, Luis Vaz de
See also DLB 287; RGWL 2, 3

Campana, Dino 1885-1932 .... **TCLC 20**
See also CA 117; DLB 114; EWL 3

Campanella, Tommaso 1568-1639 .... **LC 32**
See also RGWL 2, 3

Campbell, John W(ood, Jr.)
1910-1971 .... **CLC 32**
See also CA 21-22; 29-32R; CANR 34; CAP 2; DLB 8; MTCW 1; SCFW; SFW 4

Campbell, Joseph 1904-1987 .... **CLC 69; TCLC 140**
See also AAYA 3; BEST 89:2; CA 1-4R; 124; CANR 3, 28, 61, 107; DA3; MTCW 1, 2

Campbell, Maria 1940- .... **CLC 85; NNAL**
See also CA 102; CANR 54; CCA 1; DAC

Chang, Eileen 1921-1995 .... **AAL; SSC 28**
See Chang Ai-Ling; Zhang Ailing
See also CA 166

Chang, Jung 1952- .... **CLC 71**
See also CA 142

Chang Ai-Ling
See Chang, Eileen
See also EWL 3

Channing, William Ellery
1780-1842 .... **NCLC 17**
See also DLB 1, 59, 235; RGAL 4

Chao, Patricia 1955- .... **CLC 119**
See also CA 163

Chaplin, Charles Spencer
1889-1977 .... **CLC 16**
See Chaplin, Charlie
See also CA 81-84; 73-76

Chaplin, Charlie
See Chaplin, Charles Spencer
See also DLB 44

Chapman, George 1559(?)-1634 . **DC 19; LC 22, 116**
See also BRW 1; DAM DRAM; DLB 62, 121; LMFS 1; RGEL 2

Chapman, Graham 1941-1989 .... **CLC 21**
See Monty Python
See also CA 116; 129; CANR 35, 95

Chapman, John Jay 1862-1933 .... **TCLC 7**
See also AMWS 14; CA 104; 191

Chapman, Lee
See Bradley, Marion Zimmer
See also GLL 1

Chapman, Walker
See Silverberg, Robert

Chappell, Fred (Davis) 1936- .... **CLC 40, 78, 162**
See also CA 5-8R, 198; CAAE 198; CAAS 4; CANR 8, 33, 67, 110; CN 7; CP 7; CSW; DLB 6, 105; HGG

Char, Rene(-Emile) 1907-1988 .... **CLC 9, 11, 14, 55; PC 56**
See also CA 13-16R; 124; CANR 32; DAM POET; DLB 258; EWL 3; GFL 1789 to the Present; MTCW 1, 2; RGWL 2, 3

Charby, Jay
See Ellison, Harlan (Jay)

Chardin, Pierre Teilhard de
See Teilhard de Chardin, (Marie Joseph) Pierre

Chariton fl. 1st cent. (?)- .... **CMLC 49**

Charlemagne 742-814 .... **CMLC 37**

Charles I 1600-1649 .... **LC 13**

Charriere, Isabelle de 1740-1805 .. **NCLC 66**

Chartier, Alain c. 1392-1430 .... **LC 94**
See also DLB 208

Chartier, Emile-Auguste
See Alain

Charyn, Jerome 1937- .... **CLC 5, 8, 18**
See also CA 5-8R; CAAS 1; CANR 7, 61, 101; CMW 4; CN 7; DLBY 1983; MTCW 1

Chase, Adam
See Marlowe, Stephen

Chase, Mary (Coyle) 1907-1981 .... **DC 1**
See also CA 77-80; 105; CAD; CWD; DFS 11; DLB 228; SATA 17; SATA-Obit 29

Chase, Mary Ellen 1887-1973 .... **CLC 2; TCLC 124**
See also CA 13-16; 41-44R; CAP 1; SATA 10

Chase, Nicholas
See Hyde, Anthony
See also CCA 1

Chateaubriand, Francois Rene de
1768-1848 .... **NCLC 3, 134**
See also DLB 119; EW 5; GFL 1789 to the Present; RGWL 2, 3; TWA

Chatterje, Sarat Chandra 1876-1936(?)
See Chatterji, Saratchandra
See also CA 109

Chatterji, Bankim Chandra
1838-1894 .... **NCLC 19**

Chatterji, Saratchandra .... **TCLC 13**
See Chatterje, Sarat Chandra
See also CA 186; EWL 3

Chatterton, Thomas 1752-1770 .... **LC 3, 54**
See also DAM POET; DLB 109; RGEL 2

Chatwin, (Charles) Bruce
1940-1989 .... **CLC 28, 57, 59**
See also AAYA 4; BEST 90:1; BRWS 4; CA 85-88; 127; CPW; DAM POP; DLB 194, 204; EWL 3

Chaucer, Daniel
See Ford, Ford Madox
See also RHW

Chaucer, Geoffrey 1340(?)-1400 .. **LC 17, 56; PC 19, 58; WLCS**
See also BRW 1; BRWC 1; BRWR 2; CD-BLB Before 1660; DA; DA3; DAB; DAC; DAM MST, POET; DLB 146; LAIT 1; PAB; PFS 14; RGEL 2; TEA; WLIT 3; WP

Chavez, Denise (Elia) 1948- .... **HLC 1**
See also CA 131; CANR 56, 81; DAM MULT; DLB 122; FW; HW 1, 2; LLW 1; MTCW 2

Chaviaras, Strates 1935-
See Haviaras, Stratis
See also CA 105

Chayefsky, Paddy .... **CLC 23**
See Chayefsky, Sidney
See also CAD; DLB 7, 44; DLBY 1981; RGAL 4

Chayefsky, Sidney 1923-1981
See Chayefsky, Paddy
See also CA 9-12R; 104; CANR 18; DAM DRAM

Chedid, Andree 1920- .... **CLC 47**
See also CA 145; CANR 95; EWL 3

Cheever, John 1912-1982 ..... **CLC 3, 7, 8, 11, 15, 25, 64; SSC 1, 38, 57; WLC**
See also AMWS 1; BPFB 1; CA 5-8R; 106; CABS 1; CANR 5, 27, 76; CDALB 1941-1968; CPW; DA; DA3; DAB; DAC; DAM MST, NOV, POP; DLB 2, 102, 227; DLBY 1980, 1982; EWL 3; EXPS; INT CANR-5; MTCW 1, 2; RGAL 4; RGSF 2; SSFS 2, 14; TUS

Cheever, Susan 1943- .... **CLC 18, 48**
See also CA 103; CANR 27, 51, 92; DLBY 1982; INT CANR-27

Chekhonte, Antosha
See Chekhov, Anton (Pavlovich)

Chekhov, Anton (Pavlovich)
1860-1904 ...... **DC 9; SSC 2, 28, 41, 51; TCLC 3, 10, 31, 55, 96, 163; WLC**
See also BYA 14; CA 104; 124; DA; DA3; DAB; DAC; DAM DRAM, MST; DFS 1, 5, 10, 12; DLB 277; EW 7; EWL 3; EXPS; LAIT 3; LATS 1:1; RGSF 2; RGWL 2, 3; SATA 90; SSFS 5, 13, 14; TWA

Cheney, Lynne V. 1941- .... **CLC 70**
See also CA 89-92; CANR 58, 117; SATA 152

Chernyshevsky, Nikolai Gavrilovich
See Chernyshevsky, Nikolay Gavrilovich
See also DLB 238

Chernyshevsky, Nikolay Gavrilovich
1828-1889 .... **NCLC 1**
See Chernyshevsky, Nikolai Gavrilovich

Cherry, Carolyn Janice 1942-
See Cherryh, C. J.
See also CA 65-68; CANR 10

Cherryh, C. J. .... **CLC 35**
See Cherry, Carolyn Janice
See also AAYA 24; BPFB 1; DLBY 1980; FANT; SATA 93; SCFW 2; SFW 4; YAW

Chesnutt, Charles W(addell)
1858-1932 .... **BLC 1; SSC 7, 54; TCLC 5, 39**
See also AFAW 1, 2; AMWS 14; BW 1, 3; CA 106; 125; CANR 76; DAM MULT; DLB 12, 50, 78; EWL 3; MTCW 1, 2; RGAL 4; RGSF 2; SSFS 11

Chester, Alfred 1929(?)-1971 .... **CLC 49**
See also CA 196; 33-36R; DLB 130

Chesterton, G(ilbert) K(eith)
1874-1936 . **PC 28; SSC 1, 46; TCLC 1, 6, 64**
See also AAYA 57; BRW 6; CA 104; 132; CANR 73, 131; CDBLB 1914-1945; CMW 4; DAM NOV, POET; DLB 10, 19, 34, 70, 98, 149, 178; EWL 3; FANT; MSW; MTCW 1, 2; RGEL 2; RGSF 2; SATA 27; SUFW 1

Chettle, Henry c. 1564-c. 1606 .... **LC 112**
See also DLB 136; RGEL 2

Chiang, Pin-chin 1904-1986
See Ding Ling
See also CA 118

Chief Joseph 1840-1904 .... **NNAL**
See also CA 152; DA3; DAM MULT

Chief Seattle 1786(?)-1866 .... **NNAL**
See also DA3; DAM MULT

Ch'ien, Chung-shu 1910-1998 .... **CLC 22**
See Qian Zhongshu
See also CA 130; CANR 73; MTCW 1, 2

Chikamatsu Monzaemon 1653-1724 ... **LC 66**
See also RGWL 2, 3

Child, L. Maria
See Child, Lydia Maria

Child, Lydia Maria 1802-1880 .. **NCLC 6, 73**
See also DLB 1, 74, 243; RGAL 4; SATA 67

Child, Mrs.
See Child, Lydia Maria

Child, Philip 1898-1978 .... **CLC 19, 68**
See also CA 13-14; CAP 1; DLB 68; RHW; SATA 47

Childers, (Robert) Erskine
1870-1922 .... **TCLC 65**
See also CA 113; 153; DLB 70

Childress, Alice 1920-1994 . **BLC 1; CLC 12, 15, 86, 96; DC 4; TCLC 116**
See also AAYA 8; BW 2, 3; BYA 2; CA 45-48; 146; CAD; CANR 3, 27, 50, 74; CLR 14; CWD; DA3; DAM DRAM, MULT, NOV; DFS 2, 8, 14; DLB 7, 38, 249; JRDA; LAIT 5; MAICYA 1, 2; MAICYAS 1; MTCW 1, 2; RGAL 4; SATA 7, 48, 81; TUS; WYA; YAW

Chin, Frank (Chew, Jr.) 1940- ...... **CLC 135; DC 7**
See also CA 33-36R; CANR 71; CD 5; DAM MULT; DLB 206; LAIT 5; RGAL 4

Chin, Marilyn (Mei Ling) 1955- .... **PC 40**
See also CA 129; CANR 70, 113; CWP

Chislett, (Margaret) Anne 1943- ...... **CLC 34**
See also CA 151

Chitty, Thomas Willes 1926- .... **CLC 11**
See Hinde, Thomas
See also CA 5-8R; CN 7

Chivers, Thomas Holley
1809-1858 .... **NCLC 49**
See also DLB 3, 248; RGAL 4

Choi, Susan 1969- .... **CLC 119**
See also CA 223

Chomette, Rene Lucien 1898-1981
See Clair, Rene
See also CA 103

Chomsky, (Avram) Noam 1928- ..... **CLC 132**
See also CA 17-20R; CANR 28, 62, 110, 132; DA3; DLB 246; MTCW 1, 2

Chona, Maria 1845(?)-1936 .... **NNAL**
See also CA 144

Chopin, Kate .... **SSC 8, 68; TCLC 127; WLCS**
See Chopin, Katherine
See also AAYA 33; AMWR 2; AMWS 1; BYA 11, 15; CDALB 1865-1917; DA; DAB; DLB 12, 78; EXPN; EXPS; FW; LAIT 3; MAWW; NFS 3; RGAL 4; RGSF 2; SSFS 17; TUS

Chopin, Katherine 1851-1904
See Chopin, Kate
See also CA 104; 122; DA3; DAC; DAM MST, NOV

Chretien de Troyes c. 12th cent. - . **CMLC 10**
See also DLB 208; EW 1; RGWL 2, 3; TWA

Christie
See Ichikawa, Kon

Christie, Agatha (Mary Clarissa)
1890-1976 .. **CLC 1, 6, 8, 12, 39, 48, 110**
See also AAYA 9; AITN 1, 2; BPFB 1; BRWS 2; CA 17-20R; 61-64; CANR 10, 37, 108; CBD; CDBLB 1914-1945; CMW 4; CPW; CWD; DA3; DAB; DAC; DAM NOV; DFS 2; DLB 13, 77, 245; MSW; MTCW 1, 2; NFS 8; RGEL 2; RHW; SATA 36; TEA; YAW

Christie, Philippa .... **CLC 21**
See Pearce, Philippa
See also BYA 5; CANR 109; CLR 9; DLB 161; MAICYA 1; SATA 1, 67, 129

Christine de Pizan 1365(?)-1431(?) .... **LC 9**
See also DLB 208; RGWL 2, 3

Chuang Tzu c. 369B.C.-c.
286B.C. .... **CMLC 57**

Chubb, Elmer
See Masters, Edgar Lee

Chulkov, Mikhail Dmitrievich
1743-1792 .... **LC 2**
See also DLB 150

Churchill, Caryl 1938- .... **CLC 31, 55, 157; DC 5**
See Churchill, Chick
See also BRWS 4; CA 102; CANR 22, 46, 108; CBD; CWD; DFS 12, 16; DLB 13; EWL 3; FW; MTCW 1; RGEL 2

Churchill, Charles 1731-1764 .... **LC 3**
See also DLB 109; RGEL 2

Churchill, Chick
See Churchill, Caryl
See also CD 5

Churchill, Sir Winston (Leonard Spencer)
1874-1965 .... **TCLC 113**
See also BRW 6; CA 97-100; CDBLB 1890-1914; DA3; DLB 100; DLBD 16; LAIT 4; MTCW 1, 2

Chute, Carolyn 1947- .... **CLC 39**
See also CA 123; CANR 135

Ciardi, John (Anthony) 1916-1986 . **CLC 10, 40, 44, 129**
See also CA 5-8R; 118; CAAS 2; CANR 5, 33; CLR 19; CWRI 5; DAM POET; DLB 5; DLBY 1986; INT CANR-5; MAICYA 1, 2; MTCW 1, 2; RGAL 4; SAAS 26; SATA 1, 65; SATA-Obit 46

Cibber, Colley 1671-1757 .... **LC 66**
See also DLB 84; RGEL 2

Cicero, Marcus Tullius
106B.C.-43B.C. .... **CMLC 3**
See also AW 1; CDWLB 1; DLB 211; RGWL 2, 3

Cimino, Michael 1943- .... **CLC 16**
See also CA 105

Cioran, E(mil) M. 1911-1995 .... **CLC 64**
See also CA 25-28R; 149; CANR 91; DLB 220; EWL 3

Cisneros, Sandra 1954- .... **CLC 69, 118, 193; HLC 1; PC 52; SSC 32, 72**
See also AAYA 9, 53; AMWS 7; CA 131; CANR 64, 118; CWP; DA3; DAM MULT; DLB 122, 152; EWL 3; EXPN; FW; HW 1, 2; LAIT 5; LATS 1:2; LLW 1; MAICYA 1; MTCW 2; NFS 2; PFS 19; RGAL 4; RGSF 2; SSFS 3, 13; WLIT 1; YAW

Cixous, Helene 1937- .... **CLC 92**
See also CA 126; CANR 55, 123; CWW 2; DLB 83, 242; EWL 3; FW; GLL 2; MTCW 1, 2; TWA

Clair, Rene .... **CLC 20**
See Chomette, Rene Lucien

Clampitt, Amy 1920-1994 .... **CLC 32; PC 19**
See also AMWS 9; CA 110; 146; CANR 29, 79; DLB 105

Clancy, Thomas L., Jr. 1947-
See Clancy, Tom
See also CA 125; 131; CANR 62, 105; DA3; INT CA-131; MTCW 1, 2

Clancy, Tom .... **CLC 45, 112**
See Clancy, Thomas L., Jr.
See also AAYA 9, 51; BEST 89:1, 90:1; BPFB 1; BYA 10, 11; CANR 132; CMW 4; CPW; DAM NOV, POP; DLB 227

Clare, John 1793-1864 .. **NCLC 9, 86; PC 23**
See also DAB; DAM POET; DLB 55, 96; RGEL 2

Clarin
See Alas (y Urena), Leopoldo (Enrique Garcia)

Clark, Al C.
See Goines, Donald

Clark, (Robert) Brian 1932- .... **CLC 29**
See also CA 41-44R; CANR 67; CBD; CD 5

Clark, Curt
See Westlake, Donald E(dwin)

Clark, Eleanor 1913-1996 .... **CLC 5, 19**
See also CA 9-12R; 151; CANR 41; CN 7; DLB 6

Clark, J. P.
See Clark Bekederemo, J(ohnson) P(epper)
See also CDWLB 3; DLB 117

Clark, John Pepper
See Clark Bekederemo, J(ohnson) P(epper)
See also AFW; CD 5; CP 7; RGEL 2

Clark, Kenneth (Mackenzie)
1903-1983 .... **TCLC 147**
See also CA 93-96; 109; CANR 36; MTCW 1, 2

Clark, M. R.
See Clark, Mavis Thorpe

Clark, Mavis Thorpe 1909-1999 ...... **CLC 12**
See also CA 57-60; CANR 8, 37, 107; CLR 30; CWRI 5; MAICYA 1, 2; SAAS 5; SATA 8, 74

Clark, Walter Van Tilburg
1909-1971 .... **CLC 28**
See also CA 9-12R; 33-36R; CANR 63, 113; DLB 9, 206; LAIT 2; RGAL 4; SATA 8

Clark Bekederemo, J(ohnson) P(epper)
1935- .... **BLC 1; CLC 38; DC 5**
See Clark, J. P.; Clark, John Pepper
See also BW 1; CA 65-68; CANR 16, 72; DAM DRAM, MULT; DFS 13; EWL 3; MTCW 1

Clarke, Arthur C(harles) 1917- .... **CLC 1, 4, 13, 18, 35, 136; SSC 3**
See also AAYA 4, 33; BPFB 1; BYA 13; CA 1-4R; CANR 2, 28, 55, 74, 130; CN 7; CPW; DA3; DAM POP; DLB 261; JRDA; LAIT 5; MAICYA 1, 2; MTCW 1, 2; SATA 13, 70, 115; SCFW; SFW 4; SSFS 4, 18; YAW

Clarke, Austin 1896-1974 .... **CLC 6, 9**
See also CA 29-32; 49-52; CAP 2; DAM POET; DLB 10, 20; EWL 3; RGEL 2

Clarke, Austin C(hesterfield) 1934- .. **BLC 1; CLC 8, 53; SSC 45**
See also BW 1; CA 25-28R; CAAS 16; CANR 14, 32, 68; CN 7; DAC; DAM MULT; DLB 53, 125; DNFS 2; RGSF 2

Clarke, Gillian 1937- .... **CLC 61**
See also CA 106; CP 7; CWP; DLB 40

Clarke, Marcus (Andrew Hislop)
1846-1881 .... **NCLC 19**
See also DLB 230; RGEL 2; RGSF 2

Clarke, Shirley 1925-1997 .... **CLC 16**
See also CA 189

Clash, The
See Headon, (Nicky) Topper; Jones, Mick; Simonon, Paul; Strummer, Joe

Claudel, Paul (Louis Charles Marie)
1868-1955 .... **TCLC 2, 10**
See also CA 104; 165; DLB 192, 258; EW 8; EWL 3; GFL 1789 to the Present; RGWL 2, 3; TWA

Claudian 370(?)-404(?) .... **CMLC 46**
See also RGWL 2, 3

Claudius, Matthias 1740-1815 .... **NCLC 75**
See also DLB 97

Clavell, James (duMaresq)
1925-1994 .... **CLC 6, 25, 87**
See also BPFB 1; CA 25-28R; 146; CANR 26, 48; CPW; DA3; DAM NOV, POP; MTCW 1, 2; NFS 10; RHW

Clayman, Gregory .... **CLC 65**

Cleaver, (Leroy) Eldridge
1935-1998 .... **BLC 1; CLC 30, 119**
See also BW 1, 3; CA 21-24R; 167; CANR 16, 75; DA3; DAM MULT; MTCW 2; YAW

Cleese, John (Marwood) 1939- .... **CLC 21**
See Monty Python
See also CA 112; 116; CANR 35; MTCW 1

Cleishbotham, Jebediah
See Scott, Sir Walter

Cleland, John 1710-1789 .... **LC 2, 48**
See also DLB 39; RGEL 2

Clemens, Samuel Langhorne 1835-1910
See Twain, Mark
See also CA 104; 135; CDALB 1865-1917; DA; DA3; DAB; DAC; DAM MST, NOV; DLB 12, 23, 64, 74, 186, 189; JRDA; LMFS 1; MAICYA 1, 2; NCFS 4; NFS 20; SATA 100; SSFS 16; YABC 2

Clement of Alexandria
150(?)-215(?) .... **CMLC 41**

Cleophil
See Congreve, William

Clerihew, E.
See Bentley, E(dmund) C(lerihew)

Clerk, N. W.
See Lewis, C(live) S(taples)

Cleveland, John 1613-1658 .... **LC 106**
See also DLB 126; RGEL 2

Cliff, Jimmy .... **CLC 21**
See Chambers, James
See also CA 193

Cliff, Michelle 1946- .... **BLCS; CLC 120**
See also BW 2; CA 116; CANR 39, 72; CD-WLB 3; DLB 157; FW; GLL 2

Clifford, Lady Anne 1590-1676 .... **LC 76**
See also DLB 151

Clifton, (Thelma) Lucille 1936- .... **BLC 1; CLC 19, 66, 162; PC 17**
See also AFAW 2; BW 2, 3; CA 49-52; CANR 2, 24, 42, 76, 97; CLR 5; CP 7; CSW; CWP; CWRI 5; DA3; DAM MULT, POET; DLB 5, 41; EXPP; MAICYA 1, 2; MTCW 1, 2; PFS 1, 14; SATA 20, 69, 128; WP

Clinton, Dirk
  See Silverberg, Robert
Clough, Arthur Hugh 1819-1861 ... **NCLC 27**
  See also BRW 5; DLB 32; RGEL 2
Clutha, Janet Paterson Frame 1924-2004
  See Frame, Janet
  See also CA 1-4R; 224; CANR 2, 36, 76, 135; MTCW 1, 2; SATA 119
Clyne, Terence
  See Blatty, William Peter
Cobalt, Martin
  See Mayne, William (James Carter)
Cobb, Irvin S(hrewsbury)
  1876-1944 .... **TCLC 77**
  See also CA 175; DLB 11, 25, 86
Cobbett, William 1763-1835 .... **NCLC 49**
  See also DLB 43, 107, 158; RGEL 2
Coburn, D(onald) L(ee) 1938- .... **CLC 10**
  See also CA 89-92
Cocteau, Jean (Maurice Eugene Clement)
  1889-1963 ...... **CLC 1, 8, 15, 16, 43; DC 17; TCLC 119; WLC**
  See also CA 25-28; CANR 40; CAP 2; DA; DA3; DAB; DAC; DAM DRAM, MST, NOV; DLB 65, 258; EW 10; EWL 3; GFL 1789 to the Present; MTCW 1, 2; RGWL 2, 3; TWA
Codrescu, Andrei 1946- .... **CLC 46, 121**
  See also CA 33-36R; CAAS 19; CANR 13, 34, 53, 76, 125; DA3; DAM POET; MTCW 2
Coe, Max
  See Bourne, Randolph S(illiman)
Coe, Tucker
  See Westlake, Donald E(dwin)
Coen, Ethan 1958- .... **CLC 108**
  See also AAYA 54; CA 126; CANR 85
Coen, Joel 1955- .... **CLC 108**
  See also AAYA 54; CA 126; CANR 119
The Coen Brothers
  See Coen, Ethan; Coen, Joel
Coetzee, J(ohn) M(axwell) 1940- ..... **CLC 23, 33, 66, 117, 161, 162**
  See also AAYA 37; AFW; BRWS 6; CA 77-80; CANR 41, 54, 74, 114, 133; CN 7; DA3; DAM NOV; DLB 225; EWL 3; LMFS 2; MTCW 1, 2; WLIT 2; WWE 1
Coffey, Brian
  See Koontz, Dean R(ay)
Coffin, Robert P(eter) Tristram
  1892-1955 .... **TCLC 95**
  See also CA 123; 169; DLB 45
Cohan, George M(ichael)
  1878-1942 .... **TCLC 60**
  See also CA 157; DLB 249; RGAL 4
Cohen, Arthur A(llen) 1928-1986 ...... **CLC 7, 31**
  See also CA 1-4R; 120; CANR 1, 17, 42; DLB 28
Cohen, Leonard (Norman) 1934- ...... **CLC 3, 38**
  See also CA 21-24R; CANR 14, 69; CN 7; CP 7; DAC; DAM MST; DLB 53; EWL 3; MTCW 1
Cohen, Matt(hew) 1942-1999 .... **CLC 19**
  See also CA 61-64; 187; CAAS 18; CANR 40; CN 7; DAC; DLB 53
Cohen-Solal, Annie 19(?)- .... **CLC 50**
Colegate, Isabel 1931- .... **CLC 36**
  See also CA 17-20R; CANR 8, 22, 74; CN 7; DLB 14, 231; INT CANR-22; MTCW 1
Coleman, Emmett
  See Reed, Ishmael
Coleridge, Hartley 1796-1849 .... **NCLC 90**
  See also DLB 96
Coleridge, M. E.
  See Coleridge, Mary E(lizabeth)

Coleridge, Mary E(lizabeth)
  1861-1907 .... **TCLC 73**
  See also CA 116; 166; DLB 19, 98
Coleridge, Samuel Taylor
  1772-1834 ...... **NCLC 9, 54, 99, 111; PC 11, 39; WLC**
  See also BRW 4; BRWR 2; BYA 4; CD-BLB 1789-1832; DA; DA3; DAB; DAC; DAM MST, POET; DLB 93, 107; EXPP; LATS 1:1; LMFS 1; PAB; PFS 4, 5; RGEL 2; TEA; WLIT 3; WP
Coleridge, Sara 1802-1852 .... **NCLC 31**
  See also DLB 199
Coles, Don 1928- .... **CLC 46**
  See also CA 115; CANR 38; CP 7
Coles, Robert (Martin) 1929- .... **CLC 108**
  See also CA 45-48; CANR 3, 32, 66, 70, 135; INT CANR-32; SATA 23
Colette, (Sidonie-Gabrielle)
  1873-1954 .... **SSC 10; TCLC 1, 5, 16**
  See Willy, Colette
  See also CA 104; 131; DA3; DAM NOV; DLB 65; EW 9; EWL 3; GFL 1789 to the Present; MTCW 1, 2; RGWL 2, 3; TWA
Collett, (Jacobine) Camilla (Wergeland)
  1813-1895 .... **NCLC 22**
Collier, Christopher 1930- .... **CLC 30**
  See also AAYA 13; BYA 2; CA 33-36R; CANR 13, 33, 102; JRDA; MAICYA 1, 2; SATA 16, 70; WYA; YAW 1
Collier, James Lincoln 1928- .... **CLC 30**
  See also AAYA 13; BYA 2; CA 9-12R; CANR 4, 33, 60, 102; CLR 3; DAM POP; JRDA; MAICYA 1, 2; SAAS 21; SATA 8, 70; WYA; YAW 1
Collier, Jeremy 1650-1726 .... **LC 6**
Collier, John 1901-1980 . **SSC 19; TCLC 127**
  See also CA 65-68; 97-100; CANR 10; DLB 77, 255; FANT; SUFW 1
Collier, Mary 1690-1762 .... **LC 86**
  See also DLB 95
Collingwood, R(obin) G(eorge)
  1889(?)-1943 .... **TCLC 67**
  See also CA 117; 155; DLB 262
Collins, Hunt
  See Hunter, Evan
Collins, Linda 1931- .... **CLC 44**
  See also CA 125
Collins, Tom
  See Furphy, Joseph
  See also RGEL 2
Collins, (William) Wilkie
  1824-1889 .... **NCLC 1, 18, 93**
  See also BRWS 6; CDBLB 1832-1890; CMW 4; DLB 18, 70, 159; MSW; RGEL 2; RGSF 2; SUFW 1; WLIT 4
Collins, William 1721-1759 .... **LC 4, 40**
  See also BRW 3; DAM POET; DLB 109; RGEL 2
Collodi, Carlo .... **NCLC 54**
  See Lorenzini, Carlo
  See also CLR 5; WCH
Colman, George
  See Glassco, John
Colman, George, the Elder
  1732-1794 .... **LC 98**
  See also RGEL 2
Colonna, Vittoria 1492-1547 .... **LC 71**
  See also RGWL 2, 3
Colt, Winchester Remington
  See Hubbard, L(afayette) Ron(ald)
Colter, Cyrus J. 1910-2002 .... **CLC 58**
  See also BW 1; CA 65-68; 205; CANR 10, 66; CN 7; DLB 33
Colton, James
  See Hansen, Joseph
  See also GLL 1

Colum, Padraic 1881-1972 .... **CLC 28**
  See also BYA 4; CA 73-76; 33-36R; CANR 35; CLR 36; CWRI 5; DLB 19; MAICYA 1, 2; MTCW 1; RGEL 2; SATA 15; WCH
Colvin, James
  See Moorcock, Michael (John)
Colwin, Laurie (E.) 1944-1992 .... **CLC 5, 13, 23, 84**
  See also CA 89-92; 139; CANR 20, 46; DLB 218; DLBY 1980; MTCW 1
Comfort, Alex(ander) 1920-2000 .... **CLC 7**
  See also CA 1-4R; 190; CANR 1, 45; CP 7; DAM POP; MTCW 1
Comfort, Montgomery
  See Campbell, (John) Ramsey
Compton-Burnett, I(vy)
  1892(?)-1969 .... **CLC 1, 3, 10, 15, 34**
  See also BRW 7; CA 1-4R; 25-28R; CANR 4; DAM NOV; DLB 36; EWL 3; MTCW 1; RGEL 2
Comstock, Anthony 1844-1915 ...... **TCLC 13**
  See also CA 110; 169
Comte, Auguste 1798-1857 .... **NCLC 54**
Conan Doyle, Arthur
  See Doyle, Sir Arthur Conan
  See also BPFB 1; BYA 4, 5, 11
Conde (Abellan), Carmen
  1901-1996 .... **HLCS 1**
  See also CA 177; CWW 2; DLB 108; EWL 3; HW 2
Conde, Maryse 1937- ..... **BLCS; CLC 52, 92**
  See also BW 2, 3; CA 110; 190; CAAE 190; CANR 30, 53, 76; CWW 2; DAM MULT; EWL 3; MTCW 1
Condillac, Etienne Bonnot de
  1714-1780 .... **LC 26**
Condon, Richard (Thomas)
  1915-1996 .... **CLC 4, 6, 8, 10, 45, 100**
  See also BEST 90:3; BPFB 1; CA 1-4R; 151; CAAS 1; CANR 2, 23; CMW 4; CN 7; DAM NOV; INT CANR-23; MTCW 1, 2
Condorcet 1743-1794 .... **LC 104**
  See also GFL Beginnings to 1789
Confucius 551B.C.-479B.C. .... **CMLC 19, 65; WLCS**
  See also DA; DA3; DAB; DAC; DAM MST
Congreve, William 1670-1729 ... **DC 2; LC 5, 21; WLC**
  See also BRW 2; CDBLB 1660-1789; DA; DAB; DAC; DAM DRAM, MST, POET; DFS 15; DLB 39, 84; RGEL 2; WLIT 3
Conley, Robert J(ackson) 1940- .... **NNAL**
  See also CA 41-44R; CANR 15, 34, 45, 96; DAM MULT
Connell, Evan S(helby), Jr. 1924- . **CLC 4, 6, 45**
  See also AAYA 7; AMWS 14; CA 1-4R; CAAS 2; CANR 2, 39, 76, 97; CN 7; DAM NOV; DLB 2; DLBY 1981; MTCW 1, 2
Connelly, Marc(us Cook) 1890-1980 . **CLC 7**
  See also CA 85-88; 102; CANR 30; DFS 12; DLB 7; DLBY 1980; RGAL 4; SATA-Obit 25
Connor, Ralph .... **TCLC 31**
  See Gordon, Charles William
  See also DLB 92; TCWW 2
Conrad, Joseph 1857-1924 ..... **SSC 9, 67, 69, 71; TCLC 1, 6, 13, 25, 43, 57; WLC**
  See also AAYA 26; BPFB 1; BRW 6; BRWC 1; BRWR 2; BYA 2; CA 104; 131; CANR 60; CDBLB 1890-1914; DA; DA3; DAB; DAC; DAM MST, NOV; DLB 10, 34, 98, 156; EWL 3; EXPN; EXPS; LAIT 2; LATS 1:1; LMFS 1; MTCW 1, 2; NFS 2, 16; RGEL 2; RGSF 2; SATA 27; SSFS 1, 12; TEA; WLIT 4

Conrad, Robert Arnold
See Hart, Moss

Conroy, (Donald) Pat(rick) 1945- ... **CLC 30, 74**
See also AAYA 8, 52; AITN 1; BPFB 1; CA 85-88; CANR 24, 53, 129; CPW; CSW; DA3; DAM NOV, POP; DLB 6; LAIT 5; MTCW 1, 2

Constant (de Rebecque), (Henri) Benjamin 1767-1830 .... **NCLC 6**
See also DLB 119; EW 4; GFL 1789 to the Present

Conway, Jill K(er) 1934- .... **CLC 152**
See also CA 130; CANR 94

Conybeare, Charles Augustus
See Eliot, T(homas) S(tearns)

Cook, Michael 1933-1994 .... **CLC 58**
See also CA 93-96; CANR 68; DLB 53

Cook, Robin 1940- .... **CLC 14**
See also AAYA 32; BEST 90:2; BPFB 1; CA 108; 111; CANR 41, 90, 109; CPW; DA3; DAM POP; HGG; INT CA-111

Cook, Roy
See Silverberg, Robert

Cooke, Elizabeth 1948- .... **CLC 55**
See also CA 129

Cooke, John Esten 1830-1886 .... **NCLC 5**
See also DLB 3, 248; RGAL 4

Cooke, John Estes
See Baum, L(yman) Frank

Cooke, M. E.
See Creasey, John

Cooke, Margaret
See Creasey, John

Cooke, Rose Terry 1827-1892 ...... **NCLC 110**
See also DLB 12, 74

Cook-Lynn, Elizabeth 1930- .... **CLC 93; NNAL**
See also CA 133; DAM MULT; DLB 175

Cooney, Ray .... **CLC 62**
See also CBD

Cooper, Anthony Ashley 1671-1713 .. **LC 107**
See also DLB 101

Cooper, Dennis 1953- .... **CLC 203**
See also CA 133; CANR 72, 86; GLL 1; St. James Guide to Horror, Ghost, and Gothic Writers.

Cooper, Douglas 1960- .... **CLC 86**

Cooper, Henry St. John
See Creasey, John

Cooper, J(oan) California (?)- .... **CLC 56**
See also AAYA 12; BW 1; CA 125; CANR 55; DAM MULT; DLB 212

Cooper, James Fenimore 1789-1851 .... **NCLC 1, 27, 54**
See also AAYA 22; AMW; BPFB 1; CDALB 1640-1865; DA3; DLB 3, 183, 250, 254; LAIT 1; NFS 9; RGAL 4; SATA 19; TUS; WCH

Cooper, Susan Fenimore 1813-1894 .... **NCLC 129**
See also ANW; DLB 239, 254

Coover, Robert (Lowell) 1932- ...... **CLC 3, 7, 15, 32, 46, 87, 161; SSC 15**
See also AMWS 5; BPFB 1; CA 45-48; CANR 3, 37, 58, 115; CN 7; DAM NOV; DLB 2, 227; DLBY 1981; EWL 3; MTCW 1, 2; RGAL 4; RGSF 2

Copeland, Stewart (Armstrong) 1952- .... **CLC 26**

Copernicus, Nicolaus 1473-1543 .... **LC 45**

Coppard, A(lfred) E(dgar) 1878-1957 .... **SSC 21; TCLC 5**
See also BRWS 8; CA 114; 167; DLB 162; EWL 3; HGG; RGEL 2; RGSF 2; SUFW 1; YABC 1

Coppee, Francois 1842-1908 .... **TCLC 25**
See also CA 170; DLB 217

Coppola, Francis Ford 1939- ... **CLC 16, 126**
See also AAYA 39; CA 77-80; CANR 40, 78; DLB 44

Copway, George 1818-1869 .... **NNAL**
See also DAM MULT; DLB 175, 183

Corbiere, Tristan 1845-1875 .... **NCLC 43**
See also DLB 217; GFL 1789 to the Present

Corcoran, Barbara (Asenath) 1911- .... **CLC 17**
See also AAYA 14; CA 21-24R, 191; CAAE 191; CAAS 2; CANR 11, 28, 48; CLR 50; DLB 52; JRDA; MAICYA 2; MAIC-YAS 1; RHW; SAAS 20; SATA 3, 77; SATA-Essay 125

Cordelier, Maurice
See Giraudoux, Jean(-Hippolyte)

Corelli, Marie .... **TCLC 51**
See Mackay, Mary
See also DLB 34, 156; RGEL 2; SUFW 1

Corinna c. 225B.C.-c. 305B.C. ...... **CMLC 72**

Corman, Cid .... **CLC 9**
See Corman, Sidney
See also CAAS 2; DLB 5, 193

Corman, Sidney 1924-2004
See Corman, Cid
See also CA 85-88; 225; CANR 44; CP 7; DAM POET

Cormier, Robert (Edmund) 1925-2000 .... **CLC 12, 30**
See also AAYA 3, 19; BYA 1, 2, 6, 8, 9; CA 1-4R; CANR 5, 23, 76, 93; CDALB 1968-1988; CLR 12, 55; DA; DAB; DAC; DAM MST, NOV; DLB 52; EXPN; INT CANR-23; JRDA; LAIT 5; MAICYA 1, 2; MTCW 1, 2; NFS 2, 18; SATA 10, 45, 83; SATA-Obit 122; WYA; YAW

Corn, Alfred (DeWitt III) 1943- .... **CLC 33**
See also CA 179; CAAE 179; CAAS 25; CANR 44; CP 7; CSW; DLB 120, 282; DLBY 1980

Corneille, Pierre 1606-1684 ... **DC 21; LC 28**
See also DAB; DAM MST; DLB 268; EW 3; GFL Beginnings to 1789; RGWL 2, 3; TWA

Cornwell, David (John Moore) 1931- .... **CLC 9, 15**
See le Carre, John
See also CA 5-8R; CANR 13, 33, 59, 107, 132; DA3; DAM POP; MTCW 1, 2

Cornwell, Patricia (Daniels) 1956- . **CLC 155**
See also AAYA 16, 56; BPFB 1; CA 134; CANR 53, 131; CMW 4; CPW; CSW; DAM POP; DLB 306; MSW; MTCW 1

Corso, (Nunzio) Gregory 1930-2001 . **CLC 1, 11; PC 33**
See also AMWS 12; BG 2; CA 5-8R; 193; CANR 41, 76, 132; CP 7; DA3; DLB 5, 16, 237; LMFS 2; MTCW 1, 2; WP

Cortazar, Julio 1914-1984 ... **CLC 2, 3, 5, 10, 13, 15, 33, 34, 92; HLC 1; SSC 7, 76**
See also BPFB 1; CA 21-24R; CANR 12, 32, 81; CDWLB 3; DA3; DAM MULT, NOV; DLB 113; EWL 3; EXPS; HW 1, 2; LAW; MTCW 1, 2; RGSF 2; RGWL 2, 3; SSFS 3, 20; TWA; WLIT 1

Cortes, Hernan 1485-1547 .... **LC 31**

Corvinus, Jakob
See Raabe, Wilhelm (Karl)

Corwin, Cecil
See Kornbluth, C(yril) M.

Cosic, Dobrica 1921- .... **CLC 14**
See also CA 122; 138; CDWLB 4; CWW 2; DLB 181; EWL 3

Costain, Thomas B(ertram) 1885-1965 .... **CLC 30**
See also BYA 3; CA 5-8R; 25-28R; DLB 9; RHW

Costantini, Humberto 1924(?)-1987 . **CLC 49**
See also CA 131; 122; EWL 3; HW 1

Costello, Elvis 1954- .... **CLC 21**
See also CA 204

Costenoble, Philostene
See Ghelderode, Michel de

Cotes, Cecil V.
See Duncan, Sara Jeannette

Cotter, Joseph Seamon Sr. 1861-1949 .... **BLC 1; TCLC 28**
See also BW 1; CA 124; DAM MULT; DLB 50

Couch, Arthur Thomas Quiller
See Quiller-Couch, Sir Arthur (Thomas)

Coulton, James
See Hansen, Joseph

Couperus, Louis (Marie Anne) 1863-1923 .... **TCLC 15**
See also CA 115; EWL 3; RGWL 2, 3

Coupland, Douglas 1961- .... **CLC 85, 133**
See also AAYA 34; CA 142; CANR 57, 90, 130; CCA 1; CPW; DAC; DAM POP

Court, Wesli
See Turco, Lewis (Putnam)

Courtenay, Bryce 1933- .... **CLC 59**
See also CA 138; CPW

Courtney, Robert
See Ellison, Harlan (Jay)

Cousteau, Jacques-Yves 1910-1997 .. **CLC 30**
See also CA 65-68; 159; CANR 15, 67; MTCW 1; SATA 38, 98

Coventry, Francis 1725-1754 .... **LC 46**

Coverdale, Miles c. 1487-1569 .... **LC 77**
See also DLB 167

Cowan, Peter (Walkinshaw) 1914-2002 .... **SSC 28**
See also CA 21-24R; CANR 9, 25, 50, 83; CN 7; DLB 260; RGSF 2

Coward, Noel (Peirce) 1899-1973 . **CLC 1, 9, 29, 51**
See also AITN 1; BRWS 2; CA 17-18; 41-44R; CANR 35, 132; CAP 2; CDBLB 1914-1945; DA3; DAM DRAM; DFS 3, 6; DLB 10, 245; EWL 3; IDFW 3, 4; MTCW 1, 2; RGEL 2; TEA

Cowley, Abraham 1618-1667 .... **LC 43**
See also BRW 2; DLB 131, 151; PAB; RGEL 2

Cowley, Malcolm 1898-1989 .... **CLC 39**
See also AMWS 2; CA 5-8R; 128; CANR 3, 55; DLB 4, 48; DLBY 1981, 1989; EWL 3; MTCW 1, 2

Cowper, William 1731-1800 ..... **NCLC 8, 94; PC 40**
See also BRW 3; DA3; DAM POET; DLB 104, 109; RGEL 2

Cox, William Trevor 1928-
See Trevor, William
See also CA 9-12R; CANR 4, 37, 55, 76, 102; DAM NOV; INT CANR-37; MTCW 1, 2; TEA

Coyne, P. J.
See Masters, Hilary

Cozzens, James Gould 1903-1978 . **CLC 1, 4, 11, 92**
See also AMW; BPFB 1; CA 9-12R; 81-84; CANR 19; CDALB 1941-1968; DLB 9, 294; DLBD 2; DLBY 1984, 1997; EWL 3; MTCW 1, 2; RGAL 4

Crabbe, George 1754-1832 .... **NCLC 26, 121**
See also BRW 3; DLB 93; RGEL 2

Crace, Jim 1946- .... **CLC 157; SSC 61**
See also CA 128; 135; CANR 55, 70, 123; CN 7; DLB 231; INT CA-135

Craddock, Charles Egbert
See Murfree, Mary Noailles

Craig, A. A.
See Anderson, Poul (William)

Craik, Mrs.
See Craik, Dinah Maria (Mulock)
See also RGEL 2

Curtis, Price
 See Ellison, Harlan (Jay)
Cusanus, Nicolaus 1401-1464 .... **LC 80**
 See Nicholas of Cusa
Cutrate, Joe
 See Spiegelman, Art
Cynewulf c. 770- .... **CMLC 23**
 See also DLB 146; RGEL 2
Cyrano de Bergerac, Savinien de
 1619-1655 .... **LC 65**
 See also DLB 268; GFL Beginnings to
 1789; RGWL 2, 3
Cyril of Alexandria c. 375-c. 430 . **CMLC 59**
Czaczkes, Shmuel Yosef Halevi
 See Agnon, S(hmuel) Y(osef Halevi)
Dabrowska, Maria (Szumska)
 1889-1965 .... **CLC 15**
 See also CA 106; CDWLB 4; DLB 215;
 EWL 3
Dabydeen, David 1955- .... **CLC 34**
 See also BW 1; CA 125; CANR 56, 92; CN
 7; CP 7
Dacey, Philip 1939- .... **CLC 51**
 See also CA 37-40R; CAAS 17; CANR 14,
 32, 64; CP 7; DLB 105
Dacre, Charlotte c. 1772-1825? ... **NCLC 151**
Dafydd ap Gwilym c. 1320-c. 1380 ..... **PC 56**
Dagerman, Stig (Halvard)
 1923-1954 .... **TCLC 17**
 See also CA 117; 155; DLB 259; EWL 3
D'Aguiar, Fred 1960- .... **CLC 145**
 See also CA 148; CANR 83, 101; CP 7;
 DLB 157; EWL 3
Dahl, Roald 1916-1990 .... **CLC 1, 6, 18, 79**
 See also AAYA 15; BPFB 1; BRWS 4; BYA
 5; CA 1-4R; 133; CANR 6, 32, 37, 62;
 CLR 1, 7, 41; CPW; DA3; DAB; DAC;
 DAM MST, NOV, POP; DLB 139, 255;
 HGG; JRDA; MAICYA 1, 2; MTCW 1,
 2; RGSF 2; SATA 1, 26, 73; SATA-Obit
 65; SSFS 4; TEA; YAW
Dahlberg, Edward 1900-1977 .. **CLC 1, 7, 14**
 See also CA 9-12R; 69-72; CANR 31, 62;
 DLB 48; MTCW 1; RGAL 4
Daitch, Susan 1954- .... **CLC 103**
 See also CA 161
Dale, Colin .... **TCLC 18**
 See Lawrence, T(homas) E(dward)
Dale, George E.
 See Asimov, Isaac
Dalton, Roque 1935-1975(?) ..... **HLCS 1; PC
 36**
 See also CA 176; DLB 283; HW 2
Daly, Elizabeth 1878-1967 .... **CLC 52**
 See also CA 23-24; 25-28R; CANR 60;
 CAP 2; CMW 4
Daly, Mary 1928- .... **CLC 173**
 See also CA 25-28R; CANR 30, 62; FW;
 GLL 1; MTCW 1
Daly, Maureen 1921- .... **CLC 17**
 See also AAYA 5, 58; BYA 6; CANR 37,
 83, 108; CLR 96; JRDA; MAICYA 1, 2;
 SAAS 1; SATA 2, 129; WYA; YAW
Damas, Leon-Gontran 1912-1978 .... **CLC 84**
 See also BW 1; CA 125; 73-76; EWL 3
Dana, Richard Henry Sr.
 1787-1879 .... **NCLC 53**
Daniel, Samuel 1562(?)-1619 .... **LC 24**
 See also DLB 62; RGEL 2
Daniels, Brett
 See Adler, Renata
Dannay, Frederic 1905-1982 .... **CLC 11**
 See Queen, Ellery
 See also CA 1-4R; 107; CANR 1, 39; CMW
 4; DAM POP; DLB 137; MTCW 1
D'Annunzio, Gabriele 1863-1938 ... **TCLC 6,
 40**
 See also CA 104; 155; EW 8; EWL 3;
 RGWL 2, 3; TWA

Danois, N. le
 See Gourmont, Remy(-Marie-Charles) de
Dante 1265-1321 .... **CMLC 3, 18, 39, 70; PC
 21; WLCS**
 See also DA; DA3; DAB; DAC; DAM
 MST, POET; EFS 1; EW 1; LAIT 1;
 RGWL 2, 3; TWA; WP
d'Antibes, Germain
 See Simenon, Georges (Jacques Christian)
Danticat, Edwidge 1969- .... **CLC 94, 139**
 See also AAYA 29; CA 152, 192; CAAE
 192; CANR 73, 129; DNFS 1; EXPS;
 LATS 1:2; MTCW 1; SSFS 1; YAW
Danvers, Dennis 1947- .... **CLC 70**
Danziger, Paula 1944-2004 .... **CLC 21**
 See also AAYA 4, 36; BYA 6, 7, 14; CA
 112; 115; 229; CANR 37, 132; CLR 20;
 JRDA; MAICYA 1, 2; SATA 36, 63, 102,
 149; SATA-Brief 30; WYA; YAW
Da Ponte, Lorenzo 1749-1838 .... **NCLC 50**
Dario, Ruben 1867-1916 .... **HLC 1; PC 15;
 TCLC 4**
 See also CA 131; CANR 81; DAM MULT;
 DLB 290; EWL 3; HW 1, 2; LAW;
 MTCW 1, 2; RGWL 2, 3
Darley, George 1795-1846 .... **NCLC 2**
 See also DLB 96; RGEL 2
Darrow, Clarence (Seward)
 1857-1938 .... **TCLC 81**
 See also CA 164; DLB 303
Darwin, Charles 1809-1882 .... **NCLC 57**
 See also BRWS 7; DLB 57, 166; LATS 1:1;
 RGEL 2; TEA; WLIT 4
Darwin, Erasmus 1731-1802 .... **NCLC 106**
 See also DLB 93; RGEL 2
Daryush, Elizabeth 1887-1977 ...... **CLC 6, 19**
 See also CA 49-52; CANR 3, 81; DLB 20
Das, Kamala 1934- .... **CLC 191; PC 43**
 See also CA 101; CANR 27, 59; CP 7;
 CWP; FW
Dasgupta, Surendranath
 1887-1952 .... **TCLC 81**
 See also CA 157
**Dashwood, Edmee Elizabeth Monica de la
 Pasture** 1890-1943
 See Delafield, E. M.
 See also CA 119; 154
da Silva, Antonio Jose
 1705-1739 .... **NCLC 114**
Daudet, (Louis Marie) Alphonse
 1840-1897 .... **NCLC 1**
 See also DLB 123; GFL 1789 to the Present;
 RGSF 2
d'Aulnoy, Marie-Catherine c.
 1650-1705 .... **LC 100**
Daumal, Rene 1908-1944 .... **TCLC 14**
 See also CA 114; EWL 3
Davenant, William 1606-1668 .... **LC 13**
 See also DLB 58, 126; RGEL 2
Davenport, Guy (Mattison, Jr.)
 1927-2005 .... **CLC 6, 14, 38; SSC 16**
 See also CA 33-36R; CANR 23, 73; CN 7;
 CSW; DLB 130
David, Robert
 See Nezval, Vitezslav
Davidson, Avram (James) 1923-1993
 See Queen, Ellery
 See also CA 101; 171; CANR 26; DLB 8;
 FANT; SFW 4; SUFW 1, 2
Davidson, Donald (Grady)
 1893-1968 .... **CLC 2, 13, 19**
 See also CA 5-8R; 25-28R; CANR 4, 84;
 DLB 45
Davidson, Hugh
 See Hamilton, Edmond
Davidson, John 1857-1909 .... **TCLC 24**
 See also CA 118; 217; DLB 19; RGEL 2

Davidson, Sara 1943- .... **CLC 9**
 See also CA 81-84; CANR 44, 68; DLB
 185
Davie, Donald (Alfred) 1922-1995 .... **CLC 5,
 8, 10, 31; PC 29**
 See also BRWS 6; CA 1-4R; 149; CAAS 3;
 CANR 1, 44; CP 7; DLB 27; MTCW 1;
 RGEL 2
Davie, Elspeth 1919-1995 .... **SSC 52**
 See also CA 120; 126; 150; DLB 139
Davies, Ray(mond Douglas) 1944- ... **CLC 21**
 See also CA 116; 146; CANR 92
Davies, Rhys 1901-1978 .... **CLC 23**
 See also CA 9-12R; 81-84; CANR 4; DLB
 139, 191
Davies, (William) Robertson
 1913-1995 .... **CLC 2, 7, 13, 25, 42, 75,
 91; WLC**
 See Marchbanks, Samuel
 See also BEST 89:2; BPFB 1; CA 33-36R;
 150; CANR 17, 42, 103; CN 7; CPW;
 DA; DA3; DAB; DAC; DAM MST, NOV,
 POP; DLB 68; EWL 3; HGG; INT CANR-
 17; MTCW 1, 2; RGEL 2; TWA
Davies, Sir John 1569-1626 .... **LC 85**
 See also DLB 172
Davies, Walter C.
 See Kornbluth, C(yril) M.
Davies, William Henry 1871-1940 ... **TCLC 5**
 See also CA 104; 179; DLB 19, 174; EWL
 3; RGEL 2
Da Vinci, Leonardo 1452-1519 ..... **LC 12, 57,
 60**
 See also AAYA 40
Davis, Angela (Yvonne) 1944- .... **CLC 77**
 See also BW 2, 3; CA 57-60; CANR 10,
 81; CSW; DA3; DAM MULT; FW
Davis, B. Lynch
 See Bioy Casares, Adolfo; Borges, Jorge
 Luis
Davis, Frank Marshall 1905-1987 ...... **BLC 1**
 See also BW 2, 3; CA 125; 123; CANR 42,
 80; DAM MULT; DLB 51
Davis, Gordon
 See Hunt, E(verette) Howard, (Jr.)
Davis, H(arold) L(enoir) 1896-1960 . **CLC 49**
 See also ANW; CA 178; 89-92; DLB 9,
 206; SATA 114
Davis, Natalie Z(emon) 1928- .... **CLC 204**
 See also CA 53-56; CANR 58, 100
Davis, Rebecca (Blaine) Harding
 1831-1910 .... **SSC 38; TCLC 6**
 See also CA 104; 179; DLB 74, 239; FW;
 NFS 14; RGAL 4; TUS
Davis, Richard Harding
 1864-1916 .... **TCLC 24**
 See also CA 114; 179; DLB 12, 23, 78, 79,
 189; DLBD 13; RGAL 4
Davison, Frank Dalby 1893-1970 ..... **CLC 15**
 See also CA 217; 116; DLB 260
Davison, Lawrence H.
 See Lawrence, D(avid) H(erbert Richards)
Davison, Peter (Hubert) 1928- .... **CLC 28**
 See also CA 9-12R; CAAS 4; CANR 3, 43,
 84; CP 7; DLB 5
Davys, Mary 1674-1732 .... **LC 1, 46**
 See also DLB 39
Dawson, (Guy) Fielding (Lewis)
 1930-2002 .... **CLC 6**
 See also CA 85-88; 202; CANR 108; DLB
 130; DLBY 2002
Dawson, Peter
 See Faust, Frederick (Schiller)
 See also TCWW 2, 2
Day, Clarence (Shepard, Jr.)
 1874-1935 .... **TCLC 25**
 See also CA 108; 199; DLB 11
Day, John 1574(?)-1640(?) .... **LC 70**
 See also DLB 62, 170; RGEL 2

Day, Thomas 1748-1789 .... **LC 1**
See also DLB 39; YABC 1

Day Lewis, C(ecil) 1904-1972 . **CLC 1, 6, 10; PC 11**
See Blake, Nicholas
See also BRWS 3; CA 13-16; 33-36R; CANR 34; CAP 1; CWRI 5; DAM POET; DLB 15, 20; EWL 3; MTCW 1, 2; RGEL 2

Dazai Osamu .... **SSC 41; TCLC 11**
See Tsushima, Shuji
See also CA 164; DLB 182; EWL 3; MJW; RGSF 2; RGWL 2, 3; TWA

de Andrade, Carlos Drummond
See Drummond de Andrade, Carlos

de Andrade, Mario 1892(?)-1945
See Andrade, Mario de
See also CA 178; HW 2

Deane, Norman
See Creasey, John

Deane, Seamus (Francis) 1940- ...... **CLC 122**
See also CA 118; CANR 42

de Beauvoir, Simone (Lucie Ernestine Marie Bertrand)
See Beauvoir, Simone (Lucie Ernestine Marie Bertrand) de

de Beer, P.
See Bosman, Herman Charles

de Botton, Alain 1969- .... **CLC 203**
See also CA 159; CANR 96

de Brissac, Malcolm
See Dickinson, Peter (Malcolm de Brissac)

de Campos, Alvaro
See Pessoa, Fernando (Antonio Nogueira)

de Chardin, Pierre Teilhard
See Teilhard de Chardin, (Marie Joseph) Pierre

de Crenne, Hélisenne c. 1510-c. 1560 .... **LC 113**

Dee, John 1527-1608 .... **LC 20**
See also DLB 136, 213

Deer, Sandra 1940- .... **CLC 45**
See also CA 186

De Ferrari, Gabriella 1941- .... **CLC 65**
See also CA 146

de Filippo, Eduardo 1900-1984 ... **TCLC 127**
See also CA 132; 114; EWL 3; MTCW 1; RGWL 2, 3

Defoe, Daniel 1660(?)-1731 .... **LC 1, 42, 108; WLC**
See also AAYA 27; BRW 3; BRWR 1; BYA 4; CDBLB 1660-1789; CLR 61; DA; DA3; DAB; DAC; DAM MST, NOV; DLB 39, 95, 101; JRDA; LAIT 1; LMFS 1; MAICYA 1, 2; NFS 9, 13; RGEL 2; SATA 22; TEA; WCH; WLIT 3

de Gourmont, Remy(-Marie-Charles)
See Gourmont, Remy(-Marie-Charles) de

de Gournay, Marie le Jars 1566-1645 .... **LC 98**
See also FW

de Hartog, Jan 1914-2002 .... **CLC 19**
See also CA 1-4R; 210; CANR 1; DFS 12

de Hostos, E. M.
See Hostos (y Bonilla), Eugenio Maria de

de Hostos, Eugenio M.
See Hostos (y Bonilla), Eugenio Maria de

Deighton, Len .... **CLC 4, 7, 22, 46**
See Deighton, Leonard Cyril
See also AAYA 6; BEST 89:2; BPFB 1; CD-BLB 1960 to Present; CMW 4; CN 7; CPW; DLB 87

Deighton, Leonard Cyril 1929-
See Deighton, Len
See also AAYA 57; CA 9-12R; CANR 19, 33, 68; DA3; DAM NOV, POP; MTCW 1, 2

Dekker, Thomas 1572(?)-1632 ..... **DC 12; LC 22**
See also CDBLB Before 1660; DAM DRAM; DLB 62, 172; LMFS 1; RGEL 2

de Laclos, Pierre Ambroise Franois
See Laclos, Pierre Ambroise Francois

Delacroix, (Ferdinand-Victor-)Eugene 1798-1863 .... **NCLC 133**
See also EW 5

Delafield, E. M. .... **TCLC 61**
See Dashwood, Edmee Elizabeth Monica de la Pasture
See also DLB 34; RHW

de la Mare, Walter (John) 1873-1956 . **SSC 14; TCLC 4, 53; WLC**
See also CA 163; CDBLB 1914-1945; CLR 23; CWRI 5; DA3; DAB; DAC; DAM MST, POET; DLB 19, 153, 162, 255, 284; EWL 3; EXPP; HGG; MAICYA 1, 2; MTCW 1; RGEL 2; RGSF 2; SATA 16; SUFW 1; TEA; WCH

de Lamartine, Alphonse (Marie Louis Prat)
See Lamartine, Alphonse (Marie Louis Prat) de

Delaney, Franey
See O'Hara, John (Henry)

Delaney, Shelagh 1939- .... **CLC 29**
See also CA 17-20R; CANR 30, 67; CBD; CD 5; CDBLB 1960 to Present; CWD; DAM DRAM; DFS 7; DLB 13; MTCW 1

Delany, Martin Robison 1812-1885 .... **NCLC 93**
See also DLB 50; RGAL 4

Delany, Mary (Granville Pendarves) 1700-1788 .... **LC 12**

Delany, Samuel R(ay), Jr. 1942- .... **BLC 1; CLC 8, 14, 38, 141**
See also AAYA 24; AFAW 2; BPFB 1; BW 2, 3; CA 81-84; CANR 27, 43, 115, 116; CN 7; DAM MULT; DLB 8, 33; FANT; MTCW 1, 2; RGAL 4; SATA 92; SCFW; SFW 4; SUFW 2

De la Ramee, Marie Louise (Ouida) 1839-1908
See Ouida
See also CA 204; SATA 20

de la Roche, Mazo 1879-1961 .... **CLC 14**
See also CA 85-88; CANR 30; DLB 68; RGEL 2; RHW; SATA 64

De La Salle, Innocent
See Hartmann, Sadakichi

de Laureamont, Comte
See Lautreamont

Delbanco, Nicholas (Franklin) 1942- .... **CLC 6, 13, 167**
See also CA 17-20R, 189; CAAE 189; CAAS 2; CANR 29, 55, 116; DLB 6, 234

del Castillo, Michel 1933- .... **CLC 38**
See also CA 109; CANR 77

Deledda, Grazia (Cosima) 1875(?)-1936 .... **TCLC 23**
See also CA 123; 205; DLB 264; EWL 3; RGWL 2, 3

Deleuze, Gilles 1925-1995 .... **TCLC 116**
See also DLB 296

Delgado, Abelardo (Lalo) B(arrientos) 1930-2004 .... **HLC 1**
See also CA 131; CAAS 15; CANR 90; DAM MST, MULT; DLB 82; HW 1, 2

Delibes, Miguel .... **CLC 8, 18**
See Delibes Setien, Miguel
See also EWL 3

Delibes Setien, Miguel 1920-
See Delibes, Miguel
See also CA 45-48; CANR 1, 32; CWW 2; HW 1; MTCW 1

DeLillo, Don 1936- ...... **CLC 8, 10, 13, 27, 39, 54, 76, 143, 210**
See also AMWC 2; AMWS 6; BEST 89:1; BPFB 1; CA 81-84; CANR 21, 76, 92, 133; CN 7; CPW; DA3; DAM NOV, POP; DLB 6, 173; EWL 3; MTCW 1, 2; RGAL 4; TUS

de Lisser, H. G.
See De Lisser, H(erbert) G(eorge)
See also DLB 117

De Lisser, H(erbert) G(eorge) 1878-1944 .... **TCLC 12**
See de Lisser, H. G.
See also BW 2; CA 109; 152

Deloire, Pierre
See Peguy, Charles (Pierre)

Deloney, Thomas 1543(?)-1600 .... **LC 41**
See also DLB 167; RGEL 2

Deloria, Ella (Cara) 1889-1971(?) ..... **NNAL**
See also CA 152; DAM MULT; DLB 175

Deloria, Vine (Victor), Jr. 1933- ...... **CLC 21, 122; NNAL**
See also CA 53-56; CANR 5, 20, 48, 98; DAM MULT; DLB 175; MTCW 1; SATA 21

del Valle-Inclan, Ramon (Maria)
See Valle-Inclan, Ramon (Maria) del

Del Vecchio, John M(ichael) 1947- .. **CLC 29**
See also CA 110; DLBD 9

de Man, Paul (Adolph Michel) 1919-1983 .... **CLC 55**
See also CA 128; 111; CANR 61; DLB 67; MTCW 1, 2

DeMarinis, Rick 1934- .... **CLC 54**
See also CA 57-60, 184; CAAE 184; CAAS 24; CANR 9, 25, 50; DLB 218

de Maupassant, (Henri Rene Albert) Guy
See Maupassant, (Henri Rene Albert) Guy de

Dembry, R. Emmet
See Murfree, Mary Noailles

Demby, William 1922- .... **BLC 1; CLC 53**
See also BW 1, 3; CA 81-84; CANR 81; DAM MULT; DLB 33

de Menton, Francisco
See Chin, Frank (Chew, Jr.)

Demetrius of Phalerum c. 307B.C.- .... **CMLC 34**

Demijohn, Thom
See Disch, Thomas M(ichael)

De Mille, James 1833-1880 .... **NCLC 123**
See also DLB 99, 251

Deming, Richard 1915-1983
See Queen, Ellery
See also CA 9-12R; CANR 3, 94; SATA 24

Democritus c. 460B.C.-c. 370B.C. . **CMLC 47**

de Montaigne, Michel (Eyquem)
See Montaigne, Michel (Eyquem) de

de Montherlant, Henry (Milon)
See Montherlant, Henry (Milon) de

Demosthenes 384B.C.-322B.C. ...... **CMLC 13**
See also AW 1; DLB 176; RGWL 2, 3

de Musset, (Louis Charles) Alfred
See Musset, (Louis Charles) Alfred de

de Natale, Francine
See Malzberg, Barry N(athaniel)

de Navarre, Marguerite 1492-1549 ..... **LC 61**
See Marguerite d'Angouleme; Marguerite de Navarre

Denby, Edwin (Orr) 1903-1983 .... **CLC 48**
See also CA 138; 110

de Nerval, Gerard
See Nerval, Gerard de

Denham, John 1615-1669 .... **LC 73**
See also DLB 58, 126; RGEL 2

Denis, Julio
See Cortazar, Julio

Dr. A
See Asimov, Isaac; Silverstein, Alvin; Silverstein, Virginia B(arbara Opshelor)

Drabble, Margaret 1939- ...... **CLC 2, 3, 5, 8, 10, 22, 53, 129**
See also BRWS 4; CA 13-16R; CANR 18, 35, 63, 112, 131; CDBLB 1960 to Present; CN 7; CPW; DA3; DAB; DAC; DAM MST, NOV, POP; DLB 14, 155, 231; EWL 3; FW; MTCW 1, 2; RGEL 2; SATA 48; TEA

Drakulic, Slavenka 1949- .... **CLC 173**
See also CA 144; CANR 92

Drakulic-Ilic, Slavenka
See Drakulic, Slavenka

Drapier, M. B.
See Swift, Jonathan

Drayham, James
See Mencken, H(enry) L(ouis)

Drayton, Michael 1563-1631 .... **LC 8**
See also DAM POET; DLB 121; RGEL 2

Dreadstone, Carl
See Campbell, (John) Ramsey

Dreiser, Theodore (Herman Albert) 1871-1945 .... **SSC 30; TCLC 10, 18, 35, 83; WLC**
See also AMW; AMWC 2; AMWR 2; BYA 15, 16; CA 106; 132; CDALB 1865-1917; DA; DA3; DAC; DAM MST, NOV; DLB 9, 12, 102, 137; DLBD 1; EWL 3; LAIT 2; LMFS 2; MTCW 1, 2; NFS 8, 17; RGAL 4; TUS

Drexler, Rosalyn 1926- .... **CLC 2, 6**
See also CA 81-84; CAD; CANR 68, 124; CD 5; CWD

Dreyer, Carl Theodor 1889-1968 ...... **CLC 16**
See also CA 116

Drieu la Rochelle, Pierre(-Eugene) 1893-1945 .... **TCLC 21**
See also CA 117; DLB 72; EWL 3; GFL 1789 to the Present

Drinkwater, John 1882-1937 .... **TCLC 57**
See also CA 109; 149; DLB 10, 19, 149; RGEL 2

Drop Shot
See Cable, George Washington

Droste-Hulshoff, Annette Freiin von 1797-1848 .... **NCLC 3, 133**
See also CDWLB 2; DLB 133; RGSF 2; RGWL 2, 3

Drummond, Walter
See Silverberg, Robert

Drummond, William Henry 1854-1907 .... **TCLC 25**
See also CA 160; DLB 92

Drummond de Andrade, Carlos 1902-1987 .... **CLC 18; TCLC 139**
See Andrade, Carlos Drummond de
See also CA 132; 123; DLB 307; LAW

Drummond of Hawthornden, William 1585-1649 .... **LC 83**
See also DLB 121, 213; RGEL 2

Drury, Allen (Stuart) 1918-1998 .... **CLC 37**
See also CA 57-60; 170; CANR 18, 52; CN 7; INT CANR-18

Druse, Eleanor
See King, Stephen (Edwin)

Dryden, John 1631-1700 ..... **DC 3; LC 3, 21, 115; PC 25; WLC**
See also BRW 2; CDBLB 1660-1789; DA; DAB; DAC; DAM DRAM, MST, POET; DLB 80, 101, 131; EXPP; IDTP; LMFS 1; RGEL 2; TEA; WLIT 3

du Bellay, Joachim 1524-1560 .... **LC 92**
See also GFL Beginnings to 1789; RGWL 2, 3

Duberman, Martin (Bauml) 1930- ..... **CLC 8**
See also CA 1-4R; CAD; CANR 2, 63; CD 5

Dubie, Norman (Evans) 1945- .... **CLC 36**
See also CA 69-72; CANR 12, 115; CP 7; DLB 120; PFS 12

Du Bois, W(illiam) E(dward) B(urghardt) 1868-1963 ..... **BLC 1; CLC 1, 2, 13, 64, 96; HR 2; WLC**
See also AAYA 40; AFAW 1, 2; AMWC 1; AMWS 2; BW 1, 3; CA 85-88; CANR 34, 82, 132; CDALB 1865-1917; DA; DA3; DAC; DAM MST, MULT; DLB 47, 50, 91, 246, 284; EWL 3; EXPP; LAIT 2; LMFS 2; MTCW 1, 2; NCFS 1; PFS 13; RGAL 4; SATA 42

Dubus, Andre 1936-1999 ..... **CLC 13, 36, 97; SSC 15**
See also AMWS 7; CA 21-24R; 177; CANR 17; CN 7; CSW; DLB 130; INT CANR-17; RGAL 4; SSFS 10

Duca Minimo
See D'Annunzio, Gabriele

Ducharme, Rejean 1941- .... **CLC 74**
See also CA 165; DLB 60

du Chatelet, Emilie 1706-1749 .... **LC 96**

Duchen, Claire .... **CLC 65**

Duclos, Charles Pinot- 1704-1772 .... **LC 1**
See also GFL Beginnings to 1789

Dudek, Louis 1918-2001 .... **CLC 11, 19**
See also CA 45-48; 215; CAAS 14; CANR 1; CP 7; DLB 88

Duerrenmatt, Friedrich 1921-1990 ... **CLC 1, 4, 8, 11, 15, 43, 102**
See Durrenmatt, Friedrich
See also CA 17-20R; CANR 33; CMW 4; DAM DRAM; DLB 69, 124; MTCW 1, 2

Duffy, Bruce 1953(?)- .... **CLC 50**
See also CA 172

Duffy, Maureen 1933- .... **CLC 37**
See also CA 25-28R; CANR 33, 68; CBD; CN 7; CP 7; CWD; CWP; DFS 15; DLB 14; FW; MTCW 1

Du Fu
See Tu Fu
See also RGWL 2, 3

Dugan, Alan 1923-2003 .... **CLC 2, 6**
See also CA 81-84; 220; CANR 119; CP 7; DLB 5; PFS 10

du Gard, Roger Martin
See Martin du Gard, Roger

Duhamel, Georges 1884-1966 .... **CLC 8**
See also CA 81-84; 25-28R; CANR 35; DLB 65; EWL 3; GFL 1789 to the Present; MTCW 1

Dujardin, Edouard (Emile Louis) 1861-1949 .... **TCLC 13**
See also CA 109; DLB 123

Duke, Raoul
See Thompson, Hunter S(tockton)

Dulles, John Foster 1888-1959 .... **TCLC 72**
See also CA 115; 149

Dumas, Alexandre (pere) 1802-1870 .... **NCLC 11, 71; WLC**
See also AAYA 22; BYA 3; DA; DA3; DAB; DAC; DAM MST, NOV; DLB 119, 192; EW 6; GFL 1789 to the Present; LAIT 1, 2; NFS 14, 19; RGWL 2, 3; SATA 18; TWA; WCH

Dumas, Alexandre (fils) 1824-1895 ...... **DC 1; NCLC 9**
See also DLB 192; GFL 1789 to the Present; RGWL 2, 3

Dumas, Claudine
See Malzberg, Barry N(athaniel)

Dumas, Henry L. 1934-1968 .... **CLC 6, 62**
See also BW 1; CA 85-88; DLB 41; RGAL 4

du Maurier, Daphne 1907-1989 .. **CLC 6, 11, 59; SSC 18**
See also AAYA 37; BPFB 1; BRWS 3; CA 5-8R; 128; CANR 6, 55; CMW 4; CPW; DA3; DAB; DAC; DAM MST, POP; DLB 191; HGG; LAIT 3; MSW; MTCW 1, 2; NFS 12; RGEL 2; RGSF 2; RHW; SATA 27; SATA-Obit 60; SSFS 14, 16; TEA

Du Maurier, George 1834-1896 ..... **NCLC 86**
See also DLB 153, 178; RGEL 2

Dunbar, Paul Laurence 1872-1906 ... **BLC 1; PC 5; SSC 8; TCLC 2, 12; WLC**
See also AFAW 1, 2; AMWS 2; BW 1, 3; CA 104; 124; CANR 79; CDALB 1865-1917; DA; DA3; DAC; DAM MST, MULT, POET; DLB 50, 54, 78; EXPP; RGAL 4; SATA 34

Dunbar, William 1460(?)-1520(?) .... **LC 20**
See also BRWS 8; DLB 132, 146; RGEL 2

Dunbar-Nelson, Alice .... **HR 2**
See Nelson, Alice Ruth Moore Dunbar

Duncan, Dora Angela
See Duncan, Isadora

Duncan, Isadora 1877(?)-1927 .... **TCLC 68**
See also CA 118; 149

Duncan, Lois 1934- .... **CLC 26**
See also AAYA 4, 34; BYA 6, 8; CA 1-4R; CANR 2, 23, 36, 111; CLR 29; JRDA; MAICYA 1, 2; MAICYAS 1; SAAS 2; SATA 1, 36, 75, 133, 141; SATA-Essay 141; WYA; YAW

Duncan, Robert (Edward) 1919-1988 .... **CLC 1, 2, 4, 7, 15, 41, 55; PC 2**
See also BG 2; CA 9-12R; 124; CANR 28, 62; DAM POET; DLB 5, 16, 193; EWL 3; MTCW 1, 2; PFS 13; RGAL 4; WP

Duncan, Sara Jeannette 1861-1922 .... **TCLC 60**
See also CA 157; DLB 92

Dunlap, William 1766-1839 .... **NCLC 2**
See also DLB 30, 37, 59; RGAL 4

Dunn, Douglas (Eaglesham) 1942- .... **CLC 6, 40**
See also BRWS 10; CA 45-48; CANR 2, 33, 126; CP 7; DLB 40; MTCW 1

Dunn, Katherine (Karen) 1945- .... **CLC 71**
See also CA 33-36R; CANR 72; HGG; MTCW 1

Dunn, Stephen (Elliott) 1939- .. **CLC 36, 206**
See also AMWS 11; CA 33-36R; CANR 12, 48, 53, 105; CP 7; DLB 105; PFS 21

Dunne, Finley Peter 1867-1936 .... **TCLC 28**
See also CA 108; 178; DLB 11, 23; RGAL 4

Dunne, John Gregory 1932-2003 ..... **CLC 28**
See also CA 25-28R; 222; CANR 14, 50; CN 7; DLBY 1980

Dunsany, Lord .... **TCLC 2, 59**
See Dunsany, Edward John Moreton Drax Plunkett
See also DLB 77, 153, 156, 255; FANT; IDTP; RGEL 2; SFW 4; SUFW 1

Dunsany, Edward John Moreton Drax Plunkett 1878-1957
See Dunsany, Lord
See also CA 104; 148; DLB 10; MTCW 1

Duns Scotus, John 1266(?)-1308 ... **CMLC 59**
See also DLB 115

du Perry, Jean
See Simenon, Georges (Jacques Christian)

Durang, Christopher (Ferdinand) 1949- .... **CLC 27, 38**
See also CA 105; CAD; CANR 50, 76, 130; CD 5; MTCW 1

Fox, William Price (Jr.) 1926- .... **CLC 22**
See also CA 17-20R; CAAS 19; CANR 11;
CSW; DLB 2; DLBY 1981

Foxe, John 1517(?)-1587 .... **LC 14**
See also DLB 132

Frame, Janet .. **CLC 2, 3, 6, 22, 66, 96; SSC
29**
See Clutha, Janet Paterson Frame
See also CN 7; CWP; EWL 3; RGEL 2;
RGSF 2; TWA

France, Anatole .... **TCLC 9**
See Thibault, Jacques Anatole Francois
See also DLB 123; EWL 3; GFL 1789 to
the Present; MTCW 1; RGWL 2, 3;
SUFW 1

Francis, Claude .... **CLC 50**
See also CA 192

Francis, Richard Stanley 1920- ... **CLC 2, 22,
42, 102**
See also AAYA 5, 21; BEST 89:3; BPFB 1;
CA 5-8R; CANR 9, 42, 68, 100; CDBLB
1960 to Present; CMW 4; CN 7; DA3;
DAM POP; DLB 87; INT CANR-9;
MSW; MTCW 1, 2

Francis, Robert (Churchill)
1901-1987 .... **CLC 15; PC 34**
See also AMWS 9; CA 1-4R; 123; CANR
1; EXPP; PFS 12

Francis, Lord Jeffrey
See Jeffrey, Francis
See also DLB 107

Frank, Anne(lies Marie)
1929-1945 .... **TCLC 17; WLC**
See also AAYA 12; BYA 1; CA 113; 133;
CANR 68; CLR 101; DA; DA3; DAB;
DAC; DAM MST; LAIT 4; MAICYA 1;
MAICYAS 1; MTCW 1, 2; NCFS 2;
SATA 87; SATA-Brief 42; WYA; YAW

Frank, Bruno 1887-1945 .... **TCLC 81**
See also CA 189; DLB 118; EWL 3

Frank, Elizabeth 1945- .... **CLC 39**
See also CA 121; 126; CANR 78; INT CA-
126

Frankl, Viktor E(mil) 1905-1997 ...... **CLC 93**
See also CA 65-68; 161

Franklin, Benjamin
See Hasek, Jaroslav (Matej Frantisek)

Franklin, Benjamin 1706-1790 .... **LC 25;
WLCS**
See also AMW; CDALB 1640-1865; DA;
DA3; DAB; DAC; DAM MST; DLB 24,
43, 73, 183; LAIT 1; RGAL 4; TUS

**Franklin, (Stella Maria Sarah) Miles
(Lampe)** 1879-1954 .... **TCLC 7**
See also CA 104; 164; DLB 230; FW;
MTCW 2; RGEL 2; TWA

Franzen, Jonathan 1959- .... **CLC 202**
See also CA 129; CANR 105

Fraser, Antonia (Pakenham) 1932- . **CLC 32,
107**
See also AAYA 57; CA 85-88; CANR 44,
65, 119; CMW; DLB 276; MTCW 1, 2;
SATA-Brief 32

Fraser, George MacDonald 1925- ...... **CLC 7**
See also AAYA 48; CA 45-48; 180; CAAE
180; CANR 2, 48, 74; MTCW 1; RHW

Fraser, Sylvia 1935- .... **CLC 64**
See also CA 45-48; CANR 1, 16, 60; CCA
1

Frayn, Michael 1933- . **CLC 3, 7, 31, 47, 176**
See also BRWC 2; BRWS 7; CA 5-8R;
CANR 30, 69, 114, 133; CBD; CD 5; CN
7; DAM DRAM, NOV; DLB 13, 14, 194,
245; FANT; MTCW 1, 2; SFW 4

Fraze, Candida (Merrill) 1945- .... **CLC 50**
See also CA 126

Frazer, Andrew
See Marlowe, Stephen

Frazer, J(ames) G(eorge)
1854-1941 .... **TCLC 32**
See also BRWS 3; CA 118; NCFS 5

Frazer, Robert Caine
See Creasey, John

Frazer, Sir James George
See Frazer, J(ames) G(eorge)

Frazier, Charles 1950- .... **CLC 109**
See also AAYA 34; CA 161; CANR 126;
CSW; DLB 292

Frazier, Ian 1951- .... **CLC 46**
See also CA 130; CANR 54, 93

Frederic, Harold 1856-1898 .... **NCLC 10**
See also AMW; DLB 12, 23; DLBD 13;
RGAL 4

Frederick, John
See Faust, Frederick (Schiller)
See also TCWW 2

Frederick the Great 1712-1786 .... **LC 14**

Fredro, Aleksander 1793-1876 .... **NCLC 8**

Freeling, Nicolas 1927-2003 .... **CLC 38**
See also CA 49-52; 218; CAAS 12; CANR
1, 17, 50, 84; CMW 4; CN 7; DLB 87

Freeman, Douglas Southall
1886-1953 .... **TCLC 11**
See also CA 109; 195; DLB 17; DLBD 17

Freeman, Judith 1946- .... **CLC 55**
See also CA 148; CANR 120; DLB 256

Freeman, Mary E(leanor) Wilkins
1852-1930 .... **SSC 1, 47; TCLC 9**
See also CA 106; 177; DLB 12, 78, 221;
EXPS; FW; HGG; MAWW; RGAL 4;
RGSF 2; SSFS 4, 8; SUFW 1; TUS

Freeman, R(ichard) Austin
1862-1943 .... **TCLC 21**
See also CA 113; CANR 84; CMW 4; DLB
70

French, Albert 1943- .... **CLC 86**
See also BW 3; CA 167

French, Antonia
See Kureishi, Hanif

French, Marilyn 1929- .. **CLC 10, 18, 60, 177**
See also BPFB 1; CA 69-72; CANR 3, 31,
134; CN 7; CPW; DAM DRAM, NOV,
POP; FW; INT CANR-31; MTCW 1, 2

French, Paul
See Asimov, Isaac

Freneau, Philip Morin 1752-1832 .. **NCLC 1,
111**
See also AMWS 2; DLB 37, 43; RGAL 4

Freud, Sigmund 1856-1939 .... **TCLC 52**
See also CA 115; 133; CANR 69; DLB 296;
EW 8; EWL 3; LATS 1:1; MTCW 1, 2;
NCFS 3; TWA

Freytag, Gustav 1816-1895 .... **NCLC 109**
See also DLB 129

Friedan, Betty (Naomi) 1921- .... **CLC 74**
See also CA 65-68; CANR 18, 45, 74; DLB
246; FW; MTCW 1, 2; NCFS 5

Friedlander, Saul 1932- .... **CLC 90**
See also CA 117; 130; CANR 72

Friedman, B(ernard) H(arper)
1926- .... **CLC 7**
See also CA 1-4R; CANR 3, 48

Friedman, Bruce Jay 1930- ...... **CLC 3, 5, 56**
See also CA 9-12R; CAD; CANR 25, 52,
101; CD 5; CN 7; DLB 2, 28, 244; INT
CANR-25; SSFS 18

Friel, Brian 1929- .... **CLC 5, 42, 59, 115; DC
8; SSC 76**
See also BRWS 5; CA 21-24R; CANR 33,
69, 131; CBD; CD 5; DFS 11; DLB 13;
EWL 3; MTCW 1; RGEL 2; TEA

Friis-Baastad, Babbis Ellinor
1921-1970 .... **CLC 12**
See also CA 17-20R; 134; SATA 7

Frisch, Max (Rudolf) 1911-1991 ... **CLC 3, 9,
14, 18, 32, 44; TCLC 121**
See also CA 85-88; 134; CANR 32, 74; CD-
WLB 2; DAM DRAM, NOV; DLB 69,
124; EW 13; EWL 3; MTCW 1, 2; RGWL
2, 3

Fromentin, Eugene (Samuel Auguste)
1820-1876 .... **NCLC 10, 125**
See also DLB 123; GFL 1789 to the Present

Frost, Frederick
See Faust, Frederick (Schiller)
See also TCWW 2

Frost, Robert (Lee) 1874-1963 .. **CLC 1, 3, 4,
9, 10, 13, 15, 26, 34, 44; PC 1, 39;
WLC**
See also AAYA 21; AMW; AMWR 1; CA
89-92; CANR 33; CDALB 1917-1929;
CLR 67; DA; DA3; DAB; DAC; DAM
MST, POET; DLB 54, 284; DLBD 7;
EWL 3; EXPP; MTCW 1, 2; PAB; PFS 1,
2, 3, 4, 5, 6, 7, 10, 13; RGAL 4; SATA
14; TUS; WP; WYA

Froude, James Anthony
1818-1894 .... **NCLC 43**
See also DLB 18, 57, 144

Froy, Herald
See Waterhouse, Keith (Spencer)

Fry, Christopher 1907- .... **CLC 2, 10, 14**
See also BRWS 3; CA 17-20R; CAAS 23;
CANR 9, 30, 74, 132; CBD; CD 5; CP 7;
DAM DRAM; DLB 13; EWL 3; MTCW
1, 2; RGEL 2; SATA 66; TEA

Frye, (Herman) Northrop
1912-1991 .... **CLC 24, 70; TCLC 165**
See also CA 5-8R; 133; CANR 8, 37; DLB
67, 68, 246; EWL 3; MTCW 1, 2; RGAL
4; TWA

Fuchs, Daniel 1909-1993 .... **CLC 8, 22**
See also CA 81-84; 142; CAAS 5; CANR
40; DLB 9, 26, 28; DLBY 1993

Fuchs, Daniel 1934- .... **CLC 34**
See also CA 37-40R; CANR 14, 48

Fuentes, Carlos 1928- .. **CLC 3, 8, 10, 13, 22,
41, 60, 113; HLC 1; SSC 24; WLC**
See also AAYA 4, 45; AITN 2; BPFB 1;
CA 69-72; CANR 10, 32, 68, 104; CD-
WLB 3; CWW 2; DA; DA3; DAB; DAC;
DAM MST, MULT, NOV; DLB 113;
DNFS 2; EWL 3; HW 1, 2; LAIT 3; LATS
1:2; LAW; LAWS 1; LMFS 2; MTCW 1,
2; NFS 8; RGSF 2; RGWL 2, 3; TWA;
WLIT 1

Fuentes, Gregorio Lopez y
See Lopez y Fuentes, Gregorio

Fuertes, Gloria 1918-1998 .... **PC 27**
See also CA 178; 180; DLB 108; HW 2;
SATA 115

Fugard, (Harold) Athol 1932- . **CLC 5, 9, 14,
25, 40, 80, 211; DC 3**
See also AAYA 17; AFW; CA 85-88; CANR
32, 54, 118; CD 5; DAM DRAM; DFS 3,
6, 10; DLB 225; DNFS 1, 2; EWL 3;
LATS 1:2; MTCW 1; RGEL 2; WLIT 2

Fugard, Sheila 1932- .... **CLC 48**
See also CA 125

Fukuyama, Francis 1952- .... **CLC 131**
See also CA 140; CANR 72, 125

Fuller, Charles (H.), (Jr.) 1939- .... **BLC 2;
CLC 25; DC 1**
See also BW 2; CA 108; 112; CAD; CANR
87; CD 5; DAM DRAM, MULT; DFS 8;
DLB 38, 266; EWL 3; INT CA-112;
MTCW 1

Fuller, Henry Blake 1857-1929 .... **TCLC 103**
See also CA 108; 177; DLB 12; RGAL 4

Fuller, John (Leopold) 1937- .... **CLC 62**
See also CA 21-24R; CANR 9, 44; CP 7;
DLB 40

Garrigue, Jean 1914-1972 .... **CLC 2, 8**
See also CA 5-8R; 37-40R; CANR 20
Garrison, Frederick
See Sinclair, Upton (Beall)
Garrison, William Lloyd
1805-1879 .... **NCLC 149**
See also CDALB 1640-1865; DLB 1, 43, 235
Garro, Elena 1920(?)-1998 .. **HLCS 1; TCLC 153**
See also CA 131; 169; CWW 2; DLB 145; EWL 3; HW 1; LAWS 1; WLIT 1
Garth, Will
See Hamilton, Edmond; Kuttner, Henry
Garvey, Marcus (Moziah, Jr.)
1887-1940 .... **BLC 2; HR 2; TCLC 41**
See also BW 1; CA 120; 124; CANR 79; DAM MULT
Gary, Romain .... **CLC 25**
See Kacew, Romain
See also DLB 83, 299
Gascar, Pierre .... **CLC 11**
See Fournier, Pierre
See also EWL 3
Gascoigne, George 1539-1577 .... **LC 108**
See also DLB 136; RGEL 2
Gascoyne, David (Emery)
1916-2001 .... **CLC 45**
See also CA 65-68; 200; CANR 10, 28, 54; CP 7; DLB 20; MTCW 1; RGEL 2
Gaskell, Elizabeth Cleghorn
1810-1865 .... **NCLC 5, 70, 97, 137; SSC 25**
See also BRW 5; CDBLB 1832-1890; DAB; DAM MST; DLB 21, 144, 159; RGEL 2; RGSF 2; TEA
Gass, William H(oward) 1924- . **CLC 1, 2, 8, 11, 15, 39, 132; SSC 12**
See also AMWS 6; CA 17-20R; CANR 30, 71, 100; CN 7; DLB 2, 227; EWL 3; MTCW 1, 2; RGAL 4
Gassendi, Pierre 1592-1655 .... **LC 54**
See also GFL Beginnings to 1789
Gasset, Jose Ortega y
See Ortega y Gasset, Jose
Gates, Henry Louis, Jr. 1950- ... **BLCS; CLC 65**
See also BW 2, 3; CA 109; CANR 25, 53, 75, 125; CSW; DA3; DAM MULT; DLB 67; EWL 3; MTCW 1; RGAL 4
Gautier, Theophile 1811-1872 .. **NCLC 1, 59; PC 18; SSC 20**
See also DAM POET; DLB 119; EW 6; GFL 1789 to the Present; RGWL 2, 3; SUFW; TWA
Gawsworth, John
See Bates, H(erbert) E(rnest)
Gay, John 1685-1732 .... **LC 49**
See also BRW 3; DAM DRAM; DLB 84, 95; RGEL 2; WLIT 3
Gay, Oliver
See Gogarty, Oliver St. John
Gay, Peter (Jack) 1923- .... **CLC 158**
See also CA 13-16R; CANR 18, 41, 77; INT CANR-18
Gaye, Marvin (Pentz, Jr.)
1939-1984 .... **CLC 26**
See also CA 195; 112
Gebler, Carlo (Ernest) 1954- .... **CLC 39**
See also CA 119; 133; CANR 96; DLB 271
Gee, Maggie (Mary) 1948- .... **CLC 57**
See also CA 130; CANR 125; CN 7; DLB 207
Gee, Maurice (Gough) 1931- .... **CLC 29**
See also AAYA 42; CA 97-100; CANR 67, 123; CLR 56; CN 7; CWRI 5; EWL 3; MAICYA 2; RGSF 2; SATA 46, 101
Geiogamah, Hanay 1945- .... **NNAL**
See also CA 153; DAM MULT; DLB 175

Gelbart, Larry (Simon) 1928- .... **CLC 21, 61**
See Gelbart, Larry
See also CA 73-76; CANR 45, 94
Gelbart, Larry 1928-
See Gelbart, Larry (Simon)
See also CAD; CD 5
Gelber, Jack 1932-2003 ...... **CLC 1, 6, 14, 79**
See also CA 1-4R; 216; CAD; CANR 2; DLB 7, 228
Gellhorn, Martha (Ellis)
1908-1998 .... **CLC 14, 60**
See also CA 77-80; 164; CANR 44; CN 7; DLBY 1982, 1998
Genet, Jean 1910-1986 . **DC 25; CLC 1, 2, 5, 10, 14, 44, 46; TCLC 128**
See also CA 13-16R; CANR 18; DA3; DAM DRAM; DFS 10; DLB 72; DLBY 1986; EW 13; EWL 3; GFL 1789 to the Present; GLL 1; LMFS 2; MTCW 1, 2; RGWL 2, 3; TWA
Gent, Peter 1942- .... **CLC 29**
See also AITN 1; CA 89-92; DLBY 1982
Gentile, Giovanni 1875-1944 .... **TCLC 96**
See also CA 119
Gentlewoman in New England, A
See Bradstreet, Anne
Gentlewoman in Those Parts, A
See Bradstreet, Anne
Geoffrey of Monmouth c.
1100-1155 .... **CMLC 44**
See also DLB 146; TEA
George, Jean
See George, Jean Craighead
George, Jean Craighead 1919- .... **CLC 35**
See also AAYA 8; BYA 2, 4; CA 5-8R; CANR 25; CLR 1; 80; DLB 52; JRDA; MAICYA 1, 2; SATA 2, 68, 124; WYA; YAW
George, Stefan (Anton) 1868-1933 . **TCLC 2, 14**
See also CA 104; 193; EW 8; EWL 3
Georges, Georges Martin
See Simenon, Georges (Jacques Christian)
Gerald of Wales c. 1146-c. 1223 ... **CMLC 60**
Gerhardi, William Alexander
See Gerhardie, William Alexander
Gerhardie, William Alexander
1895-1977 .... **CLC 5**
See also CA 25-28R; 73-76; CANR 18; DLB 36; RGEL 2
Gerson, Jean 1363-1429 .... **LC 77**
See also DLB 208
Gersonides 1288-1344 .... **CMLC 49**
See also DLB 115
Gerstler, Amy 1956- .... **CLC 70**
See also CA 146; CANR 99
Gertler, T. .... **CLC 34**
See also CA 116; 121
Gertsen, Aleksandr Ivanovich
See Herzen, Aleksandr Ivanovich
Ghalib .... **NCLC 39, 78**
See Ghalib, Asadullah Khan
Ghalib, Asadullah Khan 1797-1869
See Ghalib
See also DAM POET; RGWL 2, 3
Ghelderode, Michel de 1898-1962 ..... **CLC 6, 11; DC 15**
See also CA 85-88; CANR 40, 77; DAM DRAM; EW 11; EWL 3; TWA
Ghiselin, Brewster 1903-2001 .... **CLC 23**
See also CA 13-16R; CAAS 10; CANR 13; CP 7
Ghose, Aurabinda 1872-1950 .... **TCLC 63**
See Ghose, Aurobindo
See also CA 163
Ghose, Aurobindo
See Ghose, Aurabinda
See also EWL 3

Ghose, Zulfikar 1935- .... **CLC 42, 200**
See also CA 65-68; CANR 67; CN 7; CP 7; EWL 3
Ghosh, Amitav 1956- .... **CLC 44, 153**
See also CA 147; CANR 80; CN 7; WWE 1
Giacosa, Giuseppe 1847-1906 .... **TCLC 7**
See also CA 104
Gibb, Lee
See Waterhouse, Keith (Spencer)
Gibbon, Edward 1737-1794 .... **LC 97**
See also BRW 3; DLB 104; RGEL 2
Gibbon, Lewis Grassic .... **TCLC 4**
See Mitchell, James Leslie
See also RGEL 2
Gibbons, Kaye 1960- .... **CLC 50, 88, 145**
See also AAYA 34; AMWS 10; CA 151; CANR 75, 127; CSW; DA3; DAM POP; DLB 292; MTCW 1; NFS 3; RGAL 4; SATA 117
Gibran, Kahlil 1883-1931 . **PC 9; TCLC 1, 9**
See also CA 104; 150; DA3; DAM POET, POP; EWL 3; MTCW 2
Gibran, Khalil
See Gibran, Kahlil
Gibson, William 1914- .... **CLC 23**
See also CA 9-12R; CAD 2; CANR 9, 42, 75, 125; CD 5; DA; DAB; DAC; DAM DRAM, MST; DFS 2; DLB 7; LAIT 2; MTCW 2; SATA 66; YAW
Gibson, William (Ford) 1948- ... **CLC 39, 63, 186, 192; SSC 52**
See also AAYA 12, 59; BPFB 2; CA 126; 133; CANR 52, 90, 106; CN 7; CPW; DA3; DAM POP; DLB 251; MTCW 2; SCFW 2; SFW 4
Gide, Andre (Paul Guillaume)
1869-1951 ..... **SSC 13; TCLC 5, 12, 36; WLC**
See also CA 104; 124; DA; DA3; DAB; DAC; DAM MST, NOV; DLB 65; EW 8; EWL 3; GFL 1789 to the Present; MTCW 1, 2; RGSF 2; RGWL 2, 3; TWA
Gifford, Barry (Colby) 1946- .... **CLC 34**
See also CA 65-68; CANR 9, 30, 40, 90
Gilbert, Frank
See De Voto, Bernard (Augustine)
Gilbert, W(illiam) S(chwenck)
1836-1911 .... **TCLC 3**
See also CA 104; 173; DAM DRAM, POET; RGEL 2; SATA 36
Gilbreth, Frank B(unker), Jr.
1911-2001 .... **CLC 17**
See also CA 9-12R; SATA 2
Gilchrist, Ellen (Louise) 1935- .. **CLC 34, 48, 143; SSC 14, 63**
See also BPFB 2; CA 113; 116; CANR 41, 61, 104; CN 7; CPW; CSW; DAM POP; DLB 130; EWL 3; EXPS; MTCW 1, 2; RGAL 4; RGSF 2; SSFS 9
Giles, Molly 1942- .... **CLC 39**
See also CA 126; CANR 98
Gill, Eric 1882-1940 .... **TCLC 85**
See Gill, (Arthur) Eric (Rowton Peter Joseph)
Gill, (Arthur) Eric (Rowton Peter Joseph)
1882-1940
See Gill, Eric
See also CA 120; DLB 98
Gill, Patrick
See Creasey, John
Gillette, Douglas .... **CLC 70**
Gilliam, Terry (Vance) 1940- .... **CLC 21, 141**
See Monty Python
See also AAYA 19, 59; CA 108; 113; CANR 35; INT CA-113
Gillian, Jerry
See Gilliam, Terry (Vance)

Gilliatt, Penelope (Ann Douglass)
1932-1993 .... **CLC 2, 10, 13, 53**
See also AITN 2; CA 13-16R; 141; CANR
49; DLB 14

Gilligan, Carol 1936- .... **CLC 208**
See also CA 142; CANR 121; FW

Gilman, Charlotte (Anna) Perkins (Stetson)
1860-1935 ...... **SSC 13, 62; TCLC 9, 37,
117**
See also AMWS 11; BYA 11; CA 106; 150;
DLB 221; EXPS; FW; HGG; LAIT 2;
MAWW; MTCW 1; RGAL 4; RGSF 2;
SFW 4; SSFS 1, 18

Gilmour, David 1946- .... **CLC 35**

Gilpin, William 1724-1804 .... **NCLC 30**

Gilray, J. D.
See Mencken, H(enry) L(ouis)

Gilroy, Frank D(aniel) 1925- .... **CLC 2**
See also CA 81-84; CAD; CANR 32, 64,
86; CD 5; DFS 17; DLB 7

Gilstrap, John 1957(?)- .... **CLC 99**
See also CA 160; CANR 101

Ginsberg, Allen 1926-1997 .... **CLC 1, 2, 3, 4,
6, 13, 36, 69, 109; PC 4, 47; TCLC
120; WLC**
See also AAYA 33; AITN 1; AMWC 1;
AMWS 2; BG 2; CA 1-4R; 157; CANR
2, 41, 63, 95; CDALB 1941-1968; CP 7;
DA; DA3; DAB; DAC; DAM MST,
POET; DLB 5, 16, 169, 237; EWL 3; GLL
1; LMFS 2; MTCW 1, 2; PAB; PFS 5;
RGAL 4; TUS; WP

Ginzburg, Eugenia .... **CLC 59**
See Ginzburg, Evgeniia

Ginzburg, Evgeniia 1904-1977
See Ginzburg, Eugenia
See also DLB 302

Ginzburg, Natalia 1916-1991 .... **CLC 5, 11,
54, 70; SSC 65; TCLC 156**
See also CA 85-88; 135; CANR 33; DFS
14; DLB 177; EW 13; EWL 3; MTCW 1,
2; RGWL 2, 3

Giono, Jean 1895-1970 .... **CLC 4, 11; TCLC
124**
See also CA 45-48; 29-32R; CANR 2, 35;
DLB 72; EWL 3; GFL 1789 to the
Present; MTCW 1; RGWL 2, 3

Giovanni, Nikki 1943- ...... **BLC 2; CLC 2, 4,
19, 64, 117; PC 19; WLCS**
See also AAYA 22; AITN 1; BW 2, 3; CA
29-32R; CAAS 6; CANR 18, 41, 60, 91,
130; CDALBS; CLR 6, 73; CP 7; CSW;
CWP; CWRI 5; DA; DA3; DAB; DAC;
DAM MST, MULT, POET; DLB 5, 41;
EWL 3; EXPP; INT CANR-18; MAICYA
1, 2; MTCW 1, 2; PFS 17; RGAL 4;
SATA 24, 107; TUS; YAW

Giovene, Andrea 1904-1998 .... **CLC 7**
See also CA 85-88

Gippius, Zinaida (Nikolaevna) 1869-1945
See Hippius, Zinaida (Nikolaevna)
See also CA 106; 212

Giraudoux, Jean(-Hippolyte)
1882-1944 .... **TCLC 2, 7**
See also CA 104; 196; DAM DRAM; DLB
65; EW 9; EWL 3; GFL 1789 to the
Present; RGWL 2, 3; TWA

Gironella, Jose Maria (Pous)
1917-2003 .... **CLC 11**
See also CA 101; 212; EWL 3; RGWL 2, 3

Gissing, George (Robert)
1857-1903 .... **SSC 37; TCLC 3, 24, 47**
See also BRW 5; CA 105; 167; DLB 18,
135, 184; RGEL 2; TEA

Gitlin, Todd 1943- .... **CLC 201**
See also CA 29-32R; CANR 25, 50, 88

Giurlani, Aldo
See Palazzeschi, Aldo

Gladkov, Fedor Vasil'evich
See Gladkov, Fyodor (Vasilyevich)
See also DLB 272

Gladkov, Fyodor (Vasilyevich)
1883-1958 .... **TCLC 27**
See Gladkov, Fedor Vasil'evich
See also CA 170; EWL 3

Glancy, Diane 1941- .... **CLC 210; NNAL**
See also CA 136, 225; CAAE 225; CAAS
24; CANR 87; DLB 175

Glanville, Brian (Lester) 1931- .... **CLC 6**
See also CA 5-8R; CAAS 9; CANR 3, 70;
CN 7; DLB 15, 139; SATA 42

Glasgow, Ellen (Anderson Gholson)
1873-1945 .... **SSC 34; TCLC 2, 7**
See also AMW; CA 104; 164; DLB 9, 12;
MAWW; MTCW 2; RGAL 4; RHW;
SSFS 9; TUS

Glaspell, Susan 1882(?)-1948 ..... **DC 10; SSC
41; TCLC 55**
See also AMWS 3; CA 110; 154; DFS 8,
18; DLB 7, 9, 78, 228; MAWW; RGAL
4; SSFS 3; TCWW 2; TUS; YABC 2

Glassco, John 1909-1981 .... **CLC 9**
See also CA 13-16R; 102; CANR 15; DLB
68

Glasscock, Amnesia
See Steinbeck, John (Ernst)

Glasser, Ronald J. 1940(?)- .... **CLC 37**
See also CA 209

Glassman, Joyce
See Johnson, Joyce

Gleick, James (W.) 1954- .... **CLC 147**
See also CA 131; 137; CANR 97; INT CA-
137

Glendinning, Victoria 1937- .... **CLC 50**
See also CA 120; 127; CANR 59, 89; DLB
155

Glissant, Edouard (Mathieu)
1928- .... **CLC 10, 68**
See also CA 153; CANR 111; CWW 2;
DAM MULT; EWL 3; RGWL 3

Gloag, Julian 1930- .... **CLC 40**
See also AITN 1; CA 65-68; CANR 10, 70;
CN 7

Glowacki, Aleksander
See Prus, Boleslaw

Gluck, Louise (Elisabeth) 1943- .. **CLC 7, 22,
44, 81, 160; PC 16**
See also AMWS 5; CA 33-36R; CANR 40,
69, 108, 133; CP 7; CWP; DA3; DAM
POET; DLB 5; MTCW 2; PFS 5, 15;
RGAL 4

Glyn, Elinor 1864-1943 .... **TCLC 72**
See also DLB 153; RHW

Gobineau, Joseph-Arthur
1816-1882 .... **NCLC 17**
See also DLB 123; GFL 1789 to the Present

Godard, Jean-Luc 1930- .... **CLC 20**
See also CA 93-96

Godden, (Margaret) Rumer
1907-1998 .... **CLC 53**
See also AAYA 6; BPFB 2; BYA 2, 5; CA
5-8R; 172; CANR 4, 27, 36, 55, 80; CLR
20; CN 7; CWRI 5; DLB 161; MAICYA
1, 2; RHW; SAAS 12; SATA 3, 36; SATA-
Obit 109; TEA

Godoy Alcayaga, Lucila 1899-1957 .. **HLC 2;
PC 32; TCLC 2**
See Mistral, Gabriela
See also BW 2; CA 104; 131; CANR 81;
DAM MULT; DNFS 1; HW 1, 2; MTCW 1,
2

Godwin, Gail (Kathleen) 1937- ..... **CLC 5, 8,
22, 31, 69, 125**
See also BPFB 2; CA 29-32R; CANR 15,
43, 69, 132; CN 7; CPW; CSW; DA3;
DAM POP; DLB 6, 234; INT CANR-15;
MTCW 1, 2

Godwin, William 1756-1836 .. **NCLC 14, 130**
See also CDBLB 1789-1832; CMW 4; DLB
39, 104, 142, 158, 163, 262; HGG; RGEL
2

Goebbels, Josef
See Goebbels, (Paul) Joseph

Goebbels, (Paul) Joseph
1897-1945 .... **TCLC 68**
See also CA 115; 148

Goebbels, Joseph Paul
See Goebbels, (Paul) Joseph

Goethe, Johann Wolfgang von
1749-1832 . **DC 20; NCLC 4, 22, 34, 90,
154; PC 5; SSC 38; WLC**
See also CDWLB 2; DA; DA3; DAB;
DAC; DAM DRAM, MST, POET; DLB
94; EW 5; LATS 1; LMFS 1:1; RGWL 2,
3; TWA

Gogarty, Oliver St. John
1878-1957 .... **TCLC 15**
See also CA 109; 150; DLB 15, 19; RGEL
2

Gogol, Nikolai (Vasilyevich)
1809-1852 .... **DC 1; NCLC 5, 15, 31;
SSC 4, 29, 52; WLC**
See also DA; DAB; DAC; DAM DRAM,
MST; DFS 12; DLB 198; EW 6; EXPS;
RGSF 2; RGWL 2, 3; SSFS 7; TWA

Goines, Donald 1937(?)-1974 ... **BLC 2; CLC
80**
See also AITN 1; BW 1, 3; CA 124; 114;
CANR 82; CMW 4; DA3; DAM MULT,
POP; DLB 33

Gold, Herbert 1924- ... **CLC 4, 7, 14, 42, 152**
See also CA 9-12R; CANR 17, 45, 125; CN
7; DLB 2; DLBY 1981

Goldbarth, Albert 1948- .... **CLC 5, 38**
See also AMWS 12; CA 53-56; CANR 6,
40; CP 7; DLB 120

Goldberg, Anatol 1910-1982 .... **CLC 34**
See also CA 131; 117

Goldemberg, Isaac 1945- .... **CLC 52**
See also CA 69-72; CAAS 12; CANR 11,
32; EWL 3; HW 1; WLIT 1

Golding, Arthur 1536-1606 .... **LC 101**
See also DLB 136

Golding, William (Gerald)
1911-1993 ..... **CLC 1, 2, 3, 8, 10, 17, 27,
58, 81; WLC**
See also AAYA 5, 44; BPFB 2; BRWR 1;
BRWS 1; BYA 2; CA 5-8R; 141; CANR
13, 33, 54; CDBLB 1945-1960; CLR 94;
DA; DA3; DAB; DAC; DAM MST, NOV;
DLB 15, 100, 255; EWL 3; EXPN; HGG;
LAIT 4; MTCW 1, 2; NFS 2; RGEL 2;
RHW; SFW 4; TEA; WLIT 4; YAW

Goldman, Emma 1869-1940 .... **TCLC 13**
See also CA 110; 150; DLB 221; FW;
RGAL 4; TUS

Goldman, Francisco 1954- .... **CLC 76**
See also CA 162

Goldman, William (W.) 1931- ...... **CLC 1, 48**
See also BPFB 2; CA 9-12R; CANR 29,
69, 106; CN 7; DLB 44; FANT; IDFW 3,
4

Goldmann, Lucien 1913-1970 .... **CLC 24**
See also CA 25-28; CAP 2

Goldoni, Carlo 1707-1793 .... **LC 4**
See also DAM DRAM; EW 4; RGWL 2, 3

Goldsberry, Steven 1949- .... **CLC 34**
See also CA 131

Goldsmith, Oliver 1730-1774 .... **DC 8; LC 2,
48; WLC**
See also BRW 3; CDBLB 1660-1789; DA;
DAB; DAC; DAM DRAM, MST, NOV,
POET; DFS 1; DLB 39, 89, 104, 109, 142;
IDTP; RGEL 2; SATA 26; TEA; WLIT 3

Goldsmith, Peter
See Priestley, J(ohn) B(oynton)

Grove, Frederick Philip .... **TCLC 4**
See Greve, Felix Paul (Berthold Friedrich)
See also DLB 92; RGEL 2

Grubb
See Crumb, R(obert)

Grumbach, Doris (Isaac) 1918- . **CLC 13, 22, 64**
See also CA 5-8R; CAAS 2; CANR 9, 42, 70, 127; CN 7; INT CANR-9; MTCW 2

Grundtvig, Nikolai Frederik Severin 1783-1872 .... **NCLC 1, 158**
See also DLB 300

Grunge
See Crumb, R(obert)

Grunwald, Lisa 1959- .... **CLC 44**
See also CA 120

Gryphius, Andreas 1616-1664 .... **LC 89**
See also CDWLB 2; DLB 164; RGWL 2, 3

Guare, John 1938- .... **CLC 8, 14, 29, 67; DC 20**
See also CA 73-76; CAD; CANR 21, 69, 118; CD 5; DAM DRAM; DFS 8, 13; DLB 7, 249; EWL 3; MTCW 1, 2; RGAL 4

Guarini, Battista 1537-1612 .... **LC 102**

Gubar, Susan (David) 1944- .... **CLC 145**
See also CA 108; CANR 45, 70; FW; MTCW 1; RGAL 4

Gudjonsson, Halldor Kiljan 1902-1998
See Halldor Laxness
See also CA 103; 164

Guenter, Erich
See Eich, Gunter

Guest, Barbara 1920- .... **CLC 34; PC 55**
See also BG 2; CA 25-28R; CANR 11, 44, 84; CP 7; CWP; DLB 5, 193

Guest, Edgar A(lbert) 1881-1959 ... **TCLC 95**
See also CA 112; 168

Guest, Judith (Ann) 1936- .... **CLC 8, 30**
See also AAYA 7; CA 77-80; CANR 15, 75; DA3; DAM NOV, POP; EXPN; INT CANR-15; LAIT 5; MTCW 1, 2; NFS 1

Guevara, Che .... **CLC 87; HLC 1**
See Guevara (Serna), Ernesto

Guevara (Serna), Ernesto
1928-1967 .... **CLC 87; HLC 1**
See Guevara, Che
See also CA 127; 111; CANR 56; DAM MULT; HW 1

Guicciardini, Francesco 1483-1540 ..... **LC 49**

Guild, Nicholas M. 1944- .... **CLC 33**
See also CA 93-96

Guillemin, Jacques
See Sartre, Jean-Paul

Guillen, Jorge 1893-1984 . **CLC 11; HLCS 1; PC 35**
See also CA 89-92; 112; DAM MULT, POET; DLB 108; EWL 3; HW 1; RGWL 2, 3

Guillen, Nicolas (Cristobal)
1902-1989 .... **BLC 2; CLC 48, 79; HLC 1; PC 23**
See also BW 2; CA 116; 125; 129; CANR 84; DAM MST, MULT, POET; DLB 283; EWL 3; HW 1; LAW; RGWL 2, 3; WP

Guillen y Alvarez, Jorge
See Guillen, Jorge

Guillevic, (Eugene) 1907-1997 .... **CLC 33**
See also CA 93-96; CWW 2

Guillois
See Desnos, Robert

Guillois, Valentin
See Desnos, Robert

Guimaraes Rosa, Joao 1908-1967 .... **HLCS 2**
See Rosa, Joao Guimaraes
See also CA 175; LAW; RGSF 2; RGWL 2, 3

Guiney, Louise Imogen
1861-1920 .... **TCLC 41**
See also CA 160; DLB 54; RGAL 4

Guinizelli, Guido c. 1230-1276 ...... **CMLC 49**

Guiraldes, Ricardo (Guillermo)
1886-1927 .... **TCLC 39**
See also CA 131; EWL 3; HW 1; LAW; MTCW 1

Gumilev, Nikolai (Stepanovich)
1886-1921 .... **TCLC 60**
See Gumilyov, Nikolay Stepanovich
See also CA 165; DLB 295

Gumilyov, Nikolay Stepanovich
See Gumilev, Nikolai (Stepanovich)
See also EWL 3

Gump, P. Q.
See Card, Orson Scott

Gunesekera, Romesh 1954- .... **CLC 91**
See also BRWS 10; CA 159; CN 7; DLB 267

Gunn, Bill .... **CLC 5**
See Gunn, William Harrison
See also DLB 38

Gunn, Thom(son William)
1929-2004 . **CLC 3, 6, 18, 32, 81; PC 26**
See also BRWS 4; CA 17-20R; 227; CANR 9, 33, 116; CDBLB 1960 to Present; CP 7; DAM POET; DLB 27; INT CANR-33; MTCW 1; PFS 9; RGEL 2

Gunn, William Harrison 1934(?)-1989
See Gunn, Bill
See also AITN 1; BW 1, 3; CA 13-16R; 128; CANR 12, 25, 76

Gunn Allen, Paula
See Allen, Paula Gunn

Gunnars, Kristjana 1948- .... **CLC 69**
See also CA 113; CCA 1; CP 7; CWP; DLB 60

Gunter, Erich
See Eich, Gunter

Gurdjieff, G(eorgei) I(vanovich)
1877(?)-1949 .... **TCLC 71**
See also CA 157

Gurganus, Allan 1947- .... **CLC 70**
See also BEST 90:1; CA 135; CANR 114; CN 7; CPW; CSW; DAM POP; GLL 1

Gurney, A. R.
See Gurney, A(lbert) R(amsdell), Jr.
See also DLB 266

Gurney, A(lbert) R(amsdell), Jr.
1930- .... **CLC 32, 50, 54**
See Gurney, A. R.
See also AMWS 5; CA 77-80; CAD; CANR 32, 64, 121; CD 5; DAM DRAM; EWL 3

Gurney, Ivor (Bertie) 1890-1937 ... **TCLC 33**
See also BRW 6; CA 167; DLBY 2002; PAB; RGEL 2

Gurney, Peter
See Gurney, A(lbert) R(amsdell), Jr.

Guro, Elena (Genrikhovna)
1877-1913 .... **TCLC 56**
See also DLB 295

Gustafson, James M(oody) 1925- ... **CLC 100**
See also CA 25-28R; CANR 37

Gustafson, Ralph (Barker)
1909-1995 .... **CLC 36**
See also CA 21-24R; CANR 8, 45, 84; CP 7; DLB 88; RGEL 2

Gut, Gom
See Simenon, Georges (Jacques Christian)

Guterson, David 1956- .... **CLC 91**
See also CA 132; CANR 73, 126; DLB 292; MTCW 2; NFS 13

Guthrie, A(lfred) B(ertram), Jr.
1901-1991 .... **CLC 23**
See also CA 57-60; 134; CANR 24; DLB 6, 212; SATA 62; SATA-Obit 67

Guthrie, Isobel
See Grieve, C(hristopher) M(urray)

Guthrie, Woodrow Wilson 1912-1967
See Guthrie, Woody
See also CA 113; 93-96

Guthrie, Woody .... **CLC 35**
See Guthrie, Woodrow Wilson
See also DLB 303; LAIT 3

Gutierrez Najera, Manuel
1859-1895 .... **HLCS 2; NCLC 133**
See also DLB 290; LAW

Guy, Rosa (Cuthbert) 1925- .... **CLC 26**
See also AAYA 4, 37; BW 2; CA 17-20R; CANR 14, 34, 83; CLR 13; DLB 33; DNFS 1; JRDA; MAICYA 1, 2; SATA 14, 62, 122; YAW

Gwendolyn
See Bennett, (Enoch) Arnold

H. D. .... **CLC 3, 8, 14, 31, 34, 73; PC 5**
See Doolittle, Hilda

H. de V.
See Buchan, John

Haavikko, Paavo Juhani 1931- .. **CLC 18, 34**
See also CA 106; CWW 2; EWL 3

Habbema, Koos
See Heijermans, Herman

Habermas, Juergen 1929- .... **CLC 104**
See also CA 109; CANR 85; DLB 242

Habermas, Jurgen
See Habermas, Juergen

Hacker, Marilyn 1942- ...... **CLC 5, 9, 23, 72, 91; PC 47**
See also CA 77-80; CANR 68, 129; CP 7; CWP; DAM POET; DLB 120, 282; FW; GLL 2; PFS 19

Hadewijch of Antwerp fl. 1250- ... **CMLC 61**
See also RGWL 3

Hadrian 76-138 .... **CMLC 52**

Haeckel, Ernst Heinrich (Philipp August)
1834-1919 .... **TCLC 83**
See also CA 157

Hafiz c. 1326-1389(?) .... **CMLC 34**
See also RGWL 2, 3

Hagedorn, Jessica T(arahata)
1949- .... **CLC 185**
See also CA 139; CANR 69; CWP; RGAL 4

Haggard, H(enry) Rider
1856-1925 .... **TCLC 11**
See also BRWS 3; BYA 4, 5; CA 108; 148; CANR 112; DLB 70, 156, 174, 178; FANT; LMFS 1; MTCW 2; RGEL 2; RHW; SATA 16; SCFW; SFW 4; SUFW 1; WLIT 4

Hagiosy, L.
See Larbaud, Valery (Nicolas)

Hagiwara, Sakutaro 1886-1942 .... **PC 18; TCLC 60**
See Hagiwara Sakutaro
See also CA 154; RGWL 3

Hagiwara Sakutaro
See Hagiwara, Sakutaro
See also EWL 3

Haig, Fenil
See Ford, Ford Madox

Haig-Brown, Roderick (Langmere)
1908-1976 .... **CLC 21**
See also CA 5-8R; 69-72; CANR 4, 38, 83; CLR 31; CWRI 5; DLB 88; MAICYA 1, 2; SATA 12

Haight, Rip
See Carpenter, John (Howard)

Hailey, Arthur 1920- .... **CLC 5**
See also AITN 2; BEST 90:3; BPFB 2; CA 1-4R; CANR 2, 36, 75; CCA 1; CN 7; CPW; DAM NOV, POP; DLB 88; DLBY 1982; MTCW 1, 2

Hailey, Elizabeth Forsythe 1938- ..... **CLC 40**
See also CA 93-96; 188; CAAE 188; CAAS 1; CANR 15, 48; INT CANR-15

Harris, George Washington
1814-1869 .... **NCLC 23**
See also DLB 3, 11, 248; RGAL 4

Harris, Joel Chandler 1848-1908 ..... **SSC 19;**
TCLC 2
See also CA 104; 137; CANR 80; CLR 49;
DLB 11, 23, 42, 78, 91; LAIT 2; MAI-
CYA 1, 2; RGSF 2; SATA 100; WCH;
YABC 1

Harris, John (Wyndham Parkes Lucas)
Beynon 1903-1969
See Wyndham, John
See also CA 102; 89-92; CANR 84; SATA
118; SFW 4

Harris, MacDonald .... **CLC 9**
See Heiney, Donald (William)

Harris, Mark 1922- .... **CLC 19**
See also CA 5-8R; CAAS 3; CANR 2, 55,
83; CN 7; DLB 2; DLBY 1980

Harris, Norman .... **CLC 65**

Harris, (Theodore) Wilson 1921- .... **CLC 25,**
159
See also BRWS 5; BW 2, 3; CA 65-68;
CAAS 16; CANR 11, 27, 69, 114; CD-
WLB 3; CN 7; CP 7; DLB 117; EWL 3;
MTCW 1; RGEL 2

Harrison, Barbara Grizzuti
1934-2002 .... **CLC 144**
See also CA 77-80; 205; CANR 15, 48; INT
CANR-15

Harrison, Elizabeth (Allen) Cavanna
1909-2001
See Cavanna, Betty
See also CA 9-12R; 200; CANR 6, 27, 85,
104, 121; MAICYA 2; SATA 142; YAW

Harrison, Harry (Max) 1925- .... **CLC 42**
See also CA 1-4R; CANR 5, 21, 84; DLB
8; SATA 4; SCFW 2; SFW 4

Harrison, James (Thomas) 1937- ...... **CLC 6,**
14, 33, 66, 143; SSC 19
See Harrison, Jim
See also CA 13-16R; CANR 8, 51, 79; CN
7; CP 7; DLBY 1982; INT CANR-8

Harrison, Jim
See Harrison, James (Thomas)
See also AMWS 8; RGAL 4; TCWW 2;
TUS

Harrison, Kathryn 1961- .... **CLC 70, 151**
See also CA 144; CANR 68, 122

Harrison, Tony 1937- .... **CLC 43, 129**
See also BRWS 5; CA 65-68; CANR 44,
98; CBD; CD 5; CP 7; DLB 40, 245;
MTCW 1; RGEL 2

Harriss, Will(ard Irvin) 1922- .... **CLC 34**
See also CA 111

Hart, Ellis
See Ellison, Harlan (Jay)

Hart, Josephine 1942(?)- .... **CLC 70**
See also CA 138; CANR 70; CPW; DAM
POP

Hart, Moss 1904-1961 .... **CLC 66**
See also CA 109; 89-92; CANR 84; DAM
DRAM; DFS 1; DLB 7, 266; RGAL 4

Harte, (Francis) Bret(t)
1836(?)-1902 ... **SSC 8, 59; TCLC 1, 25;**
WLC
See also AMWS 2; CA 104; 140; CANR
80; CDALB 1865-1917; DA; DA3; DAC;
DAM MST; DLB 12, 64, 74, 79, 186;
EXPS; LAIT 2; RGAL 4; RGSF 2; SATA
26; SSFS 3; TUS

Hartley, L(eslie) P(oles) 1895-1972 ... **CLC 2,**
22
See also BRWS 7; CA 45-48; 37-40R;
CANR 33; DLB 15, 139; EWL 3; HGG;
MTCW 1, 2; RGEL 2; RGSF 2; SUFW 1

Hartman, Geoffrey H. 1929- .... **CLC 27**
See also CA 117; 125; CANR 79; DLB 67

Hartmann, Sadakichi 1869-1944 ... **TCLC 73**
See also CA 157; DLB 54

Hartmann von Aue c. 1170-c.
1210 .... **CMLC 15**
See also CDWLB 2; DLB 138; RGWL 2, 3

Hartog, Jan de
See de Hartog, Jan

Haruf, Kent 1943- .... **CLC 34**
See also AAYA 44; CA 149; CANR 91, 131

Harvey, Caroline
See Trollope, Joanna

Harvey, Gabriel 1550(?)-1631 .... **LC 88**
See also DLB 167, 213, 281

Harwood, Ronald 1934- .... **CLC 32**
See also CA 1-4R; CANR 4, 55; CBD; CD
5; DAM DRAM, MST; DLB 13

Hasegawa Tatsunosuke
See Futabatei, Shimei

Hasek, Jaroslav (Matej Frantisek)
1883-1923 .... **SSC 69; TCLC 4**
See also CA 104; 129; CDWLB 4; DLB
215; EW 9; EWL 3; MTCW 1, 2; RGSF
2; RGWL 2, 3

Hass, Robert 1941- ... **CLC 18, 39, 99; PC 16**
See also AMWS 6; CA 111; CANR 30, 50,
71; CP 7; DLB 105, 206; EWL 3; RGAL
4; SATA 94

Hastings, Hudson
See Kuttner, Henry

Hastings, Selina .... **CLC 44**

Hathorne, John 1641-1717 .... **LC 38**

Hatteras, Amelia
See Mencken, H(enry) L(ouis)

Hatteras, Owen .... **TCLC 18**
See Mencken, H(enry) L(ouis); Nathan,
George Jean

Hauptmann, Gerhart (Johann Robert)
1862-1946 .... **SSC 37; TCLC 4**
See also CA 104; 153; CDWLB 2; DAM
DRAM; DLB 66, 118; EW 8; EWL 3;
RGSF 2; RGWL 2, 3; TWA

Havel, Vaclav 1936- ..... **CLC 25, 58, 65, 123;**
DC 6
See also CA 104; CANR 36, 63, 124; CD-
WLB 4; CWW 2; DA3; DAM DRAM;
DFS 10; DLB 232; EWL 3; LMFS 2;
MTCW 1, 2; RGWL 3

Haviaras, Stratis .... **CLC 33**
See Chaviaras, Strates

Hawes, Stephen 1475(?)-1529(?) .... **LC 17**
See also DLB 132; RGEL 2

Hawkes, John (Clendennin Burne, Jr.)
1925-1998 .. **CLC 1, 2, 3, 4, 7, 9, 14, 15,**
27, 49
See also BPFB 2; CA 1-4R; 167; CANR 2,
47, 64; CN 7; DLB 2, 7, 227; DLBY
1980, 1998; EWL 3; MTCW 1, 2; RGAL
4

Hawking, S. W.
See Hawking, Stephen W(illiam)

Hawking, Stephen W(illiam) 1942- . **CLC 63,**
105
See also AAYA 13; BEST 89:1; CA 126;
129; CANR 48, 115; CPW; DA3; MTCW
2

Hawkins, Anthony Hope
See Hope, Anthony

Hawthorne, Julian 1846-1934 .... **TCLC 25**
See also CA 165; HGG

Hawthorne, Nathaniel 1804-1864 ... **NCLC 2,**
10, 17, 23, 39, 79, 95, 158; SSC 3, 29,
39; WLC
See also AAYA 18; AMW; AMWC 1;
AMWR 1; BPFB 2; BYA 3; CDALB
1640-1865; DA; DA3; DAB; DAC; DAM
MST, NOV; DLB 1, 74, 183, 223, 269;
EXPN; EXPS; HGG; LAIT 1; NFS 1, 20;
RGAL 4; RGSF 2; SSFS 1, 7, 11, 15;
SUFW 1; TUS; WCH; YABC 2

Hawthorne, Sophia Peabody
1809-1871 .... **NCLC 150**
See also DLB 183, 239

Haxton, Josephine Ayres 1921-
See Douglas, Ellen
See also CA 115; CANR 41, 83

Hayaseca y Eizaguirre, Jorge
See Echegaray (y Eizaguirre), Jose (Maria
Waldo)

Hayashi, Fumiko 1904-1951 .... **TCLC 27**
See Hayashi Fumiko
See also CA 161

Hayashi Fumiko
See Hayashi, Fumiko
See also DLB 180; EWL 3

Haycraft, Anna (Margaret) 1932-
See Ellis, Alice Thomas
See also CA 122; CANR 85, 90; MTCW 2

Hayden, Robert E(arl) 1913-1980 ..... **BLC 2;**
CLC 5, 9, 14, 37; PC 6
See also AFAW 1, 2; AMWS 2; BW 1, 3;
CA 69-72; 97-100; CABS 2; CANR 24,
75, 82; CDALB 1941-1968; DA; DAC;
DAM MST, MULT, POET; DLB 5, 76;
EWL 3; EXPP; MTCW 1, 2; PFS 1;
RGAL 4; SATA 19; SATA-Obit 26; WP

Haydon, Benjamin Robert
1786-1846 .... **NCLC 146**
See also DLB 110

Hayek, F(riedrich) A(ugust von)
1899-1992 .... **TCLC 109**
See also CA 93-96; 137; CANR 20; MTCW
1, 2

Hayford, J(oseph) E(phraim) Casely
See Casely-Hayford, J(oseph) E(phraim)

Hayman, Ronald 1932- .... **CLC 44**
See also CA 25-28R; CANR 18, 50, 88; CD
5; DLB 155

Hayne, Paul Hamilton 1830-1886 . **NCLC 94**
See also DLB 3, 64, 79, 248; RGAL 4

Hays, Mary 1760-1843 .... **NCLC 114**
See also DLB 142, 158; RGEL 2

Haywood, Eliza (Fowler)
1693(?)-1756 .... **LC 1, 44**
See also DLB 39; RGEL 2

Hazlitt, William 1778-1830 ...... **NCLC 29, 82**
See also BRW 4; DLB 110, 158; RGEL 2;
TEA

Hazzard, Shirley 1931- .... **CLC 18**
See also CA 9-12R; CANR 4, 70, 127; CN
7; DLB 289; DLBY 1982; MTCW 1

Head, Bessie 1937-1986 ...... **BLC 2; CLC 25,**
67; SSC 52
See also AFW; BW 2, 3; CA 29-32R; 119;
CANR 25, 82; CDWLB 3; DA3; DAM
MULT; DLB 117, 225; EWL 3; EXPS;
FW; MTCW 1, 2; RGSF 2; SSFS 5, 13;
WLIT 2; WWE 1

Headon, (Nicky) Topper 1956(?)- ..... **CLC 30**

Heaney, Seamus (Justin) 1939- ..... **CLC 5, 7,**
14, 25, 37, 74, 91, 171; PC 18; WLCS
See also BRWR 1; BRWS 2; CA 85-88;
CANR 25, 48, 75, 91, 128; CDBLB 1960
to Present; CP 7; DA3; DAB; DAM
POET; DLB 40; DLBY 1995; EWL 3;
EXPP; MTCW 1, 2; PAB; PFS 2, 5, 8,
17; RGEL 2; TEA; WLIT 4

Hearn, (Patricio) Lafcadio (Tessima Carlos)
1850-1904 .... **TCLC 9**
See also CA 105; 166; DLB 12, 78, 189;
HGG; RGAL 4

Hearne, Samuel 1745-1792 .... **LC 95**
See also DLB 99

Hearne, Vicki 1946-2001 .... **CLC 56**
See also CA 139; 201

Hearon, Shelby 1931- .... **CLC 63**
See also AITN 2; AMWS 8; CA 25-28R;
CANR 18, 48, 103; CSW

Hesse, Hermann 1877-1962 ... **CLC 1, 2, 3, 6, 11, 17, 25, 69; SSC 9, 49; TCLC 148; WLC**
See also AAYA 43; BPFB 2; CA 17-18; CAP 2; CDWLB 2; DA; DA3; DAB; DAC; DAM MST, NOV; DLB 66; EW 9; EWL 3; EXPN; LAIT 1; MTCW 1, 2; NFS 6, 15; RGWL 2, 3; SATA 50; TWA

Hewes, Cady
See De Voto, Bernard (Augustine)

Heyen, William 1940- .... **CLC 13, 18**
See also CA 33-36R; 220; CAAE 220; CAAS 9; CANR 98; CP 7; DLB 5

Heyerdahl, Thor 1914-2002 .... **CLC 26**
See also CA 5-8R; 207; CANR 5, 22, 66, 73; LAIT 4; MTCW 1, 2; SATA 2, 52

Heym, Georg (Theodor Franz Arthur) 1887-1912 .... **TCLC 9**
See also CA 106; 181

Heym, Stefan 1913-2001 .... **CLC 41**
See also CA 9-12R; 203; CANR 4; CWW 2; DLB 69; EWL 3

Heyse, Paul (Johann Ludwig von) 1830-1914 .... **TCLC 8**
See also CA 104; 209; DLB 129

Heyward, (Edwin) DuBose 1885-1940 .... **HR 2; TCLC 59**
See also CA 108; 157; DLB 7, 9, 45, 249; SATA 21

Heywood, John 1497(?)-1580(?) .... **LC 65**
See also DLB 136; RGEL 2

Heywood, Thomas 1573(?)-1641 .... **LC 111**
See also DLB 62; DAM DRAM; LMFS 1; RGEL 2; TWA

Hibbert, Eleanor Alice Burford 1906-1993 .... **CLC 7**
See Holt, Victoria
See also BEST 90:4; CA 17-20R; 140; CANR 9, 28, 59; CMW 4; CPW; DAM POP; MTCW 2; RHW; SATA 2; SATA-Obit 74

Hichens, Robert (Smythe) 1864-1950 .... **TCLC 64**
See also CA 162; DLB 153; HGG; RHW; SUFW

Higgins, Aidan 1927- .... **SSC 68**
See also CA 9-12R; CANR 70, 115; CN 7; DLB 14

Higgins, George V(incent) 1939-1999 .... **CLC 4, 7, 10, 18**
See also BPFB 2; CA 77-80; 186; CAAS 5; CANR 17, 51, 89, 96; CMW 4; CN 7; DLB 2; DLBY 1981, 1998; INT CANR-17; MSW; MTCW 1

Higginson, Thomas Wentworth 1823-1911 .... **TCLC 36**
See also CA 162; DLB 1, 64, 243

Higgonet, Margaret ed. .... **CLC 65**

Highet, Helen
See MacInnes, Helen (Clark)

Highsmith, (Mary) Patricia 1921-1995 .... **CLC 2, 4, 14, 42, 102**
See Morgan, Claire
See also AAYA 48; BRWS 5; CA 1-4R; 147; CANR 1, 20, 48, 62, 108; CMW 4; CPW; DA3; DAM NOV, POP; DLB 306; MSW; MTCW 1, 2

Highwater, Jamake (Mamake) 1942(?)-2001 .... **CLC 12**
See also AAYA 7; BPFB 2; BYA 4; CA 65-68; 199; CAAS 7; CANR 10, 34, 84; CLR 17; CWRI 5; DLB 52; DLBY 1985; JRDA; MAICYA 1, 2; SATA 32, 69; SATA-Brief 30

Highway, Tomson 1951- ...... **CLC 92; NNAL**
See also CA 151; CANR 75; CCA 1; CD 5; DAC; DAM MULT; DFS 2; MTCW 2

Hijuelos, Oscar 1951- .... **CLC 65; HLC 1**
See also AAYA 25; AMWS 8; BEST 90:1; CA 123; CANR 50, 75, 125; CPW; DA3; DAM MULT, POP; DLB 145; HW 1, 2; LLW 1; MTCW 2; NFS 17; RGAL 4; WLIT 1

Hikmet, Nazim 1902(?)-1963 .... **CLC 40**
See also CA 141; 93-96; EWL 3

Hildegard von Bingen 1098-1179 . **CMLC 20**
See also DLB 148

Hildesheimer, Wolfgang 1916-1991 .. **CLC 49**
See also CA 101; 135; DLB 69, 124; EWL 3

Hill, Geoffrey (William) 1932- ...... **CLC 5, 8, 18, 45**
See also BRWS 5; CA 81-84; CANR 21, 89; CDBLB 1960 to Present; CP 7; DAM POET; DLB 40; EWL 3; MTCW 1; RGEL 2

Hill, George Roy 1921-2002 .... **CLC 26**
See also CA 110; 122; 213

Hill, John
See Koontz, Dean R(ay)

Hill, Susan (Elizabeth) 1942- ...... **CLC 4, 113**
See also CA 33-36R; CANR 29, 69, 129; CN 7; DAB; DAM MST, NOV; DLB 14, 139; HGG; MTCW 1; RHW

Hillard, Asa G. III .... **CLC 70**

Hillerman, Tony 1925- .... **CLC 62, 170**
See also AAYA 40; BEST 89:1; BPFB 2; CA 29-32R; CANR 21, 42, 65, 97, 134; CMW 4; CPW; DA3; DAM POP; DLB 206, 306; MSW; RGAL 4; SATA 6; TCWW 2; YAW

Hillesum, Etty 1914-1943 .... **TCLC 49**
See also CA 137

Hilliard, Noel (Harvey) 1929-1996 ... **CLC 15**
See also CA 9-12R; CANR 7, 69; CN 7

Hillis, Rick 1956- .... **CLC 66**
See also CA 134

Hilton, James 1900-1954 .... **TCLC 21**
See also CA 108; 169; DLB 34, 77; FANT; SATA 34

Hilton, Walter (?)-1396 .... **CMLC 58**
See also DLB 146; RGEL 2

Himes, Chester (Bomar) 1909-1984 .. **BLC 2; CLC 2, 4, 7, 18, 58, 108; TCLC 139**
See also AFAW 2; BPFB 2; BW 2; CA 25-28R; 114; CANR 22, 89; CMW 4; DAM MULT; DLB 2, 76, 143, 226; EWL 3; MSW; MTCW 1, 2; RGAL 4

Himmelfarb, Gertrude 1922- .... **CLC 202**
See also CA 49-52; CANR 28, 66, 102;

Hinde, Thomas .... **CLC 6, 11**
See Chitty, Thomas Willes
See also EWL 3

Hine, (William) Daryl 1936- .... **CLC 15**
See also CA 1-4R; CAAS 15; CANR 1, 20; CP 7; DLB 60

Hinkson, Katharine Tynan
See Tynan, Katharine

Hinojosa(-Smith), Rolando (R.) 1929- .... **HLC 1**
See Hinojosa-Smith, Rolando
See also CA 131; CAAS 16; CANR 62; DAM MULT; DLB 82; HW 1, 2; LLW 1; MTCW 2; RGAL 4

Hinton, S(usan) E(loise) 1950- .. **CLC 30, 111**
See also AAYA 2, 33; BPFB 2; BYA 2, 3; CA 81-84; CANR 32, 62, 92, 133; CDALBS; CLR 3, 23; CPW; DA; DA3; DAB; DAC; DAM MST, NOV; JRDA; LAIT 5; MAICYA 1, 2; MTCW 1, 2; NFS 5, 9, 15, 16; SATA 19, 58, 115; WYA; YAW

Hippius, Zinaida (Nikolaevna) .... **TCLC 9**
See Gippius, Zinaida (Nikolaevna)
See also DLB 295; EWL 3

Hiraoka, Kimitake 1925-1970
See Mishima, Yukio
See also CA 97-100; 29-32R; DA3; DAM DRAM; GLL 1; MTCW 1, 2

Hirsch, E(ric) D(onald), Jr. 1928- .... **CLC 79**
See also CA 25-28R; CANR 27, 51; DLB 67; INT CANR-27; MTCW 1

Hirsch, Edward 1950- .... **CLC 31, 50**
See also CA 104; CANR 20, 42, 102; CP 7; DLB 120

Hitchcock, Alfred (Joseph) 1899-1980 .... **CLC 16**
See also AAYA 22; CA 159; 97-100; SATA 27; SATA-Obit 24

Hitchens, Christopher (Eric) 1949- .... **CLC 157**
See also CA 152; CANR 89

Hitler, Adolf 1889-1945 .... **TCLC 53**
See also CA 117; 147

Hoagland, Edward 1932- .... **CLC 28**
See also ANW; CA 1-4R; CANR 2, 31, 57, 107; CN 7; DLB 6; SATA 51; TCWW 2

Hoban, Russell (Conwell) 1925- ... **CLC 7, 25**
See also BPFB 2; CA 5-8R; CANR 23, 37, 66, 114; CLR 3, 69; CN 7; CWRI 5; DAM NOV; DLB 52; FANT; MAICYA 1, 2; MTCW 1, 2; SATA 1, 40, 78, 136; SFW 4; SUFW 2

Hobbes, Thomas 1588-1679 .... **LC 36**
See also DLB 151, 252, 281; RGEL 2

Hobbs, Perry
See Blackmur, R(ichard) P(almer)

Hobson, Laura Z(ametkin) 1900-1986 .... **CLC 7, 25**
See Field, Peter
See also BPFB 2; CA 17-20R; 118; CANR 55; DLB 28; SATA 52

Hoccleve, Thomas c. 1368-c. 1437 ...... **LC 75**
See also DLB 146; RGEL 2

Hoch, Edward D(entinger) 1930-
See Queen, Ellery
See also CA 29-32R; CANR 11, 27, 51, 97; CMW 4; DLB 306; SFW 4

Hochhuth, Rolf 1931- .... **CLC 4, 11, 18**
See also CA 5-8R; CANR 33, 75; CWW 2; DAM DRAM; DLB 124; EWL 3; MTCW 1, 2

Hochman, Sandra 1936- .... **CLC 3, 8**
See also CA 5-8R; DLB 5

Hochwaelder, Fritz 1911-1986 .... **CLC 36**
See Hochwalder, Fritz
See also CA 29-32R; 120; CANR 42; DAM DRAM; MTCW 1; RGWL 3

Hochwalder, Fritz
See Hochwaelder, Fritz
See also EWL 3; RGWL 2

Hocking, Mary (Eunice) 1921- .... **CLC 13**
See also CA 101; CANR 18, 40

Hodgins, Jack 1938- .... **CLC 23**
See also CA 93-96; CN 7; DLB 60

Hodgson, William Hope 1877(?)-1918 .... **TCLC 13**
See also CA 111; 164; CMW 4; DLB 70, 153, 156, 178; HGG; MTCW 2; SFW 4; SUFW 1

Hoeg, Peter 1957- .... **CLC 95, 156**
See also CA 151; CANR 75; CMW 4; DA3; DLB 214; EWL 3; MTCW 2; NFS 17; RGWL 3; SSFS 18

Hoffman, Alice 1952- .... **CLC 51**
See also AAYA 37; AMWS 10; CA 77-80; CANR 34, 66, 100; CN 7; CPW; DAM NOV; DLB 292; MTCW 1, 2

Hoffman, Daniel (Gerard) 1923- . **CLC 6, 13, 23**
See also CA 1-4R; CANR 4; CP 7; DLB 5

Hoffman, Eva 1945- .... **CLC 182**
See also CA 132

Hoffman, Stanley 1944- .... **CLC 5**
See also CA 77-80

Hoffman, William 1925- .... **CLC 141**
See also CA 21-24R; CANR 9, 103; CSW;
DLB 234

Hoffman, William M(oses) 1939- ..... **CLC 40**
See Hoffman, William M.
See also CA 57-60; CANR 11, 71

Hoffmann, E(rnst) T(heodor) A(madeus)
1776-1822 .... **NCLC 2; SSC 13**
See also CDWLB 2; DLB 90; EW 5; RGSF
2; RGWL 2, 3; SATA 27; SUFW 1; WCH

Hofmann, Gert 1931- .... **CLC 54**
See also CA 128; EWL 3

Hofmannsthal, Hugo von 1874-1929 ... **DC 4;
TCLC 11**
See also CA 106; 153; CDWLB 2; DAM
DRAM; DFS 17; DLB 81, 118; EW 9;
EWL 3; RGWL 2, 3

Hogan, Linda 1947- ..... **CLC 73; NNAL; PC
35**
See also AMWS 4; ANW; BYA 12; CA 120,
226; CAAE 226; CANR 45, 73, 129;
CWP; DAM MULT; DLB 175; SATA
132; TCWW 2

Hogarth, Charles
See Creasey, John

Hogarth, Emmett
See Polonsky, Abraham (Lincoln)

Hogarth, William 1697-1764 .... **LC 112**
See also AAYA 56

Hogg, James 1770-1835 .... **NCLC 4, 109**
See also BRWS 10; DLB 93, 116, 159;
HGG; RGEL 2; SUFW 1

Holbach, Paul Henri Thiry Baron
1723-1789 .... **LC 14**

Holberg, Ludvig 1684-1754 .... **LC 6**
See also DLB 300; RGWL 2, 3

Holcroft, Thomas 1745-1809 .... **NCLC 85**
See also DLB 39, 89, 158; RGEL 2

Holden, Ursula 1921- .... **CLC 18**
See also CA 101; CAAS 8; CANR 22

Holderlin, (Johann Christian) Friedrich
1770-1843 .... **NCLC 16; PC 4**
See also CDWLB 2; DLB 90; EW 5; RGWL
2, 3

Holdstock, Robert
See Holdstock, Robert P.

Holdstock, Robert P. 1948- .... **CLC 39**
See also CA 131; CANR 81; DLB 261;
FANT; HGG; SFW 4; SUFW 2

Holinshed, Raphael fl. 1580- .... **LC 69**
See also DLB 167; RGEL 2

Holland, Isabelle (Christian)
1920-2002 .... **CLC 21**
See also AAYA 11; CA 21-24R; 205; CAAE
181; CANR 10, 25, 47; CLR 57; CWRI
5; JRDA; LAIT 4; MAICYA 1, 2; SATA
8, 70; SATA-Essay 103; SATA-Obit 132;
WYA

Holland, Marcus
See Caldwell, (Janet Miriam) Taylor
(Holland)

Hollander, John 1929- .... **CLC 2, 5, 8, 14**
See also CA 1-4R; CANR 1, 52; CP 7; DLB
5; SATA 13

Hollander, Paul
See Silverberg, Robert

Holleran, Andrew 1943(?)- .... **CLC 38**
See Garber, Eric
See also CA 144; GLL 1

Holley, Marietta 1836(?)-1926 .... **TCLC 99**
See also CA 118; DLB 11

Hollinghurst, Alan 1954- .... **CLC 55, 91**
See also BRWS 10; CA 114; CN 7; DLB
207; GLL 1

Hollis, Jim
See Summers, Hollis (Spurgeon, Jr.)

Holly, Buddy 1936-1959 .... **TCLC 65**
See also CA 213

Holmes, Gordon
See Shiel, M(atthew) P(hipps)

Holmes, John
See Souster, (Holmes) Raymond

Holmes, John Clellon 1926-1988 ...... **CLC 56**
See also BG 2; CA 9-12R; 125; CANR 4;
DLB 16, 237

Holmes, Oliver Wendell, Jr.
1841-1935 .... **TCLC 77**
See also CA 114; 186

Holmes, Oliver Wendell
1809-1894 .... **NCLC 14, 81**
See also AMWS 1; CDALB 1640-1865;
DLB 1, 189, 235; EXPP; RGAL 4; SATA
34

Holmes, Raymond
See Souster, (Holmes) Raymond

Holt, Victoria
See Hibbert, Eleanor Alice Burford
See also BPFB 2

Holub, Miroslav 1923-1998 .... **CLC 4**
See also CA 21-24R; 169; CANR 10; CD-
WLB 4; CWW 2; DLB 232; EWL 3;
RGWL 3

Holz, Detlev
See Benjamin, Walter

Homer c. 8th cent. B.C.- .... **CMLC 1, 16, 61;
PC 23; WLCS**
See also AW 1; CDWLB 1; DA; DA3;
DAB; DAC; DAM MST, POET; DLB
176; EFS 1; LAIT 1; LMFS 1; RGWL 2,
3; TWA; WP

Hongo, Garrett Kaoru 1951- .... **PC 23**
See also CA 133; CAAS 22; CP 7; DLB
120; EWL 3; EXPP; RGAL 4

Honig, Edwin 1919- .... **CLC 33**
See also CA 5-8R; CAAS 8; CANR 4, 45;
CP 7; DLB 5

Hood, Hugh (John Blagdon) 1928- . **CLC 15,
28; SSC 42**
See also CA 49-52; CAAS 17; CANR 1,
33, 87; CN 7; DLB 53; RGSF 2

Hood, Thomas 1799-1845 .... **NCLC 16**
See also BRW 4; DLB 96; RGEL 2

Hooker, (Peter) Jeremy 1941- .... **CLC 43**
See also CA 77-80; CANR 22; CP 7; DLB
40

Hooker, Richard 1554-1600 .... **LC 95**
See also BRW 1; DLB 132; RGEL 2

hooks, bell
See Watkins, Gloria Jean

Hope, A(lec) D(erwent) 1907-2000 .... **CLC 3,
51; PC 56**
See also BRWS 7; CA 21-24R; 188; CANR
33, 74; DLB 289; EWL 3; MTCW 1, 2;
PFS 8; RGEL 2

Hope, Anthony 1863-1933 .... **TCLC 83**
See also CA 157; DLB 153, 156; RGEL 2;
RHW

Hope, Brian
See Creasey, John

Hope, Christopher (David Tully)
1944- .... **CLC 52**
See also AFW; CA 106; CANR 47, 101;
CN 7; DLB 225; SATA 62

Hopkins, Gerard Manley
1844-1889 .... **NCLC 17; PC 15; WLC**
See also BRW 5; BRWR 2; CDBLB 1890-
1914; DA; DA3; DAB; DAC; DAM MST,
POET; DLB 35, 57; EXPP; PAB; RGEL
2; TEA; WP

Hopkins, John (Richard) 1931-1998 .. **CLC 4**
See also CA 85-88; 169; CBD; CD 5

Hopkins, Pauline Elizabeth
1859-1930 .... **BLC 2; TCLC 28**
See also AFAW 2; BW 2, 3; CA 141; CANR
82; DAM MULT; DLB 50

Hopkinson, Francis 1737-1791 .... **LC 25**
See also DLB 31; RGAL 4

Hopley-Woolrich, Cornell George 1903-1968
See Woolrich, Cornell
See also CA 13-14; CANR 58; CAP 1;
CMW 4; DLB 226; MTCW 2

Horace 65B.C.-8B.C. .... **CMLC 39; PC 46**
See also AW 2; CDWLB 1; DLB 211;
RGWL 2, 3

Horatio
See Proust, (Valentin-Louis-George-Eugene)
Marcel

**Horgan, Paul (George Vincent
O'Shaughnessy)** 1903-1995 .. **CLC 9, 53**
See also BPFB 2; CA 13-16R; 147; CANR
9, 35; DAM NOV; DLB 102, 212; DLBY
1985; INT CANR-9; MTCW 1, 2; SATA
13; SATA-Obit 84; TCWW 2

Horkheimer, Max 1895-1973 .... **TCLC 132**
See also CA 216; 41-44R; DLB 296

Horn, Peter
See Kuttner, Henry

Horne, Frank (Smith) 1899-1974 .... **HR 2**
See also BW 1; CA 125; 53-56; DLB 51;
WP

Horne, Richard Henry Hengist
1802(?)-1884 .... **NCLC 127**
See also DLB 32; SATA 29

Hornem, Horace Esq.
See Byron, George Gordon (Noel)

**Horney, Karen (Clementine Theodore
Danielsen)** 1885-1952 .... **TCLC 71**
See also CA 114; 165; DLB 246; FW

Hornung, E(rnest) W(illiam)
1866-1921 .... **TCLC 59**
See also CA 108; 160; CMW 4; DLB 70

Horovitz, Israel (Arthur) 1939- .... **CLC 56**
See also CA 33-36R; CAD; CANR 46, 59;
CD 5; DAM DRAM; DLB 7

Horton, George Moses
1797(?)-1883(?) .... **NCLC 87**
See also DLB 50

Horvath, odon von 1901-1938
See von Horvath, Odon
See also EWL 3

Horvath, Oedoen von -1938
See von Horvath, Odon

Horwitz, Julius 1920-1986 .... **CLC 14**
See also CA 9-12R; 119; CANR 12

Hospital, Janette Turner 1942- .... **CLC 42,
145**
See also CA 108; CANR 48; CN 7; DLBY
2002; RGSF 2

Hostos, E. M. de
See Hostos (y Bonilla), Eugenio Maria de

Hostos, Eugenio M. de
See Hostos (y Bonilla), Eugenio Maria de

Hostos, Eugenio Maria
See Hostos (y Bonilla), Eugenio Maria de

Hostos (y Bonilla), Eugenio Maria de
1839-1903 .... **TCLC 24**
See also CA 123; 131; HW 1

Houdini
See Lovecraft, H(oward) P(hillips)

Houellebecq, Michel 1958- .... **CLC 179**
See also CA 185

Hougan, Carolyn 1943- .... **CLC 34**
See also CA 139

Household, Geoffrey (Edward West)
1900-1988 .... **CLC 11**
See also CA 77-80; 126; CANR 58; CMW
4; DLB 87; SATA 14; SATA-Obit 59

Housman, A(lfred) E(dward)
1859-1936 .... **PC 2, 43; TCLC 1, 10;
WLCS**
See also BRW 6; CA 104; 125; DA; DA3;
DAB; DAC; DAM MST, POET; DLB 19,
284; EWL 3; EXPP; MTCW 1, 2; PAB;
PFS 4, 7; RGEL 2; TEA; WP

Housman, Laurence 1865-1959 .... **TCLC 7**
　　See also CA 106; 155; DLB 10; FANT;
　　RGEL 2; SATA 25
Houston, Jeanne (Toyo) Wakatsuki
　　1934- .... **AAL**
　　See also AAYA 49; CA 103; CAAS 16;
　　CANR 29, 123; LAIT 4; SATA 78
Howard, Elizabeth Jane 1923- ..... **CLC 7, 29**
　　See also CA 5-8R; CANR 8, 62; CN 7
Howard, Maureen 1930- .... **CLC 5, 14, 46,**
　　151
　　See also CA 53-56; CANR 31, 75; CN 7;
　　DLBY 1983; INT CANR-31; MTCW 1, 2
Howard, Richard 1929- .... **CLC 7, 10, 47**
　　See also AITN 1; CA 85-88; CANR 25, 80;
　　CP 7; DLB 5; INT CANR-25
Howard, Robert E(rvin)
　　1906-1936 .... **TCLC 8**
　　See also BPFB 2; BYA 5; CA 105; 157;
　　FANT; SUFW 1
Howard, Warren F.
　　See Pohl, Frederik
Howe, Fanny (Quincy) 1940- .... **CLC 47**
　　See also CA 117, 187; CAAE 187; CAAS
　　27; CANR 70, 116; CP 7; CWP; SATA-
　　Brief 52
Howe, Irving 1920-1993 .... **CLC 85**
　　See also AMWS 6; CA 9-12R; 141; CANR
　　21, 50; DLB 67; EWL 3; MTCW 1, 2
Howe, Julia Ward 1819-1910 .... **TCLC 21**
　　See also CA 117; 191; DLB 1, 189, 235;
　　FW
Howe, Susan 1937- .... **CLC 72, 152; PC 54**
　　See also AMWS 4; CA 160; CP 7; CWP;
　　DLB 120; FW; RGAL 4
Howe, Tina 1937- .... **CLC 48**
　　See also CA 109; CAD; CANR 125; CD 5;
　　CWD
Howell, James 1594(?)-1666 .... **LC 13**
　　See also DLB 151
Howells, W. D.
　　See Howells, William Dean
Howells, William D.
　　See Howells, William Dean
Howells, William Dean 1837-1920 ... **SSC 36;**
　　TCLC 7, 17, 41
　　See also AMW; CA 104; 134; CDALB
　　1865-1917; DLB 12, 64, 74, 79, 189;
　　LMFS 1; MTCW 2; RGAL 4; TUS
Howes, Barbara 1914-1996 .... **CLC 15**
　　See also CA 9-12R; 151; CAAS 3; CANR
　　53; CP 7; SATA 5
Hrabal, Bohumil 1914-1997 ...... **CLC 13, 67;**
　　TCLC 155
　　See also CA 106; 156; CAAS 12; CANR
　　57; CWW 2; DLB 232; EWL 3; RGSF 2
Hrabanus Maurus c. 776-856 .... **CMLC 78**
　　See also DLB 148
Hrotsvit of Gandersheim c. 935-c.
　　1000 .... **CMLC 29**
　　See also DLB 148
Hsi, Chu 1130-1200 .... **CMLC 42**
Hsun, Lu
　　See Lu Hsun
Hubbard, L(afayette) Ron(ald)
　　1911-1986 .... **CLC 43**
　　See also CA 77-80; 118; CANR 52; CPW;
　　DA3; DAM POP; FANT; MTCW 2; SFW
　　4
Huch, Ricarda (Octavia)
　　1864-1947 .... **TCLC 13**
　　See also CA 111; 189; DLB 66; EWL 3
Huddle, David 1942- .... **CLC 49**
　　See also CA 57-60; CAAS 20; CANR 89;
　　DLB 130
Hudson, Jeffrey
　　See Crichton, (John) Michael

Hudson, W(illiam) H(enry)
　　1841-1922 .... **TCLC 29**
　　See also CA 115; 190; DLB 98, 153, 174;
　　RGEL 2; SATA 35
Hueffer, Ford Madox
　　See Ford, Ford Madox
Hughart, Barry 1934- .... **CLC 39**
　　See also CA 137; FANT; SFW 4; SUFW 2
Hughes, Colin
　　See Creasey, John
Hughes, David (John) 1930- .... **CLC 48**
　　See also CA 116; 129; CN 7; DLB 14
Hughes, Edward James
　　See Hughes, Ted
　　See also DA3; DAM MST, POET
Hughes, (James Mercer) Langston
　　1902-1967 ..... **BLC 2; CLC 1, 5, 10, 15,**
　　35, 44, 108; DC 3; HR 2; PC 1, 53;
　　SSC 6; WLC
　　See also AAYA 12; AFAW 1, 2; AMWR 1;
　　AMWS 1; BW 1, 3; CA 1-4R; 25-28R;
　　CANR 1, 34, 82; CDALB 1929-1941;
　　CLR 17; DA; DA3; DAB; DAC; DAM
　　DRAM, MST, MULT, POET; DFS 6, 18;
　　DLB 4, 7, 48, 51, 86, 228; EWL 3; EXPP;
　　EXPS; JRDA; LAIT 3; LMFS 2; MAI-
　　CYA 1, 2; MTCW 1, 2; PAB; PFS 1, 3, 6,
　　10, 15; RGAL 4; RGSF 2; SATA 4, 33;
　　SSFS 4, 7; TUS; WCH; WP; YAW
Hughes, Richard (Arthur Warren)
　　1900-1976 .... **CLC 1, 11**
　　See also CA 5-8R; 65-68; CANR 4; DAM
　　NOV; DLB 15, 161; EWL 3; MTCW 1;
　　RGEL 2; SATA 8; SATA-Obit 25
Hughes, Ted 1930-1998 . **CLC 2, 4, 9, 14, 37,**
　　119; PC 7
　　See Hughes, Edward James
　　See also BRWC 2; BRWR 2; BRWS 1; CA
　　1-4R; 171; CANR 1, 33, 66, 108; CLR 3;
　　CP 7; DAB; DAC; DLB 40, 161; EWL 3;
　　EXPP; MAICYA 1, 2; MTCW 1, 2; PAB;
　　PFS 4, 19; RGEL 2; SATA 49; SATA-
　　Brief 27; SATA-Obit 107; TEA; YAW
Hugo, Richard
　　See Huch, Ricarda (Octavia)
Hugo, Richard F(ranklin)
　　1923-1982 .... **CLC 6, 18, 32**
　　See also AMWS 6; CA 49-52; 108; CANR
　　3; DAM POET; DLB 5, 206; EWL 3; PFS
　　17; RGAL 4
Hugo, Victor (Marie) 1802-1885 .... **NCLC 3,**
　　10, 21; PC 17; WLC
　　See also AAYA 28; DA; DA3; DAB; DAC;
　　DAM DRAM, MST, NOV, POET; DLB
　　119, 192, 217; EFS 2; EW 6; EXPN; GFL
　　1789 to the Present; LAIT 1, 2; NFS 5,
　　20; RGWL 2, 3; SATA 47; TWA
Huidobro, Vicente
　　See Huidobro Fernandez, Vicente Garcia
　　See also DLB 283; EWL 3; LAW
Huidobro Fernandez, Vicente Garcia
　　1893-1948 .... **TCLC 31**
　　See Huidobro, Vicente
　　See also CA 131; HW 1
Hulme, Keri 1947- .... **CLC 39, 130**
　　See also CA 125; CANR 69; CN 7; CP 7;
　　CWP; EWL 3; FW; INT CA-125
Hulme, T(homas) E(rnest)
　　1883-1917 .... **TCLC 21**
　　See also BRWS 6; CA 117; 203; DLB 19
Humboldt, Wilhelm von
　　1767-1835 .... **NCLC 134**
　　See also DLB 90
Hume, David 1711-1776 .... **LC 7, 56**
　　See also BRWS 3; DLB 104, 252; LMFS 1;
　　TEA
Humphrey, William 1924-1997 .... **CLC 45**
　　See also AMWS 9; CA 77-80; 160; CANR
　　68; CN 7; CSW; DLB 6, 212, 234, 278;
　　TCWW 2

Humphreys, Emyr Owen 1919- .... **CLC 47**
　　See also CA 5-8R; CANR 3, 24; CN 7;
　　DLB 15
Humphreys, Josephine 1945- ..... **CLC 34, 57**
　　See also CA 121; 127; CANR 97; CSW;
　　DLB 292; INT CA-127
Huneker, James Gibbons
　　1860-1921 .... **TCLC 65**
　　See also CA 193; DLB 71; RGAL 4
Hungerford, Hesba Fay
　　See Brinsmead, H(esba) F(ay)
Hungerford, Pixie
　　See Brinsmead, H(esba) F(ay)
Hunt, E(verette) Howard, (Jr.)
　　1918- .... **CLC 3**
　　See also AITN 1; CA 45-48; CANR 2, 47,
　　103; CMW 4
Hunt, Francesca
　　See Holland, Isabelle (Christian)
Hunt, Howard
　　See Hunt, E(verette) Howard, (Jr.)
Hunt, Kyle
　　See Creasey, John
Hunt, (James Henry) Leigh
　　1784-1859 .... **NCLC 1, 70**
　　See also DAM POET; DLB 96, 110, 144;
　　RGEL 2; TEA
Hunt, Marsha 1946- .... **CLC 70**
　　See also BW 2, 3; CA 143; CANR 79
Hunt, Violet 1866(?)-1942 .... **TCLC 53**
　　See also CA 184; DLB 162, 197
Hunter, E. Waldo
　　See Sturgeon, Theodore (Hamilton)
Hunter, Evan 1926- .... **CLC 11, 31**
　　See McBain, Ed
　　See also AAYA 39; BPFB 2; CA 5-8R;
　　CANR 5, 38, 62, 97; CMW 4; CN 7;
　　CPW; DAM POP; DLB 306; DLBY 1982;
　　INT CANR-5; MSW; MTCW 1; SATA
　　25; SFW 4
Hunter, Kristin
　　See Lattany, Kristin (Elaine Eggleston)
　　Hunter
Hunter, Mary
　　See Austin, Mary (Hunter)
Hunter, Mollie 1922- .... **CLC 21**
　　See McIlwraith, Maureen Mollie Hunter
　　See also AAYA 13; BYA 6; CANR 37, 78;
　　CLR 25; DLB 161; JRDA; MAICYA 1,
　　2; SAAS 7; SATA 54, 106, 139; SATA-
　　Essay 139; WYA; YAW
Hunter, Robert (?)-1734 .... **LC 7**
Hurston, Zora Neale 1891-1960 .... **BLC 2;**
　　CLC 7, 30, 61; DC 12; HR 2; SSC 4,
　　80; TCLC 121, 131; WLCS
　　See also AAYA 15; AFAW 1, 2; AMWS 6;
　　BW 1, 3; BYA 12; CA 85-88; CANR 61;
　　CDALBS; DA; DA3; DAC; DAM MST,
　　MULT, NOV; DFS 6; DLB 51, 86; EWL
　　3; EXPN; EXPS; FW; LAIT 3; LATS 1:1;
　　LMFS 2; MAWW; MTCW 1, 2; NFS 3;
　　RGAL 4; RGSF 2; SSFS 1, 6, 11, 19;
　　TUS; YAW
Husserl, E. G.
　　See Husserl, Edmund (Gustav Albrecht)
Husserl, Edmund (Gustav Albrecht)
　　1859-1938 .... **TCLC 100**
　　See also CA 116; 133; DLB 296
Huston, John (Marcellus)
　　1906-1987 .... **CLC 20**
　　See also CA 73-76; 123; CANR 34; DLB
　　26
Hustvedt, Siri 1955- .... **CLC 76**
　　See also CA 137
Hutten, Ulrich von 1488-1523 .... **LC 16**
　　See also DLB 179

Jacob, (Cyprien-)Max 1876-1944 .... **TCLC 6**
See also CA 104; 193; DLB 258; EWL 3;
GFL 1789 to the Present; GLL 2; RGWL
2, 3

Jacobs, Harriet A(nn)
1813(?)-1897 .... **NCLC 67**
See also AFAW 1, 2; DLB 239; FW; LAIT
2; RGAL 4

Jacobs, Jim 1942- .... **CLC 12**
See also CA 97-100; INT CA-97-100

Jacobs, W(illiam) W(ymark)
1863-1943 .... **SSC 73; TCLC 22**
See also CA 121; 167; DLB 135; EXPS;
HGG; RGEL 2; RGSF; SSFS 2; SUFW
1

Jacobsen, Jens Peter 1847-1885 .... **NCLC 34**

Jacobsen, Josephine (Winder)
1908-2003 .... **CLC 48, 102; PC 62**
See also CA 33-36R; 218; CAAS 18; CANR
23, 48; CCA 1; CP 7; DLB 244

Jacobson, Dan 1929- .... **CLC 4, 14**
See also AFW; CA 1-4R; CANR 2, 25, 66;
CN 7; DLB 14, 207, 225; EWL 3; MTCW
1; RGSF 2

Jacqueline
See Carpentier (y Valmont), Alejo

Jacques de Vitry c. 1160-1240 ...... **CMLC 63**
See also DLB 208

Jagger, Mick 1944- .... **CLC 17**

Jahiz, al- c. 780-c. 869 .... **CMLC 25**

Jakes, John (William) 1932- .... **CLC 29**
See also AAYA 32; BEST 89:4; BPFB 2;
CA 57-60, 214; CAAE 214; CANR 10,
43, 66, 111; CPW; CSW; DA3; DAM
NOV, POP; DLB 278; DLBY 1983;
FANT; INT CANR-10; MTCW 1, 2;
RHW; SATA 62; SFW 4; TCWW 2

James I 1394-1437 .... **LC 20**
See also RGEL 2

James, Andrew
See Kirkup, James

James, C(yril) L(ionel) R(obert)
1901-1989 .... **BLCS; CLC 33**
See also BW 2; CA 117; 125; 128; CANR
62; DLB 125; MTCW 1

James, Daniel (Lewis) 1911-1988
See Santiago, Danny
See also CA 174; 125

James, Dynely
See Mayne, William (James Carter)

James, Henry Sr. 1811-1882 .... **NCLC 53**

James, Henry 1843-1916 .... **SSC 8, 32, 47;**
TCLC 2, 11, 24, 40, 47, 64; WLC
See also AMW; AMWC 1; AMWR 1; BPFB
2; BRW 6; CA 104; 132; CDALB 1865-
1917; DA; DA3; DAB; DAC; DAM MST,
NOV; DLB 12, 71, 74, 189; DLBD 13;
EWL 3; EXPS; HGG; LAIT 2; MTCW 1,
2; NFS 12, 16, 19; RGAL 4; RGEL 2;
RGSF 2; SSFS 9; SUFW 1; TUS

James, M. R.
See James, Montague (Rhodes)
See also DLB 156, 201

James, Montague (Rhodes)
1862-1936 .... **SSC 16; TCLC 6**
See James, M. R.
See also CA 104; 203; HGG; RGEL 2;
RGSF 2; SUFW 1

James, P. D. .... **CLC 18, 46, 122**
See White, Phyllis Dorothy James
See also BEST 90:2; BPFB 2; BRWS 4;
CDBLB 1960 to Present; DLB 87, 276;
DLBD 17; MSW

James, Philip
See Moorcock, Michael (John)

James, Samuel
See Stephens, James

James, Seumas
See Stephens, James

James, Stephen
See Stephens, James

James, William 1842-1910 .... **TCLC 15, 32**
See also AMW; CA 109; 193; DLB 270,
284; NCFS 5; RGAL 4

Jameson, Anna 1794-1860 .... **NCLC 43**
See also DLB 99, 166

Jameson, Fredric (R.) 1934- .... **CLC 142**
See also CA 196; DLB 67; LMFS 2

James VI of Scotland 1566-1625 .... **LC 109**

Jami, Nur al-Din 'Abd al-Rahman
1414-1492 .... **LC 9**

Jammes, Francis 1868-1938 .... **TCLC 75**
See also CA 198; EWL 3; GFL 1789 to the
Present

Jandl, Ernst 1925-2000 .... **CLC 34**
See also CA 200; EWL 3

Janowitz, Tama 1957- .... **CLC 43, 145**
See also CA 106; CANR 52, 89, 129; CN
7; CPW; DAM POP; DLB 292

Japrisot, Sebastien 1931- .... **CLC 90**
See Rossi, Jean-Baptiste
See also CMW 4; NFS 18

Jarrell, Randall 1914-1965 .... **CLC 1, 2, 6, 9,**
13, 49; PC 41
See also AMW; BYA 5; CA 5-8R; 25-28R;
CABS 2; CANR 6, 34; CDALB 1941-
1968; CLR 6; CWRI 5; DAM POET;
DLB 48, 52; EWL 3; EXPP; MAICYA 1,
2; MTCW 1, 2; PAB; PFS 2; RGAL 4;
SATA 7

Jarry, Alfred 1873-1907 .... **SSC 20; TCLC 2,**
14, 147
See also CA 104; 153; DA3; DAM DRAM;
DFS 8; DLB 192, 258; EW 9; EWL 3;
GFL 1789 to the Present; RGWL 2, 3;
TWA

Jarvis, E. K.
See Ellison, Harlan (Jay)

Jawien, Andrzej
See John Paul II, Pope

Jaynes, Roderick
See Coen, Ethan

Jeake, Samuel, Jr.
See Aiken, Conrad (Potter)

Jean Paul 1763-1825 .... **NCLC 7**

Jefferies, (John) Richard
1848-1887 .... **NCLC 47**
See also DLB 98, 141; RGEL 2; SATA 16;
SFW 4

Jeffers, (John) Robinson 1887-1962 .. **CLC 2,**
3, 11, 15, 54; PC 17; WLC
See also AMWS 2; CA 85-88; CANR 35;
CDALB 1917-1929; DA; DAC; DAM
MST, POET; DLB 45, 212; EWL 3;
MTCW 1, 2; PAB; PFS 3, 4; RGAL 4

Jefferson, Janet
See Mencken, H(enry) L(ouis)

Jefferson, Thomas 1743-1826 . **NCLC 11, 103**
See also AAYA 54; ANW; CDALB 1640-
1865; DA3; DLB 31, 183; LAIT 1; RGAL
4

Jeffrey, Francis 1773-1850 .... **NCLC 33**
See Francis, Lord Jeffrey

Jelakowitch, Ivan
See Heijermans, Herman

Jelinek, Elfriede 1946- .... **CLC 169**
See also CA 154; DLB 85; FW

Jellicoe, (Patricia) Ann 1927- .... **CLC 27**
See also CA 85-88; CBD; CD 5; CWD;
CWRI 5; DLB 13, 233; FW

Jelloun, Tahar ben 1944- .... **CLC 180**
See Ben Jelloun, Tahar
See also CA 162; CANR 100

Jemyma
See Holley, Marietta

Jen, Gish .... **AAL; CLC 70, 198**
See Jen, Lillian
See also AMWC 2

Jen, Lillian 1956(?)-
See Jen, Gish
See also CA 135; CANR 89, 130

Jenkins, (John) Robin 1912- .... **CLC 52**
See also CA 1-4R; CANR 1, 135; CN 7;
DLB 14, 271

Jennings, Elizabeth (Joan)
1926-2001 .... **CLC 5, 14, 131**
See also BRWS 5; CA 61-64; 200; CAAS
5; CANR 8, 39, 66, 127; CP 7; CWP;
DLB 27; EWL 3; MTCW 1; SATA 66

Jennings, Waylon 1937- .... **CLC 21**

Jensen, Johannes V(ilhelm)
1873-1950 .... **TCLC 41**
See also CA 170; DLB 214; EWL 3; RGWL
3

Jensen, Laura (Linnea) 1948- .... **CLC 37**
See also CA 103

Jerome, Saint 345-420 .... **CMLC 30**
See also RGWL 3

Jerome, Jerome K(lapka)
1859-1927 .... **TCLC 23**
See also CA 119; 177; DLB 10, 34, 135;
RGEL 2

Jerrold, Douglas William
1803-1857 .... **NCLC 2**
See also DLB 158, 159; RGEL 2

Jewett, (Theodora) Sarah Orne
1849-1909 .... **SSC 6, 44; TCLC 1, 22**
See also AMW; AMWC 2; AMWR 2; CA
108; 127; CANR 71; DLB 12, 74, 221;
EXPS; FW; MAWW; NFS 15; RGAL 4;
RGSF 2; SATA 15; SSFS 4

Jewsbury, Geraldine (Endsor)
1812-1880 .... **NCLC 22**
See also DLB 21

Jhabvala, Ruth Prawer 1927- . **CLC 4, 8, 29,**
94, 138
See also BRWS 5; CA 1-4R; CANR 2, 29,
51, 74, 91, 128; CN 7; DAB; DAM NOV;
DLB 139, 194; EWL 3; IDFW 3, 4; INT
CANR-29; MTCW 1, 2; RGSF 2; RGWL
2; RHW; TEA

Jibran, Kahlil
See Gibran, Kahlil

Jibran, Khalil
See Gibran, Kahlil

Jiles, Paulette 1943- .... **CLC 13, 58**
See also CA 101; CANR 70, 124; CWP

Jimenez (Mantecon), Juan Ramon
1881-1958 .... **HLC 1; PC 7; TCLC 4**
See also CA 104; 131; CANR 74; DAM
MULT, POET; DLB 134; EW 9; EWL 3;
HW 1; MTCW 1, 2; RGWL 2, 3

Jimenez, Ramon
See Jimenez (Mantecon), Juan Ramon

Jimenez Mantecon, Juan
See Jimenez (Mantecon), Juan Ramon

Jin, Ha .... **CLC 109**
See Jin, Xuefei
See also CA 152; DLB 244, 292; SSFS 17

Jin, Xuefei 1956-
See Jin, Ha
See also CANR 91, 130; SSFS 17

Joel, Billy .... **CLC 26**
See Joel, William Martin

Joel, William Martin 1949-
See Joel, Billy
See also CA 108

John, Saint 10(?)-100 .... **CMLC 27, 63**

John of Salisbury c. 1115-1180 ..... **CMLC 63**

John of the Cross, St. 1542-1591 .... **LC 18**
See also RGWL 2, 3

John Paul II, Pope 1920- .... **CLC 128**
See also CA 106; 133

Kingman, Lee .... **CLC 17**
See Natti, (Mary) Lee
See also CWRI 5; SAAS 3; SATA 1, 67
Kingsley, Charles 1819-1875 .... **NCLC 35**
See also CLR 77; DLB 21, 32, 163, 178, 190; FANT; MAICYA 2; MAICYAS 1; RGEL 2; WCH; YABC 2
Kingsley, Henry 1830-1876 .... **NCLC 107**
See also DLB 21, 230; RGEL 2
Kingsley, Sidney 1906-1995 .... **CLC 44**
See also CA 85-88; 147; CAD; DFS 14, 19; DLB 7; RGAL 4
Kingsolver, Barbara 1955- . **CLC 55, 81, 130**
See also AAYA 15; AMWS 7; CA 129; 134; CANR 60, 96, 133; CDALBS; CPW; CSW; DA3; DAM POP; DLB 206; INT CA-134; LAIT 5; MTCW 2; NFS 5, 10, 12; RGAL 4
Kingston, Maxine (Ting Ting) Hong
1940- .... **AAL; CLC 12, 19, 58, 121; WLCS**
See also AAYA 8, 55; AMWS 5; BPFB 2; CA 69-72; CANR 13, 38, 74, 87, 128; CDALBS; CN 7; DA3; DAM MULT, NOV; DLB 173, 212; DLBY 1980; EWL 3; FW; INT CANR-13; LAIT 5; MAWW; MTCW 1, 2; NFS 6; RGAL 4; SATA 53; SSFS 3
Kinnell, Galway 1927- ..... **CLC 1, 2, 3, 5, 13, 29, 129; PC 26**
See also AMWS 3; CA 9-12R; CANR 10, 34, 66, 116; CP 7; DLB 5; DLBY 1987; EWL 3; INT CANR-34; MTCW 1, 2; PAB; PFS 9; RGAL 4; WP
Kinsella, Thomas 1928- .... **CLC 4, 19, 138**
See also BRWS 5; CA 17-20R; CANR 15, 122; CP 7; DLB 27; EWL 3; MTCW 1, 2; RGEL 2; TEA
Kinsella, W(illiam) P(atrick) 1935- . **CLC 27, 43, 166**
See also AAYA 7, 60; BPFB 2; CA 97-100; 222; CAAE 222; CAAS 7; CANR 21, 35, 66, 75, 129; CN 7; CPW; DAC; DAM NOV, POP; FANT; INT CANR-21; LAIT 5; MTCW 1, 2; NFS 15; RGSF 2
Kinsey, Alfred C(harles)
1894-1956 .... **TCLC 91**
See also CA 115; 170; MTCW 2
Kipling, (Joseph) Rudyard 1865-1936 . **PC 3; SSC 5, 54; TCLC 8, 17, 167; WLC**
See also AAYA 32; BRW 6; BRWC 1, 2; BYA 4; CA 105; 120; CANR 33; CDBLB 1890-1914; CLR 39, 65; CWRI 5; DA; DA3; DAB; DAC; DAM MST, POET; DLB 19, 34, 141, 156; EWL 3; EXPS; FANT; LAIT 3; LMFS 1; MAICYA 1, 2; MTCW 1, 2; RGEL 2; RGSF 2; SATA 100; SFW 4; SSFS 8; SUFW 1; TEA; WCH; WLIT 4; YABC 2
Kirk, Russell (Amos) 1918-1994 .. **TCLC 119**
See also AITN 1; CA 1-4R; 145; CAAS 9; CANR 1, 20, 60; HGG; INT CANR-20; MTCW 1, 2
Kirkham, Dinah
See Card, Orson Scott
Kirkland, Caroline M. 1801-1864 . **NCLC 85**
See also DLB 3, 73, 74, 250, 254; DLBD 13
Kirkup, James 1918- .... **CLC 1**
See also CA 1-4R; CAAS 4; CANR 2; CP 7; DLB 27; SATA 12
Kirkwood, James 1930(?)-1989 .... **CLC 9**
See also AITN 2; CA 1-4R; 128; CANR 6, 40; GLL 2
Kirsch, Sarah 1935- .... **CLC 176**
See also CA 178; CWW 2; DLB 75; EWL 3
Kirshner, Sidney
See Kingsley, Sidney

Kis, Danilo 1935-1989 .... **CLC 57**
See also CA 109; 118; 129; CANR 61; CD-WLB 4; DLB 181; EWL 3; MTCW 1; RGSF 2; RGWL 2, 3
Kissinger, Henry A(lfred) 1923- ..... **CLC 137**
See also CA 1-4R; CANR 2, 33, 66, 109; MTCW 1
Kivi, Aleksis 1834-1872 .... **NCLC 30**
Kizer, Carolyn (Ashley) 1925- ... **CLC 15, 39, 80; PC 66**
See also CA 65-68; CAAS 5; CANR 24, 70, 134; CP 7; CWP; DAM POET; DLB 5, 169; EWL 3; MTCW 2; PFS 18
Klabund 1890-1928 .... **TCLC 44**
See also CA 162; DLB 66
Klappert, Peter 1942- .... **CLC 57**
See also CA 33-36R; CSW; DLB 5
Klein, A(braham) M(oses)
1909-1972 .... **CLC 19**
See also CA 101; 37-40R; DAB; DAC; DAM MST; DLB 68; EWL 3; RGEL 2
Klein, Joe
See Klein, Joseph
Klein, Joseph 1946- .... **CLC 154**
See also CA 85-88; CANR 55
Klein, Norma 1938-1989 .... **CLC 30**
See also AAYA 2, 35; BPFB 2; BYA 6, 7, 8; CA 41-44R; 128; CANR 15, 37; CLR 2, 19; INT CANR-15; JRDA; MAICYA 1, 2; SAAS 1; SATA 7, 57; WYA; YAW
Klein, T(heodore) E(ibon) D(onald)
1947- .... **CLC 34**
See also CA 119; CANR 44, 75; HGG
Kleist, Heinrich von 1777-1811 ...... **NCLC 2, 37; SSC 22**
See also CDWLB 2; DAM DRAM; DLB 90; EW 5; RGSF 2; RGWL 2, 3
Klima, Ivan 1931- .... **CLC 56, 172**
See also CA 25-28R; CANR 17, 50, 91; CDWLB 4; CWW 2; DAM NOV; DLB 232; EWL 3; RGWL 3
Klimentev, Andrei Platonovich
See Klimentov, Andrei Platonovich
Klimentov, Andrei Platonovich
1899-1951 .... **SSC 42; TCLC 14**
See Platonov, Andrei Platonovich; Platonov, Andrey Platonovich
See also CA 108
Klinger, Friedrich Maximilian von
1752-1831 .... **NCLC 1**
See also DLB 94
Klingsor the Magician
See Hartmann, Sadakichi
Klopstock, Friedrich Gottlieb
1724-1803 .... **NCLC 11**
See also DLB 97; EW 4; RGWL 2, 3
Kluge, Alexander 1932- .... **SSC 61**
See also CA 81-84; DLB 75
Knapp, Caroline 1959-2002 .... **CLC 99**
See also CA 154; 207
Knebel, Fletcher 1911-1993 .... **CLC 14**
See also AITN 1; CA 1-4R; 140; CAAS 3; CANR 1, 36; SATA 36; SATA-Obit 75
Knickerbocker, Diedrich
See Irving, Washington
Knight, Etheridge 1931-1991 ... **BLC 2; CLC 40; PC 14**
See also BW 1, 3; CA 21-24R; 133; CANR 23, 82; DAM POET; DLB 41; MTCW 2; RGAL 4
Knight, Sarah Kemble 1666-1727 .... **LC 7**
See also DLB 24, 200
Knister, Raymond 1899-1932 .... **TCLC 56**
See also CA 186; DLB 68; RGEL 2
Knowles, John 1926-2001 ... **CLC 1, 4, 10, 26**
See also AAYA 10; AMWS 12; BPFB 2; BYA 3; CA 17-20R; 203; CANR 40, 74, 76, 132; CDALB 1968-1988; CLR 98; CN

7; DA; DAC; DAM MST, NOV; DLB 6; EXPN; MTCW 1, 2; NFS 2; RGAL 4; SATA 8, 89; SATA-Obit 134; YAW
Knox, Calvin M.
See Silverberg, Robert
Knox, John c. 1505-1572 .... **LC 37**
See also DLB 132
Knye, Cassandra
See Disch, Thomas M(ichael)
Koch, C(hristopher) J(ohn) 1932- .... **CLC 42**
See also CA 127; CANR 84; CN 7; DLB 289
Koch, Christopher
See Koch, C(hristopher) J(ohn)
Koch, Kenneth (Jay) 1925-2002 .... **CLC 5, 8, 44**
See also CA 1-4R; 207; CAD; CANR 6, 36, 57, 97, 131; CD 5; CP 7; DAM POET; DLB 5; INT CANR-36; MTCW 2; PFS 20; SATA 65; WP
Kochanowski, Jan 1530-1584 .... **LC 10**
See also RGWL 2, 3
Kock, Charles Paul de 1794-1871 . **NCLC 16**
Koda Rohan
See Koda Shigeyuki
Koda Rohan
See Koda Shigeyuki
See also DLB 180
Koda Shigeyuki 1867-1947 .... **TCLC 22**
See Koda Rohan
See also CA 121; 183
Koestler, Arthur 1905-1983 ... **CLC 1, 3, 6, 8, 15, 33**
See also BRWS 1; CA 1-4R; 109; CANR 1, 33; CDBLB 1945-1960; DLBY 1983; EWL 3; MTCW 1, 2; NFS 19; RGEL 2
Kogawa, Joy Nozomi 1935- ...... **CLC 78, 129**
See also AAYA 47; CA 101; CANR 19, 62, 126; CN 7; CWP; DAC; DAM MST, MULT; FW; MTCW 2; NFS 3; SATA 99
Kohout, Pavel 1928- .... **CLC 13**
See also CA 45-48; CANR 3
Koizumi, Yakumo
See Hearn, (Patricio) Lafcadio (Tessima Carlos)
Kolmar, Gertrud 1894-1943 .... **TCLC 40**
See also CA 167; EWL 3
Komunyakaa, Yusef 1947- .. **BLCS; CLC 86, 94, 207; PC 51**
See also AFAW 2; AMWS 13; CA 147; CANR 83; CP 7; CSW; DLB 120; EWL 3; PFS 5, 20; RGAL 4
Konrad, George
See Konrad, Gyorgy
Konrad, Gyorgy 1933- .... **CLC 4, 10, 73**
See also CA 85-88; CANR 97; CDWLB 4; CWW 2; DLB 232; EWL 3
Konwicki, Tadeusz 1926- .... **CLC 8, 28, 54, 117**
See also CA 101; CAAS 9; CANR 39, 59; CWW 2; DLB 232; EWL 3; IDFW 3; MTCW 1
Koontz, Dean R(ay) 1945- .... **CLC 78, 206**
See also AAYA 9, 31; BEST 89:3, 90:2; CA 108; CANR 19, 36, 52, 95; CMW 4; CPW; DA3; DAM NOV, POP; DLB 292; HGG; MTCW 1; SATA 92; SFW 4; SUFW 2; YAW
Kopernik, Mikolaj
See Copernicus, Nicolaus
Kopit, Arthur (Lee) 1937- ...... **CLC 1, 18, 33**
See also AITN 1; CA 81-84; CABS 3; CD 5; DAM DRAM; DFS 7, 14; DLB 7; MTCW 1; RGAL 4
Kopitar, Jernej (Bartholomaus)
1780-1844 .... **NCLC 117**
Kops, Bernard 1926- .... **CLC 4**
See also CA 5-8R; CANR 84; CBD; CN 7; CP 7; DLB 13

Longfellow, Henry Wadsworth
1807-1882 .... **NCLC 2, 45, 101, 103; PC 30; WLCS**
See also AMW; AMWR 2; CDALB 1640-1865; CLR 99; DA; DA3; DAB; DAC; DAM MST, POET; DLB 1, 59, 235; EXPP; PAB; PFS 2, 7, 17; RGAL 4; SATA 19; TUS; WP

Longinus c. 1st cent. - .... **CMLC 27**
See also AW 2; DLB 176

Longley, Michael 1939- .... **CLC 29**
See also BRWS 8; CA 102; CP 7; DLB 40

Longus fl. c. 2nd cent. - .... **CMLC 7**

Longway, A. Hugh
See Lang, Andrew

Lonnbohm, Armas Eino Leopold 1878-1926
See Leino, Eino
See also CA 123

Lonnrot, Elias 1802-1884 .... **NCLC 53**
See also EFS 1

Lonsdale, Roger ed. .... **CLC 65**

Lopate, Phillip 1943- .... **CLC 29**
See also CA 97-100; CANR 88; DLBY 1980; INT CA-97-100

Lopez, Barry (Holstun) 1945- .... **CLC 70**
See also AAYA 9; ANW; CA 65-68; CANR 7, 23, 47, 68, 92; DLB 256, 275; INT CANR-7, -23; MTCW 1; RGAL 4; SATA 67

Lopez Portillo (y Pacheco), Jose
1920-2004 .... **CLC 46**
See also CA 129; 224; HW 1

Lopez y Fuentes, Gregorio
1897(?)-1966 .... **CLC 32**
See also CA 131; EWL 3; HW 1

Lorca, Federico Garcia
See Garcia Lorca, Federico
See also DFS 4; EW 11; PFS 20; RGWL 2, 3; WP

Lord, Audre
See Lorde, Audre (Geraldine)
See also EWL 3

Lord, Bette Bao 1938- .... **AAL; CLC 23**
See also BEST 90:3; BPFB 2; CA 107; CANR 41, 79; INT CA-107; SATA 58

Lord Auch
See Bataille, Georges

Lord Brooke
See Greville, Fulke

Lord Byron
See Byron, George Gordon (Noel)

Lorde, Audre (Geraldine)
1934-1992 .. **BLC 2; CLC 18, 71; PC 12**
See Domini, Rey; Lord, Audre
See also AFAW 1, 2; BW 1, 3; CA 25-28R; 142; CANR 16, 26, 46, 82; DA3; DAM MULT, POET; DLB 41; FW; MTCW 1, 2; PFS 16; RGAL 4

Lord Houghton
See Milnes, Richard Monckton

Lord Jeffrey
See Jeffrey, Francis

Loreaux, Nichol .... **CLC 65**

Lorenzini, Carlo 1826-1890
See Collodi, Carlo
See also MAICYA 1, 2; SATA 29, 100

Lorenzo, Heberto Padilla
See Padilla (Lorenzo), Heberto

Loris
See Hofmannsthal, Hugo von

Loti, Pierre .... **TCLC 11**
See Viaud, (Louis Marie) Julien
See also DLB 123; GFL 1789 to the Present

Lou, Henri
See Andreas-Salome, Lou

Louie, David Wong 1954- .... **CLC 70**
See also CA 139; CANR 120

Louis, Adrian C. .... **NNAL**
See also CA 223

Louis, Father M.
See Merton, Thomas (James)

Louise, Heidi
See Erdrich, Louise

Lovecraft, H(oward) P(hillips)
1890-1937 .... **SSC 3, 52; TCLC 4, 22**
See also AAYA 14; BPFB 2; CA 104; 133; CANR 106; DA3; DAM POP; HGG; MTCW 1, 2; RGAL 4; SCFW; SFW 4; SUFW

Lovelace, Earl 1935- .... **CLC 51**
See also BW 2; CA 77-80; CANR 41, 72, 114; CD 5; CDWLB 3; CN 7; DLB 125; EWL 3; MTCW 1

Lovelace, Richard 1618-1657 .... **LC 24**
See also BRW 2; DLB 131; EXPP; PAB; RGEL 2

Lowe, Pardee 1904- .... **AAL**

Lowell, Amy 1874-1925 ... **PC 13; TCLC 1, 8**
See also AMW; CA 104; 151; DAM POET; DLB 54, 140; EWL 3; EXPP; LMFS 2; MAWW; MTCW 2; RGAL 4; TUS

Lowell, James Russell 1819-1891 ... **NCLC 2, 90**
See also AMWS 1; CDALB 1640-1865; DLB 1, 11, 64, 79, 189, 235; RGAL 4

Lowell, Robert (Traill Spence, Jr.)
1917-1977 .... **CLC 1, 2, 3, 4, 5, 8, 9, 11, 15, 37, 124; PC 3; WLC**
See also AMW; AMWC 2; AMWR 2; CA 9-12R; 73-76; CABS 2; CANR 26, 60; CDALBS; DA; DA3; DAB; DAC; DAM MST, NOV; DLB 5, 169; EWL 3; MTCW 1, 2; PAB; PFS 6, 7; RGAL 4; WP

Lowenthal, Michael (Francis)
1969- .... **CLC 119**
See also CA 150; CANR 115

Lowndes, Marie Adelaide (Belloc)
1868-1947 .... **TCLC 12**
See also CA 107; CMW 4; DLB 70; RHW

Lowry, (Clarence) Malcolm
1909-1957 .... **SSC 31; TCLC 6, 40**
See also BPFB 2; BRWS 3; CA 105; 131; CANR 62, 105; CDBLB 1945-1960; DLB 15; EWL 3; MTCW 1, 2; RGEL 2

Lowry, Mina Gertrude 1882-1966
See Loy, Mina
See also CA 113

Loxsmith, John
See Brunner, John (Kilian Houston)

Loy, Mina .... **CLC 28; PC 16**
See Lowry, Mina Gertrude
See also DAM POET; DLB 4, 54; PFS 20

Loyson-Bridet
See Schwob, Marcel (Mayer Andre)

Lucan 39-65 .... **CMLC 33**
See also AW 2; DLB 211; EFS 2; RGWL 2, 3

Lucas, Craig 1951- .... **CLC 64**
See also CA 137; CAD; CANR 71, 109; CD 5; GLL 2

Lucas, E(dward) V(errall)
1868-1938 .... **TCLC 73**
See also CA 176; DLB 98, 149, 153; SATA 20

Lucas, George 1944- .... **CLC 16**
See also AAYA 1, 23; CA 77-80; CANR 30; SATA 56

Lucas, Hans
See Godard, Jean-Luc

Lucas, Victoria
See Plath, Sylvia

Lucian c. 125-c. 180 .... **CMLC 32**
See also AW 2; DLB 176; RGWL 2, 3

Lucretius c. 94B.C.-c. 49B.C. .... **CMLC 48**
See also AW 2; CDWLB 1; DLB 211; EFS 2; RGWL 2, 3

Ludlam, Charles 1943-1987 .... **CLC 46, 50**
See also CA 85-88; 122; CAD; CANR 72, 86; DLB 266

Ludlum, Robert 1927-2001 .... **CLC 22, 43**
See also AAYA 10, 59; BEST 89:1, 90:3; BPFB 2; CA 33-36R; 195; CANR 25, 41, 68, 105, 131; CMW 4; CPW; DA3; DAM NOV, POP; DLBY 1982; MSW; MTCW 1, 2

Ludwig, Ken .... **CLC 60**
See also CA 195; CAD

Ludwig, Otto 1813-1865 .... **NCLC 4**
See also DLB 129

Lugones, Leopoldo 1874-1938 .... **HLCS 2; TCLC 15**
See also CA 116; 131; CANR 104; DLB 283; EWL 3; HW 1; LAW

Lu Hsun .... **SSC 20; TCLC 3**
See Shu-Jen, Chou
See also EWL 3

Lukacs, George .... **CLC 24**
See Lukacs, Gyorgy (Szegeny von)

Lukacs, Gyorgy (Szegeny von) 1885-1971
See Lukacs, George
See also CA 101; 29-32R; CANR 62; CD-WLB 4; DLB 215, 242; EW 10; EWL 3; MTCW 2

Luke, Peter (Ambrose Cyprian)
1919-1995 .... **CLC 38**
See also CA 81-84; 147; CANR 72; CBD; CD 5; DLB 13

Lunar, Dennis
See Mungo, Raymond

Lurie, Alison 1926- ..... **CLC 4, 5, 18, 39, 175**
See also BPFB 2; CA 1-4R; CANR 2, 17, 50, 88; CN 7; DLB 2; MTCW 1; SATA 46, 112

Lustig, Arnost 1926- .... **CLC 56**
See also AAYA 3; CA 69-72; CANR 47, 102; CWW 2; DLB 232, 299; EWL 3; SATA 56

Luther, Martin 1483-1546 .... **LC 9, 37**
See also CDWLB 2; DLB 179; EW 2; RGWL 2, 3

Luxemburg, Rosa 1870(?)-1919 ..... **TCLC 63**
See also CA 118

Luzi, Mario 1914- .... **CLC 13**
See also CA 61-64; CANR 9, 70; CWW 2; DLB 128; EWL 3

L'vov, Arkady .... **CLC 59**

Lydgate, John c. 1370-1450(?) .... **LC 81**
See also BRW 1; DLB 146; RGEL 2

Lyly, John 1554(?)-1606 .... **DC 7; LC 41**
See also BRW 1; DAM DRAM; DLB 62, 167; RGEL 2

L'Ymagier
See Gourmont, Remy(-Marie-Charles) de

Lynch, B. Suarez
See Borges, Jorge Luis

Lynch, David (Keith) 1946- ...... **CLC 66, 162**
See also AAYA 55; CA 124; 129; CANR 111

Lynch, James
See Andreyev, Leonid (Nikolaevich)

Lyndsay, Sir David 1485-1555 .... **LC 20**
See also RGEL 2

Lynn, Kenneth S(chuyler)
1923-2001 .... **CLC 50**
See also CA 1-4R; 196; CANR 3, 27, 65

Lynx
See West, Rebecca

Lyons, Marcus
See Blish, James (Benjamin)

Lyotard, Jean-Francois
1924-1998 .... **TCLC 103**
See also DLB 242; EWL 3

Lyre, Pinchbeck
See Sassoon, Siegfried (Lorraine)

Mirbeau, Octave 1848-1917 .... **TCLC 55**
See also CA 216; DLB 123, 192; GFL 1789
to the Present
Mirikitani, Janice 1942- .... **AAL**
See also CA 211; RGAL 4
Mirk, John (?)-c. 1414 .... **LC 105**
See also DLB 146
Miro (Ferrer), Gabriel (Francisco Victor)
1879-1930 .... **TCLC 5**
See also CA 104; 185; EWL 3
Misharin, Alexandr .... **CLC 59**
Mishima, Yukio ... CLC 2, 4, 6, 9, 27; DC 1;
SSC 4, TCLC 161
See Hiraoka, Kimitake
See also AAYA 50; BPFB 2; GLL 1; MJW;
MTCW 2; RGSF 2; RGWL 2, 3; SSFS 5,
12
Mistral, Frederic 1830-1914 .... **TCLC 51**
See also CA 122; 213; GFL 1789 to the
Present
Mistral, Gabriela
See Godoy Alcayaga, Lucila
See also DLB 283; DNFS 1; EWL 3; LAW;
RGWL 2, 3; WP
Mistry, Rohinton 1952- ... CLC 71, 196; SSC
73
See also BRWS 10; CA 141; CANR 86,
114; CCA 1; CN 7; DAC; SSFS 6
Mitchell, Clyde
See Ellison, Harlan (Jay)
Mitchell, Emerson Blackhorse Barney
1945- .... **NNAL**
See also CA 45-48
Mitchell, James Leslie 1901-1935
See Gibbon, Lewis Grassic
See also CA 104; 188; DLB 15
Mitchell, Joni 1943- .... **CLC 12**
See also CA 112; CCA 1
Mitchell, Joseph (Quincy)
1908-1996 .... **CLC 98**
See also CA 77-80; 152; CANR 69; CN 7;
CSW; DLB 185; DLBY 1996
Mitchell, Margaret (Munnerlyn)
1900-1949 .... **TCLC 11**
See also AAYA 23; BPFB 2; BYA 1; CA
109; 125; CANR 55, 94; CDALBS; DA3;
DAM NOV, POP; DLB 9; LAIT 2;
MTCW 1, 2; NFS 9; RGAL 4; RHW;
TUS; WYAS 1; YAW
Mitchell, Peggy
See Mitchell, Margaret (Munnerlyn)
Mitchell, S(ilas) Weir 1829-1914 .... **TCLC 36**
See also CA 165; DLB 202; RGAL 4
Mitchell, W(illiam) O(rmond)
1914-1998 .... **CLC 25**
See also CA 77-80; 165; CANR 15, 43; CN
7; DAC; DAM MST; DLB 88
Mitchell, William (Lendrum)
1879-1936 .... **TCLC 81**
See also CA 213
Mitford, Mary Russell 1787-1855 ... **NCLC 4**
See also DLB 110, 116; RGEL 2
Mitford, Nancy 1904-1973 .... **CLC 44**
See also BRWS 10; CA 9-12R; DLB 191;
RGEL 2
Miyamoto, (Chujo) Yuriko
1899-1951 .... **TCLC 37**
See Miyamoto Yuriko
See also CA 170, 174
Miyamoto Yuriko
See Miyamoto, (Chujo) Yuriko
See also DLB 180
Miyazawa, Kenji 1896-1933 .... **TCLC 76**
See Miyazawa Kenji
See also CA 157; RGWL 3
Miyazawa Kenji
See Miyazawa, Kenji
See also EWL 3

Mizoguchi, Kenji 1898-1956 .... **TCLC 72**
See also CA 167
Mo, Timothy (Peter) 1950(?)- ... CLC 46, 134
See also CA 117; CANR 128; CN 7; DLB
194; MTCW 1; WLIT 4; WWE 1
Modarressi, Taghi (M.) 1931-1997 ... **CLC 44**
See also CA 121; 134; INT CA-134
Modiano, Patrick (Jean) 1945- .... **CLC 18**
See also CA 85-88; CANR 17, 40, 115;
CWW 2; DLB 83, 299; EWL 3
Mofolo, Thomas (Mokopu)
1875(?)-1948 .... **BLC 3; TCLC 22**
See also AFW; CA 121; 153; CANR 83;
DAM MULT; DLB 225; EWL 3; MTCW
2; WLIT 2
Mohr, Nicholasa 1938- .... **CLC 12; HLC 2**
See also AAYA 8, 46; CA 49-52; CANR 1,
32, 64; CLR 22; DAM MULT; DLB 145;
HW 1, 2; JRDA; LAIT 5; LLW 1; MAI-
CYA 2; MAICYAS 1; RGAL 4; SAAS 8;
SATA 8, 97; SATA-Essay 113; WYA;
YAW
Moi, Toril 1953- .... **CLC 172**
See also CA 154; CANR 102; FW
Mojtabai, A(nn) G(race) 1938- ..... CLC 5, 9,
15, 29
See also CA 85-88; CANR 88
Moliere 1622-1673 ..... DC 13; LC 10, 28, 64;
WLC
See also DA; DA3; DAB; DAC; DAM
DRAM, MST; DFS 13, 18, 20; DLB 268;
EW 3; GFL Beginnings to 1789; LATS
1:1; RGWL 2, 3; TWA
Molin, Charles
See Mayne, William (James Carter)
Molnar, Ferenc 1878-1952 .... **TCLC 20**
See also CA 109; 153; CANR 83; CDWLB
4; DAM DRAM; DLB 215; EWL 3;
RGWL 2, 3
Momaday, N(avarre) Scott 1934- ...... CLC 2,
19, 85, 95, 160; NNAL; PC 25; WLCS
See also AAYA 11; AMWS 4; ANW; BPFB
2; BYA 12; CA 25-28R; CANR 14, 34,
68, 134; CDALBS; CN 7; CPW; DA;
DA3; DAB; DAC; DAM MST, MULT,
NOV, POP; DLB 143, 175, 256; EWL 3;
EXPP; INT CANR-14; LAIT 4; LATS
1:2; MTCW 1, 2; NFS 10; PFS 2, 11;
RGAL 4; SATA 48; SATA-Brief 30; WP;
YAW
Monette, Paul 1945-1995 .... **CLC 82**
See also AMWS 10; CA 139; 147; CN 7;
GLL 1
Monroe, Harriet 1860-1936 .... **TCLC 12**
See also CA 109; 204; DLB 54, 91
Monroe, Lyle
See Heinlein, Robert A(nson)
Montagu, Elizabeth 1720-1800 .... **NCLC 7,**
117
See also FW
Montagu, Mary (Pierrepont) Wortley
1689-1762 .... LC 9, 57; PC 16
See also DLB 95, 101; RGEL 2
Montagu, W. H.
See Coleridge, Samuel Taylor
Montague, John (Patrick) 1929- ..... CLC 13,
46
See also CA 9-12R; CANR 9, 69, 121; CP
7; DLB 40; EWL 3; MTCW 1; PFS 12;
RGEL 2
Montaigne, Michel (Eyquem) de
1533-1592 .... LC 8, 105; WLC
See also DA; DAB; DAC; DAM MST; EW
2; GFL Beginnings to 1789; LMFS 1;
RGWL 2, 3; TWA
Montale, Eugenio 1896-1981 ... CLC 7, 9, 18;
PC 13
See also CA 17-20R; 104; CANR 30; DLB
114; EW 11; EWL 3; MTCW 1; RGWL
2, 3; TWA

Montesquieu, Charles-Louis de Secondat
1689-1755 .... **LC 7, 69**
See also EW 3; GFL Beginnings to 1789;
TWA
Montessori, Maria 1870-1952 ...... **TCLC 103**
See also CA 115; 147
Montgomery, (Robert) Bruce 1921(?)-1978
See Crispin, Edmund
See also CA 179; 104; CMW 4
Montgomery, L(ucy) M(aud)
1874-1942 .... **TCLC 51, 140**
See also AAYA 12; BYA 1; CA 108; 137;
CLR 8, 91; DA3; DAC; DAM MST; DLB
92; DLBD 14; JRDA; MAICYA 1, 2;
MTCW 2; RGEL 2; SATA 100; TWA;
WCH; WYA; YABC 1
Montgomery, Marion H., Jr. 1925- .... **CLC 7**
See also AITN 1; CA 1-4R; CANR 3, 48;
CSW; DLB 6
Montgomery, Max
See Davenport, Guy (Mattison, Jr.)
Montherlant, Henry (Milon) de
1896-1972 .... **CLC 8, 19**
See also CA 85-88; 37-40R; DAM DRAM;
DLB 72; EW 11; EWL 3; GFL 1789 to
the Present; MTCW 1
Monty Python
See Chapman, Graham; Cleese, John
(Marwood); Gilliam, Terry (Vance); Idle,
Eric; Jones, Terence Graham Parry; Palin,
Michael (Edward)
See also AAYA 7
Moodie, Susanna (Strickland)
1803-1885 .... **NCLC 14, 113**
See also DLB 99
Moody, Hiram (F. III) 1961-
See Moody, Rick
See also CA 138; CANR 64, 112
Moody, Minerva
See Alcott, Louisa May
Moody, Rick .... **CLC 147**
See Moody, Hiram (F. III)
Moody, William Vaughan
1869-1910 .... **TCLC 105**
See also CA 110; 178; DLB 7, 54; RGAL 4
Mooney, Edward 1951-
See Mooney, Ted
See also CA 130
Mooney, Ted .... **CLC 25**
See Mooney, Edward
Moorcock, Michael (John) 1939- ...... CLC 5,
27, 58
See Bradbury, Edward P.
See also AAYA 26; CA 45-48; CAAS 5;
CANR 2, 17, 38, 64, 122; CN 7; DLB 14,
231, 261; FANT; MTCW 1, 2; SATA 93;
SCFW 2; SFW 4; SUFW 1, 2
Moore, Brian 1921-1999 ... CLC 1, 3, 5, 7, 8,
19, 32, 90
See Bryan, Michael
See also BRWS 9; CA 1-4R; 174; CANR 1,
25, 42, 63; CCA 1; CN 7; DAB; DAC;
DAM MST; DLB 251; EWL 3; FANT;
MTCW 1, 2; RGEL 2
Moore, Edward
See Muir, Edwin
See also RGEL 2
Moore, G. E. 1873-1958 .... **TCLC 89**
See also DLB 262
Moore, George Augustus
1852-1933 .... **SSC 19; TCLC 7**
See also BRW 6; CA 104; 177; DLB 10,
18, 57, 135; EWL 3; RGEL 2; RGSF 2
Moore, Lorrie .... **CLC 39, 45, 68**
See Moore, Marie Lorena
See also AMWS 10; DLB 234; SSFS 19

Moore, Marianne (Craig)
1887-1972 .... **CLC 1, 2, 4, 8, 10, 13, 19, 47; PC 4, 49; WLCS**
See also AMW; CA 1-4R; 33-36R; CANR 3, 61; CDALB 1929-1941; DA; DA3; DAB; DAC; DAM MST, POET; DLB 45; DLBD 7; EWL 3; EXPP; MAWW; MTCW 1, 2; PAB; PFS 14, 17; RGAL 4; SATA 20; TUS; WP

Moore, Marie Lorena 1957- .... **CLC 165**
See Moore, Lorrie
See also CA 116; CANR 39, 83; CN 7; DLB 234

Moore, Thomas 1779-1852 .... **NCLC 6, 110**
See also DLB 96, 144; RGEL 2

Moorhouse, Frank 1938- .... **SSC 40**
See also CA 118; CANR 92; CN 7; DLB 289; RGSF 2

Mora, Pat(ricia) 1942- .... **HLC 2**
See also AMWS 13; CA 129; CANR 57, 81, 112; CLR 58; DAM MULT; DLB 209; HW 1, 2; LLW 1; MAICYA 2; SATA 92, 134

Moraga, Cherríe 1952- ...... **CLC 126; DC 22**
See also CA 131; CANR 66; DAM MULT; DLB 82, 249; FW; GLL 1; HW 1, 2; LLW 1

Morand, Paul 1888-1976 .... **CLC 41; SSC 22**
See also CA 184; 69-72; DLB 65; EWL 3

Morante, Elsa 1918-1985 .... **CLC 8, 47**
See also CA 85-88; 117; CANR 35; DLB 177; EWL 3; MTCW 1, 2; RGWL 2, 3

Moravia, Alberto .... **CLC 2, 7, 11, 27, 46; SSC 26**
See Pincherle, Alberto
See also DLB 177; EW 12; EWL 3; MTCW 2; RGSF 2; RGWL 2, 3

More, Hannah 1745-1833 ...... **NCLC 27, 141**
See also DLB 107, 109, 116, 158; RGEL 2

More, Henry 1614-1687 .... **LC 9**
See also DLB 126, 252

More, Sir Thomas 1478(?)-1535 .... **LC 10, 32**
See also BRWC 1; BRWS 7; DLB 136, 281; LMFS 1; RGEL 2; TEA

Moréas, Jean .... **TCLC 18**
See Papadiamantopoulos, Johannes
See also GFL 1789 to the Present

Moreton, Andrew Esq.
See Defoe, Daniel

Morgan, Berry 1919-2002 .... **CLC 6**
See also CA 49-52; 208; DLB 6

Morgan, Claire
See Highsmith, (Mary) Patricia
See also GLL 1

Morgan, Edwin (George) 1920- .... **CLC 31**
See also BRWS 9; CA 5-8R; CANR 3, 43, 90; CP 7; DLB 27

Morgan, (George) Frederick
1922-2004 .... **CLC 23**
See also CA 17-20R; 224; CANR 21; CP 7

Morgan, Harriet
See Mencken, H(enry) L(ouis)

Morgan, Jane
See Cooper, James Fenimore

Morgan, Janet 1945- .... **CLC 39**
See also CA 65-68

Morgan, Lady 1776(?)-1859 .... **NCLC 29**
See also DLB 116, 158; RGEL 2

Morgan, Robin (Evonne) 1941- .... **CLC 2**
See also CA 69-72; CANR 29, 68; FW; GLL 2; MTCW 1; SATA 80

Morgan, Scott
See Kuttner, Henry

Morgan, Seth 1949(?)-1990 .... **CLC 65**
See also CA 185; 132

Morgenstern, Christian (Otto Josef Wolfgang) 1871-1914 .... **TCLC 8**
See also CA 105; 191; EWL 3

Morgenstern, S.
See Goldman, William (W.)

Mori, Rintaro
See Mori Ogai
See also CA 110

Mori, Toshio 1910-1980 .... **SSC 83**
See also AAL; CA 116; DLB 312; RGSF 2

Moricz, Zsigmond 1879-1942 .... **TCLC 33**
See also CA 165; DLB 215; EWL 3

Morike, Eduard (Friedrich)
1804-1875 .... **NCLC 10**
See also DLB 133; RGWL 2, 3

Mori Ogai 1862-1922 .... **TCLC 14**
See Ogai
See also CA 164; DLB 180; EWL 3; RGWL 3; TWA

Moritz, Karl Philipp 1756-1793 .... **LC 2**
See also DLB 94

Morland, Peter Henry
See Faust, Frederick (Schiller)

Morley, Christopher (Darlington)
1890-1957 .... **TCLC 87**
See also CA 112; 213; DLB 9; RGAL 4

Morren, Theophil
See Hofmannsthal, Hugo von

Morris, Bill 1952- .... **CLC 76**
See also CA 225

Morris, Julian
See West, Morris L(anglo)

Morris, Steveland Judkins 1950(?)-
See Wonder, Stevie
See also CA 111

Morris, William 1834-1896 . **NCLC 4; PC 55**
See also BRW 5; CDBLB 1832-1890; DLB 18, 35, 57, 156, 178, 184; FANT; RGEL 2; SFW 4; SUFW

Morris, Wright 1910-1998 .. **CLC 1, 3, 7, 18, 37; TCLC 107**
See also AMW; CA 9-12R; 167; CANR 21, 81; CN 7; DLB 2, 206, 218; DLBY 1981; EWL 3; MTCW 1, 2; RGAL 4; TCWW 2

Morrison, Arthur 1863-1945 .... **SSC 40; TCLC 72**
See also CA 120; 157; CMW 4; DLB 70, 135, 197; RGEL 2

Morrison, Chloe Anthony Wofford
See Morrison, Toni

Morrison, James Douglas 1943-1971
See Morrison, Jim
See also CA 73-76; CANR 40

Morrison, Jim .... **CLC 17**
See Morrison, James Douglas

Morrison, Toni 1931- ...... **BLC 3; CLC 4, 10, 22, 55, 81, 87, 173, 194**
See also AAYA 1, 22; AFAW 1, 2; AMWC 1; AMWS 3; BPFB 2; BW 2, 3; CA 29-32R; CANR 27, 42, 67, 113, 124; CDALB 1968-1988; CLR 99; CN 7; CPW; DA; DA3; DAB; DAC; DAM MST, MULT, NOV, POP; DLB 6, 33, 143; DLBY 1981; EWL 3; EXPN; FW; LAIT 2, 4; LATS 1:2; LMFS 2; MAWW; MTCW 1, 2; NFS 1, 6, 8, 14; RGAL 4; RHW; SATA 57, 144; SSFS 5; TUS; YAW

Morrison, Van 1945- .... **CLC 21**
See also CA 116; 168

Morrissy, Mary 1957- .... **CLC 99**
See also CA 205; DLB 267

Mortimer, John (Clifford) 1923- ..... **CLC 28, 43**
See also CA 13-16R; CANR 21, 69, 109; CD 5; CDBLB 1960 to Present; CMW 4; CN 7; CPW; DA3; DAM DRAM, POP; DLB 13, 245, 271; INT CANR-21; MSW; MTCW 1, 2; RGEL 2

Mortimer, Penelope (Ruth)
1918-1999 .... **CLC 5**
See also CA 57-60; 187; CANR 45, 88; CN 7

Mortimer, Sir John
See Mortimer, John (Clifford)

Morton, Anthony
See Creasey, John

Morton, Thomas 1579(?)-1647(?) .... **LC 72**
See also DLB 24; RGEL 2

Mosca, Gaetano 1858-1941 .... **TCLC 75**

Moses, Daniel David 1952- .... **NNAL**
See also CA 186

Mosher, Howard Frank 1943- .... **CLC 62**
See also CA 139; CANR 65, 115

Mosley, Nicholas 1923- .... **CLC 43, 70**
See also CA 69-72; CANR 41, 60, 108; CN 7; DLB 14, 207

Mosley, Walter 1952- .... **BLCS; CLC 97, 184**
See also AAYA 57; AMWS 13; BPFB 2; BW 2; CA 142; CANR 57, 92; CMW 4; CPW; DA3; DAM MULT, POP; DLB 306; MSW; MTCW 2

Moss, Howard 1922-1987 . **CLC 7, 14, 45, 50**
See also CA 1-4R; 123; CANR 1, 44; DAM POET; DLB 5

Mossgiel, Rab
See Burns, Robert

Motion, Andrew (Peter) 1952- .... **CLC 47**
See also BRWS 7; CA 146; CANR 90; CP 7; DLB 40

Motley, Willard (Francis)
1909-1965 .... **CLC 18**
See also BW 1; CA 117; 106; CANR 88; DLB 76, 143

Motoori, Norinaga 1730-1801 .... **NCLC 45**

Mott, Michael (Charles Alston)
1930- .... **CLC 15, 34**
See also CA 5-8R; CAAS 7; CANR 7, 29

Mountain Wolf Woman 1884-1960 . **CLC 92; NNAL**
See also CA 144; CANR 90

Moure, Erin 1955- .... **CLC 88**
See also CA 113; CP 7; CWP; DLB 60

Mourning Dove 1885(?)-1936 .... **NNAL**
See also CA 144; CANR 90; DAM MULT; DLB 175, 221

Mowat, Farley (McGill) 1921- .... **CLC 26**
See also AAYA 1, 50; BYA 2; CA 1-4R; CANR 4, 24, 42, 68, 108; CLR 20; CPW; DAC; DAM MST; DLB 68; INT CANR-24; JRDA; MAICYA 1, 2; MTCW 1, 2; SATA 3, 55; YAW

Mowatt, Anna Cora 1819-1870 ..... **NCLC 74**
See also RGAL 4

Moyers, Bill 1934- .... **CLC 74**
See also AITN 2; CA 61-64; CANR 31, 52

Mphahlele, Es'kia
See Mphahlele, Ezekiel
See also AFW; CDWLB 3; DLB 125, 225; RGSF 2; SSFS 11

Mphahlele, Ezekiel 1919- ... **BLC 3; CLC 25, 133**
See Mphahlele, Es'kia
See also BW 2, 3; CA 81-84; CANR 26, 76; DA3; DAM MULT; EWL 3; MTCW 2; SATA 119

Mqhayi, S(amuel) E(dward) K(rune Loliwe) 1875-1945 .... **BLC 3; TCLC 25**
See also CA 153; CANR 87; DAM MULT

Mrozek, Slawomir 1930- .... **CLC 3, 13**
See also CA 13-16R; CAAS 10; CANR 29; CDWLB 4; CWW 2; DLB 232; EWL 3; MTCW 1

Mrs. Belloc-Lowndes
See Lowndes, Marie Adelaide (Belloc)

Mrs. Fairstar
See Horne, Richard Henry Hengist

M'Taggart, John M'Taggart Ellis
See McTaggart, John McTaggart Ellis

Okri, Ben 1959- .... **CLC 87**
See also AFW; BRWS 5; BW 2, 3; CA 130; 138; CANR 65, 128; CN 7; DLB 157, 231; EWL 3; INT CA-138; MTCW 2; RGSF 2; SSFS 20; WLIT 2; WWE 1

Olds, Sharon 1942- .. **CLC 32, 39, 85; PC 22**
See also AMWS 10; CA 101; CANR 18, 41, 66, 98, 135; CP 7; CPW; CWP; DAM POET; DLB 120; MTCW 2; PFS 17

Oldstyle, Jonathan
See Irving, Washington

Olesha, Iurii
See Olesha, Yuri (Karlovich)
See also RGWL 2

Olesha, Iurii Karlovich
See Olesha, Yuri (Karlovich)
See also DLB 272

Olesha, Yuri (Karlovich) 1899-1960 . **CLC 8; SSC 69; TCLC 136**
See Olesha, Iurii; Olesha, Iurii Karlovich; Olesha, Yury Karlovich
See also CA 85-88; EW 11; RGWL 3

Olesha, Yury Karlovich
See Olesha, Yuri (Karlovich)
See also EWL 3

Oliphant, Mrs.
See Oliphant, Margaret (Oliphant Wilson)
See also SUFW

Oliphant, Laurence 1829(?)-1888 .. **NCLC 47**
See also DLB 18, 166

Oliphant, Margaret (Oliphant Wilson) 1828-1897 .... **NCLC 11, 61; SSC 25**
See Oliphant, Mrs.
See also BRWS 10; DLB 18, 159, 190; HGG; RGEL 2; RGSF 2

Oliver, Mary 1935- .... **CLC 19, 34, 98**
See also AMWS 7; CA 21-24R; CANR 9, 43, 84, 92; CP 7; CWP; DLB 5, 193; EWL 3; PFS 15

Olivier, Laurence (Kerr) 1907-1989 . **CLC 20**
See also CA 111; 150; 129

Olsen, Tillie 1912- ... **CLC 4, 13, 114; SSC 11**
See also AAYA 51; AMWS 13; BYA 11; CA 1-4R; CANR 1, 43, 74, 132; CDALBS; CN 7; DA; DA3; DAB; DAC; DAM MST; DLB 28, 206; DLBY 1980; EWL 3; EXPS; FW; MTCW 1, 2; RGAL 4; RGSF 2; SSFS 1; TUS

Olson, Charles (John) 1910-1970 .. **CLC 1, 2, 5, 6, 9, 11, 29; PC 19**
See also AMWS 2; CA 13-16; 25-28R; CABS 2; CANR 35, 61; CAP 1; DAM POET; DLB 5, 16, 193; EWL 3; MTCW 1, 2; RGAL 4; WP

Olson, Toby 1937- .... **CLC 28**
See also CA 65-68; CANR 9, 31, 84; CP 7

Olyesha, Yuri
See Olesha, Yuri (Karlovich)

Olympiodorus of Thebes c. 375-c. 430 .... **CMLC 59**

Omar Khayyam
See Khayyam, Omar
See also RGWL 2, 3

Ondaatje, (Philip) Michael 1943- .... **CLC 14, 29, 51, 76, 180; PC 28**
See also CA 77-80; CANR 42, 74, 109, 133; CN 7; CP 7; DA3; DAB; DAC; DAM MST; DLB 60; EWL 3; LATS 1:2; LMFS 2; MTCW 2; PFS 8, 19; TWA; WWE 1

Oneal, Elizabeth 1934-
See Oneal, Zibby
See also CA 106; CANR 28, 84; MAICYA 1, 2; SATA 30, 82; YAW

Oneal, Zibby .... **CLC 30**
See Oneal, Elizabeth
See also AAYA 5, 41; BYA 13; CLR 13; JRDA; WYA

O'Neill, Eugene (Gladstone) 1888-1953 ... **DC 20; TCLC 1, 6, 27, 49; WLC**
See also AAYA 54; AITN 1; AMW; AMWC 1; CA 110; 132; CAD; CANR 131; CDALB 1929-1941; DA; DA3; DAB; DAC; DAM DRAM, MST; DFS 2, 4, 5, 6, 9, 11, 12, 16, 20; DLB 7; EWL 3; LAIT 3; LMFS 2; MTCW 1, 2; RGAL 4; TUS

Onetti, Juan Carlos 1909-1994 ... **CLC 7, 10; HLCS 2; SSC 23; TCLC 131**
See also CA 85-88; 145; CANR 32, 63; CDWLB 3; CWW 2; DAM MULT, NOV; DLB 113; EWL 3; HW 1, 2; LAW; MTCW 1, 2; RGSF 2

O Nuallain, Brian 1911-1966
See O'Brien, Flann
See also CA 21-22; 25-28R; CAP 2; DLB 231; FANT; TEA

Ophuls, Max 1902-1957 .... **TCLC 79**
See also CA 113

Opie, Amelia 1769-1853 .... **NCLC 65**
See also DLB 116, 159; RGEL 2

Oppen, George 1908-1984 ..... **CLC 7, 13, 34; PC 35; TCLC 107**
See also CA 13-16R; 113; CANR 8, 82; DLB 5, 165

Oppenheim, E(dward) Phillips 1866-1946 .... **TCLC 45**
See also CA 111; 202; CMW 4; DLB 70

Opuls, Max
See Ophuls, Max

Orage, A(lfred) R(ichard) 1873-1934 .... **TCLC 157**
See also CA 122

Origen c. 185-c. 254 .... **CMLC 19**

Orlovitz, Gil 1918-1973 .... **CLC 22**
See also CA 77-80; 45-48; DLB 2, 5

O'Rourke, P(atrick) J(ake) 1947- .. **CLC 209**
See also CA 77-80; CANR 13, 41, 67, 111; CPW; DLB 185; DAM POP

Orris
See Ingelow, Jean

Ortega y Gasset, Jose 1883-1955 ...... **HLC 2; TCLC 9**
See also CA 106; 130; DAM MULT; EW 9; EWL 3; HW 1, 2; MTCW 1, 2

Ortese, Anna Maria 1914-1998 .... **CLC 89**
See also DLB 177; EWL 3

Ortiz, Simon J(oseph) 1941- ... **CLC 45, 208; NNAL; PC 17**
See also AMWS 4; CA 134; CANR 69, 118; CP 7; DAM MULT, POET; DLB 120, 175, 256; EXPP; PFS 4, 16; RGAL 4

Orton, Joe ...... **CLC 4, 13, 43; DC 3; TCLC 157**
See Orton, John Kingsley
See also BRWS 5; CBD; CDBLB 1960 to Present; DFS 3, 6; DLB 13; GLL 1; MTCW 2; RGEL 2; TEA; WLIT 4

Orton, John Kingsley 1933-1967
See Orton, Joe
See also CA 85-88; CANR 35, 66; DAM DRAM; MTCW 1, 2

Orwell, George ...... **SSC 68; TCLC 2, 6, 15, 31, 51, 128, 129; WLC**
See Blair, Eric (Arthur)
See also BPFB 3; BRW 7; BYA 5; CDBLB 1945-1960; CLR 68; DAB; DLB 15, 98, 195, 255; EWL 3; EXPN; LAIT 4, 5; LATS 1:1; NFS 3, 7; RGEL 2; SCFW 2; SFW 4; SSFS 4; TEA; WLIT 4; YAW

Osborne, David
See Silverberg, Robert

Osborne, George
See Silverberg, Robert

Osborne, John (James) 1929-1994 .... **CLC 1, 2, 5, 11, 45; TCLC 153; WLC**
See also BRWS 1; CA 13-16R; 147; CANR 21, 56; CDBLB 1945-1960; DA; DAB; DAC; DAM DRAM, MST; DFS 4, 19; DLB 13; EWL 3; MTCW 1, 2; RGEL 2

Osborne, Lawrence 1958- .... **CLC 50**
See also CA 189

Osbourne, Lloyd 1868-1947 .... **TCLC 93**

Osgood, Frances Sargent 1811-1850 .... **NCLC 141**
See also DLB 250

Oshima, Nagisa 1932- .... **CLC 20**
See also CA 116; 121; CANR 78

Oskison, John Milton 1874-1947 .... **NNAL; TCLC 35**
See also CA 144; CANR 84; DAM MULT; DLB 175

Ossian c. 3rd cent. - .... **CMLC 28**
See Macpherson, James

Ossoli, Sarah Margaret (Fuller) 1810-1850 .... **NCLC 5, 50**
See Fuller, Margaret; Fuller, Sarah Margaret
See also CDALB 1640-1865; FW; LMFS 1; SATA 25

Ostriker, Alicia (Suskin) 1937- .... **CLC 132**
See also CA 25-28R; CAAS 24; CANR 10, 30, 62, 99; CWP; DLB 120; EXPP; PFS 19

Ostrovsky, Aleksandr Nikolaevich
See Ostrovsky, Alexander
See also DLB 277

Ostrovsky, Alexander 1823-1886 .. **NCLC 30, 57**
See Ostrovsky, Aleksandr Nikolaevich

Otero, Blas de 1916-1979 .... **CLC 11**
See also CA 89-92; DLB 134; EWL 3

O'Trigger, Sir Lucius
See Horne, Richard Henry Hengist

Otto, Rudolf 1869-1937 .... **TCLC 85**

Otto, Whitney 1955- .... **CLC 70**
See also CA 140; CANR 120

Otway, Thomas 1652-1685 ... **DC 24; LC 106**
See also DAM DRAM; DLB 80; RGEL 2

Ouida .... **TCLC 43**
See De la Ramee, Marie Louise (Ouida)
See also DLB 18, 156; RGEL 2

Ouologuem, Yambo 1940- .... **CLC 146**
See also CA 111; 176

Ousmane, Sembene 1923- ... **BLC 3; CLC 66**
See Sembene, Ousmane
See also BW 1, 3; CA 117; 125; CANR 81; CWW 2; MTCW 1

Ovid 43B.C.-17 .... **CMLC 7; PC 2**
See also AW 2; CDWLB 1; DA3; DAM POET; DLB 211; RGWL 2, 3; WP

Owen, Hugh
See Faust, Frederick (Schiller)

Owen, Wilfred (Edward Salter) 1893-1918 ... **PC 19; TCLC 5, 27; WLC**
See also BRW 6; CA 104; 141; CDBLB 1914-1945; DA; DAB; DAC; DAM MST, POET; DLB 20; EWL 3; EXPP; MTCW 2; PFS 10; RGEL 2; WLIT 4

Owens, Louis (Dean) 1948-2002 .... **NNAL**
See also CA 137, 179; 207; CAAE 179; CAAS 24; CANR 71

Owens, Rochelle 1936- .... **CLC 8**
See also CA 17-20R; CAAS 2; CAD; CANR 39; CD 5; CP 7; CWD; CWP

Oz, Amos 1939- ...... **CLC 5, 8, 11, 27, 33, 54; SSC 66**
See also CA 53-56; CANR 27, 47, 65, 113; CWW 2; DAM NOV; EWL 3; MTCW 1, 2; RGSF 2; RGWL 3

Paterson, A(ndrew) B(arton)
1864-1941 .... **TCLC 32**
See also CA 155; DLB 230; RGEL 2; SATA 97

Paterson, Banjo
See Paterson, A(ndrew) B(arton)

Paterson, Katherine (Womeldorf)
1932- .... **CLC 12, 30**
See also AAYA 1, 31; BYA 1, 2, 7; CA 21-24R; CANR 28, 59, 111; CLR 7, 50; CWRI 5; DLB 52; JRDA; LAIT 4; MAICYA 1, 2; MAICYAS 1; MTCW 1; SATA 13, 53, 92, 133; WYA; YAW

Patmore, Coventry Kersey Dighton
1823-1896 .... **NCLC 9; PC 59**
See also DLB 35, 98; RGEL 2; TEA

Paton, Alan (Stewart) 1903-1988 ...... **CLC 4, 10, 25, 55, 106; TCLC 165; WLC**
See also AAYA 26; AFW; BPFB 3; BRWS 2; BYA 1; CA 13-16; 125; CANR 22; CAP 1; DA; DA3; DAB; DAC; DAM MST, NOV; DLB 225; DLBD 17; EWL 3; EXPN; LAIT 4; MTCW 1, 2; NFS 3, 12; RGEL 2; SATA 11; SATA-Obit 56; TWA; WLIT 2; WWE 1

Paton Walsh, Gillian 1937- .... **CLC 35**
See Paton Walsh, Jill; Walsh, Jill Paton
See also AAYA 11; CANR 38, 83; CLR 2, 65; DLB 161; JRDA; MAICYA 1, 2; SAAS 3; SATA 4, 72, 109; YAW

Paton Walsh, Jill
See Paton Walsh, Gillian
See also AAYA 47; BYA 1, 8

Patterson, (Horace) Orlando (Lloyd)
1940- .... **BLCS**
See also BW 1; CA 65-68; CANR 27, 84; CN 7

Patton, George S(mith), Jr.
1885-1945 .... **TCLC 79**
See also CA 189

Paulding, James Kirke 1778-1860 ... **NCLC 2**
See also DLB 3, 59, 74, 250; RGAL 4

Paulin, Thomas Neilson 1949-
See Paulin, Tom
See also CA 123; 128; CANR 98; CP 7

Paulin, Tom .... **CLC 37, 177**
See Paulin, Thomas Neilson
See also DLB 40

Pausanias c. 1st cent. - .... **CMLC 36**

Paustovsky, Konstantin (Georgievich)
1892-1968 .... **CLC 40**
See also CA 93-96; 25-28R; DLB 272; EWL 3

Pavese, Cesare 1908-1950 .... **PC 13; SSC 19; TCLC 3**
See also CA 104; 169; DLB 128, 177; EW 12; EWL 3; PFS 20; RGSF 2; RGWL 2, 3; TWA

Pavic, Milorad 1929- .... **CLC 60**
See also CA 136; CDWLB 4; CWW 2; DLB 181; EWL 3; RGWL 3

Pavlov, Ivan Petrovich 1849-1936 . **TCLC 91**
See also CA 118; 180

Pavlova, Karolina Karlovna
1807-1893 .... **NCLC 138**
See also DLB 205

Payne, Alan
See Jakes, John (William)

Paz, Gil
See Lugones, Leopoldo

Paz, Octavio 1914-1998 . **CLC 3, 4, 6, 10, 19, 51, 65, 119; HLC 2; PC 1, 48; WLC**
See also AAYA 50; CA 73-76; 165; CANR 32, 65, 104; CWW 2; DA; DA3; DAB; DAC; DAM MST, MULT, POET; DLB 290; DLBY 1990, 1998; DNFS 1; EWL 3; HW 1, 2; LAW; LAWS 1; MTCW 1, 2; PFS 18; RGWL 2, 3; SSFS 13; TWA; WLIT 1

p'Bitek, Okot 1931-1982 .... **BLC 3; CLC 96; TCLC 149**
See also AFW; BW 2, 3; CA 124; 107; CANR 82; DAM MULT; DLB 125; EWL 3; MTCW 1, 2; RGEL 2; WLIT 2

Peacock, Molly 1947- .... **CLC 60**
See also CA 103; CAAS 21; CANR 52, 84; CP 7; CWP; DLB 120, 282

Peacock, Thomas Love
1785-1866 .... **NCLC 22**
See also BRW 4; DLB 96, 116; RGEL 2; RGSF 2

Peake, Mervyn 1911-1968 .... **CLC 7, 54**
See also CA 5-8R; 25-28R; CANR 3; DLB 15, 160, 255; FANT; MTCW 1; RGEL 2; SATA 23; SFW 4

Pearce, Philippa
See Christie, Philippa
See also CA 5-8R; CANR 4, 109; CWRI 5; FANT; MAICYA 2

Pearl, Eric
See Elman, Richard (Martin)

Pearson, T(homas) R(eid) 1956- .... **CLC 39**
See also CA 120; 130; CANR 97; CSW; INT CA-130

Peck, Dale 1967- .... **CLC 81**
See also CA 146; CANR 72, 127; GLL 2

Peck, John (Frederick) 1941- .... **CLC 3**
See also CA 49-52; CANR 3, 100; CP 7

Peck, Richard (Wayne) 1934- .... **CLC 21**
See also AAYA 1, 24; BYA 1, 6, 8, 11; CA 85-88; CANR 19, 38, 129; CLR 15; INT CANR-19; JRDA; MAICYA 1, 2; SAAS 2; SATA 18, 55, 97; SATA-Essay 110; WYA; YAW

Peck, Robert Newton 1928- .... **CLC 17**
See also AAYA 3, 43; BYA 1, 6; CA 81-84, 182; CAAE 182; CANR 31, 63, 127; CLR 45; DA; DAC; DAM MST; JRDA; LAIT 3; MAICYA 1, 2; SAAS 1; SATA 21, 62, 111; SATA-Essay 108; WYA; YAW

Peckinpah, (David) Sam(uel)
1925-1984 .... **CLC 20**
See also CA 109; 114; CANR 82

Pedersen, Knut 1859-1952
See Hamsun, Knut
See also CA 104; 119; CANR 63; MTCW 1, 2

Peele, George .... **LC 115**
See also BW 1; DLB 62, 167; RGEL 2

Peeslake, Gaffer
See Durrell, Lawrence (George)

Peguy, Charles (Pierre)
1873-1914 .... **TCLC 10**
See also CA 107; 193; DLB 258; EWL 3; GFL 1789 to the Present

Peirce, Charles Sanders
1839-1914 .... **TCLC 81**
See also CA 194; DLB 270

Pellicer, Carlos 1897(?)-1977 .... **HLCS 2**
See also CA 153; 69-72; DLB 290; EWL 3; HW 1

Pena, Ramon del Valle y
See Valle-Inclan, Ramon (Maria) del

Pendennis, Arthur Esquir
See Thackeray, William Makepeace

Penn, Arthur
See Matthews, (James) Brander

Penn, William 1644-1718 .... **LC 25**
See also DLB 24

PEPECE
See Prado (Calvo), Pedro

Pepys, Samuel 1633-1703 ... **LC 11, 58; WLC**
See also BRW 2; CDBLB 1660-1789; DA; DA3; DAB; DAC; DAM MST; DLB 101, 213; NCFS 4; RGEL 2; TEA; WLIT 3

Percy, Thomas 1729-1811 .... **NCLC 95**
See also DLB 104

Percy, Walker 1916-1990 .... **CLC 2, 3, 6, 8, 14, 18, 47, 65**
See also AMWS 3; BPFB 3; CA 1-4R; 131; CANR 1, 23, 64; CPW; CSW; DA3; DAM NOV, POP; DLB 2; DLBY 1980, 1990; EWL 3; MTCW 1, 2; RGAL 4; TUS

Percy, William Alexander
1885-1942 .... **TCLC 84**
See also CA 163; MTCW 2

Perec, Georges 1936-1982 .... **CLC 56, 116**
See also CA 141; DLB 83, 299; EWL 3; GFL 1789 to the Present; RGWL 3

Pereda (y Sanchez de Porrua), Jose Maria de 1833-1906 .... **TCLC 16**
See also CA 117

Pereda y Porrua, Jose Maria de
See Pereda (y Sanchez de Porrua), Jose Maria de

Peregoy, George Weems
See Mencken, H(enry) L(ouis)

Perelman, S(idney) J(oseph)
1904-1979 .. **CLC 3, 5, 9, 15, 23, 44, 49; SSC 32**
See also AITN 1, 2; BPFB 3; CA 73-76; 89-92; CANR 18; DAM DRAM; DLB 11, 44; MTCW 1, 2; RGAL 4

Peret, Benjamin 1899-1959 .... **PC 33; TCLC 20**
See also CA 117; 186; GFL 1789 to the Present

Peretz, Isaac Leib
See Peretz, Isaac Loeb
See also CA 201

Peretz, Isaac Loeb 1851(?)-1915 ...... **SSC 26; TCLC 16**
See Peretz, Isaac Leib
See also CA 109

Peretz, Yitzhok Leibush
See Peretz, Isaac Loeb

Perez Galdos, Benito 1843-1920 ..... **HLCS 2; TCLC 27**
See Galdos, Benito Perez
See also CA 125; 153; EWL 3; HW 1; RGWL 2, 3

Peri Rossi, Cristina 1941- .. **CLC 156; HLCS 2**
See also CA 131; CANR 59, 81; CWW 2; DLB 145, 290; EWL 3; HW 1, 2

Perlata
See Peret, Benjamin

Perloff, Marjorie G(abrielle)
1931- .... **CLC 137**
See also CA 57-60; CANR 7, 22, 49, 104

Perrault, Charles 1628-1703 .... **LC 2, 56**
See also BYA 4; CLR 79; DLB 268; GFL Beginnings to 1789; MAICYA 1, 2; RGWL 2, 3; SATA 25; WCH

Perry, Anne 1938- .... **CLC 126**
See also CA 101; CANR 22, 50, 84; CMW 4; CN 7; CPW; DLB 276

Perry, Brighton
See Sherwood, Robert E(mmet)

Perse, St.-John
See Leger, (Marie-Rene Auguste) Alexis Saint-Leger

Perse, Saint-John
See Leger, (Marie-Rene Auguste) Alexis Saint-Leger
See also DLB 258; RGWL 3

Persius 34-62 .... **CMLC 74**
See also AW 2; DLB 211; RGWL 2, 3

Perutz, Leo(pold) 1882-1957 .... **TCLC 60**
See also CA 147; DLB 81

Peseenz, Tulio F.
See Lopez y Fuentes, Gregorio

Pesetsky, Bette 1932- .... **CLC 28**
See also CA 133; DLB 130

Pliny the Elder c. 23-79 .... **CMLC 23**
See also DLB 211

Pliny the Younger c. 61-c. 112 ...... **CMLC 62**
See also AW 2; DLB 211

Plomer, William Charles Franklin
1903-1973 .... **CLC 4, 8**
See also AFW; CA 21-22; CANR 34; CAP
2; DLB 20, 162, 191, 225; EWL 3;
MTCW 1; RGEL 2; RGSF 2; SATA 24

Plotinus 204-270 .... **CMLC 46**
See also CDWLB 1; DLB 176

Plowman, Piers
See Kavanagh, Patrick (Joseph)

Plum, J.
See Wodehouse, P(elham) G(renville)

Plumly, Stanley (Ross) 1939- .... **CLC 33**
See also CA 108; 110; CANR 97; CP 7;
DLB 5, 193; INT CA-110

Plumpe, Friedrich Wilhelm
1888-1931 .... **TCLC 53**
See also CA 112

Plutarch c. 46-c. 120 .... **CMLC 60**
See also AW 2; CDWLB 1; DLB 176;
RGWL 2, 3; TWA

Po Chu-i 772-846 .... **CMLC 24**

Podhoretz, Norman 1930- .... **CLC 189**
See also AMWS 8; CA 9-12R; CANR 7,
78, 135

Poe, Edgar Allan 1809-1849 ..... **NCLC 1, 16,
55, 78, 94, 97, 117; PC 1, 54; SSC 1,
22, 34, 35, 54; WLC**
See also AAYA 14; AMW; AMWC 1;
AMWR 2; BPFB 3; BYA 5, 11; CDALB
1640-1865; CMW 4; DA; DA3; DAB;
DAC; DAM MST, POET; DLB 3, 59, 73,
74, 248, 254; EXPP; EXPS; HGG; LAIT
2; LATS 1:1; LMFS 1; MSW; PAB; PFS
1, 3, 9; RGAL 4; RGSF 2; SATA 23;
SCFW 2; SFW 4; SSFS 2, 4, 7, 8, 16;
SUFW; TUS; WP; WYA

Poet of Titchfield Street, The
See Pound, Ezra (Weston Loomis)

Pohl, Frederik 1919- .... **CLC 18; SSC 25**
See also AAYA 24; CA 61-64, 188; CAAE
188; CAAS 1; CANR 11, 37, 81; CN 7;
DLB 8; INT CANR-11; MTCW 1, 2;
SATA 24; SCFW 2; SFW 4

Poirier, Louis 1910-
See Gracq, Julien
See also CA 122; 126

Poitier, Sidney 1927- .... **CLC 26**
See also AAYA 60; BW 1; CA 117; CANR
94

Pokagon, Simon 1830-1899 .... **NNAL**
See also DAM MULT

Polanski, Roman 1933- .... **CLC 16, 178**
See also CA 77-80

Poliakoff, Stephen 1952- .... **CLC 38**
See also CA 106; CANR 116; CBD; CD 5;
DLB 13

Police, The
See Copeland, Stewart (Armstrong); Summers, Andrew James

Polidori, John William 1795-1821 . **NCLC 51**
See also DLB 116; HGG

Pollitt, Katha 1949- .... **CLC 28, 122**
See also CA 120; 122; CANR 66, 108;
MTCW 1, 2

Pollock, (Mary) Sharon 1936- .... **CLC 50**
See also CA 141; CANR 132; CD 5; CWD;
DAC; DAM DRAM, MST; DFS 3; DLB
60; FW

Pollock, Sharon 1936- .... **DC 20**

Polo, Marco 1254-1324 .... **CMLC 15**

Polonsky, Abraham (Lincoln)
1910-1999 .... **CLC 92**
See also CA 104; 187; DLB 26; INT CA-
104

Polybius c. 200B.C.-c. 118B.C. ...... **CMLC 17**
See also AW 1; DLB 176; RGWL 2, 3

Pomerance, Bernard 1940- .... **CLC 13**
See also CA 101; CAD; CANR 49, 134;
CD 5; DAM DRAM; DFS 9; LAIT 2

Ponge, Francis 1899-1988 .... **CLC 6, 18**
See also CA 85-88; 126; CANR 40, 86;
DAM POET; DLBY 2002; EWL 3; GFL
1789 to the Present; RGWL 2, 3

Poniatowska, Elena 1933- . **CLC 140; HLC 2**
See also CA 101; CANR 32, 66, 107; CD-
WLB 3; CWW 2; DAM MULT; DLB 113;
EWL 3; HW 1, 2; LAWS 1; WLIT 1

Pontoppidan, Henrik 1857-1943 .... **TCLC 29**
See also CA 170; DLB 300

Ponty, Maurice Merleau
See Merleau-Ponty, Maurice

Poole, Josephine .... **CLC 17**
See Helyar, Jane Penelope Josephine
See also SAAS 2; SATA 5

Popa, Vasko 1922-1991 . **CLC 19; TCLC 167**
See also CA 112; 148; CDWLB 4; DLB
181; EWL 3; RGWL 2, 3

Pope, Alexander 1688-1744 ...... **LC 3, 58, 60,
64; PC 26; WLC**
See also BRW 3; BRWC 1; BRWR 1; CD-
BLB 1660-1789; DA; DA3; DAB; DAC;
DAM MST, POET; DLB 95, 101, 213;
EXPP; PAB; PFS 12; RGEL 2; WLIT 3;
WP

Popov, Evgenii Anatol'evich
See Popov, Yevgeny
See also DLB 285

Popov, Yevgeny .... **CLC 59**
See Popov, Evgenii Anatol'evich

Poquelin, Jean-Baptiste
See Moliere

Porete, Marguerite c. 1250-1310 .. **CMLC 73**
See also DLB 208

Porphyry c. 233-c. 305 .... **CMLC 71**

Porter, Connie (Rose) 1959(?)- .... **CLC 70**
See also BW 2, 3; CA 142; CANR 90, 109;
SATA 81, 129

Porter, Gene(va Grace) Stratton .. **TCLC 21**
See Stratton-Porter, Gene(va Grace)
See also BPFB 3; CA 112; CWRI 5; RHW

Porter, Katherine Anne 1890-1980 ... **CLC 1,
3, 7, 10, 13, 15, 27, 101; SSC 4, 31, 43**
See also AAYA 42; AITN 2; AMW; BPFB
3; CA 1-4R; 101; CANR 1, 65; CDALBS;
DA; DA3; DAB; DAC; DAM MST, NOV;
DLB 4, 9, 102; DLBD 12; DLBY 1980;
EWL 3; EXPS; LAIT 3; MAWW; MTCW
1, 2; NFS 14; RGAL 4; RGSF 2; SATA
39; SATA-Obit 23; SSFS 1, 8, 11, 16;
TUS

Porter, Peter (Neville Frederick)
1929- .... **CLC 5, 13, 33**
See also CA 85-88; CP 7; DLB 40, 289;
WWE 1

Porter, William Sydney 1862-1910
See Henry, O.
See also CA 104; 131; CDALB 1865-1917;
DA; DA3; DAB; DAC; DAM MST; DLB
12, 78, 79; MTCW 1, 2; TUS; YABC 2

Portillo (y Pacheco), Jose Lopez
See Lopez Portillo (y Pacheco), Jose

Portillo Trambley, Estela
1927-1998 .... **HLC 2; TCLC 163**
See Trambley, Estela Portillo
See also CANR 32; DAM MULT; DLB
209; HW 1

Posey, Alexander (Lawrence)
1873-1908 .... **NNAL**
See also CA 144; CANR 80; DAM MULT;
DLB 175

Posse, Abel .... **CLC 70**

Post, Melville Davisson
1869-1930 .... **TCLC 39**
See also CA 110; 202; CMW 4

Potok, Chaim 1929-2002 ... **CLC 2, 7, 14, 26,
112**
See also AAYA 15, 50; AITN 1, 2; BPFB 3;
BYA 1; CA 17-20R; 208; CANR 19, 35,
64, 98; CLR 92; CN 7; DA3; DAM NOV;
DLB 28, 152; EXPN; INT CANR-19;
LAIT 4; MTCW 1, 2; NFS 4; SATA 33,
106; SATA-Obit 134; TUS; YAW

Potok, Herbert Harold -2002
See Potok, Chaim

Potok, Herman Harold
See Potok, Chaim

Potter, Dennis (Christopher George)
1935-1994 .... **CLC 58, 86, 123**
See also BRWS 10; CA 107; 145; CANR
33, 61; CBD; DLB 233; MTCW 1

Pound, Ezra (Weston Loomis)
1885-1972 .. **CLC 1, 2, 3, 4, 5, 7, 10, 13,
18, 34, 48, 50, 112; PC 4; WLC**
See also AAYA 47; AMW; AMWR 1; CA
5-8R; 37-40R; CANR 40; CDALB 1917-
1929; DA; DA3; DAB; DAC; DAM MST,
POET; DLB 4, 45, 63; DLBD 15; EFS 2;
EWL 3; EXPP; LMFS 2; MTCW 1, 2;
PAB; PFS 2, 8, 16; RGAL 4; TUS; WP

Povod, Reinaldo 1959-1994 .... **CLC 44**
See also CA 136; 146; CANR 83

Powell, Adam Clayton, Jr.
1908-1972 .... **BLC 3; CLC 89**
See also BW 1, 3; CA 102; 33-36R; CANR
86; DAM MULT

Powell, Anthony (Dymoke)
1905-2000 .... **CLC 1, 3, 7, 9, 10, 31**
See also BRW 7; CA 1-4R; 189; CANR 1,
32, 62, 107; CDBLB 1945-1960; CN 7;
DLB 15; EWL 3; MTCW 1, 2; RGEL 2;
TEA

Powell, Dawn 1896(?)-1965 .... **CLC 66**
See also CA 5-8R; CANR 121; DLBY 1997

Powell, Padgett 1952- .... **CLC 34**
See also CA 126; CANR 63, 101; CSW;
DLB 234; DLBY 01

Powell, (Oval) Talmage 1920-2000
See Queen, Ellery
See also CA 5-8R; CANR 2, 80

Power, Susan 1961- .... **CLC 91**
See also BYA 14; CA 160; CANR 135; NFS
11

Powers, J(ames) F(arl) 1917-1999 ..... **CLC 1,
4, 8, 57; SSC 4**
See also CA 1-4R; 181; CANR 2, 61; CN
7; DLB 130; MTCW 1; RGAL 4; RGSF
2

Powers, John J(ames) 1945-
See Powers, John R.
See also CA 69-72

Powers, John R. .... **CLC 66**
See Powers, John J(ames)

Powers, Richard (S.) 1957- .... **CLC 93**
See also AMWS 9; BPFB 3; CA 148;
CANR 80; CN 7

Pownall, David 1938- .... **CLC 10**
See also CA 89-92, 180; CAAS 18; CANR
49, 101; CBD; CD 5; CN 7; DLB 14

Powys, John Cowper 1872-1963 ... **CLC 7, 9,
15, 46, 125**
See also CA 85-88; CANR 106; DLB 15,
255; EWL 3; FANT; MTCW 1, 2; RGEL
2; SUFW

Powys, T(heodore) F(rancis)
1875-1953 .... **TCLC 9**
See also BRWS 8; CA 106; 189; DLB 36,
162; EWL 3; FANT; RGEL 2; SUFW

Prado (Calvo), Pedro 1886-1952 ... **TCLC 75**
See also CA 131; DLB 283; HW 1; LAW

Prager, Emily 1952- .... **CLC 56**
See also CA 204

Pratchett, Terry 1948- .... **CLC 197**
See also AAYA 19, 54; BPFB 3; CA 143;
CANR 87, 126; CLR 64; CN 7; CPW;
CWRI 5; FANT; SATA 82, 139; SFW 4;
SUFW 2

Pratolini, Vasco 1913-1991 .... **TCLC 124**
See also CA 211; DLB 177; EWL 3; RGWL
2, 3

Pratt, E(dwin) J(ohn) 1883(?)-1964 . **CLC 19**
See also CA 141; 93-96; CANR 77; DAC;
DAM POET; DLB 92; EWL 3; RGEL 2;
TWA

Premchand .... **TCLC 21**
See Srivastava, Dhanpat Rai
See also EWL 3

Preseren, France 1800-1849 .... **NCLC 127**
See also CDWLB 4; DLB 147

Preussler, Otfried 1923- .... **CLC 17**
See also CA 77-80; SATA 24

Prevert, Jacques (Henri Marie)
1900-1977 .... **CLC 15**
See also CA 77-80; 69-72; CANR 29, 61;
DLB 258; EWL 3; GFL 1789 to the
Present; IDFW 3, 4; MTCW 1; RGWL 2,
3; SATA-Obit 30

Prevost, (Antoine Francois)
1697-1763 .... **LC 1**
See also EW 4; GFL Beginnings to 1789;
RGWL 2, 3

Price, (Edward) Reynolds 1933- ... **CLC 3, 6,**
13, 43, 50, 63; SSC 22
See also AMWS 6; CA 1-4R; CANR 1, 37,
57, 87, 128; CN 7; CSW; DAM NOV;
DLB 2, 218, 278; EWL 3; INT CANR-
37; NFS 18

Price, Richard 1949- .... **CLC 6, 12**
See also CA 49-52; CANR 3; DLBY 1981

Prichard, Katharine Susannah
1883-1969 .... **CLC 46**
See also CA 11-12; CANR 33; CAP 1; DLB
260; MTCW 1; RGEL 2; RGSF 2; SATA
66

Priestley, J(ohn) B(oynton)
1894-1984 .... **CLC 2, 5, 9, 34**
See also BRW 7; CA 9-12R; 113; CANR
33; CDBLB 1914-1945; DA3; DAM
DRAM, NOV; DLB 10, 34, 77, 100, 139;
DLBY 1984; EWL 3; MTCW 1, 2; RGEL
2; SFW 4

Prince 1958- .... **CLC 35**
See also CA 213

Prince, F(rank) T(empleton)
1912-2003 .... **CLC 22**
See also CA 101; 219; CANR 43, 79; CP 7;
DLB 20

Prince Kropotkin
See Kropotkin, Peter (Aleksieevich)

Prior, Matthew 1664-1721 .... **LC 4**
See also DLB 95; RGEL 2

Prishvin, Mikhail 1873-1954 .... **TCLC 75**
See Prishvin, Mikhail Mikhailovich

Prishvin, Mikhail Mikhailovich
See Prishvin, Mikhail
See also DLB 272; EWL 3

Pritchard, William H(arrison)
1932- .... **CLC 34**
See also CA 65-68; CANR 23, 95; DLB
111

Pritchett, V(ictor) S(awdon)
1900-1997 ... **CLC 5, 13, 15, 41; SSC 14**
See also BPFB 3; BRWS 3; CA 61-64; 157;
CANR 31, 63; CN 7; DA3; DAM NOV;
DLB 15, 139; EWL 3; MTCW 1, 2;
RGEL 2; RGSF 2; TEA

Private 19022
See Manning, Frederic

Probst, Mark 1925- .... **CLC 59**
See also CA 130

Prokosch, Frederic 1908-1989 ...... **CLC 4, 48**
See also CA 73-76; 128; CANR 82; DLB
48; MTCW 2

Propertius, Sextus c. 50B.C.-c.
16B.C. .... **CMLC 32**
See also AW 2; CDWLB 1; DLB 211;
RGWL 2, 3

Prophet, The
See Dreiser, Theodore (Herman Albert)

Prose, Francine 1947- .... **CLC 45**
See also CA 109; 112; CANR 46, 95, 132;
DLB 234; SATA 101, 149

Proudhon
See Cunha, Euclides (Rodrigues Pimenta)
da

Proulx, Annie
See Proulx, E(dna) Annie

Proulx, E(dna) Annie 1935- ...... **CLC 81, 158**
See also AMWS 7; BPFB 3; CA 145;
CANR 65, 110; CN 7; CPW 1; DA3;
DAM POP; MTCW 2; SSFS 18

Proust, (Valentin-Louis-George-Eugene)
Marcel 1871-1922 ..... **SSC 75; TCLC 7,**
13, 33, 161; WLC
See also AAYA 58; BPFB 3; CA 104; 120;
CANR 110; DA; DA3; DAB; DAC; DAM
MST, NOV; DLB 65; EW 8; EWL 3; GFL
1789 to the Present; MTCW 1, 2; RGWL
2, 3; TWA

Prowler, Harley
See Masters, Edgar Lee

Prudentius 348-c. 410-15 .... **CMLC 78**
See also EW 1; RGWL 2, 3

Prus, Boleslaw 1845-1912 .... **TCLC 48**
See also RGWL 2, 3

Pryor, Richard (Franklin Lenox Thomas)
1940- .... **CLC 26**
See also CA 122; 152

Przybyszewski, Stanislaw
1868-1927 .... **TCLC 36**
See also CA 160; DLB 66; EWL 3

Pteleon
See Grieve, C(hristopher) M(urray)
See also DAM POET

Puckett, Lute
See Masters, Edgar Lee

Puig, Manuel 1932-1990 .... **CLC 3, 5, 10, 28,**
65, 133; HLC 2
See also BPFB 3; CA 45-48; CANR 2, 32,
63; CDWLB 3; DA3; DAM MULT; DLB
113; DNFS 1; EWL 3; GLL 1; HW 1, 2;
LAW; MTCW 1, 2; RGWL 2, 3; TWA;
WLIT 1

Pulitzer, Joseph 1847-1911 .... **TCLC 76**
See also CA 114; DLB 23

Purchas, Samuel 1577(?)-1626 .... **LC 70**
See also DLB 151

Purdy, A(lfred) W(ellington)
1918-2000 .... **CLC 3, 6, 14, 50**
See also CA 81-84; 189; CAAS 17; CANR
42, 66; CP 7; DAC; DAM MST, POET;
DLB 88; PFS 5; RGEL 2

Purdy, James (Amos) 1923- .... **CLC 2, 4, 10,**
28, 52
See also AMWS 7; CA 33-36R; CAAS 1;
CANR 19, 51, 132; CN 7; DLB 2, 218;
EWL 3; INT CANR-19; MTCW 1; RGAL
4

Pure, Simon
See Swinnerton, Frank Arthur

Pushkin, Aleksandr Sergeevich
See Pushkin, Alexander (Sergeyevich)
See also DLB 205

Pushkin, Alexander (Sergeyevich)
1799-1837 .... **NCLC 3, 27, 83; PC 10;**
SSC 27, 55; WLC
See Pushkin, Aleksandr Sergeevich
See also DA; DA3; DAB; DAC; DAM
DRAM, MST, POET; EW 5; EXPS; RGSF
2; RGWL 2, 3; SATA 61; SSFS 9; TWA

P'u Sung-ling 1640-1715 .... **LC 49; SSC 31**

Putnam, Arthur Lee
See Alger, Horatio, Jr.

Puttenham, George 1529-1590 .... **LC 116**
See also DLB 281

Puzo, Mario 1920-1999 .... **CLC 1, 2, 6, 36,**
107
See also BPFB 3; CA 65-68; 185; CANR 4,
42, 65, 99, 131; CN 7; CPW; DA3; DAM
NOV, POP; DLB 6; MTCW 1, 2; NFS 16;
RGAL 4

Pygge, Edward
See Barnes, Julian (Patrick)

Pyle, Ernest Taylor 1900-1945
See Pyle, Ernie
See also CA 115; 160

Pyle, Ernie .... **TCLC 75**
See Pyle, Ernest Taylor
See also DLB 29; MTCW 2

Pyle, Howard 1853-1911 .... **TCLC 81**
See also AAYA 57; BYA 2, 4; CA 109; 137;
CLR 22; DLB 42, 188; DLBD 13; LAIT
1; MAICYA 1, 2; SATA 16, 100; WCH;
YAW

Pym, Barbara (Mary Crampton)
1913-1980 .... **CLC 13, 19, 37, 111**
See also BPFB 3; BRWS 2; CA 13-14; 97-
100; CANR 13, 34; CAP 1; DLB 14, 207;
DLBY 1987; EWL 3; MTCW 1, 2; RGEL
2; TEA

Pynchon, Thomas (Ruggles, Jr.)
1937- ...... **CLC 2, 3, 6, 9, 11, 18, 33, 62,**
72, 123, 192; SSC 14, 84; WLC
See also AMWS 2; BEST 90:2; BPFB 3;
CA 17-20R; CANR 22, 46, 73; CN 7;
CPW 1; DA; DA3; DAB; DAC; DAM
MST, NOV, POP; DLB 2, 173; EWL 3;
MTCW 1, 2; RGAL 4; SFW 4; TUS

Pythagoras c. 582B.C.-c. 507B.C. . **CMLC 22**
See also DLB 176

Q
See Quiller-Couch, Sir Arthur (Thomas)

Qian, Chongzhu
See Ch'ien, Chung-shu

Qian, Sima 145B.C.-c. 89B.C. .... **CMLC 72**

Qian Zhongshu
See Ch'ien, Chung-shu
See also CWW 2

Qroll
See Dagerman, Stig (Halvard)

Quarles, Francis 1592-1644 .... **LC 117**
See also DLB 126; RGEL 2

Quarrington, Paul (Lewis) 1953- ..... **CLC 65**
See also CA 129; CANR 62, 95

Quasimodo, Salvatore 1901-1968 .... **CLC 10;**
PC 47
See also CA 13-16; 25-28R; CAP 1; DLB
114; EW 12; EWL 3; MTCW 1; RGWL
2, 3

Quatermass, Martin
See Carpenter, John (Howard)

Quay, Stephen 1947- .... **CLC 95**
See also CA 189

Quay, Timothy 1947- .... **CLC 95**
See also CA 189

Queen, Ellery .... **CLC 3, 11**
See Dannay, Frederic; Davidson, Avram
(James); Deming, Richard; Fairman, Paul
W.; Flora, Fletcher; Hoch, Edward
D(entinger); Kane, Henry; Lee, Manfred
B(ennington); Marlowe, Stephen; Powell,

(Oval) Talmage; Sheldon, Walter J(ames);
Sturgeon, Theodore (Hamilton); Tracy,
Don(ald Fiske); Vance, John Holbrook
See also BPFB 3; CMW 4; MSW; RGAL 4

Queen, Ellery, Jr.
See Dannay, Frederic; Lee, Manfred
B(ennington)

Queneau, Raymond 1903-1976 ..... **CLC 2, 5,
10, 42**
See also CA 77-80; 69-72; CANR 32; DLB
72, 258; EW 12; EWL 3; GFL 1789 to
the Present; MTCW 1, 2; RGWL 2, 3

Quevedo, Francisco de 1580-1645 .... **LC 23**

Quiller-Couch, Sir Arthur (Thomas)
1863-1944 .... **TCLC 53**
See also CA 118; 166; DLB 135, 153, 190;
HGG; RGEL 2; SUFW 1

Quin, Ann (Marie) 1936-1973 .... **CLC 6**
See also CA 9-12R; 45-48; DLB 14, 231

Quincey, Thomas de
See De Quincey, Thomas

Quindlen, Anna 1953- .... **CLC 191**
See also AAYA 35; CA 138; CANR 73, 126;
DA3; DLB 292; MTCW 2

Quinn, Martin
See Smith, Martin Cruz

Quinn, Peter 1947- .... **CLC 91**
See also CA 197

Quinn, Simon
See Smith, Martin Cruz

Quintana, Leroy V. 1944- ...... **HLC 2; PC 36**
See also CA 131; CANR 65; DAM MULT;
DLB 82; HW 1, 2

Quintilian c. 35-40–c. 96. .... **CMLC 77**
See also AW 2; DLB 211; RGWL 2, 3

Quiroga, Horacio (Sylvestre)
1878-1937 .... **HLC 2; TCLC 20**
See also CA 117; 131; DAM MULT; EWL
3; HW 1; LAW; MTCW 1; RGSF 2;
WLIT 1

Quoirez, Françoise 1935- .... **CLC 9**
See Sagan, Françoise
See also CA 49-52; CANR 6, 39, 73;
MTCW 1, 2; TWA

Raabe, Wilhelm (Karl) 1831-1910 . **TCLC 45**
See also CA 167; DLB 129

Rabe, David (William) 1940- .. **CLC 4, 8, 33,
200; DC 16**
See also CA 85-88; CABS 3; CAD; CANR
59, 129; CD 5; DAM DRAM; DFS 3, 8,
13; DLB 7, 228; EWL 3

Rabelais, François 1494-1553 .... **LC 5, 60;
WLC**
See also DA; DAB; DAC; DAM MST; EW
2; GFL Beginnings to 1789; LMFS 1;
RGWL 2, 3; TWA

Rabinovitch, Sholem 1859-1916
See Aleichem, Sholom
See also CA 104

Rabinyan, Dorit 1972- .... **CLC 119**
See also CA 170

Rachilde
See Vallette, Marguerite Eymery; Vallette,
Marguerite Eymery
See also EWL 3

Racine, Jean 1639-1699 .... **LC 28, 113**
See also DA3; DAB; DAM MST; DLB 268;
EW 3; GFL Beginnings to 1789; LMFS
1; RGWL 2, 3; TWA

Radcliffe, Ann (Ward) 1764-1823 ... **NCLC 6,
55, 106**
See also DLB 39, 178; HGG; LMFS 1;
RGEL 2; SUFW; WLIT 3

Radclyffe-Hall, Marguerite
See Hall, (Marguerite) Radclyffe

Radiguet, Raymond 1903-1923 ...... **TCLC 29**
See also CA 162; DLB 65; EWL 3; GFL
1789 to the Present; RGWL 2, 3

Radnoti, Miklos 1909-1944 .... **TCLC 16**
See also CA 118; 212; CDWLB 4; DLB
215; EWL 3; RGWL 2, 3

Rado, James 1939- .... **CLC 17**
See also CA 105

Radvanyi, Netty 1900-1983
See Seghers, Anna
See also CA 85-88; 110; CANR 82

Rae, Ben
See Griffiths, Trevor

Raeburn, John (Hay) 1941- .... **CLC 34**
See also CA 57-60

Ragni, Gerome 1942-1991 .... **CLC 17**
See also CA 105; 134

Rahv, Philip .... **CLC 24**
See Greenberg, Ivan
See also DLB 137

Raimund, Ferdinand Jakob
1790-1836 .... **NCLC 69**
See also DLB 90

Raine, Craig (Anthony) 1944- .. **CLC 32, 103**
See also CA 108; CANR 29, 51, 103; CP 7;
DLB 40; PFS 7

Raine, Kathleen (Jessie) 1908-2003 .. **CLC 7,
45**
See also CA 85-88; 218; CANR 46, 109;
CP 7; DLB 20; EWL 3; MTCW 1; RGEL
2

Rainis, Janis 1865-1929 .... **TCLC 29**
See also CA 170; CDWLB 4; DLB 220;
EWL 3

Rakosi, Carl .... **CLC 47**
See Rawley, Callman
See also CA 228; CAAS 5; CP 7; DLB 193

Ralegh, Sir Walter
See Raleigh, Sir Walter
See also BRW 1; RGEL 2; WP

Raleigh, Richard
See Lovecraft, H(oward) P(hillips)

Raleigh, Sir Walter 1554(?)-1618 .... **LC 31,
39; PC 31**
See Ralegh, Sir Walter
See also CDBLB Before 1660; DLB 172;
EXPP; PFS 14; TEA

Rallentando, H. P.
See Sayers, Dorothy L(eigh)

Ramal, Walter
See de la Mare, Walter (John)

Ramana Maharshi 1879-1950 .... **TCLC 84**

Ramoacn y Cajal, Santiago
1852-1934 .... **TCLC 93**

Ramon, Juan
See Jimenez (Mantecon), Juan Ramon

Ramos, Graciliano 1892-1953 .... **TCLC 32**
See also CA 167; DLB 307; EWL 3; HW 2;
LAW; WLIT 1

Rampersad, Arnold 1941- .... **CLC 44**
See also BW 2, 3; CA 127; 133; CANR 81;
DLB 111; INT CA-133

Rampling, Anne
See Rice, Anne
See also GLL 2

Ramsay, Allan 1686(?)-1758 .... **LC 29**
See also DLB 95; RGEL 2

Ramsay, Jay
See Campbell, (John) Ramsey

Ramuz, Charles-Ferdinand
1878-1947 .... **TCLC 33**
See also CA 165; EWL 3

Rand, Ayn 1905-1982 ...... **CLC 3, 30, 44, 79;
WLC**
See also AAYA 10; AMWS 4; BPFB 3;
BYA 12; CA 13-16R; 105; CANR 27, 73;
CDALBS; CPW; DA; DA3; DAC; DAM
MST, NOV, POP; DLB 227, 279; MTCW
1, 2; NFS 10, 16; RGAL 4; SFW 4; TUS;
YAW

Randall, Dudley (Felker) 1914-2000 . **BLC 3;
CLC 1, 135**
See also BW 1, 3; CA 25-28R; 189; CANR
23, 82; DAM MULT; DLB 41; PFS 5

Randall, Robert
See Silverberg, Robert

Ranger, Ken
See Creasey, John

Rank, Otto 1884-1939 .... **TCLC 115**

Ransom, John Crowe 1888-1974 .. **CLC 2, 4,
5, 11, 24; PC 61**
See also AMW; CA 5-8R; 49-52; CANR 6,
34; CDALBS; DA3; DAM POET; DLB
45, 63; EWL 3; EXPP; MTCW 1, 2;
RGAL 4; TUS

Rao, Raja 1909- .... **CLC 25, 56**
See also CA 73-76; CANR 51; CN 7; DAM
NOV; EWL 3; MTCW 1, 2; RGEL 2;
RGSF 2

Raphael, Frederic (Michael) 1931- ... **CLC 2,
14**
See also CA 1-4R; CANR 1, 86; CN 7;
DLB 14

Ratcliffe, James P.
See Mencken, H(enry) L(ouis)

Rathbone, Julian 1935- .... **CLC 41**
See also CA 101; CANR 34, 73

Rattigan, Terence (Mervyn)
1911-1977 .... **CLC 7; DC 18**
See also BRWS 7; CA 85-88; 73-76; CBD;
CDBLB 1945-1960; DAM DRAM; DFS
8; DLB 13; IDFW 3, 4; MTCW 1, 2;
RGEL 2

Ratushinskaya, Irina 1954- .... **CLC 54**
See also CA 129; CANR 68; CWW 2

Raven, Simon (Arthur Noel)
1927-2001 .... **CLC 14**
See also CA 81-84; 197; CANR 86; CN 7;
DLB 271

Ravenna, Michael
See Welty, Eudora (Alice)

Rawley, Callman 1903-2004
See Rakosi, Carl
See also CA 21-24R; CANR 12, 32, 91

Rawlings, Marjorie Kinnan
1896-1953 .... **TCLC 4**
See also AAYA 20; AMWS 10; ANW;
BPFB 3; BYA 3; CA 104; 137; CANR 74;
CLR 63; DLB 9, 22, 102; DLBD 17;
JRDA; MAICYA 1, 2; MTCW 2; RGAL
4; SATA 100; WCH; YABC 1; YAW

Ray, Satyajit 1921-1992 .... **CLC 16, 76**
See also CA 114; 137; DAM MULT

Read, Herbert Edward 1893-1968 ...... **CLC 4**
See also BRW 6; CA 85-88; 25-28R; DLB
20, 149; EWL 3; PAB; RGEL 2

Read, Piers Paul 1941- .... **CLC 4, 10, 25**
See also CA 21-24R; CANR 38, 86; CN 7;
DLB 14; SATA 21

Reade, Charles 1814-1884 .... **NCLC 2, 74**
See also DLB 21; RGEL 2

Reade, Hamish
See Gray, Simon (James Holliday)

Reading, Peter 1946- .... **CLC 47**
See also BRWS 8; CA 103; CANR 46, 96;
CP 7; DLB 40

Reaney, James 1926- .... **CLC 13**
See also CA 41-44R; CAAS 15; CANR 42;
CD 5; CP 7; DAC; DAM MST; DLB 68;
RGEL 2; SATA 43

Rebreanu, Liviu 1885-1944 .... **TCLC 28**
See also CA 165; DLB 220; EWL 3

Rechy, John (Francisco) 1934- ...... **CLC 1, 7,
14, 18, 107; HLC 2**
See also CA 5-8R, 195; CAAE 195; CAAS
4; CANR 6, 32, 64; CN 7; DAM MULT;
DLB 122, 278; DLBY 1982; HW 1, 2;
INT CANR-6; LLW 1; RGAL 4

Rulfo, Juan 1918-1986 .. **CLC 8, 80; HLC 2; SSC 25**
See also CA 85-88; 118; CANR 26; CD-WLB 3; DAM MULT; DLB 113; EWL 3; HW 1, 2; LAW; MTCW 1, 2; RGSF 2; RGWL 2, 3; WLIT 1

Rumi, Jalal al-Din 1207-1273 ...... **CMLC 20; PC 45**
See also RGWL 2, 3; WP

Runeberg, Johan 1804-1877 .... **NCLC 41**

Runyon, (Alfred) Damon
1884(?)-1946 .... **TCLC 10**
See also CA 107; 165; DLB 11, 86, 171; MTCW 2; RGAL 4

Rush, Norman 1933- .... **CLC 44**
See also CA 121; 126; CANR 130; INT CA-126

Rushdie, (Ahmed) Salman 1947- .... **CLC 23, 31, 55, 100, 191; SSC 83; WLCS**
See also BEST 89:3; BPFB 3; BRWS 4; CA 108; 111; CANR 33, 56, 108, 133; CN 7; CPW 1; DA3; DAB; DAC; DAM MST, NOV, POP; DLB 194; EWL 3; FANT; INT CA-111; LATS 1:2; LMFS 2; MTCW 1, 2; RGEL 2; RGSF 2; TEA; WLIT 4; WWE 1

Rushforth, Peter (Scott) 1945- .... **CLC 19**
See also CA 101

Ruskin, John 1819-1900 .... **TCLC 63**
See also BRW 5; BYA 5; CA 114; 129; CD-BLB 1832-1890; DLB 55, 163, 190; RGEL 2; SATA 24; TEA; WCH

Russ, Joanna 1937- .... **CLC 15**
See also BPFB 3; CA 5-28R; CANR 11, 31, 65; CN 7; DLB 8; FW; GLL 1; MTCW 1; SCFW 2; SFW 4

Russ, Richard Patrick
See O'Brian, Patrick

Russell, George William 1867-1935
See A.E.; Baker, Jean H.
See also BRWS 8; CA 104; 153; CDBLB 1890-1914; DAM POET; EWL 3; RGEL 2

Russell, Jeffrey Burton 1934- .... **CLC 70**
See also CA 25-28R; CANR 11, 28, 52

Russell, (Henry) Ken(neth Alfred)
1927- .... **CLC 16**
See also CA 105

Russell, William Martin 1947-
See Russell, Willy
See also CA 164; CANR 107

Russell, Willy .... **CLC 60**
See Russell, William Martin
See also CBD; CD 5; DLB 233

Russo, Richard 1949- .... **CLC 181**
See also AMWS 12; CA 127; 133; CANR 87, 114

Rutherford, Mark .... **TCLC 25**
See White, William Hale
See also DLB 18; RGEL 2

Ruyslinck, Ward .... **CLC 14**
See Belser, Reimond Karel Maria de

Ryan, Cornelius (John) 1920-1974 ..... **CLC 7**
See also CA 69-72; 53-56; CANR 38

Ryan, Michael 1946- .... **CLC 65**
See also CA 49-52; CANR 109; DLBY 1982

Ryan, Tim
See Dent, Lester

Rybakov, Anatoli (Naumovich)
1911-1998 .... **CLC 23, 53**
See Rybakov, Anatolii (Naumovich)
See also CA 126; 135; 172; SATA 79; SATA-Obit 108

Rybakov, Anatolii (Naumovich)
See Rybakov, Anatoli (Naumovich)
See also DLB 302

Ryder, Jonathan
See Ludlum, Robert

Ryga, George 1932-1987 .... **CLC 14**
See also CA 101; 124; CANR 43, 90; CCA 1; DAC; DAM MST; DLB 60

S. H.
See Hartmann, Sadakichi

S. S.
See Sassoon, Siegfried (Lorraine)

Sa'adawi, al- Nawal
See El Saadawi, Nawal
See also AFW; EWL 3

Saadawi, Nawal El
See El Saadawi, Nawal
See also WLIT 2

Saba, Umberto 1883-1957 .... **TCLC 33**
See also CA 144; CANR 79; DLB 114; EWL 3; RGWL 2, 3

Sabatini, Rafael 1875-1950 .... **TCLC 47**
See also BPFB 3; CA 162; RHW

Sabato, Ernesto (R.) 1911- .... **CLC 10, 23; HLC 2**
See also CA 97-100; CANR 32, 65; CD-WLB 3; CWW 2; DAM MULT; DLB 145; EWL 3; HW 1, 2; LAW; MTCW 1, 2

Sa-Carneiro, Mario de 1890-1916 . **TCLC 83**
See also DLB 287; EWL 3

Sacastru, Martin
See Bioy Casares, Adolfo
See also CWW 2

Sacher-Masoch, Leopold von
1836(?)-1895 .... **NCLC 31**

Sachs, Hans 1494-1576 .... **LC 95**
See also CDWLB 2; DLB 179; RGWL 2, 3

Sachs, Marilyn (Stickle) 1927- .... **CLC 35**
See also AAYA 2; BYA 6; CA 17-20R; CANR 13, 47; CLR 2; JRDA; MAICYA 1, 2; SAAS 2; SATA 3, 68; SATA-Essay 110; WYA; YAW

Sachs, Nelly 1891-1970 .... **CLC 14, 98**
See also CA 17-18; 25-28R; CANR 87; CAP 2; EWL 3; MTCW 2; PFS 20; RGWL 2, 3

Sackler, Howard (Oliver)
1929-1982 .... **CLC 14**
See also CA 61-64; 108; CAD; CANR 30; DFS 15; DLB 7

Sacks, Oliver (Wolf) 1933- .... **CLC 67, 202**
See also CA 53-56; CANR 28, 50, 76; CPW; DA3; INT CANR-28; MTCW 1, 2

Sackville, Thomas 1536-1608 .... **LC 98**
See also DAM DRAM; DLB 62, 132; RGEL 2

Sadakichi
See Hartmann, Sadakichi

Sa'dawi, Nawal al-
See El Saadawi, Nawal
See also CWW 2

Sade, Donatien Alphonse Francois
1740-1814 .... **NCLC 3, 47**
See also EW 4; GFL Beginnings to 1789; RGWL 2, 3

Sade, Marquis de
See Sade, Donatien Alphonse Francois

Sadoff, Ira 1945- .... **CLC 9**
See also CA 53-56; CANR 5, 21, 109; DLB 120

Saetone
See Camus, Albert

Safire, William 1929- .... **CLC 10**
See also CA 17-20R; CANR 31, 54, 91

Sagan, Carl (Edward) 1934-1996 .... **CLC 30, 112**
See also AAYA 2; CA 25-28R; 155; CANR 11, 36, 74; CPW; DA3; MTCW 1, 2; SATA 58; SATA-Obit 94

Sagan, Francoise .... **CLC 3, 6, 9, 17, 36**
See Quoirez, Francoise
See also CWW 2; DLB 83; EWL 3; GFL 1789 to the Present; MTCW 2

Sahgal, Nayantara (Pandit) 1927- .... **CLC 41**
See also CA 9-12R; CANR 11, 88; CN 7

Said, Edward W. 1935-2003 .... **CLC 123**
See also CA 21-24R; 220; CANR 45, 74, 107, 131; DLB 67; MTCW 2

Saigyō 1118-1190 .... **CMLC 77**
See also DLB 203; RGWL 3

Saint, H(arry) F. 1941- .... **CLC 50**
See also CA 127

St. Aubin de Teran, Lisa 1953-
See Teran, Lisa St. Aubin de
See also CA 118; 126; CN 7; INT CA-126

Saint Birgitta of Sweden c.
1303-1373 .... **CMLC 24**

Sainte-Beuve, Charles Augustin
1804-1869 .... **NCLC 5**
See also DLB 217; EW 6; GFL 1789 to the Present

Saint-Exupery, Antoine (Jean Baptiste Marie Roger) de 1900-1944 .... **TCLC 2, 56; WLC**
See also BPFB 3; BYA 3; CA 108; 132; CLR 10; DA3; DAM NOV; DLB 72; EW 12; EWL 3; GFL 1789 to the Present; LAIT 3; MAICYA 1, 2; MTCW 1, 2; RGWL 2, 3; SATA 20; TWA

St. John, David
See Hunt, E(verette) Howard, (Jr.)

St. John, J. Hector
See Crevecoeur, Michel Guillaume Jean de

Saint-John Perse
See Leger, (Marie-Rene Auguste) Alexis Saint-Leger
See also EW 10; EWL 3; GFL 1789 to the Present; RGWL 2

Saintsbury, George (Edward Bateman)
1845-1933 .... **TCLC 31**
See also CA 160; DLB 57, 149

Sait Faik .... **TCLC 23**
See Abasiyanik, Sait Faik

Saki .... **SSC 12; TCLC 3**
See Munro, H(ector) H(ugh)
See also BRWS 6; BYA 11; LAIT 2; MTCW 2; RGEL 2; SSFS 1; SUFW

Sala, George Augustus 1828-1895 . **NCLC 46**

Saladin 1138-1193 .... **CMLC 38**

Salama, Hannu 1936- .... **CLC 18**
See also EWL 3

Salamanca, J(ack) R(ichard) 1922- .. **CLC 4, 15**
See also CA 25-28R, 193; CAAE 193

Salas, Floyd Francis 1931- .... **HLC 2**
See also CA 119; CAAS 27; CANR 44, 75, 93; DAM MULT; DLB 82; HW 1, 2; MTCW 2

Sale, J. Kirkpatrick
See Sale, Kirkpatrick

Sale, Kirkpatrick 1937- .... **CLC 68**
See also CA 13-16R; CANR 10

Salinas, Luis Omar 1937- ... **CLC 90; HLC 2**
See also AMWS 13; CA 131; CANR 81; DAM MULT; DLB 82; HW 1, 2

Salinas (y Serrano), Pedro
1891(?)-1951 .... **TCLC 17**
See also CA 117; DLB 134; EWL 3

Salinger, J(erome) D(avid) 1919- .. **CLC 1, 3, 8, 12, 55, 56, 138; SSC 2, 28, 65; WLC**
See also AAYA 2, 36; AMW; AMWC 1; BPFB 3; CA 5-8R; CANR 39, 129; CDALB 1941-1968; CLR 18; CN 7; CPW 1; DA; DA3; DAB; DAC; DAM MST, NOV, POP; DLB 2, 102, 173; EWL 3; EXPN; LAIT 4; MAICYA 1, 2; MTCW 1, 2; NFS 1; RGAL 4; RGSF 2; SATA 67; SSFS 17; TUS; WYA; YAW

Salisbury, John
See Caute, (John) David

Schama, Simon (Michael) 1945- ..... **CLC 150**
   See also BEST 89:4; CA 105; CANR 39, 91
Schary, Jill
   See Robinson, Jill
Schell, Jonathan 1943- .... **CLC 35**
   See also CA 73-76; CANR 12, 117
Schelling, Friedrich Wilhelm Joseph von 1775-1854 .... **NCLC 30**
   See also DLB 90
Scherer, Jean-Marie Maurice 1920-
   See Rohmer, Eric
   See also CA 110
Schevill, James (Erwin) 1920- .... **CLC 7**
   See also CA 5-8R; CAAS 12; CAD; CD 5
Schiller, Friedrich von 1759-1805 ...... **DC 12; NCLC 39, 69**
   See also CDWLB 2; DAM DRAM; DLB 94; EW 5; RGWL 2, 3; TWA
Schisgal, Murray (Joseph) 1926- .... **CLC 6**
   See also CA 21-24R; CAD; CANR 48, 86; CD 5
Schlee, Ann 1934- .... **CLC 35**
   See also CA 101; CANR 29, 88; SATA 44; SATA-Brief 36
Schlegel, August Wilhelm von 1767-1845 .... **NCLC 15, 142**
   See also DLB 94; RGWL 2, 3
Schlegel, Friedrich 1772-1829 .... **NCLC 45**
   See also DLB 90; EW 5; RGWL 2, 3; TWA
Schlegel, Johann Elias (von) 1719(?)-1749 .... **LC 5**
Schleiermacher, Friedrich 1768-1834 .... **NCLC 107**
   See also DLB 90
Schlesinger, Arthur M(eier), Jr. 1917- .... **CLC 84**
   See also AITN 1; CA 1-4R; CANR 1, 28, 58, 105; DLB 17; INT CANR-28; MTCW 1, 2; SATA 61
Schlink, Bernhard 1944- .... **CLC 174**
   See also CA 163; CANR 116
Schmidt, Arno (Otto) 1914-1979 ...... **CLC 56**
   See also CA 128; 109; DLB 69; EWL 3
Schmitz, Aron Hector 1861-1928
   See Svevo, Italo
   See also CA 104; 122; MTCW 1
Schnackenberg, Gjertrud (Cecelia) 1953- .... **CLC 40; PC 45**
   See also CA 116; CANR 100; CP 7; CWP; DLB 120, 282; PFS 13
Schneider, Leonard Alfred 1925-1966
   See Bruce, Lenny
   See also CA 89-92
Schnitzler, Arthur 1862-1931 ..... **DC 17; SSC 15, 61; TCLC 4**
   See also CA 104; CDWLB 2; DLB 81, 118; EW 8; EWL 3; RGSF 2; RGWL 2, 3
Schoenberg, Arnold Franz Walter 1874-1951 .... **TCLC 75**
   See also CA 109; 188
Schonberg, Arnold
   See Schoenberg, Arnold Franz Walter
Schopenhauer, Arthur 1788-1860 . **NCLC 51, 157**
   See also DLB 90; EW 5
Schor, Sandra (M.) 1932(?)-1990 ..... **CLC 65**
   See also CA 132
Schorer, Mark 1908-1977 .... **CLC 9**
   See also CA 5-8R; 73-76; CANR 7; DLB 103
Schrader, Paul (Joseph) 1946- .... **CLC 26**
   See also CA 37-40R; CANR 41; DLB 44
Schreber, Daniel 1842-1911 .... **TCLC 123**
Schreiner, Olive (Emilie Albertina) 1855-1920 .... **TCLC 9**
   See also AFW; BRWS 2; CA 105; 154; DLB 18, 156, 190, 225; EWL 3; FW; RGEL 2; TWA; WLIT 2; WWE 1

Schulberg, Budd (Wilson) 1914- .. **CLC 7, 48**
   See also BPFB 3; CA 25-28R; CANR 19, 87; CN 7; DLB 6, 26, 28; DLBY 1981, 2001
Schulman, Arnold
   See Trumbo, Dalton
Schulz, Bruno 1892-1942 .. **SSC 13; TCLC 5, 51**
   See also CA 115; 123; CANR 86; CDWLB 4; DLB 215; EWL 3; MTCW 2; RGSF 2; RGWL 2, 3
Schulz, Charles M(onroe) 1922-2000 .... **CLC 12**
   See also AAYA 39; CA 9-12R; 187; CANR 6, 132; INT CANR-6; SATA 10; SATA-Obit 118
Schumacher, E(rnst) F(riedrich) 1911-1977 .... **CLC 80**
   See also CA 81-84; 73-76; CANR 34, 85
Schumann, Robert 1810-1856 ...... **NCLC 143**
Schuyler, George Samuel 1895-1977 .... **HR 3**
   See also BW 2; CA 81-84; 73-76; CANR 42; DLB 29, 51
Schuyler, James Marcus 1923-1991 .. **CLC 5, 23**
   See also CA 101; 134; DAM POET; DLB 5, 169; EWL 3; INT CA-101; WP
Schwartz, Delmore (David) 1913-1966 ... **CLC 2, 4, 10, 45, 87; PC 8**
   See also AMWS 2; CA 17-18; 25-28R; CANR 35; CAP 2; DLB 28, 48; EWL 3; MTCW 1, 2; PAB; RGAL 4; TUS
Schwartz, Ernst
   See Ozu, Yasujiro
Schwartz, John Burnham 1965- .... **CLC 59**
   See also CA 132; CANR 116
Schwartz, Lynne Sharon 1939- .... **CLC 31**
   See also CA 103; CANR 44, 89; DLB 218; MTCW 2
Schwartz, Muriel A.
   See Eliot, T(homas) S(tearns)
Schwarz-Bart, Andre 1928- .... **CLC 2, 4**
   See also CA 89-92; CANR 109; DLB 299
Schwarz-Bart, Simone 1938- . **BLCS; CLC 7**
   See also BW 2; CA 97-100; CANR 117; EWL 3
Schwerner, Armand 1927-1999 .... **PC 42**
   See also CA 9-12R; 179; CANR 50, 85; CP 7; DLB 165
Schwitters, Kurt (Hermann Edward Karl Julius) 1887-1948 .... **TCLC 95**
   See also CA 158
Schwob, Marcel (Mayer Andre) 1867-1905 .... **TCLC 20**
   See also CA 117; 168; DLB 123; GFL 1789 to the Present
Sciascia, Leonardo 1921-1989 .. **CLC 8, 9, 41**
   See also CA 85-88; 130; CANR 35; DLB 177; EWL 3; MTCW 1; RGWL 2, 3
Scoppettone, Sandra 1936- .... **CLC 26**
   See Early, Jack
   See also AAYA 11; BYA 8; CA 5-8R; CANR 41, 73; GLL 1; MAICYA 2; MAICYAS 1; SATA 9, 92; WYA; YAW
Scorsese, Martin 1942- .... **CLC 20, 89, 207**
   See also AAYA 38; CA 110, 114; CANR 46, 85
Scotland, Jay
   See Jakes, John (William)
Scott, Duncan Campbell 1862-1947 .... **TCLC 6**
   See also CA 104; 153; DAC; DLB 92; RGEL 2
Scott, Evelyn 1893-1963 .... **CLC 43**
   See also CA 104; 112; CANR 64; DLB 9, 48; RHW

Scott, F(rancis) R(eginald) 1899-1985 .... **CLC 22**
   See also CA 101; 114; CANR 87; DLB 88; INT CA-101; RGEL 2
Scott, Frank
   See Scott, F(rancis) R(eginald)
Scott, Joan .... **CLC 65**
Scott, Joanna 1960- .... **CLC 50**
   See also CA 126; CANR 53, 92
Scott, Paul (Mark) 1920-1978 ...... **CLC 9, 60**
   See also BRWS 1; CA 81-84; 77-80; CANR 33; DLB 14, 207; EWL 3; MTCW 1; RGEL 2; RHW; WWE 1
Scott, Ridley 1937- .... **CLC 183**
   See also AAYA 13, 43
Scott, Sarah 1723-1795 .... **LC 44**
   See also DLB 39
Scott, Sir Walter 1771-1832 .... **NCLC 15, 69, 110; PC 13; SSC 32; WLC**
   See also AAYA 22; BRW 4; BYA 2; CD-BLB 1789-1832; DA; DAB; DAC; DAM MST, NOV, POET; DLB 93, 107, 116, 144, 159; HGG; LAIT 1; RGEL 2; RGSF 2; SSFS 10; SUFW 1; TEA; WLIT 3; YABC 2
Scribe, (Augustin) Eugene 1791-1861 . **DC 5; NCLC 16**
   See also DAM DRAM; DLB 192; GFL 1789 to the Present; RGWL 2, 3
Scrum, R.
   See Crumb, R(obert)
Scudery, Georges de 1601-1667 .... **LC 75**
   See also GFL Beginnings to 1789
Scudery, Madeleine de 1607-1701 .. **LC 2, 58**
   See also DLB 268; GFL Beginnings to 1789
Scum
   See Crumb, R(obert)
Scumbag, Little Bobby
   See Crumb, R(obert)
Seabrook, John
   See Hubbard, L(afayette) Ron(ald)
Seacole, Mary Jane Grant 1805-1881 .... **NCLC 147**
   See also DLB 166
Sealy, I(rwin) Allan 1951- .... **CLC 55**
   See also CA 136; CN 7
Search, Alexander
   See Pessoa, Fernando (Antonio Nogueira)
Sebald, W(infried) G(eorg) 1944-2001 .... **CLC 194**
   See also BRWS 8; CA 159; 202; CANR 98
Sebastian, Lee
   See Silverberg, Robert
Sebastian Owl
   See Thompson, Hunter S(tockton)
Sebestyen, Igen
   See Sebestyen, Ouida
Sebestyen, Ouida 1924- .... **CLC 30**
   See also AAYA 8; BYA 7; CA 107; CANR 40, 114; CLR 17; JRDA; MAICYA 1, 2; SAAS 10; SATA 39, 140; WYA; YAW
Sebold, Alice 1963(?)- .... **CLC 193**
   See also AAYA 56; CA 203
Second Duke of Buckingham
   See Villiers, George
Secundus, H. Scriblerus
   See Fielding, Henry
Sedges, John
   See Buck, Pearl S(ydenstricker)
Sedgwick, Catharine Maria 1789-1867 .... **NCLC 19, 98**
   See also DLB 1, 74, 183, 239, 243, 254; RGAL 4
Seelye, John (Douglas) 1931- .... **CLC 7**
   See also CA 97-100; CANR 70; INT CA-97-100; TCWW 2

Sheldon, Alice Hastings Bradley
    1915(?)-1987
    See Tiptree, James, Jr.
    See also CA 108; 122; CANR 34; INT CA-
        108; MTCW 1
Sheldon, John
    See Bloch, Robert (Albert)
Sheldon, Walter J(ames) 1917-1996
    See Queen, Ellery
    See also AITN 1; CA 25-28R; CANR 10
Shelley, Mary Wollstonecraft (Godwin)
    1797-1851 ...... **NCLC 14, 59, 103; WLC**
    See also AAYA 20; BPFB 3; BRW 3;
        BRWC 2; BRWS 3; BYA 5; CDBLB
        1789-1832; DA; DA3; DAB; DAC; DAM
        MST, NOV; DLB 110, 116, 159, 178;
        EXPN; HGG; LAIT 1; LMFS 1, 2; NFS
        1; RGEL 2; SATA 29; SCFW; SFW 4;
        TEA; WLIT 3
Shelley, Percy Bysshe 1792-1822 .. **NCLC 18,**
    93, 143; PC 14; WLC
    See also BRW 4; BRWR 1; CDBLB 1789-
        1832; DA; DA3; DAB; DAC; DAM MST,
        POET; DLB 96, 110, 158; EXPP; LMFS
        1; PAB; PFS 2; RGEL 2; TEA; WLIT 3;
        WP
Shepard, Jim 1956- .... **CLC 36**
    See also CA 137; CANR 59, 104; SATA 90
Shepard, Lucius 1947- .... **CLC 34**
    See also CA 128; 141; CANR 81, 124;
        HGG; SCFW 2; SFW 4; SUFW 2
Shepard, Sam 1943- .... **CLC 4, 6, 17, 34, 41,**
    44, 169; DC 5
    See also AAYA 1, 58; AMWS 3; CA 69-72;
        CABS 3; CAD; CANR 22, 120; CD 5;
        DA3; DAM DRAM; DFS 3, 6, 7, 14;
        DLB 7, 212; EWL 3; IDFW 3, 4; MTCW
        1, 2; RGAL 4
Shepherd, Michael
    See Ludlum, Robert
Sherburne, Zoa (Lillian Morin)
    1912-1995 .... **CLC 30**
    See also AAYA 13; CA 1-4R; 176; CANR
        3, 37; MAICYA 1, 2; SAAS 18; SATA 3;
        YAW
Sheridan, Frances 1724-1766 .... **LC 7**
    See also DLB 39, 84
Sheridan, Richard Brinsley
    1751-1816 .... **DC 1; NCLC 5, 91; WLC**
    See also BRW 3; CDBLB 1660-1789; DA;
        DAB; DAC; DAM DRAM, MST; DFS
        15; DLB 89; WLIT 3
Sherman, Jonathan Marc .... **CLC 55**
Sherman, Martin 1941(?)- .... **CLC 19**
    See also CA 116; 123; CAD; CANR 86;
        CD 5; DFS 20; DLB 228; GLL 1; IDTP
Sherwin, Judith Johnson
    See Johnson, Judith (Emlyn)
    See also CANR 85; CP 7; CWP
Sherwood, Frances 1940- .... **CLC 81**
    See also CA 146, 220; CAAE 220
Sherwood, Robert E(mmet)
    1896-1955 .... **TCLC 3**
    See also CA 104; 153; CANR 86; DAM
        DRAM; DFS 11, 15, 17; DLB 7, 26, 249;
        IDFW 3, 4; RGAL 4
Shestov, Lev 1866-1938 .... **TCLC 56**
Shevchenko, Taras 1814-1861 .... **NCLC 54**
Shiel, M(atthew) P(hipps)
    1865-1947 .... **TCLC 8**
    See Holmes, Gordon
    See also CA 106; 160; DLB 153; HGG;
        MTCW 2; SFW 4; SUFW
Shields, Carol (Ann) 1935-2003 ...... **CLC 91,**
    113, 193
    See also AMWS 7; CA 81-84; 218; CANR
        51, 74, 98, 133; CCA 1; CN 7; CPW;
        DA3; DAC; MTCW 2

Shields, David (Jonathan) 1956- ...... **CLC 97**
    See also CA 124; CANR 48, 99, 112
Shiga, Naoya 1883-1971 ..... **CLC 33; SSC 23**
    See Shiga Naoya
    See also CA 101; 33-36R; MJW; RGWL 3
Shiga Naoya
    See Shiga, Naoya
    See also DLB 180; EWL 3; RGWL 3
Shilts, Randy 1951-1994 .... **CLC 85**
    See also AAYA 19; CA 115; 127; 144;
        CANR 45; DA3; GLL 1; INT CA-127;
        MTCW 2
Shimazaki, Haruki 1872-1943
    See Shimazaki Toson
    See also CA 105; 134; CANR 84; RGWL 3
Shimazaki Toson .... **TCLC 5**
    See Shimazaki, Haruki
    See also DLB 180; EWL 3
Shirley, James 1596-1666 .... **DC 25; LC 96**
    See also DLB 58; RGEL 2
Sholokhov, Mikhail (Aleksandrovich)
    1905-1984 .... **CLC 7, 15**
    See also CA 101; 112; DLB 272; EWL 3;
        MTCW 1, 2; RGWL 2, 3; SATA-Obit 36
Shone, Patric
    See Hanley, James
Showalter, Elaine 1941- .... **CLC 169**
    See also CA 57-60; CANR 58, 106; DLB
        67; FW; GLL 2
Shreve, Susan
    See Shreve, Susan Richards
Shreve, Susan Richards 1939- .... **CLC 23**
    See also CA 49-52; CAAS 5; CANR 5, 38,
        69, 100; MAICYA 1, 2; SATA 46, 95, 152;
        SATA-Brief 41
Shue, Larry 1946-1985 .... **CLC 52**
    See also CA 145; 117; DAM DRAM; DFS
        7
Shu-Jen, Chou 1881-1936
    See Lu Hsun
    See also CA 104
Shulman, Alix Kates 1932- .... **CLC 2, 10**
    See also CA 29-32R; CANR 43; FW; SATA
        7
Shuster, Joe 1914-1992 .... **CLC 21**
    See also AAYA 50
Shute, Nevil .... **CLC 30**
    See Norway, Nevil Shute
    See also BPFB 3; DLB 255; NFS 9; RHW;
        SFW 4
Shuttle, Penelope (Diane) 1947- .... **CLC 7**
    See also CA 93-96; CANR 39, 84, 92, 108;
        CP 7; CWP; DLB 14, 40
Shvarts, Elena 1948- .... **PC 50**
    See also CA 147
Sidhwa, Bapsy (N.) 1938- .... **CLC 168**
    See also CA 108; CANR 25, 57; CN 7; FW
Sidney, Mary 1561-1621 .... **LC 19, 39**
    See Sidney Herbert, Mary
Sidney, Sir Philip 1554-1586 . **LC 19, 39; PC**
    32
    See also BRW 1; BRWR 2; CDBLB Before
        1660; DA; DA3; DAB; DAC; DAM MST,
        POET; DLB 167; EXPP; PAB; RGEL 2;
        TEA; WP
Sidney Herbert, Mary
    See Sidney, Mary
    See also DLB 167
Siegel, Jerome 1914-1996 .... **CLC 21**
    See Siegel, Jerry
    See also CA 116; 169; 151
Siegel, Jerry
    See Siegel, Jerome
    See also AAYA 50
Sienkiewicz, Henryk (Adam Alexander Pius)
    1846-1916 .... **TCLC 3**
    See also CA 104; 134; CANR 84; EWL 3;
        RGSF 2; RGWL 2, 3

Sierra, Gregorio Martinez
    See Martinez Sierra, Gregorio
Sierra, Maria (de la O'LeJarraga) Martinez
    See Martinez Sierra, Maria (de la
        O'LeJarraga)
Sigal, Clancy 1926- .... **CLC 7**
    See also CA 1-4R; CANR 85; CN 7
Siger of Brabant 1240(?)-1284(?) . **CMLC 69**
    See also DLB 115
Sigourney, Lydia H.
    See Sigourney, Lydia Howard (Huntley)
    See also DLB 73, 183
Sigourney, Lydia Howard (Huntley)
    1791-1865 .... **NCLC 21, 87**
    See Sigourney, Lydia H.; Sigourney, Lydia
        Huntley
    See also DLB 1
Sigourney, Lydia Huntley
    See Sigourney, Lydia Howard (Huntley)
    See also DLB 42, 239, 243
Siguenza y Gongora, Carlos de
    1645-1700 .... **HLCS 2; LC 8**
    See also LAW
Sigurjonsson, Johann
    See Sigurjonsson, Johann
Sigurjonsson, Johann 1880-1919 ... **TCLC 27**
    See also CA 170; DLB 293; EWL 3
Sikelianos, Angelos 1884-1951 .... **PC 29;**
    TCLC 39
    See also EWL 3; RGWL 2, 3
Silkin, Jon 1930-1997 .... **CLC 2, 6, 43**
    See also CA 5-8R; CAAS 5; CANR 89; CP
        7; DLB 27
Silko, Leslie (Marmon) 1948- .... **CLC 23, 74,**
    114, 211; NNAL; SSC 37, 66; WLCS
    See also AAYA 14; AMWS 4; ANW; BYA
        12; CA 115; 122; CANR 45, 65, 118; CN
        7; CP 7; CWP 1; CWP; DA; DA3; DAC;
        DAM MST, MULT, POP; DLB 143, 175,
        256, 275; EWL 3; EXPP; EXPS; LAIT 4;
        MTCW 2; NFS 4; PFS 9, 16; RGAL 4;
        RGSF 2; SSFS 4, 8, 10, 11
Sillanpaa, Frans Eemil 1888-1964 ... **CLC 19**
    See also CA 129; 93-96; EWL 3; MTCW 1
Sillitoe, Alan 1928- .. **CLC 1, 3, 6, 10, 19, 57,**
    148
    See also AITN 1; BRWS 5; CA 9-12R; 191;
        CAAE 191; CAAS 2; CANR 8, 26, 55;
        CDBLB 1960 to Present; CN 7; DLB 14,
        139; EWL 3; MTCW 1, 2; RGEL 2;
        RGSF 2; SATA 61
Silone, Ignazio 1900-1978 .... **CLC 4**
    See also CA 25-28; 81-84; CANR 34; CAP
        2; DLB 264; EW 12; EWL 3; MTCW 1;
        RGSF 2; RGWL 2, 3
Silone, Ignazione
    See Silone, Ignazio
Silver, Joan Micklin 1935- .... **CLC 20**
    See also CA 114; 121; INT CA-121
Silver, Nicholas
    See Faust, Frederick (Schiller)
    See also TCWW 2
Silverberg, Robert 1935- .... **CLC 7, 140**
    See also AAYA 24; BPFB 3; BYA 7, 9; CA
        1-4R; 186; CAAE 186; CAAS 3; CANR
        1, 20, 36, 85; CLR 59; CN 7; CPW; DAM
        POP; DLB 8; INT CANR-20; MAICYA
        1, 2; MTCW 1, 2; SATA 13, 91; SATA-
        Essay 104; SCFW 2; SFW 4; SUFW 2
Silverstein, Alvin 1933- .... **CLC 17**
    See also CA 49-52; CANR 2; CLR 25;
        JRDA; MAICYA 1, 2; SATA 8, 69, 124
Silverstein, Shel(don Allan)
    1932-1999 .... **PC 49**
    See also AAYA 40; BW 3; CA 107; 179;
        CANR 47, 74, 81; CLR 5, 96; CWRI 5;
        JRDA; MAICYA 1, 2; MTCW 2; SATA
        33, 92; SATA-Brief 27; SATA-Obit 116

Smith, David (Jeddie) 1942-
See Smith, Dave
See also CA 49-52; CANR 1, 59, 120; CP 7; CSW; DAM POET

Smith, Florence Margaret 1902-1971
See Smith, Stevie
See also CA 17-18; 29-32R; CANR 35; CAP 2; DAM POET; MTCW 1, 2; TEA

Smith, Iain Crichton 1928-1998 .... CLC 64
See also BRWS 9; CA 21-24R; 171; CN 7; CP 7; DLB 40, 139; RGSF 2

Smith, John 1580(?)-1631 .... LC 9
See also DLB 24, 30; TUS

Smith, Johnston
See Crane, Stephen (Townley)

Smith, Joseph, Jr. 1805-1844 .... NCLC 53

Smith, Lee 1944- .... CLC 25, 73
See also CA 114; 119; CANR 46, 118; CSW; DLB 143; DLBY 1983; EWL 3; INT CA-119; RGAL 4

Smith, Martin
See Smith, Martin Cruz

Smith, Martin Cruz 1942- .. CLC 25; NNAL
See also BEST 89:4; BPFB 3; CA 85-88; CANR 6, 23, 43, 65, 119; CMW 4; CPW; DAM MULT, POP; HGG; INT CANR-23; MTCW 2; RGAL 4

Smith, Patti 1946- .... CLC 12
See also CA 93-96; CANR 63

Smith, Pauline (Urmson)
1882-1959 .... TCLC 25
See also DLB 225; EWL 3

Smith, Rosamond
See Oates, Joyce Carol

Smith, Sheila Kaye
See Kaye-Smith, Sheila

Smith, Stevie .... CLC 3, 8, 25, 44; PC 12
See Smith, Florence Margaret
See also BRWS 2; DLB 20; EWL 3; MTCW 2; PAB; PFS 3; RGEL 2

Smith, Wilbur (Addison) 1933- .... CLC 33
See also CA 13-16R; CANR 7, 46, 66, 134; CPW; MTCW 1, 2

Smith, William Jay 1918- .... CLC 6
See also AMWS 13; CA 5-8R; CANR 44, 106; CP 7; CSW; CWRI 5; DLB 5; MAICYA 1, 2; SAAS 22; SATA 2, 68, 154; SATA-Essay 154

Smith, Woodrow Wilson
See Kuttner, Henry

Smith, Zadie 1976- .... CLC 158
See also AAYA 50; CA 193

Smolenskin, Peretz 1842-1885 .... NCLC 30

Smollett, Tobias (George) 1721-1771 ... LC 2, 46
See also BRW 3; CDBLB 1660-1789; DLB 39, 104; RGEL 2; TEA

Snodgrass, W(illiam) D(e Witt)
1926- .... CLC 2, 6, 10, 18, 68
See also AMWS 6; CA 1-4R; CANR 6, 36, 65, 85; CP 7; DAM POET; DLB 5; MTCW 1, 2; RGAL 4

Snorri Sturluson 1179-1241 .... CMLC 56
See also RGWL 2, 3

Snow, C(harles) P(ercy) 1905-1980 ... CLC 1, 4, 6, 9, 13, 19
See also BRW 7; CA 5-8R; 101; CANR 28; CDBLB 1945-1960; DAM NOV; DLB 15, 77; DLBD 17; EWL 3; MTCW 1, 2; RGEL 2; TEA

Snow, Frances Compton
See Adams, Henry (Brooks)

Snyder, Gary (Sherman) 1930- . CLC 1, 2, 5, 9, 32, 120; PC 21
See also AMWS 8; ANW; BG 3; CA 17-20R; CANR 30, 60, 125; CP 7; DA3; DAM POET; DLB 5, 16, 165, 212, 237, 275; EWL 3; MTCW 2; PFS 9, 19; RGAL 4; WP

Snyder, Zilpha Keatley 1927- .... CLC 17
See also AAYA 15; BYA 1; CA 9-12R; CANR 38; CLR 31; JRDA; MAICYA 1, 2; SAAS 2; SATA 1, 28, 75, 110; SATA-Essay 112; YAW

Soares, Bernardo
See Pessoa, Fernando (Antonio Nogueira)

Sobh, A.
See Shamlu, Ahmad

Sobh, Alef
See Shamlu, Ahmad

Sobol, Joshua 1939- .... CLC 60
See Sobol, Yehoshua
See also CA 200

Sobol, Yehoshua 1939-
See Sobol, Joshua
See also CWW 2

Socrates 470B.C.-399B.C. .... CMLC 27

Soderberg, Hjalmar 1869-1941 ...... TCLC 39
See also DLB 259; EWL 3; RGSF 2

Soderbergh, Steven 1963- .... CLC 154
See also AAYA 43

Sodergran, Edith (Irene) 1892-1923
See Soedergran, Edith (Irene)
See also CA 202; DLB 259; EW 11; EWL 3; RGWL 2, 3

Soedergran, Edith (Irene)
1892-1923 .... TCLC 31
See Sodergran, Edith (Irene)

Softly, Edgar
See Lovecraft, H(oward) P(hillips)

Softly, Edward
See Lovecraft, H(oward) P(hillips)

Sokolov, Alexander V(sevolodovich) 1943-
See Sokolov, Sasha
See also CA 73-76

Sokolov, Raymond 1941- .... CLC 7
See also CA 85-88

Sokolov, Sasha .... CLC 59
See Sokolov, Alexander V(sevolodovich)
See also CWW 2; DLB 285; EWL 3; RGWL 2, 3

Solo, Jay
See Ellison, Harlan (Jay)

Sologub, Fyodor .... TCLC 9
See Teternikov, Fyodor Kuzmich
See also EWL 3

Solomons, Ikey Esquir
See Thackeray, William Makepeace

Solomos, Dionysios 1798-1857 .... NCLC 15

Solwoska, Mara
See French, Marilyn

Solzhenitsyn, Aleksandr I(sayevich)
1918- .. CLC 1, 2, 4, 7, 9, 10, 18, 26, 34, 78, 134; SSC 32; WLC
See Solzhenitsyn, Aleksandr Isaevich
See also AAYA 49; AITN 1; BPFB 3; CA 69-72; CANR 40, 65, 116; DA; DA3; DAB; DAC; DAM MST, NOV; DLB 302; EW 13; EXPS; LAIT 4; MTCW 1, 2; NFS 6; RGSF 2; RGWL 2, 3; SSFS 9; TWA

Solzhenitsyn, Aleksandr Isaevich
See Solzhenitsyn, Aleksandr I(sayevich)
See also CWW 2; EWL 3

Somers, Jane
See Lessing, Doris (May)

Somerville, Edith Oenone
1858-1949 .... SSC 56; TCLC 51
See also CA 196; DLB 135; RGEL 2; RGSF 2

Somerville & Ross
See Martin, Violet Florence; Somerville, Edith Oenone

Sommer, Scott 1951- .... CLC 25
See also CA 106

Sommers, Christina Hoff 1950- ...... CLC 197
See also CA 153; CANR 95

Sondheim, Stephen (Joshua) 1930- . CLC 30, 39, 147; DC 22
See also AAYA 11; CA 103; CANR 47, 67, 125; DAM DRAM; LAIT 4

Sone, Monica 1919- .... AAL

Song, Cathy 1955- .... AAL; PC 21
See also CA 154; CANR 118; CWP; DLB 169; EXPP; FW; PFS 5

Sontag, Susan 1933- .... CLC 1, 2, 10, 13, 31, 105, 195
See also AMWS 3; CA 17-20R; CANR 25, 51, 74, 97; CN 7; CPW; DA3; DAM POP; DLB 2, 67; EWL 3; MAWW; MTCW 1, 2; RGAL 4; RHW; SSFS 10

Sophocles 496(?)B.C.-406(?)B.C. .... CMLC 2, 47, 51; DC 1; WLCS
See also AW 1; CDWLB 1; DA; DA3; DAB; DAC; DAM DRAM, MST; DFS 1, 4, 8; LAIT 1; LATS 1:1; LMFS 1; RGWL 2, 3; TWA

Sordello 1189-1269 .... CMLC 15

Sorel, Georges 1847-1922 .... TCLC 91
See also CA 118; 188

Sorel, Julia
See Drexler, Rosalyn

Sorokin, Vladimir .... CLC 59
See Sorokin, Vladimir Georgievich

Sorokin, Vladimir Georgievich
See Sorokin, Vladimir
See also DLB 285

Sorrentino, Gilbert 1929- .. CLC 3, 7, 14, 22, 40
See also CA 77-80; CANR 14, 33, 115; CN 7; CP 7; DLB 5, 173; DLBY 1980; INT CANR-14

Soseki
See Natsume, Soseki
See also MJW

Soto, Gary 1952- ... CLC 32, 80; HLC 2; PC 28
See also AAYA 10, 37; BYA 11; CA 119; 125; CANR 50, 74, 107; CLR 38; CP 7; DAM MULT; DLB 82; EWL 3; EXPP; HW 1, 2; INT CA-125; JRDA; LLW 1; MAICYA 2; MAICYAS 1; MTCW 2; PFS 7; RGAL 4; SATA 80, 120; WYA; YAW

Soupault, Philippe 1897-1990 .... CLC 68
See also CA 116; 147; 131; EWL 3; GFL 1789 to the Present; LMFS 2

Souster, (Holmes) Raymond 1921- .... CLC 5, 14
See also CA 13-16R; CAAS 14; CANR 13, 29, 53; CP 7; DA3; DAC; DAM POET; DLB 88; RGEL 2; SATA 63

Southern, Terry 1924(?)-1995 .... CLC 7
See also AMWS 11; BPFB 3; CA 1-4R; 150; CANR 1, 55, 107; CN 7; DLB 2; IDFW 3, 4

Southerne, Thomas 1660-1746 .... LC 99
See also DLB 80; RGEL 2

Southey, Robert 1774-1843 .... NCLC 8, 97
See also BRW 4; DLB 93, 107, 142; RGEL 2; SATA 54

Southwell, Robert 1561(?)-1595 .... LC 108
See also DLB 167; RGEL 2; TEA

Southworth, Emma Dorothy Eliza Nevitte
1819-1899 .... NCLC 26
See also DLB 239

Souza, Ernest
See Scott, Evelyn

Soyinka, Wole 1934- .. BLC 3; CLC 3, 5, 14, 36, 44, 179; DC 2; WLC
See also AFW; BW 2, 3; CA 13-16R; CANR 27, 39, 82; CD 5; CDWLB 3; CN 7; CP 7; DA; DA3; DAB; DAC; DAM DRAM, MST, MULT; DFS 10; DLB 125; EWL 3; MTCW 1, 2; RGEL 2; TWA; WLIT 2; WWE 1

Spackman, W(illiam) M(ode)
1905-1990 .... **CLC 46**
See also CA 81-84; 132

Spacks, Barry (Bernard) 1931- .... **CLC 14**
See also CA 154; CANR 33, 109; CP 7;
DLB 105

Spanidou, Irini 1946- .... **CLC 44**
See also CA 185

Spark, Muriel (Sarah) 1918- ..... **CLC 2, 3, 5,**
8, 13, 18, 40, 94; SSC 10
See also BRWS 1; CA 5-8R; CANR 12, 36,
76, 89, 131; CDBLB 1945-1960; CN 7;
CP 7; DA3; DAB; DAC; DAM MST,
NOV; DLB 15, 139; EWL 3; FW; INT
CANR-12; LAIT 4; MTCW 1, 2; RGEL
2; TEA; WLIT 4; YAW

Spaulding, Douglas
See Bradbury, Ray (Douglas)

Spaulding, Leonard
See Bradbury, Ray (Douglas)

Speght, Rachel 1597-c. 1630 .... **LC 97**
See also DLB 126

Spelman, Elizabeth .... **CLC 65**

Spence, J. A. D.
See Eliot, T(homas) S(tearns)

Spencer, Anne 1882-1975 .... **HR 3**
See also BW 2; CA 161; DLB 51, 54

Spencer, Elizabeth 1921- .... **CLC 22; SSC 57**
See also CA 13-16R; CANR 32, 65, 87; CN
7; CSW; DLB 6, 218; EWL 3; MTCW 1;
RGAL 4; SATA 14

Spencer, Leonard G.
See Silverberg, Robert

Spencer, Scott 1945- .... **CLC 30**
See also CA 113; CANR 51; DLBY 1986

Spender, Stephen (Harold)
1909-1995 .... **CLC 1, 2, 5, 10, 41, 91**
See also BRWS 2; CA 9-12R; 149; CANR
31, 54; CDBLB 1945-1960; CP 7; DA3;
DAM POET; DLB 20; EWL 3; MTCW 1,
2; PAB; RGEL 2; TEA

Spengler, Oswald (Arnold Gottfried)
1880-1936 .... **TCLC 25**
See also CA 118; 189

Spenser, Edmund 1552(?)-1599 ...... **LC 5, 39,**
117; PC 8, 42; WLC
See also AAYA 60; BRW 1; CDBLB Before
1660; DA; DA3; DAB; DAC; DAM MST,
POET; DLB 167; EFS 2; EXPP; PAB;
RGEL 2; TEA; WLIT 3; WP

Spicer, Jack 1925-1965 .... **CLC 8, 18, 72**
See also BG 3; CA 85-88; DAM POET;
DLB 5, 16, 193; GLL 1; WP

Spiegelman, Art 1948- .... **CLC 76, 178**
See also AAYA 10, 46; CA 125; CANR 41,
55, 74, 124; DLB 299; MTCW 2; SATA
109; YAW

Spielberg, Peter 1929- .... **CLC 6**
See also CA 5-8R; CANR 4, 48; DLBY
1981

Spielberg, Steven 1947- .... **CLC 20, 188**
See also AAYA 8, 24; CA 77-80; CANR
32; SATA 32

Spillane, Frank Morrison 1918-
See Spillane, Mickey
See also CA 25-28R; CANR 28, 63, 125;
DA3; MTCW 1, 2; SATA 66

Spillane, Mickey .... **CLC 3, 13**
See Spillane, Frank Morrison
See also BPFB 3; CMW 4; DLB 226;
MSW; MTCW 2

Spinoza, Benedictus de 1632-1677 .. **LC 9, 58**

Spinrad, Norman (Richard) 1940- ... **CLC 46**
See also BPFB 3; CA 37-40R; CAAS 19;
CANR 20, 91; DLB 8; INT CANR-20;
SFW 4

Spitteler, Carl (Friedrich Georg)
1845-1924 .... **TCLC 12**
See also CA 109; DLB 129; EWL 3

Spivack, Kathleen (Romola Drucker)
1938- .... **CLC 6**
See also CA 49-52

Spoto, Donald 1941- .... **CLC 39**
See also CA 65-68; CANR 11, 57, 93

Springsteen, Bruce (F.) 1949- .... **CLC 17**
See also CA 111

Spurling, (Susan) Hilary 1940- .... **CLC 34**
See also CA 104; CANR 25, 52, 94

Spyker, John Howland
See Elman, Richard (Martin)

Squared, A.
See Abbott, Edwin A.

Squires, (James) Radcliffe
1917-1993 .... **CLC 51**
See also CA 1-4R; 140; CANR 6, 21

Srivastava, Dhanpat Rai 1880(?)-1936
See Premchand
See also CA 118; 197

Stacy, Donald
See Pohl, Frederik

Stael
See Stael-Holstein, Anne Louise Germaine
Necker
See also EW 5; RGWL 2, 3

Stael, Germaine de
See Stael-Holstein, Anne Louise Germaine
Necker
See also DLB 119, 192; FW; GFL 1789 to
the Present; TWA

Stael-Holstein, Anne Louise Germaine
Necker 1766-1817 .... **NCLC 3, 91**
See Stael; Stael, Germaine de

Stafford, Jean 1915-1979 .. **CLC 4, 7, 19, 68;**
SSC 26
See also CA 1-4R; 85-88; CANR 3, 65;
DLB 2, 173; MTCW 1, 2; RGAL 4; RGSF
2; SATA-Obit 22; TCWW 2; TUS

Stafford, William (Edgar)
1914-1993 .... **CLC 4, 7, 29**
See also AMWS 11; CA 5-8R; 142; CAAS
3; CANR 5, 22; DAM POET; DLB 5,
206; EXPP; INT CANR-22; PFS 2, 8, 16;
RGAL 4; WP

Stagnelius, Eric Johan 1793-1823 . **NCLC 61**

Staines, Trevor
See Brunner, John (Kilian Houston)

Stairs, Gordon
See Austin, Mary (Hunter)
See also TCWW 2

Stalin, Joseph 1879-1953 .... **TCLC 92**

Stampa, Gaspara c. 1524-1554 .... **PC 43; LC**
114
See also RGWL 2, 3

Stampflinger, K. A.
See Benjamin, Walter

Stancykowna
See Szymborska, Wislawa

Standing Bear, Luther
1868(?)-1939(?) .... **NNAL**
See also CA 113; 144; DAM MULT

Stanislavsky, Konstantin
1863-1938 .... **TCLC 167**
See also CA 118

Stannard, Martin 1947- .... **CLC 44**
See also CA 142; DLB 155

Stanton, Elizabeth Cady
1815-1902 .... **TCLC 73**
See also CA 171; DLB 79; FW

Stanton, Maura 1946- .... **CLC 9**
See also CA 89-92; CANR 15, 123; DLB
120

Stanton, Schuyler
See Baum, L(yman) Frank

Stapledon, (William) Olaf
1886-1950 .... **TCLC 22**
See also CA 111; 162; DLB 15, 255; SFW
4

Starbuck, George (Edwin)
1931-1996 .... **CLC 53**
See also CA 21-24R; 153; CANR 23; DAM
POET

Stark, Richard
See Westlake, Donald E(dwin)

Staunton, Schuyler
See Baum, L(yman) Frank

Stead, Christina (Ellen) 1902-1983 ... **CLC 2,**
5, 8, 32, 80
See also BRWS 4; CA 13-16R; 109; CANR
33, 40; DLB 260; EWL 3; FW; MTCW 1,
2; RGEL 2; RGSF 2; WWE 1

Stead, William Thomas
1849-1912 .... **TCLC 48**
See also CA 167

Stebnitsky, M.
See Leskov, Nikolai (Semyonovich)

Steele, Sir Richard 1672-1729 .... **LC 18**
See also BRW 3; CDBLB 1660-1789; DLB
84, 101; RGEL 2; WLIT 3

Steele, Timothy (Reid) 1948- .... **CLC 45**
See also CA 93-96; CANR 16, 50, 92; CP
7; DLB 120, 282

Steffens, (Joseph) Lincoln
1866-1936 .... **TCLC 20**
See also CA 117; 198; DLB 303

Stegner, Wallace (Earle) 1909-1993 .. **CLC 9,**
49, 81; SSC 27
See also AITN 1; AMWS 4; ANW; BEST
90:3; BPFB 3; CA 1-4R; 141; CAAS 9;
CANR 1, 21, 46; DAM NOV; DLB 9,
206, 275; DLBY 1993; EWL 3; MTCW
1, 2; RGAL 4; TCWW 2; TUS

Stein, Gertrude 1874-1946 .... **DC 19; PC 18;**
SSC 42; TCLC 1, 6, 28, 48; WLC
See also AMW; AMWC 2; CA 104; 132;
CANR 108; CDALB 1917-1929; DA;
DA3; DAB; DAC; DAM MST, NOV,
POET; DLB 4, 54, 86, 228; DLBD 15;
EWL 3; EXPS; GLL 1; MAWW; MTCW
1, 2; NCFS 4; RGAL 4; RGSF 2; SSFS 5;
TUS; WP

Steinbeck, John (Ernst) 1902-1968 ... **CLC 1,**
5, 9, 13, 21, 34, 45, 75, 124; SSC 11, 37,
77; TCLC 135; WLC
See also AAYA 12; AMW; BPFB 3; BYA 2,
3, 13; CA 1-4R; 25-28R; CANR 1, 35;
CDALB 1929-1941; DA; DA3; DAB;
DAC; DAM DRAM, MST, NOV; DLB 7,
9, 212, 275, 309; DLBD 2; EWL 3;
EXPS; LAIT 3; MTCW 1, 2; NFS 1, 5, 7,
17, 19; RGAL 4; RGSF 2; RHW; SATA
9; SSFS 3, 6; TCWW 2; TUS; WYA;
YAW

Steinem, Gloria 1934- .... **CLC 63**
See also CA 53-56; CANR 28, 51; DLB
246; FW; MTCW 1, 2

Steiner, George 1929- .... **CLC 24**
See also CA 73-76; CANR 31, 67, 108;
DAM NOV; DLB 67, 299; EWL 3;
MTCW 1, 2; SATA 62

Steiner, K. Leslie
See Delany, Samuel R(ay), Jr.

Steiner, Rudolf 1861-1925 .... **TCLC 13**
See also CA 107

Stendhal 1783-1842 .. **NCLC 23, 46; SSC 27;**
WLC
See also DA; DA3; DAB; DAC; DAM
MST, NOV; DLB 119; EW 5; GFL 1789
to the Present; RGWL 2, 3; TWA

Stephen, Adeline Virginia
See Woolf, (Adeline) Virginia

Stephen, Sir Leslie 1832-1904 .... **TCLC 23**
See also BRW 5; CA 123; DLB 57, 144,
190

Stephen, Sir Leslie
See Stephen, Sir Leslie

Stephen, Virginia
See Woolf, (Adeline) Virginia

Stephens, James 1882(?)-1950 .... **SSC 50; TCLC 4**
See also CA 104; 192; DLB 19, 153, 162; EWL 3; FANT; RGEL 2; SUFW

Stephens, Reed
See Donaldson, Stephen R(eeder)

Steptoe, Lydia
See Barnes, Djuna
See also GLL 1

Sterchi, Beat 1949- .... **CLC 65**
See also CA 203

Sterling, Brett
See Bradbury, Ray (Douglas); Hamilton, Edmond

Sterling, Bruce 1954- .... **CLC 72**
See also CA 119; CANR 44, 135; SCFW 2; SFW 4

Sterling, George 1869-1926 .... **TCLC 20**
See also CA 117; 165; DLB 54

Stern, Gerald 1925- .... **CLC 40, 100**
See also AMWS 9; CA 81-84; CANR 28, 94; CP 7; DLB 105; RGAL 4

Stern, Richard (Gustave) 1928- ... **CLC 4, 39**
See also CA 1-4R; CANR 1, 25, 52, 120; CN 7; DLB 218; DLBY 1987; INT CANR-25

Sternberg, Josef von 1894-1969 .... **CLC 20**
See also CA 81-84

Sterne, Laurence 1713-1768 .... **LC 2, 48; WLC**
See also BRW 3; BRWC 1; CDBLB 1660-1789; DA; DAB; DAC; DAM MST, NOV; DLB 39; RGEL 2; TEA

Sternheim, (William Adolf) Carl 1878-1942 .... **TCLC 8**
See also CA 105; 193; DLB 56, 118; EWL 3; RGWL 2, 3

Stevens, Mark 1951- .... **CLC 34**
See also CA 122

Stevens, Wallace 1879-1955 . **PC 6; TCLC 3, 12, 45; WLC**
See also AMW; AMWR 1; CA 104; 124; CDALB 1929-1941; DA; DA3; DAB; DAC; DAM MST, POET; DLB 54; EWL 3; EXPP; MTCW 1, 2; PAB; PFS 13, 16; RGAL 4; TUS; WP

Stevenson, Anne (Katharine) 1933- .. **CLC 7, 33**
See also BRWS 6; CA 17-20R; CAAS 9; CANR 9, 33, 123; CP 7; CWP; DLB 40; MTCW 1; RHW

Stevenson, Robert Louis (Balfour) 1850-1894 ...... **NCLC 5, 14, 63; SSC 11, 51; WLC**
See also AAYA 24; BPFB 3; BRW 5; BRWC 1; BRWR 1; BYA 1, 2, 4, 13; CDBLB 1890-1914; CLR 10, 11; DA; DA3; DAB; DAC; DAM MST, NOV; DLB 18, 57, 141, 156, 174; DLBD 13; HGG; JRDA; LAIT 1, 3; MAICYA 1, 2; NFS 11, 20; RGEL 2; RGSF 2; SATA 100; SUFW; TEA; WCH; WLIT 4; WYA; YABC 2; YAW

Stewart, J(ohn) I(nnes) M(ackintosh) 1906-1994 .... **CLC 7, 14, 32**
See Innes, Michael
See also CA 85-88; 147; CAAS 3; CANR 47; CMW 4; MTCW 1, 2

Stewart, Mary (Florence Elinor) 1916- .... **CLC 7, 35, 117**
See also AAYA 29; BPFB 3; CA 1-4R; CANR 1, 59, 130; CMW 4; CPW; DAB; FANT; RHW; SATA 12; YAW

Stewart, Mary Rainbow
See Stewart, Mary (Florence Elinor)

Stifle, June
See Campbell, Maria

Stifter, Adalbert 1805-1868 .. **NCLC 41; SSC 28**
See also CDWLB 2; DLB 133; RGSF 2; RGWL 2, 3

Still, James 1906-2001 .... **CLC 49**
See also CA 65-68; 195; CAAS 17; CANR 10, 26; CSW; DLB 9; DLBY 01; SATA 29; SATA-Obit 127

Sting 1951-
See Sumner, Gordon Matthew
See also CA 167

Stirling, Arthur
See Sinclair, Upton (Beall)

Stitt, Milan 1941- .... **CLC 29**
See also CA 69-72

Stockton, Francis Richard 1834-1902
See Stockton, Frank R.
See also CA 108; 137; MAICYA 1, 2; SATA 44; SFW 4

Stockton, Frank R. .... **TCLC 47**
See Stockton, Francis Richard
See also BYA 4, 13; DLB 42, 74; DLBD 13; EXPS; SATA-Brief 32; SSFS 3; SUFW; WCH

Stoddard, Charles
See Kuttner, Henry

Stoker, Abraham 1847-1912
See Stoker, Bram
See also CA 105; 150; DA; DA3; DAC; DAM MST, NOV; HGG; SATA 29

Stoker, Bram . **SSC 62; TCLC 8, 144; WLC**
See Stoker, Abraham
See also AAYA 23; BPFB 3; BRWS 3; BYA 5; CDBLB 1890-1914; DAB; DLB 304; LATS 1:1; NFS 18; RGEL 2; SUFW; TEA; WLIT 4

Stolz, Mary (Slattery) 1920- .... **CLC 12**
See also AAYA 8; AITN 1; CA 5-8R; CANR 13, 41, 112; JRDA; MAICYA 1, 2; SAAS 3; SATA 10, 71, 133; YAW

Stone, Irving 1903-1989 .... **CLC 7**
See also AITN 1; BPFB 3; CA 1-4R; 129; CAAS 3; CANR 1, 23; CPW; DA3; DAM POP; INT CANR-23; MTCW 1, 2; RHW; SATA 3; SATA-Obit 64

Stone, Oliver (William) 1946- .... **CLC 73**
See also AAYA 15; CA 110; CANR 55, 125

Stone, Robert (Anthony) 1937- ... **CLC 5, 23, 42, 175**
See also AMWS 5; BPFB 3; CA 85-88; CANR 23, 66, 95; CN 7; DLB 152; EWL 3; INT CANR-23; MTCW 1

Stone, Ruth 1915- .... **PC 53**
See also CA 45-48; CANR 2, 91; CP 7; CSW; DLB 105; PFS 19

Stone, Zachary
See Follett, Ken(neth Martin)

Stoppard, Tom 1937- ... **CLC 1, 3, 4, 5, 8, 15, 29, 34, 63, 91; DC 6; WLC**
See also BRWC 1; BRWR 2; BRWS 1; CA 81-84; CANR 39, 67, 125; CBD; CD 5; CDBLB 1960 to Present; DA; DA3; DAB; DAC; DAM DRAM, MST; DFS 2, 5, 8, 11, 13, 16; DLB 13, 233; DLBY 1985; EWL 3; LATS 1:2; MTCW 1, 2; RGEL 2; TEA; WLIT 4

Storey, David (Malcolm) 1933- . **CLC 2, 4, 5, 8**
See also BRWS 1; CA 81-84; CANR 36; CBD; CD 5; CN 7; DAM DRAM; DLB 13, 14, 207, 245; EWL 3; MTCW 1; RGEL 2

Storm, Hyemeyohsts 1935- ... **CLC 3; NNAL**
See also CA 81-84; CANR 45; DAM MULT

Storm, (Hans) Theodor (Woldsen) 1817-1888 .... **NCLC 1; SSC 27**
See also CDWLB 2; DLB 129; EW; RGSF 2; RGWL 2, 3

Storni, Alfonsina 1892-1938 . **HLC 2; PC 33; TCLC 5**
See also CA 104; 131; DAM MULT; DLB 283; HW 1; LAW

Stoughton, William 1631-1701 .... **LC 38**
See also DLB 24

Stout, Rex (Todhunter) 1886-1975 ..... **CLC 3**
See also AITN 2; BPFB 3; CA 61-64; CANR 71; CMW 4; DLB 306; MSW; RGAL 4

Stow, (Julian) Randolph 1935- ... **CLC 23, 48**
See also CA 13-16R; CANR 33; CN 7; DLB 260; MTCW 1; RGEL 2

Stowe, Harriet (Elizabeth) Beecher 1811-1896 .... **NCLC 3, 50, 133; WLC**
See also AAYA 53; AMWS 1; CDALB 1865-1917; DA; DA3; DAB; DAC; DAM MST, NOV; DLB 1, 12, 42, 74, 189, 239, 243; EXPN; JRDA; LAIT 2; MAICYA 1, 2; NFS 6; RGAL 4; TUS; YABC 1

Strabo c. 64B.C.-c. 25 .... **CMLC 37**
See also DLB 176

Strachey, (Giles) Lytton 1880-1932 .... **TCLC 12**
See also BRWS 2; CA 110; 178; DLB 149; DLBD 10; EWL 3; MTCW 2; NCFS 4

Stramm, August 1874-1915 .... **PC 50**
See also CA 195; EWL 3

Strand, Mark 1934- .. **CLC 6, 18, 41, 71; PC 63**
See also AMWS 4; CA 21-24R; CANR 40, 65, 100; CP 7; DAM POET; DLB 5; EWL 3; PAB; PFS 9, 18; RGAL 4; SATA 41

Stratton-Porter, Gene(va Grace) 1863-1924
See Porter, Gene(va Grace) Stratton
See also ANW; CA 137; CLR 87; DLB 221; DLBD 14; MAICYA 1, 2; SATA 15

Straub, Peter (Francis) 1943- ... **CLC 28, 107**
See also BEST 89:1; BPFB 3; CA 85-88; CANR 28, 65, 109; CPW; DAM POP; DLBY 1984; HGG; MTCW 1, 2; SUFW 2

Strauss, Botho 1944- .... **CLC 22**
See also CA 157; CWW 2; DLB 124

Strauss, Leo 1899-1973 .... **TCLC 141**
See also CA 101; 45-48; CANR 122

Streatfeild, (Mary) Noel 1897(?)-1986 .... **CLC 21**
See also CA 81-84; 120; CANR 31; CLR 17, 83; CWRI 5; DLB 160; MAICYA 1, 2; SATA 20; SATA-Obit 48

Stribling, T(homas) S(igismund) 1881-1965 .... **CLC 23**
See also CA 189; 107; CMW 4; DLB 9; RGAL 4

Strindberg, (Johan) August 1849-1912 ... **DC 18; TCLC 1, 8, 21, 47; WLC**
See also CA 104; 135; DA; DA3; DAB; DAC; DAM DRAM, MST; DFS 4, 9; DLB 259; EW 7; EWL 3; IDTP; LMFS 2; MTCW 2; RGWL 2, 3; TWA

Stringer, Arthur 1874-1950 .... **TCLC 37**
See also CA 161; DLB 92

Stringer, David
See Roberts, Keith (John Kingston)

Stroheim, Erich von 1885-1957 ..... **TCLC 71**

Strugatskii, Arkadii (Natanovich) 1925-1991 .... **CLC 27**
See Strugatsky, Arkadii Natanovich
See also CA 106; 135; SFW 4

Strugatskii, Boris (Natanovich) 1933- .... **CLC 27**
See Strugatsky, Boris (Natanovich)
See also CA 106; SFW 4

Strugatsky, Arkadii Natanovich
See Strugatskii, Arkadii (Natanovich)
See also DLB 302

Taine, Hippolyte Adolphe
1828-1893 .... **NCLC 15**
See also EW 7; GFL 1789 to the Present

Talayesva, Don C. 1890-(?) .... **NNAL**

Talese, Gay 1932- .... **CLC 37**
See also AITN 1; CA 1-4R; CANR 9, 58;
DLB 185; INT CANR-9; MTCW 1, 2

Tallent, Elizabeth (Ann) 1954- .... **CLC 45**
See also CA 117; CANR 72; DLB 130

Tallmountain, Mary 1918-1997 .... **NNAL**
See also CA 146; 161; DLB 193

Tally, Ted 1952- .... **CLC 42**
See also CA 120; 124; CAD; CANR 125;
CD 5; INT CA-124

Talvik, Heiti 1904-1947 .... **TCLC 87**
See also EWL 3

Tamayo y Baus, Manuel
1829-1898 .... **NCLC 1**

Tammsaare, A(nton) H(ansen)
1878-1940 .... **TCLC 27**
See also CA 164; CDWLB 4; DLB 220;
EWL 3

Tam'si, Tchicaya U
See Tchicaya, Gerald Felix

Tan, Amy (Ruth) 1952- . **AAL; CLC 59, 120, 151**
See also AAYA 9, 48; AMWS 10; BEST
89:3; BPFB 3; CA 136; CANR 54, 105,
132; CDALBS; CN 7; CPW 1; DA3;
DAM MULT, NOV, POP; DLB 173;
EXPN; FW; LAIT 3, 5; MTCW 2; NFS
1, 13, 16; RGAL 4; SATA 75; SSFS 9;
YAW

Tandem, Felix
See Spitteler, Carl (Friedrich Georg)

Tanizaki, Jun'ichiro 1886-1965 ... **CLC 8, 14, 28; SSC 21**
See Tanizaki Jun'ichiro
See also CA 93-96; 25-28R; MJW; MTCW
2; RGSF 2; RGWL 2

Tanizaki Jun'ichiro
See Tanizaki, Jun'ichiro
See also DLB 180; EWL 3

Tannen, Deborah F. 1945- .... **CLC 206**
See also CA 118; CANR 95

Tanner, William
See Amis, Kingsley (William)

Tao Lao
See Storni, Alfonsina

Tapahonso, Luci 1953- .... **NNAL; PC 65**
See also CA 145; CANR 72, 127; DLB 175

Tarantino, Quentin (Jerome)
1963- .... **CLC 125**
See also AAYA 58; CA 171; CANR 125

Tarassoff, Lev
See Troyat, Henri

Tarbell, Ida M(inerva) 1857-1944 . **TCLC 40**
See also CA 122; 181; DLB 47

Tarkington, (Newton) Booth
1869-1946 .... **TCLC 9**
See also BPFB 3; BYA 3; CA 110; 143;
CWRI 5; DLB 9, 102; MTCW 2; RGAL
4; SATA 17

Tarkovskii, Andrei Arsen'evich
See Tarkovsky, Andrei (Arsenyevich)

Tarkovsky, Andrei (Arsenyevich)
1932-1986 .... **CLC 75**
See also CA 127

Tartt, Donna 1963- .... **CLC 76**
See also AAYA 56; CA 142

Tasso, Torquato 1544-1595 .... **LC 5, 94**
See also EFS 2; EW 2; RGWL 2, 3

Tate, (John Orley) Allen 1899-1979 .. **CLC 2, 4, 6, 9, 11, 14, 24; PC 50**
See also AMW; CA 5-8R; 85-88; CANR
32, 108; DLB 4, 45, 63; DLBD 17; EWL
3; MTCW 1, 2; RGAL 4; RHW

Tate, Ellalice
See Hibbert, Eleanor Alice Burford

Tate, James (Vincent) 1943- ..... **CLC 2, 6, 25**
See also CA 21-24R; CANR 29, 57, 114;
CP 7; DLB 5, 169; EWL 3; PFS 10, 15;
RGAL 4; WP

Tate, Nahum 1652(?)-1715 .... **LC 109**
See also DLB 80; RGEL 2

Tauler, Johannes c. 1300-1361 ...... **CMLC 37**
See also DLB 179; LMFS 1

Tavel, Ronald 1940- .... **CLC 6**
See also CA 21-24R; CAD; CANR 33; CD
5

Taviani, Paolo 1931- .... **CLC 70**
See also CA 153

Taylor, Bayard 1825-1878 .... **NCLC 89**
See also DLB 3, 189, 250, 254; RGAL 4

Taylor, C(ecil) P(hilip) 1929-1981 .... **CLC 27**
See also CA 25-28R; 105; CANR 47; CBD

Taylor, Edward 1642(?)-1729 . **LC 11; PC 63**
See also AMW; DA; DAB; DAC; DAM
MST, POET; DLB 24; EXPP; RGAL 4;
TUS

Taylor, Eleanor Ross 1920- .... **CLC 5**
See also CA 81-84; CANR 70

Taylor, Elizabeth 1932-1975 ..... **CLC 2, 4, 29**
See also CA 13-16R; CANR 9, 70; DLB
139; MTCW 1; RGEL 2; SATA 13

Taylor, Frederick Winslow
1856-1915 .... **TCLC 76**
See also CA 188

Taylor, Henry (Splawn) 1942- .... **CLC 44**
See also CA 33-36R; CAAS 7; CANR 31;
CP 7; DLB 5; PFS 10

Taylor, Kamala (Purnaiya) 1924-2004
See Markandaya, Kamala
See also CA 77-80; 227; NFS 13

Taylor, Mildred D(elois) 1943- .... **CLC 21**
See also AAYA 10, 47; BW 1; BYA 3, 8;
CA 85-88; CANR 25, 115; CLR 9, 59,
90; CSW; DLB 52; JRDA; LAIT 3; MAI-
CYA 1, 2; SAAS 5; SATA 135; WYA;
YAW

Taylor, Peter (Hillsman) 1917-1994 .. **CLC 1, 4, 18, 37, 44, 50, 71; SSC 10, 84**
See also AMWS 5; BPFB 3; CA 13-16R;
147; CANR 9, 50; CSW; DLB 218, 278;
DLBY 1981, 1994; EWL 3; EXPS; INT
CANR-9; MTCW 1, 2; RGSF 2; SSFS 9;
TUS

Taylor, Robert Lewis 1912-1998 .... **CLC 14**
See also CA 1-4R; 170; CANR 3, 64; SATA
10

Tchekhov, Anton
See Chekhov, Anton (Pavlovich)

Tchicaya, Gerald Felix 1931-1988 .. **CLC 101**
See Tchicaya U Tam'si
See also CA 129; 125; CANR 81

Tchicaya U Tam'si
See Tchicaya, Gerald Felix
See also EWL 3

Teasdale, Sara 1884-1933 .... **PC 31; TCLC 4**
See also CA 104; 163; DLB 45; GLL 1;
PFS 14; RGAL 4; SATA 32; TUS

Tecumseh 1768-1813 .... **NNAL**
See also DAM MULT

Tegner, Esaias 1782-1846 .... **NCLC 2**

Fujiwara no Teika 1162-1241 .... **CMLC 73**
See also DLB 203

Teilhard de Chardin, (Marie Joseph) Pierre
1881-1955 .... **TCLC 9**
See also CA 105; 210; GFL 1789 to the
Present

Temple, Ann
See Mortimer, Penelope (Ruth)

Tennant, Emma (Christina) 1937- .. **CLC 13, 52**
See also BRWS 9; CA 65-68; CAAS 9;
CANR 10, 38, 59, 88; CN 7; DLB 14;
EWL 3; SFW 4

Tenneshaw, S. M.
See Silverberg, Robert

Tenney, Tabitha Gilman
1762-1837 .... **NCLC 122**
See also DLB 37, 200

Tennyson, Alfred 1809-1892 ... **NCLC 30, 65, 115; PC 6; WLC**
See also AAYA 50; BRW 4; CDBLB 1832-
1890; DA; DA3; DAB; DAC; DAM MST,
POET; DLB 32; EXPP; PAB; PFS 1, 2, 4,
11, 15, 19; RGEL 2; TEA; WLIT 4; WP

Teran, Lisa St. Aubin de .... **CLC 36**
See St. Aubin de Teran, Lisa

Terence c. 184B.C.-c. 159B.C. ...... **CMLC 14; DC 7**
See also AW 1; CDWLB 1; DLB 211;
RGWL 2, 3; TWA

Teresa de Jesus, St. 1515-1582 .... **LC 18**

Terkel, Louis 1912-
See Terkel, Studs
See also CA 57-60; CANR 18, 45, 67, 132;
DA3; MTCW 1, 2

Terkel, Studs .... **CLC 38**
See Terkel, Louis
See also AAYA 32; AITN 1; MTCW 2; TUS

Terry, C. V.
See Slaughter, Frank G(ill)

Terry, Megan 1932- .... **CLC 19; DC 13**
See also CA 77-80; CABS 3; CAD; CANR
43; CD 5; CWD; DFS 18; DLB 7, 249;
GLL 2

Tertullian c. 155-c. 245 .... **CMLC 29**

Tertz, Abram
See Sinyavsky, Andrei (Donatevich)
See also RGSF 2

Tesich, Steve 1943(?)-1996 .... **CLC 40, 69**
See also CA 105; 152; CAD; DLBY 1983

Tesla, Nikola 1856-1943 .... **TCLC 88**

Teternikov, Fyodor Kuzmich 1863-1927
See Sologub, Fyodor
See also CA 104

Tevis, Walter 1928-1984 .... **CLC 42**
See also CA 113; SFW 4

Tey, Josephine .... **TCLC 14**
See Mackintosh, Elizabeth
See also DLB 77; MSW

Thackeray, William Makepeace
1811-1863 .... **NCLC 5, 14, 22, 43; WLC**
See also BRW 5; BRWC 2; CDBLB 1832-
1890; DA; DA3; DAB; DAC; DAM MST,
NOV; DLB 21, 55, 159, 163; NFS 13;
RGEL 2; SATA 23; TEA; WLIT 3

Thakura, Ravindranatha
See Tagore, Rabindranath

Thames, C. H.
See Marlowe, Stephen

Tharoor, Shashi 1956- .... **CLC 70**
See also CA 141; CANR 91; CN 7

Thelwell, Michael Miles 1939- .... **CLC 22**
See also BW 2; CA 101

Theobald, Lewis, Jr.
See Lovecraft, H(oward) P(hillips)

Theocritus c. 310B.C.- .... **CMLC 45**
See also AW 1; DLB 176; RGWL 2, 3

Theodorescu, Ion N. 1880-1967
See Arghezi, Tudor
See also CA 116

Theriault, Yves 1915-1983 .... **CLC 79**
See also CA 102; CCA 1; DAC; DAM
MST; DLB 88; EWL 3

Theroux, Alexander (Louis) 1939- .... **CLC 2, 25**
See also CA 85-88; CANR 20, 63; CN 7

Vanbrugh, Sir John 1664-1726 .... **LC 21**
See also BRW 2; DAM DRAM; DLB 80;
IDTP; RGEL 2

Van Campen, Karl
See Campbell, John W(ood, Jr.)

Vance, Gerald
See Silverberg, Robert

Vance, Jack .... **CLC 35**
See Vance, John Holbrook
See also DLB 8; FANT; SCFW 2; SFW 4;
SUFW 1, 2

Vance, John Holbrook 1916-
See Queen, Ellery; Vance, Jack
See also CA 29-32R; CANR 17, 65; CMW
4; MTCW 1

**Van Den Bogarde, Derek Jules Gaspard
Ulric Niven** 1921-1999 .... **CLC 14**
See Bogarde, Dirk
See also CA 77-80; 179

Vandenburgh, Jane .... **CLC 59**
See also CA 168

Vanderhaeghe, Guy 1951- .... **CLC 41**
See also BPFB 3; CA 113; CANR 72

van der Post, Laurens (Jan)
1906-1996 .... **CLC 5**
See also AFW; CA 5-8R; 155; CANR 35;
CN 7; DLB 204; RGEL 2

van de Wetering, Janwillem 1931- ... **CLC 47**
See also CA 49-52; CANR 4, 62, 90; CMW
4

Van Dine, S. S. .... **TCLC 23**
See Wright, Willard Huntington
See also DLB 306; MSW

Van Doren, Carl (Clinton)
1885-1950 .... **TCLC 18**
See also CA 111; 168

Van Doren, Mark 1894-1972 .... **CLC 6, 10**
See also CA 1-4R; 37-40R; CANR 3; DLB
45, 284; MTCW 1, 2; RGAL 4

Van Druten, John (William)
1901-1957 .... **TCLC 2**
See also CA 104; 161; DLB 10; RGAL 4

Van Duyn, Mona (Jane) 1921- ...... **CLC 3, 7,
63, 116**
See also CA 9-12R; CANR 7, 38, 60, 116;
CP 7; CWP; DAM POET; DLB 5; PFS
20

Van Dyne, Edith
See Baum, L(yman) Frank

van Itallie, Jean-Claude 1936- .... **CLC 3**
See also CA 45-48; CAAS 2; CAD; CANR
1, 48; CD 5; DLB 7

Van Loot, Cornelius Obenchain
See Roberts, Kenneth (Lewis)

van Ostaijen, Paul 1896-1928 .... **TCLC 33**
See also CA 163

Van Peebles, Melvin 1932- .... **CLC 2, 20**
See also BW 2, 3; CA 85-88; CANR 27,
67, 82; DAM MULT

van Schendel, Arthur(-Francois-Emile)
1874-1946 .... **TCLC 56**
See also EWL 3

Vansittart, Peter 1920- .... **CLC 42**
See also CA 1-4R; CANR 3, 49, 90; CN 7;
RHW

Van Vechten, Carl 1880-1964 ... **CLC 33; HR
3**
See also AMWS 2; CA 183; 89-92; DLB 4,
9, 51; RGAL 4

van Vogt, A(lfred) E(lton) 1912-2000 . **CLC 1**
See also BPFB 3; BYA 13, 14; CA 21-24R;
190; CANR 28; DLB 8, 251; SATA 14;
SATA-Obit 124; SCFW; SFW 4

Vara, Madeleine
See Jackson, Laura (Riding)

Varda, Agnes 1928- .... **CLC 16**
See also CA 116; 122

Vargas Llosa, (Jorge) Mario (Pedro)
1939- .... **CLC 3, 6, 9, 10, 15, 31, 42, 85,
181; HLC 2**
See Llosa, (Jorge) Mario (Pedro) Vargas
See also BPFB 3; CA 73-76; CANR 18, 32,
42, 67, 116; CDWLB 3; CWW 2; DA;
DA3; DAB; DAC; DAM MST, MULT,
NOV; DLB 145; DNFS 2; EWL 3; HW 1,
2; LAIT 5; LATS 1:2; LAW; LAWS 1;
MTCW 1, 2; RGWL 2; SSFS 14; TWA;
WLIT 1

Varnhagen von Ense, Rahel
1771-1833 .... **NCLC 130**
See also DLB 90

Vasari, Giorgio 1511-1574 .... **LC 114**

Vasiliu, George
See Bacovia, George

Vasiliu, Gheorghe
See Bacovia, George
See also CA 123; 189

Vassa, Gustavus
See Equiano, Olaudah

Vassilikos, Vassilis 1933- .... **CLC 4, 8**
See also CA 81-84; CANR 75; EWL 3

Vaughan, Henry 1621-1695 .... **LC 27**
See also BRW 2; DLB 131; PAB; RGEL 2

Vaughn, Stephanie .... **CLC 62**

Vazov, Ivan (Minchov) 1850-1921 . **TCLC 25**
See also CA 121; 167; CDWLB 4; DLB
147

Veblen, Thorstein B(unde)
1857-1929 .... **TCLC 31**
See also AMWS 1; CA 115; 165; DLB 246

Vega, Lope de 1562-1635 .... **HLCS 2; LC 23**
See also EW 2; RGWL 2, 3

Vendler, Helen (Hennessy) 1933- ... **CLC 138**
See also CA 41-44R; CANR 25, 72; MTCW
1, 2

Venison, Alfred
See Pound, Ezra (Weston Loomis)

Ventsel, Elena Sergeevna 1907-2002
See Grekova, I.
See also CA 154

Verdi, Marie de
See Mencken, H(enry) L(ouis)

Verdu, Matilde
See Cela, Camilo Jose

Verga, Giovanni (Carmelo)
1840-1922 .... **SSC 21; TCLC 3**
See also CA 104; 123; CANR 101; EW 7;
EWL 3; RGSF 2; RGWL 2, 3

Vergil 70B.C.-19B.C. .... **CMLC 9, 40; PC 12;
WLCS**
See Virgil
See also AW 2; DA; DA3; DAB; DAC;
DAM MST, POET; EFS 1; LMFS 1

Vergil, Polydore c. 1470-1555 .... **LC 108**
See also DLB 132

Verhaeren, Emile (Adolphe Gustave)
1855-1916 .... **TCLC 12**
See also CA 109; EWL 3; GFL 1789 to the
Present

Verlaine, Paul (Marie) 1844-1896 .. **NCLC 2,
51; PC 2, 32**
See also DAM POET; DLB 217; EW 7;
GFL 1789 to the Present; LMFS 2; RGWL
2, 3; TWA

Verne, Jules (Gabriel) 1828-1905 ... **TCLC 6,
52**
See also AAYA 16; BYA 4; CA 110; 131;
CLR 88; DA3; DLB 123; GFL 1789 to
the Present; JRDA; LAIT 2; LMFS 2;
MAICYA 1, 2; RGWL 2, 3; SATA 21;
SCFW; SFW 4; TWA; WCH

Verus, Marcus Annius
See Aurelius, Marcus

Very, Jones 1813-1880 .... **NCLC 9**
See also DLB 1, 243; RGAL 4

Vesaas, Tarjei 1897-1970 .... **CLC 48**
See also CA 190; 29-32R; DLB 297; EW
11; EWL 3; RGWL 3

Vialis, Gaston
See Simenon, Georges (Jacques Christian)

Vian, Boris 1920-1959(?) .... **TCLC 9**
See also CA 106; 164; CANR 111; DLB
72; EWL 3; GFL 1789 to the Present;
MTCW 2; RGWL 2, 3

Viaud, (Louis Marie) Julien 1850-1923
See Loti, Pierre
See also CA 107

Vicar, Henry
See Felsen, Henry Gregor

Vicente, Gil 1465-c. 1536 .... **LC 99**
See also DLB 287; RGWL 2, 3

Vicker, Angus
See Felsen, Henry Gregor

Vidal, (Eugene Luther) Gore 1925- .. **CLC 2,
4, 6, 8, 10, 22, 33, 72, 142**
See Box, Edgar
See also AITN 1; AMWS 4; BEST 90:2;
BPFB 3; CA 5-8R; CAD; CANR 13, 45,
65, 100, 132; CD 5; CDALBS; CN 7;
CPW; DA3; DAM NOV, POP; DFS 2;
DLB 6, 152; EWL 3; INT CANR-13;
MTCW 1, 2; RGAL 4; RHW; TUS

Viereck, Peter (Robert Edwin)
1916- .... **CLC 4; PC 27**
See also CA 1-4R; CANR 1, 47; CP 7; DLB
5; PFS 9, 14

Vigny, Alfred (Victor) de
1797-1863 .... **NCLC 7, 102; PC 26**
See also DAM POET; DLB 119, 192, 217;
EW 5; GFL 1789 to the Present; RGWL
2, 3

Vilakazi, Benedict Wallet
1906-1947 .... **TCLC 37**
See also CA 168

Villa, Jose Garcia 1914-1997 .... **AAL; PC 22**
See also CA 25-28R; CANR 12, 118; EWL
3; EXPP

Villa, Jose Garcia 1914-1997
See Villa, Jose Garcia

Villa, Jose Garcia 1914-1997 .... **AAL; PC 22**
See also CA 25-28R; CANR 12, 118; EWL
3; EXPP

Villard, Oswald Garrison
1872-1949 .... **TCLC 160**
See also CA 113, 162; DLB 25, 91

Villaurrutia, Xavier 1903-1950 ...... **TCLC 80**
See also CA 192; EWL 3; HW 1; LAW

Villaverde, Cirilo 1812-1894 .... **NCLC 121**
See also LAW

Villehardouin, Geoffroi de
1150(?)-1218(?) .... **CMLC 38**

Villiers, George 1628-1687 .... **LC 107**
See also DLB 80; RGEL 2

**Villiers de l'Isle Adam, Jean Marie Mathias
Philippe Auguste** 1838-1889 ... **NCLC 3;
SSC 14**
See also DLB 123, 192; GFL 1789 to the
Present; RGSF 2

Villon, Francois 1431-1463(?) . **LC 62; PC 13**
See also DLB 208; EW 2; RGWL 2, 3;
TWA

Vine, Barbara .... **CLC 50**
See Rendell, Ruth (Barbara)
See also BEST 90:4

Vinge, Joan (Carol) D(ennison)
1948- .... **CLC 30; SSC 24**
See also AAYA 32; BPFB 3; CA 93-96;
CANR 72; SATA 36, 113; SFW 4; YAW

Viola, Herman J(oseph) 1938- .... **CLC 70**
See also CA 61-64; CANR 8, 23, 48, 91;
SATA 126

Violis, G.
See Simenon, Georges (Jacques Christian)

White, Edmund (Valentine III)
1940- .... **CLC 27, 110**
See also AAYA 7; CA 45-48; CANR 3, 19, 36, 62, 107, 133; CN 7; DA3; DAM POP; DLB 227; MTCW 1, 2

White, Hayden V. 1928- .... **CLC 148**
See also CA 128; CANR 135; DLB 246

White, Patrick (Victor Martindale)
1912-1990 ...... **CLC 3, 4, 5, 7, 9, 18, 65, 69; SSC 39**
See also BRWS 1; CA 81-84; 132; CANR 43; DLB 260; EWL 3; MTCW 1; RGEL 2; RGSF 2; RHW; TWA; WWE 1

White, Phyllis Dorothy James 1920-
See James, P. D.
See also CA 21-24R; CANR 17, 43, 65, 112; CMW 4; CN 7; CPW; DA3; DAM POP; MTCW 1, 2; TEA

White, T(erence) H(anbury)
1906-1964 .... **CLC 30**
See also AAYA 22; BPFB 3; BYA 4, 5; CA 73-76; CANR 37; DLB 160; FANT; JRDA; LAIT 1; MAICYA 1, 2; RGEL 2; SATA 12; SUFW 1; YAW

White, Terence de Vere 1912-1994 ... **CLC 49**
See also CA 49-52; 145; CANR 3

White, Walter
See White, Walter F(rancis)

White, Walter F(rancis) 1893-1955 ... **BLC 3; HR 3; TCLC 15**
See also BW 1; CA 115; 124; DAM MULT; DLB 51

White, William Hale 1831-1913
See Rutherford, Mark
See also CA 121; 189

Whitehead, Alfred North
1861-1947 .... **TCLC 97**
See also CA 117; 165; DLB 100, 262

Whitehead, E(dward) A(nthony)
1933- .... **CLC 5**
See also CA 65-68; CANR 58, 118; CBD; CD 5

Whitehead, Ted
See Whitehead, E(dward) A(nthony)

Whiteman, Roberta J. Hill 1947- ...... **NNAL**
See also CA 146

Whitemore, Hugh (John) 1936- .... **CLC 37**
See also CA 132; CANR 77; CBD; CD 5; INT CA-132

Whitman, Sarah Helen (Power)
1803-1878 .... **NCLC 19**
See also DLB 1, 243

Whitman, Walt(er) 1819-1892 .. **NCLC 4, 31, 81; PC 3; WLC**
See also AAYA 42; AMW; AMWR 1; CDALB 1640-1865; DA; DA3; DAB; DAC; DAM MST, POET; DLB 3, 64, 224, 250; EXPP; LAIT 2; LMFS 1; PAB; PFS 2, 3, 13; RGAL 4; SATA 20; TUS; WP; WYAS 1

Whitney, Phyllis A(yame) 1903- .... **CLC 42**
See also AAYA 36; AITN 2; BEST 90:3; CA 1-4R; CANR 3, 25, 38, 60; CLR 59; CMW 4; CPW; DA3; DAM POP; JRDA; MAICYA 1, 2; MTCW 2; RHW; SATA 1, 30; YAW

Whittemore, (Edward) Reed, Jr.
1919- .... **CLC 4**
See also CA 9-12R; 219; CAAE 219; CAAS 8; CANR 4, 119; CP 7; DLB 5

Whittier, John Greenleaf
1807-1892 .... **NCLC 8, 59**
See also AMWS 1; DLB 1, 243; RGAL 4

Whittlebot, Hernia
See Coward, Noel (Peirce)

Wicker, Thomas Grey 1926-
See Wicker, Tom
See also CA 65-68; CANR 21, 46

Wicker, Tom .... **CLC 7**
See Wicker, Thomas Grey

Wideman, John Edgar 1941- ... **BLC 3; CLC 5, 34, 36, 67, 122; SSC 62**
See also AFAW 1, 2; AMWS 10; BPFB 4; BW 2, 3; CA 85-88; CANR 14, 42, 67, 109; CN 7; DAM MULT; DLB 33, 143; MTCW 2; RGAL 4; RGSF 2; SSFS 6, 12

Wiebe, Rudy (Henry) 1934- .. **CLC 6, 11, 14, 138**
See also CA 37-40R; CANR 42, 67, 123; CN 7; DAC; DAM MST; DLB 60; RHW

Wieland, Christoph Martin
1733-1813 .... **NCLC 17**
See also DLB 97; EW 4; LMFS 1; RGWL 2, 3

Wiene, Robert 1881-1938 .... **TCLC 56**

Wieners, John 1934- .... **CLC 7**
See also BG 3; CA 13-16R; CP 7; DLB 16; WP

Wiesel, Elie(zer) 1928- .... **CLC 3, 5, 11, 37, 165; WLCS**
See also AAYA 7, 54; AITN 1; CA 5-8R; CAAS 8, 40, 65, 125; CDALBS; CWW 2; DA; DA3; DAB; DAC; DAM MST, NOV; DLB 83, 299; DLBY 1987; EWL 3; INT CANR-8; LAIT 4; MTCW 1, 2; NCFS 4; NFS 4; RGWL 3; SATA 56; YAW

Wiggins, Marianne 1947- .... **CLC 57**
See also BEST 89:3; CA 130; CANR 60

Wigglesworth, Michael 1631-1705 .... **LC 106**
See also DLB 24; RGAL 4

Wiggs, Susan .... **CLC 70**
See also CA 201

Wight, James Alfred 1916-1995
See Herriot, James
See also CA 77-80; SATA 55; SATA-Brief 44

Wilbur, Richard (Purdy) 1921- ..... **CLC 3, 6, 9, 14, 53, 110; PC 51**
See also AMWS 3; CA 1-4R; CABS 2; CANR 2, 29, 76, 93; CDALBS; CP 7; DA; DAB; DAC; DAM MST, POET; DLB 5, 169; EWL 3; EXPP; INT CANR-29; MTCW 1, 2; PAB; PFS 11, 12, 16; RGAL 4; SATA 9, 108; WP

Wild, Peter 1940- .... **CLC 14**
See also CA 37-40R; CP 7; DLB 5

Wilde, Oscar (Fingal O'Flahertie Wills)
1854(?)-1900 .... **DC 17; SSC 11, 77; TCLC 1, 8, 23, 41; WLC**
See also AAYA 49; BRW 5; BRWC 1, 2; BRWR 2; BYA 15; CA 104; 119; CANR 112; CDBLB 1890-1914; DA; DA3; DAB; DAC; DAM DRAM, MST, NOV; DFS 4, 8, 9; DLB 10, 19, 34, 57, 141, 156, 190; EXPS; FANT; LATS 1:1; NFS 20; RGEL 2; RGSF 2; SATA 24; SSFS 7; SUFW; TEA; WCH; WLIT 4

Wilder, Billy .... **CLC 20**
See Wilder, Samuel
See also DLB 26

Wilder, Samuel 1906-2002
See Wilder, Billy
See also CA 89-92; 205

Wilder, Stephen
See Marlowe, Stephen

Wilder, Thornton (Niven)
1897-1975 .. **CLC 1, 5, 6, 10, 15, 35, 82; DC 1, 24; WLC**
See also AAYA 29; AITN 2; AMW; CA 13-16R; 61-64; CAD; CANR 40, 132; CDALBS; DA; DA3; DAB; DAC; DAM DRAM, MST, NOV; DFS 1, 4, 16; DLB 4, 7, 9, 228; DLBY 1997; EWL 3; LAIT 3; MTCW 1, 2; RGAL 4; RHW; WYAS 1

Wilding, Michael 1942- ...... **CLC 73; SSC 50**
See also CA 104; CANR 24, 49, 106; CN 7; RGSF 2

Wiley, Richard 1944- .... **CLC 44**
See also CA 121; 129; CANR 71

Wilhelm, Kate .... **CLC 7**
See Wilhelm, Katie (Gertrude)
See also AAYA 20; BYA 16; CAAS 5; DLB 8; INT CANR-17; SCFW 2

Wilhelm, Katie (Gertrude) 1928-
See Wilhelm, Kate
See also CA 37-40R; CANR 17, 36, 60, 94; MTCW 1; SFW 4

Wilkins, Mary
See Freeman, Mary E(leanor) Wilkins

Willard, Nancy 1936- .... **CLC 7, 37**
See also BYA 5; CA 89-92; CANR 10, 39, 68, 107; CLR 5; CWP; CWRI 5; DLB 5, 52; FANT; MAICYA 1, 2; MTCW 1; SATA 37, 71, 127; SATA-Brief 30; SUFW 2

William of Malmesbury c. 1090B.C.-c. 1140B.C. .... **CMLC 57**

William of Ockham 1290-1349 ..... **CMLC 32**

Williams, Ben Ames 1889-1953 ..... **TCLC 89**
See also CA 183; DLB 102

Williams, C(harles) K(enneth)
1936- .... **CLC 33, 56, 148**
See also CA 37-40R; CAAS 26; CANR 57, 106; CP 7; DAM POET; DLB 5

Williams, Charles
See Collier, James Lincoln

Williams, Charles (Walter Stansby)
1886-1945 .... **TCLC 1, 11**
See also BRWS 9; CA 104; 163; DLB 100, 153, 255; FANT; RGEL 2; SUFW 1

Williams, Ella Gwendolen Rees
See Rhys, Jean

Williams, (George) Emlyn
1905-1987 .... **CLC 15**
See also CA 104; 123; CANR 36; DAM DRAM; DLB 10, 77; IDTP; MTCW 1

Williams, Hank 1923-1953 .... **TCLC 81**
See Williams, Hiram King

Williams, Helen Maria
1761-1827 .... **NCLC 135**
See also DLB 158

Williams, Hiram Hank
See Williams, Hank

Williams, Hiram King
See Williams, Hank
See also CA 188

Williams, Hugo (Mordaunt) 1942- ... **CLC 42**
See also CA 17-20R; CANR 45, 119; CP 7; DLB 40

Williams, J. Walker
See Wodehouse, P(elham) G(renville)

Williams, John A(lfred) 1925- . **BLC 3; CLC 5, 13**
See also AFAW 2; BW 2, 3; CA 53-56, 195; CAAE 195; CAAS 3; CANR 6, 26, 51, 118; CN 7; CSW; DAM MULT; DLB 2, 33; EWL 3; INT CANR-6; RGAL 4; SFW 4

Williams, Jonathan (Chamberlain)
1929- .... **CLC 13**
See also CA 9-12R; CAAS 12; CANR 8, 108; CP 7; DLB 5

Williams, Joy 1944- .... **CLC 31**
See also CA 41-44R; CANR 22, 48, 97

Williams, Norman 1952- .... **CLC 39**
See also CA 118

Williams, Sherley Anne 1944-1999 ... **BLC 3; CLC 89**
See also AFAW 2; BW 2, 3; CA 73-76; 185; CANR 25, 82; DAM MULT, POET; DLB 41; INT CANR-25; SATA 78; SATA-Obit 116

Williams, Shirley
See Williams, Sherley Anne

Wolfram von Eschenbach c. 1170-c. 1220 .... **CMLC 5**
See Eschenbach, Wolfram von
See also CDWLB 2; DLB 138; EW 1; RGWL 2

Wolitzer, Hilma 1930- .... **CLC 17**
See also CA 65-68; CANR 18, 40; INT CANR-18; SATA 31; YAW

Wollstonecraft, Mary 1759-1797 .... **LC 5, 50, 90**
See also BRWS 3; CDBLB 1789-1832; DLB 39, 104, 158, 252; FW; LAIT 1; RGEL 2; TEA; WLIT 3

Wonder, Stevie .... **CLC 12**
See Morris, Steveland Judkins

Wong, Jade Snow 1922- .... **CLC 17**
See also CA 109; CANR 91; SATA 112

Woodberry, George Edward 1855-1930 .... **TCLC 73**
See also CA 165; DLB 71, 103

Woodcott, Keith
See Brunner, John (Kilian Houston)

Woodruff, Robert W.
See Mencken, H(enry) L(ouis)

Woolf, (Adeline) Virginia 1882-1941 .. **SSC 7, 79; TCLC 1, 5, 20, 43, 56, 101, 123, 128; WLC**
See also AAYA 44; BPFB 3; BRW 7; BRWC 2; BRWR 1; CA 104; 130; CANR 64, 132; CDBLB 1914-1945; DA; DA3; DAB; DAC; DAM MST, NOV; DLB 36, 100, 162; DLBD 10; EWL 3; EXPS; FW; LAIT 3; LATS 1:1; LMFS 2; MTCW 1, 2; NCFS 8, 12; RGEL 2; RGSF 2; SSFS 4, 12; TEA; WLIT 4

Woollcott, Alexander (Humphreys) 1887-1943 .... **TCLC 5**
See also CA 105; 161; DLB 29

Woolrich, Cornell .... **CLC 77**
See Hopley-Woolrich, Cornell George
See also MSW

Woolson, Constance Fenimore 1840-1894 .... **NCLC 82**
See also DLB 12, 74, 189, 221; RGAL 4

Wordsworth, Dorothy 1771-1855 . **NCLC 25, 138**
See also DLB 107

Wordsworth, William 1770-1850 .. **NCLC 12, 38, 111; PC 4; WLC**
See also BRW 4; BRWC 1; CDBLB 1789-1832; DA; DA3; DAB; DAC; DAM MST, POET; DLB 93, 107; EXPP; LATS 1:1; LMFS 1; PAB; PFS 2; RGEL 2; TEA; WLIT 3; WP

Wotton, Sir Henry 1568-1639 .... **LC 68**
See also DLB 121; RGEL 2

Wouk, Herman 1915- .... **CLC 1, 9, 38**
See also BPFB 2, 3; CA 5-8R; CANR 6, 33, 67; CDALBS; CN 7; CPW; DA3; DAM NOV, POP; DLBY 1982; INT CANR-6; LAIT 4; MTCW 1, 2; NFS 7; TUS

Wright, Charles (Penzel, Jr.) 1935- .. **CLC 6, 13, 28, 119, 146**
See also AMWS 5; CA 29-32R; CAAS 7; CANR 23, 36, 62, 88, 135; CP 7; DLB 165; DLBY 1982; EWL 3; MTCW 1, 2; PFS 10

Wright, Charles Stevenson 1932- ..... **BLC 3; CLC 49**
See also BW 1; CA 9-12R; CANR 26; CN 7; DAM MULT, POET; DLB 33

Wright, Frances 1795-1852 .... **NCLC 74**
See also DLB 73

Wright, Frank Lloyd 1867-1959 .... **TCLC 95**
See also AAYA 33; CA 174

Wright, Jack R.
See Harris, Mark

Wright, James (Arlington) 1927-1980 .... **CLC 3, 5, 10, 28; PC 36**
See also AITN 2; AMWS 3; CA 49-52; 97-100; CANR 4, 34, 64; CDALBS; DAM POET; DLB 5, 169; EWL 3; EXPP; MTCW 1, 2; PFS 7, 8; RGAL 4; TUS; WP

Wright, Judith (Arundell) 1915-2000 .... **CLC 11, 53; PC 14**
See also CA 13-16R; 188; CANR 31, 76, 93; CP 7; CWP; DLB 260; EWL 3; MTCW 1, 2; PFS 8; RGEL 2; SATA 14; SATA-Obit 121

Wright, L(aurali) R. 1939- .... **CLC 44**
See also CA 138; CMW 4

Wright, Richard (Nathaniel) 1908-1960 ... **BLC 3; CLC 1, 3, 4, 9, 14, 21, 48, 74; SSC 2; TCLC 136; WLC**
See also AAYA 5, 42; AFAW 1, 2; AMW; BPFB 3; BW 1; BYA 2; CA 108; CANR 64; CDALB 1929-1941; DA; DA3; DAB; DAC; DAM MST, MULT, NOV; DLB 76, 102; DLBD 2; EWL 3; EXPN; LAIT 3, 4; MTCW 1, 2; NCFS 1; NFS 1, 7; RGAL 4; RGSF 2; SSFS 3, 9, 15, 20; TUS; YAW

Wright, Richard B(ruce) 1937- .... **CLC 6**
See also CA 85-88; CANR 120; DLB 53

Wright, Rick 1945- .... **CLC 35**

Wright, Rowland
See Wells, Carolyn

Wright, Stephen 1946- .... **CLC 33**

Wright, Willard Huntington 1888-1939
See Van Dine, S. S.
See also CA 115; 189; CMW 4; DLBD 16

Wright, William 1930- .... **CLC 44**
See also CA 53-56; CANR 7, 23

Wroth, Lady Mary 1587-1653(?) ...... **LC 30; PC 38**
See also DLB 121

Wu Ch'eng-en 1500(?)-1582(?) .... **LC 7**

Wu Ching-tzu 1701-1754 .... **LC 2**

Wulfstan c. 10th cent. -1023 .... **CMLC 59**

Wurlitzer, Rudolph 1938(?)- .... **CLC 2, 4, 15**
See also CA 85-88; CN 7; DLB 173

Wyatt, Sir Thomas c. 1503-1542 . **LC 70; PC 27**
See also BRW 1; DLB 132; EXPP; RGEL 2; TEA

Wycherley, William 1640-1716 .... **LC 8, 21, 102**
See also BRW 2; CDBLB 1660-1789; DAM DRAM; DLB 80; RGEL 2

Wyclif, John c. 1330-1384 .... **CMLC 70**
See also DLB 146

Wylie, Elinor (Morton Hoyt) 1885-1928 .... **PC 23; TCLC 8**
See also AMWS 1; CA 105; 162; DLB 9, 45; EXPP; RGAL 4

Wylie, Philip (Gordon) 1902-1971 ... **CLC 43**
See also CA 21-22; 33-36R; CAP 2; DLB 9; SFW 4

Wyndham, John .... **CLC 19**
See Harris, John (Wyndham Parkes Lucas) Beynon
See also DLB 255; SCFW 2

Wyss, Johann David Von 1743-1818 .... **NCLC 10**
See also CLR 92; JRDA; MAICYA 1, 2; SATA 29; SATA-Brief 27

Xenophon c. 430B.C.-c. 354B.C. ... **CMLC 17**
See also AW 1; DLB 176; RGWL 2, 3

Xingjian, Gao 1940-
See Gao Xingjian
See also CA 193; RGWL 3

Yakamochi 718-785 .... **CMLC 45; PC 48**

Yakumo Koizumi
See Hearn, (Patricio) Lafcadio (Tessima Carlos)

Yamada, Mitsuye (May) 1923- .... **PC 44**
See also CA 77-80

Yamamoto, Hisaye 1921- .... **AAL; SSC 34**
See also CA 214; DAM MULT; LAIT 4; SSFS 14

Yamauchi, Wakako 1924- .... **AAL**
See also CA 214

Yanez, Jose Donoso
See Donoso (Yanez), Jose

Yanovsky, Basile S.
See Yanovsky, V(assily) S(emenovich)

Yanovsky, V(assily) S(emenovich) 1906-1989 .... **CLC 2, 18**
See also CA 97-100; 129

Yates, Richard 1926-1992 .... **CLC 7, 8, 23**
See also AMWS 11; CA 5-8R; 139; CANR 10, 43; DLB 2, 234; DLBY 1981, 1992; INT CANR-10

Yau, John 1950- .... **PC 61**
See also CA 154; CANR 89; CP 7; DLB 234

Yeats, W. B.
See Yeats, William Butler

Yeats, William Butler 1865-1939 . **PC 20, 51; TCLC 1, 11, 18, 31, 93, 116; WLC**
See also AAYA 48; BRW 6; BRWR 1; CA 104; 127; CANR 45; CDBLB 1890-1914; DA; DA3; DAB; DAC; DAM MST, POET; DLB 10, 19, 98, 156; EWL 3; EXPP; MTCW 1, 2; NCFS 3; PAB; PFS 1, 2, 5, 7, 13, 15; RGEL 2; TEA; WLIT 4; WP

Yehoshua, A(braham) B. 1936- .. **CLC 13, 31**
See also CA 33-36R; CANR 43, 90; CWW 2; EWL 3; RGSF 2; RGWL 3

Yellow Bird
See Ridge, John Rollin

Yep, Laurence Michael 1948- .... **CLC 35**
See also AAYA 5, 31; BYA 7; CA 49-52; CANR 1, 46, 92; CLR 3, 17, 54; DLB 52; FANT; JRDA; MAICYA 1, 2; MAICYAS 1; SATA 7, 69, 123; WYA; YAW

Yerby, Frank G(arvin) 1916-1991 ..... **BLC 3; CLC 1, 7, 22**
See also BPFB 3; BW 1, 3; CA 9-12R; 136; CANR 16, 52; DAM MULT; DLB 76; INT CANR-16; MTCW 1; RGAL 4; RHW

Yesenin, Sergei Alexandrovich
See Esenin, Sergei (Alexandrovich)

Yesenin, Sergey
See Esenin, Sergei (Alexandrovich)
See also EWL 3

Yevtushenko, Yevgeny (Alexandrovich) 1933- ...... **CLC 1, 3, 13, 26, 51, 126; PC 40**
See Evtushenko, Evgenii Aleksandrovich
See also CA 81-84; CANR 33, 54; DAM POET; EWL 3; MTCW 1

Yezierska, Anzia 1885(?)-1970 .... **CLC 46**
See also CA 126; 89-92; DLB 28, 221; FW; MTCW 1; RGAL 4; SSFS 15

Yglesias, Helen 1915- .... **CLC 7, 22**
See also CA 37-40R; CAAS 20; CANR 15, 65, 95; CN 7; INT CANR-15; MTCW 1

Yokomitsu, Riichi 1898-1947 .... **TCLC 47**
See also CA 170; EWL 3

Yonge, Charlotte (Mary) 1823-1901 .... **TCLC 48**
See also CA 109; 163; DLB 18, 163; RGEL 2; SATA 17; WCH

York, Jeremy
See Creasey, John

York, Simon
See Heinlein, Robert A(nson)

Yorke, Henry Vincent 1905-1974 ..... **CLC 13**
See Green, Henry
See also CA 85-88; 49-52

Yosano Akiko 1878-1942 .... **PC 11; TCLC 59**
See also CA 161; EWL 3; RGWL 3

Literary Criticism Series
Cumulative Topic Index

This index lists all topic entries in Gale's *Children's Literature Review* (CLR), *Classical and Medieval Literature Criticism* (CMLC), *Contemporary Literary Criticism* (CLC), *Drama Criticism* (DC), *Literature Criticism from 1400 to 1800* (LC), *Nineteenth-Century Literature Criticism* (NCLC), *Short Story Criticism* (SSC), and *Twentieth-Century Literary Criticism* (TCLC). The index also lists topic entries in the Gale Critical Companion Collection, which includes the following publications: *The Beat Generation* (BG), and *Harlem Renaissance* (HR).

Topic Index

CMLC Cumulative Nationality Index

CMLC Cumulative Title Index

Title Index

Title Index

Title Index

Title Index

Title Index

Title Index

ISBN 0-7876-8025-7

90000

9 780787 680251